TEACHER EDITION

Houghton
Mifflin
Harcourt

FLORIDA

GO MATH

Advanced Mathematics 2

Edward B. Burger

Juli K. Dixon

Timothy D. Kanold

Matthew R. Larson

Steven J. Leinwand

Martha E. Sandoval-Martinez

Special thanks to the students, teachers, staff, and principal Cheri Godek at Gotha Middle School, Windermere, FL.

Cover Image Credit: ©Comstock/Comstock Images/Getty Images

Printed in the U.S.A

ISBN 978-0-544-14891-8

2 3 4 5 6 7 8 9 10 0914 22 21 20 19 18 17 16 15 14 13

4500425320   A B C D E F G

Florida Go Math!

Teacher's Edition, Advanced Course 2

Contents in Brief

Teacher Material

Selected Answers are provided at the back of the Student Edition.

Authors

Edward B. Burger, Ph.D., is the Francis Christopher Oakley Third Century Professor of Mathematics at Williams College, an educational and business consultant, and a former vice provost at Baylor University. He has authored or coauthored more than sixty-five articles, books, and video series; delivered over five hundred addresses and workshops throughout the world; and made more than fifty radio and television appearances. He is a Fellow of the American Mathematical Society as well as having earned many national honors, including the Robert Foster Cherry Award for Great Teaching in 2010. In 2012, Microsoft Education named him a "Global Hero in Education."

Juli K. Dixon, Ph.D., is a Professor of Mathematics Education at the University of Central Florida. She has taught mathematics in urban schools at the elementary, middle, secondary, and post-secondary levels. She is an active researcher and speaker with numerous publications and conference presentations. Key areas of focus are deepening teachers' content knowledge and communicating and justifying mathematical ideas. She is a past chair of the NCTM Student Explorations in Mathematics Editorial Panel and member of the Board of Directors for the Association of Mathematics Teacher Educators.

Timothy D. Kanold, Ph.D., is an award-winning international educator, author, and consultant. He is a former superintendent and director of mathematics and science at Adlai E. Stevenson High School District 125 in Lincolnshire, Illinois. He is a past president of the National Council of Supervisors of Mathematics (NCSM) and the Council for the Presidential Awardees of Mathematics (CPAM). He has served on several writing and leadership commissions for NCTM during the past decade. He presents motivational professional development seminars with a focus on developing professional learning communities (PLC's) to improve the teaching, assessing, and learning of students. He has recently authored nationally recognized articles, books, and textbooks for mathematics education and school leadership, including *What Every Principal Needs to Know about the Teaching and Learning of Mathematics*.

Matthew R. Larson, Ph.D., is the K-12 mathematics curriculum specialist for the Lincoln Public Schools and served on the Board of Directors for the National Council of Teachers of Mathematics from 2010-2013. He is a past chair of NCTM's Research Committee and was a member of NCTM's Task Force on Linking Research and Practice. He is the author of several books on implementing the Common Core Standards for Mathematics. He has taught mathematics at the secondary and college levels and held an appointment as an honorary visiting associate professor at Teachers College, Columbia University.

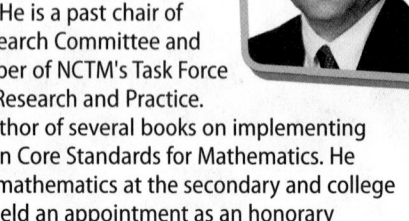

Steven J. Leinwand is a Principal Research Analyst at the American Institutes for Research (AIR) in Washington, D.C., and has over 30 years in leadership positions in mathematics education. He is past president of the National Council of Supervisors of Mathematics and served on the NCTM Board of Directors. He is the author of numerous articles, books, and textbooks and has made countless presentations with topics including student achievement, reasoning, effective assessment, and successful implementation of standards.

Martha E. Sandoval-Martinez is a mathematics instructor at El Camino College in Torrance, California. She was previously a Math Specialist at the University of California at Davis and former instructor at Santa Ana College, Marymount College, and California State University, Long Beach. In her current and former positions, she has worked extensively to improve fundamental pre-algebra and algebra skills in students who have historically struggled with mathematics.

Florida Reviewers

© Houghton Mifflin Harcourt Publishing Company

Working as a Professional Learning Community

Great teaching materials do not provide great education in and of themselves. Educators who collaborate in Professional Learning Communities can have a profound impact on their students. As a middle school mathematics teacher, your grade-level or course-based collaborative team is the engine that can drive your professional learning and the professional learning community (PLC) process. You and your colleagues hold a critical key to helping *all* students successfully learn the Florida Common Core Mathematics Standards in your middle school. Through your hard work and the work of your collaborative team, effective instruction, assessment, and intervention practices become more coherent and focused.

Coherence implies that the standards in each unit are more than a mere checklist of disconnected content; rather, they are organized into meaningful progressions of content that highlight the unity of the mathematics curriculum at your grade level, and throughout each grade of middle school.

Focus is provided in order to allow *time* for your students to master the intricate complexities of the content progressions across grades. Helping your students to better understand the coherent and focused aspects of the standards becomes one of the major benefits of working closely with your colleagues in a PLC school culture.

The National Board for Professional Teaching Standards states the following:

> Seeing themselves as partners with other teachers, [faculty members] are dedicated to improving the profession. They care about the quality of teaching in their schools, and, to this end, their collaboration with colleagues is continuous and explicit. They recognize that collaborating in a professional learning community contributes to their own professional growth, as well as to the growth of their peers, for the benefit of student learning. Teachers promote the ideal that working collaboratively increases knowledge, reflection, and quality of practice and benefits the instructional program. (*Mathematics Standards for Teachers of Students Ages 11–18+*, ©2010, p. 75)

As a highly accomplished middle school mathematics teacher you understand the value in the practice of effective collaboration with your colleagues. Teacher collaboration is not the icing on top of the proverbial cake of your work. Instead, it is the egg in the batter, holding the cake together.

As your school becomes a learning institution for the adults, it also becomes a learning institution dedicated to preparing all students for the future. The process of your collaboration in a PLC culture capitalizes on the fact that you and your colleagues come together with diverse experiences and knowledge to create a whole that is larger than the sum of the parts. Teacher collaboration is the solution to your sustained professional learning—the ongoing and never-ending process of growth necessary to meet the classroom demands of the CCSS expectations and the unit-by-unit mathematics content described in our series.

—Tim Kanold, Program Author

UNIT 1 🏴 Expressions, Equations, and Inequalities

MODULE 1 — Expressions and Equations

FL CC

MODULE 2 — Inequalities

FL CC

UNIT 2 Geometry

MODULE 3 Modeling Geometric Figures

FL CC

MODULE 4 Circumference, Area, and Volume

FL CC

UNIT 3 Statistics and Sampling

MODULE 5 Random Samples and Populations

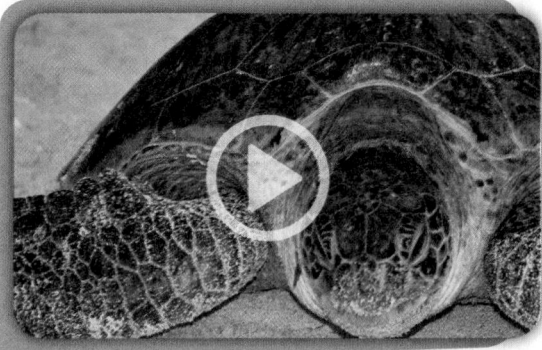

FL CC

MODULE 6 Analyzing and Comparing Data

FL CC

UNIT 4 Probability

MODULE 7 Experimental Probability

FL CC

MODULE 8 Theoretical Probability and Simulations

FL CC

UNIT 5 · Real Numbers, Exponents, and Scientific Notation

MODULE 9 — Real Numbers

MODULE 10 — Exponents and Scientific Notation

© Houghton Mifflin Harcourt Publishing Company • Image Credits: (t) ©Daniel Hershman/Getty Images; (b) ©Eyebyte/Alamy Images

UNIT 6 — Proportional and Nonproportional Relationships and Functions

MODULE 11 — Proportional Relationships

FL CC

MODULE 12 — Nonproportional Relationships

FL CC

© Houghton Mifflin Harcourt Publishing Company • Image Credits: (t) ©Angelo Giampiccolo/Shutterstock; (b) ©viappy/Shutterstock

MODULE **13** Writing Linear Equations

FL CC

MODULE **14** Functions

FL CC

© Houghton Mifflin Harcourt Publishing Company • Image Credits: (t) ©Yellow Dog Productions/Getty Images; (b) ©Huntstock/Getty Images

UNIT 7 Solving Equations and Systems of Equations

MODULE 15 Solving Linear Equations

FL CC

MODULE 16 Solving Systems of Linear Equations

FL CC

UNIT 8 Transformational Geometry

MODULE 17 Transformations and Congruence

FL CC

MODULE 18 Transformations and Similarity

FL CC

© Houghton Mifflin Harcourt Publishing Company • Image Credits: (t) ©Gregory K. Scott/Getty Images

UNIT 9 Measurement Geometry

MODULE 19 Angle Relationships in Parallel Lines and Triangles

FL CC

MODULE 20 The Pythagorean Theorem

FL CC

© Houghton Mifflin Harcourt Publishing Company • Image Credits: (t) ©Nifro Travel Images/Alamy Images; (b) ©Yuri Arcurs/Shutterstock

MODULE 21   Volume

Real-World Video. 659
Are You Ready?. 660
Reading Start-Up 661
Unpacking the Standards. . 662

FL CC

UNIT 10 Statistics: Bivariate Data

MODULE 22 Scatter Plots

FL CC

MODULE 23 Two-Way Tables

FL CC

Florida Common Core Standards for Mathematics

Correlations for HMH Florida Go Math Advanced Mathematics 2

Standard	Descriptor	Taught	Reinforced
MACC.7.EE.2 Solve real-life and mathematical problems using numerical and algebraic expressions and equations.			
MACC.7.EE.2.3	Solve multi-step real-life and mathematical problems posed with positive and negative rational numbers in any form (whole numbers, fractions, and decimals), using tools strategically. Apply properties of operations to calculate with numbers in any form; convert between forms as appropriate; and assess the reasonableness of answers using mental computation and estimation strategies.	SE: 25–28, 51–54, 271–275, 304–306, 309–312, 315–318	SE: 29–30, 31–32, 55–56, 57–58, 277–278, 291–292, 307–308, 313–314, 319–320, 321–322
MACC.7.EE.2.4	Use variables to represent quantities in a real-world or mathematical problem, and construct simple equations and inequalities to solve problems by reasoning about the quantities.	SE: 13–16, 19–22, 25, 41–42, 45–48; *See also below.*	SE: 17–18, 23–24, 28, 29–30, 31–32, 43–44, 49–50, 57–58; *See also below.*
MACC.7.EE.2.4a	Solve word problems leading to equations of the form $px + q = r$ and $p(x + q) = r$, where p, q, and r are specific rational numbers. Solve equations of these forms fluently. Compare an algebraic solution to an arithmetic solution, identifying the sequence of the operations used in each approach.	SE: 25–28	SE: 29–30, 31–32
MACC.7.EE.2.4b	Solve word problems leading to inequalities of the form $px + q > r$ or $px + q < r$, where p, q, and r are specific rational numbers. Graph the solution set of the inequality and interpret it in the context of the problem.	SE: 37–42, 51–54	SE: 43–44, 55–56, 57–58

Standard	Descriptor	Taught	Reinforced
MACC.7.G.1	**Draw, construct, and describe geometrical figures and describe the relationships between them.**		
MACC.7.G.1.1	Solve problems involving scale drawings of geometric figures, including computing actual lengths and areas from a scale drawing and reproducing a scale drawing at a different scale.	SE: 71–74	SE: 75–76, 93–94
MACC.7.G.1.3	Describe the two-dimensional figures that result from slicing three-dimensional figures, as in plane sections of right rectangular prisms and right rectangular pyramids.	SE: 81–83	SE: 83–84, 93–94
MACC.7.G.2	**Solve real-life and mathematical problems involving angle measure, area, surface area, and volume.**		
MACC.7.G.2.4	Know the formulas for the area and circumference of a circle and use them to solve problems; give an informal derivation of the relationship between the circumference and area of a circle.	SE: 99–102, 105–108	SE: 103–104, 109–110, 129–130
MACC.7.G.2.5	Use facts about supplementary, complementary, vertical, and adjacent angles in a multi-step problem to write and solve simple equations for an unknown angle in a figure.	SE: 85–90	SE: 91–92, 93–94
MACC.7.G.2.6	Solve real-world and mathematical problems involving area, volume and surface area of two- and three-dimensional objects composed of triangles, quadrilaterals, polygons, cubes, and right prisms.	SE: 111–114, 117–120, 123–126	SE: 115–116, 121–122, 127–128, 129–130

© Houghton Mifflin Harcourt Publishing Company

Standard	Descriptor	Taught	Reinforced
MACC.7.SP.1 Use random sampling to draw inferences about a population.			
MACC.7.SP.1.1	Understand that statistics can be used to gain information about a population by examining a sample of the population; generalizations about a population from a sample are valid only if the sample is representative of that population. Understand that random sampling tends to produce representative samples and support valid inferences.	SE: 145–148, 151–154	SE: 149–150, 155–156, 163–164
MACC.7.SP.1.2	Use data from a random sample to draw inferences about a population with an unknown characteristic of interest. Generate multiple samples (or simulated samples) of the same size to gauge the variation in estimates or predictions.	SE: 151–154, 157–160	SE: 155–156, 161–162, 163–164
MACC.7.SP.2 Draw informal comparative inferences about two populations.			
MACC.7.SP.2.3	Informally assess the degree of visual overlap of two numerical data distributions with similar variabilities, measuring the difference between the centers by expressing it as a multiple of a measure of variability.	SE: 170, 172, 176, 178, 181–182, 184	SE: 173–174, 179–180, 185–186, 187–188
MACC.7.SP.2.4	Use measures of center and measures of variability for numerical data from random samples to draw informal comparative inferences about two populations.	SE: 169, 171–172, 175, 177–178, 183–184	SE: 173–174, 179–180, 185–186, 187–188
MACC.7.SP.3 Investigate chance processes and develop, use, and evaluate probability models.			
MACC.7.SP.3.5	Understand that the probability of a chance event is a number between 0 and 1 that expresses the likelihood of the event occurring. Larger numbers indicate greater likelihood. A probability near 0 indicates an unlikely event, a probability around $\frac{1}{2}$ indicates an event that is neither unlikely nor likely, and a probability near 1 indicates a likely event.	SE: 201–203, 205–206	SE: 207–208
MACC.7.SP.3.6	Approximate the probability of a chance event by collecting data on the chance process that produces it and observing its long-run relative frequency, and predict the approximate relative frequency given the probability.	SE: 209, 211–212, 221–224, 235–236, 245–248	SE: 213–214, 225–226, 249–250

Standard	Descriptor	Taught	Reinforced
MACC.7.SP.3.7	Develop a probability model and use it to find probabilities of events. Compare probabilities from a model to observed frequencies; if the agreement is not good, explain possible sources of the discrepancy.	SE: 235–236; *See also below.*	SE: 237–238; *See also below.*
MACC.7.SP.3.7a	Develop a uniform probability model by assigning equal probability to all outcomes, and use the model to determine probabilities of events.	SE: 203–206, 233–234, 247–248	SE: 207–208, 227–228, 237–238, 249–250, 257–258
MACC.7.SP.3.7b	Develop a probability model (which may not be uniform) by observing frequencies in data generated from a chance process.	SE: 209–211, 212	SE: 213–214, 227–228
MACC.7.SP.3.8	Find probabilities of compound events using organized lists, tables, tree diagrams, and simulation.	SE: 215–218, 239–242, 252–254; *See also below.*	SE: 219–220, 227–228, 243–244, 255–256, 257–258; *See also below.*
MACC.7.SP.3.8a	Understand that, just as with simple events, the probability of a compound event is the fraction of outcomes in the sample space for which the compound event occurs.	SE: 215–218, 239, 242	SE: 219–220, 227–228, 243–244, 257–258
MACC.7.SP.3.8b	Represent sample spaces for compound events using methods such as organized lists, tables and tree diagrams. For an event described in everyday language (e.g., "rolling double sixes"), identify the outcomes in the sample space which compose the event.	SE: 215–218, 240–242	SE: 219–220, 227–228, 243–244
MACC.7.SP.3.8c	Design and use a simulation to generate frequencies for compound events.	SE: 217–218, 251–254	SE: 220, 255–256, 257–258

Standard	Descriptor	Taught	Reinforced
MACC.8.EE.1	**Work with radicals and integer exponents.**		
MACC.8.EE.1.1	Know and apply the properties of integer exponents to generate equivalent numerical expressions.	SE: 297–299, 300	SE: 301–302, 321, 322
MACC.8.EE.1.2	Use square root and cube root symbols to represent solutions to equations of the form $x^2 = p$ and $x^3 = p$, where p is a positive rational number. Evaluate square roots of small perfect squares and cube roots of small perfect cubes. Know that $\sqrt{2}$ is irrational.	SE: 273–275, 276	SE: 277–278, 291, 292
MACC.8.EE.1.3	Use numbers expressed in the form of a single digit times an integer power of 10 to estimate very large or very small quantities, and to express how many times as much one is than the other.	SE: 303–305, 306, 309–311, 312	SE: 307–308, 313–314, 321, 322
MACC.8.EE.1.4	Perform operations with numbers expressed in scientific notation, including problems where both decimal and scientific notation are used. Use scientific notation and choose units of appropriate size for measurements of very large or very small quantities (e.g., use millimeters per year for seafloor spreading). Interpret scientific notation that has been generated by technology.	SE: 315–317, 318	SE: 319–320, 321, 322
MACC.8.EE.2	**Understand the connections between proportional relationships, lines, and linear equations.**		
MACC.8.EE.2.5	Graph proportional relationships, interpreting the unit rate as the slope of the graph. Compare two different proportional relationships represented in different ways.	SE: 347–349, 350, 432, 434	SE: 351–352, 353, 354, 435–436
MACC.8.EE.2.6	Use similar triangles to explain why the slope m is the same between any two distinct points on a non-vertical line in the coordinate plane; derive the equation $y = mx$ for a line through the origin and the equation $y = mx + b$ for a line intercepting the vertical axis at b.	SE: 335–337, 338, 365, 367, 368, 628–629	SE: 339–340, 353, 354, 370, 385, 386, 632

Standard	Descriptor	Taught	Reinforced
MACC.8.EE.3 Analyze and solve linear equations and pairs of simultaneous linear equations.			
MACC.8.EE.3.7	Solve linear equations in one variable.	SE: 461–463, 464, 467–469, 470, 619, 622, 627–628, 630; *See also below.*	SE: 465–466, 471–472, 485, 486, 523–524, 631–632; *See also below.*
MACC.8.EE.3.7a	Give examples of linear equations in one variable with one solution, infinitely many solutions, or no solutions. Show which of these possibilities is the case by successively transforming the given equation into simpler forms, until an equivalent equation of the form $x = a$, $a = a$, or $a = b$ results (where a and b are different numbers).	SE: 479–481, 482	SE: 483–484, 485, 486
MACC.8.EE.3.7b	Solve linear equations with rational number coefficients, including equations whose solutions require expanding expressions using the distributive property and collecting like terms.	SE: 461–463, 464, 467–469, 470, 473–475, 476, 621, 622	SE: 465–466, 471–472, 477–478, 485, 486, 623–624
MACC.8.EE.3.8	Analyze and solve pairs of simultaneous linear equations.	SE: 492–495, 496; *See also below.*	SE: 497–498, 529, 530; *See also below.*
MACC.8.EE.3.8a	Understand that solutions to a system of two linear equations in two variables correspond to points of intersection of their graphs, because points of intersection satisfy both equations simultaneously.	SE: 491, 496	SE: 497–498, 529, 530
MACC.8.EE.3.8b	Solve systems of two linear equations in two variables algebraically, and estimate solutions by graphing the equations. Solve simple cases by inspection.	SE: 499–502, 504, 507–510, 512, 515–518, 520, 523–525, 526	SE: 505–506, 513–514, 521–522, 527–528, 529–530
MACC.8.EE.3.8c	Solve real-world and mathematical problems leading to two linear equations in two variables.	SE: 494–495, 496, 502–503, 504, 510–511, 512, 518–519, 520	SE: 497–498, 505–506, 513–514, 521–522, 528–530

Standard	Descriptor	Taught	Reinforced
MACC.8.F.1 Define, evaluate, and compare functions.			
MACC.8.F.1.1	Understand that a function is a rule that assigns to each input exactly one output. The graph of a function is the set of ordered pairs consisting of an input and the corresponding output.	SE: 417–421, 422, 425	SE: 423–424, 429–430, 443, 444
MACC.8.F.1.2	Compare properties of two functions each represented in a different way (algebraically, graphically, numerically in tables, or by verbal descriptions).	SE: 349, 350, 380–382, 431–433, 434	SE: 351–352, 384, 385, 386, 435–436, 443, 444
MACC.8.F.1.3	Interpret the equation $y = mx + b$ as defining a linear function, whose graph is a straight line; give examples of functions that are not linear.	SE: 359–361, 362, 371–372, 374, 377, 381, 426–427, 428	SE: 363–364, 375–376, 383, 385, 386, 429–430, 443, 444
MACC.8.F.2 Use functions to model relationships between quantities.			
MACC.8.F.2.4	Construct a function to model a linear relationship between two quantities. Determine the rate of change and initial value of the function from a description of a relationship or from two (x, y) values, including reading these from a table or from a graph. Interpret the rate of change and initial value of a linear function in terms of the situation it models, and in terms of its graph or a table of values.	SE: 341–343, 344, 347, 350, 366, 368, 372–373, 374, 378–379, 381–382, 391–393, 394, 397–399, 400, 431–432, 433, 434	SE: 340, 345–346, 351, 353, 354, 369–370, 375–376, 383–384, 385, 386, 395–396, 401–402, 411, 412, 435–436
MACC.8.F.2.5	Describe qualitatively the functional relationship between two quantities by analyzing a graph (e.g., where the function is increasing or decreasing, linear or nonlinear). Sketch a graph that exhibits the qualitative features of a function that has been described verbally.	SE: 437–439, 440	SE: 441–442, 443, 444

Standard	Descriptor	Taught	Reinforced
MACC.8.G.1 Understand congruence and similarity using physical models, transparencies, or geometry software.			
MACC.8.G.1.1a	Verify experimentally the properties of rotations, reflections, and translations: lines are taken to lines, and line segments to line segments of the same length.	SE: 543–545, 546, 549–551, 552, 555–557, 558	SE: 547–548, 553–554, 559–560, 573, 574
MACC.8.G.1.1b	Verify experimentally the properties of rotations, reflections, and translations: angles are taken to angles of the same measure.	SE: 543–545, 546, 549–551, 552, 555–557, 558	SE: 547–548, 553–554, 559–560, 573, 574
MACC.8.G.1.1c	Verify experimentally the properties of rotations, reflections, and translations: parallel lines are taken to parallel lines.	SE: 543–545, 546, 549–551, 552, 555–557, 558	SE: 547–548, 553–554, 559–560, 573, 574
MACC.8.G.1.2	Understand that a two-dimensional figure is congruent to another if the second can be obtained from the first by a sequence of rotations, reflections, and translations; given two congruent figures, describe a sequence that exhibits the congruence between them.	SE: 567–569, 570	SE: 571–572, 573, 574
MACC.8.G.1.3	Describe the effect of dilations, translations, rotations, and reflections on two-dimensional figures using coordinates.	SE: 545–546, 551–552, 557–558, 561–564, 580–581, 582, 585–587, 588	SE: 547–548, 553–554, 559–560 565–566, 583–584, 589–590, 597, 598
MACC.8.G.1.4	Understand that a two-dimensional figure is similar to another if the second can be obtained from the first by a sequence of rotations, reflections, translations, and dilations; given two similar two-dimensional figures, describe a sequence that exhibits the similarity between them.	SE: 579–580, 581–582, 591–593, 594	SE: 583–584, 595–596, 597, 598
MACC.8.G.1.5	Use informal arguments to establish facts about the angle sum and exterior angle of triangles, about the angles created when parallel lines are cut by a transversal, and the angle-angle criterion for similarity of triangles.	SE: 611–614, 617–619, 620, 622, 625–626	SE: 615–616, 623–624, 631–632, 633, 634

Standard	Descriptor	Taught	Reinforced
MACC.8.G.2 Understand and apply the Pythagorean Theorem.			
MACC.8.G.2.6	Explain a proof of the Pythagorean Theorem and its converse.	SE: 639–640, 645–647, 648	SE: 644, 649–650
MACC.8.G.2.7	Apply the Pythagorean Theorem to determine unknown side lengths in right triangles in real-world and mathematical problems in two and three dimensions.	SE: 640–642	SE: 643–644, 657, 658
MACC.8.G.2.8	Apply the Pythagorean Theorem to find the distance between two points in a coordinate system.	SE: 651–654	SE: 655–656, 657, 658
MACC.8.G.3 Solve real-world and mathematical problems involving volume of cylinders, cones, and spheres.			
MACC.8.G.3.9	Know the formulas for the volumes of cones, cylinders, and spheres and use them to solve real-world and mathematical problems.	SE: 663–665, 666, 669–671, 672, 675–677, 678	SE: 667–668, 673–674, 679–680, 681, 682
MACC.8.NS.1 Know that there are numbers that are not rational, and approximate them by rational numbers.			
MACC.8.NS.1.1	Know that numbers that are not rational are called irrational. Understand informally that every number has a decimal expansion; for rational numbers show that the decimal expansion repeats eventually, and convert a decimal expansion which repeats eventually into a rational number.	SE: 271–273, 276, 279–281, 282	SE: 277–278, 283–284, 291, 292
MACC.8.NS.1.2	Use rational approximations of irrational numbers to compare the size of irrational numbers, locate them approximately on a number line diagram, and estimate the value of expressions (e.g., π^2).	SE: 274–276, 285–287, 288	SE: 278, 289–290, 291, 292

Standard	Descriptor	Taught	Reinforced
MACC.8.SP.1 Investigate patterns of association in bivariate data.			
MACC.8.SP.1.1	Construct and interpret scatter plots for bivariate measurement data to investigate patterns of association between two quantities. Describe patterns such as clustering, outliers, positive or negative association, linear association, and nonlinear association.	SE: 406–407, 408, 697–699, 700, 703–704, 706	SE: 409–410, 411, 412, 701–702, 707–708, 709, 710
MACC.8.SP.1.2	Know that straight lines are widely used to model relationships between two quantitative variables. For scatter plots that suggest a linear association, informally fit a straight line, and informally assess the model fit by judging the closeness of the data points to the line.	SE: 403–404, 408, 703–704, 706	SE: 409–410, 707–708, 709, 710
MACC.8.SP.1.3	Use the equation of a linear model to solve problems in the context of bivariate measurement data, interpreting the slope and intercept.	SE: 404–405, 408, 704–706	SE: 409–410, 707–708, 709–710
MACC.8.SP.1.4	Understand that patterns of association can also be seen in bivariate categorical data by displaying frequencies and relative frequencies in a two-way table. Construct and interpret a two-way table summarizing data on two categorical variables collected from the same subjects. Use relative frequencies calculated for rows or columns to describe possible association between the two variables.	SE: 715–717, 718, 721–725, 726	SE: 719–720, 727–728, 729, 730

Standard	Descriptor	Citations
MP Mathematical Practices Standards		*The mathematical practices standards are integrated throughout the book. See, for example, the citations below.*
MACC.K12.MP.1.1	**Make sense of problems and persevere in solving them.** Mathematically proficient students start by explaining to themselves the meaning of a problem and looking for entry points to its solution. They analyze givens, constraints, relationships, and goals. They make conjectures about the form and meaning of the solution and plan a solution pathway rather than simply jumping into a solution attempt. They consider analogous problems, and try special cases and simpler forms of the original problem in order to gain insight into its solution. They monitor and evaluate their progress and change course if necessary. Older students might, depending on the context of the problem, transform algebraic expressions or change the viewing window on their graphing calculator to get the information they need. Mathematically proficient students can explain correspondences between equations, verbal descriptions, tables, and graphs or draw diagrams of important features and relationships, graph data, and search for regularity or trends. Younger students might rely on using concrete objects or pictures to help conceptualize and solve a problem. Mathematically proficient students check their answers to problems using a different method, and they continually ask themselves, "Does this make sense?" They can understand the approaches of others to solving complex problems and identify correspondences between different approaches.	SE: 56, 116, 158, 223, 278, 384, 442, 466, 475, 483, 506, 518–519, 572, 644, 656, 679, 719–720
MACC.K12.MP.2.1	**Reason abstractly and quantitatively.** Mathematically proficient students make sense of quantities and their relationships in problem situations. They bring two complementary abilities to bear on problems involving quantitative relationships: the ability to decontextualize—to abstract a given situation and represent it symbolically and manipulate the representing symbols as if they have a life of their own, without necessarily attending to their referents—and the ability to contextualize, to pause as needed during the manipulation process in order to probe into the referents for the symbols involved. Quantitative reasoning entails habits of creating a coherent representation of the problem at hand; considering the units involved; attending to the meaning of quantities, not just how to compute them; and knowing and flexibly using different properties of operations and objects.	SE: 52, 107, 181–182, 226, 278, 302, 346, 352, 367, 375, 417–418, 462–466, 478, 518–519, 618–619, 639–640

Standard	Descriptor	Citations
MACC.K12.MP.3.1	**Construct viable arguments and critique the reasoning of others.** Mathematically proficient students understand and use stated assumptions, definitions, and previously established results in constructing arguments. They make conjectures and build a logical progression of statements to explore the truth of their conjectures. They are able to analyze situations by breaking them into cases, and can recognize and use counterexamples. They justify their conclusions, communicate them to others, and respond to the arguments of others. They reason inductively about data, making plausible arguments that take into account the context from which the data arose. Mathematically proficient students are also able to compare the effectiveness of two plausible arguments, distinguish correct logic or reasoning from that which is flawed, and—if there is a flaw in an argument—explain what it is. Elementary students can construct arguments using concrete referents such as objects, drawings, diagrams, and actions. Such arguments can make sense and be correct, even though they are not generalized or made formal until later grades. Later, students learn to determine domains to which an argument applies. Students at all grades can listen or read the arguments of others, decide whether they make sense, and ask useful questions to clarify or improve the arguments.	SE: 44, 92, 174, 238, 284, 364, 410, 472, 522, 566, 616, 674, 708
MACC.K12.MP.4.1	**Model with mathematics.** Mathematically proficient students can apply the mathematics they know to solve problems arising in everyday life, society, and the workplace. In early grades, this might be as simple as writing an addition equation to describe a situation. In middle grades, a student might apply proportional reasoning to plan a school event or analyze a problem in the community. By high school, a student might use geometry to solve a design problem or use a function to describe how one quantity of interest depends on another. Mathematically proficient students who can apply what they know are comfortable making assumptions and approximations to simplify a complicated situation, realizing that these may need revision later. They are able to identify important quantities in a practical situation and map their relationships using such tools as diagrams, two-way tables, graphs, flowcharts and formulas. They can analyze those relationships mathematically to draw conclusions. They routinely interpret their mathematical results in the context of the situation and reflect on whether the results make sense, possibly improving the model if it has not served its purpose.	SE: 27, 104, 156, 220, 337, 393–394, 468–469, 518–519, 627–628, 677, 721–725

Standard	Descriptor	Citations
MACC.K12.MP.5.1	**Use appropriate tools strategically.** Mathematically proficient students consider the available tools when solving a mathematical problem. These tools might include pencil and paper, concrete models, a ruler, a protractor, a calculator, a spreadsheet, a computer algebra system, a statistical package, or dynamic geometry software. Proficient students are sufficiently familiar with tools appropriate for their grade or course to make sound decisions about when each of these tools might be helpful, recognizing both the insight to be gained and their limitations. For example, mathematically proficient high school students analyze graphs of functions and solutions generated using a graphing calculator. They detect possible errors by strategically using estimation and other mathematical knowledge. When making mathematical models, they know that technology can enable them to visualize the results of varying assumptions, explore consequences, and compare predictions with data. Mathematically proficient students at various grade levels are able to identify relevant external mathematical resources, such as digital content located on a website, and use them to pose or solve problems. They are able to use technological tools to explore and deepen their understanding of concepts.	SE: 25, 77–80, 157, 256, 286, 317, 461, 491–495, 549, 579, 611–612, 617, 639, 663
MACC.K12.MP.6.1	**Attend to precision.** Mathematically proficient students try to communicate precisely to others. They try to use clear definitions in discussion with others and in their own reasoning. They state the meaning of the symbols they choose, including using the equal sign consistently and appropriately. They are careful about specifying units of measure, and labeling axes to clarify the correspondence with quantities in a problem. They calculate accurately and efficiently, express numerical answers with a degree of precision appropriate for the problem context. In the elementary grades, students give carefully formulated explanations to each other. By the time they reach high school they have learned to examine claims and make explicit use of definitions.	SE: 24, 84, 180, 214, 320, 370, 407, 437–442, 478, 498, 518, 616, 668, 701

Standard	Descriptor	Citations
MACC.K12.MP.7.1	**Look for and make use of structure.** Mathematically proficient students look closely to discern a pattern or structure. Young students, for example, might notice that three and seven more is the same amount as seven and three more, or they may sort a collection of shapes according to how many sides the shapes have. Later, students will see 7×8 equals the well remembered $7 \times 5 + 7 \times 3$, in preparation for learning about the distributive property. In the expression $x^2 + 9x + 14$, older students can see the 14 as 2×7 and the 9 as $2 + 7$. They recognize the significance of an existing line in a geometric figure and can use the strategy of drawing an auxiliary line for solving problems. They also can step back for an overview and shift perspective. They can see complicated things, such as some algebraic expressions, as single objects or as being composed of several objects. For example, they can see $5 - 3(x - y)^2$ as 5 minus a positive number times a square and use that to realize that its value cannot be more than 5 for any real numbers x and y.	SE: 9, 117, 183, 244, 274–275, 297–299, 309, 397–399, 417–418, 472, 561–564, 645, 698, 703–705
MACC.K12.MP.8.1	**Look for and express regularity in repeated reasoning.** Mathematically proficient students notice if calculations are repeated, and look both for general methods and for shortcuts. Upper elementary students might notice when dividing 25 by 11 that they are repeating the same calculations over and over again, and conclude they have a repeating decimal. By paying attention to the calculation of slope as they repeatedly check whether points are on the line through $(1, 2)$ with slope 3, middle school students might abstract the equation $\frac{(y-2)}{(x-1)} = 3$. Noticing the regularity in the way terms cancel when expanding $(x - 1)(x + 1)$, $(x - 1)(x^2 + x + 1)$, and $(x - 1)(x^3 + x^2 + x + 1)$ might lead them to the general formula for the sum of a geometric series. As they work to solve a problem, mathematically proficient students maintain oversight of the process, while attending to the details. They continually evaluate the reasonableness of their intermediate results.	SE: 37–38, 99, 124, 241, 272, 297–299, 309, 371, 461, 499, 507, 515, 561–564, 652, 704

Florida Language Arts Standards

HMH Florida Go Math supports English language learners at all proficiency levels. The *HMH Florida Go Math Student Edition* provides integrated resources to assist all levels of learners, as shown in the correlation tables provided below.

In addition, students at various levels may benefit from additional program support:

Beginning—Students at a Beginning level are supported by *Spanish Student Edition, Spanish Assessment Resources,* Success for Every Learner and Leveled Practice A worksheets in *Differentiated Instruction, Math On the Spot* videos with Spanish closed captioning, and the *Multilingual Glossary.*

Intermediate—Students at the Intermediate level may use any of the resources above, and may also use Reading Strategies in *Differentiated Instruction.*

Advanced and Advanced High—Students at these levels will be successful as the *Student Edition* promotes vocabulary development through visual and context clues. The *Multilingual Glossary* may also be helpful.

Language Arts Standard	Student Edition Citations
LACC.68.RH.1.3 Identify key steps in a text's description of a process related to history/social studies (e.g., how a bill becomes law, how interest rates are raised or lowered).	This standard is met in: Essential questions in many lessons—Examples: 126, 288, 368
LACC.68.RH.2.4 Determine the meaning of words and phrases as they are used in a text, including vocabulary specific to domains related to history/social studies.	This standard is met in: Lesson instruction in all lessons— Examples: 86, 271, 336

LACC.68.WHST.1.1 Write arguments focused on *discipline-specific content.*
   a. Introduce claim(s) about a topic or issue, acknowledge and distinguish the claim(s) from alternate or opposing claims, and organize the reasons and evidence logically.
   b. Support claim(s) with logical reasoning and relevant, accurate data and evidence that demonstrate an understanding of the topic or text, using credible sources.
   c. Use words, phrases, and clauses to create cohesion and clarify the relationships among claim(s), counterclaims, reasons, and evidence.
   d. Establish and maintain a formal style.
   e. Provide a concluding statement or section that follows from and supports the argument presented.
	This standard is met in:
	Reflect questions in many lessons—Examples: 14, 71, 146, 205, 297, 299, 360, 407, 545, 567, 612, 645, 675, 697
	H.O.T. exercises in all lessons—Examples: 12, 80, 180, 238, 320, 370, 442, 514, 554, 587, 644, 674, 708

LACC.68.WHST.2.4 Produce clear and coherent writing in which the development, organization, and style are appropriate to task, purpose, and audience.	This standard is met in: Communicate Mathematical Ideas exercises in many lessons—Examples: 50, 110, 160, 238, 320, 410, 478, 548, 590, 668, 708
LACC.7.SL.1.3 Delineate a speaker's argument and specific claims, evaluating the soundness of the reasoning and the relevance and sufficiency of the evidence.	This standard is met in: Explain the Error exercises in many lessons—Examples: 30, 127, 156, 243

Progressions and Florida Common Core

Florida Go Math is designed to fully address the Florida Common Core State Standards. Concepts within each grade are organized in units that align to major domains and provide focus on key big ideas and skills. Within each unit, concepts are organized into modules that align to clusters and build connections among the individual standards.

Florida Go Math is also designed to provide coherent and focused progressions across the grades. The table below provides an overview of how important topics within each domain are developed across the grades.

	Advanced Mathematics 1	Advanced Mathematics 2	Algebra 1
Ratios and Proportionality	• Understand ratio concepts and use ratio reasoning to solve problems.	• Analyze proportional relationships and use them to solve real-world and mathematical problems.	
The Number System / Number and Quantity	• Apply and extend previous understandings of multiplication and division to divide fractions. • Compute fluently with multi-digit numbers and find common factors and multiples. • Apply and extend previous understandings of numbers to the system of rational numbers. • Apply and extend previous understandings of operations with fractions to add, subtract, multiply, and divide rational numbers.	• Know that there are numbers that are not rational, and approximate them by rational numbers.	• Extend the properties of exponents to rational exponents. • Use properties of rational and irrational numbers. • Reason quantitatively and use units to solve problems.
Expressions and Equations/ Algebra	• Apply and extend previous understandings of arithmetic to algebraic expressions. • Reason about and solve one-variable equations and inequalities. • Represent and analyze quantitative relationships between dependent and independent variables. • Use properties of operations to generate equivalent expressions.	• Solve real-life and mathematical problems using numerical and algebraic expressions and equations. • Work with radicals and integer exponents. • Understand the connections between proportional relationships, lines, and linear equations. • Analyze and solve linear equations and pairs of simultaneous linear equations.	• Interpret the structure of expressions. • Write expressions in equivalent forms to solve problems. • Perform arithmetic operations on polynomials. • Understand the relationship between zeros and factors of polynomials. • Create equations that describe numbers or relationships. • Understand solving equations as a process of reasoning and explain the reasoning. • Solve equations and inequalities in one variable. • Solve systems of equations. • Represent and solve equations and inequalities graphically.

	Advanced Mathematics 1	Advanced Mathematics 2	Algebra 1
Functions		• Define, evaluate, and compare functions. • Use functions to model relationships between quantities.	• Understand the concept of a function and use function notation. • Interpret functions that arise in applications in terms of the context. • Analyze functions using different representations. • Build a function that models a relationship between two quantities. • Build new functions from existing functions. • Construct and compare linear, quadratic, and exponential models and solve problems. • Interpret expressions for functions in terms of the situation they model.
Geometry	• Solve real-world and mathematical problems involving area, surface area, and volume.	• Draw, construct and describe geometrical figures and describe the relationships between them. • Solve real-life and mathematical problems involving angle measure, area, surface area, and volume. • Understand congruence and similarity using physical models, transparencies, or geometry software. • Understand and apply the Pythagorean theorem. • Solve real-world and mathematical problems involving volume of cylinders, cones and spheres.	
Statistics and Probability	• Develop understanding of statistical variability. • Summarize and describe distributions.	• Use random sampling to draw inferences about a population. • Draw informal comparative inferences about two populations. • Investigate chance processes and develop, use, and evaluate probability models. • Investigate patterns of association in bivariate data.	• Summarize, represent, and interpret data on a single count or measurement variable. • Summarize, represent, and interpret data on two categorical and quantitative variables. • Interpret linear models.

Succeeding with HMH Florida Go Math

Actively participate in your learning with your write-in Student Edition. Explore concepts, take notes, answer questions, and complete your homework right in your textbook!

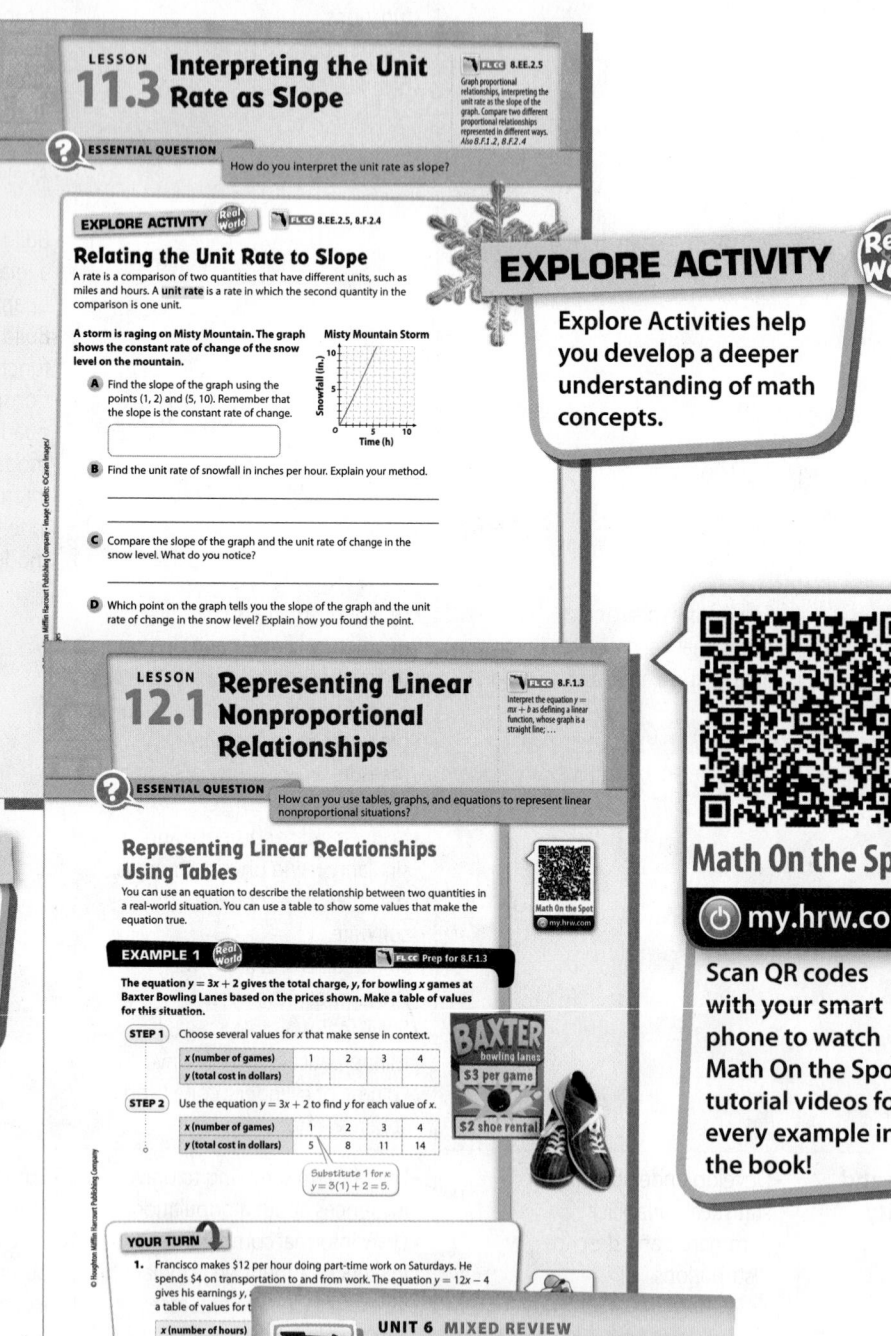

LESSON 11.3 Interpreting the Unit Rate as Slope

FL.CC 8.EE.2.5
Graph proportional relationships, interpreting the unit rate as the slope of the graph. Compare two different proportional relationships represented in different ways. Also 8.F.1.2, 8.F.2.4

? ESSENTIAL QUESTION
How do you interpret the unit rate as slope?

EXPLORE ACTIVITY Real World   FL.CC 8.EE.2.5, 8.F.2.4

Relating the Unit Rate to Slope
A rate is a comparison of two quantities that have different units, such as miles and hours. A **unit rate** is a rate in which the second quantity in the comparison is one unit.

A storm is raging on Misty Mountain. The graph shows the constant rate of change of the snow level on the mountain.

Misty Mountain Storm

A Find the slope of the graph using the points (1, 2) and (5, 10). Remember that the slope is the constant rate of change.

B Find the unit rate of snowfall in inches per hour. Explain your method.

C Compare the slope of the graph and the unit rate of change in the snow level. What do you notice?

D Which point on the graph tells you the slope of the graph and the unit rate of change in the snow level? Explain how you found the point.

EXPLORE ACTIVITY Real World

Explore Activities help you develop a deeper understanding of math concepts.

LESSON 12.1 Representing Linear Nonproportional Relationships

FL.CC 8.F.1.3
Interpret the equation y = mx + b as defining a linear function, whose graph is a straight line; ....

? ESSENTIAL QUESTION
How can you use tables, graphs, and equations to represent linear nonproportional situations?

Representing Linear Relationships Using Tables
You can use an equation to describe the relationship between two quantities in a real-world situation. You can use a table to show some values that make the equation true.

EXAMPLE 1 Real World   FL.CC Prep for 8.F.1.3

The equation $y = 3x + 2$ gives the total charge, y, for bowling x games at Baxter Bowling Lanes based on the prices shown. Make a table of values for this situation.

STEP 1 Choose several values for x that make sense in context.

x (number of games)	1	2	3	4
y (total cost in dollars)				

STEP 2 Use the equation $y = 3x + 2$ to find y for each value of x.

x (number of games)	1	2	3	4
y (total cost in dollars)	5	8	11	14

Substitute 1 for x
$y = 3(1) + 2 = 5.$

BAXTER bowling lanes
$3 per game
$2 shoe rental

YOUR TURN

1. Francisco makes $12 per hour doing part-time work on Saturdays. He spends $4 on transportation to and from work. The equation $y = 12x - 4$ gives his earnings y, [...] a table of values for t[...]

| x (number of hours) | | |
| y (earnings in dollars) | | |

YOUR TURN

Your Turn exercises check your understanding of new concepts.

Math On the Spot
⏻ my.hrw.com

Scan QR codes with your smart phone to watch Math On the Spot tutorial videos for every example in the book!

UNIT 6 MIXED REVIEW
PARCC Assessment Readiness

Check your mastery of concepts through review and practice for the PARCC test.

GO DIGITAL

my.hrw.com

Enhance Your Learning!

my.hrw.com

The Interactive Student Edition provides additional videos, activities, tools, and learning aids to support you as you study!

Practice skills and complete your homework online with the Personal Math Trainer. Your Personal Math Trainer provides a variety of learning aids that develop and improve your understanding of math concepts including videos, guided examples, and step-by-step solutions.

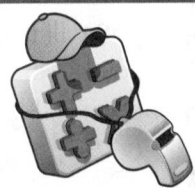

Personal Math Trainer

Online Assessment and Intervention

my.hrw.com

Math On the Spot

my.hrw.com

Math On the Spot video tutorials provide step-by-step instruction of the math concepts covered in each example.

Animated Math activities let you interactively explore and practice key math concepts and skills.

Animated Math

my.hrw.com

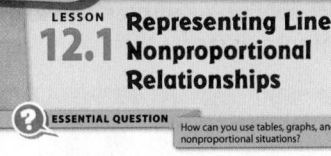

LESSON 12.1 Representing Linear Nonproportional Relationships

FL CC 8.F.1.3
Interpret the equation y = mx + b as defining a linear function, whose graph is a straight line; …

ESSENTIAL QUESTION How can you use tables, graphs, and equations to represent linear nonproportional situations?

Representing Linear Relationships Using Tables

You can use an equation to describe the relationship between two quantities in a real-world situation. You can use a table to show some values that make the equation true.

Math On the Spot
my.hrw.com

EXAMPLE 1 Real World

FL CC Prep for 8.F.1.3

The equation $y = 3x + 2$ gives the total charge, y, for bowling x games at Baxter Bowling Lanes based on the prices shown. Make a table of values for this situation.

STEP 1 Choose several values for x that make sense in context.

x (number of games)	1	2	3	4
y (total cost in dollars)				

STEP 2 Use the equation $y = 3x + 2$ to find y for each value of x.

x (number of games)	1	2	3	4
y (total cost in dollars)	5	8	11	14

BAXTER bowling lanes
$3 per game
$2 shoe rental

Substitute 1 for x.
$y = 3(1) + 2 = 5.$

YOUR TURN

1. Francisco makes $12 per hour doing part-time work on Saturdays. He spends $4 on transportation to and from work. The equation $y = 12x - 4$ gives his earnings y, after transportation costs, for working x hours. Make a table of values for this situation.

x (number of hours)				
y (earnings in dollars)				

Personal Math Trainer
Online Assessment and Intervention
my.hrw.com

Lesson 12.1 **359**

Standards for Mathematical Practice

The topics described in the Standards for Mathematical Content will vary from year to year. However, the *way* in which you learn, study, and think about mathematics will not. The Standards for Mathematical Practice describe skills that you will use in all of your math courses. These pages show some features of your book that will help you gain these skills and use them to master this year's topics.

MP.1.1   Make sense of problems and persevere in solving them.

Mathematically proficient students start by explaining to themselves the meaning of a problem… They analyze givens, constraints, relationships, and goals. They make conjectures about the form… of the solution and plan a solution pathway…

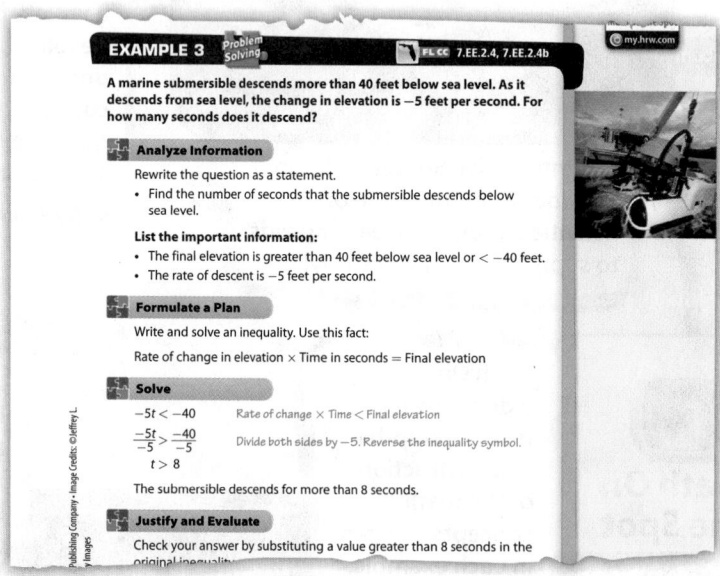

Problem-solving examples and exercises lead students through problem solving steps.

MP.2.1   Reason abstractly and quantitatively.

Mathematically proficient students… bring two complementary abilities to bear on problems…: the ability to decontextualize— to abstract a given situation and represent it symbolically… and the ability to contextualize, to pause… in order to probe into the referents for the symbols involved.

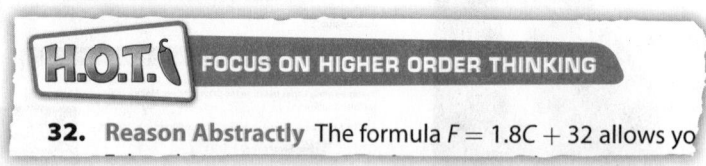

Focus on Higher Order Thinking exercises in every lesson and **Performance Tasks** in every unit require you to use logical reasoning, represent situations symbolically, use mathematical models to solve problems, and state your answers in terms of a problem context.

MP.3.1 Construct viable arguments and critique the reasoning of others.

Mathematically proficient students… justify their conclusions, [and]… distinguish correct… reasoning from that which is flawed.

Reflect

2. **Make a Conjecture** Use your results from parts **E**, **H**, and a conjecture about translations.

ESSENTIAL QUESTION CHECK-IN

Essential Question Check-in and **Reflect** in every lesson ask you to evaluate statements, explain relationships, apply mathematical principles, make conjectures, construct arguments, and justify your reasoning.

MP.4.1 Model with mathematics.

Mathematically proficient students can apply… mathematics… to… problems… in everyday life, society, and the workplace.

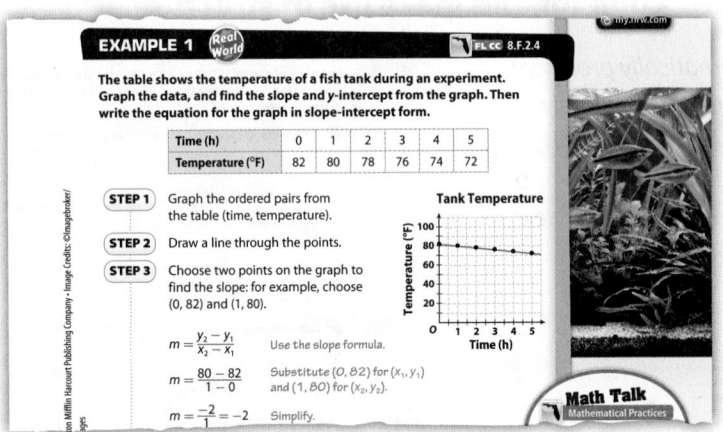

Real-world examples and **mathematical modeling** apply mathematics to other disciplines and real-world contexts such as science and business.

MP.5.1 Use appropriate tools strategically.

Mathematically proficient students consider the available tools when solving a… problem… [and] are… able to use technological tools to explore and deepen their understanding…

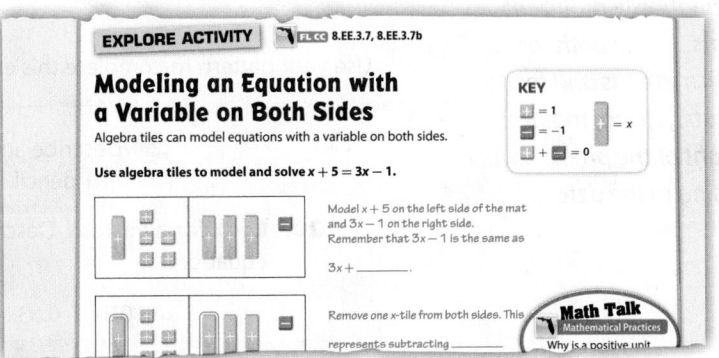

Exploration Activities in lessons use concrete and technological tools, such as manipulatives or graphing calculators, to explore mathematical concepts.

MP.6.1 Attend to precision.

Mathematically proficient students… communicate precisely… with others and in their own reasoning… [They] give carefully formulated explanations…

19. Communicate Mathematical Ideas Explain how you can fir̶ height of a cylinder if you know the diameter and the volum̶ an example with your explana̶

Key Vocabulary

slope *(pendiente)*
A measure of the steepness of a line on a graph; the rise divided by the run.

Precision refers not only to the correctness of calculations but also to the proper use of mathematical language and symbols. **Communicate Mathematical Ideas** exercises and **Key Vocabulary** highlighted for each module and unit help you learn and use the language of math to communicate mathematics precisely.

MP.7.1 Look for and make use of structure.

Mathematically proficient students… look closely to discern a pattern or structure… They can also step back for an overview and shift perspectives.

Follow the steps to informally prove the Triangle Sum Theorem. You should draw each step on your own paper. The figures below are provided for you to check your work.

A Draw a triangle and label the angles as ∠1, ∠2, and ∠3 as shown.

B Draw line *a* through the base of the triangle.

C The Parallel Postulate states that through a point not on a line ℓ, there is exactly one line parallel to line ℓ. Draw line *b* parallel to line *a*, through the vertex opposite the base of the triangle.

D Extend each of the non-base sides of the triangle to form transversal *s* and transversal *t*. Transversals *s* and *t* intersect parallel lines *a* and *b*.

E Label the angles formed by line *b* and the transversals as ∠4 and ∠5.

F Because ∠4 and _____ are alternate interior

Throughout the lessons, you will observe regularity in mathematical structures in order to make generalizations and make connections between related problems. For example, you can apply your knowledge of geometric theorems to determine when an auxiliary line would be helpful.

MP.8.1 Look for and express regularity in repeated reasoning.

Mathematically proficient students… look both for general methods and for shortcuts… [and] maintain oversight of the process, while attending to the details.

Use your pattern to complete this equation: $(7^2)^4 = 7^{\boxed{}}$.

B Describe any patterns you see. Use your pattern to deterr̶ of 1 pencil.

20. Look for a Pattern Describe the pattern in the equation. The̶ equation.

$$0.3x + 0.03x + 0.003x + 0.0003x + \ldots = 3$$

You will look for repeated calculations and mathematical patterns in examples and exercises. Recognizing patterns can help you make generalizations and obtain a better understanding of the underlying mathematics.

Review Test

Personal Math Trainer
Online Assessment and Intervention
my.hrw.com

Selected Response

1. Suppose you have developed a scale that indicates the brightness of sunlight. Each category in the table is 5 times brighter than the category above it. For example, a day that is dazzling is 5 times brighter than a day that is radiant. How many times brighter is a dazzling day than a dim day?

Sunlight Intensity	
Category	**Brightness**
Dim	2
Illuminated	3
Radiant	4
Dazzling	5

Ⓐ 125 times brighter

Ⓑ 625 times brighter

Ⓒ 3 times brighter

Ⓓ 25 times brighter

2. Patricia paid $584 for 8 nights at a hotel. Find the unit rate.

Ⓐ $\frac{\$146}{1\ night}$ Ⓒ $\frac{\$37}{1\ night}$

Ⓑ $\frac{\$584}{1\ night}$ Ⓓ $\frac{\$73}{1\ night}$

3. Valerie sold 6 tickets to the school play and Mark sold 16 tickets. What is the ratio of the number of tickets Valerie sold to the number of tickets Mark sold?

Ⓐ 16 to 6   Ⓒ 2 to 8

Ⓑ 2 to 3   Ⓓ 3 to 8

4. Grant and Pedro are comparing their stocks for the week. On Monday, their results were opposites. Explain how you would graph their results for Monday if Grant lost $4.

Ⓐ Grant's point is 4 units to the right of 0 on a number line, and Pedro's point is 4 units to the left of 0.

Ⓑ Grant's point is 4 units to the right of 0 on a number line, and Pedro's point is the same point.

Ⓒ Grant's loss is a point 4 units to the left of 0 on a number line, and Pedro's point is 4 units to the right of 0.

Ⓓ Grant's loss is a point 4 units to the left of 0 on a number line, and Pedro's point is the same point because it's already negative.

5. The fuel for a chain saw is a mix of oil and gasoline. The label says to mix 5 ounces of oil with 15 gallons of gasoline. How much oil would you use if you had 45 gallons of gasoline?

Ⓐ 21 ounces   Ⓒ 15 ounces

Ⓑ 1.67 ounces   Ⓓ 135 ounces

6. A stack of blocks is 12.3 inches tall. If there are 10 blocks stacked one on top of the other, how tall is each block?

Ⓐ 1.33 inches   Ⓒ 2.3 inches

Ⓑ 1.13 inches   Ⓓ 1.23 inches

7. Which temperature is warmest?

Ⓐ 16 °F   Ⓒ −21 °F

Ⓑ −16 °F   Ⓓ 21 °F

8. Each student needs a pencil and an eraser to take a test. If pencils come 8 in a box and erasers come 12 in a bag, what is the least number of boxes and bags needed for 24 students to each have a pencil and an eraser?

Ⓐ 3 boxes of pencils, 2 bags of erasers

Ⓑ 1 box of pencils, 1 bag of erasers

Ⓒ 8 boxes of pencils, 12 bags of erasers

Ⓓ 2 boxes of pencils, 3 bags of erasers

9. Find the quotient $7\frac{1}{6} \div \frac{5}{9}$.

Ⓐ 12   Ⓒ $12\frac{9}{10}$

Ⓑ $13\frac{1}{2}$ Ⓓ $1\frac{13}{30}$

10. Find the product 4.7×4.75.

Ⓐ 223.25   Ⓒ 22.325

Ⓑ 9.45   Ⓓ 2.2325

11. Carla is building a table out of boards that are 4.25 inches wide. She wants the table to be at least 36 inches wide. What is the least number of boards she can use?

Ⓐ 8   Ⓒ 9.5

Ⓑ 9   Ⓓ 153

12. How many centimeters are there in 740.2 millimeters?

Ⓐ 7402 cm   Ⓒ 7.402 cm

Ⓑ 74.02 cm   Ⓓ 0.7402 cm

Mini-Tasks

13. Jada is making lasagna and pizzas for a large party. Her lasagna recipe calls for $1\frac{1}{4}$ cups of tomato paste, and her pizza recipe uses $\frac{1}{2}$ cup of tomato paste per pizza. She will double her lasagna recipe and make 5 pizzas. Write and evaluate an expression for how many $\frac{3}{4}$-cup cans of tomato paste she will need in all.

 $\left(2 \cdot 1\frac{1}{4} + 5 \cdot \frac{1}{2}\right) \div \frac{3}{4} = 6\frac{2}{3}$; 7 cans

14. Explain how you can use multiplication to find the quotient $\frac{3}{5} \div \frac{3}{15}$. Then evaluate the expression.

Multiply by the reciprocal of the divisor; $\frac{3}{5} \div \frac{3}{15} = \frac{3}{5} \times \frac{15}{3} = \frac{45}{15} = 3$

15. You are working as an assistant to a chef. The chef has 8 cups of berries and will use $\frac{2}{3}$ cup of berries for each dessert he makes. How many desserts can he make?

$8 \div \frac{2}{3} = 8 \cdot \frac{3}{2} = \frac{24}{2} = 12$; 12 desserts

Performance Task

16. School A has 216 students and 12 classrooms. School B has 104 students and 4 classrooms.

Part A: What is the ratio of students to classrooms at School A?

Part B: What is the ratio of students to classrooms at School B?

Part C: How many students would have to transfer from School B to School A for the ratios of students to classrooms at both schools to be the same? Explain your reasoning.

Part A: 18 students to 1 classroom

Part B: 26 students to 1 classroom

Part C: 24 students would have to transfer from School B to School A. Since there are a total of 16 classrooms and 320 students at both schools, the ratio of students to classrooms should be 20:1. There should be 12 × 20 or 240 students at School A and 4 × 20 or 80 students at School B. 24 students must transfer.

© Houghton Mifflin Harcourt Publishing Company

Mathematics 1
Review Test

Use this test to ensure that your students have mastered the concepts from the previous course.

Scoring Guide for Performance Task

A. 1 point for correctly identifying the ratio of students to classrooms at School A.

B. 1 point for correctly identifying the ratio of students to classrooms at School B.

C. 1 point for identifying the ratio of the total number of students to the total number of classrooms. **1 point each** for finding the correct number of students at each school after the transfer. **1 point** for finding the number of students who must transfer.

Florida Common Core Standards

Items	Standards	Items	Standards
1	6.EE.1.1	9	6.NS.1.1
2	6.RP.1.2	10	6.NS.2.3
3	6.RP.1.1	11	6.NS.2.3
4	6.NS.3.5	12	6.RP.1.3d
5	6.RP.1.3	13	6.NS.1.1
6	6.NS.2.3	14	6.NS.1.1
7	6.NS.3.5	15	6.NS.1.1
8	6.NS.2.4	16	6.RP.1.1

MATHEMATICS 1 PART 2
Review Test

Personal Math Trainer
Online Assessment and Intervention
@ my.hrw.com

Selected Response

1. Kahlil is recording a beat for a song that he is working on. He wants the length of the beat to be more than 17 seconds long. His friend tells him the beat needs to be 9 seconds longer than that to match the lyrics he has written.

Write an inequality to represent the beat's length. Give three possible beat lengths that satisfy the inequality.

  Ⓐ $t < 17$
    8, 6, 5

  Ⓒ $t > 8$
    27, 35, 33

  Ⓑ $t > 26$
    27, 35, 33

  Ⓓ $t < 26$
    8, 6, 5

2. Write an expression for the missing value in the table.

Tom's Age	Kim's Age
11	14
12	15
13	16
a	?

  Ⓐ $a + 16$
  Ⓒ $a + 1$

  Ⓑ $a + 11$
  Ⓓ $a + 3$

3. A plant's height is 1.6 times its age. Write an equation for the situation. Tell what each variable you use represents.

  Ⓐ h = plant's height; y = plant's age; $1.6 = hy$

  Ⓑ h = plant's height; y = plant's age; $y = 1.6h$

  Ⓒ h = plant's age; y = plant's height; $h = 1.6y$

  Ⓓ h = plant's height; y = plant's age; $h = 1.6y$

4. A driveway is 162 feet long, 6 feet wide, and 4 inches deep. How many cubic feet of concrete will be required for the driveway?

  Ⓐ 355 ft³
  Ⓒ 3,888 ft³

  Ⓑ 324 ft³
  Ⓓ 254 ft³

5. Write the phrase as an algebraic expression.
6 less than a number times 11

  Ⓐ $6y - 11y$
  Ⓒ $11y - 6$

  Ⓑ $11 \div y$
  Ⓓ $11 + y$

6. Wilson bought gift cards for some lawyers and their assistants. Each lawyer got a gift card worth $\$\ell$. Each assistant got a gift card worth $\$a$. There are 14 lawyers. Each lawyer has 3 assistants. The expression for the total cost of the gift cards is $14\ell + 42a$. Write an expression that is equivalent to the given expression.

  Ⓐ $14(\ell + 2a)$
  Ⓒ $14(\ell + 42a)$

  Ⓑ $14(\ell + 3a)$
  Ⓓ $42(\ell + 3a)$

7. At the beginning of the year, Jason had $80 in his savings account. Each month, he added $15 to his account. Write an expression for the amount of money in Jason's savings account each month. Then use the expression to find the amount of money in his account at the end of the year.

Month	January	February	March	m
Amount	$95	$110	$125	$?

  Ⓐ $95 + 15m$; $275

  Ⓑ $95 + m$; $107

  Ⓒ $80 + 12m$; $224

  Ⓓ $15m + 80$; $260

8. In a fish tank, $\frac{6}{7}$ of the fish have a red stripe on them. If 18 of the fish have red stripes, how many total fish are in the tank?

  Ⓐ 26 fish
  Ⓒ 23 fish

  Ⓑ 21 fish
  Ⓓ 25 fish

9. Solve the equation $s + 2.8 = 6.59$.

  Ⓐ $s = 4.13$
  Ⓒ $s = 9.39$

  Ⓑ $s = 3.79$
  Ⓓ $s = 3$

10. Which question is a statistical question?

  Ⓐ How long is lunch period at your school?

  Ⓑ How old is the oldest student in your class?

  Ⓒ How many classrooms are there in your school?

  Ⓓ What are the ages of all the people in your class?

11. In a box-and-whisker plot, the *interquartile range* is a measure of the spread of the middle half of the data. Find the interquartile range for the data set: 10, 3, 7, 6, 9, 12, 13.

  Ⓐ 12
  Ⓒ 6

  Ⓑ 7
  Ⓓ 8

12. Mike was in charge of collecting contributions for the Food Bank. He received contributions of $50, $80, $60, $50, and $90. Find the mean and median of the contributions.

  Ⓐ mean: $66
    median: $60

  Ⓒ mean: $50
    median: $60

  Ⓑ mean: $50
    median: $66

  Ⓓ mean: $60
    median: $66

13. Which expression is NOT equivalent to this expression? $11y - 5$

  Ⓐ $88y - 40$
  Ⓒ $19y - 3$

  Ⓑ $5y - 11$
  Ⓓ $22y - 10$

Mini-Tasks

14. It costs $9 to go to Pete's Pottery Place to make your own bowls for $3 per bowl. Natalie goes to Pete's Pottery Place and makes b bowls. She decides to make bowls 5 days this month so she can sell them at a crafts fair.

  Part A: Write an expression that will represent Natalie's total cost for this month.

  Part B: If she makes 4 bowls each time she goes to Pete's Pottery Place, what will her total cost be?

  Part A: $5(9 + 3b)$

  Part B: $105

15. To find the mileage, or how many miles per gallon a car can travel, you can use the expression $\frac{m}{g}$, where m is the distance in miles and g is the number of gallons of gas used. Find the mileage for a car that travels 576 miles on 18 gallons of gas.

  32 mi/gal

Performance Task

16. ***Part A:*** Is $x = 6$ a solution of the equation $8x + 8 = 56$? Explain.

  Part B: Suppose the solution $x = 6$ increases to $x = 9$, and the left side of the equation stays the same. How would the right side need to change if the solution is now $x = 9$?

  Part A: Yes. When you substitute 6 for x and simplify the left side of the equation, the result is true.

  Part B: The new solution is 3 greater than the old solution. The right side of the equation $8x + 8 = 56$ should increase by $8 \cdot 3 = 24$ to result in $8x + 8 = 80$.

Florida Common Core Standards

Items	Standards		Items	Standards
1	6.EE.2.8		9	6.NS.2.3
2	6.EE.2.2		10	6.SP.1.1
3	6.EE.3.9		11	6.SP.1.2
4	6.G.1.6		12	6.SP.1.3
5	6.EE.1.2a		13	6.EE.1.4
6	6.EE.1.4		14	6.EE.1.2
7	6.EE.1.2		15	6.EE.1.2
8	6.EE.2.7		16	6.EE.2.5

Scoring Guide for Performance Task

A. 1 point for correctly answering the question.
  2 points for correctly explaining the answer.

B. 3 points for correctly explaining why the given increase in the solution produces the indicated change in the right side of the equation.

© Houghton Mifflin Harcourt Publishing Company

Selected Response

1. What are the actual dimensions of the Check-out Area?

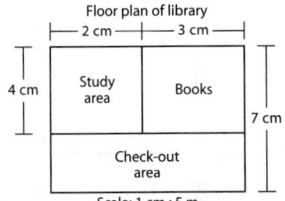

Floor plan of library

Scale: 1 cm : 5 m

Ⓐ 25 m × 15 m   Ⓒ 15 m × 35 m

Ⓑ 15 m × 20 m   Ⓓ 2 m × 4 m

2. For a history fair, a school is building a circular wooden stage that will stand 2 feet off the ground. Find the area of the stage if the radius of the stage is 19 feet. Use 3.14 for π.

Ⓐ 1,133.54 ft²   Ⓒ 2,267.08 ft²

Ⓑ 119.32 ft²   Ⓓ 4534.16 ft²

3. Find the area of the circle to the nearest tenth. Use 3.14 for π.

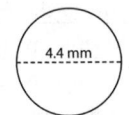

4.4 mm

Ⓐ 47.7 mm²   Ⓒ 60.8 mm²

Ⓑ 15.2 mm²   Ⓓ 13.8 mm²

4. What is the solution of the inequality $-0.4x - 1.2 > 0.8$?

Ⓐ $x < -5$ Ⓒ $x < -0.8$

Ⓑ $x < -1$ Ⓓ $x > 5$

5. Find m∠LMN.

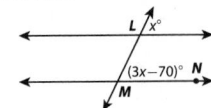

$(3x-70)°$

Ⓐ m∠LMN = 40°   Ⓒ m∠LMN = 35°

Ⓑ m∠LMN = 45°   Ⓓ m∠LMN = 50°

6. Ralph is an electrician. He charges an initial fee of $32, plus $33 per hour. If Ralph earned $197 on a job, how long did the job take?

Ⓐ 5.1 hours   Ⓒ 5 hours

Ⓑ 132 hours   Ⓓ 4 hours

7. Find the volume of the cylinder. Use 3.14 for π. Round your answer to the nearest tenth.

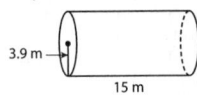

3.9 m

15 m

Ⓐ 183.7 m³   Ⓒ 2,865.6 m³

Ⓑ 716.4 m³   Ⓓ 2,755.4 m³

8. Which is the least valid way to simulate how many boys and girls are in a random sample of 20 students from a school population that is half boys and half girls?

Ⓐ Flip a coin 20 times, assigning one outcome to boys and the other to girls.

Ⓑ Drop 20 coins at once and count the number of each outcome.

Ⓒ Count how many boys and girls are in your math class and use a proportion.

Ⓓ Have a calculator generate 20 random integers and count the number of even and odd integers.

9. Roberto plays on the school baseball team. In the last 9 games, Roberto was at bat 32 times and got 11 hits. What is the experimental probability that Roberto will get a hit during his next time at bat? Express your answer as a fraction in simplest form.

Ⓐ $\frac{32}{11}$ Ⓒ $\frac{21}{32}$

Ⓑ $\frac{11}{32}$ Ⓓ $\frac{11}{21}$

10. A coin-operated machine sells plastic rings. It contains 14 pink rings, 10 green rings, 9 purple rings, and 13 black rings. Sarah puts a coin into the machine. Find the theoretical probability she gets a pink ring. Express your answer as a decimal. If necessary, round your answer to the nearest thousandth.

Ⓐ 3.286   Ⓒ 4.6

Ⓑ 0.304   Ⓓ 0.217

11. A manufacturer inspects a sample of 400 personal video players and finds that 399 of them have no defects. The manufacturer sent a shipment of 2000 video players to a distributor. Predict the number of players in the shipment that are likely to have no defects.

Ⓐ 5   Ⓒ 399

Ⓑ 1995   Ⓓ 1950

12. An experiment consists of rolling two fair number cubes. What is the probability that the sum of the two numbers will be 8? Express your answer as a fraction in simplest form.

Ⓐ $\frac{5}{36}$ Ⓒ $\frac{36}{5}$

Ⓑ $\frac{1}{9}$ Ⓓ $\frac{31}{36}$

Mini-Tasks

13. A map of Australia has a scale of 1 cm : 110 km. If the distance between Darwin and Alice Springs is 1444 kilometers, how far apart are they on the map, to the nearest tenth of a centimeter?

13.1 cm

14. The student council president wants to find out the opinion of the students on the issue of school lunch options. The president sends out a survey to a random sample of students in the school. What type of sample is this? Explain.

random sample; the students are within the population (students in school) and are randomly chosen

15. Using the following data, state the errors in the box-and-whisker plot.

33, 27, 6, 34, 31, 59, 26, 1, 30

lower quartile should be 16; upper quartile should be 33.5

Performance Task

16. The number of goals scored by a hockey team in each of its first 10 games is 2, 4, 0, 3, 4, 1, 3, 1, 1, and 5.

a. Find the mean number of goals scored.

2.4 goals

b. Find the mean absolute deviation (MAD) of the number of goals scored.

1.4

c. A second team in the same division scores a mean of 4.5 goals in its first 10 games, with the same MAD as the team above. Compare the difference in the teams' mean number of goals with the MAD in the number of goals scored.

difference in means is 2.1, which is 1.5 times MAD

Advanced Course 2
Benchmark Test

Scoring Guide for Performance Task

A. 2 points for correctly finding the mean

B. 2 points for correctly finding the mean absolute deviation

C. 2 points for correctly comparing the difference in the means with the MAD

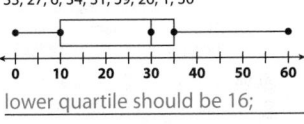

Florida Common Core Standards

Items	Standards	Items	Standards
1	7.G.1.1	9	7.RP.1.3
2	7.G.2.4	10	7.SP.3.6
3	7.G.2.4	11	7.SP.3.7
4	7.EE.2.4b	12	7.SP.3.8a
5	7.G.2.5	13	7.G.1.1
6	7.EE.2.4a	14	7.SP.1.1
7	7.G.2.6	15	7.SP.2.4
8	7.SP.1.2	16	7.SP.2.3; 7.SP.2.4

Selected Response

1. Multiply. Write the product as one power.
$a^8 \cdot a^5$

Ⓐ a^{13} Ⓒ a^{40}

Ⓑ a^3 Ⓓ Cannot combine

2. Simplify $(6^{-4})^6$.

Ⓐ -24^6 Ⓒ 6^2

Ⓑ $\frac{1}{6^{24}}$ Ⓓ $\frac{1}{6^{10}}$

3. A square mosaic is made of small glass squares. If there are 196 small squares in the mosaic, how many are along an edge?

Ⓐ 98 squares   Ⓒ 14 squares

Ⓑ 49 squares   Ⓓ 16 squares

4. Simplify $2\sqrt{-19 + 44}$.

Ⓐ 13.3   Ⓒ 10

Ⓑ 44   Ⓓ 27

5. A passenger plane travels at about 7.97×10^2 feet per second. The plane takes 1.11×10^4 seconds to reach its destination.

About how far must the plane travel to reach its destination? Write your answer in scientific notation.

Ⓐ 8.85×10^8 feet   Ⓒ 8.85×10^6 feet

Ⓑ 9.08×10^6 feet   Ⓓ 9.08×10^8 feet

6. Approximate $\sqrt{158}$ to the nearest hundredth.

Ⓐ 12.57   Ⓒ 16.57

Ⓑ 16.62   Ⓓ 8.52

7. Write a rule for the linear function.

x	y
−3	12
−2	10
3	0
5	−4

Ⓐ $y = -2x - 6$ Ⓒ $y = \frac{1}{2}x + 6$

Ⓑ $y = -2x + 6$ Ⓓ $y = \frac{1}{2}x - 6$

8. A remote-control airplane descends at a rate of 2 feet per second. After 3 seconds it is 67 feet above the ground. Write the equation in point-slope form that models the situation. Then, find the height of the plane after 8 seconds.

Ⓐ $y - 67 = -2(x - 3)$; 57 feet

Ⓑ $y - 67 = -3(x - 2)$; 49 feet

Ⓒ $y - 3 = -2(x - 67)$; 121 feet

Ⓓ $y - 2 = 67(x - 3)$; 337 feet

9. A bicyclist heads east at 19 km/h. After she has traveled 24.2 kilometers, another cyclist sets out in the same direction going 30 km/h. About how long will it take the second cyclist to catch up to the first cyclist?

Ⓐ It will take the second cyclist 3.2 hours to catch up to the first cyclist.

Ⓑ It will take the second cyclist 3.7 hours to catch up to the first cyclist.

Ⓒ It will take the second cyclist 2.2 hours to catch up to the first cyclist.

Ⓓ It will take the second cyclist 1.7 hours to catch up to the first cyclist.

10. What is the equation of the graph in slope-intercept form?

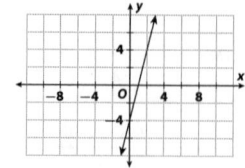

Ⓐ $y = -4x - 4$ Ⓒ $y = -5x - 4$

Ⓑ $y = 4x - 4$ Ⓓ $y = 5x - 4$

11. Solve $-2z + 3 + 7z = -12$.

Ⓐ $z = -3$ Ⓒ $z = 1$

Ⓑ $z = -15$ Ⓓ $z = -1.8$

12. Which equation has only one solution?

Ⓐ $c + 2 = c + 2$ Ⓒ $c + 2 = c - 2$

Ⓑ $c = -c + 2$ Ⓓ $c - c = 2$

13. Which ordered pair is a solution of the system of equations?
$y = 3x + 1$
$y = 5x - 1$

Ⓐ (2, 3)   Ⓒ (1, 2)

Ⓑ (0, 1)   Ⓓ (1, 4)

14. Which of these functions is *not* linear?

Ⓐ $y = x^2 - x$ Ⓒ $y = \frac{x}{3}$

Ⓑ $y = 1 - x$ Ⓓ $y = \frac{2}{3}x - 2x$

15. Which function has the greatest rate of change?

Ⓐ $y = -5x$

Ⓑ {(−1, −2), (1, 2), (3, 6), (5, 10), (7, 14)}

Ⓒ A fitness club charges a $200 membership fee plus monthly fees of $25.

Ⓓ $y = 3x - 16$

Mini-Tasks

16. The graph below shows an airplane's speed over a period of time. Describe the events.

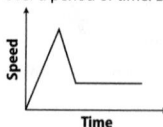

The airplane accelerates quickly on take-off, then slows down, and then proceeds at a steady speed.

17. Identify $\sqrt{\frac{169}{64}}$ as *rational* or *irrational*. Explain your reasoning.

rational; $\sqrt{\frac{169}{64}} = \frac{13}{8}$

Performance Task

18. Ashley reads 2 pages/minute for 10 minutes, takes a 10 minute break, and then reads at the same rate for 10 more minutes. Adam reads at the same rate the entire time. The equation for the number of pages he reads is $y = 1.2x$. How are these functions similar? How are they different?

Both have y-intercept 0. Adam's graph is linear, Ashley's is not. Ashley's has three parts: a line with slope 2 from (0, 0) to (10, 20), a horizontal line from (10, 20) to (20, 20) and a line with slope 2 from (20, 20) to (30, 40).

Florida Common Core Standards

Items	Standards	Items	Standards
1	8.EE.1.1	10	8.EE.2.6
2	8.EE.1.1	11	8.EE.3.7b
3	8.EE.1.2	12	8.EE.3.7a
4	8.EE.1.2	13	8.EE.3.8
5	8.EE.1.4	14	8.F.1.3
6	8.NS.1.2	15	8.F.1.2
7	8.F.1.1	16	8.F.2.5
8	8.F.2.4	17	8.NS.1.1
9	8.EE.3.8c	18	8.F.1.2

Use this test to assess students' mastery of topics in this course. The test can be used to assist with placement or as a cumulative review before high-stakes tests.

Scoring Guide for Performance Task

2 points for stating that both graphs have y-intercept 0

2 points for stating that Adam's graph is linear and Ashley's is not

2 points for correctly describing Ashley's graph

ADVANCED MATHEMATICS 2 PART 3

Benchmark Test

Personal
Math Trainer

Online
Assessment and
Intervention

my.hrw.com

Selected Response

1. In the gift shop of the History of Flight museum, Elisa bought a kit to make a model of a jet airplane. The actual plane is 21 feet long with a wingspan of 17.5 feet. If the finished model will be 12 inches long, what will the wingspan be?

Ⓐ 30.6 in.   Ⓒ 14.4 in.
Ⓑ 10 in.   Ⓓ 5 in.

2. Find the angle measures in the isosceles triangle.

Ⓐ $f = 18°$ Ⓒ $f = 68°$
Ⓑ $f = 118°$ Ⓓ $f = 11.7°$

3. Which ordered pair is a solution of the system of equations?
$y = 3x - 1$
$y = 5x + 1$

Ⓐ (4, 1)   Ⓒ (−4, −1)
Ⓑ (1, 4)   Ⓓ (−1, −4)

4. Melanie is making a piece of jewelry that is in the shape of a right triangle. The two shorter sides of the piece of jewelry are 9 mm and 12 mm. Find the perimeter of the piece of jewelry.

Ⓐ 32 mm   Ⓒ 30 mm
Ⓑ 36 mm   Ⓓ 34 mm

5. Find the distance, to the nearest tenth, from $T(4, -2)$ to $U(-2, 3)$.

Ⓐ −1.0 units   Ⓒ 0.0 units
Ⓑ 3.4 units   Ⓓ 7.8 units

6. Which of the following is *not* a congruence transformation?

Ⓐ A reflection over the *x*-axis.
Ⓑ A dilation with scale factor 0.5.
Ⓒ A translation 1 unit left.
Ⓓ A dilation with scale factor 1.

7. Harry and Selma start driving from the same location. Harry drives 42 miles north while Selma drives 144 miles east. How far apart are Harry and Selma when they stop?

Ⓐ 1,764 miles   Ⓒ 22,500 miles
Ⓑ 150 miles   Ⓓ 20,736 miles

8. Which triangle with side lengths given below is a right triangle?

Ⓐ 10, 15, 20   Ⓒ 9, 40, 41
Ⓑ 10, 24, 25   Ⓓ 16, 20, 25

9. Angles *B* and *F* are corresponding angles formed by a transversal intersecting two parallel lines. Angle *B* has a measure of 44°. What is the measure of Angle *F*?

Ⓐ 44°   Ⓒ 90°
Ⓑ 46°   Ⓓ 136°

10. Which transformation below preserves similarity between the preimage and image, but does not preserve congruence?

Ⓐ reflections   Ⓒ translations
Ⓑ rotations   Ⓓ dilations

11. An artist is creating a large conical sculpture for a park. The cone has a height of 16 m and a diameter of 25 m. Find the volume of the sculpture to the nearest hundredth.

Ⓐ 833.33 m³   Ⓒ 2,616.67 m³
Ⓑ 7,850 m³   Ⓓ 209.33 m³

12. A cylindrical barrel has a radius of 7.6 ft and a height of 10.8 ft. Tripling which dimension(s) will triple the volume of the barrel?

Ⓐ height
Ⓑ radius
Ⓒ both height and radius
Ⓓ neither height nor radius

13. Which linear equation approximates the best fit to the data?

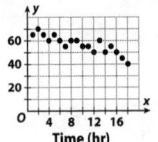

Ⓐ $y = -2x + 65$ Ⓒ $y = -x + 68$
Ⓑ $y = -5x + 100$ Ⓓ $y = -0.5x + 55$

Mini-Tasks

14. On Monday, a work group eats at Ava's café, where a lunch special is $8 and a dessert is $2. The total is $108. On Friday, the group eats at Bo's café, where a lunch special is $6 and a dessert is $3. The total is $90. Each time, the group orders the same number of lunches and the same number of desserts. How many lunches and desserts are ordered?

12 lunches, 6 desserts

15. Dilate the figure by a scale factor of 0.5 with the origin as the center of dilation.

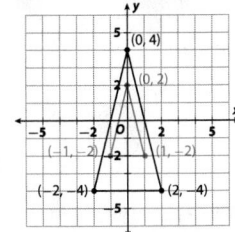

Performance Task

16. In a drought, many trees on a plot of land died. The table shows how many oak trees and pine trees survived or died.

Survived/ Died	Survived	Died	Total
Oak	60	20	80
Pine	72	48	120
Total	0	68	200

a. Create a two-way relative frequency table using decimals.

Survived/ Died	Survived	Died	TOTAL
Oak	0.30	0.10	0.40
Pine	0.36	0.24	0.60
TOTAL	0.66	0.34	1.00

b. As a percent, what was the joint relative frequency of pine trees that died?

24%

c. Compare the conditional relative frequencies, in percent form, that a tree survived given that it was an oak and that it survived given that it was a pine.

oak: 75%, pine: 60%; a greater percent of oaks survived

Florida Common Core Standards

Items	Standards		Items	Standards
1	8.G.1.4		9	8.G.1.5
2	8.G.1.5		10	8.G.1.1
3	8.EE.3.8		11	8.G.3.9
4	8.G.2.7		12	8.G.3.9
5	8.G.2.8		13	8.SP.1.2
6	8.G.1.2		14	8.EE.3.8
7	8.G.2.7		15	8.G.1.3
8	8.G.2.6		16	8.SP.1.4

Scoring Guide for Performance Task

a. 2 points for creating a correct two-way relative frequency table

b. 2 points for finding the correct joint relative frequency as a percent

c. 2 points for correctly comparing the conditional relative frequencies

UNIT 1

Expressions, Equations, and Inequalities

Contents

Unit Pacing Guide

45-Minute Classes

Module 1

DAY 1	DAY 2	DAY 3	DAY 4	DAY 5
Lesson 1.1	Lesson 1.2	Lesson 1.3	Lesson 1.4	Lesson 1.4

DAY 6				
Ready to Go On? PARCC Assessment Readiness				

Module 2

DAY 1	DAY 2	DAY 3	DAY 4	DAY 5
Lesson 2.1	Lesson 2.1	Lesson 2.2	Lesson 2.3	Ready to Go On? PARCC Assessment Readiness

DAY 6				
Study Guide PARCC Assessment Readiness				

90-Minute Classes

Module 1

DAY 1	DAY 2	DAY 3
Lesson 1.1 Lesson 1.2	Lesson 1.3 Lesson 1.4	Lesson 1.4 Ready to Go On? PARCC Assessment Readiness

Module 2

DAY 1	DAY 2	DAY 3	
Lesson 2.1	Lesson 2.2 Lesson 2.3	Ready to Go On? PARCC Assessment Readiness	Study Guide PARCC Assessment Readiness

Program Resources

⏻ Plan

Online Teacher Edition

Access a full suite of teaching resources online—plan, present, and manage classes, assignments, and activities.

ePlanner Easily plan your classes, create and view assignments, and access all program resources with your online, customizable planning tool.

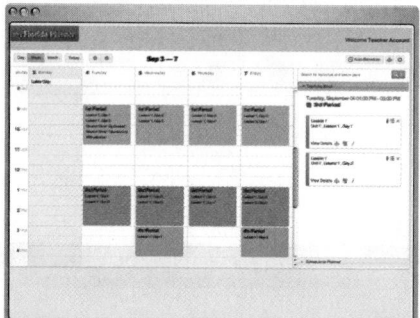

Professional Development Videos

Author Juli Dixon models successful teaching practices and strategies in actual classroom settings.

QR Codes Scan with your smart phone to jump directly from your print book to online videos and other resources.

Teacher's Edition

Support students with point-of-use Questioning Strategies, teaching tips, resources for differentiated instruction, additional activities, and more.

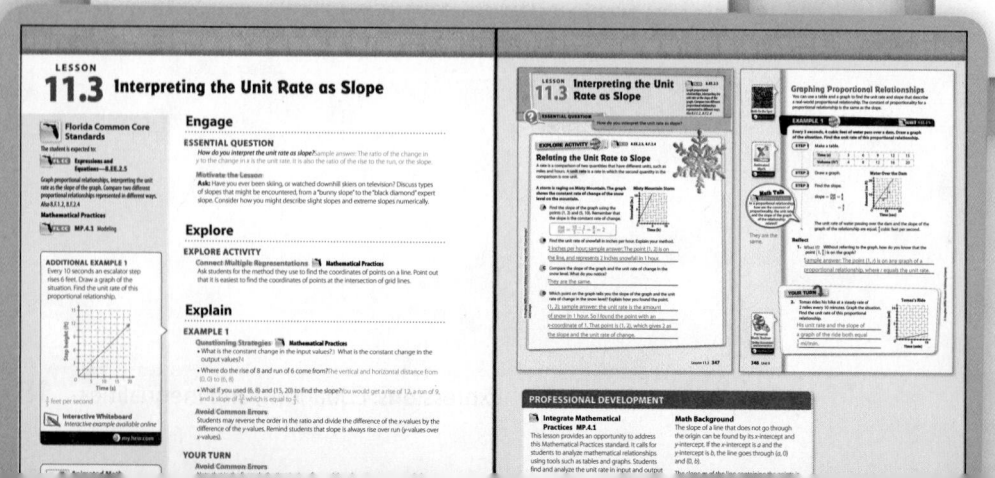

⏻ Engage and Explore

Real-World Videos Engage students with interesting and relevant applications of the mathematical content of each module.

Animated Math Online interactive simulations, tools, and games help students actively learn and practice key concepts.

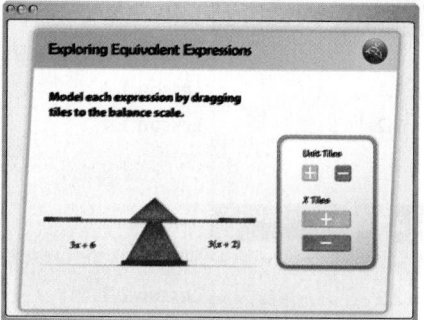

Explore Activities

Students interactively explore new concepts using a variety of tools and approaches.

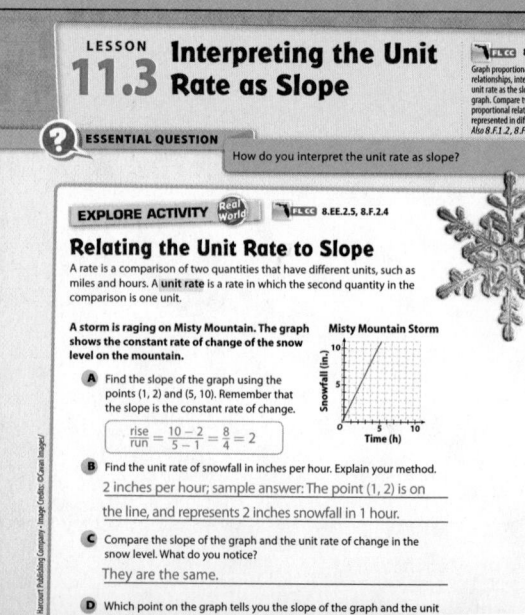

LESSON 11.3 Interpreting the Unit Rate as Slope

FL C.C 8.EE.2.5
Graph proportional relationships, interpreting the unit rate as the slope of the graph. Compare two different proportional relationships represented in different ways. Also 8.F.1.2, 8.F.2.4

? ESSENTIAL QUESTION

How do you interpret the unit rate as slope?

EXPLORE ACTIVITY Real World — FL C.C 8.EE.2.5, 8.F.2.4

Relating the Unit Rate to Slope

A rate is a comparison of two quantities that have different units, such as miles and hours. A **unit rate** is a rate in which the second quantity in the comparison is one unit.

A storm is raging on Misty Mountain. The graph shows the constant rate of change of the snow level on the mountain.

A Find the slope of the graph using the points (1, 2) and (5, 10). Remember that the slope is the constant rate of change.

$$\frac{\text{rise}}{\text{run}} = \frac{10-2}{5-1} = \frac{8}{4} = 2$$

B Find the unit rate of snowfall in inches per hour. Explain your method.

2 inches per hour; sample answer: The point (1, 2) is on the line, and represents 2 inches snowfall in 1 hour.

C Compare the slope of the graph and the unit rate of change in the snow level. What do you notice?

They are the same.

D Which point on the graph tells you the slope of the graph and the unit

⏻ Teach

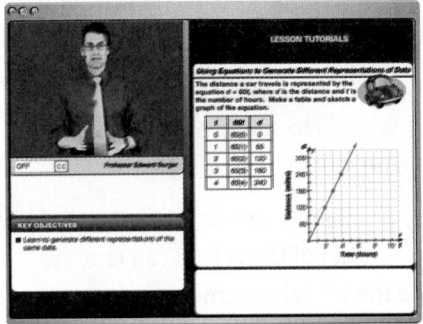

Math On the Spot video tutorials, featuring program authors Dr. Edward Burger and Martha Sandoval-Martinez, accompany every example in the textbook and give students step-by-step instructions and explanations of key math concepts.

Present engaging content on a multitude of devices, including tablets and interactive whiteboards.

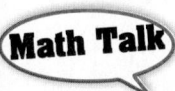

Math Talk Continually monitor and assess student progress with integrated formative assessment.

CLUSTER CONNECTION Look for exercises indicated with this icon to build connections among standards within Florida Common Core clusters.

Differentiated Instruction Print Resources

Support all learners with Differentiated Instruction Resources, including

- **Leveled Practice and Problem Solving**
- **Reteach**
- **Reading Strategies**
- **Success for English Learners**
- **Challenge**

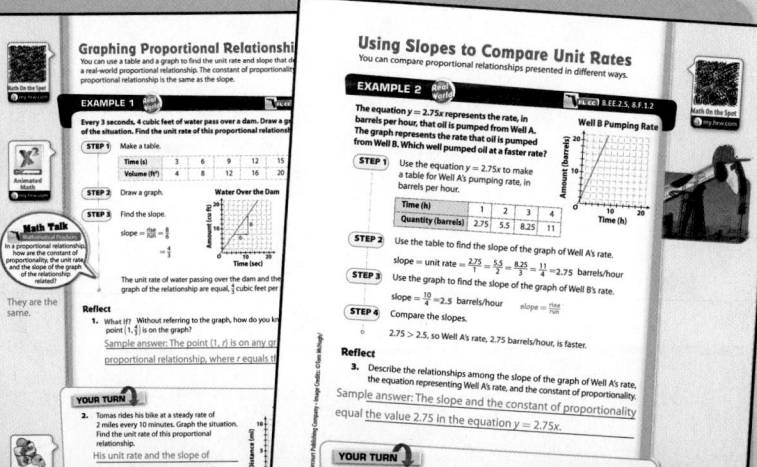

Graphing Proportional Relationship
You can use a table and a graph to find the unit rate and slope that de a real-world proportional relationship. The constant of proportionalit proportional relationship is the same as the slope.

EXAMPLE 1

Every 3 seconds, 4 cubic feet of water pass over a dam. Draw a g of the situation. Find the unit rate of this proportional relationsh

STEP 1 Make a table.

Time (s)	3	6	9	12	15
Volume (ft³)	4	8	12	16	20

STEP 2 Draw a graph.

STEP 3 Find the slope.

The unit rate of water passing over the dam and the graph of the relationship are equal, ⁴⁄₃ cubic feet per

Reflect

1. What If? Without referring to the graph, how do you k point (1, ⁴⁄₃) is on any gr
Sample answer: The point (1, r) is on any gr proportional relationship, where r equals th

YOUR TURN

2. Tomas rides his bike at a steady rate of 2 miles every 10 minutes. Graph the situation. Find the unit rate of this proportional relationship.
His unit rate and the slope of

Using Slopes to Compare Unit Rates
You can compare proportional relationships presented in different ways.

EXAMPLE 2

The equation $y = 2.75x$ represents the rate, in barrels per hour, that oil is pumped from Well A. The graph represents the rate that oil is pumped from Well B. Which well pumped oil at a faster rate?

Well B Pumping Rate

STEP 1 Use the equation $y = 2.75x$ to make a table for Well A's pumping rate, in barrels per hour.

Time (h)	1	2	3	4
Quantity (barrels)	2.75	5.5	8.25	11

STEP 2 Use the table to find the slope of the graph of Well A's rate.
slope = unit rate = $\frac{2.75}{1} = \frac{5.5}{2} = \frac{8.25}{3} = \frac{11}{4} = 2.75$ barrels/hour

STEP 3 Use the graph to find the slope of the graph of Well B's rate.
slope = $\frac{10}{4} = 2.5$ barrels/hour   slope = $\frac{rise}{run}$

STEP 4 Compare the slopes.
$2.75 > 2.5$, so Well A's rate, 2.75 barrels/hour, is faster.

Reflect

3. Describe the relationships among the slope of the graph of Well A's rate, the equation representing Well A's rate, and the constant of proportionality.
Sample answer: The slope and the constant of proportionality equal the value 2.75 in the equation $y = 2.75x$.

YOUR TURN

⏻ Assessment and Intervention

The **Personal Math Trainer** provides online practice, homework, assessments, and intervention. Monitor student progress through reports and alerts. Create and customize assignments aligned to specific lessons or standards.

- **Practice** – With dynamic items and assignments, students get unlimited practice on key concepts supported by guided examples, step-by-step solutions, and video tutorials.

- **Assessments** – Choose from course assignments or customize your own based on course content, standards, difficulty levels, and more.

- **Homework** – Students can complete online homework with a wide variety of problem types, including the ability to enter expressions, equations, and graphs. Let the system automatically grade homework, so you can focus where your students need help the most!

- **Intervention** – Let the Personal Math Trainer automatically prescribe a targeted, personalized intervention path for your students.

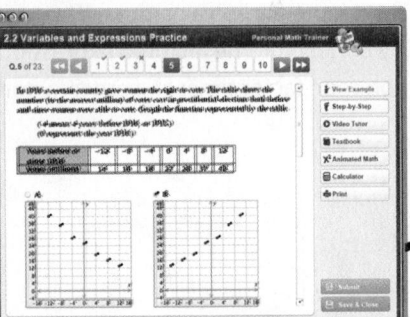

Raise the bar with homework and practice that incorporates higher-order thinking and mathematical processes in every lesson.

PARCC Assessment Readiness
Prepare students for success on the PARCC math test with practice at every module and unit.

Assessment Resources

Tailor assessments to meet the needs of all your classes and students, including

- **Leveled Module Quizzes**
- **Leveled Unit Tests**
- **Unit Performance Tasks**
- **Placement, Diagnostic, and Quarterly Benchmark Tests**

Math Background

Algebraic Expressions 7.EE.1.1
LESSON 1.1

The properties of addition can be used along with the Distributive Property to perform operations with algebraic expressions. Expressions are added by combining like terms. The Commutative and Associative Properties may be used to make combining like terms easier.

Expressions are subtracted by first rewriting the subtraction as addition of the opposite.

The Distributive Property is used to multiply an algebraic expression by a constant. Each term in the expression is multiplied by the constant, and the products are added.

Factoring a constant out of an expression is the inverse operation of multiplying an expression by a constant. The first step is finding a common factor and dividing each term by that factor. The factored expression is written as the common factor times the other factored expression.

Equations with Rational Numbers 7.EE.2.3
LESSONS 1.2 to 1.4

When solutions to equations are fractions or decimals, it is especially important that students evaluate the reasonableness of their solutions to real-world problems. For example, consider the following problem.

> It costs $6.50 to become a member of a store that rents DVDs. With a membership, it costs $2.40 to rent each DVD. Paul wants to become a member and rent DVDs, and he plans to spend a total of $20. How many DVDs can he rent?

The first step in solving the problem is choosing a variable, such as x, to represent the number of DVDs Paul can rent. Then students should write the verbal statements as an algebraic equation: $6.5 + 2.4x = 20$. The usual process may be used to solve this two-step equation, resulting in the solution $x = 5.625$.

At this point, many students will consider the problem solved. However, they should get in the habit of revisiting the original problem to see whether the solution makes sense. In this situation, it is not possible to rent part of a DVD, so the correct solution is 5 DVDs. Notice that 5.625 is not simply rounded to the nearest whole number. Rather, the solution must be interpreted thoughtfully in the context of the original problem.

Writing and Solving Two-Step Equations 7.EE.2.4, 7.EE.2.4a
LESSONS 1.3 and 1.4

A two-step linear equation may be written in the form $ax + b = c$, where a, b, and c are real numbers, $a \neq 0$ or 1, and $b \neq 0$. For example, the equation $60 = 100 - 5x$ may be written as the equivalent equation $-5x + 100 = 60$, and so $a = -5$, $b = 100$, and $c = 60$. The equation $\frac{x-4}{3} = 2.5$ is equivalent to $\frac{x}{3} - \frac{4}{3} = 2.5$ or $\frac{1}{3}x - \frac{4}{3} = 2.5$, and so $a = \frac{1}{3}$, $b = -\frac{4}{3}$, and $c = 2.5$.

Every equation of the form $ax + b = c$ with $a \neq 0$ has one solution, namely $\frac{c-b}{a}$. Recall that a solution is a value of the variable that makes the equation true. Substituting this value for x in the left side of the equation gives the following.

$$a\left(\frac{c-b}{a}\right) + b = c - b + b = c$$

In other words, $x = \frac{c-b}{a}$ makes the equation true and therefore is a solution.

It is worth noting that $x = \frac{c-b}{a}$ may be considered the "Linear Formula" because it gives the solution to any equation of the form $ax + b = c$, where $a \neq 0$, much in the same way the Quadratic Formula gives the solutions of any equation of the form $ax^2 + bx + c = 0$ with $a \neq 0$.

It still remains to be shown that $ax + b = c$ has *only one* solution. To do so, suppose that the values x_1 and x_2 are both solutions. Then it must be true that $ax_1 + b = c$ and $ax_2 + b = c$. Thus,

$$ax_1 + b = ax_2 + b$$
$$\underline{-b = \quad -b} \qquad \textit{Subtraction Property of Eq.}$$
$$ax_1 = ax_2$$
$$\frac{ax_1}{a} = \frac{ax_2}{a} \qquad \textit{Division Property of Eq.}$$
$$x_1 = x_2$$

The preceding discussion shows that every two-step linear equation has one and only one solution. Students are unlikely to question this fact, but they should realize that they will later encounter equations that have no solution, two solutions, and even infinitely many solutions.

Writing and Solving Inequalities
7.EE.2.4
LESSONS 2.1 to 2.3

Solving an inequality in one variable is similar to solving an equation in one variable. The goal is to isolate the variable on one side of the inequality by writing a series of inequalities that have the same solution set.

The Addition and Subtraction Properties of Inequality state that the same quantity may be added to or subtracted from both sides of an inequality without changing the solution set. That is, if $a > b$, then $a + c > b + c$ and $a - c > b - c$. Multiplying or dividing both sides of an inequality by a *positive* number also produces an inequality with the same solution set as the original inequality. In general terms, if $a > b$ and $c > 0$, then $ac > bc$ and $\frac{a}{b} > \frac{b}{c}$.

When multiplying or dividing both sides of an inequality by a *negative* number, however, the inequality symbol must be reversed. Thus, if $a > b$ and $c < 0$, then $ac < bc$ and $\frac{a}{c} < \frac{b}{c}$.

To see why this is the case, consider the inequality $a > b$. This inequality can be rewritten as follows by using the Subtraction Property of Inequality twice.

$$a > b$$
$$a - a > b - a$$
$$0 > b - a$$
$$0 - b > b - a - b$$
$$-b > -a$$

The final inequality can also be written as $-a < -b$, which shows that the inequality symbol is reversed when both sides of the original inequality are multiplied by -1.

Some students may benefit from seeing a similar example involving integers. It is often helpful for students to check the solution of an inequality by substituting specific values for the variable.

Expressions, Equations, and Inequalities

CAREERS IN MATH

Mechanical Engineer A mechanical engineer designs, develops, and manufactures mechanical devices and technological systems. Mechanical engineers use math to solve diverse problems, from calculating the strength of materials to determining energy consumption of a device.

If you are interested in a career in mechanical engineering, you should study these mathematical subjects:
- Algebra
- Geometry
- Trigonometry
- Statistics
- Calculus

Research other careers that require the daily use of mathematics to solve problems.

Unit 1 Performance Task

At the end of the unit, check out how **mechanical engineers** use math.

Careers in Math

Mechanical Engineer

A mechanical engineer uses her creativity to synthesize, solve problems, and innovate. Mathematics is the language of engineering. You will learn more about how mechanical engineers use math in the Performance Tasks at the end of the unit.

For more information about careers in mathematics as well as various mathematics appreciation topics, visit the American Mathematical Society at www.ams.org

Vocabulary Preview

Use the puzzle to give students a preview of important concepts in this unit. Students may work individually, in pairs, or in groups.

Unit Resources

Go online to access all your unit resources.

my.hrw.com

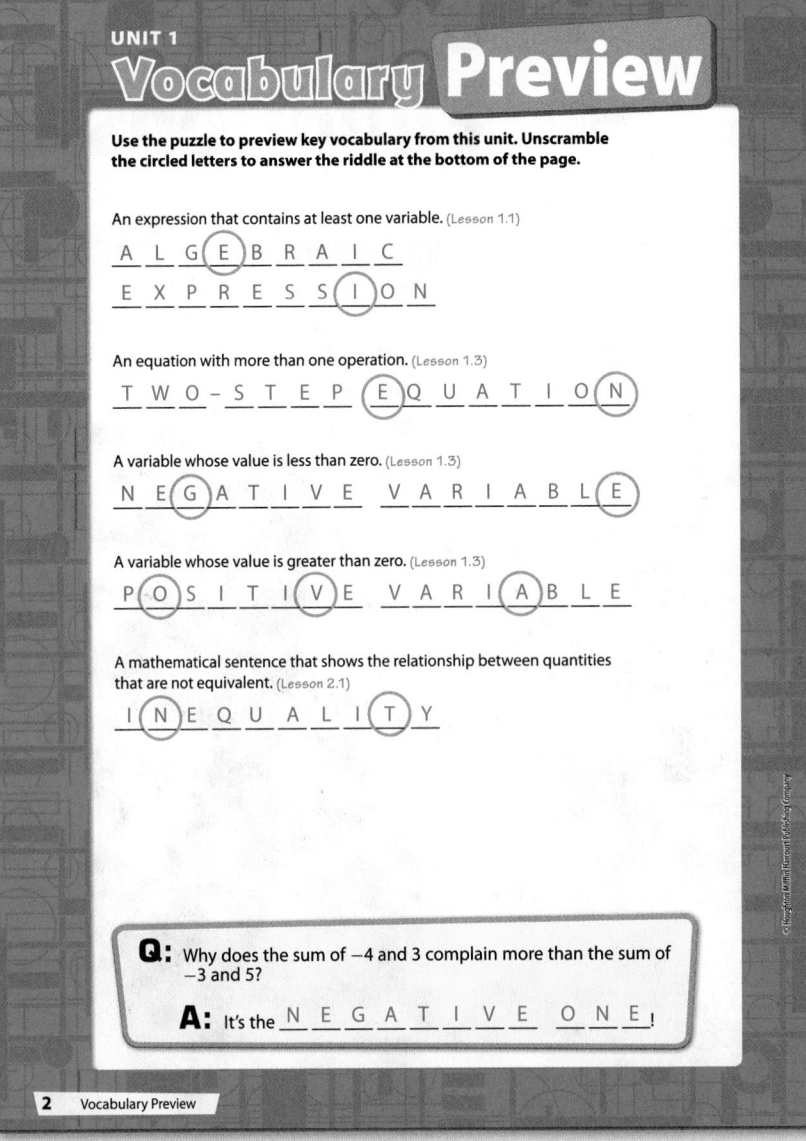

UNIT 1

Vocabulary Preview

Use the puzzle to preview key vocabulary from this unit. Unscramble the circled letters to answer the riddle at the bottom of the page.

An expression that contains at least one variable. (Lesson 1.1)

A L G E B R A I C
E X P R E S S I O N

An equation with more than one operation. (Lesson 1.3)

T W O - S T E P   E Q U A T I O N

A variable whose value is less than zero. (Lesson 1.3)

N E G A T I V E   V A R I A B L E

A variable whose value is greater than zero. (Lesson 1.3)

P O S I T I V E   V A R I A B L E

A mathematical sentence that shows the relationship between quantities that are not equivalent. (Lesson 2.1)

I N E Q U A L I T Y

Q: Why does the sum of −4 and 3 complain more than the sum of −3 and 5?

A: It's the N E G A T I V E   O N E !

Before	In this Unit	After
Students understand: • how to model and solve one-step, one-variable equations and inequalities that contain addition or subtraction • how to model and solve one-step, one-variable equations and inequalities that contain multiplication or division • how to represent a given situation using verbal descriptions, tables, graphs, and equations in the form $y = kx$ or $y = x + b$	Students will learn about: • writing and solving two-step equations • writing and solving two-step inequalities	Students will connect: • two-step equations and equations with variables on both sides and rational number coefficients and constants • two-step inequalities and inequalities with variables on both sides and rational number coefficients and constants

Expressions and Equations

ESSENTIAL QUESTION

How can you use algebraic expressions and equations to solve real-world problems?

You can model real-world problems with equations, then use algebraic rules to solve the equations.

Real-World Video

When you take a taxi, you will be charged an initial fee plus a charge per mile. To describe situations like this, you can write a two-step equation.

my.hrw.com

GO DIGITAL

my.hrw.com

my.hrw.com

Go digital with your write-in student edition, accessible on any device.

Math On the Spot

Scan with your smart phone to jump directly to the online edition, video tutor, and more.

Animated Math

Interactively explore key concepts to see how math works.

Personal Math Trainer

Get immediate feedback and help as you work through practice sets.

Are You Ready?

Assess Readiness

Use the assessment on this page to determine if students need intensive or strategic intervention for the module's prerequisite skills.

 **Response to Intervention**

Personal Math Trainer

Online Assessment and Intervention

my.hrw.com

Intervention	Enrichment

Access Are You Ready? assessment online, and receive instant scoring, feedback, and customized intervention or enrichment.

Online and Print Resources

Skills Intervention worksheets
- Skill 53 Words for Operations
- Skill 54 Evaluate Expressions
- Skill 42 Operations with Fractions

Differentiated Instruction
- Challenge worksheets **PRE-AP**
- Extend the Math **PRE-AP** Lesson Activities in TE

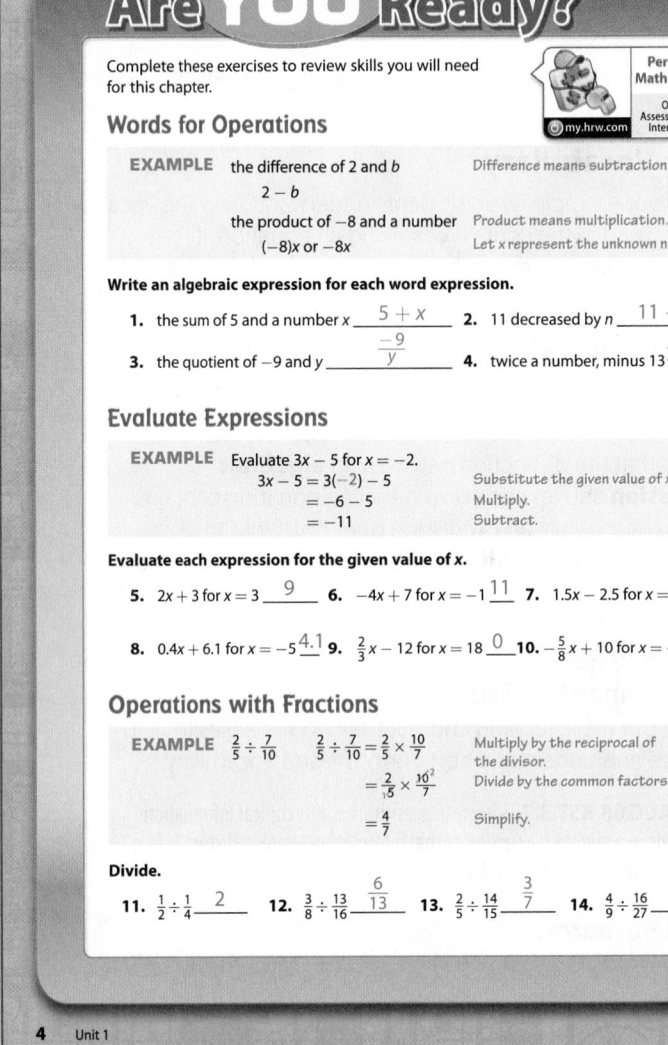

Are YOU Ready?

Complete these exercises to review skills you will need for this chapter.

Personal Math Trainer
Online Assessment and Intervention
my.hrw.com

Words for Operations

EXAMPLE	the difference of 2 and b	Difference means subtraction.
	$2 - b$	
	the product of -8 and a number	Product means multiplication.
	$(-8)x$ or $-8x$	Let x represent the unknown number.

Write an algebraic expression for each word expression.

1. the sum of 5 and a number x ___$5 + x$___
2. 11 decreased by n ___$11 - n$___
3. the quotient of -9 and y ___$\frac{-9}{y}$___
4. twice a number, minus 13 ___$2x - 13$___

Evaluate Expressions

EXAMPLE	Evaluate $3x - 5$ for $x = -2$.	
	$3x - 5 = 3(-2) - 5$	Substitute the given value of x for x.
	$= -6 - 5$	Multiply.
	$= -11$	Subtract.

Evaluate each expression for the given value of x.

5. $2x + 3$ for $x = 3$ ___9___
6. $-4x + 7$ for $x = -1$ ___11___
7. $1.5x - 2.5$ for $x = 3$ ___2___
8. $0.4x + 6.1$ for $x = -5$ ___4.1___
9. $\frac{2}{3}x - 12$ for $x = 18$ ___0___
10. $-\frac{5}{8}x + 10$ for $x = -8$ ___15___

Operations with Fractions

EXAMPLE	$\frac{2}{5} \div \frac{7}{10}$	$\frac{2}{5} \div \frac{7}{10} = \frac{2}{5} \times \frac{10}{7}$	Multiply by the reciprocal of the divisor.
		$= \frac{2}{{}_1 5} \times \frac{10^2}{7}$	Divide by the common factors.
		$= \frac{4}{7}$	Simplify.

Divide.

11. $\frac{1}{2} \div \frac{1}{4}$ ___2___
12. $\frac{3}{8} \div \frac{13}{16}$ ___$\frac{6}{13}$___
13. $\frac{2}{5} \div \frac{14}{15}$ ___$\frac{3}{7}$___
14. $\frac{4}{9} \div \frac{16}{27}$ ___$\frac{3}{4}$___

PROFESSIONAL DEVELOPMENT VIDEO

Author Juli Dixon models successful teaching practices as she explores expressions in an actual seventh-grade classroom.

Professional Development

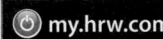 my.hrw.com

 **GO DIGITAL**
my.hrw.com

 Online Teacher Edition
Access a full suite of teaching resources online—plan, present, and manage classes and assignments.

 ePlanner
Easily plan your classes and access all your resources online.

 Interactive Answers and Solutions
Customize answer keys to print or display in the classroom. Choose to include answers only or full solutions to all lesson exercises.

 Interactive Whiteboards
Engage students with interactive whiteboard-ready lessons and activities.

 **Personal Math Trainer: Online Assessment and Intervention**
Assign automatically graded homework, quizzes, tests, and intervention activities. Prepare your students with updated practice tests aligned with Common Core.

Reading Start-Up

Have students complete the activities on this page by working alone or with others.

Visualize Vocabulary

The stepped out example helps students understand how the vocabulary terms are used in the context of solving an equation. If time permits, have students perform the same activity with a different equation.

Understand Vocabulary

Use the following explanations to help students learn the preview words.

Explain that the distinction between an **algebraic expression** and an **equation** is that an equation contains an equal sign while an expression does not. Only an equation can have a **solution**, although some expressions can be simplified.

Active Reading

Integrating Language Arts

Students can use these reading and note-taking strategies to help them organize and understand new concepts and vocabulary.

FL CC **LACC.68.RST.3.7** Integrate quantitative or technical information expressed in words in a text with a version of that information expressed visually (e.g., in a flowchart, diagram, model, graph, or table).

Additional Resources

Differentiated Instruction

• Reading Strategies **ELL**

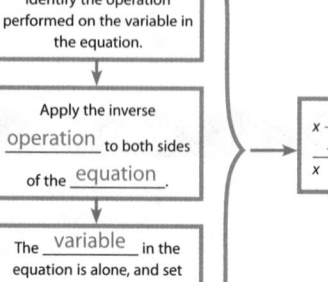

Reading Start-Up

Visualize Vocabulary

Use the ✔ words to complete the graphic. You may put more than one word in each box.

Vocabulary

Review Words
- algebraic expression *(expresión algebraica)*
- Distributive Property *(Propiedad distributiva)*
- ✔ equation *(ecuación)*
- factor *(factor)*
- ✔ operation *(operacion)*
- ✔ solution *(solución)*
- ✔ variable *(variable)*

Identify the operation performed on the variable in the equation.

↓

Apply the inverse <u>operation</u> to both sides of the <u>equation</u>.

↓

The <u>variable</u> in the equation is alone, and set equal to the <u>solution</u>.

$$x - 5.5 = 3$$
$$+5.5 \quad +5.5$$
$$x \quad = \quad 8.5$$

Add 5.5 to both sides. The solution is $x = 8.5$.

Understand Vocabulary

Complete the sentences using the review words.

1. A(n) <u>algebraic expression</u> contains at least one variable.

2. A mathematical sentence that shows that two expressions are equivalent is called a(n) <u>equation</u>.

Active Reading

Tri-Fold Before beginning the module, create a tri-fold to help you learn the concepts and vocabulary in this module. Fold the paper into three sections. Label the columns "What I Know," "What I Need to Know," and "What I Learned." Complete the first two columns before you read. After studying the module, complete the third column.

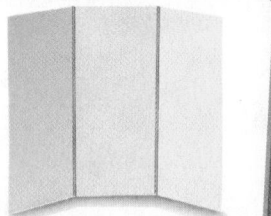

Before	In this module	After
Students understand rational numbers: • one-step, one-variable equations • how to solve one-step, one-variable equations that contain addition or subtraction • how to solve one-step, one-variable equations that contain multiplication or division	Students will learn how to: • write two-step equations to represent real-world problems, and write a real-world problem to represent an equation • solve two step equations	Students will connect: • two-step equations and equations with variables on both sides and rational number coefficients and constants.

Unpacking the Standards

Use the exercises on this page to determine if students need intensive or strategic intervention for the module's prerequisite skills.

 Florida Common Core Standards

Content Areas

 FL CC Expressions and Equations—7.EE.1

Use properties of operations to generate equivalent expressions.

FL CC Expressions and Equations—7.EE.2

Solve real-life and mathematical problems using numerical and algebraic expressions and equations.

Go online to see a complete unpacking of the Florida Common Core Standards.

my.hrw.com

MODULE 1
Unpacking the Standards

Understanding the standards and the vocabulary terms in the standards will help you know exactly what you are expected to learn in this module.

FL CC 7.EE.1.1

Apply properties of operations as strategies to add, subtract, factor, and expand linear expressions with rational coefficients.

Key Vocabulary
coefficient *(coeficiente)*
The number that is multiplied by the variable in an algebraic expression.

rational number *(número racional)* Any number that can be expressed as a ratio of two integers.

What It Means to You

You will use your knowledge of properties of operations to write equivalent expressions.

UNPACKING EXAMPLE 7.EE.1.1

Expand the expression $2(a + 7)$ using the distributive property.

$$2(a + 7) = 2 \cdot a + 2 \cdot 7 \qquad \text{Multiply each term in parentheses by 2.}$$
$$= 2a + 14$$

FL CC 7.EE.2.4a

Solve word problems leading to equations of the form $px + q = r$ and $p(x + q) = r$, where p, q, and r are specific rational numbers. Solve equations of these forms fluently.

Key Vocabulary
equation *(ecuación)*
A mathematical sentence that shows that two expressions are equivalent.

solution *(solución)*
The value for the variable that makes the equation true.

 Visit my.hrw.com to see all Florida Common Core Standards unpacked.

my.hrw.com

What It Means to You

You will write and solve real-world equations that require two steps.

UNPACKING EXAMPLE 7.EE.2.4a

Jai and Lúpe plan to rent a kayak. The rental is $12 for the first hour and $9 for each hour after that. If they have $50, for how long can they rent the kayak?

Rental Charge $= 12 + 9x$, where x is the number of hours after the first hour.

$$50 = 12 + 9x$$
$$50 - 12 = 12 - 12 + 9x \qquad \text{Subtract 12 from both sides.}$$
$$38 = 9x$$
$$\frac{38}{9} = x, \text{ or } x \approx 4.2 \qquad \text{Divide both sides by 9.}$$

They can rent the kayak for 4 hours.

Florida Common Core Standards	Lesson 1.1	Lesson 1.2	Lesson 1.3	Lesson 1.4
FL CC 7.EE.1.1 Apply properties of operations as strategies to add, subtract, factor, and expand linear expressions with rational coefficients.				
FL CC 7.EE.2.4 Use variables to represent quantities in a real-world or mathematical problem, and construct simple equations and inequalities to solve problems by reasoning about the quantities.		✓	✓	
FL CC 7.EE.2.4a Solve word problems leading to equations of the form $px + q = r$ and $p(x + q) = r$, where p, q, and r are specific rational numbers. Solve equations of these forms fluently. Compare an algebraic solution to an arithmetic solution, identifying the sequence of the operations used in each approach.				✓
FL CC 7.EE.2.4b Solve word problems leading to inequalities of the form $px + q > r$ or $px + q < r$, where p, q, and r are specific rational numbers. Graph the solution set of the inequality and interpret it in the context of the problem.		✓		

© Houghton Mifflin Harcourt Publishing Company

LESSON
1.1 Algebraic Expressions

ADDITIONAL EXAMPLE 1
Each week, Steven gets an allowance of $8 plus $3 for each chore he does. His younger sister Jill gets an allowance of $6 plus $2 per chore. Write an expression for how much their parents give Steven and Jill each week if they do the same number of chores.

$14 + 5c$

 Interactive Whiteboard
Interactive example available online

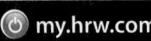 my.hrw.com

---

ADDITIONAL EXAMPLE 2
A group of 5 people go out to eat and buy appetizers and main dishes. They decide to split the bill so each person pays 20% of the total cost. Appetizers are $5 and main dishes are $10. Write an expression to show how much each person pays.

$0.2 \times (5a + 10m)$ or $a + 2m$

 Interactive Whiteboard
Interactive example available online

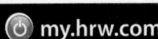 my.hrw.com

---

Engage

ESSENTIAL QUESTION
How do you add, subtract, factor, and multiply algebraic expressions? Sample answer: You can use the properties of addition and the Distributive Property to add and subtract algebraic expressions by combining like terms. You can use the Distributive Property to multiply and factor algebraic expressions.

Motivate the Lesson
Ask: Can you think of some quantities that vary and some quantities that stay the same?

Explore

Connect to Daily Life
Discuss with students how temperature and prices are examples of quantities that vary, but the length of a day and the year someone was born are examples of quantities that stay the same. Brainstorm other examples of quantities that vary and quantities that stay the same.

Explain

EXAMPLE 1
Connect Multiple Representations 🖊 Mathematical Practices
Make sure students understand that an algebraic expression is another way of representing the information from a verbal expression.

Questioning Strategies 🖊 Mathematical Practices
• Why is the Commutative Property used to simplify the expression? It allows the order of the addends to be switched so that the like terms are together.

• What property is used to combine like terms? Distributive Property

YOUR TURN
Avoid Common Errors
In Your Turn 3, students may forget to distribute the negative sign to the second term within the parentheses. Remind students to distribute the negative sign to each term.

EXAMPLE 2
Connect Multiple Representations 🖊 Mathematical Practices
Make sure students understand that a percent can be changed to a decimal or a fraction.

Questioning Strategies 🖊 Mathematical Practices
• How could you write the expression representing what the band gets to keep using a fraction instead of a decimal? $\frac{1}{4} \times (16.60a + 12.20c)$.

• What expression could you write to represent how much the band does *not* get to keep? Sample answer: $\frac{3}{4} \times (16.60a + 12.20c)$.

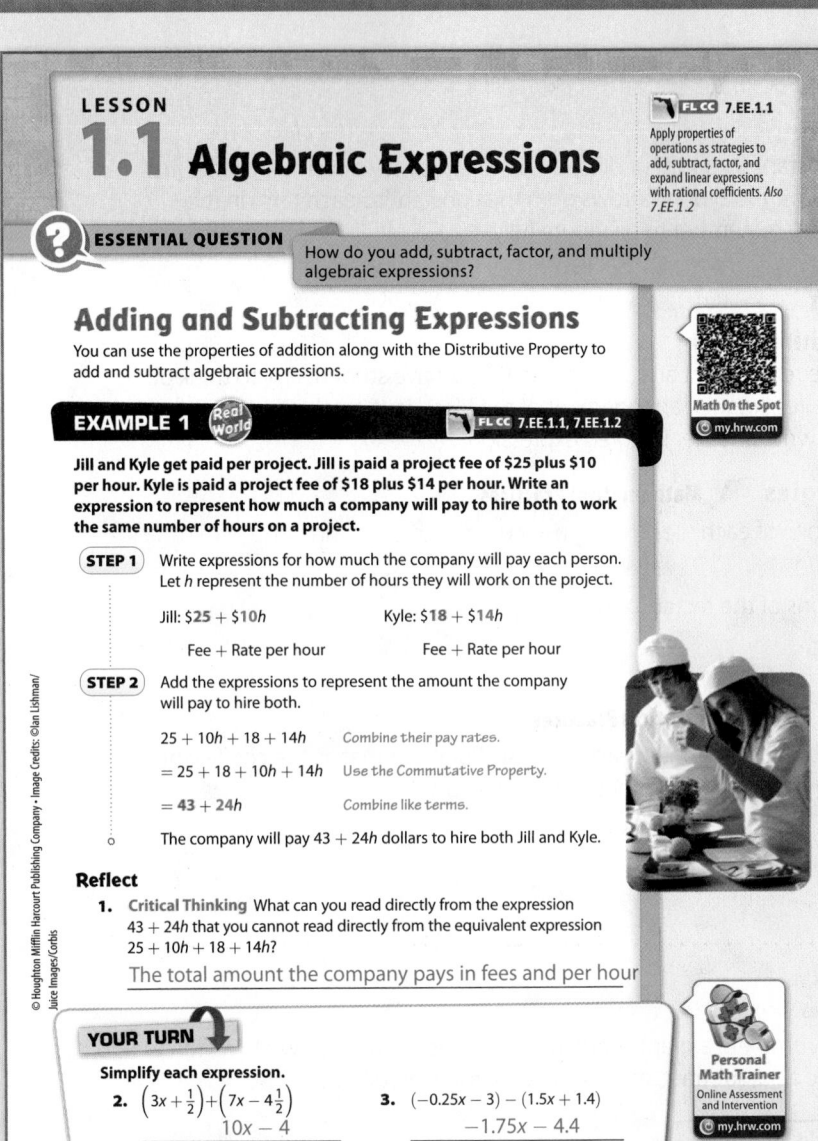

LESSON 1.1 Algebraic Expressions

FL CC 7.EE.1.1
Apply properties of operations as strategies to add, subtract, factor, and expand linear expressions with rational coefficients. Also 7.EE.1.2

? ESSENTIAL QUESTION
How do you add, subtract, factor, and multiply algebraic expressions?

Adding and Subtracting Expressions

You can use the properties of addition along with the Distributive Property to add and subtract algebraic expressions.

EXAMPLE 1 Real World   FL CC 7.EE.1.1, 7.EE.1.2

Jill and Kyle get paid per project. Jill is paid a project fee of $25 plus $10 per hour. Kyle is paid a project fee of $18 plus $14 per hour. Write an expression to represent how much a company will pay to hire both to work the same number of hours on a project.

STEP 1 Write expressions for how much the company will pay each person. Let h represent the number of hours they will work on the project.

Jill: $\$25 + \$10h$ Kyle: $\$18 + \$14h$

Fee + Rate per hour   Fee + Rate per hour

STEP 2 Add the expressions to represent the amount the company will pay to hire both.

$25 + 10h + 18 + 14h$ *Combine their pay rates.*

$= 25 + 18 + 10h + 14h$ *Use the Commutative Property.*

$= 43 + 24h$ *Combine like terms.*

The company will pay $43 + 24h$ dollars to hire both Jill and Kyle.

Reflect

1. **Critical Thinking** What can you read directly from the expression $43 + 24h$ that you cannot read directly from the equivalent expression $25 + 10h + 18 + 14h$?

   The total amount the company pays in fees and per hour

YOUR TURN

Simplify each expression.

2. $\left(3x + \frac{1}{2}\right) + \left(7x - 4\frac{1}{2}\right)$

   $10x - 4$

3. $(-0.25x - 3) - (1.5x + 1.4)$

   $-1.75x - 4.4$

Personal Math Trainer
Online Assessment and Intervention
my.hrw.com

Math On the Spot
my.hrw.com

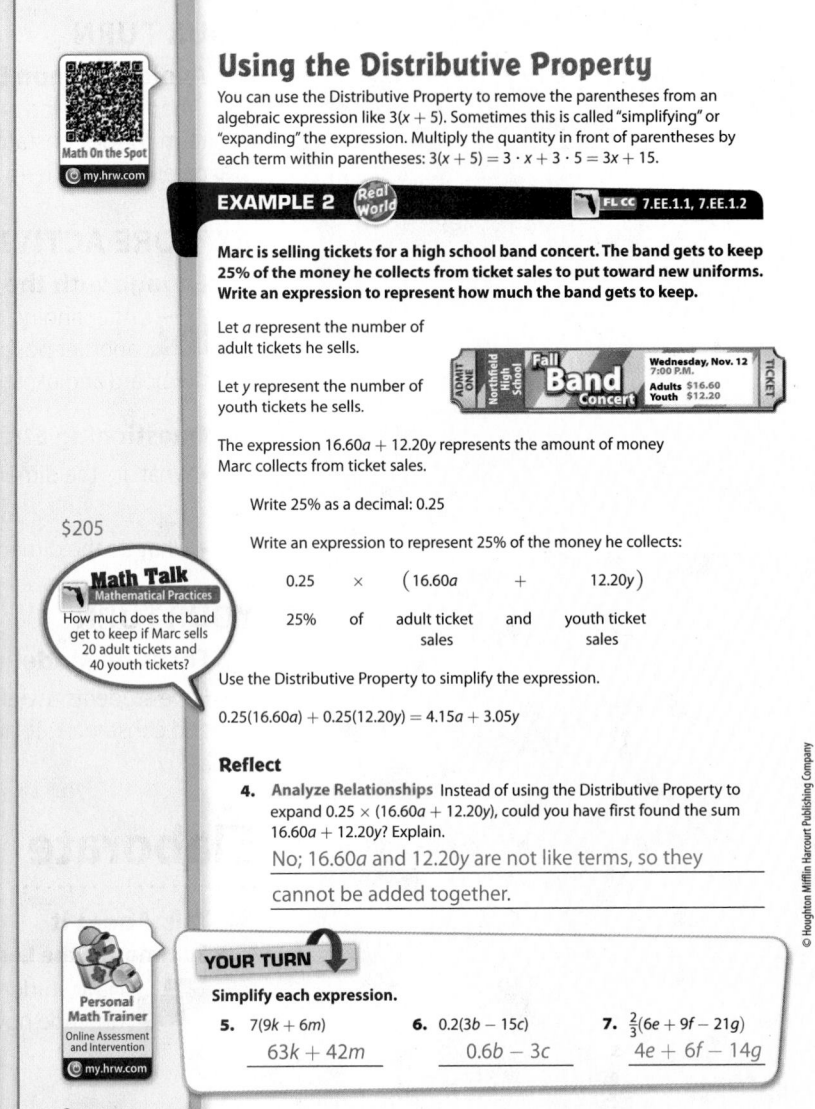

Using the Distributive Property

You can use the Distributive Property to remove the parentheses from an algebraic expression like $3(x + 5)$. Sometimes this is called "simplifying" or "expanding" the expression. Multiply the quantity in front of parentheses by each term within parentheses: $3(x + 5) = 3 \cdot x + 3 \cdot 5 = 3x + 15$.

EXAMPLE 2 Real World   FL CC 7.EE.1.1, 7.EE.1.2

Marc is selling tickets for a high school band concert. The band gets to keep 25% of the money he collects from ticket sales to put toward new uniforms. Write an expression to represent how much the band gets to keep.

Let a represent the number of adult tickets he sells.

Let y represent the number of youth tickets he sells.

The expression $16.60a + 12.20y$ represents the amount of money Marc collects from ticket sales.

Write 25% as a decimal: 0.25

Write an expression to represent 25% of the money he collects:

0.25	$\times$	$(16.60a$	$+$	$12.20y)$
25%	of	adult ticket sales	and	youth ticket sales

Use the Distributive Property to simplify the expression.

$0.25(16.60a) + 0.25(12.20y) = 4.15a + 3.05y$

Math Talk
Mathematical Practices
How much does the band get to keep if Marc sells 20 adult tickets and 40 youth tickets?

Reflect

4. **Analyze Relationships** Instead of using the Distributive Property to expand $0.25 \times (16.60a + 12.20y)$, could you have first found the sum $16.60a + 12.20y$? Explain.

   No; 16.60a and 12.20y are not like terms, so they cannot be added together.

YOUR TURN

Simplify each expression.

5. $7(9k + 6m)$
   $63k + 42m$

6. $0.2(3b - 15c)$
   $0.6b - 3c$

7. $\frac{2}{3}(6e + 9f - 21g)$
   $4e + 6f - 14g$

Personal Math Trainer
Online Assessment and Intervention
my.hrw.com

$205

Math On the Spot
my.hrw.com

PROFESSIONAL DEVELOPMENT

Integrate Mathematical Practices MP.4.1

This lesson provides an opportunity to address this Mathematical Practice standard. It calls for students to model with mathematics. Defining variables links the symbols to their real-world meanings. Substituting values for the variables allows students to interpret the results in the context of the situation. Students use the sum of expressions to model the situation, to solve the problem, and to answer the question in context.

Math Background

An algebraic expression is a mathematical statement constructed from at least one variable and possibly one or more operation symbols and one or more numbers. The table shows examples and nonexamples of algebraic expressions.

Algebraic Expressions	
Examples	$x, 3y - 5, -2xy, z^2 + 1$
Nonexamples	$7, 20 \div (4 + 1), 4x = 16$

Note that an algebraic expression must not contain an equal sign. A mathematical statement that contains an equal sign, such as $4x = 16$, is an equation.

YOUR TURN

Avoid Common Errors

When multiplying a constant by a sum or difference, students may only multiply the first term by the constant. Have them draw arrows from the constant to each term in the parentheses to help them remember to distribute fully.

EXPLORE ACTIVITY

Engage with the Whiteboard

 After finding one rectangular arrangement in Part B, have students try to think of another possible rectangular arrangement of the tiles. Have a volunteer draw it on the board and use it to write another factored expression: $2(2x + 4)$.

Questioning Strategies 🟫 Mathematical Practices

• What are the dimensions of each tile? The x-tile is x units long and 1 unit wide. The 1-tiles are 1 unit long and 1 unit wide.

• What do the dimensions of the rectangle represent? the factors

YOUR TURN

Focus on Modeling 🟫 Mathematical Practices

Have students use algebra tiles to model each exercise. Point out that as the coefficients and constants get larger, modeling becomes more unwieldy.

Elaborate

Talk About It
Summarize the Lesson

 Have students complete a graphic organizer, such as the one shown here, to describe how to add, subtract, multiply, and factor expressions.

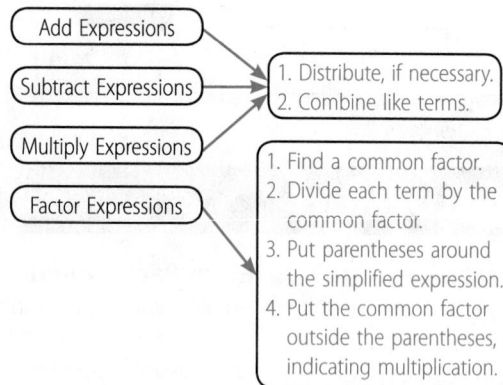

GUIDED PRACTICE

Engage with the Whiteboard

Have students volunteer to fill in the blanks in Guided Practice 1–4 and draw algebra tiles to represent the factoring for Guided Practice 5.

Avoid Common Errors

Exercise 6 Remind students that there are several ways to factor the expression. The correct answer is found by placing the greatest possible factor outside the parentheses.

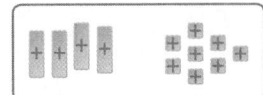
EXPLORE ACTIVITY

Factoring Expressions

A **factor** is a number that is multiplied by another number to get a product. To **factor** is to write a number or an algebraic expression as a product.

Factor $4x + 8$.

A Model the expression with algebra tiles.

Use ___4___ positive x tiles and ___8___ +1-tiles.

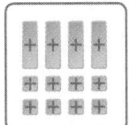

B Arrange the tiles to form a rectangle. The total area represents $4x + 8$.

Sample answer:

C Since the length multiplied by the width equals the area, the length and the width of the rectangle are the factors of $4x + 8$. Find the length and width.

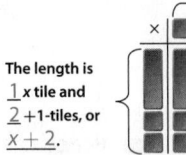 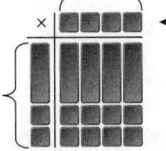

The width is $\underline{4}$ +1-tiles, or $\underline{4}$.

The length is $\underline{1}$ x tile and $\underline{2}$ +1-tiles, or $x + 2$.

D Use the expressions from the length and width of the rectangle to write the area of the rectangle, $4x + 8$, in factored form. ___$4(x + 2)$___

Reflect

8. Communicate Mathematical Ideas How could you use the Distributive Property to check your factoring?

Multiply the factors. The result should be the original expression.

YOUR TURN

Factor each expression.

9. $2x + 2$ **10.** $3x + 9$ **11.** $5x + 15$ **12.** $4x + 16$

$2(x + 1)$ $3(x + 3)$ $5(x + 3)$ $4(x + 4)$

Personal Math Trainer
Online Assessment and Intervention
my.hrw.com

---

1. The manager of a summer camp has 14 baseballs and 23 tennis balls. The manager buys some boxes of baseballs with 12 baseballs to a box and an equal number of boxes of tennis balls with 16 tennis balls to a box. Write an expression to represent the total number of balls. (Example 1)

STEP 1 Write expressions for the total number of baseballs and tennis balls. Let n represent the number of boxes of each type.

baseballs: $\underline{14} + (\underline{12})n$ tennis balls: $\underline{23} + (\underline{16})n$

STEP 2 Find an expression for the total number of balls.

$\underline{14} + \underline{12n} + \underline{23} + \underline{16n}$ Combine the two expressions.

$\underline{14} + \underline{23} + \underline{12n} + \underline{16n}$ Use the Commutative Property.

$\underline{37} + \underline{28n}$ Combine like terms.

So, the total number of baseballs and tennis balls is $\underline{37} + \underline{28n}$.

2. Use the expression you found above to find the total number of baseballs and tennis balls if the manager bought 9 boxes of each type. (Example 1) ___289___

Use the Distributive Property to expand each expression. (Example 2)

3. $0.5(12m - 22n)$

$0.5(12m - 22n) = 0.5(\underline{12m}) - 0.5(\underline{22n})$ Distribute 0.5 to both terms in parentheses.

$= \underline{6m} - \underline{11n}$ Multiply.

4. $\frac{2}{3}(18x + 6z)$

$\frac{2}{3}(\underline{18x}) + \frac{2}{3}(\underline{6z}) = \underline{12x} + \underline{4z}$

Factor each expression. (Example 3)

5. $2x + 12$ **6.** $12x + 24$ **7.** $7x + 35$

$2(x + 6)$ $12(x + 2)$ $7(x + 5)$

? ESSENTIAL QUESTION CHECK-IN

8. What is the relationship between multiplying and factoring?

You multiply numbers or expressions to produce a product. You factor a product into the numbers or expressions that were multiplied to produce it.

DIFFERENTIATE INSTRUCTION

Modeling

Provide students with algebra tiles. Have students model expressions such as the following.

$(2x + 8) + (4x - 3)$
$(7x + 5) - (3x + 1)$
$(-4x + 2) - (x + 6)$

Students should combine tiles of the same type or remove zero pairs to create simplified models of the expressions. Have the students write the simplified expressions.

Visual Cues

When multiplying a constant by a sum or difference, have students first draw arrows from the constant to each term inside the parentheses. The arrows remind students to also distribute the multiplication to the other terms. For example.

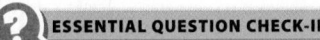

$0.4(9x + 5y) = 0.4(9x) + 0.4(5y)$

Additional Resources

Differentiated Instruction includes:

- Reading Strategies
- Success for English Learners **ELL**
- Reteach
- Challenge **PRE-AP**

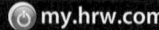
1.1 LESSON QUIZ

 **FL CC** 7.EE.1.1

A company sets up a food booth and a game booth at the county fair. The fee for the food booth is $100 plus $5 per day. The fee for the game booth is $50 plus $7 per day.

1. Write an expression for how much both booths will cost for the same number of days.

2. How much does the company pay for both booths for 5 days?

Simplify each expression.

3. $(-0.75x + 6) - (2.5x - 1.9)$

4. $8(5x - 3y)$

Factor each expression.

5. $4x + 20$

6. $6x + 54$

Lesson Quiz available online

ⓘ my.hrw.com

Answers

1. $100 + 5d + 50 + 7d$, or $150 + 12d$

2. $210

3. $-3.25x + 7.9$

4. $40x - 24y$

5. $4(x + 5)$

6. $6(x + 9)$

Evaluate

GUIDED AND INDEPENDENT PRACTICE

 **FL CC** 7.EE.1.1

Concepts & Skills	Practice
Example 1 Adding and Subtracting Expressions	Exercises 1, 2, 9, 10, 14, 15
Example 2 Using the Distributive Property	Exercises 3, 4, 13
Explore Activity Factoring Expressions	Exercises 5–9, 11, 12

Exercise	Depth of Knowledge (D.O.K.)	**FL CC** Mathematical Practices
9–10	**2** Skills/Concepts	**MP.4.1** Modeling
11–12	**2** Skills/Concepts	**MP.5.1** Using tools
13	**3** Strategic Thinking **H.O.T.**	**MP.3.1** Logic
14–15	**2** Skills/Concepts	**MP.2.1** Reasoning
16	**2** Skills/Concepts	**MP.1.1** Problem Solving
17	**2** Skills/Concepts	**MP.2.1** Reasoning
18	**3** Strategic Thinking **H.O.T.**	**MP.7.1** Using Structure
19	**3** Strategic Thinking **H.O.T.**	**MP.3.1** Logic

Additional Resources

Differentiated Instruction includes:

• Leveled Practice Worksheets

CLUSTER CONNECTION **Exercises 9 and 10** combine concepts from the Florida Common Core cluster "Use properties of operations to generate equivalent expressions."

1.1 Independent Practice

FL CC 7.EE.1.1, 7.EE.1.2

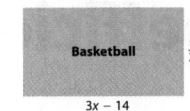
Personal Math Trainer

Online Assessment and Intervention

my.hrw.com

Write and simplify an expression for each situation.

9. A company rents out 15 food booths and 20 game booths at the county fair. The fee for a food booth is $100 plus $5 per day. The fee for a game booth is $50 plus $7 per day. The fair lasts for d days, and all the booths are rented for the entire time. Write and simplify an expression for the amount in dollars that the company is paid.

$15(100 + 5d) + 20(50 + 7d) = 2,500 + 215d$

10. A rug maker is using a pattern that is a rectangle with a length of 96 inches and a width of 60 inches. The rug maker wants to increase each dimension by a different amount. Let ℓ and w be the increases in inches of the length and width. Write and simplify an expression for the perimeter of the new pattern.

$2(96 + \ell) + 2(60 + w) = 312 + 2\ell + 2w$

In 11–12, identify the two factors that were multiplied together to form the array of tiles. Then identify the product of the two factors.

11.  3 and $x + 2$; $3x + 6$

12.  4 and $2x - 1$; $8x - 4$

13. Explain how the figure illustrates that $6(9) = 6(5) + 6(4)$.

The area is the product of the length and width (6×9). It is also the sum of the areas of the rectangles separated by the dashed line (6×5 and 6×4). So, $6(9) = 6(5) + 6(4)$.

In 14–15, the perimeter of the figure is given. Find the length of the indicated side.

14.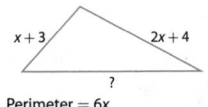
$x + 3$, $2x + 4$, ?
Perimeter = $6x$
$3x - 7$

15.
$3x - 3$, ?
Perimeter = $10x + 6$
$2x + 6$

© Houghton Mifflin Harcourt Publishing Company • Image Credits: ©Hemera Technologies/Jupiterimages/Getty Images

---

16. **Persevere in Problem Solving** The figures show the dimensions of a tennis court and a basketball court given in terms of the width x in feet of the tennis court.

Tennis x
$2x + 6$

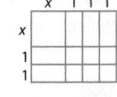
Basketball $\frac{1}{2}x + 32$
$3x - 14$

a. Write an expression for the perimeter of each court. T: $6x + 12$, B: $7x + 36$

b. Write an expression that describes how much greater the perimeter of the basketball court is than the perimeter of the tennis court. $x + 24$

c. Suppose the tennis court is 36 feet wide. Find all dimensions of the two courts. T: 36 ft by 78 ft, B: 50 ft by 94 ft

H.O.T. FOCUS ON HIGHER ORDER THINKING

Work Area

17. **Draw Conclusions** Use the figure to find the product $(x + 3)(x + 2)$. (*Hint*: Find the area of each small square or rectangle, then add.)

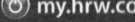
x 1 1 1
x
1
1

$(x + 3)(x + 2) = $ $x^2 + 5x + 6$

18. **Communicate Mathematical Ideas** Desmond claims that the product shown at the right illustrates the Distributive Property. Do you agree? Explain why or why not.

```
   58
 × 23
  174
 1160
1,334
```

Agree. To find 58×23, let $23 = 3 + 20$. Then find the product $58(3 + 20)$. First step: $58(3) = 174$. Second step: $58(20) = 1,160$. Third step: $174 + 1160 = 1,334$. So, $58(23) = 58(3) + 58(20)$

19. **Justify Reasoning** Describe two different ways that you could find the product 8×997 using mental math. Find the product and explain why your methods work.

(1) Think of 997 as $1,000 - 3$. So, $8 \times 997 = 8(1,000 - 3)$. By the Distributive Property, $8(1,000 - 3) = 8,000 - 24 = 7,976$. (2) Think of 997 as $900 + 90 + 7$. By the Distributive Property, $8(900 + 90 + 7) = 7,200 + 720 + 56 = 7,976$.

© Houghton Mifflin Harcourt Publishing Company

EXTEND THE MATH PRE-AP

Activity available online my.hrw.com

Challenge

A rectangle with a length of $x + 5$ has a perimeter of $4x + 14$.

1. Write the expression for the width of the rectangle in terms of x.

2. Suppose the perimeter of the rectangle is 42 inches. What are the length and width of the rectangle?

3. Write the expression for the area of the rectangle in terms of x.

4. What is the area of the rectangle when $x = 7$?

1. $x + 2$

2. length is 12 in., width is 9 in.

3. $x^2 + 7x + 10$

4. 108 in²

Florida Common Core Standards

The student is expected to:

 **Expressions and Equations—7.EE.2.4**

Use variables to represent quantities in a real-world or mathematical problem, and construct simple equations and inequalities to solve problems by reasoning about the quantities.

Mathematical Practices

 **MP.7.1** Using Structure

---

ADDITIONAL EXAMPLE 1
Use inverse operations to solve each equation.

A $x - 5.6 = -1.7$ $x = 3.9$

B $y + \frac{3}{4} = 6$ $y = 5\frac{1}{4}$

C $0.7n = -3.5$ $n = -5$

D $\frac{c}{2.5} = -4.2$ $c = -10.5$

 Interactive Whiteboard
Interactive example available online

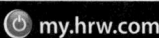 my.hrw.com

Engage

ESSENTIAL QUESTION

How do you use one-step equations with rational coefficients to solve problems?
Sample answer: You write an equation for the situation and solve the equation by using inverse operations.

Motivate the Lesson
Ask: What kinds of real-world quantities can negative numbers represent? What kinds of quantities can fractions or decimals represent?

Explore

Connect to Daily Life
Have students suggest a story or problem that might fit the equation $-8.5 + x = -2$ using a real-world context, such as owing money, degrees below zero, or feet below sea level.

Explain

EXAMPLE 1

Talk About It
Check for Understanding
 Ask: Which operation is shown in each part of the example? What is the inverse operation for each part? Part A: addition; subtraction; Part B: subtraction; addition; Part C; multiplication; division; Part D: division; multiplication.

Questioning Strategies Mathematical Practices
• Does it matter which side of the equals sign the variable is on when you solve the equation? no

• How do you check that your solution is correct? Substitute your answer for the variable in the original equation. If both sides remain equal, then it is the solution.

YOUR TURN

Engage with the Whiteboard
Have a student volunteer circle the symbol that represents the operation in each exercise and then identify the inverse operation needed to solve the equation. Be sure to note that the lack of a symbol in exercise 3 means multiplication.

Avoid Common Errors
Some students may focus on determining which inverse operation is needed to solve the equation, but only perform the inverse operation on the side of the equation that contains the variable. Remind students to perform the same operation on both sides of the equation.

FL CC 7.EE.2.4

Use variables to represent quantities in a real-world or mathematical problem, and construct simple equations ... to solve problems by reasoning about the quantities.

? ESSENTIAL QUESTION
How do you use one-step equations with rational coefficients to solve problems?

One-Step Equations

You have written and solved one-step equations involving whole numbers. Now you will learn to work with equations containing negative numbers.

Math On the Spot
my.hrw.com

EXAMPLE 1
FL CC 7.EE.2.4

Use inverse operations to solve each equation.

A $x + 3.2 = -8.5$

$x + 3.2 = -8.5$
$\underline{\quad -3.2 \quad\quad -3.2}$ Subtract -3.2 from both sides.
$x = -11.7$

B $-\frac{2}{3} + y = 8$

$-\frac{2}{3} + y = 8$
$\underline{+\frac{2}{3} \quad\quad +\frac{2}{3}}$ Add $\frac{2}{3}$ to both sides.
$y = 8\frac{2}{3}$

$-7.5 = -1.5n$

C $30 = -0.5a$

$\dfrac{30}{-0.5} = \dfrac{-0.5a}{-0.5}$ Divide both sides by -0.5.
$-60 = a$

D $-\dfrac{q}{3.5} = 9.2$

$-\dfrac{q}{3.5}(-3.5) = 9.2\,(-3.5)$ Multiply both sides by -3.5.
$q = -32.2$

YOUR TURN

Use inverse operations to solve each equation.

1. $4.9 + z = -9$
$z = -13.9$

2. $r - 17.1 = -4.8$
$r = 12.3$

3. $-3c = 36$
$c = -12$

Personal Math Trainer
Online Assessment and Intervention
my.hrw.com

Math On the Spot
my.hrw.com

Writing and Solving One-Step Addition and Subtraction Equations

Negative numbers often appear in real-world situations. For example, elevations below sea level are represented by negative numbers. When you increase your elevation, you are moving in a positive direction. When you decrease your elevation, you are moving in a negative direction.

EXAMPLE 2
FL CC 7.EE.2.4

A scuba diver is exploring at an elevation of -12.2 meters. As the diver rises to the surface, she plans to stop and rest briefly at a reef that has an elevation of -4.55 meters. Find the vertical distance that the diver traveled.

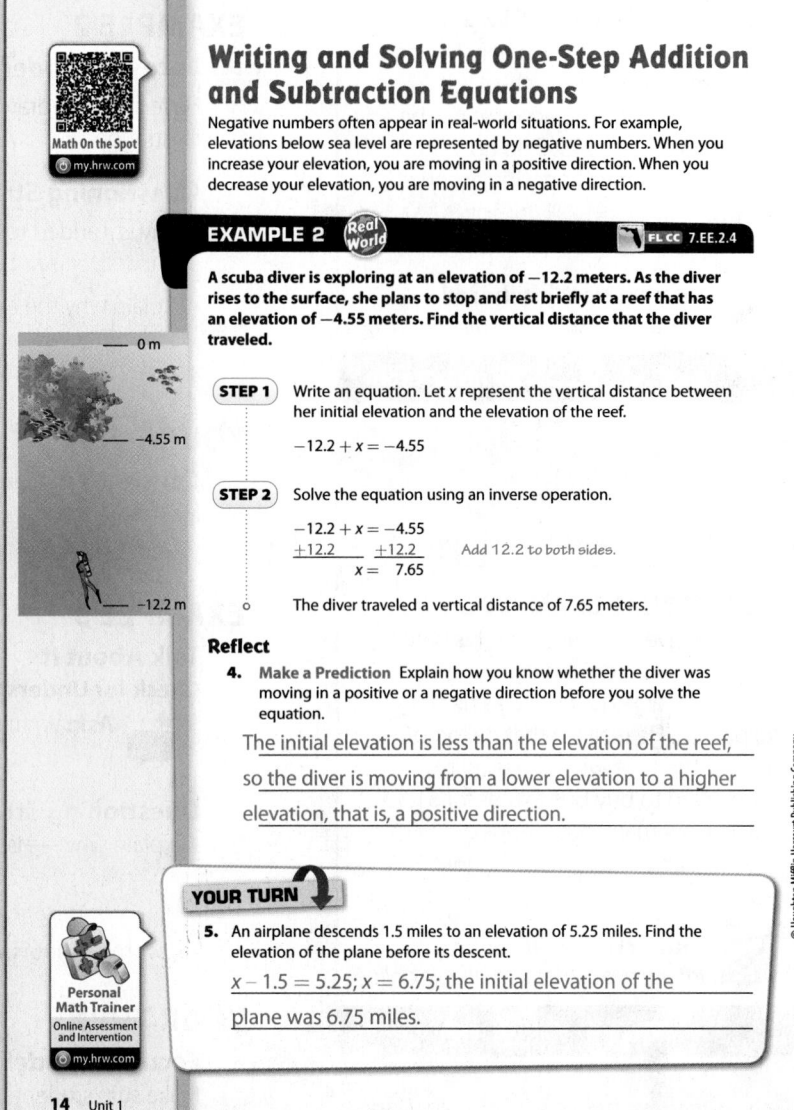

— 0 m
— -4.55 m
— -12.2 m

STEP 1 Write an equation. Let x represent the vertical distance between her initial elevation and the elevation of the reef.

$-12.2 + x = -4.55$

STEP 2 Solve the equation using an inverse operation.

$-12.2 + x = -4.55$
$\underline{+12.2 \quad\quad +12.2}$ Add 12.2 to both sides.
$x = 7.65$

The diver traveled a vertical distance of 7.65 meters.

Reflect

4. **Make a Prediction** Explain how you know whether the diver was moving in a positive or a negative direction before you solve the equation.

The initial elevation is less than the elevation of the reef,
so the diver is moving from a lower elevation to a higher
elevation, that is, a positive direction.

YOUR TURN

5. An airplane descends 1.5 miles to an elevation of 5.25 miles. Find the elevation of the plane before its descent.

$x - 1.5 = 5.25; x = 6.75;$ the initial elevation of the
plane was 6.75 miles.

Personal Math Trainer
Online Assessment and Intervention
my.hrw.com

PROFESSIONAL DEVELOPMENT

Integrate Mathematical Practices MP.7.1

This lesson provides an opportunity to address this Mathematical Practice standard. It calls for students to look for and make use of structure. When students solve one-step equations, they first look at the equation to identify the operation involved. Then they identify and use the inverse operation to solve the equation.

Math Background

A solution of an equation is the value of the variable that makes the equation true. Operations that undo each other, such as addition and subtraction, and multiplication and division, are called inverse operations. Inverse operations are used to solve equations. To solve an equation, the operation performed on the variable must be undone, leaving the variable alone, or isolated, on one side of the equation. The value on the other side of the equals sign should be the solution of the equation, if the solution process was performed properly.

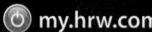

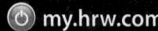
EXAMPLE 2

Focus on Modeling **Mathematical Practices**

Have students draw a diagram that illustrates the problem or explain how to use the given illustration.

Questioning Strategies **Mathematical Practices**

- Why is x added to -12.2 in the equation in Step 1? Sample answer: It indicates that the scuba diver is rising in a positive direction.

- Explain why the equation $-12.2 + x = -4.55$ can be rewritten as $x - 12.2 = -4.55$. By the Commutative Property of Addition, the addends can be switched, and subtracting is the same as adding the opposite.

YOUR TURN

Connect Vocabulary **ELL**

Make sure students understand that the word *descends* means that the airplane is going down, indicating subtraction.

EXAMPLE 3

Talk About It
Check for Understanding

 Ask: What is the product when you multiply a fraction by its reciprocal? The product is 1.

Questioning Strategies **Mathematical Practices**

- Explain why $-\frac{3}{4}$ is multiplied by $-\frac{4}{3}$ instead of being multiplied by $-\frac{3}{4}$. You need to multiply by the reciprocal of the coefficient of x to get a coefficient of 1. The product of $-\frac{3}{4}$ and $-\frac{3}{4}$ is not 1.

- How many hours will it take for the temperature to decrease by 5 °F? $6\frac{2}{3}$ hours

YOUR TURN

Focus on Modeling

Make sure students understand how to express the relationship for each situation. Remind them to use unit analysis to help them write the correct equation.

Elaborate

Talk About It
Summarize the Lesson

 Ask: Which operations are inverses of each other? Why must you perform the same operation on both sides of the equation when isolating the variable? Sample answer: Addition and subtraction are inverse operations that undo each other. Multiplication and division are inverse operations that undo each other. In order for the rewritten equation to have the same solution as the original, you must keep the equation in balance by performing exactly the same operation on both sides.

GUIDED PRACTICE

Engage with the Whiteboard

 Have a student cross out the unnecessary information in the table in Exercise 1.

Avoid Common Errors

Exercise 2 Remind students to multiply by negative two thirds, not two thirds, to isolate x.

Writing and Solving One-Step Multiplication and Division Problems

Temperatures can be both positive and negative, and they can increase or decrease during a given period of time. A decrease in temperature is represented by a negative number. An increase in temperature is represented by a positive number.

Math On the Spot
⊙ my.hrw.com

EXAMPLE 3   Real World   FL CC 7.EE.2.4

Between the hours of 10 P.M. and 6 A.M., the temperature decreases an average of $\frac{3}{4}$ of a degree per hour. How many minutes will it take for the temperature to decrease by 5 °F?

STEP 1   Write an equation. Let x represent the number of hours it takes for the temperature to decrease by 5 °F.

$$-\frac{3}{4}x = -5$$

STEP 2   Solve the equation using an inverse operation.

$$-\frac{3}{4}x = -5$$

$$-\frac{4}{3}\left(-\frac{3}{4}x\right) = -\frac{4}{3}(-5) \qquad \text{Multiply both sides by } -\frac{4}{3}.$$

$$x = \frac{20}{3}$$

STEP 3   Convert the number of hours to minutes.

$$\frac{20}{3} \text{ hours} \times \frac{60 \text{ minutes}}{1 \text{ hour}} = 400 \text{ minutes}$$

It takes 400 minutes for the temperature to decrease by 5 °F.

> **Math Talk**
> Mathematical Practices
>
> Why is multiplying by $-\frac{4}{3}$ the inverse of multiplying by $-\frac{3}{4}$?
>
> Multiplying by $-\frac{4}{3}$ is the same as dividing by $-\frac{3}{4}$.

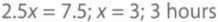

YOUR TURN

6. The value of a share of stock decreases in value at a rate of $1.20 per hour during the first 3.5 hours of trading. Write and solve an equation to find the decrease in the value of the share of stock during that time.

   $\frac{x}{3.5} = -1.2$; $x = -4.2$; $4.20

7. After a power failure, the temperature in a freezer increased at an average rate of 2.5 °F per hour. The total increase was 7.5 °F. Write and solve an equation to find the number of hours until the power was restored.

   $2.5x = 7.5$; $x = 3$; 3 hours

Personal Math Trainer
Online Assessment and Intervention
⊙ my.hrw.com

The table shows the average temperature in Barrow, Alaska, for three months during one year.

Month	Average Temperature (°F)
January	−13.4
June	34.0
November	−1.7

1. How many degrees warmer is the average temperature in November than in January? (Examples 1 and 2)

   STEP 1   Write an equation. Let x represent the number of degrees warmer the average temperature is in Nov. than in Jan.

   $$x + \underline{(-13.4)} = \underline{-1.7}, \text{ or } x - \underline{13.4} = \underline{-1.7}$$

   STEP 2   Solve the equation. Show your work.

   The average temperature in November is $\underline{11.7}$ °F warmer.

   $$\begin{aligned} x - 13.4 &= -1.7 \\ +13.4 \quad &+13.4 \\ \hline x &= 11.7 \end{aligned}$$

2. Suppose that during one period of extreme cold, the average daily temperature decreased $1\frac{1}{2}$ °F each day. How many days did it take for the temperature to decrease by 9 °F? (Examples 1 and 3)

   STEP 1   Write an equation. Let x represent the number of days it takes the average temperature to decrease by 9 °F

   $$-1\frac{1}{2}\,x = \underline{-9}$$

   STEP 2   Solve the equation. Show your work.

   It took $\underline{6}$ days for the temperature to decrease by 9 °F.

   $$\left(-\frac{2}{3}\right)\left(-\frac{3}{2}x\right) = \left(-\frac{2}{3}\right)(-9)$$
   $$x = \frac{18}{3}$$
   $$x = 6$$

Use inverse operations to solve each equation. (Example 1)

3. $-2x = 34$

   $x = -17$

4. $y - 3.5 = -2.1$

   $y = 1.4$

5. $\frac{2}{3}z = -6$

   $z = -9$

? ESSENTIAL QUESTION CHECK-IN

6. How does writing an equation help you solve a problem?

   Sample answer: It helps me describe the problem precisely and solve it using inverse operations.

DIFFERENTIATE INSTRUCTION

Manipulatives

Have students use an actual balance scale to emphasize the concept of keeping both sides equal, or balanced. Write the equation $x + 5 = 13$ on the board. Have students place 5 tiles on the left side and 13 on the right side. Have students stack tiles on the side with 5 tiles until the scale balances. When they place 8 more tiles on the scale, the scale should balance. So, the solution to $x + 5 = 13$ is $x = 8$.

Visual Cues

Suggest that students use colored pencils to circle the number that must be moved (or operated on) in order to isolate the variable. Then students can use a different color to write the step of performing the inverse operation on both sides of the equation.

Additional Resources

Differentiated Instruction includes:

- Reading Strategies
- Success for English Learners   **ELL**
- Reteach
- Challenge   **PRE-AP**

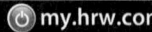
1.2 LESSON QUIZ

 **7.EE.2.4**

Use inverse operations to solve each equation.

1. $a - \frac{5}{6} = -3\frac{2}{3}$

2. $k + 7.2 = 3.4$

3. $-\frac{3}{5}d = 15$

4. $\frac{w}{-1.3} = -6.2$

5. The height of the water in an above ground pool is 3 feet. The pool needs to be drained. As the water drains, the height of the water changes at a rate of $-\frac{1}{2}$ inch per minute. Write and solve an equation to find how many minutes it will take to drain the pool.

6. The melting point of the chemical bromine is −7.2 °C. The boiling point of bromine is 58.8 °C. Write and solve an equation to find how much greater the boiling point of bromine is than the melting point.

Lesson Quiz available online

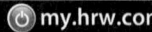 my.hrw.com

Answers

1. $a = -2\frac{5}{6}$

2. $k = -3.8$

3. $d = -25$

4. $w = 8.06$

5. $-\frac{1}{2}n = -36$; 72 minutes

6. $-7.2 + x = 58.8$; 66 °C

Evaluate

GUIDED AND INDEPENDENT PRACTICE

 FL CC 7.EE.2.4

Concepts & Skills	Practice
Example 1 One-Step Equations	Exercises 1–5
Example 2 Writing and Solving One-Step Addition and Subtraction Equations	Exercises 1, 6–9, 12–15
Example 3 Writing and Solving One-Step Multiplication and Division Equations	Exercises 2, 10, 11, 16, 18

Exercise	Depth of Knowledge (D.O.K.)	**FL CC** Mathematical Practices
7	**2** Skills/Concepts	**MP.4.1** Modeling
8	**2** Skills/Concepts	**MP.4.1** Modeling
9	**2** Skills/Concepts	**MP.4.1** Modeling
10	**2** Skills/Concepts	**MP.4.1** Modeling
11	**2** Skills/Concepts	**MP.4.1** Modeling
12	**2** Skills/Concepts	**MP.4.1** Modeling
13	**2** Skills/Concepts	**MP.4.1** Modeling
14	**2** Skills/Concepts	**MP.4.1** Modeling
15	**2** Skills/Concepts	**MP.4.1** Modeling
16	**2** Skills/Concepts	**MP.4.1** Modeling
17	**3** Strategic Thinking **H.O.T.**	**MP.7.1** Using Structure
18	**2** Skills/Concepts	**MP.4.1** Modeling
19	**3** Strategic Thinking **H.O.T.**	**MP.3.1** Logic
20	**3** Strategic Thinking **H.O.T.**	**MP.7.1** Using Structure
21	**3** Strategic Thinking **H.O.T.**	**MP.4.1** Modeling

Additional Resources

Differentiated Instruction includes:

• Leveled Practice Worksheets

1.2 Independent Practice

FL CC 7.EE.2.4

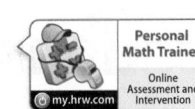

Personal Math Trainer

Online Assessment and Intervention

my.hrw.com

The table shows the elevation in feet at the peaks of several mountains. Use the table for 7–9.

Mountain	Elevation (feet)
Mt. McKinley	20,321.5
K2	28,251.31
Tupungato	22,309.71
Dom	14,911.42

7. Mt. Everest is 8,707.37 feet higher than Mt. McKinley. What is the elevation of Mt. Everest?

_____29,028.87 ft_____

8. Liam descended from the summit of K2 to an elevation of 23,201.06 feet. How many feet did Liam descend? What was his change in elevation?

_____5050.25 ft; −5050.25 ft_____

9. K2 is 11,194.21 feet higher than Mt. Kenya. Write and solve an equation to find the elevation of Mt. Kenya.

$28,251.31 − x = 11,194.21;$

$x = 17,057.1; 17,057.1$ feet

10. A hot air balloon is at an elevation of 1,250 feet. Its elevation begins to change at a rate of $−22\frac{1}{2}$ feet per minute. How many minutes will it take the balloon to descend to an elevation of 935 feet?

_____14 minutes_____

11. During another part of its flight, the balloon in Exercise 10 went from an elevation of 4,106 feet to an elevation of 3,205 feet in 34 minutes. What was its rate of descent?

_____$−26\frac{1}{2}$ feet per minute_____

The table shows the average temperatures in several states from January through March. Use the table for 12–14.

State	Average Temperature (°C)
Florida	18.1
Minnesota	−2.5
Montana	−0.7
Texas	12.5

12. Write and solve an equation to find how much warmer Montana's average 3-month temperature is than Minnesota's.

$−2.5 + x = −0.7; x = 1.8;$ 1.8 °C warmer

13. How much warmer is Florida's average 3-month temperature than Montana's?

_____18.8 °C warmer_____

14. How would the average temperature in Texas have had to change to match the average temperature in Florida?

It would have to increase by 5.6 °C.

15. A football team has a net yardage of $−26\frac{1}{3}$ yards on a series of plays. The team needs a net yardage of 10 yards to get a first down. How many yards do they have to get on their next play to get a first down?

$36\frac{1}{3}$ yards

© Houghton Mifflin Harcourt Publishing Company • Image Credits: ©Ilene MacDonald/Alamy Images

16. A diver begins at sea level and descends vertically at a rate of $−2\frac{1}{2}$ feet per second. How long does the diver take to reach −15.6 feet? _____6.24 sec_____

17. **Analyze Relationships** In Exercise 16, what is the relationship between the rate at which the diver descends, the elevation he reaches, and the time it takes to reach that elevation?

Sample answer: the elevation is the product of the rate and the time.

18. **Check for Reasonableness** Jane withdrew money from her savings account in each of 5 months. The average amount she withdrew per month was $45.50. How much did she withdraw in all during the 5 months? Show that your answer is reasonable.

$227.50; sample answer: $45.50 ≈ $50, and $50 × 5 = $250, which is close to $227.50.

H.O.T. FOCUS ON HIGHER ORDER THINKING

Work Area

19. **Justify Reasoning** Consider the two problems below. Which values in the problems are represented by negative numbers? Explain why.

(1) A diver below sea level ascends 25 feet to a reef at −35.5 feet. What was the elevation of the diver before she ascended to the reef?

(2) A plane descends 1.5 miles to an elevation of 3.75 miles. What was the elevation of the plane before its descent?

(1) The elevations of the diver and the reef; both are below sea level. (2) The change in the plane's elevation; the plane is moving from a higher to a lower elevation.

20. **Analyze Relationships** How is solving $−4x = −4.8$ different from solving $−\frac{1}{4}x = −4.8$? How are the solutions related?

In the first case, you divide both sides by −4. In the second, you multiply both sides by −4. The second solution (19.2) is 16 times the first (1.2).

21. **Communicate Mathematical Ideas** Flynn opens a savings account. In one 3-month period, he makes deposits of $75.50 and $55.25. He makes withdrawals of $25.15 and $18.65. His balance at the end of the 3-month period is $210.85. Explain how you can find his initial deposit amount.

Add the deposits and the withdrawals. Let x represent the amount of the initial deposit. Write and solve the equation $x +$ deposits − withdrawals = $210.85.

© Houghton Mifflin Harcourt Publishing Company

EXTEND THE MATH PRE-AP

Activity available online my.hrw.com

Activity Solve the equations in order. Use the value of the variables you find in each of the following equations.

1. Solve for a: $3a = −4.2$

2. Solve for b: $a + b = −7.8$

3. Solve for c: $1\frac{2}{3}c = a − b$

4. Solve for d: $\frac{a + b}{c} = −2d$

1. $a = −1.4$

2. $b = −6.4$

3. $c = 3$

4. $d = 1.3$

LESSON
1.3 Writing Two-Step Equations

 Florida Common Core Standards

The student is expected to:

 **Expressions and Equations— 7.EE.2.4**

Use variables to represent quantities in a real-world or mathematical problem, and construct simple equations... to solve problems by reasoning about the quantities.

Mathematical Practices

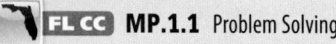 **MP.1.1** Problem Solving

---

ADDITIONAL EXAMPLE 1
A taxi driver charges $3.25 for the first mile of the trip and $1.25 for each mile after that. He charges a customer $17 for a ride. Write an equation that would help the customer find the distance she traveled in the taxi.

$3.25 + 1.25x = 17$

 Interactive Whiteboard
Interactive example available online

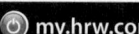 my.hrw.com

---

Engage

ESSENTIAL QUESTION

How do you write a two-step equation? Sample answer: Choose a variable for the unknown value you are trying to find. Use important words from the problem to identify the correct operations and numbers to use.

Motivate the Lesson
Ask: How have you used manipulatives in the past to help you solve math problems? Think of a way to use manipulatives to solve math problems before you begin the Explore Activity.

Explore

EXPLORE ACTIVITY

Focus on Communication Mathematical Practices
Since positive signs (and negative signs) are found on more than one algebra tile, remind students to use descriptive terms when talking about algebra tiles. Using the phrases "positive variable tile" and "−1 tile", for example, will make talking about their models easier.

Explain

EXAMPLE 1

Focus on Reasoning Mathematical Practices
Students who are proficient in mental math may be able to find the monthly fee without writing a two-step equation. Have students discuss why writing an equation can still be useful. Students should recognize that writing an equation incorporates all the important information in a compact form.

Engage with the Whiteboard
Cover up the solution in Step 3, and have students read Example 1. Then invite a student to circle all the numbers needed to solve the problem and to draw a line under any words that will help decide which operations to use in writing the two-step equation.

Questioning Strategies Mathematical Practices
• Write the equation for Example 1 in a different way. Explain what each side of the equation represents. Sample answer: $460 − 40 = 12m$; each side represents the total amount of monthly fees paid in 1 year.

• How would the equation in Example 1 be different if the gym charged $460 for a two-year membership? Explain. The equation would change to $40 + 24m = 460$; the number 24 is used in the equation because there are 24 months in 2 years.

LESSON 1.3 Writing Two-Step Equations

FL CC 7.EE.2.4
Use variables to represent quantities in a real-world or mathematical problem, and construct simple equations... to solve problems by reasoning about the quantities.

? ESSENTIAL QUESTION

How do you write a two-step equation?

EXPLORE ACTIVITY FL CC Prep for 7.EE.2.4

Modeling Two-Step Equations

You can use algebra tiles to model two-step equations.

KEY

= positive variable
= negative variable
+ = 1   - = −1

Use algebra tiles to model $3x - 4 = 5$.

A How can you model the left side of the equation?

Use three positive variable tiles and four −1-tiles.

B How can you model the right side of the equation?

Use five +1-tiles.

C Use algebra tiles or draw them to model the equation on the mat.

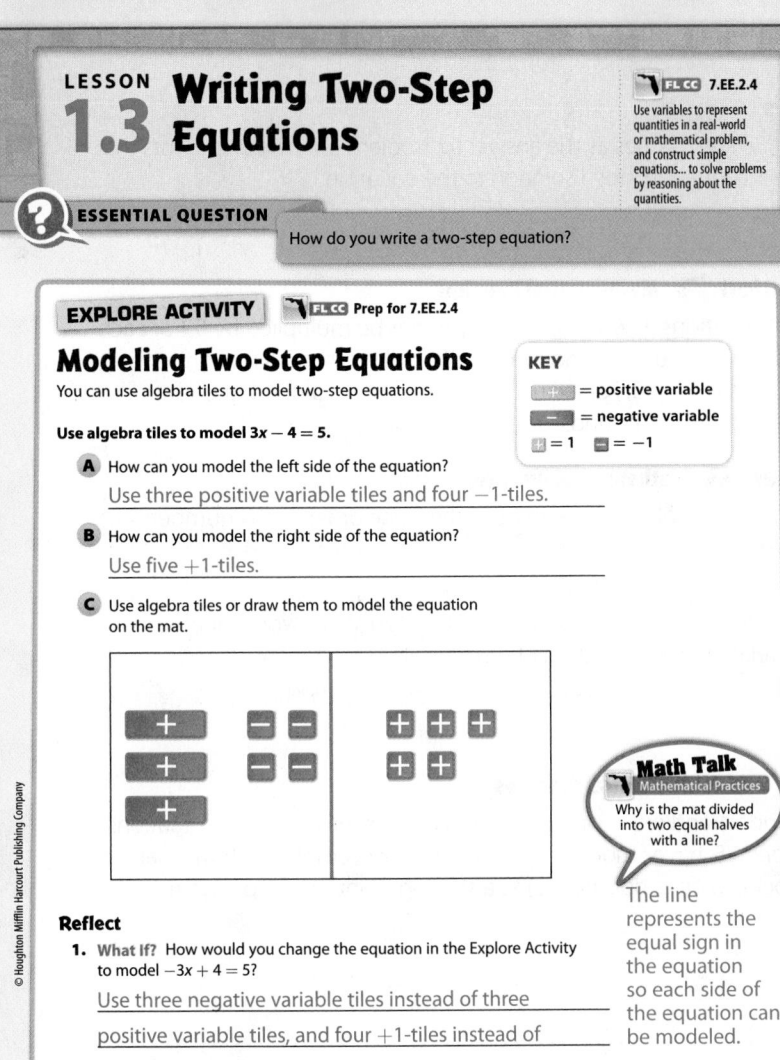

Math Talk
Mathematical Practices

Why is the mat divided into two equal halves with a line?

The line represents the equal sign in the equation so each side of the equation can be modeled.

Reflect

1. **What If?** How would you change the equation in the Explore Activity to model $-3x + 4 = 5$?

   Use three negative variable tiles instead of three positive variable tiles, and four +1-tiles instead of four −1-tiles.

Math On the Spot
my.hrw.com

Writing Two-Step Equations

You can write two-step equations to represent real-world problems by translating the words of the problems into numbers, variables, and operations.

EXAMPLE 1 Real World   FL CC 7.EE.2.4

A one-year membership to Metro Gym costs $460. There is a fee of $40 when you join, and the rest is paid monthly. Write an equation to represent what you will pay monthly for the yearlong membership. Write an equation that would help members find how much they pay per month.

STEP 1 Identify what you are trying to find. This will be the variable in the equation.

Let m represent the amount of money members pay per month.

STEP 2 Identify important information in the problem that can be used to help write an equation.

one-time joining fee: $40
fee charged for 1 year: $12 \cdot m$
total cost for the year: $460

> Convert 1 year into 12 months to find how much members pay per month.

STEP 3 Use words in the problem to tie the information together and write an equation.

One-time joining fee	plus	12	times	monthly cost	equals	$460
↓	↓	↓	↓	↓	↓	↓
$40	+	12	·	m	=	$460

The equation $40 + 12m = 460$ can help members find out their monthly fee.

Reflect

2. **Multiple Representations** Why would this equation for finding the monthly fee be difficult to model with algebra tiles?

   You would need to place 460 +1-tiles on one side of the mat.

3. Can you rewrite the equation in the form $52m = 460$? Explain.

   No, you cannot combine 40 and 12m because they are not like terms.

PROFESSIONAL DEVELOPMENT

◥ Integrate Mathematical Practices MP.1.1

This lesson provides an opportunity to address this Mathematical Practice standard. It calls for students to write equations by analyzing word problems to find the numbers to include in the equations, as well as to identify words that determine the operations to use. Then students write real-world problems by analyzing the numbers and operations used in equations, and identifying situations that correspond to the numbers and operations.

Math Background

In this lesson, two-step equations will always involve two different operations. One operation will be multiplication or division, and the other will be addition or subtraction. When one of the operations is multiplication, the equation can be written without a multiplication sign. The expression $5x$ means to multiply 5 by the value of x. This notation is often used in algebraic equations to eliminate possible confusion between the variable x and the multiplication sign $\times$.

Avoid Common Errors

Students may want to put 3 video games as the answer to Problem 4. Remind students that the correct answer will be an equation, not a solution to the equation.

EXAMPLE 2

Focus on Communication ◥ Mathematical Practices

In Step 2, students think of situations in which a quantity might be multiplied by 5. For each example, have students identify the units being measured. Students should recognize that the units should stay the same in Step 3. For example, if $5x$ represents a number of pounds, then 50 and 120 should also represent pounds.

Questioning Strategies ⚑ Mathematical Practices

• Do the numbers in a real-world problem have to be in the same order as the numbers in a corresponding equation? No; the numbers in an equation can be presented in different orders while still representing the same situation.

• Step 3 has two different problems that represent $5x + 50 = 120$. What words or phrases in each of the problems relate to the operation of multiplication? The phrases "each weighing 5 pounds" and "each week he saves $5" relate to multiplication.

YOUR TURN

Connect to Daily Life ◥ Mathematical Practices

Make sure that students understand real-world problems can be similar to actual situations in their daily lives. For Problem 5, have students think of personal examples of items that they own at least 10 of (socks, pencils, dollars, etc.) as a starting point for the problem.

Elaborate

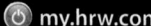

Talk About It
Summarize the Lesson

Ask: How is writing an equation that matches a problem similar to writing a problem that matches an equation? In both situations, you have to analyze the given information and decide on a different way to represent the same information.

GUIDED PRACTICE

Engage with the Whiteboard

Refer students to the different kinds of algebra tiles described in Explore Activity 1, and have students use drawings of algebra tiles to model Exercises 1 and 2. Then have other students verify that the values represented on each side of the equation are correctly represented on each side of the model.

Avoid Common Errors

Exercise 5 Remind students that Exercise 5 is not asking for a solution to the equation; it is asking for a situation that can be modeled by the equation.

Integrating Language Arts ELL

You may want to pair up English learners with a partner for Example 2 to help them develop their language skills.

 **YOUR TURN**

4. Billy has a gift card with a $150 balance. He buys several video games that cost $35 each. After the purchases, his gift card balance is $45. Write an equation to help find out how many video games Billy bought.

$$150 - 35x = 45$$

Personal Math Trainer
Online Assessment and Intervention
my.hrw.com

Math On the Spot
my.hrw.com

Writing a Verbal Description of a Two-Step Equation

You can also write a verbal description to fit a two-step equation.

EXAMPLE 2

FL CC 7.EE.2.4

Write a corresponding real-world problem to represent $5x + 50 = 120$.

STEP 1 Analyze what each part of the equation means mathematically.

x is the solution of the problem, the quantity you are looking for.

$5x$ means that, for a reason given in the problem, the quantity you are looking for is multiplied by 5.

$+ 50$ means that, for a reason given in the problem, 50 is added to $5x$.

$= 120$ means that after multiplying the solution x by 5 and adding 50 to it, the result is 120.

STEP 2 Think of some different situations in which a quantity x might be multiplied by 5.

You have x number of books, each weighing 5 pounds, and you want to know their total weight.	You save $5 each week for x weeks and want to know the total amount you have saved.

STEP 3 Build on the situation and adjust it to create a verbal description that takes all of the information of the equation into account.

- A publisher ships a package of x number of books each weighing 5 pounds, plus a second package weighing 50 pounds. The total weight of both packages is 120 pounds. How many books are being shipped?

- Leon receives a birthday gift of $50 from his parents. Each week he saves $5. How many weeks will it take for him to save $120?

My Notes

Lesson 1.3 **21**

Personal Math Trainer
Online Assessment and Intervention
my.hrw.com

 **YOUR TURN**

5. Write a real-world problem that can be represented by $10x + 40 = 100$.

Check students' answers.

Guided Practice

Draw algebra tiles to model the given two-step equation. (Explore Activity)

1. $2x + 5 = 7$

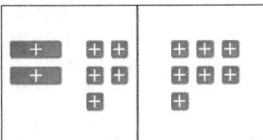

2. $-3 = 5 - 4x$

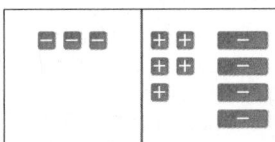

3. A group of adults plus one child attend a movie at Cineplex 15. Tickets cost $9 for adults and $6 for children. The total cost for the movie is $78. Write an equation to find the number of adults in the group. (Example 1)

$6 + 9a = 78$

4. Break down the equation $2x + 10 = 16$ to analyze each part. (Example 2)

x is ___the solution___ of the problem.

$2x$ is the quantity you are looking for ___multiplied by 2___.

$+ 10$ means 10 is ___added to $2x$___. $= 16$ means the ___result___ is 16.

5. Write a corresponding real-world problem to represent $2x - 125 = 400$.

(Example 2) Check students' answers.

 **? ESSENTIAL QUESTION CHECK-IN**

6. Describe the steps you would follow to write a two-step equation you can use to solve a real-world problem.

Choose a variable to represent what you want to find. Decide how the items of information in the problem relate to the variable and to each other. Then write an equation tying this all together.

22 Unit 1

DIFFERENTIATE INSTRUCTION

Home Connections

Have students bring in receipts showing their family's purchases. Students can use the prices on the receipts as real-world data to create word problems and challenge other students to write an equation for their word problems.

Graphic Organizers

As students create equations that correspond to word problems, have them identify the words in the problem that determined the operations in the equations. Students can make a table that lists phrases that suggest each of the operations. Students can refer to the table when writing equations that match word problems, and when writing word problems that match equations.

Additional Resources

Differentiated Instruction includes:

- Reading Strategies
- Success for English Learners **ELL**
- Reteach
- Challenge **PRE-AP**

Writing Two-Step Equations **22**

Personal Math Trainer

Online Assessment and Intervention

Online homework assignment available

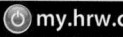 my.hrw.com

1.3 LESSON QUIZ

 **FL CC** 7.EE.2.4

1. Joaquin is ordering 5 identical sandwiches and a bag of chips. The bag of chips costs $1.25, and the entire order costs $38.75. Write an equation you can use to find the price of a sandwich.

2. The drama club is planning a field trip. Two-thirds of the drama club will attend, in addition to 8 teachers. There are 48 people going on the field trip. Write an equation you can use to find the number of students in the drama club.

3. Write a real-world problem that corresponds to the equation $200 - 7x = 95$.

4. Write a real-world problem that corresponds to the equation $10x + 30 = 100$.

Lesson Quiz available online

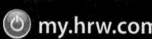 my.hrw.com

Answers

1. $5s + 1.25 = 38.75$

2. $\frac{2}{3}d + 8 = 48$

3. Sample answer: Rico made 200 cupcakes. He gave the same number of cupcakes to each of his 7 friends. When he was finished, he had 95 cupcakes left. How many cupcakes did he give to each friend?

4. Sample answer: Baxter runs 10 times in a month. Each time he runs the same distance. Ashley runs 30 miles in the same month. Together, they ran 100 miles. How many miles did Baxter travel each time he went running?

Evaluate

GUIDED AND INDEPENDENT PRACTICE

 **FL CC** 7.EE.2.4

Concepts & Skills	Practice
Explore Activity Modeling Two-Step Equations	Exercises 1–2, 7
Example 1 Writing Two-Step Equations	Exercises 3, 8–15
Example 2 Writing a Verbal Description of a Two-Step Equation	Exercises 4, 5, 14

Exercise	Depth of Knowledge (D.O.K.)	 **FL CC** Mathematical Practices
7–13	**2** Skills/Concepts	**MP.4.1** Modeling
14	**3** Strategic Thinking **H.O.T.**	**MP.6.1** Precision
15	**3** Strategic Thinking **H.O.T.**	**MP.6.1** Precision
16	**3** Strategic Thinking **H.O.T.**	**MP.8.1** Patterns
17	**3** Strategic Thinking **H.O.T.**	**MP.7.1** Using Structure
18	**3** Strategic Thinking **H.O.T.**	**MP.4.1** Modeling

Additional Resources

Differentiated Instruction includes:

• Leveled Practice Worksheets

CLUSTER CONNECTION **Exercise 15** combines concepts from the Florida Common Core cluster "Solve real-life and mathematical problems using numerical and algebraic expressions and equations."

1.3 Independent Practice

FL CC 7.EE.2.4

Personal Math Trainer
Online Assessment and Intervention
my.hrw.com

7. Describe how to model $-3x + 7 = 28$ with algebra tiles.

three negative variable tiles and seven +1-tiles on one side of a line and 28 +1-tiles on the other side.

8. Val rented a bicycle while she was on vacation. She paid a flat rental fee of $55.00, plus $8.50 each day. The total cost was $123. Write an equation you can use to find the number of days she rented the bicycle.

$$8.5d + 55 = 123$$

9. A restaurant sells a coffee refill mug for $6.75. Each refill costs $1.25. Last month Keith spent $31.75 on a mug and refills. Write an equation you can use to find the number of refills that Keith bought.

$$1.25r + 6.75 = 31.75$$

10. A gym holds one 60-minute exercise class on Saturdays and several 45-minute classes during the week. Last week all of the classes lasted a total of 285 minutes. Write an equation you can use to find the number of weekday classes.

$$45n + 60 = 285$$

11. Multiple Representations There are 172 South American animals in the Springdale Zoo. That is 45 more than half the number of African animals in the zoo. Write an equation you could use to find n, the number of African animals in the zoo.

$$\tfrac{1}{2}n + 45 = 172$$

12. A school bought $548 in basketball equipment and uniforms costing $29.50 each. The total cost was $2,023. Write an equation you can use to find the number of uniforms the school purchased.

$$29.5u + 548 = 2,023$$

13. Financial Literacy Heather has $500 in her savings account. She withdraws $20 per week for gas. Write an equation Heather can use to see how many weeks it will take her to have a balance of $220.

$$500 - 20x = 220$$

14. Critique Reasoning For $9x + 25 = 88$, Deena wrote the situation "I bought some shirts at the store for $9 each and received a $25 discount. My total bill was $88. How many shirts did I buy?"

a. What mistake did Deena make?

The equation adds 25, but Deena's scenario involves subtracting 25.

b. Rewrite the equation to match Deena's situation.

$$9x - 25 = 88$$

c. How could you rewrite the situation to make it fit the equation?

I bought some shirts at the store for $9 each and a pair of jeans for $25, making my bill a total of $88. How many shirts did I buy?

15. Multistep Sandy charges each family that she babysits a flat fee of $10 for the night and an extra $5 per child. Kimmi charges $25 per night, no matter how many children a family has.

a. Write a two-step equation that would compare what the two girls charge and find when their fees are the same. $10 + 5c = 25$

b. How many children must a family have for Sandy and Kimmi to charge the same amount? 3 children

c. The Sanderson family has five children. Which babysitter should they choose if they wish to save some money on babysitting, and why?

They should choose Kimmi, because she charges only $25. If they chose Sandy, they would pay $35.

H.O.T.  **FOCUS ON HIGHER ORDER THINKING**

16. Analyze Relationships Each student wrote a two-step equation. Peter wrote the equation $4x - 2 = 10$, and Andres wrote the equation $16x - 8 = 40$. The teacher looked at their equations and asked them to compare them. Describe one way in which the equations are similar.

To get Andres' equation, you can multiply every number in Peter's equation by 4. To get Peter's equation, you can divide every number in Andrew's equation by 4, or multiply by $\tfrac{1}{4}$.

17. What's the Error? Damon has 5 dimes and some nickels in his pocket, worth a total of $1.20. To find the number of nickels Damon has, a student wrote the equation $5n + 50 = 1.20$. Find the error in the student's equation.

Part of the equation is written in cents and part in dollars. All of the numbers in the equation should be written either in cents or in dollars.

18. Represent Real-World Problems Write a real-world problem you could answer by solving the equation $-8x + 60 = 28$.

Sample answer: Cici has a gift card with a balance of 60. She buys several T-shirts for $8 each. Her new balance is $28 after the purchases. Write an equation to help find out how many T-shirts Cici bought.

Work Area

EXTEND THE MATH   PRE-AP

Activity available online 🔘 my.hrw.com

Yvette is starting a jewelry business. She spends $120 on supplies and makes 18 necklaces. She wants to earn a profit equal to 3 times the amount she spent on supplies. Use this information to write 3 different equations that Yvette could use to determine how much she should charge for each necklace.

Sample answer:

$18n = 360 + 120$

$18n - 120 = 360$

$18n - 360 = 120$

LESSON
1.4 Solving Two-Step Equations

 Florida Common Core Standards

The student is expected to:

 **Expressions and Equations—7.EE.2.4a**

Solve word problems leading to equations of the form $px + q = r$ and $p(x + q) = r$, where p, q, and r are specific rational numbers. Solve equations of these forms fluently. Compare an algebraic solution to an arithmetic solution, identifying the sequence of the operations used in each approach.

 **Expressions and Equations—7.EE.2.4**

Use variables to represent quantities in a real-world or mathematical problem, and construct simple equations and inequalities to solve problems by reasoning about the quantities.

Mathematical Practices

 **MP.4.1** Modeling

ADDITIONAL EXAMPLE 1
Use algebra tiles to model and solve $4x + 7 = 23$. $x = 4$

 Interactive Whiteboard
Interactive example available online

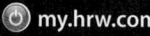 my.hrw.com

ADDITIONAL EXAMPLE 2
As a reward for winning a math competition, 26 students in the 7th grade visited a theme park. On one ride, 3 equal groups of students could be seated and 2 students were left over. Write and solve an equation to find how many students could be seated in each group. $3x + 2 = 26$; the number in each group is 8.

 Interactive Whiteboard
Interactive example available online

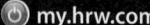 my.hrw.com

Engage

ESSENTIAL QUESTION

How do you solve a two-step equation? Sample answer: You can use models or algorithms to solve two-step equations. For both methods, isolate the variable by performing the same operation on both sides of the equation.

Motivate the Lesson
Ask: Have you ever used a see saw on a playground? Think about different ways to get on or off a see saw. What can go wrong?

Explore

Connect to Daily Life Mathematical Practices
Discuss with students the safest ways to get on or off a see saw. Relate removing weight from both sides of the see saw simultaneously to solving equations by performing the same calculation on both sides of the equation.

Explain

EXAMPLE 1

Connect Vocabulary ELL
Make sure that students understand that isolating the variable means getting the variable to be the only thing on one side of the equation. Understanding the meaning of the word *isolate* can give students a better intuitive sense of how to solve two-step equations.

Questioning Strategies Mathematical Practices
• In Step 2, explain why you cannot move the two +1 tiles from the left side of the model to the right side of the model. If you move the two +1 tiles from the left side to the right side, the two sides of the model will no longer be equal.

YOUR TURN

Avoid Common Errors
Students using algebra tiles may mistakenly remove a number of −1 tiles from one side and an equal number of +1 tiles from the other side. Remind students that for Problems 2 and 4, they can add the same number of +1-tiles or −1-tiles to both sides, and then remove pairs of +1 and −1 tiles from the same side, since $-1 + 1 = 0$.

EXAMPLE 2

Questioning Strategies Mathematical Practices
• How do the steps in the solution use inverse operations? Since 20 is subtracted in the equation, you add 20 to both sides to undo the subtraction. Since the variable is multiplied by 2 in the equation, you divide both sides by 2 to undo the multiplication.

Solving Two-Step Equations

FL CC 7.EE.2.4a
Solve word problems leading to equations of the form $px + q = r$ and $p(x + q) = r$ ... Compare an algebraic solution to an arithmetic solution ...
Also 7.EE.2.3, 7.EE.2.4

ESSENTIAL QUESTION

How do you solve a two-step equation?

Modeling and Solving Two-Step Equations

You can solve two-step equations using algebra tiles.

EXAMPLE 1
FL CC 7.EE.2.4

Use algebra tiles to model and solve $3n + 2 = 11$.

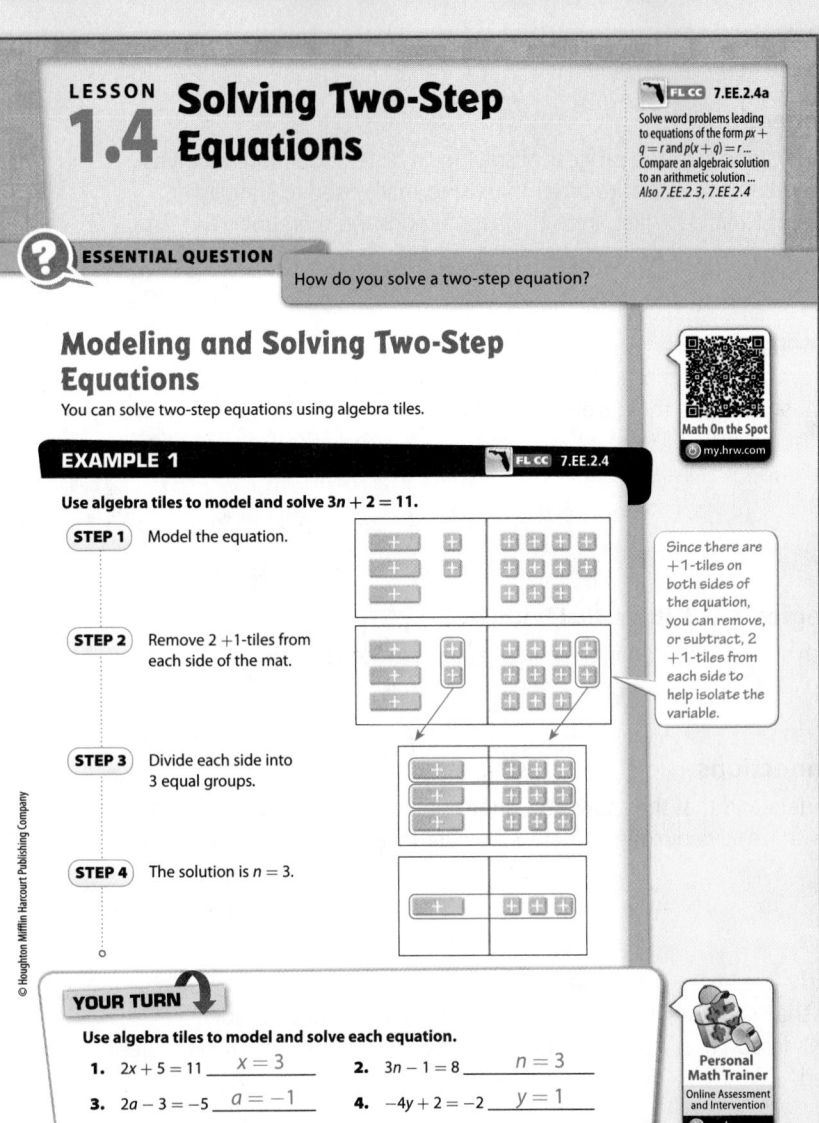

STEP 1 Model the equation.

STEP 2 Remove 2 +1-tiles from each side of the mat.

Since there are +1-tiles on both sides of the equation, you can remove, or subtract, 2 +1-tiles from each side to help isolate the variable.

STEP 3 Divide each side into 3 equal groups.

STEP 4 The solution is $n = 3$.

Math On the Spot
my.hrw.com

YOUR TURN

Use algebra tiles to model and solve each equation.

1. $2x + 5 = 11$ $x = 3$
2. $3n - 1 = 8$ $n = 3$
3. $2a - 3 = -5$ $a = -1$
4. $-4y + 2 = -2$ $y = 1$

Personal Math Trainer
Online Assessment and Intervention
my.hrw.com

© Houghton Mifflin Harcourt Publishing Company

Lesson 1.4 **25**

Math On the Spot
my.hrw.com

Solving Two-Step Equations

You can use inverse operations to solve equations with more than one operation.

EXAMPLE 2 Real World
FL CC 7.EE.2.4a

A dog sled driver added more gear to the sled, doubling its weight. This felt too heavy, so the driver removed 20 pounds to reach the final weight of 180 pounds. Write and solve an equation to find the sled's original weight.

STEP 1 Write an equation. Let w represent the original weight of the sled.

$2w - 20 = 180$.

STEP 2 Solve the equation.

$$2w - 20 = 180$$
$$\underline{+20 \quad +20} \qquad \text{Add 20 to both sides.}$$
$$2w \quad = 200$$
$$\frac{2w}{2} = \frac{200}{2} \qquad \text{Divide both sides by 2.}$$
$$w = 100$$

The sled's original weight was 100 pounds.

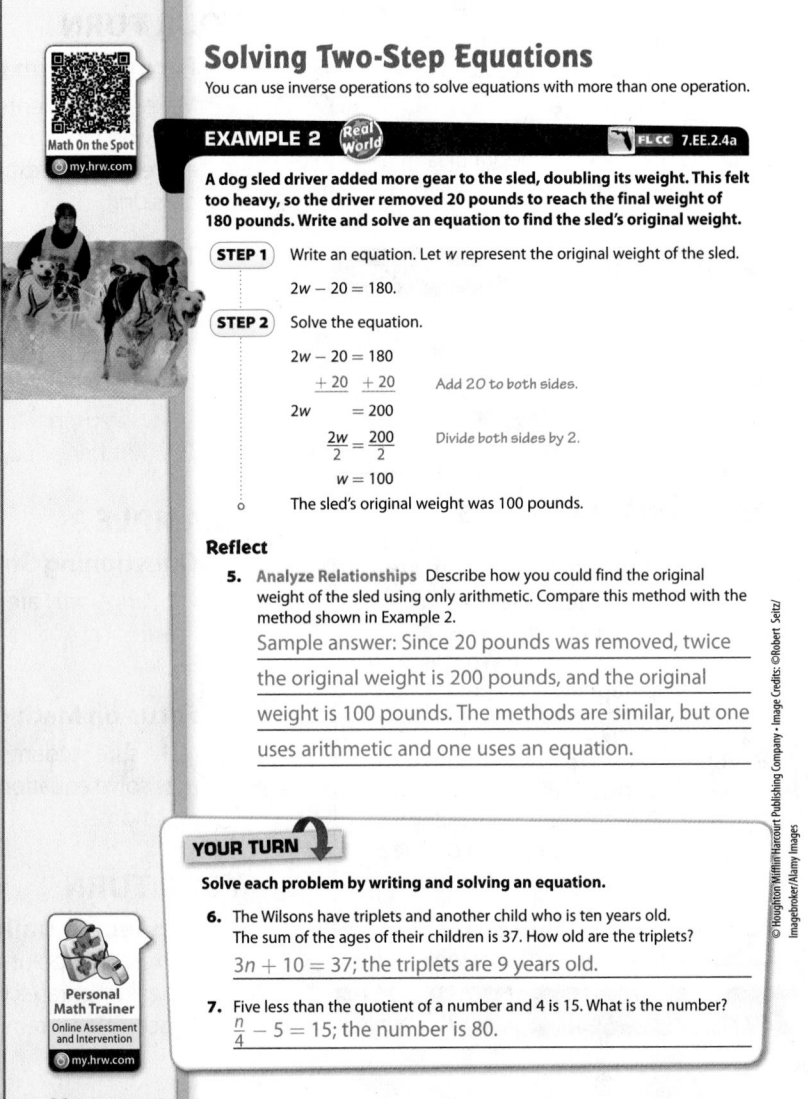

Reflect

5. **Analyze Relationships** Describe how you could find the original weight of the sled using only arithmetic. Compare this method with the method shown in Example 2.

   Sample answer: Since 20 pounds was removed, twice the original weight is 200 pounds, and the original weight is 100 pounds. The methods are similar, but one uses arithmetic and one uses an equation.

YOUR TURN

Solve each problem by writing and solving an equation.

6. The Wilsons have triplets and another child who is ten years old. The sum of the ages of their children is 37. How old are the triplets?
   $3n + 10 = 37$; the triplets are 9 years old.

7. Five less than the quotient of a number and 4 is 15. What is the number?
   $\frac{n}{4} - 5 = 15$; the number is 80.

Personal Math Trainer
Online Assessment and Intervention
my.hrw.com

© Houghton Mifflin Harcourt Publishing Company • Image Credits: ©Robert Seitz/ImageBroker/Alamy Images

---

PROFESSIONAL DEVELOPMENT

Integrate Mathematical Practices MP.4.1

This lesson provides an opportunity to address this Mathematical Practice standard. It calls for students to model with mathematics. Students learn to model and solve two-step equations using algebra tiles. They also represent and solve real-world problem situations using equations, both with and without negative numbers.

Math Background

A **monomial** is an expression that consists of a single term. Examples include 12, $3y$, 27, $4x^2$, and ab. The numbers 27 and 12 are called **constants.**
A **polynomial** can be a monomial, or it can be the sum or difference of monomials.
A **polynomial equation** is an equation with polynomials on both sides of the equation. The two-step equations in this lesson are examples of polynomial equations.

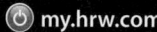
YOUR TURN

Focus on Math Connections

Make sure students understand that the process of solving two-step equations involves
applying inverse operations in the opposite order than is normally used to simplify an
expression. For example, in Exercise 7, first undo the subtraction, and then undo the
division.

Talk About It
Check for Understanding

 Ask: Andrea says she used trial and error to find that the first term of the equation
in Exercise 7 must be 20, so the number must be 80. How does her method work?
The variable term $\frac{n}{4}$ must be 20 because she knows that 5 less than the variable term is 15.
Then she used trial and error to answer the question, "What number divided by 4 is 20?"
The number is 80.

EXAMPLE 3

Questioning Strategies   Mathematical Practices

• In Part A, why are both sides of the equation multiplied by $\frac{9}{5}$ in Step 2? Since $\frac{9}{5}$ is the
reciprocal of $\frac{5}{9}$, multiplying by $\frac{9}{5}$ will clear the fractions and make the equation easier to
solve.

Focus on Math Connections

Make sure students understand that they solve equations with negative numbers just as
they solve equations with positive numbers. That is, they use inverse operations to solve the
equations.

YOUR TURN

Connect to Daily Life

In Exercise 9, point out that "she lost 4 points" is represented by a negative number.
Other key phrases in this lesson that indicate using a negative quantity in an equation are
"descend" and "removed."

Elaborate

Talk About It
Summarize the Lesson

 Ask: How can you find the solution to a two-step equation? To find the solution to
a two-step equation, perform the same operations on both sides of the equation
until the variable is isolated.

GUIDED PRACTICE

Engage with the Whiteboard

 When students identify the solution steps in Exercise 1, have them sketch how the
algebra tiles change as the steps are applied.

Avoid Common Errors

Exercises 3, 4 If students have trouble writing the correct equation, encourage them
to explicitly define the variable before attempting to translate the words into math.

Two-Step Equations with Negative Numbers

Many real-world quantities such as altitude or temperature involve negative numbers. You solve equations with negative numbers just as you did equations with positive numbers.

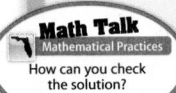 **EXAMPLE 3** FL CC 7.EE.2.4a

A To convert a temperature from degrees Fahrenheit to degrees Celsius, first subtract 32. Then multiply the result by $\frac{5}{9}$. An outdoor thermometer showed a temperature of $-10\ °C$. What was the temperature in degrees Fahrenheit?

STEP 1 Write an equation. Let x represent the temperature in degrees Fahrenheit.

$$-10 = \frac{5}{9}(x - 32)$$

STEP 2 Solve the equation.

$$\frac{9}{5}(-10) = \frac{9}{5}\left(\frac{5}{9}(x-32)\right) \qquad \text{Multiply both sides by } \frac{9}{5}.$$
$$-18 = x - 32$$
$$\underline{+32 \quad +32} \qquad\qquad \text{Add 32 to both sides.}$$
$$14 = x$$

The temperature was 14 degrees Fahrenheit.

B An airplane flies at an altitude of 38,000 feet. As it nears the airport, the plane begins to descend at a rate of 600 feet per minute. At this rate, how many minutes will the plane take to descend to 18,800 feet?

STEP 1 Write an equation. Let m represent the number of minutes.

$$38,000 - 600m = 18,800$$

STEP 2 Solve the equation. Start by isolating the term that contains the variable.

$$38,000 - 600m = 18,800$$
$$\underline{-38,000 \qquad\quad -38,000} \qquad \text{Subtract 38,000 from both sides.}$$
$$-600m = -19,200$$
$$\frac{-600m}{-600} = \frac{-19,200}{-600} \qquad \text{Divide both sides by } -600.$$
$$m = 32$$

The plane will take 32 minutes to descend to 18,800 feet.

Math Talk
Mathematical Practices

How can you check the solution?

Substitute the value into the original equation and determine whether the value makes the equation true.

Math On the Spot
my.hrw.com

Animated Math
my.hrw.com

Personal Math Trainer
Online Assessment and Intervention
my.hrw.com

YOUR TURN

Solve each problem by writing and solving an equation.

8. What is the temperature in degrees Fahrenheit of a freezer kept at $-20\ °C$?

   $-20 = \frac{5}{9}(x - 32);\ -4\ °F$

9. Jenny earned 92 of a possible 120 points on a test. She lost 4 points for each incorrect answer. How many incorrect answers did she have?

   $120 - 4x = 92;\ 7$ incorrect answers

Guided Practice

The equation $2x + 1 = 9$ is modeled below. (Example 1)

1. To solve the equation with algebra tiles, first remove one +1-tile from both sides.

   Then divide each side into two equal groups .

2. The solution is $x =$ 4 .

Solve each problem by writing and solving an equation.

3. A rectangular picture frame has a perimeter of 58 inches. The height of the frame is 18 inches. What is the width of the frame? (Example 2)

   $2(18 + w) = 58$; the width is 11 inches

4. A school store has 1200 pencils in stock, and sells an average of 24 pencils per day. The manager reorders when the number of pencils in stock is 500. In how many days will the manager have to reorder? (Example 3)

   $1200 - 25x = 500$; 28 days

? ESSENTIAL QUESTION CHECK-IN

5. How can you decide which operations to use to solve a two-step equation?

   Use the inverse operations of the operations indicated in the equation. Usually it is best to use addition and subtraction before multiplication and division.

DIFFERENTIATE INSTRUCTION

Visual Cues

Have students circle the important numbers in a word problem, as well as any words that suggest a certain operation. Students may find it easier to write an equation from a word problem if they can focus on the relevant information.

Number Sense

Students may benefit from an introduction to solving two-step equations that uses the strategy of guess, check, and revise. Have students choose a value for the variable, and substitute it in the equation. If the chosen value does not make the equation true, students make another choice and repeat the process. Using this method can give students a better sense of the reasonableness of their answers as they move to using more traditional algorithms.

Additional Resources

Differentiated Instruction includes:

- Reading Strategies
- Success for English Learners **ELL**
- Reteach
- Challenge **PRE-AP**

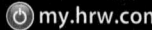
1.4 LESSON QUIZ

 **FL CC** 7.EE.2.4a

1. Solve $22 - 3b = 7$ for b.

2. Solve $4(x - 5) = 92$ for x.

3. Eya is 5 years younger than 3 times Bill's age. If Eya is 28 years old, how old is Bill?

4. What is the temperature in degrees Fahrenheit of a freezer kept at $-25\,°C$?

Lesson Quiz available online

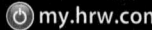
Answers

1. $b = 5$

2. $x = 28$

3. 11 years old

4. $-13\,°C$

Evaluate

GUIDED AND INDEPENDENT PRACTICE

 **FL CC** 7.EE.2.4a, 7.EE.2.4

Concepts and Skills	Practice
Example 1 Modeling and Solving Two-Step Equations	Exercises 1, 2
Example 2 Solving Two-Step Equations	Exercises 3, 18, 19, 22, 23, 24, 27
Example 3 Two-Step Equations with Negative Integers	Exercises 4, 20, 21, 25, 26

Exercise	Depth of Knowledge (D.O.K.)		**FL CC** Mathematical Practices
6–17	**1**	Recall of Information	**MP.6.1** Precision
18–24	**2**	Skills/Concepts	**MP.4.1** Modeling
25–27	**1**	Recall of Information	**MP.5.1** Using Tools
28–29	**2**	Skills/Concepts	**MP.2.1** Reasoning
30	**3**	Strategic Thinking	**MP.3.1** Logic
31	**3**	Strategic Thinking	**MP.3.1** Logic
32–33	**3**	Strategic Thinking H.O.T.	**MP.2.1** Reasoning
34	**3**	Strategic Thinking H.O.T.	**MP.7.1** Using Structure

Additional Resources

Differentiated Instruction includes:

• Leveled Practice worksheets

Name _____ **Class** _____ **Date** _____

1.4 Independent Practice

FL CC 7.EE.2.3, 7.EE.2.4, 7.EE.2.4a

Personal
Math Trainer

Online
Assessment and
Intervention

@ my.hrw.com

Solve.

6. $9s + 3 = 57$
$s = 6$

7. $4d + 6 = 42$
$d = 9$

8. $-3y + 12 = -48$
$y = 20$

9. $\frac{k}{2} + 9 = 30$
$k = 42$

10. $\frac{g}{3} - 7 = 15$
$g = 66$

11. $\frac{z}{5} + 3 = -35$
$z = -190$

12. $-9h - 15 = 93$
$h = -12$

13. $-3(n + 5) = 12$
$n = -9$

14. $-17 + \frac{b}{8} = 13$
$b = 240$

15. $7(c - 12) = -21$
$c = 9$

16. $-3 + \frac{p}{7} = -5$
$p = -14$

17. $46 = -6t - 8$
$t = -9$

18. After making a deposit, Puja had $264 in her savings account. She noticed that if she added $26 to the amount originally in the account and doubled the sum, she would get the new amount. How much did she originally have in the account?
$106

19. The current temperature in Smalltown is 20 °F. This is 6 degrees less than twice the temperature that it was six hours ago. What was the temperature in Smalltown six hours ago?
13 °F

20. One reading at an Arctic research station showed that the temperature was −35 °C. What is this temperature in degrees Fahrenheit?
−31 °F

21. Artaud noticed that if he takes the opposite of his age and adds 40, he gets the number 28. How old is Artaud?
12 years old

22. Sven has 11 more than twice as many customers as when he started selling newspapers. He now has 73 customers. How many did he have when he started?
31 customers

23. Paula bought a ski jacket on sale for $6 less than half its original price. She paid $88 for the jacket. What was the original price?
$188

24. The McIntosh family went apple picking. They picked a total of 115 apples. The family ate a total of 8 apples each day. After how many days did they have 19 apples left?
$115 - 8n = 19$; 12 days

Use a calculator to solve each equation.

25. $-5.5x + 0.56 = -1.64$
$x = 0.4$

26. $-4.2x + 31.5 = -65.1$
$x = 23$

27. $\frac{k}{5.2} + 81.9 = 47.2$
$k = -180.44$

© Houghton Mifflin Harcourt Publishing Company

---

28. Write a two-step equation that involves multiplication and subtraction, includes a negative coefficient, and has a solution of $x = 7$.
Sample answer: $-3x - 5 = -26$

29. Write a two-step equation involving division and addition that has a solution of $x = -25$
Sample answer: $\frac{x}{5} + 10 = 5$

30. Explain the Error A student's solution to the equation $3x + 2 = 15$ is shown. Describe and correct the error that the student made.

$3x + 2 = 15$　　Divide both sides by 3.

$x + 2 = 5$　　Subtract 2 from both sides.

$x = 3$

When dividing both sides by 3, the student did not divide 2 by 3. The solution should be $x + \frac{2}{3} = 5$, $x = 4\frac{1}{3}$.

31. Multiple Representations Explain how you could use the work backward problem-solving strategy to solve the equation $\frac{x}{4} - 6 = 2$.

The equation says that a number was divided by 4 and that 6 was then subtracted from the quotient, giving the result 2. So, working backward, first add 6 to 2, giving 8. Then multiply 8 by 4, giving $x = 32$.

H.O.T. FOCUS ON HIGHER ORDER THINKING

32. Reason Abstractly The formula $F = 1.8C + 32$ allows you to find the Fahrenheit (F) temperature for a given Celsius (C) temperature. Solve the equation for C to produce a formula for finding the Celsius temperature for a given Fahrenheit temperature.
$C = \frac{F - 32}{1.8}$

33. Reason Abstractly The equation $P = 2(\ell + w)$ can be used to find the perimeter P of a rectangle with length ℓ and width w. Solve the equation for w to produce a formula for finding the width of a rectangle given its perimeter and length.
$w = \frac{P - 2\ell}{2}$

34. Reason Abstractly Solve the equation $ax + b = c$ for x.
$x = \frac{c - b}{a}$

Work Area

© Houghton Mifflin Harcourt Publishing Company

EXTEND THE MATH PRE-AP

Activity available online ⏻ my.hrw.com

Explain how to solve the equation $16 + \frac{7}{x} = 24$.

First, subtract 16 from both sides of the equation, which changes the equation to $\frac{7}{x} = 8$. Next, multiply both sides of the equation by x, which changes the equation to $7 = 8x$. Last, divide both sides by 8, which changes the equation to $\frac{7}{8} = x$.

Ready to Go On?

Assess Mastery

Use the assessment on this page to determine if students have mastered the concepts and standards covered in this module.

 **RtI** **Response to Intervention**

Intervention	Enrichment

Access Ready to Go On? assessment online, and receive instant scoring, feedback, and customized intervention or enrichment.

 **Personal Math Trainer**
Online Assessment and Intervention
(*) my.hrw.com

Online and Print Resources

Differentiated Instruction	*Differentiated Instruction*
• Reteach worksheets	• Challenge worksheets
• Reading Strategies **ELL**	**PRE-AP**
• Success for English Learners **ELL**	Extend the Math **PRE-AP** Lesson Activities in TE

Additional Resources

Assessment Resources includes:
• Leveled Module Quizzes

Ready to Go On?

 Personal Math Trainer
Online Assessment and Intervention
(*) my.hrw.com

1.1 Algebraic Expressions

1. The Science Club went on a two-day field trip. The first day the members paid $60 for transportation plus $15 per ticket to the planetarium. The second day they paid $95 for transportation plus $12 per ticket to the geology museum. Write an expression to represent the total cost for two days for the n members of the club. _____ $27n + 155$

1.2 One-Step Equations with Rational Coefficients
Solve.

2. $h + 9.7 = -9.7$ _____ $h = -19.4$

3. $-\frac{3}{4} + p = \frac{1}{2}$ _____ $p = \frac{5}{4}$

4. $-15 = -0.2k$ _____ $k = 75$

5. $\frac{y}{-3} = \frac{1}{6}$ _____ $y = -\frac{1}{2}$

6. $-\frac{2}{3}m = -12$ _____ $m = 18$

7. $2.4 = -\frac{t}{4.5}$ _____ $t = -10.8$

1.3 Writing Two-Step Equations

8. Jerry started doing sit-ups every day. The first day he did 15 sit-ups. Every day after that he did 2 more sit-ups than he had done the previous day. Today Jerry did 33 sit-ups. Write an equation that could be solved to find the number of days Jerry has been doing sit-ups, not counting the first day.
_____ $2d + 15 = 33$ _____

1.4 Solving Two-Step Equations
Solve.

9. $5n + 8 = 43$ _____ $n = 7$

10. $\frac{y}{6} - 7 = 4$ _____ $y = 66$

11. $8w - 15 = 57$ _____ $w = 9$

12. $\frac{g}{3} + 11 = 25$ _____ $g = 42$

13. $\frac{f}{5} - 22 = -25$ _____ $f = -15$

14. $-4p + 19 = 11$ _____ $p = 2$

? ESSENTIAL QUESTION

15. How can you use two-step equations and inequalities to represent and solve real-world problems?
Sample answer: Analyze the situation to determine how to model it using a two-step equation. Solve the equation. Interpret the solution in the given situation.

© Houghton Mifflin Harcourt Publishing Company

 ## Florida Common Core Standards

Lesson	Exercises	 Common Core Standards
1.1	1	**7.EE.1.1**
1.2	2–7	**7.EE.2.4**
1.3	8	**7.EE.2.4a**
1.4	9–14	**7.EE.2.4a**

PARCC Assessment Readiness

Assessment Readiness Tip Students can use key words to identify the number that should be the coefficient of the variable in the equations they write.

Item 1 The key word "each" identifies the quantity $0.75 as the coefficient of the variable in the equation. The remaining quantity, $1.50, should be the constant.

Item 4 The word "each" suggests that the quantity $3.25 should be the coefficient of the variable in the equation.

Avoid Common Errors

Item 3 Remind students that under the Distributive Property, the quantity outside the parentheses must be distributed to both of the quantities inside the parentheses. If they forget this, they might choose incorrect answer choice A or D.

Item 5 Students may forget to use inverse operations, multiplying by −4.6 rather than dividing. Remind them that to solve an equation they need to "undo" the operations, not perform them again.

Additional Resources

Personal Math Trainer
Online Assessment and Intervention
my.hrw.com

MODULE 1 MIXED REVIEW

PARCC Assessment Readiness

COMMON CORE

Personal Math Trainer
Online Assessment and Intervention
my.hrw.com

Selected Response

1. A taxi cab costs $1.50 for the first mile and $0.75 for each additional mile. Which equation could be solved to find how many miles you can travel in a taxi for $10, given that x is the number of additional miles?

- Ⓐ $1.5x + 0.75 = 10$
- Ⓑ $0.75x + 1.5 = 10$
- Ⓒ $1.5x - 0.75 = 10$
- Ⓓ $0.75x - 1.5 = 10$

2. Which is the solution of $\frac{t}{2.5} = -5.2$?

- Ⓐ $t = -13$
- Ⓑ $t = -2.08$
- Ⓒ $t = 2.08$
- Ⓓ $t = 13$

3. Which expression is equivalent to $5x - 30$?

- Ⓐ $5(x - 30)$
- Ⓑ $5(x - 6)$
- Ⓒ $5x(x - 6)$
- Ⓓ $x(5 - 30)$

4. Alexander had $20 when he went to a comic store. After buying x comics at $3.25 each, he had $3.75 left. Which equation represents the situation?

- Ⓐ $20 - 3.75x = 3.25$
- Ⓑ $20 - 3.25x = 3.75$
- Ⓒ $20x + 3.25 = 3.75$
- Ⓓ $20x + 3.75 = 3.25$

5. What is the solution of $-4.6x = -11.04$?

- Ⓐ $x = -50.784$
- Ⓑ $x = -2.4$
- Ⓒ $x = 2.4$
- Ⓓ $x = 50.784$

6. Which expression factors to $5(x - 3)$?

- Ⓐ $5x + 3$
- Ⓑ $5x - 3$
- Ⓒ $5x - 8$
- Ⓓ $5x - 15$

Mini-Task

7. Casey bought 9 tickets to a concert. The total charge was $104, including a $5 service charge.

a. Write an equation you can solve to find c, the cost of one ticket.

$$9c + 5 = 104$$

b. Explain how you could estimate the solution of your equation.

Sample answer: Approximate the equation with the equation $10c = 100$, which has as its solution $c = 10$.

c. Solve the equation. How much did each ticket cost?

$c = 11$, so each ticket cost $11.

Florida Common Core Standards

Items	Grade 7 Standards	Mathematical Practices
1	7.EE.2.4	MP.4.1
2	7.EE.2.4	MP.6.1
3*	7.EE.1.1	MP.7.1
4	7.EE.2.4	MP.4.1
5	7.EE.2.4a	MP.2.1
6	7.EE.1.1	MP.7.1
7	7.EE.2.4, 7.EE.2.4a	MP.2.1, MP.4.1, MP.6.1

* Item integrates mixed review concepts from previous modules or a previous course.

Inequalities

ESSENTIAL QUESTION

How can you use inequalities to solve real-world problems?

You can model real-world problems with inequalities, then use algebraic rules to solve the inequalities.

my.hrw.com

Real-World Video

Many school groups and other organizations hold events to raise money. Members can write and solve inequalities to represent the financial goals they are trying to achieve.

GO DIGITAL

my.hrw.com

my.hrw.com

Go digital with your write-in student edition, accessible on any device.

Math On the Spot

Scan with your smart phone to jump directly to the online edition, video tutor, and more.

Animated Math

Interactively explore key concepts to see how math works.

Personal Math Trainer

Get immediate feedback and help as you work through practice sets.

Are You Ready?

Assess Readiness

Use the assessment on this page to determine if students need intensive or strategic intervention for the module's prerequisite skills.

Response to Intervention

Intervention	Enrichment
Access Are You Ready? assessment online, and receive instant scoring, feedback, and customized intervention or enrichment.	

Online and Print Resources

Skills Intervention worksheets
- Skill 57 Inverse Operations
- Skill 61 Locate Points on a Number Line
- Skill 47 Integer Operations

Differentiated Instruction
- Challenge worksheets **PRE-AP**
- Extend the Math **PRE-AP** Lesson Activities in TE

Personal Math Trainer

Online Assessment and Intervention

my.hrw.com

Are YOU Ready?

Complete these exercises to review skills you will need for this module.

Personal Math Trainer
Online Assessment and Intervention
my.hrw.com

Inverse Operations

EXAMPLE	$3x = 24$	x is multiplied by 3.
	$\frac{3x}{3} = \frac{24}{3}$	Use the inverse operation, division.
	$x = 8$	Divide both sides by 3.
	$z + 6 = 4$	6 is added to z.
	$\underline{-6} = \underline{-6}$	Use the inverse operation, subtraction.
	$z = -2$	Subtract 6 from both sides.

Solve each equation, using inverse operations.

1. $9w = -54$ $w = -6$
2. $b - 12 = 3$ $b = 15$
3. $\frac{n}{4} = -11$ $n = -44$

Locate Points on a Number Line

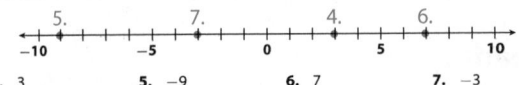

EXAMPLE
Graph $+2$ by starting at O and counting 2 units to the *right*.

Graph -4 by starting at O and counting 4 units to the *left*.

Graph each number on the number line.

4. 3
5. -9
6. 7
7. -3

Integer Operations

EXAMPLE	$-7 - (-4) = -7 + 4$	To subtract an integer, add its opposite.
	$= |-7| - |4|$	The signs are different, so find the difference of the absolute values.
	$= 7 - 4$, or 3	
	$= -3$	Use the sign of the number with the greater absolute value.

8. $3 - (-5)$ 8
9. $-4 - 5$ -9
10. $6 - 10$ -4
11. $-5 - (-3)$ -2
12. $8 - (-8)$ 16
13. $9 - 5$ 4
14. $-3 - 9$ -12
15. $0 - (-6)$ 6

PROFESSIONAL DEVELOPMENT VIDEO

Author Juli Dixon models successful teaching practices as she explores two-step equations and inequalities in an actual seventh-grade classroom.

Professional Development

my.hrw.com

GO DIGITAL
my.hrw.com

Online Teacher Edition
Access a full suite of teaching resources online—plan, present, and manage classes and assignments.

ePlanner
Easily plan your classes and access all your resources online.

Interactive Answers and Solutions
Customize answer keys to print or display in the classroom. Choose to include answers only or full solutions to all lesson exercises.

Interactive Whiteboards
Engage students with interactive whiteboard-ready lessons and activities.

Personal Math Trainer: Online Assessment and Intervention
Assign automatically graded homework, quizzes, tests, and intervention activities. Prepare your students with updated practice tests aligned with Common Core.

Reading Start-Up

Have students complete the activities on this page by working alone or with others.

Visualize Vocabulary

The definitions and examples in the graphic organizer help students review vocabulary associated with expressions and inequalities. As a class, add boxes to the graphic organizer and brainstorm additional terms and definitions related to the content in this module.

Understand Vocabulary

Use the following explanations to help students learn the review words.

An expression includes numbers and operations. An **algebraic expression** includes at least one variable. A **variable** represents an unknown value. The word *variable* means "able to change." A **constant** is a fixed number and the word means "unchanging."

Active Reading

Integrating Language Arts

Students can use these reading and note-taking strategies to help them organize and understand new concepts and vocabulary.

FL CC **LACC.68.RST.3.7** Integrate quantitative or technical information expressed in words in a text with a version of that information expressed visually (e.g., in a flowchart, diagram, model, graph, or table).

Additional Resources

Differentiated Instruction

• Reading Strategies **ELL**

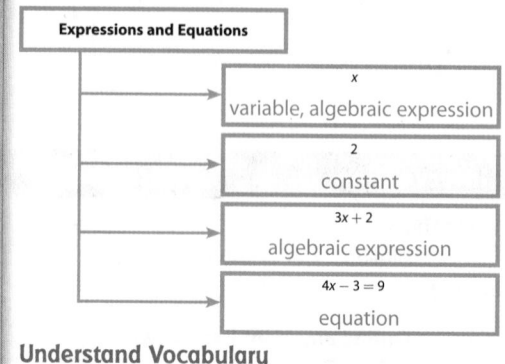

Reading Start-Up

Visualize Vocabulary

Use the ✔ words to complete the graphic. You may put more than one word in each box.

Vocabulary

Review Words
- ✔ algebraic expression *(expresión algebraica)*
- coefficient *(coeficiente)*
- ✔ constant *(contante)*
- ✔ equation *(ecuación)*
- greater than *(mayor que)*
- ✔ inequality *(desigualdad)*
- integers *(enteros)*
- less than *(menor que)*
- operations *(operaciones)*
- solution *(solución)*
- ✔ variable *(variable)*

Expressions and Equations

x
variable, algebraic expression

2
constant

$3x + 2$
algebraic expression

$4x - 3 = 9$
equation

Understand Vocabulary

Complete each sentence, using the review words.

1. A value of the variable that makes the equation true is a __solution__.

2. The set of all whole numbers and their opposites are __integers__.

3. An __algebraic expression__ is an expression that contains at least one variable.

Active Reading

Layered Book Before beginning the module, create a layered book to help you learn the concepts in this module. At the top of the first flap, write the title of the module, "Inequalities." Then label each flap with one of the lesson titles in this module. As you study each lesson, write important ideas, such as vocabulary and processes, under the appropriate flap.

© Houghton Mifflin Harcourt Publishing Company

Module 2 **35**

Before	**In this module**	**After**
Students understand:	Students will learn how to:	Students will connect:
• one-step, one-variable inequalities	• write two-step inequalities to represent real-world problems, and write a real-world problem to represent an inequality	• two-step inequalities and inequalities with variables on both sides and rational number coefficients and constants
• how to solve one-step, one-variable inequalities that contain addition or subtraction	• solve two-step inequalities	
• how to solve one-step, one-variable inequalities that contain multiplication or division		

Unpacking the Standards

Use the examples on the page to help students know exactly what they are expected to learn in this module.

Florida Common Core Standards

Content Areas

 FL CC Expressions and Equations—7.EE.2

Solve real-life and mathematical problems using numerical and algebraic expressions and equations.

Go online to see a complete unpacking of the Florida Common Core Standards.

⏻ my.hrw.com

MODULE 2
Unpacking the Standards

Understanding the standards and the vocabulary terms in the standards will help you know exactly what you are expected to learn in this module.

FL CC 7.EE.2.4

Use variables to represent quantities in a real-world or mathematical problem, and construct simple equations and inequalities to solve problems by reasoning about the quantities.

Key Vocabulary

inequality *(desigualdad)*
A mathematical sentence that shows that two quantities are not equal.

What It Means to You

You will write an inequality to solve a real-world problem.

UNPACKING EXAMPLE 7.EE.2.4

To rent a certain car for a day costs $39 plus $0.29 for every mile the car is driven. Write an inequality to show the maximum number of miles you can drive and keep the rental cost under $100.

The expression for the cost of the rental is $39 + 0.29m$. The total cost of the rental must be under $100. So the inequality is as shown.

$$39 + 0.29m < 100$$

FL CC 7.EE.2.4b

Solve word problems leading to inequalities of the form $px + q > r$ or $px + q < r$, where p, q, and r are specific rational numbers. Graph the solution set of the inequality and interpret it in the context of the problem.

Key Vocabulary

solution *(solución)*
The value(s) for the variable that makes the inequality true.

What It Means to You

You will solve inequalities that involve two steps and interpret the solutions.

UNPACKING EXAMPLE 7.EE.2.4b

Solve and graph the solution of $-3x + 7 > -8$.

$$-3x + 7 > -8$$

$-3x > -7 - 8$	Subtract 7 from both sides.
$-3x > -15$	Simplify.
$x < 5$	Divide both sided by -5, and reverse the inequality.

All numbers less than 5 are solutions for this inequality.

Visit my.hrw.com to see all Florida Common Core Standards unpacked.

⏻ my.hrw.com

36 Unit 1

 Florida Common Core Standards	Lesson 2.1	Lesson 2.2	Lesson 2.3
FL CC 7.EE.2.4 Use variables to represent quantities in a real-world or mathematical problem, and construct simple equations and inequalities to solve problems by reasoning about the quantities.	🏴	🏴	
FL CC 7.EE.2.4b Solve word problems leading to inequalities of the form $px + q > r$ or $px + q < r$, where p, q, and r are specific rational numbers. Graph the solution set of the inequality and interpret it in the context of the problem.	🏴		🏴

Florida Common Core Standards

The student is expected to:

 **FL CC** Expressions and Equations—7.EE.2.4b

Solve word problems leading to inequalities of the form $px + q > r$ or $px + q < r$, where p, q, and r are specific rational numbers. Graph the solution set of the inequality and interpret it in the context of the problem.

Mathematical Practices

 **FL CC** MP.1.1 Problem Solving

---

ADDITIONAL EXAMPLE 1

Solve each inequality. Graph and check the solution.

A $x - 11 < -7$ $x < 4$

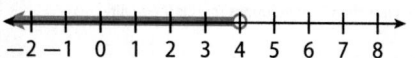

B $9 \le y + 7$ $y \ge 2$

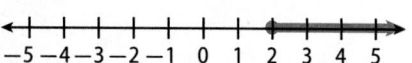

 Interactive Whiteboard
Interactive example available online

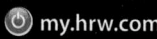 my.hrw.com

---

 Animated Math
Subtraction Inequalities

Students model subtraction inequality solutions on a number line.

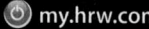 my.hrw.com

---

Engage

ESSENTIAL QUESTION

How do you write and solve one-step inequalities? Sample answer: You can list the important information from the problem and use this information to write an inequality. You can then use the properties of inequality and inverse operations to solve.

Motivate the Lesson
Ask: How can you use what you know about solving equations to help you solve inequalities? Take a guess. Begin the Explore Activity to find out.

Explore

EXPLORE ACTIVITY

Focus on Reasoning 🌴 Mathematical Practices
Students complete tables to show that addition and division can be performed on an inequality and have it still be true. Have students use these tables to justify their conclusions to Exercises 1–3.

Explain

EXAMPLE 1

Focus on Patterns 🌴 Mathematical Practices
Make sure students understand that the inequality symbol is not reversed when adding (or subtracting) the same number on both sides of the inequality unless the inequality is being rewritten so that the variable is moved from one side to the other side.

Questioning Strategies 🌴 Mathematical Practices
• How does graphing the solution help you to be sure you have the correct solution? The graph can help you see values to use when checking the solution. The shaded values that are part of the number line and the value at a closed circle should make the inequality true.

• Why is it helpful to rewrite an inequality with the variable on the left side? It is generally easier to read and understand the inequality with the variable on the left. "x is less than 6" is more straightforward to most people than "6 is greater than x."

2.1 Writing and Solving One-Step Inequalities

 **FL CC** 7.EE.2.4b

Use variables to represent quantities in a real-world or mathematical problem, and construct simple ... inequalities to solve problems by reasoning about the quantities.

ESSENTIAL QUESTION

How do you write and solve one-step inequalities?

 **EXPLORE ACTIVITY** **FL CC** Prep. for 7.EE.2.4b

Investigating Inequalities

You know that when you perform any of the four basic operations on both sides of an equation, the resulting equation is still true. What effect does performing these operations on both sides of an *inequality* have?

A Complete the table.

Inequality	Add to both sides:	New Inequality	Is new inequality true or false?
$2 \geq -3$	3	$5 \geq 0$	true
$-1 \leq 6$	-1	$-2 \leq 5$	true
$-8 > -10$	-8	$-16 > -18$	true

Reflect

1. **Make a Conjecture** When you add the same number to both sides of an inequality, is the inequality still true? Explain how you know that your conjecture holds for *subtracting* the same number.

   Yes; subtracting a number is the same as adding its opposite.

B Complete the table.

Inequality	Divide both sides by:	New Inequality	Is new inequality true or false?
$4 < 8$	4	$1 < 2$	true
$12 \geq -15$	3	$4 \geq -5$	true
$-16 \leq 12$	-4	$4 \leq -3$	false
$15 > 5$	-5	$-3 > -1$	false

What do you notice when you divide both sides of an inequality by the same negative number?

The inequality is no longer true.

EXPLORE ACTIVITY (cont'd)

Reflect

2. **Make a Conjecture** What could you do to make the inequalities that are not true into true statements?

   Reverse the inequality symbol.

3. **Communicate Mathematical Ideas** Explain how you know that your conjecture holds for multiplying both sides of an inequality by a negative number.

   Multiplying a number is the same as dividing by its reciprocal.

Math On the Spot
my.hrw.com

Solving Inequalities Involving Addition and Subtraction

You can use properties of inequality to solve inequalities involving addition and subtraction with rational numbers.

Addition and Subtraction Properties of Inequality	
Addition Property of Inequality	**Subtraction Property of Inequality**
You can add the same number to both sides of an inequality and the inequality will remain true.	You can subtract the same number from both sides of an inequality and the inequality will remain true.

Animated Math
my.hrw.com

EXAMPLE 1 **FL CC** 7.EE.2.4b

Solve each inequality. Graph and check the solution.

A $x + 5 < -12$

STEP 1 Solve the inequality.

$x + 5 < -12$ Use the Subtraction Property of Inequality.

$\dfrac{-5}{x} < \dfrac{-5}{-17}$ Subtract 5 from both sides.

STEP 2 Graph the solution.

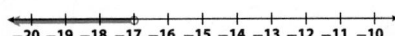

$-20\ -19\ -18\ -17\ -16\ -15\ -14\ -13\ -12\ -11\ -10$

STEP 3 Check the solution. Substitute a solution from the shaded part of your number line into the original inequality.

$-18 + 5 \overset{?}{<} -12$ Substitute -18 for x into $x + 5 < -12$.

$-13 < -12$ The inequality is true.

PROFESSIONAL DEVELOPMENT

Integrate Mathematical Practices MP.1.1

This lesson provides an opportunity to address this Mathematical Practice standard. It calls for students to make sense of problems and persevere in solving them. Students write and solve inequalities to make sense of, and then solve, real-world problems. They make sense of a real-world problem by applying a 4-step problem-solving plan: Analyze information, Formulate a plan, Solve, and Justify and Evaluate.

Math Background

An inequality such as $|x| > -1$ has no solutions because the absolute value of a number can never have a negative value. But an inequality such as $x > -1$ has an infinite number of solutions. Graphing the solution to an inequality on a number line includes values for x other than just integers. It also includes all rational and irrational numbers that fulfill the terms of the inequality. For example, any positive real number is a solution of $x > 0$.

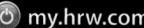

YOUR TURN

Avoid Common Errors

For Exercise 5, remind students to check which side of the inequality symbol is oriented toward the variable before it is moved. That side should be oriented toward the variable when the variable is moved to the left side. So for $9 > x$, the closed side is oriented toward x, the same as it is in $x < 9$.

EXAMPLE 2

Focus on Modeling 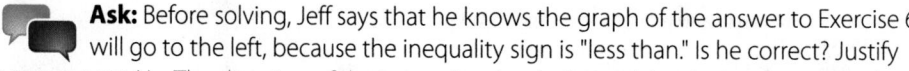 Mathematical Practices

Make sure students understand how to choose the scale for the number line on which they will graph the solution. Be sure students understand the location of the positive and negative numbers on the scale and when it might be necessary to change the increment of the scale to something other than 1.

Questioning Strategies ◤ Mathematical Practices

• How do you indicate on a number line that the greatest value a variable can have is -13? The graph will have a closed circle at -13 and will be shaded to the left of -13.

• How could you eliminate dividing by a negative number in Step 1 of Part B? You could add $4x$ to each side. The result would be $0 > 52 + 4x$ and the result after subtracting 52 would be $-52 > 4x$. Dividing by 4 results in $-13 > x$ or $x < -13$.

YOUR TURN

Engage with the Whiteboard

For Exercises 6 and 7, have volunteers demonstrate how to solve each inequality. Have another volunteer graph the solutions.

Talk About It
Check for Understanding

Ask: Before solving, Jeff says that he knows the graph of the answer to Exercise 6 will go to the left, because the inequality sign is "less than." Is he correct? Justify your answer. No. The direction of the inequality sign before solving is not necessarily the same as the direction of the solution. In this case, the "less than" sign flips to "greater than," so the graph actually points to the right.

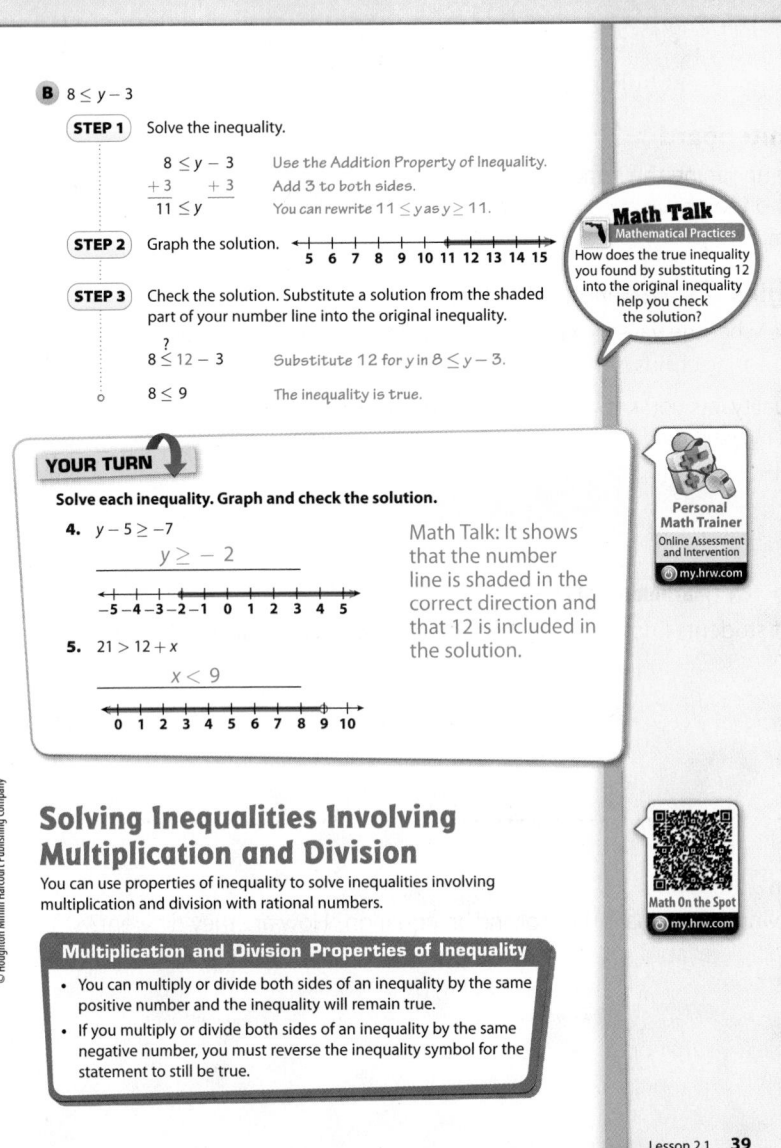

B $8 \le y - 3$

STEP 1 Solve the inequality.

$$8 \le y - 3 \qquad \text{Use the Addition Property of Inequality.}$$
$$\underline{+3 \quad +3} \qquad \text{Add 3 to both sides.}$$
$$11 \le y \qquad \text{You can rewrite } 11 \le y \text{ as } y \ge 11.$$

STEP 2 Graph the solution.

5 6 7 8 9 10 11 12 13 14 15

STEP 3 Check the solution. Substitute a solution from the shaded part of your number line into the original inequality.

$$8 \overset{?}{\le} 12 - 3 \qquad \text{Substitute 12 for } y \text{ in } 8 \le y - 3.$$
$$8 \le 9 \qquad \text{The inequality is true.}$$

Math Talk
Mathematical Practices

How does the true inequality you found by substituting 12 into the original inequality help you check the solution?

YOUR TURN

Solve each inequality. Graph and check the solution.

4. $y - 5 \ge -7$

$y \ge -2$

−5 −4 −3 −2 −1 0 1 2 3 4 5

5. $21 > 12 + x$

$x < 9$

0 1 2 3 4 5 6 7 8 9 10

Math Talk: It shows that the number line is shaded in the correct direction and that 12 is included in the solution.

Personal Math Trainer
Online Assessment and Intervention
my.hrw.com

Solving Inequalities Involving Multiplication and Division

You can use properties of inequality to solve inequalities involving multiplication and division with rational numbers.

Multiplication and Division Properties of Inequality

- You can multiply or divide both sides of an inequality by the same positive number and the inequality will remain true.
- If you multiply or divide both sides of an inequality by the same negative number, you must reverse the inequality symbol for the statement to still be true.

Math On the Spot
my.hrw.com

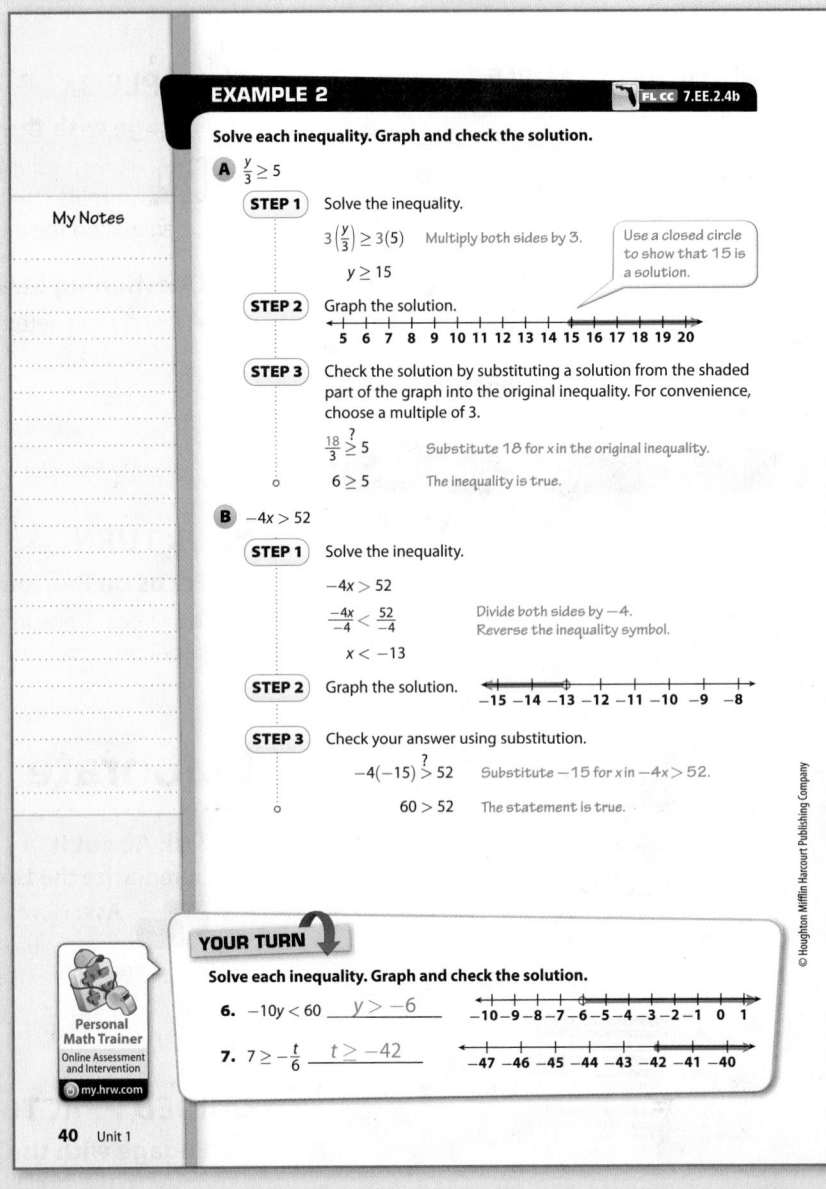

My Notes

EXAMPLE 2   FL CC 7.EE.2.4b

Solve each inequality. Graph and check the solution.

A $\frac{y}{3} \ge 5$

STEP 1 Solve the inequality.

$$3\left(\frac{y}{3}\right) \ge 3(5) \qquad \text{Multiply both sides by 3.}$$
$$y \ge 15$$

Use a closed circle to show that 15 is a solution.

STEP 2 Graph the solution.

5 6 7 8 9 10 11 12 13 14 15 16 17 18 19 20

STEP 3 Check the solution by substituting a solution from the shaded part of the graph into the original inequality. For convenience, choose a multiple of 3.

$$\frac{18}{3} \overset{?}{\ge} 5 \qquad \text{Substitute 18 for } x \text{ in the original inequality.}$$
$$6 \ge 5 \qquad \text{The inequality is true.}$$

B $-4x > 52$

STEP 1 Solve the inequality.

$$-4x > 52$$
$$\frac{-4x}{-4} < \frac{52}{-4} \qquad \text{Divide both sides by } -4. \text{ Reverse the inequality symbol.}$$
$$x < -13$$

STEP 2 Graph the solution.

−15 −14 −13 −12 −11 −10 −9 −8

STEP 3 Check your answer using substitution.

$$-4(-15) \overset{?}{>} 52 \qquad \text{Substitute } -15 \text{ for } x \text{ in } -4x > 52.$$
$$60 > 52 \qquad \text{The statement is true.}$$

YOUR TURN

Solve each inequality. Graph and check the solution.

6. $-10y < 60$ $y > -6$

−10 −9 −8 −7 −6 −5 −4 −3 −2 −1 0 1

7. $7 \ge -\frac{t}{6}$ $t \ge -42$

−47 −46 −45 −44 −43 −42 −41 −40

Personal Math Trainer
Online Assessment and Intervention
my.hrw.com

DIFFERENTIATE INSTRUCTION

Critical Thinking

Have small groups of students determine which value an inequality can never be multiplied or divided by when solving an inequality. Then have students justify the value they chose by using examples. Students may find multiplication by zero, division by zero, or multiplication or division by the variable to not be possible for various reasons.

Visual Cues

Once an inequality is simplified with the variable on the left side, the inequality symbol indicates which way to shade the graph of the solution. Show students visual cues similar to the ones below.

x 9

 $y \ge -2$

Additional Resources

Differentiated Instruction includes:

- Reading Strategies
- Success for English Learners **ELL**
- Reteach
- Challenge **PRE-AP**

ADDITIONAL EXAMPLE 3

Every month, Tracie writes a check for $25 to pay off part of a loan. She has enough in her checking account to pay no more than $450 towards the loan. For how many months can Tracie send payments for the loan? $m \leq 18$; Tracie can pay for no more than 18 months.

 Interactive Whiteboard
Interactive example available online

⏻ my.hrw.com

EXAMPLE 3

Engage with the Whiteboard

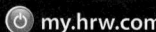 Have a volunteer underline the important information in the problem. Discuss the formula $rt = d$, and then have another volunteer circle the values to use for r and d when writing the inequality.

Questioning Strategies 🖊 Mathematical Practices

• How do you determine what the variable stands for in the inequality? The question asks for the number of seconds. Seconds is a unit of time. So, time is t, the unknown.

• What part of the inequality lets you know you must reverse the inequality symbol? The coefficient of t is a negative number, so the inequality symbol is reversed when dividing by -5 on both sides.

YOUR TURN

Focus on Reasoning 🖊 Mathematical Practices

In Exercise 8, ensure that students know how to check their answer using substitution to justify their conclusion.

Elaborate

. . . .

Talk About It
Summarize the Lesson

 Ask: How is solving an inequality like solving an equation? How are they different? The general principle of applying inverse operations to isolate the variable is the same. One difference is that when multiplying or dividing by a negative number, the inequality symbol is reversed. Another difference is that an inequality can have an infinite number of solutions while an equation usually does not.

GUIDED PRACTICE

Engage with the Whiteboard

In the space to the right of Exercises 1–4, have volunteers show and explain the process of arriving at the resulting inequality.

Avoid Common Errors

Exercises 5–8 Remind students to check a value in the shaded region of their graph to be sure they have not made an error in reversing the inequality symbol.

Exercise 9a Alert students to the third sentence. This sentence provides them with the relationship between the rate of change, number of seconds, and the final temperature to be used when they write an inequality to represent the situation.

Solving a Real-World Problem

Although elevations below sea level are represented by negative numbers, we often use absolute values to describe these elevations. For example, −50 feet relative to sea level might be described as 50 feet below sea level.

Math On the Spot
my.hrw.com

EXAMPLE 3 *Problem Solving* FL CC 7.EE.2.4, 7.EE.2.4b

A marine submersible descends more than 40 feet below sea level. As it descends from sea level, the change in elevation is −5 feet per second. For how many seconds does it descend?

Analyze Information

Rewrite the question as a statement.
- Find the number of seconds that the submersible descends below sea level.

List the important information:
- The final elevation is greater than 40 feet below sea level or < −40 feet.
- The rate of descent is −5 feet per second.

Formulate a Plan

Write and solve an inequality. Use this fact:

Rate of change in elevation × Time in seconds = Final elevation

Solve

$-5t < -40$ *Rate of change × Time < Final elevation*

$\dfrac{-5t}{-5} > \dfrac{-40}{-5}$ *Divide both sides by −5. Reverse the inequality symbol.*

$t > 8$

The submersible descends for more than 8 seconds.

Justify and Evaluate

Check your answer by substituting a value greater than 8 seconds in the original inequality.

$-5(9) \overset{?}{<} -40$ *Substitute 9 for t in the inequality −5t < −40.*

$-45 < -40$ *The statement is true.*

YOUR TURN

8. Every month, $35 is withdrawn from Tony's savings account to pay for his gym membership. He has enough savings to withdraw no more than $315. For how many months can Tony pay for his gym membership?

$m \le 9$; Tony can pay for no more than 9 months of his gym membership using this account.

Personal Math Trainer
Online Assessment and Intervention
my.hrw.com

Write the resulting inequality. (Explore Activity)

1. $-5 \le -2$; Add 7 to both sides _____ $2 \le 5$

2. $-6 < -3$; Divide both sides by −3 _____ $2 > 1$

3. $7 > -4$; Subtract 7 from both sides _____ $0 > -11$

4. $-1 \ge -8$; Multiply both sides by −2 _____ $2 \le 16$

Solve each inequality. Graph and check the solution. (Examples 1 and 2)

5. $n - 5 \ge -2$ _____ $n \ge 3$

   −5 −4 −3 −2 −1 0 1 2 3 4 5

6. $3 + x < 7$ _____ $x < 4$

   −2 −1 0 1 2 3 4 5 6 7 8

7. $-7y \le 14$ _____ $y \ge -2$

   −7 −6 −5 −4 −3 −2 −1 0 1 2 3

8. $\dfrac{b}{5} > -1$ _____ $b > -5$

   −8 −7 −6 −5 −4 −3 −2 −1 0 1 2

9. For a scientific experiment, a physicist must make sure that the temperature of a metal at 0 °C gets no colder than −80 °C. The physicist changes the metal's temperature at a steady rate of −4 °C per hour. For how long can the physicist change the temperature? (Example 3)

   a. Let t represent temperature in degrees Celsius. Write an inequality. Use the fact that the rate of change in temperature times the number of hours equals the final temperature.

   $-4t \ge -80$

   b. Solve the inequality in part **a**. How long can the physicist change the temperature of the metal?

   20 or fewer hours

   c. The physicist has to repeat the experiment if the metal gets cooler than −80 °C. How many hours would the physicist have to cool the metal for this to happen?

   more than 20 hours

? ESSENTIAL QUESTION CHECK-IN

10. Suppose you are solving an inequality. Under what circumstances do you reverse the inequality symbol?

   when you divide or multiply both sides by a negative number

2.1 LESSON QUIZ

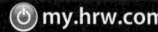 7.EE.2.4b

Write the resulting inequality.

1. $-3 \le 6$ Add 8 to both sides.

2. $2 > -4$ Multiply both sides by -3.

Solve each inequality. Graph and check the solution.

3. $x + 8 > 3$

4. $-9x \le 18$

5. To cover her rectangular screened-in porch with outdoor carpet, Kendra needs at least 67.1 square feet of carpet. The length of Kendra's porch is 12.2 feet. What are the possible widths of Kendra's porch?

Lesson Quiz available online

⏻ my.hrw.com

Answers

1. $5 \le 14$

2. $-6 < 12$

3. $x > -5$

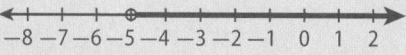

4. $x \ge -2$

5. $12.2w \ge 67.1$; $w \ge 5.5$; the width of Kendra's porch is at least 5.5 feet.

Evaluate

GUIDED AND INDEPENDENT PRACTICE

 **FL CC** 7.EE.2.4b

Concepts and Skills	Practice
Explore Activity Investigating Inequalities	Exercises 1–4
Example 1 Solving Inequalities Involving Addition and Subtraction	Exercises 5, 6, 11, 12, 15
Example 2 Solving Inequalities Involving Multiplication and Division	Exercises 7, 8, 13, 14, 16
Example 3 Solving a Real-World Problem	Exercises 9, 17–25

Exercise	Depth of Knowledge (D.O.K.)	**FL CC** Mathematical Practices
11–16	**1** Recall	**MP.2.1** Reasoning
17	**2** Skills/Concepts	**MP.4.1** Modeling
18	**2** Skills/Concepts	**MP.4.1** Modeling
19	**2** Skills/Concepts	**MP.4.1** Modeling
20	**2** Skills/Concepts	**MP.4.1** Modeling
21	**2** Skills/Concepts	**MP.4.1** Modeling
22	**2** Skills/Concepts	**MP.4.1** Modeling
23	**2** Skills/Concepts	**MP.4.1** Modeling
24	**2** Skills/Concepts	**MP.4.1** Modeling
25	**3** Strategic Thinking **H.O.T.**	**MP.3.1** Logic
26	**3** Strategic Thinking **H.O.T.**	**MP.3.1** Logic
27	**3** Strategic Thinking **H.O.T.**	**MP.8.1** Patterns
28	**3** Strategic Thinking **H.O.T.**	**MP.1.1** Problem Solving

Additional Resources

Differentiated Instruction includes:

• Leveled Practice worksheets

2.1 Independent Practice

FL CC 7.EE.2.4, 7.EE.2.4b

Personal Math Trainer

Online Assessment and Intervention

© my.hrw.com

In 11–16, solve each inequality. Graph and check the solution.

11. $x - 35 > 15$ _____ $x > 50$

0 10 20 30 40 50 60 70 80 90 100

12. $193 + y \geq 201$ _____ $y \geq 8$

0 1 2 3 4 5 6 7 8 9 10

13. $-\frac{q}{7} \geq -1$ _____ $q \leq 7$

0 1 2 3 4 5 6 7 8 9 10

14. $-12x < 60$ _____ $x > -5$

-10 -9 -8 -7 -6 -5 -4 -3 -2 -1 0

15. $5 > z - 3$ _____ $z < 8$

0 1 2 3 4 5 6 7 8 9 10

16. $0.5 \leq \frac{y}{8}$ _____ $y \geq 4$

0 1 2 3 4 5 6 7 8 9 10

17. The vet says that Lena's puppy will grow to be at most 28 inches tall. Lena's puppy is currently 1 foot tall. How many more inches will the puppy grow?

at most 16 inches

18. In a litter of 7 kittens, each kitten weighs less than 3.5 ounces. Find all the possible values of the combined weights of the kittens.

any nonzero weight < 24.5 oz

19. Geometry The sides of the hexagon shown are equal in length. The perimeter of the hexagon is at most 42 inches. Find the possible side lengths of the hexagon.

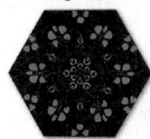

at most 7 inches

20. To get a free meal at his favorite restaurant, Tom needs to spend $50 or more at the restaurant. He has already spent $30.25. How much more does Tom need to spend to get his free meal?

at least $19.75

21. To cover a rectangular region of her yard, Penny needs at least 170.5 square feet of sod. The length of the region is 15.5 feet. What are the possible widths of the region?

at least 11 feet

22. Draw Conclusions A submarine descends from sea level to the entrance of an underwater cave. The elevation of the entrance is -120 feet. The rate of change in the submarine's elevation is no greater than -12 feet per second. Can the submarine reach the entrance to the cave in less than 10 seconds? Explain.

No; let t be the number of seconds the descent takes; $-12t < -120$ and $t > 10$; the descent takes 10 seconds or more.

The sign shows some prices at a produce stand.

23. Selena has $10. What is the greatest amount of spinach she can buy?

$3\frac{1}{3}$ pounds

Produce	Price per Pound
Onions	$1.25
Yellow Squash	$0.99
Spinach	$3.00
Potatoes	$0.50

24. Gary has enough money to buy at most 5.5 pounds of potatoes. How much money does Gary have?

at most $2.75

25. Florence wants to spend no more than $3 on onions. Will she be able to buy 2.5 pounds of onions? Explain.

No; $1.25x \leq 3$; $x \leq 2.4$ so 2.4 pounds of onions is the most Florence can buy. $2.4 < 2.5$, so she cannot buy 2.5 pounds.

H.O.T. FOCUS ON HIGHER ORDER THINKING

Work Area

26. Counterexamples John says that if one side of an inequality is 0, you don't have to reverse the inequality symbol when you multiply or divide both sides by a negative number. Find an inequality that you can use to disprove John's statement. Explain your thinking.

If you divide both sides of $-7z \geq 0$ by -7, you get $z \geq 0$. This is incorrect because if you choose a value from the possible solutions, such as $z = 1$, and substitute it into the original equation, you get $-7 \geq 0$, which is not true.

27. Look for a Pattern Solve $x + 1 > 10$, $x + 11 > 20$, and $x + 21 > 30$. Describe a pattern. Then use the pattern to predict the solution of $x + 9,991 > 10,000$.

$x > 9$ for each inequality; in each case the number added to x is 9 less than the number on the right side of each inequality, so $x > 9$ is the solution.

28. Persevere in Problem Solving The base of a rectangular prism has a length of 13 inches and a width of $\frac{1}{2}$ inch. The volume of the prism is less than 65 cubic inches. Find all possible heights of the prism. Show your work.

All heights greater than 0 in. and less than 10 in.; $13\left(\frac{1}{2}\right)h \leq 65$; $6.5h \leq 65$; $h \leq 10$. A height cannot be 0 or less than 0, so $h > 0$ and $h \leq 10$.

EXTEND THE MATH PRE-AP

Activity available online © my.hrw.com

Activity Let $a \leq 2$ and $a \geq -2$. Between what two values will the solution to $ay < 6$ be found? Justify your answer and graph it on a number line.

y is between 3 and -3. Test the two extremes of a: The maximum value of a occurs when $a = 2$. Then, $2y < 6$ and $y < 3$. The minimum value of a occurs when $a = -2$. In this case, $-2y < 6$ and $y > -3$. Therefore, $y < 3$ and $y > -3$.

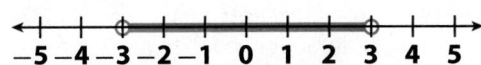

-5 -4 -3 -2 -1 0 1 2 3 4 5

Florida Common Core Standards

The student is expected to:

 **FL CC** **Expressions and Equations—7.EE.2.4**

Use variables to represent quantities in a real-world or mathematical problem, and construct simple equations and inequalities to solve problems by reasoning about the quantities.

Mathematical Practices

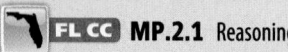 **FL CC** **MP.2.1** Reasoning

ADDITIONAL EXAMPLE 1

Trevor is writing a paper that must be at least 50,000 words long. He has already written 23,210 words. Write an inequality to find the average number of words Trevor must write per week if he wants to finish the paper in the next 5 weeks.

$23{,}210 + 5w \geq 50{,}000$

 Interactive Whiteboard
Interactive example available online

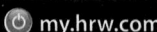 my.hrw.com

Engage

ESSENTIAL QUESTION

How do you write a two-step inequality? Sample answer: Identify the important numbers in the problem, and use words and phrases from the problem to decide what operations and symbols to use in the inequality.

Motivate the Lesson

Ask: How can you use algebra tiles to model equations? inequalities? Think about the steps you would use before you start the Explore Activity.

Explore

EXPLORE ACTIVITY

Focus on Math Connections Mathematical Practices

Students may not recall the symbols $\leq$ and $\geq$. Make sure that students understand that $\leq$ is read as "less than or equal to" and $\geq$ is read as "greater than or equal to."

Explain

EXAMPLE 1

Connect Vocabulary **ELL**

Remind students that an equation is a mathematical statement containing an equal sign, and that an **inequality** is a mathematical statement containing one of these symbols: $<, >, \leq,$ or $\geq$. Understanding the difference between equations and inequalities will be important when students solve two-step inequalities.

Engage with the Whiteboard

Cover up the equation in Step 3, and have students provide the numbers, operations, and symbols that correspond to the descriptions.

Questioning Strategies Mathematical Practices

• In the inequality $18{,}460 + 6d \geq 29{,}029$, how would the corresponding problem be different if the $\geq$ symbol was changed to an equal sign? The amount of time the climbing team takes to reach the summit would change from 6 days or less to exactly 6 days.

• Why is the $\geq$ symbol used if the mountain climbing team cannot go higher than the summit of the mountain? The $\geq$ symbol is used because the daily amount climbed should be greater than or equal to the daily amount needed to reach the summit in exactly 6 days.

YOUR TURN

Focus on Reasoning Mathematical Practices

Have students justify their reasons for choosing the inequality symbol in the inequalities they have written. Students should be able to identify words or phrases in the problem that determined which symbol to use in the inequality, as well as explain which side of the inequality should represent the greater amount.

Writing Two-Step Inequalities

 7.EE.2.4

Use variables to represent quantities in a real-world or mathematical problem, and construct simple... inequalities...

? ESSENTIAL QUESTION

How do you write a two-step inequality?

EXPLORE ACTIVITY | FL CC Prep for 7.EE.2.4

Modeling Two-Step Inequalities

You can use algebra tiles to model two-step inequalities.

Use algebra tiles to model $2k + 5 \geq -3$.

A Using the line on the mat, draw in the inequality symbol shown in the inequality.

B How can you model the left side of the inequality?

Use 2 positive variable tiles and 5 + 1-tiles.

C How can you model the right side of the inequality?

Use 3 − 1-tiles.

D Use algebra tiles or draw them to model the inequality on the mat.

Reflect

1. **Multiple Representations** How does your model differ from the one you would draw to model the equation $2k + 5 = -3$?

The tiles would be the same, but the line now represents an inequality symbol instead of an equal sign.

2. Why might you need to change the inequality sign when you solve an inequality using algebra tiles?

If you multiply or divide both sides of the inequality by a negative number, you will change the direction of the inequality sign.

© Houghton Mifflin Harcourt Publishing Company

Math On the Spot
my.hrw.com

Writing Two-Step Inequalities

You can write two-step inequalities to represent real-world problems by translating the words of the problems into numbers, variables, and operations.

EXAMPLE 1 Real World | FL CC 7.EE.2.4

A mountain climbing team is camped at an altitude of 18,460 feet on Mount Everest. The team wants to reach the 29,029-foot summit within 6 days. Write an inequality to find the average number of feet per day the team must climb to accomplish its objective.

STEP 1 Identify what you are trying to find. This will be the variable in the inequality.

Let d represent the average altitude the team must gain each day.

STEP 2 Identify important information in the problem that you can use to write an inequality.

starting altitude: **18,460 ft**   target altitude: **29,029 ft**
number of days times altitude gained to reach target altitude: $6 \cdot d$

STEP 3 Use words in the problem to tie the information together and write an inequality.

The solution will give d, the minimum amount the team must gain each day. Any amount greater than d will also get the team to the summit in 6 days or less.

Math Talk
Mathematical Practices

Why is the inequality sign $\geq$ used, rather than an equal sign?

starting altitude	+	number of days	times	altitude gain	is greater than or equal to	target altitude
↓	↓	↓	↓	↓	↓	↓
18,460	+	6	×	d	≥	29,029

$18,460 + 6d \geq 29,029$

YOUR TURN

3. The 45 members of the glee club are trying to raise $6,000 so they can compete in the state championship. They already have $1,240. What inequality can you write to find the amount each member must raise, on average, to meet the goal? $1,240 + 45a \geq 6,000$

4. Ella has $40 to spend at the State Fair. Admission is $6 and each ride costs $3. Write an inequality to find the greatest number of rides she can go on.

$6 + 3n \leq 40$

Personal Math Trainer
Online Assessment and Intervention
my.hrw.com

© Houghton Mifflin Harcourt Publishing Company • Image Credits: ©Photographers Choice RF/SuperStock

---

PROFESSIONAL DEVELOPMENT

Integrate Mathematical Practices MP.2.1

This lesson provides an opportunity to address this Mathematical Practice standard. It calls for students to communicate mathematical ideas … using multiple representations, including symbols, diagrams … and language as appropriate. Students use algebra tiles to model two-step inequalities. Then students write two-step inequalities that correspond to word problems. Finally, students analyze word problems to identify the important information, and use that information to write a corresponding two-step inequality.

Math Background

While the study of mathematics dates back thousands of years, several features of modern mathematics are only a few hundred years old. Abū al-Hasan ibn Alī al-Qalasādī, who lived from 1412 to 1486, was the first mathematician to use symbols for the mathematical operations. Athough the symbols he used were different from modern mathematical notation, his ideas led to the introduction of algebraic symbolism.

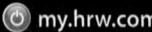
EXAMPLE 2

Connect to Daily Life 🖊 Mathematical Practices

Discuss with students situations from their personal life where 50 is the maximum value that an amount can be. Students may think of budgets, inviting guests to a party, and other situations that could be used in writing future word problems.

Questioning Strategies 🖊 Mathematical Practices

- Do the numbers in an inequality have to be presented in the same order in the corresponding word problem? Explain. No; the numbers can be presented in any order, as long as the inequality is equivalent to the situation in the word problem.

- Is the inequality $20 + 2x \leq 50$ the same as the inequality $2x + 20 \leq 50$? Explain. Yes; the order in which the two quantities are added does not change the inequality.

YOUR TURN

Avoid Common Errors

Students can easily confuse the inequality symbols $>$ and $\geq$, and the symbols $<$ and $\leq$. Have students reread their word problems to make sure they have used words or phrases that match the symbols used in each inequality.

Elaborate

. . . .

Talk About It
Summarize the Lesson

Ask: How is the process of writing an inequality similar to the process of writing an equation? How is the process of writing an inequality different from the process of writing an equation? Both involve reading a word problem to identify important numbers and phrases that determine which operations to use. When writing inequalities, there is an extra step of deciding which of the four inequality symbols corresponds to the word problem.

GUIDED PRACTICE

Engage with the Whiteboard

Have students draw the algebra tiles needed to model the inequalities in Exercises 1 and 2. Make sure students realize that they have to include the inequality symbol from the equation as part of the model.

Avoid Common Errors

Exercise 3 Some word problems will mention a specific variable to use. Remind students that when a variable is mentioned in a word problem, they must use that variable in their inequality.

Writing a Verbal Description of a Two-Step Inequality

You can also write a verbal description to fit a two-step inequality.

Math On the Spot
my.hrw.com

EXAMPLE 2   Real World   FL CC 7.EE.2.4

Write a corresponding real-world problem to represent $2x + 20 \leq 50$.

STEP 1 Analyze what each part of the inequality means mathematically.

x is the solution of the problem, the quantity you are looking for.

$2x$ means that, for a reason given in the problem, the quantity you are looking for is multiplied by 2.

$+ 20$ means that, for a reason given in the problem, 20 is added to $2x$.

≤ 50 means that after multiplying the solution x by 2 and adding 20 to it, the result can be no greater than 50.

STEP 2 Think of some different situations in which a quantity x is multiplied by 2.

You run x miles per day for 2 days. So, $2x$ is the total distance run.	You buy 2 items each costing x dollars. So, $2x$ is the total cost.

STEP 3 Build on the situation and adjust it to create a verbal description that takes all of the information into account.

- Tomas has run 20 miles so far this week. If he intends to run 50 miles or less, how many miles on average should he run on each of the 2 days remaining in the week?

- Manny buys 2 work shirts that are each the same price. After using a $20 gift card, he can spend no more than $50. What is the maximum amount he can spend on each shirt?

YOUR TURN

Write a real-world problem for each inequality.

5. $3x + 10 > 30$

Check students' answers.

_____

_____

6. $5x - 50 \leq 100$

Check students' answers.

_____

_____

Personal Math Trainer
Online Assessment and Intervention
my.hrw.com

My Notes

Draw algebra tiles to model each two-step inequality. (Explore Activity)

1. $4x - 5 < 7$

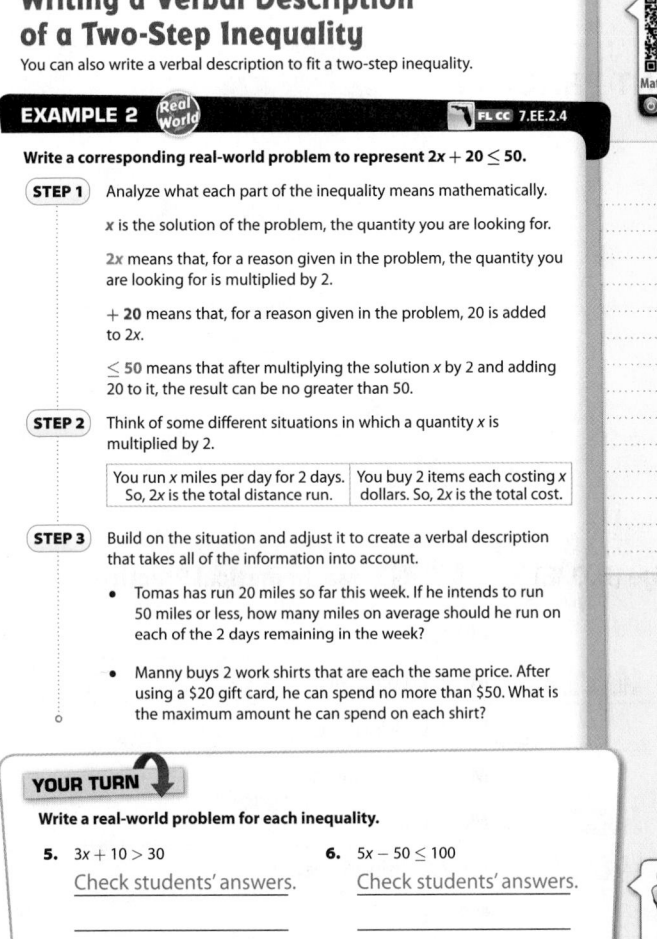

2. $-3x + 6 > 9$

3. The booster club needs to raise at least $7,000 for new football uniforms. So far, they have raised $1,250. Write an inequality to find the average amounts each of the 92 members can raise to meet the club's objective. (Example 1)

Let a represent the amount each member must raise.

amount to be raised:	amount already raised:	number of members:
$7,000	$1,250	92

Use clues in the problem to write an equation.

amount already raised	plus	number of members	times	amount each member raises	is greater than or equal to	target amount
1,250	+	92	×	a	≥	7,000

The inequality that represents the situation is $1{,}250 + 92a \geq 7{,}000$.

4. Analyze what each part of $7x - 18 \leq 32$ means mathematically. (Example 2)

x is the solution of the problem $7x$ is the solution multiplied by 7

-18 means that 18 is subtracted from $7x$

≤ 32 means that the result can be no greater than 32.

5. Write a real-world problem to represent $7x - 18 \leq 32$.

Check students' answers.

_____

 **ESSENTIAL QUESTION CHECK-IN**

6. Describe the steps you would follow to write a two-step inequality you can use to solve a real-world problem.

Sample answer: Choose a variable to represent what you want to find. Decide how the information in the problem is related to the variable. Then write an inequality.

DIFFERENTIATE INSTRUCTION

Multiple Representations

Have students discuss different words and phrases that they feel correspond to one of the four inequality symbols: $<$, $>$, $\leq$, and $\geq$. Have students create separate word walls that list the different words and phrases that students can refer to as they write two-step inequalities and their corresponding word problems.

Graphic Organizers

Have students use maps to measure the distances between their hometown and several surrounding cities, and record the values in a table. Knowing the actual distances between cities can make it easier to write inequalities involving traveling between those cities.

Additional Resources

Differentiated Instruction includes:

- Reading Strategies
- Success for English Learners **ELL**
- Reteach
- Challenge **PRE-AP**

Personal Math Trainer

Online Assessment and Intervention

Online homework assignment available

 my.hrw.com

2.2 LESSON QUIZ

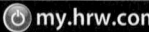 **7.EE.2.4**

1. Draw algebra tiles to model $5t - 6 \geq 2$.

2. Connie's dog Fido weighs 35 pounds. Her vet placed Fido on a diet. What inequality can you write to find the average number of pounds Fido must lose monthly to reach a healthier weight of 28 pounds within 6 months?

3. Jerome spent $20 on supplies to make 50 cookies for a bake sale. What inequality can you write to find the price Jerome should charge for each cookie if he wants to have a profit of more than $60?

4. Write a real-world problem for the inequality $8 - 2x \leq 5$.

Lesson Quiz available online

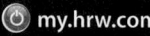 my.hrw.com

Answers

1.

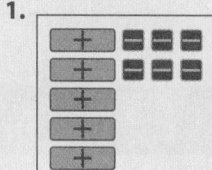  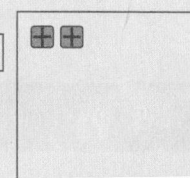

2. $35 - 6m \leq 28$

3. $50c - 20 > 60$

4. Bob and Tino have 8 pounds of grapes and a bag that can hold at most 5 pounds. If Bob and Tino both eat the same amount, how many pounds of grapes can each eat so that the remaining grapes will fit in the bag?

Evaluate

GUIDED AND INDEPENDENT PRACTICE

 **7.EE.2.4**

Concepts & Skills	Practice
Explore Activity Modeling Two-Step Inequalities	Exercises 1, 2
Example 1 Writing Two-Step Inequalities	Exercises 3, 7–14
Example 2 Writing a Verbal Description of a Two-Step Inequality	Exercises 4, 5, 15

Exercise	Depth of Knowledge (D.O.K.)		FL CC Mathematical Practices
7–14	**2** Skills/Concepts		**MP.4.1** Modeling
15	**3** Strategic Thinking	H.O.T.	**MP.7.1** Using Structure
16–21	**1** Recall of Information		**MP.7.1** Using Structure
22	**2** Skills/Concepts		**MP.2.1** Reasoning
23	**3** Strategic Thinking	H.O.T.	**MP.3.1** Logic
24	**3** Strategic Thinking	H.O.T.	**MP.7.1** Using Structure
25	**2** Skills/Concepts		**MP.7.1** Using Structure

Additional Resources

Differentiated Instruction includes:

• Leveled Practice worksheets

2.2 Independent Practice

FL CC 7.EE.2.4

Personal Math Trainer

Online Assessment and Intervention

my.hrw.com

7. Three friends earned more than $200 washing cars. They paid their parents $28 for supplies and divided the rest of money equally. Write an inequality to find possible amounts each friend earned. Identify what your variable represents.

$3a + 28 > 200$; $a =$ possible amounts each friend earned

8. Nick has $7.00. Bagels cost $0.75 each, and a small container of cream cheese costs $1.29. Write an inequality to find the numbers of bagels Nick can buy. Identify what your variable represents.

$0.75n + 1.29 \leq 7.00$; $n =$ the number of bagels Nick can buy

9. Chet needs to buy 4 work shirts, all costing the same amount. After he uses a $25 gift certificate, he can spend no more than $75. Write an inequality to find the possible costs for a shirt. Identify what your variable represents.

$4a - 25 \leq 75$; $a =$ the maximum amount each shirt can cost

10. Due to fire laws, no more than 720 people may attend a performance at Metro Auditorium. The balcony holds 120 people. There are 32 rows on the ground floor, each with the same number of seats. Write an inequality to find the numbers of people that can sit in a ground-floor row if the balcony is full. Identify what your variable represents.

$120 + 32n \leq 720$; $n =$ the number of people in each row

11. Liz earns a salary of $2,100 per month, plus a commission of 5% of her sales. She wants to earn at least $2,400 this month. Write an inequality to find amounts of sales that will meet her goal. Identify what your variable represents.

$2,100 + 0.05s \geq 2,400$; $s =$ the amount of her sales

12. Lincoln Middle School plans to collect more than 2,000 cans of food in a food drive. So far, 668 cans have been collected. Write an inequality to find numbers of cans the school can collect on each of the final 7 days of the drive to meet this goal. Identify what your variable represents.

$668 + 7n > 2,000$; $n =$ the average number of cans each day

13. Joanna joins a CD club. She pays $7 per month plus $10 for each CD that she orders. Write an inequality to find how many CDs she can purchase in a month if she spends no more than $100. Identify what your variable represents.

$7 + 10c \leq 100$; $c =$ the number of CDs she buys

14. Lionel wants to buy a belt that costs $22. He also wants to buy some shirts that are on sale for $17 each. He has $80. What inequality can you write to find the number of shirts he can buy? Identify what your variable represents.

$22 + 17n \leq 80$; $n =$ the number of shirts he can buy

15. Write a situation for $15x - 20 \leq 130$ and solve.

Sample answer: Mr. Craig is buying pizzas for the 7th grade field day. He can spend up to $130 and needs 15 pizzas. He has a $20 coupon. How much can he spend per pizza?; $10 or less per pizza

Analyze Relationships Write $>$, $<$, $\geq$, or $\leq$ in the blank to express the given relationship.

16. m is at least 25 $m \underline{\geq} 25$

17. k is no greater than 9 $k \underline{\leq} 9$

18. p is less than 48 $p \underline{<} 48$

19. b is no more than -5 $b \underline{\leq} -5$

20. h is at most 56 $h \underline{\leq} 56$

21. w is no less than 0 $w \underline{\geq} 0$

22. **Critical Thinking** Marie scored 95, 86, and 89 on three science tests. She wants her average score for 6 tests to be at least 90. What inequality can you write to find the average scores that she can get on her next three tests to meet this goal? Use s to represent the lowest average score.

$95 + 86 + 89 + 3s \geq 540$ or $270 + 3s \geq 540$

or $\frac{95 + 86 + 89 + 3s}{6} \geq 90$

H.O.T. FOCUS ON HIGHER ORDER THINKING

Work Area

23. **Communicate Mathematical Ideas** Write an inequality that expresses the reason the lengths 5 feet, 10 feet, and 20 feet could not be used to make a triangle. Explain how the inequality demonstrates that fact.

$5 + 10 < 20$; sample answer: If the combined length of two sides of a triangle is less than the length of the third side, the two shorter sides will not be long enough to form a triangle with the third side. Here, the combined length of 5 ft and 10 ft is 15 ft, not enough to make a triangle.

24. **Analyze Relationships** The number m satisfies the relationship $m < 0$. Write an inequality expressing the relationship between $-m$ and 0. Explain your reasoning.

$-m > 0$; sample answer: Since m is less than 0, it must be a negative number. $-m$ represents the opposite of m, which must be a positive number since the opposite of a negative number is positive. So, $-m > 0$.

25. **Analyze Relationships** The number n satisfies the relationship $n > 0$. Write three inequalities to express the relationship between n and $\frac{1}{n}$.

$n > \frac{1}{n}$ if $n > 1$; $n < \frac{1}{n}$ if $n < 1$; $n = \frac{1}{n}$ if $n = 1$

EXTEND THE MATH PRE-AP

Activity available online my.hrw.com

Cheryl is thinking of three consecutive numbers whose average is less than or equal to half of the smallest number. Write an inequality that Cheryl could use to identify the smallest of the three numbers.

If x is the smallest of three consecutive numbers, then the next two numbers are $(x + 1)$ and $(x + 2)$. To find the average of these numbers, find their sum and divide by 3. The average of x, $(x + 1)$, and $(x + 2)$ is $\frac{x + (x + 1) + (x + 2)}{3}$. Since the average is less than or equal to half of the smallest number, you can write the inequality $\frac{x + (x + 1) + (x + 2)}{3} \leq \frac{x}{2}$.

LESSON
2.3 Solving Two-Step Inequalities

 Florida Common Core Standards

The student is expected to:

 **Expressions and Equations—7.EE.2.4b**

Solve word problems leading to inequalities of the form $px + q > r$ or $px + q > r$, where p, q, and r are specific rational numbers. Graph the solution set of the inequality and interpret it in the context of the problem.

Mathematical Practices

 **MP.5.1** Using Tools

ADDITIONAL EXAMPLE 1
Use algebra tiles to model and solve $5f + 11 \leq -4$.

$f \leq -3$

 Interactive Whiteboard
Interactive example available online

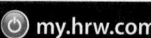 my.hrw.com

ADDITIONAL EXAMPLE 2
Ed wants to bicycle at least 75 miles this week. The inequality $11 + 4b \geq 75$ can be used to find b, the average number of miles he should bike on his remaining 4 bike rides this week. Solve the inequality, and graph the solution set on a number line.

$b \geq 16$

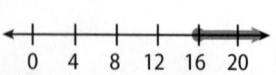

 Interactive Whiteboard
Interactive example available online

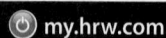 my.hrw.com

Engage

ESSENTIAL QUESTION
How do you solve a two-step inequality? Sample answer: Isolate the variable by performing the same operation on both sides of the inequality. If you divide both sides of the inequality by a negative number, reverse the inequality sign.

Motivate the Lesson
Ask: How many different numbers do you think could be the solution to the inequality $2x - 1 > 10$? Take a guess. Begin the Explore Activity to find out.

Explore

Focus on Math Connections  Mathematical Practices
To introduce students to multistep inequalities, review how to solve multistep equations. Then, discuss $x = 2$ and $x \geq 2$. How many values of x satisfy each statement?

Explain

EXAMPLE 1
Focus on Math Connections Mathematical Practices
Students may think it's unnecessary to perform the same operation to both sides of an inequality. Make sure students understand that using different operations produces a different inequality and causes their answers to be incorrect.

Engage with the Whiteboard
Cover up the mats shown in Steps 1–5, and have students draw the algebra tiles that belong on each side of the mat based on the descriptions in each step.

Questioning Strategies Mathematical Practices
• Why is adding three +1 tiles to both sides a better strategy than adding nine −1 tiles to both sides? Adding three +1 tiles to both sides isolates $4d$ on one side of the inequality.

YOUR TURN
Avoid Common Errors
Students often express a solution for an inequality using an equal sign. Have students verify that the sign that was used in the inequality is also present in their solution.

EXAMPLE 2
Connect Vocabulary **ELL**
Have students understand **open** and **closed** refer to the circle as unshaded and shaded.

Questioning Strategies Mathematical Practices
• How can you tell if a specific number is a solution to an inequality by looking at the graph of the solution on a number line? If the arrow passes through the number on the number line, or if there is a closed circle above that number, then the number is a solution.

LESSON 2.3 Solving Two-Step Inequalities

7.EE.2.4b
Solve...inequalities of the form $px + q > r$ or $px + q < r$, where p, q, and r are specific rational numbers. Graph the solution set...and interpret it in the context of the problem.
Also 7.EE.2.3

? ESSENTIAL QUESTION

How do you solve a two-step inequality?

Modeling and Solving Two-Step Inequalities

You can solve two-step inequalities using algebra tiles. The method is similar to the one you used to solve two-step equations.

EXAMPLE 1

FL CC Prep for 7.EE.2.4b

Use algebra tiles to model and solve $4d - 3 \geq 9$.

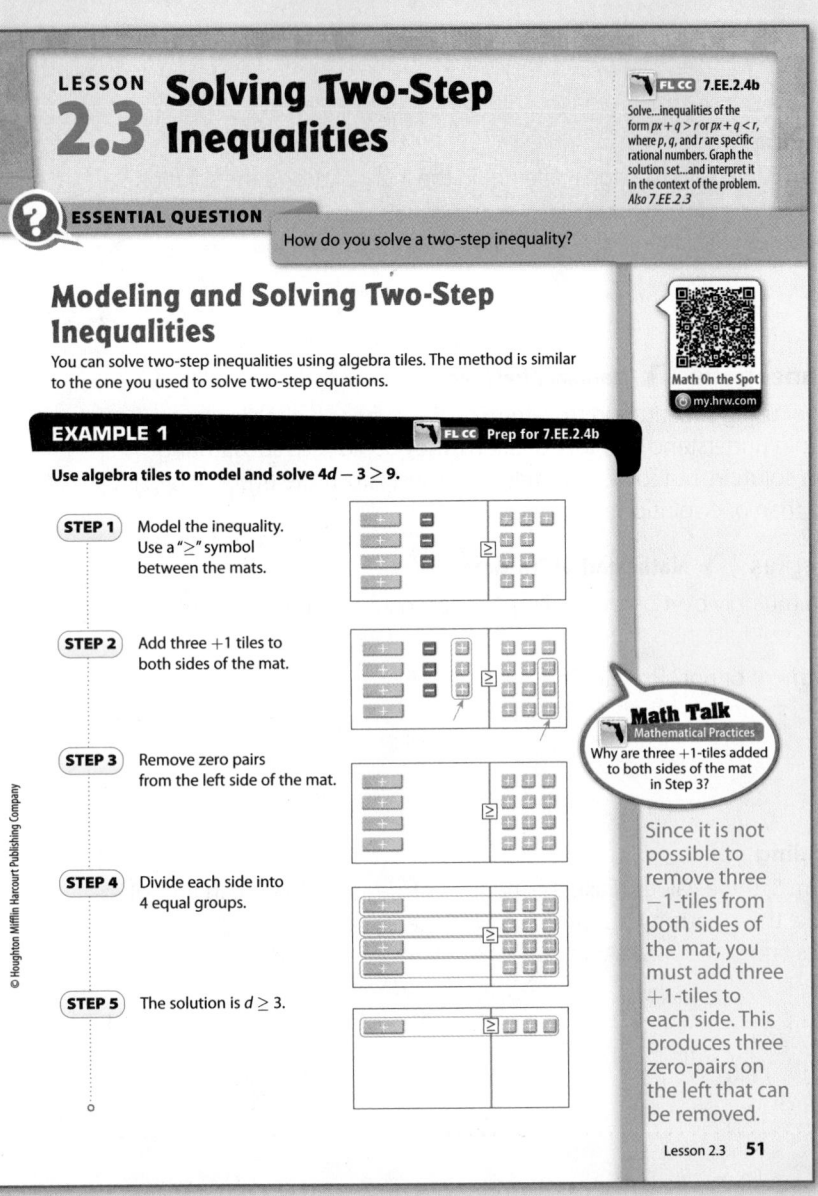

STEP 1 Model the inequality. Use a "$\geq$" symbol between the mats.

STEP 2 Add three +1 tiles to both sides of the mat.

STEP 3 Remove zero pairs from the left side of the mat.

STEP 4 Divide each side into 4 equal groups.

STEP 5 The solution is $d \geq 3$.

Math Talk
Mathematical Practices

Why are three +1-tiles added to both sides of the mat in Step 3?

Since it is not possible to remove three −1-tiles from both sides of the mat, you must add three +1-tiles to each side. This produces three zero-pairs on the left that can be removed.

Lesson 2.3 **51**

Math On the Spot
my.hrw.com

Personal Math Trainer
Online Assessment and Intervention
my.hrw.com

Math On the Spot
my.hrw.com

My Notes

YOUR TURN

Use algebra tiles to model and solve each inequality.

1. $2x + 7 > 11$ $x > 2$
2. $5h - 4 \geq 11$ $h \geq 3$

Solving and Interpreting Solutions

You can apply what you know about solving two-step equations and one-step inequalities to solving two-step inequalities.

EXAMPLE 2 (Real World)

FL CC 7.EE.2.4b

Serena wants to complete the first 3 miles of a 10-mile run in 45 minutes or less running at a steady pace. The inequality $10 - 0.75p \leq 7$ can be used to find p, the pace, in miles per hour, she can run to reach her goal. Solve the inequality. Then graph and interpret the solution.

STEP 1 Use inverse operations to solve the inequality.

$$10 - 0.75p \leq 7 \quad \text{Subtract 10 from both sides.}$$
$$\underline{-10 \qquad\quad -10}$$
$$-0.75p \leq -3$$
$$\frac{-0.75p}{-0.75} \geq \frac{-3}{-0.75} \quad \text{Divide both sides by −0.75. Reverse the inequality symbol.}$$
$$n \geq 4$$

STEP 2 Graph the inequality and interpret the circle and the arrow.

Serena can meet her goal by running at a pace of 4 miles per hour.

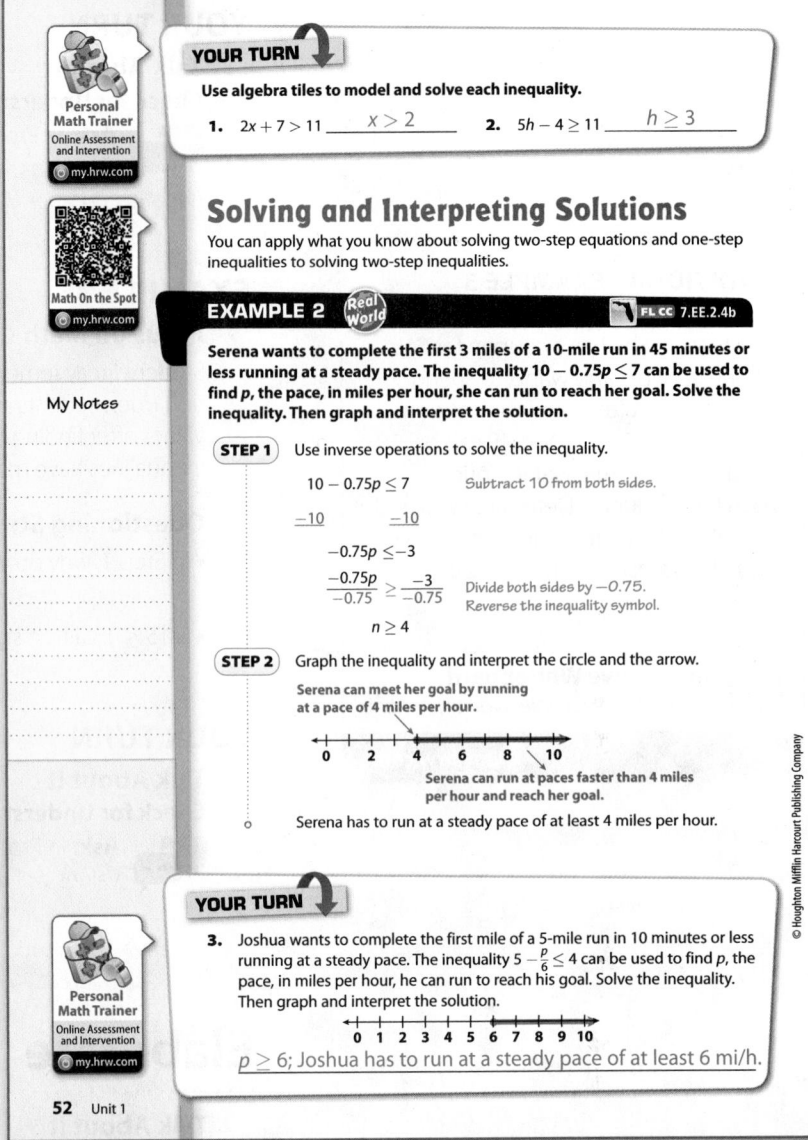

Serena can run at paces faster than 4 miles per hour and reach her goal.

Serena has to run at a steady pace of at least 4 miles per hour.

YOUR TURN

3. Joshua wants to complete the first mile of a 5-mile run in 10 minutes or less running at a steady pace. The inequality $5 - \frac{p}{6} \leq 4$ can be used to find p, the pace, in miles per hour, he can run to reach his goal. Solve the inequality. Then graph and interpret the solution.

$p \geq 6$; Joshua has to run at a steady pace of at least 6 mi/h.

Personal Math Trainer
Online Assessment and Intervention
my.hrw.com

52 Unit 1

© Houghton Mifflin Harcourt Publishing Company

PROFESSIONAL DEVELOPMENT

Integrate Mathematical Practices MP.5.1

This lesson provides an opportunity to address this Mathematical Practice standard. It calls for students to select tools, including real objects, manipulatives, paper and pencil, and technology as appropriate, and techniques, including … number sense as appropriate, to solve problems. Students use algebra tiles to model and solve inequalities. Then students use paper and pencil to solve inequalities, and graph their answers on number lines.

Math Background

The Addition and Subtraction Properties of Inequality state that the same quantity may be added to or subtracted from both sides of an inequality without changing the solution set. That is, if $a > b$ then and $a + c > b + c$ and $a - c > b - c$. Multiplying or dividing both sides of an inequality by a positive number also produces an inequality with the same solution set as the original inequality. In general terms, if $a > b$ and $b > c$, then and $ac > bc$ and $\frac{a}{c} > \frac{b}{c}$.

YOUR TURN

Talk About It
Check for Understanding

 Ask: In Problem 3, why are the signs different in the inequality and the solution? The signs are different because both sides of the equation were divided by a negative number. Both sides were multipled by -3, so the sign was reversed, from $\leq$ to $\geq$.

EXAMPLE 3

Focus on Math Connections   Mathematical Practices

Students may remember using substitution to determine if a given value makes an equation true. Students should understand that for equations, they could stop substituting values after finding one solution, but for inequalities, they must substitute every value, since inequalities have more than one solution.

Questioning Strategies   Mathematical Practices

• In Step 1, why do you multiply by 4 before adding 12 in each inequality? The order of operations states that multiplication should be performed before addition.

• Is $15 \leq 15$ a true statement or not? Explain. The inequality $15 \leq 15$ is a true statement, because the symbol $\leq$ means "less than or equal to."

YOUR TURN

Talk About It
Check for Understanding

Ask: In Problem 5, three values make the inequality true. Does this mean that all values will make the inequality true? Explain. No, for any inequality, there are some values that are solutions and some values that are not solutions.

Elaborate

Talk About It
Summarize the Lesson

Ask: How is solving a two-step equation similar to solving a two-step inequality? How are they different? For solving both equations and inequalities, you have to isolate the variable by performing the same operation on both sides of the equation or inequality. When solving inequalities, you have to remember to reverse the sign if you multipy or divide both sides by a negative number, but when solving an equation, the sign always stays the same.

GUIDED PRACTICE

Engage with the Whiteboard

For Exercises 2 and 3, have students graph each solution on the number line. Students should be able to explain why they chose an open or closed circle, and why they chose the direction of the arrow on the number line.

Avoid Common Errors

Exercises 4, 5 Remind students that they have to check each value to see if it makes the inequality true, because inequalities can have more than one solution.

Determining if a Given Value Makes the Inequality True

You can use substitution to decide whether a given value is the solution of an inequality.

EXAMPLE 3 Real World

FL CC 7.EE.2.4b

CAR WASH

At Gas 'n' Wash, gasoline sells for $4.00 a gallon and a car wash costs $12. Harika wants to have her car washed and keep her total purchase under $60. The inequality $4g + 12 < 60$ can be used to find g, the number of gallons of gas she can buy. Determine which, if any, of these values is a solution: $g = 10$; $g = 11$; $g = 12$.

STEP 1 Substitute each value for g in the inequality $4g + 12 < 60$.

$g = 10$	$g = 11$	$g = 12$
$4(10) + 12 < 60$	$4(11) + 12 < 60$	$4(12) + 12 < 60$

STEP 2 Evaluate each expression to see if a true inequality results.

$4(10) + 12 \overset{?}{<} 60$	$4(11) + 12 \overset{?}{<} 60$	$4(12) + 12 \overset{?}{<} 60$
$40 + 12 \overset{?}{<} 60$	$44 + 12 \overset{?}{<} 60$	$48 + 12 \overset{?}{<} 60$
$52 \overset{?}{<} 60$	$56 \overset{?}{<} 60$	$60 \overset{?}{<} 60$
true ✓	true ✓	not true ✗

So, Harika can buy 10 or 11 gallons of gas but not 12 gallons.

Check: Solve and graph the inequality.

$4g + 12 < 60$

$4g < 48$

$g < 12$

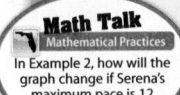
0 2 4 6 8 10 12 14 16 18 20

The closed circle at zero represents the minimum amount she can buy, zero gallons. She cannot buy a negative number of gallons. The open circle at 12 means that she can buy any amount up to but not including 12 gallons.

Math Talk
Mathematical Practices
In Example 2, how will the graph change if Serena's maximum pace is 12 miles per hour?

There will be a closed circle at 12 with no shading beyond it.

© Houghton Mifflin Harcourt Publishing Company

YOUR TURN

Circle any given values that make the inequality true.

4. $3v - 8 > 22$
$v = 9$; $v = 10$; $\boxed{v = 11}$

5. $5h + 12 \leq -3$
$\boxed{h = -3; h = -4; h = -5}$

Guided Practice

1. Describe how to solve the inequality $3x + 4 < 13$ using algebra tiles. (Example 1)

Remove $4 + 1$-tiles from both sides, then divide each side into 3 equal groups; $x < 3$

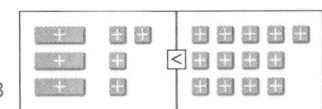

Solve each inequality. Graph and check the solution. (Example 2)

2. $5d - 13 < 32$ ___$d < 9$___

0 2 4 6 8 10 12 14 16 18 20

3. $-4b + 9 \leq -7$ ___$b \geq 4$___

0 2 4 6 8 10 12 14 16 18 20

Circle any given values that make the inequality true. (Example 3)

4. $2m + 18 > -4$
$m = -12$; $m = -11$; $\boxed{m = -10}$

5. $-6y + 3 \geq 0$
$y = 1$; $\boxed{y = \frac{1}{2}}$; $y = 0$

0   0.5   1   1.5   2   2.5

6. Lizzy has 6.5 hours to tutor 4 students and spend 1.5 hours in a lab. She plans to tutor each student the same amount of time. The inequality $6.5 - 4t \geq 1.5$ can be used to find t, the amount of time in hours Lizzy could spend with each student. Solve the inequality. Graph and interpret the solution. Can Lizzy tutor each student for 1.5 hours? Explain. (Examples 2 and 3)

$t \leq 1.25$; Lizzy can spend from 0 to 1.25 h with each student.

No; 1.5 h per student will exceed Lizzy's available time.

? ESSENTIAL QUESTION CHECK-IN

7. How do you solve a two-step inequality?

Sample answer: Apply inverse operations until you have isolated the variable. If you multiply or divide both sides of the inequality by a negative number, reverse the direction of the inequality symbol.

© Houghton Mifflin Harcourt Publishing Company

DIFFERENTIATE INSTRUCTION

Curriculum Integration

Have students create inequalities that they can use to track their progress in other school subjects. For example, students can write inequalities to figure out the number of pages they would have to read weekly in order to finish a book by a certain date. Students can record how many pages they have actually read and write a new inequality every week to help track their progress.

Graphic Organizers

Have students create Venn diagrams that show the ways in which solving equations and solving inequalities are similar and the ways in which they are different. The overlapping section of the Venn diagram should contain the ways the two processes are similar, and the ways in which they are different should be placed in one of the two other sections of the Venn diagram.

Additional Resources

Differentiated Instruction includes:

- Reading Strategies
- Success for English Learners **ELL**
- Reteach
- Challenge **PRE-AP**

Personal Math Trainer

Online Assessment and Intervention

Online homework assignment available

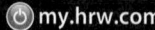
my.hrw.com

2.3 LESSON QUIZ

 **FL CC** 7.EE.2.4b

1. Solve $\frac{x}{3} - 10 \leq 11$.

2. Solve $52 > -12 + 8d$.

3. Solve $-16p + 111 \geq -65$.

4. Charlene is a writer who is going on a trip. She has brought several copies of her latest book in her suitcase. The suitcase itself weighs 5 pounds, and each book weighs 3 pounds. If her full suitcase can weigh no more than 50 pounds, how many books can she bring?

5. Carl is having a party. He has bought 24 brownies and is making 6 more batches of brownies. The inequality $24 + 6b \geq 138$ can be used to determine how many brownies, b, must be in each batch so that all 138 guests get at least 1 brownie. Determine which of the given values, if any, make the inequality true: $b = 10$; $b = 15$; $b = 20$.

Lesson Quiz available online

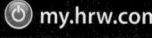 my.hrw.com

Answers

1. $x \leq 63$

2. $d < 8$

3. $p \leq 11$

4. at most 15 books

5. $b = 20$

Evaluate

GUIDED AND INDEPENDENT PRACTICE

 **FL CC** 7.EE.2.4b

Concepts & Skills	Practice
Example 1 Modeling and Solving Two-Step Inequalities	Exercise 1
Example 2 Representing Solutions on a Number Line	Exercises 2, 3, 6, 8–17, 21
Example 3 Determining if a Given Value Makes the Inequality True	Exercises 4–6

Exercise	Depth of Knowledge (D.O.K.)	 **FL CC** Mathematical Practices
8–17	**2** Skills/Concepts	**MP.5.1** Using Tools
18–20	**3** Strategic Thinking **H.O.T.**	**MP.7.1** Using Structure
21	**3** Strategic Thinking **H.O.T.**	**MP.3.1** Logic
22	**3** Strategic Thinking **H.O.T.**	**MP.7.1** Using Structure

Additional Resources

Differentiated Instruction includes:

• Leveled Practice Worksheets

CLUSTER CONNECTION **Exercise 19** combines concepts from the Florida Common Core cluster "Solve real-life and mathematical problems using numerical and algebraic expressions and equations."

2.3 Independent Practice

FL CC 7.EE.2.3, 7.EE.2.4b

Solve each inequality. Graph and check the solution.

8. $2s + 5 \geq 49$ ____ $s \geq 22$

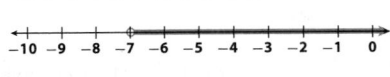

9. $-3t + 9 \geq -21$ ____ $t \leq 10$

10. $55 > -7v + 6$ ____ $v > -7$

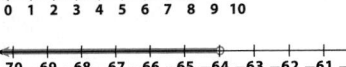

11. $41 > 6m - 7$ ____ $m < 8$

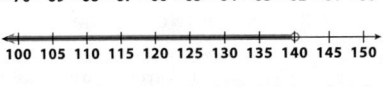

12. $\frac{a}{-8} + 15 > 23$ ____ $a < -64$

13. $\frac{f}{2} - 22 < 48$ ____ $f < 140$

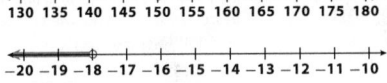

14. $-25 + \frac{t}{2} \geq 50$ ____ $t \geq 150$

15. $10 + \frac{g}{-9} > 12$ ____ $g < -18$

16. $25.2 \leq -1.5y + 1.2$ ____ $y \leq -16$

17. $-3.6 \geq -0.3a + 1.2$ ____ $a \geq 16$

18. What If? The perimeter of a rectangle is at most 80 inches. The length of the rectangle is 25 inches. The inequality $80 - 2w \geq 50$ can be used to find w, the width of the rectangle in inches. Solve the inequality and interpret the solution. How will the solution change if the width must be at least 10 inches and a whole number?

$w \leq 15$; the width is a positive number no greater than 15 inches; the possible widths, in inches, will be 10, 11, 12, 13, 14, and 15.

Lesson 2.3 **55**

19. Interpret the Answer Grace earns $7 for each car she washes. She always saves $25 of her weekly earnings. This week, she wants to have at least $65 in spending money. How many cars must she wash? Write and solve an inequality to represent this situation. Interpret the solution in context.

$7n - 25 \geq 65$; $n \geq 12\frac{6}{7}$; Grace must wash at least 13 cars, because n must be a whole number.

H.O.T. FOCUS ON HIGHER ORDER THINKING

Work Area

20. Critical Thinking Is there any value of x with the property that $x < x - 1$? Explain your reasoning.

No; sample answer: If $x < x - 1$, then, subtracting x from both sides of the inequality, $0 < -1$. That is untrue, so no value of x can be less than $x - 1$.

21. Analyze Relationships A *compound inequality* consists of two simple equalities joined by the word "*and*" or "*or*." Graph the solution sets of each of these compound inequalities.

a. $x > 2$ and $x < 7$

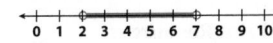

b. $x < 2$ or $x > 7$

c. Describe the solution set of the compound inequality $x < 2$ and $x > 7$.

There is no number that satisfies both inequalities.

d. Describe the solution set of the compound inequality $x > 2$ or $x < 7$.

The solution set is all numbers.

22. Communicate Mathematical Ideas Joseph used the problem-solving strategy Work Backward to solve the inequality $2n + 5 < 13$. Shawnee solved the inequality using the algebraic method you used in this lesson. Compare the two methods.

Sample answer: Joseph might have reasoned that n was first multiplied by 2, then increased by 5 to give a result less than 13. Working backward, he would have subtracted 5 from 13 (8), then divided by 2 (4), giving $n < 4$. Shawnee would have followed these same steps but would have used a variable and inverse operations.

56 Unit 1

EXTEND THE MATH PRE-AP

Activity available online my.hrw.com

The equation $-y(x) + y^y \geq -y$ has the solution $x \leq 10$ for a certain value of y. Use substitution and guess-and-check to find the correct value for y. Explain how you know your answer is correct.

$y = 3$; if you substitute 3 for y in the equation, you get $-3x + 3^3 \geq -3$. When you evaluate the power, the equation can be written as $-3x + 27 \geq -3$. Subtract 27 from both sides, and the equation can be written as $-3x \geq -30$. When you divide both sides by -3, you will have to reverse the inequality sign, and the solution is $x \leq 10$.

Ready to Go On?

Assess Mastery

Use the assessment on this page to determine if students have mastered the concepts and standards covered in this module.

 **Response to Intervention**

Personal Math Trainer
Online Assessment and Intervention
my.hrw.com

Intervention	Enrichment
Access Ready to Go On? assessment online, and receive instant scoring, feedback, and customized intervention or enrichment.	

Online and Print Resources

Differentiated Instruction
• Reteach worksheets
• Reading Strategies **ELL**
• Success for English Learners **ELL**

Differentiated Instruction
• Challenge worksheets **PRE-AP**
• Extend the Math **PRE-AP** Lesson Activities in TE

Additional Resources

Assessment Resources includes:
• Leveled Module Quizzes

MODULE QUIZ

Ready to Go On?

 Personal Math Trainer
Online Assessment and Intervention
my.hrw.com

2.1 Writing and Solving One-Step Inequalities

Solve each inequality.

1. $n + 7 < -3$ ___ $n < -10$

2. $5p \geq -30$ ___ $p \geq -6$

3. $14 < k + 11$ ___ $k > 3$

4. $\frac{d}{-3} \leq -6$ ___ $d \geq 18$

5. $c - 2.5 \leq 2.5$ ___ $c \leq 5$

6. $12 \geq -3b$ ___ $b \geq -4$

7. Jose has scored 562 points on his math tests so far this semester. To get an A for the semester, he must score at least 650 points. Write and solve an inequality to find the minimum number of points he must score on the remaining tests in order to get an A.

$562 + n \geq 650; n \geq 88$

2.2 Writing Two-Step Inequalities

8. During a scuba dive, Lainey descended to a point 20 feet below the ocean surface. She continued her descent at a rate of 20 feet per minute. Write an inequality you could solve to find the number of minutes she can continue to descend if she does not want to reach a point more than 100 feet below the ocean surface.

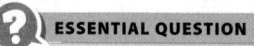 $-20 - 20t \geq -100$

2.3 Solving Two-Step Inequalities

Solve.

9. $2s + 3 > 15$ ___ $s > 6$

10. $-\frac{d}{12} - 6 < 1$ ___ $d > -84$

11. $-6w - 18 \geq 36$ ___ $w \leq -9$

12. $\frac{z}{4} + 22 \leq 38$ ___ $z \leq 64$

13. $\frac{b}{9} - 34 < -36$ ___ $b < -18$

14. $-2p + 12 > 8$ ___ $p < 2$

? ESSENTIAL QUESTION

15. How can you recognize whether a real-world situation should be represented by an equation or an inequality?

Sample answer: Look for key words or phrases that indicate inequality, such as "greater than," "less than," "at most," or "at least."

© Houghton Mifflin Harcourt Publishing Company

Module 2 **57**

 Florida Common Core Standards

Lesson	Exercises	Common Core Standards
2.1	1–7	**7.EE.2.4b**
2.2	8	**7.EE.2.4**
2.3	9–14	**7.EE.2.4b**

PARCC Assessment Readiness

Assessment Readiness Tip Students can use their knowledge of inequality symbols and inequality graphing to eliminate answer choices.

Item 5 The given inequality contains the > symbol. The students should eliminate answer choices B and D because they contain the ≤ and ≥ symbols.

Item 6 The graph has an open dot at −2, which means the answer will not contain a ≤ or ≥ symbol allowing students to eliminate answer choices A and C.

Avoid Common Errors

Item 2 Some students will have trouble deciding which number goes with the variable and which number stands alone. Remind students to look for the word "each" or "per" to discover which number is paired with the variable.

Item 4 Some students will have difficulty deciding which inequality symbol to use to model the real-world situation. Remind the students to look for "at least," "more than," "less than," and other key phrases to help guide them in which to choose.

Additional Resources

Personal Math Trainer

Online Assessment and Intervention

my.hrw.com

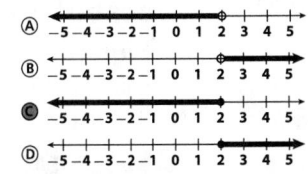

MODULE 2 MIXED REVIEW

PARCC Assessment Readiness

Personal Math Trainer

Online Assessment and Intervention

my.hrw.com

Selected Response

1. Which graph models the solution of the inequality $-6 \le -3x$?

Ⓐ ![number line -5 to 5](−5−4−3−2−1 0 1 2 3 4 5)

Ⓑ ![number line -5 to 5](−5−4−3−2−1 0 1 2 3 4 5)

Ⓒ ![number line -5 to 5](−5−4−3−2−1 0 1 2 3 4 5)

Ⓓ ![number line -5 to 5](−5−4−3−2−1 0 1 2 3 4 5)

2. A taxi cab costs $1.75 for the first mile and $0.75 for each additional mile. You have $20 to spend on your ride. Which inequality could be solved to find how many miles you can travel, if n is the number of additional miles?

Ⓐ $1.75n + 0.75 \ge 20$

Ⓑ $1.75n + 0.75 \le 20$

Ⓒ $0.75n + 1.75 \ge 20$

Ⓓ $0.75n + 1.75 \le 20$

3. The inequality $\frac{9}{5}C + 32 < -40$ can be used to find Celsius temperatures that are less than $-40°$ Fahrenheit. What is the solution of the inequality?

Ⓐ $C < 40$

Ⓑ $C < -\frac{40}{9}$

Ⓒ $C < -40$

Ⓓ $C < -\frac{72}{5}$

4. The 30 members of a choir are trying to raise at least $1,500 to cover travel costs to a singing camp. They have already raised $600. Which inequality could you solve to find the average amounts each member can raise that will at least meet the goal?

Ⓐ $30x + 600 > 1,500$

Ⓑ $30x + 600 \ge 1,500$

Ⓒ $30x + 600 < 1,500$

Ⓓ $30x + 600 \le 1,500$

5. Which represents the solution for the inequality $3x - 7 > 5$?

Ⓐ $x < 4$

Ⓑ $x \le 4$

Ⓒ $x > 4$

Ⓓ $x \ge 4$

6. Which inequality has the following graphed solution?

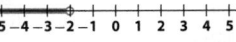

![number line -5 to 5](−5−4−3−2−1 0 1 2 3 4 5)

Ⓐ $3x + 8 \le 2$

Ⓑ $4x + 12 < 4$

Ⓒ $2x + 5 \le 1$

Ⓓ $3x + 6 < 3$

7. What is the solution of $x - 3.2 = 11.5$?

Ⓐ $x = 14.7$

Ⓑ $x = 8.3$

Ⓒ $x = -8.3$

Ⓓ $x = -14.2$

8. What expression is equivalent to $3y - 21$?

Ⓐ $3(y - 21)$

Ⓑ $3(3y - 7)$

Ⓒ $3(3y - 21)$

Ⓓ $3(y - 7)$

Mini-Task

9. In golf, the lower your score, the better. Negative scores are best of all. Teri scored $+1$ on each of the first three holes at a nine-hole miniature golf course. Her goal is a total score of -9 or better after she has completed the final six holes.

a. Let h represent the score Teri must average on each of the last six holes in order to meet her goal. Write a two-step inequality you can solve to find h.

$$6h + 3 \le -9$$

b. Solve the inequality.

$$h \le -2$$

Florida Common Core Standards

Items	🏴 Grade 7 Standards	🏴 Mathematical Practices
1	7.EE.2.4	MP.2.1
2	7.EE.2.4	MP.4.1
3	7.EE.2.4b	MP.4.1
4	7.EE.2.4	MP.2.1
5	7.EE.2.4	MP.2.1
6	7.EE.2.4	MP.2.1
7*	7.EE.2.4	MP.2.1
8*	7.EE.1.1	MP.2.1
9	7.EE.2.4, 7.EE.2.4b	MP.4.1

* Item integrates mixed review concepts from previous modules or a previous course.

Study Guide Review

Vocabulary Development

Integrating Language Arts

Encourage students to practice using the unit vocabulary as they talk and write about mathematics. Understanding vocabulary will aid their understanding of the concepts.

 **LACC.68.RST.2.4** Determine the meaning of symbols, key terms, and other domain-specific words and phrases as they are used in a specific scientific or technical context relevant to grades 6–8 texts and topics.

MODULE 1 Expressions and Equations

FL.CC **7.EE.1.1, 7.EE.2.4, 7.EE.2.4a, 7.EE.2.4b**

Key Concepts

• The form of the rational numbers used in an expression can simplify the choice of strategies used in adding, subtracting, factoring, and expanding linear expressions. *(Lesson 1.1)*

• Solve word problems by using an equation or inequality and interpret the meaning of the solution when represented on a number line. *(Lesson 1.2)*

• To solve a two-step equation, use inverse operations. *(Lesson 1.3)*

• Use substitution to check if a given value is a solution of an equation. *(Lesson 1.4)*

Study Guide Review

MODULE 1 ► Expressions and Equations

Key Vocabulary
algebraic expression
(*expresión algebraica*)
equation (*ecuación*)

❓ ESSENTIAL QUESTION

How can you use equations to solve real-world problems?

EXAMPLE 1

Huang and Belita both repair computers. Huang makes $50 a day plus $25 per repair. Belita makes $20 a day plus $35 per repair. Write an expression for Huang and Belita's total daily earnings if they make the same number of repairs r.

Huang: $50 + $25r

Belita: $20 + $35r

Together: $(50 + 25r) + (20 + 35r) = 50 + 20 + 25r + 35r$

$$= 70 + 60r$$

Huang and Belita earn $70 + $60r together.

EXAMPLE 2

A skydiver's parachute opens at a height of 2,790 feet. He then falls at a rate of $-15\frac{1}{2}$ feet per second. How long will it take the skydiver to reach the ground?

Let x represent the number of seconds it takes to reach the ground.

$$-15\frac{1}{2}x = -2,790$$

$$-\frac{31}{2}x = -2,790 \qquad \text{Write as a fraction.}$$

$$\left(-\frac{2}{32}\right)\left(-\frac{31}{2}x\right) = \left(-\frac{2}{32}\right)(-2,790) \qquad \text{Multiply both sides by the reciprocal.}$$

$$x = 180$$

It takes 180 seconds for the skydiver to reach the ground.

EXAMPLE 3

A clothing store sells clothing for 2 times the wholesale cost plus $10. The store sells a pair of pants for $48. How much did the store pay for the pants? Represent the solution on a number line.

Let w represent the wholesale cost of the pants, or the price paid by the store.

$2w + 10 = 48$

$2w = 38$ Subtract 10 from both sides.

$w = 19$ Divide both sides by 2.

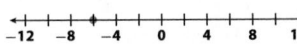

The store paid $19 for the pants.

EXERCISES

Simplify each expression. (Lesson 1.1)

1. $(2x + 3\frac{2}{5}) + (5x - \frac{4}{5})$ $7x + 2\frac{3}{5}$ **2.** $(-0.5x - 4) - (1.5x + 2.3)$ $-2x - 6.3$

3. $9(3t + 4b)$ $27t + 36b$ **4.** $0.7(5a - 13p)$ $-0.35a - 0.91p$

Factor each expression. (Lesson 1.1)

5. $8x + 56$ $8(x + 7)$ **6.** $3x + 57$ $3(x + 19)$

Use inverse operations to solve each equation. (Lesson 1.2)

7. $1.6 + y = -7.3$ $y = -8.9$ **8.** $-\frac{2}{3}n = 12$ $n = -18$

9. The cost of a ticket to an amusement park is $42 per person. For groups of up to 8 people, the cost per ticket decreases by $3 for each person in the group. Marcos's ticket cost $30. Write and solve an equation to find the number of people in Marcos's group. (Lesson 1.3, 1.4)

$42 - 3n = 30; n = 4$

Solve each equation. Graph the solution on a number line. (Lesson 1.4)

10. $8x - 28 = 44$

$x = 9$

11. $-5z + 4 = 34$

$x = -6$

MODULE 2 Inequalities

FL CC 7.EE.2.4, 7.EE.2.4b

Key Concepts

- The direction of the inequality symbol is reversed when multiplying or dividing both sides of an inequality by a negative quantity. *(Lesson 2.1)*
- To solve a two-step inequality, use inverse operations. *(Lesson 2.2)*
- Use substitution to check if a given value is a solution of an inequality. *(Lesson 2.3)*

Unit 1 Performance Tasks

The Performance Tasks provide students with the opportunity to apply concepts from this unit in real-world problem situations.

CAREERS IN MATH

Mechanical Engineer In Performance Task item 1, students can see how a mechanical engineer uses mathematics on the job.

SCORING GUIDES FOR PERFORMANCE TASKS

1. MATHEMATICAL PRACTICES **FL CC** MP.1.1, MP.4.1, MP.6.1

Task	Possible Points (Total: 6)
a	**1 point** for correct expression and stretch: $2.5x$; 15 mm.
b	**1 point** for correct expression and stretch: $0.25x$; 1.5 cm. **1 point** for correct answer yes and explanation: 1.5 cm is the same length as 15 mm.
c	**1 point** for correct equation, description of the variable, and answer: $7 = 0.25x + 4$ (or $70 = 2.5x + 40$) where x is the force in Newtons; $x = 12$ N
d	**1 point** for correct expression: $-0.25c + 4$ or $-2.5c + 40$ **1 point** for correct answer: 2.5 cm or 25 mm

2. MATHEMATICAL PRACTICES **FL CC** MP.2.1, MP.3.1, MP.4.1

Task	Possible Points (Total: 6)
a	**1 point** for writing the inequality: $70 + 25w > 200$. **1 point** for solving the inequality: $w > 5.2$. **1 point** for correctly answering that Yolanda must save for 6 or more full weeks.
b	**1 point** for correctly answering no. **2 points** for correct explanation: Yolanda will have $70 + \$25(6) = \$220$ in 6 weeks. After buying the phone, she will only have $\$220 - \$200 = \$20$ left.

CAREERS IN MATH

For more information about careers in mathematics as well as various mathematics appreciation topics, visit the American Mathematical Society at http://www.ams.org.

MODULE 2 Inequalities

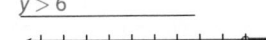 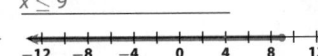

Key Vocabulary
inequalities
(desigualdad)

? ESSENTIAL QUESTION

How can you use inequalities to solve real-world problems?

EXAMPLE 1

Amy is having her birthday party at a roller skating rink. The rink charges a fee of $50 plus $8 per person. If Amy wants to spend at most $170 for the party at the rink, how many people can she invite to her party?

Let p represent the number of people skating at the party.

$50 + 8p \leq 170$

$\begin{aligned} 8p &\leq 120 & \text{Subtract 50 from both sides.}\\ \frac{8p}{8} &\leq \frac{120}{8} & \text{Divide both sides by 8.}\\ p &\leq 15 \end{aligned}$

Up to 15 people can skate, so Amy can invite up to 14 people to her party.

EXAMPLE 2

Determine which, if any, of these values makes the inequality $-7x + 42 \leq 28$ true: $x = -1$, $x = 2$, $x = 5$.

$-7(-1) + 42 \leq 28 \qquad -7(2) + 42 \leq 28 \qquad -7(5) + 42 \leq 28$

Substitute each value for x in the inequality and evaluate the expression to see if a true inequality results.

$x = 2$ and $x = 5$

EXERCISES

1. Prudie needs $90 or more to be able to take her family out to dinner. She has already saved $30 and wants to take her family out to eat in 4 days. (Lesson 2.2)

   a. Suppose that Prudie earns the same each day. Write an inequality to find how much she needs to earn each day.

   $30 + 4x \geq 90$

   b. Suppose that Prudie earns $18 each day. Will she have enough money to take her family to dinner in 4 days? Explain.

   Yes, $x = 18$ is a solution of the inequality.

Solve each inequality. Graph and check the solution. (Lesson 2.3)

2. $11 - 5y < -19$

   $y > 6$

3. $7x - 2 \leq 61$

   $x \leq 9$

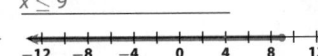

Unit 1 Performance Tasks

1. **CAREERS IN MATH** | **Mechanical Engineer** A mechanical engineer is testing how different springs stretch for a given force. Force is measured in units called *Newtons*, abbreviated N. A spring stretches 2.5 millimeters for each 1-N force applied.

   a. Write an expression for the stretch of this spring in millimeters for a given force x in Newtons. Use your expression to find how much the spring stretches for a 6-N force.

   $2.5x$; 15 mm

   b. Write an expression for the stretch of this spring in *centimeters* for a given force x in Newtons. Use your expression to find how much the spring stretches for a 6-N force. Does the spring stretch the same length as in part a? Explain.

   $0.25x$; 1.5 cm; Yes, the spring stretches 1.5 cm which is the same as 15 mm.

   c. The spring is 4 cm long when unloaded. Write and solve an equation for the force needed to stretch the spring to a length of 7 cm. Include a description of the variable.

   $7 = 0.25x + 4$ or $70 = 2.5x + 40$ where x is the force in Newtons; $x = 12$ N

   The amount a spring stretches for a 1-N force is called the *spring constant*, and depends on the spring's construction and material. The spring constant applies when the spring is compressed, which reduces its length, as well as when it is stretched.

   d. Write an expression for the 4-centimeter spring under a compressive force c. Then find the length of the spring under a 6-N compressive force.

   $-0.25c + 4$ or $-2.5c + 40$ where x is a positive compressive force in Newtons; 2.5 cm or 25 mm

2. Yolanda saves money to buy a $200 cell phone. She has $70, and saves $25 each week.

   a. Write and solve an inequality to find out how many full weeks Yolanda must save to have at least enough money to buy the cell phone.

   $70 + 25w > 200$; $w > 5.2$; 6 full weeks or more

   b. Yolanda buys her phone when she has enough money saved. Will she also have enough to buy a $35 protective case? Explain.

   No; in 6 weeks, she has $70 + $25 \times 6 = 220; $220 - $200 = 20

MIXED REVIEW

PARCC Assessment Readiness

Assessment Readiness Tip If students notice that their original solution method is time-consuming, encourage them to consider whether a faster solution method might be available.

Item 7 Students may start by attempting to solve each equation individually. However, because the solution is given in the problem statement, students can instead substitute the solution into the answer choices and simplify. This will generally be a faster technique.

Avoid Common Errors

Item 2 Some students have a hard time distinguishing which number is the coefficient of the variable. Remind them to look for words like *each* or *every* to see which number is the coefficient. In this case, the coefficient is $2.25, because it says that is the price for *each* meal.

Item 11 Students may attempt to solve each answer choice inequality to find the solution. Point out that due to the closed point on the graph, they can immediately eliminate choices A and B without solving, saving time and reducing the chance of making an error.

 Florida Common Core Standards

Items	Grade 7 Standards	Mathematical Practices
1*	7.EE.1.1	MP.5.1
2	7.EE.2.4, 7.EE.2.4b	MP.4.1
3	7.EE.1.1	MP.5.1
4	7.EE.2.4	MP.4.1
5	7.EE.2.4, 7.EE.2.4b	MP.4.1
6	7.EE.1.1	MP.4.1
7	7.EE.2.4b	MP.5.1
8	7.EE.2.4	MP.4.1
9	7.EE.2.4b	MP.2.1
10	7.EE.2.4b	MP.2.1
11	7.EE.2.4b	MP.2.1
12	7.EE.2.4a	MP.4.1
13	7.EE.2.4	MP.2.1
14	7.EE.2.4b	MP.2.1
15	7.EE.2.4, 7.EE.2.4b	MP.1.1

* Item integrates mixed review concepts from previous modules or a previous course.

PARCC Assessment Readiness

Personal Math Trainer

my.hrw.com

Online Assessment and Intervention

Selected Response

1. Which expression is equivalent to $(9x - 3\frac{1}{8}) - (7x + 1\frac{3}{8})$?

Ⓐ $2x - 4\frac{1}{2}$ Ⓒ $2x - 1\frac{3}{4}$

Ⓑ $16x - 4\frac{1}{2}$ Ⓓ $16x - 1\frac{3}{4}$

2. Timothy began the week with $35. He bought lunch at school, paying $2.25 for each meal. Let x be the number of meals he bought at school and y be the amount of money he had left at the end of the week. Which equation represents the relationship in the situation?

Ⓐ $y = 2.25x + 35$

Ⓑ $y = 35 - 2.25x$

Ⓒ $x = 35 - 2.25y$

Ⓓ $y = 2.25x - 35$

3. Which expression factors to $8(x + 2)$?

Ⓐ $8x + 2$ Ⓒ $16x$

Ⓑ $8x + 10$ Ⓓ $8x + 16$

4. Ramón's toll pass account has a value of $32. Each time he uses the toll road, $1.25 is deducted from the account. When the value drops below $10, he must add value to the toll pass. Which inequality represents how many times Ramón can use the toll road without having to add value to the toll pass?

Ⓐ $10 - 1.25t \geq 0$

Ⓑ $-1.25t + 32 < 10$

Ⓒ $32 - 1.25t \geq 10$

Ⓓ $32 - 10t \geq 1.25$

5. A taxi costs $1.65 for the first mile and $0.85 for each additional mile. Which equation could be solved to find the number x of additional miles traveled in a taxi given that the total cost of the trip is $20?

Ⓐ $1.65x + 0.85 = 20$

Ⓑ $0.85x + 1.65 = 20$

Ⓒ $1.65x - 0.85 = 20$

Ⓓ $0.85x - 1.65 = 20$

6. A sales tax of 6% is added to the price of an item. If Marisa buys an item, which expression indicates how much she will pay in all?

Ⓐ $n + 0.06$ Ⓒ $n + 0.06n$

Ⓑ $0.06n$ Ⓓ $0.06 + 0.06n$

7. Which equation has the solution $x = 12$?

Ⓐ $4x + 3 = 45$

Ⓑ $3x + 6 = 42$

Ⓒ $2x - 5 = 29$

Ⓓ $5x - 8 = 68$

8. The 23 members of the school jazz band are trying to raise at least $1,800 to cover the cost of traveling to a competition. The members have already raised $750. Which inequality could you solve to find the amount that each member should raise to meet the goal?

Ⓐ $23x + 750 > 1,800$

Ⓑ $23x + 750 \geq 1,800$

Ⓒ $23x + 750 < 1,800$

Ⓓ $23x + 750 \leq 1,800$

9. What is the solution of the inequality $2x - 9 < 7$?

Ⓐ $x < 8$

Ⓑ $x \leq 8$

Ⓒ $x > 8$

Ⓓ $x \geq 8$

10. Which inequality has the solution $n < 5$?

Ⓐ $4n + 11 > -9$

Ⓑ $4n + 11 < -9$

Ⓒ $-4n + 11 < -9$

Ⓓ $-4n + 11 > -9$

11. Which inequality has the solution shown?

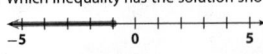

Ⓐ $3x + 5 < 2$

Ⓑ $4x + 12 < 4$

Ⓒ $2x + 5 \leq 1$

Ⓓ $3x + 6 \leq 3$

12. A bike rental costs $8 plus $3 per hour. Ravi spent a total of $29 for a bike rental. For how many hours did he rent the bike?

Ⓐ 3 hours

Ⓑ 7 hours

Ⓒ 8 hours

Ⓓ 29 hours

13. Which equation has the solution $x = -5$?

Ⓐ $3x - 5 = -10$

Ⓑ $6x + 2 = 32$

Ⓒ $-2x + 3 = 13$

Ⓓ $-4x - 8 = -28$

14. What is the solution of the inequality $-4z < -20$?

Ⓐ $z < 5$ Ⓒ $z > 5$

Ⓑ $z < -5$ Ⓓ $z > -5$

Mini-Task

15. Max wants to buy some shorts that are priced at $8 each. He decided to buy a pair of sneakers for $39, but the total cost of the shorts and the sneakers must be less than $75.

a. Write an inequality to find out how many pairs of shorts Max can buy.

$39 + 8s < 75$

b. Suppose that Max wants to buy 6 pairs of shorts. Will he have enough money? Explain.

No; 6 is not a solution of the inequality: $39 + 8(6) = 39 + 48 = 87$, which is greater than $75.

c. Solve the inequality to find the greatest number of pairs of shorts that Max can buy. Show your work.

$39 + 8s < 75$

$8s < 36$

$s < 4.5$

The greatest number of pairs of shorts Max can buy is 4.

UNIT 2

Geometry

Contents

Unit Pacing Guide

45-Minute Classes

Module 3

DAY 1	DAY 2	DAY 3	DAY 4	DAY 5
Lesson 3.1	Lesson 3.2	Lesson 3.3	Lesson 3.4	Lesson 3.4

DAY 6				
Ready to Go On? PARCC Assessment Readiness				

Module 4

DAY 1	DAY 2	DAY 3	DAY 4	DAY 5
Lesson 4.1	Lesson 4.2	Lesson 4.3	Lesson 4.4	Lesson 4.5

DAY 6	DAY 7			
Ready to Go On? PARCC Assessment Readiness	Study Guide PARCC Assessment Readiness			

90-Minute Classes

Module 3

DAY 1	DAY 2	DAY 3
Lesson 3.1 Lesson 3.2	Lesson 3.3 Lesson 3.4	Lesson 3.4 Ready to Go On? PARCC Assessment Readiness

Module 4

DAY 1	DAY 2	DAY 3	DAY 4	
Lesson 4.1 Lesson 4.2	Lesson 4.3 Lesson 4.4	Lesson 4.5	Ready to Go On? PARCC Assessment Readiness	Study Guide PARCC Assessment Readiness

Program Resources

⏻ Plan

Online Teacher Edition

Access a full suite of teaching resources online—plan, present, and manage classes, assignments, and activities.

ePlanner Easily plan your classes, create and view assignments, and access all program resources with your online, customizable planning tool.

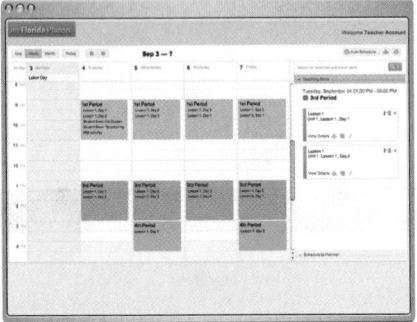

Professional Development Videos

Author Juli Dixon models successful teaching practices and strategies in actual classroom settings.

QR Codes Scan with your smart phone to jump directly from your print book to online videos and other resources.

Teacher's Edition

Support students with point-of-use Questioning Strategies, teaching tips, resources for differentiated instruction, additional activities, and more.

⏻ Engage and Explore

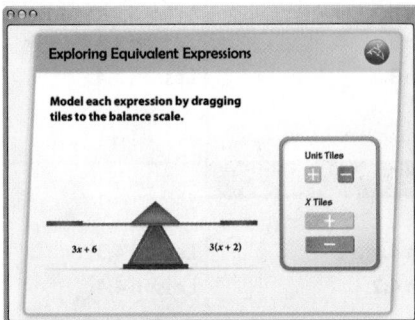

Real-World Videos Engage students with interesting and relevant applications of the mathematical content of each module.

Animated Math Online interactive simulations, tools, and games help students actively learn and practice key concepts.

Exploring Equivalent Expressions

Model each expression by dragging tiles to the balance scale.

Unit Tiles
+ −

X Tiles
+ −

$3x + 6$ $3(x + 2)$

Explore Activities

Students interactively explore new concepts using a variety of tools and approaches.

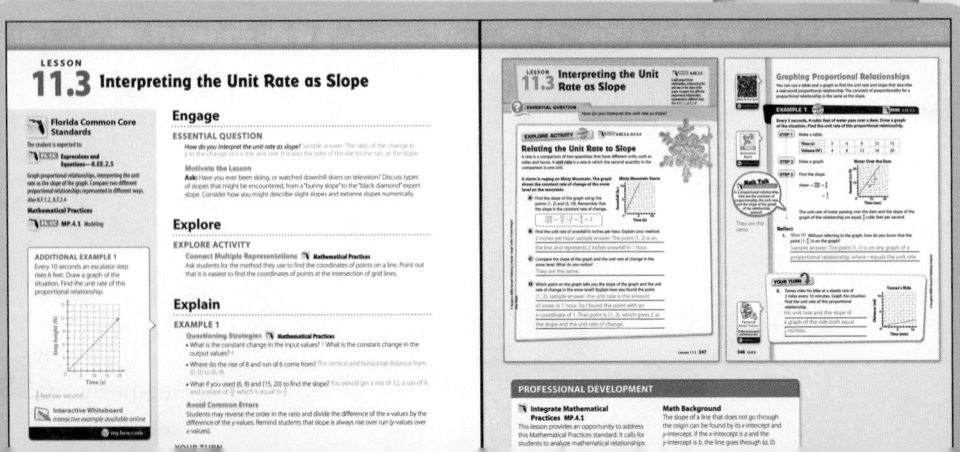

LESSON
11.3 Interpreting the Unit Rate as Slope

8.EE.2.5

Graph proportional relationships, interpreting the unit rate as the slope of the graph. Compare two different proportional relationships represented in different ways. *Also 8.F.1.2, 8.F.2.4*

? ESSENTIAL QUESTION

How do you interpret the unit rate as slope?

EXPLORE ACTIVITY *Real World*   8.EE.2.5, 8.F.2.4

Relating the Unit Rate to Slope

A rate is a comparison of two quantities that have different units, such as miles and hours. A **unit rate** is a rate in which the second quantity in the comparison is one unit.

A storm is raging on Misty Mountain. The graph shows the constant rate of change of the snow level on the mountain.

A Find the slope of the graph using the points (1, 2) and (5, 10). Remember that the slope is the constant rate of change.

$$\frac{\text{rise}}{\text{run}} = \frac{10 - 2}{5 - 1} = \frac{8}{4} = 2$$

Misty Mountain Storm

Snowfall (in.) vs *Time (h)*

B Find the unit rate of snowfall in inches per hour. Explain your method.

2 inches per hour; sample answer: The point (1, 2) is on the line, and represents 2 inches snowfall in 1 hour.

C Compare the slope of the graph and the unit rate of change in the snow level. What do you notice?

They are the same.

D Which point on the graph tells you the slope of the graph and the unit

Teach

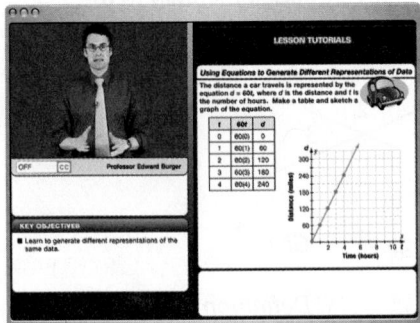

Math On the Spot video tutorials, featuring program authors Dr. Edward Burger and Martha Sandoval-Martinez, accompany every example in the textbook and give students step-by-step instructions and explanations of key math concepts.

Present engaging content on a multitude of devices, including tablets and interactive whiteboards.

Math Talk Continually monitor and assess student progress with integrated formative assessment.

CLUSTER CONNECTION Look for exercises indicated with this icon to build connections among standards within Florida Common Core clusters.

Differentiated Instruction Print Resources

Support all learners with Differentiated Instruction Resources, including

- **Leveled Practice and Problem Solving**
- **Reteach**
- **Reading Strategies**
- **Success for English Learners**
- **Challenge**

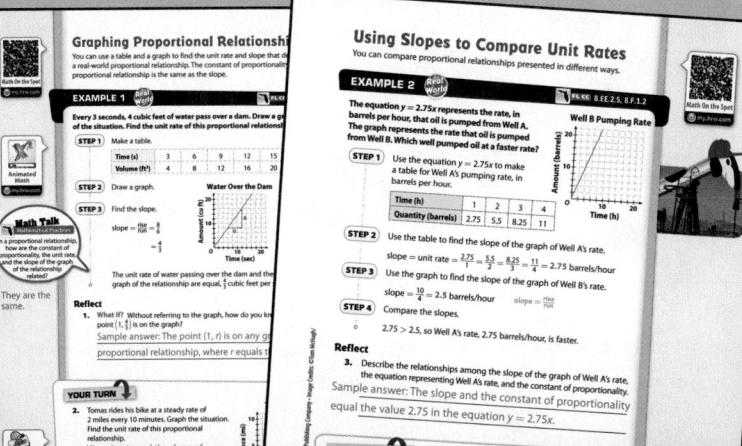

Assessment and Intervention

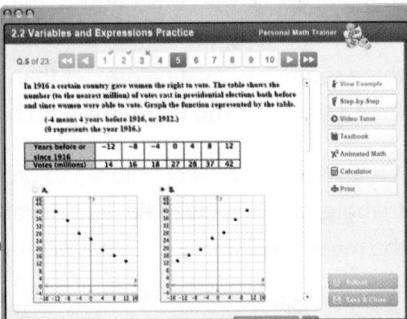

The **Personal Math Trainer** provides online practice, homework, assessments, and intervention. Monitor student progress through reports and alerts. Create and customize assignments aligned to specific lessons or standards.

- **Practice** – With dynamic items and assignments, students get unlimited practice on key concepts supported by guided examples, step-by-step solutions, and video tutorials.

- **Assessments** – Choose from course assignments or customize your own based on course content, standards, difficulty levels, and more.

- **Homework** – Students can complete online homework with a wide variety of problem types, including the ability to enter expressions, equations, and graphs. Let the system automatically grade homework, so you can focus where your students need help the most!

- **Intervention** – Let the Personal Math Trainer automatically prescribe a targeted, personalized intervention path for your students.

Raise the bar with homework and practice that incorporates higher-order thinking and mathematical processes in every lesson.

PARCC Assessment Readiness
Prepare students for success on the PARCC math test with practice at every module and unit.

Assessment Resources

Tailor assessments to meet the needs of all your classes and students, including

- **Leveled Module Quizzes**
- **Leveled Unit Tests**
- **Unit Performance Tasks**
- **Placement, Diagnostic, and Quarterly Benchmark Tests**

Math Background

Geometric Drawings 7.G.1.2
LESSON 3.2

Using line segments of given lengths, angles of given measures, and related conditions, students will notice how relationships among the givens may determine or preclude the existence of a triangle. They will notice whether no triangle is possible, or whether one or more triangles are possible.

Although students will not recognize it at this point, they will be anticipating geometric postulates and theorems. For instance, the measures of two angles and the length of a segment included between the angles determine a unique triangle. Similarly, the lengths of two segments and the measure of the angle between them determine a unique triangle. The lengths of three segments determine a unique triangle, within the constraints of the Triangle Inequality Theorem. That is, the sum of the lengths of any two of the three segments must be greater than the length of the third. Otherwise, no triangle is possible.

It is also possible for conditions to produce more than one triangle, as when given the lengths of two segments and the measure of an angle that is *not* included between them.

Cross Sections 7.G.1.3
LESSON 3.3

In this lesson, students will investigate the two-dimensional figures that result when three dimensional figures are intersected by planes. In high school, they will investigate conic sections. After studying circles, ellipses, parabolas, and hyperbolas, students will discover that each of these curves can be produced by a plane that intersects a double-napped cone.

Angle Relationships 7.G.2.5
LESSON 3.4

In this lesson, students learn that vertical angles are congruent. This relationship is formally known as the Vertical Angles Theorem, and its proof is shown below. This proof makes use of the Congruent Supplements Theorem, which states that if two angles are supplementary to the same angle, then the two angles are congruent.

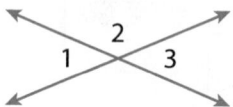

∠1 and ∠3 are vertical angles.	*Given*
∠1 and ∠3 are formed by intersecting lines.	*Definition of vert. angles*
∠1 and ∠2 are a linear pair; ∠2 and ∠3 are a linear pair.	*Definition of linear pair*
∠1 and ∠2 are supp.; ∠2 and ∠3 are supp.	*Linear Pair Theorem*
∠1 ≅ ∠3	*Congruent Supps. Theorem*

Understanding Pi 7.G.2.4
LESSON 4.1

The constant π can be defined in various ways. Most commonly, π is defined as the ratio of the circumference of a circle to the diameter of the circle, or $\pi = \frac{C}{d}$.

The value of π can also be defined as the area of a circle with a radius of one unit (commonly called a *unit circle*). Students can explore this definition by using a compass and grid paper. For example, have students draw a circle with a radius of 10 grid squares, where each grid square represents $\frac{1}{100}$ of a square unit. Students can count grid squares to estimate the area of the circle. Their estimates should be close to 3.14 square units.

Students should understand that π is irrational. That is, π cannot be represented as the ratio of two integers or as a terminating or repeating decimal. One consequence of this is that a circle cannot have both a diameter and a circumference that are rational. Students will learn the proof that π is irrational in future math courses.

Emphasize that 3.14 and $\frac{22}{7}$, the values most commonly associated with π, are only approximations. With the aid of computers, mathematicians have calculated more accurate approximations of π that have more than 200 billion decimal places!

Circumference and Area 7.G.2.4, 7.G.2.6
LESSONS 4.1 to 4.3

Since all circles are similar, and the ratio of distances between corresponding points in similar figures is constant, we know that the ratio of the circumference to the diameter is the same for all circles. This ratio is denoted by the symbol π. So, if C is the circumference and d is the diameter of a circle, then $\frac{C}{d} = \pi$. From this we obtain the well-known formula $C = \pi d$. Given a circle with radius r, we have $d = 2r$ and $C = \pi(2r) = 2\pi r$.

The number π is an irrational number whose decimal expansion begins $\pi = 3.1415926....$ In applications, the approximations $\pi \approx 3.14$ and $\pi \approx \frac{22}{7}$ are often useful. The decimal form of $\frac{22}{7}$, $3.\overline{142857}$, is accurate to two decimal places and is slightly more accurate than 3.14. Fifth-century Chinese mathematicians developed an approximation of π that is accurate to 6 decimal places: $\pi \approx \frac{355}{113} \approx 3.1415929....$

One way to arrive at a formula for the area of a circle is a limit approach. Consider regular polygons of increasing numbers of sides circumscribed about a circle of radius r. If such a polygon has n sides, each with a side length of s, the polygon can be divided into n triangles, each with a vertex at the center, altitude r, and base length of s. Since each of these triangles has area $\frac{1}{2}rs$, the polygon has area $n \cdot \frac{1}{2}rs = \frac{1}{2}r(ns) = \frac{1}{2}rP$, where P is the perimeter of the polygon.

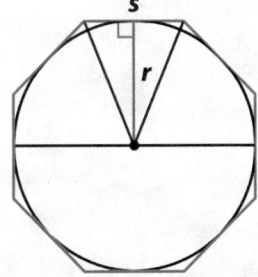

The diagram shows a circle inscribed in a regular polygon with 8 sides.

When the number n of sides is very large, the perimeter of the polygon is very close to the circumference of the circle, so $P \approx 2\pi r$. Therefore, the area $\frac{1}{2}rP$ of the polygon is close to $\frac{1}{2}r(2\pi r) = \pi r^2$. But for large n, the area of the polygon is close to that of the circle, so it is reasonable to expect that the area of the circle is given by $A = \pi r^2$.

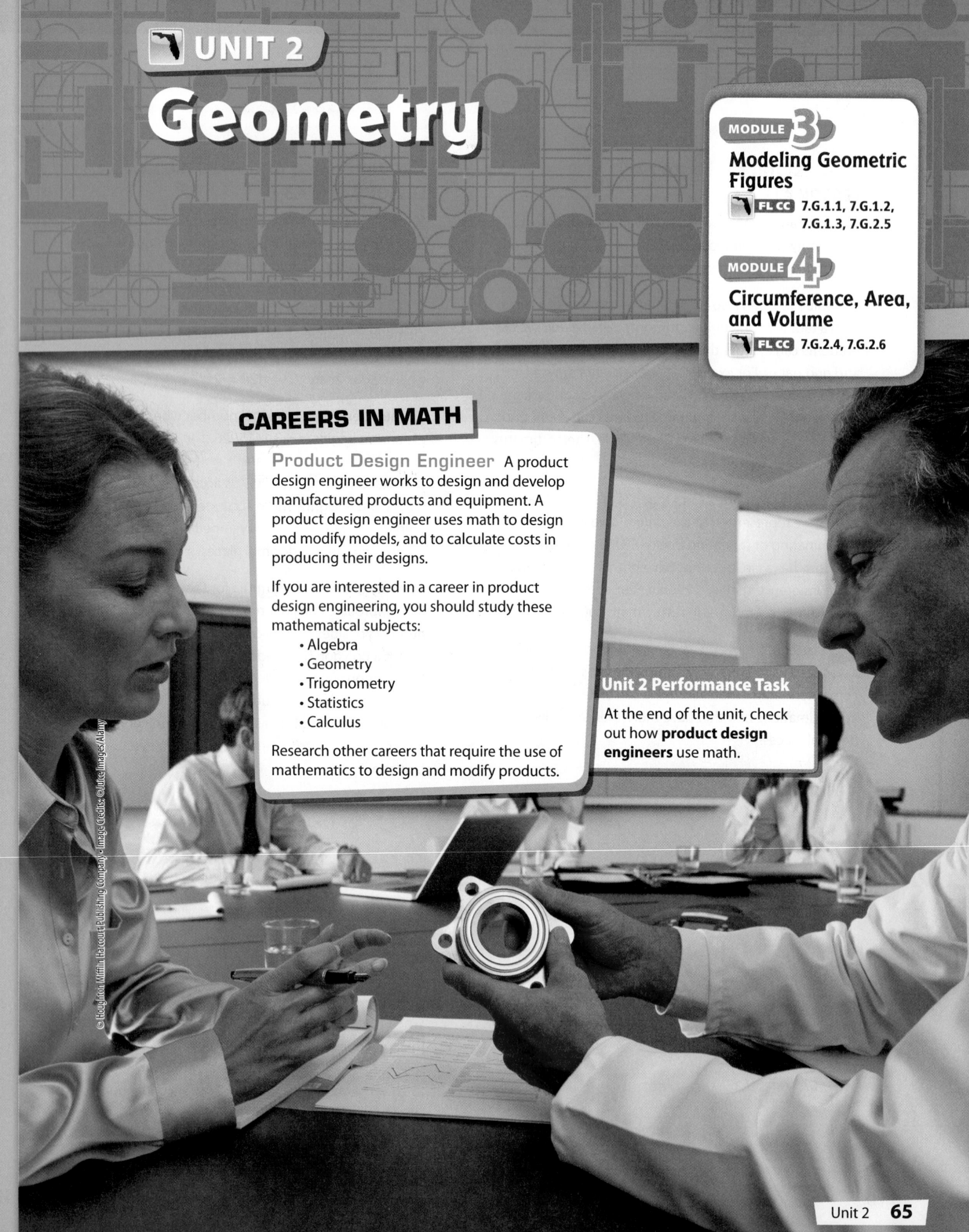

Geometry

MODULE 3

Modeling Geometric Figures

FL CC 7.G.1.1, 7.G.1.2, 7.G.1.3, 7.G.2.5

MODULE 4

Circumference, Area, and Volume

FL CC 7.G.2.4, 7.G.2.6

CAREERS IN MATH

Product Design Engineer A product design engineer works to design and develop manufactured products and equipment. A product design engineer uses math to design and modify models, and to calculate costs in producing their designs.

If you are interested in a career in product design engineering, you should study these mathematical subjects:
- Algebra
- Geometry
- Trigonometry
- Statistics
- Calculus

Research other careers that require the use of mathematics to design and modify products.

Unit 2 Performance Task

At the end of the unit, check out how **product design engineers** use math.

Careers in Math

Product Design Engineer

Product design engineers combine artistic talent with mathematics to create manufactured products. You will learn more about product design engineering in the Performance Tasks at the end of the unit.

For more information about careers in mathematics as well as various mathematics appreciation topics, visit the American Mathematical Society at www.ams.org

Vocabulary Preview

Use the puzzle to give students a preview of important concepts in this unit. Students may work individually, in pairs, or in groups.

Unit Resources

Go online to access all your unit resources.

my.hrw.com

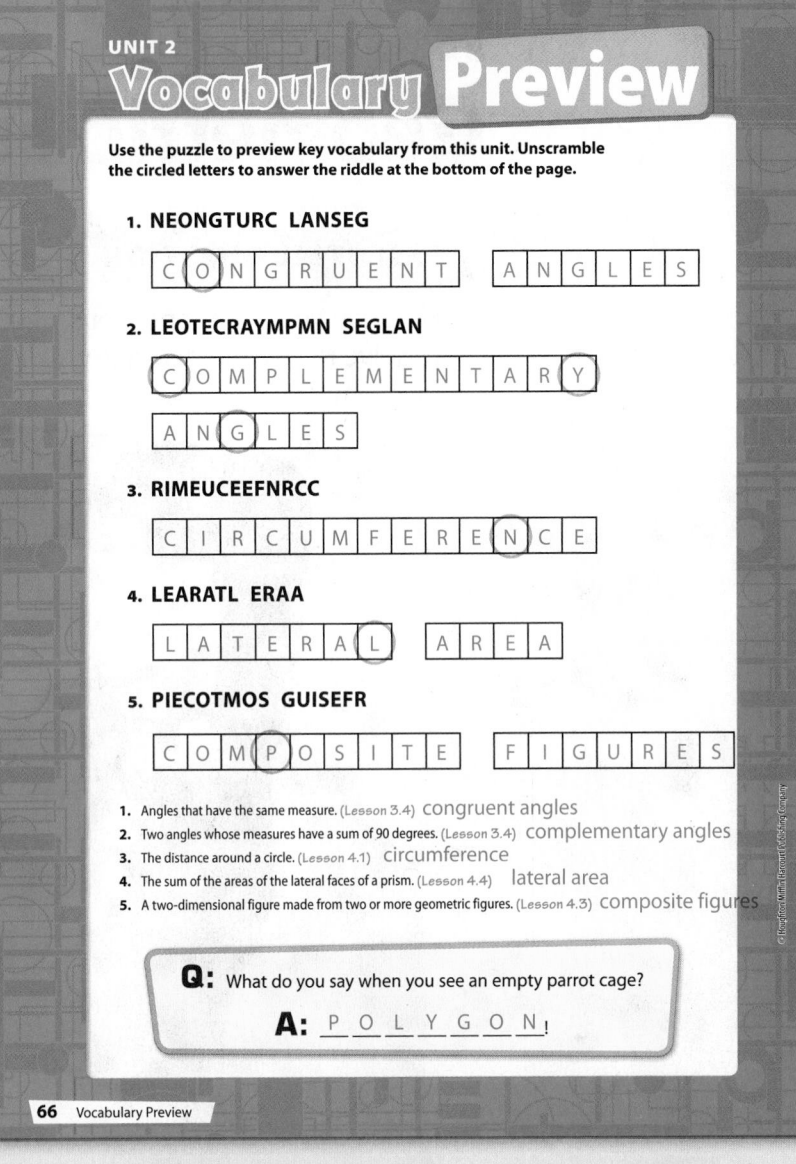

UNIT 2

Vocabulary Preview

Use the puzzle to preview key vocabulary from this unit. Unscramble the circled letters to answer the riddle at the bottom of the page.

1. **NEONGTURC LANSEG**

   C O N G R U E N T   A N G L E S

2. **LEOTECRAYMPMN SEGLAN**

   C O M P L E M E N T A R Y

   A N G L E S

3. **RIMEUCEEFNRCC**

   C I R C U M F E R E N C E

4. **LEARATL ERAA**

   L A T E R A L   A R E A

5. **PIECOTMOS GUISEFR**

   C O M P O S I T E   F I G U R E S

1. Angles that have the same measure. (Lesson 3.4) congruent angles
2. Two angles whose measures have a sum of 90 degrees. (Lesson 3.4) complementary angles
3. The distance around a circle. (Lesson 4.1) circumference
4. The sum of the areas of the lateral faces of a prism. (Lesson 4.4) lateral area
5. A two-dimensional figure made from two or more geometric figures. (Lesson 4.3) composite figures

Q: What do you say when you see an empty parrot cage?

A: P O L Y G O N !

66 Vocabulary Preview

Before

Students understand:

- how to use the relationships between side lengths and between angle measures in a triangle to solve problems
- how to write equations that represent problems related to the area of rectangles, parallelograms, trapezoids, and triangles
- how to write equations that represent problems related to the volume of right rectangular prisms

In this Unit

Students will learn about:

- angle pair relationships
- circumference and area of a circle
- area of composite figures
- volume and surface area of prisms and pyramids

After

Students will connect:

- angle pairs and angles formed by parallel lines that are cut by a transversal
- formulas for lateral and total surface area of prisms

Modeling Geometric Figures

? ESSENTIAL QUESTION

How can you use proportions to solve real-world geometry problems?

You can find the lengths of unknown sides of similar figures by writing and solving proportions involving corresponding sides of the figures.

© Houghton Mifflin Harcourt Publishing Company • Image Credits: ©Photo Researchers/Getty Images

Real-World Video

Architects make blueprints and models of their designs to show clients and contractors. These scale drawings and scale models have measurements in proportion to those of the project when built.

⏻ my.hrw.com

GO DIGITAL
my.hrw.com

my.hrw.com

Go digital with your write-in student edition, accessible on any device.

Math On the Spot

Scan with your smart phone to jump directly to the online edition, video tutor, and more.

Animated Math

Interactively explore key concepts to see how math works.

Personal Math Trainer

Get immediate feedback and help as you work through practice sets.

Are You Ready?

Assess Readiness

Use the assessment on this page to determine if students need intensive or strategic intervention for the module's prerequisite skills.

 **Response to Intervention**

Personal Math Trainer
Online Assessment and Intervention
my.hrw.com

Intervention	Enrichment

Access Are You Ready? assessment online, and receive instant scoring, feedback, and customized intervention or enrichment.

Online and Print Resources

Skills Intervention worksheets	*Differentiated Instruction*
• Skill 60 Solving Two-Step Equations	• Challenge worksheets **PRE-AP**
• Skill 65 Solve Proportions	Extend the Math **PRE-AP** Lesson Activities in TE

Are YOU Ready?

Complete these exercises to review skills you will need for this module.

Personal Math Trainer
Online Assessment and Intervention
my.hrw.com

Solve Two-Step Equations

EXAMPLE		
	$5x + 3 = -7$	
	$5x + 3 - 3 = -7 - 3$	Subtract 3 from both sides.
	$5x = -10$	Simplify.
	$\frac{5x}{5} = \frac{-10}{5}$	Divide both sides by 5.
	$x = -2$	

Solve.

1. $3x + 4 = 10$ 2

2. $5x - 11 = 34$ 9

3. $-2x + 5 = -9$ 7

4. $-11 = 8x + 13$ -3

5. $4x - 7 = -27$ -5

6. $\frac{1}{2}x + 16 = 39$ 46

7. $12 = 2x - 16$ 14

8. $5x - 15 = -65$ -10

Solve Proportions

EXAMPLE		
	$\frac{a}{4} = \frac{27}{18}$	
	$a \times 18 = 4 \times 27$	Write the cross products.
	$18a = 108$	Simplify.
	$\frac{18a}{18} = \frac{108}{18}$	Divide both sides by 18.
	$a = 6$	

Solve for x.

9. $\frac{x}{5} = \frac{18}{30}$ 3

10. $\frac{x}{12} = \frac{24}{36}$ 8

11. $\frac{3}{9} = \frac{x}{3}$ 1

12. $\frac{14}{15} = \frac{x}{75}$ 70

13. $\frac{8}{x} = \frac{14}{7}$ 4

14. $\frac{14}{x} = \frac{2}{5}$ 35

15. $\frac{5}{6} = \frac{x}{15}$ 12.5

16. $\frac{81}{33} = \frac{x}{5.5}$ 13.5

© Houghton Mifflin Harcourt Publishing Company

68   Unit 2

PROFESSIONAL DEVELOPMENT VIDEO

Author Juli Dixon models successful teaching practices as she explores the concept of proportions in an actual seventh-grade classroom.

Professional Development
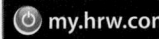
my.hrw.com

GO DIGITAL
my.hrw.com

 Online Teacher Edition
Access a full suite of teaching resources online—plan, present, and manage classes and assignments.

ePlanner
Easily plan your classes and access all your resources online.

 Interactive Answers and Solutions
Customize answer keys to print or display in the classroom. Choose to include answers only or full solutions to all lesson exercises.

 Interactive Whiteboards
Engage students with interactive whiteboard-ready lessons and activities.

 Personal Math Trainer: Online Assessment and Intervention
Assign automatically graded homework, quizzes, tests, and intervention activities. Prepare your students with updated practice tests aligned with Common Core.

Reading Start-Up

Have students complete the activities on this page by working alone or with others.

Visualize Vocabulary

The word magnet helps students review vocabulary associated with comparing similar shapes. Encourage students to draw examples of each word used in the graphic. If time allows, have students work in groups to add lines to the word magnet and additional related words.

Understand Vocabulary

Use the following explanation to help students learn the preview words.

> **Complementary angles** sum to 90 degrees and **supplementary angles** sum to 180 degrees. To remember which is which, just remember that "c" (complementary) comes before "s" (for supplementary), just like 90 comes before 180.

Active Reading

Integrating Language Arts

Students can use these reading and note-taking strategies to help them organize and understand new concepts and vocabulary.

FL CC **LACC.68.RST.3.7** Integrate quantitative or technical information expressed in words in a text with a version of that information expressed visually (e.g., in a flowchart, diagram, model, graph, or table).

Additional Resources

Differentiated Instruction

• Reading Strategies **ELL**

Reading Start-Up

Visualize Vocabulary

Use the ✔ words to complete the graphic. You may put more than one word on each line.

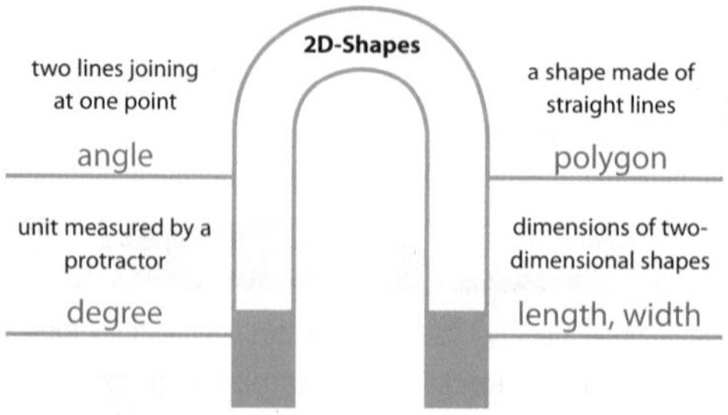

	2D-Shapes	
two lines joining at one point		a shape made of straight lines
angle		polygon
unit measured by a protractor		dimensions of two-dimensional shapes
degree		length, width

Vocabulary

Review Words
✔ angle (ángulo)
✔ degree (grado)
   dimension (dimensión)
✔ length (longitud)
   proportion (proporción)
✔ polygon (polígono)
   ratio (razón)
✔ width (ancho)

Preview Words
   adjacent angles (ángulos adyacentes)
   complementary angles (ángulos complementarios)
   congruent angles (ángulos congruentes)
   cross section (sección transversal)
   intersection (intersección)
   scale (escala)
   scale drawing (dibujo a escala)
   supplementary angles (ángulos suplementarios)
   vertical angles (ángulos verticales)

Understand Vocabulary

Complete each sentence using a preview word.

1. What is a proportional two-dimensional drawing of an object?
   <u>scale drawing</u>

2. <u>Congruent angles</u> are angles that have the same measure.

3. <u>Complementary angles</u> are angles whose measures have a sum of 90°.

Active Reading

Key-Term Fold Before beginning the module, create a key-term fold to help you learn the vocabulary in this module. Write each highlighted vocabulary word on one side of a flap. Write the definition for each word on the other side of the flap. Use the key-term fold to quiz yourself on the definitions in this module.

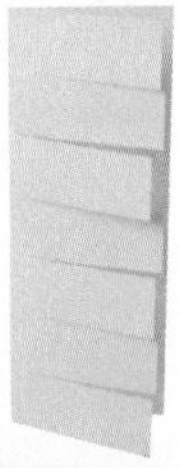

Before	In this module	After
Students understand: • ratios • equivalent fractions • plane figures	Students describe and solve problems involving proportional relationships in geometry: • use ratios to determine if two figures are similar • use similar shapes to find unknown measures • understand the relationship between different types of angle pairs.	Students will connect: • proportional relationships and similarity • angle pairs and angle measurements

Unpacking the Standards

Use the exercises on this page to determine if students need intensive or strategic intervention for the module's prerequisite skills.

 Florida Common Core Standards

Content Areas

 FL CC Geometry—7.G.1

Draw, construct, and describe geometrical figures and describe the relationship between them.

Go online to see a complete unpacking of the Florida Common Core Standards.

⏻ my.hrw.com

 MODULE 3

Unpacking the Standards

Understanding the standards and the vocabulary terms in the standards will help you know exactly what you are expected to learn in this module.

FL CC 7.G.1.1

Solve problems involving scale drawings of geometric figures, including computing actual lengths and areas from a scale drawing and reproducing a scale drawing at a different scale.

Key Vocabulary

scale (*escala*)
The ratio between two sets of measurements.

What It Means to You

You will learn how to calculate actual measurements from a scale drawing.

UNPACKING EXAMPLE 7.G.1.1

A photograph of a painting has dimensions 5.4 cm and 4 cm. The scale factor is $\frac{1}{15}$. Find the length and width of the actual painting.

$$\frac{1}{15} = \frac{5.4}{\ell} \qquad \frac{1}{15} = \frac{4}{w}$$

$$\frac{1 \times 5.4}{15 \times 5.4} = \frac{5.4}{\ell} \qquad \frac{1 \times 4}{15 \times 4} = \frac{4}{w}$$

$$15 \times 5.4 = \ell \qquad 15 \times 4 = w$$

$$81 = \ell \qquad 60 = w$$

The painting is 81 cm long and 60 cm wide.

FL CC 7.G.2.5

Use facts about supplementary, complementary, vertical, and adjacent angles in a multi-step problem to write and solve simple equations for an unknown angle in a figure.

Key Vocabulary

supplementary angles
(*ángulos suplementarios*)
Two angles whose measures have a sum of 180°.

Visit my.hrw.com to see all Florida Common Core Standards unpacked.

⏻ my.hrw.com

What It Means to You

You will learn about supplementary, complementary, vertical, and adjacent angles. You will solve simple equations to find the measure of an unknown angle in a figure.

UNPACKING EXAMPLE 7.G.2.5

Suppose $m\angle 1 = 55°$.

Adjacent angles formed by two intersecting lines are supplementary.

$$m\angle 1 + m\angle 2 = 180°$$

$$55° + m\angle 2 = 180° \qquad \text{Substitute.}$$

$$m\angle 2 = 180° - 55°$$

$$= 125°$$

© Houghton Mifflin Harcourt Publishing Company

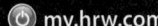 **Florida Common Core Standards**	Lesson 3.1	Lesson 3.2	Lesson 3.3	Lesson 3.4
FL CC 7.G.1.1 Solve problems involving scale drawings of geometric figures, including computing actual lengths and areas from a scale drawing and reproducing a scale drawing at a different scale.	🏴			
FL CC 7.G.1.2 Draw (freehand, with ruler and protractor, and with technology) geometric shapes with given conditions. Focus on constructing triangles from three measures of angles or sides, noticing when the conditions determine a unique triangle, more than one triangle, or no triangle.		🏴		
FL CC 7.G.1.3 Describe the two-dimensional figures that result from slicing three-dimensional figures, as in plane sections of right rectangular prisms and right rectangular pyramids.			🏴	
FL CC 7.G.2.5 Use facts about supplementary, complementary, vertical, and adjacent angles in a multi-step problem to write and solve simple equations for an unknown angle in a figure.				🏴

LESSON
3.1 Similar Shapes and Scale Drawings

Florida Common Core Standards

The student is expected to:

 **FL CC** Geometry—7.G.1.1

Solve problems involving scale drawings of geometric figures, including computing actual lengths and areas from a scale drawing and reproducing a scale drawing at a different scale.

Mathematical Practices

 **FL CC** MP.4.1 Modeling

Engage

ESSENTIAL QUESTION

How can you use scale drawings to solve problems? Sample answer: You use scale drawings to represent measurements of actual objects or places. You can find dimensions of actual objects by making and completing a table, or by writing and solving proportions.

Motivate the Lesson

Ask: Have you ever seen a floor plan of a room or a house? Can you draw a floor plan of our classroom? Try to sketch an overhead view of the room, with doors and windows clearly marked. Then begin the Explore Activity.

Explore

EXPLORE ACTIVITY 1

Focus on Patterns Mathematical Practices

Discuss with students any patterns they may see in the table. Students may notice the addition pattern where numbers increase by 4 and the addition pattern were numbers increase by 3. Make sure that students realize that the values in the table for the actual length increase by 3 because the values for the blueprint length increase by 4.

Explain

EXAMPLE 1

Connect Vocabulary ELL

Remind students that a **scale drawing** must be proportional to a life-size drawing of the same object. Since a scale drawing and a life-size drawing are proportional, they are similar: any corresponding angles will have equivalent measures, and the ratios of the lengths of corresponding sides are proportional.

Questioning Strategies Mathematical Practices

- Are the scales 2 in:3 ft and 1:18 the same scale? Explain. Yes; since there are 12 inches in a foot, the scale 2 in:3 ft can be rewritten as 2 in:36 in., or 2:36. The ratio 2:36 is equivalent to the ratio 1:18.

- Can you multiply the numerator and denominator of $\frac{2 \text{ in.}}{3 \text{ ft}}$ by the same number to show that $\frac{2 \text{ in.}}{3 \text{ ft}} = \frac{11 \text{ in.}}{16.5 \text{ ft}}$? Explain. Yes; multiply the numerator and the denominator by 5.5.

Integrating Language Arts ELL

Encourage a broad class discussion on the Math Talk. English learners will benefit from hearing and participating in classroom discussions.

ADDITIONAL EXAMPLE 1
Joanne has a scale drawing of her backyard that includes a garden bed that measures 16 inches long and 25 inches wide. What is the area of the actual garden bed? 625 ft²

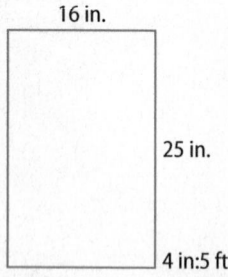

16 in.

25 in.

4 in:5 ft

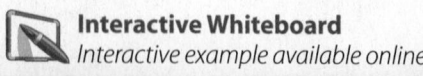 **Interactive Whiteboard**
Interactive example available online

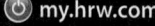 my.hrw.com

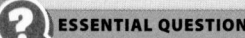

LESSON 3.1 Similar Shapes and Scale Drawings

FL CC 7.G.1.1
Solve problems involving scale drawings of geometric figures, including computing actual lengths and areas from a scale drawing and reproducing a scale drawing at a different scale.

? ESSENTIAL QUESTION
How can you use scale drawings to solve problems?

EXPLORE ACTIVITY 1 Real World    **FL CC** 7.G.1.1

Finding Dimensions

Scale drawings and scale models are used in mapmaking, construction, and other trades.

A blueprint is a technical drawing that usually displays architectural plans. Pete's blueprint shows a layout of a house. Every 4 inches in the blueprint represents 3 feet of the actual house. One of the walls in the blueprint is 24 inches long. What is the actual length of the wall?

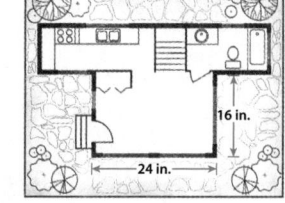

16 in.

24 in.

A Complete the table to find the actual length of the wall.

Blueprint length (in.)	4	8	12	16	20	24
Actual length (ft)	3	6	9	12	15	18

Reflect

1. In Pete's blueprint the length of a side wall is 16 inches. Find the actual length of the wall.

   12 feet

2. The back wall of the house is 33 feet long. What is the length of the back wall in the blueprint?

   44 inches

3. **Check for Reasonableness** How do you know your answer to **2** is reasonable?

   Sample answer: For 18 feet of actual length, the blueprint shows 24 inches. 2 times 18 feet gives 36 feet, which would be shown as 24 times 2, or 48 inches in the blueprint. Thus, for 33 feet, 44 inches is reasonable.

© Houghton Mifflin Harcourt Publishing Company

Lesson 3.1 **71**

Math On the Spot
my.hrw.com

Using a Scale Drawing to Find Area

A **scale drawing** is a proportional two-dimensional drawing of an object. Scale drawings can represent objects that are smaller or larger than the actual object.

A **scale** is a ratio between 2 sets of measurements. It shows how a dimension in a scale drawing is related to the actual object. Scales are usually shown as two numbers separated by a colon such as 1:20 or 1 cm:1 m. Scales can be shown in the same unit or in different units.

You can solve scale-drawing problems by using proportional reasoning.

My Notes

EXAMPLE 1 Real World   **FL CC** 7.G.1.1

The art class is planning to paint a mural on an outside wall. This figure is a scale drawing of the wall. What is the area of the actual wall?

28 in.

11 in.

2 in.:3 ft

STEP 1 Find the number of feet represented by 1 inch in the drawing.

$\frac{2 \text{ in.} \div 2}{3 \text{ ft} \div 2} = \frac{1 \text{ in.}}{1.5 \text{ ft}}$

1 inch in this drawing equals 1.5 feet on the actual wall.

STEP 2 Find the height of the actual wall labeled 11 inches in the drawing.

$\frac{1 \text{ in.} \times 11}{1.5 \text{ ft} \times 11} = \frac{11 \text{ in.}}{16.5 \text{ ft}}$

The height of the actual wall labeled 11 in. is 16.5 ft.

STEP 3 Find the length of the actual wall labeled 28 inches in the drawing.

$\frac{1 \text{ in.} \times 28}{1.5 \text{ ft} \times 28} = \frac{28 \text{ in.}}{42 \text{ ft}}$

The length of the actual wall is 42 ft.

STEP 4 Since area is length times width, the area of the actual wall is 16.5 ft × 42 ft = 693 ft².

Math Talk
Mathematical Practices

How can use a scale to determine whether the drawing or the object is larger?

Put both parts of the scale in the same unit. If the first number is greater, then the drawing is larger. If the second number is greater, then the object is larger.

Reflect

4. **Analyze Relationships** How could you solve the example without having to determine the number of feet represented by 1 inch?

   Sample answer: For the side labeled 28 in., set up the proportion $\frac{2 \text{ in.}}{3 \text{ ft}} = \frac{28 \text{ in.}}{x \text{ ft}}$, and solve to find x = 42. Set up and solve a similar proportion for the side labeled 11 inches.

© Houghton Mifflin Harcourt Publishing Company

72 Unit 2

PROFESSIONAL DEVELOPMENT

Integrate Mathematical Practices MP.4.1

This lesson provides an opportunity to address this Mathematical Practice standard. It calls for students to apply mathematics to problems arising in everyday life, society, and the workplace. Students use blueprint measurements to find actual measurements by using tables and proportional reasoning. Then students use the scale of a scale drawing to find the actual measurements, by writing and solving proportions. Finally, students learn how to take an object drawn to one scale and redraw it in another scale.

Math Background

Scale factors are used to classify maps, which are scale drawings of a geographical region. Small scale maps have a scale of 1:2,000,000 or greater and are usually world maps or larger regional maps. Large scale maps have a scale of 1:600,000 or less and are usually county or city maps.

Similar Shapes and Scale Drawings **72**

YOUR TURN

Focus on Modeling Mathematical Practices

Remind students that drawing a picture helps solve a problem. Demonstrate translating the dimensions in the problem into a scale drawing with a scale. Draw a rectangle, label the longer side 13.2 in., and label the shorter side 6 in. Include the scale 3 in:5 ft.

Talk About It
Check for Understanding

Ask: How can you use the drawing of a room with a scale 2 in:5 ft to find the actual dimensions of the room? Write the scale as a ratio in fraction form, divide both numerator and denominator by 2 to show that 1 inch represents 2.5 feet, then multiply the number of inches of each dimension by 2.5 to find the actual length in feet.

EXPLORE ACTIVITY 2

Avoid Common Errors

Students may think that using a scale of 1 cm:6 m creates a larger image than a scale of 1 cm:3 m. Have students find more measurements using both scales. Ask students what 4 centimeters or 8 centimeters represents in each scale. After working with several sample measurements, students should reason that the new scale will result in a smaller drawing.

Engage with the Whiteboard

Use a grid to draw a more complicated shape using the 1 cm:3 m scale. Have students take turns drawing a side of the polygon in the 1 cm:6 m scale.

Questioning Strategies Mathematical Practices

• What ratio equivalent to 1 cm:3 m shows that the new drawing should have dimensions that are half the original drawing? Explain. 2 cm:6 m; the equivalent ratio of 2 cm:6 m shows that every 6 m is represented by 2 cm. In the second scale, every 6 m is represented by 1 cm, which is half as long as 6 m represented using the original scale.

• One square centimeter in the new scale drawing represents the same actual area as how many square centimeters in the old scale drawing? Explain. 4; 1 square cm in the original drawing represents a square that measures 3 meters on each side and has an area of 9 square meters, and 1 square cm in the new drawing represents a square that measures 6 meters on each side and has an area of 36 square meters. $36 \div 9 = 4$

Elaborate

Talk About It
Summarize the Lesson

Ask: How do you use the scale on a scale drawing to find the measurements of the actual object? Write the scale as a ratio in fraction form. Use the ratio to write a proportion that uses measurements from the scale drawing. Use proportional reasoning to solve for the actual measurements in the proportion.

GUIDED PRACTICE

Engage with the Whiteboard

Allow students to use the drawing given in Exercise 4a to problem solve. Some students may not extract the dimensions of the cafeteria before attempting the second drawing. First count the squares and then apply the 1 cm:4 m scale.

Avoid Common Errors

Exercise 4 Remind students that using a new scale with larger numbers does not mean that a new scale drawing will have larger measurements.

YOUR TURN

5. Find the length and width of the actual room, shown in the scale drawing. Then find the area of the actual room. Round your answer to the nearest tenth.

length: about 17.3 feet; width: about

13.3 feet; area: 230.1 square feet.

6.5 in.

5 in.

3 in.:8 ft

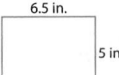

Personal Math Trainer
Online Assessment and Intervention
© my.hrw.com

6. The drawing plan for an art studio shows a rectangle that is 13.2 inches by 6 inches. The scale in the plan is 3 in.:5 ft. Find the length and width of the actual studio. Then find the area of the actual studio.

The length is 22 feet, and the width is 10 feet.

The area is 22 feet × 10 feet, or 220 square feet.

EXPLORE ACTIVITY 2   Real World   FL CC 7.G.1.1

Drawing in Different Scales

A A scale drawing of a meeting hall is drawn on centimeter grid paper as shown. The scale is 1 cm:3 m.

Suppose you redraw the rectangle on centimeter grid paper using a scale of 1 cm:6 m. In the new scale, 1 cm

represents (more than/less) than 1 cm in the old scale.

The measurement of each side of the new drawing will

be (twice/half) as long as the measurement of the

original drawing.

B Draw the rectangle for the new scale 1 cm:6 m.

Reflect

7. Find the actual length of each side of the hall using the original drawing. Then find the actual length of each side of the hall using the your new drawing and the new scale. How do you know your answers are correct?

The lengths of the hall are 8 × 3 = 24 m and 6 × 3 =

18 m. Using the new drawing and scale, the lengths are

4 × 6 = 24 m and 3 × 6 = 18 m. The answers are correct

because both scales give the same actual lengths.

Guided Practice

1. The scale of a room in a blueprint is 3 in : 5 ft. A wall in the same blueprint is 18 in. Complete the table. (Explore Activity 1)

Blueprint length (in.)	3	6	9	12	15	18
Actual length (ft)	5	10	15	20	25	30

a. How long is the actual wall? _The wall is 30 feet long._

b. A window in the room has an actual width of 2.5 feet. Find the width of the window in the blueprint. _1.5 in._

2. The scale in the drawing is 2 in. : 4 ft. What are the length and width of the actual room? Find the area of the actual room. (Example 1)

The length is 28 feet, and the width is 14 feet.

The area is 28 feet × 14 feet, or 392 square feet.

14 in.

7 in.

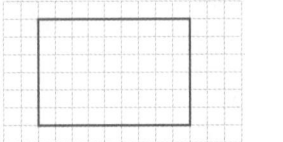

3. The scale in the drawing is 2 cm : 5 m. What are the length and width of the actual room? Find the area of the actual room. (Example 1)

length: 25 meters; width: 15 meters; area: 375 square meters

10 cm

6 cm

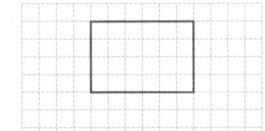

4. A scale drawing of a cafeteria is drawn on centimeter grid paper as shown. The scale is 1 cm : 4 m. (Explore Activity 2)

a. Redraw the rectangle on centimeter grid paper using a scale of 1 cm:6 m.

b. What is the actual length and width of the cafeteria using the original scale? What are the actual dimensions of the cafeteria using the new scale?

Length is 36 m and width is 24 m, using both scales.

? ESSENTIAL QUESTION CHECK-IN

5. If you have an accurate, complete scale drawing and the scale, which measurements of the object of the drawing can you find?

If the scale drawing is complete and accurate, you can use

it to find any length or area of the object of the drawing.

DIFFERENTIATE INSTRUCTION

Modeling

Have students create scale drawings of their classroom. Students will have to take actual measurements and choose a scale to use in their drawing. Each student should check another student's scale drawing to verify that the scale used in the drawing matches the actual measurements of the classroom.

Kinesthetic Experience

Students may have trouble visualizing how a scale relates a small measurement like 2 cm to a larger measurement like 5 ft. Have students create "scale rulers" to better understand the concept of scale. Use strips of paper divided into 2 cm sections: label the mark at 2 cm, 4 cm, 6 cm, and every 2 cm thereafter. Underneath each mark, write the corresponding number of feet: write 5 ft under 2 cm, write 10 ft under 4 cm, and continue until the entire scale ruler is completed. Students can use the scale ruler to find actual measurements on drawings that use that scale.

Additional Resources

Differentiated Instruction includes:

- Reading Strategies
- Success for English Learners **ELL**
- Reteach
- Challenge **PRE-AP**

3.1 LESSON QUIZ

 **FL CC** 7.G.1.1

1. A scale drawing of a billboard uses the scale 4 cm:9 ft. The length of the billboard in the drawing is 11 cm. How long is the actual billboard?

2. A scale drawing of a dance floor is shown. What is the area of the actual dance floor?

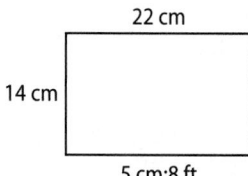

22 cm

14 cm

5 cm:8 ft

3. A bookcase measures 13 feet wide and 24 feet tall. What would the bookcase's measurements be on a scale drawing using the scale 3 cm:2 ft?

4. Bob makes a scale drawing of a statue using the scale 1 cm:5 ft. His drawing measures 12 cm. Kia makes a scale drawing of the same statue using the scale 1 cm:4 ft. How many centimeters tall is the statue in Kia's drawing?

Lesson Quiz available online

ⓘ my.hrw.com

Answers
1. 24.75 ft
2. 788.48 ft²
3. 19.5 cm wide, 36 cm tall
4. 15 cm

Evaluate

GUIDED AND INDEPENDENT PRACTICE

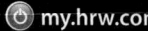 **FL CC** 7.G.1.1

Concepts & Skills	Practice
Explore Activity 1 Finding Dimensions	Exercises 1, 6
Example 1 Using a Scale Drawing to Find Area	Exercises 2, 3, 6
Explore Activity 2 Drawing in Different Scales	Exercises 4, 8

Exercise	Depth of Knowledge (D.O.K.)		**FL CC** Mathematical Practices
6	**2** Skills/Concepts		**MP.4.1** Modeling
7	**2** Skills/Concepts		**MP.4.1** Modeling
8	**3** Strategic Thinking	H.O.T.	**MP.4.1** Modeling
9	**3** Strategic Thinking	H.O.T.	**MP.7.1** Using Structure
10	**3** Strategic Thinking	H.O.T.	**MP.8.1** Patterns
11	**3** Strategic Thinking	H.O.T.	**MP.4.1** Modeling
12	**3** Strategic Thinking	H.O.T.	**MP.1.1** Problem Solving
13	**3** Strategic Thinking	H.O.T.	**MP.2.1** Reasoning
14	**4** Extending Thinking	H.O.T.	**MP.4.1** Modeling

Additional Resources
Differentiated Instruction includes:
• Leveled Practice Worksheets

3.1 Independent Practice

FL.CC 7.G.1.1

Personal Math Trainer

Online Assessment and Intervention

my.hrw.com

6. **Art** Marie has a small copy of Rene Magritte's famous painting, *The Schoolmaster*. Her copy has dimensions 2 inches by 1.5 inches. The scale of the copy is 1 in:40 cm.

   a. Find the dimensions of the original painting.

   80 cm by 60 cm

   b. Find the area of the original painting.

   4,800 cm^2

   c. Since 1 inch is 2.54 centimeters, find the dimensions of the original painting in inches.

   31.5 in. by 23.6 in.

   d. Find the area of the original painting in square inches.

   approximately 743 in^2

7. A game room has a floor that is 120 feet by 75 feet. A scale drawing of the floor on grid paper uses a scale of 1 unit:5 feet. What are the dimensions of the scale drawing?

   The scale drawing is 24 units by 15 units.

8. **Multiple Representations** The length of a table is 6 feet. On a scale drawing, the length is 2 inches. Write three possible scales for the drawing.

   Sample answer: 2 in.:6 ft, 1 in.:3 ft, and 1 in.:1 yd

9. **Analyze Relationships** A scale for a scale drawing is 10 cm:1 mm. Which is larger, the actual object or the scale drawing? Explain.

   Because the scale is 10 cm:1 mm and because 10 cm is longer than 1 mm, the drawing will be larger.

10. **Architecture** The scale model of a building is 5.4 feet tall.

    a. If the original building is 810 meters tall, what was the scale used to make the model?

    1 ft = 150 m

    b. If the model is made out of tiny bricks each measuring 0.4 inch in height, how many bricks tall is the model?

    162 tiny bricks tall

11. You have been asked to build a scale model of your school out of toothpicks. Imagine your school is 30 feet tall. Your scale is 1 ft:1.26 cm.

    a. If a toothpick is 6.3 cm tall, how many toothpicks tall will your model be?

    6 toothpicks tall

    b. Your mother is out of toothpicks, and suggests you use cotton swabs instead. You measure them, and they are 7.6 cm tall. How many cotton swabs tall will your model be?

    approximately 5 cotton swabs tall

H.O.T. FOCUS ON HIGHER ORDER THINKING

Work Area

12. **Draw Conclusions** The area of a square floor on a scale drawing is 100 square centimeters, and the scale of the drawing is 1 centimeter:2 ft, What is the area of the actual floor? What is the ratio of the area in the drawing to the actual area?

    400 square feet; 1 square centimeter:4 square feet

13. **Multiple Representations** Describe how to redraw a scale drawing with a new scale.

    Decide on the new scale you'd like to use. Then, find the ratio between the old scale and the new scale, and redraw the scale drawing accordingly. For example, the ratio could be 1:3. In that case, you would redraw the dimensions at three times the original size.

14. **Represent Real-World Problems** Describe how several jobs or professions might use scale drawings at work.

    Possible answer: architects drawing plans for buildings and houses; engineers planning bridges and roads; office designers planning the use of building space; ship designers drawing blueprints for builders; carpenters and construction workers following plans; interior designers measuring for wall and window coverings; gardeners installing beds in public parks.

EXTEND THE MATH PRE-AP

Activity available online ⏻ my.hrw.com

A billboard is 2.5 times as long as it is wide. The area of the billboard is 2,250 ft^2. A scale drawing is made of the billboard, and the area of the scale drawing is 160 in^2. What is the scale used in the scale drawing? Explain.

4 in:15 feet; Since the length of the billboard is 2.5 times the width, the equation for the area of the billboard is $(w)(2.5w) = 2,250$ ft^2, where w is the width and $2.5w$ is the length. Using trial and error, students can find that the width is 30 ft and the length is 75 ft. Since the scale drawing is similar in shape to the billboard, the drawing is also 2.5 times as long as it is wide, and $(w)(2.5w) = 160$ in^2. Students can find the width is 8 inches, and the length is 20 inches. Since the drawing and the billboard are similar, 8 inches on the drawing corresponds to 30 feet on the billboard. The scale used is 8 in:30 ft, which can be simplified as 4 in:15 ft.

LESSON
3.2 Geometric Drawings

Engage

ESSENTIAL QUESTION

How can you draw shapes that satisfy given conditions? Sample answer: You can use a ruler, protractor, compass, and software to help you draw shapes. Some conditions result in unique triangles, while other conditions create more than one triangle, or no triangle at all.

Motivate the Lesson
Ask: Can any three line segments be put together to form a triangle? Take a guess. Begin the Explore Activity to find out.

Explore

EXPLORE ACTIVITY 1

Focus on Technology
If geometry software is not available, have students use a ruler to measure and cut out a thin strip of paper the length of each segment. Have students label each segment and then manipulate the segments to form a triangle.

Explain

EXPLORE ACTIVITY 2

Questioning Strategies Mathematical Practices
- How do you know that the triangles in this activity are unique? No matter the position or orientation that you begin constructing each triangle, you will always end up with a triangle with the same shape and size.

- Would the triangle be unique if you knew the measure of all three angles, but did not know the measure of any of the sides? Explain your answer. It would not be unique. As long as the angles have a sum of 180°, there are an infinite number of triangles that can be formed with them. The triangles would have the same shape but not the same size.

Engage with the Whiteboard
On the whiteboard, have a volunteer use a protractor and show the steps for drawing the triangle in Part B.

Avoid Common Errors
Students may think there are other triangles that can be formed with the same two angles and included side as the triangle in Part A. Ask students to test their assumption by trying to draw a different triangle. Suggest they draw the 80° angle first, and then the 30° angle. They should see that the two triangles are, in fact, the same triangle.

Animated Math
Exploring Side Length Relationships

Students explore Triangle Inequality by adjusting the side lengths of a dynamic triangle.

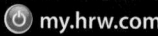 my.hrw.com

LESSON
3.2 Geometric Drawings

FL CC 7.G.1.2
Draw... geometric shapes with given conditions. Focus on constructing triangles...

? ESSENTIAL QUESTION

How can you draw shapes that satisfy given conditions?

EXPLORE ACTIVITY 1 FL CC 7.G.1.2

Drawing Three Sides

Use geometry software to draw a triangle whose sides have the following lengths: 2 units, 3 units, and 4 units.

A Draw the segments.

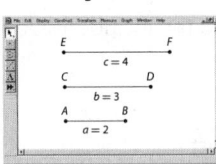

B Let $\overline{AB}$ be the base of the triangle. Place point C on top of point B and point E on top of point A.

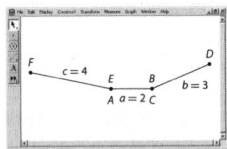

C Using the points C and E as fixed vertices, rotate points F and D to see if they will meet in a single point.

Note that the line segments form a triangle.

D Repeat **A** and **B**, but use a different segment as the base. Do the segments form a triangle? If so, is it the same as the original triangle?

Yes; the triangle has the same size and shape as the original.

E Use geometry software to draw a triangle with sides of length 2, 3, and 6 units, and one with sides of length 2, 3, and 5 units. Do the line segments form triangles? How does the sum of the lengths of the two shorter sides of each triangle compare to the length of the third side?

1st: no, $2 + 3 < 6$; 2nd: no; $2 + 3 = 5$

X² Animated Math my.hrw.com

Reflect

1. Conjecture Do two segments of lengths a and b units and a longer segment of length c units form one triangle, more than one, or none?

One triangle if $a + b > c$; none if $a + b \leq c$.

Lesson 3.2 **77**

EXPLORE ACTIVITY 2 FL CC 7.G.1.2

Two Angles and Their Included Side

Use a ruler and a protractor to draw each triangle.

Triangle 1	Triangle 2
Angles: 30° and 80°	Angles: 55° and 50°
Length of included side: 2 inches	Length of included side: 1 inch

A Draw Triangle 1.

STEP 1 Use a ruler to draw a line that is 2 inches long. This will be the included side.

STEP 2 Place the center of the protractor on the left end of the 2-in. line. Then make a 30°-angle mark.

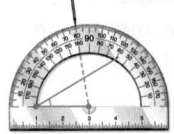

STEP 3 Draw a line connecting the left side of the 2-in. line and the 30°-angle mark. This will be the 30° angle.

STEP 4 Repeat Step 2 on the right side of the triangle to construct the 80° angle.

STEP 5 The side of the 80° angle and the side of the 30° angle will intersect. This is Triangle 1 with angles of 30° and 80° and an included side of 2 inches.

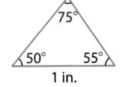

B Use the steps in A to draw Triangle 2.

75°
50° 55°
1 in.

Reflect

2. Conjecture When you are given two angle measures and the length of the included side, do you get a unique triangle?

Yes, the two angles and the length of the included side determine the point at which the sides meet. The triangle is unique.

78 Unit 2

DIFFERENTIATE INSTRUCTION

Critical Thinking

Have small groups construct triangles in which the following sets of measurements have been given to them. Have them report back about which conditions produce a unique triangle. (All except #5 should produce a unique triangle.)

1. SSS (side-side-side)
2. ASA (angle-side-angle)
3. SAS (side-angle-side)
4. AAS (angle-angle-side)
5. SSA (side-side-angle)
6. HL (hypotenuse-leg) (for a right triangle)

Kinesthetic Experience

Provide each group of students with 6 drinking straws cut to different whole-inch lengths and labeled A–F. Have groups measure the length of each straw to the nearest inch and record the lengths in a table. Then ask students to record the different combinations of three straws they think will form triangles. Finally, have students test their list by arranging each set of the three straws to form a triangle.

Additional Resources

Differentiated Instruction includes:
• Reading Strategies
• Success for English Learners **ELL**
• Reteach
• Challenge **PRE-AP**

Geometric Drawings **78**

Elaborate

Talk About It
Summarize the Lesson

Ask: How can you determine whether three segments will form a unique triangle or no triangle? If the sum of the measures of the two shorter segments is greater than the measure of the third segment, the triangle formed is unique. If the sum of the two shorter segments is less than or equal to the measure of the third segment, a triangle cannot be formed.

GUIDED PRACTICE

Engage with the Whiteboard
In Exercises 1 and 3, have volunteers indicate the two angles and the included side that make the triangle unique.

Avoid Common Errors
Exercises 2 and 4 Remind students to find the sum of the two shortest sides before drawing a conclusion about the uniqueness of the triangles.

Evaluate

GUIDED AND INDEPENDENT PRACTICE

 7.G.1.2

Concepts and Skills	Practice
Explore Activity 1 Drawing Three Sides	Exercises 2, 4, 7
Explore Activity 2 Two Angles and Their Included Side	Exercises 1, 3, 6

Exercise	Depth of Knowledge (D.O.K.)	 Mathematical Practices
6	**2** Skills/Concepts	**MP.4.1** Modeling
7	**3** Strategic Thinking **H.O.T.**	**MP.3.1** Logic
8	**3** Strategic Thinking **H.O.T.**	**MP.3.1** Logic
9	**3** Strategic Thinking **H.O.T.**	**MP.7.1** Using Structure
10	**3** Strategic Thinking **H.O.T.**	**MP.3.1** Logic

Additional Resources
Differentiated Instruction includes:
• Leveled Practice worksheets

CLUSTER CONNECTION **Exercise 9** combines concepts from the Florida Common Core cluster "Draw, construct, and describe geometrical figures and describe the relationships between them."

3.2 LESSON QUIZ

FL CC 7.G.1.2

Tell whether each figure creates the conditions to form a unique triangle, more than one triangle, or no triangle.

1.
3 in.
6 in.
10 in.

2.
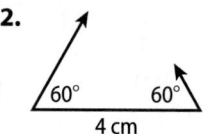
60°   60°
4 cm

3.
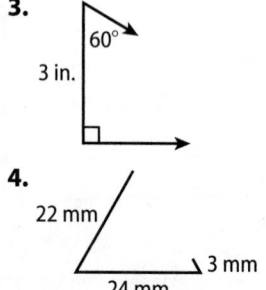
60°
3 in.

4.
22 mm
3 mm
24 mm
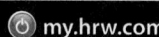

5. The angles of a triangle are 30°, 60°, and 90°. Is this a unique triangle? Justify your answer.

Lesson Quiz example available online

🕐 my.hrw.com

Answers
1. no triangle

2. a unique triangle

3. a unique triangle

4. a unique triangle

5. It is not a unique triangle. More than one triangle can have these angle measures and have corresponding sides that are different lengths.

 **Personal Math Trainer** Online Assessment and Intervention

Online homework assignment available

🕐 my.hrw.com

Guided Practice

Name_____ Class_____ Date_____

Tell whether each figure creates the conditions to form a unique triangle, more than one triangle, or no triangle. (Explore Activities 1 and 2)

1.

8 cm
45°

_____a unique triangle_____

2.

4 cm   3 cm
11 cm

_____no triangle_____

3.

40°   30°
7 cm

_____a unique triangle_____

4.

6 cm
12 cm
7 cm

_____a unique triangle_____

ESSENTIAL QUESTION CHECK-IN

5. Describe lengths of three segments that could **not** be used to form a triangle.

Sample answer: segments with lengths of 5 in., 5 in., and 100 in.

3.2 Independent Practice

FL CC 7.G.1.2

Personal Math Trainer
Online Assessment and Intervention
my.hrw.com

6. On a separate piece of paper, try to draw a triangle with side lengths of 3 centimeters and 6 centimeters, and an included angle of 120°. Determine whether the given segments and angle produce a unique triangle, more than one triangle, or no triangle.

A unique triangle; check students' work.

7. A landscape architect submitted a design for a triangle-shaped flower garden with side lengths of 21 feet, 37 feet, and 15 feet to a customer. Explain why the architect was not hired to create the flower garden.

The side lengths proposed are 15, 21, and 37 ft, and

$15 + 21 < 37$. No such triangle can be created.

8. Make a Conjecture The angles in an actual triangle-shaped traffic sign all have measures of 60°. The angles in a scale drawing of the sign all have measures of 60°. Explain how you can use this information to decide whether three given angle measures can be used to form a unique triangle or more than one triangle.

More than one triangle; the sign and the scale drawing are

two different-sized triangles with the same angle measures.

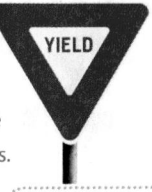

Work Area

H.O.T. FOCUS ON HIGHER ORDER THINKING

9. Communicate Mathematical Ideas The figure on the left shows a line segment 2 inches long forming a 45° angle with a dashed line whose length is not given. The figure on the right shows a compass set at a width of $1\frac{1}{2}$ inches with its point on the top end of the 2-inch segment. An arc is drawn intersecting the dashed line twice.

2 in.   2 in.
45°   45°

Explain how you can use this figure to decide whether two sides and an angle **not** included between them can be used to form a unique triangle, more than one triangle, or no triangle.

More than one triangle; two triangles can be created by

connecting the top of the 2-in. segment with the dashed

line, once in each spot where the arc intersects the

dashed line. The triangles are different, but both have

sides with lengths of 2 in. and $1\frac{1}{2}$ in., and a 45° angle

not included between them.

10. Critical Thinking Two sides of an isosceles triangle have lengths of 6 inches and 15 inches, respectively. Find the length of the third side. Explain your reasoning.

15 in.; The third side must be congruent to one of the

other two sides because the triangle is isosceles. The third

side cannot measure 6 in. because $6 + 6$ is not greater

than 15. So the third side must measure 15 in.

© Houghton Mifflin Harcourt Publishing Company

© Houghton Mifflin Harcourt Publishing Company • Image Credits: ©David Frazier/Corbis

EXTEND THE MATH   PRE-AP

Activity available online my.hrw.com

Activity A triangle has a perimeter of 25 inches. The measures of the lengths of its sides are whole numbers. What are the possible lengths of the longest side of the triangle? Justify your answer.

The longest side could be 12, 11, 10, or 9 inches long. When it is 12 inches long, the sum of the two shorter sides will be 13. The two shorter sides could be 5 and 8 inches. When it is 9 inches long, the sum of the two shorter sides will be 16. The two shorter sides could be 8 and 8. If the longest side were 13 inches long, the sum of the two shorter sides would be 12, so a triangle would not be formed. If the longest side were 8 inches long, the sum of the two shorter sides would be 17. A triangle could be formed but the 8-inch side would not be the longest side.

LESSON
3.3 Cross Sections

 Florida Common Core Standards

The student is expected to:

 **Geometry—7.G.1.3**

Describe the two-dimensional figures that result from slicing three-dimensional figures, as in plane sections of right rectangular prisms and right rectangular pyramids.

Mathematical Practices

 **MP.4.1** Modeling

Engage

ESSENTIAL QUESTION

How can you identify cross sections of three-dimensional figures? Sample answer: You visualize the shape of an intersection created by a flat plane cutting into a three-dimensional object.

Motivate the Lesson

Ask: What two-dimensional shapes can you make when slicing through a rectangular solid? Take a guess. Begin the Explore Activity to find out.

Explore

EXPLORE ACTIVITY 1

Focus on Modeling

Use a dry floral foam brick to demonstrate various cross sections of a rectangular solid. Floral foam cuts cleanly and evenly allowing you to demonstrate the various cross sections shown in Parts A–D of this activity.

Explain

EXPLORE ACTIVITY 2

Questioning Strategies Mathematical Practices

• What causes a cross section of a pyramid to have a different shape? The angle of the slice changes the size and shape of a cross section. A horizontal slice makes a rectangle, while a vertical slice forms either a triangle or a trapezoid.

• Does any possible cross section of a right rectangular pyramid include a curved line? Explain. No. All edges and sides of the pyramid are straight, so there is no way for a flat plane to create a cross section that includes a curved line.

Engage with the Whiteboard

In Part C, have student volunteers sketch a few additional pyramids and cross sections. Point out that the plane does not have to be perfectly horizontal or vertical.

Avoid Common Errors

Students may initially believe that a square cross section is possible. Explain that the only cross sections that include right angles are horizontal, and every horizontal cross section is a rectangle that is similar to the base of the pyramid.

LESSON
3.3 Cross Sections

FL CC 7.G.1.3
Describe the two-dimensional figures that result from slicing three-dimensional figures ...

? **ESSENTIAL QUESTION**

How can you identify cross sections of three-dimensional figures?

EXPLORE ACTIVITY 1 FL CC 7.G.1.3

Cross Sections of a Right Rectangular Prism

An **intersection** is a point or set of points common to two or more geometric figures. A **cross section** is the intersection of a three-dimensional figure and a plane. Imagine a plane slicing through the pyramid shown, or through a cone or a prism.

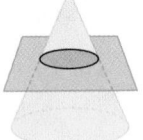

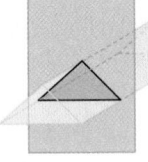

This figure shows the intersection of the cone and a plane. The cross section is a circle.

This figure shows the intersection of a triangular prism and a plane. The cross section is a triangle.

A three-dimensional figure can have several different cross sections depending on the position and the direction of the slice. For example, if the intersection of the plane and cone were vertical, the cross section would form a triangle.

Describe each cross section of the right rectangular prism with the name of its shape.

 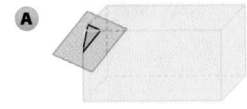

A

B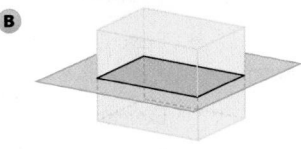

triangle

rectangle

Lesson 3.3 **81**

EXPLORE ACTIVITY 1 *(cont'd)*

C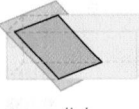

D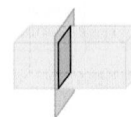

parallelogram

rectangle

Reflect

1. **Conjecture** Is it possible to have a circular cross section in a right rectangular prism?

No, there are no curves in a right rectangular prism.

EXPLORE ACTIVITY 2 FL CC 7.G.1.3

Describing Cross Sections

A right rectangular pyramid with a non-square base is shown.

A The shape of the base is a _____ rectangle

The shape of each side is a _____ triangle

B Is it possible for a cross section of the pyramid to have each shape?

square	rectangle	triangle	circle	trapezoid
no	yes	yes	no	yes

C Sketch the cross sections of the right rectangular pyramid below.

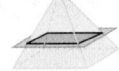

Math Talk: Both cross sections are rectangles. They have the same shape but different sizes. The rectangle farther from the base of the pyramid is the smaller rectangle.

Reflect

2. **What If?** Suppose the figure in **B** had a square base. Would your answers in **B** be the same? Explain.

All the answers but the first would be the same.

The cross section could be a square.

Math Talk
Mathematical Practices

Describe and compare the cross sections created when two horizontal planes intersect a right rectangular pyramid.

82 Unit 2

DIFFERENTIATE INSTRUCTION

Curriculum Integration

Set a large cone on the floor. Have students stand over the cone "mountain", look down on it and then draw a contour map on a piece of paper to represent the height and shape of the "mountain." Students should draw several concentric circles to represent horizontal cross sections of the cone. Explain that topographical maps (also called relief maps) use this same idea to show hills and valleys on a flat map. If possible show students an image of a topographical map.

Kinesthetic Experience

Provide each group of students with about 25 index cards. Have students cut the index cards into squares that are a variety of sizes. Then, have the students stack the squares from largest to smallest. Have students identify the three-dimensional shape represented by the cards. If they have trouble, ask them to imagine the stack made out of hundreds of cards, with each square only barely smaller than the previous square. The cards represent a square pyramid.

Additional Resources

Differentiated Instruction includes:

- Reading Strategies
- Success for English Learners **ELL**
- Reteach
- Challenge **PRE-AP**

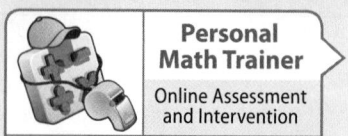

Personal Math Trainer

Online Assessment and Intervention

Online homework assignment available

⏻ my.hrw.com

3.3 LESSON QUIZ

 **FL CC** 7.G.1.3

Describe each cross section.

1.

2.

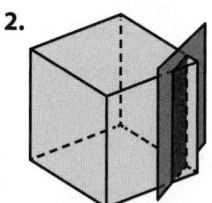

3.

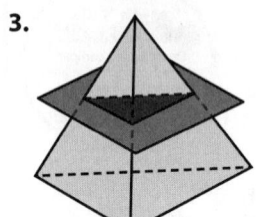

4.

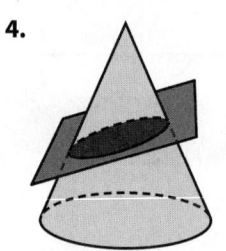

5. Is it possible for a cross section of a cylinder to have a triangular shape?

Lesson Quiz example available online

⏻ my.hrw.com

Answers

1. oval

2. rectangle

3. triangle

4. oval

5. No

Elaborate

Talk About It
Summarize the Lesson

 **Ask:** What happens when a plane intersects a solid? The plane slices the solid so that a cross section of the solid can be seen. In the case of a cylinder intersected by a vertical plane, the cross section has a rectangular shape.

GUIDED PRACTICE

Engage with the Whiteboard

 In Exercises 1–4, have volunteers outline the cross sections they see.

Avoid Common Errors

Exercise 3 Remind students that a plane slicing a solid figure parallel to the figure's base will create a cross section the same shape as the base of the figure.

Evaluate

GUIDED AND INDEPENDENT PRACTICE

 **FL CC** 7.G.1.3

Concepts and Skills	Practice
Explore Activity 1 Cross Sections of a Right Rectangular Prism	Exercise 1
Explore Activity 2 Describing Cross Sections	Exercises 2–4, 6, 7

Exercise	Depth of Knowledge (D.O.K.)	FL CC Mathematical Practices
6	**2** Skills/Concepts	**MP.4.1** Modeling
7	**2** Skills/Concepts	**MP.7.1** Using Structure
8	**2** Skills/Concepts	**MP.4.1** Modeling
9	**3** Strategic Thinking **H.O.T.**	**MP.4.1** Modeling
10	**3** Strategic Thinking **H.O.T.**	**MP.4.1** Modeling

Additional Resources

Differentiated Instruction includes:

• Leveled Practice worksheets

 **CLUSTER CONNECTION** **Exercise 10** combines concepts from the Florida Common Core cluster "Draw, construct, and describe geometrical figures and describe the relationships between them."

Guided Practice

Describe each cross section.

1.

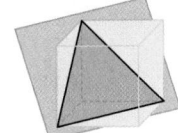

(Explore Activity 1)

triangle or equilateral triangle

2.

(Explore Activity 2)

rectangle

3.

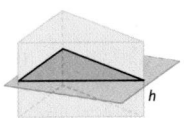

(Explore Activity 2)

triangle

4.

(Explore Activity 2)

rainbow-shaped curve

? ESSENTIAL QUESTION CHECK-IN

5. What is the first step in describing what figure results when a given plane intersects a given three-dimensional figure?

Sample answer: Draw the figure and the plane.

3.3 Independent Practice

FL CC 7.G.1.3

Personal Math Trainer
Online Assessment and Intervention
my.hrw.com

6. Describe different ways in which a plane might intersect the cylinder, and the cross section that results.

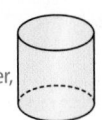

Sample answers: Horizontally, a circle; slanted between horizontal and vertical, an oval; vertically through the cylinder, a rectangle; vertically along an edge of the cylinder, a line.

7. Make a Conjecture What cross sections might you see when a plane intersects a cone that you would **not** see when a plane intersects a pyramid or a prism? ____Circles or ovals____

H.O.T. FOCUS ON HIGHER ORDER THINKING

8. Critical Thinking The two figures on the left below show that you can form a cross section of a cube that is a pentagon. Think of a plane cutting the cube at an angle in such a way as to slice through five of the cube's six faces. Draw dotted lines on the third cube to show how to form a cross section that is a hexagon.

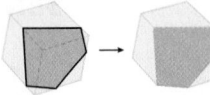

9. Analyze Relationships A sphere has a radius of 12 inches. A horizontal plane passes through the center of the sphere.

a. Describe the cross section formed by the plane and the sphere.

It is a circle with a radius of 12 in.

b. Describe the cross sections formed as the plane intersects the interior of the sphere but moves away from the center.

The cross sections will still be circles, but their radii will decrease as the plane moves away from the sphere's center.

10. Communicate Mathematical Ideas A right rectangular prism is intersected by a horizontal plane and a vertical plane. The cross section formed by the horizontal plane and the prism is a rectangle with dimensions 8 in. and 12 in. The cross section formed by the vertical plane and the prism is a rectangle with dimensions 5 in. and 8 in. Describe the faces of the prism, including their dimensions. Then find its volume.

Two faces are 12 in. by 8 in., two are 8 in. by 5 in., and two are 12 in. by 5 in.; 480 in³

11. Represent Real-World Problems Describe a real-world situation that could be represented by planes slicing a three-dimensional figure to form cross sections.

Sample answer: If you think of a building shaped like a rectangular prism, you can think of horizontal planes slicing the prism to form the different floors.

Work Area

EXTEND THE MATH PRE-AP

Activity available online 🔅 my.hrw.com

Activity A conic section (circle, ellipse, parabola, or hyperbola) can be made by making various cross sections at different angles on a double cone. A hyperbola is formed when the plane slices both cones. The other conic sections are made when the plane slices one or the other of the cones. Identify each cross section below as a circle, ellipse, parabola, or a hyperbola.

A: ellipse; B: hyperbola; C: circle; D: parabola

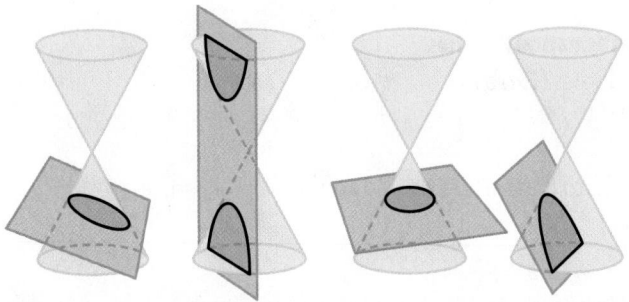

LESSON
3.4 Angle Relationships

 Florida Common Core Standards

The student is expected to:

 FL CC Geometry—7.G.2.5

Use facts about supplementary, complementary, vertical, and adjacent angles in a multi-step problem to write and solve simple equations for an unknown angle in a figure.

Mathematical Practices

 **FL CC** MP.2.1 Reasoning

---

ADDITIONAL EXAMPLE 1
Use the diagram.

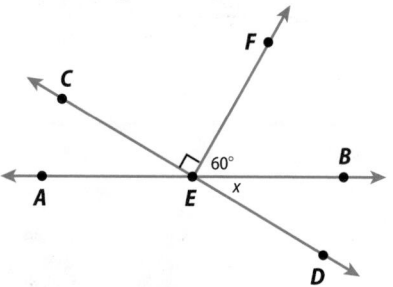

A Name a pair of vertical angles.
∠AEC and ∠BED

B Name a pair of adjacent angles.
Sample answer: ∠BEF and ∠AEF

C Name a pair of complementary angles. ∠BEF and ∠BED

D Name a pair of supplementary angles. Sample answer: ∠AEF and ∠BEF

 Interactive Whiteboard
Interactive example available online

 my.hrw.com

---

Engage

ESSENTIAL QUESTION

How can you use angle relationships to solve problems? Sample answer: You can use the relationships about angle pairs, such as supplementary, complementary, or vertical angles, to write and solve an equation to find the unknown measure of an angle.

Motivate the Lesson
Ask: How would you measure the opposite angles formed by two intersecting lines, like the angles made by two intersecting streets? Take a guess. Begin the Explore Activity to find out.

Explore

EXPLORE ACTIVITY

Focus on Modeling 🔲 Mathematical Practices
Point out that congruent angles are angles that have the same measure. Two intersecting lines form two pairs of opposite congruent angles. Also, the two measures of each pair of adjacent angles formed by the lines add up to 180°.

Explain

EXAMPLE 1

Connect Vocabulary ELL
Remind students that **congruent angles** are angles having the same measure, **vertical angles** are opposite angles formed by two intersecting lines, **adjacent angles** are pairs of angles that share a vertex and one side but do not overlap, **complementary angles** are two angles whose measures have a sum of 90°, and **supplementary angles** are two angles whose measures have a sum of 180°. Point out that they will use these definitions to solve a variety of angle problems.

Avoid Common Errors
Some students may confuse complementary and supplementary angles, especially when both types of angle pairs appear in a diagram. Help students associate the correct angle measure with each term by pointing out that the letter *c* comes before the letter *s* in the alphabet just as 90° comes numerically before 180°.

Questioning Strategies 🔲 Mathematical Practices
• Are angles ∠BFC and ∠DFE vertical angles? Explain. No. Vertical angles are opposite angles formed by two intersecting lines, and these angles are not formed by a pair of intersecting lines.

• What angle relationship could you use to find m∠CFE? Using supplementary angles, m∠BFC + m∠CFE = 180°.

3.4 Angle Relationships

FL CC 7.G.2.5

Use facts about supplementary, complementary, vertical, and adjacent angles in a multi-step problem to write and solve simple equations for an unknown angle in a figure.

ESSENTIAL QUESTION

How can you use angle relationships to solve problems?

EXPLORE ACTIVITY FL CC Prep. for 7.G.2.5

Measuring Angles

It is useful to work with pairs of angles and to understand how pairs of angles relate to each other. **Congruent angles** are angles that have the same measure.

STEP 1 Using a ruler, draw a pair of intersecting lines. Label each angle from 1 to 4.

Step 2: Sample answers given.

STEP 2 Use a protractor to help you complete the chart.

Sample answer:

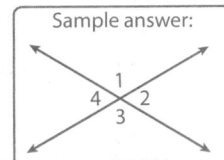

Angle	Measure of Angle
m∠1	120°
m∠2	60°
m∠3	120°
m∠4	60°
m∠1 + m∠2	180°
m∠2 + m∠3	180°
m∠3 + m∠4	180°
m∠4 + m∠1	180°

Reflect

1. **Make a Conjecture** Share your results with other students. Make a conjecture about pairs of angles that are opposite each other.

Sample answer: Pairs of opposite angles are congruent.

2. **Make a Conjecture** When two lines intersect to form two angles, what conjecture can you make about the pairs of angles that are next to each other?

Sample answer: Their measures have a sum of 180°.

Angle Pairs and One-Step Equations

Vertical angles are the opposite angles formed by two intersecting lines. Vertical angles are congruent because the angles have the same measure.

Adjacent angles are pairs of angles that share a vertex and one side but do not overlap.

Complementary angles are two angles whose measures have a sum of 90°.

Supplementary angles are two angles whose measures have a sum of 180°. You discovered in the Explore Activity that adjacent angles formed by two intersecting lines are supplementary.

Math On the Spot
my.hrw.com

EXAMPLE 1 FL CC 7.G.2.5

Use the diagram.

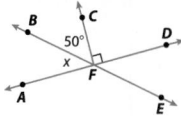

Math Talk
Mathematical Practices

Are ∠BFD and ∠AFE vertical angles? Why or why not?

Yes; they are opposite angles formed by intersecting lines.

A **Name a pair of vertical angles.**

Vertical angles are opposite angles formed by intersecting lines.

∠AFB and ∠DFE are vertical angles.

B **Name a pair of adjacent angles.**

Adjacent angles share a vertex and a side but do not overlap.

∠AFB and ∠BFD are adjacent angles.

C **Name a pair of supplementary angles.**

Adjacent angles formed by intersecting lines are supplementary.

∠AFB and ∠BFD are supplementary angles.

D **Name two pairs of supplementary angles that include ∠DFE.**

Any angle that forms a line with ∠DFE is a supplementary angle to ∠DFE.

∠DFE and ∠EFA are supplementary angles, as are ∠DFE and ∠DFB.

PROFESSIONAL DEVELOPMENT

Integrate Mathematical Practices MP.2.1

This lesson provides an opportunity to address this Mathematical Practice standard. It calls for students to communicate mathematical ideas, …, using multiple representations, including symbols, diagrams, … . Students use symbols and diagrams to represent angle relationships. They solve one-step and two-step equations relating to angle pairs and their relationships. Students also find the measures of angles in real-world triangles using the property that the sum of the measures of the angles of a triangle is 180°. In these ways, students have communicated the mathematical relationships between angle pairs and the angles of a triangle.

Math Background

Many of the equations in this lesson make use of the Angle Addition Postulate, which states that if a point S is in the interior of ∠PQR, then m∠PQS + m∠SQR = m∠PQR.

Other angle relationships follow from the Angle Addition Postulate. For example, a *linear pair* of angles is a pair of adjacent angles whose noncommon sides form a straight line and are therefore supplementary.

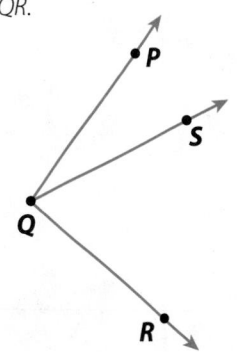

YOUR TURN

Talk About It
Check for Understanding

Ask: Must supplementary angles be adjacent? Justify your answer. No; ∠AGB and ∠EGD are congruent because they are vertical angles. So both angles are right angles. They are supplementary angles because their measures add to 180°, but they are not adjacent angles.

EXAMPLE 2

Questioning Strategies 🖊 Mathematical Practices

• What fact about the angle pair do you use to find the angle measure in part A? The two angles are supplementary.

• What fact about the angle pair do you use to find the angle measure in part B? The two angles are complementary.

Focus on Reasoning 🏴 Mathematical Practices

In part B, ask students to make a conjecture about the measure of ∠ZXY before beginning the calculations to find the measure. Then ask them to complete the steps to determine the validity of their conjecture.

Engage with the Whiteboard

Cover the calculations in Step 2 of part A, and invite a volunteer to do the calculations. Invite a second student to find the measure of ∠EHF without finding the value of x first. Discuss the differences and similarities in the two methods.

YOUR TURN

Avoid Common Errors

Some students might believe that the value of x is the measure of ∠JML. Remind students that they have to multiply x by 3 to get m∠JML. Ask them to verify their result by adding the measure of ∠JML to 54 to see if the sum is 180°.

Questioning Strategies 🖊 Mathematical Practices

• What knowledge do you use to write the equation needed to find the value of x? The two angles are supplementary, so the equation shows the sum of their measures is equal to 180°: m∠JML + m∠LMN = 180°.

Engage with the Whiteboard

Invite a volunteer to complete the steps for finding the value of x and m∠JML. Invite a second volunteer to show how to find the measure of ∠JML without finding the value of x first. Discuss the differences and similarities in the two methods.

D Find the measure of ∠AFB.

Use the fact that ∠AFB and ∠BFD in the diagram are supplementary angles to find m∠AFB.

m∠AFB + m∠BFD = 180°	They are supplementary angles.
x + 140° = 180°	m∠BFD = 50° + 90° = 140°
$\underline{-140° \quad -140°}$	Subtract 140 from both sides.
x = 40°	

The measure of ∠AFB is 40°.

Reflect

3. Analyze Relationships What is the relationship between ∠AFB and ∠BFC? Explain.

They are complementary angles; the sum of their

measures is 90°.

4. Draw Conclusions Are ∠AFC and ∠BFC adjacent angles? Why or why not?

No; ∠AFC and ∠BFC share a vertex and one side, but

they overlap.

YOUR TURN

Use the diagram.

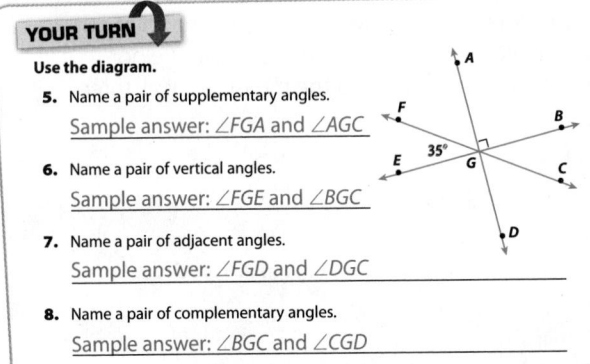

5. Name a pair of supplementary angles.

Sample answer: ∠FGA and ∠AGC

6. Name a pair of vertical angles.

Sample answer: ∠FGE and ∠BGC

7. Name a pair of adjacent angles.

Sample answer: ∠FGD and ∠DGC

8. Name a pair of complementary angles.

Sample answer: ∠BGC and ∠CGD

9. Find the measure of ∠CGD. _____ 55° _____

Personal Math Trainer
Online Assessment and Intervention
my.hrw.com

Math On the Spot
my.hrw.com

My Notes

Angle Pairs and Two-Step Equations

Sometimes solving an equation is only the first step in using an angle relationship to solve a problem.

EXAMPLE 2 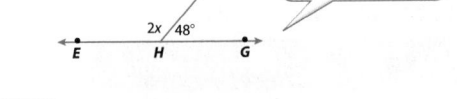 FL CC 7.G.2.5

A Find the measure of ∠EHF.

∠EHF and ∠FHG form a straight line.

STEP 1 Identify the relationship between ∠EHF and ∠FHG.

Since angles ∠EHF and ∠FHG form a straight line, the sum of the measures of the angles is 180°.

∠EHF and ∠FHG are supplementary angles.

STEP 2 Write and solve an equation to find x.

m∠EHF + m∠FHG = 180°	The sum of the measures of supplementary angles is 180°.
2x + 48° = 180°	
$\underline{-48° \quad -48°}$	Subtract 48 from both sides.
2x = 132°	Divide both sides by 2.
x = 66°	

STEP 3 Find the measure of ∠EHF.

m∠EHF = 2x	
= 2(66°)	Substitute 66° for x.
= 132°	Multiply.

The measure of ∠EHF is 132°.

Check Confirm that ∠EHF and ∠FHG are supplementary.

$$m\angle EHF + m\angle FHG \overset{?}{=} 180°$$
$$132° + 48° \overset{?}{=} 180°$$
$$180° = 180°$$

DIFFERENTIATE INSTRUCTION

Visual Cues

Ask students to make a list of all the complementary, supplementary, and vertical angle pairs they see in the diagram below.

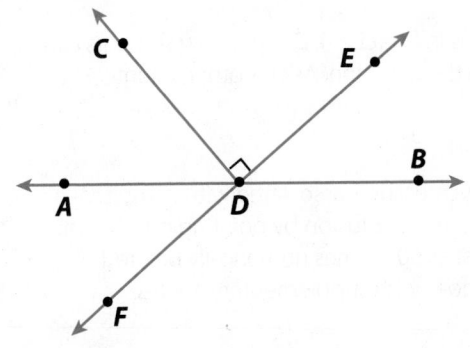

Graphic Organizers

Have groups of students write the vocabulary words for this lesson on index cards. Instruct each group to place the cards face down on a desk. One student in the group then selects a card, verbally defines the term, and draws an example of the term on the card. That student then chooses another person to repeat the activity. Challenge students to include angle pairs that are both supplementary and vertical, adjacent and complementary, or complementary and nonadjacent, in addition to those that exhibit just one type of angle pair.

Additional Resources

Differentiated Instruction includes

- Reading Strategies
- Success for English Learners **ELL**
- Reteach
- Challenge **PRE-AP**

EXAMPLE 3

Questioning Strategies 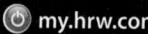 Mathematical Practices

• What fact about isosceles triangles do you need to find the measure of a base angle? The base angles of an isosceles triangle have the same measure.

• If the measure of the angle at the top of the triangle doubles, would the measure of each base angle be multiplied by $\frac{1}{2}$? Justify your answer. No. For example, if the measure of the angle at the top of the A-frame house triangle doubled to be 140°, then the base angles would each be 20°, which is not one-half of 55°.

Talk About It
Check for Understanding

💬 **Ask:** How do you find the measure of the unknown angles of an isosceles triangle if you know the measure of one base angle? The other base angle has the same measure. Subtract twice the measure of a base angle from 180° to find the measure of the third angle.

YOUR TURN

Avoid Common Errors

A common error is to assume the unknown angles in $\angle ABC$ are complementary. Point out that these two measures must have a sum of 180° − 80°, or 100°, so the angles are not complementary. Instruct students to check their work by adding the measures of all three angles to verify that the sum is 180°.

Elaborate

Talk About It
Summarize the Lesson

💬 Ask students to draw an example of each type of angle pair in the graphic organizer below. Check students' drawings.

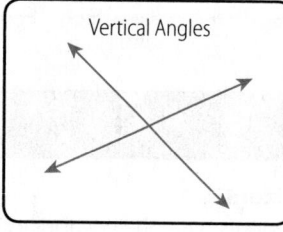
Vertical Angles

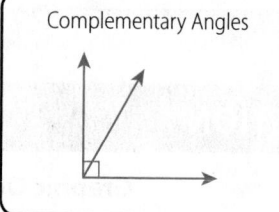
Complementary Angles

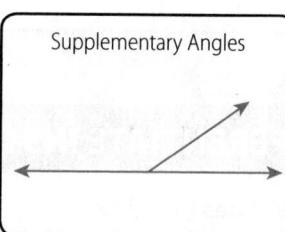
Supplementary Angles

GUIDED PRACTICE

Engage with the Whiteboard

 Ask student volunteers to complete the steps in Exercise 4. Discuss how students can use vertical angles to find m∠DGE for use in the equation. Ask for other volunteers to complete the steps in Exercise 5.

Avoid Common Errors

Exercise 1 Some students may confuse the degree measures associated with complementary and supplementary angles. Help students avoid this confusion by pointing out that the letter *c* comes before the letter *s* in the alphabet just as 90° comes numerically before 180°, so 90° goes with complementary angles and 180° goes with supplementary angles.

B Find the measure of ∠ZXY.

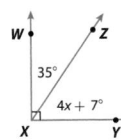

STEP 1 Identify the relationship between ∠WXZ and ∠ZXY.

∠WXZ and ∠ZXY are complementary angles.

STEP 2 Write and solve an equation to find x.

m∠WXZ + m∠ZXY = 90°   The sum of the measures of complementary angles is 90°.

4x + 7° + 35° = 90°   Substitute the values.

4x + 42° = 90°   Combine like terms.

$\underline{-42° \quad -42°}$ Subtract 42 from both sides.

4x = 48°   Divide both sides by 4.

x = 12°

STEP 3 Find the measure of ∠ZXY.

m∠ZXY = 4x + 7°

= 4(12°) + 7°   Substitute 12° for x.

= 55°   Use the Order of Operations.

The measure of ∠ZXY is 55°.

Add m∠WXZ and m∠ZXY to make sure the sum is 90°: 35° + 55° = 90°.

Math Talk
Mathematical Practices
How can you check that your answer is reasonable?

YOUR TURN

10. Write and solve an equation to find the measure of ∠JML.

54° + 3x = 180°

3x = 126°

x = 42°

m∠JML = 3x

= 126°

11. **Critique Reasoning** Cory says that to find m∠JML above, you can stop when you get to the solution step 3x = 126°. Explain why this works.

Sample answer: You can stop at the solution step where you find the value of 3x because the measure of ∠JML is equal to 3x.

Personal Math Trainer
Online Assessment and Intervention
my.hrw.com

For 1–2, use the figure. (Example 1)

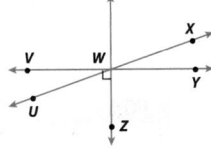

1. **Vocabulary** The sum of the measures of ∠UWV and ∠UWZ is 90°, so ∠UWV and ∠UWZ are ___complementary___ angles.

2. **Vocabulary** ∠UWV and ∠VWX share a vertex and one side. They do not overlap, so ∠UWV and ∠VWX are ___adjacent___ angles.

For 3–4, use the figure.

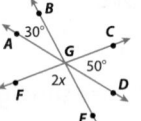

3. ∠AGB and ∠DGE are ___vertical___ angles, so m∠DGE = ___30°___. (Example 1)

4. Find the measure of ∠EGF. (Example 2)

m∠CGD + m∠DGE + m∠EGF = 180°

$\underline{50°} + \underline{30°} + \underline{2x} = 180°$

$\underline{80°} + 2x = 180°$

$2x = \underline{100°}$

m∠EGF = 2x = $\underline{100°}$

5. Find the value of x and the measure of ∠MNQ (Example 2)

m∠MNQ + m∠QNP = 90°

$\underline{3x - 13°} + \underline{58°} = 90°$, so 3x + $\underline{45°}$ = 90°.

Then 3x = $\underline{45°}$, and x = $\underline{15°}$.

m∠MNQ = 3x - 13° = 3($\underline{15°}$) - 13°

= $\underline{45°}$ - 13°

= $\underline{32°}$

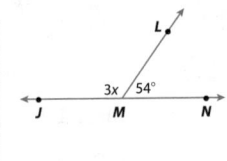

? ESSENTIAL QUESTION CHECK-IN

6. Suppose that you know that ∠T and ∠S are supplementary, and that m∠T = 3(m∠S). How can you find m∠T?

Sample answer: Let m∠S = x. Write and solve the equation (x + 3x = 180°) to find the value of x; then multiply the value by 3.

© Houghton Mifflin Harcourt Publishing Company

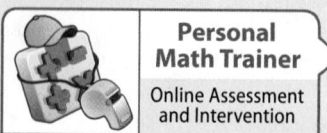
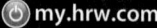
3.4 LESSON QUIZ

 **FL CC** 7.G.2.5

For Exercises 1–3, use the figure.

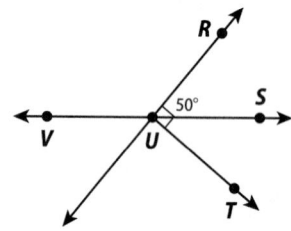

1. Name a pair of adjacent angles. Explain why they are adjacent.

2. Name a pair of complementary angles.

3. Find m∠VUR. Justify your answer.

4. Find the value of *x* and m∠HKL.

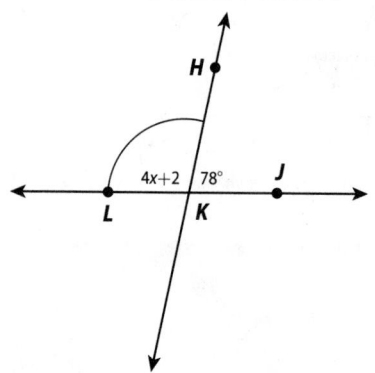

For Exercises 5 and 6, use the figure.

5. m∠VUW

6. m∠TUW

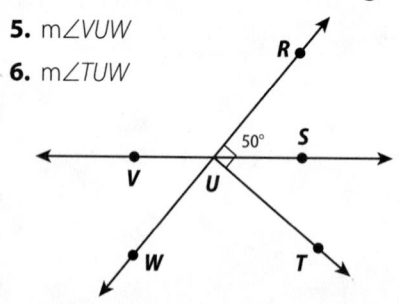

Lesson Quiz available online

 my.hrw.com

Evaluate

GUIDED AND INDEPENDENT PRACTICE

FL CC 7.G.2.5

Concepts & Skills	Practice
Explore Activity Measuring Angles	Exercises 1–3
Example 1 Angle Pairs and One-Step Equations	Exercises 7–13
Example 2 Angle Pairs and Two-Step Equations	Exercises 4–5, 17–18
Example 3 Using Angle Measures in Triangles	Exercises 14–18

Exercise	Depth of Knowledge (D.O.K.)		**FL CC** Mathematical Practices
6	**3** Strategic Thinking	H.O.T.	**MP.8.1** Patterns
7–9	**1** Recall of Information		**MP.8.1** Patterns
10–11	**3** Strategic Thinking	H.O.T.	**MP.3.1** Logic
12–16	**1** Recall of Information		**MP.5.1** Using Tools
17–20	**3** Strategic Thinking	H.O.T.	**MP.8.1** Patterns
21–22	**3** Strategic Thinking	H.O.T.	**MP.3.1** Logic

Additional Resources

Extra Practice includes:

• Leveled Practice Worksheets

Answers

1. Sample answer: ∠RUV and ∠RUS are adjacent angles because they share a vertex and one side and do not overlap.

2. Sample answer: ∠RUS and ∠SUT

3. 130°; ∠VUR and ∠RUS are supplementary, so their sum is 180°. 130° + 50° = 180°.

4. $x = 25$; m∠HKL = 102°

5. m∠VUW = 50°

6. m∠TUW = 90°

Name_____ Class_____ Date_____

3.4 Independent Practice

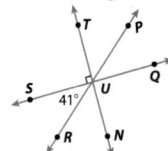

FL.CC 7.G.2.5

Personal Math Trainer

Online Assessment and Intervention

my.hrw.com

For 7–11, use the figure.

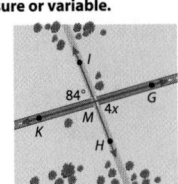

7. Name a pair of adjacent angles. Explain why they are adjacent.

Sample answer: ∠SUR and ∠QUR are adjacent. They share a vertex and a side.

8. Name a pair of acute vertical angles.

Sample answer: ∠SUR and ∠QUP

9. Name a pair of supplementary angles.

Sample answer: ∠TUS and ∠QUN

10. Justify Reasoning Find m∠QUR. Justify your answer.

139°; Sample answer: ∠SUR and ∠SUP are supp., so m∠SUP = 180° − 41° = 139°. ∠SUP and ∠QUR are vert. angles, so they are congruent and m∠QUR = m∠SUP = 139°.

11. Draw Conclusions Which is greater, m∠TUR or m∠RUQ? Explain.

m∠RUQ; Sample answer: ∠SUR and ∠NUR are complementary, so m∠NUR = 90° − 41° = 49°. m∠TUR = 41° + 90°, which is less than m∠RUQ = 49° + 90°.

For 12–13, use the figure. A bike path crosses a road as shown. Solve for each indicated angle measure or variable.

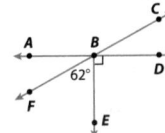

12. x _____ 21°

13. m∠KMH _____ 96°

For 14–16, use the figure. Solve for each indicated angle measure.

14. m∠CBE _____ 118°

15. m∠ABF _____ 28°

16. m∠CBA _____ 152°

17. The measure of ∠A is 4° greater than the measure of ∠B. The two angles are complementary. Find the measure of each angle.

m∠A = 47°, m∠B = 43°

18. The measure of ∠D is 5 times the measure of ∠E. The two angles are supplementary. Find the measure of each angle.

m∠D = 150°, m∠E = 30°

Lesson 3.4 **91**

---

19. Astronomy Astronomers sometimes use angle measures divided into degrees, minutes, and seconds. One degree is equal to 60 minutes, and one minute is equal to 60 seconds. Suppose that ∠J and ∠K are complementary, and that the measure of ∠J is 48 degrees, 26 minutes, 8 seconds. What is the measure of ∠K?

41 degrees, 33 minutes, 52 seconds

H.O.T. FOCUS ON HIGHER ORDER THINKING

20. Represent Real-World Problems The railroad tracks meet the road as shown. The town will allow a parking lot at angle K if the measure of angle K is greater than 38°. Can a parking lot be built at angle K? Why or why not?

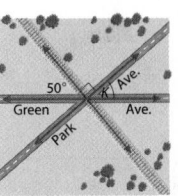

Yes, a parking lot can be built because the measure of angle K is 180° − (50° + 90°), or 40°, which is greater than 38°.

21. Justify Reasoning Kendra says that she can draw ∠A and ∠B so that m∠A is 119° and ∠A and ∠B are complementary angles. Do you agree or disagree? Explain your reasoning.

Disagree; The sum of the measures of a pair of complementary angles is 90°. So, the measure of each angle must be less than 90°. But m∠A = 119°, and 119° > 90°.

Work Area

22. Draw Conclusions If two angles are complementary, each angle is called a *complement* of the other. If two angles are supplementary, each angle is called a *supplement* of the other.

a. Suppose m∠A = 77°. What is the measure of a complement of a complement of ∠A? Explain.

77°; a complement of ∠A has a measure of 13°, and a complement of that angle has a measure of 77°.

b. What conclusion can you draw about a complement of a complement of an angle? Explain.

A complement of a complement of an angle has the same measure as the angle itself. Let x° be the measure of the angle. The measure of a complement of the angle is (90 − x)°. A complement of that angle has a measure of (90 − (90 − x))° = (90 − 90 + x)° = x°.

92 Unit 2

EXTEND THE MATH PRE-AP

Activity available online my.hrw.com

Activity Word Search: Find each of the words from this lesson.

adjacent

angle

base

complementary

congruent

isosceles

sum

supplementary

triangle

vertical

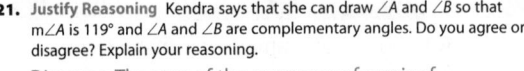

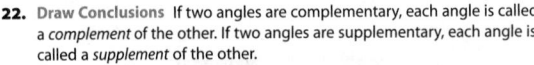

Angle Relationships **92**

Ready to Go On?

. . . .

Assess Mastery

Use the assessment on this page to determine if students have mastered the concepts and standards covered in this module.

 **RtI** Response to Intervention

Personal Math Trainer

Online Assessment and Intervention

 my.hrw.com

Intervention	Enrichment
Access Ready to Go On? assessment online, and receive instant scoring, feedback, and customized intervention or enrichment.	

Online and Print Resources

Differentiated Instruction
• Reteach worksheets
• Reading Strategies **ELL**
• Success for English Learners **ELL**

Differentiated Instruction
• Challenge worksheets **PRE-AP**
• Extend the Math **PRE-AP** Lesson Activities in TE

Additional Resources

Assessment Resources includes:
• Leveled Module Quizzes

MODULE QUIZ

Ready to Go On?

Personal Math Trainer
Online Assessment and Intervention
my.hrw.com

3.1 Similar Shapes and Scale Drawings

1. A house blueprint has a scale of 1 in. : 4 ft. The length and width of each room in the actual house are shown in the table. Complete the table by finding the length and width of each room on the blueprint.

	Living room	Kitchen	Office	Bedroom	Bedroom	Bathroom
Actual $\ell \times w$ (ft)	16×20	12×12	8×12	20×12	12×12	6×8
Blueprint $\ell \times w$ (in.)	4×5	3×3	2×3	5×3	3×3	1.5×2

3.2 Geometric Drawings

2. Can a triangle be formed with the side lengths of 8 cm, 4 cm, and 12 cm? __no__

3. A triangle has side lengths of 11 cm and 9 cm. Which could be the value of the third side, 20 cm or 15 cm? _____ 15 cm

3.3 Cross Sections Sample answers are given.

4. Name one possible cross section of a sphere. ___circle, point___

5. Name at least two shapes that are cross sections of a cylinder.
circle, rectangle, oval, line

3.4 Angle Relationships

6. $\angle BGC$ and $\angle FGE$ are __vertical__ angles, so $m\angle FGE = $ ___50°___

7. Suppose you know that $\angle S$ and $\angle Y$ are complementary, and that $m\angle S = 2(m\angle Y) - 30°$. Find $m\angle Y$. __$m\angle Y = 40$__

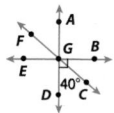

 ESSENTIAL QUESTION

8. How can you model geometry figures to solve real-world problems?
Sample answer: You can use scale drawings to plan rooms or gardens.

Module 3   93

Florida Common Core Standards

Lesson	Exercises	Common Core Standards
3.1	1–2	**7.G.1.1**
3.2	3–4	**7.G.1.2**
3.3	5–6	**7.G.1.3**
3.4	7–8	**7.G.2.5**

PARCC Assessment Readiness

Assessment Readiness Tip Students can draw a diagram, graph, or picture to help organize information from a test item.

Item 2 A sketch of the backdrop with side lengths labeled and a similar sketch of the scale drawing can help students to stay organized while finding the measurements of the scale drawing.

Avoid Common Errors

Item 6 Students may have noticed the pattern that complementary angles are always both acute and therefore guess that these two angles are complementary. Remind them that some angle terms refer to the spatial relationship of the angles and can apply to angles of any size.

Item 7 If students do not read carefully, they may select the expression that represents the tip rather than the expression that represents the full price. Encourage them to pay close attention to the wording of exercises.

Additional Resources

Personal Math Trainer

Online Assessment and Intervention

my.hrw.com

MODULE 3 MIXED REVIEW

PARCC Assessment Readiness

Personal Math Trainer

Online Assessment and Intervention

my.hrw.com

Selected Response

1. Which expression factors to $-2(x + 8)$?

- (A) $-2x + 16$
- (C) $-2x + 8$
- (B) $-2x - 16$
- (D) $-2x - 8$

2. Students are painting the backdrop for the school play. The backdrop is 15 feet wide and 10 feet high. Every 16 inches on the scale drawing represents 5 feet on the backdrop. What is the area of the scale drawing?

- (A) 150 in²
- (C) 3,096 in²
- (B) 6 in²
- (D) 1,536 in²

3. What is the solution of the inequality $3x + 5 > 2$?

- (A) $x > 3$
- (C) $x > 1$
- (B) $x > -3$
- (D) $x > -1$

4. A cross section is the intersection of a three-dimensional figure and a _____.

- (A) point
- (C) line
- (B) plane
- (D) set

For 5–6, use the diagram.

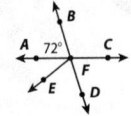

5. What is the measure of $\angle BFC$?

- (A) 18°
- (C) 72°
- (B) 108°
- (D) 144°

6. Which describes the relationship between $\angle BFA$ and $\angle CFD$?

- (A) adjacent angles
- (B) complementary angles
- (C) supplementary angles
- (D) vertical angles

7. Simon adds a 15% tip to a meal. If the meal originally cost n dollars, which expression indicates how much it costs with the tip?

- (A) $n - 0.15n$
- (C) $n + 0.15$
- (B) $n + 0.15n$
- (D) $0.15n$

Mini-Task

8. Ira built a model of the Great Pyramid in Egypt for a school project. The Great Pyramid has a square base with sides of length 756 feet. The height of the Great Pyramid is 481 feet. Ira made his model pyramid using a scale of 1 inch : 20 feet.

a. What is the length of each side of the base of Ira's pyramid?

37.8 in.

b. What is the area of the base of Ira's pyramid?

1,428.84 in²

c. What is the height of Ira's pyramid?

24.05 in.

d. Ira built his model using cross sections that were cut parallel to the base. What shape was each cross section?

square

Florida Common Core Standards

Items	Grade 7 Standards	Mathematical Practices
1*	7.EE.1.1	MP.7.1
2	7.G.1.1	MP.4.1
3*	7.EE.2.4b	MP.2.1
4	7.G.1.3	MP.6.1
5	7.G.2.5	
6	7.G.2.5	MP.6.1
7*	7.EE.1.1	MP.4.1
8	7.G.1.1, 7.G.1.3	MP.4.1

* Item integrates mixed review concepts from previous modules or a previous course.

Circumference, Area, and Volume

ESSENTIAL QUESTION

How can you apply geometry concepts to solve real-world problems?

You can use geometry concepts to find areas, perimeters, volumes, and surface areas of real-world objects.

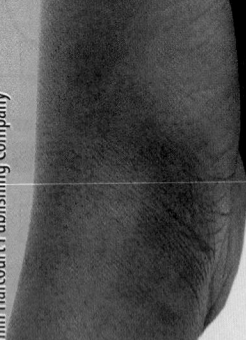

Real-World Video

A 16-inch pizza has a diameter of 16 inches. You can use the diameter to find circumference and area of the pizza. You can also determine how much pizza in one slice of different sizes of pizzas.

my.hrw.com

GO DIGITAL
my.hrw.com

my.hrw.com
Go digital with your write-in student edition, accessible on any device.

Math On the Spot
Scan with your smart phone to jump directly to the online edition, video tutor, and more.

Animated Math
Interactively explore key concepts to see how math works.

Personal Math Trainer
Get immediate feedback and help as you work through practice sets.

© Houghton Mifflin Harcourt Publishing Company

Are You Ready?

Use the assessment on this page to determine if students need intensive or strategic intervention for the module's prerequisite skills.

 **Response to Intervention**

Personal Math Trainer
Online Assessment and Intervention
my.hrw.com

Intervention	Enrichment
Access Are You Ready? assessment online, and receive instant scoring, feedback, and customized intervention or enrichment.	

Online and Print Resources

Skills Intervention worksheets	*Differentiated Instruction*
• Skill 45 Multiply with Fractions and Decimals **PRE-AP**	• Challenge worksheets **PRE-AP**
• Skill 85 Area of Squares, Rectangles, and Triangles	Extend the Math **PRE-AP** Lesson Activities in TE

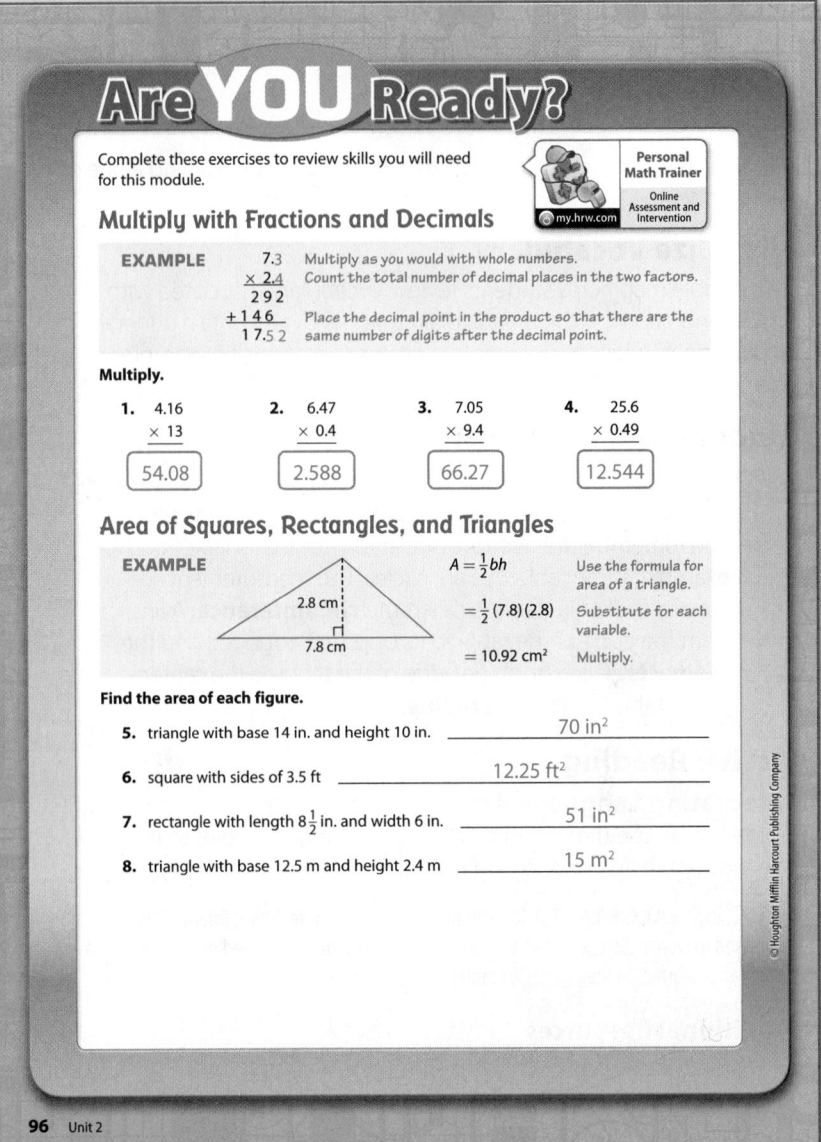

Are YOU Ready?

Complete these exercises to review skills you will need for this module.

Personal Math Trainer
Online Assessment and Intervention
my.hrw.com

Multiply with Fractions and Decimals

EXAMPLE

$$
\begin{array}{r}
7.3 \\
\times\ 2.4 \\
\hline
292 \\
+146 \\
\hline
17.52
\end{array}
$$

Multiply as you would with whole numbers.
Count the total number of decimal places in the two factors.
Place the decimal point in the product so that there are the same number of digits after the decimal point.

Multiply.

1. $\begin{array}{r} 4.16 \\ \times\ 13 \\ \hline \end{array}$ 54.08

2. $\begin{array}{r} 6.47 \\ \times\ 0.4 \\ \hline \end{array}$ 2.588

3. $\begin{array}{r} 7.05 \\ \times\ 9.4 \\ \hline \end{array}$ 66.27

4. $\begin{array}{r} 25.6 \\ \times\ 0.49 \\ \hline \end{array}$ 12.544

Area of Squares, Rectangles, and Triangles

EXAMPLE

2.8 cm
7.8 cm

$A = \frac{1}{2}bh$ Use the formula for area of a triangle.

$= \frac{1}{2}(7.8)(2.8)$ Substitute for each variable.

$= 10.92 \text{ cm}^2$ Multiply.

Find the area of each figure.

5. triangle with base 14 in. and height 10 in. _____ 70 in²

6. square with sides of 3.5 ft _____ 12.25 ft²

7. rectangle with length $8\frac{1}{2}$ in. and width 6 in. _____ 51 in²

8. triangle with base 12.5 m and height 2.4 m _____ 15 m²

PROFESSIONAL DEVELOPMENT VIDEO

Author Juli Dixon models successful teaching practices as she explores area of composite figures in an actual seventh-grade classroom.

 **Professional Development**

my.hrw.com

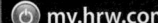

GO DIGITAL
my.hrw.com

 **Online Teacher Edition**
Access a full suite of teaching resources online—plan, present, and manage classes and assignments.

 ePlanner
Easily plan your classes and access all your resources online.

 Interactive Answers and Solutions
Customize answer keys to print or display in the classroom. Choose to include answers only or full solutions to all lesson exercises.

 Interactive Whiteboards
Engage students with interactive whiteboard-ready lessons and activities.

 Personal Math Trainer: Online Assessment and Intervention
Assign automatically graded homework, quizzes, tests, and intervention activities. Prepare your students with updated practice tests aligned with Common Core.

Reading Start-Up

Have students complete the activities on this page by working alone or with others.

Visualize Vocabulary

The bubble map helps students review vocabulary associated with measuring geometric figures. Explain that the ovals contain general explanations, while the rectangle contains more specific examples of the concepts.

Understand Vocabulary

Use the following explanation to help students learn the preview words.

> Sometimes thinking of a shape in the real world can help you remember the words associated with that shape. For example, some tabletops are circles. The measurement around the entire table is called the **circumference.** A line from the edge of the table to its opposite edge is called the **diameter.** A line from the edge of the table to the center of the table is called the **radius.**

Active Reading

Integrating Language Arts

Students can use these reading and note-taking strategies to help them organize and understand new concepts and vocabulary.

LACC.68.RST.3.7 Integrate quantitative or technical information expressed in words in a text with a version of that information expressed visually (e.g., in a flowchart, diagram, model, graph, or table).

Additional Resources

Differentiated Instruction

- Reading Strategies **ELL**

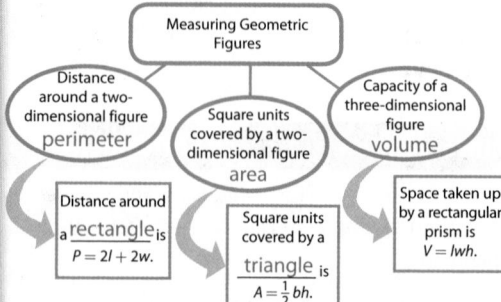

Before	In this module	After
Students understand: • how to model area formulas for parallelograms, rhombuses, and trapezoids • how to write equations related to the area of rectangles, parallelograms, trapezoids, and triangles	Students write and solve equations using formulas and geometry concepts: • find the circumference of a circle • find the area of a circle • find the area of composite figures	Students will connect: • the areas of individual two-dimensional figures with the area of composite figures

Unpacking the Standards

Use the examples on the page to help students know exactly what they are expected to learn in this module.

Florida Common Core Standards

Content Areas

 FL CC Geometry—7.G.2

Solve real-life mathematical problems involving angle measure, area, surface area, and volume.

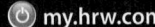

Go online to see a complete unpacking of the Florida Common Core Standards.

⏻ my.hrw.com

MODULE 4
Unpacking the Standards

Understanding the standards and the vocabulary terms in the standards will help you know exactly what you are expected to learn in this module.

FL CC 7.G.2.4

Know the formulas for the area and circumference of a circle and use them to solve problems; give an informal derivation of the relationship between the circumference and area of a circle.

Key Vocabulary

circumference *(circunferencia)*
The distance around a circle.

What It Means to You

You will use formulas to solve problems involving the area and circumference of circles.

UNPACKING EXAMPLE 7.G.2.4

Lily is drawing plans for a circular fountain. The diameter of the fountain is 20 feet. What is the approximate circumference?

$$C = \pi d$$
$$C \approx 3.14 \cdot 20 \quad \text{Substitute.}$$
$$C \approx 62.8$$

The circumference of the fountain is about 62.8 feet.

FL CC 7.G.2.6

Solve real-world and mathematical problems involving area, volume and surface area of two- and three-dimensional objects composed of triangles, quadrilaterals, polygons, cubes, and right prisms.

Key Vocabulary

volume *(volumen)*
The number of cubic units inside a three-dimensional solid.

surface area *(área total)*
The sum of the areas of all the surfaces of a three-dimensional solid.

What It Means to You

You will find area, volume and surface area of real-world objects.

UNPACKING EXAMPLE 7.G.2.6

Find the volume and the surface area of a tissue box before the hole is cut in the top.

The tissue box is a right rectangular prism. The base is $4\frac{3}{8}$ in. by $4\frac{3}{8}$ in. and the height is 5 in.

Use the volume and surface area formulas:

B is the area of the base, h is the height of the box, and P is the perimeter of the base.

$$V = Bh \qquad\qquad S = 2B + Ph$$
$$= \left(4\frac{3}{8} \cdot 4\frac{3}{8}\right)5 \qquad = 2\left(4\frac{3}{8} \cdot 4\frac{3}{8}\right) + \left(4 \cdot 4\frac{3}{8}\right)5$$
$$= 95\frac{45}{64} \text{ in}^3 \qquad = 125\frac{25}{32} \text{ in}^2$$

The volume is $95\frac{45}{64}$ in³ and the surface area is $125\frac{25}{32}$ in².

Visit my.hrw.com to see all Florida Common Core Standards unpacked.
⏻ my.hrw.com

98 Unit 2

Florida Common Core Standards	Lesson 4.1	Lesson 4.2	Lesson 4.3	Lesson 4.4	Lesson 4.5
FL CC 7.G.2.4 Know the formulas for the area and circumference of a circle and use them to solve problems; give an informal derivation of the relationship between the circumference and area of a circle.	✓	✓			
FL CC 7.G.2.6 Solve real-world and mathematical problems involving area, volume and surface area of two- and three-dimensional objects composed of triangles, quadrilaterals, polygons, cubes, and right prisms.			✓	✓	✓

LESSON 4.1 Circumference

Florida Common Core Standards

The student is expected to:

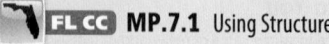 **FL CC** Geometry—7.G.2.4

Know the formulas for the area and circumference of a circle and use them to solve problems; given an informal derivation of the relationship between the circumference and area of a circle.

Mathematical Practices

FL CC MP.7.1 Using Structure

ADDITIONAL EXAMPLE 1
A circular wading pool at a park has a radius of 21 feet. Find the circumference of the pool. Use $\frac{22}{7}$ for π.
about 132 ft

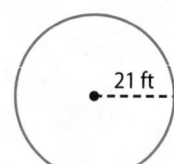

21 ft

 **Interactive Whiteboard**
Interactive example available online

 my.hrw.com

Engage

ESSENTIAL QUESTION
How do you find and use the circumference of a circle? Sample answer: Use $C = \pi d$ or $C = 2\pi r$, where C is the circumference, d is the diameter, and r is the radius. Use 3.14 for π.

Motivate the Lesson
Ask: Which do you think is greater, the circumference of a basketball rim or the total circumference of two basketballs?

Explore

EXPLORE ACTIVITY

Avoid Common Errors
Using small circular objects will make it more difficult to take precise measurements of the diameter and the circumference of the object. Imprecise measurements may lead students to infer that $\frac{C}{d}$ is not a constant, or that $\frac{C}{d}$ is not close to 3. Using larger objects, like a mixing bowl or a bicycle wheel, will make it easier to take precise measurements.

Engage with the Whiteboard
Have several students list their measured values for the circumference and diameter of a single circular object: sizable errors in measurement will be more obvious when compared to other students' measurements.

Explain

EXAMPLE 1

Avoid Common Errors
Encourage students to notice whether they are given the diameter of the circle or its radius.

Questioning Strategies 🖊 Mathematical Practices
• If you double the radius of a circle, what will happen to the circumference? Justify your reasoning. It will also double; $2\pi(2r) = 4\pi r$, and $4\pi r = 2(2\pi r)$.

YOUR TURN

Talk About It
Check for Understanding
Ask: How did you find the circumference of the circle? Multiply 11 cm by 3.14, an approximation for π.

LESSON
4.1 Circumference

 **FL CC** 7.G.2.4
Know the formulas for the area and circumference of a circle and use them to solve problems ...

ESSENTIAL QUESTION
How do you find and use the circumference of a circle?

EXPLORE ACTIVITY **FL CC** 7.G.2.4

Exploring Circumference

A circle is a set of points in a plane that are a fixed distance from the center.

A **radius** is a line segment with one endpoint at the center of the circle and the other endpoint on the circle. The length of a radius is called the radius of the circle.

A **diameter** of a circle is a line segment that passes through the center of the circle and whose endpoints lie on the circle. The length of the diameter is twice the length of the radius. The length of a diameter is called the diameter of the circle.

The **circumference** of a circle is the distance around the circle.

A Use a measuring tape to find the circumference of five circular objects. Then measure the distance across each item to find its diameter. Record the measurements of each object in the table below. Check students' work.

Object	Circumference C	Diameter d	$\frac{C}{d}$

B Divide the circumference of each object by its diameter. Record your answer, rounded to the nearest hundredth, in the table above.

Reflect

1. **Make a Conjecture** Describe what you notice about the ratio $\frac{C}{d}$ in your table.
   Sample answer: $\frac{C}{d}$ is always close to or a little more than 3.

Math On the Spot
@ my.hrw.com

Finding Circumference

The ratio of the circumference to the diameter $\frac{C}{d}$ is the same for all circles. This ratio is called π or *pi*, and you can approximate it as 3.14 or as $\frac{22}{7}$. You can use π to find a formula for circumference.

For any circle, $\frac{C}{d} = \pi$. Solve the equation for C to give an equation for the circumference of a circle in terms of the diameter.

$\frac{C}{d} = \pi$ *The ratio of the circumference to the diameter is π.*

$\frac{C}{d} \times d = \pi \times d$ *Multiply both sides by d.*

$C = \pi d$ *Simplify.*

The diameter of a circle is twice the radius. You can use the equation $C = \pi d$ to find a formula for the circumference C in terms of the radius r.

$C = \pi d = \pi(2r) = 2\pi r$

The two equivalent formulas for circumference are $C = \pi d$ and $C = 2\pi r$.

EXAMPLE 1 **FL CC** 7.G.2.4

An irrigation sprinkler waters a circular region with a radius of 14 feet. Find the circumference of the region watered by the sprinkler. Use $\frac{22}{7}$ for π.

Use the formula.

$C = 2\pi r$ [The radius is 14 feet.]

$C = 2\pi(14)$ *Substitute 14 for r.*

$C \approx 2\left(\frac{22}{7}\right)(14)$ *Substitute $\frac{22}{7}$ for π.*

$C \approx 88$ *Multiply.*

The circumference of the region watered by the sprinkler is about 88 feet.

Reflect

2. **Analyze Relationships** When is it logical to use $\frac{22}{7}$ instead of 3.14 for π?
   when the radius or diameter is a multiple of 7

Personal Math Trainer
Online Assessment and Intervention
@ my.hrw.com

YOUR TURN

3. Find the circumference of the circle to the nearest hundredth.
   about 34.54 cm

11 cm

PROFESSIONAL DEVELOPMENT

Integrate Mathematical Practices MP.7.1

This lesson provides an opportunity to address this mathematical Practice standard. It calls for students to look for and make use of structure. Students initially examine the measurements of several circular objects, reaching the conclusion that the relationship between the circumference and the diameter is a constant ratio, pi. They then use this underlying structure to solve problems involving the radius, diameter, and circumference of a circle.

Math Background

Although π is an irrational number, its value can be shown to be between 3 and 4. Consider the following, a hexagon is inscribed in a circle that is inscribed in a square.

The diagonals of the hexagon divide it into six equilateral triangles. The length of each side of these triangles is equal to the radius of the circle. So the perimeter of the hexagon is 6 times the radius of the circle, or 6r. Since the circumference of the circle is $2\pi r$ and the hexagon is inscribed in the circle, $2\pi r$ must be greater than 6r. If $2\pi r > 6r$, then $\pi > 3$. The width of the square is 2r, so the perimeter of the square is 8r. Since the circle is inscribed in the square, 8r must be greater than $2\pi r$. If $8r > 2\pi r$, then $4 > \pi$. Therefore, $3 < \pi < 4$.

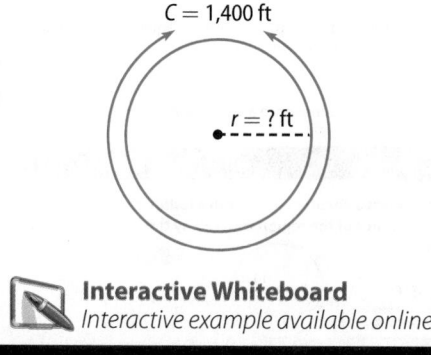
EXAMPLE 2

Questioning Strategies Mathematical Practices

• If the speed of the model boat doubled, would it take one-half the time to reach the center of the pond from the edge? Justify your reasoning. Yes; the radius of the pond is still about 100 feet, and $100 \div 10 = 10$ seconds. This is one-half of 20 seconds.

Focus on Technology Mathematical Practices

Point out that if students key in $628/(2\pi)$ on their calculator, the result will be 99.94930426, which rounds to a radius of about 100 feet. The calculator result is slightly lower because the value of π is slightly greater than 3.14.

Engage with the Whiteboard

After working through Example 3, have a student volunteer use $\frac{22}{7}$ for π and perform the calculations to find the radius of the pond. Discuss the differences that occur when using the two approximations for π. For this solution, which method was easier?

YOUR TURN

Talk About It
Check for Understanding

 Ask: How do you find the radius of the garden? Divide 44 yards by 6.28.

Elaborate

Talk About It
Summarize the Lesson

Ask students to add the formulas to the graphic organizer below.

Shape	Measurement	Formulas
Circle	Circumference	$C = \pi d$ or $C = 2\pi r$

GUIDED PRACTICE

Engage with the Whiteboard

Ask student volunteers to complete Exercises 3–5, showing the formula they use and the steps for finding the circumference.

Avoid Common Errors

Exercises 7–8 Students sometimes use the wrong formula when finding the radius or diameter when given the circumference. Instruct students to find the radius first here.

Using Circumference

Given the circumference of a circle, you can use the appropriate circumference formula to find the radius or the diameter of the circle. You can use that information to solve problems.

EXAMPLE 2  FL CC 7.G.2.4

A circular pond has a circumference of 628 feet. A model boat is moving directly across the pond, along a radius, at a rate of 5 feet per second. How long does it take the boat to get from the edge of the pond to the center?

STEP 1 Find the radius of the pond.

$C = 2\pi r$	Use the circumference formula.
$628 \approx 2(3.14)r$	Substitute for the circumference and for π.
$\frac{628}{6.28} \approx \frac{6.28r}{6.28}$	Divide both sides by 6.28.
$100 \approx r$	Simplify.

$C = 628$ ft
$r = ?$ ft

The radius is about 100 feet.

STEP 2 Find the time it takes the boat to get from the edge of the pond to the center along the radius. Divide the radius of the pond by the speed of the model boat.

$$100 \div 5 = 20$$

It takes the boat about 20 seconds to get to the center of the pond.

Reflect

4. **Analyze Relationships** Dante checks the answer to Step 1 by multiplying it by 6 and comparing it with the given circumference. Explain why Dante's estimation method works. Use it to check Step 1.

   $\pi \approx 3$, so $C = 2\pi r \approx 6r$; $6(100) = 600$ is close to 628.

5. **What If?** Suppose the model boat were traveling at a rate of 4 feet per second. How long would it take the model boat to get from the edge of the pond to the center? _about 25 seconds_

 **YOUR TURN**

6. A circular garden has a circumference of 44 yards. Lars is digging a straight line along a diameter of the garden at a rate of 7 yards per hour. How many hours will it take him to dig across the garden?

   about 2 hours

Math Talk
Mathematical Practices
Would it be reasonable to solve Example 2 using $\frac{22}{7}$ for π? Explain.

Yes; 168 is a multiple of 7 ($168 = 7 \cdot 24$).

Math On the Spot
@ my.hrw.com

My Notes

Personal Math Trainer
Online Assessment and Intervention
@ my.hrw.com

Find the circumference of each circle. (Example 1)

1. $C = \pi d$
   $C \approx$ _3.14(9)_
   $C \approx$ _28.26_ inches
    9 in.

2. $C = 2\pi r$
   $C \approx 2\left(\frac{22}{7}\right)($ _7_ $)$
   $C \approx$ _44_ cm
   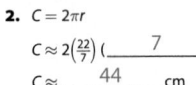 7 cm

Find the circumference of each circle. Use 3.14 or $\frac{22}{7}$ for π. Round to the nearest hundredth, if necessary. (Example 1)

3. 25 m — _78.5 m_
4. 4.8 yd — _30.14 yd_
5. 7.5 in. — _47.1 in._

6. A round swimming pool has a circumference of 66 feet. Carlos wants to buy a rope to put across the diameter of the pool. The rope costs $0.45 per foot, and Carlos needs 4 feet more than the diameter of the pool. How much will Carlos pay for the rope? (Example 2)

   Find the diameter.
   $C = \pi d$
   _66_ $\approx 3.14d$
   $\frac{\boxed{66}}{3.14} \approx \frac{3.14d}{3.14}$
   _21_ $\approx d$

   Find the cost.
   Carlos needs _21 + 4 = 25_ feet of rope.
   _25_ $\times \$0.45 =$ _$11.25_
   Carlos will pay _$11.25_ for the rope.

Find each missing measurement to the nearest hundredth. Use 3.14 for π. (Examples 1 and 2)

7. $r =$ _0.5 yd_
   $d =$ _1 yd_
   $C = \pi$ yd

8. $r \approx$ _12.55 ft_
   $d \approx$ _25.10 ft_
   $C = 78.8$ ft

9. $r \approx$ _1.7 in._
   $d \approx 3.4$ in.
   $C =$ _10.68 in._

? ESSENTIAL QUESTION CHECK-IN

10. Norah knows that the diameter of a circle is 13 meters. How would you tell her to find the circumference?

    Use the formula $C = \pi d$, and substitute 3.14 for π and 13 for the diameter.

DIFFERENTIATE INSTRUCTION

Home Connection

Ask students to work with a family member to identify several circular items in their home. Some possibilities are a tabletop, a wall clock, and a mirror. Have them measure the diameter of each item, and then calculate its circumference using the formula $C = \pi d$. Instruct them to make a table listing each item, its diameter, and its circumference.

Critical Thinking

Point out to students that 3.14 and $\frac{22}{7}$ are only two approximations for π. Discuss the Leibniz formula for π, which states that $1 - \frac{1}{3} + \frac{1}{5} - \frac{1}{7} + \frac{1}{9} - \frac{1}{11} + \ldots = \frac{\pi}{4}$, or $4 - \frac{4}{3} + \frac{4}{5} - \frac{4}{7} + \frac{4}{9} - \frac{4}{11} + \ldots = \pi$. Challenge students to find the sum of the first 25 numbers in the series, and compare that approximation to 3.14 and $\frac{22}{7}$. Calculating an approximation for π can help students see that π is a non-repeating, non-terminating decimal.

Additional Resources

Differentiated Instruction includes:

• Reading Strategies
• Success for English Learners **ELL**
• Reteach
• Challenge **PRE-AP**

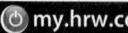
4.1 LESSON QUIZ

FL CC 7.G.2.4

For 1–3, find the circumference of each circle. Use 3.14 or $\frac{22}{7}$ for π. Round to the nearest hundredth if necessary.

1. a circle with radius 63 mm

2. a circle with diameter 6.2 in.

3. a circle with diameter 18 in.

4. A circular satellite dish antenna has a circumference of about 62.8 inches. Find its diameter.

5. The diameter of a bicycle's tires is 2.5 feet. How many revolutions of the tires does it take to travel 1 mile? Use 5,280 feet = 1 mile. Round to the nearest tenth.

6. **a.** The Jones family wants to enclose their circular garden with a fence. To the nearest foot, what is the minimum length of fencing they need to buy?

   b. If the fence costs $2.50 per foot, what will be the total cost?

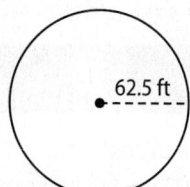

62.5 ft

Lesson Quiz available online

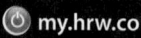
Answers

1. about 396 mm

2. about 19.47 in.

3. about 56.52 in.

4. 20 in.

5. 672.6 revolutions

6. **a.** 393 ft

   b. $982.50

Evaluate

GUIDED AND INDEPENDENT PRACTICE

FL CC 7.G.2.4

Concepts & Skills	Practice
Explore Activity Exploring Circumference	
Example 1 Finding Circumference	Exercises 1–5, 7–9, 11–13
Example 2 Using Circumference	Exercises 6–9, 15–22

Exercise	Depth of Knowledge (D.O.K.)		**FL CC** Mathematical Practices
11–13	**1** Recall of Information		**MP.2.1** Reasoning
14	**3** Strategic Thinking	H.O.T.	**MP.2.1** Reasoning
15–19	**2** Skills/Concepts		**MP.4.1** Modeling
20	**3** Strategic Thinking	H.O.T.	**MP.4.1** Modeling
21	**2** Skills/Concepts		**MP.4.1** Modeling
22	**2** Skills/Concepts		**MP.4.1** Modeling
23	**2** Skills/Concepts		**MP.4.1** Modeling
24	**2** Skills/Concepts		**MP.4.1** Modeling
25	**2** Skills/Concepts		**MP.4.1** Modeling
26	**3** Strategic Thinking	H.O.T.	**MP.3.1** Logic
27	**3** Strategic Thinking	H.O.T.	**MP.4.1** Modeling

Additional Resources

Extra Practice includes:

• Leveled Practice Worksheets

Name_____ Class_____ Date_____

4.1 Independent Practice

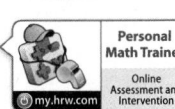

FL CC 7.G.2.4

Personal Math Trainer
Online Assessment and Intervention
⊙ my.hrw.com

For 11–13, find the circumference of each circle. Use 3.14 or $\frac{22}{7}$ for π. Round to the nearest hundredth, if necessary.

11.

(5.9 ft)

18.53 ft

12.

(•——56 cm)

352 cm

13.

(35 in.)

110 in.

14. In Exercises 11–13, for which problems did you use $\frac{22}{7}$ for π? Explain your choice.

Sample answer: In exercises 12 and 13; the radius or diameter is a multiple of 7.

15. A circular fountain has a radius of 9.4 feet. Find its diameter and circumference to the nearest tenth.

$d = 18.8$ ft; $C \approx 59.0$ ft

16. Find the radius and circumference of a CD with a diameter of 4.75 inches.

$r = 2.375$ in.; $C \approx 14.915$ in.

17. A dartboard has a diameter of 18 inches. What are its radius and circumference?

$r = 9$ in.; $C \approx 56.52$ in.

18. Multistep Randy's circular garden has a radius of 1.5 feet. He wants to enclose the garden with edging that costs $0.75 per foot. About how much will the edging cost? Explain.

$7.07; C \approx 2(3.14)(1.5) \approx 9.42$ ft; $9.42 \cdot 0.75 = 7.065$ or $7.07

19. Represent Real-World Problems The Ferris wheel shown makes 12 revolutions per ride. How far would someone travel during one ride?

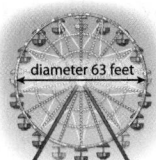

diameter 63 feet

about 2,376 feet

20. The diameter of a bicycle wheel is 2 feet. About how many revolutions does the wheel make to travel 2 kilometers? Explain. Hint: 1 km ≈ 3,280 ft

about 1,045 revolutions; 2 km $\approx 6,560$ ft; $C \approx \pi(2) \approx 6.28$ ft; $6,560$ ft $\div 6.28$ ft $\approx 1,044.59$

21. Multistep A map of a public park shows a circular pond. There is a bridge along a diameter of the pond that is 0.25 mi long. You walk across the bridge, while your friend walks halfway around the pond to meet you at the other side of the bridge. How much farther does your friend walk?

about 0.14 mi

22. Architecture The Capitol Rotunda connects the House and the Senate sides of the U.S. Capitol. Complete the table. Round your answers to the nearest foot.

Capitol Rotunda Dimensions	
Height	180 ft
Circumference	301.5 ft
Radius	48 ft
Diameter	96 ft

H.O.T. FOCUS ON HIGHER ORDER THINKING

Work Area

23. Multistep A museum groundskeeper is creating a semicircular statuary garden with a diameter of 30 feet. There will be a fence around the garden. The fencing costs $9.25 per linear foot. About how much will the fencing cost altogether?

about $713.18

24. Critical Thinking Sam is placing rope lights around the edge of a circular patio with a diameter of 18 feet. The lights come in lengths of 54 inches. How many strands of lights does he need to surround the patio edge?

13 strands

25. Represent Real-World Problems A circular path 2 feet wide has an inner diameter of 150 feet. How much farther is it around the outer edge of the path than around the inner edge?

12.56 feet

26. Critique Reasoning A gear on a bicycle has the shape of a circle. One gear has a diameter of 4 inches, and a smaller one has a diameter of 2 inches. Justin says that the circumference of the larger gear is 2 inches more than the circumference of the smaller gear. Do you agree? Explain your answer.

No. The circumference of the larger gear is about 12.56 inches. The circumference of the smaller gear is about 6.28 inches. So the circumference of the larger gear is 6.28 inches more than the circumference of the smaller gear.

27. Persevere in Problem Solving Consider two circular swimming pools. Pool A has a radius of 12 feet, and Pool B has a diameter of 7.5 meters. Which pool has a greater circumference? How much greater? Justify your answers.

Pool B; about 0.57 m or 1.84 ft; Sample answer: 24 feet ≈ 7.32 m, so the diameter of Pool B is greater, and the circumference is greater. 3.14(7.5) − 3.14(7.32) = 3.14(0.18) = 0.57; 0.57 m ≈ 1.84 ft

EXTEND THE MATH PRE-AP

Activity available online ⊙ my.hrw.com

Activity Suppose a piece of rope is wrapped around Earth at its equator and that Earth's equator is a perfect circle.

A If the equator is 25,000 miles long, what is the length of the rope in feet? Use 5,280 ft = 1 mile. 132,000,000 ft

B What is the radius of the circle made by the rope in part A? Use 3.14 for π, and do not round. 21,019,108.28 ft

C Suppose the length of the rope is increased by 3 feet. What is the new length of the rope in feet? 132,000,003 ft

D What is the radius of the circle made by the rope in part C? Use 3.14 for π, and do not round. 21,019,108.76 ft

E How far above Earth is the new rope? Hint: Find the difference in the radii. about 0.48 ft, or about 5.76 in.

© Houghton Mifflin Harcourt Publishing Company

4.2 Area of Circles

 Florida Common Core Standards

The student is expected to:

 **Geometry—7.G.2.4**

Know the formulas for the area and circumference of a circle and use them to solve problems; given an informal derivation of the relationship between the circumference and area of a circle.

Mathematical Practices

 **MP.4.1** Modeling

ADDITIONAL EXAMPLE 1
A remodeling project calls for sanding a chair with a disk sander. The sanding disk used on the sander has a radius of 4.5 inches. Find the area of the disk. Use 3.14 for π. about 63.59 in²

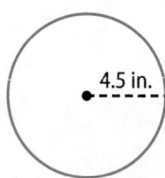

4.5 in.

 Interactive Whiteboard
Interactive example available online

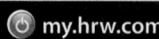 **my.hrw.com**

Engage

ESSENTIAL QUESTION

How do you find the area of a circle? Sample answer: Use the formula $A = \pi r^2$, where A is the area and r is the radius. Use 3.14 or $\frac{22}{7}$ for π.

Motivate the Lesson
Ask: How do you find the area of any circular object like a pizza? Take a guess. Begin Explore Activity 1 to find out.

Explore

EXPLORE ACTIVITY 1

Focus on Math Connections Mathematical Practices
Point out that using a parallelogram as a model to find the area of a circle is appropriate because the wedges used to make the parallelogram can be made so small that the "curves" essentially disappear. The sides of the parallelogram then become straight.

Explain

EXAMPLE 1

Engage with the Whiteboard
Cover up the solution steps after the given equation, and have a volunteer complete the calculations for the area. Discuss how the calculations depend on the size of the radius of the biscuit.

Focus on Patterns Mathematical Practices
Emphasize that the length of the radius is squared in the formula for the area of a circle and that squaring this length is the reason that the units for area are squared.

Questioning Strategies Mathematical Practices
• How can you check for the reasonableness of the answer for the area of a circle? You could substitute 3 for π and multiply by the square of the radius.

• Explain how to find the area of a semicircle and the area of a quarter circle. Multiply the area of the full circle by one-half to find the area of the semicircle and by one-fourth to find the area of the quarter circle.

YOUR TURN

Talk About It
Check for Understanding
Ask: How do you find the area of a circle when its diameter is given? You must first divide the diameter by 2 in order to determine the radius of the circle; then you square the radius and multiply by 3.14, an approximation for π.

LESSON

4.2 Area of Circles

FL CC 7.G.2.4

Know the formulas for the area and circumference of a circle and use them to solve problems; give an informal derivation of the relationship between the circumference and area of a circle.

ESSENTIAL QUESTION

How do you find the area of a circle?

EXPLORE ACTIVITY 1 FL CC 7.G.2.4

Exploring Area of Circles

You can use what you know about circles and π to help find the formula for the area of a circle.

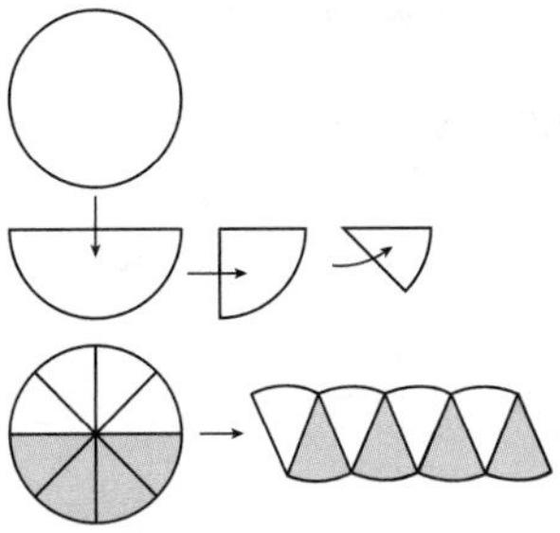

STEP 1 Use a compass to draw a circle and cut it out.

STEP 2 Fold the circle three times as shown to get equal wedges.

STEP 3 Unfold and shade one-half of the circle.

STEP 4 Cut out the wedges, and fit the pieces together to form a figure that looks like a parallelogram.

The base and height of the parallelogram relate to the parts of the circle.

base b = $\frac{1}{2}$ the circumference of the circle, or $\underline{\pi r}$

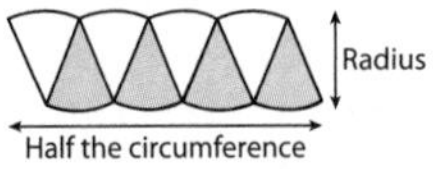

height h = the <u>radius</u> of the circle, or <u>r</u>

To find the area of a parallelogram, the equation is A = <u>bh</u>.

To find the area of the circle, substitute for b and h in the area formula.

$A = bh$

$A = \pi r \, h$ Substitute πr for b.

$A = \pi r \, r$ Substitute r for h.

$A = \pi \, r^2$ $r \cdot r = r^2$

Reflect

1. How can you make the wedges look more like a parallelogram?

   Sample answer: Make the wedges smaller so the base looks more like a straight line than curves.

Math On the Spot my.hrw.com

Finding the Area of a Circle

Area of a Circle

The area of a circle is equal to π times the radius squared.

$A = \pi r^2$

Remember that area is given in square units.

EXAMPLE 1 Real World FL CC 7.G.2.4

A biscuit recipe calls for the dough to be rolled out and circles to be cut from the dough. The biscuit cutter has a radius of 4 cm. Find the area of the biscuit once it is cut. Use 3.14 for π.

$A = \pi r^2$ Use the formula.

$A = \pi(4)^2$ Substitute. Use 4 for r.

$A \approx 3.14 \times 4^2$ Substitute. Use 3.14 for π.

$A \approx 3.14 \times 16$ Evaluate the power.

$A \approx 50.24$ Multiply.

The area of the biscuit is about 50.24 cm^2.

Math Talk Mathematical Practices

If the radius increases by 1 centimeter, how does the area of the top of the biscuit change?

The area increases by about 28.26 cm^2.

Reflect

2. Compare finding the area of a circle when given the radius with finding the area when given the diameter.

   The formula for area of a circle uses the radius of the circle. If you are given the diameter of the circle, you must first divide it by two to get the radius.

3. Why do you evaluate the power in the equation before multiplying?

   Sample answer: You must follow the order of operations and evaluate the exponents before multiplying.

Personal Math Trainer Online Assessment and Intervention my.hrw.com

YOUR TURN

4. A circular pool has a radius of 10 feet. What is the area of the pool? Use 3.14 for π. <u>314 ft^2</u>

PROFESSIONAL DEVELOPMENT

Integrate Mathematical Practices MP.4.1

This lesson provides an opportunity to address this Mathematical Practice standard. It calls for students to apply mathematics to problems arising in everyday life, society, and the workplace. Students develop the formula for the area of a circle by using a parallelogram as a model, and then use the formula to find the area of real-life circles in real-life situations. Students also explore the relationship between the circumference of a circle and its area, and then use that relationship to solve problems. In this way, students have applied mathematics to problems involving the area of circular figures.

Math Background

Although $A = \pi r^2$ is the most common formula used to find the area of a circle with radius r, you can also use the formula $A = \frac{1}{2}Cr$, where C is the circumference and r is the radius.

$$C = 2\pi r$$

$$\frac{1}{2}Cr = \frac{1}{2}(2\pi r)r$$

$$\frac{1}{2}Cr = \pi r^2$$

$$= A$$

So, $A = \frac{1}{2}Cr = \pi r^2$.

EXPLORE ACTIVITY 2

Avoid Common Errors
Students sometimes make the error of multiplying the radius by 2 rather than squaring it when finding the area of a circle. Remind students that area is a "squared" measurement as a way to remember to square r.

Engage with the Whiteboard
 Invite a group of volunteers to complete the steps for showing the relationship between the circumference of a circle and the area. Discuss how students can use multiple formulas containing A, the area, and C, the circumference.

Questioning Strategies Mathematical Practices
- What does it mean to solve $C = 2\pi r$ for r? It means to get r on one side of the equation; the expression on the other side can then be substituted for r in the next step.
- How do you find the square of $\frac{C}{2\pi}$? Square both the numerator and denominator, being sure to square both factors in the denominator: $\left(\frac{C}{2\pi}\right)^2 = \frac{C^2}{2^2\pi^2} = \frac{C^2}{4\pi^2}$.

Elaborate

Talk About It
Summarize the Lesson
Ask students to add the formulas to the graphic organizer below.

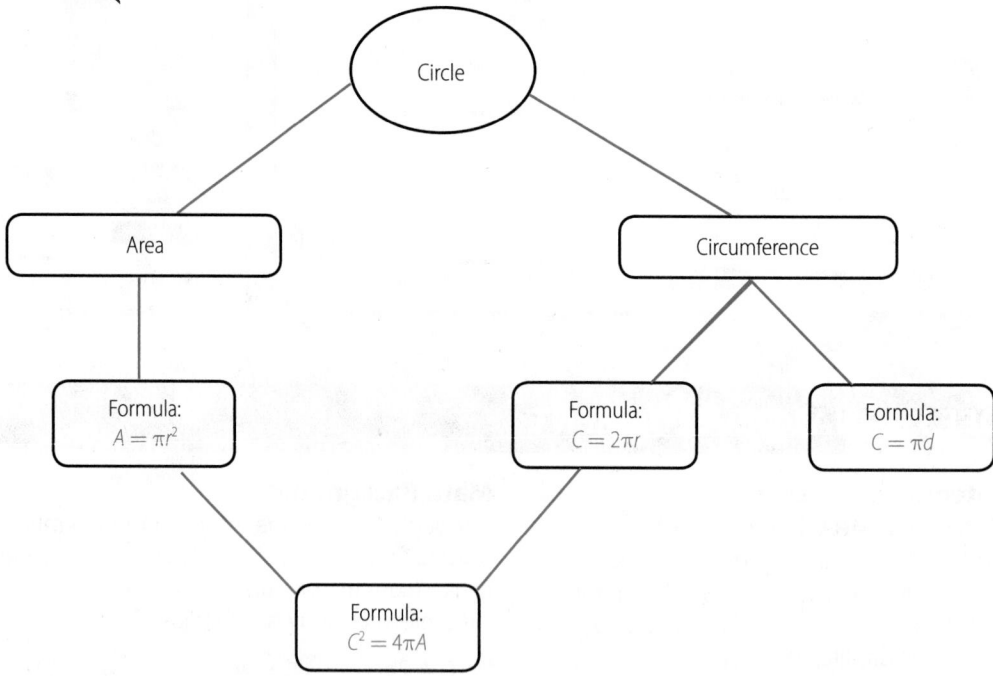

GUIDED PRACTICE

Engage with the Whiteboard
 Ask volunteers to complete Exercises 1–6 by showing their steps for finding the area.

Avoid Common Errors
Exercises 5–6 A common error is to substitute the diameter directly into the area formula. Explain that students must always use the radius when finding the area of a circle.

EXPLORE ACTIVITY 2 FL CC 7.G.2.4

Finding the Relationship between Circumference and Area

You can use what you know about circumference and area of circles to find a relationship between them.

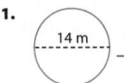

Find the relationship between the circumference and area of a circle.

Start with a circle that has radius r.
Solve the equation $C = 2\pi r$ for r.

$$r = \frac{\boxed{C}}{\boxed{2\pi}}$$

Substitute your expression for r in the formula for area of a circle.

$$A = \pi \left(\frac{\boxed{C}}{\boxed{2\pi}} \right)^2$$

> Remember: Because the exponent is outside the parentheses, you must apply it to the numerator and to each factor of the denominator.

Square the term in the parentheses.

$$A = \pi \left(\frac{\boxed{C}^2}{\boxed{2}^2 \cdot \boxed{\pi}^2} \right)$$

Evaluate the power.

$$A = \frac{\boxed{\pi} \cdot \boxed{C}^2}{\boxed{4} \cdot \boxed{\pi}^2}$$

Simplify.

$$A = \frac{\boxed{C}^2}{\boxed{4} \cdot \boxed{\pi}}$$

Solve for C^2.

$$C^2 = 4 \boxed{\pi} \boxed{A}$$

The circumference of the circle squared is equal to

<u>four times π times the area</u>.

EXPLORE ACTIVITY 2 *(cont'd)*

Reflect

5. Does this formula work for a circle with a radius of 3 inches? Show your work.

Yes; $A = \pi r^2 \qquad C = 2\pi r \qquad C^2 \overset{?}{=} 4\pi A$

$\quad = \pi \times 3^2 \qquad = 2\pi 3 \qquad 18.84^2 \overset{?}{=} 4 \times 3.14 \times 28.26$

$\quad = 9\pi \qquad\quad = 6\pi \qquad 354.9456 = 354.9456$

$\quad \approx 28.26 \qquad \approx 18.84$

Guided Practice

Find the area of each circle. Round to the nearest tenth if necessary. Use 3.14 for π.
(Explore Activity 1)

1.  14 m 153.9 m²

2. 12 mm 452.2 mm²

3. 20 yd 314 yd²

Solve. Use 3.14 for π. (Example 1)

4. A clock face has a radius of 8 inches. What is the area of the clock face? Round your answer to the nearest hundredth.   200.96 in²

5. A DVD has a diameter of 12 centimeters. What is the area of the DVD? Round your answer to the nearest hundredth.   113.04 cm²

6. A company makes steel lids that have a diameter of 13 inches. What is the area of each lid? Round your answer to the nearest hundredth.   132.67 in²

Find the area of each circle. Give your answers in terms of π.
(Explore Activity 2)

7. $C = 4\pi$
   $A =$ <u>4π square units</u>

8. $C = 12\pi$
   $A =$ <u>36π square units</u>

9. $C = \dfrac{\pi}{2}$
   $A =$ <u>$\dfrac{\pi}{16}$ square units</u>

10. A circular pen has an area of 64π square yards. What is the circumference of the pen? Give your answer in terms of π.
(Explore Activity 2) 16π yd

❓ ESSENTIAL QUESTION CHECK-IN

11. What is the formula for the area A of a circle in terms of the radius r? $A = \pi r^2$

DIFFERENTIATE INSTRUCTION

Multiple Representations

Ask groups of students to use a centimeter ruler to measure the radius of several circular objects in the room or that you bring to class. Have them fill in the table below and compare the values in the last two columns.

Object	Radius (cm)	$C^2 = (2 \cdot 3.14r)^2$ (cm²)	$A = 3.14r^2$ (cm²)	$A = \dfrac{C^2}{4(3.14)}$ (cm²)
Can	4	631.01	50.24	50.24
Counter	1	39.44	3.14	3.14
Quarter	1.2	56.79	4.52	4.52

Critical Thinking

Have students work in pairs. Have one student in the pair make up a circumference problem, including a solution showing the formula and steps. Have the other student in the pair make up an area problem, including a solution showing the formula and steps. Then have them exchange problems and solve the problem they receive. Ask them to justify how to find the area given the circumference, and how to find the circumference given the area.

Additional Resources

Differentiated Instruction includes:

• Reading Strategies

• Success for English Learners **ELL**

• Reteach

• Challenge **PRE-AP**

4.2 LESSON QUIZ

 **FL CC** 7.G.2.4

For 1–3, find the area of each circle. Use 3.14 for π. Round to the nearest tenth if necessary.

1. a circle with radius 48 mm

2. a circle with diameter 8.4 ft

3. a circle with diameter 14 in.

4. The diameter of the face-off circle on an ice-hockey rink is 30 feet. Find its area.

5. A circle has a circumference of 16π yards. Find the area in terms of π.

6. The Garcia family bought 400 yards of fencing to enclose a circular wildflower garden. They will use all of the fencing.

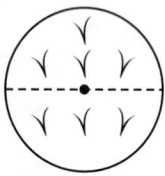

   a. What is the diameter of the garden?

   b. Use your answer to part **a** to find the area enclosed by the fence?

Lesson Quiz available online

 my.hrw.com

Answers

1. 7,234.56 mm²

2. 55.39 ft²

3. 153.86 in²

4. 706.5 ft²

5. 64π yd²

6. **a.** about 127.39 yd

   b. about 12,739.15 yd²

Evaluate

GUIDED AND INDEPENDENT PRACTICE

 **FL CC** 7.G.2.4

Concepts & Skills	Practice
Explore Activity 1 Exploring Area of Circles	Exercises 1–3
Example 1 Finding the Area of a Circle	Exercises 4–6, 12–17, 19, 21–22
Explore Activity 2 Finding the Relationship Between Circumference and Area	Exercises 7–10, 18, 20

Exercise	Depth of Knowledge (D.O.K.)		**FL CC** Mathematical Practices
12–17	**2** Skills/Concepts		**MP.4.1** Modeling
18	**3** Strategic Thinking	H.O.T.	**MP.3.1** Logic
19	**3** Strategic Thinking	H.O.T.	**MP.7.1** Using Structure
20–21	**3** Strategic Thinking	H.O.T.	**MP.3.1** Logic
22	**2** Skills/Concepts		**MP.4.1** Modeling
23–24	**3** Strategic Thinking	H.O.T.	**MP.7.1** Using Structure
25	**3** Strategic Thinking	H.O.T.	**MP.3.1** Logic

Additional Resources

Extra Practice includes:

• Leveled Practice Worksheets

4.2 Independent Practice

FL CC 7.G.2.4

Personal Math Trainer

my.hrw.com
Online Assessment and Intervention

12. The most popular pizza at Pavone's Pizza is the 10-inch personal pizza with one topping. What is the area of a pizza with a diameter of 10 inches? Round your answer to the nearest hundredth.

78.5 in²

13. A hubcap has a radius of 16 centimeters. What is the area of the hubcap? Round your answer to the nearest hundredth.

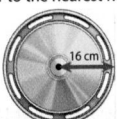
16 cm

803.84 cm²

14. A stained glass window is shaped like a semicircle. The bottom edge of the window is 36 inches long. What is the area of the stained glass window? Round your answer to the nearest hundredth.

508.68 in²

15. Analyze Relationships The point (3, 0) lies on a circle with the center at the origin. What is the area of the circle to the nearest hundredth?

28.26 square units

16. Multistep A radio station broadcasts a signal over an area with a radius of 50 miles. The station can relay the signal and broadcast over an area with a radius of 75 miles. How much greater is the area of the broadcast region when the signal is relayed? Round your answer to the nearest square mile.

9,813 mi²

17. Multistep The sides of a square field are 12 meters. A sprinkler in the center of the field sprays a circular area with a diameter that corresponds to a side of the field. How much of the field is **not** reached by the sprinkler? Round your answer to the nearest hundredth.

30.96 m²

18. Justify Reasoning A small silver dollar pancake served at a restaurant has a circumference of 2π inches. A regular pancake has a circumference of 4π inches. Is the area of the regular pancake twice the area of the silver dollar pancake? Explain.

No; the area of the regular pancake is 4π in² and the area of the silver dollar pancake is π in², so the area of the regular pancake is 4 times the area of the silver dollar pancake.

19. Analyze Relationships A bakery offers a small circular cake with a diameter of 8 inches. It also offers a large circular cake with a diameter of 24 inches. Does the top of the large cake have three times the area of that of the small cake? If not, how much greater is its area? Explain.

No; the top of the large cake has an area 9 times that of the small cake. The area of the top of the large cake is 144π in² and that of the small cake is 16π in².

20. Communicate Mathematical Ideas You can use the formula $A = \frac{C^2}{4\pi}$ to find the area of a circle given the circumference. Describe another way to find the area of a circle when given the circumference.

Sample answer: First find the radius of the circle by using the formula $C = 2\pi r$. Then substitute the radius into the formula for the area of a circle.

21. Draw Conclusions Mark wants to order a pizza. Which is the better deal? Explain.

The 18-inch pizza is a better deal because it costs about 8¢ per square inch while the 12-inch pizza costs about 9¢ per square inch.

Donnie's Pizza Palace

Diameter (in.)	12	18
Cost ($)	10	20

22. Multistep A bear was seen near a campground. Searchers were dispatched to the region to find the bear.

a. Assume the bear can walk in any direction at a rate of 2 miles per hour. Suppose the bear was last seen 4 hours ago. How large an area must the searchers cover? Use 3.14 for π. Round your answer to the nearest square mile. _____ 201 mi²

b. **What If?** How much additional area would the searchers have to cover if the bear were last seen 5 hours ago? _____ 113 mi²

H.O.T. FOCUS ON HIGHER ORDER THINKING

Work Area

23. Analyze Relationships Two circles have the same radius. Is the combined area of the two circles the same as the area of a circle with twice the radius? Explain.

No; the combined area is $2\pi r^2$ while the area of a circle with twice the radius is $4\pi r^2$.

24. Look for a Pattern How does the area of a circle change if the radius is multiplied by a factor of n, where n is a whole number?

The area is multiplied by a factor of n^2.

25. Represent Real World Problems The bull's-eye on a target has a diameter of 3 inches. The whole target has a diameter of 15 inches. What part of the whole target is the bull's-eye? Explain.

$\frac{\pi(1.5)^2}{\pi(7.5)^2} = \frac{2.25}{56.25} = \frac{1}{25}$ or 0.04 or 4%

EXTEND THE MATH PRE-AP

Activity available online my.hrw.com

Activity Use the figure at the right to see how close you can estimate the area of a circle using squares.

A The diameter of the circle is equal to the side length of the larger square in the figure. What is the area of the larger square if the diameter of the circle is 10 cm? 100 cm²

B The diameter of the circle is also equal to the diagonal of the smaller square shown in the figure. The side length of the smaller square is about 7.07 cm. What is the area of the smaller square? about 50 cm²

C Estimate the area of the circle. Justify your reasoning. Sample answer: 75 cm²; 75 cm² is the average of 100 cm² and 50 cm².

D Find the actual area of the circle. Use $\pi = 3.14$.
$A = \pi(5)^2 = 3.14(25) = 78.5$; about 78.5 cm²

E How does your estimated area of the circle compare to its actual area? Sample answer: The estimate is close to the actual area.

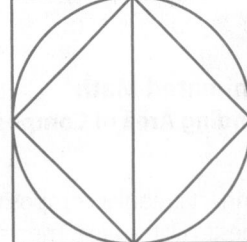

LESSON
4.3 Area of Composite Figures

ADDITIONAL EXAMPLE 1
Find the area of the figure. 50.8 m²

5.5 m

5.5 m

3 m   8.2 m

5.5 m

Interactive Whiteboard
Interactive example available online

⏻ my.hrw.com

Engage

ESSENTIAL QUESTION

How do you find the area of composite figures? Sample answer: Divide the figure into simpler nonoverlapping figures. Find the area of each simpler figure, and then add the areas together to find the total area of the composite figure.

Motivate the Lesson
Ask: How do you find the area of a shape that is irregular? Take a guess. Begin the Explore Activity to find out.

Explore

EXPLORE ACTIVITY

Focus on Critical Thinking   Mathematical Practices
Tell students that they may divide up the shape in a way that makes sense to them. Stress that most composite figures can be divided up in several different ways. Point out that there is more than one way to divide up the given figure. Students should be able to justify that each method of dividing up the figure will result in the same total area.

Explain

EXAMPLE 1

Engage with the Whiteboard
Cover up the area calculations, and have student volunteers show the calculations for the area of each shape. Ask other volunteers to divide up the composite figure differently, and then ask them if they can determine (without estimating) all of the dimensions of their simpler figures needed to find each area.

Avoid Common Errors
Students may forget how to find the height of the trapezoid or parallelogram. Point out that the height always forms a right angle with the base(s). Have students highlight the height and base(s) before beginning the calculations.

Questioning Strategies   Mathematical Practices
• Which measurements given in the figure are not used to find the area of the composite figure? 3 cm, 4 cm, 2 cm

X² Animated Math
Finding Area of Composite Figures

Students connect irregular composite shapes with the shapes they are made up of by dragging familiar shapes to fill the area. Then students find the areas of each piece to find the total area.

Area of Composite Figures

FL CC 7.G.2.6

Solve real-world and mathematical problems involving area, . . . of . . . objects composed of triangles, quadrilaterals, polygons, ...

? ESSENTIAL QUESTION

How do you find the area of composite figures?

EXPLORE ACTIVITY Real World | FL CC 7.G.2.6

Exploring Areas of Composite Figures

Aaron was plotting the shape of his garden on grid paper. While it was an irregular shape, it was perfect for his yard. Each square on the grid represents 1 square meter.

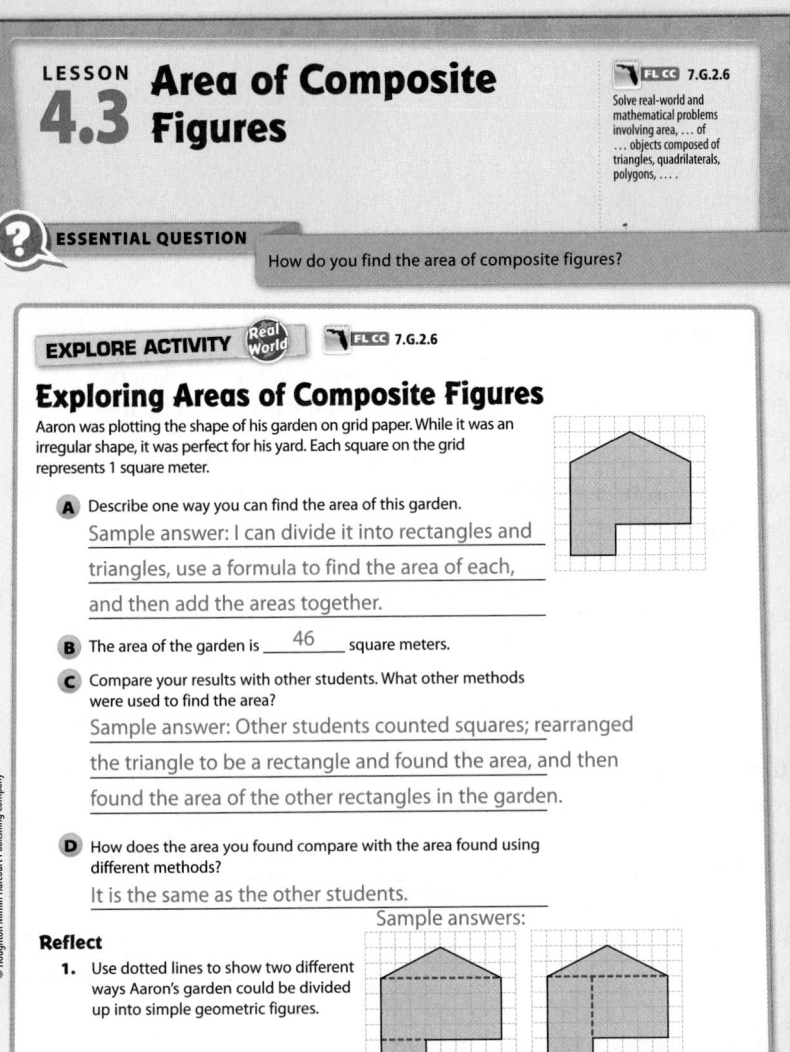

A Describe one way you can find the area of this garden.

Sample answer: I can divide it into rectangles and triangles, use a formula to find the area of each, and then add the areas together.

B The area of the garden is _____46_____ square meters.

C Compare your results with other students. What other methods were used to find the area?

Sample answer: Other students counted squares; rearranged the triangle to be a rectangle and found the area, and then found the area of the other rectangles in the garden.

D How does the area you found compare with the area found using different methods?

It is the same as the other students.

Reflect

1. Use dotted lines to show two different ways Aaron's garden could be divided up into simple geometric figures.

Sample answers:

Math On the Spot
my.hrw.com

Finding the Area of a Composite Figure

A composite figure is made up of simple geometric shapes. To find the area of a composite figure or other irregular-shaped figure, divide it into simple, nonoverlapping figures. Find the area of each simpler figure, and then add the areas together to find the total area of the composite figure.

Use the chart below to review some common area formulas.

Shape	Area Formula
triangle	$A = \frac{1}{2}bh$
square	$A = s^2$
rectangle	$A = \ell w$
parallelogram	$A = bh$
trapezoid	$A = \frac{1}{2}h(b_1 + b_2)$

X^2
Animated Math
my.hrw.com

EXAMPLE 1 Real World | FL CC 7.G.2.6

Find the area of the figure.

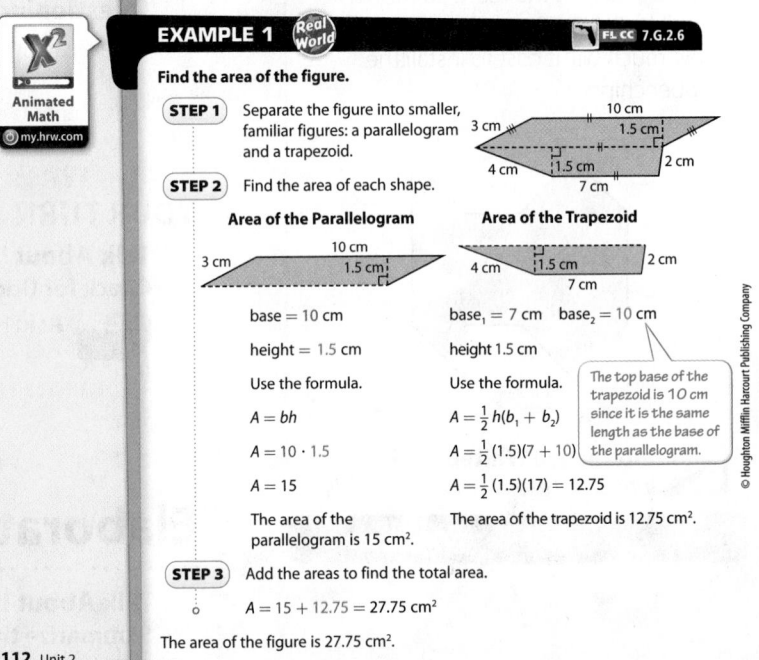

STEP 1 Separate the figure into smaller, familiar figures: a parallelogram and a trapezoid.

STEP 2 Find the area of each shape.

Area of the Parallelogram

base = 10 cm

height = 1.5 cm

Use the formula.

$A = bh$

$A = 10 \cdot 1.5$

$A = 15$

The area of the parallelogram is 15 cm².

Area of the Trapezoid

base₁ = 7 cm   base₂ = 10 cm

$base_1 = 7$ cm $base_2 = 10$ cm

height 1.5 cm

Use the formula.

$A = \frac{1}{2}h(b_1 + b_2)$

$A = \frac{1}{2}(1.5)(7 + 10)$

$A = \frac{1}{2}(1.5)(17) = 12.75$

The area of the trapezoid is 12.75 cm².

The top base of the trapezoid is 10 cm since it is the same length as the base of the parallelogram.

STEP 3 Add the areas to find the total area.

$A = 15 + 12.75 = 27.75$ cm²

The area of the figure is 27.75 cm².

PROFESSIONAL DEVELOPMENT

Integrate Mathematical Practices MP.5.1

This lesson provides an opportunity to address this Mathematical Practice standard. It calls for students to select tools, including paper and pencil, and techniques…to solve problems. Students find the area of a composite figure by dividing it into simpler figures for which they know the area formulas. Then they find the area of each simpler figure and add these areas together to find the total area of the composite figure. They apply this technique to real-life figures. In this way, students have used a technique to solve a problem involving a real-world, composite figure.

Math Background

You can estimate the area of an irregular figure by placing a grid over the figure, as shown below.

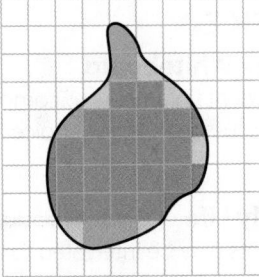

20 full squares shaded blue,
5 nearly full squares shaded green,
5 red squares shaded very little,
6 half-squares shaded yellow.

So, an estimate of the area of the irregular figure is 20 + 5 + 3, or 28 square units.

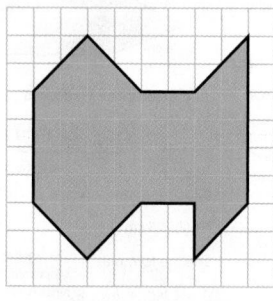

YOUR TURN

Talk About It
Check for Understanding

 Ask: How do you find the area of the figure in Exercise 3? Sample answer: Add the area of the square with side length 10 m to the area of a semicircle with radius 5 m.

EXAMPLE 2

Engage with the Whiteboard

Cover up the area calculations, and have student volunteers show the calculations for the area of each shape. Then have another volunteer add the results to find the total area of the banquet room.

Questioning Strategies ⚑ Mathematical Practices

• Are there any other ways to find the area of the composite figure? Explain. Sample answer: Yes; you could enclose the entire area in a rectangle, and then subtract the areas of the simpler figures that are not shaded from the area of that rectangle. You can also count the shaded squares directly, combining partial squares to make whole squares where possible.

YOUR TURN

Talk About It
Check for Understanding

 Ask: How do you find the area of the window? Sample answer: Divide the window into one circle (equal to two semicircles) and one rectangle. Then find the total area of the parts in square feet.

Elaborate

Talk About It
Summarize the Lesson

Ask students to complete the graphic organizer below, which gives the steps for finding the area of a composite figure.

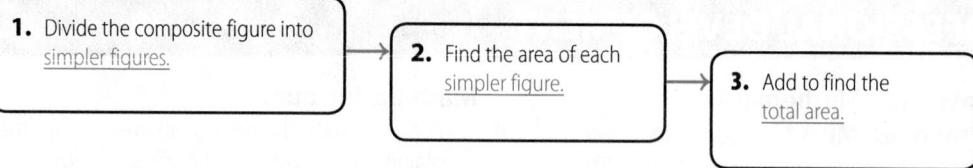

1. Divide the composite figure into simpler figures.

2. Find the area of each simpler figure.

3. Add to find the total area.

GUIDED PRACTICE

Engage with the Whiteboard

Ask two student volunteers to complete Exercise 2 using different ways for finding the area. Discuss the various choices for separating a composite figure into simpler figures.

Connect to Daily Life ⚑ Mathematical Practices

Exercise 3 Students may be interested to know that to purchase the exact amount of tile needed to cover the area would be a mistake. This floor plan requires many tiles to be cut to fit the angles involved. An experienced tile installer will order 10% more to allow for waste and breakage.

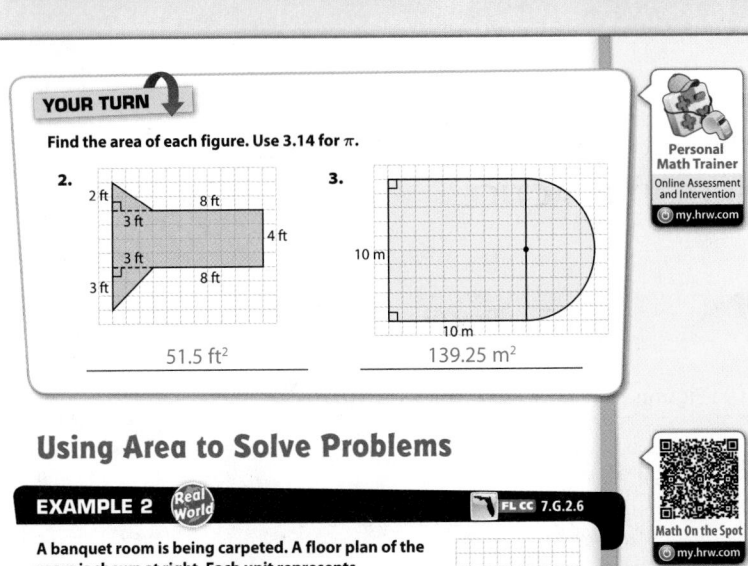

YOUR TURN

Find the area of each figure. Use 3.14 for π.

2.
2 ft
8 ft
3 ft
4 ft
3 ft
3 ft
3 ft
8 ft

51.5 ft²

3.

10 m

10 m

139.25 m²

Personal Math Trainer
Online Assessment and Intervention
my.hrw.com

Math On the Spot
my.hrw.com

Using Area to Solve Problems

EXAMPLE 2 Real World
FL CC 7.G.2.6

A banquet room is being carpeted. A floor plan of the room is shown at right. Each unit represents 1 yard. The carpet costs $23.50 per square yard. How much will it cost to carpet the room?

STEP 1 Separate the composite figure into simpler shapes as shown by the dashed lines: a parallelogram, a rectangle, and a triangle.

STEP 2 Find the area of the simpler figures. Count units to find the dimensions.

Parallelogram	Rectangle	Triangle
$A = bh$	$A = \ell w$	$A = \frac{1}{2}bh$
$A = 4 \cdot 2$	$A = 6 \cdot 4$	$A = \frac{1}{2}(1)(2)$
$A = 8$ yd²	$A = 24$ yd²	$A = 1$ yd²

STEP 3 Find the area of the composite figure.

$A = 8 + 24 + 1 = 33$ square yards

STEP 4 Calculate the cost to carpet the room.

Area · Cost per yard = Total cost

33 · $23.50 = $775.50

The cost to carpet the banquet room is $775.50.

Math Talk
Mathematical Practices

Describe how you can estimate the cost to carpet the room.

Sample answer: Draw a bigger rectangle around the room and overestimate the area. Round the price of the carpet to $20 per square yard.

Lesson 4.3 **113**

YOUR TURN

Personal Math Trainer
Online Assessment and Intervention
my.hrw.com

4. A window is being replaced with tinted glass. The plan at the right shows the design of the window. Each unit length represents 1 foot. The glass costs $28 per square foot. How much will it cost to replace the glass? Use 3.14 for π.

$911.68

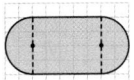

Guided Practice

1. A tile installer plots an irregular shape on grid paper. Each square on the grid represents 1 square centimeter. What is the area of the irregular shape? (Explore Activity, Example 2)

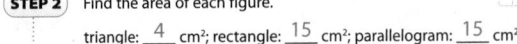

STEP 1 Separate the figure into a triangle, a ___rectangle___, and a parallelogram.

STEP 2 Find the area of each figure.

triangle: __4__ cm²; rectangle: __15__ cm²; parallelogram: __15__ cm²

STEP 3 Find the area of the composite figure: __4__ + __15__ + __15__ = __34__ cm²

The area of the irregular shape is __34__ cm².

2. Show two different ways to divide the composite figure. Find the area both ways. Show your work below. (Example 1)

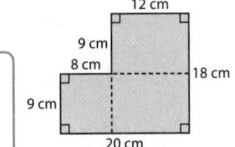
12 cm
9 cm
8 cm
18 cm
9 cm
20 cm

Method 1		Method 2	
$A_1 = \ell w$	$A_2 = \ell w$	$A_1 = \ell w$	$A_2 = \ell w$
$= 12 \cdot 9$	$= 20 \cdot 9$	$= 9 \cdot 8$	$= 12 \cdot 18$
$= 108$	$= 180$	$= 72$	$= 216$
total area = 288 cm²		total area = 288 cm²	

3. Sal is tiling his entryway. The floor plan is drawn on a unit grid. Each unit length represents 1 foot. Tile costs $2.25 per square foot. How much will Sal pay to tile his entryway? (Example 2)

$97.88

? **ESSENTIAL QUESTION CHECK-IN**

4. What is the first step in finding the area of a composite figure?

___separating the composite figure into simpler figures___

114 Unit 2

DIFFERENTIATE INSTRUCTION

Cooperative Learning

Ask pairs of students to find the areas of composite figures. Have each student draw a figure on a grid and then trade the figure with his or her partner. The partner should divide the figure into simpler figures, calculate the areas of these simpler figures, and then add to find the total area of the composite figure.

Visual Cues

Have students use the problem-solving technique of drawing a diagram for problems that do not include a figure. Suggest that they sketch the figure on a grid whenever possible, using a scale appropriate for the dimensions included in the problem. Have them add the dimensions to the diagram and highlight the measures needed in the area formulas.

Additional Resources

Differentiated Instruction includes:

• Reading Strategies
• Success for English Learners **ELL**
• Reteach
• Challenge **PRE-AP**

4.3 LESSON QUIZ

 FL CC 7.G.2.6

For 1 and 2, find the area of each figure. Use 3.14 for π.

1. a patio shaped like the figure shown below with the length of each square equal to 1 meter

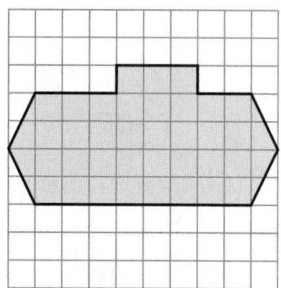

2. a field shaped like the figure shown

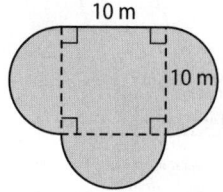

3. Juan wants to carpet the floor of a bedroom. A floor plan is shown.

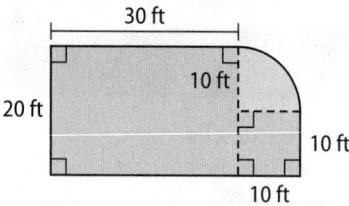

a. How much carpet does he need?

b. The carpet costs $3 per square foot. How much will it cost to carpet the bedroom?

Lesson Quiz available online

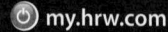
Evaluate

GUIDED AND INDEPENDENT PRACTICE

FL CC 7.G.2.6

Concepts & Skills	Practice
Explore Activity Exploring Areas of Composite Figures	Exercise 1
Example 1 Finding the Area of a Composite Figure	Exercises 2, 5, 7
Example 2 Using Area to Solve Problems	Exercises 3, 6, 8–10

Exercise	Depth of Knowledge (D.O.K.)	FL CC Mathematical Practices
5–6	**2** Skills/Concepts	**MP.4.1** Modeling
7	**2** Skills/Concepts	**MP.5.1** Using Tools
8–10	**2** Skills/Concepts	**MP.7.1** Using Structure
11	**3** Strategic Thinking H.O.T.	**MP.7.1** Using Structure
12	**3** Strategic Thinking H.O.T.	**MP.3.1** Logic
13	**3** Strategic Thinking H.O.T.	**MP.7.1** Using Structure
14–15	**2** Skills/Concepts	**MP.5.1** Using Tools

Additional Resources

Extra Practice includes:

• Leveled Practice Worksheets

Answers

1. 39 m²

2. 217.75 m²

3. a. 778.5 ft²

   b. $2,335.50

4.3 Independent Practice

FL CC 7.G.2.6

Personal Math Trainer

Online Assessment and Intervention

my.hrw.com

5. A banner is made of a square and a semicircle. The square has side lengths of 26 inches. One side of the square is also the diameter of the semicircle. What is the total area of the banner? Use 3.14 for π.

941.33 in²

6. Multistep Erin wants to carpet the floor of her closet. A floor plan of the closet is shown.

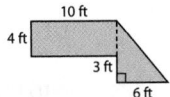

10 ft
4 ft
3 ft
6 ft

a. How much carpet does Erin need?

61 ft²

b. The carpet Erin has chosen costs $2.50 per square foot. How much will it cost her to carpet the floor?

$152.50

7. Multiple Representations Hexagon ABCDEF has vertices A(−2, 4), B(0, 4), C(2, 1), D(5, 1), E(5, −2), and F(−2, −2). Sketch the figure on a coordinate plane. What is the area of the hexagon?

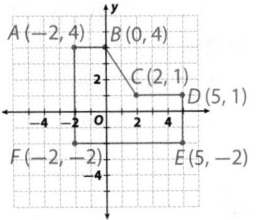

A (−2, 4) B (0, 4)
2   C (2, 1)
        D (5, 1)
−4 −2 O 2 4
F (−2, −2)   E (5, −2)
−4

30 square units

8. A field is shaped like the figure shown. What is the area of the field? Use 3.14 for π.

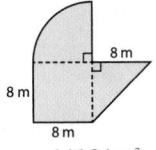

8 m
8 m
8 m

146.24 m²

9. A bookmark is shaped like a rectangle with a semicircle attached at both ends. The rectangle is 12 cm long and 4 cm wide. The diameter of each semicircle is the width of the rectangle. What is the area of the bookmark? Use 3.14 for π.

60.56 cm²

10. Multistep Alex is making 12 pennants for the school fair. The pattern he is using to make the pennants is shown in the figure. The fabric for the pennants costs $1.25 per square foot. How much will it cost Alex to make 12 pennants?

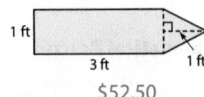

1 ft
3 ft   1 ft

$52.50

11. Reasoning A composite figure is formed by combining a square and a triangle. Its total area is 32.5 ft². The area of the triangle is 7.5 ft². What is the length of each side of the square? Explain.

5 ft; 32.5 ft² − 7.5 ft² = 25 ft²; 25 ft² is area of the square, so each side of the square is 5 ft because 5 × 5 = 25

H.O.T. FOCUS ON HIGHER ORDER THINKING

Work Area

12. Represent Real-World Problems Christina plotted the shape of her garden on graph paper. She estimates that she will get about 15 carrots from each square unit. She plans to use the entire garden for carrots. About how many carrots can she expect to grow? Explain.

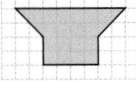

The area of the garden is 20 square units. Each square unit will grow about 15 carrots. So Christina will grow about 20(15), or 300, carrots.

13. Analyze Relationships The figure shown is made up of a triangle and a square. The perimeter of the figure is 56 inches. What is the area of the figure? Explain.

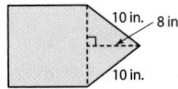

10 in. 8 in.
10 in.

The total length of three sides of the square is 56 − 20 = 36 in., so the side length of the square is 12 in. The area of the triangle is 48 in², and the area of the square is 144 in², so the total area is 192 in².

14. Critical Thinking The pattern for a scarf is shown at right. What is the area of the scarf? Use 3.14 for π.

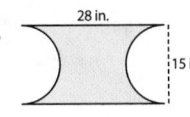

28 in.
15 in.

$243\frac{3}{8}$ in²

15. Persevere in Problem Solving The design for the palladium window shown includes a semicircular shape at the top. The bottom is formed by squares of equal size. A shade for the window will extend 4 inches beyond the perimeter of the window, shown by the dashed line around the window. Each square in the window has an area of 100 in².

a. What is the area of the window? Use 3.14 for π.

2,228 in²

b. What is the area of the shade? Round your answer to the nearest whole number.

3,016 in²

EXTEND THE MATH PRE-AP

Activity available online my.hrw.com

Activity Carol wants to build a mailbox like the one on the right. She designs the mailbox as a net consisting of simple shapes.

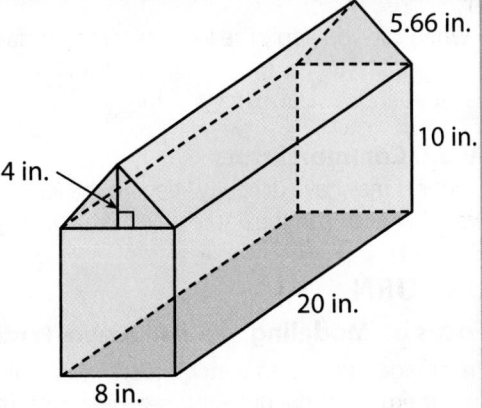

5.66 in.
10 in.
4 in.
20 in.
8 in.

A What is the area of the bottom? 160 in²

B What is the area of the front and back, including the triangular parts? 192 in²

C What is the total area of the two sides? 400 in²

D What is the total area of the roof? 226.4 in²

E What is the total area of the mailbox? 978.4 in²

F The wood is sold by the square foot and costs $8 per square foot. Rounded up to the nearest dollar, how much will it cost to buy the wood to build the mailbox? Hint: 1 ft² = 144 in². $54

LESSON
4.4 Solving Surface Area Problems

 Florida Common Core Standards

The student is expected to:

 **Geometry—7.G.2.6**

Solve real-world and mathematical problems involving area, volume and surface area of two- and three-dimensional objects composed of triangles, quadrilaterals, polygons, cubes, and right prisms.

Mathematical Practices

 **MP.4.1** Modeling

Engage

ESSENTIAL QUESTION

How can you find the surface area of a figure made up of cubes and prisms? Sample answer: Find the surface area of each of the cubes and prisms that make up the solid. Add the surface areas, and subtract the areas of any parts that are not on the surface.

Motivate the Lesson
Ask: How can you use the height of a prism and the perimeter and area of its base to find its total surface area? Take a guess. Begin the Explore Activity to find out.

Explore

EXPLORE ACTIVITY

Focus on Reasoning Mathematical Practices
You may wish to have students examine the formula for surface area algebraically. When finding the surface area by adding each face you get $(2)(8)(15) + (2)(20)(8) + (2)(20)(15)$. Using the Distributive Property you can rewrite this expression as $(2)(8)(15) + 20[(2)(8) + (2)(15)]$, which is the total area of both bases plus the height times the perimeter of the prism.

Explain

EXAMPLE 1

Questioning Strategies Mathematical Practices
• How do you decide which dimension is the length, width and height of the prism? First determine which side is a base. The longer edge on a base is commonly called the length, the shorter edge is commonly called the width, and the other edge is commonly called the height.

• When can you apply the formula for the surface area of a prism? This formula can be applied any time you want to find the surface area of any prism, as long as you know the height and the dimensions of the prism's base.

Avoid Common Errors
Students may have difficulty keeping the length, width, and height straight. Suggest they write l, w, and h on the figure next to the given dimensions.

YOUR TURN

Focus on Modeling Mathematical Practices
Encourage students to sketch a rectangular solid and label the given dimensions. This will help them insert the different measurements into the formula correctly.

ADDITIONAL EXAMPLE 1
Henry stores the arrowheads he has found in a box the shape of a rectangular prism. The box is 12 inches long, 12 inches wide and 2 inches high. He plans to paint the exterior of the box. How many square inches does he have to paint?

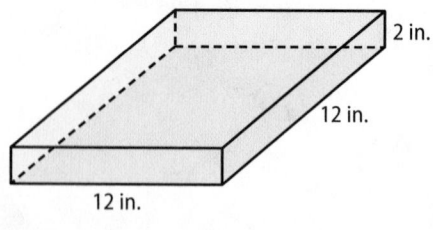

2 in.

12 in.

12 in.

384 in²

 Interactive Whiteboard
Interactive example available online

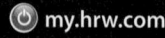 my.hrw.com

LESSON 4.4 Solving Surface Area Problems

FL CC 7.G.2.6
Solve real-world and mathematical problems involving ... surface area of ... three-dimensional objects composed of ... cubes and right prisms.

? ESSENTIAL QUESTION
How can you find the surface area of a figure made up of cubes and prisms?

EXPLORE ACTIVITY **FL CC 7.G.2.6**

Modeling Surface Area of a Prism

The surface area of a three-dimensional figure is the sum of the areas of all its surfaces. You know how to use the net of a figure to find its surface area. Now you will discover a formula that you can use.

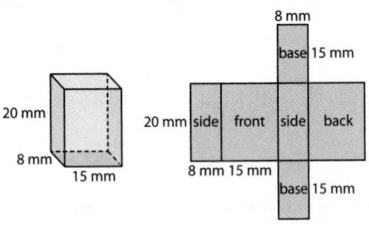

A The lateral area L of a prism is the area of all faces except the bases.

$L = 2(\underline{160 \text{ mm}^2}) + 2(\underline{300 \text{ mm}^2}) = \underline{920 \text{ mm}^2}$.

B The area B of each base is $\underline{120 \text{ mm}^2}$.

C The surface area S of the prism is the sum of the lateral area L and the total area of the bases, or $\underline{1,160 \text{ mm}^2}$.

Reflect

1. **Analyze Relationships** Use the net above to answer this question: How does the product of the perimeter P of the base of the prism and the height h of the prism compare to the lateral area L?

$$Ph = L$$

2. **Critical Thinking** How can you express the surface area S of the prism in terms of P, h, and B? Use your answer to Question 1.

$$S = Ph + 2B$$

Math On the Spot
my.hrw.com

Finding the Surface Area of a Prism

Given a prism's dimensions, you can use a formula to find the surface area.

Surface Area of a Prism

The surface area S of a prism with base perimeter P, height h, and base area B is $S = Ph + 2B$.

My Notes

EXAMPLE 1 Real World **FL CC 7.G.2.6**

Erin is making a jewelry box of wood in the shape of a rectangular prism. The jewelry box will have the dimensions shown. She plans to spray paint the exterior of the box. How many square inches will she have to paint?

6 in.
15 in.
12 in.

STEP 1 Make a sketch of the box. Drawing a diagram helps you understand and solve the problem.

STEP 2 Identify a base, and find its area and perimeter.

Any pair of opposite faces can be the bases. For example, you can choose the bottom and top of the box as the bases.

$B = \ell \times w$	$P = 2(12) + 2(15)$
$= 12 \times 15$	$= 24 + 30$
$= 180$ square inches	$= 54$ inches

STEP 3 Identify the height, and find the surface area.

The height h of the prism is 6 inches. Use the formula to find the surface area.

$S = Ph + 2B$

$S = 54(6) + 2(180) = 684$ square inches

Erin will have to spray paint 684 square inches of wood.

Math Talk Anno:
$S = 2\ell w + 2\ell h + 2wh$

Math Talk
Mathematical Practices

How can you express the formula for the surface area S of a rectangular prism in terms of its dimensions ℓ, w, and h?

Personal Math Trainer
Online Assessment and Intervention
my.hrw.com

YOUR TURN

3. A brand of uncooked spaghetti comes in a box that is a rectangular prism with a length of 9 inches, a width of 2 inches, and a height of $1\frac{1}{2}$ inches.

What is the surface area of the box? $\underline{69 \text{ in}^2}$

PROFESSIONAL DEVELOPMENT

Integrate Mathematical Practices MP.4.1

This lesson provides an opportunity to address this Mathematical Practice standard. It calls for students to model with mathematics. Students find the surface area of a prism by adding the area of each of its sides. They then analyze the relationship between the dimensions of the prism to find that the lateral area is equal to the product of the perimeter of a base and the height. Finally, they apply this knowledge to solve problems involving the surface area of prisms and composite figures.

Math Background

To visualize the faces of a prism and their dimensions, you can use a net. A net is a two-dimensional representation of a three-dimensional figure. When cut out, folded, and taped together the net should form a prism. There may be more than one way to draw a net for a prism. For example, there are 11 different nets that correctly represent a cube if you do not include mirror images.

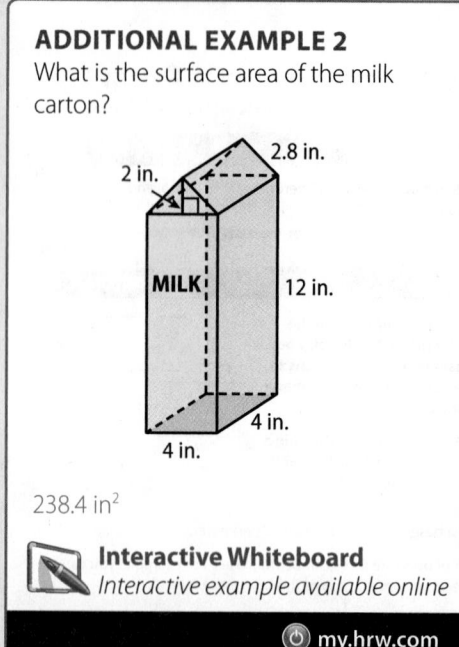
EXAMPLE 2

Questioning Strategies Mathematical Practices

• Once the circle for the opening in the birdhouse is cut out, what would you do to calculate the new surface area? Find the area of the circle and then subtract that from 3,720 cm².

• If you were to let the pentagonal faces be the bases, how could you find the perimeter of the base? All five lengths are given, so you would find 2(17) + 2(18) + 30 to get 100 cm.

YOUR TURN

Engage with the Whiteboard

For Exercise 4, have a series of volunteers each identify one flat surface of the stand that will be stained, then write and simplify an expression that represents the area of the surface. Have a final volunteer find the sum of the surfaces.

Elaborate

Talk About It
Summarize the Lesson

Ask: How does knowing how to find the surface area of prisms help you when finding the surface area of a composite solid? When a composite solid is made up of more than one prism, adding the surface area of each of the prisms and then subtracting any area not on the surface allows you to find the total surface area.

GUIDED PRACTICE

Engage with the Whiteboard

For Exercises 1 and 2, have volunteers show and explain the process of arriving at the correct values to input on the write-on lines.

Avoid Common Errors

Exercise 1 Remind students that the bases are the same size and shape, so the sides of the triangular base are 5 ft, 5 ft, and 8 ft. Because the triangular faces are the only two faces opposite each other, they are the only faces that can be used as bases.

Exercises 1 and 2 Explain to students that the dashed lines are lines that cannot be seen when looking at the solid from the perspective shown. They are the edges behind the solid. Knowing this should help students identify the bases and faces of these two figures more easily.

Finding the Surface Area of a Composite Solid

A composite solid is made up of two or more solid figures. To find the surface area of a composite solid, find the surface area of each figure. Subtract any area not on the surface.

Math On the Spot
my.hrw.com

EXAMPLE 2 · Problem Solving

FL CC 7.G.2.6

Daniel built the birdhouse shown. What was the surface area of the birdhouse before the hole was drilled?

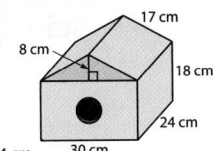
17 cm
8 cm
18 cm
24 cm
30 cm

Analyze Information

Identify the important information.

- The top is a triangular prism with $h = 24$ cm. The base is a triangle with height 8 cm and base 30 cm.
- The bottom is a rectangular prism with $h = 18$ cm. The base is a 30 cm by 24 cm rectangle.
- One face of each prism is not on the surface of the figure.

Formulate a Plan

Find the surface area of each prism.

Add the areas. Subtract the areas of the parts not on the surface.

Solve

Find the area of the triangular prism.

Perimeter $= 17 + 17 + 30 = 64$ cm; Base area $= \frac{1}{2}(30)(8) = 120$ cm²

Surface area $= Ph + 2B$

$= 64(24) + 2(120) = 1,776$ cm²

Find the area of the rectangular prism.

Perimeter $= 2(30) + 2(24) = 108$ cm; Base area $= 30(24) = 720$ cm²

Surface area $= Ph + 2B$

$= 108(18) + 2(720) = 3,384$ cm²

Add. Then subtract twice the areas of the parts not on the surface.

Surface area $= 1,776 + 3,384 - 2(720) = 3,720$ cm²

The surface area before the hole was drilled was 3,720 cm².

Justify and Evaluate

You can check your work by using a net to find the surface areas.

The bases are pentagons with $B = 660$ cm², the prism has $h = 24$ cm and $P = 100$ cm. So, $S = 100(24) + 2(660) = 3,720$ cm².

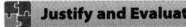
Math Talk
Mathematical Practices

How could you find the surface area by letting the front and back of the prism be the bases?

Lesson 4.4 **119**

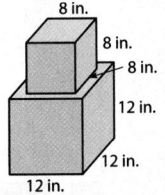
Personal Math Trainer
Online Assessment and Intervention
my.hrw.com

YOUR TURN

4. Dara is building a plant stand. She wants to stain the plant stand, except for the bottom of the larger prism. Find the surface area of the part of the plant stand she will stain. ___976 in²___

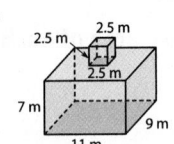
8 in.
8 in.
8 in.
12 in.
12 in.
12 in.

Guided Practice

Find the surface area of each solid figure. (Examples 1 and 2)

1.
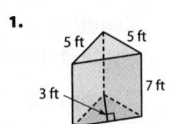
5 ft 5 ft
3 ft
7 ft
8 ft

Perimeter of base = ___18 ft___

Height = ___7 ft___

Base area = ___12 ft²___

Surface area:

$S = ($ ___18 ft___ $)($ ___7 ft___ $) + 2($ ___12 ft²___ $)$

$=$ ___150 ft²___

2.
2.5 m   2.5 m
2.5 m
7 m
11 m
9 m

Surface area of cube:

$S =$ ___37.5 m²___

Surface area of rectangular prism:

$S =$ ___478 m²___

Overlapping area: $A =$ ___6.25 m²___

Surface area of composite figure:

$=$ ___37.5___ $+$ ___478___ $- 2($ ___6.25___ $) =$

___503___ m²

? ESSENTIAL QUESTION CHECK-IN

3. How can you find the surface area of a composite solid made up of prisms?

Find the surface area of each of the prisms that make up the solid. Add the surface areas, and subtract the areas of any parts that are not on the surface.

120 Unit 2

DIFFERENTIATE INSTRUCTION

Curriculum Integration

Surface area is an important factor in the study of human biological systems. For example, humans often curl up their hands into fists when cold. In doing so they reduce the size of the surface area exposed to the cold air, thus reducing heat loss. Also, inside of a human pair of lungs, there are alveoli that have a total surface area of about 90 to 120 m². This large surface area means that carbon dioxide and oxygen can be released and absorbed more efficiently.

Kinesthetic Experience

Have students create their own composite solid. On grid paper have students draw the net for two solids, cut the nets out, and tape them together. Then have students glue the two solids together to form a composite solid. Have students find the surface area three ways: by counting the number of square units on the surface of their composite solid, by calculating and then adding/subtracting the area of each face, and finally by using the formula $S = Ph + 2B$.

Additional Resources

Differentiated Instruction includes:

- Reading Strategies
- Success for English Learners **ELL**
- Reteach
- Challenge **PRE-AP**

Solving Surface Area Problems **120**

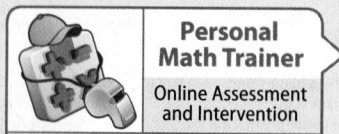
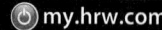
4.4 LESSON QUIZ

 **FL CC** 7.G.2.6

Find the surface area of each solid figure.

1.

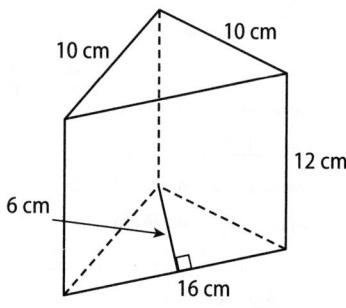

10 cm
10 cm
12 cm
6 cm
16 cm

2.

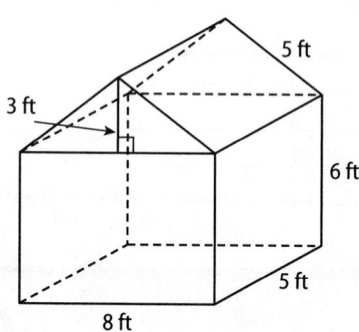

5 ft
3 ft
6 ft
5 ft
8 ft

3.

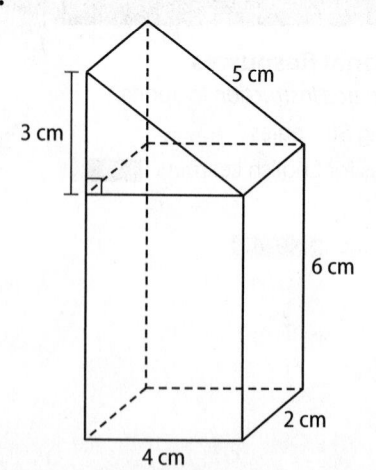

5 cm
3 cm
6 cm
2 cm
4 cm

Lesson Quiz available online

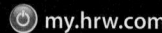 my.hrw.com

Evaluate

GUIDED AND INDEPENDENT PRACTICE

 **FL CC** 7.G.2.6

Concepts and Skills	Practice
Explore Activity Modeling Surface Area of a Prism	
Example 1 Finding the Surface Area of a Prism	Exercises 1, 4–5
Example 2 Finding the Surface Area of a Composite Solid	Exercises 2, 6–11

Exercise	Depth of Knowledge (D.O.K.)	**FL CC** Mathematical Practices
4–7	**2** Skills/Concepts	**MP.4.1** Modeling
8	**3** Strategic Thinking **H.O.T.**	**MP.7.1** Using Structure
9	**2** Skills/Concepts	**MP.4.1** Modeling
10	**2** Skills/Concepts	**MP.4.1** Modeling
11	**3** Strategic Thinking **H.O.T.**	**MP.3.1** Logic
12	**2** Skills/Concepts	**MP.4.1** Modeling
13	**3** Strategic Thinking **H.O.T.**	**MP.7.1** Using Structure
14	**2** Skills/Concepts	**MP.4.1** Modeling
15	**2** Skills/Concepts	**MP.4.1** Modeling
16	**3** Strategic Thinking **H.O.T.**	**MP.2.1** Reasoning

Additional Resources

Differentiated Instruction includes:
• Leveled Practice Worksheets

CLUSTER CONNECTION **Exercise 15** combines concepts from the Florida Common Core cluster "Solve real-life and mathematical problems involving angle measure, area, surface area, and volume."

Answers
1. 528 cm^2
2. 270 ft^2
3. 108 cm^2

Name _____ Class _____ Date _____

4.4 Independent Practice

FL CC 7.G.2.6

4. Carla is wrapping a present in the box shown. How much wrapping paper does she need, not including overlap?

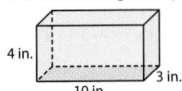

4 in. 10 in. 3 in.

164 in²

5. Dmitri wants to cover the top and sides of the box shown with glass tiles that are 5 mm square. How many tiles does he need?

9 cm 20 cm 15 cm

3,720 tiles

6. Shera is building a cabinet. She is making wooden braces for the corners of the cabinet. Find the surface area of each brace.

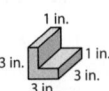

1 in. 3 in. 1 in. 3 in. 3 in.

46 in²

7. The doghouse shown has a floor, but no windows. Find the total surface area of the doghouse, including the door.

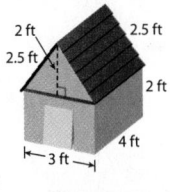

2 ft 2.5 ft 2.5 ft 2 ft 3 ft 4 ft

66 ft²

Eddie built the ramp shown to train his puppy to do tricks. Use the figure for 8–9.

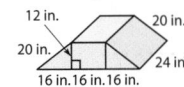

12 in. 20 in. 20 in. 24 in. 16 in. 16 in. 16 in.

8. **Analyze Relationships** Describe two ways to find the surface area of the ramp.

Treat the figure as (1) a composite of two triangular prisms and one rectangular prism, or (2) a prism with a base that is a trapezoid.

9. What is the surface area of the ramp?

3,264 in²

Marco and Elaine are building a stand like the one shown to display trophies. Use the figure for 10–11.

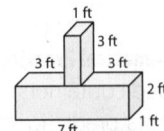

1 ft 3 ft 3 ft 3 ft 3 ft 2 ft 1 ft 7 ft 1 ft

10. What is the surface area of the stand?

58 ft²

11. **Critique Reasoning** Marco and Elaine want to paint the entire stand silver. A can of paint covers 25 square feet and costs $6.79. They set aside $15 for paint. Is that enough? Explain.

No; they need 3 cans, which will cost 3($6.79) = $20.37.

Lesson 4.4 **121**

12. Henry wants to cover the box shown with paper without any overlap. How many square centimeters will be covered with paper?

10 cm 27 cm 24 cm

2,316 cm²

13. **What If?** Suppose the length and width of the box in Exercise 12 double. Does the surface area S double? Explain.

No; Ph doubles, and 2B quadruples. S more than doubles.

H.O.T. FOCUS ON HIGHER ORDER THINKING

Work Area

14. **Persevere in Problem Solving** Enya is building a storage cupboard in the shape of a rectangular prism. The rectangular prism has a square base with side lengths of 2.5 feet and a height of 3.5 feet. Compare the amount of paint she would use to paint all but the bottom surface of the prism to the amount she would use to paint the entire prism.

Sample answer: She would be painting about 87% of the total surface area, so she would use about 87% of the amount of paint.

15. **Interpret the Answer** The oatmeal box shown is shaped like a cylinder. Use a net to find the surface area S of the oatmeal box to the nearest tenth. Then find the number of square feet of cardboard needed for 1,500 oatmeal boxes. Round your answer to the nearest whole number.

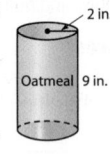

2 in. Oatmeal 9 in.

138.2 in²; 1,440 ft² of cardboard

16. **Analyze Relationships** A prism is made of centimeter cubes. How can you find the surface area of the prism in Figure 1 without using a net or a formula? How does the surface area change in Figures 2, 3, and 4? Explain.

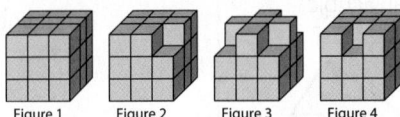

Figure 1 Figure 2 Figure 3 Figure 4

Each face has 9 squares 1 cm by 1 cm, so S = 54 cm². The surface area stays the same when one or more corner cubes are removed (Fig. 2, 3), because the number of faces showing is still the same. In Fig. 4, S increases because 2 more faces show.

EXTEND THE MATH PRE-AP

Activity available online my.hrw.com

Activity Describe what happens to the surface area of a cube when the edge lengths are doubled, tripled, quadrupled, or increased by a factor of n.

When the edge length is doubled, the surface area is 4 times as large. When the edge length is tripled, the surface area is 9 times as large. When the edge length is quadrupled, the surface area is 16 times as large. When the edge length is increased by a factor of n, the surface area is n^2 times as large.

LESSON 4.5 Solving Volume Problems

Florida Common Core Standards

The student is expected to:

 **Geometry—7.G.2.6**

Solve real-world and mathematical problems involving area, volume and surface area of two- and three-dimensional objects composed of triangles, quadrilaterals, polygons, cubes, and right prisms.

Mathematical Practices

 **MP.7.1** Using Structure

---

ADDITIONAL EXAMPLE 1

A shipping carton is in the shape of a triangular prism. How many cubic inches of space are in the carton?

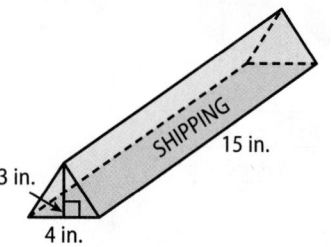

90 in^3

 Interactive Whiteboard
Interactive example available online

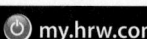 my.hrw.com

---

ADDITIONAL EXAMPLE 2

A box is in the shape of a trapezoidal prism. How many cubic centimeters of space are in the box?

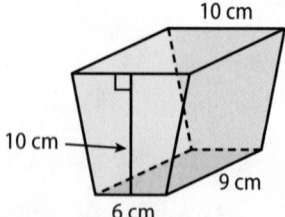

720 cm^3

 Interactive Whiteboard
Interactive example available online

 my.hrw.com

---

Engage

ESSENTIAL QUESTION

How can you find the volume of a figure made of cubes and prisms? Sample answer: Find the volume of each individual cube and prism that makes up the solid using the formula $V = Bh$. Then add the volumes of all the cubes and prisms to find the total volume.

Motivate the Lesson

Ask: What do you use to represent how much space something takes up? How do you compare the capacities of different containers? Take a guess. Begin the lesson to find out.

Explore

Focus on Reasoning ⚐ Mathematical Practices

Show students different prism-shaped containers and ask them to speculate as to which container can hold more. Test students' predictions by filling one container with rice and then pouring that rice into the other containers to determine which holds the most.

Explain

EXAMPLE 1

Questioning Strategies ⚐ Mathematical Practices

• How do you determine which edge is the height of the prism? First find the bases of the prism. The height is any edge perpendicular to the bases.

Avoid Common Errors

Given the orientation of the prism, students may think that the face it is sitting on is the base. Review with students how to identify the base of a prism.

YOUR TURN

Engage with the Whiteboard

Have a volunteer draw additional lines on the prism to turn it into a rectangular prism that is 7 m × 24 m × 22 m. Discuss with students how visualizing this can help them check that their answer is reasonable.

EXAMPLE 2

Questioning Strategies ⚐ Mathematical Practices

• How is the variable B different from b_1 or b_2? B stands for the area of the base. The base is a trapezoid with two linear bases called b_1 and b_2 in the formula for the area of a trapezoid.

Avoid Common Errors

Students may think that the variable h in Steps 1 and 2 has the same value. Point out that in Step 1 h is the height of the base, while in Step 2 h is the height of the prism.

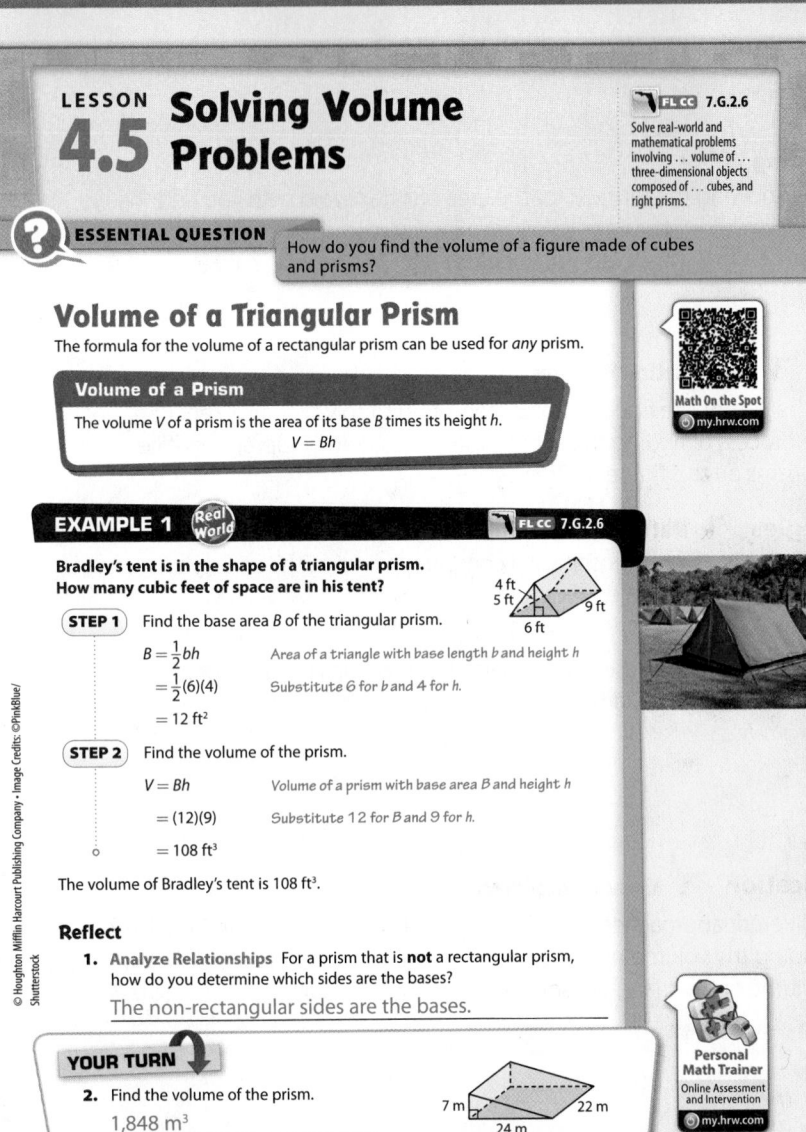

LESSON 4.5 Solving Volume Problems

FL CC 7.G.2.6
Solve real-world and mathematical problems involving ... volume of ... three-dimensional objects composed of ... cubes, and right prisms.

? ESSENTIAL QUESTION How do you find the volume of a figure made of cubes and prisms?

Volume of a Triangular Prism

The formula for the volume of a rectangular prism can be used for *any* prism.

Volume of a Prism

The volume V of a prism is the area of its base B times its height h.
$$V = Bh$$

EXAMPLE 1 Real World **FL CC** 7.G.2.6

Bradley's tent is in the shape of a triangular prism. How many cubic feet of space are in his tent?

STEP 1 Find the base area B of the triangular prism.

$B = \frac{1}{2}bh$ Area of a triangle with base length b and height h

$= \frac{1}{2}(6)(4)$ Substitute 6 for b and 4 for h.

$= 12 \text{ ft}^2$

STEP 2 Find the volume of the prism.

$V = Bh$ Volume of a prism with base area B and height h

$= (12)(9)$ Substitute 12 for B and 9 for h.

$= 108 \text{ ft}^3$

The volume of Bradley's tent is 108 ft³.

Reflect

1. **Analyze Relationships** For a prism that is **not** a rectangular prism, how do you determine which sides are the bases?

   The non-rectangular sides are the bases.

YOUR TURN

2. Find the volume of the prism.

   1,848 m³

Math On the Spot
my.hrw.com

Lesson 4.5 **123**

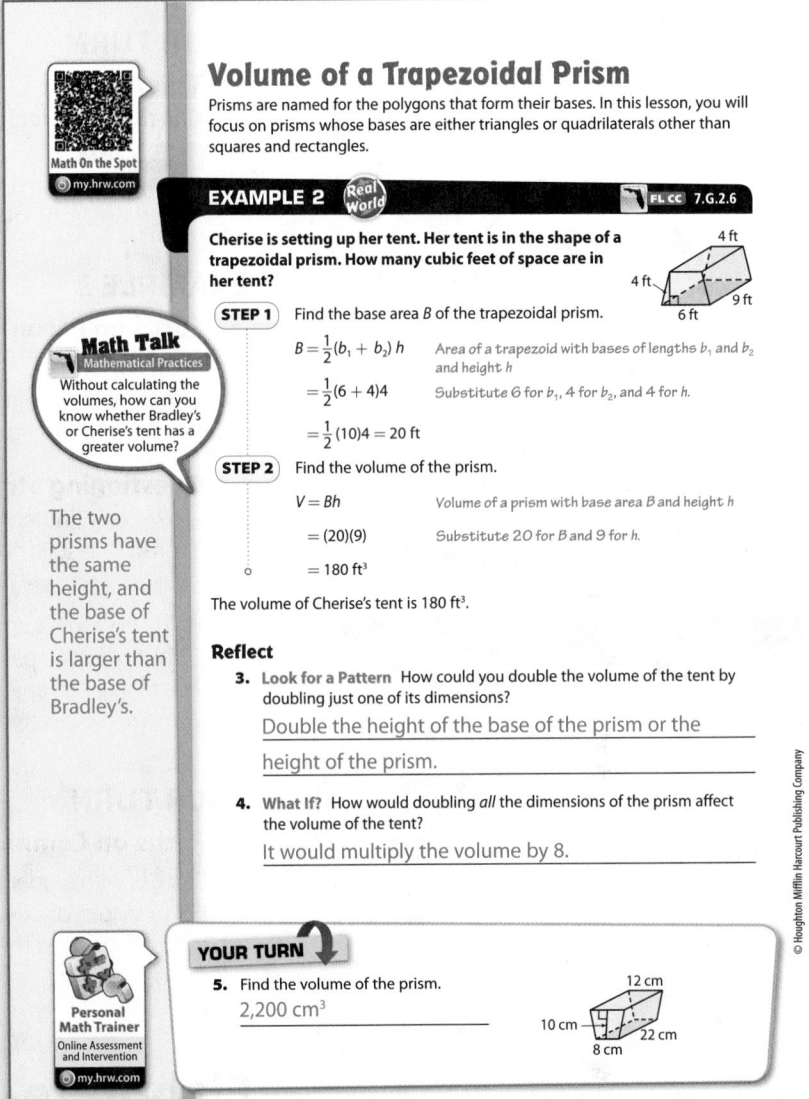

Volume of a Trapezoidal Prism

Prisms are named for the polygons that form their bases. In this lesson, you will focus on prisms whose bases are either triangles or quadrilaterals other than squares and rectangles.

Math On the Spot
my.hrw.com

EXAMPLE 2 Real World **FL CC** 7.G.2.6

Cherise is setting up her tent. Her tent is in the shape of a trapezoidal prism. How many cubic feet of space are in her tent?

STEP 1 Find the base area B of the trapezoidal prism.

$B = \frac{1}{2}(b_1 + b_2)h$ Area of a trapezoid with bases of lengths b_1 and b_2 and height h

$= \frac{1}{2}(6 + 4)4$ Substitute 6 for b_1, 4 for b_2, and 4 for h.

$= \frac{1}{2}(10)4 = 20 \text{ ft}$

STEP 2 Find the volume of the prism.

$V = Bh$ Volume of a prism with base area B and height h

$= (20)(9)$ Substitute 20 for B and 9 for h.

$= 180 \text{ ft}^3$

The volume of Cherise's tent is 180 ft³.

Math Talk
Mathematical Practices

Without calculating the volumes, how can you know whether Bradley's or Cherise's tent has a greater volume?

The two prisms have the same height, and the base of Cherise's tent is larger than the base of Bradley's.

Reflect

3. **Look for a Pattern** How could you double the volume of the tent by doubling just one of its dimensions?

   Double the height of the base of the prism or the height of the prism.

4. **What If?** How would doubling *all* the dimensions of the prism affect the volume of the tent?

   It would multiply the volume by 8.

YOUR TURN

5. Find the volume of the prism.

   2,200 cm³

Personal Math Trainer
Online Assessment and Intervention
my.hrw.com

124 Unit 2

PROFESSIONAL DEVELOPMENT

Integrate Mathematical Practices MP.7.1

This lesson provides an opportunity to address this Mathematical Practice standard. It calls for students to look for and make use of structure. Students are shown a general formula for finding the volume of any prism. This allows students to see the structure of various volume formulas they may have learned in the past. They develop an understanding of the connection between the area of a prism's 2-dimensional base and its 3-dimensional volume.

Math Background

To convert from one unit of volume to another, you can use conversion factors. For example, to convert cubic yards to cubic feet, you can cube both sides of the conversion factor 1 yd = 3 ft to find that $1 \text{ yd}^3 = (3 \text{ ft})^3$ or 27 ft³. Thus, to find the number of cubic feet in a number of cubic yards, you must multiply by 27.

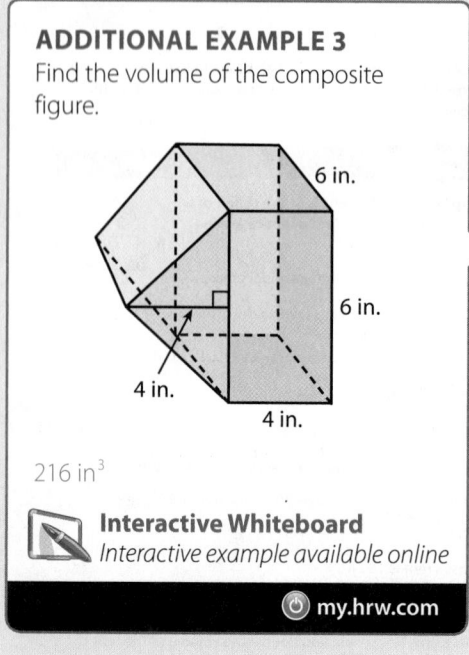
YOUR TURN

Talk About It
Check for Understanding

💬 **Ask:** How does knowing the formula for the area of a trapezoid help you find the volume of the prism? The volume of prism is found by multiplying the area of its base times its height. The prism in Exercise 5 is a trapezoidal prism. Its base is a trapezoid.

EXAMPLE 3

Focus on Patterns 🏴 Mathematical Practices

Explain that analyzing the composite figure before attempting to solve the problem can sometimes shorten the process of finding the solution. In this case, it is helpful to notice that the left and right prisms on this figure are identical.

Questioning Strategies 🏴 Mathematical Practices

• How does finding the volume of a composite solid compare to finding the surface area of a composite solid? In both cases you add each part to get the whole. However, when finding the total volume you do not subtract as you do when finding the total surface area.

• Why do you have a choice of bases to use in each part of the composite figure for Example 3 but only one pair of bases to use in Example 2? All sides of a rectangular prism are rectangles, so any pair of sides that are opposite each other can be the bases. A trapezoidal prism only has two sides that are trapezoids, so those two sides must be the bases.

YOUR TURN

Focus on Communication 🏴 Mathematical Practices

Discuss with students different approaches to finding the volume of the figure in Exercise 7. For example, discuss finding the volume of a 13 in. × 22 in. × 30 in. rectangular solid and then subtracting the volume of the triangular solid as a method for finding the volume of the given figure.

Elaborate

Talk About It
Summarize the Lesson

💬 **Ask:** How does knowing how to find the volume of prisms help you when finding the volume of a composite solid? When a composite solid is made up of multiple prisms, the volumes of the individual prisms can be added to find the total volume.

GUIDED PRACTICE

Engage with the Whiteboard

 For Exercises 1 and 2, have volunteers label different parts of the figure with the appropriate variables from both formulas.

Avoid Common Errors

Exercise 4 Suggest that students break down the volume of the composite figure into the two prisms whose volume they must find, as was done in Exercise 3.

Volume of a Composite Solid

You can use the formula for the volume of a prism to find the volume of a composite figure that is made up of prisms.

EXAMPLE 3 FL CC 7.G.2.6

Allie has two aquariums connected by a small square prism. Find the volume of the double aquarium.

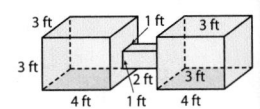

STEP 1 Find the volume of each of the larger aquariums.

$V = Bh$ Volume of a prism

    $= (12)(3)$ Substitute $3 \times 4 = 12$ for B and 3 for h.

    $= 36$ ft³

STEP 2 Find the volume of the connecting prism.

$V = Bh$ Volume of a prism

    $= (1)(2)$ Substitute $1 \times 1 = 1$ for B and 2 for h.

    $= 2$ ft³

STEP 3 Add the volumes of the three parts of the aquarium.

$V = 36 + 36 + 2 = 74$ ft³

The volume of the aquarium is 74 ft³.

Reflect

6. What If? Find the volume of one of the large aquariums on either end using another pair of opposite sides as the bases. Do you still get the same volume? Explain.

Yes; to find the volume *V*, you still multiply the same

dimensions: 3, 3, and 4.

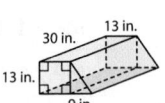

YOUR TURN

7. The figure is composed of a rectangular prism and a triangular prism. Find the volume of the figure.

6,825 in³

Personal Math Trainer
Online Assessment and Intervention
my.hrw.com

Math On the Spot
my.hrw.com

My Notes

---

1. Find the volume of the triangular prism. (Example 1)

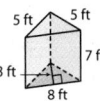

$B = \frac{1}{2}bh = \frac{1}{2}(8)(3) = 12$ ft²   [2]

$V = Bh = \left(\boxed{12} \times \boxed{7}\right)$ ft³   [3] $= \boxed{84}$ ft³

2. Find the volume of the trapezoidal prism. (Example 2)

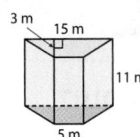

$B = \frac{1}{2}(b_1 + b_2)h = \frac{1}{2}(15 + 5)(3) = 30$ m²   [2]

$V = Bh = \left(\boxed{30} \times \boxed{11}\right)$ m³   [3] $= \boxed{330}$ m³

3. Find the volume of the composite figure. (Example 3)

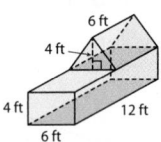

Volume of rectangular prism = 288 ft³

Volume of triangular prism = 72 ft³

Volume of composite figure = 360 ft³

Find the volume of each figure. (Examples 2 and 3)

4. The figure shows a barn that Mr. Fowler is building for his farm.

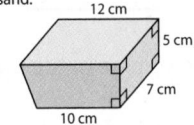

40,000 ft³

5. The figure shows a container that Pete filled with sand.

385 cm³

❓ ESSENTIAL QUESTION CHECK-IN

6. How do you find the volume of a composite solid formed by two or more prisms?

Find the volume of each prism using the formula

$V = Bh$. Then add the volumes of all the prisms.

DIFFERENTIATE INSTRUCTION

Number Sense

Computing a volume involves multiplying three dimensions. Sometimes the order in which you multiply those dimensions can make the computation easier. Sometimes the order does not matter at all. For example, if a rectangular solid had a length of 15, width of 23, and a height of 9, you multiply 15(23)(9) to get the volume. Multiplying these factors in any order does not make a difference in the difficulty of the computation. However, if the solid had had a length of 25, width of 16, and a height of 4, you would want to multiply in this order 25(4)(16) because 25(4) = 100 and you can finish the computation mentally to get 1,600.

Visual Cues

Have students create their own "cue sheet" of area formulas on an index card. They can use this sheet to help them recall the formulas for the area of the bases in prisms for which they are asked to find the volumes. Including a sketch of the two-dimensional shapes will also be helpful.

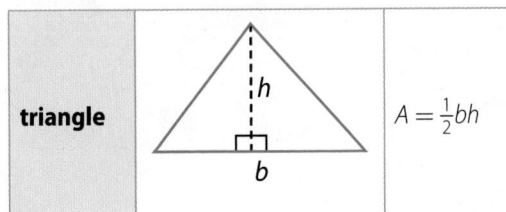

triangle $A = \frac{1}{2}bh$

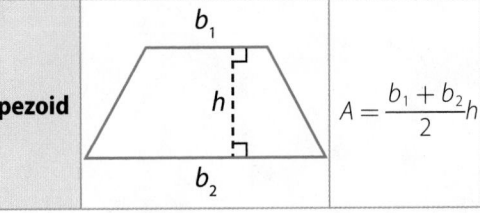

trapezoid $A = \frac{b_1 + b_2}{2}h$

Additional Resources

Differentiated Instruction includes:

• Reading Strategies
• Success for English Learners **ELL**
• Reteach
• Challenge **PRE-AP**

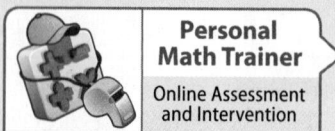

1. Find the volume of the triangular prism.

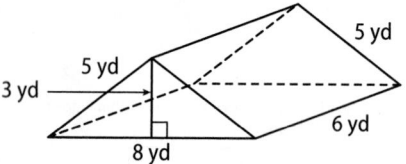

2. Find the volume of the trapezoidal prism.

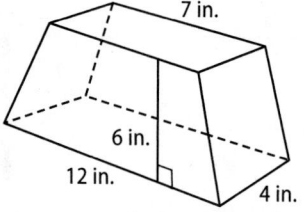

3. How many cubic feet of water can the in-ground swimming pool design below hold?

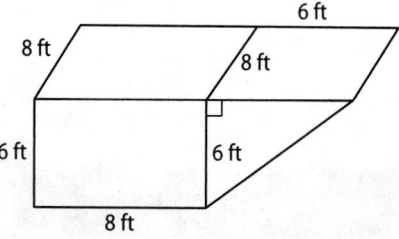

Lesson Quiz available online

⏻ my.hrw.com

Answers

1. 72 yd³

2. 228 in³

3. 528 ft³

Evaluate

GUIDED AND INDEPENDENT PRACTICE

 FL CC **7.G.2.6**

Concepts and Skills	Practice
Example 1 Finding the Volume of a Triangular Prism	Exercises 1, 7–9, 11, 14, 15
Example 2 Finding the Volume of a Trapezoidal Prism	Exercises 2, 5, 10, 15
Example 3 Finding the Volume of a Composite Solid	Exercises 3, 4, 10, 12, 13

Exercise	Depth of Knowledge (D.O.K.)	FL CC Mathematical Practices
7–10	**2** Skills/Concepts	**MP.4.1** Modeling
11	**3** Strategic Thinking H.O.T.	**MP.3.1** Logic
12–13	**2** Skills/Concepts	**MP.4.1** Modeling
14	**2** Skills/Concepts	**MP.2.1** Reasoning
15	**3** Strategic Thinking H.O.T.	**MP.2.1** Reasoning
16	**2** Skills/Concepts	**MP.2.1** Reasoning
17	**2** Skills/Concepts	**MP.4.1** Modeling
18	**3** Strategic Thinking H.O.T.	**MP.7.1** Using Structure
19	**2** Skills/Concepts	**MP.2.1** Reasoning

Additional Resources

Differentiated Instruction includes:

• Leveled Practice worksheets

 **CLUSTER CONNECTION**

Exercise 18 combines concepts from the Florida Common Core cluster "Solve real-life and mathematical problems involving angle measure, area, surface area, and volume."

Name _____ Class _____ Date _____

4.5 Independent Practice

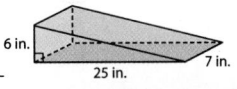 FL CC 7.G.2.6

Personal Math Trainer
Online Assessment and Intervention
my.hrw.com

7. A trap for insects is in the shape of a triangular prism. The area of the base is 3.5 in² and the height of the prism is 5 in. What is the volume of this trap?

17.5 in³

8. Arletta built a cardboard ramp for her little brothers' toy cars. Identify the shape of the ramp. Then find its volume.

triangular prism; 525 in³

6 in.
25 in.
7 in.

9. Alex made a sketch for a homemade soccer goal he plans to build. The goal will be in the shape of a triangular prism. The legs of the right triangles at the sides of his goal measure 4 ft and 8 ft, and the opening along the front is 24 ft. How much space is contained within this goal?

384 ft³

10. A gift box is in the shape of a trapezoidal prism with base lengths of 7 inches and 5 inches and a height of 4 inches. The height of the gift box is 8 inches. What is the volume of the gift box?

192 in³

11. **Explain the Error** A student wrote this statement: "A triangular prism has a height of 15 inches and a base area of 20 square inches. The volume of the prism is 300 square inches." Identify and correct the error.

The units for volume are incorrect; the volume is 300 cubic inches.

Find the volume of each figure. Round to the nearest hundredth if necessary.

12. B ≈ 23.4 in²

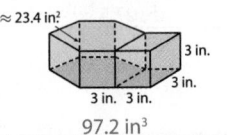
3 in.
3 in.
3 in. 3 in.

97.2 in³

13.

7.5 m
7.5 m
3.75 m
15 m
3.75 m

316.41 m³

14. **Multi-Step** Josie has 260 cubic centimeters of candle wax. She wants to make a hexagonal prism candle with a base area of 21 square centimeters and a height of 8 centimeters. She also wants to make a triangular prism candle with a height of 14 centimeters. Can the base area of the triangular prism candle be 7 square centimeters? Explain.

No; the area must be less than or equal to about 6.57 cm².

Lesson 4.5 **127**

---

15. A movie theater offers popcorn in two different containers for the same price. One container is a trapezoidal prism with a base area of 36 square inches and a height of 5 inches. The other container is a triangular prism with a base area of 32 square inches and a height of 6 inches. Which container is the better deal? Explain.

Triangular prism; you get 192 in³ for the same price you would pay for 180 in³ with the trapezoidal prism.

H.O.T. FOCUS ON HIGHER ORDER THINKING

Work Area

16. **Critical Thinking** The wading pool shown is a trapezoidal prism with a total volume of 286 cubic feet. What is the missing dimension?

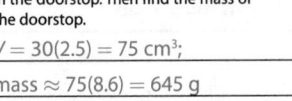
13 ft
2 ft
?
8 ft

3.5 ft

17. **Persevere in Problem Solving** Lynette has a metal doorstop with the dimensions shown. Each cubic centimeter of the metal in the doorstop has a mass of about 8.6 grams. Find the volume of the metal in the doorstop. Then find the mass of the doorstop.

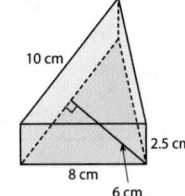
10 cm
2.5 cm
8 cm
6 cm

$V = 30(2.5) = 75$ cm³;

mass ≈ 75(8.6) = 645 g

18. **Analyze Relationships** What effect would tripling all the dimensions of a triangular prism have on the volume of the prism? Explain your reasoning.

If both the base and height of the triangular base are tripled, the area of the base is multiplied by 9. Tripling the height of the prism as well means the volume of the prism is multiplied by 27.

19. **Persevere in Problem Solving** Each of two trapezoidal prisms has a volume of 120 cubic centimeters. The prisms have no dimensions in common. Give possible dimensions for each prism.

Sample answers: (1) height of trapezoid = 4 cm, base lengths = 2 cm and 6 cm, height of prism = 7.5 cm (2) height of trapezoid = 2.5 cm, base lengths = 1 cm and 7 cm, height of prism = 12 cm

128 Unit 2

EXTEND THE MATH   PRE-AP

Activity available online ⊙ my.hrw.com

Activity The edge of a cube is 4 cm. What happens to the volume of the cube if its height doubles? What if its height and length both double? Or its height, length, and width all double?

If the height doubles, the volume also doubles from 64 cm³ to 128 cm³. If the height and length both double, the volume is multiplied by 4, from 64 cm³ to 256 cm³. If the height, length, and width all double, the volume is multiplied by 8, from 64 cm³ to 512 cm³.

Solving Volume Problems **128**

Ready to Go On?

Assess Mastery

Use the assessment on this page to determine if students have mastered the concepts and standards covered in this module.

 **Response to Intervention**

 Personal Math Trainer
Online Assessment and Intervention
⏱ my.hrw.com

Intervention	Enrichment
Access Ready to Go On? Assessment online, and receive instant scoring, feedback, and customized intervention or enrichment.	

Online and Print Resources

Differentiated Instruction
- Reteach worksheets
- Reading Strategies **ELL**
- Success for English Learners **ELL**

Differentiated Instruction
- Challenge worksheets **PRE-AP**
- Extend the Math **PRE-AP** Lesson Activities in TE

Additional Resources

Assessment Resources includes:
- Leveled Module Quizzes

Ready to Go On?

 Personal Math Trainer
Online Assessment and Intervention
⏱ my.hrw.com

4.1, 4.2 Circumference and Area of Circles
Find the circumference and area of each circle. Use 3.14 for π.

1.
 7 m
43.96 m; 153.86 m²

2.
12 ft
37.68 ft; 113.04 ft²

4.3 Area of Composite Figures
Find the area of each figure. Use 3.14 for π.

3.
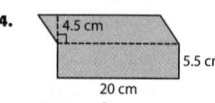 10 m, 16 m
180.48 m²

4.
4.5 cm, 5.5 cm, 20 cm
200 cm²

4.4, 4.5 Solving Surface Area and Volume Problems
Find the surface area and volume of each figure.

5.
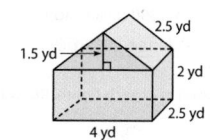 5 cm, 10 cm, 3 cm, 4 cm
132 cm²; 60 cm³

6.
2.5 yd, 1.5 yd, 2 yd, 2.5 yd, 4 yd
54.5 yd²; 27.5 yd³

 **ESSENTIAL QUESTION**

7. How can you use geometry figures to solve real-world problems?
Sample answer: You can use a composite figure to model a room, then find surface area to decide how much paint you need to paint the room.

© Houghton Mifflin Harcourt Publishing Company

 Florida Common Core Standards

Lesson	Exercises	🏴 Common Core Standards
4.1	1–2	**7.G.2.4**
4.2	1–2	**7.G.2.4**
4.3	3–4	**7.G.2.6**
4.4	5–6	**7.G.2.6**
4.5	5–6	**7.G.2.6**

PARCC Assessment Readiness

Assessment Readiness Tip In addition to knowing various geometric formulas, students must be prepared to modify the formulas or the measurements they are given in order to correctly answer problems.

Item 1 Students can use the formula $C = \pi d$ for finding the circumference of a circle but must remember to first double the radius to find the diameter.

Item 3 Students can use the formula for the area of a circle and the formula for the area of a rectangle, but they will have to adapt them. They should multiply the area of the circle by 0.25, and they need to realize that a square is a type of rectangle.

Avoid Common Errors

Item 2 Some students may forget that they are given the diameter and need to divide it by 2 to find the radius before finding the area of the circle. Remind students to be sure they have all of the elements of a formula before plugging things in.

Item 5 Some students may simply multiply the three measurements together, treating the prism as if it were rectangular. Remind them that the area of the base of a triangular prism is *half* of the product of the base and the height of the triangle.

Additional Resources

Personal Math Trainer

Online Assessment and Intervention

my.hrw.com

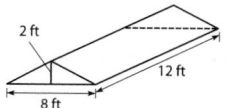

PARCC Assessment Readiness

Personal Math Trainer

Online Assessment and Intervention

my.hrw.com

Selected Response

1. What is the circumference of the circle?

11 m

- Ⓐ 34.54 m
- Ⓑ 69.08 m
- Ⓒ 379.94 m
- Ⓓ 1,519.76 m

2. What is the area of the circle?

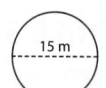

15 m

- Ⓐ 23.55 m²   Ⓒ 176.625 m²
- Ⓑ 47.1 m²   Ⓓ 706.5 m²

3. What is the area of the figure?

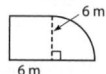

6 m

6 m

- Ⓐ 28.26 m²   Ⓒ 64.26 m²
- Ⓑ 36 m²   Ⓓ 92.52 m²

4. A one-year membership to a health club costs $480. This includes a $150 fee for new members that is paid when joining. Which equation represents the monthly cost x in dollars for a new member?

- Ⓐ $12x + 150 = 480$
- Ⓑ $\frac{x}{12} + 150 = 480$
- Ⓒ $12x + 480 = 150$
- Ⓓ $\frac{x}{12} + 480 = 150$

5. What is the volume of the prism?

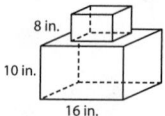

2 ft

12 ft

8 ft

- Ⓐ 192 ft³
- Ⓑ 48 ft³
- Ⓒ 69 ft³
- Ⓓ 96 ft³

6. The price of mailing a small package is $0.32 for the first ounce and $0.21 for each additional ounce. Sandra paid $1.16 to mail her package. How much did it weigh?

- Ⓐ 4 ounces
- Ⓑ 5 ounces
- Ⓒ 6 ounces
- Ⓓ 7 ounces

Mini-Task

7. Each dimension of the smaller prism is half the corresponding dimension of the larger prism.

8 in.

10 in.

16 in.

a. What is the surface area of the figure?

856 in²

b. What is the volume of the figure?

1,440 in³

 Florida Common Core Standards

Items	🏴 Grade 7 Standards	🏴 Mathematical Practices
1	7.G.2.4	MP.2.1
2	7.G.2.4	MP.2.1
3	7.G.2.6	MP.2.1
4*	7.EE.2.4	MP.4.1
5	7.G.2.6	MP.2.1
6*	7.EE.2.4a	MP.4.1
7	7.G.2.6	MP.4.1

* Item integrates mixed review concepts from previous modules or a previous course.

Study Guide Review

Vocabulary Development

Integrating Language Arts

Encourage students to practice using the unit vocabulary as they talk and write about mathematics. Understanding vocabulary will aid their understanding of the concepts.

🏴 **FL CC** **LACC.68.RST.2.4** Determine the meaning of symbols, key terms, and other domain-specific words and phrases as they are used in a specific scientific or technical context relevant to grades 6–8 texts and topics.

MODULE 3 Modeling Geometric Figures

🏴 **FL CC** **7.G.1.1, 7.G.1.2, 7.G.1.3, 7.G.2.5**

Key Concepts
• In a scale drawing, the dimensions of an object are related to the dimensions of the actual object by a ratio called the scale factor. *(Lesson 3.1)*
• The sum of the angles of a triangle is 180° *(Lesson 3.2)*
• Two-dimensional figures are formed when a plane slices through a three-dimensional object. *(Lesson 3.3)*
• The sum of the measures of a pair of complementary angles is 90°, and the sum of the measures of a pair of supplementary angles is 180°. *(Lesson 3.4)*
• Vertical angles are the opposite angles formed by two intersecting lines that are congruent. *(Lesson 3.4)*

Study Guide Review

MODULE 3 **Modeling Geometric Figures**

? ESSENTIAL QUESTION

How can you apply geometry concepts to solve real-world problems?

EXAMPLE 1

Use the scale drawing to find the perimeter of Tim's yard.

15 cm

4 cm

2 cm : 14 ft

$\frac{2\text{ cm}}{14\text{ ft}} = \frac{1\text{ cm}}{7\text{ ft}}$ 1 cm in the drawing equals 7 feet in the actual yard.

$\frac{1\text{ cm} \times 15}{7\text{ ft} \times 15} = \frac{15\text{ cm}}{105\text{ ft}}$ 15 cm in the drawing equals 105 feet in the actual yard. Tim's yard is 105 feet long.

$\frac{1\text{ cm} \times 4}{7\text{ ft} \times 4} = \frac{4\text{ cm}}{28\text{ ft}}$ 4 cm in the drawing equals 7 feet in the actual yard. Tim's yard is 28 feet wide.

Perimeter is twice the sum of the length and the width. So the perimeter of Tim's yard is 2(105 + 28) = 2(133), or 266 feet.

EXAMPLE 2

Find (a) the value of x and (b) the measure of ∠APY.

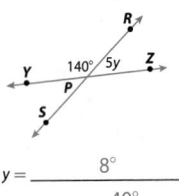

3x 78°

a. ∠XPB and ∠YPB are supplementary.

$3x + 78° = 180°$

$3x = 102°$

$x = 34°$

b. ∠APY and ∠XPB are vertical angles.

$m\angle APY = m\angle XPB = 3x = 102°$

Key Vocabulary

adjacent angles (*ángulos adyacentes*)
complementary angles (*ángulos complementarios*)
congruent angles (*ángulos congruentes*)
cross section (*sección transversal*)
intersection (*intersección*)
scale (*escala*)
scale drawing (*dibujo a escala*)
supplementary angles (*ángulos suplementarios*)
vertical angles (*ángulos opuestos por el vértice*)

---

1. In the scale drawing of a park, the scale is 1 cm : 10 m. Find the area of the actual park.

(Lesson 3.1) _____ 450 m² _____

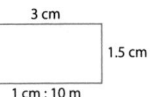

3 cm

1.5 cm

1 cm : 10 m

2. Find the value of y and the measure of ∠YPS (Lesson 3.4)

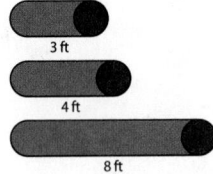

140° 5y

$y = $ _____ 8° _____

$m\angle YPS = $ _____ 40° _____

3. Kanye wants to make a triangular flower bed using logs with the lengths shown below to form the border. Can Kanye form a triangle with the logs without cutting any of them? Explain. (Lesson 3.2)

3 ft

4 ft

8 ft

No, he will not be able to make a triangle, because the sum of the lengths of the two shorter logs is less than the length of the longest log.

4. In shop class, Adriana makes a pyramid with a 4-inch square base and a height of 6 inches. She then cuts the pyramid vertically in half as shown. What is the area of each cut surface? (Lesson 3.3)

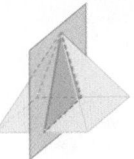

12 in²

MODULE 4 Circumference, Area, and Volume

FL CC 7.G.2.4, 7.G.2.6

Key Concepts

- To find the circumference of a circle, or the distance around the circle, use the formula $C = \pi d$ or $C = 2\pi r$. *(Lesson 4.1)*

- To find the area of a circle, use the formula $A = \pi r^2$. *(Lesson 4.2)*

- The area of a complex shape can be found by finding the sum of the areas of known geometric shapes that conform to the complex shape. *(Lesson 4.3)*

- The total surface area of a figure is the area of all the faces of the figure. *(Lesson 4.4)*

- To find the volume of a prism, use the formula $V = Bh$, where B is the area of the base. *(Lesson 4.5)*

 MODULE 4

Circumference, Area, and Volume

? ESSENTIAL QUESTION

How can you use geometry concepts to solve real-world problems?

Key Vocabulary

circumference *(circunferencia)*

composite figure *(figura compuesta)*

diameter *(diámetro)*

radius *(radio)*

EXAMPLE 1

Find the area of the composite figure. It consists of a semicircle and a rectangle.

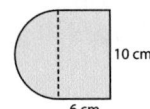

10 cm

6 cm

Area of semicircle $= 0.5(\pi r^2)$

$\approx 0.5(3.14)25$

$\approx 39.25 \text{ cm}^2$

Area of rectangle $= \ell w$

$= 10(6)$

$= 60 \text{ cm}^2$

The area of the composite figure is approximately 99.25 square centimeters.

EXAMPLE 2

Find the volume and surface area of the regular hexagonal prism hat box shown. Each side of the hexagonal base is 20 inches.

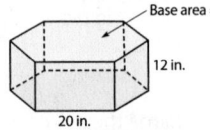

Base area = 1,039 in.²

12 in.

20 in.

Use the formulas for volume and surface area of a prism.

$V = Bh$

$= 1,039(12)$

$= 12,468 \text{ in}^3$

$S = Ph + 2B$

$= 120(12) + 2(1,039)$

$= 1,440 + 2,078$

$= 3,518 \text{ in}^2$

Perimeter $= 6(20) = 120$ in.

Unit 2 **133**

EXERCISES

Find the circumference and area of each circle. Round to the nearest hundredth. (Lessons 4.1, 4.2)

1.

22 in.

$C \approx 69.08 \text{ in., } A \approx 379.94 \text{ in}^2$

2.

4.5 m

$C \approx 28.26 \text{ m, } A \approx 63.59 \text{ m}^2$

Find the area of each composite figure. Round to the nearest hundredth if necessary. (Lesson 4.3)

3.

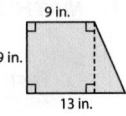

9 in.

9 in.

13 in.

Area _____99 in²_____

4.

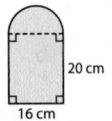

20 cm

16 cm

Area _____420.48 cm²_____

5. Find the volume of the figure. (Lesson 4.5)

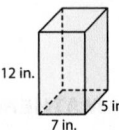

12 in.

5 in.

7 in.

_____420 in³_____

6. The volume of a triangular prism is 264 cubic feet. The area of a base of the prism is 48 square feet. Find the height of the prism.

(Lesson 4.5) _____5.5 ft_____

134 Unit 2

Geometry **134**

Unit 2 Performance Tasks

The Performance Tasks provide students with the opportunity to apply concepts from this unit in real-world problem situations.

CAREERS IN MATH

For more information about careers in mathematics as well as various mathematics appreciation topics, visit the American Mathematical Society at www.ams.org.

CAREERS IN MATH

Product Design Engineer In Performance Task Item 1, students can see how a product design engineer uses mathematics on the job.

SCORING GUIDES FOR PERFORMANCE TASKS

1. MATHEMATICAL PRACTICES FL CC **MP.2.1, MP.3.1, MP.4.1, MP.6.1**

Task	Possible Points (Total: 6)
a	**2 points** for correctly finding the surface area of 261.75 square feet and showing work: $2\left(\frac{1}{2}\right)(8)(6) + 2\left(9\frac{1}{2}\right)\left(7\frac{1}{4}\right) + \left(9\frac{1}{2}\right)(8) = 48 + 137.75 + 76 = 261.75$
b	**2 points** for correctly finding the volume of 228 cubic feet and showing work: $\left(\frac{1}{2}\right)(8)(6)\left(9\frac{1}{2}\right) = 228$
c	**1 point** for describing what modification needs to be made: change the length, 9.5 ft, so that the new volume is $\left(1\frac{1}{10}\right)(228) = 250\frac{4}{5}$ ft^3 **1 point** for finding the new length: $250\frac{4}{5} = \left(\frac{1}{2}\right)(8)(6)\ell$, so $\ell = 10\frac{9}{20}$ ft

2. MATHEMATICAL PRACTICES FL CC **MP.2.1, MP.4.1, MP.6.1**

Task	Possible Points (Total: 6)
a	**2 points** for calculating the volume, 135,000 cm^3, with appropriate unit conversions
b	**2 points** for calculating that Li will need 116,702 cm^3 of sand, and **2 points** for a suitable explanation for how they found their answer, including how they calculated the dimensions of the interior of the stand. For example: The dimensions of the interior are $(45 - 2)$ cm, $(120 - 2)$ cm, and $(25 - 2)$ cm, because each piece of wood is 1 cm thick. The interior volume is $V = (43$ cm$)(118$ cm$)(23$ cm$) = 116,702$ cm^3.

3. MATHEMATICAL PRACTICES FL CC **MP.3.1, MP.4.1, MP.6.1**

Task	Possible Points (Total: 6)
a	**2 points** for finding the correct area: 5,980.8125 ft^2
b	**1 point** for correct answer: no. **3 points** for correct explanation: 2 cm = 12 ft is equivalent to 1 cm = 6 ft. At the new scale, each centimeter of the drawing represents more of the house, so the plans will get smaller.

A glass paperweight has a composite shape: a square pyramid fitting exactly on top of an 8 centimeter cube. The pyramid has a height of 3 cm. Each triangular face has a height of 5 centimeters. (Lessons 4.4, 4.5)

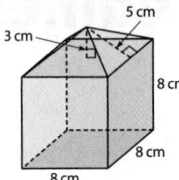

7. What is the volume of the prism? $\underline{576 \text{ cm}^3}$

8. What is the total surface area of the prism? $\underline{400 \text{ cm}^2}$

Unit 2 Performance Tasks

1. **CAREERS IN MATH** | Product Design Engineer   Miranda is a product design engineer working for a sporting goods company. She designs a tent in the shape of a triangular prism. The dimensions of the tent are shown in the diagram.

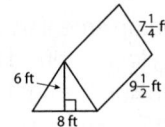

a. How many square feet of material does Miranda need to make the tent (including the floor)? Show your work.

$2\left(\frac{1}{2}\right)(8)(6) + 2\left(9\frac{1}{2}\right)\left(7\frac{1}{4}\right) + \left(9\frac{1}{2}\right)(8) = 48 + 137.75 + 76 = 261.75 \text{ ft}^2$

b. What is the volume of the tent? Show your work.

$\left(\frac{1}{2}\right)(8)(6)\left(9\frac{1}{2}\right) = 228 \text{ ft}^3$

c. Suppose Miranda wants to increase the volume of the tent by 10%. The specifications for the height (6 feet) and the width (8 feet) must stay the same. How can Miranda meet this new requirement? Explain.

She will need to change the length, $9\frac{1}{2}$ ft, so that the new volume is $\left(1\frac{1}{10}\right)(228) = 250\frac{4}{5} \text{ ft}^3$. That is $\left(\frac{1}{2}\right)(8)(6)\ell = 250\frac{4}{5}$, so $\ell = 10\frac{9}{20}$ ft .

2. Li is making a stand to display a sculpture made in art class. The stand will be 45 centimeters wide, 25 centimeters long, and 1.2 meters high.

a. What is the volume of the stand? Write your answer in cubic centimeters.

$V = (45 \text{ cm})(25 \text{ cm})(1.2 \text{ m}) \left(\frac{100 \text{ cm}}{\text{m}}\right) = 135{,}000 \text{ cm}^3$

b. Li needs to fill the stand with sand so that it is heavy and stable. Each piece of wood is 1 centimeter thick. The boards are put together as shown in the figure, which is not drawn to scale. How many cubic centimeters of sand does she need to fill the stand? Explain how you found your answer.

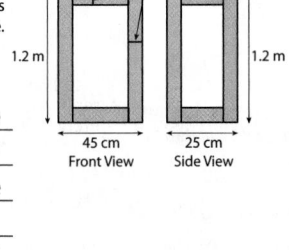

The dimensions of the interior of the stand are $(45 - 2)$ cm, $(120 - 2)$ cm, and $(25 - 2)$ cm, because each piece of wood is 1 cm thick. The interior volume is $V = (43 \text{ cm}) (118 \text{ cm}) (23 \text{ cm}) = 116{,}702 \text{ cm}^3$.

3. Lucia is designing her dream house. The plans shown represent the dimensions of the house's exterior. They are drawn to a scale of 1 cm = 5 ft.

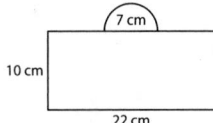

a. What is the area of house? Use 3.14 for π.

$5{,}980.8125 \text{ ft}^2$

b. Lucia wants to change the scale of the plans so that they are larger. She is considering using a scale of 2 cm = 12 ft. Will this scale produce a larger set of plans? Justify your answer.

No. 2 cm = 12 ft is equivalent to 1 cm = 6 ft. At the new scale, each centimeter of the drawing represents more of the house, so the plans will get smaller.

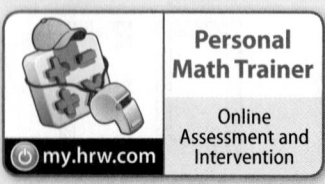
MIXED REVIEW

PARCC Assessment Readiness

Assessment Readiness Tip Students can use the provided formula chart to find formulas they may have forgotten.

Item 7 Students can look on their formula charts to see that the volume of a prism is found with the formula Bh, where B represents the area of the base (in this case, a triangle). Since the area of the base is given as 30, students need simply multiply 30 by 75 to get the correct answer.

Item 10 Students can use the formula chart to look up the formulas for finding the area of a square and a triangle so they might find the area of this composite figure.

Avoid Common Errors

Item 12 Students sometimes confuse supplementary and complementary angles. Have the students double check which angle they should be solving for by using a letter trick. The 'c' in 'complementary' can be turned into a 9 by placing a line on the right side, linking complementary to 90 degrees. The 's' in 'supplementary' can be turned into an 8 with one line, linking supplementary to 180 degrees.

Florida Common Core Standards

Items	Grade 7 Standards	Mathematical Practices
1	7.G.2.5	MP.2.1
2	7.G.1.1	MP.4.1
3	7.G.2.6	MP.1.1
4*	7.EE.2.4a	MP.2.1
5*	7.EE.2.4	MP.4.1
6*	7.EE.2.4	MP.4.1
7	7.G.2.6	MP.2.1
8	7.G.1.3	MP.6.1
9	7.G.2.4	MP.2.1
10	7.G.2.6	MP.2.1
11	7.G.2.4	MP.4.1
12	7.G.2.5	MP.2.1
13	7.G.2.6	MP.2.1
14	7.G.2.4	MP.2.1
15	7.G.2.6	MP.1.1, MP.5.1

* Item integrates mixed review concepts from previous modules or a previous course.

PARCC Assessment Readiness

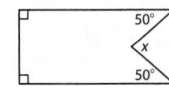

Personal
Math Trainer
my.hrw.com
Online
Assessment and
Intervention

Selected Response

1. A school flag is in the shape of a rectangle with a triangle removed as shown.

What is the measure of angle *x*?

Ⓐ 50°
Ⓒ 90°
Ⓑ 80°
Ⓓ 100°

2. On a map with a scale of 2 cm = 1 km, the distance from Beau's house to the beach is 4.6 centimeters. What is the actual distance?

Ⓐ 2.3 km
Ⓒ 6.5 km
Ⓑ 4.6 km
Ⓓ 9.2 km

3. Lalasa and Yasmin are designing a triangular banner to hang in the school gymnasium. They first draw the design on paper. The triangle has a base of 5 inches and a height of 7 inches. If 1 inch on the drawing is equivalent to 1.5 feet on the actual banner, what will the area of the actual banner be?

Ⓐ 17.5 ft²
Ⓒ 39.375 ft²
Ⓑ 52.5 ft²
Ⓓ 78.75 ft²

4. Which has the same solution as $4x + 5 = -11$?

Ⓐ $-5x = 25$
Ⓑ $x + 6 = 2$
Ⓒ $7 - x = -2$
Ⓓ $\frac{x}{3} = 2$

5. A one-topping pizza costs $15.00. Each additional topping costs $1.25. Let *x* be the number of additional toppings. You have $20 to spend. Which equation can you solve to find the number of additional toppings you can get on your pizza?

Ⓐ $15x + 1.25 = 20$
Ⓑ $1.25x + 15 = 20$
Ⓒ $15x - 1.25 = 20$
Ⓓ $1.25x - 15 = 20$

6. Which inequality can be used to find how many $1.25 snack packs can be purchased for $10.00?

Ⓐ $1.25s \geq 10.00$
Ⓒ $\frac{s}{1.25} \geq 10.00$
Ⓑ $1.25s \leq 10.00$
Ⓓ $\frac{s}{1.25} \leq 10.00$

7. What is the volume of a triangular prism that is 75 centimeters long and that has a base with an area of 30 square centimeters?

Ⓐ 2.5 cubic centimeters
Ⓑ 750 cubic centimeters
Ⓒ 1,125 cubic centimeters
Ⓓ 2,250 cubic centimeters

8. Consider the right circular cone shown.

If a vertical plane slices through the cone to create two identical half cones, what is the shape of the cross section?

Ⓐ a rectangle
Ⓒ a triangle
Ⓑ a square
Ⓓ a circle

9. The radius of the circle is given in meters. What is the circumference of the circle? Use 3.14 for π.

8 m

Ⓐ 25.12 meters
Ⓑ 50.24 meters
Ⓒ 200.96 meters
Ⓓ 803.84 meters

10. The dimensions of the figure are given in millimeters. What is the area of the two-dimensional figure?

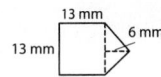

13 mm
13 mm
6 mm

Ⓐ 39 square millimeters
Ⓑ 169 square millimeters
Ⓒ 208 square millimeters
Ⓓ 247 square millimeters

11. A forest ranger wants to determine the radius of the trunk of a tree. She measures the circumference to be 8.6 feet. What is the trunk's radius to the nearest tenth of a foot?

Ⓐ 1.4 ft
Ⓑ 4.3 ft
Ⓒ 2.7 ft
Ⓓ 17.2 ft

> **Hot Tip!** It is helpful to draw or redraw a figure. Answers to geometry problems may become clearer as you redraw the figure.

12. What is the measure in degrees of an angle that is supplementary to a 74° angle?

Ⓐ 16°
Ⓑ 74°
Ⓒ 90°
Ⓓ 106°

13. What is the volume in cubic centimeters of a rectangular prism that has a length of 6.2 centimeters, a width of 3.5 centimeters, and a height of 10 centimeters?

Ⓐ 19.7 cm³
Ⓒ 217.0 cm³
Ⓑ 108.5 cm³
Ⓓ 237.4 cm³

14. A patio is the shape of a circle with diameter shown.

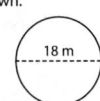

18 m

What is the area of the patio? Use 3.14 for π.

Ⓐ 9.00 m²
Ⓑ 28.26 m²
Ⓒ 254.34 m²
Ⓓ 1,017.36 m²

Mini-Task

15. Petra fills a small cardboard box with sand. The dimensions of the box are 3 inches by 4 inches by 2 inches.

a. What is the volume of sand the box can hold?

24 in³

b. Petra decides to cover the box by gluing on wrapping paper. How much wrapping paper does she need to cover all six sides of the box?

52 in²

c. Petra has a second, larger box that is 6 inches by 8 inches by 4 inches. How many times larger is the volume of this second box? The surface area?

Volume: 8 times; SA: 4 times

Statistics and Sampling

Contents

Unit Pacing Guide

45-Minute Classes

Module 5

DAY 1	DAY 2	DAY 3	DAY 4	DAY 5
Lesson 5.1	Lesson 5.1	Lesson 5.2	Lesson 5.3	Ready to Go On? PARCC Assessment Readiness

Module 6

DAY 1	DAY 2	DAY 3	DAY 4	DAY 5
Lesson 6.1	Lesson 6.2	Lesson 6.2	Lesson 6.3	Lesson 6.3

DAY 6	DAY 7
Ready to Go On? PARCC Assessment Readiness	Study Guide PARCC Assessment Readiness

90-Minute Classes

Module 5

DAY 1	DAY 2
Lesson 5.1 Lesson 5.2	Lesson 5.3 Ready to Go On? PARCC Assessment Readiness

Module 6

DAY 1	DAY 2	DAY 3	
Lesson 6.1 Lesson 6.2	Lesson 6.3	Ready to Go On? PARCC Assessment Readiness	Study Guide PARCC Assessment Readiness

Program Resources

⏻ Plan

Online Teacher Edition

Access a full suite of teaching resources online—plan, present, and manage classes, assignments, and activities.

ePlanner **Easily plan your classes, create and view assignments, and access all program resources with your online, customizable planning tool.**

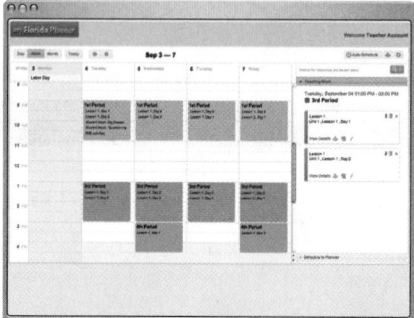

Professional Development Videos

Author Juli Dixon models successful teaching practices and strategies in actual classroom settings.

QR Codes **Scan with your smart phone to jump directly from your print book to online videos and other resources.**

Teacher's Edition

Support students with point-of-use Questioning Strategies, teaching tips, resources for differentiated instruction, additional activities, and more.

⏻ Engage and Explore

Real-World Videos **Engage students with interesting and relevant applications of the mathematical content of each module.**

Animated Math **Online interactive simulations, tools, and games help students actively learn and practice key concepts.**

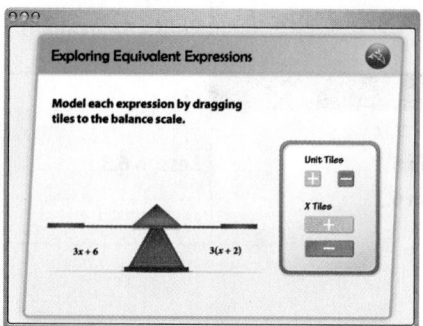

Explore Activities

Students interactively explore new concepts using a variety of tools and approaches.

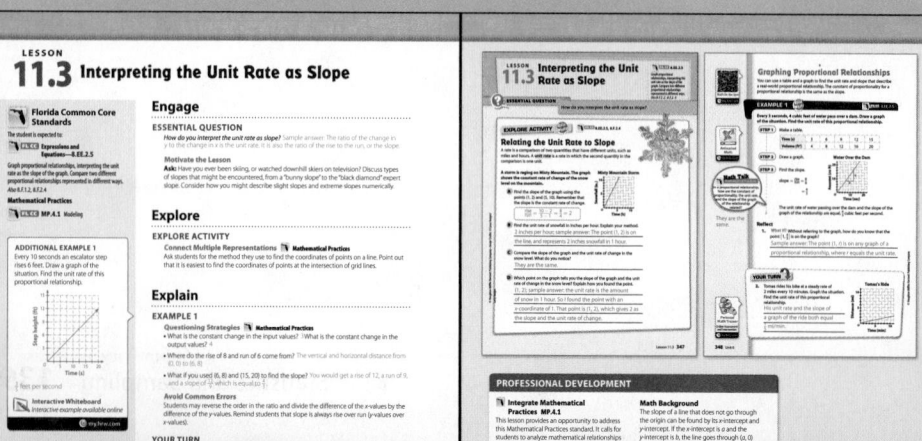

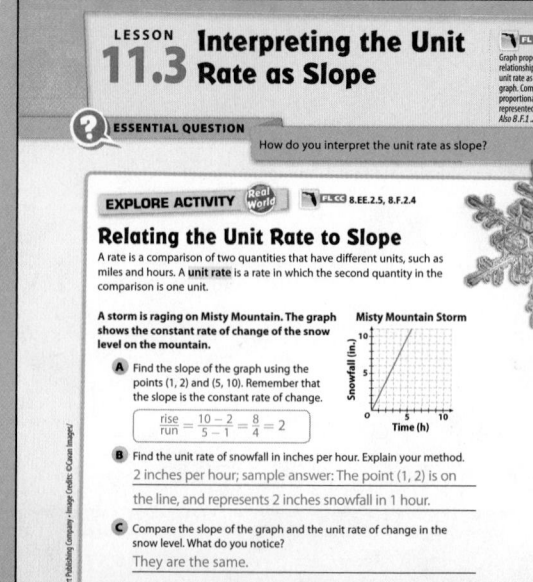

LESSON
11.3 **Interpreting the Unit Rate as Slope**

FL.CC 8.EE.2.5

Graph proportional relationships, interpreting the unit rate as the slope of the graph. Compare two different proportional relationships represented in different ways. Also 8.F.1.2, 8.F.2.4

? ESSENTIAL QUESTION

How do you interpret the unit rate as slope?

EXPLORE ACTIVITY (Real World)   FL.CC 8.EE.2.5, 8.F.2.4

Relating the Unit Rate to Slope

A rate is a comparison of two quantities that have different units, such as miles and hours. A **unit rate** is a rate in which the second quantity in the comparison is one unit.

A storm is raging on Misty Mountain. The graph shows the constant rate of change of the snow level on the mountain.

A Find the slope of the graph using the points (1, 2) and (5, 10). Remember that the slope is the constant rate of change.

$$\frac{\text{rise}}{\text{run}} = \frac{10 - 2}{5 - 1} = \frac{8}{4} = 2$$

B Find the unit rate of snowfall in inches per hour. Explain your method.

2 inches per hour; sample answer: The point (1, 2) is on the line, and represents 2 inches snowfall in 1 hour.

C Compare the slope of the graph and the unit rate of change in the snow level. What do you notice?

They are the same.

⏻ Teach

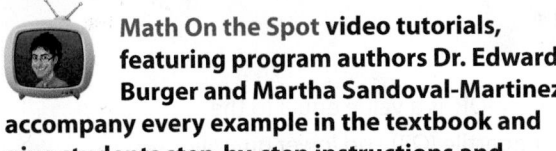

Math On the Spot video tutorials, featuring program authors Dr. Edward Burger and Martha Sandoval-Martinez, accompany every example in the textbook and give students step-by-step instructions and explanations of key math concepts.

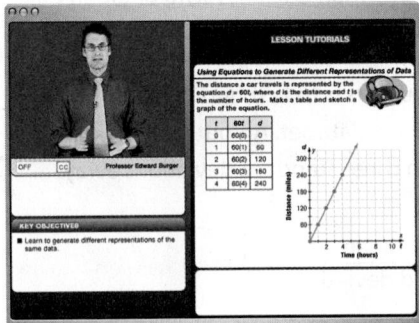

Present engaging content on a multitude of devices, including tablets and interactive whiteboards.

Math Talk Continually monitor and assess student progress with integrated formative assessment.

CLUSTER CONNECTION Look for exercises indicated with this icon to build connections among standards within Florida Common Core clusters.

Differentiated Instruction Print Resources

Support all learners with Differentiated Instruction Resources, including

- **Leveled Practice and Problem Solving**
- **Reteach**
- **Reading Strategies**
- **Success for English Learners**
- **Challenge**

⏻ Assessment and Intervention

The **Personal Math Trainer** provides online practice, homework, assessments, and intervention. Monitor student progress through reports and alerts. Create and customize assignments aligned to specific lessons or standards.

- **Practice** – With dynamic items and assignments, students get unlimited practice on key concepts supported by guided examples, step-by-step solutions, and video tutorials.

- **Assessments** – Choose from course assignments or customize your own based on course content, standards, difficulty levels, and more.

- **Homework** – Students can complete online homework with a wide variety of problem types, including the ability to enter expressions, equations, and graphs. Let the system automatically grade homework, so you can focus where your students need help the most!

- **Intervention** – Let the Personal Math Trainer automatically prescribe a targeted, personalized intervention path for your students.

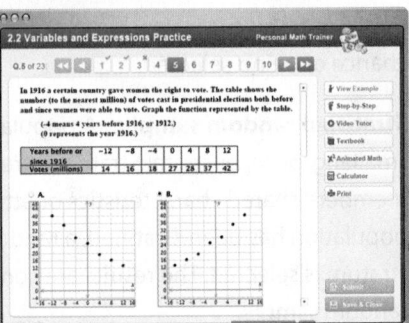

Raise the bar with homework and practice that incorporates higher-order thinking and mathematical processes in every lesson.

PARCC Assessment Readiness
Prepare students for success on the PARCC math test with practice at every module and unit.

Assessment Resources

Tailor assessments to meet the needs of all your classes and students, including

- **Leveled Module Quizzes**
- **Leveled Unit Tests**
- **Unit Performance Tasks**
- **Placement, Diagnostic, and Quarterly Benchmark Tests**

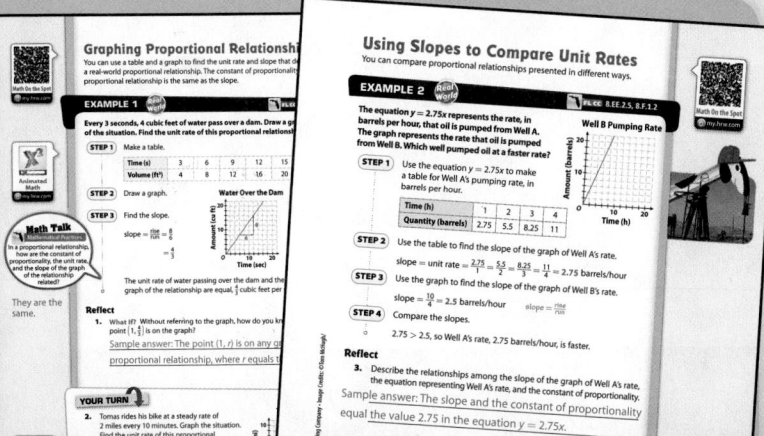

Math Background

Populations and Samples 7.SP.1.1
LESSON 5.1

Sampling is the area of statistics concerned with choosing a subset of a population in order to make statistical inferences about the population. Suppose you want to survey voters to predict the results of an upcoming statewide election. It would be necessary to use a sample because it is not practical to identify and survey every potential voter.

The way in which the sample is selected can have a profound effect on the data that are collected. There are many different ways to sample a given population. Some of the most common are described here.

Simple random sample: A sample of the population is selected, and each member of the sample is chosen entirely by chance. This means each member has an equally likely chance of being selected.

Stratified random sample: A population is divided into smaller groups, or strata. Strata are created based on members' shared characteristics or attributes. Once the population has been stratified, a random sample from each stratum is selected. The results are combined to obtain a random sample.

Convenience sample: A sampling of a population is selected based on ease or convenience, such as shoppers in a grocery store. A convenience sample does not represent the entire population; therefore, it is a biased sample.

Cluster sampling: The population is divided into groups, or clusters. A random sample of these clusters is then selected.

Systematic sample: In a systematic sample, every nth item is included in the sample, where n is a natural number. For example, choosing every 6th name on a list of students is a systematic sample.

Voluntary response sample: This sample consists of people who are self-selected and respond to a general appeal.

Making Inferences From a Random Sample 7.SP.1.2
LESSON 5.2

The interquartile range, or IQR, is a value equal to the difference of the upper quartile (Q3) and lower quartile (Q1). The interquartile range can be used to find outliers in a data set. Values that are less than $Q1 - 1.5(IQR)$ or greater than $Q3 + 1.5(IQR)$ are considered outliers.

Another method to find outliers is to first find the mean and standard deviation of the data set. An outlier is any value x that is greater than three standard deviations away from the mean.

$$\frac{|x - \text{mean}|}{\text{standard deviation}} > 3$$

Generating Random Samples 7.SP.1.2
LESSON 5.3

When a population is too large to be studied easily, a representative sample of the population may be studied instead. Random sampling is a way to select a group that represents the larger group. Statistics based on a study of the smaller group can be used as a basis for inferring the results for the entire population. In this lesson, students learn to simulate samples both with and without technology. The technology method involves generating random numbers using a graphing calculator. Random number tables may be used if graphing calculators are not readily available.

Comparing Data Displayed in Dot Plots 7.SP.2.4
LESSON 6.1

A Cleveland dot plot shows categorical labels on the vertical axis and continuous values on the horizontal axis.

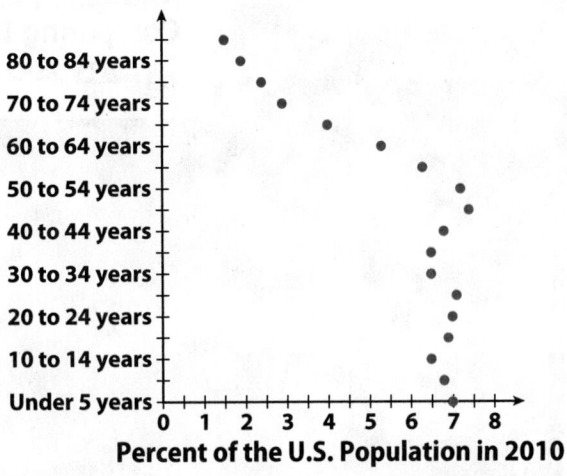

There are two categories of dot plots. A Wilkinson dot plot shows the data points plotted above a horizontal scale.

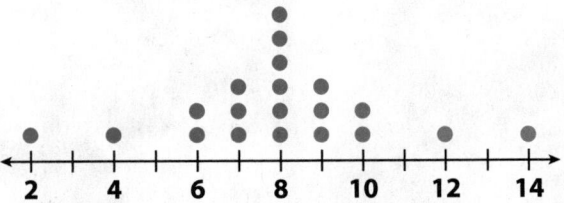

Comparing Data Displayed in Box Plots 7.SP.2.3
LESSON 6.2

The box plot was originally developed by John Tukey, an American mathematician. It was introduced in his book "Exploratory Data Analysis," published in 1977.

The minimum or maximum value of a data set may be an outlier. An outlier is described as a value that is very high or very low compared to the other values in the set. It is sometimes specifically defined as any value that is more than 1.5 times the interquartile range either below the first quartile or above the third quartile. An outlier can have a great effect on the mean and range of a data set, but does not affect the median.

Statistics and Sampling

MODULE **5**

Random Samples and Populations

 **FL CC** 7.RP.1.2c, 7.SP.1.1, 7.SP.1.2

MODULE **6**

Analyzing and Comparing Data

FL CC 7.SP.2.3, 7.SP.2.4

CAREERS IN MATH

Entomologist An entomologist is a biologist who studies insects. These scientists analyze data and use mathematical models to understand and predict the behavior of insect populations.

If you are interested in a career in entomology, you should study these mathematical subjects:
- Algebra
- Trigonometry
- Probability and Statistics
- Calculus

Research other careers that require the analysis of data and use of mathematical models.

Unit 3 Performance Task

At the end of the unit, check out how **entomologists** use math.

Careers in Math

Entomologist

An entomologist collects and analyzes data about the life cycles and behaviors of different insects, as well as ways of controlling insect populations. You will learn more about how entomologists analyze data in the Performance Tasks at the end of the unit.

For more information about careers in mathematics as well as various mathematics appreciation topics, visit the American Mathematical Society at www.ams.org.

Vocabulary Preview

Use the puzzle to give students a preview of important concepts in this unit. Students may work individually, in pairs, or in groups.

Unit Resources

Go online to access all your unit resources.

my.hrw.com

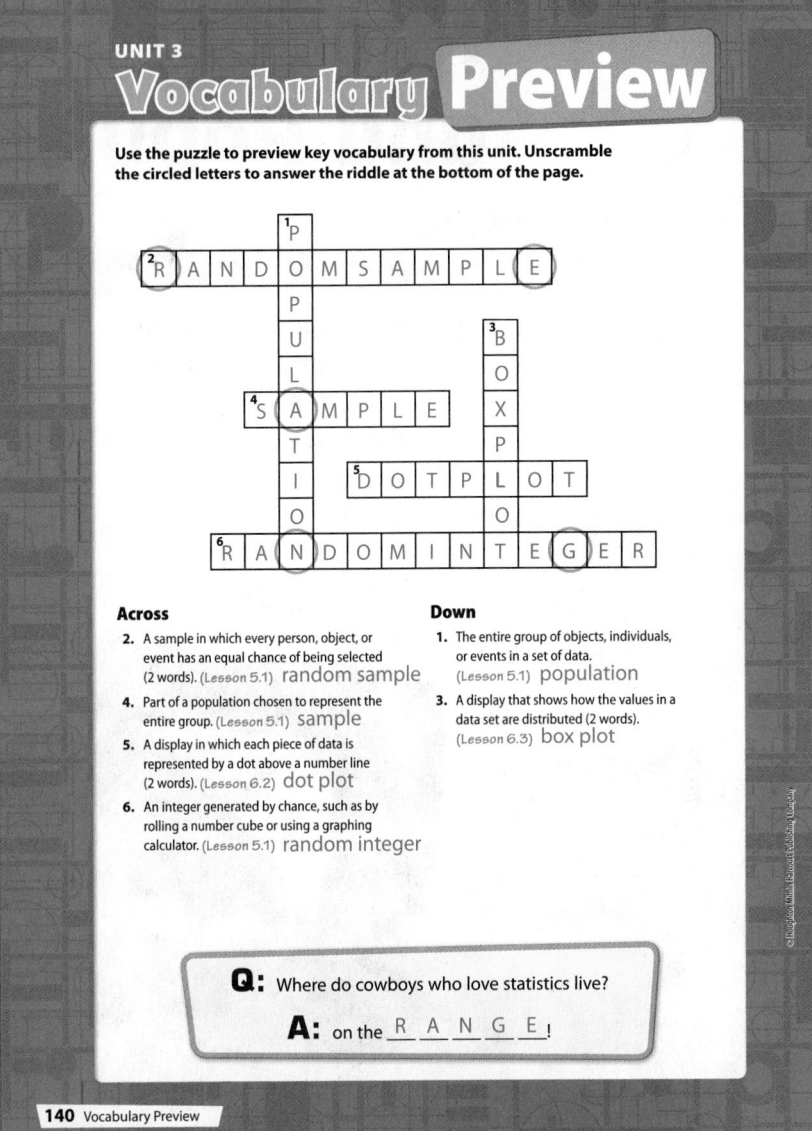

UNIT 3
Vocabulary Preview

Use the puzzle to preview key vocabulary from this unit. Unscramble the circled letters to answer the riddle at the bottom of the page.

Across

2. A sample in which every person, object, or event has an equal chance of being selected (2 words). (Lesson 5.1) random sample

4. Part of a population chosen to represent the entire group. (Lesson 5.1) sample

5. A display in which each piece of data is represented by a dot above a number line (2 words). (Lesson 6.2) dot plot

6. An integer generated by chance, such as by rolling a number cube or using a graphing calculator. (Lesson 5.1) random integer

Down

1. The entire group of objects, individuals, or events in a set of data. (Lesson 5.1) population

3. A display that shows how the values in a data set are distributed (2 words). (Lesson 6.3) box plot

Q: Where do cowboys who love statistics live?

A: on the R A N G E !

140 Vocabulary Preview

Before	In this Unit	After
Students understand: • numeric data • how to represent numeric data graphically • how to interpret numeric data from a dot plot • categorical data	Students will learn about: • ways to analyze data about a population • making inferences from random samples • ways to compare two sets of data	Students will learn about: • mean absolute deviation • random samples

Random Samples and Populations

MODULE 5

? ESSENTIAL QUESTION

How can you use random samples and populations to solve real-world problems?

You can solve problems involving large populations by modeling them with smaller random samples and then analyzing the samples.

Real-World Video

Scientists place radio frequency tags on some animals within a population of that species. Then they track data, such as migration patterns, about the animals.

my.hrw.com

© Houghton Mifflin Harcourt Publishing Company • Image Credits: ©Mike Veitch/

GO DIGITAL

my.hrw.com

my.hrw.com

Go digital with your write-in student edition, accessible on any device.

Math On the Spot

Scan with your smart phone to jump directly to the online edition, video tutor, and more.

Animated Math

Interactively explore key concepts to see how math works.

Personal Math Trainer

Get immediate feedback and help as you work through practice sets.

Are You Ready?

Assess Readiness

Use the assessment on this page to determine if students need intensive or strategic intervention for the module's prerequisite skills.

 **Response to Intervention**

Personal Math Trainer
Online Assessment and Intervention
⏻ my.hrw.com

Intervention	Enrichment
Access *Are You Ready?* assessment online, and receive instant scoring, feedback, and customized intervention or enrichment.	

Online and Print Resources

Skills Intervention worksheets
- Skill 65 Solve Proportions
- Skill 91 Find the Range
- Skill 93 Find the Mean

Differentiated Instruction
- Challenge worksheets **PRE-AP**
- Extend the Math **PRE-AP** Lesson Activities in TE

Are YOU Ready?

Complete these exercises to review skills you will need for this module.

 **Personal Math Trainer**
Online Assessment and Intervention
⏻ my.hrw.com

Solve Proportions

EXAMPLE	$\frac{a}{1} = \frac{30}{1.5}$	
	$a \times 1.5 = 1 \times 30$	Write the cross products.
	$1.5a = 30$	Simplify.
	$\frac{1.5a}{1.5} = \frac{30}{1.5}$	Divide both sides by 1.5.
	$a = 20$	

Solve for *x*.

1. $\frac{x}{16} = \frac{45}{40}$ __18__   2. $\frac{x}{5} = 1\frac{1}{4}$ __$\frac{5}{4} = 1.25$__   3. $\frac{2.5}{10} = \frac{x}{50}$ __12.5__   4. $\frac{x}{6} = \frac{2}{9}$ __$\frac{4}{3}$__

Find the Range

EXAMPLE	29, 26, 21, 30, 32, 19	Order the data from least to greatest.
	19, 21, 26, 29, 30, 32	
	range = 32 − 19	The range is the difference between the greatest and the least data items.
	= 13	

Find the range of the data.

5. 52, 48, 57, 47, 49, 60, 59, 51 __13__   6. 5, 9, 13, 6, 4, 5, 8, 12, 12, 6 __9__

7. 97, 106, 99, 97, 115, 95, 108, 100 __20__   8. 27, 13, 35, 19, 71, 12, 66, 47, 39 __59__

Find the Mean

EXAMPLE	21, 15, 26, 19, 25, 14	
	mean = $\frac{21 + 15 + 26 + 19 + 25 + 14}{6}$	The mean is the sum of the data items divided by the number of items.
	= $\frac{120}{6}$	
	= 20	

Find the mean of each set of data.

9. 3, 5, 7, 3, 6, 4, 8, 6, 9, 5 __5.6__   10. 8.1, 9.4, 11.3, 6.7, 6.2, 7.5 __8.2__

© Houghton Mifflin Harcourt Publishing Company

PROFESSIONAL DEVELOPMENT VIDEO

Author Juli Dixon models successful teaching practices as she explores random samples in an actual seventh-grade classroom.

 **Professional Development**
⏻ my.hrw.com

GO DIGITAL
my.hrw.com

 Online Teacher Edition
Access a full suite of teaching resources online—plan, present, and manage classes and assignments.

 ePlanner
Easily plan your classes and access all your resources online.

Interactive Answers and Solutions
Customize answer keys to print or display in the classroom. Choose to include answers only or full solutions to all lesson exercises.

Interactive Whiteboards
Engage students with interactive whiteboard-ready lessons and activities.

Personal Math Trainer: Online Assessment and Intervention
Assign automatically graded homework, quizzes, tests, and intervention activities. Prepare your students with updated practice tests aligned with Common Core.

Reading Start-Up

Have students complete the activities on this page by working alone or with others.

Visualize Vocabulary

The chart helps students review vocabulary associated with box plots. As a class, review the process for creating a box plot.

Understand Vocabulary

Use the following explanations to help students learn the preview words.

In statistics, a **population** is the entire group of people that you want to know something about. A **random sample** of the population can be used to represent the whole population. In a random sample, every person in the population has the same chance of being part of the sample. A **biased sample** does not accurately represent the entire population.

Active Reading

Integrating Language Arts

Students can use these reading and note-taking strategies to help them organize and understand new concepts and vocabulary.

FL CC **LACC.68.RST.3.7** Integrate quantitative or technical information expressed in words in a text with a version of that information expressed visually (e.g., in a flowchart, diagram, model, graph, or table).

Additional Resources

Differentiated Instruction

• Reading Strategies **ELL**

Reading Start-Up

Visualize Vocabulary

Use the ✔ words to complete the right column of the chart.

Box Plots to Display Data

Definition	Review Word
A display that uses values from a data set to show how the values are spread out.	box plot
The middle value of a data set.	median
The median of the lower half of the data.	lower quartile
The median of the upper half of the data.	upper quartile

Vocabulary

Review Words
✔ box plot (*diagrama de caja*)
  data (*datos*)
  dot plot (*diagrama de puntos*)
  interquartile range (*rango entre cuartiles*)
✔ lower quartile (*cuartil inferior*)
✔ median (*mediana*)
  spread (*dispersión*)
  survey (*estudio*)
✔ upper quartile (*cuartil superior*)

Preview Words
  biased sample (*muestra sesgada*)
  population (*población*)
  random sample (*muestra aleatoria*)
  sample (*muestra*)

Understand Vocabulary

Complete each sentence, using the preview words.

1. An entire group of objects, individuals, or events is a ___population___.

2. A ___sample___ is part of the population chosen to represent the entire group.

3. A sample that does not accurately represent the population is a ___biased sample___.

Active Reading

Tri-Fold Before beginning the module, create a tri-fold to help you learn the concepts and vocabulary in this module. Fold the paper into three sections. Label the columns "What I Know," "What I Need to Know," and "What I Learned." Complete the first two columns before you read. After studying the module, complete the third column.

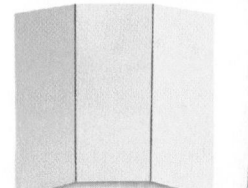

Before	In this module	After
Students understand: • how to represent numeric data graphically, including box plots, stem-and-leaf plots, and histograms • how to interpret numeric data summarized in dot plots	Students will learn how to: • use a sample to gain information about a population using random and nonrandom sampling • make inferences from dot plots and box plots • use data about a sample and proportional reasoning to make inferences or predictions about a population	Students will connect: • simulations and random samples • mean absolute deviation and measures of variability

Unpacking the Standards

Use the examples on the page to help students know exactly what they are expected to learn in this module.

 Florida Common Core Standards

Content Areas

 **Statistics and Probability—7.SP.1**

Use random sampling to draw inferences about a population.

Go online to see a complete unpacking of the Florida Common Core Standards.
⏻ my.hrw.com

MODULE 5
Unpacking the Standards
Understanding the standards and the vocabulary terms in the standards will help you know exactly what you are expected to learn in this module.

FL CC 7.SP.1.1

Understand that statistics can be used to gain information about a population by examining a sample of the population; generalizations about a population from a sample are valid only if the sample is representative of that population. Understand that random sampling tends to produce representative samples and support valid inferences.

What It Means to You

You will learn how a random sample can be representative of a population.

UNPACKING EXAMPLE 7.SP.1.1

Avery wants to survey residents who live in an apartment building. She writes down all of the apartment numbers on slips of paper, and draws slips from a box without looking to decide who to survey. Will this produce a random sample?

The population is all of the residents or people who live in the apartment building. The sample is a valid random sample because every apartment number has the same chance of being selected.

FL CC 7.SP.1.2

Use data from a random sample to draw inferences about a population with an unknown characteristic of interest. Generate multiple samples (or simulated samples) of the same size to gauge the variation in estimates or predictions.

Key Vocabulary

population *(población)*
The entire group of objects or individuals considered for a survey.

sample *(muestra)*
A part of the population.

What It Means to You

You will use data collected from a random sample to make inferences about a population.

UNPACKING EXAMPLE 7.SP.1.2

Alexi surveys a random sample of 80 students at his school and finds that 22 of them usually walk to school. There are 1,760 students at the school. Predict the number of students who usually walk to school.

$$\frac{\text{number in sample who walk}}{\text{size of sample}} = \frac{\text{number in population who walk}}{\text{size of population}}$$

$$\frac{22}{80} = \frac{x}{1,760}$$

$$x = \frac{22}{80} \cdot 1,760$$

$$x = \frac{38,720}{80} = 484$$

Approximately 484 students usually walk to school.

Visit my.hrw.com to see all Florida Common Core Standards unpacked.
⏻ my.hrw.com

Florida Common Core Standards	Lesson 5.1	Lesson 5.2	Lesson 5.3
FL CC 7.RP.1.2c Represent proportional relationships by equations.		🔲	
FL CC 7.SP.1.1 Understand that statistics can be used to gain information about a population by examining a sample of the population; generalizations about a population from a sample are valid only if the sample is representative of that population. Understand that random sampling tends to produce representative samples and support valid inferences.	🔲	🔲	
FL CC 7.SP.1.2 Use data from a random sample to draw inferences about a population with an unknown characteristic of interest. Generate multiple samples (or simulated samples) of the same size to gauge the variation in estimates or predictions.		🔲	🔲

LESSON 5.1 Populations and Samples

Florida Common Core Standards

The student is expected to:

 **Statistics and Probability— 7.SP.1.1**

Understand that statistics can be used to gain information about a population by examining a sample of the population; generalizations about a population from a sample are valid only if the sample is representative of that population.

Mathematical Practices

 **MP.6.1** Precision

---

ADDITIONAL EXAMPLE 1
Identify the population. Determine whether each sample is a random sample or a biased sample. Explain your reasoning.

A Gino wants to know how most people in his neighborhood get to work. He surveys 100 people getting off the bus at a bus stop near his house. The population is people in Gino's neighborhood. The sample is biased because people at a bus stop are likely to say they take the bus to work.

B Raylene wants to know the favorite ice cream flavor of the employees at her company. She surveys 150 employees chosen at random from a list of all employees. The population is employees at Raylene's company. The sample is not biased because every employee has the same chance to be selected.

 Interactive Whiteboard
Interactive example available online

ⓑ my.hrw.com

Engage

ESSENTIAL QUESTION

How can you use a sample to gain information about a population? Sample answer: Select a sample that represents the population, and survey the sample using an unbiased question.

Motivate the Lesson
Ask: How could you determine the most popular movie among students in your school? Think of how you could find the most popular movie before you begin the Explore Activity.

Explore

EXPLORE ACTIVITY

Focus on Critical Thinking Mathematical Practices
Students may feel that the actual average of all the numbers will give the gardener a better answer. Discuss the differences between having a table of data like the one shown and randomly selecting plants from a garden where the number of tomatoes on every plant is not known.

Explain

EXAMPLE 1

Connect Vocabulary ELL
Students may use the word *random* in a nonmath context as a synonym for "unexpected." Remind students that **random** has a very specific definition in mathematics, referring to the way in which things are selected for a sample.

Engage with the Whiteboard
Cover up the answers, and have students underline the part of each problem that identifies the population and the part that identifies the sample. Have students compare the sample to the population to decide whether the sample is biased.

Questioning Strategies Mathematical Practices
• How could Roberto change his sampling method so that his sample was not biased? He could survey people at a location where most people are not likely to prefer a certain sport.

• Can a sample be both random and biased? Justify your answer. Yes; if a random sample is too small, it may be biased if it does not accurately represent the population.

LESSON 5.1 Populations and Samples

… Understand that random sampling tends to produce representative samples and support valid inferences.

ESSENTIAL QUESTION How can you use a sample to gain information about a population?

EXPLORE ACTIVITY (Real World) FL CC 7.SP.1.1

Random and Non-Random Sampling

When information is being gathered about a group, the entire group of objects, individuals, or events is called the **population**. A **sample** is part of the population that is chosen to represent the entire group.

A vegetable garden has 36 tomato plants arranged in a 6-by-6 array. The gardener wants to know the average number of tomatoes on the plants. Each white cell in the table represents a plant. The number in the cell tells how many tomatoes are on that particular plant.

Because counting the number of tomatoes on all of the plants is too time-consuming, the gardener decides to choose plants at random to find the average number of tomatoes on them.

To simulate the random selection, roll two number cubes 10 times. Find the cell in the table identified by the first and second number cubes. Record the number in each randomly selected cell.

						First Number Cube
8	9	13	18	24	15	1
34	42	46	20	13	41	2
29	21	14	45	27	43	3
22	45	46	41	22	33	4
12	42	44	17	42	11	5
18	26	43	32	33	26	6
Second Number Cube						
1	2	3	4	5	6	

A What is the average number of tomatoes on the 10 plants that were randomly selected?

Answers will vary based on each student's results.

B Alternately, the gardener decides to choose the plants in the first row. What is the average number of tomatoes on these plants?

31.5 tomatoes

Math Talk
Mathematical Practices
How do the averages you got with each sampling method compare?

Sample answer: The random sample average is greater than the average of the first row.

Lesson 5.1 **145**

EXPLORE ACTIVITY (cont'd)

Reflect

1. How do the averages you got with each sampling method compare to the average for the entire population, which is 28.25?

Sample answer: The random sample is closer to the actual average. The first row average is much lower.

2. Why might the first method give a closer average than the second method?

The plants in the first row seem to have fewer tomatoes than the plants in other rows, so it is not representative of the whole plot.

Math On the Spot
my.hrw.com

Random Samples and Biased Samples

A sample in which every person, object, or event has an equal chance of being selected is called a **random sample**. A random sample is more likely to be representative of the entire population than other sampling methods. When a sample does not accurately represent the population, it is called a **biased sample**.

EXAMPLE 1 (Real World) FL CC 7.SP.1.1

Identify the population. Determine whether each sample is a random sample or a biased sample. Explain your reasoning.

A Roberto wants to know the favorite sport of adults in his hometown. He surveys 50 adults at a baseball game.

The population is adults in Roberto's hometown.

The sample is biased.

Think: People who don't like baseball will not be represented in this sample.

B Paula wants to know the favorite type of music for students in her class. She puts the names of all students in a hat, draws 8 names, and surveys those students.

The population is students in Paula's class.

The sample is random.

Think: Each student has an equal chance of being selected.

Math Talk
Mathematical Practices
Why do you think samples are used? Why not survey each member of the population?

Samples save the time, expense, and difficulty of surveying everyone in a given population.

Reflect

3. How might you choose a sample of size 20 to determine the preferred practice day of all the players in a soccer league?

Sample answer: Place the names of all the players in a hat. Draw 20 names.

146 Unit 3

PROFESSIONAL DEVELOPMENT

Integrate Mathematical Practices MP.6.1

This lesson provides an opportunity to address this Mathematical Practice standard. It calls for students to explain mathematical ideas and arguments using precise mathematical language in written or oral communication. Students use mathematical definitions to explain whether a given sample is random or biased. Then students explain whether survey questions could be biased based on the language used in the questions.

Math Background

Sampling is the area of statistics concerned with choosing a subset of a population in order to make statistical inferences about the population as a whole. For example, suppose you want to survey voters to predict the results of an upcoming statewide election. It would be necessary to use a sample because it would be impossible to identify and survey every potential voter. The way in which the sample is selected can have a profound effect on the data that are collected.

ADDITIONAL EXAMPLE 2
Local residents were surveyed about adding stoplights at the corner of Main Street and Perry Avenue. Determine whether each survey question may be biased. Explain.

A Are stoplights needed at the intersection of Main and Perry? Not biased; the question does not lead people to give a particular answer.

B Fewer accidents occur at intersections with stoplights than at intersections that do not have them. Would you be in favor of having stoplights installed to make the intersection at Main and Perry safer? Biased; the question encourages people to answer yes to the question by mentioning safety.

C Installing a new stoplight will require detours that will decrease traffic to local businesses for up to a month. Should stoplights be installed at the corner of Main and Perry? Biased; the question discourages people from answering yes to the question by mentioning a decrease in business customers.

D Should stoplights be installed at the corner of Main and Perry? Not biased; the question does not include an opinion on the stoplight.

 Interactive Whiteboard
Interactive example available online

⏻ my.hrw.com

YOUR TURN

Talk About It
Check for Understanding

Ask: If you want to know how often people in your town travel as part of their job, why will surveying people at the airport produce a biased sample? People at the airport might be more likely to travel as part of their job, so they would not accurately represent the entire town's population.

EXAMPLE 2

Avoid Common Errors
Students may be inclined to say a question is not biased if they agree with the implications in the question. Have students underline any words that have unnecessary negative or positive connotations to help them determine whether a question is biased.

Questioning Strategies 🏴 **Mathematical Practices**

• Can a survey question be biased if the information included is true? Justify your answer. Yes, true information can still be used to influence people to respond a certain way to a question. For example, "A glass of water has less calories than a glass of soda. What's the best drink to have with meals?" is a biased question.

• What could be the negative effects of using a biased survey question? The biased survey question could produce answers that are not truly representative of the entire population.

YOUR TURN

Focus on Communication
Discuss situations where the question in Exercise 5 might be used in a survey where most people would answer that they prefer dogs, such as surveying people at a dog park. Be sure students understand that unbiased samples and unbiased questions are both important when conducting a survey.

Elaborate

Talk About It
Summarize the Lesson

Ask: How can you make sure you are using unbiased samples and unbiased questions when surveying people? To have an unbiased sample, select people who are unlikely to answer the survey with a certain response. To write an unbiased question, make sure the words you choose do not make it more likely that people will respond with a certain answer.

GUIDED PRACTICE

Engage with the Whiteboard
Have students display their data for both Method 1 and Method 2 for Exercise 1. Discuss with students how they chose the students for their random sample, and whether they could have selected a sample that better represented the average male, seventh grade student.

Avoid Common Errors
Exercise 4 Some students may not consider the question to be biased if green is their favorite color. Remind students that they must not include information in the question that appears to lead to any particular response.

4. For a survey, a company manager assigned a number to each of the company's 500 employees, and put the numbers in a bag. The manager chose 20 numbers and surveyed the employees with those numbers. Did the manager choose a random sample?

Yes; every employee had an equal chance of being

selected.

Bias in Survey Questions

Once you have selected a representative sample of the population, be sure that the data is gathered without bias. Make sure that the survey questions themselves do not sway people to respond a certain way.

EXAMPLE 2 *Real World*   FL CC 7.SP.1.1

In Madison County, residents were surveyed about a new skateboard park. Determine whether each survey question may be biased. Explain.

A Would you like to waste the taxpayers' money to build a frivolous skateboard park?

This question is biased. It discourages residents from saying yes to a new skateboard park by implying it is a waste of money.

B Do you favor a new skateboard park?

This question is not biased. It does not include an opinion on the skateboard park.

C Studies have shown that having a safe place to go keeps kids out of trouble. Would you like to invest taxpayers' money to build a skateboard park?

This question is biased. It leads people to say yes because it mentions having a safe place for kids to go and to stay out of trouble.

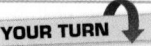

Determine whether each question may be biased. Explain.

5. When it comes to pets, do you prefer cats?

The question is biased since cats are suggested.

6. What is your favorite season?

The question is not biased. It does not lead people to

pick a particular season.

Personal Math Trainer
Online Assessment and Intervention
my.hrw.com

Math On the Spot
my.hrw.com

Personal Math Trainer
Online Assessment and Intervention
my.hrw.com

Guided Practice

1. Follow each method described below to collect data to estimate the average shoe size of seventh grade boys. (Explore Activity)

Method 1

A Randomly select 6 seventh grade boys and ask each his shoe size. Record your results in a table like the one shown.
Check students' work.

Random Sample of Seventh Grade Male Students	
Student	Shoe Size

B Find the mean of this data. Mean:
Answers will vary.

Method 2

A Find the 6 boys in your math class with the largest shoes and ask their shoe size. Record your results in a table like the one shown in Method 1.
Check students' work.

B Find the mean of this data. Mean: _____ Answers will vary.

2. Method 1 produces results that are (more)/ less representative of the entire student population because it is a (random)/ biased sample. (Example 1)

3. Method 2 produces results that are more /(less) representative of the entire student population because it is a random /(biased) sample. (Example 1)

4. Heidi decides to use a random sample to determine her classmates' favorite color. She asks, "Is green your favorite color?" Is Heidi's question biased? If so, give an example of an unbiased question that would serve Heidi better. (Example 2)
Yes; Sample answer: What is your favorite color?

 **ESSENTIAL QUESTION CHECK-IN**

5. How can you select a sample so that the information gained represents the entire population?
Select a random sample of sufficient size that represents the

population and ask each participant unbiased questions.

DIFFERENTIATE INSTRUCTION

Cooperative Learning

Have students work in groups to develop a way to survey a random sample of students from the whole school. Have groups share their plans and vote on the best one. Then have the class develop a questionnaire to be used and carry out the plan. Sample answer: Visit each classroom and assign a number to each row of desks. Write the numbers on slips of paper, and choose one at random. Have students in that row fill out the questionnaire. Randomly choose a slip of paper at each classroom.

Critical Thinking

Using bags containing 50 blue counters and 50 red counters, have students collect data by drawing (then returning) a sample of 6 counters. Then have students repeat this selection process 10 times. Have students collect similar data with samples of 12 counters and 18 counters. Discuss with students how often their samples were close to being 50% red and 50% blue. Also discuss if larger samples were more likely or less likely to be representative of the population.

Additional Resources

Differentiated Instruction includes:
- Reading Strategies
- Success for English Learners **ELL**
- Reteach
- Challenge **PRE-AP**

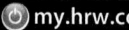
5.1 LESSON QUIZ

 **FL CC** 7.SP.1.1

Determine whether each sample is a random sample or a biased sample. Explain.

1. Carlos chooses 50 movies at random from a list of all his movies to determine the average runtime of the movies in his collection.

2. Lisa asks 75 people at a neighborhood fast food restaurant about the last meal they ate, in order to find out the eating habits of people in her neighborhood.

3. To determine the favorite subject of students at his school, Jason surveys 30 students who ride his bus about their favorite subject.

Determine whether each question may be biased. Explain.

4. Would a theme park with expensive ticket prices be a good place for a field trip?

5. What is your favorite horror movie?

Lesson Quiz available online

 my.hrw.com

Answers

1. Random; the movies were selected at random.

2. Biased; eating habits of people at a fast food restaurant might not accurately represent the population.

3. Biased; most of the students at his school have no chance to be surveyed.

4. Biased; the use of the word *expensive* in the question discourages people from answering yes.

5. Not biased; the question does not suggest a certain answer.

Evaluate

GUIDED AND INDEPENDENT PRACTICE

 **FL CC** 7.SP.1.1

Concepts & Skills	Practice
Explore Activity Random and Nonrandom Sampling	Exercise 1
Example 1 Random Samples and Biased Samples	Exercises 2–3, 6–11
Example 2 Bias in Survey Questions	Exercises 4, 12–13

Exercise	Depth of Knowledge (D.O.K.)	**FL CC** Mathematical Practices
6–7	**3** Strategic Thinking H.O.T.	**MP.4.1** Problem Solving
8–13	**3** Strategic Thinking H.O.T.	**MP.7.1** Using Structure
14	**3** Strategic Thinking H.O.T.	**MP.3.1** Logic
15	**3** Strategic Thinking H.O.T.	**MP.1.1** Problem Solving
16	**3** Strategic Thinking H.O.T.	**MP.3.1** Logic

Additional Resources

Extra Practice includes:

• Leveled Practice Worksheets

5.1 Independent Practice

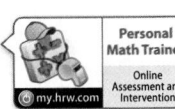

FL CC 7.SP.1.1

Personal Math Trainer
Online Assessment and Intervention
my.hrw.com

6. Paul and his friends average their test grades and find that the average is 95. The teacher announces that the average grade of all of her classes is 83. Why are the averages so different?

Sample answer: Paul's sample was biased. Maybe his friends studied more than others.

7. Nancy hears a report that the average price of gasoline is $2.82. She averages the prices of stations near her home. She finds the average price of gas to be $3.03. Why are the averages different?

Sample answer: Nancy sampled only stations near her, not in other parts of the nation.

For 8–10, determine whether each sample is a random sample or a biased sample. Explain.

8. Carol wants to find out the favorite foods of students at her middle school. She asks the boys' basketball team about their favorite foods.

It is a biased sample. Students who aren't on the team won't be selected.

9. Dallas wants to know what elective subjects the students at his school like best. He surveys students who are leaving band class.

It is biased because students who aren't in that class won't be selected.

10. To choose a sample for a survey of seventh graders, the student council puts pieces of paper with the names of all the seventh graders in a bag, and selects 20 names.

It is a random sample because all seventh graders have an equal chance of being selected.

11. Members of a polling organization survey 700 of the 7,453 registered voters in a town by randomly choosing names from a list of all registered voters. Is their sample likely to be representative?

Sample answer: Yes; the sample is random.

For 12–13, determine whether each question may be biased. Explain.

12. Joey wants to find out what sport seventh grade girls like most. He asks girls, "Is basketball your favorite sport?"

It is biased because basketball is mentioned.

13. Jae wants to find out what type of art her fellow students enjoy most. She asks her classmates, "What is your favorite type of art?"

Jae's question is not biased since it does not suggest a type of art to students.

H.O.T. FOCUS ON HIGHER ORDER THINKING

Work Area

14. **Draw Conclusions** Determine which sampling method will better represent the entire population. Justify your answer.

Student Attendance at Football Games	
Sampling Method	**Results of Survey**
Collin surveys 78 students by randomly choosing names from the school directory.	63% attend football games.
Karl surveys 25 students that were sitting near him during lunch.	82% attend football games.

Collin's method better represents the entire student population because he used a random sample. Karl's method picked people that could all be friends that go to football games together. The sample may not best represent the entire student population.

15. **Multistep** Barbara surveyed students in her school by looking at an alphabetical list of the 600 student names, dividing them into groups of 10, and randomly choosing one from each group.

a. How many students did she survey? What type of sample is this?

60; a random sample

b. Barbara found that 35 of the survey participants had pets. About what percent of the students she surveyed had pets? Is it safe to believe that about the same percent of students in the school have pets? Explain your thinking.

58%; it appears reasonable because Barbara used a random sample and surveyed a significant percent of the students.

16. **Communicating Mathematical Ideas** Carlo said a population can have more than one sample associated with it. Do you agree or disagree with his statement? Justify your answer.

Carlo is correct. There are many valid ways to select a representative sample from a population.

EXTEND THE MATH   PRE-AP

Activity available online my.hrw.com

Activity Have you ever wondered what the 10 most frequently used letters in the English language are? Use a book to select a random sample of English words. Open the book to any page. Write the first complete word that appears on the page. Repeat the process until you have a list of 200 words, some of which could be the same word. Find the 10 letters that occur most often in your sample, and determine the percent of the total sample for each of the 10 most frequent letters.

Check students' work. The actual relative frequencies for the 10 most common letters in the English language are shown in the table below.

Letter	Relative Frequency	Letter	Relative Frequency
E	12.702%	N	6.749%
T	9.056%	S	6.327%
A	8.167%	H	6.094%
O	7.507%	R	5.987%
I	6.966%	D	4.253%

LESSON 5.2 Making Inferences from a Random Sample

 Florida Common Core Standards

The student is expected to:

 **Statistics and Probability— 7.SP.1.2**

Use data from a random sample to draw inferences about a population with an unknown characteristic of interest. Generate multiple samples (or simulated samples) of the same size to gauge the variation in estimates or predictions.

 **Ratio and Proportional Relationships—7.RP.1.2c**

Represent proportional relationships by equations.

 **Statistics and Probability— 7.SP.1.1**

Understand that statistics can be used to gain information about a population by examining a sample of the population; generalizations about a population from a sample are valid only if the sample is representative of that population. Understand that random sampling tends to produce representative samples and support valid inferences.

Mathematical Practices

 MP.4.1 Modeling

Engage

ESSENTIAL QUESTION

How can you use a sample to gain information about a population? Sample answer: If the sample is random, you can write a proportion that relates the number of items in the sample with a certain trait to the number of items in the population with the same trait.

Motivate the Lesson

Ask: If you conducted a survey about how many pens people have in their backpack, what number of pens do you think would be the most frequent answer? Take a guess before you begin Explore Activity 1.

Explore

EXPLORE ACTIVITY 1

Avoid Common Errors

Students sometimes leave a data value off a dot plot when the data set is not presented in numerical order. Have students cross out each data value after they place the dot on the plot for that value. Also encourage students to count the data values in the set and the dots in their finished dot plot to verify that the totals are the same.

Explain

EXPLORE ACTIVITY 2

Connect Vocabulary ELL

Make a connection between the word *quarter* and the vocabulary terms **lower quartile** and **upper quartile.** Be sure students realize that the lower quartile, upper quartile, and median divide the data set into four sections that each contain the same number of data values.

Engage with the Whiteboard

For Steps 2 and 3, have students determine a scale for the number line, then plot the median and the upper and lower quartiles. Make sure students only draw vertical lines through the upper and lower quartiles and through the median.

Questioning Strategies Mathematical Practices

• How do you find the median of a set of numbers? Write the numbers in order from least to greatest. If there is an odd number of values, the median is the middle value in the list. If there is an even number of values, there will be two middle values and the median is the average of these two numbers.

• What is the difference between the median and the mean for a set of numbers? The median is the middle value when the set of numbers is written in order. The mean is found by dividing the sum of all the values in the set by the number of values in the set.

Making Inferences from a Random Sample

 FL CC 7.SP.1.2
Use data from a random sample to draw inferences about a population with an unknown characteristic of interest ... *Also 7.RP.1.2c, 7.SP.1.1*

? ESSENTIAL QUESTION How can you use a sample to gain information about a population?

EXPLORE ACTIVITY 1 *Real World* **FL CC** 7.SP.1.2, 7.SP.1.1

Using Dot Plots to Make Inferences

After obtaining a random sample of a population, you can make inferences about the population. Random samples are usually representative and support valid inferences.

Rosee asked students on the lunch line how many books they had in their backpacks. She recorded the data as a list: 2, 6, 1, 0, 4, 1, 4, 2, 2. Make a dot plot for the books carried by this sample of students.

STEP 1 Order the data from least to greatest. Find the least and greatest values in the data set.

STEP 2 Draw a number line from 0 to 6. Place a dot above each number on the number line for each time it appears in the data set.

[dot plot: 0 1 2 3 4 5 6]

Notice that the dot plot puts the data values in order.

Sample answer: No, most of the students have between 1 and 4 books, so some would likely have 3.

Math Talk
Mathematical Practices
No students in Rosee's sample carry 3 books. Do you think this is true of all the students at the school? Explain.

Reflect

1. **Critical Thinking** How are the number of dots you plotted related to the number of data values?

   They are the same. Each dot represents one data value.

2. **Draw Conclusions** Complete each qualitative inference about the population.
   Sample answers are given.

   Most students have __at least__ 1 book in their backpacks.

   Most students have fewer than __5__ books in their backpacks.

   Most students have between __1 and 4__ books in their backpacks.

3. **Analyze Relationships** What could Rosee do to improve the quality of her data?

   Rosee could increase the size of her sample.

Lesson 5.2 **151**

EXPLORE ACTIVITY 2 *Real World* **FL CC** 7.SP.1.2

Using Box Plots to Make Inferences

You can also analyze box plots to make inferences about a population.

The number of pets owned by a random sample of students at Park Middle school is shown below. Use the data to make a box plot.

9, 2, 0, 4, 6, 3, 3, 2, 5

STEP 1 Order the data from least to greatest. Then find the least and greatest values, the median, and the lower and upper quartiles.

STEP 2 The lower and upper quartiles can be calculated by finding the medians of each "half" of the number line that includes all the data.

[number line: 0 2 2 3 3 4 5 6 9]

The lower quartile is the mean of 2 and 2. The upper quartile is the mean of 5 and 6.

Least value | Lower quartile | Median | Upper quartile | Greatest value
0 | 2 | 3 | 5.5 | 9

Draw a number line that includes all the data values.

Plot a point for each of the values found in Step 1.

[box plot: 0 5 10]

STEP 3 Draw a box from the lower to upper quartile. Inside the box, draw a vertical line through the median. Finally, draw the whiskers by connecting the least and greatest values to the box.

The median value and the interquartile range

Math Talk
Mathematical Practices
What can you see from a box plot that is not readily apparent in a dot plot?

Reflect

4. **Draw Conclusions** Complete each qualitative inference about the population.

   A good measure for the most likely number of pets is __3__.

   50% of the students have between __0__ and 3 pets.

   Almost every student in Parkview has at least __1__ pet.

152 Unit 3

PROFESSIONAL DEVELOPMENT

Integrate Mathematical Practices MP.4.1

This lesson provides an opportunity to address this Mathematical Practice standard. It calls for students to model with mathematics. Students learn to model sets of data using dot plots and box plots, and then use the representations to make inferences. They learn to represent and solve real-world problems using proportions.

Math Background

The interquartile range, or IQR, is a value equal to the difference between the upper quartile (also called Q3) and lower quartile (also called Q1). The interquartile range can be used to find outliers in a data set. Values that are less than $Q1 - 1.5(IQR)$ or greater than $Q3 + 1.5(IQR)$ are considered outliers.

EXAMPLE 1

Focus on Communication

Review the different methods students have already learned for solving proportions. Remind students that when solving proportions, they may want to write one of the ratios in simplest terms to make calculations easier.

Focus on Critical Thinking 🖊 **Mathematical Practices**

Discuss with students other correct proportions that could be made using the same numbers, such as $\frac{50}{3,500} = \frac{3}{x}$. In this proportion, the ratio on the left is the ratio of sample size to population size and the ratio on the right is the ratio of defective MP3s in the sample to defective MP3s in the entire population. Help students realize that some proportions may have more obvious methods for finding a solution, but every correct proportion can be solved to obtain the same correct result.

Questioning Strategies 🖊 **Mathematical Practices**

• What division problem can be used to find the number by which both the numerator and the denominator need to be multiplied? $3,500 \div 50 = 70$

• If the manager concluded that 21 MP3 players were likely to be defective, what error did he make? The manager did not correctly multiply 3×70.

YOUR TURN

Talk About It
Check for Understanding

Ask: What proportion did you use to find the total number of damaged MP3 players in the shipment when six MP3 players in the sample had been damaged? $\frac{6}{50} = \frac{x}{3,500}$

Elaborate

. . . .

Talk About It
Summarize the Lesson

Ask: Can random samples and proportional reasoning be used to determine precise information about a population? Explain. No, random samples and proportional reasoning can only be used to make predictions. While these predictions are likely to be close to the actual value, it is possible for a prediction to be inaccurate.

GUIDED PRACTICE

Engage with the Whiteboard

For Exercise 1, have students decide on an appropriate scale and then have volunteers plot the points on the dot plot. For Exercise 2, have the class discuss whether using the same scale for the box plot will make it easy to compare both plots. Then have volunteers identify the key values and use them to construct the various parts of the box plot.

Avoid Common Errors

Exercise 1 Suggest students cross out each data value as they add dots to the dot plot. This will help them be sure that none of the values in the data set were overlooked as they constructed the dot plot.

Using Proportions to Make Inferences

You can use data based on a random sample, along with proportional reasoning, to make inferences or predictions about the population.

 Math On the Spot
my.hrw.com

EXAMPLE 1 Real World   FL CC 7.SP.1.2, 7.RP.1.2c

A shipment to a warehouse consists of 3,500 MP3 players. The manager chooses a random sample of 50 MP3 players and finds that 3 are defective. How many MP3 players in the shipment are likely to be defective?

It is reasonable to make a prediction about the population because this sample is random.

STEP 1 Set up a proportion.

$$\frac{\text{defective MP3s in sample}}{\text{size of sample}} = \frac{\text{defective MP3s in population}}{\text{size of population}}$$

STEP 2 Substitute values into the proportion.

$\frac{3}{50} = \frac{x}{3,500}$ Substitute known values. Let x be the number of defective MP3 players in the population.

$\frac{3 \cdot 70}{50 \cdot 70} = \frac{x}{3,500}$ $50 \cdot 70 = 3,500$, so multiply the numerator and denominator by 70.

$\frac{210}{3,500} = \frac{x}{3,500}$

$210 = x$

Based on the sample, you can predict that 210 MP3 players in the shipment would be defective.

Animated Math
my.hrw.com

YOUR TURN

5. What If? How many MP3 players in the shipment would you predict to be damaged if 6 MP3s in the sample had been damaged?

420 damaged MP3s

Reflect

6. Check for Reasonableness How could you use estimation to check if your answer is reasonable?

Sample answer: 6 is a little more than 10% of 50. 10% of 3,500 is 350, and 420 is a little more than that.

Personal Math Trainer
Online Assessment and Intervention
my.hrw.com

Patrons in the children's section of a local branch library were randomly selected and asked their ages. The librarian wants to use the data to infer the ages of all patrons of the children's section so he can select age appropriate activities. In 3–6, complete each inference. (Explore Activity 1 and 2)

7, 4, 7, 5, 4, 10, 11, 6, 7, 4

1. Make a dot plot of the sample population data.

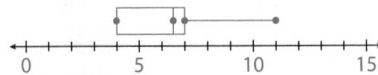

2. Make a box plot of the sample population data.

3. The most common ages of children that use the library are __4__ and __7__.

4. The range of ages of children that use the library is from __4__ to __11__.

5. The median age of children that use the library is __6.5__.

6. A manufacturer fills an order for 4,200 smart phones. The quality inspector selects a random sample of 60 phones and finds that 4 are defective. How many smart phones in the order are likely to be defective? (Example 1)

About __280__ smart phones in the order are likely to be defective.

7. Part of the population of 4,500 elk at a wildlife preserve is infected with a parasite. A random sample of 50 elk shows that 8 of them are infected. How many elk are likely to be infected? (Example 1)

720 elk

? ESSENTIAL QUESTION CHECK-IN

8. How can you use a random sample of a population to make predictions?

You can set up proportions using information obtained in a random sample of the population. For instance, the number of defective parts in a batch can be used to predict how many parts will be defective in a different-size batch.

DIFFERENTIATE INSTRUCTION

Kinesthetic Experience

When students use data sets to make box plots, write the data values on index cards. Have students place the cards in numerical order on a flat surface. Have them identify the cards representing the extremes, lower quartile, median, and upper quartile by rotating them a quarter turn. The final arrangement should help students visualize the box plot. You can also use the final arrangement to illustrate that although the box plot does divide the data into four equal-sized groups, the range of data values in each group will probably be different.

Curriculum Integration

Students can collect data from their class about various exercises, such as the number of pushups each person can do in a minute. Students can display the data in a box plot and collect more data about the same exercise at regular intervals. By comparing box plots from different time periods, students can make inferences about the progress of the class as a whole.

Additional Resources

Differentiated Instruction includes:
- Reading Strategies
- Success for English Learners **ELL**
- Reteach
- Challenge **PRE-AP**

Personal Math Trainer

Online Assessment and Intervention

Online homework assignment available

 my.hrw.com

5.2 LESSON QUIZ

 **FL CC** 7.SP.1.2

1. A random sample of 25 of the 400 members of the Bigtime Theater Company is surveyed about how many plays each has acted in. Make a box plot of the data. Then make a qualitative statement about the population. 3, 5, 5, 3, 4, 4, 1, 3, 6, 10, 1, 3, 4, 5, 1, 2, 4, 2, 3, 2, 5, 5, 5, 5, 6

2. Gerald buys a bag of 7,500 assorted beads online. A random sample of 150 beads contains 17 red beads. Predict the number of red beads in the bag of assorted beads that Gerald bought.

3. A store manager selects 30 cartons of eggs and finds 4 cartons that have cracked eggs. If the store has 105 cartons of eggs, how many cartons can she expect to have cracked eggs in them?

4. Jon finds a box of 350 postcards. He selects a random sample of 75 postcards and finds that 27 already have a stamp on them. Predict the total number of postcards in the box with stamps on them.

Lesson Quiz available online

 my.hrw.com

Answers

1. Sample answer: The most common number of plays to have acted in is between 4 and 5 plays.

2. 850 red beads

3. 14 cartons

4. 126 postcards

Evaluate

GUIDED AND INDEPENDENT PRACTICE

 **FL CC** 7.SP.1.1, 7.SP.1.2, 7.RP.1.2c

Concepts & Skills	Practice
Explore Activity 1 Using Dot Plots to Make Inferences	Exercises 1, 3–5, 13–15
Explore Activity 2 Using Box Plots to Make Inferences	Exercises 2, 3–5, 13–14, 16–17
Example 1 Using Proportions to Make Inferences	Exercises 6–7, 9–12

Exercise	Depth of Knowledge (D.O.K.)	**FL CC** Mathematical Practices
9–12	**2** Skills/Concepts	**MP.4.1** Modeling
13–14	**3** Strategic Thinking **H.O.T.**	**MP.3.1** Logic
15–16	**3** Strategic Thinking **H.O.T.**	**MP.2.1** Reasoning
17	**3** Strategic Thinking **H.O.T.**	**MP.3.1** Logic
18	**3** Strategic Thinking **H.O.T.**	**MP.7.1** Using Structure
19	**3** Strategic Thinking **H.O.T.**	**MP.4.1** Modeling
20	**3** Strategic Thinking **H.O.T.**	**MP.2.1** Reasoning

Additional Resources

Extra Practice includes:

• Leveled Practice Worksheets

5.2 Independent Practice

FL CC 7.RP.1.2c, 7.SP.1.1, 7.SP.1.2

Personal Math Trainer

Online Assessment and Intervention

my.hrw.com

9. A manager samples the receipts of every fifth person who goes through the line. Out of 50 people, 4 had a mispriced item. If 600 people go to this store each day, how many people would you expect to have a mispriced item?

48 people

10. Jerry randomly selects 20 boxes of crayons from the shelf and finds 2 boxes with at least one broken crayon. If the shelf holds 130 boxes, how many would you expect to have at least one broken crayon?

13 boxes

11. A random sample of dogs at different animal shelters in a city shows that 12 of the 60 dogs are puppies. The city's animal shelters collectively house 1,200 dogs each year. About how many dogs in all of the city's animal shelters are puppies?

240 puppies

12. Part of the population of 10,800 hawks at a national park are building a nest. A random sample of 72 hawks shows that 12 of them are building a nest. Estimate the number of hawks building a nest in the population.

1,800 hawks

13. In a wildlife preserve, a random sample of the population of 150 raccoons was caught and weighed. The results, given in pounds, were 17, 19, 20, 21, 23, 27, 28, 28, 28 and 32. Jean made the qualitative statement, "The average weight of the raccoon population is 25 pounds." Is her statement reasonable? Explain.

Yes, this seems reasonable

because 25 is the median of

the data.

14. Greta collects the number of miles run each week from a random sample of female marathon runners. Her data are shown below. She made the qualitative statement, "25% of female marathoners run 13 or more miles a week." Is her statement reasonable? Explain. Data: 13, 14, 18, 13, 12, 17, 15, 12, 13, 19, 11, 14, 14, 18, 22, 12

No. The statement should say

that 75% of female marathoners

run 13 or more miles a week.

15. A random sample of 20 of the 200 students at Garland Elementary is asked how many siblings each has. The data are ordered as shown. Make a dot plot of the data. Then make a qualitative statement about the population. Data: 0, 1, 1, 1, 1, 1, 1, 2, 2, 2, 2, 2, 3, 3, 3, 3, 4, 4, 4, 6

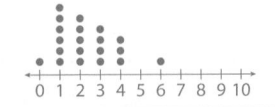

Sample answer: Most students at

Garland have 2 or fewer siblings.

16. Linda collects a random sample of 12 of the 98 Wilderness Club members' ages. She makes an inference that most wilderness club members are between 20 and 40 years old. Describe what a box plot that would confirm Linda's inference should look like.

The box plot should show that at

least 50% of the ages are between

20 and 40 years of age.

17. What's the Error? Kudrey was making a box plot. He first plotted the least and greatest data values. He then divided the distance into half, and then did this again for each half. What did Kudrey do wrong and what did his box plot look like?

Kudrey needs to find the median and the lower and

upper quartiles and plot those points. He assumed all

quartiles would be equally long when each quartile

represents an equal number of data values.

H.O.T. FOCUS ON HIGHER ORDER THINKING

Work Area

18. Communicating Mathematical Ideas A dot plot includes all of the actual data values. Does a box plot include any of the actual data values?

Yes, the least and greatest data values. The median and

quartiles may or may not be actual data values,

depending on how many values are in the data.

19. Make a Conjecture Sammy counted the peanuts in several packages of roasted peanuts. He found that the bags had 102, 114, 97, 85, 106, 120, 107, and 111 peanuts. Should he make a box plot or dot plot to represent the data? Explain your reasoning.

A box plot; Since every number is different, a dot

plot would only have one dot over each value, which

doesn't give much information. The box plot would

show the median, the range, and where data values are

concentrated if in fact they are.

20. Represent Real-World Problems The salaries for the eight employees at a small company are $20,000, $20,000, $22,000, $24,000, $24,000, $29,000, $34,000 and $79,000. Make a qualitative inference about a typical salary at this company. Would an advertisement that stated that the average salary earned at the company is $31,500 be misleading? Explain.

The typical salary at this company is $24,000, the median.

Yes, it is misleading; the average is thrown off by the

outlier value of $79,000.

EXTEND THE MATH PRE-AP

Activity available online my.hrw.com

Scientists often use random samples to estimate the size of an animal population. For example, to estimate the size of a population of deer, scientists can capture a random sample of 100 deer and place an identifying mark on each deer's left ear. All 100 deer are then released back into the wild. A month later, another sample of 50 deer is captured. If 4 deer in this sample already have the identifying mark on their left ear, how large is the deer population? Explain how you found your answer.

1,250 deer; to find the size of the total population, write a proportion.

$$\frac{\text{marked in first sample}}{\text{total size of population}} = \frac{\text{marked in second sample}}{\text{total size of second sample}}$$

$$\frac{100}{x} = \frac{4}{50}$$

$$\frac{100}{x} = \frac{4 \times 25}{50 \times 25}$$

$$\frac{100}{x} = \frac{100}{1,250}$$

So, $x = 1,250$.

5.3 Generating Random Samples

Florida Common Core Standards

The student is expected to:

 **FL CC** **Statistics and Probability— 7.SP.1.2**

Use data from a random sample to draw inferences about a population with an unknown characteristic of interest. Generate multiple samples (or simulated samples) of the same size to gauge the variation in estimates or predictions.

Mathematical Practices

FL CC **MP.5.1** Using Tools

Engage

ESSENTIAL QUESTION

How can you generate and use random samples to represent a population? Sample answer: Generate random samples using a calculator or other technique for producing random numbers. Use random samples as representative populations to make predictions.

Motivate the Lesson

Ask: How can you select a number between 1 and 1000, where every number has the same likelihood of being selected? Try to think of a method before starting the Explore Activity.

Explore

EXPLORE ACTIVITY 1

Focus on Communication 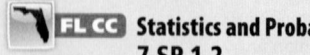 Mathematical Practices

Students may expect a series of random numbers to be somewhat evenly distributed or to not include the lower or upper limit of the range (1 or 200 in this case). Students should understand that randomly generated numbers may or may not be distributed evenly within the given range, can repeat, and can include any number in the given range.

Questioning Strategies

• When generating a random sample, can the same value appear more than once? Explain.
 Yes; since a random sample is one where every value has an equal chance of being selected, then any value in the range, even one already selected, could be selected.

Focus on Technology 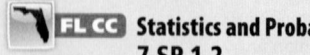 Mathematical Practices

Another possible syntax for the randInt command is randInt (x, y, z), where x is the smallest value, y is the largest value, and z is the number of random integers generated.

Focus on Critical Thinking 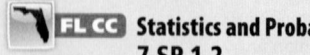 Mathematical Practices

Students may feel that a larger sample will always give more accurate results than a smaller sample. Discuss with students how a larger sample is more likely to be representative of the population than a smaller sample, but there will still be cases where a smaller sample can produce the more accurate results.

Avoid Common Errors

Several graphing calculator functions have similar names to the randInt function. Students must choose the randInt function to produce a usable random sample.

© Houghton Mifflin Harcourt Publishing Company • Image Credits: ©Richard Bingham II/Alamy Images

LESSON 5.3
Generating Random Samples

 FL CC 7.SP.1.2

Use data from a random sample ... Generate multiple samples (or simulated samples) of the same size to gauge the variation in estimates or predictions.

? ESSENTIAL QUESTION How can you generate and use random samples to represent a population?

EXPLORE ACTIVITY 1 *Real World* FL CC 7.SP.1.2

Generating a Random Sample Using Technology

In an earlier lesson, you generated random samples by rolling number cubes. You can also generate random samples by using technology. In Explore Activity 1, you will generate samples using a graphing calculator.

Each of the 200 students in a school will have a chance to vote on one of two names, Tigers or Bears, for the school's athletic teams. A group of students decides to select a random sample of 20 students and ask them for which name they intend to vote. How can the group choose a random sample to represent the entire population of 200 students?

A One way to identify a random sample is to use a graphing calculator to generate random integers.

To simulate choosing 20 students at random from among 200 students:

- Press **MATH**, scroll right and select **PRB**, then select **5: randInt(**.

- Enter the least value, comma, greatest possible value.

In this specific case, the students will enter **randInt** (1 , 200)

because there are ___200___ students in school.

- Hit **ENTER** __20__ times to generate __20__ random numbers.

randInt (1, 200)
            43
            93
            75
           178

The group gets a list of all the students in the school and assigns a number to each one. The group surveys the students with the given numbers.

Of the 20 students surveyed, 9 chose Tigers. The percent choosing

Tigers was __45%__. What might the group infer?

<u>The group might infer that the name Bears will probably</u>
<u>win, or that both names are almost equally likely to win.</u>

Lesson 5.3 **157**

EXPLORE ACTIVITY 1 *(cont'd)*

B You can simulate multiple random samples to see how much statistical measures vary for different samples of size 20.

Assume that the 200 students are evenly divided among those voting for Tigers and those voting for Bears. You can generate random numbers and let each number represent a vote. Let numbers from 1 to 100 represent votes for Tigers, and numbers from 101 to 200 represent votes for Bears. For each simulated sample, use randInt(1, 200) and generate 20 numbers.

Perform the simulation 10 times and record how many numbers from 1 to 100 are generated. How many of the samples indicated that there were 9 or fewer votes for Tigers?

Check students' results.

Combine your results with those of your classmates. Make a dot plot showing the number of numbers from 1 to 100 generated in each simulation.

Check students' results.

Reflect

1. **Communicate Mathematical Reasoning** Assume that it was accurate to say that the 200 students are evenly divided among those voting for Tigers and those voting for Bears. Based on your results, does it seem likely that in a sample of size 20, there would be 9 or fewer votes for Tigers?

Check students' results.

2. **Make a Prediction** Based on your answers, do you think it is likely that Tigers will win? Explain.

Check students' results.

3. **Multiple Representations** Suppose you wanted to simulate a random sample for the situation in Explore Activity 1 without using technology. One way would be to use marbles of two different colors to represent students choosing the different names. Describe how you could perform a simulation.

Let one color, say white, represent a vote for Tigers

and another, say, black represent a vote for Bears.

Place 100 white marbles and 100 black marbles in

a bag. Draw one without looking, record the color,

replace the marble and repeat till you've drawn

20 marbles.

© Houghton Mifflin Harcourt Publishing Company

158 Unit 3

PROFESSIONAL DEVELOPMENT

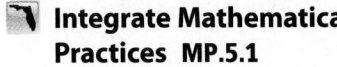 Integrate Mathematical Practices MP.5.1

This lesson provides an opportunity to address this Mathematical Practice standard. It calls for students to use appropriate tools strategically. Students use graphing calculators to randomly generate samples, then use paper and pencil to make predictions about the entire population. Then students use real objects dropped on an array of values to simulate a random selection of numbers, and go on to use pencil and paper to make predictions using the values in the random sample.

Math Background

Before the introduction of computers that easily generate random numbers, random numbers were usually found using random number tables. Random number tables were designed so that numbers chosen from a given row, column, or diagonal would be just as random as numbers selected irregularly. The numbers used in random number tables were collected from places such as the numbers used in census registers, and the numbers in logarithm tables.

Explain

EXPLORE ACTIVITY 2

Questioning Strategies

- Could the problem in Explore Activity 2 be solved using a calculator to generate random numbers? Explain. Yes; the calculator could be used to randomly generate 10 numbers between 1 and 100. Each of those numbers corresponds to a certain value in the chart. Calculate the mean of those 10 values.

- Could you use pencils as the objects you drop on the array? Explain. Sample answer: No; a pencil would cover several cells at the same time, so it would not produce a random individual selection.

Focus on Communication ⬛ Mathematical Practices

The randomness of the sample is dependent on using objects that can easily simulate randomness. A flipped coin results in unpredictable movement when it lands, but a heavier object might not. Discuss with students what objects seem likely to produce a random sample.

Integrating Language Arts ELL

Encourage a broad class discussion on the Math Talk question. English Learners will benefit from hearing and participating in classroom discussions.

Engage with the Whiteboard

Before performing the experiment, have a student circle ten numbers in the array, attempting to choose cells at random. Compare the outcome of the experiment to the student's circled numbers. Discuss whether the student's selection seems random compared to the actually random selection. How are they different?

Elaborate

Talk About It
Summarize the Lesson

Ask: Compare and contrast generating a random sample using a calculator, and generating a random sample by performing an experiment. With both methods, it is important to select a large enough sample to accurately represent the population. When generating a random sample by performing an experiment, it is important to make sure the experiment involves random selection.

GUIDED PRACTICE

Engage with the Whiteboard

For exercises 2–3, have a volunteer generate their own list of 20 random numbers and write them on the whiteboard. Have another student analyze the list. Is the sample reasonable in this case?

Avoid Common Errors

Exercise 2 Encourage students to go through the list carefully and circle the numbers that represent defective batteries as they go. Missing even one or two numbers makes a large difference to the final calculation.

Generating a Random Sample without Technology

A tree farm has a 100 acre square field arranged in a 10-by-10 array. The farmer wants to know the average number of trees per acre. Each cell in the table represents an acre. The number in each cell represents the number of trees on that acre.

22	24	27	29	31	24	27	29	30	25
37	22	60	53	62	42	64	53	41	62
61	54	57	34	44	66	39	60	65	40
45	33	64	36	33	51	62	66	42	42
37	34	57	33	47	43	66	33	61	66
66	45	46	67	60	59	51	46	67	48
53	46	35	35	55	56	61	46	38	64
55	51	54	62	55	58	51	45	41	53
61	38	48	48	43	59	64	48	49	47
41	53	53	59	58	48	62	53	45	59

The farmer decides to choose a random sample of 10 of the acres.

A To simulate the random selection, number the table columns 1–10 from left to right, and the rows 1–10 from top to bottom. Write the numbers 1–10 on identical pieces of paper. Place the pieces into a bag. Draw one at random, replace it, and draw another. Let the first number represent a table column, and the second represent a row. For instance, a draw of 2 and then 3 represents the cell in the second column and third row of the table, an acre containing 54 trees. Repeat this process 9 more times.

B Based on your sample, predict the average number of trees per acre. How does your answer compare with the actual mean number, 48.4?

Check students' answers. They may not be very close to the

actual mean because the sample was so small.

C Compare your answer to **B** with several of your classmates' answers. Do they vary a lot? Is it likely that you can make a valid prediction about the average number of trees per acre? Explain.

Check students' answers.

EXPLORE ACTIVITY 2 (cont'd)

Reflect

4. **Communicate Mathematical Ideas** Suppose that you use the method in **A** to collect a random sample of 25 acres. Do you think any resulting prediction would be more or less reliable than your original one? Explain.

Sample answer: More reliable; the larger sample should be

more representative of the population.

5. **Multiple Representations** How could you use technology to select the acres for your sample?

Number the acres in the grid from 1 to 100. Use the formula randInt (1, 100)

to generate numbers. Sample the acres with those numbers.

Guided Practice

A manufacturer gets a shipment of 600 batteries of which 50 are defective. The store manager wants to be able to test random samples in future shipments. She tests a random sample of 20 batteries in this shipment to see whether a sample of that size produces a reasonable inference about the entire shipment. (Explore Activities 1 and 2)

1. The manager selects a random sample using the formula

   randInt (1 , 600) to generate ___20___ random numbers.

2. She lets numbers from 1 to ___50___ represent defective batteries, and ___51___ to ___600___ represent working batteries. She generates this list: 120, 413, 472, 564, 38, 266, 344, 476, 486, 177, 26, 331, 358, 131, 352, 227, 31, 253, 31, 277.

3. Does the sample produce a reasonable inference?

   No, it has 4 defective batteries, or 20%. For the shipment, $\frac{50}{600}$, or

   about 8% of the batteries are defective.

? **ESSENTIAL QUESTION CHECK-IN**

4. What can happen if a sample is too small or is not random?

   Sample answer: A too-small or non-random sample is

   likely to pick unrepresentative data values.

DIFFERENTIATE INSTRUCTION

Manipulatives

Have students use a set of playing cards to generate sets of random numbers. Students will need 10 cards: an ace to represent the number 1, cards to represent numbers 2 through 9, and a joker to represent 0. Draw shuffled cards one at a time and replace them to create a random number. For example, to find a random number between 1 and 50, draw and replace a card to represent the first digit, then draw and replace a card to represent the second digit. If the number selected is over 50, discard that number from the sample. Students can repeat the process until they have collected the desired sample size.

Critical Thinking

Have students try to generate a set of numbers that seem random by writing down any five numbers between 1 and 100. Have students compare their random numbers with each other. Discuss with students ways to determine if the numbers selected by students are random, or if students are more likely to choose numbers in a certain range or with certain characteristics. Point out that truly random numbers are as likely to be one number five times in a row as they are to be any specific set of five different numbers.

Additional Resources

Differentiated Instruction includes:

• Reading Strategies
• Success for English Learners **ELL**
• Reteach
• Challenge **PRE-AP**

Personal Math Trainer

Online Assessment and Intervention

Online homework assignment available

 my.hrw.com

---

5.3 LESSON QUIZ

 **FL CC** 7.SP.1.2

Carter orders 120 glass ornaments online without knowing that 16 ornaments in the order are cracked. He decides to test a random sample of 20 ornaments to predict the number of cracked ornaments in the order.

1. What graphing calculator function could be used to generate random numbers to simulate this problem?

2. How many random numbers should be generated to simulate this problem?

3. Explain which randomly generated numbers should represent cracked ornaments, and which randomly generated numbers should represent noncracked ornaments.

4. How many cracked ornaments would Carter expect to find in the order based on this sample: 60, 5, 99, 88, 61, 19, 57, 50, 21, 49, 78, 94, 80, 2, 109, 14, 79, 41, 90, 114? Explain.

Lesson Quiz available online

 my.hrw.com

Answers

1. randInt(1,120).

2. 20

3. Sample answer: Numbers from 1 to 16 could represent cracked ornaments, and numbers 17 to 120 could represent intact ornaments.

4. 18 cracked ornaments; $\frac{3}{20}$ of the sample is between 1 and 16, so $\frac{3}{20}$ of the sample represents cracked ornaments. $\frac{3}{20}$ of 120 gives 18 cracked ornaments in the entire shipment.

Evaluate

GUIDED AND INDEPENDENT PRACTICE

 **FL CC** 7.SP.1.2

Concepts & Skills	Practice
Explore Activity 1 Generating a Random Sample Using Technology	Exercises 1–3, 8
Explore Activity 2 Generating a Random Sample without Technology	Exercises 1–3, 9

Exercise	Depth of Knowledge (D.O.K.)	**FL CC** Mathematical Practices
5–7	**2** Skills/Concepts	**MP.3.1** Logic
8–9	**2** Skills/Concepts	**MP.4.1** Modeling
10	**3** Strategic Thinking H.O.T.	**MP.4.1** Modeling
11	**3** Strategic Thinking H.O.T.	**MP.2.1** Reasoning
12	**3** Strategic Thinking H.O.T.	**MP.3.1** Logic

Additional Resources

Differentiated Instruction includes:

• Leveled Practice Worksheets

 **CLUSTER CONNECTION**   **Exercises 5–7** combine concepts from the Florida Common Core cluster "Use random sampling to draw inferences about a population."

5.3 Independent Practice

FL CC 7.SP.1.2

Maureen owns three bagel shops. Each shop sells 500 bagels per day. Maureen asks her store managers to use a random sample to see how many whole-wheat bagels are sold at each store each day. The results are shown in the table. Use the table for 5–7.

	Total bagels in sample	Whole-wheat bagels
Shop A	50	10
Shop B	100	23
Shop C	25	7

5. If you assume the samples are representative, how many whole-wheat bagels might you infer are sold at each store?

Shop A sells 100; Shop B sells 115; Shop C sells 140.

6. Rank the samples for the shops in terms of how representative they are likely to be. Explain your rankings.

From most to least likely: B, A, C; Shop B sold the most

bagels. Shop C sold the fewest bagels.

7. Which sample or samples should Maureen use to tell her managers how many whole-wheat bagels to make each day? Explain.

Shop A or Shop B; Both samples are large enough to

produce a reasonably valid inference. Shop C's sample is

too small.

8. In a shipment of 1,000 T-shirts, 75 do not meet quality standards. The table below simulates a manager's random sample of 20 T-shirts to inspect. For the simulation, the integers 1 to 75 represent the below-standard shirts.

124	876	76	79	12	878	86	912	435	91
340	213	45	678	544	271	714	777	812	80

In the sample, how many of the shirts are below quality standards? ___2___

If someone used the sample to predict the number of below standard shirts in the shipment, how far off would the prediction be?

The prediction would be that 100 of the shirts are below-

standard. That is $1\frac{1}{3}$ times the actual count of 75.

9. Multistep A 64 acre coconut farm is arranged in an 8-by-8 array. Mika wants to know the average number of coconut palms on each acre. Each cell in the table represents an acre of land. The number in each cell tells how many coconut palms grow on that particular acre.

56	54	40	34	44	66	43	65
66	33	42	36	33	51	62	63
33	34	66	33	47	43	66	61
46	35	48	67	60	59	52	67
46	32	64	35	55	47	61	38
45	51	53	62	55	58	51	41
48	38	47	48	43	59	64	54
53	67	59	59	58	48	62	45

a. The numbers in green represent Mika's random sample of 10 acres. What is the average number of coconut palms on the randomly selected acres?

49.8 palms

b. Project the number of palms on the entire farm.

about 3187 palms

H.O.T. FOCUS ON HIGHER ORDER THINKING

Work Area

10. Draw Conclusions A random sample of 15 of the 78 competitors at a middle school gymnastics competition are asked their height. The data set lists the heights in inches: 55, 57, 57, 58, 59, 59, 59, 59, 59, 61, 62, 62, 63, 64, 66. What is the mean height of the sample? Do you think this is a reasonable prediction of the mean height of all competitors? Explain.

60 inches; Sample answer: yes; the sample is random and of

a good size. But taking more samples to gauge the variability

among the samples would make for a more valid estimate.

11. Critical Thinking The six-by-six grid contains the ages of actors in a youth Shakespeare festival. Describe a method for randomly selecting 8 cells by using number cubes. Then calculate the average of the 8 values you found.

12	15	16	9	21	11
9	10	14	10	13	12
16	21	14	12	8	14
16	20	9	16	19	18
17	14	12	15	10	15
12	20	14	10	12	9

Sample answer: Roll two six-

sided number cubes, with one

cube representing the row and

the other representing the column. Select the cell represented

by the row and column shown on the cubes. Answers will vary

based on each student's results but should be about 13 or 14.

12. Communicating Mathematical Ideas Describe how the size of a random sample affects how well it represents a population as a whole.

Sample answer: The larger a random sample is, the more

likely it is to represent the population accurately.

EXTEND THE MATH PRE-AP

Activity available online my.hrw.com

Allison buys 1000 hair clips for $275 without knowing that 160 of the clips are broken. She selects a random sample of 100 clips to predict how many clips will be broken in all. The random numbers in the chart represent her sample. If Allison wants to make a profit of at least $225 by selling all the nonbroken clips, what is the lowest price Allison can charge per clip? Justify your answer.

$0.58; there are 13 values between 1 and 160 in the table, so the sample is 13% broken. Allison can estimate that 130 clips are broken and 870 are not broken. She must earn a profit of $225 plus the cost of her supplies, $275. She should charge $0.58 a piece.

925	224	278	884	273	246	442	761	882	267
317	95	364	853	282	46	741	591	662	18
986	638	395	275	269	583	357	411	58	614
285	254	294	194	952	740	143	334	349	275
316	422	271	79	552	784	759	879	134	645
235	468	299	539	848	178	613	179	817	471
698	226	927	160	970	756	136	540	663	693
207	269	856	431	298	617	343	656	238	231
279	597	909	58	859	289	481	80	518	961
962	906	576	546	355	795	426	68	762	135

Ready to Go On?

Assess Mastery

Use the assessment on this page to determine if students have mastered the concepts and standards covered in this module.

Response to Intervention

Intervention	Enrichment

Personal Math Trainer
Online Assessment and Intervention
my.hrw.com

Access Ready to Go On? assessment online, and receive instant scoring, feedback, and customized intervention or enrichment.

Online and Print Resources

Differentiated Instruction
• Reteach worksheets
• Reading Strategies **ELL**
• Success for English Learners **ELL**

Differentiated Instruction
• Challenge worksheets **PRE-AP**
Extend the Math **PRE-AP** Lesson Activities in TE

Additional Resources

Assessment Resources includes:
• Leveled Module Quizzes

Ready to Go On?

Personal Math Trainer
Online Assessment and Intervention
my.hrw.com

5.1 Populations and Samples

1. A company uses a computer to identify their 600 most loyal customers from its database and then surveys those customers to find out how they like their service. Identify the population and determine whether the sample is random or biased.

   Customers in the company's database; biased; loyal customers are likely to value their service.

5.2 Making Inferences from a Random Sample

2. A university has 30,330 students. In a random sample of 270 students, 18 speak three or more languages. Predict the number of students at the university who speak three or more languages.

   2,022 students

5.3 Generating Random Samples

A store receives a shipment of 5,000 MP3 players. In a previous shipment of 5,000 MP3 players, 300 were defective. A store clerk generates random numbers to simulate a random sample of this shipment. The clerk lets the numbers 1 through 300 represent defective MP3 players, and the numbers 301 through 5,000 represent working MP3 players. The results are given.

   13   2,195   3,873   525   900   167   1,094   1,472   709   5,000

3. Based on the sample, how many of the MP3 players might the clerk predict would be defective?

   1000 MP3 players

4. Can the manufacturer assume the prediction is valid? Explain.

   No; the sample is too small compared to the size of the shipment.

? ESSENTIAL QUESTION

5. How can you use random samples to solve real-world problems?

   Sample answer: You can make predictions about populations that are too large to survey.

Module 5 **163**

 ## Florida Common Core Standards

Lesson	Exercises	Common Core Standards
5.1	1	**7.SP.1.1**
5.2	2	**7.RP.1.2c, 7.SP.1.1, 7.SP.1.2**
5.3	3–4	**7.SP.1.2**

PARCC Assessment Readiness

Item 2 24 is a little less than half of 60, so the answer should be a little less than half of 490. Choice A is too small, choice C is exactly half of 490, and choice D is too large. The only possible answer is B.

Item 3 Students can quickly estimate the circumference by multiplying 3 for pi and 20 for the diameter, finding that the distance around the garden is about 60 meters. The only reasonable answer is B.

Avoid Common Errors

Item 4 Students may choose answer choice D because it has a large number of people, but surveying by email about using the Internet would be biased. The correct answer choice is C because they are choosing randomly from a very large pool of people.

Additional Resources

Personal Math Trainer

Online Assessment and Intervention

my.hrw.com

MODULE 5 MIXED REVIEW

PARCC Assessment Readiness

Personal Math Trainer
Online Assessment and Intervention
my.hrw.com

Selected Response

1. A farmer is using a random sample to predict the number of broken eggs in a shipment of 3,000 eggs. Using a calculator, the farmer generates the following random numbers. The numbers 1–250 represent broken eggs.

| 477 | 2,116 | 1,044 | 81 | 619 | 755 |
| 2,704 | 900 | 238 | 1,672 | 187 | 1,509 |

Based on this sample, how many broken eggs might the farmer expect?

- Ⓐ 250 broken eggs
- Ⓑ 375 broken eggs
- Ⓒ 750 broken eggs
- Ⓓ 900 broken eggs

2. A middle school has 490 students. Mae surveys a random sample of 60 students and finds that 24 of them have pet dogs. How many students are likely to have pet dogs?

- Ⓐ 98
- Ⓑ 196
- Ⓒ 245
- Ⓓ 294

3. A circular garden has a diameter of 18 meters. What is the circumference of the garden?

- Ⓐ 28.26 meters
- Ⓑ 56.52 meters
- Ⓒ 254.34 meters
- Ⓓ 1,017.36 meters

4. Which of the following is a random sample?

- Ⓐ A radio DJ asks the first 10 listeners who call in if they liked the last song.
- Ⓑ 20 customers at a chicken restaurant are surveyed on their favorite food.
- Ⓒ A polling organization numbers all registered voters, then generates 800 random integers. The polling organization interviews the 800 voters assigned those numbers.
- Ⓓ Rebecca used an email poll to survey 100 students about how often they use the internet.

Mini-Task

5. Each cell in the table represents the number of people who work in one 25-square-block section of the town of Middleton. The mayor uses a random sample to estimate the average number of workers per block.

47	61	56	48	(56)
(60)	39	63	60	46
51	58	49	63	45
55	58	(50)	(43)	48
(62)	(53)	44	66	55

a. The circled numbers represent the mayor's random sample. What is the mean number of workers on the 6 blocks that were randomly selected?

_____ 54 _____

b. Predict the number of workers in the entire 25-block section of Middleton.

_____ 1,350 workers _____

© Houghton Mifflin Harcourt Publishing Company

 ## Florida Common Core Standards

Items	Grade 7 Standards	Mathematical Practices
1	7.SP.1.2	MP.4.1
2	7.SP.1.2	MP.4.1
3*	7.G.2.4	MP.4.1
4	7.SP.1.1	MP.6.1
5	7.SP.1.2	MP.4.1

* Item integrates mixed review concepts from previous modules or a previous course.

Analyzing and Comparing Data

 ESSENTIAL QUESTION

How can you use solve real-world problems by analyzing and comparing data?

You can find measures of the data such as the mean and the median, and use them to solve the problems.

© Houghton Mifflin Harcourt Publishing Company • Image Credits: ©Kevin Schafer/ Alamy

Real-World Video

Scientists study animals like dolphins to learn more about characteristics such as behavior, diet, and communication. Acoustical data (recordings of dolphin sounds) can reveal the species that made the sound.

⏀ my.hrw.com

GO DIGITAL
my.hrw.com

 **my.hrw.com**

Go digital with your write-in student edition, accessible on any device.

 **Math On the Spot**

Scan with your smart phone to jump directly to the online edition, video tutor, and more.

 **Animated Math**

Interactively explore key concepts to see how math works.

 **Personal Math Trainer**

Get immediate feedback and help as you work through practice sets.

Are You Ready?

Assess Readiness

Use the assessment on this page to determine if students need intensive or strategic intervention for the module's prerequisite skills.

 **Response to Intervention**

Personal Math Trainer
Online Assessment and Intervention
⏱ my.hrw.com

Intervention	Enrichment

Access Are You Ready? assessment online, and receive instant scoring, feedback, and customized intervention or enrichment.

Online and Print Resources

Skills Intervention worksheets
- Skill 31 Fractions, Decimals, and Percents
- Skill 92 Find the Median and Mode
- Skill 93 Find the Mean

Differentiated Instruction
- Challenge worksheets **PRE-AP**
- Extend the Math **PRE-AP** Lesson Activities in TE

Are YOU Ready?

Complete these exercises to review skills you will need for this module.

 **Personal Math Trainer**
Online Assessment and Intervention
⏱ my.hrw.com

Fractions, Decimals, and Percents

EXAMPLE

Write $\frac{13}{20}$ as a decimal and a percent.

$$\begin{array}{r} 0.65 \\ 20\overline{)13.00} \\ -12\,0 \\ \hline 1\,00 \\ -1\,00 \\ \hline 0 \end{array}$$

$0.65 = 65\%$

Write the fraction as a division problem.
Write a decimal point and zeros in the dividend.
Place a decimal point in the quotient.

Write the decimal as a percent.

Write each fraction as a decimal and a percent.

1. $\frac{7}{8}$ 0.875; 87.5%
2. $\frac{4}{5}$ 0.8; 80%
3. $\frac{1}{4}$ 0.25; 25%
4. $\frac{3}{10}$ 0.3; 30%
5. $\frac{19}{20}$ 0.95; 95%
6. $\frac{7}{25}$ 0.28; 28%
7. $\frac{37}{50}$ 0.74; 74%
8. $\frac{29}{100}$ 0.29; 29%

Find the Median and Mode

EXAMPLE

17, 14, 13, 16, 13, 11
11, 13, 13, 14, 16, 17

median $= \frac{13 + 14}{2}$
$= 13.5$

Order the data from least to greatest.

The median is the middle item or the average of the two middle items.

Find the median and the mode of the data.

9. 11, 17, 7, 6, 7, 4, 15, 9   8; 7
10. 43, 37, 49, 51, 56, 40, 44, 50, 36   44; none

Find the Mean

EXAMPLE

17, 14, 13, 16, 13, 11

mean $= \frac{17 + 14 + 13 + 16 + 13 + 11}{6}$
$= \frac{84}{6}$
$= 14$

The mean is the sum of the data items divided by the number of items.

Find the mean of the data.

11. 9, 16, 13, 14, 10, 16, 17, 9   13
12. 108, 95, 104, 96, 97, 106, 94   100

© Houghton Mifflin Harcourt Publishing Company

PROFESSIONAL DEVELOPMENT VIDEO

Author Juli Dixon models successful teaching practices as she demonstrates how to analyze and compare data in an actual seventh-grade classroom.

 **Professional Development**
⏱ my.hrw.com

GO DIGITAL
my.hrw.com

 **Online Teacher Edition**
Access a full suite of teaching resources online—plan, present, and manage classes and assignments.

 ePlanner
Easily plan your classes and access all your resources online.

 Interactive Answers and Solutions
Customize answer keys to print or display in the classroom. Choose to include answers only or full solutions to all lesson exercises.

 Interactive Whiteboards
Engage students with interactive whiteboard-ready lessons and activities.

 Personal Math Trainer: Online Assessment and Intervention
Assign automatically graded homework, quizzes, tests, and intervention activities. Prepare your students with updated practice tests aligned with Common Core.

Analyzing and Comparing Data **166**

Reading Start-Up

Have students complete the activities on this page by working alone or with others.

Visualize Vocabulary

The chart helps students review vocabulary associated with statistical data. As a class, discuss other terms that can be added to the chart. Add those terms, their definitions, and an example for each to the chart.

Understand Vocabulary

Use the following explanations to help students learn the preview words.

A **box plot** shows the minimum, maximum, median, and quartiles of a data set, but does not show all of the individual values that make up the set. A **dot plot** shows every piece of data in a set.

Active Reading

Integrating Language Arts

Students can use these reading and note-taking strategies to help them organize and understand new concepts and vocabulary.

FL CC LACC.68.RST.3.7 Integrate quantitative or technical information expressed in words in a text with a version of that information expressed visually (e.g., in a flowchart, diagram, model, graph, or table).

Additional Resources

Differentiated Instruction

• Reading Strategies **ELL**

Reading Start-Up

Visualize Vocabulary

Use the ✔ words to complete the right column of the chart.

Statistical Data

Definition	Example	Review Word
A group of facts.	Grades on history exams: 85, 85, 90, 92, 94	data
The middle value of a data set.	85, 85, 90, 92, 94	median
A value that summarizes a set of values, found through addition and division.	Results of the survey show that students typically spend 5 hours a week studying.	mean

Understand Vocabulary

Complete each sentence using the preview words.

1. A display that uses values from a data set to show how the values are spread out is a ___box plot___.

2. A ___dot plot___ uses a number line to display data.

Vocabulary

Review Words
✔ data *(datos)*
interquartile range *(rango entre cuartiles)*
✔ mean *(media)*
measure of center *(medida central)*
measure of spread *(medida de dispersión)*
✔ median *(mediana)*
survey *(encuesta)*

Preview Words
box plot *(diagrama de caja)*
dot plot *(diagrama de puntos)*
mean absolute deviation (MAD) *(desviación absoluta media, (DAM))*

Active Reading

Layered Book Before beginning the module, create a layered book to help you learn the concepts in this module. Label the first flap with the module title. Label the remaining flaps with the lesson titles. As you study each lesson, write important ideas, such as vocabulary and formulas, under the appropriate flap. Refer to your finished layered book as you work on exercises from this module.

Module 6 **167**

© Houghton Mifflin Harcourt Publishing Company

Before	In this module	After
Students understand: • how to summarize numeric data with numerical summaries, including the mean and median • how to represent numeric data graphically, including box plots, stem-and-leaf plots, and histograms • how to interpret numeric data summarized in dot plots • how to summarize categorical data with numerical and graphical summaries	Students will learn how to: • compare two sets of data displayed in dot plots • compare two sets of data displayed in box plots	Students will connect: • the types of data analysis that can be performed with different data representations

Unpacking the Standards

Use the examples on the page to help students know exactly what they are expected to learn in this module.

 Florida Common Core Standards

Content Areas

 Statistics and Probability—7.SP.2

Draw informal comparative inferences about two populations.

Go online to see a complete unpacking of the Florida Common Core Standards.

(button) my.hrw.com

MODULE 6

Unpacking the Standards

Understanding the standards and the vocabulary terms in the standards will help you know exactly what you are expected to learn in this module.

FL CC 7.SP.2.3

Informally assess the degree of visual overlap of two numerical data distributions with similar variabilities, measuring the difference between the centers by expressing it as a multiple of a measure of variability.

Key Vocabulary

measure of center *(medida de centro)*
A measure used to describe the middle of a data set; the mean and median are measures of center.

What It Means to You

You will compare two populations based on random samples.

UNPACKING EXAMPLE 7.SP.2.3

Melinda surveys a random sample of 16 students from two college dorms to find the average number of hours of sleep they get. Use the results shown in the dot plots to compare the two populations.

Average Daily Hours of Sleep

Anderson Hall	Jones Hall
5 6 7 8 9 10 11	5 6 7 8 9 10 11

Students in Jones Hall tend to sleep more than students in Anderson Hall, but the variation in the data sets is similar.

FL CC 7.SP.2.3

Informally assess... distributions with similar variabilities, measuring the difference between the centers by expressing it as a multiple of a measure of variability.

Key Vocabulary

measure of spread *(medida de la dispersión)*
A measure used to describe how much a data set varies; the range, IQR, and mean absolute deviation are measures of spread.

Visit my.hrw.com to see all Florida Common Core Standards unpacked.
(button) my.hrw.com

What It Means to You

You will compare two groups of data by comparing the difference in the means to the variability.

UNPACKING EXAMPLE 7.SP.2.3

The tables show the number of items that students in a class answered correctly on two different math tests. How does the difference in the means of the data sets compare to the variability?

Items Correct on Test 1
20, 13, 18, 19, 15, 18, 20, 20, 15, 15, 19, 18

Mean: 17.5; Mean absolute deviation: 2

Items Correct on Test 2
8, 12, 12, 8, 15, 16, 14, 12, 13, 9, 14, 11

Mean: 12; Mean absolute deviation: 2

The means of the two data sets differ by $\frac{17.5-12}{2}=2.75$ times the variability of the data sets.

168 Unit 3

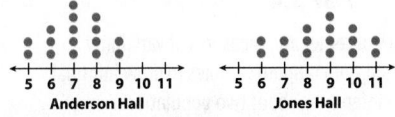

Florida Common Core Standards	Lesson 6.1	Lesson 6.2	Lesson 6.3
FL CC 7.SP.2.3 Informally assess the degree of visual overlap of two numerical data distributions with similar variabilities, measuring the difference between the centers by expressing it as a multiple of a measure of variability.	✓	✓	✓
FL CC 7.SP.2.4 Use measures of center and measures of variability for numerical data from random samples to draw informal comparative inferences about two populations.	✓	✓	✓

LESSON
6.1 Comparing Data Displayed in Dot Plots

Florida Common Core Standards

The student is expected to:

 Statistics and Probability—
7.SP.2.4

Use measures of center and measures of variability for numerical data from random samples to draw informal comparative inferences about two populations.
Also **7.SP.2.3**

Mathematical Practices

 **MP.7.1** Using Structure

---

ADDITIONAL EXAMPLE 1
Visually compare the dot plots of the scores for 25 science tests to the scores for 25 math tests.

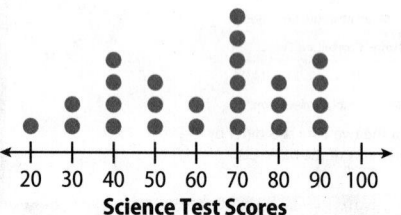

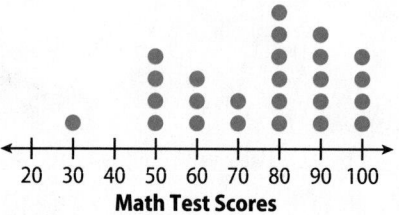

As a group, the science test scores are lower than the math test scores.

Science: The data is centered around 70. Math: The data is centered around 80.

Science: The spread is from 20 to 90. Math: The spread is from 30 to 100. The spread is the same 70 points.

 Interactive Whiteboard
Interactive example available online

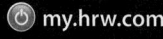 my.hrw.com

Engage

ESSENTIAL QUESTION

How do you compare two sets of data displayed in dot plots? Sample answer: You can compare the shapes, the centers, and the spread of the dots in the two plots. You can also compare the median and the range of the dot plots numerically.

Motivate the Lesson
Ask: How did the customary units of length, inch, foot, and yard, originate? Take a guess. Begin the Explore Activity to find out.

Explore

EXPLORE ACTIVITY

Focus on Modeling 🖊 Mathematical Practices
Point out that the shape of the dot plot is used to visualize whether the values in the data set are evenly distributed or grouped on one side. The mean, median, and range of the data help describe the spread of the data.

Explain

EXAMPLE 1

Focus on Math Connections 🖊 Mathematical Practices
Point out that because there are no outliers in the softball players' heights, the mean may be a useful statistic to find. The mean height is about 5'3".

Avoid Common Errors
Students may use the dot plot to make conclusions that are not valid. For example, the dot plot cannot be used to conclude that the basketball players are older than the softball players because they are taller. Caution students to only use the dot plot for information about the heights of the players.

Questioning Strategies 🖊 Mathematical Practices
• Why is the spread a useful way to compare the dot plots? The spread can tell you which team has more variability in the heights of its players.

• Why is the center a useful way to compare the dot plots? The center can compare the most common height for each group of players.

YOUR TURN

Focus on Math Connections 🖊 Mathematical Practices
Point out that because the center for field hockey players is lower than the center for either the softball players or the basketball players, in general, the heights of the field hockey players may be less than the corresponding heights of the softball or basketball players.

LESSON
6.1 Comparing Data Displayed in Dot Plots

FL CC 7.SP.2.4
Use measures of center and measures of variability ... to draw informal comparative inferences about two populations. *Also 7.SP.2.3*

ESSENTIAL QUESTION

How do you compare two sets of data displayed in dot plots?

EXPLORE ACTIVITY Real World

FL CC 7.SP.2.4

Analyzing Dot Plots

You can use dot plots to analyze a data set, especially with respect to its center and spread.

People once use body parts for measurements. For example, an inch was the width of a man's thumb. In the 12th century, King Henry I of England stated that a yard was the distance from his nose to his outstretched arm's thumb. The dot plot shows the different lengths, in inches, of the "yards" for students in a 7th grade class.

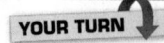

Length from Nose to Thumb (in.)

A Describe the shape of the dot plot. Are the dots evenly distributed or grouped on one side?

The dots are fairly evenly spread out with most in the middle.

B Describe the center of the dot plot. What single dot would best represent the data?

The most dots occur at 31 inches. The center with an equal number of dots on each side is around 31.5 in.

C Describe the spread of the dot plot. Are there any outliers?

The data values start at 28 in. and end at 35 in. Most of the data is between 29 in. and 34 in. 28 and 35 do not look like outliers.

Reflect

1. Calculate the mean, median, and range of the data in the dot plot.

Mean: about 31.6 in.; median: 31.5 in.; range: 7 in.

Lesson 6.1 **169**

Comparing Dot Plots Visually

You can compare dot plots visually using various characteristics, such as center, spread, and shape.

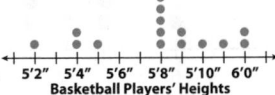

EXAMPLE 1 Real World

FL CC 7.SP.2.3

The dot plots show the heights of 15 high school basketball players and the heights of 15 high school softball players.

5'0" 5'2" 5'4" 5'6"
Softball Players' Heights

5'2" 5'4" 5'6" 5'8" 5'10" 6'0"
Basketball Players' Heights

A Visually compare the shapes of the dot plots.

Softball: All the data is 5'6" or less.
Basketball: Most of the data is 5'8" or greater.
As a group, the softball players are shorter than the basketball players.

B Visually compare the centers of the dot plots.

Softball: The data is centered around 5'4".
Basketball: The data is centered around 5'8".
This means that the most common height for the softball players is 5 feet 4 inches, and for the basketball players 5 feet 8 inches.

C Visually compare the spreads of the dot plots.

Softball: The spread is from 4'11" to 5'6".
Basketball: The spread is from 5'2" to 6'0".
There is a greater spread in heights for the basketball players.

Math Talk
Mathematical Practices

How do the heights of field hockey players compare with the heights of softball and basketball players?

Field hockey players as a group are about the same height as softball players.

YOUR TURN

2. Visually compare the dot plot of heights of field hockey players to the dot plots for softball and basketball players.

5'0" 5'2" 5'4" 5'6"
Field Hockey Players' Heights

Shape: dot plots for field hockey players and softball players have a similar spread.

Center: center of the field hockey dot plot is less than the center for softball or basketball players.

Spread: dot plots for field hockey players and softball players have a similar spread.

Personal Math Trainer
Online Assessment and Intervention
my.hrw.com

170 Unit 3

PROFESSIONAL DEVELOPMENT

Integrate Mathematical Practices MP.7.1

This lesson provides an opportunity to address this Mathematical Practice standard. It calls for students to analyze mathematical relationships to connect and communicate mathematical ideas. Students analyze pairs of dot plots, both visually and numerically. They also find and compare the medians and the ranges of the dot plots. In this way, students have analyzed mathematical relationships to communicate mathematical ideas.

Math Background

The median of a data set is one of the measures of central tendency. The others are the mean and mode. Here are some guidelines for choosing which measure to use to describe a data set.

Mean: The mean is the sum of the data values divided by the number of values. It is useful for describing data that are close in value and data that are normally distributed. The mean is not useful if the data contains outliers, which can skew the mean to the right or left of the center.

Median: The median is the middle value of the data when it is in numerical order. It is easy to calculate and is useful for describing a data set that is not normally distributed or that has outliers.

Mode: The mode is the data value that occurs most often. It is useful for describing a data set when the data clusters around certain values. It is the only measure of the three that can be used to describe nonnumerical, categorical data.

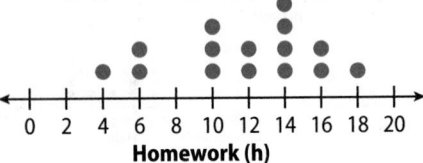
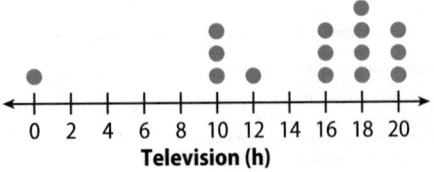
EXAMPLE 2

Questioning Strategies 🏴 Mathematical Practices

• Why do outliers affect the range of the dot plots but not the median? The range depends on the high and low values, while the median only depends on the number of data.

• When does it make sense to use the median to compare two data sets? Using the median makes sense when the center of the data gives a good description of the data or when there are outliers.

Focus on Modeling 🏴 Mathematical Practices

Point out that although graphing calculators can be used to find and compare the medians, the dot plots make finding the medians simply a matter of counting dots. The displays also give a way to visualize the medians in relation to the other data values.

Engage with the Whiteboard

Invite a student volunteer to compare the dot plots numerically. Have other volunteers discuss how to use the shapes, the centers, and the spread of the dot plots to visually compare the data sets.

YOUR TURN

Focus on Math Connections 🏴 Mathematical Practices

Point out that removing the outliers always affects the range greatly because outliers are extreme values.

Questioning Strategies 🏴 Mathematical Practices

• Why can you compare the data represented in the dot plot for Internet usage with the two dot plots in Example 2? Each of the dot plots represents data collected from the same students, and each of them uses the same units, hours.

Elaborate

Talk About It
Summarize the Lesson

Ask: In what ways can you compare data displayed in a pair of dot plots? You can compare the shapes, centers, and spread of the dot plots. You can also calculate the means and ranges of the dot plots and compare them.

GUIDED PRACTICE

Engage with the Whiteboard

Ask student volunteers to do the calculations for Exercises 4 and 5. Discuss the importance of comparing dot plots numerically as well as visually.

Avoid Common Errors

Exercise 4 Some students may write 7 as the median because it is halfway between 0 and 14 miles. Stress that the median is an actual data point. It is represented by the dot that has an equal number of dots in front of and behind it. Emphasize that the dot plot allows you to visually count the dots from each extreme in order to identify the dot representing the median value.

Integrating Language Arts ELL

Encourage a broad class discussion on the Math Talk. English learners will benefit from hearing and participating in classroom discussions.

Comparing Dot Plots Numerically

You can also compare the shape, center, and spread of two dot plots numerically by calculating values related to the center and spread. Remember that outliers can affect your calculations.

EXAMPLE 2

FL CC 7.SP.2.4

Numerically compare the dot plots of the number of hours a class of students exercises each week to the number of hours they play video games each week.

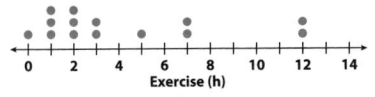
Exercise (h)

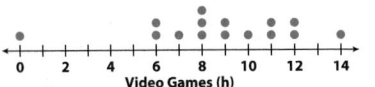
Video Games (h)

A Compare the shapes of the dot plots.

Exercise: Most of the data is less than 4 hours.
Video games: Most of the data is 6 hours or greater.

B Compare the centers of the dot plots by finding the medians.

Median for exercise: 2.5 hours. Even though there are outliers at 12 hours, most of the data is close to the median.
Median for video games: 9 hours. Even though there is an outlier at 0 hours, these values do not seem to affect the median.

C Compare the spreads of the dot plots by calculating the range.

Exercise range with outlier: $12 - 0 = 12$ hours
Exercise range without outlier: $7 - 0 = 7$ hours
Video games range with outlier: $14 - 0 = 14$ hours
Video games range without outlier: $14 - 6 = 8$ hours

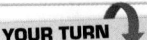

3. Calculate the median and range of the data in the dot plot. Then compare the results to the dot plot for Exercise in Example 2.

Internet Usage (h)

median: 6 h, range: 10 h; If you remove the outliers, the range is 4 hours. The median is greater than the median for exercise. The range is less than exercise.

Math Talk
Mathematical Practices

How do outliers affect the results of this data?

The outliers do not affect the median, but they greatly increase the range.

Math On the Spot
my.hrw.com

Animated Math
my.hrw.com

Personal Math Trainer
Online Assessment and Intervention
my.hrw.com

Guided Practice

The dot plots show the number of miles run per week for two different classes. For 1–5, use the dot plots shown.

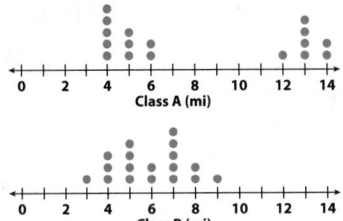
Class A (mi)

Class B (mi)

1. Compare the shapes of the dot plots.
Class A: clustered around two areas.
Class B: clustered in the middle

2. Compare the centers of the dot plots.
Class A: two peaks at 4 and 13 mi.
Class B: looks centered around 7 mi

3. Compare the spreads of the dot plots.
Class A: spread from 4 to 14 mi, a wide gap no data.
Class B: spread from 3 to 9 mi

4. Calculate the medians of the dot plots.
The median for both dot plots is 6 miles.

5. Calculate the ranges of the dot plots.
Range for Class A: 10 mi; range for Class B: 6 mi

ESSENTIAL QUESTION CHECK-IN

6. What do the medians and ranges of two dot plots tell you about the data?
The medians allow you to compare the centers. The ranges allow you to compare the spreads.

DIFFERENTIATE INSTRUCTION

Multiple Representations

Ask students to categorize the data for the Guided Practice exercises on page 358 using a table like the one shown below. Ask them if the table can be used effectively to compare the two data sets.

Miles	Class A	Class B
0–2	0	0
3–5	8	8
6–8	2	9
9–11	0	1
12–14	7	0

Kinesthetic Experience

Divide students into random groups A and B. Draw congruent number lines at the front and at the back of the room with heights as labels. Be sure the range of the number line is greater than the range of heights of the students. Ask the students in each group to line up along the number lines by height, group A in the front and group B in the back. Have each student draw a dot identifying their height. Then have each group find the median height and the range of heights for their group. Finally, have the entire class compare the shape, center, and spread of the two dot plots.

Additional Resources

Differentiated Instruction includes:

- Reading Strategies
- Success for English Learners **ELL**
- Reteach
- Challenge **PRE-AP**

6.1 LESSON QUIZ

MP.7.1

For 1–3, use the dot plots representing the number of siblings of students in each class.

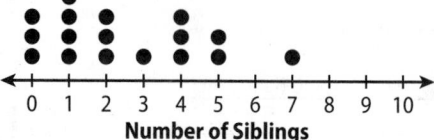

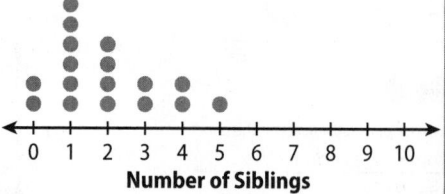

1. Visually compare the dot plots.

2. Compare the centers of the dot plots by finding the medians.

3. Compare the spreads of the dot plots by calculating the range.

For 4–5, use the dot plot.

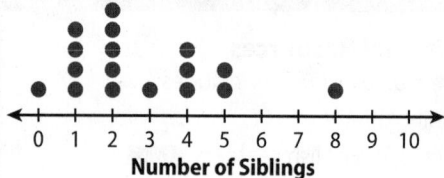

4. How does the shape of the dot plot for Mr. Barrett's class compare to the shape of the dot plot for Ms. White's class above?

5. How do the ranges of the dot plots compare for Mr. Barrett's and Mr. Walker's classes.

Lesson Quiz available online

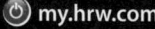
my.hrw.com

Evaluate

GUIDED AND INDEPENDENT PRACTICE

MP.7.1

Concepts & Skills	Practice
Explore Activity Analyzing Dot Plots	Exercises 1–5, 14, 18
Example 1 Comparing Dot Plots Visually	Exercises 1–3, 7–9, 11–13, 15
Example 2 Comparing Dot Plots Numerically	Exercises 4–5, 10, 16–17

Exercise	Depth of Knowledge (D.O.K.)	FL CC Mathematical Practices
7–9	**3** Strategic Thinking H.O.T.	**MP.8.1** Patterns
10	**2** Skills/Concepts	**MP.5.1** Using Tools
11–14	**3** Strategic Thinking H.O.T.	**MP.4.1** Modeling
15–20	**3** Strategic Thinking H.O.T.	**MP.8.1** Patterns

Additional Resources

Extra Practice includes:
• Leveled Practice Worksheets

Answers

1. Mr. Walker's class: All the data are 7 siblings or less. Ms. White's class: All the data are 5 siblings or less. So, as a group, students in Ms. White's class have fewer siblings. The data are centered around 2, so the most common number of siblings in both classes is 2. The spread for Mr. Walker's class is from 0 to 7 siblings, while the spread for Ms. White's class is 0 to 5 siblings. There is a greater spread in the number of siblings in Mr. Walker's class.

2. The median for each class is 2.

3. The range for Mr. Walker's class is 7 siblings; the range for Ms. White's class is 5 siblings.

4. The data in Ms. White's class are clustered around 1 or 2 siblings. The data in Mr. Barrett's have an outlier of 8, but the rest of the data are also clustered around 1 or 2 siblings.

5. The range for Mr. Barrett's class is 8 siblings, while the range for Mr. Walker's class is 7 siblings. The ranges are nearly the same.

6.1 Independent Practice

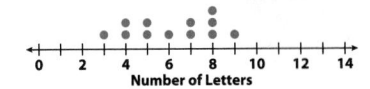

FL CC 7.SP.2.3, 7.SP.2.4

Personal Math Trainer
Online Assessment and Intervention
my.hrw.com

The dot plot shows the number of letters in the spellings of the 12 months. Use the dot plot for 7–10.

Number of Letters
0 2 4 6 8 10 12 14

7. Describe the shape of the dot plot.

The dots have a relatively even spread, with a peak at 8 letters.

8. Describe the center of the dot plot.

The center of the graph is between 6 and 7 letters.

9. Describe the spread of the dot plot.

The dots spread from 3 to 9 letters.

10. Calculate the mean, median, and range of the data in the dot plot.

mean ≈ 6.17; median = 6.5; range = 6

The dot plots show the mean number of days with rain per month for two cities.

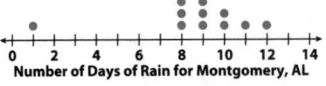
Number of Days of Rain for Montgomery, AL
0 2 4 6 8 10 12 14

Number of Days of Rain for Lynchburg, VA
0 2 4 6 8 10 12 14

11. Compare the shapes of the dot plots.

AL: clustered in one small interval with an outlier to the left;

VA: relatively uniform in height over the same interval

12. Compare the centers of the dot plots.

AL: centered between 8 and 9 days of rain;

VA: centered around 10 days of rain

13. Compare the spreads of the dot plots.

AL: spreads from 1 to 12 days of rain, an outlier at 1;

VA: spreads from 8 to 12 days of rain

14. What do the dot plots tell you about the two cities with respect to their average monthly rainfall?

Lynchburg, VA, has more consistent levels of rain, and more rain per month, compared to Montgomery, AL.

© Houghton Mifflin Harcourt Publishing Company

The dot plots show the shoe sizes of two different groups of people.

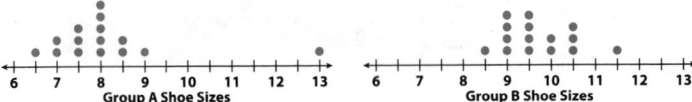
Group A Shoe Sizes
6 7 8 9 10 11 12 13

Group B Shoe Sizes
6 7 8 9 10 11 12 13

15. Compare the shapes of the dot plots.

Group A: clustered to the left of size 9;

Group B: clustered to the right of size 9

16. Compare the medians of the dot plots.

Group A: median at size 8; Group B: median at size 9.5

17. Compare the ranges of the dot plots (with and without the outliers).

Group A: range with outlier = 6.5, without outlier = 2.5;

Group B: range = 3

18. **Make A Conjecture** Provide a possible explanation for the results of the dot plots.

Sample answer: Group A could be children and Group B could be adults.

H.O.T. FOCUS ON HIGHER ORDER THINKING

Work Area

19. **Analyze Relationships** Can two dot plots have the same median and range but have completely different shapes? Justify your answer using examples.

Yes; one group of five students could have the following number of pets: 1, 2, 3, 4, 5. Another group of five students could have the following number of pets: 1, 3, 3, 3, 5. For both groups of students, the median would be 3 and the range would be 4.

20. **Draw Conclusions** What value is most affected by an outlier, the median or the range? Explain. Can you see these effects in a dot plot?

range; an outlier greatly increases the range whereas the median will generally not be greatly affected, as it is in the middle of all the values. A dot plot will show both.

© Houghton Mifflin Harcourt Publishing Company

EXTEND THE MATH PRE-AP

Activity available online my.hrw.com

Activity Suppose you and a friend want to use a dot plot to display the number of points you each made during the 15 games of the basketball season. Use the number lines shown to draw two dot plots with the following characteristics.

1. Your median score is 16 points, while your friend's median score is 12 points.

2. The range of your scores is 16 points, while the range of your friend's scores is 14 points.

3. The shape of your dot plot is evenly distributed on the right. The shape of your friend's dot plot is evenly distributed around the center, if the one outlier in her data is removed.

4. You have no outliers in your dot plot, but your friend only scored 2 points in one of her games.

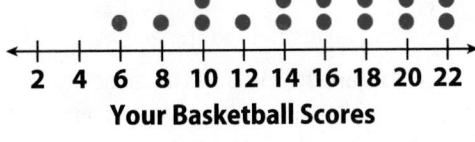
Your Basketball Scores
2 4 6 8 10 12 14 16 18 20 22

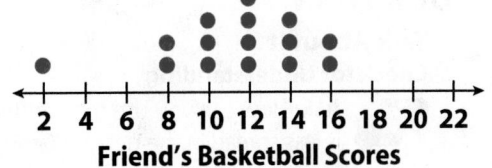
Friend's Basketball Scores
2 4 6 8 10 12 14 16 18 20 22

LESSON 6.2 Comparing Data Displayed in Box Plots

 Florida Common Core Standards

The student is expected to:

 **Statistics and Probability— 7.SP.2.3**

Informally assess the degree of visual overlap of two numerical data distributions with similar variabilities, measuring the difference between the centers by expressing it as a multiple of a measure of variability. *Also* **7.SP.2.4**

Mathematical Practices

 **MP.2.1** Reasoning

---

ADDITIONAL EXAMPLE 1
The box plots show the distribution of days spent at a national park by two different groups of visitors.

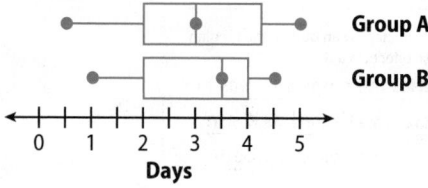

A Compare the shapes of the box plots. The position and lengths of the boxes appear to be similar. In both plots, the rightmost whisker is shorter than the leftmost whisker.

B Compare the centers of the box plots. Group B has a higher median of 3.5, while Group A has a median of 3. This means the median visitor in Group B spends 0.5 day longer at the park.

C Compare the spreads of the box plots. The box shows the interquartile range, and each box is similar. Group A = 2.25 days; Group B = 2 days. The whiskers are similar lengths, with Group A having slightly more extreme values than Group B.

 Interactive Whiteboard
Interactive example available online

⏻ my.hrw.com

Engage

ESSENTIAL QUESTION

How do you compare two sets of data displayed in box plots? Sample answer: You can compare the shapes, the centers, and the spreads of the box plots.

Motivate the Lesson
Ask: What are whiskers on a box plot, and what do they represent? Take a guess. Begin the Explore Activity to find out.

Explore

EXPLORE ACTIVITY

Focus on Math Connections 🏴 **Mathematical Practices**
Point out that while the median is displayed in a box plot, the mean and mode are not. Also point out that you cannot tell how many values there are in a data set by looking at its box plot. The shape of the box plot is used to visualize whether the data values are evenly distributed or grouped on one side of the median. Stress that evenly distributed data are modeled by a box plot whose quartiles (the two whiskers and the two parts of the box) are all about the same length.

Explain

EXAMPLE 1

Focus on Modeling 🏴 **Mathematical Practices**
Remind students that box plots model five key values that can be used to visually and numerically compare data sets. Box plots with similar key values indicate similar variability in the data sets, while box plots with very different key values indicate more variability in the data sets.

Questioning Strategies 🏴 **Mathematical Practices**
• How is the interquartile range used to compare the spread of the data in the box plots? The interquartile ranges of the box plots are computed and then compared. The wider the box, the greater the spread of the data around the median.

• How are the measures of variability in the data compared in the box plots? The sizes of the boxes and the lengths of the corresponding whiskers are compared.

YOUR TURN

Talk About It
Check for Understanding
Ask: How can you use the widths of the boxes in the box plots to know that there is less spread in the data for Group B than in the data for Group A? Group B has a shorter box than Group A.

LESSON 6.2 Comparing Data Displayed in Box Plots

FL CC 7.SP.2.3
Informally assess the degree of visual overlap of two numerical data distributions with similar variabilities, … *Also 7.SP.2.4*

? ESSENTIAL QUESTION

How do you compare two sets of data displayed in box plots?

EXPLORE ACTIVITY *Real World*   **FL CC 7.SP.2.4**

Analyzing Box Plots

Box plots show five key values to represent a set of data, the least and greatest values, the lower and upper quartile, and the median. To create a box plot, arrange the data in order, and divide them into four equal-size parts or quarters. Then draw the box and the whiskers as shown.

The number of points a high school basketball player scored during the games he played this season are organized in the box plot shown.

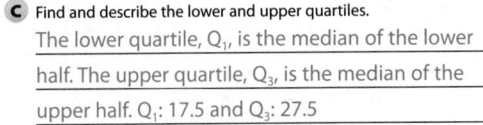

Points Scored

A Find the least and greatest values.

Least value: ___15 points___   Greatest value: ___30 points___

B Find the median and describe what it means for the data.

Median: 21 points; the median, or second quartile, Q_2, divides the data values into two halves, a lower half and an upper half.

C Find and describe the lower and upper quartiles.

The lower quartile, Q_1, is the median of the lower half. The upper quartile, Q_3, is the median of the upper half. Q_1: 17.5 and Q_3: 27.5

D The interquartile range is the difference between the lower and upper quartiles, which is represented by the length of the box. Find the interquartile range.

$Q_3 - Q_1 =$ ___27.5___ $-$ ___17.5___ $=$ ___10 points___

The whiskers are about the same length, which means that both quarters of the data have about the same range.

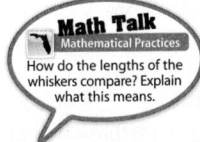
Math Talk
Mathematical Practices
How do the lengths of the whiskers compare? Explain what this means.

Lesson 6.2 **175**

EXPLORE ACTIVITY (cont'd)

Reflect

1. Why is one-half of the box wider than the other half of the box?

The quarter of data to the right of the median is more spread out than the quarter of data to the left of the median.

Box Plots with Similar Variability

You can compare two box plots numerically according to their centers, or medians, and their spreads, or variability. Range and interquartile range (IQR) are both measures of spread. Box plots with similar variability should have similar boxes and whiskers.

Math On the Spot
my.hrw.com

My Notes

EXAMPLE 1 *Real World*   **FL CC 7.SP.2.3**

The box plots show the distribution of times spent shopping by two different groups.

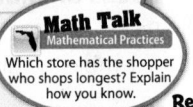

Shopping Time (min)

A Compare the shapes of the box plots.

The positions and lengths of the boxes and whiskers appear to be very similar. In both plots, the right whisker is shorter than the left whisker.

B Compare the centers of the box plots.

Group A's median, 47.5, is greater than Group B's, 40. This means that the median shopping time for Group A is 7.5 minutes more.

C Compare the spreads of the box plots.

The box shows the interquartile range. The boxes are similar.

Group A: $55 - 30 = 25$ min   Group B: About $59 - 32 = 26$ min

The whiskers have similar lengths, with Group A's slightly shorter than Group B's.

Math Talk
Mathematical Practices
Which store has the shopper who shops longest? Explain how you know.

Group B because it has a greater maximum.

Reflect

2. Which group has the greater variability in the bottom 50% of shopping times? The top 50% of shopping times? Explain how you know.

Group A; Group B; look at which box plot has a greater distance from the median to the minimum or maximum value, respectively.

176 Unit 3

PROFESSIONAL DEVELOPMENT

Integrate Mathematical Practices MP.2.1

This lesson provides an opportunity to address this Mathematical Practice standard. It calls for students to create and use representations to organize, record, and communicate mathematical ideas. Students analyze pairs of box plots, both with similar and with different variability. They compare the shapes, the centers, and the spreads of the box plots as a way to compare the data sets. In this way, students use representations to communicate mathematical ideas.

Math Background

The minimum or maximum value of a data set may be an outlier. An outlier is described as a value that is very high or very low compared to the other values in the set. However, it is often quantified further as any value that is more than 1.5 times the interquartile range either below the first quartile or above the third quartile. An outlier can have a great effect on the mean and range of a data set, but does not affect the median.

© Houghton Mifflin Harcourt Publishing Company • Image Credits: ©Rim Light/ PhotoLink/Photodisc/Getty Images

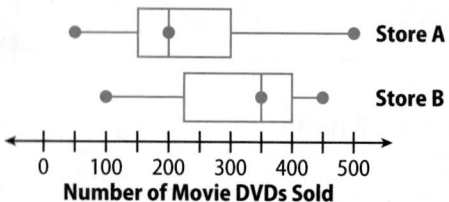

EXAMPLE 2

Focus on Reasoning 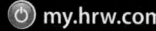 Mathematical Practices

Point out that the actual data values other than the maximum, minimum, and quartiles,
cannot be compared for the two box plots as they can for dot plots.

Engage with the Whiteboard

Invite a volunteer to mark the five key values for each box plot along the top of the
plot. Then have other volunteers discuss how these numbers relate to the shapes,
the centers, and the spreads of the box plots when comparing them.

Questioning Strategies Mathematical Practices

• Why do outliers affect the range of the box plots but not the interquartile range? The
range depends on the high and low values, while the interquartile range only depends
on the upper and lower quartiles of the data.

• Suppose you randomly pick a number of wristbands sold by Store A and by Store B. Can
the number of wristbands sold by Store A be higher? Explain. Yes; for any given day, the
sales for Store A can be higher than the sales for Store B.

• How are the range and the interquartile range different? Why do you often compare the
plots using the interquartile range? The range is the difference between the highest and
lowest values, while the interquartile range is the difference between the upper and lower
quartiles. You often use the interquartile range because it shows how widely the data are
spread around the median.

YOUR TURN

Focus on Math Connections Mathematical Practices

Point out that the shape, center, and spread of the data for this box plot more closely
resemble the distribution for Store A.

Talk About It
Check for Understanding

Ask: How do you determine the variability of this box plot? Find the spread of the
box plot by computing its range and interquartile range. If there is little spread,
then the data have less variability. If there is a great spread, then they have more variability.

Elaborate

Talk About It
Summarize the Lesson

Ask: How do you compare data modeled by a pair of box plots? You compare the
shapes, centers, and spreads of the box plots.

GUIDED PRACTICE

Avoid Common Errors

Exercise 6 Stress that the quartiles are single values. The first quartile is the median of the
lower half of the data, the second quartile is the median of all the data (or the middle half of
the data), and the third quartile is the median of the upper half of the data. Each quartile
represents one quarter of the data.

Engage with the Whiteboard

 Ask student volunteers to complete Exercises 4–6. Discuss how comparing the
distribution of a pair of box plots can help you make predictions about the data.

YOUR TURN

3. The box plots show the distribution of weights in pounds of two different groups of football players. Compare the shapes, centers, and spreads of the box plots.

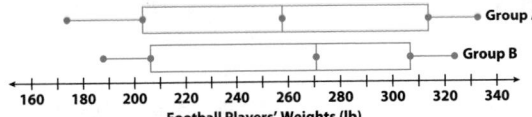

Football Players' Weights (lb)

Sample: The boxes have similar shapes, although
Group B has a shorter box and shorter whiskers.
Group B's median is greater than Group A's. Group B's
shorter box means the middle 50% of its data are
closer together than the middle 50% of Group A's.

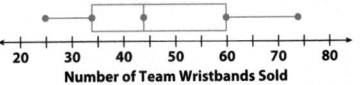

Personal Math Trainer
Online Assessment and Intervention
my.hrw.com

Box Plots with Different Variability

You can compare box plots with greater variability, where there is less overlap of the median and interquartile range.

EXAMPLE 2 · Real World

FL CC 7.SP.2.4

Math On the Spot
my.hrw.com

The box plots show the distribution of the number of team wristbands sold daily by two different stores over the same time period.

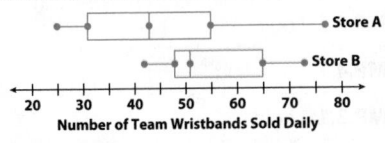

Number of Team Wristbands Sold Daily

A Compare the shapes of the box plots.
Store A's box and right whisker are longer than Store B's.

B Compare the centers of the box plots.
Store A's median is about 43, and Store B's is about 51. Store A's median is close to Store B's minimum value, so about 50% of Store A's daily sales were less than sales on Store B's worst day.

C Compare the spreads of the box plots.
Store A has a greater spread. Its range and interquartile range are both greater. Four of Store B's key values are greater than Store A's corresponding value. Store B had a greater number of sales overall.

Lesson 6.2 **177**

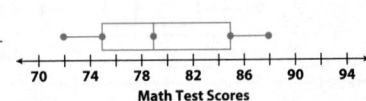

Personal Math Trainer
Online Assessment and Intervention
my.hrw.com

YOUR TURN

4. Compare the shape, center, and spread of the data in the box plot with the data for Stores A and B in the two box plots in Example 2.

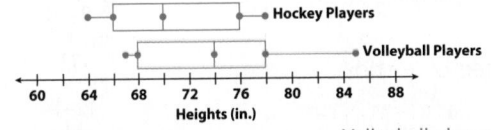

Number of Team Wristbands Sold

Sample answer: The shape is similar to Store A's. The median is
greater than Store A's and less than Store B's. The interquartile
range is about the same as Store A's and longer than B's.

Guided Practice

For 1–3, use the box plot Terrence created for his math test scores. Find each value. (Explore Activity)

1. Minimum = __72__   Maximum = __88__

2. Median = __79__

3. Range = __16__   IQR = __10__

Math Test Scores

For 4–7, use the box plots showing the distribution of the heights of hockey and volleyball players. (Examples 1 and 2)

Heights (in.)

4. Which group has a greater median height? __Volleyball players__

5. Which group has the shortest player? __Hockey players__

6. Which group has an interquartile range of about 10? __Both groups__

? ESSENTIAL QUESTION CHECK-IN

7. What information can you use to compare two box plots?
Sample: Minimum and maximum values, median, range, and IQRs.

178 Unit 3

DIFFERENTIATE INSTRUCTION

Visual Cues

Ask students to visualize the median of a four-lane interstate highway dividing the lanes of traffic into two halves. Extend the visual comparison further by thinking of the white lines between lanes dividing the traffic into quartiles.

Cooperative Learning

Divide students into groups. Have each group write the numbers of a data set onto separate pieces of paper. Have them arrange the papers in ascending order. Then have each group separate the ordered pieces of paper into quarters and identify the maximum, minimum, lower quartile, median, and upper quartile values. Finally, have them draw a box plot modeling the group's data set. After the plots are complete, have pairs of groups compare their box plots by shapes, centers, and spreads.

Additional Resources

Differentiated Instruction includes:

• Reading Strategies

• Success for English Learners **ELL**

• Reteach

• Challenge **PRE-AP**

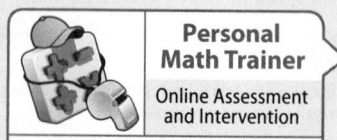

Personal Math Trainer

Online Assessment and Intervention

Online homework assignment available

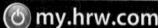
my.hrw.com

6.2 LESSON QUIZ

 **FL CC** 7.SP.2.3

For 1–3, use the box plots.

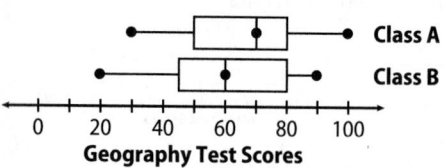

Class A

Class B

0   20   40   60   80   100
Geography Test Scores

1. Compare the shapes of the box plots.

2. Compare the centers of the box plots.

3. Compare the spreads of the box plots.

For 4–6, use the box plots.

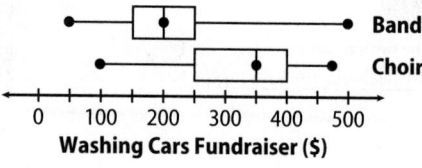

Band

Choir

0   100   200   300   400   500
Washing Cars Fundraiser ($)

4. Compare the shapes of the box plots.

5. Compare the centers of the box plots.

6. Compare the spreads of the box plots.

Lesson Quiz available online

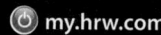
my.hrw.com

Answers

1. The position of Class A is higher, and the ranges of the box plots appear to be very similar.

2. The median score for Class A is 10 points higher than for Class B.

3. The boxes show that the interquartile ranges are similar. Class A has an IQR of 30, and Class B has an IQR of 35. The range of Class A is 70. The range of Class B is 70.

Evaluate

GUIDED AND INDEPENDENT PRACTICE

 **FL CC** 7.SP.2.3

Concepts & Skills	Practice
Explore Activity Analyzing Box Plots	Exercises 1–3
Example 1 Box Plots with Similar Variability	Exercises 4–6, 8–11
Example 2 Box Plots with Different Variability	Exercises 4–6, 12–15

Exercise	Depth of Knowledge (D.O.K.)	**FL CC** Mathematical Practices
8–10	3 Strategic Thinking H.O.T.	**MP.7.1** Using Structure
11	3 Strategic Thinking H.O.T.	**MP.3.1** Logic
12–14	3 Strategic Thinking H.O.T.	**MP.4.1** Modeling
15	3 Strategic Thinking H.O.T.	**MP.3.1** Logic
16	3 Strategic Thinking H.O.T.	**MP.7.1** Using Structure
17	3 Strategic Thinking H.O.T.	**MP.3.1** Logic
18	3 Strategic Thinking H.O.T.	**MP.7.1** Using Structure

Additional Resources

Extra Practice includes:

• Leveled Practice Worksheets

CLUSTER CONNECTION **Exercises 8–11** combine concepts from the Florida Common Core cluster "Draw informal comparative inferences about two populations."

4. The choir's box is longer than the band's box, and the band's right whisker is much longer than the choir's right whisker.

5. The band has a median of about $200, while the choir has a median of about $350. The choir has 75% of its values greater than the upper quartile of the band's values.

6. The IQR of the band's plot is about $100, while the IQR of the choir's plot is about $150. The position of the choir's box is much higher on the number line, meaning they earned more money during the fundraiser.

6.2 Independent Practice

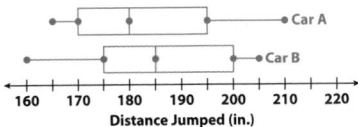

FL CC 7.SP.2.3, 7.SP.2.4

Personal Math Trainer
Online Assessment and Intervention
my.hrw.com

For 8–11, use the box plots of the distances traveled by two toy cars that were jumped from a ramp.

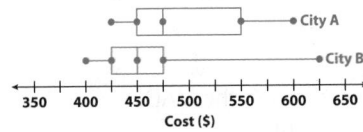

Car A
Car B

160 170 180 190 200 210 220
Distance Jumped (in.)

8. Compare the minimum, maximum, and median of the box plots.

Car A has a minimum of 165 in. and a maximum of 210 in. Car B has a minimum of 160 in. and a maximum of 205 in. Car A has a median of 180 in. Car B has a median of 185 in.

9. Compare the ranges and interquartile ranges of the data in box plots.

Both cars have ranges of 45 in. Both cars have interquartile ranges of 25 in.

10. What do the box plots tell you about the jump distances of two cars?

Car B has a greater median distance than Car A. The interquartile ranges are the same, so the middle 50% of the jump distances for the two cars have the same variability.

11. Critical Thinking What do the whiskers tell you about the two data sets?

Car A has less variability in the lowest quarter of its data and greater variability in the highest quarter of its data. The variability is reversed for Car B.

For 12–14, use the box plots to compare the costs of leasing cars in two different cities.

City A
City B

350 400 450 500 550 600 650
Cost ($)

12. In which city could you spend the least amount of money to lease a car? The greatest?

City B has the lowest price of $400 and also has highest price of $625.

13. Which city has a higher median price? How much higher is it?

City A; $25

14. Make a Conjecture A car in one of the cities costs $440 to lease. Which city do you think it is more likely to be? Why?

Sample answer: City B; that amount is less than 75% of the lease prices in City A.

15. Summarize Look back at the box plots for 12–14 on the previous page. What do the box plots tell you about the costs of leasing cars in those two cities?

Sample answer: City A has a greater median car leasing cost than City B. City A has a greater IQR of car leasing costs than City B. City B has a more predictable car leasing cost than City A for the middle 50% of data values.

H.O.T. **FOCUS ON HIGHER ORDER THINKING**

16. Draw Conclusions Two box plots have the same median and equally long whiskers. If one box plot has a longer box than the other box plot, what does this tell you about the difference between the data sets?

The box plot with the longer box has more variability in the middle 50% of the values.

17. Communicate Mathematical Ideas What you can learn about a data set from a box plot? How is this information different from a dot plot?

You can identify the minimum and maximum values and the range of the data. You can identify the quartiles, including the lower and upper quartiles and the median, as well as the interquartile range. Together, these values help you to recognize the center of the data, both the median and the middle 50%. It helps you to recognize how spread out the data are overall and how spread out the middle 50% of the values are around the median. A dot plot contains all the data values, which a box plot does not.

18. Analyze Relationships In mathematics, *central tendency* is the tendency of data values to cluster around some central value. What does a measure of variability tell you about the central tendency of a set of data? Explain.

Sample answer: The range tells you very little, but the interquartile range tells you how closely the middle half of the data cluster around the median.

Work Area

EXTEND THE MATH PRE-AP

Activity available online 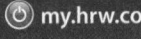 my.hrw.com

Activity Use a graphing calculator to graph the test scores shown in the table below as box plots on the same screen. Then find the key values (maximum, minimum, lower quartile Q_1, median Q_2, and upper quartile Q_3) by tracing each graph.

Math Test 1 Scores	Math Test 2 Scores
72, 86, 86, 58, 67, 78, 92, 98, 100, 81, 82, 85, 71, 70, 68	85, 87, 91, 78, 78, 90, 92, 91, 88, 87, 79, 90, 71, 80, 70

Step 1 Enter the values for Test 1 into list 1 (L1) by pressing STAT **1:Edit**. Enter each value into L1 and press ENTER after each number. Exit the list by pressing 2nd QUIT MODE.

Step 2 Press 2nd Y= . Press ENTER to choose Plot1. Turn the plot on and use the arrow keys to choose the fifth entry, the box plot. Repeat the process to activate Plot 2.

Step 3 Press ZOOM and choose **9:ZoomStat** to see the box plots.

Step 4 Press TRACE and use the arrow keys to find the key values for each box plot.

Plot 1: min = 58, Q_1 = 70, Q_2 = 81, Q_3 = 86, max = 100; Plot 2: min = 70, Q_1 = 78, Q_2 = 87, Q_3 = 90, max = 92

Comparing Data Displayed in Box Plots **180**

LESSON 6.3 Using Statistical Measures to Compare Populations

ADDITIONAL EXAMPLE 1

The test scores of two students are shown below. What is the difference of the means as a multiple of the mean absolute deviation?

Test Scores for Student A
78, 99, 80, 85, 95, 79, 85, 95, 96

Test Scores for Student B
100, 80, 79, 75, 92, 93, 75, 78, 84

Student A: mean = 88; MAD is about 7.3; Student B: mean = 84; MAD is about 7.3. The means of the two data sets differ by about 0.5 times the variability of the two data sets.

 Interactive Whiteboard
Interactive example available online

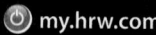 my.hrw.com

---

Engage

ESSENTIAL QUESTION

How can you use statistical measures to compare populations? Sample answer: You can compare data sets by finding measures of center and variability. If the variabilities are similar, you can express the difference in centers as a multiple of the variabilities. You can also take multiple samples from populations and compare the distributions of the medians or the means of the samples.

Motivate the Lesson

Ask: How can you use the mean and the MAD of two data sets to compare the sets? Take a guess. Begin the lesson to find out.

Explore

Focus on Communication

Write the data set 3, 7, and 8 on the board. Have a student volunteer find the mean of the data set (6), another find the distance of each data point from the mean (3, 1, and 2), and a third find the mean of the distances (2). Ask the class to name the final number. If they do not remember, identify it as the mean absolute deviation, or MAD.

Explain

EXAMPLE 1

Questioning Strategies 🟦 Mathematical Practices

• How does the *A* in MAD help you recall how to calculate the MAD? The *A* stands for "absolute." One step in finding the MAD is to find the absolute value of the difference between each data value and the mean of the data set.
• What does the term *deviation* mean outside of statistics? A deviation is a change or difference from what is accepted as usual or normal.

Focus on Modeling 🟦 Mathematical Practices

Point out that the MAD values found in Steps 2 and 4 are about the same. Not all sets of data being compared will have similar MAD values. Only when the MAD values are nearly the same can the difference of the means as a multiple of the MAD be calculated.

YOUR TURN

Avoid Common Errors

Finding the MAD involves a lengthy series of calculations, and errors can easily sneak in. Point out that if students find MADs that are significantly different from each other, they have made an error and need to recalculate.

Using Statistical Measures to Compare Populations

FL CC 7.SP.2.3
Informally assess . . . two numerical data distributions . . . measuring the difference between the centers by expressing it as a multiple of a measure of variability. *Also* 7.SP.2.4

? ESSENTIAL QUESTION

How can you use statistical measures to compare populations?

Comparing Differences in Centers to Variability

Recall that to find the mean absolute deviation (MAD) of a data set, first find the mean of the data. Next, take the absolute value of the difference between the mean and each data point. Finally, find the mean of those absolute values.

Math On the Spot
my.hrw.com

EXAMPLE 1 Real World

FL CC 7.SP.2.3

The tables show the number of minutes per day students in a class spend exercising and playing video games. What is the difference of the means as a multiple of the mean absolute deviations?

Minutes Per Day Exercising
0, 7, 7, 18, 20, 38, 33, 24, 22, 18, 11, 6

Minutes Per Day Playing Video Games
13, 18, 19, 30, 32, 46, 50, 34, 36, 30, 23, 19

STEP 1 Calculate the mean number of minutes per day exercising.

$0 + 7 + 7 + 18 + 20 + 38 + 33 + 24 + 22 + 18 + 11 + 6 = 204$

$204 \div 12 = 17$ *Divide the sum by the number of students.*

STEP 2 Calculate the mean absolute deviation for the number of minutes exercising.

$|0-17| = 17$	$|7-17| = 10$	$|7-17| = 10$	$|18-17| = 1$
$|20-17| = 3$	$|38-17| = 21$	$|33-17| = 16$	$|24-17| = 7$
$|22-17| = 5$	$|18-17| = 1$	$|11-17| = 6$	$|6-17| = 11$

Find the mean of the absolute values.

$17 + 10 + 10 + 1 + 3 + 21 + 16 + 7 + 5 + 1 + 6 + 11 = 108$

$108 \div 12 = 9$ *Divide the sum by the number of students.*

My Notes

STEP 3 Calculate the mean number of minutes per day playing video games. Round to the nearest tenth.

$13 + 18 + 19 + 30 + 32 + 46 + 50 + 34 + 36 + 30 + 23 + 19 = 350$

$350 \div 12 \approx 29.2$ *Divide the sum by the number of students.*

STEP 4 Calculate the mean absolute deviation for the numbers of minutes playing video games.

$|13-29.2| = 16.2$	$|18-29.2| = 11.2$	$|19-29.2| = 10.2$
$|30-29.2| = 0.8$	$|32-29.2| = 2.8$	$|46-29.2| = 16.8$
$|50-29.2| = 20.8$	$|34-29.2| = 4.8$	$|36-29.2| = 6.8$
$|30-29.2| = 0.8$	$|23-29.2| = 6.2$	$|19-29.2| = 10.2$

Find the mean of the absolute values. Round to the nearest tenth.

$16.2 + 11.2 + 10.2 + 0.8 + 2.8 + 16.8 + 20.8 + 4.8 + 6.8 + 0.8 + 6.2 + 10.2 = 107.6$

$107.6 \div 12 \approx 9$ *Divide the sum by the number of students.*

STEP 5 Find the difference in the means.

$29.2 - 17 = 12.2$ *Subtract the lesser mean from the greater mean.*

STEP 6 Write the difference of the means as a multiple of the mean absolute deviations, which are similar but not identical.

$12.2 \div 9 \approx 1.36$ *Divide the difference of the means by the MAD.*

The means of the two data sets differ by about 1.4 times the variability of the two data sets.

YOUR TURN

1. The high jumps in inches of the students on two intramural track and field teams are shown below. What is the difference of the means as a multiple of the mean absolute deviations?

High Jumps for Students on Team 1 (in.)
44, 47, 67, 89, 55, 76, 85, 80, 87, 69, 47, 58

High Jumps for Students on Team 2 (in.)
40, 32, 52, 75, 65, 70, 72, 61, 54, 43, 29, 32

Personal Math Trainer
Online Assessment and Intervention
my.hrw.com

About 1.1 times the MAD.

PROFESSIONAL DEVELOPMENT

Integrate Mathematical Practices MP.6.1

This lesson provides an opportunity to address this Mathematical Practice standard. It calls for students to attend to precision. Students must be precise in their calculations with data values. They must be especially careful to include every value in the multiple-step process of finding the MAD. When given the distribution of measures of center from multiple random samples, they must describe the relationship shown by the distribution correctly and precisely.

Math Background

The mean absolute deviation (MAD) is the average distance of the data set from its mean. It is a measure of statistical dispersion of quantitative data. A data set with a smaller MAD has data values that clustered closer to the mean than a data set with a greater MAD. This should not be confused with the *median* absolute deviation, the median of the absolute deviations from the median.

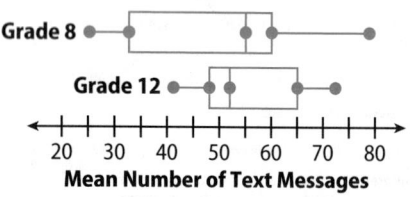

EXAMPLE 2

Focus on Modeling 🏴 Mathematical Practices

Point out that the median is the point through which a vertical line has been drawn for each box plot. Also, remind students that the shape of the box plot is used to visualize whether the data values are evenly distributed (the whiskers and the two parts of the box will be about the same length) or grouped more on one side of the median.

Questioning Strategies 🏴 Mathematical Practices

• What five key values are shown in every box plot? The upper and lower extremes, upper and lower quartiles, and the median are shown in every box plot.

• How did the statistician calculate the medians of the 10 random samples of size 10 that were used to create the Grade 7 box plots in Step 2? The ten recorded number of actual hours spent doing homework for each of the 10 samples were arranged in order, and the average of the two middle numbers provided the median.

YOUR TURN

Engage with the Whiteboard

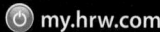 Invite a volunteer to mark the five key values along the top of each box plot in this exercise and in Step 2 of Example 2. Then ask a volunteer to discuss how the shapes of these box plots compare to the shapes of the box plots in Step 2.

Elaborate

Talk About It
Summarize the Lesson

 Ask: How do you use the mean to find the difference of two sets of data as a multiple of the MAD? First, find the mean and the MAD of both sets of data. Then, if the MADs of both sets are similar, divide the difference of the two means by the MAD.

GUIDED PRACTICE

Engage with the Whiteboard

For Exercises 1–2, have volunteers show and explain the process of arriving at the correct values to input on the write-on lines.

Avoid Common Errors

Exercise 3 Remind students that they should compare the medians of School A to the medians of School B, and the means of School A to the means of School B. Tell them that making box plots will help them to see the relationships.

Using Multiple Samples to Compare Populations

Many different random samples are possible for any given population, and their measures of center can vary. Using multiple samples can give us an idea of how reliable any inferences or predictions we make are.

Math On the Spot
my.hrw.com

EXAMPLE 2 *Real World*

FL CC 7.SP.2.4

A group of about 250 students in grade 7 and about 250 students in grade 11 were asked, "How many hours per month do you volunteer?" Responses from one random sample of 10 students in grade 7 and one random sample of 10 students in grade 11 are summarized in the box plots.

Two Random Samples of Size 10

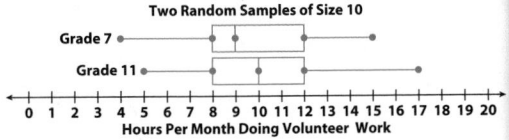

How can we tell if the grade 11 students do more volunteer work than the grade 7 students?

STEP 1 The median is higher for the students in grade 11. But there is a great deal of variation. To make an inference for the entire population, it is helpful to consider how the medians vary among multiple samples.

STEP 2 The box plots below show how the medians from 10 different random samples for each group vary.

Distribution of Medians from 10 Random Samples of Size 10

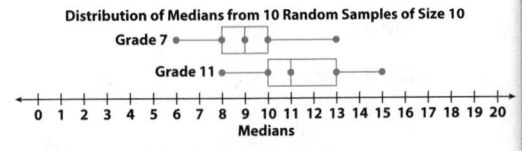

The medians vary less than the actual data. Half of the grade 7 medians are within 1 hour of 9. Half of the grade 11 medians are within 1 or 2 hours of 11. Although the distributions overlap, the middle halves of the data barely overlap. This is fairly convincing evidence that the grade 11 students volunteer more than the grade 7 students.

Math Talk
Mathematical Practices

Why doesn't the first box plot establish that students in grade 11 volunteer more than students in grade 7?

Possible answer: The two samples are relatively small and have a high degree of overlap.

Personal Math Trainer
Online Assessment and Intervention
my.hrw.com

YOUR TURN

2. The box plots show the variation in the means for 10 different random samples for the groups in the example. Why do these data give less convincing evidence that the grade 11 students volunteer more?

Distribution of Means from 10 Random Samples of Size 10

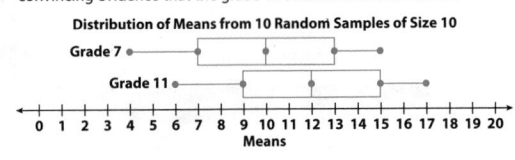

There is much more overlap between the two distributions.

Guided Practice

The tables show the numbers of miles run by the students in two classes. Use the tables in 1–2. (Example 1)

Miles Run by Class 1 Students
12, 1, 6, 10, 1, 2, 3, 10, 3, 8, 3, 9, 8, 6, 8

Miles Run by Class 2 Students
11, 14, 11, 13, 6, 7, 8, 6, 8, 13, 8, 15, 13, 17, 15

1. For each class, what is the mean? What is the mean absolute deviation?

   Class 1: 6, Class 2: 11; Class 1: 3, Class 2: 3

2. The difference of the means is about ___1.67___ times the mean absolute deviations.

3. Mark took 10 random samples of 10 students from two schools. He asked how many minutes they spend per day going to and from school. The tables show the medians and the means of the samples. Compare the travel times using distributions of the medians and means. (Example 2)

School A		
Medians: 28, 22, 25, 10, 40, 36, 30, 14, 20, 25		
Means: 27, 24, 27, 15, 42, 36, 32, 18, 22, 29		

School B		
Medians: 22, 25, 20, 14, 20, 18, 21, 18, 26, 19		
Means: 24, 30, 22, 15, 20, 17, 22, 15, 36, 27		

Both distributions show longer travel times for school A. The distribution of the medians shows less overlap, so is more convincing.

? ESSENTIAL QUESTION CHECK-IN

4. Why is it a good idea to use multiple random samples when making comparative inferences about two populations?

   To see how statistical measures vary among the different samples.

DIFFERENTIATE INSTRUCTION

Technology

For long lists of data, it is helpful to use a spreadsheet program to find the MAD. The first column can hold the data values, the second column the mean, the third column the difference between the data and the mean, and the fourth column the absolute value of the difference. Students will need to use the following formulas:

- "=AVERAGE(A1:A10)" finds the average of cells A1 through A10
- "=A1–B1" finds the difference between cells A1 and B1
- "=ABS(C1)" finds the absolute value of cell C1

Cooperative Learning

Have groups of at least five students generate their own data sets. Have each student randomly select a sentence out of a book and count how many letters are in that sentence. Then have the group find the mean and the MAD of their data set. If the MADs of any two groups are similar, have the two groups combine to find the difference in the means of each data set as a multiple of the MAD.

Additional Resources

Differentiated Instruction includes:

- Reading Strategies
- Success for English Learners **ELL**
- Reteach
- Challenge **PRE-AP**

Personal Math Trainer

Online Assessment and Intervention

Online homework assignment available

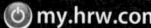 my.hrw.com

6.3 LESSON QUIZ

 7.SP.2.3

The data shows the number of pairs of shoes owned by a random sample of people in two coffee shops.

Pairs of Shoes for People in Shop A
7, 6, 2, 8, 3, 9, 5, 4, 6, 10

Pairs of Shoes for People in Shop B
5, 10, 8, 9, 10, 4, 5, 8, 11, 10

1. Find the mean and the MAD of the number of pairs of shoes owned for each shop.

2. What is the difference of the means as a multiple of the mean absolute deviation?

3. Jess took 10 random samples of 10 students from two schools and asked them how many minutes they spent per day reading. The medians and the means of the samples are shown below. Compare the distributions of the medians and means to compare the reading times for the two populations.

School A
Medians: 30, 30, 40, 50, 40, 35, 35, 45, 60, 60
Means: 25, 25, 45, 60, 50, 45, 45, 35, 40, 50

School B
Medians: 10, 20, 15, 25, 35, 40, 50, 25, 50, 30
Means: 15, 10, 20, 30, 15, 40, 50, 25, 40, 25

Lesson Quiz available online

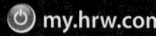 my.hrw.com

Evaluate

GUIDED AND INDEPENDENT PRACTICE

 7.SP.2.3, 7.SP.2.4

Concepts & Skills	Practice
Example 1 Comparing Differences in Centers to Variability	Exercises 1, 2
Example 2 Using Multiple Samples to Compare Populations	Exercises 3

Exercise	Depth of Knowledge (D.O.K.)	FL CC Mathematical Practices
4	**3** Strategic Thinking H.O.T.	**MP.2.1** Reasoning
5–6	**2** Skills/Concepts	**MP.4.1** Modeling
7	**3** Strategic Thinking H.O.T.	**MP.7.1** Using Structure
8	**2** Skills/Concepts	**MP.4.1** Modeling
9	**3** Strategic Thinking H.O.T.	**MP.3.1** Logic
10	**3** Strategic Thinking H.O.T.	**MP.4.1** Modeling
11	**2** Skills/Concepts	**MP.4.1** Modeling
12	**3** Strategic Thinking H.O.T.	**MP.3.1** Logic
13	**3** Strategic Thinking H.O.T.	**MP.4.1** Modeling
14	**2** Skills/Concepts	**MP.3.1** Logic

Additional Resources

Differentiated Instruction includes:

• Leveled Practice worksheets

Answers

1. Shop A: mean = 6; MAD = 2

2. Shop B: mean = 8; MAD = 2

3. 1

4. Both the medians and the means show that the reading times for the students at School A are longer.

6.3 Independent Practice

FL CC 7.SP.2.3, 7.SP.2.4

Josie recorded the average monthly temperatures for two cities in the state where she lives. Use the data for 5–7.

Average Monthly Temperatures for City 1 (°F)
23, 38, 39, 48, 55, 56, 71, 86, 57, 53, 43, 31

Average Monthly Temperatures for City 2 (°F)
8, 23, 24, 33, 40, 41, 56, 71, 42, 38, 28, 16

5. For City 1, what is the mean of the average monthly temperatures? What is the mean absolute deviation of the average monthly temperatures?

The mean is 50°F, and the MAD is 13°F.

6. What is the difference between each average monthly temperature for City 1 and the corresponding temperature for City 2? _____ 15°F

7. Draw Conclusions Based on your answers to Exercises 5 and 6, what do you think the mean of the average monthly temperatures for City 2 is? What do you think the mean absolute deviation of the average monthly temperatures for City 2 is? Give your answers without actually calculating the mean and the mean absolute deviation. Explain your reasoning.

35°F, 13°F; the mean for City 2 must be 15°F less than the mean for City 1, and the MAD must be the same.

8. What is the difference in the means as a multiple of the mean absolute deviations? _____ ≈ 1.2(MAD)

9. Make a Conjecture The box plots show the distributions of mean weights of 10 samples of 10 football players from each of two leagues, A and B. What can you say about any comparison of the weights of the two populations? Explain.

Distribution of Means from 10 Random Samples of Size 10

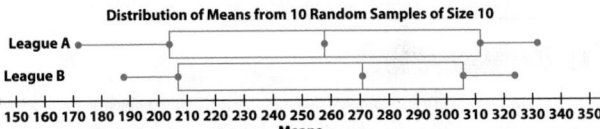

League A
League B

150 160 170 180 190 200 210 220 230 240 250 260 270 280 290 300 310 320 330 340 350
Means

The variation and overlap in the distributions make it hard to make any convincing comparison.

10. Justify Reasoning Statistical measures are shown for the ages of middle school and high school teachers in two states.

State A: Mean age of middle school teachers = 38, mean age of high school teachers = 48, mean absolute deviation for both = 6

State B: Mean age of middle school teachers = 42, mean age of high school teachers = 50, mean absolute deviation for both = 4

In which state is the difference in ages between members of the two groups more significant? Support your answer.

State A if you look only at the differences in mean ages, but State B if you consider the variability as well.

11. Analyze Relationships The tables show the heights in inches of all the adult grandchildren of two sets of grandparents, the Smiths and the Thompsons. What is the difference in the medians as a multiple of the ranges?

Heights of the Smiths' Adult Grandchildren (in.)	Heights of the Thompsons' Adult Grandchildren (in.)
64, 65, 68, 66, 65, 68, 69, 66, 70, 67	75, 80, 78, 77, 79, 76, 75, 79, 77, 74

1.75 × range

H.O.T. FOCUS ON HIGHER ORDER THINKING

Work Area

12. Critical Thinking Jill took many samples of 10 tosses of a standard number cube. What might she reasonably expect the median of the medians of the samples to be? Why?

≈ 3.5; it should be close to the median of the population, which should be ≈ 3.5. (The outcomes are equally likely.)

13. Analyze Relationships Elly and Ramon are both conducting surveys to compare the average numbers of hours per month that men and women spend shopping. Elly plans to take many samples of size 10 from both populations and compare the distributions of both the medians and the means. Ramon will do the same, but will use a sample size of 100. Whose results will probably produce more reliable inferences? Explain.

Ramon's; the larger the sample size, the less variability there should be in the distributions of the medians and means.

14. Counterexamples Seth believes that it is always possible to compare two populations of numerical values by finding the difference in the means of the populations as a multiple of the mean absolute deviations. Describe a situation that explains why Seth is incorrect.

Any situation in which the MADs of the population are not very similar.

EXTEND THE MATH PRE-AP

Activity available online ⏻ my.hrw.com

Activity The mean absolute deviation is the summation of the absolute value of each deviation. The formula for MAD is $\frac{1}{n}\left(\sum_{i=1}^{n}|x_i - \mu|\right)$ where n = the number of items in the data set, x_i = the ith number in the data set, and μ = the mean of the data set. For example, to use this formula with the data set {8, 9, 6, 5}, first you find that $n = 4$, $\mu = 7$, $x_1 = 8$, $x_2 = 9$, $x_3 = 6$, and $x_4 = 5$. So, the MAD is

$$\frac{1}{4}\left(\sum_{i=1}^{4}|x_i - \mu|\right) = \frac{1}{4}(|8 - 7| + |9 - 7| + |6 - 7| + |5 - 7|) = \frac{6}{4} = 1.5.$$

Using this example as a guide, use the formula to find the MAD of {69, 70, 72, 73, 74, 75, 75, 76}. $n = 8$, $\mu = 73$, MAD = 2

Ready to Go On?

Assess Mastery

Use the assessment on this page to determine if students have mastered the concepts and standards covered in this module.

 **Response to Intervention**

Intervention	Enrichment

Access Ready to Go On? assessment online, and receive instant scoring, feedback, and customized intervention or enrichment.

Personal Math Trainer
Online Assessment and Intervention
⏻ my.hrw.com

Online and Print Resources

Differentiated Instruction
• Reteach worksheets
• Reading Strategies **ELL**
• Success for English Learners **ELL**

Differentiated Instruction
• Challenge worksheets
  PRE-AP
• Extend the Math **PRE-AP**
  Lesson Activities in TE

Additional Resources

Assessment Resources includes:
• Leveled Module Quizzes

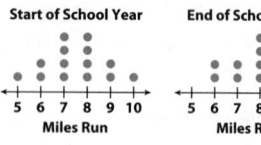 to Go On?

Personal Math Trainer
Online Assessment and Intervention
⏵ my.hrw.com

6.1 Comparing Data Displayed in Dot Plots

The two dot plots show the number of miles run by 14 students at the start and at the end of the school year. Compare each measure for the two dot plots. Use the data for 1–3.

Start of School Year — Miles Run (5 6 7 8 9 10)
End of School Year — Miles Run (5 6 7 8 9 10)

1. means __Start: 7.5 mi; End: ≈ 8.2 mi__

2. medians __Start: 7.5 mi, End: 8 mi__   3. ranges __Start: 5 mi, End: 4 mi__

6.2 Comparing Data Displayed in Box Plots

The box plots show lengths of flights in inches flown by two model airplanes. Use the data for 4–5.

Airplane A
Airplane B
Length of Flight (in.) — 180 190 200 210 220 230 240 250

4. Which has a greater median flight length? __Airplane A__

5. Which has a greater interquartile range? __Airplane B__

6.3 Using Statistical Measures to Compare Populations

6. Roberta grows pea plants, some in shade and some in sun. She picks 8 plants of each type at random and records the heights.

Shade plant heights (in.)	7	11	11	12	9	12	8	10
Sun plant heights (in.)	21	24	19	19	22	23	24	24

Express the difference in the means as a multiple of their ranges.
__2.4 times the ranges__

? ESSENTIAL QUESTION

7. How can you use and compare data to solve real-world problems?
__Sample answer: You can identify similarities and differences in groups.__

© Houghton Mifflin Harcourt Publishing Company

 Florida Common Core Standards

Lesson	Exercises	Common Core Standards
6.1	1–3	**7.SP.2.3, 7.SP.2.4**
6.2	4–5	**7.SP.2.3, 7.SP.2.4**
6.3	6	**7.SP.2.3, 7.SP.2.4**

PARCC Assessment Readiness

Assessment Readiness Tip Encourage students to write on graphical representations whenever it could be helpful.

Item 1 Writing the minimum, maximum, median, and quartiles of each box plot directly above the appropriate points will help students to quickly evaluate each of the four answer choices.

Item 4 Students can locate the median in a dot plot by working from the outside in. Place a tick mark on the outermost dot, alternating from left to right until arriving at the location of the median.

Avoid Common Errors

Item 2 Each answer choice is about a different characteristic of the data, and the city being referred to changes as well. Caution students to proceed carefully and consider each answer choice in isolation in order to avoid careless errors.

Additional Resources

Personal Math Trainer
Online Assessment and Intervention
my.hrw.com

PARCC Assessment Readiness

Personal Math Trainer
Online Assessment and Intervention
my.hrw.com

Selected Response

1. Which statement about the data is true?

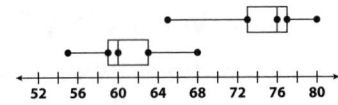

Ⓐ The difference between the medians is about 4 times the range.

Ⓑ The difference between the medians is about 4 times the IQR.

Ⓒ The difference between the medians is about 2 times the range.

Ⓓ The difference between the medians is about 2 times the IQR.

2. Which is a true statement based on the box plots below?

City A
City B

Ⓐ The data for City A has the greater range.

Ⓑ The data for City B is more symmetric.

Ⓒ The data for City A has the greater interquartile range.

Ⓓ The data for City B has the greater median.

3. Which of the following is **not** a possible cross section of a cylinder?

Ⓐ a circle

Ⓑ an oval

Ⓒ a rectangle

Ⓓ a triangle

4. Which is a true statement based on the dot plots below?

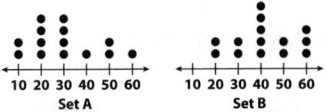
Set A   Set B

Ⓐ Set A has the lesser range.

Ⓑ Set B has the greater median.

Ⓒ Set A has the greater mean.

Ⓓ Set B is less symmetric than Set A.

Mini-Task

5. The dot plots show the lengths of a random sample of words in a fourth-grade book and a seventh-grade book.

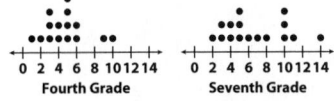
Fourth Grade   Seventh Grade

a. Compare the shapes of the plots.

Sample answer: Grade 4 data mostly clustered around 3-5; Grade 7 data more spread out.

b. Compare the ranges of the plots. Explain what your answer means in terms of the situation.

Grade 7 range > Grade 4 range (12 > 9); more variation in word length in Grade 7 book.

© Houghton Mifflin Harcourt Publishing Company

Florida Common Core Standards

Items	Grade 7 Standards	Mathematical Practice
1	7.SP.2.3	MP.2.1
2	7.SP.2.4	MP.4.1
3*	7.G.1.3	MP.7.1
4	7.SP.2.4	MP.2.1
5	7.SP.2.4	MP.3.1, MP.4.1

* Item integrates mixed review concepts from previous modules or a previous course.

Study Guide Review

Vocabulary Development

Integrating Language Arts

Encourage students to practice using the unit vocabulary as they talk and write about mathematics. Understanding vocabulary will aid their understanding of the concepts.

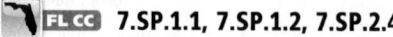 **FL CC** **LACC.68.RST.2.4** Determine the meaning of symbols, key terms, and other domain-specific words and phrases as they are used in a specific scientific or technical context relevant to grades 6–8 texts and topics.

MODULE 5 Random Samples and Populations

FL CC **7.SP.1.1, 7.SP.1.2, 7.SP.2.4**

Key Concepts

• A random sample is a sample in which every member of your population has an equal chance of being selected. If a sample is not random, it is called a biased sample. *(Lesson 5.1)*

• Dot plots and box plots can be used to represent data from a random sample and to make inferences about data from a random sample. *(Lesson 5.2)*

• Technology can be used to model a random sample by generating random numbers. *(Lesson 5.3)*

Study Guide Review

MODULE 5 **Random Samples and Populations**

Key Vocabulary

biased sample *(muestra sesgada)*

population *(población)*

random sample *(muestra aleatoria)*

sample *(muestra)*

? ESSENTIAL QUESTION

How can you use random samples and populations to solve real-world problems?

EXAMPLE 1

An engineer at a lightbulb factory chooses a random sample of 100 lightbulbs from a shipment of 2,500 and finds that 2 of them are defective. How many lightbulbs in the shipment are likely to be defective?

$$\frac{\text{defective lightbulbs}}{\text{size of sample}} = \frac{\text{defective lightbulbs in population}}{\text{size of population}}$$

$$\frac{2}{100} = \frac{x}{2,500}$$

$$\frac{2 \cdot 25}{100 \cdot 25} = \frac{x}{2,500}$$

$$x = 50$$

In a shipment of 2,500 lightbulbs, 50 are likely to be defective.

EXAMPLE 2

The 300 students in a school are about to vote for student body president. There are two candidates, Jay and Serena, and each candidate has about the same amount of support. Use a simulation to generate a random sample. Interpret the results.

Step 1: Write the digits 0 through 9 on 10 index cards, one digit per card. Draw and replace a card three times to form a 3-digit number. For example, if you draw 0-4-9, the number is 49. If you draw 1-0-8, the number is 108. Repeat this process until you have a sample of 30 3-digit numbers.

Step 2: Let the numbers from 1 to 150 represent votes for Jay and the numbers from 151 to 300 represent votes for Serena. For example:

Jay: 83, 37, 16, 4, 127, 93, 9, 62, 91, 75, 13, 35, 94, 26, 60, 120, 36, 73

Serena: 217, 292, 252, 186, 296, 218, 284, 278, 209, 296, 190, 300

Step 3: Notice that 18 of the 30 numbers represent votes for Jay. The results suggest that Jay will receive $\frac{18}{30}$ = 60% of the 300 votes, or 180 votes.

Step 4: Based on this one sample, Jay will win the election. The results of samples can vary. Repeating the simulation many times and looking at the pattern across the different samples will produce more reliable results.

EXERCISES

1. Molly uses the school directory to select, at random, 25 students from her school for a survey on which sports people like to watch on television. She calls the students and asks them, "Do you think basketball is the best sport to watch on television?" *(Lesson 5.1)*

   a. Did Molly survey a random sample or a biased sample of the students at her school?

   <u>random</u>

   b. Was the question she asked an unbiased question? Explain your answer.

   <u>No. Sample answer: It assumes the person watches basketball on television.</u>

2. There are 2,300 licensed dogs in Clarkson. A random sample of 50 of the dogs in Clarkson shows that 8 have ID microchips implanted. How many dogs in Clarkson are likely to have ID microchips implanted? *(Lesson 5.2)*

   <u>368 dogs</u>

3. A store gets a shipment of 500 MP3 players. Twenty-five of the players are defective, and the rest are working. A graphing calculator is used to generate 20 random numbers to simulate a random sample of the players. *(Lesson 5.3)*

   A list of 20 randomly generated numbers representing MP3 players is:

474	77	101	156	378	188	116	458	230	333
78	19	67	5	191	124	226	496	481	161

   a. Let numbers 1 to 25 represent players that are <u>defective</u>.

   b. Let numbers 21 to 500 represent players that are <u>working</u>.

   c. How many players in this sample are expected to be defective? <u>2</u>

   d. If 300 players are chosen at random from the shipment, how many are expected to be defective based on the sample? Does the sample provide a reasonable inference? Explain.

   <u>30 defective players; no; you might expect 25 out of 500, or 5%, of the 300 players to be defective, which is only 15 players. A single small sample is not necessarily representative.</u>

MODULE 6 Analyzing and Comparing Data

FL CC 7.SP.2.3, 7.SP.2.4

Key Concepts
- To compare dot plots, look at the shape, center, and spread of the dot plots. *(Lesson 6.1)*
- To compare box plots, look at the median, interquartile range, and shape of the box plots. *(Lesson 6.2)*
- If the mean absolute deviations of two data sets are similar, then the data sets can be compared by expressing the difference of their means as a multiple of their mean absolute deviations. *(Lesson 6.3)*

Unit 3 Performance Tasks

The Performance Tasks provide students with the opportunity to apply concepts from this unit in real-world problem situations.

CAREERS IN MATH

Entomologist In Performance Task item 1, students can see how an entomologist uses mathematics on the job.

SCORING GUIDES FOR PERFORMANCE TASKS

1. MATHEMATICAL PRACTICES   **FL CC** MP.3.1, MP.4.1, MP.6.1

Task	Possible Points (Total: 6)
a	**1 point** for the correct medians of 11 for Type A and 11 for Type B, **1 point** for the correct ranges of 4 for Type A and 10 for Type B, and **1 point** for the correct interquartile ranges of 3 for Type A and 2 for Type B.
b	**1 point** for the answer: range makes Type A appear more consistent, **1 point** for the answer: interquartile range makes Type B appear more consistent, and **1 point** for any reasonable choice and explanation, for example: Type A is actually more consistent because it has a much smaller range, while its IQR is only slightly larger.

MODULE 6 Analyzing and Comparing Data

Key Vocabulary
mean absolute deviation (MAD) *(desviación absoluta media, (DAM))*

? ESSENTIAL QUESTION

How can you solve real-world problems by analyzing and comparing data?

EXAMPLE

The box plots show amounts donated to two charities at a fundraising drive. Compare the shapes, centers and spreads of the box plots.

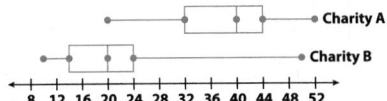

Shapes: The lengths of the boxes and overall plot lengths are fairly similar, but while the whiskers for Charity A are similar in length, Charity B has a very short whisker and a very long whisker.

Centers: The median for Charity A is $40, and for Charity B is $20.

Spreads: The interquartile range for Charity A is $44 - 32 = 12$. The interquartile range for Charity B is slightly less, $24 - 14 = 10$.

The donations varied more for Charity B and were lower overall.

EXERCISES

The dot plots show the number of hours a group of students spends online each week, and how many hours they spend reading. Compare the dot plots visually. (Lesson 6.1)

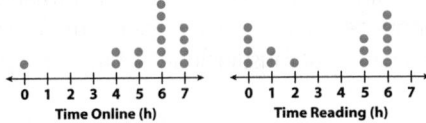

1. Compare the shapes, centers, and spreads of the dot plots.

   Shape: Online: The data are clustered to the right. Reading: The data have two clusters, one at the left and one at the right.

   Center: Online: The data have a single peak at 6. Reading: The data have two peaks, at 0 and 6.

   Spread: Online: The data are spread from 4 to 7 with an outlier at 0. Reading: The data are spread from 0 to 6 with a gap from 3 to 4.

2. Calculate the medians of the dot plots. Online: 6; Reading: 5

3. Calculate the ranges of the dot plots. Online: 7; Reading: 6

4. The average times (in minutes) a group of students spends studying and watching TV per school day are given. (Lesson 6.3)

   Studying: 25, 30, 35, 45, 60, 60, 70, 75
   Watching TV: 0, 35, 35, 45, 50, 50, 70, 75

   a. Find the mean times for studying and for watching TV.

      Studying: 50 minutes; Watching TV: 45 minutes

   b. Find the mean absolute deviations (MADs) for each data set.

      Studying: 16.25; Watching TV: 16.25

   c. Find the difference of the means as a multiple of the MAD, to two decimal places.

      0.31

Unit 3 Performance Tasks

1. **CAREERS IN MATH** Entomologist An entomologist is studying how two different types of flowers appeal to butterflies. The box-and-whisker plots show the number of butterflies that visited one of two different types of flowers in a field. The data were collected over a two-week period, for one hour each day.

   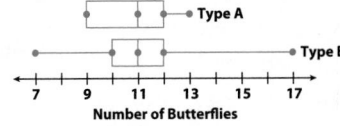

   a. Find the median, range, and interquartile range for each data set.

      Type A: median = 11; range = 4; IQR = 3

      Type B: median = 11; range = 10; IQR = 2

   b. Which measure makes it appear that flower type A had a more consistent number of butterfly visits? Which measure makes it appear that flower type B did? If you had to choose one flower as having the more consistent visits, which would you choose? Explain your reasoning.

      The range makes Type A appear more consistent. The interquartile range makes Type B appear more consistent. Possible explanation: Type A is actually more consistent because it has a much smaller range, while its IQR is only slightly larger.

MIXED REVIEW

PARCC Assessment Readiness

Assessment Readiness Tip Students can rewrite information given to them in a chart or graph in a different form to help them solve problems.

Item 1 Some students might be more comfortable with the data presented in list form rather than as dot plots. Remind them that each dot represents one data value, so many values in the lists will be repeated.

Avoid Common Errors

Item 5 When students divide an inequality by a negative number, they may only remember to flip the inequality sign or reverse the sign of the constant. Remind them that they must do both to get the correct answer.

Item 7 Some students may not know how to translate the information in the box plots into statements in everyday language. Point out that since the median value is the middle value, any statement using the word *most* must include half the box plot up to the median, and a little more.

 Florida Common Core Standards

Items	Grade 7 Standards	Mathematical Practices
1	7.SP.2.3	MP.2.1
2*	7.EE.2.4a	MP.2.1
3	7.SP.2.3	MP.4.1
4	7.SP.1.2	MP.6.1
5*	7.EE.2.4b	MP.2.1
6	7.SP.1.2, 7.SP.2.3	MP.6.1
7	7.SP.2.3	MP.4.1
8*	7.G.2.5	MP.2.1
9	7.SP.1.2, 7.SP.2.3	MP.1.1

* Item integrates mixed review concepts from previous modules or a previous course.

PARCC Assessment Readiness

Personal Math Trainer

Online Assessment and Intervention

my.hrw.com

Selected Response

1. Which is a true statement based on the dot plots below?

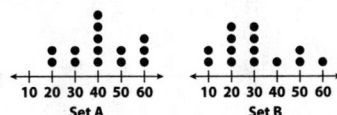

Set A   Set B

Ⓐ Set B has the greater range.

Ⓑ Set B has the greater median.

Ⓒ Set B has the greater mean.

Ⓓ Set A is less symmetric than Set B.

2. Which is a solution to the equation $7g - 2 = 47$?

Ⓐ $g = 5$

Ⓑ $g = 6$

Ⓒ $g = 7$

Ⓓ $g = 8$

3. Which is a true statement based on the box plots below?

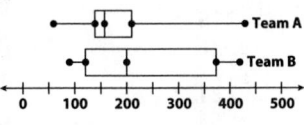

Ⓐ The data for Team B have the greater range.

Ⓑ The data for Team A are more symmetric.

Ⓒ The data for Team B have the greater interquartile range.

Ⓓ The data for Team A have the greater median.

4. Which is the best way to choose a random sample of people from a sold-out movie audience for a survey?

Ⓐ Survey all audience members who visit the restroom during the movie.

Ⓑ Assign each seat a number, write each number on a slip of paper, and then draw several slips from a hat. Survey the people in those seats.

Ⓒ Survey all of the audience members who sit in the first or last row of seats in the movie theater.

Ⓓ Before the movie begins, ask for volunteers to participate in a survey. Survey the first twenty people who volunteer.

5. What is the solution of $-3x + 2 < 11$?

Ⓐ $x < 3$ Ⓒ $x > 3$

Ⓑ $x < -3$ Ⓓ $x > -3$

6. A survey asked 100 students in a school to name the temperature at which they feel most comfortable. The box plot below shows the results for temperatures in degrees Fahrenheit. Which could you infer based on the box plot below?

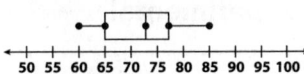

50 55 60 65 70 75 80 85 90 95 100

Ⓐ Most students prefer a temperature less than 65 degrees.

Ⓑ Most students prefer a temperature of at least 70 degrees.

Ⓒ Almost no students prefer a temperature of less than 75 degrees.

Ⓓ Almost no students prefer a temperature of more than 65 degrees.

Unit 3 **193**

7. The box plots below show data from a survey of students under 14 years old. They were asked on how many days in a month they read and draw. Based on the box plots, which is a true statement about students?

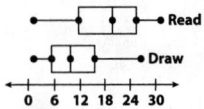

0 6 12 18 24 30

Ⓐ Most students draw at least 12 days a month.

Ⓑ Most students read less than 12 days a month.

Ⓒ Most students read more often than they draw.

Ⓓ Most students draw more often than they read.

Hot Tip! Use logic to eliminate answer choices that are incorrect. This will help you to make an educated guess if you are having trouble with the question.

8. Which describes the relationship between $\angle NOM$ and $\angle JOK$ in the diagram?

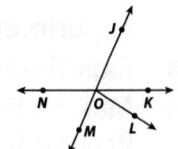

Ⓐ adjacent angles

Ⓑ complementary angles

Ⓒ supplementary angles

Ⓓ vertical angles

Mini-Task

9. The tables show the typical number of minutes spent exercising each week for a group of fourth-grade students and a group of seventh-grade students.

Weekly Exercising (minutes), 4th Grade
120, 75, 30, 30, 240, 90, 100, 180, 125, 300

Weekly Exercising (minutes), 7th Grade
410, 145, 240, 250, 125, 95, 210, 190, 245, 300

a. What is the mean number of minutes spent exercising for fourth graders? For seventh graders?

4th grade: 129; 7th grade: 221

b. What is the mean absolute deviation of each data set?

4th grade: 66.6; 7th grade: 68

c. Compare the two data sets with respect to their measures of center and their measures of variability.

Sample answer: The means are very far apart, with a difference of nearly 100. The MADs are very close.

d. How many times the MADs is the difference between the means, to the nearest tenth?

The difference between the means is about 1.4 times the MAD.

194 Unit 3

UNIT 4

Probability

COMMON CORE

Contents

Unit Pacing Guide

45-Minute Classes

Module 7

DAY 1	DAY 2	DAY 3	DAY 4	DAY 5
Lesson 7.1	Lesson 7.1	Lesson 7.2	Lesson 7.3	Lesson 7.4

DAY 6	DAY 7			
Lesson 7.4	Ready to Go On? PARCC Assessment Readiness			

Module 8

DAY 1	DAY 2	DAY 3	DAY 4	DAY 5
Lesson 8.1	Lesson 8.2	Lesson 8.2	Lesson 8.3	Lesson 8.3

DAY 6	DAY 7	DAY 8		
Lesson 8.4	Ready to Go On? PARCC Assessment Readiness	Study Guide PARCC Assessment Readiness		

90-Minute Classes

Module 7

DAY 1	DAY 2	DAY 3
Lesson 7.1	Lesson 7.2 Lesson 7.3	Lesson 7.4 Ready to Go On? PARCC Assessment Readiness

Module 8

DAY 1	DAY 2	DAY 3	DAY 4	
Lesson 8.1 Lesson 8.2	Lesson 8.2 Lesson 8.3	Lesson 8.3 Lesson 8.4	Ready to Go On? PARCC Assessment Readiness	Study Guide PARCC Assessment Readiness

Program Resources

⏻ Plan

Online Teacher Edition

Access a full suite of teaching resources online—plan, present, and manage classes, assignments, and activities.

ePlanner Easily plan your classes, create and view assignments, and access all program resources with your online, customizable planning tool.

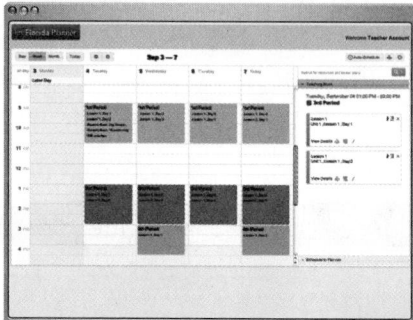

Professional Development Videos

Author Juli Dixon models successful teaching practices and strategies in actual classroom settings.

QR Codes Scan with your smart phone to jump directly from your print book to online videos and other resources.

Teacher's Edition

Support students with point-of-use Questioning Strategies, teaching tips, resources for differentiated instruction, additional activities, and more.

⏻ Engage and Explore

Real-World Videos Engage students with interesting and relevant applications of the mathematical content of each module.

Animated Math Online interactive simulations, tools, and games help students actively learn and practice key concepts.

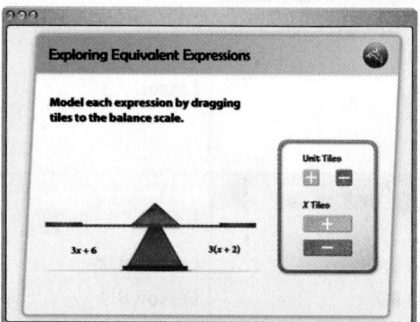

Explore Activities

Students interactively explore new concepts using a variety of tools and approaches.

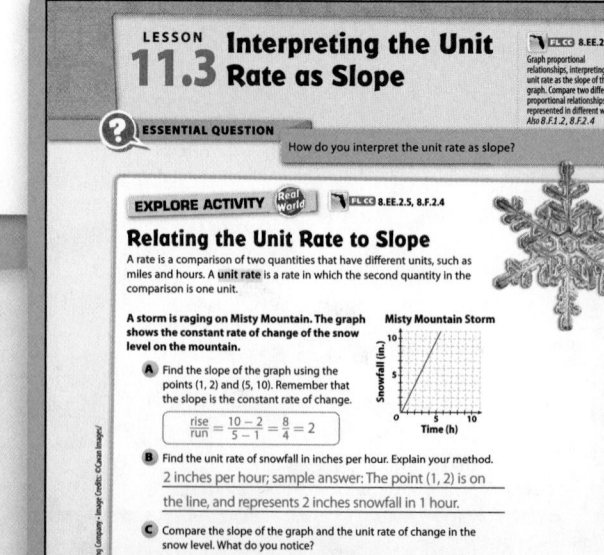

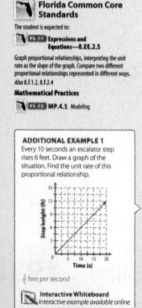

⏻ Teach

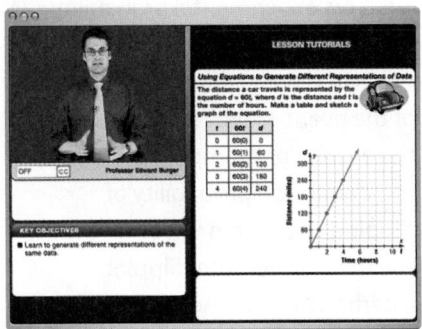

Math On the Spot video tutorials, featuring program authors Dr. Edward Burger and Martha Sandoval-Martinez, accompany every example in the textbook and give students step-by-step instructions and explanations of key math concepts.

Present engaging content on a multitude of devices, including tablets and interactive whiteboards.

Math Talk Continually monitor and assess student progress with integrated formative assessment.

CLUSTER CONNECTION Look for exercises indicated with this icon to build connections among standards within Florida Common Core clusters.

Differentiated Instruction Print Resources

Support all learners with Differentiated Instruction Resources, including

- Leveled Practice and Problem Solving
- Reteach
- Reading Strategies
- Success for English Learners
- Challenge

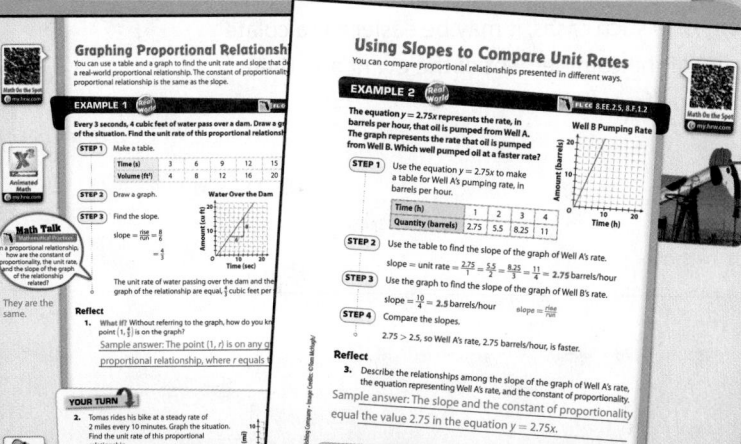

⏻ Assessment and Intervention

The **Personal Math Trainer** provides online practice, homework, assessments, and intervention. Monitor student progress through reports and alerts. Create and customize assignments aligned to specific lessons or standards.

- **Practice** – With dynamic items and assignments, students get unlimited practice on key concepts supported by guided examples, step-by-step solutions, and video tutorials.

- **Assessments** – Choose from course assignments or customize your own based on course content, standards, difficulty levels, and more.

- **Homework** – Students can complete online homework with a wide variety of problem types, including the ability to enter expressions, equations, and graphs. Let the system automatically grade homework, so you can focus where your students need help the most!

- **Intervention** – Let the Personal Math Trainer automatically prescribe a targeted, personalized intervention path for your students.

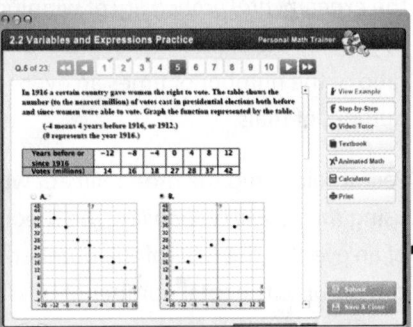

 Raise the bar with homework and practice that incorporates higher-order thinking and mathematical processes in every lesson.

 **PARCC Assessment Readiness**
Prepare students for success on the PARCC math test with practice at every module and unit.

Assessment Resources

Tailor assessments to meet the needs of all your classes and students, including

- Leveled Module Quizzes
- Leveled Unit Tests
- Unit Performance Tasks
- Placement, Diagnostic, and Quarterly Benchmark Tests

Math Background

Probability 7.SP.3.5, 7.SP.3.6, 7.SP.3.7a, 7.SP.3.7b
LESSONS 7.1 and 7.2

The birth of modern probability theory can be traced to a famous letter. In 1654, a French nobleman, the Chevalier de Méré, wrote to the renowned philosopher and mathematician Blaise Pascal to seek his advice about a gambling situation. The Chevalier de Méré sometimes bet his friends that he could roll at least one 6 in four rolls of a die. His experience told him that this tended to be a winning proposition, but he asked Pascal to provide a mathematical explanation.

This situation provides a good illustration of experimental probability versus theoretical probability. The Chevalier de Méré might have recorded his results and found that he won 52 times out of a total of 100 bets. In this case, the *experimental probability* of winning is 0.52 or 52%. In general, the experimental probability of an event is the ratio of the number of times an event occurs to the total number of trials.

Pascal calculated the probability of winning the bet using *theoretical probability*. The theoretical probability of an event is the ratio of the number of ways the event can occur to the total number of possible outcomes. For the Chevalier de Méré's situation, this ratio works out to $\frac{671}{1296}$ or approximately 0.5177, confirming the chevalier's experience that the chances of winning the bet were slightly in his favor.

A probability may be expressed as a ratio, a decimal, or a percent. In some situations, one representation may be more enlightening than another. For instance, the probability of rolling a 3 on a number cube is $\frac{1}{6}$, or $16.\overline{66}\%$. The ratio makes it easy to see that rolling a 3 is one out of six possible outcomes. When comparing two or more probabilities, it may be most useful to express the probabilities as decimals or percents. Regardless of how probabilities are expressed, students should understand that a probability is always a real number between 0 and 1, inclusive, or a percent between 0% and 100%, inclusive.

Note that if an event is impossible, then it has a probability of 0. If an event is certain, then it has a probability of 1. In the case of a finite sample space, the converses of these statements are also true. That is, if an event has a probability of 0, then it is impossible. If an event has a probability of 1, then it is certain.

The Law of Large Numbers relates experimental probability and theoretical probability. The basic idea of the theorem is that as an experiment is repeated many times, the experimental probability of the event approaches the theoretical probability of the event. For example, consider flipping a coin ten times. The theoretical probability of heads is $\frac{1}{2}$. The individual flipping of the coin ten times may not get five heads and five tails. However, after flipping the coin many more times, perhaps 1,000 times, the experimental probability will tend to get closer to $\frac{1}{2}$.

Theoretical Probability of Simple Events 7.SP.3.7a
LESSON 8.1

Calculating theoretical probabilities is primarily an exercise in counting. Students must count the number of outcomes in the sample space and the number of outcomes in the relevant event. Considering the complement of an event can sometimes offer a shortcut.

Given an event E, the complement of the event is the set of all outcomes that are not included in the event. The complement of the event E can be represented in various ways, such as $\sim E$, E', or E^c. In the following text, the symbol $\sim E$ will be used. An event and its complement are disjoint (that is, they have no events in common), and together they form the entire sample space. Therefore, $P(E) + P(\sim E) = 1$ and consequently, $P(E) = 1 - P(\sim E)$. This last fact is often useful in calculating probabilities of events that contain many outcomes. In such cases, it may be easier to calculate the probability of the complement of the event and then subtract this value from 1.

Compound Events 7.SP.3.8, 7.SP.3.8a, 7.SP.3.8b
LESSONS 7.3 and 8.2

Two events are *independent events* if the occurrence of one event does not affect the occurrence of the other. For independent events, $P(A \text{ and } B) = P(A) \cdot P(B)$. A specific example illustrates why the probabilities are multiplied.

Consider the following independent events.

Event A: Spinning a 1 or 2 on a spinner with five congruent sectors labeled 1 through 5

Event B: Rolling a 1, 2, or 3 on a number cube

Clearly, $P(A) = \frac{2}{5}$ and $P(B) = \frac{3}{6}$. To find $P(A \text{ and } B)$, notice that the sample space, shown below, consists of $5 \times 6 = 30$ outcomes. The event "A and B," shown by the green rectangle, consists of $2 \times 3 = 6$ outcomes. Thus, $P(A \text{ and } B) = \frac{2 \times 3}{5 \times 6} = \frac{2}{5} \times \frac{3}{6} = P(A) \cdot P(B)$.

Event B

Event A	1	2	3	4	5	6
1	1, 1	1, 2	1, 3	1, 4	1, 5	1, 6
2	2, 1	2, 2	2, 3	2, 4	2, 5	2, 6
3	3, 1	3, 2	3, 3	3, 4	3, 5	3, 6
4	4, 1	4, 2	4, 3	4, 4	4, 5	4, 6
5	5, 1	5, 2	5, 3	5, 4	5, 5	5, 6

Two events are *dependent events* if the occurrence of one event affects the occurrence of the other event. In this case, $P(A \text{ and } B) = P(A) \cdot P(B \text{ after } A)$, where $P(B \text{ after } A)$ means the probability of event B given that event A has already occurred. Note that $P(B \text{ after } A)$ is sometimes written $P(B|A)$.

Sometimes it is difficult to determine the total number of outcomes for an event. Tree diagrams, organized lists, and tables, while useful ways to record the number of outcomes, can become unwieldy when the sample space is large. The Fundamental Counting Principle provides a more succinct way to count the number of outcomes. If event A can occur in m ways and event B can occur in n ways, the events occur together a total of $m \cdot n$ ways. Note that the principle easily extends to more than two events.

Making Predictions with Probability
7.SP.3.6
LESSONS 7.4 and 8.3

In future courses, students will encounter probability distributions. These distributions are used to make predictions in real-life situations. Two well-known distributions are the binomial distribution and the normal distribution. The binomial distribution is a discrete probability distribution while the normal distribution is a continuous distribution. Discrete and continuous refer to the types of values the random variables can assume. A discrete random variable has a finite or countably infinite number of possible values. Discrete random variables are often counts, such as the number of possible heads when a coin is tossed. Continuous random variables have an uncountably infinite number of possible values. Measurements, such as speed or height, are examples of continuous random variables.

Using Technology to Conduct a Simulation 7.SP.3.6
LESSON 8.4

A simulation can be useful to model experimental probabilities when an actual trial is too difficult, time consuming, or costly to perform. A simulation is designed such that its outcomes represent the outcomes for the event in the real world. Many simulations involve generating random numbers, and assigning one or more random numbers to each possible outcome. The random numbers may be generated using coins, number cubes, spinners, random number tables, graphing calculators, or computer software. Note that as more trials of the simulation are performed, the experimental probabilities will more closely approximate the theoretical probabilities associated with the experiment.

UNIT 4
Probability

MODULE 7

Experimental Probability

FL CC 7.SP.3.5, 7.SP.3.6, 7.SP.3.7a, 7.SP.3.7b, 7.SP.3.8, 7.SP.3.8a, 7.SP.3.8b, 7.SP.3.8c

MODULE 8

Theoretical Probability and Simulations

FL CC 7.SP.3.6, 7.SP.3.7, 7.SP.3.7a, 7.SP.3.8, 7.SP.3.8a, 7.SP.3.8b, 7.SP.3.8c

CAREERS IN MATH

Meteorologist Meteorologists use scientific principles to explain, understand, observe, and forecast atmospheric phenomena and how the atmosphere affects us. They use math in many ways, such as calculating wind velocities, computing the probabilities of weather conditions, and creating and using mathematical models to predict weather patterns. If you are interested in a career as a meteorologist, you should study these mathematical subjects:

- Algebra
- Geometry
- Trigonometry
- Calculus
- Probability and Statistics

Research other careers that require computing probabilities and using mathematical models.

Unit 4 Performance Task

At the end of the unit, check out how **meteorologists** use math.

© Houghton Mifflin Harcourt Publishing Company • Image Credits: Oima7/Alamy Images

Careers in Math

Meteorologist

A meteorologist uses probability calculations to predict the weather. You will learn more about this in the Performance Tasks at the end of the unit.

For more information about careers in mathematics as well as various mathematics appreciation topics, visit the American Mathematical Society at www.ams.org

Vocabulary Preview

Use the puzzle to give students a preview of important concepts in this unit. Students may work individually, in pairs, or in groups.

Unit Resources

Go online to access all your unit resources.

my.hrw.com

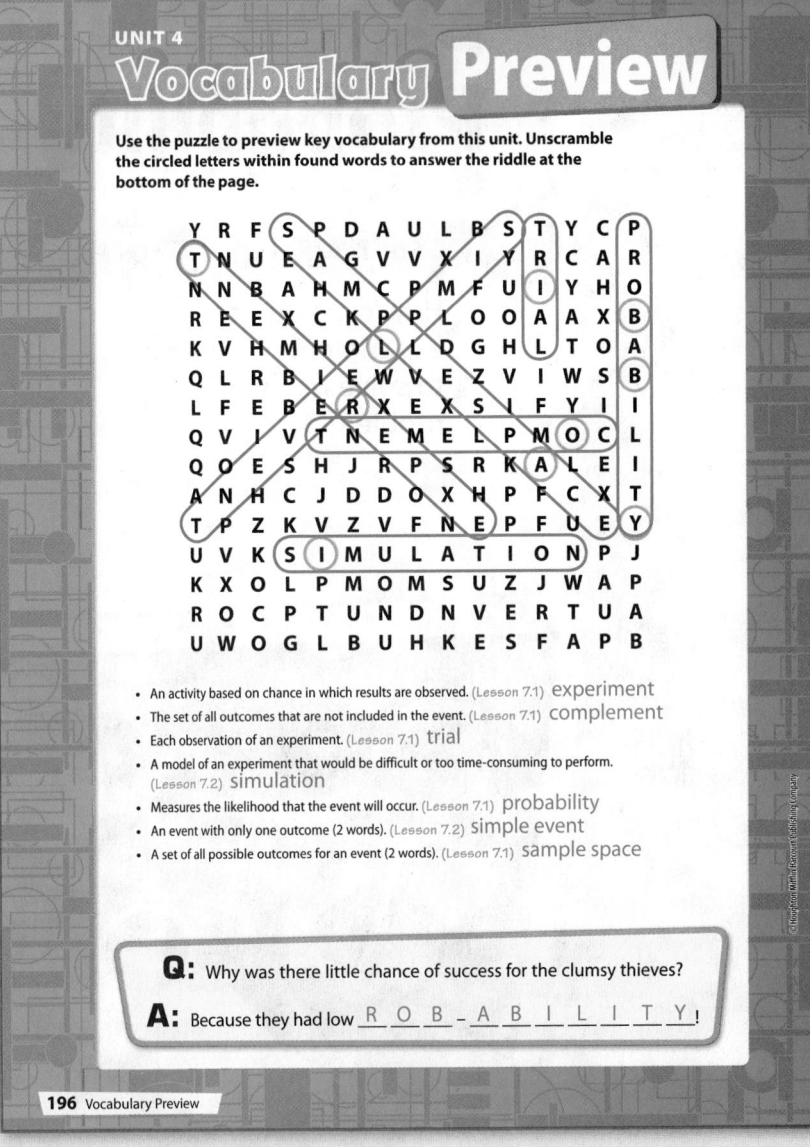

UNIT 4
Vocabulary Preview

Use the puzzle to preview key vocabulary from this unit. Unscramble the circled letters within found words to answer the riddle at the bottom of the page.

```
Y R F S P D A U L B S T Y C P
T N U E A G V V X I Y R C A R
N N B A H M C P M F U I Y H O
R E E X C K P P L O O A A X B
K V H M H O L L D G H L T O A
Q L R B J E W V E Z V I W S B
L F E B E R X E X S I F Y I I
Q V I V T N E M E L P M O C L
Q O E S H J R P S R K A L E I
A N H C J D D O X H P F C X T
T P Z K V Z V F N E P F U E Y
U V K S I M U L A T I O N P J
K X O L P M O M S U Z J W A P
R O C P T U N D N V E R T U A
U W O G L B U H K E S F A P B
```

- An activity based on chance in which results are observed. (Lesson 7.1) experiment
- The set of all outcomes that are not included in the event. (Lesson 7.1) complement
- Each observation of an experiment. (Lesson 7.1) trial
- A model of an experiment that would be difficult or too time-consuming to perform. (Lesson 7.2) simulation
- Measures the likelihood that the event will occur. (Lesson 7.1) probability
- An event with only one outcome (2 words). (Lesson 7.2) simple event
- A set of all possible outcomes for an event (2 words). (Lesson 7.1) sample space

Q: Why was there little chance of success for the clumsy thieves?

A: Because they had low R O B _ A B I L I T Y !

196 Vocabulary Preview

Before	In this Unit	After
Students understand ratios and fractions: • write ratios • simplify fractions	Students will learn about: • experimental probability • theoretical probability	Students will connect: • probability and the fundamental counting principle • probability and permutations and combinations • probability and predictions • probability and odds

Experimental Probability

 **MODULE 7**

 **ESSENTIAL QUESTION**

How can you use experimental probability to solve real-world problems?

You can conduct experiments to model real-world situations, and use the results of those experiments to make predictions about the situations.

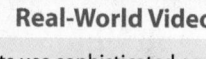
my.hrw.com

Real-World Video

Meteorologists use sophisticated equipment to gather data about the weather. Then they use experimental probability to forecast, or predict, what the weather conditions will be.

GO DIGITAL
my.hrw.com

my.hrw.com
Go digital with your write-in student edition, accessible on any device.

Math On the Spot
Scan with your smart phone to jump directly to the online edition, video tutor, and more.

Animated Math
Interactively explore key concepts to see how math works.

Personal Math Trainer
Get immediate feedback and help as you work through practice sets.

Are You Ready?

Assess Readiness

Use the assessment on this page to determine if students need intensive or strategic intervention for the module's prerequisite skills.

 **RtI** Response to Intervention

Personal Math Trainer

Online Assessment and Intervention

my.hrw.com

Intervention	Enrichment

Access Are You Ready? assessment online, and receive instant scoring, feedback, and customized intervention or enrichment.

Online and Print Resources

Skills Intervention worksheets
- Skill 19 Simplify Fractions
- Skill 26 Write Fractions as Decimals
- Skill 30 Percents and Decimals

Differentiated Instruction
- Challenge worksheets **PRE-AP**
- Extend the Math **PRE-AP** Lesson Activities in TE

Are YOU Ready?

Complete these exercises to review skills you will need for this module.

 **Personal Math Trainer**
Online Assessment and Intervention
my.hrw.com

Simplify Fractions

EXAMPLE Simplify $\frac{12}{21}$.

12: 1, 2, ③ 4, 6, 12   List all the factors of the numerator and denominator.
21: 1, ③ 7, 21   Circle the greatest common factor (GCF).

$\frac{12 \div 3}{21 \div 3} = \frac{4}{7}$ Divide the numerator and denominator by the GCF.

Write each fraction in simplest form.

1. $\frac{6}{10}$ $\frac{3}{5}$ 2. $\frac{9}{15}$ $\frac{3}{5}$ 3. $\frac{16}{24}$ $\frac{2}{3}$ 4. $\frac{9}{36}$ $\frac{1}{4}$

5. $\frac{45}{54}$ $\frac{5}{6}$ 6. $\frac{30}{42}$ $\frac{5}{7}$ 7. $\frac{36}{60}$ $\frac{3}{5}$ 8. $\frac{14}{42}$ $\frac{1}{3}$

Write Fractions as Decimals

EXAMPLE $\frac{13}{25} \rightarrow$

$$25)\overline{13.00}$$
$$\underline{-12.5}$$
$$50$$
$$\underline{-50}$$
$$0$$

Write the fraction as a division problem.
Write a decimal point and a zero in the dividend.
Place a decimal point in the quotient.
Write more zeros in the dividend if necessary.

Write each fraction as a decimal.

9. $\frac{3}{4}$ 0.75   10. $\frac{7}{8}$ 0.875   11. $\frac{3}{20}$ 0.15   12. $\frac{19}{50}$ 0.38

Percents and Decimals

EXAMPLE $109\% = 100\% + 9\%$
$= \frac{100}{100} + \frac{9}{100}$
$= 1 + 0.09$
$= 1.09$

Write the percent as the sum of 1 whole and a percent remainder.
Write the percents as fractions.
Write the fractions as decimals.
Simplify.

Write each percent as a decimal.

13. 67%   0.67   14. 31%   0.31   15. 7%   0.07   16. 146%   1.46

Write each decimal as a percent.

17. 0.13   13%   18. 0.55   55%   19. 0.08   8%   20. 1.16   116%

© Houghton Mifflin Harcourt Publishing Company

 **PROFESSIONAL DEVELOPMENT VIDEO**

 Author Juli Dixon models successful teaching practices as she explores experimental probability in an actual seventh-grade classroom.

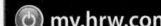

Professional Development

my.hrw.com

GO DIGITAL my.hrw.com

 **Online Teacher Edition**
Access a full suite of teaching resources online—plan, present, and manage classes and assignments.

 ePlanner
Easily plan your classes and access all your resources online.

 Interactive Answers and Solutions
Customize answer keys to print or display in the classroom. Choose to include answers only or full solutions to all lesson exercises.

 Interactive Whiteboards
Engage students with interactive whiteboard-ready lessons and activities.

 Personal Math Trainer: Online Assessment and Intervention
Assign automatically graded homework, quizzes, tests, and intervention activities. Prepare your students with updated practice tests aligned with Common Core.

Reading Start-Up

Have students complete the activities on this page by working alone or with others.

Visualize Vocabulary

The decision tree helps students review vocabulary associated with making mathematical predictions using experimental probability. If time allows, have students rewrite definitions in their own words and think of real-world examples of the words. Some students may benefit from a class discussion of students' prior knowledge related to the words.

Understand Vocabulary

Use the following explanation to help students learn the preview words.

> You may have taken part in a raffle, in which a ticket is drawn at random and a prize given to the ticket holder. You can determine the **probability** of winning a raffle if you know the number of tickets sold. A **simple event** would occur if one ticket was drawn in the raffle.

Active Reading

Integrating Language Arts

Students can use these reading and note-taking strategies to help them organize and understand new concepts and vocabulary.

FL CC **LACC.68.RST.3.7** Integrate quantitative or technical information expressed in words in a text with a version of that information expressed visually (e.g., in a flowchart, diagram, model, graph, or table).

Additional Resources

Differentiated Instruction

• Reading Strategies ELL

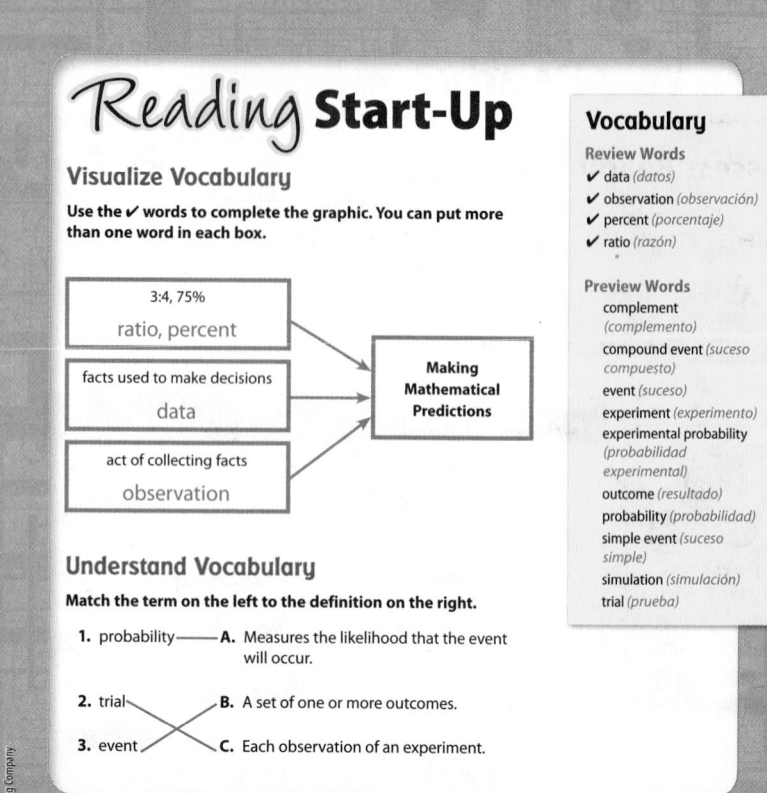

Before	In this module	After
Students understand ratios and fractions: • write ratios • simplify fractions	Students find probabilities of events: • find the probability of a simple event and its complement • find experimental probabilities of simple and compound events • use experimental probability to make a prediction	Students will connect: • simple and compound events • probability and predictions

Unpacking the Standards

Use the exercises on this page to determine if students need intensive or strategic intervention for the module's prerequisite skills.

 Florida Common Core Standards

Content Areas

 **Statistics and Probability—7.SP.3**

Investigate chance processes and develop, use, and evaluate probability models.

Go online to see a complete unpacking of the Florida Common Core Standards.

my.hrw.com

MODULE 7

Unpacking the Standards

Understanding the standards and the vocabulary terms in the standards will help you know exactly what you are expected to learn in this module.

FL CC 7.SP.3.6

Approximate the probability of a chance event by collecting data on the chance process that produces it and observing its long-run relative frequency, and predict the approximate relative frequency given the probability.

Key Vocabulary

simple event *(suceso simple)*
An event consisting of only one outcome.

experimental probability *(probabilidad experimental)*
The ratio of the number of times an event occurs to the total number of trials, or times that the activity is performed.

What It Means to You

You will use experimental probabilities to make predictions and solve problems.

UNPACKING EXAMPLE 7.SP.3.6

Caitlyn finds that the experimental probability of her making a goal in hockey is 30%. Out of 500 attempts to make a goal, about how many could she predict she would make?

$$\frac{3}{10} \cdot 500 = x$$

$$150 = x$$

Caitlyn can predict that she will make about 150 of the 500 goals that she attempts.

FL CC 7.SP.3.7b

Develop a probability model (which may not be uniform) by observing frequencies in data generated from a chance process.

Key Vocabulary

sample space *(espacio muestral)*
All possible outcomes of an experiment.

What It Means to You

You will use data to determine experimental probabilities.

UNPACKING EXAMPLE 7.SP.3.7b

Anders buys a novelty coin that is weighted more heavily on one side. He flips the coin 60 times and a head comes up 36 times. Based on his results, what is the experimental probability of flipping a head?

$$\text{experimental probability} = \frac{\text{number of times event occurs}}{\text{total number of trials}}$$

$$= \frac{36}{60} = \frac{3}{5}$$

The experimental probability of flipping a head is $\frac{3}{5}$.

Visit my.hrw.com to see all Florida Common Core Standards unpacked.

my.hrw.com

200 Unit 4

Florida Common Core Standards	Lesson 7.1	Lesson 7.2	Lesson 7.3	Lesson 7.4
FL CC 7.SP.3.5 Understand that the probability of a chance event is a number between 0 and 1 that expresses the likelihood of the event occurring.	▪			
FL CC 7.SP.3.6 Approximate the probability of a chance event by collecting data on the chance process that produces it and observing its long-run relative frequency, and predict the approximate relative frequency given the probability.		▪		▪
FL CC 7.SP.3.7.a Develop a uniform probability model by assigning equal probability to all outcomes, and use the model to determine probabilities of events.	▪			
FL CC 7.SP.3.7.b Develop a probability model ... by observing frequencies in data generated from a chance process.		▪		
FL CC 7.SP.3.8.a Understand that, just as with simple events, the probability of a compound event is the fraction of outcomes in the sample space for which the compound event occurs.			▪	
FL CC 7.SP.3.8.b Represent sample spaces for compound events using methods such as organized lists, tables and tree diagrams. For an event described in everyday language ..., identify the outcomes in the sample space which compose the event.			▪	
FL CC 7.SP.3.8c Design and use a simulation to generate frequencies for compound events.			▪	

LESSON
7.1 Probability

Florida Common Core Standards

The student is expected to:

 **FL CC** **Statistics and Probability—7.SP.3.5**

Understand that the probability of a chance event is a number between 0 and 1 that expresses the likelihood of the event occurring.

 **FL CC** **Statistics and Probability—7.SP.3.7a**

Develop a uniform probability model by assigning equal probability to all outcomes, and use the model to determine probabilities of events.

Mathematical Practices

 FL CC **MP.6.1** Precision

ADDITIONAL EXAMPLE 1
Tell whether each event is impossible, unlikely, as likely as not, likely, or certain. Then tell whether the probability is 0, close to 0, $\frac{1}{2}$, close to 1, or 1.

A You roll a six-sided number and the number is less than 2. unlikely; close to 0

B You roll two number cubes and the sum of the numbers is 1. impossible; 0

C A bag contains 3 blue marbles and 3 red marbles. You select a red marble from the bag at random. as likely as not; $\frac{1}{2}$

D A spinner has 5 equal sections marked 1 through 5. You spin and land on a number less than 5. likely; close to 1

 Interactive Whiteboard
Interactive example available online

 my.hrw.com

Engage

ESSENTIAL QUESTION

How can you describe the likelihood of an event? Sample answer: I can describe the likelihood as certain, likely, as likely as not, unlikely, or impossible.

Motivate the Lesson
Ask: How can you decide the likelihood that you will win in a game of chance? Begin the Explore Activity to find out.

Explore

EXPLORE ACTIVITY

Focus on Reasoning
Encourage students to list the possible numbers that correspond to each event. Discuss how and why they can compare the numbers that correspond to each event to help order the events.

Explain

EXAMPLE 1

Connect Vocabulary ELL
Check that students understand the difference between an *outcome* and an *event*. In the experiment of rolling a six-sided number cube, rolling a 1 is both a possible outcome and an event. Rolling a 1 or a 2 is a different event that includes two possible outcomes, 1 and 2.

Questioning Strategies   Mathematical Practices

• The event for the experiment in A is certain. What is an event that is impossible? Justify your answer. Rolling any number greater than 6 is impossible since any number greater than 6 is not a possible outcome.

• How can you find the possible outcomes to support the claim in B, that the sum of the numbers is 3 when you roll two number cubes is unlikely? What are the possible sums? Sample answer: Make an organized list to show all the sums possible when rolling two number cubes. Possible sums: 2, 3, 4, 5, 6, 7, 8, 9, 10, 11, 12

• How do you know that both the events in **C** and **D** are as likely as not? If there are as many ways for an event to occur as not to occur, then the event is as likely as not. For C, 2, 4, 6, 8, and 10 are even while 1, 3, 5, 7, and 9 are odd. For D, 2, 3, 5, and 7 are prime while 0, 1, 4, and 6 are not prime.

FL CC 7.SP.3.5
Understand that the probability of a chance event is a number between 0 and 1 that expresses the likelihood of the event occurring. Larger numbers indicate greater likelihood. ... Also 7.SP.3.7a

? ESSENTIAL QUESTION

How can you describe the likelihood of an event?

EXPLORE ACTIVITY FL CC 7.SP.3.5

Finding the Likelihood of an Event

Each time you roll a number cube, a number from 1 to 6 lands face up. This is called an *event*.

Work with a partner to decide how many of the six possible results of rolling a number cube match the described event.

Then order the events from least likely (1) to most likely (9) by writing a number in each box to the right.

Rolling a number less than 7 <u>1, 2, 3, 4, 5, 6; 6 of 6 possible rolls</u> [9]

Rolling an 8 <u>0 of 6 possible rolls</u> [1]

Rolling a number greater than 4 <u>5, 6; 2 of 6 possible rolls</u> [3/4]

Rolling a 5 <u>5; 1 of 6 possible rolls</u> [2]

Rolling a number other than 6 <u>1, 2, 3, 4, 5; 5 of 6 possible rolls</u> [8]

Rolling an even number <u>2, 4, 6; 3 of 6 possible rolls</u> [5/6]

Rolling a number less than 5 <u>1, 2, 3, 4; 4 of 6 possible rolls</u> [7]

Rolling an odd number <u>1, 3, 5; 3 of 6 possible rolls</u> [5/6]

Rolling a number divisible by 3 <u>3, 6; 2 of 6 possible rolls</u> [3/4]

Reflect

1. Are any of the events impossible? <u>Sample answer: Rolling an 8 is impossible because there is no 8 on the number cube.</u>

Math On the Spot
my.hrw.com

Describing Events

An **experiment** is an activity involving chance in which results are observed. Each observation of an experiment is a **trial**, and each result is an **outcome**. A set of one or more outcomes is an **event**.

The **probability** of an event, written P(event), measures the likelihood that the event will occur. Probability is a measure between 0 and 1 as shown on the number line, and can be written as a fraction, a decimal, or a percent.

If the event is not likely to occur, the probability of the event is close to 0. If an event is likely to occur, the event's probability is closer to 1.

Impossible	Unlikely	As likely as not	Likely	Certain
0		$\frac{1}{2}$		1
0		0.5		1.0
0%		50%		100%

EXAMPLE 1 Real World   FL CC 7.SP.3.5

Tell whether each event is impossible, unlikely, as likely as not, likely, or certain. Then, tell whether the probability is 0, close to 0, $\frac{1}{2}$, close to 1, or 1.

A You roll a six-sided number cube and the number is 1 or greater.

This event is certain to happen. Its probability is 1.

> Because you can roll the numbers 1, 2, 3, 4, 5, and 6 on a number cube, there are 6 possible outcomes.

B You roll two number cubes and the sum of the numbers is 3.

This event is unlikely to happen. Its probability is close to 0.

C A bowl contains disks marked with the numbers 1 through 10. You close your eyes and select a disk at random. You pick an odd number.

This event is as likely as not. The probability is $\frac{1}{2}$.

D A spinner has 8 equal sections marked 0 through 7. You spin and land on a prime number.

This event is as likely as not. The probability is $\frac{1}{2}$.

> Remember that a prime number is a whole number greater than 1 and has exactly 2 divisors, 1 and itself.

Math Talk
Mathematical Practices

Is an event that is *not* certain an impossible event? Explain.

Sample answer: No; it is unlikely that I will draw a blue marble at random out of a jar containing 35 yellow marbles and one blue one, but it could happen.

Reflect

2. The probability of event A is $\frac{1}{3}$. The probability of event B is $\frac{1}{4}$. What can you conclude about the two events?

<u>Neither is very likely, but event A is more likely to happen than event B, because $\frac{1}{3} > \frac{1}{4}$.</u>

PROFESSIONAL DEVELOPMENT

Integrate Mathematical Practices MP.6.1

This lesson provides an opportunity to address this Mathematical Practice standard. It calls for students to display, explain, and justify mathematical ideas … using precise mathematical language in written or oral communication. Students learn the definitions for probabilistic events and connect the likelihood of an event to probabilities. Next, they identify the sample space for an event and use a ratio to find the probability of a simple event. Finally, students find the complement of an event. In this way, students are able to use precise language to communicate about probability.

Math Background

Considering the complement of an event can sometimes offer a shortcut when calculating theoretical probabilities. Given an event E, the complement of the event (denoted $\bar{E}$) is the set of all outcomes not included in the event. An event and its complement are disjoint and together form the entire sample space. Hence, $P(E) + P(\bar{E}) = 1$ and so $P(E) = 1 - P(\bar{E})$. The difference is often useful in calculating probabilities of events that contain many outcomes. In such cases, it may be easier to calculate the probability of the complement and then subtract this value from 1.

YOUR TURN

Talk About It
Check for Understanding

 Ask: For the hat experiment, what is an event that is likely? unlikely? How do you know? Sample answer: A likely event is picking a number greater than 3 because there are more numbers from 4 to 16 than from 1 to 3. An unlikely event is picking a number less than 3 because there are fewer numbers less than 3 than from 3 to 16.

EXAMPLE 2

Questioning Strategies  Mathematical Practices

- Why do you find the sample space for an experiment to find the probability of an event? The sample space lists the total number of possible outcomes for an experiment. This is the denominator of the probability ratio.

- How do you decide which outcomes are the favorable outcomes? The favorable outcomes are the outcomes that correspond to the event.

Engage with the Whiteboard

Invite a student volunteer to rewrite the probabilty of rollling an even number as a decimal and as a percent.

Talk About It
Check for Understanding

Ask: How does the probability of rolling an odd number compare to the probability of rolling an even number? Explain. It is the same. There are still 3 favorable outcomes (1, 3, and 5) and 6 possible outcomes.

Avoid Common Errors

Students may write the probability ratio with the number of unfavorable outcomes in the denominator. Remind them that the total number of possible outcomes should go in the denominator.

YOUR TURN

Focus on Modeling Mathematical Practices

Encourage students to list the sample spaces involved in Problems 5 and 6. This will help them in setting up the probability ratios that represents each event.

Integrating the ELPS ELL

Encourage English learners to take notes on new terms or concepts and to write them in familiar language.

EXAMPLE 3

Questioning Strategies 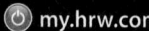 Mathematical Practices

- The probability of choosing a card with an even number at random from a deck of 52 cards is $\frac{20}{52}$ or $\frac{5}{13}$. Can you use the probability of the complement to find the probability of choosing a card with an odd number at random? Justify your answer. No, the complement includes both the cards with odd numbers and the face cards.

Engage with the Whiteboard

Ask a volunteer to first simplify the probability of getting a red jack. Then have the student use the formula to verify that the probability of the complement is the same.

Focus on Reasoning Mathematical Practices

Connect the likelihood of an event to its complement. Discuss why events that are impossible have complements that are certain, events that are unlikely have complements that are likely, and so on.

ADDITIONAL EXAMPLE 2
What is the probability of rolling a multiple of 3 on a standard number cube? $\frac{1}{3}$

 Interactive Whiteboard
Interactive example available online

⏻ my.hrw.com

ADDITIONAL EXAMPLE 3
There are 4 aces in a standard deck of 52 cards. $\frac{4}{52}$ What is the probability of not getting an ace if you select one card at random? $\frac{12}{13}$

 Interactive Whiteboard
Interactive example available online

⏻ my.hrw.com

YOUR TURN

3. A hat contains pieces of paper marked with the numbers 1 through 16. Tell whether picking an even number is impossible, unlikely, as likely as not, likely, or certain. Tell whether the probability is 0, close to 0, $\frac{1}{2}$, close to 1, or 1.

as likely as not; $\frac{1}{2}$

Personal Math Trainer
Online Assessment and Intervention
my.hrw.com

Math On the Spot
my.hrw.com

Finding Probability

The **sample space** is a set of all possible outcomes for an event. A sample space can be small, such as the 2 outcomes when a coin is flipped. Or a sample space can be large, such as the possible number of Texas Classic automobile license plates. Identifying the sample space can help you calculate the probability of an event.

Probability of An Event

$$P(\text{event}) = \frac{\text{number of times the event occurs}}{\text{total number of equally likely possible outcomes}}$$

EXAMPLE 2 *Real World*

FL CC 7.SP.3.7a

What is the probability of rolling an even number on a standard number cube?

STEP 1 Find the sample space for a standard number cube.

{1, 2, 3, 4, 5, 6}   *There are 6 possible outcomes.*

STEP 2 Find the number of ways to roll an even number.

2, 4, 6   *The event can occur 3 ways.*

STEP 3 Find the probability of rolling an even number.

$$P(\text{even}) = \frac{\text{number of ways to roll an even number}}{\text{number of faces on a number cube}}$$

$$= \frac{3}{6} = \frac{1}{2} \qquad \text{Substitute values and simplify.}$$

The probability of rolling an even number is $\frac{1}{2}$.

Personal Math Trainer
Online Assessment and Intervention
my.hrw.com

Math On the Spot
my.hrw.com

YOUR TURN

Find each probability. Write your answer in simplest form.

4. Picking a purple marble from a jar with 10 green and 10 purple marbles. $\frac{1}{2}$

5. Rolling a number greater than 4 on a standard number cube. $\frac{1}{3}$

Using the Complement of an Event

The **complement** of an event is the set of all outcomes in the sample space that are *not* included in the event. For example, in the event of rolling a 3 on a number cube, the complement is rolling any number other than 3, which means the complement is rolling a 1, 2, 4, 5, or 6.

An Event and Its Complement

The sum of the probabilities of an event and its complement equals 1.

$$P(\text{event}) + P(\text{complement}) = 1$$

You can apply probabilities to situations involving random selection, such as drawing a card out of a shuffled deck or pulling a marble out of a closed bag.

EXAMPLE 3 *Real World*

FL CC 7.SP.3.7a

There are 2 red jacks in a standard deck of 52 cards. What is the probability of not getting a red jack if you select one card at random?

$$P(\text{event}) + P(\text{complement}) = 1$$

$$P(\text{red jack}) + P(\text{not a red jack}) = 1 \qquad \text{The probability of getting a red jack is } \frac{2}{52}.$$

$$\frac{2}{52} + P(\text{not a red jack}) = 1 \qquad \text{Substitute } \frac{2}{52} \text{ for } P(\text{red jack}).$$

$$\frac{2}{52} + P(\text{not a red jack}) = \frac{52}{52} \qquad \text{Subtract } \frac{2}{52} \text{ from both sides.}$$

$$\underline{\quad -\frac{2}{52} \qquad\qquad\qquad -\frac{2}{52}\quad}$$

$$P(\text{not a red jack}) = \frac{50}{52}$$

$$P(\text{not a red jack}) = \frac{25}{26} \qquad \text{Simplify.}$$

The probability that you will not draw a red jack is $\frac{25}{26}$. It is likely that you will not select a red jack.

DIFFERENTIATE INSTRUCTION

Communicating Math

Have students suggest events that are impossible, unlikely, as likely as not, likely, or certain. Do all students agree with the likelihoods of the suggested events? Discuss the reasons for any differences. When possible, work with students to find the probabilities of their suggested simple events. Contrast the precision of the numerical probability with the intuitive likelihood description of the event.

Home Connection

Encourage students to play a game at home with family members and then to write responses to the following questions on notebook paper. Discuss students' answers in class.

What game did you play?

Before starting the game, did every player have an equal chance or likelihood of winning the game? How do you know?

How do skill and strategy affect the outcome of the game?

What other factors affect the outcome of the game?

Additional Resources

Differentiated Instruction includes:

- Reading Strategies
- Success for English Learners **ELL**
- Reteach
- Challenge **PRE-AP**

YOUR TURN

Focus on Communication **Mathematical Practices**

Discuss the advantages of using the rule for the complement to find each probability.

Elaborate

Talk About It
Summarize the Lesson

Ask: How are the probability and the likelihood of an event related? If the probability is 0, the event is impossible. If the probability is close to 0, the event is unlikely. If the probability is $\frac{1}{2}$, the event is as likely as not. If the probability is close to 1, the event is likely. If the probability is 1, the event is certain.

GUIDED PRACTICE

Engage with the Whiteboard

Have students list the numbers that correspond to each event in Exercises 1–5.

Avoid Common Errors

Exercise 6 Students are used to even numbers having a probability of $\frac{1}{2}$ in other contexts and may give that incorrect answer here. Remind them to read each item carefully.

Exercises 8–11 Remind students to use the rule for the complement to find each probability.

Reflect

6. Why do the probability of an event and the probability of its complement add up to 1?

The complement is made up of all outcomes not in the event. When you put the outcomes of an event and its complement together, you get all possible outcomes of an event. The probability of getting all the possible outcomes equals 1.

YOUR TURN

Personal Math Trainer
Online Assessment and Intervention
🔵 my.hrw.com

7. A jar contains 8 marbles marked with the numbers 1 through 8. You pick a marble at random. What is the probability of not picking the marble marked with the number 5? $\frac{7}{8}$

8. You roll a standard number cube. Use the probability of rolling an even number to find the probability of rolling an odd number. $\frac{1}{2}$

Guided Practice

1. In a hat, you have index cards with the numbers 1 through 10 written on them. Order the events from least likely to happen (1) to most likely to happen (8) when you pick one card at random. In the boxes, write a number from 1 to 8 to order the eight different events. (Explore Activity)

You pick a number greater than 0.	8
You pick an even number.	5
You pick a number that is at least 2.	7
You pick a number that is at most 0.	1
You pick a number divisible by 3.	3
You pick a number divisible by 5.	2
You pick a prime number.	4
You pick a number less than the greatest prime number.	6

Guided Practice

Determine whether each event is impossible, unlikely, as likely as not, likely, or certain. Then, tell whether the probability is 0, close to 0, $\frac{1}{2}$, close to 1, or 1. (Example 1)

2. randomly picking a green card from a standard deck of playing cards.
impossible; 0

3. randomly picking a red card from a standard deck of playing cards
as likely as not; $\frac{1}{2}$

4. picking a number less than 15 from a jar with papers labeled from 1 to 12
certain; 1

5. picking a number that is divisible by 5 from a jar with papers labeled from 1 to 12
unlikely; close to 0

Find each probability. Write your answer in simplest form. (Example 2)

6. Spinning a spinner that has 5 equal sections marked 1 through 5 and landing on an even number. $\frac{2}{5}$

7. Picking a diamond from a standard deck of playing cards which has 13 cards in each of four suits: spades, hearts, diamonds and clubs. $\frac{1}{4}$

Use the complement to find each probability. (Example 3)

8. What is the probability of not rolling a 5 on a standard number cube? $\frac{5}{6}$

9. A spinner has 3 equal sections that are red, white, and blue. What is the probability of not landing on blue? $\frac{2}{3}$

10. A spinner has 5 equal sections marked 1 through 5. What is the probability of not landing on 4? $\frac{4}{5}$

11. There are 4 queens in a standard deck of 52 cards. You pick one card at random. What is the probability of not picking a queen? $\frac{12}{13}$

? ESSENTIAL QUESTION CHECK-IN

12. Describe an event that has a probability of 0% and an event that has a probability of 100%.

Sample answer: pulling a red marble out of a bag that contains only blue marbles; pulling a white marble out of a bag that contains only white marbles.

Personal Math Trainer

Online Assessment and Intervention

Online homework assignment available

⏻ my.hrw.com

7.1 LESSON QUIZ

FL CC 7.SP.3.5

Tell whether each event is impossible, unlikely, as likely as not, likely, or certain. Then tell whether the probability is 0, close to 0, $\frac{1}{2}$, close to 1, or 1.

1. rolling a number less than 4 on a standard number cube

2. randomly picking a king from a standard deck of playing cards

A bag has 2 blue, 3 red, and 5 yellow tiles. Find each probability. Write your answer in simplest form.

3. picking a blue tile

4. picking a yellow tile

5. not picking a red tile

Lesson Quiz available online

⏻ my.hrw.com

Answers
1. as likely as not; $\frac{1}{2}$

2. unlikely; close to 0

3. $\frac{1}{5}$

4. $\frac{1}{2}$

5. $\frac{7}{10}$

Evaluate

GUIDED AND INDEPENDENT PRACTICE

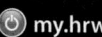 **FL CC** 7.SP.3.5, 7.SP.3.7a

Concepts & Skills	Practice
Explore Activity Finding the Likelihood of an Event	Exercises 1, 16
Example 1 Describing Events	Exercises 2–5, 15, 18
Example 2 Finding Probability	Exercises 6–7, 13, 17, 19
Example 3 Using the Complement of an Event	Exercises 8–11, 14, 18

Exercise	Depth of Knowledge (D.O.K.)	**FL CC** Mathematical Practices
13	**2** Skills/Concepts	**MP.4.1** Problem Solving
14	**3** Strategic Thinking H.O.T.	**MP.4.1** Problem Solving
15	**3** Strategic Thinking H.O.T.	**MP.4.1** Problem Solving
16	**3** Strategic Thinking H.O.T.	**MP.6.1** Precision
17	**3** Strategic Thinking H.O.T.	**MP.4.1** Problem Solving
18	**3** Strategic Thinking H.O.T.	**MP.6.1** Precision
19	**2** Skills/Concepts	**MP.8.1** Patterns
20	**3** Strategic Thinking H.O.T.	**MP.8.1** Patterns
21	**3** Strategic Thinking H.O.T.	**MP.8.1** Patterns
22	**3** Strategic Thinking H.O.T.	**MP.6.1** Precision

Additional Resources
Differentiated Instruction includes:
• Leveled Practice Worksheets

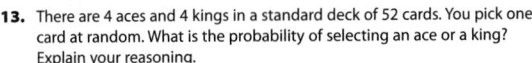

7.1 Independent Practice

FL CC 7.SP.3.5, 7.SP.3.7a

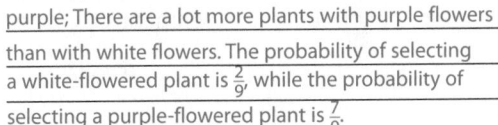
Personal Math Trainer
Online Assessment and Intervention
my.hrw.com

13. There are 4 aces and 4 kings in a standard deck of 52 cards. You pick one card at random. What is the probability of selecting an ace or a king? Explain your reasoning.

$\frac{2}{13}$; The event can occur in 8 ways. There are 52 outcomes in the sample space. $\frac{8}{52} = \frac{2}{13}$.

14. There are 12 pieces of fruit in a bowl. Seven of the pieces are apples and two are peaches. What is the probability that a randomly selected piece of fruit will not be an apple or a peach? Justify your answer.

$\frac{1}{4}$; Since 7 pieces of fruit are apples and 2 are peaches, 3 pieces are not apples or peaches. $P(\text{not an apple or a peach}) = \frac{3}{12} = \frac{1}{4}$.

15. Critique Reasoning For breakfast, Clarissa can choose from oatmeal, cereal, French toast, or scrambled eggs. She thinks that if she selects a breakfast at random, it is likely that it will be oatmeal. Is she correct? Explain your reasoning.

No, it is unlikely that she will have oatmeal for breakfast. Since there are 4 choices, the probability that she will choose oatmeal is $\frac{1}{4}$, or 25%.

16. Draw Conclusions A researcher's garden contains 90 sweet pea plants, which have either white or purple flowers. About 70 of the plants have purple flowers, and about 20 have white flowers. Would you expect that one plant randomly selected from the garden will have purple or white flowers? Explain.

purple; There are a lot more plants with purple flowers than with white flowers. The probability of selecting a white-flowered plant is $\frac{2}{9}$, while the probability of selecting a purple-flowered plant is $\frac{7}{9}$.

17. The power goes out as Sandra is trying to get dressed. If she has 4 white T-shirts and 10 colored T-shirts in her drawer, is it likely that she will pick a colored T-shirt in the dark? What is the probability she will pick a colored T-shirt? Explain your answers.

Because she has more colored T-shirts than white T-shirts, it is likely that she will pick a colored T-shirt; $\frac{\text{colored T-shirts}}{\text{total T-shirts}} = \frac{10}{10+4} = \frac{5}{7}$

18. James counts the hair colors of the 22 people in his class, including himself. He finds that there are 4 people with blonde hair, 8 people with brown hair, and 10 people with black hair. What is the probability that a randomly chosen student in the class does not have red hair? Explain.

1; None of the students in the class have red hair, so it is certain that a randomly chosen student will not have red hair.

19. Persevere in Problem Solving A bag contains 8 blue coins and 6 red coins. A coin is removed at random and replaced by three of the other color.

a. What is the probability that the removed coin is blue?

$\frac{8}{14} = \frac{4}{7}$

b. If the coin removed is blue, what is the probability of drawing a red coin after three red coins are put in the bag to replace the blue one?

$8 - 1 = 7$ blue coins and $6 + 3 = 9$ red coins; $\frac{9}{16}$

c. If the coin removed is red, what is the probability of drawing a red coin after three blue coins are put in the bag to replace the red one?

$8 + 3 = 11$ blue coins and $6 - 1 = 5$ red coins; $\frac{5}{16}$

H.O.T. FOCUS ON HIGHER ORDER THINKING

Work Area

20. Draw Conclusions Give an example of an event in which all of the outcomes are not equally likely. Explain.

Sample answer: If some marbles in a jar are heavier than others, then the heavier marbles would sink and be less likely to be selected.

21. Critique Reasoning A box contains 150 black pens and 50 red pens. Jose said the sum of the probability that a randomly selected pen will not be black and the probability that the pen will not be red is 1. Explain whether you agree.

Yes; Because there are only two colors, selecting not black is equal to selecting not red. So, $P(\text{not black}) + P(\text{black}) = P(\text{not black}) + P(\text{not red}) = 1$.

22. Communicate Mathematical Ideas A spinner has 7 identical sections. Two sections are blue, 1 is red, and 4 of the sections are green. Suppose the probability of an event happening is $\frac{2}{7}$. What does each number in the ratio represent? What outcome matches this probability?

2 is the number of ways the event can happen; 7 is the number of outcomes in the sample space; landing on blue

EXTEND THE MATH PRE-AP

Activity available online ⏻ my.hrw.com

A sample space consists of 26 separate events. Each event is equally likely.

a. What is the probability of each event? $\frac{1}{26}$

b. What is the probability of the complement of each event? $\frac{25}{26}$

c. Is the probability of each event highly likely or highly unlikely? Explain. The probability is highly unlikely because $\frac{1}{26}$ is close to 0.

d. Describe a sample space that consists of 26 separate events. Sample answer: the 26 letters of the English alphabet

e. For the sample space, describe an experiment with an event that is as likely as not. Sample answer: Draw, at random, any letter from A through M from a hat containing the 26 letters of the alphabet.

f. Write and answer a different probability question based on your sample space. Sample answer: What is the probability of drawing a vowel from a hat that contains every letter of the alphabet? $\frac{5}{26}$

LESSON 7.2 Experimental Probability of Simple Events

 Florida Common Core Standards

The student is expected to:

 **Statistics and Probability—7.SP.3.6**

Approximate the probability of a chance event by collecting data on the chance process that produces it and observing its long-run relative frequency, and predict the approximate frequency given the probability.

 **Statistics and Probability—7.SP.3.7b**

Develop a probability model (which may not be uniform) by observing frequencies in data generated from a chance process.

Mathematical Practices

 **MP.4.1** Modeling

---

ADDITIONAL EXAMPLE 1

A bag has tiles with pictures of different shapes. The table shows the results of drawing one tile at random from the bag, recording the shape, and then placing the tile back in the bag. Find the probability of each shape.

Shape	Frequency
circle	11
square	6
triangle	8

circle: $\frac{11}{25}$; square: $\frac{6}{25}$; triangle: $\frac{8}{25}$

 Interactive Whiteboard
Interactive example available online

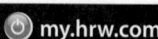 my.hrw.com

---

Engage

ESSENTIAL QUESTION

How do you find the experimental probability of a simple event? Sample answer: Repeat an experiment several times. Write the ratio of the number of successful outcomes to the total number of times the experiment was conducted.

Motivate the Lesson

Ask: What does it mean when a meteorologist makes a weather forecast that includes a probability of precipitation? Begin the Explore Activity to find out.

Explore

EXPLORE ACTIVITY

Focus on Cooperative Learning

Have students work with a partner or in small groups to conduct the experiment. Combine class results to extend the experiment to include more trials.

Explain

EXAMPLE 1

Connect Vocabulary ELL

Point out that **experimental probability** is always based on events that have already occurred.

Focus on Math Connections Mathematical Practices

However, determining the experimental probability of an event can, and will, yield any number of outcomes. That is why the definition of experimental probability uses an *approximation* symbol in its statement rather than an equal sign. Experimental probability is only an estimate.

Questioning Strategies Mathematical Practices

• Do you need to know the total number of marbles in the bag to find the experimental probability? Explain. No, you only need the total number of trials and the number of times the event occurs.

• What should the total of the experimental probabilities be equal to? Justify your answer. The total should be 1 since the sum of the results in the numerators should equal the total number of trials in the denominator.

Animated Math
Simulate Experimental Probability

Students simulate a simple event to find its experimental probability, then guess whether the next event will occur based on their analysis.

LESSON 7.2 Experimental Probability of Simple Events

FL CC 7.SP.3.6
Approximate the probability of a chance event by collecting data on the chance process that produces it and observing its long-run relative frequency ... *Also* 7.SP.3.b

? ESSENTIAL QUESTION
How do you find the experimental probability of a simple event?

EXPLORE ACTIVITY **FL CC** 7.SP.3.6, 7.SP.3.7b

Finding Experimental Probability

You can toss a paper cup to demonstrate *experimental probability*.

A Consider tossing a paper cup. Fill in the Outcome column of the table with the three different ways the cup could land.

B Toss a paper cup twenty times. Record your observations in the table.

B and 3, below: Check students' answers.

Outcome	Number of Times
Open-end up	
Open-end down	
On its side	

Reflect

1. Do the outcomes appear to be equally likely? ___No___

2. Describe the three outcomes using the words *likely* and *unlikely*.
   Sample answer: On its side, most likely; open-end down, somewhat likely; open-end up, unlikely

3. Use the number of times each event occurred to approximate the probability of each event.

4. **Make a Prediction** What do you think would happen if you performed more trials?
   Sample answer: The probability of the cup landing on its side would increase.

Outcome	Experimental Probability
Open-end up	$\dfrac{\text{open-end up}}{20} = \dfrac{\boxed{}}{20}$
Open-end down	$\dfrac{\text{open-end down}}{20} = \dfrac{\boxed{}}{20}$
On its side	$\dfrac{\text{on its side}}{20} = \dfrac{\boxed{}}{20}$

5. What is the sum of the probabilities in 3?
   The sum is 1.

Calculating Experimental Probability

You can use *experimental probability* to approximate the probability of an event. An **experimental probability** of an event is found by comparing the number of times the event occurs to the total number of trials. When there is only one outcome for an event, it is called a **simple event**.

> **Experimental Probability**
>
> For a given experiment:
> Experimental probability $= \dfrac{\text{number of times the event occurs}}{\text{total number of trials}}$

EXAMPLE 1 (Real World) **FL CC** 7.SP.3.7b

Martin has a bag of marbles. He removed one marble at random, recorded the color and then placed it back in the bag. He repeated this process several times and recorded his results in the table. Find the experimental probability of drawing each color.

Color	Frequency
Red	12
Blue	10
Green	15
Yellow	13

STEP 1 Identify the number of trials: $12 + 10 + 15 + 13 = 50$

STEP 2 Complete the table of experimental probabilities. Write each answer as a fraction in simplest form.

Color	Experimental Probability	
Red	$\dfrac{\text{frequency of the event}}{\text{total number of trials}} = \dfrac{12}{50} = \dfrac{6}{25}$	*Substitute the results recorded in the table. You can also write each probability as a decimal or as a percent.*
Blue	$\dfrac{\text{frequency of the event}}{\text{total number of trials}} = \dfrac{10}{50} = \dfrac{1}{5}$	
Green	$\dfrac{\text{frequency of the event}}{\text{total number of trials}} = \dfrac{15}{50} = \dfrac{3}{10}$	
Yellow	$\dfrac{\text{frequency of the event}}{\text{total number of trials}} = \dfrac{13}{50}$	

Reflect

6. **Communicate Mathematical Ideas** What are two different ways you could find the experimental probability of the event that Martin does **not** draw a red marble?
   Sample answer: (1) Add the frequencies for blue, green, and yellow and then find the ratio of the sum to the total number of trials. (2) Use the complement by subtracting the probability of red from 1.

PROFESSIONAL DEVELOPMENT

Integrate Mathematical Practices MP.4.1

This lesson provides an opportunity to address this Mathematical Practice standard. It calls for students to model with mathematics. Students learn to use experimental data to create a probability model for the likelihood of an event. They also use these probability models to make predictions about future events.

Math Background

The birth of modern probability can be traced to a letter written by a French nobleman, the Chevalier de Méré, to Blaise Pascal, a French philosopher and mathematician. The Chevalier sometimes bet his friends that he could roll a 6 in four rolls of a number cube. In the letter, he asked Pascal to provide a mathematical explanation. The Chevalier might have recorded his results to find that the experimental probability was greater than 50%. Pascal calculated the theoretical probability as 0.5177, confirming the Chevalier's experience that the chances of winning the bet were slightly in his favor.

YOUR TURN

Focus on Reasoning  Mathematical Practices
Ask students to suggest which section on the spinner might be the largest, the smallest.

Avoid Common Errors
Students may attempt to write an experimental probability using only two colors. Remind students to find the total number of trials and use that as the denominator.

EXAMPLE 2

Questioning Strategies  Mathematical Practices
- When you perform the simulation and put the card back in the deck, what should you do before drawing the next card? Justify your answer. Put the card back in the deck, reshuffle, and draw the next card so that each draw is random.

- Would you expect another simulation to have the same result? Explain. The experimental probability would most likely differ because drawing cards from the deck is random.

Engage with the Whiteboard
Use a deck of cards to repeat the simulation. Have one student draw the cards while another lists the results. Ask other volunteers to circle the hearts in the list and compute the experimental probability for this simulation.

Focus on Critical Thinking  Mathematical Practices
Challenge students to suggest other models that could be used to perform the simulation. For example, a spinner divided into four equal sections where one section represents a "hit."

YOUR TURN

Talk About It

Check for Understanding
Ask: What is the probability that each boy will get the next text message? How is this used to create the model for the prediction? $\frac{1}{3}$; each boy is equally likely to get the next text, so there must be three equal groups of two numbers.

Elaborate

Talk About It
Summarize the Lesson
Ask: How can you use an experiment to find probability? Repeat an experiment many times, and record the number of favorable outcomes. Then find the ratio of the number of favorable outcomes to the total number of trials.

GUIDED PRACTICE

Engage with the Whiteboard
Have a student volunteer solve Exercise 2 on the whiteboard. Have other volunteers find how the answer changes if Rachel used 5 cards, 20 cards, or 100 cards.

Avoid Common Errors
Exercise 1 Remind students to use the total number of trials as the denominator.
Exercise 2 Students may have difficulty with the model. Point out that 60% of 10 is 6.

ADDITIONAL EXAMPLE 2
Typically, a soccer player gets an assist every other game. Describe how you can use a standard deck of cards to model this situation. Then use a simulation to predict how many times in the next 12 games the soccer player will get an assist. Sample answer: Let two suits (such as both red suits) represent an "assist" and the other two suits (such as both black suits) represent "no assist." Simulation results will vary.

 **Interactive Whiteboard**
Interactive example available online

⏻ my.hrw.com

YOUR TURN

7. A spinner has three unequal sections: red, yellow, and blue. The table shows the results of Nolan's spins. Find the experimental probability of landing on each color. Write your answers in simplest form.

Color	Frequency
Red	10
Yellow	14
Blue	6

red: $\frac{1}{3}$, yellow: $\frac{7}{15}$, blue: $\frac{1}{5}$

Math Talk
Mathematical Practices

Will everyone who does this experiment get the same results?

No, probably not. Each set of trials results in a different set of data.

Math On the Spot
my.hrw.com

Making Predictions with Experimental Probability

A **simulation** is a model of an experiment that would be difficult or inconvenient to actually perform. You can use a simulation to find an experimental probability and make a prediction.

EXAMPLE 2

FL CC 7.SP.3.6

A baseball team has a batting average of 0.250 so far this season. This means that the team's players get hits in 25% of their chances at bat. Use a simulation to predict the number of hits the team's players will have in their next 34 chances at bat.

STEP 1 Choose a model.

Batting average $= 0.250 = \frac{250}{1,000} = \frac{1}{4}$

A standard deck of cards has four suits, hearts, diamonds, spades, and clubs. Since $\frac{1}{4}$ of the cards are hearts, you can let hearts represent a "hit." Diamonds, clubs, and spades then represent "no hit."

STEP 2 Perform the simulation.

Draw a card at random from the deck, record the result, and put the card back into the deck. Continue until you have drawn and replaced 34 cards in all.

(H = heart, D = diamond, C = club, S = spade)

Since the team has 34 chances at bat, you must draw a card 34 times.

H D D S H C H S D H C D C C D H H
S D D H C C H C H H D S S S C H D

STEP 3 Make a prediction.

Count the number of hearts in the simulation.

Since there are 11 hearts, you can predict that the team will have 11 hits in its next 34 chances at bat.

My Notes

Lesson 7.2 **211**

Personal Math Trainer
Online Assessment and Intervention
my.hrw.com

YOUR TURN

8. A toy machine has equal numbers of red, white, and blue foam balls which it releases at random. Ross wonders which color ball will be released next. Describe how you could use a standard number cube to predict the answer.

Sample answer: Let 1 and 2 represent red, 3 and 4 represent white, and 5 and 6 represent blue. Toss the cube 50 times to determine the experimental probability for each color. Predict that the next ball will be the color with the greatest experimental probability.

Guided Practice

1. A spinner has four sections lettered A, B, C, and D. The table shows the results of several spins. Find the experimental probability of spinning each letter as a fraction in simplest form, a decimal, and a percent. *(Explore Activity and Example 1)*

Letter	A	B	C	D
Frequency	14	7	11	8

A: $\frac{7}{20}$, 0.35, 35%   B: $\frac{7}{40}$, 0.175, 17.5%

C: $\frac{11}{40}$, 0.275, 27.5%   D: $\frac{1}{5}$, 0.2, 20%

2. Rachel's free-throw average for basketball is 60%. She wants to predict how many times in the next 50 tries she will make a free throw. Describe how she could use 10 index cards to predict the answer. *(Example 2)*

Sample answer: Write "yes" on 6 cards and "no" on 4. Draw a card at random 50 times. Use the number of "yes" cards drawn as her prediction.

? ESSENTIAL QUESTION CHECK-IN

3. **Essential Question Follow Up** How do you find an experimental probability of a simple event?

Use an experiment to find the number of times the event occurs for a certain number of trials.

212 Unit 4

DIFFERENTIATE INSTRUCTION

Curriculum Integration

Students may be familiar with the scientific method from their science classes. In the scientific method, a hypothesis is formulated and then tested. Have students discuss observations and results from their science classes that are related to experimental probability. How are the results similar, and how are they different? How are the probability experiments in the lesson similar to, and different from, science experiments students have conducted?

Critical Thinking

Tell students that the probability defined in the previous lesson is based on the likelihood of the event. Ask: Are the probability of an event based on its likelihood and the experimental probability of an event always the same? Explain. No, they may be different. Probability-based likelihood is based on the structure of an experiment while experimental probability is based on the results of an experiment. The experimental results may differ from the likelihood of the event because they are real observations of outcomes, not likelihoods.

Additional Resources

Differentiated Instruction includes:

• Reading Strategies
• Success for English Learners **ELL**
• Reteach
• Challenge **PRE-AP**

7.2 LESSON QUIZ

FL CC 7.SP.3.6, 7.SP.3.7b

1. A spinner has four lettered sections. The table shows the results of an experiment spinning the pointer.

Letter	Frequency
Q	15
R	8
S	3
T	24

a. Find the probability of each letter. Write your answer in simplest form.

b. Do you think the spinner is divided into equal sections? Explain.

2. When playing tennis, Dylan gets his first serve in play 75% of the time. Describe how you can use 12 index cards to model this situation. Then use a simulation to predict how many times in the next 20 serves Dylan will get his first serve in play.

Lesson Quiz available online

Answers

1. a. $Q: \frac{3}{10}$; $R: \frac{4}{25}$; $S: \frac{3}{50}$; $T: \frac{12}{25}$

b. No, the probabilities are very different. If the spinner had equal sections, each probability would be close to $\frac{1}{4}$.

2. Write "in" on 9 cards and "out" on 3 cards. Results will vary.

Evaluate

GUIDED AND INDEPENDENT PRACTICE

FL CC 7.SP.3.6, 7.SP.3.7b

Concepts & Skills	Practice
Explore Activity Finding Experimental Probability	Exercise 1
Example 1 Calculating Experimental Probability	Exercises 1, 4, 5, 7
Example 2 Making Predictions with Experimental Probability	Exercises 2, 6, 8, 9

Exercise	Depth of Knowledge (D.O.K.)	**FL CC** Mathematical Practices
4	**3** Strategic Thinking H.O.T.	**MP.4.1** Modeling
5	**3** Strategic Thinking H.O.T.	**MP.2.1** Reasoning
6	**3** Strategic Thinking H.O.T.	**MP.3.1** Logic
7	**2** Skills/Concepts	**MP.2.1** Reasoning
8	**3** Strategic Thinking H.O.T.	**MP.4.1** Modeling
9	**2** Skills/Concepts	**MP.4.1** Modeling
10	**2** Skills/Concepts	**MP.4.1** Modeling
11	**3** Strategic Thinking H.O.T.	**MP.3.1** Logic
12	**3** Strategic Thinking H.O.T.	**MP.4.1** Modeling
13	**3** Strategic Thinking H.O.T.	**MP.3.1** Logic

Additional Resources

Differentiated Instruction includes:

• Leveled Practice Worksheets

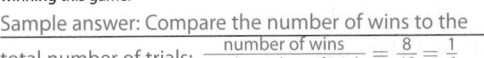

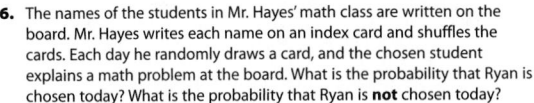

7.2 Independent Practice

FL CC 7.SP.3.6, 7.SP.3.7b

Personal
Math Trainer

Online
Assessment and
Intervention

my.hrw.com

4. Dree rolls a strike in 6 out of the 10 frames of bowling. What is the experimental probability that Dree will roll a strike in the first frame of the next game? Explain why a number cube would not be a good way to simulate this situation.

There is no way to accurately represent $\frac{3}{5}$ on a number

cube with 6 faces.

5. To play a game, you spin a spinner like the one shown. You win if the arrow lands in one of the areas marked "WIN". Lee played this game many times and recorded her results. She won 8 times and lost 40 times. Use Lee's data to explain how to find the experimental probability of winning this game.

Sample answer: Compare the number of wins to the

total number of trials; $\frac{\text{number of wins}}{\text{total number of trials}} = \frac{8}{48} = \frac{1}{6}$

6. The names of the students in Mr. Hayes' math class are written on the board. Mr. Hayes writes each name on an index card and shuffles the cards. Each day he randomly draws a card, and the chosen student explains a math problem at the board. What is the probability that Ryan is chosen today? What is the probability that Ryan is **not** chosen today?

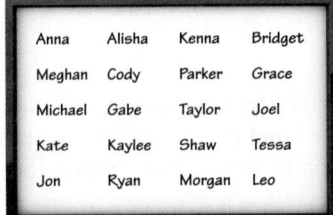

Anna	Alisha	Kenna	Bridget
Meghan	Cody	Parker	Grace
Michael	Gabe	Taylor	Joel
Kate	Kaylee	Shaw	Tessa
Jon	Ryan	Morgan	Leo

$\frac{1}{20}, \frac{19}{20}$

7. Critique Reasoning A meteorologist reports an 80% chance of precipitation. Is this an example of experimental probability, written as a percent? Explain your reasoning.

Yes, because it is based on actual data of weather patterns.

8. Mica and Joan are on the same softball team. Mica got 8 hits out of 48 times at bat, while Joan got 12 hits out of 40 times at bat. Who do you think is more likely to get a hit her next time at bat? Explain.

Joan; Mica hit about 17% of the times she was at bat,

while Joan hit 30% of the times she was at bat.

9. Make a Prediction In tennis, Gabby serves an ace, a ball that can't be returned, 4 out of the 10 times she serves. What is the experimental probability that Gabby will serve an ace in the first match of the next game? Make a prediction about how many aces Gabby will have for the next 40 serves. Justify your reasoning.

$\frac{2}{5}$; 16 aces; $\frac{2}{5}$ of 40 is 16.

10. Represent Real-World Problems Patricia finds that the experimental probability that her dog will want to go outside between 4 P.M. and 5 P.M. is $\frac{7}{12}$. About what percent of the time does her dog **not** want to go out between 4 P.M. and 5 P.M.?

$\frac{5}{12}$ or about 41.7%

H.O.T. FOCUS ON HIGHER ORDER THINKING

11. Explain the Error Talia tossed a penny many times. She got 40 heads and 60 tails. She said the experimental probability of getting heads was $\frac{40}{60}$. Explain and correct her error.

No; there were 40 heads in 100 trials; $P(\text{heads}) = \frac{40}{100}$.

12. Communicate Mathematical Ideas A high school has 438 students, with about the same number of males as females. Describe a simulation to predict how many of the first 50 students who leave school at the end of the day are female.

Sample answer: coin toss; Heads represents male, and

tails represents female; Toss the coin 50 times, and use

the results to make a prediction.

13. Critical Thinking For a scavenger hunt, Chessa put one coin in each of 10 small boxes. Four coins are quarters, 4 are dimes, and 2 are nickels. How could you simulate choosing one box at random? Would you use the same simulation if you planned to put these coins in your pocket and choose one? Explain your reasoning.

Sample answer: Make an index card to represent each

coin, then pick one card at random. No; since the coins

are different sizes, they do not each have the same

probability of getting pulled out of my pocket.

Work Area

EXTEND THE MATH PRE-AP

Activity available online my.hrw.com

a. Roll a 1 through 6 number cube 25 times. Record the result of each roll in a frequency table. Then find the experimental probability of each number.

b. Repeat for another 25 rolls. Find the experimental probability of each number for 50 rolls.

c. Repeat for another 25 rolls. Find the experimental probability of each number for 75 rolls.

d. Compare the experimental probabilities of each number for 25, 50, and 75 rolls. What do you notice?

Answers may vary. The probabilities for each number will likely get closer to $\frac{1}{6}$ with the increase in the number of trials.

Experimental Probability of Compound Events

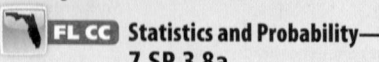
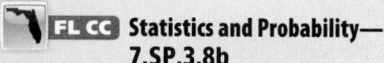
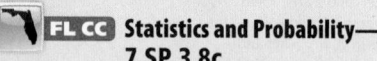

ADDITIONAL EXAMPLE 1
A breakfast cart offers plain and multigrain bagels with three different toppings: butter, cream cheese, or jam. The orders one morning were recorded in the table. What is the experimental probability that the next customer wants a multigrain bagel with cream cheese?

	Butter	Cream cheese	Jam
Plain	6	15	3
Multigrain	5	12	9

$\frac{6}{25} = 24\%$

 Interactive Whiteboard
Interactive example available online

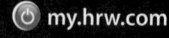 my.hrw.com

Engage

ESSENTIAL QUESTION

How do you find the experimental probability of a compound event? Sample answer: Write a ratio of the number of ways the event happens in an experiment to the total number of times the experiment was performed.

Motivate the Lesson
Ask: How can you find the experimental probability of getting both heads when you flip two coins? Take a guess. Begin the Explore Activity to find out.

Explore

EXPLORE ACTIVITY

Connect Vocabulary ELL
Point out that a **compound event** is an event defined by two or more separate simple events, such as rolling a 1 and a 2 when rolling two different number cubes. Emphasize that this is different from an event that is defined by two or more outcomes, such as rolling a 1 or a 2 when rolling a single number cube.

Explain

EXAMPLE 1

Focus on Math Connections   Mathematical Practices
Discuss how to recognize that the compound events in the table are independent. Note that the compound events in all the examples and exercises in this lesson are independent.

Questioning Strategies   Mathematical Practices
• How does the total of the 2-piece and 3-piece orders compare to the total of the orders that have different sides? Explain. The totals are the same. They are different ways of categorizing the same orders, by size or by sides.

• Why do you think the owner of the food trailer might be interested in finding this experimental probability? Sample answer: It gives the owner an idea of the ingredients to have on hand to fill orders each day.

YOUR TURN

Engage with the Whiteboard
Ask a volunteer to find the total for all row. Then ask another student to find the total for all columns. Finally, have a student explain why the total of the rows and the total of the columns is the same.

Talk About It
Check for Understanding
Ask: Why is it useful to write the experimental probability as a percent? A percent makes it easier to recognize whether a probability is high or low.

Experimental Probability of Compound Events

FL CC 7.SP.3.8
Find probabilities of compound events using... tables, ..., and simulation. Also 7.SP.3.8a, 7.SP.3.8b, 7.SP.3.8c

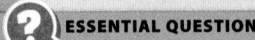

? ESSENTIAL QUESTION

How do you find the experimental probability of a compound event?

EXPLORE ACTIVITY FL CC 7.SP.3.8a, 7.SP.3.8b

Exploring Compound Probability

A **compound event** is an event that includes two or more simple events, such as flipping a coin *and* rolling a number cube. A compound event can include events that depend on each other or are independent. Events are independent if the occurrence of one event does not affect the probability of the other event, such as flipping a coin and rolling a number cube.

A What are the possible outcomes of flipping a coin once? Heads, Tails

B What are the possible outcomes of rolling a standard number cube once? 1, 2, 3, 4, 5, 6

C Complete the list for all possible outcomes for flipping a coin *and* rolling a number cube.

H1, H2, __H3__, __H4__, __H5__, __H6__, T1, __T2__, __T3__, __T4__, __T5__, __T6__

There are __12__ possible outcomes for this compound event.

> H1 would mean the coin landed on heads, and the number cube showed a 1.

D Flip a coin and roll a number cube 50 times. Use tally marks to record your results in the table. Check students' answers.

	1	2	3	4	5	6
H						
T						

E Based on your data, which compound event had the greatest experimental probability and what was it? The least experimental probability? Check students' answers.

F **Draw Conclusions** Did you expect to have the same probability for each possible combination of flips and rolls? Why or why not?

Sample answer: No; 50 trials is not enough for the results to be close.

Math On the Spot
my.hrw.com

No; 8 is the number of possible outcomes. The total number of orders is 330.

Math Talk
Mathematical Practices
Javier said the total number of orders is 8 and not 330. Is he correct? Explain.

Personal Math Trainer
Online Assessment and Intervention
my.hrw.com

Calculating Experimental Probability of Compound Events

The experimental probability of a compound event can be found using recorded data.

EXAMPLE 1 Real World FL CC 7.SP.3.8, 7.SP.3.8a

A food trailer serves chicken and records the order size and sides on their orders, as show in the table. What is the experimental probability that the next order is for 3-pieces with cole slaw?

	Green Salad	Macaroni & Cheese	French Fries	Cole Slaw
2 pieces	33	22	52	35
3 pieces	13	55	65	55

STEP 1 Find the total number of trials, or orders.

$33 + 22 + 52 + 35 + 13 + 55 + 65 + 55 = 330$

STEP 2 Find the number of orders that are for 3 pieces with cole slaw: 55.

STEP 3 Find the experimental probability.

$$P(3 \text{ piece} + \text{slaw}) = \frac{\text{number of 3 piece} + \text{slaw}}{\text{total number of orders}}$$

$$= \frac{55}{330} \quad \text{Substitute the values.}$$

$$= \frac{1}{6} \quad \text{Simplify.}$$

The experimental probability that the next order is for 3 pieces of chicken with cole slaw is $\frac{1}{6}$.

YOUR TURN

1. Drink sales for an afternoon at the school carnival were recorded in the table. What is the experimental probability that the next drink is a small cocoa?

	Soda	Water	Cocoa
Small	77	98	60
Large	68	45	52

$\frac{60}{400} = \frac{3}{20} = 15\%$

PROFESSIONAL DEVELOPMENT

Integrate Mathematical Practices MP.2.1

This lesson provides an opportunity to address this Mathematical Practice standard. It calls for students to create and use representations to organize, record, and communicate mathematical ideas. Students use lists to find the sample space for a compound event. They use data in tables to find the experimental probability of a compound event. Next, students choose a model for a simulation, perform the simulation, and use a table to record the results. Finally, they use the simulation results to make a prediction. In this way, students create and use a variety of representations to organize, record, and interpret experimental probability in real-world situations.

Math Background

In probability, two events are independent if the occurrence of one or any does not affect the probability of the occurrence of the other. If events are not independent, they are dependent. These definitions lead to two different multiplication rules for the theoretical probability of events A and B. For independent events, $P(A \text{ and } B) = P(A) \cdot P(B)$. For dependent events, $P(A \text{ and } B) = P(A) \cdot P(B|A)$, where $P(B|A)$ denotes the probability of event B given the occurrence of event A. Sometimes it can be difficult to determine whether events are independent or not. In these cases, the multiplication rules can be used to confirm or deny independence.

EXAMPLE 2

Questioning Strategies Mathematical Practices

- How could you use a coin and a number cube as the simulation model? Use the coin to model the two vehicles and different pairs of numbers (1 and 2, 3 and 4, 5 and 6) to model the three directions.

- Why is a simulation a good way to collect the data for this problem? It is much quicker and easier than standing on the street corner to observe and record the data.

- If you found the experimental probability of each compound event identified in the table, what would the sum of the probabilities be? How do you know? 1; each compound event will be a numerator with a denominator that is the total number of trials. The total of the numerators will equal the denominator.

- How can you use the data in the simulation to find the experimental probability that the next vehicle will be a car? The total of the car data is the numerator: $\frac{23}{50}$.

- If the simulation were repeated more times, how different would you expect the results to be? Explain. The results would likely be different but not drastically different. The simulation shows about the same number for each outcome, as stated in the problem. Most likely the results would be close.

Focus on Math Connections Mathematical Practices
In the Reflect question, point out that the prediction is based on the simulation, not on the theoretical likelihood of each vehicle and direction of turn. Discuss why this is the case and how the two are related.

YOUR TURN

Focus on Reasoning Mathematical Practices
Assuming that about equal numbers of each type of necklace are sold, have students suggest models that could be used to perform the simulation. Review the necessity of the assumption of "equal numbers of each type of necklace" to create the simulation model.

Avoid Common Errors
Students may attempt to find the total trials by only adding the numbers in a single row or column. Emphasize that *total* means total, and they need to add all of the numbers in the table to find the total number of trials.

Elaborate

Talk About It
Summarize the Lesson
Ask: How can you find the probability of a compound event using data recorded from an experiment or a simulation? Find the total number of trials in the experiment. Then find the number of occurrences of the compound event. The experimental probability is the ratio of the number of occurrences to the total number of trials.

GUIDED PRACTICE

Avoid Common Errors
Exercise 1 Make sure students understand that while the numerator is represented by a single cell in the table, the denominator of the experimental probability ratio is the total of all the cells.

Engage with the Whiteboard
For Exercise 1, ask a volunteer to circle the part of the table that represents females, age 22–39. Then, to reinforce finding the total trials, have another student circle the part of the table that represents the number of trials.

Using a Simulation to Make a Prediction

You can use a simulation or model of an experiment to find the experimental probability of compound events.

Math On the Spot
my.hrw.com

EXAMPLE 2

FL CC 7.SP.3.8c

At a street intersection, a vehicle is classified either as a *car* or a *truck*, and it can turn *left*, *right*, or go *straight*. About an equal number of cars and trucks go through the intersection and turn in each direction. Use a simulation to find the experimental probability that the next vehicle will be a car that turns right.

STEP 1 Choose a model.
Use a coin toss to model the two vehicle types.
Let Heads = Car and Tails = Truck

Use a spinner divided into 3 equal sectors to represent the *three* directions as shown.

STEP 2 Find the sample space for the compound event.

There are 6 possible outcomes: **CL, CR, CS, TL, TR, TS**

STEP 3 Perform the simulation.

A coin was tossed and a spinner spun 50 times.
The results are shown in the table.

	Car	Truck
Left	8	9
Right	6	11
Straight	9	7

STEP 4 Find the experimental probability that a car turns right.

$$P(\text{Car turns right}) = \frac{\text{frequency of compound event}}{\text{total number of trials}}$$

$$= \frac{6}{50} \quad \text{Substitute the values.}$$

$$= \frac{3}{25} \quad \text{Simplify.}$$

Based on the simulation, the experimental probability is $\frac{3}{25}$ that the next vehicle will be a car that turns right.

Reflect

2. **Make a Prediction** Predict the number of cars that turn right out of 100 vehicles that enter the intersection. Explain your reasoning.

<u>12; The data shows that 6 out of 50 vehicles are cars</u>

<u>that turn right. An equivalent ratio is 12 out of 100.</u>

My Notes

Personal Math Trainer
Online Assessment and Intervention
my.hrw.com

YOUR TURN

3. A jeweler sells necklaces made in three sizes and two different metals. Use the data from a simulation to find the experimental probability that the next necklace sold is a 20-inch gold necklace.

	Silver	Gold
12 in.	12	22
16 in.	16	8
20 in.	5	12

$$\frac{12}{75} = \frac{4}{25}$$

Guided Practice

1. A dentist has 400 male and female patients that range in ages from 10 years old to 50 years old and up as shown in the table. What is the experimental probability that the next patient will be female and in the age range 22–39? (Explore Activity and Example 1)

	Range: 10–21	Range: 22–39	Range: 40–50	Range: 50+
Male	44	66	32	53
Female	36	50	45	74

$$\frac{50}{400} = \frac{1}{8}$$

2. At a car wash, customers can choose the type of wash and whether to use the interior vacuum. Customers are equally likely to choose each type of wash and whether to use the vacuum. Use a simulation to find the experimental probability that the next customer purchases a deluxe wash and no interior vacuum. Describe your simulation. (Example 2)

Check student's work.

CAR WASH
Standard
Deluxe
Superior
Vacuum
yes   no

? ESSENTIAL QUESTION CHECK-IN

3. How do you find the experimental probability of a compound event?

<u>Find the number of occurrences of the compound event</u>

<u>and divide it by the total number of trials.</u>

DIFFERENTIATE INSTRUCTION

Cooperative Learning

Have students work in pairs to find the experimental probabilities of the other compound events in Example 2. Ask students to identify each compound event, find the experimental probability in simplest form, and then use the probability to make a prediction based on the simulation. $P(\text{car turns left}) = \frac{4}{25}$; $P(\text{car goes straight}) = \frac{9}{50}$; $P(\text{truck turns left}) = \frac{9}{50}$; $P(\text{truck turns right}) = \frac{11}{50}$; $P(\text{truck goes straight}) = \frac{7}{50}$

Visual Cues

Have students create a total for each row and column in the tables showing the experimental results in the Examples and the Exercises. Elicit that the sum of the row totals and the column totals must be the same and is equal to the total number of trials in the experiment. Point out that this is a good way to both check the total number of trials in the experiment and to remember that this is the total needed for the denominator of the experimental probability ratio. Students can also circle the compound event of interest in the table to identify the numerator of the experimental probability ratio.

Additional Resources

Differentiated Instruction includes:
- Reading Strategies
- Success for English Learners **ELL**
- Reteach
- Challenge **PRE-AP**

7.3 LESSON QUIZ

FL CC 7.SP.3.8

An attendant recorded the data in the table showing the types and colors of vehicles that parked in a parking lot.

	Red	Blue	Black	White
SUV	5	3	13	4
Car	14	6	19	18
Van	3	1	6	8

1. What is the experimental probability that the next vehicle in the lot is a red car?

2. What is the experimental probability that the next vehicle in the lot is a black van?

3. What is the experimental probability that the next vehicle in the lot is a white SUV?

4. A café offers iced tea in three sizes: small, medium, and large. The tea is served plain or sweetened. Each option is ordered with about the same frequency. Use a simulation to find the experimental probability that the next customer who orders tea orders a medium, sweetened tea.

Lesson Quiz available online

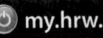 my.hrw.com

Answers
1. $\frac{14}{100} = \frac{7}{50}$
2. $\frac{6}{100} = \frac{3}{50}$
3. $\frac{4}{100} = \frac{1}{25}$
4. Check students' work.

Evaluate

GUIDED AND INDEPENDENT PRACTICE

FL CC 7.SP.3.8, 7.SP.3.8a, 7.SP.3.8b, 7.SP.3.8c

Concepts & Skills	Practice
Explore Activity Exploring Compound Probability	Exercise 1
Example 1 Calculating Experimental Probability of Compound Events	Exercises 1, 4–9
Example 2 Using a Simulation to Make a Prediction	Exercise 2

Exercise	Depth of Knowledge (D.O.K.)	**FL CC** Mathematical Practices
4	**3** Strategic Thinking H.O.T.	**MP.4.1** Modeling
5	**2** Skills/Concepts	**MP.2.1** Reasoning
6	**3** Strategic Thinking H.O.T.	**MP.8.1** Patterns
7	**3** Strategic Thinking H.O.T.	**MP.8.1** Patterns
8	**3** Strategic Thinking H.O.T.	**MP.8.1** Patterns
9	**3** Strategic Thinking H.O.T.	**MP.8.1** Patterns
10	**3** Strategic Thinking H.O.T.	**MP.4.1** Modeling
11	**3** Strategic Thinking H.O.T.	**MP.2.1** Reasoning
12	**3** Strategic Thinking H.O.T.	**MP.8.1** Patterns
13	**3** Strategic Thinking H.O.T.	**MP.5.1** Using Tools
14	**3** Strategic Thinking H.O.T.	**MP.8.1** Patterns

Additional Resources

Differentiated Instruction includes:

• Leveled Practice Worksheets

 **CLUSTER CONNECTION**

Exercises 12–13 combine concepts from the Florida Common Core cluster "Investigate chance processes and develop, use, and evaluate probability models."

7.3 Independent Practice

FL.CC 7.SP.3.8, 7.SP.3.8a, 7.SP.3.8b, 7.SP.3.8c

Personal Math Trainer
Online Assessment and Intervention
my.hrw.com

4. Represent Real-World Problems For the same food trailer mentioned in Example 1, explain how to find the experimental probability that the next order is two pieces of chicken with a green salad.

Divide the number of 2 piece + salad, 33, by the total number of

2 piece + salad orders, 330: $P = \dfrac{\text{number of 2 piece + salad}}{\text{total number of orders}} = \dfrac{33}{330} = \dfrac{1}{10}$

The school store sells spiral notebooks in four colors and three different sizes. The table shows the sales by size and color for 400 notebooks.

	Red	Green	Blue	Yellow
100 Pages	55	37	26	12
150 Pages	60	44	57	27
200 Pages	23	19	21	19

5. What is the experimental probability that the next customer buys a red notebook with 150 pages?

$\dfrac{60}{400} = \dfrac{3}{20}$

6. What is the experimental probability that the next customer buys any red notebook?

$P(\text{red notebook}) = \dfrac{\text{number of red notebooks}}{\text{total number of notebooks}} = \dfrac{138}{400} = \dfrac{69}{200}$

7. Analyze Relationships How many possible combined page count and color choices are possible? How does this number relate to the number of page size choices and to the number of color choices?

12; The total is the product of 3 page count choices and 4 color choices, which is 12.

A middle school English teacher polled random students about how many pages of a book they read per week.

	6th	7th	8th
75 Pages	24	18	22
100 Pages	22	32	24
150 Pages	30	53	25

8. Critique Reasoning Jennie says the experimental probability that a 7th grade student reads at least 100 pages per week is $\dfrac{16}{125}$. What is her error and the correct experimental probability?

She left out the 53 students that read 150 pages; $\dfrac{85}{250} = \dfrac{17}{50}$

9. Analyze Relationships Based on the data, which group(s) of students should be encouraged to read more? Explain your reasoning.

Sample answer: 8th grade; 8th grade students are least likely to have read 150 pages.

Work Area

10. Make a Conjecture Would you expect the probability for the simple event "rolling a 6" to be greater than or less than the probability of the compound event "rolling a 6 and getting heads on a coin"? Explain.

Greater; heads occurs on about half the occasions that you roll a 6, so the compound event is half as likely.

11. Critique Reasoning Donald says he uses a standard number cube for simulations that involve 2, 3, or 6 equal outcomes. Explain how Donald can do this.

Sample answer: For 2 outcomes, he could use even and odd numbers. For 3 outcomes, he could use 1 or 2, 3 or 4, and 5 or 6. For 6 outcomes, he could use each number once.

12. Draw Conclusions Data collected in a mall recorded the shoe styles worn by 150 male and for 150 female customers. What is the probability that the next customer is male and has an open-toe shoe (such as a sandal)? What is the probability that the next male customer has an open-toe shoe? Are the two probabilities the same? Explain.

	Male	Female
Open toe	11	92
Closed toe	139	58

$P(\text{male and open toe}) = \dfrac{11}{300}$; $P(\text{male has open toe}) = \dfrac{11}{150}$;

No, the first scenario includes females, and the second does not.

13. What If? Suppose you wanted to perform a simulation to model the shoe style data shown in the table. Could you use two coins? Explain.

No, because coins are fair and the probabilities do not appear to be equally likely.

14. Represent Real-World Problems A middle school is made up of grades 6, 7, and 8, and has about the same number of male and female students in each grade. Explain how to use a simulation to find the experimental probability that the first 50 students who arrive at school are male and 7th graders.

Sample answer: On a coin, heads = male and tails = female. On a number cube, (1 or 2) = 6th grade, (3 or 4) = 7th grade, and (5 or 6) = 8th grade. Toss the coin and roll the number cube 50 times each. Record the number of outcomes that are heads and 3 or 4.

EXTEND THE MATH PRE-AP

Activity available online my.hrw.com

Activity Provide students with a pair of number cubes. Ask them to name their three favorite types of sandwiches and their three favorite types of fruit to have for lunch. Have them assume that they are equally likely to get each option for lunch tomorrow, then have them use a simulation to find the experimental probability of getting:

a) a particular combination of one sandwich and one fruit

b) either of two sandwiches and one particular fruit

c) either of two sandwiches and either of two fruits

Check students' work. With a sufficient number of trials, Part a should be close to $\dfrac{1}{9}$, Part b should be close to $\dfrac{2}{9}$, and Part c should be close to $\dfrac{4}{9}$.

LESSON 7.4 Making Predictions with Experimental Probability

 Florida Common Core Standards

The student is expected to:

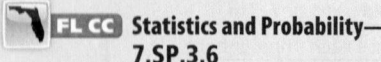 **Statistics and Probability— 7.SP.3.6**

Approximate the probability of a chance event by collecting data on the chance process that produces it and observing its long-run relative frequency, and predict the approximate frequency given the probability.

Mathematical Practices

 **MP.4.1** Modeling

Engage

ESSENTIAL QUESTION

How do you make predictions using experimental probability? Sample answer: Write an equation to find the likelihood of the event. Use the likelihood to make the prediction.

Motivate the Lesson
Ask: How can you use your past performance to predict your future performance?

Explore

Focus on Reasoning **Mathematical Practices**
Have students roll a number cube 20 times, recording multiples of 3 rolled. How can you use the experimental probability of a success to predict the number of successes in 100 rolls? Multiply the experimental probability of a success by 100.

Explain

EXAMPLE 1

Focus on Math Connections **Mathematical Practices**
Discuss why the first method can be rewritten as the second method.

Questioning Strategies **Mathematical Practices**
• In 75 throws, will Danae match her prediction? She will be close but not match it exactly.

YOUR TURN

Talk About It
Check for Understanding
Ask: How can you use 1% and mental math to predict the number of defective chips in Your Turn 2? 1% of 2,500 is 25, and 25(4) = 100.

EXAMPLE 2

Connect to Daily Life **Mathematical Practices**
Discuss why a doctor should be interested in rescheduling patient appointments.

Questioning Strategies **Mathematical Practices**
• Why is 11% an experimental probability? It is based on collected data.

YOUR TURN

Avoid Common Errors
Make sure students who set up a proportion are able to solve the proportion. Remind students that another way to solve a proportion is to cross multiply. Eliminating any common factor in numerators and denominators makes for easier calculations.

ADDITIONAL EXAMPLE 1
Lorenzo found that his experimental probability of getting a hit is 40%. Out of 350 at bats, about how many hits could he predict he would make?
about 140 hits

 Interactive Whiteboard
Interactive example available online

 my.hrw.com

---

ADDITIONAL EXAMPLE 2
The owner of a rafting company notices that 16% of customers call to cancel before a guided rafting trip. The owner predicts that of 850 customers booked for the week, 102 will cancel. Do you agree with the prediction? Explain. No, about 136 customers will cancel. The prediction is low.

 Interactive Whiteboard
Interactive example available online

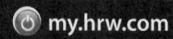 my.hrw.com

---

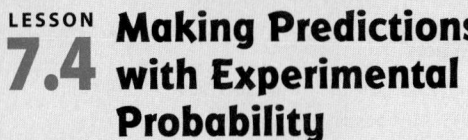

LESSON 7.4 Making Predictions with Experimental Probability

FL CC 7.SP.3.6
Approximate the probability of a chance event by collecting data on the chance process that produces it..., and predict the approximate relative frequency given the probability.

? ESSENTIAL QUESTION
How do you make predictions using experimental probability?

Using Experimental Probability to Make a Prediction

Scientists study data to make predictions. You can use probabilities to make predictions in your daily life.

EXAMPLE 1 *Real World*   FL CC 7.SP.3.6

Danae found that the experimental probability of her making a bull's-eye when throwing darts is $\frac{2}{10}$, or 20%. Out of 75 throws, about how many bull's-eyes could she predict she would make?

Method 1: Use a proportion.

$\frac{2}{10} = \frac{x}{75}$ Write a proportion. 2 out of 10 is how many out of 75?

$\frac{2}{10} = \frac{x}{75}$

$\frac{2}{10} \overset{\times 7.5}{=} \frac{15}{75}$ Since 10 times 7.5 is 75, multiply 2 times 7.5 to find the value of x.

$x = 15$

Method 2: Use a percent equation.

$0.20 \cdot 75 = x$ Find 20% of 75.

$15 = x$

> You can write probabilities as ratios, decimals, or percents.

Danae can predict that she will make about 15 bull's-eye throws out of 75.

YOUR TURN

1. A car rental company sells accident insurance to 24% of its customers. Out of 550 customers, about how many customers are predicted to purchase insurance? __132 customers__

Math On the Spot
my.hrw.com

Personal Math Trainer
Online Assessment and Intervention
my.hrw.com

Lesson 7.4 **221**

Math On the Spot
my.hrw.com

Using Experimental Probability to Make a Qualitative Prediction

A prediction is something you reasonably expect to happen in the future. A qualitative prediction helps you decide which situation is more likely in general.

EXAMPLE 2 *Real World*   FL CC 7.SP.3.6

A doctor's office records data and concludes that, on average, 11% of patients call to reschedule their appointments per week. The office manager predicts that 23 appointments will be rescheduled out of the 240 total appointments during next week. Explain whether the prediction is reasonable.

Method 1: Use a proportion.

$\frac{11}{100} = \frac{x}{240}$ Write a proportion. 11 out of 100 is how many out of 240?

$\frac{11}{100} = \frac{x}{240}$

$\frac{11}{100} \overset{\times 2.4}{\underset{\times 2.4}{=}} \frac{26.4}{240}$ Since 100 times 2.4 is 240, multiply 11 times 2.4 to find the value of x.

$x = 26.4$

> 26.4 is the average number of patients that would call to reschedule.

Method 2: Use a percent equation.

$0.11 \cdot 240 = x$ Find 11% of 240.

$26.4 = x$ Solve for x.

The prediction of 23 is reasonable but a little low, because 23 is a little less than 26.4.

Reflect

2. Does 26.4 make sense for the number of patients?
   The number of patients should be a whole number, so to be more accurate you should round to the nearest whole number.

YOUR TURN

3. In emails to monthly readers of a newsletter 3% of the emails come back undelivered. The editor predicts that if he sends out 12,372 emails, he will receive 437 notices for undelivered email. Do you agree with his prediction?

   Explain. No; About 371 emails out of 12,372 will come back undelivered. The prediction is high.

Personal Math Trainer
Online Assessment and Intervention
my.hrw.com

222 Unit 4

PROFESSIONAL DEVELOPMENT

Integrate Mathematical Practices MP.4.1

This lesson provides an opportunity to address this Mathematical Practice standard. It calls for students to apply mathematics to problems arising in everyday life, society, and the workplace. Students use proportions and equations to make a prediction about playing darts in everyday life. Then students use experimental probability to make qualitative predictions that relate to a doctor's office. Finally, students use proportional reasoning to make a quantitative prediction and compare the prediction to determine the validity of a claim about a real-world situation.

Math Background

Experimental probability plays an important role in measuring uncertainty and providing a way to make useful predictions based on data. The examples in this lesson are somewhat similar to what an actuary does. Actuaries apply probability and statistics to create models of real-world situations and then use the models to make predictions that can be useful in determining risks, assessing costs for investments and insurance, and drawing conclusions about real-life situations.

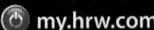
EXAMPLE 3

Questioning Strategies Mathematical Practices

• Is there another way to use experimental probability to determine if the movie site's claim is accurate? If so, how does this method lead to the same conclusion? Write the ratio of the number of people who liked the movie to the total number surveyed: $\frac{104}{150} = 69\frac{1}{3}\%$. $69\frac{1}{3}\%$ is close to the 72% of people who liked the movie according to the online poll.

Engage with the Whiteboard

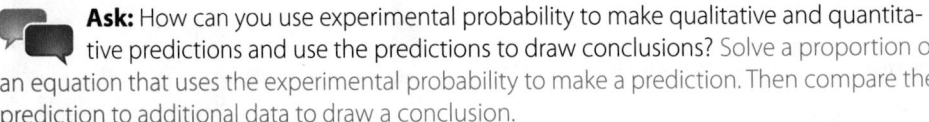 Ask a volunteer to set up and solve an equation for the Solve section.

YOUR TURN

Avoid Common Errors

Make sure that students understand that the problem has two parts: make a prediction and then use the prediction to draw a conclusion. Point out that the total number of customers in the problem is paired with the percent to make the prediction, while the number of customers that bought two or more pairs is used for the comparison. Discuss why.

Elaborate

Talk About It
Summarize the Lesson

 Ask: How can you use experimental probability to make qualitative and quantitative predictions and use the predictions to draw conclusions? Solve a proportion or an equation that uses the experimental probability to make a prediction. Then compare the prediction to additional data to draw a conclusion.

GUIDED PRACTICE

Engage with the Whiteboard

Invite student volunteers to circle the predictions in Exercises 3–6, and then circle the information used for the comparisons.

Avoid Common Errors

Exercises 1–6 Students may get stuck or make more mistakes using one method instead of the other. Remind students to use the method they find easiest and that they can calculate most accurately to make their predictions.

Exercises 3–6 Emphasize that students must use the prediction to support their conclusions about the accuracy of the claims.

Making a Quantitative Prediction

You can use proportional reasoning to make quantitative predictions and compare options in real-world situations.

Math On the Spot
my.hrw.com

EXAMPLE 3   Problem Solving   **FL CC** 7.SP.3.6

An online poll for a movie site shows its polling results for a new movie. If a newspaper surveys 150 people leaving the movie, how many people can it predict will like the movie based on the online poll? Is the movie site's claim accurate if the newspaper has 104 people say they like the movie?

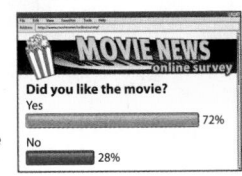

MOVIE NEWS
online survey

Did you like the movie?
Yes   72%
No   28%

Analyze Information

The **answer** is a prediction for how many people out of 150 will like the movie based on the online poll. Also tell whether the 104 people that say they like the movie is enough to support the movie site's claim.

List the important information:
- The online poll says 72% of movie goers like the new movie.
- A newspaper surveys 150 people.

Formulate a Plan

Use a proportion to calculate 72% of the 150 people surveyed.

Solve

$\frac{72}{100} = \frac{x}{150}$ Set up a proportion. 72 out of 100 is how many out of 150?

$\frac{72}{100} = \frac{x}{150}$ ×1.5

$\frac{72}{100} = \frac{108}{150}$ ×1.5   Since 100 times 1.5 is 150, multiply 72 times 1.5 to find the value of x.

$x = 108$

The newspaper can predict that 108 out of 150 people will say they like the movie, based on the online poll.

Justify and Evaluate

Since 108 is close to 104, the newspaper survey and the online poll show that about the same percent of people like the movie.

My Notes

Personal
Math Trainer
Online Assessment
and Intervention
my.hrw.com

YOUR TURN

4. On average, 24% of customers who buy shoes in a particular store buy two or more pairs. One weekend, 350 customers purchased shoes. How many can be predicted to buy two or more pairs? If 107 customers buy more than two pairs, did more customers than normal buy two or more pairs?

    84 customers; Yes, 107 > 84, so more customers than normal bought two or more pairs.

Guided Practice

1. A baseball player reaches first base 30% of the times he is at bat. Out of 50 times at bat, about how many times will the player reach first base? (Example 1)

    15 times

2. The experimental probability that it will rain on any given day in Houston, Texas, is about 15%. Out of 365 days, about how many days can residents predict rain? (Example 1)

    about 55 days

3. A catalog store has 6% of its orders returned for a refund. The owner predicts that a new candle will have 812 returns out of the 16,824 sold. Do you agree with this prediction? Explain. (Example 2)

    No, about 1,009 candles out of 16,824 will be returned. The prediction is low.

4. On a toy assembly line, 3% of the toys are found to be defective. The quality control officer predicts that 872 toys will be found defective out of 24,850 toys made. Do you agree with this prediction? Explain. (Example 2)

    No, about 746 toys out of 24,850 will be defective. The prediction is high.

5. A light-rail service claims to be on time 98% of the time. Jeanette takes the light-rail 40 times one month, how many times can she predict she will be on time? Is the light-rail's claim accurate if she is late 6 times? (Example 3)

    39 times; The light-rail's claim is higher than the actual 85%.

6. On average, a college claims to accept 18% of its applicants. If the college has 5,000 applicants, predict how many will be accepted. If 885 applicants are accepted, is the college's claim accurate? (Example 3)

    900 students; The college's claim is close to the number actually accepted.

? ESSENTIAL QUESTION CHECK-IN

7. How do you make predictions using experimental probability?

    Solve a proportion using the experimental probability to find an expected number of events to happen. Make a prediction based on the expected number of events.

DIFFERENTIATE INSTRUCTION

Kinesthetic Experience

Have students perform a simple activity, such as tossing a paper clip into a cup from a set distance. Each student keeps track of the number of times the paper clip goes in the cup out of 20 tries. Ask students to use the data to predict how many successes they will have in 10 more tries. Then have students test their predictions.

Communicating Math

Ask students to find examples of claims from magazines, newspapers, television, and the Internet. Have students note whether any data is given to support the claims. Discuss how to determine the validity of the claims.

Additional Resources

Differentiated Instruction includes:
- Reading Strategies
- Success for English Learners **ELL**
- Reteach
- Challenge **PRE-AP**

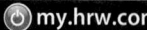
7.4 LESSON QUIZ

FL CC 7.SP.3.6

1. A librarian noticed that 60% of seventh graders checked out fantasy books. About how many of 240 seventh graders would check out fantasy books?

2. A tennis player gets an ace 35% of his serves. Out of 80 serves, about how many aces will he get?

3. A light bulb manufacturer finds that 4% of the bulbs it makes are defective. The quality control officer predicts that 700 bulbs will be defective out of 15,500 bulbs made. Do you agree? Explain.

4. A delivery service claims that orders arrive before noon 90% of the time. If Amy uses the delivery service 20 times, how many times can she predict the deliveries will arrive before noon? Is the claim accurate if her packages arrive after noon 4 times?

Lesson Quiz available online

🔘 my.hrw.com

Answers

1. 144 seventh graders

2. 28 aces

3. No, about 620 will be defective. The prediction is high.

4. She can predict the packages will arrive before noon 18 times. No, the claim is not accurate if 4 packages arrive after noon.

Evaluate

GUIDED AND INDEPENDENT PRACTICE

 **FL CC** 7.SP.3.6

Concepts & Skills	Practice
Example 1 Using Experimental Probability to Make a Prediction	Exercises 1, 2, 8, 10, 11
Example 2 Using Experimental Probability to Make a Qualitative Prediction	Exercises 3, 4, 14–16
Example 3 Making a Quantitative Prediction	Exercises 5, 6, 8–13

Exercise	Depth of Knowledge (D.O.K.)	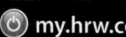 **FL CC** Mathematical Practices
8	**3** Strategic Thinking **H.O.T.**	**MP.2.1** Reasoning
9	**3** Strategic Thinking **H.O.T.**	**MP.2.1** Reasoning
10	**3** Strategic Thinking **H.O.T.**	**MP.4.1** Modeling
11	**2** Skills/Concepts	**MP.4.1** Modeling
12	**3** Strategic Thinking **H.O.T.**	**MP.3.1** Logic
13	**3** Strategic Thinking **H.O.T.**	**MP.7.1** Using Structure
14	**2** Skills/Concepts	**MP.4.1** Modeling
15	**3** Strategic Thinking **H.O.T.**	**MP.3.1** Logic
16	**3** Strategic Thinking **H.O.T.**	**MP.7.1** Using Structure

Additional Resources

Differentiated Instruction includes:

• Leveled Practice Worksheets

7.4 Independent Practice

FL CC 7.SP.3.6

Personal Math Trainer
Online Assessment and Intervention
my.hrw.com

The table shows the number of students in a middle school at the beginning of the year and the percentage that can be expected to move out of the area by the end of the year.

	6th	7th	8th
Number of Students	250	200	150
% Moves	2%	4%	8%

8. How many 7th grade students are expected to move by the end of the year? If 12 students actually moved, did more or fewer 7th grade students move than expected? Justify your answer.

8; more; $\frac{4}{100} = \frac{x}{200} \rightarrow x = 8$; Because $8 < 12$, more 7th grade

students moved than expected.

9. **Critique Reasoning** The middle school will lose some of its funding if 50 or more students move away in any year. The principal claims he only loses about 30 students a year. Do the values in the table support his claim? Explain.

Yes; 6th grade: $\frac{2}{100} = \frac{x}{250} \rightarrow x = 5$; 7th grade: $\frac{4}{100} = \frac{x}{200} \rightarrow x = 8$;

8th grade: $\frac{8}{100} = \frac{x}{150} \rightarrow x = 12$; Since $5 + 8 + 12 = 25$,

the values in the table support his claim.

10. **Represent Real-World Problems** An airline knows that, on average, the probability that a passenger will not show up for a flight is 6%. If an airplane is fully booked and holds 300 passengers, how many seats are expected to be empty? If the airline overbooked the flight by 10 passengers, about how many passengers are expected to show up for the flight? Justify your answer.

18 seats; about 291 passengers; $\frac{6}{100} = \frac{x}{300} \rightarrow x = 18$, so

18 passengers are not expected to show up. If overbooked,

94% of 310 are expected to show up.

$310 \times 94\% = 291.4 \approx 291$.

11. **Draw Conclusions** In a doctor's office, an average of 94% of the clients pay on the day of the appointment. If the office has 600 clients per month, how many are expected not to pay on the day of the appointment? If 40 clients do not pay on the day of their appointment in a month, did more or fewer than the average not pay?

36 clients; more than would be expected on average

12. **Counterexamples** The soccer coach claimed that, on average, only 80% of the team come to practice each day. The table shows the number of students that came to practice for 8 days. If the team has 20 members, how many team members should come to practice to uphold the coach's claim? Was the coach's claim accurate? Explain your reasoning.

	1	2	3	4	5	6	7	8
Number of Students	18	15	18	17	17	19	20	20

16 team members; The coach's claim is not accurate because

the average number of students at practice is $\frac{144}{8} = 18$.

13. **What's the Error?** Ronnie misses the school bus 1 out of every 30 school days. He sets up the proportion $\frac{1}{30} = \frac{180}{x}$ to predict how many days he will miss the bus in the 180-day school year. What is Ronnie's error?

He set up the fraction incorrectly; it should be $\frac{1}{30} = \frac{x}{180}$.

H.O.T. **FOCUS ON HIGHER ORDER THINKING**

14. **Persevere in Problem Solving** A gas pump machine rejects 12% of credit card transactions. If this is twice the normal rejection rate for a normal gas pump, how many out of 500 credit cards transactions would a normal gas pump machine reject? _____30 transactions_____

15. **Make Predictions** An airline's weekly flight data showed a 98% probability of being on time. If this airline has 15,000 flights in a year, how many flights would you predict to arrive on time? Explain whether you can use the data to predict whether a specific flight with this airline will be on time.

14,700 on-time flights; Sample answer: No, one week

of data could be misleading and not representative of

the yearly on-time probability (because it ignores bad

weather, etc.).

16. **Draw Conclusions** An average response rate for a marketing letter is 4%, meaning that 4% of the people who receive the letter respond to it. A company writes a new type of marketing letter, sends out 2,400 of them, and gets 65 responses. Explain whether the new type of letter would be considered to be a success.

Sample answer: No; They could expect to get $\frac{4}{100} = \frac{x}{2,400}$,

$x = 96$ responses with the old letter. The new letter

received fewer responses.

Work Area

EXTEND THE MATH PRE-AP

Activity available online my.hrw.com

A hotel manager finds that on average 86% of customers keep their reservations each week. The manager predicts that out of 2,200 reservations next week, 300 customers will cancel. He thinks they should overbook the hotel by 42 reservations each day. Do you agree with the manager? Explain.

Sample answer: On average, 14% will cancel. This is 308 of the 2,200 reservations next week or 44 per day. So the manager's estimate of 42 is reasonable. However, there is no data to suggest that the people who cancel, cancel at the same rate each day of the week. The manager should look at additional data before deciding how many to overbook or risk having unhappy customers.

Ready to Go On?

Assess Mastery

Use the assessment on this page to determine if students have mastered the concepts and standards covered in this module.

 **Response to Intervention**

Intervention	Enrichment
Access Ready to Go On? assessment online, and receive instant scoring, feedback, and customized intervention or enrichment.	

Personal Math Trainer
Online Assessment and Intervention
⏻ my.hrw.com

Online and Print Resources

Differentiated Instruction
• Reteach worksheets
• Reading Strategies **ELL**
• Success for English Learners **ELL**

Differentiated Instruction
• Challenge worksheets
  PRE-AP
• Extend the Math **PRE-AP**
  Lesson Activities in TE

Additional Resources

Assessment Resources
• Leveled Module Quizzes

Ready to Go On?

Personal Math Trainer
Online Assessment and Intervention
my.hrw.com

7.1 Probability

1. Josue tosses a coin and spins the spinner at the right. What are all the possible outcomes?

H1, H2, T1, T2

7.2 Experimental Probability of Simple Events

2. While bowling with friends, Brandy rolls a strike in 6 out of 10 frames. What is the experimental probability that Brandy will roll a strike in the first frame of the next game?

$\frac{3}{5}$

3. Ben is greeting customers at a music store. Of the first 20 people he sees enter the store, 13 are wearing jackets and 7 are not. What is the experimental probability that the next person to enter the store will be wearing a jacket?

$\frac{13}{20}$

7.3 Experimental Probability of Compound Events

4. Auden rolled two number cubes and recorded the results.

Roll #1	Roll #2	Roll #3	Roll #4	Roll #5	Roll #6	Roll #7
2, 1	4, 5	3, 2	2, 2	1, 3	6, 2	5, 3

What is the experimental probability that the sum of the next two numbers rolled is greater than 5?

$\frac{3}{7}$

7.4 Making Predictions with Experimental Probability

5. A player on a school baseball team reaches first base $\frac{3}{10}$ of the time he is at bat. Out of 80 times at bat, about how many times would you predict he will reach first base?

24

? ESSENTIAL QUESTION

6. How is experimental probability used to make predictions?

You can use the experimental probability based on observation or simulation to set up a proportion and use the proportion to predict a value.

Module 7 **227**

 Florida Common Core Standards

Lesson	Exercises	🚩 Common Core Standards
7.1	1	**7.SP.3.5**
7.2	2, 3	**7.SP.3.6, 7.SP.3.7, 7.SP.3.7a, 7.SP.3.7b**
7.3	4	**7.SP.3.8a, 7.SP.3.8b**
7.4	5	**7.SP.3.6**

PARCC Assessment Readiness

Assessment Readiness Tip Students can draw a diagram, graph, or picture to help organize information from a test item.

Item 1 Students can sketch a tree diagram to find the answer. The first level has three branches, one for each type of cone. Then, on the second level, each original branch splits into five additional branches, one for each flavor. The total number of branches in the second level is the answer.

Item 4 Sketching two rectangles and labeling the sides with the appropriate lengths can help students to write the correct proportion.

Avoid Common Errors

Item 2 Students may find the probability of either of the nonpink colors, instead of both of them. Remind them that the word *not* means complement in probability, and the complement is found by subtracting the probability of drawing a pink bead from 1.

Item 7 In part b, students are likely to provide the theoretical probability because information was provided about the sample space. Emphasize that if the item asks for the experimental probability, they must provide it, and their calculations must be based on the outcomes, not the possible outcomes.

Additional Resources

Selected Response

1. A frozen yogurt shop offers scoops in cake cones, waffle cones, or cups. You can get vanilla, chocolate, strawberry, pistachio, or coffee flavored frozen yogurt. If you order a single scoop, how many outcomes are in the sample space?

   Ⓐ 3　　Ⓒ 8
   Ⓑ 5　　Ⓓ 15

2. A bag contains 7 purple beads, 4 blue beads, and 4 pink beads. What is the probability of **not** drawing a pink bead?

   Ⓐ $\frac{4}{15}$　　Ⓒ $\frac{8}{15}$
   Ⓑ $\frac{7}{15}$　　Ⓓ $\frac{11}{15}$

3. During the month of June, Ava kept track of the number of days she saw birds in her garden. She saw birds on 18 days of the month. What is the experimental probability that she will see birds in her garden on July 1?

   Ⓐ $\frac{1}{18}$　　Ⓒ $\frac{1}{2}$
   Ⓑ $\frac{2}{5}$　　Ⓓ $\frac{3}{5}$

4. A rectangle has a width of 4 inches and a length of 6 inches. A similar rectangle has a width of 12 inches. What is the length of the similar rectangle?

   Ⓐ 8 inches　　Ⓒ 14 inches
   Ⓑ 12 inches　　Ⓓ 18 inches

5. The experimental probability of hearing thunder on any given day in Ohio is 30%. Out of 600 days, on about how many days can Ohioans expect to hear thunder?

   Ⓐ 90 days　　Ⓒ 210 days
   Ⓑ 180 days　　Ⓓ 420 days

6. Isidro tossed two coins several times and then recorded the results in the table below.

Toss 1	Toss 2	Toss 3	Toss 4	Toss 5
H; T	T; T	T; H	H; T	H; T

   What is the experimental probability that both coins will land on the same side on Isidro's next toss?

   Ⓐ $\frac{1}{5}$　　Ⓒ $\frac{3}{5}$
   Ⓑ $\frac{2}{5}$　　Ⓓ $\frac{4}{5}$

Mini-Task

7. Magdalena had a spinner that was evenly divided into sections of red, blue, and green. She spun the spinner and tossed a coin several times. The table below shows the results.

Trial 1	Trial 2	Trial 3	Trial 4	Trial 5
blue; T	green; T	green; H	red; T	blue; H

   a. What are all the possible outcomes?

      R, tails; B, tails; G, tails; R, heads; B, heads; G, heads

   b. What experimental probability did Magdalena find for spinning blue? Give your answer as a fraction in simplest form, as a decimal, and as a percent.

      $\frac{2}{5}$, 0.4, 40%

   c. Out of 90 trials, how many times should Magdalena predict she will spin green while tossing tails?

      18 times

🔲 Florida Common Core Standards

Items	🏴 Grade 7 Standards	🏴 Mathematical Practices
1	7.SP.3.8b	MP.4.1
2	7.SP.3.7a	MP.4.1
3	7.SP.3.7b	MP.4.1
4*	7.G.1.1	MP.4.1
5	7.SP.3.6	MP.4.1
6	7.SP.3.7b	MP.4.1
7	7.SP.3.7b, 7.SP.3.8b	MP.4.1

* Item integrates mixed review concepts from previous modules or a previous course.

Theoretical Probability and Simulations

MODULE 8

COMMON CORE

ESSENTIAL QUESTION

How can you use theoretical probability to solve real-world problems?

You can use theoretical models to make predictions about the solutions to real-world problems that would be difficult to simulate using experimental probability.

© Houghton Mifflin Harcourt Publishing Company • Image Credits: ©Monashee Frantz/Alamy Images

⏻ my.hrw.com

Real-World Video

Many carnival games rely on theoretical probability to set the chance of winning fairly low. Understanding how the game is set up might help you be more likely to win.

GO DIGITAL

my.hrw.com

my.hrw.com

Go digital with your write-in student edition, accessible on any device.

Math On the Spot

Scan with your smart phone to jump directly to the online edition, video tutor, and more.

Animated Math

Interactively explore key concepts to see how math works.

Personal Math Trainer

Get immediate feedback and help as you work through practice sets.

Are You Ready?

Assess Readiness

Use the assessment on this page to determine if students need intensive or strategic intervention for the module's prerequisite skills.

 **Response to Intervention**

Intervention	Enrichment

Personal Math Trainer

Online Assessment and Intervention

my.hrw.com

Access Are You Ready? assessment online, and receive instant scoring, feedback, and customized intervention or enrichment.

Online and Print Resources

Skills Intervention worksheets
- Skill 31 Fractions, Decimals, and Percents
- Skill 42 Operations with Fractions
- Skill 44 Multiply Fractions

Differentiated Instruction
- Challenge worksheets **PRE-AP**
- Extend the Math **PRE-AP** Lesson Activities in TE

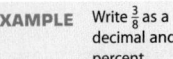

Are YOU Ready?

Complete these exercises to review skills you will need for this module.

Personal Math Trainer — Online Assessment and Intervention — my.hrw.com

Fractions, Decimals, and Percents

EXAMPLE Write $\frac{3}{8}$ as a decimal and a percent.

$$8\overline{)3.000}$$
$$-24$$
$$60$$
$$-56$$
$$40$$
$$-40$$
$$0$$

Write the fraction as a division problem.
Write a decimal point and zeros in the dividend.
Place a decimal point in the quotient.
Divide as with whole numbers.

$0.375 = 37.5\%$. Write the decimal as a percent.

Write each fraction as a decimal and a percent.

1. $\frac{3}{4}$ _0.75; 75%_   2. $\frac{2}{5}$ _0.4; 40%_   3. $\frac{9}{10}$ _0.9; 90%_   4. $\frac{7}{20}$ _0.35; 35%_

5. $\frac{7}{8}$ _0.875; 87.5%_   6. $\frac{1}{20}$ _0.05; 5%_   7. $\frac{19}{25}$ _0.76; 76%_   8. $\frac{23}{50}$ _0.46; 46%_

Operations with Fractions

EXAMPLE
$$1 - \frac{7}{12} = \frac{12}{12} - \frac{7}{12}$$
$$= \frac{12-7}{12}$$
$$= \frac{5}{12}$$

Use the denominator of the fraction to write 1 as a fraction.
Subtract the numerators.
Simplify.

Find each difference.

9. $1 - \frac{1}{5}$ _$\frac{4}{5}$_   10. $1 - \frac{2}{9}$ _$\frac{7}{9}$_   11. $1 - \frac{8}{13}$ _$\frac{5}{13}$_   12. $1 - \frac{3}{20}$ _$\frac{17}{20}$_

Multiply Fractions

EXAMPLE
$$\frac{4}{15} \times \frac{5}{6} = \frac{2\cancel{4}}{\cancel{15}_3} \times \frac{\cancel{5}^1}{\cancel{6}_3}$$
$$= \frac{2}{9}$$

Divide by the common factors.
Simplify.

Multiply. Write each product in simplest form.

13. $\frac{8}{15} \times \frac{5}{8}$ _$\frac{1}{3}$_   14. $\frac{2}{9} \times \frac{3}{4}$ _$\frac{1}{6}$_   15. $\frac{9}{16} \times \frac{12}{13}$ _$\frac{27}{52}$_   16. $\frac{7}{10} \times \frac{5}{28}$ _$\frac{1}{8}$_

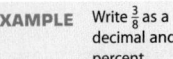

© Houghton Mifflin Harcourt Publishing Company

PROFESSIONAL DEVELOPMENT VIDEO

 Author Juli Dixon models successful teaching practices as she explores theoretical probability in an actual seventh-grade classroom.

 **Professional Development**

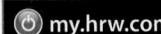 my.hrw.com

GO DIGITAL my.hrw.com

 Online Teacher Edition
Access a full suite of teaching resources online—plan, present, and manage classes and assignments.

 ePlanner
Easily plan your classes and access all your resources online.

Interactive Answers and Solutions
Customize answer keys to print or display in the classroom. Choose to include answers only or full solutions to all lesson exercises.

 Interactive Whiteboards
Engage students with interactive whiteboard-ready lessons and activities.

 Personal Math Trainer: Online Assessment and Intervention
Assign automatically graded homework, quizzes, tests, and intervention activities. Prepare your students with updated practice tests aligned with Common Core.

Reading Start-Up

Have students complete the activities on this page by working alone or with others.

Visualize Vocabulary

The main idea web helps students review vocabulary associated with probability. After students complete the web, discuss the vocabulary as a class. Students can also add other review words and their definitions to the web.

Understand Vocabulary

Use the following explanation to help students learn the preview words.

> **Theoretical probability** is the ratio of the number of equally likely outcomes in an event to the total number of possible outcomes. For example, if you are playing a board game and you need a 4 to come up, you have a 1 in 6 chance of rolling a 4.

Active Reading

Integrating Language Arts

Students can use these reading and note-taking strategies to help them organize and understand new concepts and vocabulary.

FL CC LACC.68.RST.3.7 Integrate quantitative or technical information expressed in words in a text with a version of that information expressed visually (e.g., in a flowchart, diagram, model, graph, or table).

Additional Resources

Differentiated Instruction
• Reading Strategies **ELL**

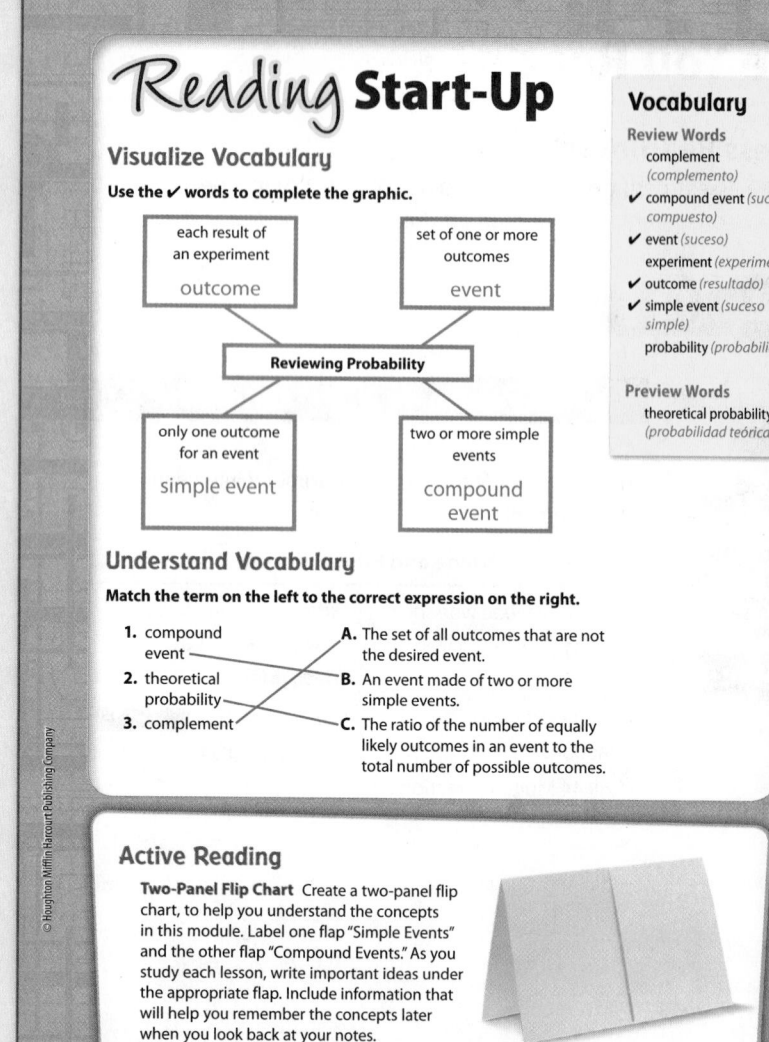

Before	In this module	After
Students understand ratios and fractions: • write ratios • simplify fractions	Students find probabilities of events: • find theoretical probability of simple and compound events • compare theoretical and experimental probabilities • use theoretical probability to make a prediction • use technology to conduct different simulations for simple and compound events	Students will connect: • simple and compound events • theoretical and experimental probabilities • random numbers and simulations

Unpacking the Standards

Use the exercises on this page to determine if students need intensive or strategic intervention for the module's prerequisite skills.

 Florida Common Core Standards

Content Areas

 Statistics and Probability—7.SP.3

Investigate chance processes and develop, use, and evaluate probability models.

Go online to see a complete unpacking of the Florida Common Core Standards.

⏻ my.hrw.com

MODULE 8

Unpacking the Standards

Understanding the standards and the vocabulary terms in the standards will help you know exactly what you are expected to learn in this module.

FL CC 7.SP.3.7a

Develop a uniform probability model by assigning equal probability to all outcomes, and use the model to determine probabilities of events.

What It Means to You

You will find the probabilities of a simple event and its complement.

UNPACKING EXAMPLE 7.SP.3.7A

Tara has a bag that contains 8 white marbles, 10 green marbles, and 7 red marbles. She selects a marble at random. Find the probability that the marble is red, and the probability that it is **not** red.

$$P(\text{red}) = \frac{\text{number of red marbles}}{\text{total number of marbles}}$$

$$= \frac{7}{25}$$

$$P(\text{not red}) = 1 - P(\text{red}) = 1 - \frac{7}{25} = \frac{25}{25} - \frac{7}{25} = \frac{18}{25}$$

The probability that the marble is red is $\frac{7}{25}$, and the probability that it is not red is $\frac{18}{25}$.

FL CC 7.SP.3.8b

Represent sample spaces for compound events using methods such as organized lists, tables and tree diagrams. For an event described in everyday language (e.g., "rolling double sixes"), identify the outcomes in the sample space which compose the event.

Key Vocabulary

compound event *(suceso compuesto)*
An event made of two or more simple events.

What It Means to You

You will identify the outcomes in the sample space of a compound event.

UNPACKING EXAMPLE 7.SP.3.8B

Identify the sample space for flipping a coin and rolling a number cube.

Make a table to organize the information.

		Number Cube Outcomes					
		1	2	3	4	5	6
C O I N	H	H1	H2	H3	H4	H5	H6
	T	T1	T2	T3	T4	T5	T6

The sample space includes 12 possible outcomes:
H1, H2, H3, H4, H5, H6, T1, T2, T3, T4, T5, and T6.

Visit **my.hrw.com** to see all **Florida Common Core Standards** unpacked.

⏻ my.hrw.com

Florida Common Core Standards	Lesson 8.1	Lesson 8.2	Lesson 8.3	Lesson 8.4
FL CC 7.SP.3.6 Approximate the probability of a chance event by collecting data … and observing its long-run relative frequency, and predict the approximate relative frequency given the probability.			🏴	
FL CC 7.SP.3.7 Develop a probability model and use it to find probabilities of events.	🏴			
FL CC 7.SP.3.7.a Develop a uniform probability model by assigning equal probability to all outcomes, and use the model to determine probabilities of events.	🏴		🏴	
FL CC 7.SP.3.7.b Develop a probability model … by observing frequencies in data generated from a chance process.				
FL CC 7.SP.3.8 Find probabilities of compound events using organized lists, tables, tree diagrams, and simulation.		🏴		🏴
FL CC 7.SP.3.8.a Understand that, just as with simple events, the probability of a compound event is the fraction of outcomes in the sample space for which the compound event occurs.		🏴		
FL CC 7.SP.3.8.b Represent sample spaces for compound events … identify the outcomes in the sample space which compose the event.		🏴		
FL CC 7.SP.3.8.c Design and use a simulation to generate frequencies for compound events.				🏴

8.1 Theoretical Probability of Simple Events

 Florida Common Core Standards

The student is expected to:

 **Statistics and Probability—7.SP.3.7a**

Develop a uniform probability model by assigning equal probability to all outcomes, and use the model to determine probabilities of events.

 **Statistics and Probability—7.SP.3.6**

Approximate the probability of a chance event by collecting data on the chance process that produces it and observing its long-run relative frequency, and predict the approximate relative frequency given the probability. *Also* **7.SP.3.7**

Mathematical Practices

 MP.7.1 Using Structure

ADDITIONAL EXAMPLE 1

A bag contains 4 white tiles and 8 black tiles. You select one tile at random from the bag. What is the probability that you select a black tile? Write your answer in simplest form.
$$\frac{8}{12} = \frac{2}{3}$$

 Interactive Whiteboard
Interactive example available online

my.hrw.com

Engage

ESSENTIAL QUESTION

How can you find the theoretical probability of a simple event? Sample answer: Write the ratio of the number of ways the event can occur to the total number of possible outcomes.

Motivate the Lesson

Ask: How can you use probability to help your chances of winning a game? Take a guess. Begin the Explore Activity to find out.

Explore

EXPLORE ACTIVITY 1

Focus on Modeling 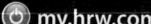 Mathematical Practices

Make sure students connect the total number of outcomes to the total number of sections on each spinner. Note that each spinner is divided into sections of equal size.

Explain

EXAMPLE 1

Focus on Math Connections 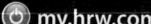 Mathematical Practices

Compare the definitions of theoretical and experimental probability. Stress that both are between 0 and 1. Discuss why the theoretical probability of an event is fixed while the experimental probability will change based on the experiment. Elicit that the formula for the complement is the same for both probability definitions.

Questioning Strategies 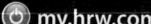 Mathematical Practices

• How do you know the outcomes are equally likely? Any marble is as likely as any other to be drawn from the bag at random.

• Why doesn't the fact that the outcomes are equally likely mean that a red marble is as likely to be drawn as a blue marble? There are different numbers of red and blue marbles. Although each marble is equally likely to be chosen, the color that appears in the bag most often also has the probability of being drawn most often.

YOUR TURN

Avoid Common Errors

Emphasize the importance of counting the total number of equally likely outcomes separately from the number of ways the event can occur so students write the correct ratio.

Talk About It
Check for Understanding

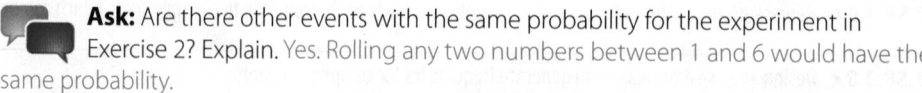 **Ask:** Are there other events with the same probability for the experiment in Exercise 2? Explain. Yes. Rolling any two numbers between 1 and 6 would have the same probability.

Theoretical Probability of Simple Events

FL CC 7.SP.3.7a
Develop a uniform probability model by assigning equal probability to all outcomes, and use the model to determine probabilities of events. *Also 7.SP.3.6, 7.SP.3.7*

? ESSENTIAL QUESTION

How can you find the theoretical probability of a simple event?

EXPLORE ACTIVITY 1    FL CC 7.SP.3.7a

Finding Theoretical Probability

In previous lessons, you found probabilities based on observing data, or experimental probabilities. In this lesson, you will find *theoretical probabilities*.

At a school fair, you have a choice of spinning Spinner A or Spinner B. You win an MP3 player if the spinner lands on a section with a star in it. Which spinner should you choose if you want a better chance of winning?

A Complete the table.

	Spinner A	Spinner B
Total number of outcomes	8	16
Number of sections with stars	3	5
P(winning MP3) = number of sections with stars / total number of outcomes	$\frac{3}{8}$	$\frac{5}{16}$

Spinner A

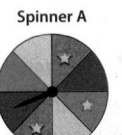

Spinner B

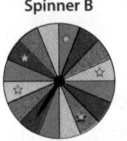

B Compare the ratios for Spinner A and Spinner B.

The ratio for Spinner ___A___ is greater than the ratio for Spinner ___B___.

I should choose ___Spinner A___ for a better chance of winning.

Reflect

1. *Theoretical probability* is a way to describe how you found the chance of winning an MP3 player in the scenario above. Using the spinner example to help you, explain in your own words how to find the theoretical probability of an event.

   Sample answer: The theoretical probability of an event is a ratio comparing the number of ways the event can occur to the total number of outcomes for the experiment.

Math Talk
Mathematical Practices

Describe a way to change Spinner B to make your chances of winning equal to your chances of not winning? Explain.

Add a star to each of 3 sections without stars. Then the probability of winning would be $\frac{8}{16}$ or $\frac{1}{2}$, which is the same probability as not winning.

Math On the Spot
my.hrw.com

Calculating Theoretical Probability of Simple Events

Theoretical probability is the probability that an event occurs when all of the outcomes of the experiment are equally likely.

> **Theoretical Probability**
>
> $$P(\text{event}) = \frac{\text{number of ways the event can occur}}{\text{total number of equally likely outcomes}}$$

Probability can be written as a fraction, a decimal, or a percent. For example, the probability you win with Spinner B is $\frac{5}{16}$. You can also write that as 0.3125 or as 31.25%.

EXAMPLE 1   FL CC 7.SP.3.7a

A bag contains 6 red marbles and 12 blue ones. You select one marble at random from the bag. What is the probability that you select a red marble? Write your answer in simplest form.

STEP 1 Find the number of ways the event can occur, that is, the number of red marbles: 6

STEP 2 Add to find the total number of equally likely outcomes.

number of red marbles	+	number of blue marbles	=	total number of marbles
6	+	12	=	**18**

There are 18 possible outcomes in the sample space.

STEP 3 Find the probability of selecting a red marble.

$$P(\text{red marble}) = \frac{\text{number of red marbles}}{\text{total number of marbles}} = \frac{6}{18}$$

The probability that you select a red marble is $\frac{6}{18}$, or $\frac{1}{3}$.

Math Talk
Mathematical Practices

Describe a situation that has a theoretical probability of $\frac{1}{4}$.

YOUR TURN

2. You roll a number cube one time. What is the probability that you roll a 3 or 4? Write your answer in simplest form.

   $$P(\text{rolling a 3 or 4}) = \frac{\text{number of sides with 3 or 4}}{\text{total number of sides on cube}} = \frac{2}{6} = \frac{1}{3}$$

3. How is the sample space for an event related to the formula for theoretical probability? The total number of outcomes in the sample space is the denominator of the formula for theoretical probability.

Personal Math Trainer
Online Assessment and Intervention
my.hrw.com

Sample answer: spinning a 2 on a spinner with 4 equal sections marked 1 through 4

PROFESSIONAL DEVELOPMENT

Integrate Mathematical Practices MP.7.1

This lesson provides an opportunity to address this Mathematical Practice standard. It calls for students to analyze mathematical relationships to connect and communicate mathematical ideas. Students find and compare the theoretical probability of simple events. They also use the probability of an event to find the probability of its complement. Finally, students perform an experiment to compare the theoretical and experimental probability of an event.

Math Background

The Law of Large Numbers is an interesting theorem in probability theory. The theorem relates experimental probability and theoretical probability. The basic idea of the theorem is that as an experiment is repeated many times, the experimental probability of the event approaches the theoretical probability of the event. For example, consider flipping a coin ten times. The theoretical probability of heads is $\frac{1}{2}$. The individual flipping of the coin ten times may not get five heads and five tails. However, after flipping the coin many more times, perhaps 100 times, the experimental probability will tend to get closer to $\frac{1}{2}$.

EXPLORE ACTIVITY 2

Questioning Strategies Mathematical Practices

- How does the number cube represent the students? Assign each student a different number from the number cube.

- How do you predict the number of times each number will be rolled out of 30 rolls? Use the theoretical probability to set up a proportion $\left(\frac{1}{6} = \frac{x}{30}\right)$, or write an equation $\left(\frac{1}{6} \cdot 30 = x\right)$.

Engage with the Whiteboard

Have a student volunteer complete the frequency row of the table in Step 3 with the combined results from the class. Have other volunteers calculate experimental probabilities and fill in the appropriate cells.

Focus on Reasoning Mathematical Practices

As students work to combine their tables in Step 3, pause after every four or five students add their results. Compute and compare the experimental probabilities of each number. Discuss how the new data affect the experimental probabilities.

YOUR TURN

Focus on Communication

Make sure students understand the difference between theoretical and experimental probability. Elicit that theoretical probability is based on the structure of an experiment while experimental probability is based on the results of the experiment.

Elaborate

Talk About It
Summarize the Lesson

Ask: How do you find the theoretical probability of an event? Write the ratio of the number of ways the event can occur to the total number of equally likely outcomes to find the probability.

GUIDED PRACTICE

Engage with the Whiteboard

Ask a volunteer to complete the chart in Exercise 1 as students work together to provide the data from the problem and perform calculations.

Avoid Common Errors

Exercise 1 Students may still be confused by the vocabulary of probability. Point out that the total number of outcomes is the same as the sample space, the equally likely outcomes, or the set of all possible outcomes, and in this case, all of the marbles in the bag.

Exercise 6 Remind students that theoretical probability is based on the structure of an experiment while experimental probability is based on the results of the experiment.

Reflect

4. Could the experimental probabilities ever be exactly equal to the theoretical probability? If so, how likely is it? If not, why not?

   Sample answer: Yes, the experimental probabilities could be exactly equal to the theoretical probabilities, but it is very unlikely.

EXPLORE ACTIVITY 2 FL CC 7.SP.3.7, 7.SP.3.6

Comparing Theoretical and Experimental Probability

Now that you have calculated theoretical probabilities, you may wonder how theoretical and experimental probabilities compare.

Six students are performing in a talent contest. You roll a number cube to determine the order of the performances.

STEP 1 You roll the number cube once. Complete the table of theoretical probabilities for the different outcomes.

Number	1	2	3	4	5	6
Theoretical probability	$\frac{1}{6}$	$\frac{1}{6}$	$\frac{1}{6}$	$\frac{1}{6}$	$\frac{1}{6}$	$\frac{1}{6}$

STEP 2 Predict the number of times each number will be rolled out of 30 total rolls.

1: 5 times   3: 5 times   5: 5 times

2: 5 times   4: 5 times   6: 5 times

STEP 3 Roll a number cube 30 times. Complete the table for the frequency of each number and then find its experimental probability. Check students' tables.

Number	1	2	3	4	5	6
Frequency						
Experimental probability						

STEP 4 Look at the tables you completed. How do the experimental probabilities compare with the theoretical probabilities?

Sample answer: The experimental probabilities are not close to the theoretical probabilities.

STEP 5 **Conjecture** By performing more trials, you tend to get experimental results that are closer to the theoretical probabilities. Combine your table from **Step 3** with those of your classmates to make one table for the class. How do the class experimental probabilities compare with the theoretical probabilities?

Sample answer: The experimental probabilities are closer to the theoretical probabilities.

Guided Practice

At a school fair, you have a choice of randomly picking a ball from Basket A or Basket B. Basket A has 5 green balls, 3 red balls, and 8 yellow balls. Basket B has 7 green balls, 4 red balls, and 9 yellow balls. You can win a digital book reader if you pick a red ball. (Explore Activity 1)

1. Complete the chart. Write each answer in simplest form.

2. Which basket should you choose if you want the better chance of winning? ___Basket B___

	Basket A	Basket B
Total number of outcomes	16	20
Number of red balls	3	4
P(win) = $\frac{\text{number of red balls}}{\text{total number of outcomes}}$	$\frac{3}{16}$	$\frac{4}{20} = \frac{1}{5}$

A spinner has 11 equal-sized sections marked 1 through 11. Find each probability. (Example 1)

3. You spin once and land on an odd number.

   $P(\text{odd}) = \frac{\text{number of odd sections}}{\text{total number of sections}} = \frac{6}{11}$

4. You spin once and land on an even number.

   $P(\text{even}) = \frac{\text{number of even sections}}{\text{total number of sections}} = \frac{5}{11}$

You roll a number cube once.

5. What is the theoretical probability that you roll a 3 or 4? (Example 1) $\frac{2}{6} = \frac{1}{3}$

6. Suppose you rolled the number cube 199 more times. Would you expect the experimental probability of rolling a 3 or 4 to be the same as your answer to Exercise 5? (Explore Activity 2)

   Sample answer: No, but it might be reasonably close.

? **ESSENTIAL QUESTION CHECK-IN**

7. How can you find the probability of a simple event if the total number of equally likely outcomes is 20?

   Divide the number of ways the event can occur by 20.

DIFFERENTIATE INSTRUCTION

Kinesthetic Experience

Offer students another opportunity to compare theoretical and experimental probabilities using a number cube.

a. Ask students to find the theoretical probability of rolling a number less than 6. $\frac{5}{6}$

b. Have them roll the number cube 30 times, record the results, and find the experimental probability of rolling a number less than 6. Answers will vary.

c. Finally ask: Based on the probability, is it certain that you will roll a number less than 6 in 10 rolls? Explain. No, while it is very likely, the probability is not 1. The probability must be 1 for the event to be certain.

Critical Thinking

Discuss with students whether they would prefer to use theoretical or experimental probability to make a prediction. Ask them to explain their thinking. Under what circumstances might theoretical probability appear to be a good choice, but actually be misleading? Sample answers: a weighted die, an unbalanced spinner, etc.

Additional Resources

Differentiated Instruction includes:

- Reading Strategies
- Success for English Learners **ELL**
- Reteach
- Challenge **PRE-AP**

Personal Math Trainer

Online Assessment and Intervention

Online homework assignment available

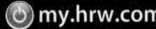

⏻ my.hrw.com

8.1 LESSON QUIZ

 **FL CC** 7.SP.3.7a

Each card in a set of cards has one of the letters from the word *mathematics*. The cards are shuffled.

1. What is the probability of drawing the letter *m*?

2. What is the probability of drawing a vowel?

3. What is the probability of drawing a consonant?

4. Suppose you draw a card from the set of cards, record the letter, return the card to the set, and shuffle the cards. You repeat this experiment 22 times. Would you expect the experimental probability of drawing a vowel to be the same as the theoretical probability? Explain.

Lesson Quiz available online

⏻ my.hrw.com

Answers

1. $\frac{2}{11}$

2. $\frac{4}{11}$

3. $\frac{7}{11}$

4. Sample answer: No, it is possible but not likely. It is not very many trials, so the experimental probability could be quite different.

Evaluate

GUIDED AND INDEPENDENT PRACTICE

FL CC 7.SP.3.6, 7.SP.3.7, 7.SP.3.7a

Concepts & Skills	Practice
Explore Activity 1 Finding Theoretical Probability	Exercises 1, 2
Example 1 Calculating Theoretical Probability of Simple Events	Exercises 3–5, 7–14, 16
Explore Activity 2 Comparing Theoretical and Experimental Probability	Exercise 6

Exercise	Depth of Knowledge (D.O.K.)	**FL CC** Mathematical Practices
8–14	**2** Skills/Concepts	**MP.4.1** Modeling
15	**3** Strategic Thinking **H.O.T.**	**MP.8.1** Patterns
16	**3** Strategic Thinking **H.O.T.**	**MP.3.1** Logic
17	**3** Strategic Thinking **H.O.T.**	**MP.8.1** Patterns
18	**3** Strategic Thinking **H.O.T.**	**MP.3.1** Logic
19	**3** Strategic Thinking **H.O.T.**	**MP.3.1** Logic
20	**3** Strategic Thinking **H.O.T.**	**MP.8.1** Patterns

Additional Resources

Differentiated Instruction includes:

• Leveled Practice Worksheets

Name_____ Class_____ Date_____

8.1 Independent Practice

FL CC 7.SP.3.7, 7.SP.3.7a

Personal Math Trainer
Online Assessment and Intervention
my.hrw.com

Find the probability of each event. Write each answer as a fraction in simplest form, as a decimal to the nearest hundredth, and as a percent to the nearest whole number.

8. You spin the spinner shown. The spinner lands on yellow.

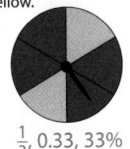

$\frac{1}{3}$, 0.33, 33%

9. You spin the spinner shown. The spinner lands on blue or green.

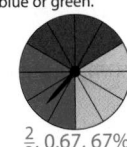

$\frac{2}{3}$, 0.67, 67%

10. A jar contains 4 cherry cough drops and 10 honey cough drops. You choose one cough drop without looking. The cough drop is cherry.

$\frac{2}{7}$, 0.29, 29%

11. You pick one card at random from a standard deck of 52 playing cards. You pick a black card.

$\frac{1}{2}$, 0.50, 50%

12. There are 12 pieces of fruit in a bowl. Five are lemons and the rest are limes. You choose a piece of fruit without looking. The piece of fruit is a lime.

$\frac{7}{12}$, 0.58, 58%

13. You choose a movie CD at random from a case containing 8 comedy CDs, 5 science fiction CDs, and 7 adventure CDs. The CD is **not** a comedy.

$\frac{3}{5}$, 0.60, 60%

14. You roll a number cube. You roll a number that is greater than 2 and less than 5.

$\frac{1}{3}$, 0.33, 33%

15. Communicate Mathematical Ideas The theoretical probability of a given event is $\frac{9}{13}$. Explain what each number represents.

9 represents the ways the event can occur; 13 represents the number of equally likely outcomes.

16. Leona has 4 nickels, 6 pennies, 4 dimes, and 2 quarters in a change purse. Leona lets her little sister Daisy pick a coin at random. If Daisy is equally likely to pick each type of coin, what is the probability that her coin is worth more than five cents? Explain.

$\frac{6}{16} = \frac{3}{8}$; the event is choosing a dime or a quarter, and 6 of the 16 coins are dimes or quarters.

H.O.T. FOCUS ON HIGHER ORDER THINKING

Work Area

17. Critique Reasoning A bowl of flower seeds contains 5 petunia seeds and 15 begonia seeds. Riley calculated the probability that a randomly selected seed is a petunia seed as $\frac{1}{3}$. Describe and correct Riley's error.

Sample answer: Riley divided the number of petunia seeds by the number of begonia seeds, rather than the total number of seeds. The correct probability is $\frac{5}{5+15} = \frac{5}{20} = \frac{1}{4}$.

18. There are 20 seventh graders and 15 eighth graders in a club. A club president will be chosen at random.

a. Analyze Relationships Compare the probabilities of choosing a seventh grader or an eighth grader.

P(seventh grader) $= \frac{4}{7}$; P(eighth grader) $= \frac{3}{7}$; since $\frac{4}{7} > \frac{3}{7}$, choosing a seventh grader is more likely.

b. Critical Thinking If a student from one grade is more likely to be chosen than a student from the other, is the method unfair? Explain.

No; each student has the same probability of being selected, $\frac{1}{35}$.

A jar contains 8 red marbles, 10 blue ones, and 2 yellow ones. One marble is chosen at random. The color is recorded in the table, and then it is returned to the jar. This is repeated 40 times.

Red	Blue	Yellow
14	16	10

19. Communicate Mathematical Ideas Use proportional reasoning to explain how you know that for each color, the theoretical and experimental probabilities are not the same.

Sample answer: The number of trials is twice the number of marbles in the jar. If the probabilities for each color were the same, the number of times that color was drawn would be twice the number of marbles with that color in the jar.

20. Persevere in Problem Solving For which color marble is the experimental probability closest to the theoretical probability? Explain.

Red; red: difference is $\frac{2}{5} - \frac{7}{20} = \frac{1}{20}$; blue: difference is $\frac{1}{2} - \frac{2}{5} = \frac{1}{10}$; yellow: difference is $\frac{1}{4} - \frac{1}{10} = \frac{3}{20}$.

EXTEND THE MATH PRE-AP

Activity available online my.hrw.com

Two events are mutually exclusive if they cannot occur at the same time. The events rolling a 1 or rolling a 2 on a number cube are mutually exclusive. However, the events rolling a 2 or rolling an even number are not mutually exclusive since 2 is an even number. For mutually exclusive events A and B, $P(A \text{ or } B) = P(A) + P(B)$. If two events are not mutually exclusive, $P(A \text{ or } B) = P(A) + P(B) - P(A \text{ and } B)$. In this case, $P(A \text{ and } B)$ means the probability of rolling a 2 and the 2 is even.

You roll a number cube once.

a. Use the definition of theoretical probability to find the probability of rolling a 1 or a 2. $\frac{2}{6} = \frac{1}{3}$

b. Use $P(A \text{ or } B) = P(A) + P(B)$ to find the probability of rolling a 1 or a 2. $\frac{1}{6} + \frac{1}{6} = \frac{2}{6} = \frac{1}{3}$

c. Use the definition of theoretical probability to find the probability of rolling a 2 or an even number. $\frac{3}{6} = \frac{1}{2}$

d. Use the definition of theoretical probability to find the probability of rolling a 2 and an even number. $\frac{3}{6} = \frac{1}{2}$

e. Use $P(A \text{ or } B) = P(A) + P(B) - P(A \text{ and } B)$ to find the probability of rolling a 2 or an even number. $\frac{1}{6} + \frac{3}{6} - \frac{1}{6} = \frac{3}{6} = \frac{1}{2}$

Theoretical Probability of Simple Events **238**

LESSON 8.2 Theoretical Probability of Compound Events

ADDITIONAL EXAMPLE 1

Brianna is ordering a taco. She can order a corn tortilla or a flour tortilla. She can choose beef, fish, chicken, or zucchini as the filling. She can also choose sour cream or guacamole. Each combination is equally likely. Find the probability that a taco she chooses at random has a corn tortilla, fish, and guacamole. $\frac{1}{16}$

 Interactive Whiteboard
Interactive example available online

⏻ my.hrw.com

Engage

ESSENTIAL QUESTION

How do you find the probability of a compound event? Sample answer: Write the ratio of the number of ways the event can happen to the total number of possible outcomes.

Motivate the Lesson
Ask: How can probability help you improve your chances when you play a game with two number cubes? Begin the Explore Activity to find out.

Explore

EXPLORE ACTIVITY

Focus on Modeling Mathematical Practices
Have students look for and describe the pattern of the sums within the table. How does the probability of the sum being 3 relate to the probability of the sum being 11 or the sums being 2 and 12?

Explain

EXAMPLE 1

Questioning Strategies 🏳 Mathematical Practices

• How does a tree diagram help you find the probability? It shows all the possible outcomes and makes it easy to find the number of ways the compound event can happen.

• If you wrote the parts of the sandwich in a different order in the tree diagram—for example, cheese, then meat, then bread—would you find a different probability? Explain. No. Changing the order of the parts does not change anything about the actual situation; it just makes the tree diagram look different.

Engage with the Whiteboard
Ask about probabilities of other events. Have volunteers circle the parts of the event in the tree diagram and then state the corresponding probability. Example: ham on wheat with either cheddar or swiss has a probability of $\frac{2}{12} = \frac{1}{6}$.

YOUR TURN

Avoid Common Errors
In Your Turn 3, help students to properly use the tree diagram. Point out that Ham appears twice in the Meat column. But each of those choices can have Cheddar or Swiss, for a total of four ham sandwiches in the last column.

Talk About It
Check for Understanding
Ask: Are any of the sandwiches in the last branch of your tree diagram the same? Explain. No, they are all different because each branch has at least one element that is different from the other branches.

Theoretical Probability of Compound Events

FL CC 7.SP.3.8
Find probabilities of compound events using organized lists, tables, tree diagrams, ... 7.SP.3.8a, 7.SP.3.8b

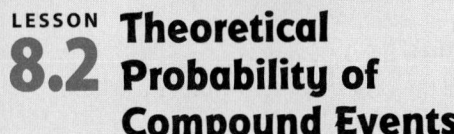

? **ESSENTIAL QUESTION**

How do you find the probability of a compound event?

EXPLORE ACTIVITY FL CC 7.SP.3.8, 7.SP.3.8a, 7.SP.3.8b

Finding Probability Using a Table

Recall that a compound event consists of two or more simple events. To find the probability of a compound event, you write a ratio of the number of ways the compound event can happen to the total number of equally likely possible outcomes.

Jacob rolls two fair number cubes. Find the probability that the sum of the numbers he rolls is 8.

STEP 1 Use the table to find the sample space for rolling a particular sum on two number cubes. Each cell is the sum of the first number in that row and column.

STEP 2 How many possible outcomes are in the sample space? __36__

STEP 3 Circle the outcomes that give the sum of 8.

STEP 4 How many ways are there to roll a sum of 8? __5__

STEP 5 What is the probability of rolling a sum of 8? __$\frac{5}{36}$__

	1	2	3	4	5	6
1	2	3	4	5	6	7
2	3	4	5	6	7	⑧
3	4	5	6	7	⑧	9
4	5	6	7	⑧	9	10
5	6	7	⑧	9	10	11
6	7	⑧	9	10	11	12

Reflect

1. Give an example of an event that is more likely than rolling a sum of 8.

   Sample answer: rolling a sum of 7

2. Give an example of an event that is less likely than rolling a sum of 8.

   Sample answer: rolling a sum of 2 or a sum of 12

Finding Probability Using a Tree Diagram

You can also use a tree diagram to calculate theoretical probabilities of compound events.

EXAMPLE 1 Real World FL CC 7.SP.3.8, 7.SP.3.8b

A deli prepares sandwiches with one type of bread (white or wheat), one type of meat (ham, turkey, or chicken), and one type of cheese (cheddar or Swiss). Each combination is equally likely. Find the probability of choosing a sandwich at random and getting turkey and Swiss on wheat bread.

STEP 1 Make a tree diagram to find the sample space for the compound event.

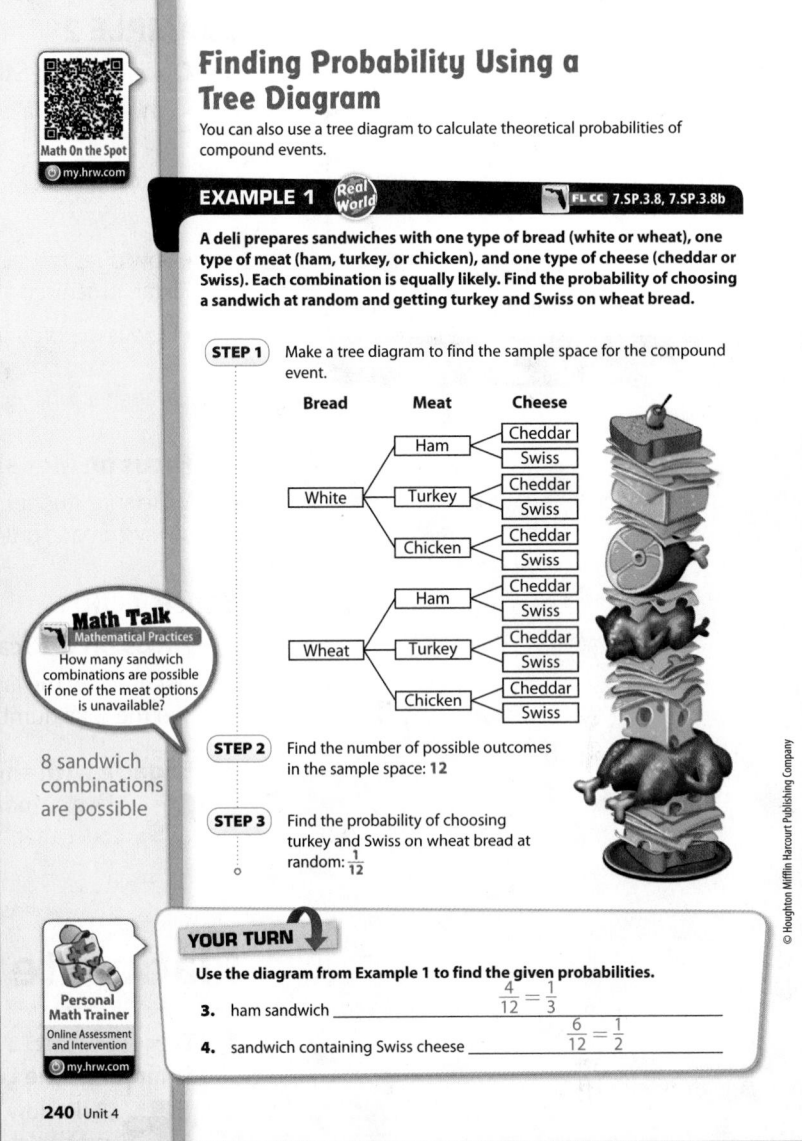

Math Talk
Mathematical Practices

How many sandwich combinations are possible if one of the meat options is unavailable?

8 sandwich combinations are possible

STEP 2 Find the number of possible outcomes in the sample space: **12**

STEP 3 Find the probability of choosing turkey and Swiss on wheat bread at random: $\frac{1}{12}$

YOUR TURN

Use the diagram from Example 1 to find the given probabilities.

3. ham sandwich _____ $\frac{4}{12} = \frac{1}{3}$

4. sandwich containing Swiss cheese _____ $\frac{6}{12} = \frac{1}{2}$

Personal Math Trainer
Online Assessment and Intervention
my.hrw.com

PROFESSIONAL DEVELOPMENT

Integrate Mathematical Practices MP.2.1

This lesson provides an opportunity to address this Mathematical Practice standard. It calls for students to create and use representations to organize, record, and communicate mathematical ideas. Students make a table to model a sample space. Then students use a tree diagram to find the sample space. Finally, students make an organized list to describe a sample space. In all three situations, students create and use different representations to find the probability of compound events based on real-world situations.

Math Background

Sometimes it can be difficult to determine the total number of outcomes for a probability experiment. Tree diagrams, organized lists, and tables, while useful ways to record the number of outcomes, can become unwieldy when the sample space is large. The Fundamental Counting Principle provides a more succinct way to count the number of outcomes: if event A can occur in m ways and event B can occur in n ways, the events occur together a total of $m \cdot n$ ways. Note that the principle easily extends to more than two events.

EXAMPLE 2

Questioning Strategies Mathematical Practices

- Why do you have to repeat the steps after listing all the codes that start with 1? You have to find all the possible codes that start with the remaining numbers.

- How does the organized list help you find the sample space? It provides an organized way to keep track of all the possible codes.

- How does the sample space change if none of the numbers may be repeated? Give them in an organized list. It is reduced to 6 possible outcomes: 123, 132, 213, 231, 312, 321.

- How is the organized list similar to a tree diagram? How is it different? Both methods are ways to keep track of different events in an organized manner. A tree diagram uses branches while a list organizes the events in a table.

Focus on Modeling Mathematical Practices

Make sure students understand how to set up and interpret the organized list. Emphasize the systematic ordering of the numerals in each section of the list.

YOUR TURN

Focus on Critical Thinking 🟠 Mathematical Practices

Discuss how the fact that a four-position code utilizing only two numbers can be used to find the total number of outcomes: $2 \cdot 2 \cdot 2 \cdot 2 = 2^4 = 16$.

Engage with the Whiteboard

Have a student list the possible codes that start with 1 and another list the possible codes that start with 0. Have a volunteer circle the codes that have exactly two zeros.

Elaborate

Talk About It
Summarize the Lesson

Ask: How can a table, a tree diagram, or an organized list help you find the probability of a compound event? A table, tree diagram, or organized list shows all the possible outcomes in the sample space. This number is the denominator of the probability ratio in unsimplified form. It also shows the number of ways the event can occur, which is the numerator of the ratio.

GUIDED PRACTICE

Engage with the Whiteboard

Ask one student to complete the table in Exercise 1. Then have others circle the favorable outcomes for Exercises 2 and 3. Similarly, have a student complete the tree diagram in Exercise 4. Have others circle the favorable outcomes for Exercises 7 and 8.

Avoid Common Errors

Exercises 2, 3, 7, 8 Point out that these exercises ask for a probability, not the total number of outcomes in the sample space, so the answers will be fractions. Suggest that students list the events that correspond to the favorable outcomes so they are sure to count the total number of ways the event can happen.

Integrating Language Arts ELL

English learners understand the organized list in Example 2. You may want to emphasize that these are all the outcomes in the sample space.

Finding Probability Using a List

One way to provide security for a locker or personal account is to assign it an access code number known only to the owner.

EXAMPLE 2

FL CC 7.SP.3.8, 7.SP.3.8b

The combination for Khiem's locker is a 3-digit code that uses the numbers 1, 2, and 3. Any of these numbers may be repeated. Find the probability that Khiem's randomly-assigned number is 222.

Make an organized list to find the sample space.

STEP 1 List all the codes that start with 1 and have 1 as a second digit.

1	1	1
1	1	2
1	1	3

STEP 2 List all the codes that start with 1 and have 2 as a second digit.

STEP 3 List all the codes that start with 1 and have 3 as a second digit.

1	2	1
1	2	2
1	2	3

STEP 4 You have now listed all the codes that start with 1. Repeat Steps 1–3 for codes that start with 2, and then for codes that start with 3.

1	3	1
1	3	2
1	3	3

2	1	1	2	2	1	2	3	1
2	1	2	2	2	2	2	3	2
2	1	3	2	2	3	2	3	3

3	1	1	3	2	1	3	3	1
3	1	2	3	2	2	3	3	2
3	1	3	3	2	3	3	3	3

> Notice that there are 3 possible first numbers, 3 possible second numbers, and 3 possible third numbers, or $3 \times 3 \times 3 = 27$ numbers in all.

STEP 5 Find the number of outcomes in the sample space by counting all the possible codes. There are **27** such codes.

STEP 6 Find the probability that Khiem's locker code is 222.

$$P(\text{Code } 222) = \frac{\text{number of favorable outcomes}}{\text{total number of possible outcomes}} = \frac{1}{27}$$

Math Talk
Mathematical Practices

How could you find the probability that Khiem's locker code includes exactly two 1s?

YOUR TURN

5. Martha types a 4-digit code into a keypad to unlock her car doors. The code uses the numbers 1 and 0. If the digits are selected at random, what is the probability of getting a code with exactly two 0s? $\frac{3}{8}$

Personal Math Trainer
Online Assessment and Intervention
my.hrw.com

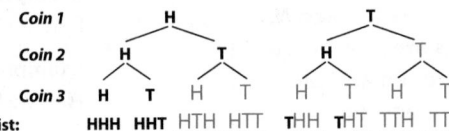
Math On the Spot
my.hrw.com

My Notes

> Math Talk Anno:
> Count the codes with exactly two 1s and divide by 27: $\frac{6}{27} = \frac{2}{9}$

Drake rolls two fair number cubes. (Explore Activity)

1. Complete the table to find the sample space for rolling a particular product on two number cubes.

	1	2	3	4	5	6
1	1	2	3	4	5	6
2	2	4	6	8	10	12
3	3	6	9	12	15	18
4	4	8	12	16	20	24
5	5	10	15	20	25	30
6	6	12	18	24	30	36

2. What is the probability that the product of the two numbers Drake rolls is a multiple of 4? $\frac{15}{36}$

3. What is the probability that the product of the two numbers Drake rolls is less than 13? $\frac{23}{36}$

You flip three coins and want to explore probabilities of certain events. (Examples 1 and 2)

4. Complete the tree diagram and make a list to find the sample space.

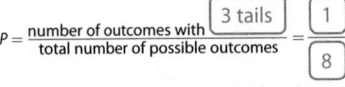

Coin 1 ... H ... T
Coin 2 ... H ... T ... H ... T
Coin 3 ... H T ... H T ... H T ... H T
List: HHH HHT HTH HTT THH THT TTH TTT

5. How many outcomes are in the sample space? **8**

6. List all the ways to get three tails. **TTT**

7. Complete the expression to find the probability of getting three tails.

$$P = \frac{\text{number of outcomes with } \boxed{3 \text{ tails}}}{\text{total number of possible outcomes}} = \frac{\boxed{1}}{\boxed{8}}$$

The probability of getting three tails when three coins are flipped is $\frac{1}{8}$.

8. What is the probability of getting exactly two heads?

There are ___**3**___ way(s) to obtain exactly two heads: HHT, **HTH, THH**

$$P = \frac{\text{number of outcomes with } \boxed{\text{exactly 2 heads}}}{\text{total number of possible outcomes}} = \frac{\boxed{3}}{\boxed{8}}$$

? ESSENTIAL QUESTION CHECK-IN

9. There are 6 ways a given compound event can occur. What else do you need to know to find the theoretical probability of the event?

the number of equally likely outcomes in the sample space

DIFFERENTIATE INSTRUCTION

Cooperative Learning

Have students discuss different ways to find the sample space for a compound event, such as spinning a spinner with five equal areas twice. Ask them to choose a method and demonstrate it to each other.

Student 1: I make a table to list all the possible outcomes.

Student 2: I use a tree diagram to keep track of the possible outcomes.

Student 3: I make an organized list to find the elements of the sample space.

Modeling

Provide small groups of students with four different colored markers, pencils, or crayons. Ask the groups to draw circles, rectangles, and triangles using each of the different colors once. Then have students find different probabilities, such as the probability of a red circle, a red shape, a circle, a polygon, a red or blue circle, and so on. Vary the activity using fewer or more markers and shapes. Discuss the strategies groups used to find the probabilities.

Additional Resources

Differentiated Instruction includes:

- Reading Strategies
- Success for English Learners **ELL**
- Reteach
- Challenge **PRE-AP**

Theoretical Probability of Compound Events **242**

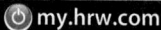

8.2 LESSON QUIZ

FL CC 7.SP.3.8

In a game, four cards are labeled *N, S, E,* and *W.* Two tiles are numbered 1 and 2. Two discs are red and blue. A player randomly selects one card, one tile, and one disc.

1. Find the probability the player selects a card with *S,* a tile with 1, and a blue disc.

2. Find the probability the player selects a card with *S* or *E,* a tile with 2, and a red disc.

A three-character code uses the letters *D* and *Q.* Either of the letters may be repeated.

3. Find the probability of the code *QDQ.*

4. Find the probability of a code with exactly two *D*'s.

Lesson Quiz available online

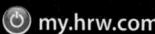 my.hrw.com

Answers
1. $\frac{1}{16}$
2. $\frac{1}{8}$
3. $\frac{1}{8}$
4. $\frac{3}{8}$

Evaluate

GUIDED AND INDEPENDENT PRACTICE

 **FL CC** 7.SP.3.8, 7.SP.3.8a, 7.SP.3.8b

Concepts & Skills	Practice
Explore Activity Finding Probability Using a Table	Exercises 1–3, 15
Example 1 Finding Probability Using a Tree Diagram	Exercises 4–8, 10–12, 14, 16
Example 2 Finding Probability Using a List	Exercises 4–8, 13, 19

Exercise	Depth of Knowledge (D.O.K.)		**FL CC** Mathematical Practices
10–12	**2** Skills/Concepts		**MP.2.1** Reasoning
13–15	**2** Skills/Concepts		**MP.4.1** Modeling
16	**2** Skills/Concepts		**MP.2.1** Reasoning
17	**3** Strategic Thinking	H.O.T.	**MP.3.1** Logic
18	**2** Skills/Concepts	H.O.T.	**MP.4.1** Modeling
19	**3** Strategic Thinking	H.O.T.	**MP.4.1** Modeling
20	**3** Strategic Thinking	H.O.T.	**MP.3.1** Logic

Additional Resources
Differentiated Instruction includes:
• Leveled Practice Worksheets

8.2 Independent Practice

FL CC 7.SP.3.8, 7.SP.3.8a, 7.SP.3.8b

Personal Math Trainer
Online Assessment and Intervention
my.hrw.com

In Exercises 10–12, use the following information. Mattias gets dressed in the dark one morning and chooses his clothes at random. He chooses a shirt (green, red, or yellow), a pair of pants (black or blue), and a pair of shoes (checkered or red).

10. Use the space below to make a tree diagram to find the sample space.

Shirt	Pants	Shoes
Green	Blue	Checkered / Red
	Black	Checkered / Red
Red	Blue	Checkered / Red
	Black	Checkered / Red
Yellow	Blue	Checkered / Red
	Black	Checkered / Red

11. What is the probability that Mattias picks an outfit at random that includes red shoes? _____ $\frac{1}{2}$

12. What is the probability that no part of Mattias's outfit is red? _____ $\frac{1}{3}$

13. Rhee and Pamela are two of the five members of a band. Every week, the band picks two members at random to play on their own for five minutes. What is the probability that Rhee and Pamela are chosen this week? _____ $\frac{1}{10}$

14. Ben rolls two number cubes. What is the probability that the sum of the numbers he rolls is less than 6? _____ $\frac{5}{18}$

15. Nhan is getting dressed. He considers two different shirts, three pairs of pants, and three pairs of shoes. He chooses one of each of the articles at random. What is the probability that he will wear his jeans but not his sneakers?

Shirt	Pants	Shoes
collared	khakis	sneakers
T-shirt	jeans	flip-flops
	shorts	sandals

$\frac{2}{9}$

16. Communicate Mathematical Ideas A ski resort has 3 chair lifts, each with access to 6 ski trails. Explain how you can find the number of possible outcomes when choosing a chair lift and a ski trail without making a list, a tree diagram, or table.

For each chair lift, there are 6 possible trails. So you can multiply the number of choices of chair lifts (3) by the number of trails (6).

17. Explain the Error For breakfast, Sarah can choose eggs, granola or oatmeal as a main course, and orange juice or milk for a drink. Sarah says that the sample space for choosing one of each contains $3^2 = 9$ outcomes. What is her error? Explain.

Because there are 3 choices for the first item and 2 for the second, there are $3 \cdot 2 = 6$ possible outcomes.

18. Represent Real-World Problems A new shoe comes in two colors, black or red, and in sizes from 5 to 12, including half sizes. If a pair of the shoes chosen at random for a store display, what is the probability it will be red and size 9 or larger? _____ $\frac{7}{30}$

H.O.T. FOCUS ON HIGHER ORDER THINKING

19. Analyze Relationships At a diner, Sondra tells the server, "Give me one item from each column." Gretchen says, "Give me one main dish and a vegetable." Who has a greater probability of getting a meal that includes salmon? Explain.

Main Dish	Vegetable	Side
Pasta	Carrots	Tomato soup
Salmon	Peas	Tossed salad
Beef	Asparagus	
Pork	Sweet potato	

Neither; sample answer: Sondra: $P(\text{salmon}) = \frac{8}{32} = \frac{1}{4}$; Gretchen: $P(\text{salmon}) = \frac{4}{16} = \frac{1}{4}$.

20. The digits 1 through 5 are used for a set of locker codes.

a. Look for a Pattern Suppose the digits cannot repeat. Find the number of possible two-digit codes and three-digit codes. Describe any pattern and use it to predict the number of possible five-digit codes.

20 two-digit codes, 60 three-digit codes, 120 five-digit codes; students may base their descriptions on tree diagrams, lists, or multiplication.

b. Look for a Pattern Repeat part a, but allow digits to repeat.

25 two-digit codes, 125 three-digit codes, 3,125 five-digit codes; students may base their descriptions on tree diagrams, lists, or multiplication.

c. Justify Reasoning Suppose that a gym plans to issue numbered locker codes by choosing the digits at random. Should the gym use codes in which the digits can repeat or not? Justify your reasoning.

Sample answer: repeat; there are more unique codes with repeated digits than without, so it is harder to guess the code for a locker.

Work Area

EXTEND THE MATH PRE-AP

Activity available online my.hrw.com

A computer byte is a sequence of 8 bits. Each bit is a 0 or 1. What is the probability of randomly selecting the following byte: 0001000? Explain. [Hint: It will be very time-consuming to use a list or tree diagram to find the answer directly. Instead, try finding the number of possibilities for 2 bits, 3 bits, and 4 bits, and extend the pattern.]

$\frac{1}{256}$; using lists or tree diagrams, we find that 2 bits can occur in 4 different combinations, 3 bits in 8 combinations, and 4 bits in 16 combinations. Extending the pattern: 5 bits is 32, 6 bits is 64, 7 bits is 128, and 8 bits is 256. Since there are a total of 256 possibilities, the probability of getting one particular combination is $\frac{1}{256}$.

Florida Common Core Standards

The student is expected to:

 **FL CC** **Statistics and Probability—7.SP.3.6**

Approximate the probability of a chance event by collecting data on the chance process that produces it and observing its long-run relative frequency, and predict the approximate relative frequency given the probability.

 FL CC **Statistics and Probability—7.SP.3.7a**

Develop a uniform probability model by assigning equal probability to all outcomes, and use the model to determine probabilities of events.

Mathematical Practices

 FL CC **MP.4.1** Modeling

ADDITIONAL EXAMPLE 1

A A spinner has eight equal sections numbered from 1–8. Predict how many times the pointer will land on a multiple of 3 in 300 spins. about 75

B Blake volunteers at the animal shelter. He has an equally likely chance of being assigned to the dog, cat, bird, or reptile section. If he volunteers 30 times, about how many times should he expect to be assigned to the cat or reptile section? about 15 times

 Interactive Whiteboard
Interactive example available online

 my.hrw.com

Engage

ESSENTIAL QUESTION

How do you make predictions using theoretical probability? Sample answer: Use the theoretical probability to write an equation or use a proportion to make the prediction for a given experiment.

Motivate the Lesson

Ask: How can you use probability to predict how well you will do in a game of chance?

Explore

Focus on Modeling Mathematical Practices

Provide students with a coin. Have them predict how many times they will toss heads in ten tosses. Ask them to conduct the experiment and compare their results with their predictions. Discuss the reasoning behind the students' predictions.

Explain

EXAMPLE 1

Questioning Strategies Mathematical Practices

• Why are there two different methods to make the prediction in part A? They are different but equivalent ways of using the probability and the total to find the prediction.

• How can you use the prediction in part A to predict how many times a number 1 through 4 will be rolled in 150 tries? Explain. Multiply the prediction by two since 1 and 2 are two additional equally likely outcomes. So, you can expect 1–4 about 100 times out of 150.

• How could you predict the number of times a number 2 through 5 will be rolled in 150 tries? Explain. The prediction is the same as for 1–4 because there are also 4 numbers in the group from 2–5.

Engage with the Whiteboard

 Have a student use an equation to solve part B. Have them explain their choice of decimal or fraction to represent the probability.

YOUR TURN

Avoid Common Errors

Students may initially include 5 as a favorable outcome. Remind them that "less than 5" does not include the number 5.

Making Predictions with Theoretical Probability

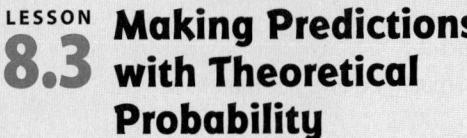

FL CC 7.SP.3.6

... predict the approximate relative frequency given the probability. *Also 7.SP.3.7a*

ESSENTIAL QUESTION

How do you make predictions using theoretical probability?

Using Theoretical Probability to Make a Quantitative Prediction

You can make quantitative predictions based on theoretical probability just as you did with experimental probability earlier.

EXAMPLE 1 *Real World*

FL CC 7.SP.3.6

A You roll a standard number cube 150 times. Predict how many times you will roll a 3 or a 4.

The probability of rolling a 3 or a 4 is $\frac{2}{6} = \frac{1}{3}$.

Method 1: Set up a proportion.

$$\frac{1}{3} = \frac{x}{150}$$ Write a proportion. 1 out of 3 is how many out of 150?

$$\frac{1}{3} = \frac{x}{150}$$
   $\times 50$

$$\frac{1}{3} = \frac{50}{150}$$ Since 3 times 50 is 150, multiply 1 times 50 to find the value of x.
   $\times 50$

$$x = 50$$

Method 2: Set up an equation and solve.

p(rolling a 3 or 4) · Number of events = Prediction

$$\frac{1}{3} \cdot 150 = x$$ Multiply the probability by the total number of rolls.

$$50 = x$$ Solve for x.

You can expect to roll a 3 or a 4 about 50 times out of 150.

My Notes

Math On the Spot
my.hrw.com

B Celia volunteers at her local animal shelter. She has an equally likely chance to be assigned to the dog, cat, bird, or reptile section. If she volunteers 24 times, about how many times should she expect to be assigned to the dog section?

Set up a proportion. The probability of being assigned to the dog section is $\frac{1}{4}$.

$$\frac{1}{4} = \frac{x}{24}$$ Write a proportion. 1 out of 4 is how many out of 24?

$$\frac{1}{4} = \frac{x}{24}$$
   $\times 6$

$$\frac{1}{4} = \frac{x}{24}$$ Since 4 times 6 is 24, multiply 1 times 6 to find the value of x.
   $\times 6$

$$x = 6$$

Celia can expect to be assigned to the dog section about 6 times out of 24.

Personal Math Trainer
Online Assessment and Intervention
my.hrw.com

YOUR TURN

1. Predict how many times you will roll a number less than 5 if you roll a standard number cube 250 times.

about 167 times

2. You flip a fair coin 18 times. About how many times would you expect heads to appear?

about 9 times

Using Theoretical Probability to Make a Qualitative Prediction

Earlier, you learned how to make predictions using experimental probability. You can use theoretical probabilities in the same way to help you predict or compare how likely events are.

Math On the Spot
my.hrw.com

PROFESSIONAL DEVELOPMENT

Integrate Mathematical Practices MP.4.1

This lesson provides an opportunity to address this Mathematical Practice standard. It calls for students to apply mathematics to problems arising in everyday life. Students use theoretical probability to write a proportion and an equation, which model a game, to make a quantitative prediction about the game. Then they use probability to make a quantitative prediction based on volunteer options. Next, students use probability to make qualitative predictions based on probabilities in real-world situations. In this way, students use mathematical models to make both quantitative and qualitative predictions that arise in everyday life.

Math Background

In future courses, students will encounter probability distributions. These distributions are widely used to make predictions in real-life situations. The most encountered distributions are likely the binomial distribution and the normal distribution. The binomial distribution is a discrete probability distribution while the normal distribution is a continuous distribution. Discrete and continuous refer to the types of outcomes the random variables can assume. For example, tossing a coin has two discrete outcomes (heads or tails). Measurements, such as speed or height, are examples of continuous, random variables.

EXAMPLE 2

Questioning Strategies 🔲 Mathematical Practices

• In part A, why do you find the probability of both matching and not matching socks? to compare the likelihoods of matching and not matching

• How can you use inverse operations to solve the proportion in part B? Multiply both sides of the proportion equation by 2,000.

• Explain how to interpret the completed proportion in part B. One out of every 125 people will likely have the same code. This is the same as 16 out of 2,000 people.

Focus on Modeling 🔲 Mathematical Practices

In part B, make sure students understand how to find the total number of possible security codes. Check that they recognize there are five digits in 0 through 4. Discuss how to start a tree diagram or an organized list to determine the number of codes in the sample space.

YOUR TURN

Focus on Critical Thinking 🔲 Mathematical Practices

After students find the answer to Exercise 4, have them discuss whether this result definitely means the grab bag is a bad deal. What if the $100 bill were actually a $1,000,000 check?

Elaborate

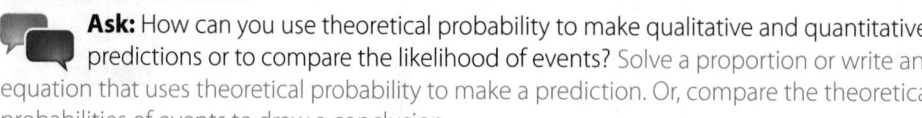

Talk About It
Summarize the Lesson

 Ask: How can you use theoretical probability to make qualitative and quantitative predictions or to compare the likelihood of events? Solve a proportion or write an equation that uses theoretical probability to make a prediction. Or, compare the theoretical probabilities of events to draw a conclusion.

GUIDED PRACTICE

Engage with the Whiteboard

Have a student set up a table to summarize the data in Exercise 3.

Avoid Common Errors

Exercise 2 Students may assume the answer is one-third of the ticket holders. Remind students that only half of the 300 ticket holders will receive a prize.

Exercise 3 Point out that students must find the probability of each eye color to draw a conclusion.

EXAMPLE 2  FL CC 7.SP.3.6, 7.SP.3.7a

A Herschel pulls a sock out of his drawer without looking and puts it on. The sock is black. There are 7 black socks, 8 white socks, and 5 striped socks left in the drawer. He pulls out a second sock without looking. Is it likely that he will be wearing matching socks to school?

Find the theoretical probability that Herschel picks a matching sock and the probability that he picks one that does not match.

$P(\text{matching}) = \frac{7}{20}$ $P(\text{not matching}) = 1 - \frac{7}{20} = \frac{13}{20}$

> $P(\text{not matching}) = 1 - P(\text{matching})$

The probability that Herschel picks a matching sock is about half the probability that he picks one that does not match. It is likely that he will **not** be wearing matching socks to school.

B All 2,000 customers at a gym are randomly assigned a 3-digit security code that they use to access their online accounts. The codes are made up of the digits 0 through 4, and the digits can be repeated. Is it likely that fewer than 10 of the customers are issued the code 103?

Set up a proportion. The probability of the code 103 is $\frac{1}{125}$.

$\frac{1}{125} = \frac{x}{2,000}$

> Write a proportion. 1 out of 125 is how many out of 2,000?

$\frac{1}{125} \overset{\times 16}{\underset{\times 16}{=}} \frac{16}{2,000}$

> Since 125 times 16 is 2,000, multiply 1 times 125 to find the value of x.

> There are 5 possible first numbers, 5 possible second numbers, and 5 possible third numbers. So, the probability of any one code is $\frac{1}{5} \cdot \frac{1}{5} \cdot \frac{1}{5} = \frac{1}{125}$.

It is **not** likely that fewer than 10 of the customers get the same code. It is more likely that 16 members get the code 103.

YOUR TURN

3. A bag of marbles contains 8 red marbles, 4 blue marbles, and 5 white marbles. Tom picks a marble at random. Is it more likely that he picks a red marble or a marble of another color?

more likely that he picks a marble of another color

4. At a fundraiser, a school group charges $6 for tickets for a "grab bag." You choose one bill at random from a bag that contains 40 $1 bills, 20 $5 bills, 5 $10 bills, 5 $20 bills, and 1 $100 bill. Is it likely that you will win enough to pay for your ticket? Justify your answer.

No; sample answer: You would need to pick a $10, $20, or $100 bill. $P(\text{bill worth \$6 or more}) = \frac{5+5+1}{71} = \frac{11}{71}$, or about 15%.

Personal Math Trainer
Online Assessment and Intervention
my.hrw.com

---

1. Bob works at a construction company. He has an equally likely chance to be assigned to work different crews every day. He can be assigned to work on crews building apartments, condominiums, or houses. If he works 18 days a month, about how many times should he expect to be assigned to the house crew? (Example 1)

STEP 1 Find the probabilities of being assigned to each crew.

Apartment $\frac{1}{3}$ Condo $\frac{1}{3}$ House $\frac{1}{3}$

The probability of being assigned to the house crew is $\frac{1}{3}$.

STEP 2 Set up and solve a proportion.

$\frac{1}{3} = \frac{x}{18}$ $x = 6$

Bob can expect to be assigned to the house crew about 6 times out of 18.

2. During a raffle drawing, half of the ticket holders will receive a prize. The winners are equally likely to win one of three prizes: a book, a gift certificate to a restaurant, or a movie ticket. If there are 300 ticket holders, predict the number of people who will win a movie ticket. (Example 1) 50 people

3. In Mr. Jawarani's first period math class, there are 9 students with hazel eyes, 10 students with brown eyes, 7 students with blue eyes, and 2 students with green eyes. Mr. Jawarani picks a student at random. Which color eyes is the student most likely to have? Explain. (Example 2)

brown; $P(\text{hazel}) = \frac{9}{28}$, $P(\text{brown}) = \frac{10}{28}$, $P(\text{blue}) = \frac{7}{28}$, and $P(\text{green}) = \frac{2}{28}$. The event with the greatest probability is choosing a person with brown eyes.

? ESSENTIAL QUESTION CHECK-IN

4. How do you make predictions using theoretical probability?

You can find and compare probabilities. Or, you can use probability to set up and solve a proportion or an equation that relates the probability to the unknown quantity.

DIFFERENTIATE INSTRUCTION

Cooperative Learning

Provide students with 10 to 12 playing cards. Have them work in small groups to describe different outcomes of drawing two cards. Ask them to make a prediction based on the theoretical probability of one of their outcomes. Then have them perform the experiment and compare their prediction to their results.

Graphic Organizers

Encourage students to create tables to display data sets in probability problems. For example, the data in Your Turn Exercise 4 may be easier for students to interpret if the data are displayed in a table. Discuss how the table makes it easier to determine both the favorable outcomes and the total number of outcomes needed to write a probability ratio.

Additional Resources

Differentiated Instruction includes:

• Reading Strategies
• Success for English Learners **ELL**
• Reteach
• Challenge **PRE-AP**

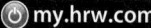
8.3 LESSON QUIZ

 **FL CC** 7.SP.3.6

1. You roll a six-sided number cube 270 times. Predict how many times you will roll a number less than 3.

2. The equal sections of a spinner have one of the following letters: *A*, *B*, *A*, *C*, *B*. Predict how many times the pointer will land on a consonant in 60 spins.

3. In Kim's homeroom, 4 students have no siblings, 9 students have 1 sibling, 8 students have 2 siblings, and 2 students have 3 or more siblings. Is it likely that a student chosen at random will have 2 or more siblings? Explain.

4. Drew rolls two number cubes 75 times. Is it likely that she will get a sum of 3 more than 5 times? Explain.

Lesson Quiz available online

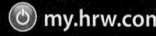 my.hrw.com

Answers

1. about 90 times

2. about 36 times

3. no; $P(2 \text{ or more}) = \frac{10}{23}$, $P(0 \text{ or } 1) = \frac{13}{23}$, and $\frac{10}{23} < \frac{13}{23}$.

4. No, it is likely she will get the sum about 4 times since $\frac{1}{18} \cdot 75 = 4\frac{1}{6}$.

Evaluate

GUIDED AND INDEPENDENT PRACTICE

 **FL CC** 7.SP.3.6, 7.SP.3.7a

Concepts & Skills	Practice
Example 1 Using Theoretical Probability to Make a Quantitative Prediction	Exercises 1–2, 5, 8, 9–12
Example 2 Using Theoretical Probability to Make a Qualitative Prediction	Exercises 3, 6, 7, 10

Exercise	Depth of Knowledge (D.O.K.)	**FL CC** Mathematical Practices
5	**2** Skills/Concepts	**MP.4.1** Modeling
6	**2** Skills/Concepts	**MP.2.1** Reasoning
7–9	**2** Skills/Concepts	**MP.4.1** Modeling
10	**3** Strategic Thinking H.O.T.	**MP.8.1** Patterns
11–12	**2** Skills/Concepts	**MP.4.1** Modeling
13	**3** Strategic Thinking H.O.T.	**MP.3.1** Logic
14	**3** Strategic Thinking H.O.T.	**MP.2.1** Reasoning
15	**3** Strategic Thinking H.O.T.	**MP.8.1** Patterns
16	**3** Strategic Thinking H.O.T.	**MP.8.1** Patterns
17	**3** Strategic Thinking H.O.T.	**MP.3.1** Logic

Additional Resources

Differentiated Instruction includes:

• Leveled Practice Worksheets

 **CLUSTER CONNECTION**   **Exercise 11** combines concepts from the Florida Common Core cluster "Investigate chance processes and develop, use, and evaluate probability models."

8.3 Independent Practice

FL CC 7.SP.3.6, 7.SP.3.7a

Personal
Math Trainer
my.hrw.com
Online
Assessment and
Intervention

5. A bag contains 6 red marbles, 2 white marbles, and 1 gray marble. You randomly pick out a marble, record its color, and put it back in the bag. You repeat this process 45 times. How many white or gray marbles do you expect to get?

15 white or gray marbles

6. Using the blank circle below, draw a spinner with 8 equal sections and 3 colors—red, green, and yellow. The spinner should be such that you are equally likely to land on green or yellow, but more likely to land on red than either on green or yellow.

Sample answer:

Use the following for Exercises 7–9.
In a standard 52-card deck, half of the cards are red and half are black. The 52 cards are divided evenly into 4 suits: spades, hearts, diamonds, and clubs. Each suit has three face cards (jack, queen, king), and an ace. Each suit also has 9 cards numbered from 2 to 10.

7. Dawn draws 1 card, replaces it, and draws another card. Is it more likely that she draws 2 red cards or 2 face cards?

It is more likely that she draws
2 red cards.

8. Luis draws 1 card from a deck, 39 times. Predict how many times he draws an ace.

3 times

9. Suppose a solitaire player has played 1,000 games. Predict how many times the player turned over a red card as the first card.

500 times

10. John and O'Neal are playing a board game in which they roll two number cubes. John needs to get a sum of 8 on the number cubes to win. O'Neal needs a sum of 11. If they take turns rolling the number cube, who is more likely to win? Explain.

John; there is a higher probability
of rolling a sum of 8, $\frac{5}{36}$, than a
sum of 11, $\frac{2}{36}$.

11. Every day, Navya's teacher randomly picks a number from 1 to 20 to be the number of the day. The number of the day can be repeated. There are 180 days in the school year. Predict how many days the number of the day will be greater than 15. _45 days_

12. Eben rolls two standard number cubes 36 times. Predict how many times he will roll a sum of 4. _3 times_

13. **Communicate Mathematical Ideas** Can you always show that a prediction based on theoretical probability is true by performing the event often enough? If so, explain why. If not, describe a situation that justifies your response.

Sample answer: No; Every time
you flip a coin, the probability of
heads is $\frac{1}{2}$, but in reality you
could flip a coin many times and
have it land heads up every time.

14. **Represent Real-World Problems** Give a real-world example of an experiment in which all of the outcomes are not equally likely. Can you make a prediction for this experiment, using theoretical probability?

Sample answer: A bag of marbles contains red and blue
marbles that are different sizes. Since it is easy to feel the
difference between the two colors, all of the outcomes
are not equally likely. You cannot make a prediction
using theoretical probability.

H.O.T. FOCUS ON HIGHER ORDER THINKING

Work Area

15. **Critical Thinking** Pierre asks Sherry a question involving the theoretical probability of a compound event in which you flip a coin and draw a marble from a bag of marbles. The bag of marbles contains 3 white marbles, 8 green marbles, and 9 black marbles. Sherry's answer, which is correct, is $\frac{12}{40}$. What was Pierre's question?

Sample answer: What is the theoretical probability that
the coin lands on heads, and you pick a marble that is
not green?

16. **Make a Prediction** Horace is going to roll a standard number cube and flip a coin. He wonders if it is more likely that he rolls a 5 **and** the coin lands on heads, or that he rolls a 5 **or** the coin lands on heads. Which event do you think is more likely to happen? Find the probability of both events to justify or reject your initial prediction.

Sample answer: It is much more likely that he rolls a 5 or
the coin lands on heads. That probability is $\frac{7}{12}$, while the
probability that he rolls a 5 and the coin lands on heads
is $\frac{1}{12}$.

17. **Communicate Mathematical Ideas** Cecil solved a theoretical prediction problem and got this answer: "The spinner will land on the red section 4.5 times." Is it possible to have a prediction that is not a whole number? If so, give an example.

Yes, but only theoretically because in reality, nothing
can occur 0.5 time. Sample answer: The probability that
a flipped coin lands heads up is $\frac{1}{2}$, so in 75 flips, you can
expect heads about $\frac{75}{2}$ or 37.5 times.

EXTEND THE MATH PRE-AP

Activity available online ⓞ my.hrw.com

A probability model for an event gives all the possible outcomes of the event and the probabilities for that event.

a. Use a table to create a probability model for drawing a card of any of the four equal suits using a standard deck of 52 cards.

b. Each probability in a probability model must be between 0 and 1 inclusive. The total of the probabilities must be 1. Verify that these conditions are true for your model. $0 \le \frac{1}{4} \le 1; 4\left(\frac{1}{4}\right) = 1$

c. Josh draws a card randomly from a deck, records the suit, returns the card to the deck, and then shuffles the deck. He repeats this experiment 500 times. Explain how to use the probability model to predict about how many times Josh can expect to draw a card that is not a spade. Sample answer: The probability of a card that is not a spade is $\frac{3}{4}$. In 500 draws there will be about 375 cards that are not spades.

LESSON
8.4 Using Technology to Conduct a Simulation

ADDITIONAL EXAMPLE 1
The probability of spinning the winning letter in a game show is 20%. What is the experimental probability that a contestant will spin exactly four times before spinning the winning letter? Check students' work. Note that the winning letter can be represented by 2 numbers out of 10 or 1 out of 5 and each trial will end when the designated number that identifies the winning number is generated.

 Interactive Whiteboard
Interactive example available online

 **⏻ my.hrw.com**

 Animated Math
Conducting a Simulation

Students explore designing and conducting simulations by using an interactive tool that allows them to preform trials, record results, and calculate the probability.

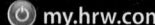 **⏻ my.hrw.com**

Engage

ESSENTIAL QUESTION

How can you use technology simulations to estimate probabilities? Sample answer: Use a calculator or computer to generate random numbers to simulate an experiment. Use the results to estimate probabilities.

Motivate the Lesson
Ask: How can flipping a coin or tossing a number cube help you model a random event?

Explore

Focus on Patterns Mathematical Practices

Ask the students in the class to each write three one-digit numbers on a sheet of paper. Collect the papers, and have a volunteer record the numbers on the board. Ask the class to discuss whether the numbers are random or not.

Explain

EXAMPLE 1

Focus on Modeling 🔖 Mathematical Practices

Discuss how to generate a set of random numbers using technology. Students can access lists from a graphing calculator or on the Internet. Also discuss how the table helps organize the trials in the experiment and is used to identify the favorable trial. Note that coins and number cubes are low tech methods of generating random number lists.

Questioning Strategies 🔖 Mathematical Practices

• Do you have to use the numbers 1, 2, 3 to represent the winning code? Explain. No, any three numbers could represent the winning code and the remaining seven the nonwinning code.

• Why does the trial stop when you get a winning code? The numbers up to and including the winning code represent the number of boxes. After the winning code is found, no additional boxes need to be bought, so the trial ends.

• Could you perform more trials? Would this change the probability? Explain. Yes, you can continue the experiment. The number of trials in the denominator of the experimental probability ratio would change. It is likely the experimental probability would also change.

YOUR TURN

Avoid Common Errors
Make sure students understand that a successful trial will be represented by 0001 and will have a total of 4 calves. Suggest that students perform 20 trials in the simulation.

Engage with the Whiteboard
Have a student create a table to record the simulation results. Ask several volunteers to record the results of their simulations. Find the probabilities after each additional set of data is added to the table.

8.4 Using Technology to Conduct a Simulation

FL CC 7.SP.3.8c

Design and use a simulation to generate frequencies for compound events. *Also* 7.SP.3.8

? ESSENTIAL QUESTION How can you use technology simulations to estimate probabilities?

Designing and Conducting a Simulation for a Simple Event

You can use a graphing calculator or computer to generate random numbers and conduct a simulation.

Math On the Spot
my.hrw.com

EXAMPLE 1 Real World

FL CC 7.SP.3.8c

A cereal company is having a contest. There are codes for winning prizes in 30% of its cereal boxes. Find an experimental probability that you have to buy *exactly* 3 boxes of cereal before you find a winning code.

STEP 1 Choose a model.

The probability of finding a winning code is $30\% = \frac{3}{10}$.

Use whole numbers from 1 to 10.
Let three numbers represent buying a box with a winning code.

Winning code: 1, 2, 3   Nonwinning code: 4, 5, 6, 7, 8, 9, 10

STEP 2 Generate random numbers from 1 to 10 until you get one that represents a box with a winning code. Record how many boxes you bought before finding a winning code.

5 numbers generated: 9, 6, 7, 8, 1 — *1 represents a box with a winning code.*

STEP 3 Perform multiple trials by repeating Step 2.

STEP 4 Find the experimental probability.

In 1 of 10 trials, you bought exactly 3 boxes of cereal before finding a winning code. The experimental probability is $\frac{1}{10}$, or 10%.

Trial	Numbers generated	Boxes bought
1	9, 6, 7, 8, 1	5
2	2	1
3	10, 4, 8, 1	4
4	4, 10, 7, 1	4
5	2	1
6	4, 3	2
7	3	1
8	7, 5, 2	3
9	8, 5, 4, 8, 10, 3	6
10	9, 1	2

Trial 8 represents a winning code after buying 3 boxes.

Animated Math
my.hrw.com

Personal Math Trainer
Online Assessment and Intervention
my.hrw.com

YOUR TURN

1. An elephant has a 50% chance of giving birth to a male or a female calf. Use a simulation to find an experimental probability that the elephant gives birth to 3 male calves before having a female calf. (*Hint*: Use 0s and 1s. Let 0 represent a male calf, and 1 represent a female calf. Generate random numbers until you get a 1.)

Trial	Numbers generated	3 Males first		Trial	Numbers generated	3 Males first
1				6		
2				7		
3				8		
4				9		
5				10		

Check students' work.

Math Talk
Mathematical Practices

Could you generate random numbers from a list of more than 2 numbers? Explain.

You could choose any even number of numbers, so that half can represent males and half females. 2 is the least possible number.

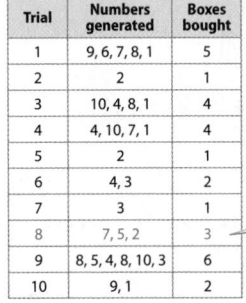
Math On the Spot
my.hrw.com

Designing and Conducting a Simulation for a Compound Event

You can use random numbers to simulate compound events as well as simple events.

EXAMPLE 2 Real World

FL CC 7.SP.3.8c, 7.SP.3.8

Suppose that there is a 20% chance that a particular volcano will erupt in any given decade. Find an experimental probability that the volcano will erupt in at least 1 of the next 5 decades.

STEP 1 Choose a model.

The probability of an eruption is $20\% = \frac{1}{5}$.
Use whole numbers from 1 to 5.

Let 1 represent a decade with an eruption.

Let 2, 3, 4, and 5 represent a decade without an eruption.

PROFESSIONAL DEVELOPMENT

Integrate Mathematical Practices MP.5.1

This lesson provides an opportunity to address this Mathematical Practice standard. It calls for students to select tools, including real objects and technology as appropriate, and to solve problems. Students use a random number generator of a graphing calculator or computer to help them perform a simulation. Thus, the students use technology to find experimental probabilities of events that would otherwise be difficult to find.

Math Background

A simulation is useful in modeling experimental probabilities when an actual trial is too difficult, time consuming, or costly to perform.
A simulation is designed so that its outcomes reflect ways that outcomes occur in the real world. Each possible outcome must be linked to one or more random numbers. Coins, number cubes, spinners, random number tables, and random number generators can be used to generate random numbers for a simulation. Note that as more trials of the simulation are performed, the experimental probabilities will more closely approximate the theoretical probabilities associated with the experiment.

EXAMPLE 2

Questioning Strategies 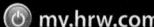 Mathematical Practices

• How does the 20% chance of an eruption help you choose a simulation model? Since 20% means 1 out of 5, it suggests the numbers to use in the model.

• Why do you generate five random numbers for each trial? Each trial represents five decades, so you need a random number for each decade.

Focus on Communication

Stress that a simulation must reflect the circumstances of the problem. Make sure students understand that the number 1 represents a 20% chance of an eruption and not "1 of the next 5 decades." Note how Example 2 differs from Example 1.

YOUR TURN

Engage with the Whiteboard

Perform a simulation of ten trials with the class. After the numbers are generated, ask a volunteer to identify the trials with two or more correct answers. Have the student draw a circle around the numbers that correspond to the favorable outcomes. Have another student calculate the experimental probability.

Talk About It
Check for Understanding

Ask: Why does each trial need to have a total of five 0's and 1's? There are five True/False questions. The 0's and 1's represent the incorrect and correct answers on the quiz represented by the trial.

Elaborate

Talk About It
Summarize the Lesson

Ask: How can you use a simulation to find the experimental probability of an event? Use the chance of an event to choose a model and define what the numbers in the model will represent. Generate random numbers to create a trial simulation, and record the results of several trials. Write the ratio of the number of favorable outcomes to the total number of trials.

GUIDED PRACTICE

Engage with the Whiteboard

Ask a volunteer to describe the model they created in Exercise 1 and use the model to complete the table in Exercise 2. Have the student circle the drought years in each trial before recording the number of drought years in the corresponding column.

Avoid Common Errors

Exercise 3 Remind students to count the number of trials with drought years, not the total number of drought years. Also point out that the total number of trials is ten, not the total number of numbers generated.

STEP 2 Generate 5 random numbers from 1 to 5. Record the number of decades with an eruption.

5 numbers generated: 3, 1, 3, 4, 2   Eruption decades: 1

STEP 3 Perform multiple trials by repeating Step 2. Calculate the percent of trials in which there was an eruption in at least 1 of the 5 decades.

Trial	Numbers generated	Eruption decades
1	3, 1, 3, 4, 2	1
2	3, 2, 2, 4, 5	0
3	1, 3, 3, 2, 5	1
4	5, 3, 4, 5, 4	0
5	5, 5, 3, 2, 4	0

Trial	Numbers generated	Eruption decades
6	2, 3, 3, 4, 2	0
7	1, 2, 4, 1, 4	2
8	1, 3, 2, 1, 5	2
9	1, 2, 4, 2, 5	1
10	5, 5, 3, 2, 4	0

In 5 out of the 10 trials, there was an eruption in at least 1 of the 5 decades. The experimental probability of an eruption in at least 1 of the next 5 decades is $\frac{5}{10} = 50\%$.

YOUR TURN

2. Matt guesses the answers on a quiz with 5 true-false questions. The probability of guessing a correct answer on each question is 50%. Use a simulation to find an experimental probability that he gets at least 2 questions right. (*Hint:* Use 0s and 1s. Let 0s represent incorrect answers, and 1s represent correct answers. Perform 10 trials, generating 5 random numbers in each, and count the number of 1s.)

Trial	Numbers generated	Correct answers
1		
2		
3		
4		
5		

Trial	Numbers generated	Correct answers
6		
7		
8		
9		
10		

Check students' work.

Personal Math Trainer
Online Assessment and Intervention
my.hrw.com

Lesson 8.4 **253**

 (right margin copyright text, vertical)

Guided Practice

There is a 30% chance that T'Shana's county will have a drought during any given year. She performs a simulation to find the experimental probability of a drought in at least 1 of the next 4 years. (Examples 1 and 2)

1. T'Shana's model involves the whole numbers from 1 to 10. Complete the description of her model.

   Let the numbers 1 to 3 represent [years with a drought]

   and the numbers 4 to 10 represent [years without a drought.]

   Perform multiple trials, generating [4] random numbers each time.

2. Suppose T'Shana used the model described in Exercise 1 and got the results shown in the table. Complete the table.

Trial	Numbers generated	Drought years
1	10, 3, 5, 1	2
2	10, 4, 6, 5	0
3	3, 2, 10, 3	3
4	2, 10, 4, 4	1
5	7, 3, 6, 3	2

Trial	Numbers generated	Drought years
6	8, 4, 8, 5	0
7	6, 2, 2, 8	2
8	6, 5, 2, 4	1
9	2, 2, 3, 2	4
10	6, 3, 1, 5	2

3. According to the simulation, what is the experimental probability that there will be a drought in the county in at least 1 of the next 4 years? ___80%___

ESSENTIAL QUESTION CHECK-IN

4. You want to generate random numbers to simulate an event with a 75% chance of occurring. Describe a model you could use.

   Sample answer: Generate whole numbers from 1 to 4.

   Let 1 to 3 represent the event occurring, and 4 represent

   the event not occurring.

   _____

254 Unit 4

DIFFERENTIATE INSTRUCTION

Cooperative Learning

Have students work in pairs or in small groups to create additional simulations for Examples 1 and 2. If possible, have students use a variety of different random number generators, or even random letters. They can use calculators, the Internet, or a spreadsheet. Discuss which method they prefer.

Graphic Organizers

Have students use a coin to create a list of 0's and 1's. Point out that students have generated a set of random numbers. Discuss how students could use their results to find the experimental probabilities in Your Turn 1 and 2. Then challenge students to explain how they could use number cubes to generate random numbers for Example 2.

Additional Resources

Differentiated Instruction includes:

- Reading Strategies
- Success for English Learners **ELL**
- Reteach
- Challenge **PRE-AP**

8.4 LESSON QUIZ

 **7.SP.3.8c**

At a restaurant, 60% of customers typically order a salad with their meal. What is the experimental probability that the next 4 customers will order a salad?

1. Describe a model to simulate the event.

2. Use a simulation to find the probability.

There is a 10% chance that a box of tiles in a shipment will contain broken tiles. What is the experimental probability that there will be broken tiles in a box in at least 1 of the next 5 shipments?

3. Describe a model to simulate the event.

4. Use a simulation to find the probability.

Lesson Quiz available online

 my.hrw.com

Answers

1. Sample model: $60\% = \frac{3}{5}$; Let 1, 2, and 3 represent customers who order a salad. Let 4 and 5 represent customers who do not order a salad. For each trial, generate 4 random numbers. Count the number of trials where all four numbers are 1, 2, or 3.

2. Check students' work.

3. Sample model: $10\% = \frac{1}{10}$; Let 1 represent a box with broken tiles. Let 2–10 represent a box with unbroken tiles. For each trial, generate 5 random numbers. Count the number of trials that contain at least one 1.

4. Check students' work.

Evaluate

GUIDED AND INDEPENDENT PRACTICE

 **7.SP.3.8, 7.SP.3.8c**

Concepts & Skills	Practice
Example 1 Designing and Conducting a Simulation for a Simple Event	Exercises 1–3, 5, 6, 10
Example 2 Designing and Conducting a Simulation for a Compound Event	Exercises 1–3, 7, 8

Exercise	Depth of Knowledge (D.O.K.)	 Mathematical Practices
5	**2** Skills/Concepts	**MP.2.1** Reasoning
6	**2** Skills/Concepts	**MP.2.1** Reasoning
7	**2** Skills/Concepts	**MP.4.1** Modeling
8	**3** Strategic Thinking **H.O.T.**	**MP.7.1** Using Structure
9	**3** Strategic Thinking **H.O.T.**	**MP.3.1** Logic
10	**2** Skills/Concepts	**MP.4.1** Modeling
11	**3** Strategic Thinking **H.O.T.**	**MP.4.1** Modeling
12	**3** Strategic Thinking **H.O.T.**	**MP.7.1** Using Structure

Additional Resources

Differentiated Instruction includes:

• Leveled Practice Worksheets

CLUSTER CONNECTION **Exercise 11** combines concepts from the Florida Common Core cluster "Investigate chance processes and develop, use, and evaluate probability models."

8.4 Independent Practice

FL CC 7.SP.3.8, 7.SP.3.8c

Personal Math Trainer

Online Assessment and Intervention

my.hrw.com

Every contestant on a game show has a 40% chance of winning. In the simulation below, the numbers 1–4 represent a winner, and the numbers 5–10 represent a nonwinner. Numbers were generated until one that represented a winner was produced.

Trial	Numbers generated	Trial	Numbers generated
1	7, 4	6	8, 8, 6, 2
2	6, 5, 2	7	2
3	1	8	5, 9, 4
4	9, 1	9	10, 3
5	3	10	1

5. In how many of the trials did it take exactly 4 contestants to get a winner? ___1 trial___

6. Based on the simulation, what is the experimental probability that it will take exactly 4 contestants to get a winner? ___10%___

Over a 100-year period, the probability that a hurricane struck Rob's city in any given year was 20%. Rob performed a simulation to find an experimental probability that a hurricane would strike the city in at least 4 of the next 10 years. In Rob's simulation, 1 represents a year with a hurricane.

Trial	Numbers generated	Trial	Numbers generated
1	2, 5, 3, 2, 5, 5, 1, 4, 5, 2	6	1, 1, 5, 5, 1, 4, 2, 2, 3, 4
2	1, 1, 5, 2, 2, 1, 3, 1, 1, 5	7	2, 1, 5, 3, 1, 5, 1, 2, 1, 4
3	4, 5, 4, 5, 5, 4, 3, 5, 1, 1	8	2, 4, 3, 2, 4, 4, 2, 1, 3, 1
4	1, 5, 5, 5, 1, 2, 2, 3, 5, 3	9	3, 2, 1, 4, 5, 3, 5, 5, 1, 2
5	5, 1, 5, 3, 5, 3, 4, 5, 3, 2	10	3, 4, 2, 4, 3, 5, 2, 3, 5, 1

7. According to Rob's simulation, what was the experimental probability that a hurricane would strike the city in at least 4 of the next 10 years? ___20%___

8. **Analyze Relationships** Suppose that over the 10 years following Rob's simulation, there was actually 1 year in which a hurricane struck. How did this compare to the results of Rob's simulation?

It is fewer than expected based on the simulation.

9. **Communicate Mathematical Ideas** You generate three random whole numbers from 1 to 10. Do you think that it is unlikely or even impossible that all of the numbers could be 10? Explain?

It is unlikely but it is not impossible. Each of the 3 numbers could be any number from 1 to 10. However, there are 10 possible first numbers, 10 possible second numbers, and 10 possible third numbers, or a total of 1,000 possible numbers when generating three numbers from 1 to 10. The probability of three 10s is $\frac{1}{1,000}$.

10. Erika collects baseball cards, and 60% of the packs contain a player from her favorite team. Use a simulation to find an experimental probability that she has to buy exactly 2 packs before she gets a player from her favorite team.

Check students' work.

H.O.T. FOCUS ON HIGHER ORDER THINKING

Work Area

11. **Represent Real-World Problems** When Kate plays basketball, she usually makes 37.5% of her shots. Design and conduct a simulation to find the experimental probability that she makes at least 3 of her next 10 shots. Justify the model for your simulation.

Sample answer: The probability that she makes a shot is 37.5% = $\frac{3}{8}$. Use the whole numbers from 1 to 8, with 1–3 representing shots she makes, and 4–8 representing shots she misses. For each trial, generate 10 random numbers. Count the number of times 1, 2, or 3 appears in each trial. Divide the number of trials in which she made at least 3 shots by the total number of trials.

12. **Justify Reasoning** George and Susannah used a simulation to simulate the flipping of 8 coins 50 times. In all of the trials, at least 5 heads came up. What can you say about their simulation? Explain.

Sample answer: Their simulation was not appropriate, perhaps because they chose an incorrect model. You would expect there to have been exactly 4 heads on more of the trials, and more variation in the number of heads in general.

EXTEND THE MATH PRE-AP

Activity available online my.hrw.com

Recall from Your Turn Exercise 1 that an elephant has a 50% chance of giving birth to a male or female calf. Use a simulation to determine the number of male calves in three births. Use the results of your simulation to complete the table.

Probability Model				
Number of males in 3 births	0	1	2	3
Probability				

Check students' work.

How many trials did you perform in your experiment? Why?

Answers may vary.

What do you notice about the frequencies of the different numbers of male births?

Answers may vary. In most simulations, there will be a noticeably larger number of outcomes with 1 or 2 males than with 0 or 3 males.

© Houghton Mifflin Harcourt Publishing Company

Ready to Go On?

Assess Mastery

Use the assessment on this page to determine if students have mastered the concepts and standards covered in this module.

 **Response to Intervention**

Personal Math Trainer
Online Assessment and Intervention
my.hrw.com

Intervention	Enrichment
Access Ready to Go On? assessment online, and receive instant scoring, feedback, and customized intervention or enrichment.	

Online and Print Resources

Differentiated Instruction
- Reteach worksheets
- Reading Strategies **ELL**
- Success for English Learners **ELL**

Differentiated Instruction
- Challenge worksheets **PRE-AP**
- Extend the Math **PRE-AP** Lesson Activities in TE

Additional Resources

Assessment Resources:
- Leveled Module Quizzes

MODULE QUIZ

Ready to Go On?

Personal Math Trainer
Online Assessment and Intervention
my.hrw.com

8.1, 8.2 Theoretical Probability of Simple and Compound Events

Find the probability of each event. Write your answer as a fraction, as a decimal, and as a percent.

1. You choose a marble at random from a bag containing 12 red, 12 blue, 15 green, 9 yellow, and 12 black marbles. The marble is red. $\frac{1}{5}$, 0.2, 20%

2. You draw a card at random from a shuffled deck of 52 cards. The deck has four 13-card suits (diamonds, hearts, clubs, spades). The card is a diamond or a spade. $\frac{1}{2}$, 0.5, 50%

8.3 Making Predictions with Theoretical Probability

3. A bag contains 23 red marbles, 25 green marbles, and 18 blue marbles. You choose a marble at random from the bag. What color marble will you most likely choose?   green

8.4 Using Technology to Conduct a Simulation

4. Bay City has a 25% chance of having a flood in any given decade. The table shows the results of a simulation using random numbers to find the experimental probability that there will be a flood in Bay City in at least 1 of the next 5 decades. In the table, the number 1 represents a decade with a flood. The numbers 2 through 5 represent a decade without a flood.

Trial	Numbers generated	Trial	Numbers generated
1	2, 2, 5, 5, 5	6	4, 2, 2, 5, 4
2	3, 2, 3, 5, 4	7	1, 3, 2, 4, 4
3	5, 5, 5, 4, 3	8	3, 5, 5, 2, 1
4	5, 1, 3, 3, 5	9	4, 3, 3, 2, 5
5	4, 5, 5, 3, 2	10	5, 4, 1, 2, 1

According to the simulation, what is the experimental probability of a flood in Bay City in at least 1 of the next 5 decades?   40%

 **ESSENTIAL QUESTION**

5. How can you use theoretical probability to make predictions in real-world situations?

Sample answer: You can find the theoretical probability of an event and then use it to make a prediction by setting up a proportion.

Module 8 **257**

 ## Florida Common Core Standards

Lesson	Exercises	Common Core Standards
8.1	1–2	7.SP.3.6, 7.SP.3.7, 7.SP.3.7a
8.2	1–2	7.SP.3.8, 7.SP.3.8a, 7.SP.3.8b
8.3	3	7.SP.3.6, 7.SP.3.7a
8.4	4	7.SP.3.8, 7.SP.3.8c

PARCC Assessment Readiness

Assessment Readiness Tip Students can draw a model or make a list to help them visualize a problem.

Item 3 Students can list all of the numbers on a number cube, then circle the number or numbers that are both even and less than 4. This will make the probability more clear.

Item 7 Students can draw a model of the tennis balls in the bag fairly quickly. Once it is drawn, students can visualize the situation and more easily choose which color ball would be the least likely.

Avoid Common Errors

Item 4 If students do not read this question carefully, they may miss the word *not* and give the probability that a card is green. Remind them to read carefully and look for words like "not" to indicate they need to look for opposites.

Item 6 If students examine each answer choice in turn, they may not be able to visualize a way to make a particular cross section, and incorrectly answer C or D. Instead, encourage students to think about straight and curved lines. Since a rectangular prism is made up of straight lines, its cross sections will never include curved lines. Therefore, a circle is impossible.

Additional Resources

Personal Math Trainer
Online Assessment and Intervention
my.hrw.com

MODULE 8 MIXED REVIEW

PARCC Assessment Readiness

COMMON CORE

Personal Math Trainer
Online Assessment and Intervention
my.hrw.com

Selected Response

1. What is the probability of flipping two fair coins and having both show tails?
   - (A) $\frac{1}{8}$
   - (B) $\frac{1}{4}$
   - (C) $\frac{1}{3}$
   - (D) $\frac{1}{2}$

2. A bag contains 8 white marbles and 2 black marbles. You pick out a marble, record its color, and put the marble back in the bag. If you repeat this process 45 times, how many times would you expect to remove a white marble from the bag?
   - (A) 9
   - (B) 32
   - (C) 36
   - (D) 40

3. Philip rolls a standard number cube 24 times. Which is the best prediction for the number of times he will roll a number that is even and less than 4?
   - (A) 2
   - (B) 3
   - (C) 4
   - (D) 6

4. A set of cards includes 24 yellow cards, 18 green cards, and 18 blue cards. What is the probability that a card chosen at random is **not** green?
   - (A) $\frac{3}{10}$
   - (B) $\frac{4}{10}$
   - (C) $\frac{3}{5}$
   - (D) $\frac{7}{10}$

5. A rectangle made of square tiles measures 10 tiles long and 8 tiles wide. What is the width of a similar rectangle whose length is 15 tiles?
   - (A) 3 tiles
   - (B) 12 tiles
   - (C) 13 tiles
   - (D) 18.75 tiles

6. Which of the following could NOT be a cross section of a rectangular prism?
   - (A) rectangle
   - (B) circle
   - (C) parallelogram
   - (D) triangle

7. There are 20 tennis balls in a bag. Five are orange, 7 are white, 2 are yellow, and 6 are green. You choose one at random. Which color ball are you **least** likely to choose?
   - (A) green
   - (B) orange
   - (C) white
   - (D) yellow

Mini-Task

8. Center County has had a 1 in 6 (or about 16.7%) chance of a tornado in any given decade. In a simulation to consider the probability of tornadoes in the next 5 decades, Ava rolled a number cube. She let a 1 represent a decade with a tornado, and 2–6 represent decades without tornadoes. What experimental probability did Ava find for each event?

Trial	Numbers Generated	Trial	Numbers Generated
1	2, 2, 3, 1, 5	6	4, 5, 2, 2, 4
2	3, 5, 6, 4, 5	7	5, 1, 6, 3, 1
3	1, 3, 3, 2, 2	8	1, 2, 1, 2, 4
4	6, 3, 3, 5, 4	9	1, 4, 4, 1, 4
5	4, 1, 4, 4, 4	10	3, 6, 5, 3, 6

a. Center County has a tornado in at least one of the next five decades.

60%

b. Center County has a tornado in exactly one of the next five decades.

30%

© Houghton Mifflin Harcourt Publishing Company

🌴 Florida Common Core Standards

Items	🌴 Grade 7 Standards	🌴 Mathematical Practices
1	7.SP.3.8	MP.4.1
2	7.SP.3.6	MP.4.1
3	7.SP.3.6	MP.4.1
4	7.SP.3.7a	MP.4.1
5*	7.G.1.1	MP.7.1
6*	7.G.1.3	MP.7.1
7*	7.RP.1.2c	MP.4.1
8	7.SP.3.7a	MP.4.1
9	7.SP.3.8c	MP.4.1

* Item integrates mixed review concepts from previous modules or a previous course.

Study Guide Review

Vocabulary Development

Integrating Language Arts

Encourage students to practice using the unit vocabulary as they talk and write about mathematics. Understanding vocabulary will aid their understanding of the concepts.

FL CC LACC.68.RST.2.4 Determine the meaning of symbols, key terms, and other domain-specific words and phrases as they are used in a specific scientific or technical context relevant to grades 6–8 texts and topics.

MODULE 7 Experimental Probability

FL CC 7.SP.3.5, 7.SP.3.6, 7.SP.3.7a, 7.SP.3.7b, 7.SP.3.8, 7.SP.3.8a, 7.SP.3.8b, 7.SP.3.8c

Key Concepts
- The probability of an event, or $\frac{\text{number of favorable outcomes}}{\text{total number of possible outcomes}}$, measures the likelihood that the event will occur. *(Lesson 7.1)*
- The probability of an event can be from 0 to 1, inclusive. *(Lesson 7.1)*
- The experimental probability of an event can be found by comparing the number of times an event occurs to the total number of trials. *(Lesson 7.2)*
- A compound event is an event that includes two or more simple events. *(Lesson 7.3)*
- Proportions and equations can be used to make predictions. *(Lesson 7.4)*

MODULE 8 Theoretical Probability and Simulations

FL CC 7.SP.3.6, 7.SP.3.7, 7.SP.3.7a, 7.SP.3.8, 7.SP.3.8a, 7.SP.3.8b, 7.SP.3.8c

Key Concepts
- Theoretical probability is the probability that an event occurs when all the outcomes of the experiment are equally likely. *(Lesson 8.1)*
- To find the theoretical probability, compare the number of ways the event can occur to the total number of equally likely outcomes. *(Lesson 8.1)*
- A tree diagram can be used to calculate the theoretical probability of a compound event. *(Lesson 8.2)*
- The event with the higher probability, experimental or theoretical, is more likely to occur. *(Lesson 8.3)*
- Calculators and computers can generate random numbers that can be used to simulate simple or compound events. *(Lesson 8.4)*

UNIT 4

Study Guide Review

MODULE 7 — Experimental Probability

? ESSENTIAL QUESTION

How can you use experimental probability to solve real-world problems?

EXAMPLE 1

What is the probability of picking a red marble from a jar with 5 green marbles and 2 red marbles?

$P(\text{picking a red marble}) = \dfrac{\text{number of red marbles}}{\text{number of total marbles}}$

$= \dfrac{2}{7}$ There are 2 red marbles.
The total number of marbles is $2 + 5 = 7$.

EXAMPLE 2

For one month, a doctor recorded information about new patients as shown in the table.

	Senior	Adult	Young adult	Child
Female	5	8	2	14
Male	3	10	1	17

What is the experimental probability that his next new patient is a female adult?

$P\left(\begin{array}{c}\text{new patient is a}\\\text{female adult}\end{array}\right) = \dfrac{\text{number of female adults}}{\text{total number of patients}}$

$P = \dfrac{8}{60} = \dfrac{2}{15}$

What is the experimental probability that his next new patient is a child?

$P\left(\begin{array}{c}\text{new patient is}\\\text{a child}\end{array}\right) = \dfrac{\text{number of children}}{\text{total number of patients}}$

$P = \dfrac{31}{60}$

Key Vocabulary

complement *(complemento)*
compound event *(suceso compuesto)*
event *(suceso)*
experiment *(experimento)*
experimental probability *(probabilidad experimental)*
outcome *(resultado)*
probability *(probabilidad)*
sample space *(espacio muestral)*
simple event *(suceso simple)*
simulation *(simulación)*
trial *(prueba)*

EXERCISES

Find the probability of each event. (Lesson 7.1)

1. Rolling a 5 on a fair number cube.

$P = \dfrac{1}{6}$

2. Picking a 7 from a standard deck of 52 cards. A standard deck includes 4 cards of each number from 2 to 10.

$P = \dfrac{4}{52} = \dfrac{1}{13}$

3. Picking a blue marble from a bag of 4 red marbles, 6 blue marbles, and 1 white marble.

$P = \dfrac{6}{11}$

4. Rolling a number greater than 7 on a 12-sided number cube.

$P = \dfrac{5}{12}$

---

5. Christopher picked coins randomly from his piggy bank and got the numbers of coins shown in the table. Find each experimental probability. (Lessons 7.2, 7.3)

Penny	Nickel	Dime	Quarter
7	2	8	6

a. The next coin that Christopher picks is a quarter. $\dfrac{6}{23}$

b. The next coin that Christopher picks is not a quarter. $\dfrac{17}{23}$

c. The next coin that Christopher picks is a penny or a nickel. $\dfrac{9}{23}$

6. A grocery store manager found that 54% of customers usually bring their own bags. In one afternoon, 82 out of 124 customers brought their own grocery bags. Did a greater or lesser number of people than usual bring their own bags? (Lesson 7.4)

$\dfrac{54}{100} < \dfrac{82}{124}$; more customers than usual brought their own bags.

MODULE 8 — Theoretical Probability

Key Vocabulary
theoretical probability *(probabilidad teórica)*

? ESSENTIAL QUESTION

How can you use theoretical probability to solve real-world problems?

EXAMPLE 1

A. Lola rolls two fair number cubes. What is the probability that the two numbers Lola rolls include at least one 4 and have a product of at least 16?

There are 5 pairs of numbers that include a 4 and have a product of at least 16:

(4, 4), (4, 5), (4, 6), (5, 4), (6, 4)

Find the probability.

$P = \dfrac{\text{number of possible ways}}{\text{total number of possible outcomes}} = \dfrac{5}{36}$

	1	2	3	4	5	6
1	1	2	3	4	5	6
2	2	4	6	8	10	12
3	3	6	9	12	15	18
4	4	8	12	16	20	24
5	5	10	15	20	25	30
6	6	12	18	24	30	36

B. Suppose Lola rolls the two number cubes 180 times. Predict how many times she will roll two numbers that include a pair of numbers like the ones described above.

One way to answer is to write and solve an equation.

$\dfrac{5}{36} \times 180 = x$ Multiply the probability by the total number of rolls.

$25 = x$ Solve for x.

Lola can expect to roll two numbers that include at least one 4 and have a product of 16 or more about 25 times.

Unit 4 Performance Tasks

The Performance Tasks provide students with the opportunity to apply concepts from this unit in real-world problem situations.

CAREERS IN MATH

Meteorologist In Performance Task Item 1, students can see how a meteorologist uses mathematics on the job.

SCORING GUIDES FOR PERFORMANCE TASKS

1. MATHEMATICAL PRACTICES 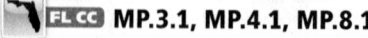 **MP.3.1, MP.4.1, MP.8.1**

Task	Possible Points (Total: 6)
a	**1 point** for correct answer: the third night **1 point** for noting that a probability of 75% means that it is likely to rain.
b	**1 point** for correct answer: Tara should go camping. **3 points** for explanation that shows a calculation of the probability of rain all three nights: $(0.2)(0.2)(0.75) = 0.03$, noting that the probability, 0.03, is very low.

2. MATHEMATICAL PRACTICES 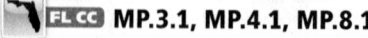 **MP.2.1, MP.6.1, MP.7.1**

Task	Possible Points (Total: 6)
a	**2 points** for the correct answer: $6 \div 50 = 0.12$
b	**1 point** for correct answer: no **1 point** for correct explanation: Not enough information is given to determine exactly how many times the coins showed no heads.
c	**1 point** for correct answer: 15 times **1 point** for correct work, for example solving the proportion $\frac{6}{50} = \frac{x}{125}$

EXAMPLE 2

A store has a sale bin of soup cans. There are 6 cans of chicken noodle soup, 8 cans of split pea soup, 8 cans of minestrone, and 13 cans of vegetable soup. Find the probability of picking each type of soup at random. Then predict what kind of soup a customer is most likely to pick.

$P(\text{chicken noodle}) = \frac{6}{35}$ $\qquad$ $P(\text{split pea}) = \frac{8}{35}$

$P(\text{minestrone}) = \frac{8}{35}$ $\qquad$ $P(\text{vegetable}) = \frac{13}{35}$

The customer is most likely to pick vegetable soup. That is the event that has the greatest probability.

EXERCISES

Find the probability of each event. (Lessons 8.1, 8.2)

1. Graciela picks a white mouse at random from a bin of 8 white mice, 2 gray mice, and 2 brown mice.
$$P = \frac{8}{12} = \frac{2}{3}$$

2. Theo spins a spinner that has 12 equal sections marked 1 through 12. It does **not** land on 1.
$$P = \frac{11}{12}$$

3. Tania flips a coin three times. The coin lands on heads twice and on tails once, not necessarily in that order.
$$P = \frac{3}{8}$$

4. Students are randomly assigned two-digit codes. Each digit is either 1, 2, 3, or 4. Guy is given the number 11.
$$P = \frac{1}{16}$$

5. Patty tosses a coin and rolls a number cube. (Lesson 8.3)

a. Find the probability that the coin lands on heads and the cube lands on an even number.
$$P = \frac{1}{4}$$

b. Patty tosses the coin and rolls the number cube 60 times. Predict how many times the coin will land on heads and the cube will land on an even number.

15 times

6. Rajan's school is having a raffle. The school sold raffle tickets with 3-digit numbers. Each digit is either 1, 2, or 3. The school also sold 2 tickets with the number 000. Which number is more likely to be picked, 123 or 000? (Lesson 8.3)

000

---

7. Suppose you know that over the last 10 years, the probability that your town would have at least one major storm was 40%. Describe a simulation that you could use to find the experimental probability that your town will have at least one major storm in at least 3 of the next 5 years. (Lesson 8.4)

Sample answer: Use whole numbers from 1 to 5. Let 1 and 2 represent a year with a major storm and 3, 4, and 5 represent a year without a major storm. Perform 10 trials by randomly generating 10 sets of 5 numbers. Count the sets that model 3 or more storms and divide by 10.

Unit 4 Performance Tasks

1. CAREERS IN MATH | Meteorologist A meteorologist predicts a 20% chance of rain for the next two nights, and a 75% chance of rain on the third night.

a. On which night is it most likely to rain? On that night, is it *likely* to rain or *unlikely* to rain?

the third night; likely

b. Tara would like to go camping for the next 3 nights, but will not go if it is likely to rain on all 3 nights. Should she go? Use probability to justify your answer.

Yes; the probability of its raining on all 3 nights is $0.2 \cdot 0.2 \cdot 0.75 =$ 0.03, or only a 3% chance. It is very unlikely to rain on all 3 nights.

2. Sinead tossed 4 coins at the same time. She did this 50 times, and 6 of those times, all 4 coins showed the same result (heads or tails).

a. Find the experimental probability that all 4 coins show the same result when tossed.

0.12

b. Can you determine the experimental probability that **no** coin shows heads? Explain.

No; we aren't told how many times all tails came up.

c. Suppose Sinead tosses the coins 125 more times. Use experimental probability to predict the number of times that all 4 coins will show heads or tails. Show your work.

$125 \cdot 0.12 = 15$ times

MIXED REVIEW
PARCC Assessment Readiness

Assessment Readiness Tip Students should underline or highlight the word "not" when it appears in a problem.

> **Item 2** The problem statement is relatively lengthy, which may cause students to scan it for important information rather than reading carefully. Missing the word "not" would cause students to select the wrong answer.

Avoid Common Errors

> **Item 7** Some students may choose answer choice B because, with two coins together, there are four sides in all. Remind students to think about possible outcomes carefully, listing them whenever possible. Here, listing outcomes would show that half of the outcomes have exactly one coin land tails up.

> **Item 12** If students do not read carefully, they may count the number 5 as part of the positive outcomes. Remind them the phrase "less than 5" means that 5 itself is not included in the set.

 Florida Common Core Standards

Items	Grade 7 Standards	Mathematical Practices
1	7.SP.3.8b	MP.4.1
2	7.SP.3.7	MP.4.1
3	7.SP.3.7	MP.1.1
4	7.SP.3.6	MP.4.1
5*	7.G.2.5	MP.6.1
6	7.SP.3.6	MP.4.1
7	7.SP.3.8	MP.2.1
8*	7.EE.2.4	MP.4.1
9	7.SP.3.6	MP.2.1
10	7.SP.3.7a	MP.2.1
11	7.SP.3.8	MP.1.1
12	7.SP.3.7	MP.2.1
13	7.SP.3.6	MP.2.1
14	7.SP.3.7a	MP.2.1
15	7.SP.3.7a, 7.SP.3.7b	MP.1.1
16	7.SP.3.8a, 7.SP.3.8b	MP.4.1, MP.1.1

* Item integrates mixed review concepts from previous modules or a previous course.

Personal Math Trainer

Online Assessment and Intervention

my.hrw.com

Selected Response

1. A pizza parlor offers thin, thick, and traditional style pizza crusts. You can get pepperoni, beef, mushrooms, olives, or peppers for toppings. You order a one-topping pizza. How many outcomes are in the sample space?

Ⓐ 3 Ⓒ 8
Ⓑ 5 Ⓓ 15

2. A bag contains 9 purple marbles, 2 blue marbles, and 4 pink marbles. The probability of randomly drawing a blue marble is $\frac{2}{15}$. What is the probability of **not** drawing a blue marble?

Ⓐ $\frac{2}{15}$ Ⓒ $\frac{11}{15}$
Ⓑ $\frac{4}{15}$ Ⓓ $\frac{13}{15}$

3. During the month of April, Dora kept track of the bugs she saw in her garden. She saw a ladybug on 23 days of the month. What is the experimental probability that she will see a ladybug on May 1?

Ⓐ $\frac{1}{23}$ Ⓒ $\frac{1}{2}$
Ⓑ $\frac{7}{30}$ Ⓓ $\frac{23}{30}$

4. Ryan flips a coin 8 times and gets tails all 8 times. What is the experimental probability that Ryan will get heads the next time he flips the coin?

Ⓐ 1 Ⓒ $\frac{1}{8}$
Ⓑ $\frac{1}{2}$ Ⓓ 0

5. Angle D is a vertical angle to $\angle F$. The measure of $\angle D$ is 53°. What is the measure of $\angle F$?

Ⓐ 3° Ⓒ 43°
Ⓑ 37° Ⓓ 53°

6. Jay tossed two coins several times and then recorded the results in the table below.

Coin Toss Results				
Toss 1	Toss 2	Toss 3	Toss 4	Toss 5
H; H	H; T	T; H	T; T	T; H

What is the experimental probability that the coins will land on different sides on his next toss?

Ⓐ $\frac{1}{5}$ Ⓒ $\frac{3}{5}$
Ⓑ $\frac{2}{5}$ Ⓓ $\frac{4}{5}$

7. What is the probability of tossing two fair coins and having exactly one land tails side up?

Ⓐ $\frac{1}{8}$ Ⓒ $\frac{1}{3}$
Ⓑ $\frac{1}{4}$ Ⓓ $\frac{1}{2}$

8. Which inequality can be used to find how many $0.35 pencils can be purchased for $5.00?

Ⓐ $0.35p \geq 5$ Ⓒ $5p \geq 0.25$
Ⓑ $0.35p \leq 5$ Ⓓ $5p \leq 0.35$

9. A bag contains 6 white beads and 4 black beads. You pick out a bead, record its color, and put the bead back in the bag. You repeat this process 35 times. Which is the best prediction of how many times you would expect to remove a white bead from the bag?

Ⓐ 6 Ⓒ 18
Ⓑ 10 Ⓓ 21

10. A set of cards includes 20 yellow cards, 16 green cards, and 24 blue cards. What is the probability that a blue card is chosen at random?

Ⓐ 0.04 Ⓒ 0.4
Ⓑ 0.24 Ⓓ 0.66

11. Jason, Erik, and Jamie are friends in art class. The teacher randomly chooses 2 of the 21 students in the class to work together on a project. What is the probability that two of these three friends will be chosen?

Ⓐ $\frac{1}{105}$
Ⓑ $\frac{1}{70}$
Ⓒ $\frac{34}{140}$
Ⓓ $\frac{4}{50}$

12. Philip rolls a number cube 12 times. Which is the best prediction for the number of times that he will roll a number that is odd and less than 5?

Ⓐ 2 Ⓒ 4
Ⓑ 3 Ⓓ 6

Hot Tip!

Estimate your answer before solving the problem. Use your estimate to check the reasonableness of your answer.

13. A survey reveals that one airline's flights have a 92% probability of being on time. Based on this, out of 4000 flights in a year, how many flights would you predict will arrive on time?

Ⓐ 368 Ⓒ 3,680
Ⓑ 386 Ⓓ 3,860

14. Matt's house number is a two-digit number. Neither of the digits is 0 and the house number is even. What is the probability that Matt's house number is 18?

Ⓐ $\frac{1}{45}$ Ⓒ $\frac{1}{18}$
Ⓑ $\frac{1}{36}$ Ⓓ $\frac{1}{16}$

Mini-Tasks

15. Laura picked a crayon randomly from a box, recorded the color, and then placed it back in the box. She repeated the process and recorded the results in the table.

Red	Blue	Yellow	Green
5	6	7	2

Find each experimental probability. Write your answers in simplest form.

a. The next crayon Laura picks is red.

$\frac{1}{4}$

b. The next crayon Laura picks is **not** red.

$\frac{3}{4}$

16. For breakfast, Trevor has a choice of 3 types of bagels (plain, sesame, or multigrain), 2 types of eggs (scrambled or poached), and 2 juices (orange or apple).

a. Use the space below to make a tree diagram to find the sample space.

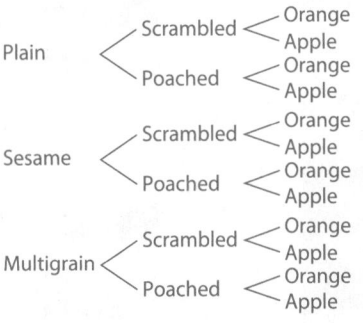

b. If he chooses at random, what is the probability that Trevor eats a breakfast that has orange juice?

$\frac{1}{2}$

UNIT 5

COMMON CORE

Real Numbers, Exponents, and Scientific Notation

Contents

Unit Pacing Guide

45-Minute Classes

Module 9

DAY 1	DAY 2	DAY 3	DAY 4	DAY 5
Lesson 9.1	Lesson 9.1	Lesson 9.2	Lesson 9.3	Ready to Go On? PARCC Assessment Readiness

Module 10

DAY 1	DAY 2	DAY 3	DAY 4	DAY 5
Lesson 10.1	Lesson 10.2	Lesson 10.3	Lesson 10.4	Ready to Go On? PARCC Assessment Readiness

DAY 6				
Study Guide PARCC Assessment Readiness				

90-Minute Classes

Module 9

DAY 1	DAY 2
Lesson 9.1 Lesson 9.2	Lesson 9.3 Ready to Go On? PARCC Assessment Readiness

Module 10

DAY 1	DAY 2	DAY 3	
Lesson 10.1 Lesson 10.2	Lesson 10.3 Lesson 10.4	Ready to Go On? PARCC Assessment Readiness	Study Guide PARCC Assessment Readiness

Program Resources

⏻ Plan

Online Teacher Edition

Access a full suite of teaching resources online—plan, present, and manage classes, assignments, and activities.

 **ePlanner** Easily plan your classes, create and view assignments, and access all program resources with your online, customizable planning tool.

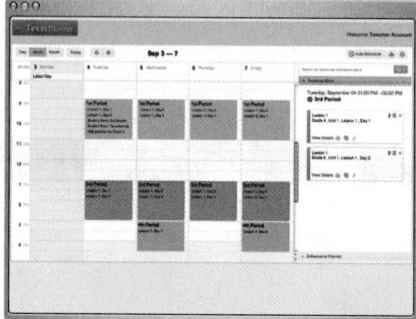

Professional Development Videos

Author Juli Dixon models successful teaching practices and strategies in actual classroom settings.

 **QR Codes** Scan with your smart phone to jump directly from your print book to online videos and other resources.

Teacher's Edition

Support students with point-of-use Questioning Strategies, teaching tips, resources for differentiated instruction, additional activities, and more.

⏻ Engage and Explore

 **Real-World Videos Engage** students with interesting and relevant applications of the mathematical content of each module.

 **Animated Math** Online interactive simulations, tools, and games help students actively learn and practice key concepts.

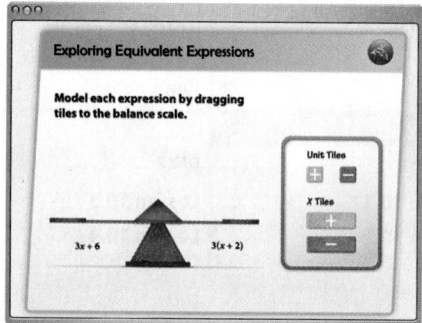

Explore Activities

Students interactively explore new concepts using a variety of tools and approaches.

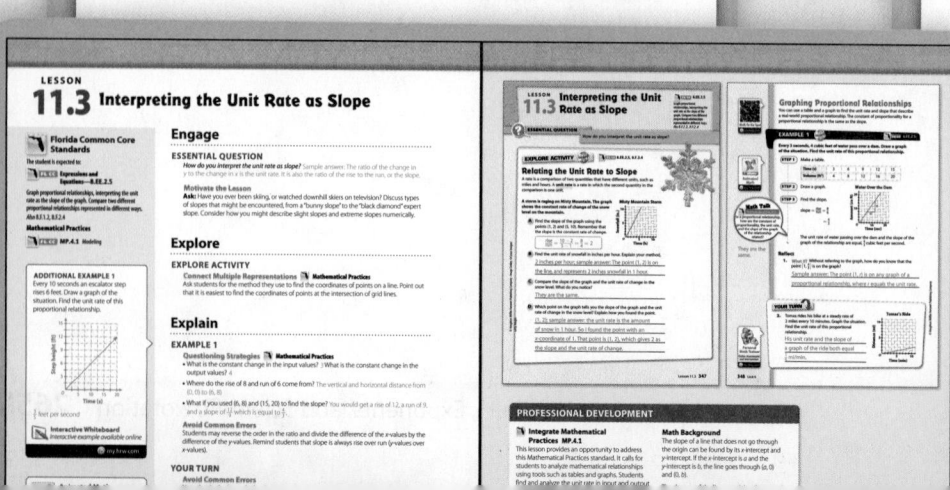

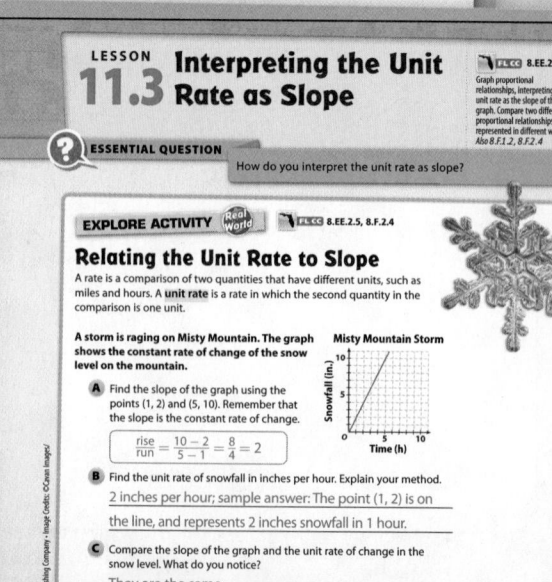

LESSON 11.3 Interpreting the Unit Rate as Slope

FL.C 8.EE.2.5
Graph proportional relationships, interpreting the unit rate as the slope of the graph. Compare two different proportional relationships represented in different ways. Also 8.F.1.2, 8.F.2.4

ESSENTIAL QUESTION How do you interpret the unit rate as slope?

EXPLORE ACTIVITY Real World   FL.C 8.EE.2.5, 8.F.2.4

Relating the Unit Rate to Slope

A rate is a comparison of two quantities that have different units, such as miles and hours. A **unit rate** is a rate in which the second quantity in the comparison is one unit.

A storm is raging on Misty Mountain. The graph shows the constant rate of change of the snow level on the mountain.

A Find the slope of the graph using the points (1, 2) and (5, 10). Remember that the slope is the constant rate of change.

$$\frac{\text{rise}}{\text{run}} = \frac{10-2}{5-1} = \frac{8}{4} = 2$$

B Find the unit rate of snowfall in inches per hour. Explain your method.

2 inches per hour; sample answer: The point (1, 2) is on the line, and represents 2 inches snowfall in 1 hour.

C Compare the slope of the graph and the unit rate of change in the snow level. What do you notice?

They are the same.

D Which point on the graph tells you the slope of the graph and the unit

Response to
Intervention

Teach

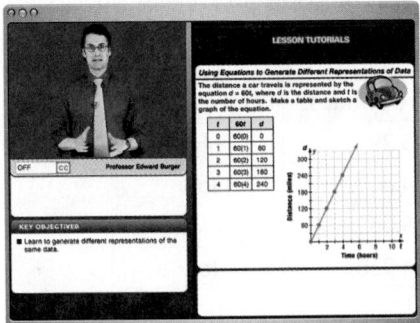

Math On the Spot video tutorials, featuring program authors Dr. Edward Burger and Martha Sandoval-Martinez, accompany every example in the textbook and give students step-by-step instructions and explanations of key math concepts.

Present engaging content on a multitude of devices, including tablets and interactive whiteboards.

Continually monitor and assess student progress with integrated formative assessment.

CLUSTER CONNECTION Look for exercises indicated with this icon to build connections among standards within Florida Common Core clusters.

Differentiated Instruction Print Resources

Support all learners with Differentiated Instruction Resources, including

- **Leveled Practice and Problem Solving**
- **Reteach**
- **Reading Strategies**
- **Success for English Learners**
- **Challenge**

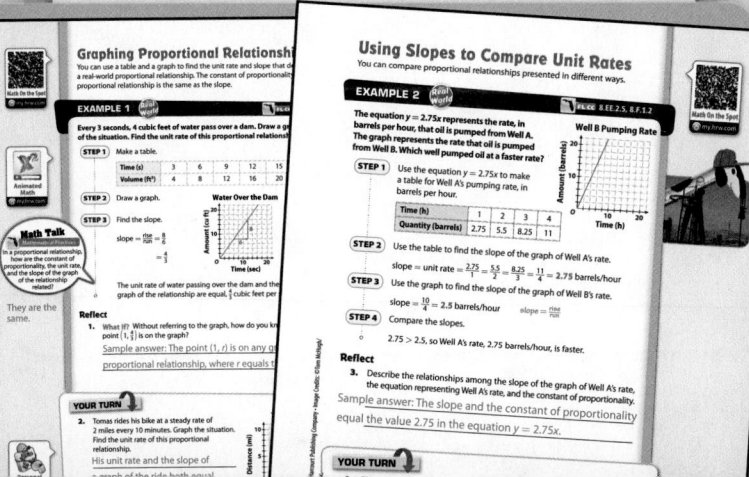

Assessment and Intervention

The **Personal Math Trainer** provides online practice, homework, assessments, and intervention. Monitor student progress through reports and alerts. Create and customize assignments aligned to specific lessons or standards.

- **Practice** – With dynamic items and assignments, students get unlimited practice on key concepts supported by guided examples, step-by-step solutions, and video tutorials.
- **Assessments** – Choose from course assignments or customize your own based on course content, standards, difficulty levels, and more.
- **Homework** – Students can complete online homework with a wide variety of problem types, including the ability to enter expressions, equations, and graphs. Let the system automatically grade homework, so you can focus where your students need help the most!
- **Intervention** – Let the Personal Math Trainer automatically prescribe a targeted, personalized intervention path for your students.

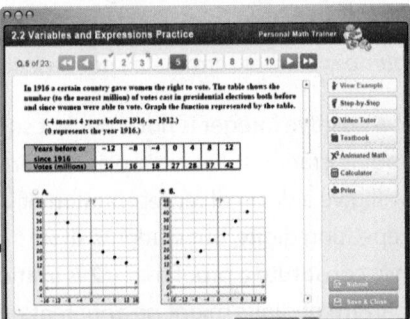

Raise the bar with homework and practice that incorporates higher-order thinking and mathematical processes in every lesson.

PARCC Assessment Readiness
Prepare students for success on the PARCC math test with practice at every module and unit.

Assessment Resources

Tailor assessments to meet the needs of all your classes and students, including

- **Leveled Module Quizzes**
- **Leveled Unit Tests**
- **Unit Performance Tasks**
- **Placement, Diagnostic, and Quarterly Benchmark Tests**

Real Numbers, Exponents, and Scientific Notation **265D**

Math Background

Rational and Irrational Numbers

8.NS.1.1, 8.NS.1.2, 8.EE.1.2

LESSON 9.1

Given a square with side length x, the area of the square is x^2. Given a square with area a, the side length of the square is a *square root* of a. For $a > 0$, if x is a solution of $x^2 = a$, then x is a square root of a. Note that this equation has two solutions that are opposites of each other. For example, $x^2 = 121$ has the solutions 11 and -11. The radical symbol $\sqrt{}$ is used to represent the nonnegative, or principal, square root. Thus, the solutions of $x^2 = a$ are $\sqrt{a}$ and $-\sqrt{a}$.

If $a > 0$, then $\sqrt{a^2} = a$. If $a < 0$, then $\sqrt{a^2} = -a$ because the principal square root must be nonnegative. In general, $\sqrt{a^2} = |a|$.

Working with square roots gives students exposure to irrational numbers. The decimal form of an *irrational number* neither terminates nor repeats.

If a positive integer is not a perfect square, then its square root is irrational. For example, $\sqrt{2}$ is irrational. A calculator will give a decimal representation of $\sqrt{2}$ that exhibits no repeating digits, but students should realize that this does not constitute a proof that $\sqrt{2}$ is irrational. (A repeating pattern of digits might be apparent only after the fiftieth decimal place!) The essential idea for students at this level is that there are vast quantities of irrational numbers and that they will encounter specific examples, like π and e, throughout their study of mathematics.

In some problem-solving situations, it is helpful to be able to estimate the value of a square root. The first step uses logical reasoning. Notice that $\sqrt{5}$ is between $\sqrt{4} = 2$ and $\sqrt{9} = 3$. A reasonable rough estimate might be 2.2 or 2.3 since $\sqrt{5}$ should be closer to 2 than 3.

Then you can use a guess-and-check method. Make a guess, square the guess, and compare it to 5. Revise your guess and repeat, as shown.

Guess	Square of Guess	High or Low?
2.3	5.29	high
2.2	4.84	low
2.25	5.0625	high
2.22	4.9284	low

Because this method uses squaring, it uses the definition of square root, which can reinforce the concept of square roots.

Some students find generating examples of irrational numbers interesting. One way to find a nonrepeating, nonterminating decimals is to place several zeros after the decimal point, then replace the first, fourth, ninth, and sixteenth places and all other places that are perfect squares:

$$0.100100001000001000000001000....$$

Variations of non repeating patterns like this are limitless.

Scientific Notation 8.EE.1.3, 8.EE.1.4
LESSONS 10.2 to 10.4

Scientific notation is an efficient way to write very large and very small numbers. The distance from Earth to the sun is approximately 93 million miles or 93,000,000 miles. The key step in the translation to scientific notation is to recognize that

$$93,000,000 = 9.3 \times 10,000,000$$

and to see that 10,000,000 is a power of 10, namely 10^7. Thus, $93,000,000 = 9.3 \times 10^7$.

In general, every positive real number may be written in scientific notation as $a \times 10^n$, where $1 \leq a < 10$ and n is an integer. The value of a is called the *coefficient*.

Numbers greater than or equal to 1 but less than 10 are written in scientific notation with an exponent of 0. For example,

$$3.8 = 3.8 \times 1 = 3.8 \times 10^0.$$

Numbers greater than 0 but less than 1 are written with negative exponents. Again, a specific example shows why this makes sense:

$$0.0041 = 4.1 \times 0.001 = 4.1 \times \frac{1}{1000} = 4.1 \times 10^{-3}.$$

Changing the sign of the coefficient changes a positive number to its opposite. Thus, any negative real number may be written in scientific notation.

Another advantage of using scientific notation is clearly indicating the precision of a measurement by the number of significant figures (also called significant digits). If you see the measurement 4,000 m, it is unclear whether the trailing zeros are significant. Writing this value in scientific notation alleviates this uncertainty.

Writing 4,000 as 4.000×10^3 m shows that this measurement has four significant digits. If the measurement only has two significant digits, it will be written as 4.0×10^3 m.

Scientific notation is also useful is when doing order-of-magnitude calculations. Suppose you would like to know approximately how long it takes for light to travel from the Sun to Earth. Light travels at 3.0×10^8 m/s, and the distance from the Sun to Earth is about 1.5×10^{11} m. To find the time it takes light to travel that distance, divide the distance by the speed of light.

$$\frac{1.5 \times 10^{11} \text{ m}}{3.0 \times 10^8 \text{ m/s}}$$

First divide the coefficients: $1.5 \div 3.0 = 0.5$

Next, use the properties of exponents:

$$\frac{a^m}{a^n} = a^{m-n} \rightarrow \frac{10^{11}}{10^8} - 10^{11-8} = 10^3$$

$\frac{1.5 \times 10^{11} \text{ m}}{3.0 \times 10^8 \text{ m/s}} = 0.5 \times 10^3$, so it takes about 500 seconds (a little over 8 minutes) for light to travel from the Sun to Earth.

Engineering notation is similar to scientific notation, except the powers of 10 are in multiples of 3. Often, engineers use prefixes instead of powers of 10. For example, one may refer to 1,000 meters as a kilometer. A partial list of prefixes is shown in the table.

Prefix	Symbol	Power
exa	E	10^{18}
peta	P	10^{15}
tera	T	10^{12}
giga	G	10^9
mega	M	10^6
kilo	k	10^3
milli	m	10^{-3}
micro	μ	10^{-6}
nano	n	10^{-9}
pico	p	10^{-12}
femto	f	10^{-15}
atto	a	10^{-18}

Real Numbers, Exponents, and Scientific Notation

MODULE 9

Real Numbers

FL CC 8.NS.1.1, 8.NS.1.2, 8.EE.1.2

MODULE 10

Exponents and Scientific Notation

FL CC 8.EE.1.1, 8.EE.1.3, 8.EE.1.4

CAREERS IN MATH

Astronomer An astronomer is a scientist who studies and tries to interpret the universe beyond Earth. Astronomers use math to calculate distances to celestial objects and to create mathematical models to help them understand the dynamics of systems from stars and planets to black holes. If you are interested in a career as an astronomer, you should study the following mathematical subjects:

- Algebra
- Geometry
- Trigonometry
- Calculus

Research other careers that require creating mathematical models to understand physical phenomena.

Unit 5 Performance Task

At the end of the unit, check out how **astronomers** use math.

© Houghton Mifflin Harcourt Publishing Company • Image Credits: Larry Landolfi/Getty Images

Careers in Math

Astronomer

Astronomers use math to understand and predict the physical properties and motion of objects in space. They also use math as a tool to help them form and test theories about the laws that govern the Universe. You will learn more about this in the Performance Tasks at the end of the unit.

For more information about careers in mathematics as well as various mathematics appreciation topics, visit the American Mathematical Society at www.ams.org

Vocabulary Preview

Use the puzzle to give students a preview of important concepts in this unit. Students may work individually, in pairs, or in groups.

Unit Resources

Go online to access all your unit resources.

my.hrw.com

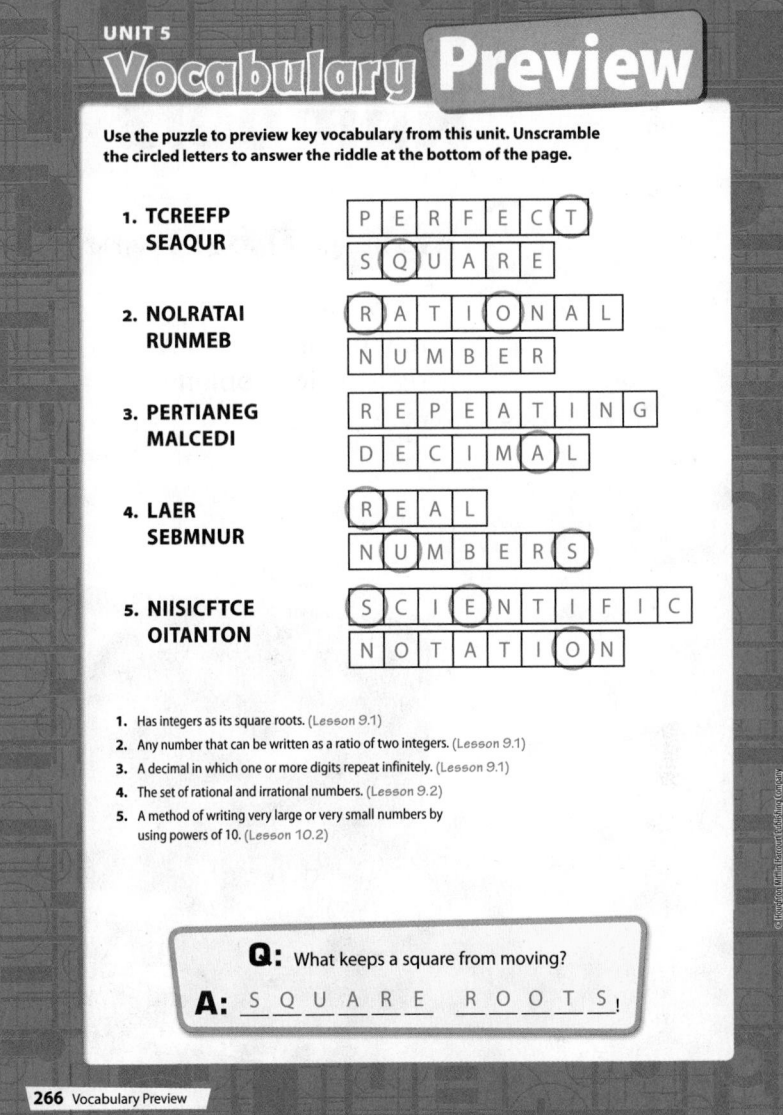

UNIT 5
Vocabulary Preview

Use the puzzle to preview key vocabulary from this unit. Unscramble the circled letters to answer the riddle at the bottom of the page.

1. **TCREEFP SEAQUR**
   P E R F E C T
   S Q U A R E

2. **NOLRATAI RUNMEB**
   R A T I O N A L
   N U M B E R

3. **PERTIANEG MALCEDI**
   R E P E A T I N G
   D E C I M A L

4. **LAER SEBMNUR**
   R E A L
   N U M B E R S

5. **NIISICFTCE OITANTON**
   S C I E N T I F I C
   N O T A T I O N

1. Has integers as its square roots. (Lesson 9.1)
2. Any number that can be written as a ratio of two integers. (Lesson 9.1)
3. A decimal in which one or more digits repeat infinitely. (Lesson 9.1)
4. The set of rational and irrational numbers. (Lesson 9.2)
5. A method of writing very large or very small numbers by using powers of 10. (Lesson 10.2)

Q: What keeps a square from moving?

A: S Q U A R E   R O O T S

Before	In this Unit	After
Students understand: • sets and subsets of rational numbers • operations with rational numbers • exponents	Students will learn about: • relationships between sets of real numbers • irrational numbers including π • ordering irrational and rational numbers • scientific notation • properties of integer exponents • scientific notation • operations with scientific notation	Students will connect: • rational and irrational numbers • irrational numbers and a number line • decimal notation and scientific notation

Real Numbers

ESSENTIAL QUESTION

How can you use real numbers to solve real-world problems?

Since every rational and irrational number is a real number, any real-world problem that can be modeled and solved with rational or irrational numbers can be modeled and solved with real numbers.

Real-World Video

Living creatures can be classified into groups. The sea otter belongs to the kingdom Animalia and class Mammalia. Numbers can also be classified into groups such as rational numbers and integers.

ⓞ my.hrw.com

© Houghton Mifflin Harcourt Publishing Company • Image Credits: ©Daniel Hershman/Getty Images

GO DIGITAL

my.hrw.com

my.hrw.com

Go digital with your write-in student edition, accessible on any device.

Math On the Spot

Scan with your smart phone to jump directly to the online edition, video tutor, and more.

Animated Math

Interactively explore key concepts to see how math works.

Personal Math Trainer

Get immediate feedback and help as you work through practice sets.

Are You Ready?

Assess Readiness

Use the assessment on this page to determine if students need intensive or strategic intervention for the module's prerequisite skills.

Response to Intervention

Personal Math Trainer

Online Assessment and Intervention

⏻ my.hrw.com

Intervention	Enrichment

Access Are You Ready? assessment online, and receive instant scoring, feedback, and customized intervention or enrichment.

Online and Print Resources

Skills Intervention worksheets
- Skill 11 Find the Square of a Number
- Skill 12 Exponents
- Skill 22 Write a Mixed Number as an Improper Fraction

Differentiated Instruction
- Challenge worksheets **PRE-AP**
- Extend the Math **PRE-AP** Lesson Activities in TE

Are YOU Ready?

Complete these exercises to review skills you will need for this module.

Personal Math Trainer

Online Assessment and Intervention

⏻ my.hrw.com

Find the Square of a Number

EXAMPLE Find the square of $\frac{2}{3}$.

$\frac{2}{3} \times \frac{2}{3} = \frac{2 \times 2}{3 \times 3}$ Multiply the number by itself.

$= \frac{4}{9}$ Simplify.

Find the square of each number.

1. 7   49
2. 21   441
3. −3   9
4. $\frac{4}{5}$ $\frac{16}{25}$
5. 2.7   7.29
6. $-\frac{1}{4}$ $\frac{1}{16}$
7. −5.7   32.49
8. $1\frac{2}{5}$ $1\frac{24}{25}$ or 1.96

Exponents

EXAMPLE $5^3 = 5 \times 5 \times 5$ Use the base, 5, as a factor 3 times.

$= 25 \times 5$ Multiply from left to right.

$= 125$

Simplify each exponential expression.

9. 9^2 81
10. 2^4 16
11. $\left(\frac{1}{3}\right)^2$ $\frac{1}{9}$
12. $(-7)^2$ 49
13. 4^3 64
14. $(-1)^5$ −1
15. 4.5^2 20.25
16. 10^5 100,000

Write a Mixed Number as an Improper Fraction

EXAMPLE $2\frac{2}{5} = 2 + \frac{2}{5}$ Write the mixed number as a sum of a whole number and a fraction.

$= \frac{10}{5} + \frac{2}{5}$ Write the whole number as an equivalent fraction with the same denominator as the fraction in the mixed number.

$= \frac{12}{5}$ Add the numerators.

Write each mixed number as an improper fraction.

17. $3\frac{1}{3}$ $\frac{10}{3}$
18. $1\frac{5}{8}$ $\frac{13}{8}$
19. $2\frac{3}{7}$ $\frac{17}{7}$
20. $5\frac{5}{6}$ $\frac{35}{6}$

© Houghton Mifflin Harcourt Publishing Company

PROFESSIONAL DEVELOPMENT VIDEO

Author Juli Dixon models successful teaching practices as she explores the concept of real numbers in an actual eighth-grade classroom.

Professional Development

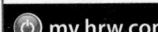 ⏻ my.hrw.com

GO DIGITAL
my.hrw.com

Online Teacher Edition
Access a full suite of teaching resources online—plan, present, and manage classes and assignments.

ePlanner
Easily plan your classes and access all your resources online.

Interactive Answers and Solutions
Customize answer keys to print or display in the classroom. Choose to include answers only or full solutions to all lesson exercises.

Interactive Whiteboards
Engage students with interactive whiteboard-ready lessons and activities.

Personal Math Trainer: Online Assessment and Intervention
Assign automatically graded homework, quizzes, tests, and intervention activities. Prepare your students with updated practice tests aligned with Common Core.

Reading Start-Up

Have students complete the activities on this page by working alone or with others.

Visualize Vocabulary

The summary triangle helps students review the concepts related to integers. Students should write one or more review words to match the examples in each section of the triangle.

Understand Vocabulary

Use the following explanations to help students learn the preview words.

To terminate something means to end it. A **terminating decimal** has an ending, or a limited amount of digits. To repeat something means to do it over again. A **repeating decimal** has one or more digits that repeat and never ends.

Real numbers include **rational numbers** and **irrational numbers.**

Active Reading

Integrating Language Arts
Students can use these reading and note-taking strategies to help them organize and understand new concepts and vocabulary.

FL CC **LACC.68.RST.3.7** Integrate quantitative or technical information expressed in words in a text with a version of that information expressed visually (e.g., in a flowchart, diagram, model, graph, or table).

Additional Resources
Differentiated Instruction
• Reading Strategies **ELL**

Reading Start-Up

Visualize Vocabulary

Use the ✔ words to complete the graphic. You can put more than one word in each section of the triangle.

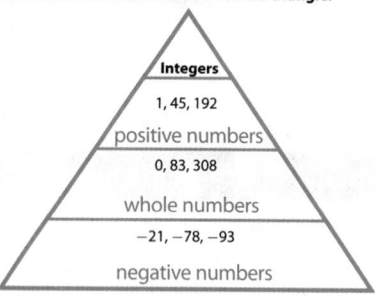

- **Integers** — 1, 45, 192
- positive numbers — 0, 83, 308
- whole numbers — −21, −78, −93
- negative numbers

Understand Vocabulary

Complete the sentences using the preview words.

1. One of the two equal factors of a number is a ___square root___.

2. A ___perfect square___ has integers as its square roots.

3. The ___principal square root___ is the nonnegative square root of a number.

© Houghton Mifflin Harcourt Publishing Company

Vocabulary

Review Words
- integers *(enteros)*
- ✔ negative numbers *(números negativos)*
- ✔ positive numbers *(números positivos)*
- ✔ whole number *(número entero)*

Preview Words
- cube root *(raíz cúbica)*
- irrational numbers *(número irracional)*
- perfect cube *(cubo perfecto)*
- perfect square *(cuadrado perfecto)*
- principal square root *(raíz cuadrada principal)*
- rational number *(número racional)*
- real numbers *(número real)*
- repeating decimal *(decimal periódico)*
- square root *(raíz cuadrada)*
- terminating decimal *(decimal finito)*

Active Reading

Layered Book Before beginning the lessons in this module, create a layered book to help you learn the concepts in this module. Label the flaps "Rational Numbers," "Irrational Numbers," "Square Roots," and "Real Numbers." As you study each lesson, write important ideas such as vocabulary, models, and sample problems under the appropriate flap.

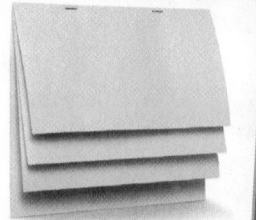

Before	In this module	After
Students understand:	Students will learn how to:	Students will connect that:
• write rational numbers as decimals	• express a rational number as a decimal	• the rational numbers are those with decimal expansions that terminate in 0s or eventually repeat
• describe relationships between sets and subsets of rational numbers	• approximate the value of an irrational number	
• compare rational numbers	• describe the relationship between sets of real numbers	• non-rational numbers are called irrational numbers
	• order a set of real numbers arising from mathematical and real-world contexts	

Unpacking the Standards

Use the examples on the page to help students know exactly what they are expected to learn in this module.

 Florida Common Core Standards

Content Areas

 The Number System—8.NS.1

Know that there are numbers that are not rational, and approximate them by rational numbers.

 **Go online to see a complete unpacking of the Florida Common Core Standards.**

⏻ my.hrw.com

MODULE 9

Unpacking the Standards

Understanding the standards and the vocabulary terms in the standards will help you know exactly what you are expected to learn in this module.

FL CC 8.NS.1.1

Know that numbers that are not rational are called irrational. Understand informally that every number has a decimal expansion; for rational numbers show that the decimal expansion repeats eventually, and convert a decimal expansion which repeats eventually into a rational number.

Key Vocabulary

rational number *(número racional)*
A number that can be expressed as a ratio of two integers.

irrational number *(número irracional)*
A number that cannot be expressed as a ratio of two integers or as a repeating or terminating decimal.

What It Means to You

You will recognize a number as rational or irrational by looking at its fraction or decimal form.

UNPACKING EXAMPLE 8.NS.1.1

Classify each number as rational or irrational.

$0.\overline{3} = \frac{1}{3}$ $\qquad$ $0.25 = \frac{1}{4}$

These numbers are rational because they can be written as ratios of integers or as repeating or terminating decimals.

$\pi \approx 3.141592654\ldots$ $\qquad$ $\sqrt{5} \approx 2.236067978\ldots$

These numbers are irrational because they cannot be written as ratios of integers or as repeating or terminating decimals.

FL CC 8.NS.1.2

Use rational approximations of irrational numbers to compare the size of irrational numbers, locate them approximately on a number line diagram, and estimate the value of expressions (e.g., π^2).

 Visit my.hrw.com to see all Florida Common Core Standards unpacked.

⏻ my.hrw.com

What It Means to You

You will learn to estimate the values of irrational numbers.

UNPACKING EXAMPLE 8.NS.1.2

Estimate the value of $\sqrt{8}$.

8 is not a perfect square. Find the two perfect squares closest to 8.

8 is between the perfect squares 4 and 9.
So $\sqrt{8}$ is between $\sqrt{4}$ and $\sqrt{9}$.
  $\sqrt{8}$ is between 2 and 3.

8 is closer to 9, so $\sqrt{8}$ is closer to 3.
$2.8^2 = 7.84$ $\quad$ $2.9^2 = 8.41$
$\sqrt{8}$ is between 2.8 and 2.9
A good estimate for $\sqrt{8}$ is 2.85.

Florida Common Core Standards	Lesson 9.1	Lesson 9.2	Lesson 9.3
FL CC 8.NS.1.1 Know that numbers that are not rational are called irrational. Understand informally that every number has a decimal expansion; for rational numbers show that the decimal expansion repeats eventually, and convert a decimal expansion which repeats eventually into a rational number.	▨	▨	
FL CC 8.NS.1.2 Use rational approximations of irrational numbers to compare the size of irrational numbers, locate them approximately on a number line diagram, and estimate the value of expressions (e.g., π^2).	▨		▨
FL CC 8.EE.1.2 Use square root and cube root symbols to represent solutions to equations of the form $x^2 = p$ and $x^3 = p$, where p is a positive rational number. Evaluate square roots of small perfect squares and cube roots of small perfect cubes. Know that $\sqrt{2}$ is irrational.	▨		

LESSON
9.1 Rational and Irrational Numbers

 Florida Common Core Standards

The student is expected to:

 FL CC The Number System—8.NS.1.1

Know that numbers that are not rational are called irrational. Understand informally that every number has a decimal expansion; for rational numbers show that the decimal expansion repeats eventually, and convert a decimal expansion which repeats eventually into a rational number.

 FL CC The Number System—8.NS.1.2

Use rational approximations of irrational numbers to compare the size of irrational numbers, locate them approximately on a number line diagram, and estimate the value of expressions (e.g. π^2).

FL CC Expressions and Equations—8.EE.1.2

Use square root and cube root symbols to represent solutions to equations of the form $x^2 = p$ and $x^3 = p$, where p is a positive rational number. Evaluate square roots of small perfect squares and cube roots of small perfect cubes. Know that $\sqrt{2}$ is irrational.

Mathematical Practices

 **FL CC MP.6.1** Precision

ADDITIONAL EXAMPLE 1
Write each fraction as a decimal.

A $\frac{2}{5}$ 0.4   **B** $\frac{5}{9}$ $0.\overline{5}$

 Interactive Whiteboard
Interactive example available online

 my.hrw.com

ADDITIONAL EXAMPLE 2
Write each decimal as a fraction in simplest form.

A 0.355 $\frac{71}{200}$

B $0.\overline{43}$ $\frac{43}{99}$

 Interactive Whiteboard
Interactive example available online

 my.hrw.com

Engage

ESSENTIAL QUESTION

How do you rewrite rational numbers and decimals, take square roots and cube roots, and approximate irrational numbers? To express as a decimal, divide the numerator by the denominator. To take a square root or cube root of a number, find the number that when squared or cubed equals the original number. To approximate an irrational number, estimate a number between two consecutive perfect squares.

Motivate the Lesson
Ask: Which type of rational number do you see more often, fractions or decimals? Which do you prefer to use? Why?

Explore

Have students write examples of ratios, and then share with the class the various notations for ratios that they used (for example 2:5, 2 to 5, $\frac{2}{5}$). Point out the connection between the word *ratio* and the meaning of *rational number*. See also Explore Activity in student text.

Explain

EXAMPLE 1
Questioning Strategies Mathematical Practices
• How does the denominator of a fraction in simplest form tell whether the decimal equivalent of the fraction is a terminating decimal? The decimal will terminate if the denominator is an even number, a multiple of 5, or a multiple of 10.

Avoid Common Errors
To avoid interpreting $\frac{1}{4}$ as 4 divided by 1, tell students to start at the top of the fraction and read the bar as "divided by."

YOUR TURN
Talk About It
Check for Understanding
Ask: Can an improper fraction be written as a decimal? Give an example to support your answer. Yes; $\frac{5}{4} = 1.25$.

EXAMPLE 2
Questioning Strategies  Mathematical Practices
• How can you use place value to write a terminating decimal as a fraction with a power of ten in the denominator? Start by identifying the place value of the decimal's last digit, and then use the corresponding power of 10 as the denominator of the fraction.

• How can you tell if a decimal can be written as a rational number? If the decimal is a terminating or repeating decimal, then it can be written as a rational number.

LESSON 9.1 Rational and Irrational Numbers

FL CC 8.NS.1.1
Know that numbers that are not rational are called irrational. Understand informally that every number has a decimal expansion; ... Also 8.NS.1.2, 8.EE.1.2

? ESSENTIAL QUESTION

How do you rewrite rational numbers and decimals, take square roots and cube roots, and approximate irrational numbers?

Expressing Rational Numbers as Decimals

A **rational number** is any number that can be written as a ratio in the form $\frac{a}{b}$, where a and b are integers and b is not 0. Examples of rational numbers are 6 and 0.5.

6 can be written as $\frac{6}{1}$.   0.5 can be written as $\frac{1}{2}$.

Every rational number can be written as a terminating decimal or a repeating decimal. A **terminating decimal**, such as 0.5, has a finite number of digits. A **repeating decimal** has a block of one or more digits that repeat indefinitely.

EXAMPLE 1   FL CC 8.NS.1.1

Write each fraction as a decimal.

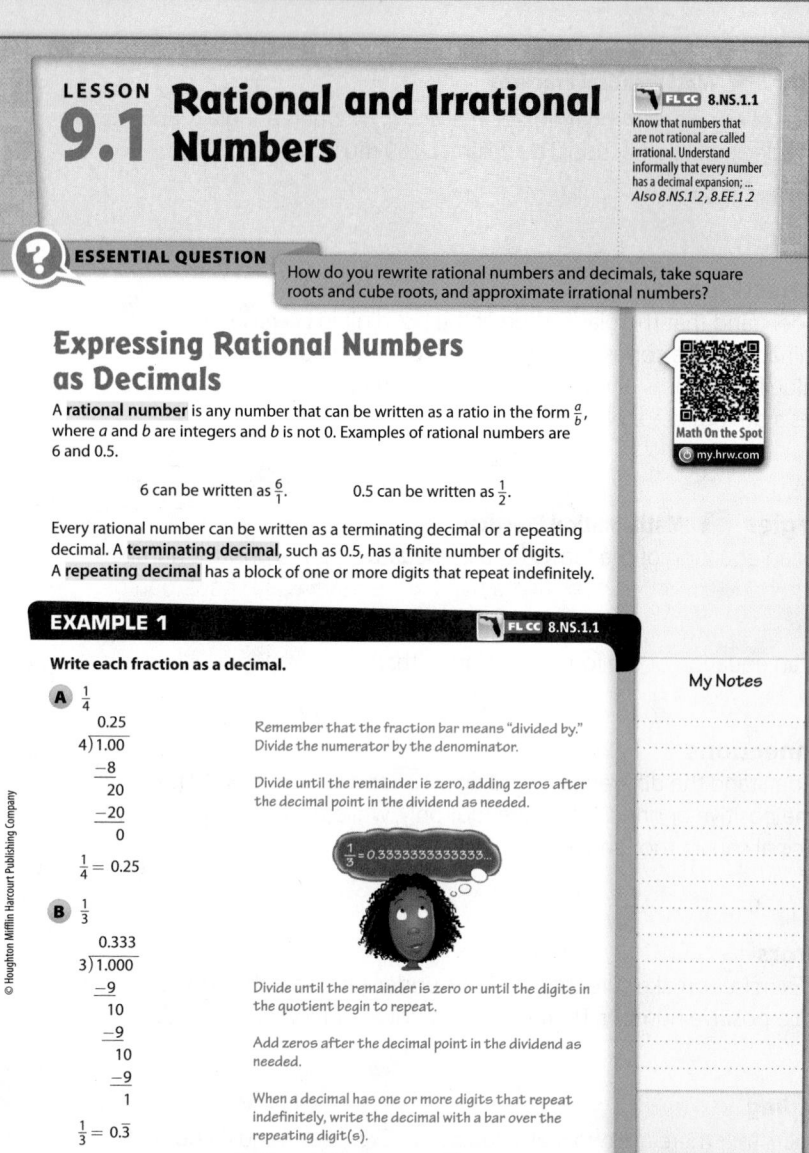

A $\frac{1}{4}$

$$4)\overline{1.00}$$
$$0.25$$
$$\underline{-8}$$
$$20$$
$$\underline{-20}$$
$$0$$

$\frac{1}{4} = 0.25$

Remember that the fraction bar means "divided by." Divide the numerator by the denominator.

Divide until the remainder is zero, adding zeros after the decimal point in the dividend as needed.

$\frac{1}{3} = 0.3333333333333...$

B $\frac{1}{3}$

$$3)\overline{1.000}$$
$$0.333$$
$$\underline{-9}$$
$$10$$
$$\underline{-9}$$
$$10$$
$$\underline{-9}$$
$$1$$

$\frac{1}{3} = 0.\overline{3}$

Divide until the remainder is zero or until the digits in the quotient begin to repeat.

Add zeros after the decimal point in the dividend as needed.

When a decimal has one or more digits that repeat indefinitely, write the decimal with a bar over the repeating digit(s).

Personal Math Trainer
Online Assessment and Intervention
@ my.hrw.com

Math On the Spot
@ my.hrw.com

My Notes

Math On the Spot
@ my.hrw.com

YOUR TURN

Write each fraction as a decimal.

1. $\frac{5}{11}$ $0.\overline{45}$ 2. $\frac{1}{8}$ 0.125 3. $2\frac{1}{3}$ $2.\overline{3}$

Expressing Decimals as Rational Numbers

You can express terminating and repeating decimals as rational numbers.

EXAMPLE 2   FL CC 8.NS.1.1

Write each decimal as a fraction in simplest form.

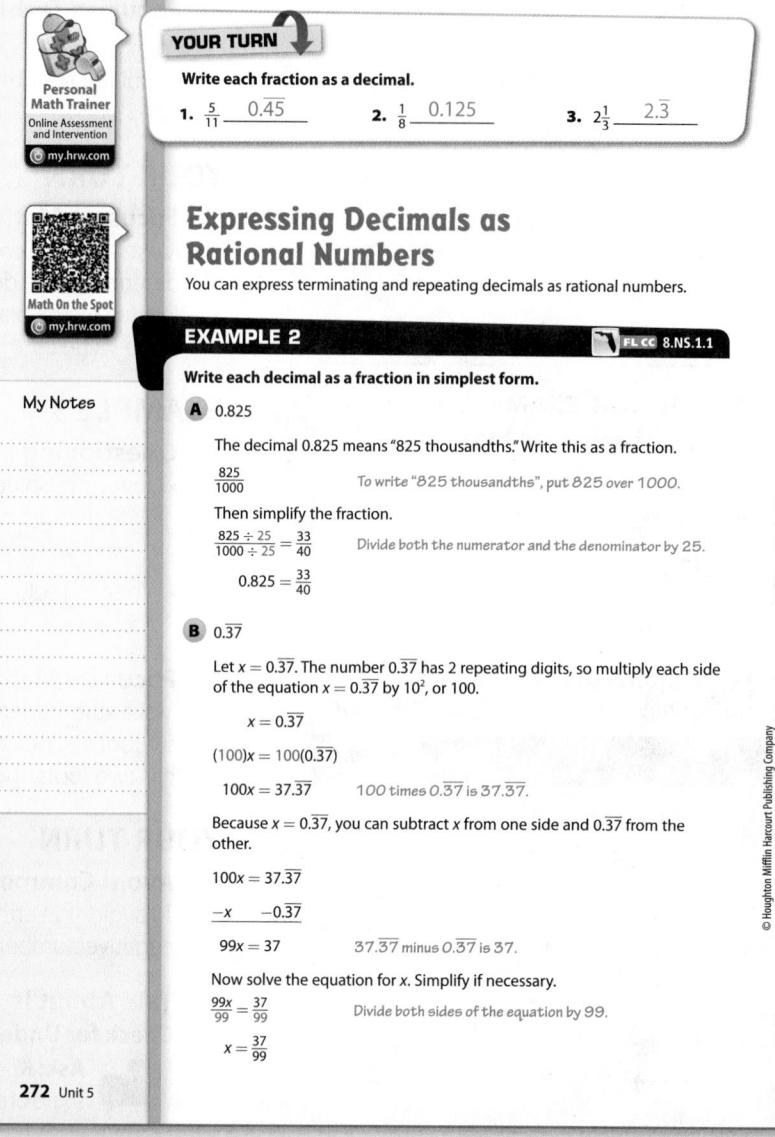

A 0.825

The decimal 0.825 means "825 thousandths." Write this as a fraction.

$\frac{825}{1000}$ To write "825 thousandths", put 825 over 1000.

Then simplify the fraction.

$\frac{825 \div 25}{1000 \div 25} = \frac{33}{40}$ Divide both the numerator and the denominator by 25.

$0.825 = \frac{33}{40}$

B $0.\overline{37}$

Let $x = 0.\overline{37}$. The number $0.\overline{37}$ has 2 repeating digits, so multiply each side of the equation $x = 0.\overline{37}$ by 10^2, or 100.

$x = 0.\overline{37}$

$(100)x = 100(0.\overline{37})$

$100x = 37.\overline{37}$ 100 times $0.\overline{37}$ is $37.\overline{37}$.

Because $x = 0.\overline{37}$, you can subtract x from one side and $0.\overline{37}$ from the other.

$100x = 37.\overline{37}$
$\underline{-x \qquad -0.\overline{37}}$
$99x = 37$ $37.\overline{37}$ minus $0.\overline{37}$ is 37.

Now solve the equation for x. Simplify if necessary.

$\frac{99x}{99} = \frac{37}{99}$ Divide both sides of the equation by 99.

$x = \frac{37}{99}$

My Notes

PROFESSIONAL DEVELOPMENT

Integrate Mathematical Practices MP.6.1

This lesson provides an opportunity to address this Mathematical Practices standard. It calls for students to attend to precision. Students learn to express rational numbers accurately and precisely in both fractional and decimal forms, and learn to translate from one form to the other. They also learn how to precisely represent and communicate ideas about irrational numbers, square roots, and cube roots.

Math Background

Some decimals may have a pattern but still not be a repeating decimal that is rational. For example, in 3.12112111211112…, you can predict the next digit, and describe the pattern. (There is one more 1 each time before the 2.) However, this is not a terminating decimal, nor is it a repeating decimal, and it is therefore NOT a rational number.

YOUR TURN

Focus on Math Connections

Make sure students understand that the place value of the last digit in Exercises 4 and 6 determines the denominator of the corresponding fraction or mixed number. So, for Exercise 4, the place value hundredths gives a denominator of 100, and for Exercise 6, the place value tenths gives a denominator of 10.

ADDITIONAL EXAMPLE 3
Solve each equation for x.

A $x^2 = 324$ $18, -18$

B $x^2 = \frac{25}{144}$ $\frac{5}{12}, -\frac{5}{12}$

C $343 = x^3$ 7

D $x^3 = \frac{125}{512}$ $\frac{5}{8}$

 Interactive Whiteboard
Interactive example available online

🔵 my.hrw.com

EXAMPLE 3

Questioning Strategies  Mathematical Practices

• How can a solution of an equation of the form $x^2 = p$ be negative if p is a positive number? Since the square of a negative number is positive, a negative number is also a solution of x^2 equals a positive number.

• When is a solution of an equation of the form $x^3 = p$ larger than p? The solution is larger than p if p is a number between 0 and 1.

Focus on Math Connections

Make sure students understand the difference in finding $\sqrt{121}$ and solving $x^2 = 121$. The symbol $\sqrt{}$ indicates the positive or principal square root only, while the equation $x^2 = 121$ has two roots, the principal square root and its opposite.

YOUR TURN

Avoid Common Errors

To avoid sign errors in Exercise 9, make sure that students understand that the cube of a negative number is not a positive number. Therefore, -8 is not a solution of $x^3 = 512$.

Talk About It
Check for Understanding

Ask: Kris predicts that there are two real solutions for Exercises 7 and 8 and that there are three real solutions for Exercises 9 and 10. Is his prediction correct? Explain. His prediction is correct for Exercises 7 and 8 because there are two numbers whose squares are the same positive number given in the exercises. His prediction is not correct for Exercises 9 and 10, however, because there is only one real number whose cube is the same positive number given in the exercises.

EXPLORE ACTIVITY

Questioning Strategies  Mathematical Practices

• Compare the values for 13^2 and 1.3^2. The digits are the same, but 1.3^2 has two decimal places (1.69), while 13^2 has none (169).

• How do you know whether $\sqrt{2}$ will be closer to 1 or closer to 2? It will be closer to 1 because 2 is between the perfect squares of 1 and 4, but closer to 1 than it is to 4.

Connect Vocabulary **ELL**

Explain to students that the word *irrational,* when used as an ordinary word in English, means without logic or reason. In mathematics, when we say that a number is irrational it means only that the number cannot be written as the quotient of two integers.

Engage with the Whiteboard

Have students extend the number line in both directions and label the locations of the whole numbers 2 and 3. These are the roots of the consecutive perfect squares 4 and 9 used to estimate $\sqrt{7}$.

Write each decimal as a fraction in simplest form.

4. 0.12 ___ $\frac{3}{25}$ **5.** $0.\overline{57}$ ___ $\frac{19}{33}$ **6.** 1.4 ___ $1\frac{2}{5}$

Personal Math Trainer
Online Assessment and Intervention
my.hrw.com

Finding Square Roots and Cube Roots

The **square root** of a positive number p is x if $x^2 = p$. There are two square roots for every positive number. For example, the square roots of 36 are 6 and −6 because $6^2 = 36$ and $(-6)^2 = 36$. The square roots of $\frac{1}{25}$ are $\frac{1}{5}$ and $-\frac{1}{5}$. You can write the square roots of $\frac{1}{25}$ as $\pm\frac{1}{5}$. The symbol $\sqrt{\ }$ indicates the positive, or **principal square root**.

A number that is a **perfect square** has square roots that are integers. The number 81 is a perfect square because its square roots are 9 and −9.

The **cube root** of a positive number p is x if $x^3 = p$. There is one cube root for every positive number. For example, the cube root of 8 is 2 because $2^3 = 8$. The cube root of $\frac{1}{27}$ is $\frac{1}{3}$ because $\left(\frac{1}{3}\right)^3 = \frac{1}{27}$. The symbol $\sqrt[3]{\ }$ indicates the cube root.

A number that is a **perfect cube** has a cube root that is an integer. The number 125 is a perfect cube because its cube root is 5.

Math On the Spot
my.hrw.com

EXAMPLE 3   FL CC 8.EE.1.2

Solve each equation for x.

A $x^2 = 121$

$x^2 = 121$ Solve for x by taking the square root of both sides.

$x = \pm\sqrt{121}$ Apply the definition of square root.

$x = \pm 11$ Think: What numbers squared equal 121?

The solutions are 11 and −11.

B $x^2 = \frac{16}{169}$

$x^2 = \frac{16}{169}$ Solve for x by taking the square root of both sides.

$x = \pm\sqrt{\frac{16}{169}}$ Apply the definition of square root.

$x = \pm\frac{4}{13}$ Think: What numbers squared equal $\frac{16}{169}$?

The solutions are $\frac{4}{13}$ and $-\frac{4}{13}$.

Math Talk
Mathematical Practices

Can you square an integer and get a negative number? What does this indicate about whether negative numbers have square roots?

No; the square of a positive integer is positive, the square of a negative integer is positive, and the square of 0 is 0. So negative numbers do not have (real) square roots.

Lesson 9.1 **273**

C $729 = x^3$

$\sqrt[3]{729} = \sqrt[3]{x^3}$ Solve for x by taking the cube root of both sides.

$\sqrt[3]{729} = x$ Apply the definition of cube root.

$9 = x$ Think: What number cubed equals 729?

The solution is 9.

D $x^3 = \frac{8}{125}$

$\sqrt[3]{x^3} = \sqrt[3]{\frac{8}{125}}$ Solve for x by taking the cube root of both sides.

$x = \sqrt[3]{\frac{8}{125}}$ Apply the definition of cube root.

$x = \frac{2}{5}$ Think: What number cubed equals $\frac{8}{125}$?

The solution is $\frac{2}{5}$.

Personal Math Trainer
Online Assessment and Intervention
my.hrw.com

Solve each equation for x.

7. $x^2 = 196$ ___ $x = \pm 14$ **8.** $x^2 = \frac{9}{256}$ ___ $x = \pm\frac{3}{16}$

9. $x^3 = 512$ ___ $x = 8$ **10.** $x^3 = \frac{64}{343}$ ___ $x = \frac{4}{7}$

EXPLORE ACTIVITY   FL CC 8.NS.1.2, 8.EE.1.2

Estimating Irrational Numbers

Irrational numbers are numbers that are not rational. In other words, they cannot be written in the form $\frac{a}{b}$, where a and b are integers and b is not 0. Square roots of perfect squares are rational numbers. Square roots of numbers that are not perfect squares are irrational. The number $\sqrt{3}$ is irrational because 3 is not a perfect square of any rational number.

Estimate the value of $\sqrt{2}$.

A Since 2 is not a perfect square, $\sqrt{2}$ is irrational.

B To estimate $\sqrt{2}$, first find two consecutive perfect squares that 2 is between. Complete the inequality by writing these perfect squares in the boxes.

$\boxed{1} < 2 < \boxed{4}$

C Now take the square root of each number.

$\sqrt{\boxed{1}} < \sqrt{2} < \sqrt{\boxed{4}}$

D Simplify the square roots of perfect squares.

$\boxed{1} < \sqrt{2} < \boxed{2}$

$\sqrt{2}$ is between ___ 1 ___ and ___ 2 ___ .

274 Unit 5

DIFFERENTIATE INSTRUCTION

Critical Thinking

In the Explore Activity, students estimated the location of $\sqrt{2}$ on a number line. Ask students whether they think that it is possible to locate more precisely the point that represents $\sqrt{2}$. In other words, can you graph irrational numbers exactly on a number line, along with rational numbers? Students should understand that $\sqrt{2}$ is a real number, and all real numbers can be located on a real number line. A more precise estimate will allow more precise placement on a number line.

The Modeling note tells one way to do this.

Modeling

Have students use a ruler to represent a number line with a unit that is one inch long. Have them draw a square with a side of one inch, and draw the diagonal to make two isosceles triangles. Lead students to understand that the length of the diagonal (or hypotenuse) is $\sqrt{2}$.

Have them copy the length of their diagonal onto their ruler, or number line, starting at zero. The end point of the diagonal represents the exact point for the irrational number $\sqrt{2}$ on a number line.

Additional Resources

Differentiated Instruction includes:

- Reading Strategies
- Success for English Learners **ELL**
- Reteach
- Challenge **PRE-AP**

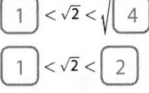

Elaborate

Talk About It
Summarize the Lesson

Ask: If someone claims that a certain number is irrational but you know it is actually rational, how could you prove to that person that the number is rational? You could find a fraction equal to the number, such that the number is the ratio of two integers, with the denominator not equal to zero.

GUIDED PRACTICE

Engage with the Whiteboard

Have students plot each number in Exercises 16–18 on a number line. Students should label each point with the irrational number written as a radical and as a decimal.

Avoid Common Errors

Exercises 1–6 To avoid reversing the order of the dividend and divisor, tell students to start at the top of the fraction and read the bar as "divided by."

Focus on Technology

Have students use a calculator to investigate the decimal equivalents of such fractions as $\frac{1}{9}, \frac{2}{9}, \cdots, \frac{8}{9}$ and $\frac{1}{11}, \frac{2}{11}, \cdots, \frac{10}{11}$. Ask them to describe the patterns they find as a result of these investigations.

E Estimate that $\sqrt{2} \approx 1.5$.

$\sqrt{2} \approx 1.5$

0 1 2 3 4

F To find a better estimate, first choose some numbers between 1 and 2 and square them. For example, choose 1.3, 1.4, and 1.5.

$1.3^2 = \underline{1.69}$ $1.4^2 = \underline{1.96}$ $1.5^2 = \underline{2.25}$

Is $\sqrt{2}$ between 1.3 and 1.4? How do you know?

No; 2 is not between 1.69 and 1.96.

Is $\sqrt{2}$ between 1.4 and 1.5? How do you know?

Yes; 2 is between 1.96 and 2.25.

$\sqrt{2}$ is between $\underline{1.4}$ and $\underline{1.5}$, so $\sqrt{2} \approx \underline{1.45}$.

G Locate and label this value on the number line.

$\sqrt{2} \approx 1.45$

1.1 1.2 1.3 1.4 1.5

Reflect

11. How could you find an even better estimate of $\sqrt{2}$?

Test the squares of numbers between 1.4 and 1.5.

12. Find a better estimate of $\sqrt{2}$. Draw a number line and locate and label your estimate.

$\sqrt{2}$ is between $\underline{1.41}$ and $\underline{1.42}$, so $\sqrt{2} \approx \underline{1.415}$.

$\sqrt{2} \approx 1.415$

1.41 1.42 1.43 1.44 1.45

13. Estimate the value of $\sqrt{7}$ to two decimal places. Draw a number line and locate and label your estimate.

$\sqrt{7}$ is between $\underline{2.6}$ and $\underline{2.7}$, so $\sqrt{7} \approx \underline{2.65}$.

$\sqrt{7} \approx 2.65$

2.5 2.6 2.7 2.8 2.9

© Houghton Mifflin Harcourt Publishing Company

Write each fraction or mixed number as a decimal. (Example 1)

1. $\frac{2}{5}$ $\underline{0.4}$ **2.** $\frac{8}{9}$ $\underline{0.\overline{8}}$ **3.** $3\frac{3}{4}$ $\underline{3.75}$

4. $\frac{7}{10}$ $\underline{0.7}$ **5.** $2\frac{3}{8}$ $\underline{2.375}$ **6.** $\frac{5}{6}$ $\underline{0.8\overline{3}}$

Write each decimal as a fraction or mixed number in simplest form. (Example 2)

7. 0.675 $\underline{\frac{27}{40}}$ **8.** 5.6 $\underline{5\frac{3}{5}}$ **9.** 0.44 $\underline{\frac{11}{25}}$

10. $0.\overline{4}$

$10x = \boxed{4.\overline{4}}$

$-x \quad -\boxed{0.\overline{4}}$

$\boxed{9}\,x = \boxed{4}$

$x = \underline{\frac{4}{9}}$

11. $0.\overline{26}$

$100x = \boxed{26.\overline{26}}$

$-x \quad -\boxed{0.\overline{26}}$

$\boxed{99}\,x = \boxed{26}$

$x = \underline{\frac{26}{99}}$

12. $0.\overline{325}$

$1000x = \boxed{325.\overline{325}}$

$-x \quad -\boxed{0.\overline{325}}$

$\boxed{999}\,x = \boxed{325}$

$x = \underline{\frac{325}{999}}$

Solve each equation for x. (Example 3)

13. $x^2 = 144$

$x = \pm\sqrt{\boxed{144}} = \pm\boxed{12}$

14. $x^2 = \frac{25}{289}$

$x = \pm\sqrt{\boxed{\dfrac{25}{289}}} = \pm\boxed{\dfrac{5}{17}}$

15. $x^3 = 216$

$x = \sqrt[3]{\boxed{216}} = \boxed{6}$

Approximate each irrational number to two decimal places without a calculator.
(Explore Activity)

16. $\sqrt{5} \approx \boxed{2.25}$ **17.** $\sqrt{3} \approx \boxed{1.75}$ **18.** $\sqrt{10} \approx \boxed{3.15}$

? ESSENTIAL QUESTION CHECK-IN

19. What is the difference between rational and irrational numbers?

Rational numbers can be written in the form $\frac{a}{b}$, where a and b are integers and $b \neq 0$. Irrational numbers cannot be written in this form.

© Houghton Mifflin Harcourt Publishing Company

9.1 LESSON QUIZ

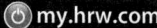 **FL CC** 8.NS.1.1, 8.NS.1.2, 8.EE.1.2

1. Write as a decimal: $2\frac{5}{8}$, $1\frac{7}{12}$

2. Write as a fraction: 0.34, $1.\overline{24}$

3. Solve $x^2 = \frac{9}{49}$ for x.

4. Solve $x^3 = 216$ for x.

5. Estimate the value of $\sqrt{13}$ to the nearest 0.05 without using a calculator.

Lesson Quiz example available online

⏻ my.hrw.com

Answers
1. 2.625, $1.58\overline{3}$

2. $\frac{17}{50}$, $1\frac{8}{33}$

3. $x = \pm\frac{3}{7}$

4. $x = 6$

5. 3.60

Evaluate

GUIDED AND INDEPENDENT PRACTICE

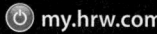 **FL CC** 8.NS.1.1, 8.NS.1.2, 8.EE.1.2

Concepts & Skills	Practice
Example 1 Expressing Rational Numbers as Decimals	Exercises 1–6, 20–21, 24–25
Example 2 Expressing Decimals as Rational Numbers	Exercises 7–12, 22–23, 26–27
Example 3 Finding Square Roots and Cube Roots	Exercises 13–15, 28, 31
Explore Activity Estimating Irrational Numbers	Exercises 16–18, 29–30

Exercise	Depth of Knowledge (D.O.K.)	**FL CC** Mathematical Practices
20–27	**2** Skills/Concepts	**MP.4.1** Modeling
28	**3** Strategic Thinking **H.O.T.**	**MP.4.1** Modeling
29	**3** Strategic Thinking **H.O.T.**	**MP.7.1** Using Structure
30	**2** Skills/Concepts	**MP.3.1** Logic
31	**2** Skills/Concepts	**MP.4.1** Modeling
32	**3** Strategic Thinking **H.O.T.**	**MP.3.1** Logic
33	**3** Strategic Thinking **H.O.T.**	**MP.7.1** Using Structure
34	**3** Strategic Thinking **H.O.T.**	**MP.2.1** Reasoning

Additional Resources
Differentiated Instruction includes:

• Leveled Practice worksheets

Name _____ Class _____ Date _____

9.1 Independent Practice

FL CC 8.NS.1.1, 8.NS.1.2, 8.EE.1.2

Personal Math Trainer

Online Assessment and Intervention

my.hrw.com

20. A $\frac{7}{16}$-inch-long bolt is used in a machine. What is the length of the bolt written as a decimal?

___0.4375 in.___

21. The weight of an object on the moon is $\frac{1}{6}$ its weight on Earth. Write $\frac{1}{6}$ as a decimal.

___$0.1\overline{6}$___

22. The distance to the nearest gas station is $2\frac{4}{5}$ kilometers. What is this distance written as a decimal?

___2.8 km___

23. A baseball pitcher has pitched $98\frac{2}{3}$ innings. What is the number of innings written as a decimal?

___$98.\overline{6}$___

24. A heartbeat takes 0.8 seconds. How many seconds is this written as a fraction?

___$\frac{4}{5}$ seconds___

25. There are 26.2 miles in a marathon. Write the number of miles using a fraction.

___$26\frac{1}{5}$ mi___

26. The average score on a biology test was $72.\overline{1}$. Write the average score using a fraction.

___$72\frac{1}{9}$___

27. The metal in a penny is worth about 0.505 cents. How many cents is this written as a fraction?

___$\frac{101}{200}$ cents___

28. **Multistep** An artist wants to frame a square painting with an area of 400 square inches. She wants to know the length of the wood trim that is needed to go around the painting.

a. If x is the length of one side of the painting, what equation can you set up to find the length of a side? ___$x^2 = 400$___

b. Solve the equation you wrote in part a. How many solutions does the equation have?

$x = \pm 20$; The equation has 2 solutions.

c. Do all of the solutions that you found in part b make sense in the context of the problem? Explain.

The solution $x = 20$ makes sense, but the solution $x = -20$ doesn't, because a painting cannot have a side length of -20 inches.

d. What is the length of the wood trim needed to go around the painting?

$4 \times 20 = 80$ inches

29. **Analyze Relationships** To find $\sqrt{15}$, Beau found $3^2 = 9$ and $4^2 = 16$. He said that since 15 is between 9 and 16, $\sqrt{15}$ must be between 3 and 4. He thinks a good estimate for $\sqrt{15}$ is $\frac{3+4}{2} = 3.5$. Is Beau's estimate high, low, or correct? Explain.

His estimate is low because 15 is very close to 16, so $\sqrt{15}$ is very close to $\sqrt{16}$, or 4. A better estimate would be 3.8 or 3.9.

30. **Justify Reasoning** What is a good estimate for the solution to the equation $x^3 = 95$? How did you come up with your estimate?

Sample answer: A good estimate is $x \approx 4.5$. Because $4^3 = 64$ and $5^3 = 125$ and 95 is about halfway between 64 and 125, $\sqrt[3]{95}$ is probably closer to 4.5 than to 4 or 5.

31. The volume of a sphere is 36π ft^3. What is the radius of the sphere? Use the formula $V = \frac{4}{3}\pi r^3$ to find your answer.

3 feet

H.O.T. FOCUS ON HIGHER ORDER THINKING

Work Area

32. **Draw Conclusions** Can you find the cube root of a negative number? If so, is it positive or negative? Explain your reasoning.

Yes; the cube root of a negative number is negative, because a negative number cubed is always negative, and a nonnegative number cubed is always nonnegative.

33. **Make a Conjecture** Evaluate and compare the following expressions.

$$\sqrt{\frac{4}{25}} \text{ and } \frac{\sqrt{4}}{\sqrt{25}} \qquad \sqrt{\frac{16}{81}} \text{ and } \frac{\sqrt{16}}{\sqrt{81}} \qquad \sqrt{\frac{36}{49}} \text{ and } \frac{\sqrt{36}}{\sqrt{49}}$$

Use your results to make a conjecture about a division rule for square roots. Since division is multiplication by the reciprocal, make a conjecture about a multiplication rule for square roots.

$\sqrt{\frac{4}{25}} = \frac{2}{5} = \frac{\sqrt{4}}{\sqrt{25}} \qquad \sqrt{\frac{16}{81}} = \frac{4}{9} = \frac{\sqrt{16}}{\sqrt{81}} \qquad \sqrt{\frac{36}{49}} = \frac{6}{7} = \frac{\sqrt{36}}{\sqrt{49}},$

$\frac{\sqrt{a}}{\sqrt{b}} = \sqrt{\frac{a}{b}}; \sqrt{a} \cdot \sqrt{b} = \sqrt{a \cdot b}$

34. **Persevere in Problem Solving** The difference between the solutions to the equation $x^2 = a$ is 30. What is a? Show that your answer is correct.

225; the solutions to $x^2 = a$ are $x = \pm 15$, and $15 - (-15) = 30$.

EXTEND THE MATH PRE-AP

Activity available online my.hrw.com

Activity Write $\sqrt{0.9}$ on the board and invite students to conjecture what the value might be. Have them check their conjectures by squaring. Invite them to suggest ways to estimate $\sqrt{0.9}$. As a hint, point out that 0.9 is close to 1.0, and so they might use that to help guide their estimates. Lead them to see that, since 0.9^2 is 0.81 and 1.0^2 is 1, the value of $\sqrt{0.9}$ is greater than 0.9 and less than 1.0. Try squaring 0.95 to get 0.9025. A good estimate for $\sqrt{0.9}$ is 0.95.

LESSON
9.2 Sets of Real Numbers

Florida Common Core Standards

The student is expected to:

 FL CC **The Number System—8.NS.1.1**

Know that numbers that are not rational are called irrational. Understand informally that every number has a decimal expansion; for rational numbers show that the decimal expansion repeats eventually, and convert a decimal expansion which repeats eventually into a rational number.

Mathematical Practices

 FL CC **MP.7.1** Using Structure

Engage

ESSENTIAL QUESTION

How can you describe relationships between sets of real numbers? Sample answer: Describe them as two different sets, or one set as being a subset of another.

Motivate the Lesson
Ask: How many different types of tigers can you name? How does the set of Bengal tigers relate to the set of tigers?

Explore

Point to different locations in the Animals diagram and ask for examples for that classification. Do the same for the Real Numbers diagram. Students should understand that everything within a region is part of the set, for example both −3 and 2 are integers.

Explain

EXAMPLE 1

Questioning Strategies Mathematical Practices

• In A, why is 5 not a perfect square? It does not have rational numbers as its square roots.

• Can the number in B be written as a fraction? Why or why not? Yes; it is a terminating decimal, so it is a rational number.

Engage with the Whiteboard
Have students place the numbers in Example 1 and Additional Example 1 in the Venn diagram for numbers.

YOUR TURN

Avoid Common Errors
Be sure that students read Exercise 5 carefully before answering. The number given in the problem, 10, is the area, not the side length.

EXAMPLE 2

Questioning Strategies Mathematical Practices

• What two major sets are the real numbers composed of? rational and irrational numbers

• What is the location of the set of whole numbers in the Venn diagram in relation to the set of rational numbers? Explain. Inside it; whole numbers are rational numbers.

Focus on Reasoning Mathematical Practices
Remind students that it takes only one counterexample to show that a statement is false.

9.2 Sets of Real Numbers

FL CC 8.NS.1.1
Know that numbers that are not rational are called irrational. . . .

? ESSENTIAL QUESTION

How can you describe relationships between sets of real numbers?

Classifying Real Numbers

Biologists classify animals based on shared characteristics. A cardinal is an animal, a vertebrate, a bird, and a passerine.

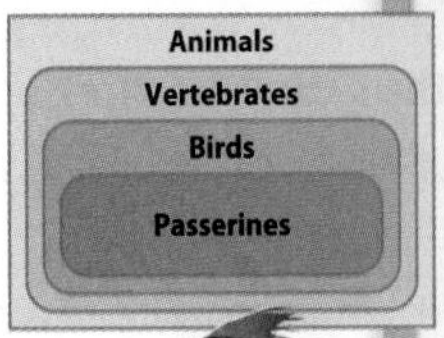

You already know that the set of rational numbers consists of whole numbers, integers, and fractions. The set of **real numbers** consists of the set of rational numbers and the set of irrational numbers.

Animals
Vertebrates
Birds
Passerines

Math On the Spot
my.hrw.com

Real Numbers

Rational Numbers	Irrational Numbers
$\frac{27}{4}$ $0.\overline{3}$ $-\frac{6}{7}$	$\sqrt{17}$
Integers −3 **Whole Numbers** −2	$-\sqrt{11}$
−1 0 1 3 $\sqrt{4}$	$\sqrt{2}$
4.5	π

Passerines, such as the cardinal, are also called "perching birds."

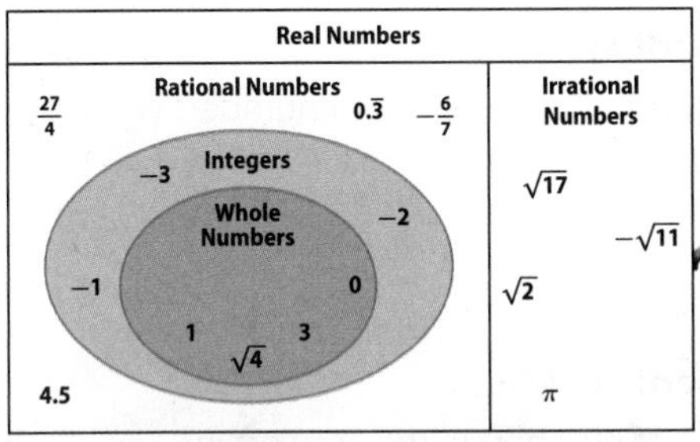

EXAMPLE 1
FL CC 8.NS.1.1

Write all names that apply to each number.

A $\sqrt{5}$
irrational, real

5 is a whole number that is not a perfect square.

B −17.84
rational, real

−17.84 is a terminating decimal.

C $\frac{\sqrt{81}}{9}$
whole, integer, rational, real

$\frac{\sqrt{81}}{9} = \frac{9}{9} = 1$

X²
Animated Math
my.hrw.com

Math Talk
Mathematical Practices

What types of numbers are between 3.1 and 3.9 on a number line?

rational, irrational, real

Lesson 9.2 **279**

Personal Math Trainer
Online Assessment and Intervention
my.hrw.com

YOUR TURN

Write all names that apply to each number.

1. A baseball pitcher has pitched $12\frac{2}{3}$ innings.
   rational, real

2. The length of the side of a square that has an area of 10 square yards. irrational, real

Math On the Spot
my.hrw.com

Sample answer: 8; $8 = \frac{8}{1}$

Understanding Sets and Subsets of Real Numbers

By understanding which sets are subsets of types of numbers, you can verify whether statements about the relationships between sets are true or false.

EXAMPLE 2
FL CC 8.NS.1.1

Tell whether the given statement is true or false. Explain your choice.

A All irrational numbers are real numbers.

True. Every irrational number is included in the set of real numbers. Irrational numbers are a subset of real numbers.

B No rational numbers are whole numbers.

False. A whole number can be written as a fraction with a denominator of 1, so every whole number is included in the set of rational numbers. Whole numbers are a subset of rational numbers.

Math Talk
Mathematical Practices

Give an example of a rational number that is a whole number. Show that the number is both whole and rational.

YOUR TURN

Tell whether the given statement is true or false. Explain your choice.

3. All rational numbers are integers.
   False. Every integer is a rational number, but not every rational number is an integer. Rational numbers such as $\frac{3}{5}$ and $-\frac{5}{2}$ are not integers.

4. Some irrational numbers are integers.
   False. Real numbers are either rational or irrational numbers. Integers are rational numbers, so no integers are irrational numbers.

Personal Math Trainer
Online Assessment and Intervention
my.hrw.com

280 Unit 5

PROFESSIONAL DEVELOPMENT

Integrate Mathematical Practices MP.7.1

This lesson provides an opportunity to address this Mathematical Practices standard. It calls for students to discern structure to connect and communicate mathematical ideas.

Students use a Venn diagram to structure relationships between sets of numbers. They connect and communicate mathematical ideas when they make logical statements about the sets and describe which set best describes numbers applied to real-life situations.

Math Background

The relationships between sets of numbers extend to include *complex numbers*. A complex number can be written as a sum of a real number, *a*, and an imaginary number, *bi*.

$$a + bi$$

An imaginary number is a special number that, when squared gives a negative value. When you square a real number, you get a nonnegative number. When you square an imaginary number, you get a negative value. The imaginary unit is *i*.

$$i = \sqrt{-1}$$

ADDITIONAL EXAMPLE 3
Identify the set of numbers that best describes the situation. Explain your choice.

A the amount of time that has passed since midnight

The set of real numbers; time is continuous, so the amount of time can be rational or irrational.

B the number of tickets sold to a basketball game

The set of whole numbers; the number of tickets sold may be 0 or a counting number

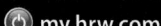 **Interactive Whiteboard**
Interactive example available online

⏻ my.hrw.com

YOUR TURN

Avoid Common Errors
Students may see the word "*All*" or "*No*" in Exercises 3 and 4 and immediately assume that any absolute statements like these are false. Remind them that there are true statements that begin with these words, and encourage them to provide examples.

EXAMPLE 3

Questioning Strategies Mathematical Practices
- In A, how does the phrase "*number of*" give you a clue about the number classification? It indicates a counting number.

- What is the relationship between the circumference of a circle and the diameter? The circumference is diameter times π.

Focus on Critical Thinking Mathematical Practices
In B, suppose the diameters in inches were $\frac{25}{\pi}$, $\frac{28}{\pi}$, $\frac{31}{\pi}$, and so on. What set of numbers would best describe the circumferences? Explain. Whole numbers; the circumferences would be the whole numbers 25, 28, 31, and so on.

YOUR TURN

Focus on Critical Thinking Mathematical Practices
Have students compare and contrast the classification of numbers in the answers in Exercises 5 and 6. Point out that the numbers in both exercises are real numbers, but the numbers in Exercise 5 are nonnegative real numbers while the numbers in Exercise 6 are negative real numbers.

Elaborate

Talk About It
Summarize the Lesson

Ask: What are some ways that number sets can be related? Sets may be subsets of other sets or they may be separate from other sets.

GUIDED PRACTICE

Engage with the Whiteboard
Have students place the numbers in Exercises 1–8 in the Venn diagram for numbers at the beginning of the lesson.

Integrating Language Arts **ELL**
Encourage English learners to ask for clarification on any terms or phrases that they do not understand.

Avoid Common Errors
Exercise 7 Remind students that a repeating decimal is a rational number.
Exercises 9–10 Remind students that it only takes one counterexample to show that a statement is false.

Identifying Sets for Real-World Situations

Real numbers can be used to represent real-world quantities. Highways have posted speed limit signs that are represented by natural numbers such as 55 mph. Integers appear on thermometers. Rational numbers are used in many daily activities, including cooking. For example, ingredients in a recipe are often given in fractional amounts such as $\frac{2}{3}$ cup flour.

Math On the Spot
@ my.hrw.com

 EXAMPLE 3  FL CC 8.NS.1.1

Identify the set of numbers that best describes each situation. Explain your choice.

A the number of people wearing glasses in a room

The set of whole numbers best describes the situation. The number of people wearing glasses may be 0 or a counting number.

B the circumference of a flying disk has a diameter of 8, 9, 10, 11, or 14 inches

The set of irrational numbers best describes the situation. Each circumference would be a product of π and the diameter, and any multiple of π is irrational.

My Notes

YOUR TURN

Identify the set of numbers that best describes the situation. Explain your choice.

5. the amount of water in a glass as it evaporates

Real numbers; the amount can be any number greater than 0.

6. the number of seconds remaining when a song is playing, displayed as a negative number

Real numbers; the number of seconds left can be any number less than 0.

Personal Math Trainer
Online Assessment and Intervention
@ my.hrw.com

Lesson 9.2 **281**

Write all names that apply to each number. (Example 1)

1. $\frac{7}{8}$
   rational, real

2. $\sqrt{36}$
   whole, integer, rational, real

3. $\sqrt{24}$
   irrational, real

4. 0.75
   rational, real

5. 0
   whole, integer, rational, real

6. $-\sqrt{100}$
   integer, rational, real

7. $5.\overline{45}$
   rational, real

8. $-\frac{18}{6}$
   integer, rational, real

Tell whether the given statement is true or false. Explain your choice. (Example 2)

9. All whole numbers are rational numbers.

   True. Whole numbers are a subset of the set of rational numbers and can be written as a ratio of the whole number to 1.

10. No irrational numbers are whole numbers.

    True. Whole numbers are rational numbers.

Identify the set of numbers that best describes each situation. Explain your choice. (Example 3)

11. the change in the value of an account when given to the nearest dollar

    Integers; the change can be a whole dollar amount and can be positive, negative, or zero.

    $\frac{1}{16}$ inch

12. the markings on a standard ruler
    Rational numbers; the ruler is marked every $\frac{1}{16}$th inch.

IN.   1

❓ ESSENTIAL QUESTION CHECK-IN

13. What are some ways to describe the relationships between sets of numbers?

    Sample answer: Describe one set as being a subset of another, or show their relationships in a Venn diagram.

282 Unit 5

DIFFERENTIATE INSTRUCTION

Graphic Organizers

Give students a list of numbers (including terminating and repeating decimals, fractions, integers, and rational and irrational square roots) and a graphic organizer as shown below.

Real Numbers	
Rational numbers	Irrational numbers
Integer numbers	
Whole numbers	

Ask students to write each number in the list in the correct section of the organizer.

Number Sense

Point out to students that knowing the types of numbers to expect in different situations can alert them to incorrect math as well as to impossible situations. For example, 13.5 shots made in basketballs is not possible, but an average number of shots can equal 13.5.

Additional Resources

Differentiated Instruction includes:
- Reading Strategies
- Success for English Learners **ELL**
- Reteach
- Challenge **PRE-AP**

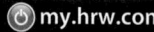
9.2 LESSON QUIZ

 **8.NS.1.1**

1. Write all the names that apply to the number $-1.\overline{5}$.

2. Tell whether the given statement is true or false. Explain your choice.
All numbers between 1 and 2 are rational numbers.

3. Identify the set of numbers that best describes the situation. Explain your choice.
The choices on a survey question change the total points for the survey by -2, -1, 0, 1, or 2 points.

Lesson Quiz available online

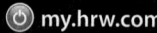
my.hrw.com

Answers

1. rational, real

2. False; $\sqrt{2}$ is an example of an irrational number between 1 and 2

3. Integers; each number is an integer, but only three are whole numbers.

Evaluate

GUIDED AND INDEPENDENT PRACTICE

 **8.NS.1.1**

Concepts & Skills	Practice
Example 1 Classifying Real Numbers	Exercises 1–8, 14–19, 22–24
Example 2 Understanding Sets and Subsets of Real Numbers	Exercises 9–10
Example 3 Identifying Sets for Real-World Situations	Exercises 11–12, 20–21, 25

Exercise	Depth of Knowledge (D.O.K.)		Mathematical Practices
14–19	**2** Skills/Concepts		**MP.7.1** Using Structure
20–21	**2** Skills/Concepts		**MP.6.1** Precision
22–23	**2** Skills/Concepts		**MP.3.1** Logic
24	**1** Recall of Information		**MP.7.1** Using Structure
25	**2** Skills/Concepts		**MP.2.1** Reasoning
26–27	**3** Strategic Thinking	H.O.T.	**MP.3.1** Logic
28	**3** Strategic Thinking	H.O.T.	**MP.8.1** Patterns
29	**3** Strategic Thinking	H.O.T.	**MP.3.1** Logic

Additional Resources

Differentiated Instruction includes:

• Leveled Practice worksheets

 **CLUSTER CONNECTION** **Exercise 29** combines concepts from the Florida Common Core cluster "Know that there are numbers that are not rational, and approximate them by rational numbers."

9.2 Independent Practice

FL CC 8.NS.1.1

Personal Math Trainer
Online Assessment and Intervention
my.hrw.com

Write all names that apply to each number. Then place the numbers in the correct location on the Venn diagram.

14. $\sqrt{9}$ _whole, integer, rational, real_

15. 257 _whole, integer, rational, real_

16. $\sqrt{50}$ _irrational, real_

17. $8\frac{1}{2}$ _rational, real_

18. 16.6 _rational, real_

19. $\sqrt{16}$ _whole, integer, rational, real_

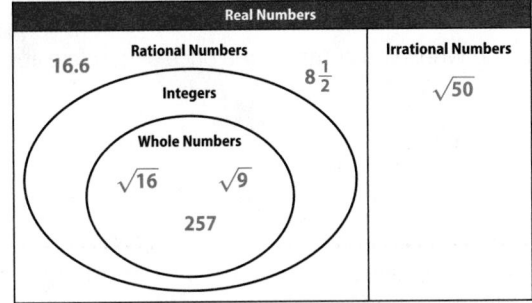

Real Numbers

Rational Numbers — 16.6 — $8\frac{1}{2}$

Irrational Numbers — $\sqrt{50}$

Integers

Whole Numbers — $\sqrt{16}$ — $\sqrt{9}$ — 257

Identify the set of numbers that best describes each situation. Explain your choice.

20. the height of an airplane as it descends to an airport runway

Real numbers; the height can be any number greater than zero.

21. the score with respect to par of several golfers: 2, −3, 5, 0, −1

Integers; the scores are counting numbers, their opposites, and zero.

22. **Critique Reasoning** Ronald states that the number $\frac{1}{11}$ is not rational because, when converted into a decimal, it does not terminate. Nathaniel says it is rational because it is a fraction. Which boy is correct? Explain.

Nathaniel is correct. A rational number is a number that can be written as a fraction, and $\frac{1}{11}$ is a fraction.

© Houghton Mifflin Harcourt Publishing Company

Lesson 9.2 **283**

23. **Critique Reasoning** The circumference of a circular region is shown. What type of number best describes the diameter of the circle? Explain your answer. Whole; the diameter is $\frac{\pi}{\pi} = 1$ mile.

π mi

24. **Critical Thinking** A number is not an integer. What type of number can it be?

It can be a rational number that is not an integer, or an irrational number.

25. A grocery store has a shelf with half-gallon containers of milk. What type of number best represents the total number of gallons?

rational number

H.O.T. FOCUS ON HIGHER ORDER THINKING

26. **Explain the Error** Katie said, "Negative numbers are integers." What was her error?

The set of negative numbers also includes non-integer rational numbers and irrational numbers.

27. **Justify Reasoning** Can you ever use a calculator to determine if a number is rational or irrational? Explain.

Sample answer: If the calculator shows a decimal that terminates in fewer digits than what the calculator screen allows, then you can tell that the number is rational. If not, you cannot tell from the calculator display whether the number terminates because you see a limited number of digits. It may be a repeating decimal (rational), or non-terminating non-repeating decimal (irrational).

28. **Draw Conclusions** The decimal $0.\overline{3}$ represents $\frac{1}{3}$. What type of number best describes $0.\overline{9}$, which is $3 \cdot 0.\overline{3}$? Explain.

Whole; $3 \cdot 0.\overline{3}$ represents $3 \cdot \frac{1}{3} = 1$, so $0.\overline{9}$ is exactly 1.

29. **Communicate Mathematical Ideas** Irrational numbers can never be precisely represented in decimal form. Why is this?

Sample answer: In decimal form, irrational numbers never terminate and never repeat. Therefore, no matter how many decimal places you include, the number will never be precisely represented. There are always more digits.

Work Area

© Houghton Mifflin Harcourt Publishing Company

284 Unit 5

EXTEND THE MATH PRE-AP
Activity available online ⏻ my.hrw.com

Activity Have students consider the concept of *restricted domain* for the sets of numbers that describe situations. For example, the number of sisters a person has can best be described by whole numbers, but no one has ever had 1,500 sisters. An area code is an integer or whole number between 200 and 999.

Have students use a source, such as the *Guinness Book of World Records*, and give examples of sets of numbers that describe situations where the domain is restricted. Ask whether the restriction may be changed in the future.

Sets of Real Numbers **284**

LESSON
9.3 Ordering Real Numbers

Florida Common Core Standards

The student is expected to:

 **The Number System—8.NS.1.2**

Use rational approximations of irrational numbers to compare the size of irrational numbers, locate them approximately on a number line diagram, and estimate the value of expressions (e.g. π^2)

Mathematical Practices

 **MP.4.1** Modeling

---

ADDITIONAL EXAMPLE 1
Compare. Write $<$, $>$, or $=$.

A $\sqrt{8} - 2 \bigcirc 4 - \sqrt{8}$ $<$

B $\sqrt{20} + 1 \bigcirc 3 + \sqrt{2}$ $>$

 Interactive Whiteboard
Interactive example available online

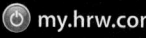 my.hrw.com

---

ADDITIONAL EXAMPLE 2
Order 3π, $\sqrt{10}$, and 3.25 from greatest to least.

3π, 3.25, $\sqrt{10}$

 Interactive Whiteboard
Interactive example available online

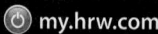 my.hrw.com

---

Engage

ESSENTIAL QUESTION

How do you order a set of real numbers? Sample answer: Find their approximate decimal values and order them.

Motivate the Lesson

Ask: What kind of numbers are you comparing when you compare the price of gasoline at two different gas stations?

Explore

Give students two rational numbers and ask them to name a number between them. Repeat a few times and then give them two irrational numbers and ask them to name a number between them.

Explain

EXAMPLE 1

Questioning Strategies Mathematical Practices

• Which is greater, the difference between 5 and 3, or the difference between $\sqrt{5}$ and $\sqrt{3}$? The difference between 5 and 3 is 2; the difference between $\sqrt{5}$ and $\sqrt{3}$ is approximately 1. So the difference between 5 and 3 is greater.

Avoid Common Errors

Caution students to read the problem carefully and think about what the radical sign means so that they do not misread the problem and answer that the two sides are equal.

YOUR TURN

Focus on Technology

Calculators should not be used at this point, because developing number sense is the goal.

EXAMPLE 2

Questioning Strategies Mathematical Practices

• How do you determine whether $\sqrt{22}$ is less than or greater than 4.5? The square of 4.5 is 20.25, which is less than 22, so the square root of 22 must be greater than 4.5.

Engage with the Whiteboard

Have students graph and label various real numbers between 4.2 and 4.4 and between 4.7 and 5.

YOUR TURN

Focus on Modeling Mathematical Practices

Have students label the integers on the number line with their equivalent square root. For example, 1, 2, and 3 on the number line would be labeled $\sqrt{1}$, $\sqrt{4}$, and $\sqrt{9}$.

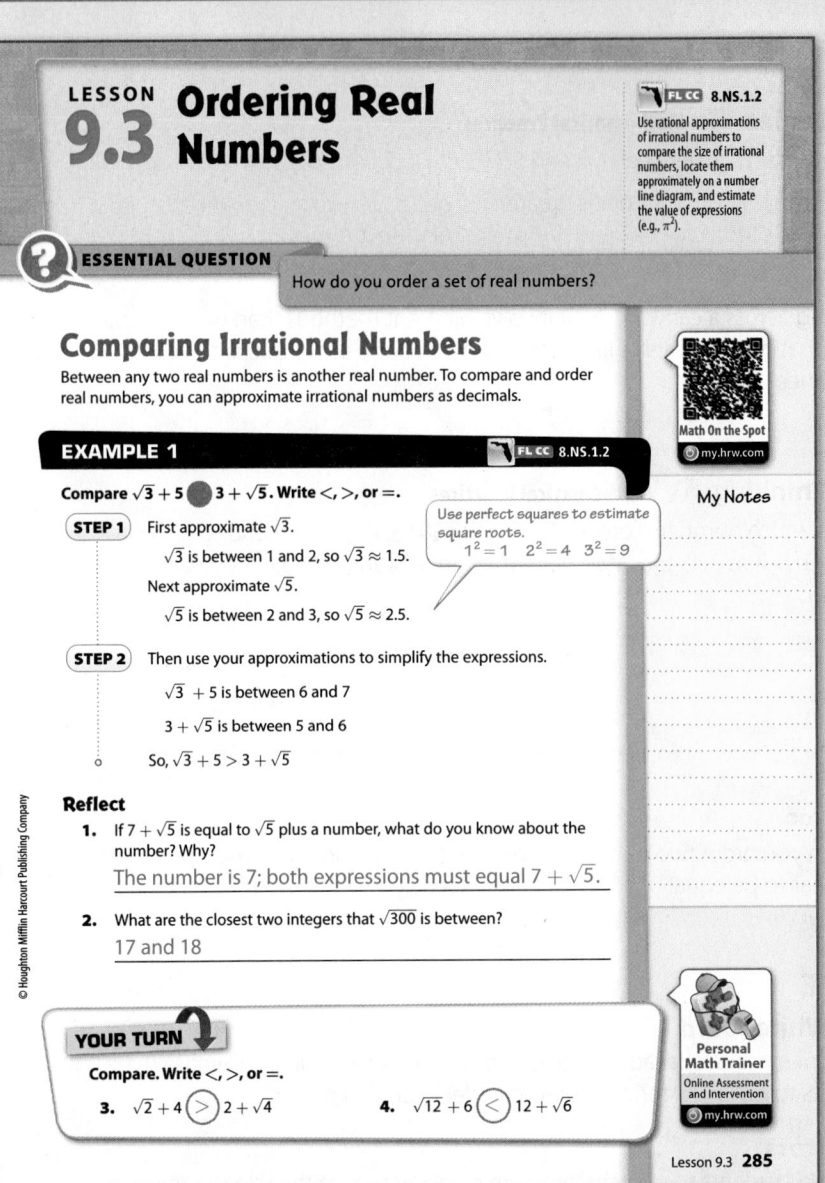

LESSON 9.3 Ordering Real Numbers

FL CC 8.NS.1.2
Use rational approximations of irrational numbers to compare the size of irrational numbers, locate them approximately on a number line diagram, and estimate the value of expressions (e.g., π^2).

ESSENTIAL QUESTION

How do you order a set of real numbers?

Comparing Irrational Numbers

Between any two real numbers is another real number. To compare and order real numbers, you can approximate irrational numbers as decimals.

EXAMPLE 1 — FL CC 8.NS.1.2

Compare $\sqrt{3} + 5$ ⬤ $3 + \sqrt{5}$. Write $<$, $>$, or $=$.

STEP 1 First approximate $\sqrt{3}$.

$\sqrt{3}$ is between 1 and 2, so $\sqrt{3} \approx 1.5$.

Next approximate $\sqrt{5}$.

$\sqrt{5}$ is between 2 and 3, so $\sqrt{5} \approx 2.5$.

> Use perfect squares to estimate square roots.
> $1^2 = 1 \quad 2^2 = 4 \quad 3^2 = 9$

STEP 2 Then use your approximations to simplify the expressions.

$\sqrt{3} + 5$ is between 6 and 7

$3 + \sqrt{5}$ is between 5 and 6

So, $\sqrt{3} + 5 > 3 + \sqrt{5}$

Reflect

1. If $7 + \sqrt{5}$ is equal to $\sqrt{5}$ plus a number, what do you know about the number? Why?

   The number is 7; both expressions must equal $7 + \sqrt{5}$.

2. What are the closest two integers that $\sqrt{300}$ is between?

   17 and 18

YOUR TURN

Compare. Write $<$, $>$, or $=$.

3. $\sqrt{2} + 4$ ⬤$>$ $2 + \sqrt{4}$

4. $\sqrt{12} + 6$ ⬤$<$ $12 + \sqrt{6}$

Personal Math Trainer
Online Assessment and Intervention
my.hrw.com

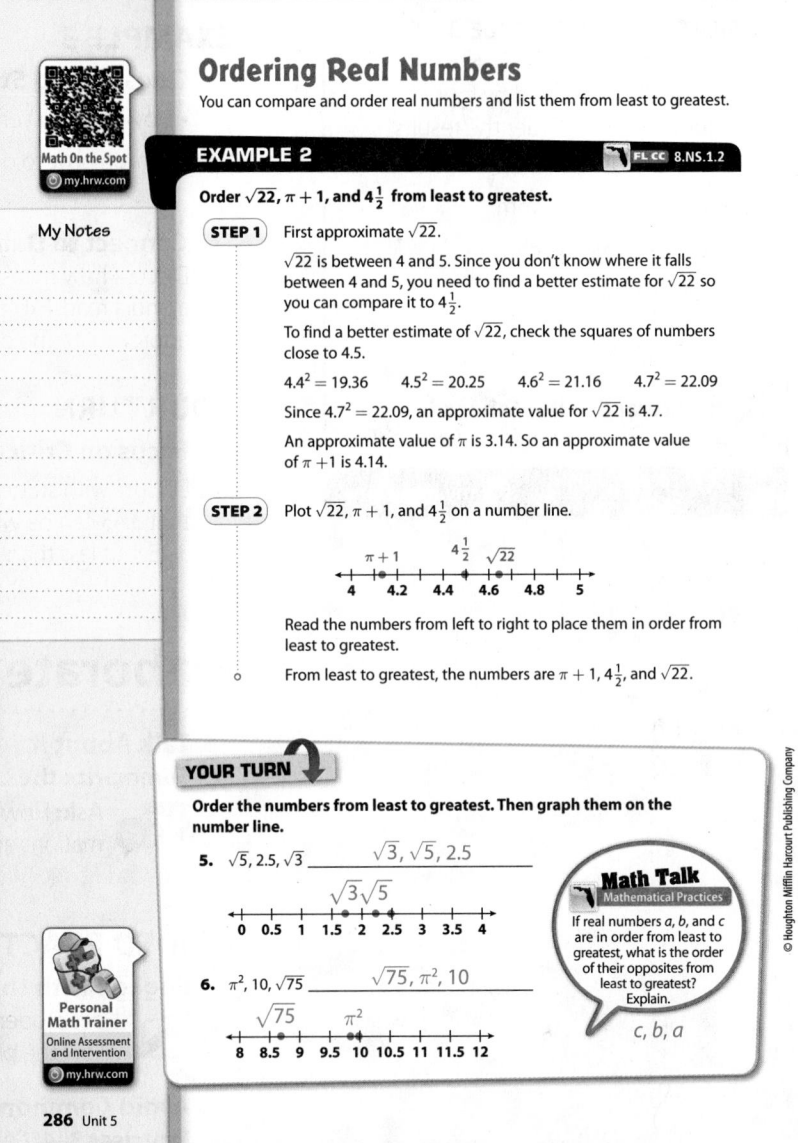

Ordering Real Numbers

You can compare and order real numbers and list them from least to greatest.

EXAMPLE 2 — FL CC 8.NS.1.2

Order $\sqrt{22}$, $\pi + 1$, and $4\frac{1}{2}$ from least to greatest.

STEP 1 First approximate $\sqrt{22}$.

$\sqrt{22}$ is between 4 and 5. Since you don't know where it falls between 4 and 5, you need to find a better estimate for $\sqrt{22}$ so you can compare it to $4\frac{1}{2}$.

To find a better estimate of $\sqrt{22}$, check the squares of numbers close to 4.5.

$4.4^2 = 19.36 \quad 4.5^2 = 20.25 \quad 4.6^2 = 21.16 \quad 4.7^2 = 22.09$

Since $4.7^2 = 22.09$, an approximate value for $\sqrt{22}$ is 4.7.

An approximate value of π is 3.14. So an approximate value of $\pi + 1$ is 4.14.

STEP 2 Plot $\sqrt{22}$, $\pi + 1$, and $4\frac{1}{2}$ on a number line.

Read the numbers from left to right to place them in order from least to greatest.

From least to greatest, the numbers are $\pi + 1$, $4\frac{1}{2}$, and $\sqrt{22}$.

YOUR TURN

Order the numbers from least to greatest. Then graph them on the number line.

5. $\sqrt{5}$, 2.5, $\sqrt{3}$ ___ $\sqrt{3}$, $\sqrt{5}$, 2.5

6. π^2, 10, $\sqrt{75}$ ___ $\sqrt{75}$, π^2, 10

> **Math Talk**
> Mathematical Practices
>
> If real numbers a, b, and c are in order from least to greatest, what is the order of their opposites from least to greatest? Explain.
>
> c, b, a

Personal Math Trainer
Online Assessment and Intervention
my.hrw.com

PROFESSIONAL DEVELOPMENT

Integrate Mathematical Practices MP.4.1

This lesson provides an opportunity to address this Mathematical Practices standard. It calls for students to model relationships using multiple representations, including diagrams, graphs, and language as appropriate. Students use multiple representations when they use number lines to estimate the locations of and order rational and irrational numbers given as symbols.

Math Background

In this lesson, students estimate irrational numbers in the form of square roots of nonperfect squares by finding two perfect squares between which the number falls. A more precise method involves repeated division. For example, to find $\sqrt{28}$, find a whole number whose perfect square is close to 28, such as 5. Divide 28 by that number: $28 \div 5 = 5.6$. Find the average of the quotient and divisor: $\frac{5 + 5.6}{2} = 5.3$. Continue dividing 28 by each result and averaging until you get the desired accuracy.

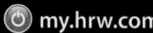
EXAMPLE 3

Questioning Strategies Mathematical Practices

• How can you verify that $\sqrt{28}$ is between 5.2 and 5.3? $5.2^2 = 27.04$ and $5.3^2 = 28.09$

• Explain how to determine which number is greater: $5.\overline{5}$ or 5.5. When the repeating decimal is rounded to the nearest tenth or hundredth, you can see that it is greater.

Connect to Daily Life

Discuss how measuring across a canyon might involve different methods than measuring along a road. Explain that measurements like these are often done using calculations that approximate the distance.

YOUR TURN

Focus on Critical Thinking Mathematical Practices

Discuss with students which number is greater, $3.\overline{45}$ or 3.450? $3.\overline{45}$ or 3.455 and why. Explain that $3.\overline{45}$ can be written out as 3.4545…Make sure they understand that $3.\overline{45}$ is greater than 3.45, but less than 3.455.

Elaborate

....

Talk About It
Summarize the Lesson

Ask: How can you order two numbers in different forms whose decimal approximations appear to be equal? Approximate one or both numbers to an additional number of decimal places.

GUIDED PRACTICE

Engage with the Whiteboard

Have students place and label additional points on the number line in Exercise 9. Allow the points to be in any format other than decimal.

Avoid Common Errors

Exercises 3–4 Caution students to read the problem carefully so that they do not misread the problem as the same numbers combined by addition on each side of the circle.

Exercise 10 Remind students that the calculations have units.

Ordering Real Numbers in a Real-World Context

Calculations and estimations in the real world may differ. It can be important to know not only which are the most accurate but which give the greatest or least values, depending upon the context.

Math On the Spot
my.hrw.com

EXAMPLE 3 Real World

FL CC 8.NS.1.2

Four people have found the distance in kilometers across a canyon using different methods. Their results are given in the table. Order the distances from greatest to least.

Distance Across Quarry Canyon (km)			
Juana	Lee Ann	Ryne	Jackson
$\sqrt{28}$	$\frac{23}{4}$	$5.\overline{5}$	$5\frac{1}{2}$

STEP 1 Approximate $\sqrt{28}$.

$\sqrt{28}$ is between 5.2 and 5.3, so $\sqrt{28} \approx 5.25$.

$\frac{23}{4} = 5.75$

$5.\overline{5}$ is 5.555..., so $5.\overline{5}$ to the nearest hundredth is 5.56.

$5\frac{1}{2} = 5.5$

STEP 2 Plot $\sqrt{28}$, $\frac{23}{4}$, $5.\overline{5}$, and $5\frac{1}{2}$ on a number line.

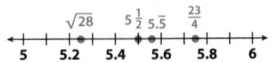

From greatest to least, the distances are:

$\frac{23}{4}$ km, $5.\overline{5}$ km, $5\frac{1}{2}$ km, $\sqrt{28}$ km.

YOUR TURN

7. Four people have found the distance in miles across a crater using different methods. Their results are given below.

Jonathan: $\frac{10}{3}$, Elaine: $3.\overline{45}$, José: $3\frac{1}{2}$, Lashonda: $\sqrt{10}$

Order the distances from greatest to least.

$3\frac{1}{2}$ mi, $3.\overline{45}$ mi, $\frac{10}{3}$ mi, $\sqrt{10}$ mi

Personal Math Trainer
Online Assessment and Intervention
my.hrw.com

Guided Practice

Compare. Write <, >, or =. (Example 1)

1. $\sqrt{3} + 2$ ⟨<⟩ $\sqrt{3} + 3$

2. $\sqrt{11} + 15$ ⟨>⟩ $\sqrt{8} + 15$

3. $\sqrt{6} + 5$ ⟨<⟩ $6 + \sqrt{5}$

4. $\sqrt{9} + 3$ ⟨<⟩ $9 + \sqrt{3}$

5. $\sqrt{17} - 3$ ⟨>⟩ $-2 + \sqrt{5}$

6. $10 - \sqrt{8}$ ⟨<⟩ $12 - \sqrt{2}$

7. $\sqrt{7} + 2$ ⟨>⟩ $\sqrt{10} - 1$

8. $\sqrt{17} + 3$ ⟨>⟩ $3 + \sqrt{11}$

9. Order $\sqrt{3}$, 2π, and 1.5 from least to greatest. Then graph them on the number line. (Example 2)

$\sqrt{3}$ is between ___1.7___ and ___1.8___, so $\sqrt{3} \approx$ ___1.75___.

$\pi \approx 3.14$, so $2\pi \approx$ ___6.28___.

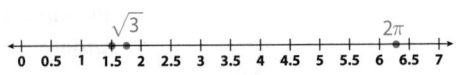

From least to greatest, the numbers are ___1.5___, ___$\sqrt{3}$___

___2π___.

10. Four people have found the perimeter of a forest using different methods. Their results are given in the table. Order their calculations from greatest to least. (Example 3)

$1 + \frac{\pi}{2}$ km, 2.5 km, $\frac{12}{5}$ km, $\sqrt{17} - 2$ km

Forest Perimeter (km)			
Leon	Mika	Jason	Ashley
$\sqrt{17} - 2$	$1 + \frac{\pi}{2}$	$\frac{12}{5}$	2.5

ESSENTIAL QUESTION CHECK-IN

11. Explain how to order a set of real numbers.

Sample answer: Convert each number to a decimal equivalent, using estimation to find equivalents for irrational numbers. Graph each number on a number line. Read the numbers from left to right for least to greatest. Read the numbers from right to left for greatest to least.

DIFFERENTIATE INSTRUCTION

Modeling

Place papers around the room with the numbers from 1 to 5, one per sheet. Give each student a card showing a number between 1 and 5 in different forms. Have students place his or her card between the correct integers, and decide where the number goes in relation to any numbers already placed.

Multiple Representations

Give students a vertical number line, which some students might find easier to use than a horizontal one. Have them decide whether to place points for rational and irrational numbers above or below existing points.

Additional Resources

Differentiated Instruction includes:

• Reading Strategies

• Success for English Learners **ELL**

• Reteach

• Challenge **PRE-AP**

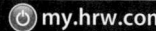
9.3 LESSON QUIZ

 **FL CC** 8.NS.1.2

1. Compare. Write $<$, $>$, or $=$.

$\sqrt{95} - 5 \bigcirc \sqrt{62} - 2$

2. Order 10.5, $\sqrt{105}$, and $3\pi + 1$ from greatest to least.

3. A length in centimeters is calculated differently by four different people. Order their calculations from least to greatest.

K.D.: $\frac{11}{2}$ cm, Silvio: $\frac{5}{3}\pi$ cm,

Paula: $5.\overline{4}$ cm, Luis: $\sqrt{33}$ cm

Lesson Quiz available online

 my.hrw.com

Answers

1. $\sqrt{95} - 5 < \sqrt{62} - 2$

2. $\sqrt{105}$, $3\pi + 1$, 10.5

3. Silvio: $\frac{5}{3}\pi$ cm, Paula: $5.\overline{4}$ cm,

K.D.: $\frac{11}{2}$ cm, Luis: $\sqrt{33}$ cm

Evaluate

GUIDED AND INDEPENDENT PRACTICE

 **FL CC** 8.NS.1.2

Concepts & Skills	Practice
Example 1 Comparing Irrational Numbers	Exercises 1–8
Example 2 Ordering Real Numbers	Exercises 9, 12–15, 18–21
Example 3 Ordering Real Numbers in a Real-World Context	Exercises 10, 16–17

Exercise	Depth of Knowledge (D.O.K.)		**FL CC** Mathematical Practices
12–15	**1** Recall of Information		**MP.5.1** Using Tools
16	**2** Skills/Concepts		**MP.2.1** Reasoning
17	**2** Skills/Concepts		**MP.6.1** Precision
18–21	**2** Skills/Concepts		**MP.2.1** Reasoning
22	**3** Strategic Thinking	H.O.T.	**MP.4.1** Modeling
23–24	**3** Strategic Thinking	H.O.T.	**MP.3.1** Logic

Additional Resources

Differentiated Instruction includes:

• Leveled Practice worksheets

9.3 Independent Practice

FL CC 8.NS.1.2

Personal Math Trainer

Online Assessment and Intervention

my.hrw.com

Order the numbers from least to greatest.

12. $\sqrt{7}, 2, \frac{\sqrt{8}}{2}$

$\frac{\sqrt{8}}{2}, 2, \sqrt{7}$

13. $\sqrt{10}, \pi, 3.5$

$\pi, \sqrt{10}, 3.5$

14. $\sqrt{220}, -10, \sqrt{100}, 11.5$

$-10, \sqrt{100}, 11.5, \sqrt{220}$

15. $\sqrt{8}, -3.75, 3, \frac{9}{4}$

$-3.75, \frac{9}{4}, \sqrt{8}, 3$

16. Your sister is considering two different shapes for her garden. One is a square with side lengths of 3.5 meters, and the other is a circle with a diameter of 4 meters.

   a. Find the area of the square. _____ 12.25 m²

   b. Find the area of the circle. _____ 4π m², or approximately 12.6 m²

   c. Compare your answers from parts **a** and **b**. Which garden would give your sister the most space to plant?

   The circle would give her more space to plant because it has a larger area.

17. Winnie measured the length of her father's ranch four times and got four different distances. Her measurements are shown in the table.

Distance Across Father's Ranch (km)			
1	2	3	4
$\sqrt{60}$	$\frac{58}{8}$	$7.\overline{3}$	$7\frac{3}{5}$

   a. To estimate the actual length, Winnie first approximated each distance to the nearest hundredth. Then she averaged the four numbers. Using a calculator, find Winnie's estimate.

   $\sqrt{60} \approx 7.75, \frac{58}{8} = 7.25, 7.\overline{3} \approx 7.33, 7\frac{3}{5} = 7.60$, so the average is 7.4825 km.

   b. Winnie's father estimated the distance across his ranch to be $\sqrt{56}$ km. How does this distance compare to Winnie's estimate?

   They are nearly identical. $\sqrt{56}$ is approximately 7.4833... .

Give an example of each type of number.

18. a real number between $\sqrt{13}$ and $\sqrt{14}$ _____ Sample answer: 3.7

19. an irrational number between 5 and 7 _____ Sample answer: $\sqrt{31}$

© Houghton Mifflin Harcourt Publishing Company

---

20. A teacher asks his students to write the numbers shown in order from least to greatest. Paul thinks the numbers are already in order. Sandra thinks the order should be reversed. Who is right?

Neither student is correct. The answer should be $\frac{115}{11}$, 10.5624, $\sqrt{115}$.

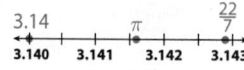
$\sqrt{115}, \frac{115}{11}$, and 10.5624

21. Math History There is a famous irrational number called Euler's number, symbolized with an *e*. Like π, its decimal form never ends or repeats. The first few digits of *e* are 2.7182818284.

   a. Between which two square roots of integers could you find this number?

   between $\sqrt{7} \approx 2.65$ and $\sqrt{8} \approx 2.83$

   b. Between which two square roots of integers can you find π?

   between $\sqrt{9} \approx 3$ and $\sqrt{10} \approx 3.16$

H.O.T. FOCUS ON HIGHER ORDER THINKING

22. Analyze Relationships There are several approximations used for π, including 3.14 and $\frac{22}{7}$. π is approximately 3.14159265358979...

   a. Label π and the two approximations on the number line.

   3.14 π $\frac{22}{7}$
   |—+—+—+—+—+—|
   3.140 3.141 3.142 3.143

   b. Which of the two approximations is a better estimate for π? Explain.

   $\frac{22}{7}$; it is closer to π on the number line.

   c. Find a whole number *x* in $\frac{x}{113}$ so that the ratio is a better estimate for π than the two given approximations. _____ 355

23. Communicate Mathematical Ideas If a set of six numbers that include both rational and irrational numbers is graphed on a number line, what is the fewest number of distinct points that need to be graphed? Explain.

   2; rational numbers can have the same location, and irrational numbers can have the same location, but they cannot share a location.

24. Critique Reasoning Jill says that $12.\overline{6}$ is less than 12.63. Explain her error.

   She did not consider the repeating digit. 12.66... .

Work Area

© Houghton Mifflin Harcourt Publishing Company • Image Credits: ©3DStock/ iStockPhoto.com

---

EXTEND THE MATH PRE-AP

Activity available online my.hrw.com

Activity Have students investigate whether there are infinitely many numbers between two numbers by giving examples for each of the following.

- Between any two rational numbers there is at least one other rational number.
  Sample answer: 4.5 is between 4.1 and 4.8

- Between any two irrational numbers there is at least one rational number.
  Sample answer: 4.5 is between $\sqrt{11}$ and $\sqrt{29}$

- Between any two rational numbers there is at least one irrational number.
  Sample answer: $\sqrt{11}$ is between 3.1 and 3.6

- Between any two irrational numbers there is at least one irrational number.
  Sample answer: $\sqrt{17}$ is between $\sqrt{11}$ and $\sqrt{29}$

Ready to Go On?

Assess Mastery

Use the assessment on this page to determine if students have mastered the concepts and standards covered in this module.

  **RtI** **Response to Intervention**

Intervention	Enrichment

Access Ready to Go On? assessment online, and receive instant scoring, feedback, and customized intervention or enrichment.

Personal Math Trainer

Online Assessment and Intervention

⏻ my.hrw.com

Online and Print Resources

Differentiated Instruction
• Reteach worksheets
• Reading Strategies **ELL**
• Success for English Learners **ELL**

Differentiated Instruction
• Challenge worksheets
  PRE-AP
• Extend the Math **PRE-AP**
  Lesson Activities in TE

Additional Resources

Assessment Resources includes

• Leveled Module Quizzes

Ready to Go On?

Personal Math Trainer
Online Assessment and Intervention
ⓐ my.hrw.com

9.1 Rational and Irrational Numbers

Write each fraction as a decimal or each decimal as a fraction.

1. $\frac{7}{20}$ ___0.35___
2. $1.\overline{27}$ ___$\frac{14}{11}$___
3. $1\frac{7}{8}$ ___1.875___

Solve each equation for x.

4. $x^2 = 81$ ___9, −9___
5. $x^3 = 343$ ___7___
6. $x^2 = \frac{1}{100}$ ___$\frac{1}{10}, -\frac{1}{10}$___

7. A square patio has an area of 200 square feet. How long is each side of the patio to the nearest 0.05? ___14.15 ft___

9.2 Sets of Real Numbers

Write all names that apply to each number.

8. $\frac{121}{\sqrt{121}}$ whole, integer, rational, real

9. $\frac{\pi}{2}$ irrational, real

10. Tell whether the statement "All integers are rational numbers" is true or false. Explain your choice.
True; integers can be written as the quotient of two integers.

9.3 Ordering Real Numbers

Compare. Write $<$, $>$, or $=$.

11. $\sqrt{8} + 3$ $<$ $8 + \sqrt{3}$
12. $\sqrt{5} + 11$ $>$ $5 + \sqrt{11}$

Order the numbers from least to greatest.

13. $\sqrt{99}, \pi^2, 9.\overline{8}$ ___$\pi^2, 9.\overline{8}, \sqrt{99}$___
14. $\sqrt{\frac{1}{25}}, \frac{1}{4}, 0.\overline{2}$ ___$\sqrt{\frac{1}{25}}, 0.\overline{2}, \frac{1}{4}$___

 ESSENTIAL QUESTION

15. How are real numbers used to describe real-world situations?
Sample answer: Real numbers, such as the rational number $\frac{1}{4}$, can describe amounts used in cooking.

© Houghton Mifflin Harcourt Publishing Company

 ## Florida Common Core Standards

Lesson	Exercises	🏴 Common Core Standards
9.1	1–7	**8.NS.1.1, 8.NS.1.2, 8.EE.1.2**
9.2	8–10	**8.NS.1.1**
9.3	11–14	**8.NS.1.2**

PARCC Assessment Readiness

PARCC Assessment Readiness
MODULE 9 MIXED REVIEW

Personal Math Trainer
Online Assessment and Intervention
my.hrw.com

Assessment Readiness Tip Students can use estimation to eliminate some or all of the answer choices.

Item 2 24 is close to 20, and 20 squared is 400. 400 is much less than 4840, so A is not likely to be correct. 242 is close to 200, and 200 squared is 40,000, which is much greater than 4840. C is not correct, and since D is greater than C, D is also incorrect.

Item 8 π is about 3.14, so $\pi + 3$ is about 6.14, which is much lower than the point on the graph. $6.\overline{14}$ is nearby and therefore also much too low. Answer choices A and D can be eliminated.

Avoid Common Errors

Item 4 Students commonly confuse real numbers and rational numbers, which may lead them to believe that C is true. Remind them that real numbers include rational and irrational numbers.

Item 6 If students do not read the item carefully, they may mistakenly look for a true statement and choose any of the distractors. Remind them to always read carefully.

Additional Resources

Personal Math Trainer
Online Assessment and Intervention
my.hrw.com

Selected Response

1. The square root of a number is 9. What is the other square root?
- (A) −9
- (B) −3
- (C) 3
- (D) 81

2. A square acre of land is 4840 square yards. Between which two integers is the length of one side?
- (A) between 24 and 25 yards
- (B) between 69 and 70 yards
- (C) between 242 and 243 yards
- (D) between 695 and 696 yards

3. Which of the following is an integer but not a whole number?
- (A) −9.6
- (B) −4
- (C) 0
- (D) 3.7

4. Which statement is false?
- (A) No integers are irrational numbers.
- (B) All whole numbers are integers.
- (C) No real numbers are irrational numbers.
- (D) All integers greater than 0 are whole numbers.

5. An eighth-grade class has 120 students. Gavin surveys a random sample of 30 students and finds that 17 of them have brown eyes. How many students in the class are likely to have brown eyes?
- (A) 17
- (B) 30
- (C) 52
- (D) 68

6. Which of the following is **not** true?
- (A) $\pi^2 < 2\pi + 4$
- (B) $3\pi > 9$
- (C) $\sqrt{27} + 3 > \frac{17}{2}$
- (D) $5 - \sqrt{24} < 1$

7. Which number is between $\sqrt{21}$ and $\frac{3\pi}{2}$?
- (A) $\frac{14}{3}$
- (B) $2\sqrt{6}$
- (C) 5
- (D) $\pi + 1$

8. What number is shown on the graph?

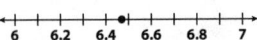

- (A) $\pi + 3$
- (B) $\frac{129}{20}$
- (C) $\sqrt{20} + 2$
- (D) $6.\overline{14}$

9. Which is in order from least to greatest?
- (A) $3.3, \frac{10}{3}, \pi, \frac{11}{4}$
- (B) $\frac{10}{3}, 3.3, \frac{11}{4}, \pi$
- (C) $\pi, \frac{10}{3}, \frac{11}{4}, 3.3$
- (D) $\frac{11}{4}, \pi, 3.3, \frac{10}{3}$

Mini-Task

10. The volume of a cube is given by $V = x^3$, where x is the length of an edge of the cube. The area of a square is given by $A = x^2$, where x is the length of a side of the square. A given cube has a volume of 1,728 cubic inches.

a. Find the length of an edge.

_____12 in._____

b. Find the area of one side of the cube.

_____144 in²_____

c. Find the surface area of the cube.

_____864 in²_____

d. What is the surface area in square feet?

_____6 ft²_____

© Houghton Mifflin Harcourt Publishing Company

 ## Florida Common Core Standards

Items	Grade 8 Standards	Mathematical Practices
1	8.EE.1.2	MP.7.1
2*	7.G.2.6, 8.NS.1.2	MP.4.1
3	8.NS.1.1	
4	8.NS.1.1	
5*	7.SP.3.6	MP.4.1
6	8.NS.1.2	MP.6.1
7	8.NS.1.2	MP.6.1
8	8.NS.1.2	MP.6.1
9	8.NS.1.2	MP.6.1
10*	7.G.2.6, 8.EE.1.2	MP.4.1

* Item integrates mixed review concepts from previous modules or a previous course.

Exponents and Scientific Notation

COMMON CORE

 **ESSENTIAL QUESTION**

How can you use scientific notation to solve real-world problems?

You can simplify calculations with very large and very small numbers by first writing them in scientific notation.

Real-World Video

The distance from Earth to other planets, moons, and stars is a very great number of kilometers. To make it easier to write very large and very small numbers, we use scientific notation.

⏱ my.hrw.com

GO DIGITAL

my.hrw.com

my.hrw.com

Go digital with your write-in student edition, accessible on any device.

Math On the Spot

Scan with your smart phone to jump directly to the online edition, video tutor, and more.

Animated Math

Interactively explore key concepts to see how math works.

Personal Math Trainer

Get immediate feedback and help as you work through practice sets.

Are You Ready?

Assess Readiness

Use the assessment on this page to determine if students need intensive or strategic intervention for the module's prerequisite skills.

 **Response to Intervention**

Personal Math Trainer
Online Assessment and Intervention
my.hrw.com

Intervention	Enrichment
Access Are You Ready? assessment online, and receive instant scoring, feedback, and customized intervention or enrichment.	

Online and Print Resources

Skills Intervention worksheets
• Skill 12 Exponents
• Skill 37 Multiply and Divide by Powers of 10

Differentiated Instruction
• Challenge worksheets **PRE-AP**
Extend the Math **PRE-AP** Lesson Activities in TE

Are YOU Ready?

Complete these exercises to review skills you will need for this module.

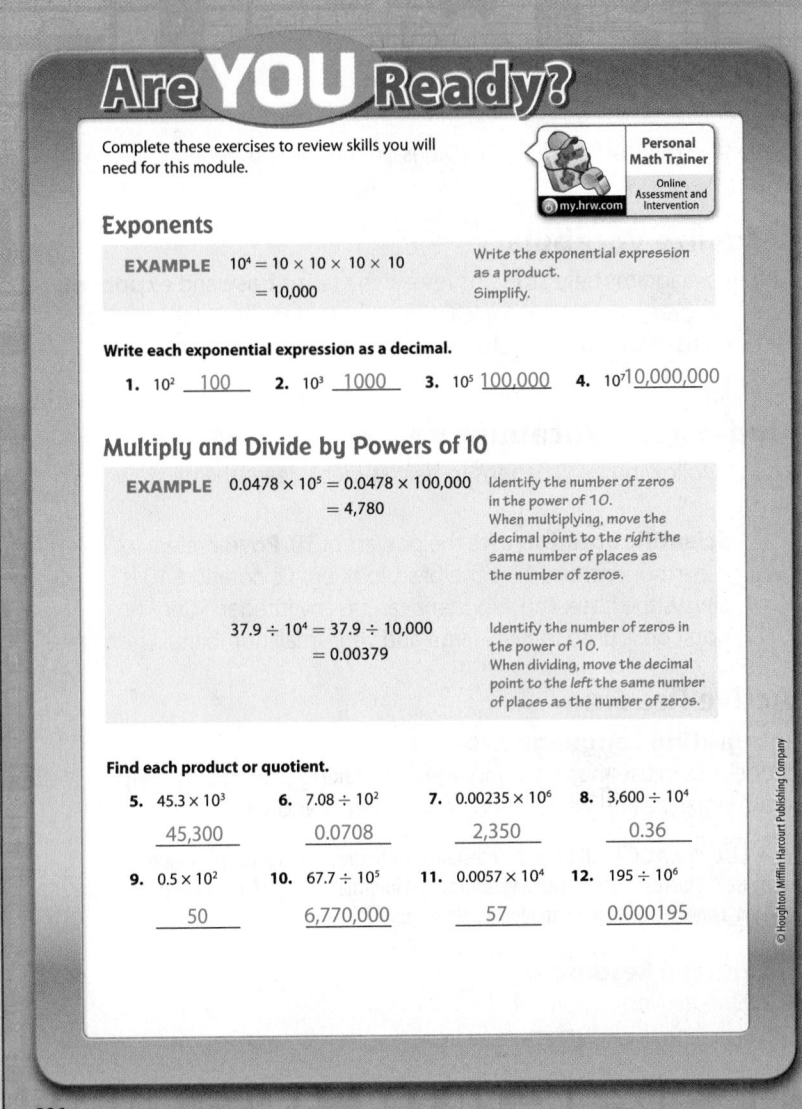

Personal Math Trainer
Online Assessment and Intervention
my.hrw.com

Exponents

EXAMPLE	$10^4 = 10 \times 10 \times 10 \times 10$ $= 10,000$	Write the exponential expression as a product. Simplify.

Write each exponential expression as a decimal.

1. 10^2 __100__   2. 10^3 __1000__   3. 10^5 __100,000__   4. 10^7 __10,000,000__

Multiply and Divide by Powers of 10

EXAMPLE	$0.0478 \times 10^5 = 0.0478 \times 100,000$ $= 4,780$	Identify the number of zeros in the power of 10. When multiplying, move the decimal point to the *right* the same number of places as the number of zeros.
	$37.9 \div 10^4 = 37.9 \div 10,000$ $= 0.00379$	Identify the number of zeros in the power of 10. When dividing, move the decimal point to the *left* the same number of places as the number of zeros.

Find each product or quotient.

5. 45.3×10^3 __45,300__   6. $7.08 \div 10^2$ __0.0708__   7. 0.00235×10^6 __2,350__   8. $3,600 \div 10^4$ __0.36__

9. 0.5×10^2 __50__   10. $67.7 \div 10^5$ __6,770,000__   11. 0.0057×10^4 __57__   12. $195 \div 10^6$ __0.000195__

294 Unit 5

© Houghton Mifflin Harcourt Publishing Company

PROFESSIONAL DEVELOPMENT VIDEO

Author Juli Dixon models successful teaching practices as she explores the concept of scientific notation in an actual eighth-grade classroom.

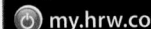
Professional Development
my.hrw.com

GO DIGITAL
my.hrw.com

Online Teacher Edition
Access a full suite of teaching resources online—plan, present, and manage classes and assignments.

ePlanner
Easily plan your classes and access all your resources online.

Interactive Answers and Solutions
Customize answer keys to print or display in the classroom. Choose to include answers only or full solutions to all lesson exercises.

Interactive Whiteboards
Engage students with interactive whiteboard-ready lessons and activities.

Personal Math Trainer: Online Assessment and Intervention
Assign automatically graded homework, quizzes, tests, and intervention activities. Prepare your students with updated practice tests aligned with Common Core.

Reading Start-Up

Have students complete the activities on this page by working alone or with others.

Visualize Vocabulary

The two diagrams help students review the terms **base** and **exponent,** and help prepare students for learning about scientific notation which is the focus of this module. Students should write more than one review word in each box.

Understand Vocabulary

Use the following explanations to help students learn the preview words.

> **Scientific notation** uses the powers of 10. **Power** refers to the exponent, and 10 is the base. In scientific notation, 10 is always the base. The exponent can be any integer. Scientific notation is used for very large and very small numbers.

Active Reading

Integrating Language Arts

Students can use these reading and note-taking strategies to help them organize and understand new concepts and vocabulary.

FL CC LACC.68.RST.3.7 Integrate quantitative or technical information expressed in words in a text with a version of that information expressed visually (e.g., in a flowchart, diagram, model, graph, or table).

Additional Resources

Differentiated Instruction

• Reading Strategies **ELL**

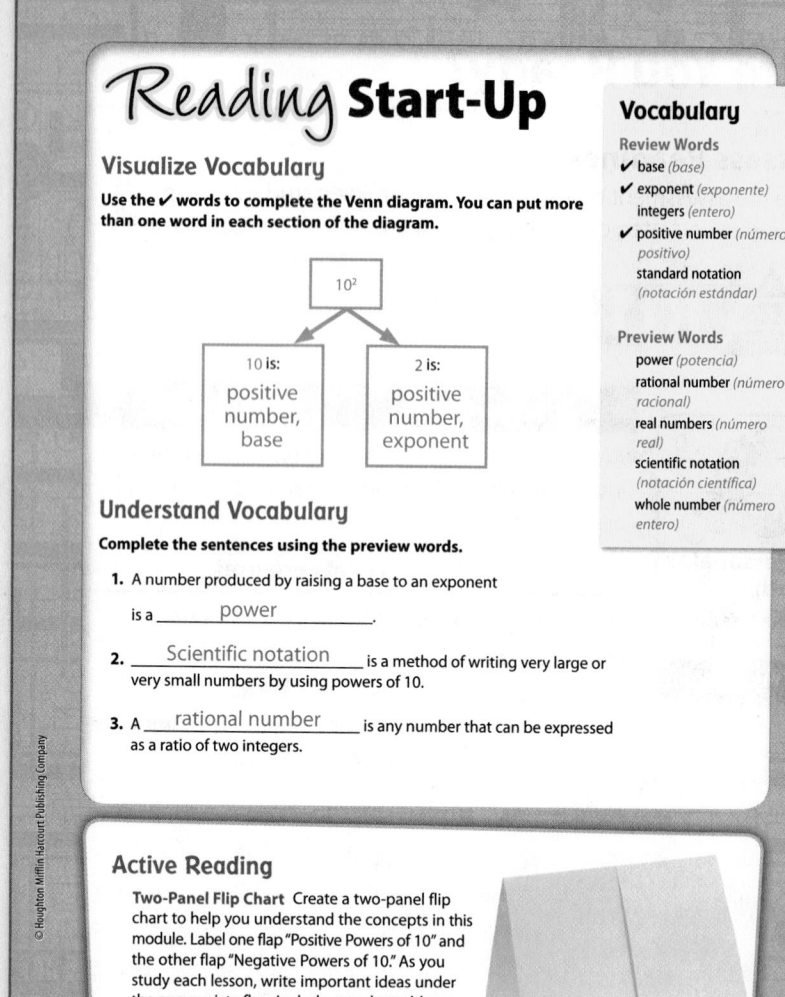

Vocabulary

Review Words
✔ base *(base)*
✔ exponent *(exponente)*
   integers *(entero)*
✔ positive number *(número positivo)*
   standard notation *(notación estándar)*

Preview Words
   power *(potencia)*
   rational number *(número racional)*
   real numbers *(número real)*
   scientific notation *(notación científica)*
   whole number *(número entero)*

Reading Start-Up

Visualize Vocabulary

Use the ✔ words to complete the Venn diagram. You can put more than one word in each section of the diagram.

10^2

10 is:
positive number, base

2 is:
positive number, exponent

Understand Vocabulary

Complete the sentences using the preview words.

1. A number produced by raising a base to an exponent is a ___power___.

2. ___Scientific notation___ is a method of writing very large or very small numbers by using powers of 10.

3. A ___rational number___ is any number that can be expressed as a ratio of two integers.

Active Reading

Two-Panel Flip Chart Create a two-panel flip chart to help you understand the concepts in this module. Label one flap "Positive Powers of 10" and the other flap "Negative Powers of 10." As you study each lesson, write important ideas under the appropriate flap. Include sample problems that will help you remember the concepts later when you look back at your notes.

Module 10 **295**

Before	In this module	After
Students understand how to: • write decimals • use exponents • add, subtract, multiply, and divide rational numbers	Students will learn how to: • apply properties of integer exponents to evaluate expressions • convert between large numbers in standard decimal notation and scientific notation • convert between small numbers in standard decimal notation and scientific notation • add, subtract, multiply, and divide numbers expressed with scientific notation	Students will connect that: • positive numbers written in scientific notation with negative exponents represent numbers between 0 and 1 • measurements written in scientific notation often use significant digits to show the precision of a measurement

Unpacking the Standards

Use the examples on the page to help students know exactly what they are expected to learn in this module.

 Florida Common Core Standards

Content Areas

 FL CC Expressions and Equations—8.EE.1

Work with radicals and integer exponents.

Go online to see a complete unpacking of the Florida Common Core Standards.

my.hrw.com

FL CC 8.EE.1.1

Know and apply the properties of integer exponents to generate equivalent numerical expressions.

Key Vocabulary

integer *(entero)*
The set of whole numbers and their opposites

exponent *(exponente)*
The number that indicates how many times the base is used as a factor.

What It Means to You

You will use the properties of integer exponents to find equivalent expressions.

UNPACKING EXAMPLE 8.EE.1.1

Evaluate two different ways.

$$\frac{8^3}{8^5} \qquad \frac{8^3}{8^5} = \frac{8 \cdot 8 \cdot 8}{8 \cdot 8 \cdot 8 \cdot 8 \cdot 8} = \frac{1}{8 \cdot 8} = \frac{1}{64}$$

$$\frac{8^3}{8^5} = 8^{(3-5)} = 8^{-2} = \frac{1}{8^2} = \frac{1}{8 \cdot 8} = \frac{1}{64}$$

$$(3^2)^4 \qquad (3^2)^4 = (3^2)(3^2)(3^2)(3^2) = 3^{2+2+2+2} = 3^8 = 6{,}561$$

$$(3^2)^4 = 3^{(2 \cdot 4)} = 3^8 = 6{,}561$$

FL CC 8.EE.1.3

Use numbers expressed in the form of a single digit times an integer power of 10 to estimate very large or very small quantities, and to express how many times as much one is than the other.

Key Vocabulary

scientific notation *(notación científica)*
A method of writing very large or very small numbers by using powers of 10.

What It Means to You

You will convert very large numbers to scientific notation.

UNPACKING EXAMPLE 8.EE.1.3

There are about 55,000,000,000 cells in an average-sized adult. Write this number in scientific notation.

Move the decimal point to the left until you have a number that is greater than or equal to 1 and less than 10.

5.5 0 0 0 0 0 0 0 0 0   *Move the decimal point 10 places to the left.*

5.5   *Remove the extra zeros.*

You would have to multiply 5.5 by 10^{10} to get 55,000,000,000.

$$55{,}000{,}000{,}000 = 5.5 \times 10^{10}$$

Visit my.hrw.com to see all Florida Common Core Standards unpacked.

my.hrw.com

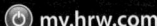 Florida Common Core Standards	Lesson 10.1	Lesson 10.2	Lesson 10.3	Lesson 10.4
FL CC 8.EE.1.1 Know and apply the properties of integer exponents to generate equivalent numerical expressions.	✓			
FL CC 8.EE.1.3 Use numbers expressed in the form of a single digit times a whole-number power of 10 to estimate very large or very small quantities, and to express how many times as much one is than the other.		✓	✓	
FL CC 8.EE.1.4 Perform operations with numbers expressed in scientific notation, including problems where both decimal and scientific notation are used. Use scientific notation and choose units of appropriate size for measurements of very large or very small quantities (e.g., use millimeters per year for seafloor spreading). Interpret scientific notation that has been generated by technology.				✓

LESSON
10.1 Integer Exponents

 Florida Common Core Standards

The student is expected to:

 **FL CC** **Expressions and Equations—8.EE.1.1**

Know and apply the properties of integer exponents to generate equivalent numerical expressions.

Mathematical Practices

 **FL CC** **MP.8.1** Patterns

Engage

ESSENTIAL QUESTION

How can you develop and use the properties of integer exponents? Sample answer: To develop the properties of integer exponents, look for patterns in a powers table and in the multiplication and division of powers with the same base. The properties can be used to simplify complicated expressions.

Motivate the Lesson

Ask: How can patterns help you simplify numbers involving negative exponents? Take a guess. Begin Explore Activity 1 to find out.

Explore

EXPLORE ACTIVITY 1

Focus on Patterns Mathematical Practices

If students have trouble seeing the patterns, point out that they should look at one row of the table at a time, and examine the two sides of the equation separately. Ask them to identify what changes on the left side and what changes on the right side.

Explain

EXPLORE ACTIVITY 2

Questioning Strategies Mathematical Practices

• In Part B, why are there five factors of 4 in the numerator and only three in the denominator? 4^5 means 4 is a factor five times. 4^3 means 4 is a factor three times.

• In Part C, could $(5^3)^2$ be thought of as $(5^3)(5^3)$? Justify your answer. Yes, the base is (5^3), and the exponent 2 means that (5^3) is used as a factor two times, so $(5^3)^2 = (5^3)(5^3)$.

Engage with the Whiteboard

For each equation in Part A, have volunteers circle each factor as they count aloud. Then have students write the total number of factors in the box provided.

LESSON
10.1 Integer Exponents

FL CC 8.EE.1.1
Know and apply the properties of integer exponents to generate equivalent numerical expressions.

? **ESSENTIAL QUESTION**
How can you develop and use the properties of integer exponents?

EXPLORE ACTIVITY 1 FL CC 8.EE.1.1

Using Patterns of Integer Exponents

The table below shows powers of 5, 4, and 3.

$5^4 = 625$	$5^3 = 125$	$5^2 = 25$	$5^1 = 5$	$5^0 = \boxed{1}$	$5^{-1} = \boxed{\frac{1}{5}}$	$5^{-2} = \boxed{\frac{1}{25}}$
$4^4 = 256$	$4^3 = 64$	$4^2 = 16$	$4^1 = 4$	$4^0 = \boxed{1}$	$4^{-1} = \boxed{\frac{1}{4}}$	$4^{-2} = \boxed{\frac{1}{16}}$
$3^4 = 81$	$3^3 = 27$	$3^2 = 9$	$3^1 = 3$	$3^0 = \boxed{1}$	$3^{-1} = \boxed{\frac{1}{3}}$	$3^{-2} = \boxed{\frac{1}{9}}$

A What pattern do you see in the powers of 5?

As the exponent decreases by 1, the value of the power is divided by 5.

B What pattern do you see in the powers of 4?

As the exponent decreases by 1, the value of the power is divided by 4.

C What pattern do you see in the powers of 3?

As the exponent decreases by 1, the value of the power is divided by 3.

D Complete the table for the values of $5^0, 5^{-1}, 5^{-2}$. See table above.
E Complete the table for the values of $4^0, 4^{-1}, 4^{-2}$. See table above.
F Complete the table for the values of $3^0, 3^{-1}, 3^{-2}$. See table above.

Reflect

1. **Make a Conjecture** Write a general rule for the value of a^0.

2. **Make a Conjecture** Write a general rule for the value of a^{-n}.

$$a^0 = 1$$
$$a^{-n} = \frac{1}{a^n}$$

EXPLORE ACTIVITY 2 FL CC 8.EE.1.1

Exploring Properties of Integer Exponents

A Complete the following equations.

$3 \cdot 3 \cdot 3 \cdot 3 \cdot 3 = 3^{\boxed{5}}$

$(3 \cdot 3 \cdot 3 \cdot 3) \cdot 3 = 3^{\boxed{4}} \cdot 3^{\boxed{1}} = 3^{\boxed{5}}$

$(3 \cdot 3 \cdot 3) \cdot (3 \cdot 3) = 3^{\boxed{3}} \cdot 3^{\boxed{2}} = 3^{\boxed{5}}$

What pattern do you see when multiplying two powers with the same base?

The result has the same base with an exponent equal to the sum of the exponents in the powers.

Use your pattern to complete this equation: $5^2 \cdot 5^5 = 5^{\boxed{7}}$.

B Complete the following equation:

$\frac{4^5}{4^3} = \frac{4 \cdot 4 \cdot 4 \cdot 4 \cdot 4}{4 \cdot 4 \cdot 4} = \frac{\cancel{4} \cdot \cancel{4} \cdot \cancel{4} \cdot 4 \cdot 4}{\cancel{4} \cdot \cancel{4} \cdot \cancel{4}} = 4 \cdot 4 = 4^{\boxed{2}}$

What pattern do you see when dividing two powers with the same base?

The result has the same base with an exponent equal to the difference of the exponent in the numerator and exponent in the denominator.

Use your pattern to complete this equation: $\frac{6^8}{6^3} = 6^{\boxed{5}}$.

C Complete the following equations:

$(5^3)^2 = (5 \cdot 5 \cdot 5)^{\boxed{2}} = (5 \cdot 5 \cdot 5) \cdot (5 \cdot 5 \cdot 5) = 5^{\boxed{6}}$

What pattern do you see when raising a power to a power?

The result has the same base with an exponent equal to the product of the exponents.

Use your pattern to complete this equation: $(7^2)^4 = 7^{\boxed{8}}$.

Yes;
$5^{-1} \cdot 5^{-2} =$
$\frac{1}{5} \cdot \frac{1}{25} = \frac{1}{125} = \frac{1}{5^3}$
$= 5^{-3} = 5^{-1 + (-2)}$;

$\frac{2^{-5}}{2^{-3}} = \frac{2^3}{2^5}$
$= \frac{2 \cdot 2 \cdot 2}{2 \cdot 2 \cdot 2 \cdot 2 \cdot 2}$
$= 2^{-2} = 2^{-5 - (-3)}$

$(3^{-2})^{-3} = \left(\frac{1}{3^2}\right)^{-3}$
$= (3^2)^3 = 3^6$
$= 3^{-2 \cdot (-3)}$

Math Talk
Mathematical Practices
Do the patterns you found apply if the exponents are negative? If so, give an example of each.

PROFESSIONAL DEVELOPMENT

Integrate Mathematical Practices MP.8.1

This lesson provides an opportunity to address this Mathematical Practices standard. It calls for students to notice if calculations are repeated. Students learn to recognize how repeated division defines the use of negative exponents. They then use repeated multiplication and division to discover properties of exponents and find shortcuts for solving expressions.

Math Background

Using patterns, you can intuitively see that any nonzero number raised to the zero power equals 1. For example, $2^4 = 16$; $2^3 = 8$; $2^2 = 4$; $2^1 = 2$; $2^0 = 1$. The exponent decreases by 1 as the value of the exponential expression is divided by the value of the base. Another way to understand this is to use the fact that any number (other than 0) divided by itself is 1 and the property of exponents that tells us that is $a^x \div a^y = a^{x-y}$, for $a \neq 0$. Therefore, since $a^x \div a^x = a^{x-x}$ or a^0 and $a^x \div a^x = 1$, we can conclude that $a^0 = 1$, for $a \neq 0$.

EXAMPLE 1

Questioning Strategies  Mathematical Practices

• How can you use your knowledge of the order of operations to help simplify expressions involving exponents? Start by simplifying what you can inside parentheses, and then use the properties of exponents to simplify terms with exponents.

• How else could you find the product of 3^5 and 3^{-8}? Evaluate each exponent separately and then multiply the numbers 243 and $\frac{1}{6561}$.

Focus on Critical Thinking

Make sure students understand that for expressions such as $(3 + 1)^2$ in Part B, they do not distribute the exponent to each term inside the parentheses but rather simplify inside the parentheses and then apply the exponent. That is, $(3 + 1)^2 \neq 3^2 + 1^2$ but rather $(3 + 1)^2 = 4^2$.

YOUR TURN

Avoid Common Errors

To avoid calculation errors in expressions like those in Exercise 6, make sure that students understand that simplifying terms with common bases usually makes calculating easier. For example, $[(6 - 1)^2]^2 = 5^4 = 625$ and $(3 + 2)^3 = 5^3 = 125$. It is much easier to mentally simplify $\frac{5^4}{5^3} = 5$ than it is to simplify $\frac{625}{125}$.

Talk About It
Check for Understanding

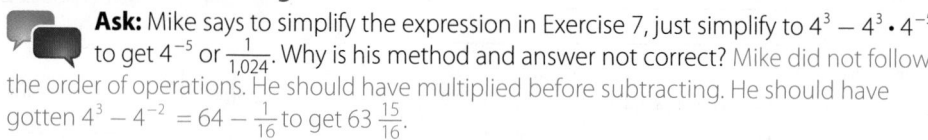 **Ask:** Mike says to simplify the expression in Exercise 7, just simplify to $4^3 - 4^3 \cdot 4^{-5}$ to get 4^{-5} or $\frac{1}{1,024}$. Why is his method and answer not correct? Mike did not follow the order of operations. He should have multiplied before subtracting. He should have gotten $4^3 - 4^{-2} = 64 - \frac{1}{16}$ to get $63\frac{15}{16}$.

Elaborate

Talk About It
Summarize the Lesson

Ask: How can you simplify an expression with exponents by applying the properties of exponents? The order of operations must always be followed. Each expression within brackets or parentheses must be simplified first. Then terms with the same base that are being multiplied or divided can be simplified using the properties of exponents. Finally, any terms being added or subtracted are simplified.

GUIDED PRACTICE

Engage with the Whiteboard

For Exercises 18 and 19, have students underline each expression inside parentheses and then write the value of each underlined expression below it while explaining how to simplify each part of the expression.

Avoid Common Errors

Exercises 1–2, 6–7, 9 Remind students that a negative exponent does not mean the answer will be a negative number.

Exercise 10 Remind students that when no exponent is given, it is understood that the number is raised to the power of 1.

Reflect

3. **Make a Conjecture** Write a general rule for the value of $a^m \cdot a^n$.

$$a^m \cdot a^n = a^{m+n}$$

4. **Make a Conjecture** Write a general rule for the value of $\frac{a^m}{a^n}$.

$$\frac{a^m}{a^n} = a^{m-n}$$

5. **Make a Conjecture** Write a general rule for the value of $(a^m)^n$.

$$(a^m)^n = a^{m \cdot n}$$

Applying Properties of Integer Exponents

You can use the general rules you found in the Explore Activities to simplify more complicated expressions.

Math On the Spot
my.hrw.com

EXAMPLE 1   FL CC 8.EE.1.1

Simplify each expression.

A $(5-2)^5 \cdot 3^{-8} + (5+2)^0$

$(3)^5 \cdot 3^{-8} + (7)^0$	Simplify within parentheses.
$3^{5+(-8)} + 1$	Use properties of exponents.
$3^{-3} + 1$	Simplify.
$\frac{1}{27} + 1 = 1\frac{1}{27}$	Apply the rule for negative exponents and add.

B $\frac{[(3+1)^2]^3}{(7-3)^2}$

$\frac{(4^2)^3}{4^2}$	Simplify within parentheses.
$\frac{4^6}{4^2}$	Use properties of exponents.
4^{6-2}	Use properties of exponents.
$4^4 = 256$	Simplify.

YOUR TURN

Simplify each expression.

6. $\frac{[(6-1)^2]^2}{(3+2)^3}$

   5

7. $(2^2)^3 - (10-6)^3 \cdot 4^{-5}$

   $63\frac{15}{16}$

Personal Math Trainer
Online Assessment and Intervention
my.hrw.com

My Notes

Find the value of each power. (Explore Activity 1)

1. $8^{-1} = \underline{\frac{1}{8}}$

2. $6^{-2} = \underline{\frac{1}{36}}$

3. $256^0 = \underline{1}$

4. $10^2 = \underline{100}$

5. $5^4 = \underline{625}$

6. $2^{-5} = \underline{\frac{1}{32}}$

7. $4^{-5} = \underline{\frac{1}{1024}}$

8. $89^0 = \underline{1}$

9. $11^{-3} = \underline{\frac{1}{1331}}$

Use properties of exponents to write an equivalent expression. (Explore Activity 2)

10. $4 \cdot 4 \cdot 4 = 4^{\boxed{3}}$

11. $(2 \cdot 2) \cdot (2 \cdot 2 \cdot 2) = 2^{\boxed{2}} \cdot 2^{\boxed{3}} = 2^{\boxed{5}}$

12. $\frac{6^7}{6^5} = \frac{6 \cdot 6 \cdot 6 \cdot 6 \cdot 6 \cdot 6 \cdot 6}{6 \cdot 6 \cdot 6 \cdot 6 \cdot 6} = 6^{\boxed{2}}$

13. $\frac{8^{12}}{8^9} = 8^{\boxed{12} - \boxed{9}} = 8^{\boxed{3}}$

14. $5^{10} \cdot 5 \cdot 5 = 5^{\boxed{12}}$

15. $7^8 \cdot 7^5 = 7^{\boxed{13}}$

16. $(6^2)^4 = (6 \cdot 6)^{\boxed{4}}$

$= (6 \cdot 6) \cdot (6 \cdot 6) \cdot \boxed{(6 \cdot 6)} \cdot \underline{(6 \cdot 6)}$

$= 6^{\boxed{8}}$

17. $(3^3)^3 = (3 \cdot 3 \cdot 3)^3$

$= (3 \cdot 3 \cdot 3) \cdot \boxed{(3 \cdot 3 \cdot 3)} \cdot \underline{(3 \cdot 3 \cdot 3)}$

$= 3^{\boxed{9}}$

Simplify each expression. (Example 1)

18. $(10-6)^3 \cdot 4^2 + (10+2)^2$ ___1168___

19. $\frac{(12-5)^7}{[(3+4)^2]^2}$ ___343___

? ESSENTIAL QUESTION CHECK-IN

20. Summarize the rules for multiplying powers with the same base, dividing powers with the same base, and raising a power to a power.

When multiplying powers with the same base, you add the exponents. When dividing powers with the same base, you subtract the exponents. When raising a power to a power, you multiply the exponents.

DIFFERENTIATE INSTRUCTION

Multiple Representations

Working in pairs, each student creates two expressions involving exponents that can be simplified. Encourage students to use negative exponents. Have students in each pair exchange problems and simplify each other's expressions. Sample expressions: $(-4)^{-2} = \frac{1}{(-4)^2} = \frac{1}{16}$; $\frac{6^2}{6^5} = 6^{-3} = \frac{1}{6^3} = \frac{1}{216}$

Critical Thinking

Have students discuss whether $(-a)^2$ for $a \neq 0$ will always have a positive value or a negative value. Then have them do the same for $-a^2$ for $a \neq 0$. Students should recognize that $(-a)^2$ is always positive because the square of any nonzero number is always positive. Students should recognize that the order of operations means $-a^2 = -(a^2)$, and its value will always be negative.

Additional Resources

Differentiated Instruction includes:

- Reading Strategies
- Success for English Learners **ELL**
- Reteach
- Challenge **PRE-AP**

Personal Math Trainer

Online Assessment
and Intervention

Online homework
assignment available

 my.hrw.com

---

10.1 LESSON QUIZ

 **FL CC** 8.EE.1.1

Find the value of each power.

1. 5^{-2}

2. 3^4

Use properties of exponents to write an equivalent expression.

3. $(5 \cdot 5) \cdot (5 \cdot 5 \cdot 5 \cdot 5)$

4. $\frac{(7^4)^2}{7^5}$

Simplify each expression.

5. $(8 - 6)^5 \cdot (2)^{-4} + (2)^0$

6. $\frac{[(9 - 1)]^5}{(6 + 2)^3}$

Lesson Quiz available online

 my.hrw.com

Answers

1. $\frac{1}{25}$

2. 81

3 5^6

4. 7^3

5. 3

6. 64

Evaluate

GUIDED AND INDEPENDENT PRACTICE

 **FL CC** 8.EE.1.1

Concepts & Skills	Practice
Explore Activity 1 Using Patterns of Integer Exponents	Exercises 1–9
Explore Activity 2 Exploring Properties of Integer Exponents	Exercises 10–17, 21–27, 29–30
Example 1 Applying Properties of Integer Exponents	Exercises 18–19

Exercise	Depth of Knowledge (D.O.K.)	**FL CC** Mathematical Practices
21–22	**2** Skills/Concepts	**MP.7.1** Using Structure
23	**2** Skills/Concepts	**MP.4.1** Modeling
24	**2** Skills/Concepts	**MP.3.1** Logic
25–27	**2** Skills/Concepts	**MP.5.1** Using Tools
28	**3** Strategic Thinking **H.O.T.**	**MP.3.1** Logic
29–30	**2** Skills/Concepts	**MP.4.1** Modeling
31	**3** Strategic Thinking **H.O.T.**	**MP.3.1** Logic
32–34	**2** Skills/Concepts	**MP.7.1** Using Structure
35–36	**3** Strategic Thinking **H.O.T.**	**MP.3.1** Logic
37	**3** Strategic Thinking **H.O.T.**	**MP.1.1** Problem Solving

Additional Resources

Differentiated Instruction includes:

• Leveled Practice worksheets

Lesson 10.1

Name _____ Class _____ Date _____

10.1 Independent Practice

FL CC 8.EE.1.1

Personal Math Trainer
Online Assessment and Intervention
my.hrw.com

21. Explain why the exponents cannot be added in the product $12^3 \cdot 11^3$.

The exponents cannot be added because the bases are not the same.

22. List three ways to express 3^5 as a product of powers.

$3^5 \cdot 3^0; \quad 3^4 \cdot 3^1; \quad 3^3 \cdot 3^2$

23. **Astronomy** The distance from Earth to the moon is about 22^4 miles. The distance from Earth to Neptune is about 22^7 miles. Which distance is the greater distance and about how many times greater is it?

Earth to Neptune; 22^3, or 10,648, times greater.

24. **Critique Reasoning** A student claims that $8^3 \cdot 8^{-5}$ is greater than 1. Explain whether the student is correct or not.

The student is not correct because $8^3 \cdot 8^{-5} = 8^{3+(-5)} = 8^{-2} = \frac{1}{8^2} = \frac{1}{64}$, which is less than 1.

Find the missing exponent.

25. $(b^2)^{\boxed{-3}} = b^{-6}$

26. $x^{\boxed{3}} \cdot x^6 = x^9$

27. $\frac{y^{25}}{y^{\boxed{19}}} = y^6$

28. **Communicate Mathematical Ideas** Why do you subtract exponents when dividing powers with the same base?

Dividing is the same as multiplying by the reciprocal. So when dividing powers with the same base, you add the opposite of the exponent in the denominator. This is the same as subtracting the exponents.

29. **Astronomy** The mass of the Sun is about 2×10^{27} metric tons, or 2×10^{30} kilograms. How many kilograms are in one metric ton?

10^3 kg, or 1000 kg

30. **Represent Real-World Problems** In computer technology, a kilobyte is 2^{10} bytes in size. A gigabyte is 2^{30} bytes in size. The size of a terabyte is the product of the size of a kilobyte and the size of a gigabyte. What is the size of a terabyte?

2^{40} bytes

31. Write equivalent expressions for $x^7 \cdot x^{-2}$ and $\frac{x^7}{x^2}$. What do you notice? Explain how your results relate to the properties of integer exponents.

Both expressions equal x^5, so $x^7 \cdot x^{-2} = \frac{x^7}{x^2}$. When multiplying powers with the same base, you add exponents; $7 + (-2) = 5$. When dividing powers with the same base, you subtract exponents; $7 - 2 = 5$. In cases like this, $x^n \cdot x^{-m} = \frac{x^n}{x^m}$.

A toy store is creating a large window display of different colored cubes stacked in a triangle shape. The table shows the number of cubes in each row of the triangle, starting with the top row.

Row	1	2	3	4
Number of cubes in each row	3	3^2	3^3	3^4

32. **Look for a Pattern** Describe any pattern you see in the table.

The number of cubes in each row is 3 raised to the row number.

33. Using exponents, how many cubes will be in Row 6? How many times as many cubes will be in Row 6 than in Row 3?

$3^6; 3^3$

34. **Justify Reasoning** If there are 6 rows in the triangle, what is the total number of cubes in the triangle? Explain how you found your answer.

1092; I evaluated $3^6, 3^5, 3^4, 3^3, 3^2$, and 3^1 and added these numbers together.

H.O.T. FOCUS ON HIGHER ORDER THINKING

Work Area

35. **Critique Reasoning** A student simplified the expression $\frac{6^2}{36^2}$ as $\frac{1}{3}$. Do you agree with this student? Explain why or why not.

No; $\frac{6^2}{36^2} = \frac{6 \cdot 6}{36 \cdot 36} = \frac{6 \cdot 6}{6 \cdot 6 \cdot 6 \cdot 6} = \frac{1}{6 \cdot 6} = \frac{1}{36}$

36. **Draw Conclusions** Evaluate $-a^n$ when $a = 3$ and $n = 2, 3, 4$, and 5. Now evaluate $(-a)^n$ when $a = 3$ and $n = 2, 3, 4$, and 5. Based on this sample, does it appear that $-a^n = (-a)^n$? If not, state the relationships, if any, between $-a^n$ and $(-a)^n$.

For $-a^n$, you get $-9, -27, -81, -243$. For $(-a)^n$, you get $9, -27, 81, -243$. In general, $-a^n \neq (-a)^n$. When n is even, the two expressions are opposites; when n is odd, the two expressions are equal.

37. **Persevere in Problem Solving** A number to the 12th power divided by the same number to the 9th power equals 125. What is the number?

The number is 5.

EXTEND THE MATH PRE-AP

Activity available online my.hrw.com

Activity Describe the following pattern:

$(-1)^{-1} = \boxed{}$

$(-1)^{-2} = \boxed{}$

$(-1)^{-3} = \boxed{}$

$(-1)^{-4} = \boxed{}$

Determine what $(-1)^{-100}$ would be. Justify your thinking.

$(-1)^{-1} = -1; (-1)^{-2} = 1; (-1)^{-3} = -1; (-1)^{-4} = 1$; so the pattern is $-1, 1, -1, 1$, etc. -1 raised to an odd number equals -1, and -1 raised to an even number equals 1. Since -100 is an even number, then $(-1)^{-100} = 1$.

Scientific Notation with Positive Powers of 10

ADDITIONAL EXAMPLE 1
The average distance from Earth to Mars is about 140,000,000 miles. Write this distance in scientific notation.
1.4×10^8

 Interactive Whiteboard
Interactive example available online

 my.hrw.com

Engage

ESSENTIAL QUESTION

How can you use scientific notation to express very large quantities? Sample answer: Write the large quantity as the product of a number greater than or equal to 1 and less than 10 and a power of 10.

Motivate the Lesson
Ask: If you were given the weight of a whale in pounds as 2×10^5, how many pounds do you think that is? Begin the Explore Activity to find out.

Explore

EXPLORE ACTIVITY

Talk About It
Check for Understanding

 Ask: In 250,000, what place is the 2 in? hundred thousands What digit is in the ten thousands place? 5

Integrating Language Arts ELL
You may want to pair English learners with a partner for Explore Activity 1 to help them develop their language skills.

Explain

EXAMPLE 1

Questioning Strategies Mathematical Practices

• When you write 9×10^7 in standard notation, how many zeros do you write? 7 If you were to write 9×10^2 in standard notation, how many zeros would you write? 2

• The standard notation for 9.3×10^7 is 93,000,000. Why are there 6 zeros instead of 7 zeros in the standard notation? One of the 7 factors of 10 moves the decimal to the right of 3. The remaining 6 factors of 10 moves the decimal 6 places, represented with zeros.

Avoid Common Errors
A dot used for multiplication can sometimes be confused as a decimal point when using scientific notation. Encourage students to use X instead.

YOUR TURN

Talk About It
Check for Understanding

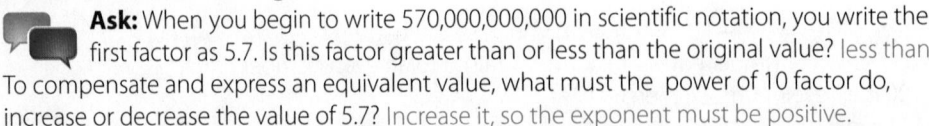 **Ask:** When you begin to write 570,000,000,000 in scientific notation, you write the first factor as 5.7. Is this factor greater than or less than the original value? less than To compensate and express an equivalent value, what must the power of 10 factor do, increase or decrease the value of 5.7? Increase it, so the exponent must be positive.

LESSON 10.2 Scientific Notation with Positive Powers of 10

FL CC 8.EE.1.3 Use numbers expressed in the form of a single digit times an integer power of 10 to estimate very large or very small quantities, ….

? ESSENTIAL QUESTION

How can you use scientific notation to express very large quantities?

EXPLORE ACTIVITY (Real World) FL CC 8.EE.1.3

Using Scientific Notation

Scientific notation is a method of expressing very large and very small numbers as a product of a number greater than or equal to 1 and less than 10, and a power of 10.

The weights of various sea creatures are shown in the table. Write the weight of the blue whale in scientific notation.

Sea Creature	Blue whale	Gray whale	Whale shark
Weight (lb)	250,000	68,000	41,200

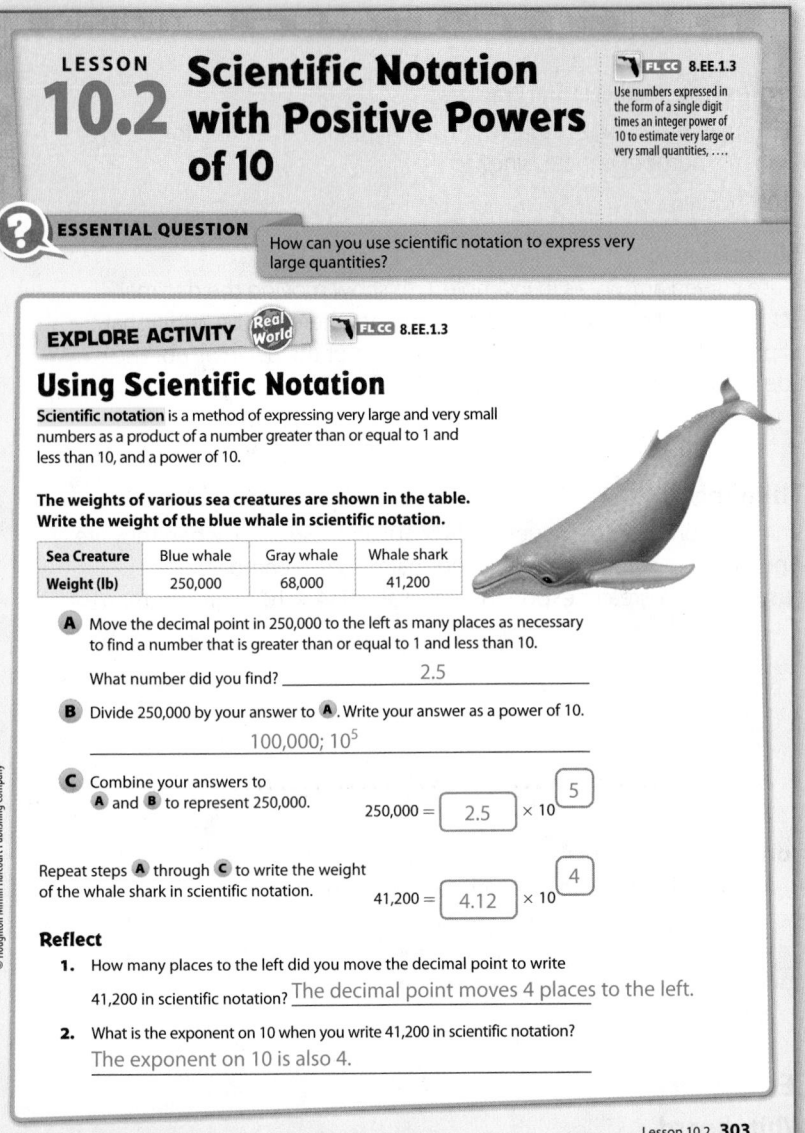

A Move the decimal point in 250,000 to the left as many places as necessary to find a number that is greater than or equal to 1 and less than 10.

What number did you find? _____2.5_____

B Divide 250,000 by your answer to **A**. Write your answer as a power of 10.

_____100,000; 10^5_____

C Combine your answers to **A** and **B** to represent 250,000.

$250,000 = \boxed{2.5} \times 10^{\boxed{5}}$

Repeat steps **A** through **C** to write the weight of the whale shark in scientific notation.

$41,200 = \boxed{4.12} \times 10^{\boxed{4}}$

Reflect

1. How many places to the left did you move the decimal point to write 41,200 in scientific notation? The decimal point moves 4 places to the left.

2. What is the exponent on 10 when you write 41,200 in scientific notation? The exponent on 10 is also 4.

Lesson 10.2 **303**

Writing a Number in Scientific Notation

To translate between standard notation and scientific notation, you can count the number of places the decimal point moves.

Writing Numbers in Scientific Notation		
When the number is greater than or equal to 10, use a positive exponent.	$84,000 = 8.4 \times 10^4$	The decimal point moves 4 places.

EXAMPLE 1 (Real World) FL CC 8.EE.1.3

The distance from Earth to the Sun is about 93,000,000 miles. Write this distance in scientific notation.

STEP 1 Move the decimal point in 93,000,000 to the left until you have a number that is greater than or equal to 1 and less than 10.

9.3 0 0 0 0 0 0.   *Move the decimal point 7 places to the left.*

9.3   *Remove extra zeros.*

STEP 2 Divide the original number by the result from Step 1.

10,000,000   *Divide 93,000,000 by 9.3.*

10^7 *Write your answer as a power of 10.*

STEP 3 Write the product of the results from Steps 1 and 2.

$93,000,000 = 9.3 \times 10^7$ miles   *Write a product to represent 93,000,000 in scientific notation.*

Math Talk
Mathematical Practices

Is 12×10^7 written in scientific notation? Explain.

No, because the first factor must be greater than or equal to 1 and less than 10.

YOUR TURN

Write each number in scientific notation.

3. 6,400
_____6.4×10^3_____

4. 570,000,000,000
_____5.7×10^{11}_____

5. A light-year is the distance that light travels in a year and is equivalent to 9,461,000,000,000 km. Write this distance in scientific notation.
_____9.461×10^{12} km_____

304 Unit 5

PROFESSIONAL DEVELOPMENT

Integrate Mathematical Practices MP.4.1

This lesson provides an opportunity to address this Mathematical Practices standard. It calls for students to solve problems arising in everyday life, society, and the workplace. Students use scientific notation to write very large numbers to express facts about the natural world, and they see how this notation is used by scientists in reporting scientific information.

Math Background

Scientific notation is used to represent very large numbers. One very large named number is a googol–the number 1 followed by 100 zeros. An even larger named number is the googolplex–the number 1 followed by a googol (10^{100}) of zeros. This massive number can be represented as 10^{googol}. This idea has been extended even further to name a googolplexian, which is the number 1 followed by a googolplex of zeros. The googol (also spelled google) was named by the nine-year-old nephew of the American mathematician Edward Kasner.

Scientific Notation with Positive Powers of 10   **304**

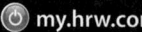
EXAMPLE 2

Questioning Strategies Mathematical Practices

• Is the value of 3.5×10^6 greater than or less than than 3.5? greater Which direction does a decimal point move when a number is increasing? to the right

• What is the value of 10^0? Explain. $10^0 = 1$. Any number to the zero power is equal to 1.

Engage with the Whiteboard

Have a student use curved arrows, as in Example 1, to show moving the decimal point the correct number of places. Ask students whether there can be additional zeros after the decimal point. Remind them that it is the location of the decimal, not the number of zeros, that determines the value.

YOUR TURN

Focus on Critical Thinking

Discuss with students how to compare the values 7.034×10^9 and 2.36×10^5 when they are expressed in scientific notation. Be sure they understand that they can compare the exponents of 10. Because 10^9 has a greater exponent than 10^5, 7.034×10^9 is greater than 2.36×10^5.

Elaborate

Talk About It
Summarize the Lesson

Ask: How can you write a very large number such as 51,200,000 in scientific notation? First, move the decimal point 7 places to the left to determine the first factor, which must be greater than or equal to 1 and less than 10. Then write the power of 10 factor with the exponent equal to 7, which is the number of places you moved the decimal to determine the first factor.

GUIDED PRACTICE

Engage with the Whiteboard

For Exercises 1–12, have students draw and count curved arrows to show moving the decimal point the correct number of places.

Avoid Common Errors

Exercises 1–6 Remind students to draw arrows to avoid counting errors as they move the decimal point.

Exercises 7, 11–12 To avoid decimal placement errors, suggest that students place the decimal point to the right of the whole number factor before converting to standard notation.

Writing a Number in Standard Notation

To translate between scientific notation and standard notation, move the decimal point the number of places indicated by the exponent in the power of 10. When the exponent is positive, move the decimal point to the right and add placeholder zeros as needed.

Math On the Spot
my.hrw.com

EXAMPLE 2   FL CC 8.EE.1.3

Write 3.5×10^6 in standard notation.

STEP 1 Use the exponent of the power of 10 to see how many places to move the decimal point.   6 places

STEP 2 Place the decimal point. Since you are going to write a number greater than 3.5, move the decimal point to the *right*. Add placeholder zeros if necessary.   3 5 0 0 0 0 0

The number 3.5×10^6 written in standard notation is 3,500,000.

My Notes

Reflect

6. Explain why the exponent in 3.5×10^6 is 6, while there are only 5 zeros in 3,500,000.

   The decimal point moves 6 places to the right, but one of those places is the 5 tenths in 3.5, so only 5 placeholder zeros are needed.

7. What is the exponent on 10 when you write 5.3 in scientific notation?

   The exponent on 10 is 0. $5.3 = 5.3 \times 10^0$.

YOUR TURN

Write each number in standard notation.

8. 7.034×10^9

   7,034,000,000

9. 2.36×10^5

   236,000

10. The mass of one roosting colony of Monarch butterflies in Mexico was estimated at 5×10^6 grams. Write this mass in standard notation.

    5,000,000 g

Personal Math Trainer
Online Assessment and Intervention
my.hrw.com

Guided Practice

Write each number in scientific notation. (Explore Activity and Example 1)

1. 58,927
   Hint: Move the decimal left 4 places.
   5.8927×10^4

2. 1,304,000,000
   Hint: Move the decimal left 9 places.
   1.304×10^9

3. 6,730,000
   6.73×10^6

4. 13,300
   1.33×10^4

5. An ordinary quarter contains about 97,700,000,000,000,000,000,000 atoms.
   9.77×10^{22}

6. The distance from Earth to the Moon is about 384,000 kilometers.
   3.84×10^5

Write each number in standard notation. (Example 2)

7. 4×10^5
   Hint: Move the decimal right 5 places.
   400,000

8. 1.8499×10^9
   Hint: Move the decimal right 9 places.
   1,849,900,000

9. 6.41×10^3
   6,410

10. 8.456×10^7
    84,560,000

11. 8×10^5
    800,000

12. 9×10^{10}
    90,000,000,000

13. Diana calculated that she spent about 5.4×10^4 seconds doing her math homework during October. Write this time in standard notation. (Example 2)
    54,000 s

14. The town recycled 7.6×10^6 cans this year. Write the number of cans in standard notation. (Example 2)
    7,600,000 cans

 ESSENTIAL QUESTION CHECK-IN

15. Describe how to write 3,482,000,000 in scientific notation.

    First move the decimal point 9 places to the left to find 3.482, a number that is greater than or equal to 1 and less than 10. Then multiply 3.482 by 10^9, using an exponent on 10 that equals the number of places you moved the decimal.

DIFFERENTIATE INSTRUCTION

Cognitive Strategies

Suggest that students visualize how the final answer will look before writing anything down.

If the question says "Write in scientific notation," realize that the answer will be the product of a number greater than or equal to 1 and less than 10, and a power of 10.

If the question says "Write in standard notation," be aware that an answer may have zeros as placeholders to show the number's size.

Technology

Have students use a graphing calculator and enter 3,500,000. Then have them multiply that number by 1,000,000. Ask what the answer in the display, 3.5E12, means. 3.5×10^{12} Ask them to predict the answer display on a calculator for 10 million times 3 million. Then have them check their prediction using the calculator. 3E13 Have them investigate when their calculator changes to scientific notation. Sample answer: when there are more than 11 digits in the combined factors

Additional Resources

Differentiated Instruction includes:

- Reading Strategies
- Success for English Learners ELL
- Reteach
- Challenge PRE-AP

Personal Math Trainer

Online Assessment and Intervention

Online homework assignment available

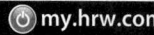
my.hrw.com

10.2 LESSON QUIZ

 **FL CC** 8.EE.1.3

1. The approximate mass of Mars is 6.42×10^{23} kilograms. Write this mass in standard notation.

2. An adult blue whale can eat about 40,000,000 krill a day. Write this number in scientific notation.

3. Write 9 in scientific notation.

4. Write 1.0×10^5 in standard notation and in words.

5. Is 10.2×10^5 written in scientific notation? Explain.

Lesson Quiz available online

 my.hrw.com

Answers

1. 642,000,000,000,000,000,000,000 kg

2. 4×10^7 krill

3. 9×10^0

4. 100,000; one hundred thousand

5. No; the first number is not more than 1 and less than 10.

Evaluate

GUIDED AND INDEPENDENT PRACTICE

 **FL CC** 8.EE.1.3

Concepts & Skills	Practice
Explore Activity Using Scientific Notation	Exercises 1–6
Example 1 Writing a Number in Scientific Notation	Exercises 1–6, 16–22, 24–27
Example 2 Writing a Number in Standard Notation	Exercises 7–14, 23–24, 25

Exercise	Depth of Knowledge (D.O.K.)	**FL CC** Mathematical Practices
16–25	**2** Skills/Concepts	**MP.4.1** Modeling
26	**1** Recall of Information	**MP.7.1** Using Structure
27	**2** Skills/Concepts	**MP.3.1** Logic
28	**3** Strategic Thinking H.O.T.	**MP.3.1** Logic
29–30	**3** Strategic Thinking H.O.T.	**MP.4.1** Modeling
31	**3** Strategic Thinking H.O.T.	**MP.7.1** Using Structure

Additional Resources

Differentiated Instruction includes:

• Leveled Practice worksheets

10.2 Independent Practice

FL CC 8.EE.1.3

Personal Math Trainer
Online Assessment and Intervention
my.hrw.com

Paleontology Use the table for problems 16–21. Write the estimated weight of each dinosaur in scientific notation.

Estimated Weight of Dinosaurs	
Name	**Pounds**
Argentinosaurus	220,000
Brachiosaurus	100,000
Apatosaurus	66,000
Diplodocus	50,000
Camarasaurus	40,000
Cetiosauriscus	19,850

16. Apatosaurus _____ 6.6×10^4 lb

17. Argentinosaurus _____ 2.2×10^5 lb

18. Brachiosaurus _____ 1×10^5 lb

19. Camarasaurus _____ 4×10^4 lb

20. Cetiosauriscus _____ 1.985×10^4 lb

21. Diplodocus _____ 5×10^4 lb

22. A single little brown bat can eat up to 1000 mosquitoes in a single hour. Express in scientific notation how many mosquitoes a little brown bat might eat in 10.5 hours.

    1.05×10^4 mosquitoes

23. **Multistep** Samuel can type nearly 40 words per minute. Use this information to find the number of hours it would take him to type 2.6×10^5 words.

    $108\frac{1}{3}$ hours or 108 hours and 20 minutes

24. **Entomology** A tropical species of mite named *Archegozetes longisetosus* is the record holder for the strongest insect in the world. It can lift up to 1.182×10^3 times its own weight.

    a. If you were as strong as this insect, explain how you could find how many pounds you could lift.

       Write 1.182×10^3 in standard
       notation, 1182, and then
       multiply by your weight.

    b. Complete the calculation to find how much you could lift, in pounds, if you were as strong as an *Archegozetes longisetosus* mite. Express your answer in both scientific notation and standard notation.

       Answers will vary. Sample
       answer: 94,560 lb; 9.456×10^4

25. During a discussion in science class, Sharon learns that at birth an elephant weighs around 230 pounds. In four herds of elephants tracked by conservationists, about 20 calves were born during the summer. In scientific notation, express approximately how much the calves weighed all together.

    4.6×10^3 lb

26. **Classifying Numbers** Which of the following numbers are written in scientific notation?

    0.641×10^3 9.999×10^4
    2×10^1 4.38×5^{10}

    9.999×10^4 and 2×10^1

27. **Explain the Error** Polly's parents' car weighs about 3500 pounds. Samantha, Esther, and Polly each wrote the weight of the car in scientific notation. Polly wrote 35.0×10^2, Samantha wrote 0.35×10^4, and Esther wrote 3.5×10^4.

    a. Which of these girls, if any, is correct?

       None of the girls has the correct answer.

    b. Explain the mistakes of those who got the question wrong.

       Neither Polly nor Samantha moved the decimal point
       to the correct place. Esther moved the decimal point to
       the correct place, but wrote the wrong power of 10.

28. **Justify Reasoning** If you were a biologist counting very large numbers of cells as part of your research, give several reasons why you might prefer to record your cell counts in scientific notation instead of standard notation.

    Sample answer: Scientific notation is shorter to write,
    easier to read (you see how many zeros), used by scientists
    everywhere, and easier to compare sizes of large numbers.

H.O.T. 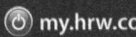 **FOCUS ON HIGHER ORDER THINKING**

29. **Draw Conclusions** Which measurement would be least likely to be written in scientific notation: number of stars in a galaxy, number of grains of sand on a beach, speed of a car, or population of a country? Explain your reasoning.

    The speed of a car because it is likely to be less than 100.

30. **Analyze Relationships** Compare the two numbers to find which is greater. Explain how you can compare them without writing them in standard notation first.

    4.5×10^6 2.1×10^8

    2.1×10^8 is greater because the exponent 8 is greater
    than the exponent 6.

31. **Communicate Mathematical Ideas** To determine whether a number is written in scientific notation, what test can you apply to the first factor, and what test can you apply to the second factor?

    Is the first factor greater than or equal to 1 and less than
    10? Is the second factor a power of 10?

Work Area

EXTEND THE MATH PRE-AP

Activity available online my.hrw.com

Activity Ask students to consider the three numbers and compare each pair.

$$3.2 \times 10^3 \qquad 8.7 \times 10^3 \qquad 2.4 \times 10^4$$

When comparing two numbers written in scientific notation, should students compare the coefficient or the power of 10 first? the power of 10. Which pair of numbers have the same power of 10? 3.2×10^3 and 8.7×10^3 When the power of 10 is the same, how do you compare the numbers? by comparing the coefficient When the power of 10 is different, do you need to compare the coefficient? no

Have students write their own set of rules to describe how to compare two numbers written in scientific notation.

Florida Common Core Standards

The student is expected to:

 **FL CC** Expressions and Equations—8.EE.1.3

Use numbers expressed in the form of a single digit times an integer power of 10 to estimate very large or very small quantities, and to express how many times as much one is than the other.

Mathematical Practices

 **FL CC** MP.2.1 Reasoning

 **Animated Math**
Powers of 10

Students will explore and visualize powers of ten through virtual manipulatives.

 my.hrw.com

ADDITIONAL EXAMPLE 1
The weight of one of the smaller species of butterflies was measured at 0.0007 ounces. Write the weight of this butterfly in scientific notation.
7.0×10^{-4} ounces

 Interactive Whiteboard
Interactive example available online

 my.hrw.com

Engage

ESSENTIAL QUESTION

How can you use scientific notation to express very small quantities? Write the small quantity as the product of a number greater than or equal to 1 and less than 10 times a power of 10 with a negative exponent.

Motivate the Lesson
Ask: Have you ever seen a large number of insects in flight? Monarch butterflies migrating through Texas travel in huge numbers; as many as 22,410,000 butterflies in an area about the size of two and a half football fields. You have written very large numbers like this in scientific notation. What is a shorter way to write very small numbers, such as the weight of a butterfly egg? A single Monarch egg may weigh as little as 0.00046 grams.

Explore

EXPLORE ACTIVITY

Focus on Patterns
Discuss with students the relationship between moving a decimal point to the left and dividing by 10. Ask them the following questions. What does moving a decimal point one place to the left do to a number? divides the number by 10 What does dividing a number by 10 do to an exponent with a base of 10? reduces the exponent by 1

Explain

EXAMPLE 1

Questioning Strategies  Mathematical Practices
• How do you know whether to move a decimal point left or right? Move it left if the number is greater than or equal to 10, right if the number is less than 1.

• Where does moving the decimal point 8 places right in 0.00000003 put the decimal point? after the 3

Avoid Common Errors
To prevent writing the wrong exponent, students should first predict how the answer will look. Think: 0.00000003 is a very small number. When you multiply 3.0 times a power of 10, the exponent must be negative to equal this very small value.

YOUR TURN

Talk About It
Check for Understanding
Ask: With 0.0000829, after you write the first part as 8.29, have you made the original number larger or smaller? larger So you must multiply by a power of 10 make the number larger or smaller? smaller What will be the sign of the exponent? negative

Scientific Notation with Negative Powers of 10

  8.EE.1.3
Use numbers expressed in the form of a single digit times an integer power of 10 to estimate very large or very small quantities, ...

? ESSENTIAL QUESTION How can you use scientific notation to express very small quantities?

EXPLORE ACTIVITY (Real World) 8.EE.1.3

Animated Math
my.hrw.com

Negative Powers of 10

You can use what you know about writing very large numbers in scientific notation to write very small numbers in scientific notation.

A typical human hair has a diameter of 0.000025 meter. Write this number in scientific notation.

A Notice how the decimal point moves in the list below. Complete the list.

2.345×10^0	= 2.345	It moves one place to the right with each increasing power of 10.
2.345×10^1	= 23.45	
2.345×10^2	= 234.5	
$2.345 \times 10^{\boxed{3}}$	= 2345.	

2.345×10^0	= 2.345	It moves one place to the left with each decreasing power of 10.
2.345×10^{-1}	= 0.2345	
2.345×10^{-2}	= 0.02345	
$2.345 \times 10^{\boxed{-3}}$	= 0.002345	

B Move the decimal point in 0.000025 to the right as many places as necessary to find a number that is greater than or equal to 1 and less than 10. What number did you find? ___2.5___

C Divide 0.000025 by your answer to **B**. ___0.00001___

Write your answer as a power of 10. ___10^{-5}___

D Combine your answers to **B** and **C** to represent 0.000025 in scientific notation. ___$0.000025 = 2.5 \times 10^{-5}$___

Reflect

1. When you move the decimal point, how can you know whether you are increasing or decreasing the number?

   Moving left is a decrease; moving right is an increase.

2. Explain how the two steps of moving the decimal and multiplying by a power of 10 leave the value of the original number unchanged.

   One increases and the other decreases the number.

Math On the Spot
my.hrw.com

Writing a Number in Scientific Notation

To write a number less than 1 in scientific notation, move the decimal point right and use a negative exponent.

Writing Numbers in Scientific Notation

When the number is less than 1, use a negative exponent.	$0.0783 = 7.83 \times 10^{-2}$	The decimal point moves 2 places.

EXAMPLE 1 (Real World)  8.EE.1.3

The average size of an atom is about 0.00000003 centimeter across. Write the average size of an atom in scientific notation.

Move the decimal point as many places as necessary to find a number that is greater than or equal to 1 and less than 10.

STEP 1 Place the decimal point. 3.0

STEP 2 Count the number of places you moved the decimal point. 8 $\boxed{-8}$

STEP 3 Multiply 3.0 times a power of 10. 3.0×10^{-8}

Since 0.00000003 is less than 1, you moved the decimal point to the right and the exponent on 10 is negative.

The average size of an atom in scientific notation is 3.0×10^{-8}.

Reflect

3. **Critical Thinking** When you write a number that is less than 1 in scientific notation, how does the power of 10 differ from when you write a number greater than 1 in scientific notation?

   The exponent is negative instead of positive.

YOUR TURN

Personal Math Trainer
Online Assessment and Intervention
my.hrw.com

Write each number in scientific notation.

4. 0.0000829 ___8.29×10^{-5}___

5. 0.000000302 ___3.02×10^{-7}___

6. A typical red blood cell in human blood has a diameter of approximately 0.000007 meter. Write this diameter in scientific notation. ___7×10^{-6} m___

PROFESSIONAL DEVELOPMENT

Integrate Mathematical Practices MP.2.1

This lesson provides an opportunity to address this Mathematical Practices standard. It calls for students to represent a situation symbolically. Students write very small numbers in two forms of symbolic representation: standard form and scientific notation. Students also use mathematical language to express the processes they use to convert from one representation to the other.

Math Background

Scientific notation is used to represent very small numbers in an efficient way which is easy to write and easy to read. Later, students will use this form as they compare and combine very large and very small numbers.

There may be confusion about whether "a very small" number might indicate a number that is negative with a large absolute value, such as −999,999 (a debt, for instance). In this context "very small" indicates a number that is very close to zero (has a very small absolute value).

© Houghton Mifflin Harcourt Publishing Company

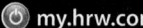
EXAMPLE 2

Questioning Strategies Mathematical Practices

- Is the value of 2.33×10^{-6} greater than or less than 2.33? less Which direction does the decimal point move when a number is decreasing? to the left

- How could you check your answer? Convert 0.00000233 back to scientific notation by moving the decimal right 6 places and writing the number times 10^{-6}.

Engage with the Whiteboard

In Exercise 7, rewrite 0.9×10^{-5} in standard notation, then convert it to scientific notation. Draw curved arrows as you move the decimal point.

YOUR TURN

Focus on Communication Mathematical Practices

- Compare the number of places that a decimal point moves with the number of zeros in the resulting standard notation form. Discuss with students, in Exercise 9 for example, why the decimal moves 6 places, but there are only 5 zeros in the decimal part of the answer. Help them to communicate that one of the 6 factors of 10^{-1} moves the decimal point to the left of the digit 1. The remaining 5 factors of 10^{-1} move the decimal point leftward 5 spaces, and those spaces are filled with zeros.

Elaborate

. . . .

Talk About It
Summarize the Lesson

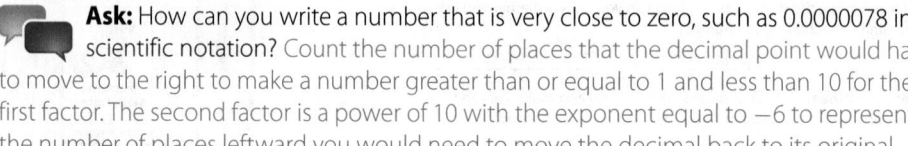 **Ask:** How can you write a number that is very close to zero, such as 0.0000078 in scientific notation? Count the number of places that the decimal point would have to move to the right to make a number greater than or equal to 1 and less than 10 for the first factor. The second factor is a power of 10 with the exponent equal to −6 to represent the number of places leftward you would need to move the decimal back to its original position.

GUIDED PRACTICE

Engage with the Whiteboard

For Exercises 1–14, have students draw and count curved arrows to show moving the decimal point the correct number of places.

Integrating Language Arts ELL

Encourage a broad class discussion on the Math Talk. English learners will benefit from hearing and participating in classroom discussions.

Avoid Common Errors

Exercises 1–6 Remind students to avoid counting errors as they move the decimal point by drawing arrows and counting a second time to check.

Writing a Number in Standard Notation

To translate between scientific notation and standard notation with very small numbers, you can move the decimal point the number of places indicated by the exponent on the power of 10. When the exponent is negative, move the decimal point to the left.

Math On the Spot
my.hrw.com

EXAMPLE 2 Real World
FL CC 8.EE.1.3

Platelets are one component of human blood. A typical platelet has a diameter of approximately 2.33×10^{-6} meter. Write 2.33×10^{-6} in standard notation.

STEP 1 Use the exponent of the power of 10 to see how many places to move the decimal point.   6 places

STEP 2 Place the decimal point. Since you are going to write a number less than 2.33, move the decimal point to the *left*. Add placeholder zeros if necessary. 0.00000233

The number 2.33×10^{-6} in standard notation is 0.00000233.

Reflect

7. **Justify Reasoning** Explain whether 0.9×10^{-5} is written in scientific notation. If not, write the number correctly in scientific notation.

   No, because the first factor is less than 1. The decimal point should move to the right and the exponent should decrease by 1: 9×10^{-6}

8. Which number is larger, 2×10^{-3} or 3×10^{-2}? Explain.

   3×10^{-2} because it's exponent is greater.

Math Talk
Mathematical Practices

Describe the two factors that multiply together to form a number written in scientific notation.

The first factor is a number greater than or equal to 1 and less than 10, and the second factor is a power of 10.

YOUR TURN

Write each number in standard notation.

9. 1.045×10^{-6}

   0.000001045

10. 9.9×10^{-5}

   0.000099

11. Jeremy measured the length of an ant as 1×10^{-2} meter. Write this length in standard notation.

   0.01 m

Personal Math Trainer
Online Assessment and Intervention
my.hrw.com

Write each number in scientific notation. (Explore Activity and Example 1)

1. 0.000487
   Hint: Move the decimal right 4 places.
   4.87×10^{-4}

2. 0.000028
   Hint: Move the decimal right 5 places.
   2.8×10^{-5}

3. 0.000059
   5.9×10^{-5}

4. 0.0417
   4.17×10^{-2}

5. Picoplankton can be as small as 0.00002 centimeter.
   2×10^{-5}

6. The average mass of a grain of sand on a beach is about 0.000015 gram.
   1.5×10^{-5}

Write each number in standard notation. (Example 2)

7. 2×10^{-5}
   Hint: Move the decimal left 5 places.
   0.00002

8. 3.582×10^{-6}
   Hint: Move the decimal left 6 places.
   0.000003582

9. 8.3×10^{-4}
   0.00083

10. 2.97×10^{-2}
   0.0297

11. 9.06×10^{-5}
   0.0000906

12. 4×10^{-5}
   0.00004

13. The average length of a dust mite is approximately 0.0001 meter. Write this number in scientific notation. (Example 1)
   1×10^{-4}

14. The mass of a proton is about 1.7×10^{-24} gram. Write this number in standard notation. (Example 2)
   0.0000000000000000000000017

 **ESSENTIAL QUESTION CHECK-IN**

15. Describe how to write 0.0000672 in scientific notation.

   Move the decimal point 5 places right to find 6.72, a number greater than or equal to 1 and less than 10. Then multiply 6.72 by 10^{-5}, using a negative exponent on 10 that equals the number of places you moved the decimal.

DIFFERENTIATE INSTRUCTION

Cognitive Strategies

Suggest that students, before writing anything, think about where the number would be on a number line.

When a number that is very close to zero is written in scientific notation, the exponent will be a negative number.

A number that is very close to zero when written in standard notation will have zeros as placeholders after the decimal point.

Number Sense

Have students use a graphing calculator and type 0.000000000099 and press ENTER. Ask what the answer in the display, 9.9E–11, means. 9.9×10^{-11} This number has 10 zeros after the decimal point. Have students compare what happens when they enter the number 0.0099 with what happens when they enter 0.00099. Ask them to draw some conclusions, based on their investigations, about the rules in the programming software for their calculator.

Additional Resources

Differentiated Instruction includes:

• Reading Strategies
• Success for English Learners **ELL**
• Reteach
• Challenge **PRE-AP**

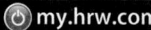
10.3 LESSON QUIZ

 **8.EE.1.3**

1. The weight of an ant is about 1.7×10^{-5} pounds. Write 1.7×10^{-5} in standard notation.

2. A bee sting delivers about 0.00005 grams of venom. Write this number in scientific notation.

3. Write 0.77 in scientific notation.

4. Write 1.0×10^{-3} in standard notation and in words.

5. Is 0.1×10^{-4} written in scientific notation? Explain.

Lesson Quiz available online

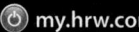 my.hrw.com

Answers
1. 0.000017
2. 5×10^{-5}
3. 7.7×10^{-1}
4. 0.001; one thousandth
5. No; the first number is not more than 1 and less than 10.

Evaluate

GUIDED AND INDEPENDENT PRACTICE

 **8.EE.1.3**

Concepts & Skills	Practice
Explore Activity Negative Powers of 10	Exercises 1–6
Example 1 Writing a Number in Scientific Notation	Exercises 1–6, 13, 16–21, 23, 26, 28, 30, 32
Example 2 Writing a Number in Standard Notation	Exercises 7–12, 14, 29, 31, 33

Exercise	Depth of Knowledge (D.O.K.)	FL CC Mathematical Practices
16–21	**2** Skills/Concepts	**MP.4.1** Modeling
22	**2** Skills/Concepts	**MP.3.1** Logic
23	**2** Skills/Concepts	**MP.2.1** Reasoning
24–26	**2** Skills/Concepts	**MP.4.1** Modeling
27	**2** Skills/Concepts	**MP.3.1** Logic
28–34	**2** Skills/Concepts	**MP.4.1** Modeling
35	**3** Strategic Thinking **H.O.T.**	**MP.5.1** Using Tools
36–37	**3** Strategic Thinking **H.O.T.**	**MP.3.1** Logic

Additional Resources
Differentiated Instruction includes:
• Leveled Practice worksheets

10.3 Independent Practice

FL CC 8.EE.1.3

Personal Math Trainer

Online Assessment and Intervention

my.hrw.com

Use the table for problems 16–21. Write the diameter of the fibers in scientific notation.

Average Diameter of Natural Fibers

Animal	Fiber Diameter (cm)
Vicuña	0.0008
Angora rabbit	0.0013
Alpaca	0.00277
Angora goat	0.0045
Llama	0.0035
Orb web spider	0.015

16. Alpaca

2.77×10^{-3} cm

17. Angora rabbit

1.3×10^{-3} cm

18. Llama

3.5×10^{-3} cm

19. Angora goat

4.5×10^{-3} cm

20. Orb web spider

1.5×10^{-2} cm

21. Vicuña

8×10^{-4} cm

22. Make a Conjecture Which measurement would be least likely to be written in scientific notation: the thickness of a dog hair, the radius of a period on this page, the ounces in a cup of milk? Explain your reasoning.

The ounces in a cup of milk; it is more than 1 but less than 10.

23. Multiple Representations Convert the length 7 centimeters to meters. Compare the numerical values when both numbers are written in scientific notation.

7 cm = 0.07 m , 7 cm = 7×10^{0} cm;

0.07 m = 7×10^{-2} m. The first

factors are the same; the

exponents differ by 2.

24. Draw Conclusions A graphing calculator displays 1.89×10^{12} as 1.89E12. How do you think it would display 1.89×10^{-12}? What does the E stand for?

1.89E–12; the exponent on 10

25. Communicate Mathematical Ideas When a number is written in scientific notation, how can you tell right away whether or not it is greater than or equal to 1?

If the exponent on 10 is

nonnegative, the number is

greater than or equal to 1.

26. The volume of a drop of a certain liquid is 0.000047 liter. Write the volume of the drop of liquid in scientific notation.

4.7×10^{-5} L

27. Justify Reasoning If you were asked to express the weight in ounces of a ladybug in scientific notation, would the exponent of the 10 be positive or negative? Justify your response.

Negative, because a ladybug

would weigh less than 1 ounce.

Physical Science The table shows the length of the radii of several very small or very large items. Complete the table.

	Item	Radius in Meters (Standard Notation)	Radius in Meters (Scientific Notation)
28.	The Moon	1,740,000	1.74×10^{6}
29.	Atom of silver	0.000000000125	1.25×10^{-10}
30.	Atlantic wolfish egg	0.0028	2.8×10^{-3}
31.	Jupiter	71,490,000	7.149×10^{7}
32.	Atom of aluminum	0.000000000182	1.82×10^{-10}
33.	Mars	3,397,000	3.397×10^{6}

34. List the items in the table in order from the smallest to the largest.

Atom of silver, atom of aluminum, Atlantic wolfish egg,

the Moon, Mars, Jupiter

H.O.T. FOCUS ON HIGHER ORDER THINKING

35. Analyze Relationships Write the following diameters from least to greatest.
1.5×10^{-2} m 1.2×10^{2} m 5.85×10^{-3} m 2.3×10^{-2} m 9.6×10^{-1} m

5.85×10^{-3} m, 1.5×10^{-2} m, 2.3×10^{-2} m,

9.6×10^{-1} m, 1.2×10^{2} m

36. Critique Reasoning Jerod's friend Al had the following homework problem:

Express 5.6×10^{-7} in standard form.

Al wrote 56,000,000. How can Jerod explain Al's error and how to correct it?

Al treated the exponent as if it were positive instead

of negative and moved the decimal in the wrong

direction. The answer should be 0.00000056.

37. Make a Conjecture Two numbers are written in scientific notation. The number with a positive exponent is divided by the number with a negative exponent. Describe the result. Explain your answer.

The result will be greater than the number with the

positive exponent because the divisor is less than 1.

Work Area

EXTEND THE MATH PRE-AP

Activity available online my.hrw.com

Activity Have students write 0.008 and 800 in scientific notation. Notice that both of these numbers have two zeros that are essential (since 0.008 can be written as .008). Do both exponents have the same absolute value when the numbers are written in scientific notation? Explain.

Sample answer: No; 0.008 = 8.0×10^{-3} and 800 = 8.0×10^{2}. When you move the decimal to the left, the 8 counts as one place. When you move to the right, the 8 is not included in the count of the number of moves.

10.4 Operations with Scientific Notation

Florida Common Core Standards

The student is expected to:

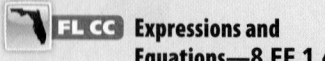 **Expressions and Equations—8.EE.1.4**

Perform operations with numbers expressed in scientific notation, including problems where both decimal and scientific notation are used. Use scientific notation and choose units of appropriate size for measurements of very large or very small quantities .... Interpret scientific notation that has been generated by technology.

Mathematical Practices

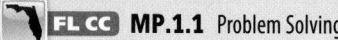 **MP.1.1** Problem Solving

---

ADDITIONAL EXAMPLE 1

Use the population table in Example 1 on the student page. How many more people live in the United States than in Canada? 2.762×10^8 people

 Interactive Whiteboard
Interactive example available online

 my.hrw.com

---

ADDITIONAL EXAMPLE 2

When Neptune makes an orbit around the Sun, it travels about 2.82×10^{10} km. Neptune travels at a rate of about 470,000 km/day. How many days does one orbit of Neptune take? Write your answer in scientific notation.

about 6.0×10^4 days

 Interactive Whiteboard
Interactive example available online

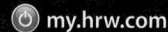 my.hrw.com

---

Engage

ESSENTIAL QUESTION

How do you add, subtract, multiply, and divide using scientific notation? Sample answer: To add or subtract, rewrite the numbers to the same power of 10, add or subtract the multipliers, and rewrite in scientific notation. To multiply or divide, multiply or divide the multipliers, multiply or divide the powers of 10, and rewrite the answer in scientific notation.

Motivate the Lesson

Ask: How do you think you could add or subtract numbers in scientific notation without rewriting them in standard notation? What about if you wanted to multiply or divide?

Explore

Explain to students that operations with scientific notation can be handled either by converting the numbers into standard notation or by keeping them in scientific notation and rewriting the powers of 10 using the properties of exponents. Discuss with students the advantages and disadvantages of each method.

Explain

EXAMPLE 1

Questioning Strategies Mathematical Practices

• In which method would you expect more errors to be made? Justify your answer. When the exponents are very large or small, Method 2 could introduce more errors because it would be easy to write an incorrect number of 0s when converting between notations.

Focus on Critical Thinking

Make sure students understand why the table figure for Canada has been written with a different exponent in Method 1, Step 1.

YOUR TURN

Avoid Common Errors

Students may compare the multipliers and think Canada has a greater population than Mexico. Remind students that the power of 10 must be the same in order to compare and subtract these numbers.

EXAMPLE 2

Questioning Strategies Mathematical Practices

• How is dividing two values with scientific notation a matter of solving two division problems? The multipliers are divided and the powers of 10 are divided.

Avoid Common Errors

Make sure students understand that the powers of 10 do not need to be the same when multiplying or dividing.

LESSON 10.4 Operations with Scientific Notation

FL CC 8.EE.1.4

Perform operations ... in scientific notation. ... choose units of appropriate size for measurements .... Interpret scientific notation ... generated by technology.

ESSENTIAL QUESTION How do you add, subtract, multiply, and divide using scientific notation?

Adding and Subtracting with Scientific Notation

Numbers in scientific notation can be added and subtracted, either directly or by rewriting them in standard form.

Math On the Spot
my.hrw.com

EXAMPLE 1 Real World

FL CC 8.EE.1.4

The table below shows the population of the three largest countries in North America in 2011. Find the total population of these countries.

Country	United States	Canada	Mexico
Population	3.1×10^8	3.38×10^7	1.1×10^8

Method 1:

STEP 1 First, write each population with the same power of 10.

United States: 3.1×10^8

Canada: 0.338×10^8

Mexico: 1.1×10^8

STEP 2 Add the multipliers for each population.

$3.1 + 0.338 + 1.1 = 4.538$

STEP 3 Write the final answer in scientific notation: 4.538×10^8.

Method 2:

STEP 1 First, write each number in standard notation.

United States: 310,000,000

Canada: 33,800,000

Mexico: 110,000,000

STEP 2 Find the sum of the numbers in standard notation.

$310,000,000 + 33,800,000 + 110,000,000 = 453,800,000$

STEP 3 Write the answer in scientific notation: 4.538×10^8.

Lesson 10.4 **315**

Personal Math Trainer
Online Assessment and Intervention
my.hrw.com

Math On the Spot
my.hrw.com

YOUR TURN

1. Using the population table above, how many more people live in Mexico than in Canada? Write your answer in scientific notation.

7.62×10^7 more people

Multiplying and Dividing with Scientific Notation

Numbers in scientific notation can be multiplied and divided directly by using properties of exponents.

EXAMPLE 2 Problem Solving

FL CC 8.EE.1.4

When the Sun makes an orbit around the center of the Milky Way, it travels 2.025×10^{14} kilometers. The orbit takes 225 million years. At what rate does the Sun travel? Write your answer in scientific notation.

Analyze Information

The answer is the number of kilometers per year that the Sun travels around the Milky Way.

Formulate a Plan

Set up a division problem using Rate $= \frac{Distance}{Time}$ to represent the situation.

Solve

STEP 1 Substitute the values from the problem into the Rate formula.

Rate $= \frac{2.025 \times 10^{14} \text{ kilometers}}{225,000,000 \text{ years}}$

STEP 2 Write the expression for rate with years in scientific notation.

Rate $= \frac{2.025 \times 10^{14} \text{ kilometers}}{2.25 \times 10^8 \text{ years}}$ 225 million $= 2.25 \times 10^8$

STEP 3 Find the quotient by dividing the decimals and using the laws of exponents.

$2.025 \div 2.25 = 0.9$ *Divide the multipliers.*

$\frac{10^{14}}{10^8} = 10^{14-8} = 10^6$ *Divide the powers of 10.*

STEP 4 Combine the answers to write the rate in scientific notation.

Rate $= 0.9 \times 10^6 = 9.0 \times 10^5$ km per year

Justify and Evaluate

Check your answer using multiplication.

$900,000 \times 225,000,000 = 202,500,000,000,000$, or 2.025×10^{14}.
The answer is correct.

Math Talk
Mathematical Practices

Could you write 2.025×10^{14} in standard notation to do the division? Would this be a good way to solve the problem?

Yes; no; 2.025×10^{14} in standard notation is 202,500,000,000,000. Dividing this by 225,000,000 is more complicated than doing the division using scientific notation.

316 Unit 5

PROFESSIONAL DEVELOPMENT

Integrate Mathematical Practices MP.1.1

This lesson provides an opportunity to address this Mathematical Practice standard. It calls for students to make sense of problems and persevere in solving them. Example 2 uses a four-step problem-solving process to determine the speed of the sun as it moves in the Milky Way. Students analyze the information, formulate a plan, solve the problem, and justify and evaluate the solution.

Math Background

The rules of exponents are used when performing operations with numbers in scientific notation:

1. Product Rule: $a^m \cdot a^n = a^{m+n}$, for $a \neq 0$.

   Example: $4^3 \cdot 4^{-1} = 4^{(3+-1)} = 4^2$

2. Quotient Rule: $a^m \div a^n = a^{m-n}$, for $a \neq 0$.

   Example: $4^3 \div 4^{-1} = 4^{3-(-1)} = 4^4$

3. Power Rule: $(a^m)^n = a^{m \times n}$, for $a \neq 0$.

   Example: $(4^3)^{-1} = 4^{3 \cdot (-1)} = 4^{-3}$

YOUR TURN

Engage with the Whiteboard

 For Exercises 2 and 3, have volunteers demonstrate the solution method while they explain how to multiply or divide the multipliers and the powers of 10.

EXAMPLE 3

Questioning Strategies  Mathematical Practices

• How does the situation inform you as to which values you will be operating on and which operation(s) you will use? The phrase "total area of these three continents" tells you to add the areas of Asia, Africa, and Europe.

• How can you access the EE feature on a calculator when it is printed next to a key but not on a key? You must first enter the "2nd" or "shift" key, then the key next to EE.

Focus on Technology 🖊 Mathematical Practices

Scientific calculators handle scientific notation in a variety of ways. Before beginning Example 3, review with students how their calculators display very large and very small numbers and how best to input numbers in scientific notation. Note that e^x and e are not used for entering scientific notation.

YOUR TURN

Focus on Modeling Mathematical Practices

In Exercises 4–6, expressions that model scientific notation are to be rewritten in calculator notation and vice versa for Exercises 7–9. Ensure that students can locate the multiplier, the base, and the exponent in each.

Elaborate

· ·

Talk About It
Summarize the Lesson

 Ask: When must the powers of 10 be the same when operating on numbers written in scientific notation? If the expressions are to be added or subtracted, the powers of 10 must be the same.

GUIDED PRACTICE

Engage with the Whiteboard

For Exercises 1–2, have volunteers explain the process of arriving at the correct value as they complete the write-in boxes for each exercise.

Avoid Common Errors
Exercises 5–8 Remind students that the multipliers are operated on separately from the powers of 10.

Exercises 9–11 Remind students that the exponent is not written as a superscript to E but rather the same size as and to the right of E.

YOUR TURN

2. Light travels at a speed of 1.86×10^5 miles per second. It takes light from the Sun about 4.8×10^3 seconds to reach Saturn. Find the approximate distance from the Sun to Saturn. Write your answer in scientific notation. $\underline{8.928 \times 10^8 \text{ miles}}$

3. Light travels at the speed of 1.17×10^7 miles per minute. Pluto's average distance from the Sun is 3,670,000,000 miles. On average, how long does it take sunlight to reach Pluto? Write your answer in scientific notation. $\underline{3.14 \times 10^2 \text{ minutes}}$

Scientific Notation on a Calculator

On many scientific calculators, you can enter numbers in scientific notation by using a function labeled "ee" or "EE". Usually, the letter "E" takes the place of "×10". So, the number 4.1×10^9 would appear as 4.1E9 on the calculator.

EXAMPLE 3 (Real World)   FL CC 8.EE.1.4

The table shows the approximate areas for three continents given in square meters. What is the total area of these three continents? Write the answer in scientific notation using more appropriate units.

Continent	Asia	Africa	Europe
Area (m²)	4.4×10^{13}	3.02×10^{13}	1.04×10^{13}

Find $4.4 \times 10^{13} + 3.02 \times 10^{13} + 1.04 \times 10^{13}$.

Enter 4.4E13 + 3.02E13 + 1.04E13 on your calculator.

Write the results from your calculator: 8.46E13.

Write this number in scientific notation: 8.46×10^{13}.

Square kilometers is more appropriate: 8.46×10^7 km².

Because 1 km = 1,000 m, 1 km² = 1,000² m², or 10⁶ m²

YOUR TURN

Write each number using calculator notation.

4. 7.5×10^5 $\underline{7.5E5}$

5. 3×10^{-7} $\underline{3E-7}$

6. 2.7×10^{13} $\underline{2.7E13}$

Write each number using scientific notation.

7. 4.5E−1 $\underline{4.5 \times 10^{-1}}$

8. 5.6E12 $\underline{5.6 \times 10^{12}}$

9. 6.98E−8 $\underline{6.98 \times 10^{-8}}$

Lesson 10.4   317

Guided Practice

Add or subtract. Write your answer in scientific notation. (Example 1)

1. $4.2 \times 10^6 + 2.25 \times 10^5 + 2.8 \times 10^6$

$4.2 \times 10^6 + \boxed{0.225} \times 10^{\boxed{6}} + 2.8 \times 10^6$

$4.2 + \boxed{0.225} + \boxed{2.8}$

$\boxed{7.225} \times 10^{\boxed{6}}$

2. $8.5 \times 10^3 - 5.3 \times 10^3 - 1.0 \times 10^2$

$8.5 \times 10^3 - 5.3 \times 10^3 - \boxed{0.10} \times 10^{\boxed{3}}$

$\boxed{8.5} - \boxed{5.3} - \boxed{0.10}$

$\boxed{3.1} \times 10^{\boxed{3}}$

3. $1.25 \times 10^2 + 0.50 \times 10^2 + 3.25 \times 10^2$
$\underline{\qquad 5 \times 10^2 \qquad}$

4. $6.2 \times 10^5 - 2.6 \times 10^4 - 1.9 \times 10^2$
$\underline{\qquad 5.9381 \times 10^5 \qquad}$

Multiply or divide. Write your answer in scientific notation. (Example 2)

5. $\left(1.8 \times 10^9\right)\left(6.7 \times 10^{12}\right)$ $\underline{1.206 \times 10^{22}}$

6. $\dfrac{3.46 \times 10^{17}}{2 \times 10^9}$ $\underline{1.73 \times 10^8}$

7. $\left(5 \times 10^{12}\right)\left(3.38 \times 10^6\right)$ $\underline{1.69 \times 10^{19}}$

8. $\dfrac{8.4 \times 10^{21}}{4.2 \times 10^{14}}$ $\underline{2 \times 10^7}$

Write each number using calculator notation. (Example 3)

9. 3.6×10^{11}
$\underline{3.6E11}$

10. 7.25×10^{-5}
$\underline{7.25E-5}$

11. 8×10^{-1}
$\underline{8E-1}$

Write each number using scientific notation. (Example 3)

12. 7.6E−4
$\underline{7.6 \times 10^{-4}}$

13. 1.2E16
$\underline{1.2 \times 10^{16}}$

14. 9E1
$\underline{9 \times 10^1}$

? ESSENTIAL QUESTION CHECK-IN

15. How do you add, subtract, multiply, and divide numbers written in scientific notation?

To add or subtract, rewrite the numbers to the same power of 10, add or subtract the multipliers, and rewrite the answer in scientific notation. To multiply or divide, multiply or divide the multipliers, use the rules of exponents to multiply or divide the powers of 10, and rewrite the answer in scientific notation.

318 Unit 5

DIFFERENTIATE INSTRUCTION

Cooperative Learning

Have pairs of students solve a list of four or five addition and subtraction problems similar to 34,000,000 × 18,000,000 and 0.0000000015 ÷ 0.0006. Have one student solve a problem using standard notation and the other student solve the same problem using scientific notation. Have the students compare answers and discuss which method is faster for that particular problem. Then switch roles to solve the next problem.

Visual Cues

Have students solve multiplication and division of scientific notation by splitting the factors into separate problems. Students can circle the multipliers in red and the powers of 10 in blue.

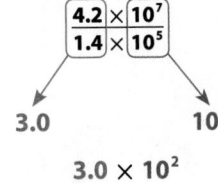

$$\frac{4.2 \times 10^7}{1.4 \times 10^5}$$

3.0 10^2

$$3.0 \times 10^2$$

Additional Resources

Differentiated Instruction includes:

• Reading Strategies
• Success for English Learners **ELL**
• Reteach
• Challenge **PRE-AP**

Operations with Scientific Notation   **318**

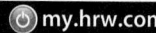
10.4 LESSON QUIZ

FL CC 8.EE.1.4

Add or subtract. Write your answer in scientific notation.

1. $3.2 \times 10^{-2} + 3.2 \times 10^{-4} + 2.8 \times 10^{-2}$

2. $5.2 \times 10^{4} - 1.5 \times 10^{2} - 4.6 \times 10^{4}$

Multiply or divide. Write your answer in scientific notation.

3. $(1.25 \times 10^{4})(4 \times 10^{4})$

4. $\dfrac{4.5 \times 10^{28}}{3 \times 10^{15}}$

5. Write 7.18×10^{-2} using calculator notation.

6. Write 2.898E15 using scientific notation.

Lesson Quiz example available online

⊙ my.hrw.com

Answers

1. 6.032×10^{-2}

2. 5.85×10^{3}

3. 5×10^{8}

4. 1.5×10^{13}

5. 7.18E−2

6. 2.898×10^{15}

Evaluate

GUIDED AND INDEPENDENT PRACTICE

 FL CC 8.EE.1.4

Concepts & Skills	Practice
Example 1 Adding and Subtracting with Scientific Notation	Exercises 1–4, 18–20, 22
Example 2 Multiplying and Dividing with Scientific Notation	Exercises 5–8, 16–17, 21, 23–27
Example 3 Scientific Notation on a Calculator	Exercises 9–14

Exercise	Depth of Knowledge (D.O.K.)	FL CC Mathematical Practices
16–27	2 Skills/Concepts	**MP.4.1** Modeling
28	3 Strategic Thinking H.O.T.	**MP.6.1** Precision
29	3 Strategic Thinking H.O.T.	**MP.3.1** Logic
30	3 Strategic Thinking H.O.T.	**MP.6.1** Precision

Additional Resources

Differentiated Instruction includes:

• Leveled Practice worksheets

 CLUSTER CONNECTION **Exercises 18–21** combine concepts from the Florida Common Core cluster "Work with radicals and integer exponents."

10.4 Independent Practice

FL CC 8.EE.1.4

16. An adult blue whale can eat 4.0×10^7 krill in a day. At that rate, how many krill can an adult blue whale eat in 3.65×10^2 days?

1.46×10^{10} krill

17. A newborn baby has about 26,000,000,000 cells. An adult has about 4.94×10^{13} cells. How many times as many cells does an adult have than a newborn? Write your answer in scientific notation.

about 1.9×10^3 as many

Represent Real-World Problems The table shows the number of tons of waste generated and recovered (recycled) in 2010.

	Paper	Glass	Plastics
Tons generated	7.131×10^7	1.153×10^7	3.104×10^7
Tons recovered	4.457×10^7	0.313×10^7	0.255×10^7

18. What is the total amount of paper, glass, and plastic waste generated?

11.388×10^7, or in scientific notation 1.1388×10^8 tons

19. What is the total amount of paper, glass, and plastic waste recovered?

5.025×10^7 tons

20. What is the total amount of paper, glass, and plastic waste *not* recovered?

6.363×10^7 tons

21. Which type of waste has the lowest recovery ratio?

Plastics

Social Studies The table shows the approximate populations of three countries.

Country	China	France	Australia
Population	1.3×10^9	6.48×10^7	2.15×10^7

22. How many more people live in France than in Australia?

4.33×10^7 more people

23. The area of Australia is 2.95×10^6 square miles. What is the approximate average number of people per square mile in Australia?

about 7 people per square mile

24. How many times greater is the population of China than the population of France? Write your answer in standard notation.

about 20.1 times as great

25. Mia is 7.01568×10^6 minutes old. Convert her age to more appropriate units using years, months, and days. Assume every other month has 30 days, instead of 31.

13 years, 4 months, 5 days

26. Courtney takes 2.4×10^4 steps during her a long-distance run. Each step covers an average of 810 mm. What total distance (in mm) did Courtney cover during her run? Write your answer in scientific notation. Then convert the distance to the more appropriate unit kilometers. Write that answer in standard form.

1.944×10^7 mm; 19.44 km

27. **Social Studies** The U.S. public debt as of October 2010 was $\$9.06 \times 10^{12}$. What was the average U.S. public debt per American if the population in 2010 was 3.08×10^8 people?

$\$2.94 \times 10^4$, or $29,400 per person

H.O.T. FOCUS ON HIGHER ORDER THINKING

28. **Communicate Mathematical Ideas** How is multiplying and dividing numbers in scientific notation different from adding and subtracting numbers in scientific notation?

You can add or subtract numbers written in scientific notation only if their powers of 10 are the same. You can multiply and divide numbers written in scientific notation that have different powers. The laws of exponents are used to combine the powers.

29. **Explain the Error** A student found the product of 8×10^6 and 5×10^9 to be 4×10^{15}. What is the error? What is the correct product?

The student is off by a power of ten. The correct product is 40×10^{15} or 4.0×10^{16}.

30. **Communicate Mathematical Ideas** Describe a procedure that can be used to simplify $\dfrac{\left(4.87 \times 10^{12}\right) - \left(7 \times 10^{10}\right)}{\left(3 \times 10^7\right) + \left(6.1 \times 10^8\right)}$. Write the expression in scientific notation in simplified form.

First, simplify the numerator by rewriting both numbers to the same power of 10 (10^{10}) and subtracting to get 480×10^{10} or 4.8×10^{12}. Then, simplify the denominator by rewriting both numbers to the same power of 10 (10^7) and adding to get 64×10^7 or 6.4×10^8. Finally, divide the multipliers ($4.8 \div 6.4$) to get 0.75, use the division rule for exponents $\left(\dfrac{10^{12}}{10^8}\right)$ to get 10^4, and rewrite 0.75×10^4 in scientific notation as 7.5×10^3.

Work Area

EXTEND THE MATH PRE-AP

Activity available online my.hrw.com

Activity Assume $1 \le a < 10$. When the quotient of $(6 \times 10^6) \div (a \times 10^2)$ is written in scientific notation, the power of 10 is 4. What are the possible values of a? Justify your answer.

$1 \le a \le 6$; Since $(6 \times 10^6) \div (a \times 10^2) = (6 \div a) \times 10^4$, if a is any number between 6 and 10, the value of $6 \div a$ would be less than 1. You could not write this expression in scientific notation with an exponent of 4.

Ready to Go On?

Assess Mastery

Use the assessment on this page to determine if students have mastered the concepts and standards covered in this module.

 **Response to Intervention**

Intervention	Enrichment

Personal Math Trainer
Online Assessment and Intervention
my.hrw.com

Access Ready to Go On? assessment online, and receive instant scoring, feedback, and customized intervention or enrichment.

Online and Print Resources

Differentiated Instruction
- Reteach worksheets
- Reading Strategies **ELL**
- Success for English Learners **ELL**

Differentiated Instruction
- Challenge worksheets **PRE-AP**
- Extend the Math **PRE-AP** Lesson Activities in TE

Additional Resources

Assessment Resources includes
- Leveled Module Quizzes

Ready to Go On?

Personal Math Trainer
Online Assessment and Intervention
my.hrw.com

10.1 Integer Exponents

Find the value of each power.

1. 3^{-4} ___$\frac{1}{81}$___ **2.** 35^0 ___1___ **3.** 4^4 ___256___

Use the properties of exponents to write an equivalent expression.

4. $8^3 \cdot 8^7$ ___8^{10}___ **5.** $\frac{12^6}{12^2}$ ___12^4___ **6.** $(10^3)^5$ ___10^{15}___

10.2 Scientific Notation with Positive Powers of 10

Convert each number to scientific notation or standard notation.

7. 2,000 ___2×10^3___   **8.** 91,007,500 ___9.10075×10^7___

9. 1.0395×10^9 ___1,039,500,000___   **10.** 4×10^2 ___400___

10.3 Scientific Notation with Negative Powers of 10

Convert each number to scientific notation or standard notation.

11. 0.02 ___2×10^{-2}___   **12.** 0.000701 ___7.01×10^{-4}___

13. 8.9×10^{-5} ___0.000089___   **14.** 4.41×10^{-2} ___0.0441___

10.4 Operations with Scientific Notation

Perform the operation. Write your answer in scientific notation.

15. $7 \times 10^6 - 5.3 \times 10^6$ ___1.7×10^6___   **16.** $3.4 \times 10^4 + 7.1 \times 10^5$ ___7.44×10^5___

17. $(2 \times 10^4)(5.4 \times 10^6)$ ___1.08×10^{11}___   **18.** $\frac{7.86 \times 10^9}{3 \times 10^4}$ ___2.62×10^5___

19. Neptune's average distance from the Sun is 4.503×10^9 km. Mercury's average distance from the Sun is 5.791×10^7 km. About how many times farther from the Sun is Neptune than Mercury? Write your answer in scientific notation.

___about 7.776×10^1 times farther___

? ESSENTIAL QUESTION

20. How is scientific notation used in the real world?
Sample answer: Very large numbers, such as distances in space, and very small numbers, such as the sizes of atomic particles, can be written in scientific notation.

© Houghton Mifflin Harcourt Publishing Company

 **Florida Common Core Standards**

Lessons	Exercises	Common Core Standards
10.1	1–6	**8.EE.1.1**
10.2	7–10	**8.EE.1.3**
10.3	11–14	**8.EE.1.3**
10.4	15–19	**8.EE.1.4**

PARCC Assessment Readiness

Assessment Readiness Tip Students can often eliminate some answer choices of multiple-choice questions using logic.

Item 3 1.584 doesn't make sense as a population figure, since it's not possible to have part of a person, and 1,584 people is a very small figure for the population of a country. Therefore answers A and B can be eliminated.

Item 5 The salary of several account executives must be much larger than the salary of a single executive. Answer choices A and B are smaller, while answer choice C is only slightly larger. Therefore, only answer choice D makes sense in the context.

Avoid Common Errors

Item 2 Caution students not to simply count the zeros in the number and select answer choice A. Remind them that they must count the number of places that the decimal point is moved to determine the correct exponent.

Item 8 To avoid losing their place when counting many zeros, encourage students to use the point of a pen or pencil to keep track of where they are when counting, and also to repeat counting to confirm that it is correct.

Additional Resources

Personal Math Trainer

Online Assessment and Intervention

my.hrw.com

MODULE 10 MIXED REVIEW

PARCC Assessment Readiness

Personal Math Trainer

Online Assessment and Intervention

my.hrw.com

Selected Response

1. Which of the following is equivalent to 6^{-3}?

   (A) 216
   (B) $\frac{1}{216}$
   (C) $-\frac{1}{216}$
   (D) -216

2. About 786,700,000 passengers traveled by plane in the United States in 2010. What is this number written in scientific notation?

   (A) 7.867×10^5 passengers
   (B) 7.867×10^2 passengers
   (C) 7.867×10^8 passengers
   (D) 7.867×10^9 passengers

3. In 2011, the population of Mali was about 1.584×10^7 people. What is this number written in standard notation?

   (A) 1.584 people
   (B) 1,584 people
   (C) 15,840,000 people
   (D) 158,400,000 people

4. The square root of a number is between 7 and 8. Which could be the number?

   (A) 72
   (B) 83
   (C) 51
   (D) 66

5. Each entry-level account executive in a large company makes an annual salary of 3.48×10^4. If there are 5.2×10^2 account executives in the company, how much do they make in all?

   (A) 6.69×10^1
   (B) 3.428×10^4
   (C) 3.532×10^4
   (D) 1.8096×10^7

6. Place the numbers in order from least to greatest.
   0.24, 4×10^{-2}, 0.042, 2×10^{-4}, 0.004

   (A) 2×10^{-4}, 4×10^{-2}, 0.004, 0.042, 0.24
   (B) 0.004, 2×10^{-4}, 0.042, 4×10^{-2}, 0.24
   (C) 0.004, 2×10^{-4}, 4×10^{-2}, 0.042, 0.24
   (D) 2×10^{-4}, 0.004, 4×10^{-2}, 0.042, 0.24

7. Guillermo is $5\frac{5}{6}$ feet tall. What is this number of feet written as a decimal?

   (A) 5.7 feet
   (B) $5.\overline{7}$ feet
   (C) 5.83 feet
   (D) $5.8\overline{3}$ feet

8. A human hair has a width of about 6.5×10^{-5} meter. What is this width written in standard notation?

   (A) 0.00000065 meter
   (B) 0.0000065 meter
   (C) 0.000065 meter
   (D) 0.00065 meter

Mini-Task

9. Consider the following numbers: 7000, 700, 70, 0.7, 0.07, 0.007

   a. Write the numbers in scientific notation.
   7×10^3, 7×10^2, 7×10^1,
   7×10^{-1}, 7×10^{-2}, 7×10^{-3}

   b. Look for a pattern in the given list and the list in scientific notation. Which numbers are missing from the lists?
   7 and 7×10^0

   c. Make a conjecture about the missing numbers.
   7×10^0 is 7 written in scientific notation.

© Houghton Mifflin Harcourt Publishing Company

Florida Common Core Standards

Items	Grade 8 Standards	Mathematical Practices
1	8.EE.1.1	
2	8.EE.1.3	MP.4.1
3	8.EE.1.3	MP.4.1
4*	8.NS.1.2	MP.6.1
5	8.EE.1.4	MP.4.1
6	8.EE.1.3	
7*	8.NS.1.1	MP.4.1
8	8.EE.1.3	MP.4.1
9	8.EE.1.3	MP.7.1, MP.8.1

* Item integrates mixed review concepts from previous modules or a previous course.

UNIT 5 Real Numbers, Exponents, and Scientific Notation

Study Guide Review

Additional Resources

Personal Math Trainer

Online Assessment and Intervention

⏻ my.hrw.com

Assessment Resources
- Leveled Unit Tests: A, B, C, D
- Performance Assessment

Vocabulary Development

Integrating Language Arts

Encourage students to practice using the unit vocabulary as they talk and write about mathematics. Understanding vocabulary will aid their understanding of the concepts.

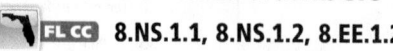 **LACC.68.RST.2.4** Determine the meaning of symbols, key terms, and other domain-specific words and phrases as they are used in a specific scientific or technical context relevant to grades 6–8 texts and topics.

MODULE 9 Real Numbers

FL CC 8.NS.1.1, 8.NS.1.2, 8.EE.1.2

Key Concepts
- An irrational number is a number that is not rational and cannot be written in the form $\frac{a}{b}$ where a and b are integers and $b \neq 0$. *(Lesson 9.1)*
- The square root of a number is the number that when multiplied by itself has the original number as the product. Every positive number has a positive and negative square root. *(Lesson 9.1)*
- The set of real numbers consists of the set of rational numbers and the set of irrational numbers. *(Lesson 9.2)*
- Between any two real numbers is another real number. *(Lesson 9.3)*

Study Guide Review

MODULE 9 Real Numbers

Key Vocabulary
cube root *(raíz cúbica)*
irrational number *(número irracional)*
perfect cube *(cubo perfecto)*
perfect square *(cuadrado perfecto)*
principal square root *(raíz cuadrada principal)*
rational number *(número racional)*
real number *(número real)*
repeating decimal *(decimal periódico)*
square root *(raíz cuadrada)*
terminating decimal *(decimal finito)*

? ESSENTIAL QUESTION
How can you use real numbers to solve real-world problems?

EXAMPLE 1
Write $0.\overline{81}$ as a fraction in simplest form.

$$x = 0.\overline{81}$$
$$100x = 81.\overline{81}$$
$$\underline{-x \quad -0.\overline{81}}$$
$$99x = 81$$
$$x = \frac{81}{99}$$
$$x = \frac{9}{11}$$

EXAMPLE 2
Solve each equation for x.

A $x^2 = 289$

$x = \pm\sqrt{289}$

$x = \pm 17$

The solutions are 17 and -17.

B $x^3 = 1,000$

$x = \sqrt[3]{1,000}$

$x = 10$

The solution is 10.

EXAMPLE 3
Write all names that apply to each number.

A $5.\overline{4}$
rational, real

$5.\overline{4}$ is a repeating decimal.

B $\frac{8}{4}$
whole, integer, rational, real

$\frac{8}{4} = 2$

C $\sqrt{13}$
irrational, real

13 is a whole number that is not a perfect square.

EXAMPLE 4
Order 6, 2π, and $\sqrt{38}$ from least to greatest.

2π is approximately equal to 2×3.14, or 6.28.

$\sqrt{38}$ is approximately 6.15 based on the following reasoning.

$$\sqrt{36} < \sqrt{38} < \sqrt{49} \quad 6 < \sqrt{38} < 7 \quad 6.1^2 = 37.21 \quad 6.2^2 = 38.44$$

From least to greatest, the numbers are 6, $\sqrt{38}$, and 2π.

EXERCISES
Find the two square roots of each number. If the number is not a perfect square, approximate the values to the nearest 0.05.
(Lesson 9.1)

1. 16 _____ 4, −4

2. $\frac{4}{25}$ _____ $\frac{2}{5}$, $-\frac{2}{5}$

3. 225 _____ 15, −15

4. $\frac{1}{49}$ _____ $\frac{1}{7}$, $-\frac{1}{7}$

5. $\sqrt{10}$ _____ 3.15, −3.15

6. $\sqrt{18}$ _____ 4.25, −4.25

Write each decimal as a fraction in simplest form. (Lesson 9.1)

7. $0.\overline{5}$ _____ $\frac{5}{9}$

8. $0.\overline{63}$ _____ $\frac{7}{11}$

9. $0.\overline{214}$ _____ $\frac{214}{999}$

Solve each equation for x. (Lesson 9.1)

10. $x^2 = 361$
$x = 19$

11. $x^3 = 1,728$
$x = 12$

12. $x^2 = \frac{49}{121}$
$x = \frac{7}{11}$

Write all names that apply to each number. (Lesson 9.2)

13. $\frac{2}{3}$
rational, real

14. $-\sqrt{100}$
integer, rational, real

15. $\frac{15}{5}$
whole, integer, rational, real

16. $\sqrt{21}$
irrational, real

Compare. Write <, >, or =. (Lesson 9.3)

17. $\sqrt{7} + 5$ ⟨<⟩ $7 + \sqrt{5}$

18. $6 + \sqrt{8}$ ⟨<⟩ $\sqrt{6} + 8$

19. $\sqrt{4} - 2$ ⟨<⟩ $4 - \sqrt{2}$

Order the numbers from least to greatest. (Lesson 9.3)

20. $\sqrt{81}, \frac{72}{7}, 8.9$ _____ $8.9, \sqrt{81}, \frac{72}{7}$

21. $\sqrt{7}, 2.55, \frac{7}{3}$ _____ $\frac{7}{3}, 2.55, \sqrt{7}$

MODULE 10 Exponents and Scientific Notation

FL CC 8.EE.1.1, 8.EE.1.3, 8.EE.1.4

Key Concepts

- Expressions with integer exponents can be simplified using the properties of integer exponents. (Lesson 10.1)

- Scientific notation is a method of expressing very large and very small numbers as a product of a number greater than or equal to 1 and less than 10, and a power of 10. (Lesson 10.2)

- To multiply a number by 10, move the decimal one place to the right, and to divide a number by 10, move the decimal one place to the left. (Lessons 10.2, 10.3)

- Numbers expressed in scientific notation can be added or subtracted by rewriting them in standard form. (Lesson 10.4)

- Numbers expressed in scientific notation can be multiplied or divided by applying properties of exponents. (Lesson 10.4)

Unit 5 Performance Tasks

The Performance Tasks provide students with the opportunity to apply concepts from this unit in real-world problem situations.

CAREERS IN MATH

Astronomer In Performance Task Item 1, students can see how an astronomer uses mathematics on the job.

SCORING GUIDES FOR PERFORMANCE TASKS

1. MATHEMATICAL PRACTICES   FL CC MP.1.1, MP.4.1, MP.6.1

Task	Possible Points (Total: 6)
a	**1 point** for writing the correct number: 3.99×10^{16} m
b	**2 points** for explanation, for example: since $d = rt$, divide the distance from Earth by the speed of light and **1 point** for the correct answer: $s = 13,300,000$ or $s = 133 \times 10^8$ s
c	**1 point** for dividing answer to **b** by 3.1536×10^7 s, **1 point** for the correct answer: 4.22 years

2. MATHEMATICAL PRACTICES   FL CC MP.3.1, MP.4.1, MP.7.1

Task	Possible Points (Total: 6)
a	**2 points** for choosing correct numbers: $\sqrt{200}$ and 8π
b	**2 points** for correct order: 3.14, $\sqrt{200}$, $\frac{122}{5}$, 8π, 4^3
c	**2 points** for correct explanation: Because 3.14 is a terminating decimal, it can be written as a ratio of two numbers: $\frac{314}{100} = \frac{157}{50}$. On the other hand, π is irrational because it is a nonterminating, nonrepeating decimal: 3.141592654…

Key Vocabulary
scientific notation
(notación científica)

? ESSENTIAL QUESTION

How can you use scientific notation to solve real-world problems?

EXAMPLE 1

Write each measurement in scientific notation.

A The diameter of Earth at the equator is approximately 12,700 kilometers.

Move the decimal point in 12,700 four places to the left: 1.2 7 0 0.

$12{,}700 = 1.27 \times 10^4$

B The diameter of a human hair is approximately 0.00254 centimeters.

Move the decimal point in 0.00254 three places to the right: 0.0 0 2.5 4

$0.00254 = 2.54 \times 10^{-3}$

EXAMPLE 2

Find the quotient: $\dfrac{2.4 \times 10^7}{9.6 \times 10^3}$

Divide the multipliers: $2.4 \div 9.6 = 0.25$

Divide the powers of ten: $\dfrac{10^7}{10^3} = 10^{7-3} = 10^4$

Combine the answers and write the product in scientific notation.

$0.25 \times 10^4 = 0.25 \times (10 \times 10^3) = (0.25 \times 10) \times 10^3 = 2.5 \times 10^3$

EXERCISES

Write each number in scientific notation. (Lessons 10.2, 10.3)

1. 25,500,000 2.55×10^7 2. 0.00734 7.34×10^{-3}

Write each number in standard notation. (Lessons 10.2, 10.3)

3. 5.23×10^4 52,300   4. 1.33×10^{-5} 0.0000133

Simplify each expression. (Lessons 10.1, 10.4)

5. $(9-7)^3 \cdot 5^0 + (8+3)^2$ 129   6. $\dfrac{(4+2)^2}{[(9-3)^3]^2}$ $\dfrac{1}{1{,}296}$

7. $3.2 \times 10^5 + 1.25 \times 10^4 + 2.9 \times 10^5$

     6.225×10^5

8. $(2{,}600)(3.24 \times 10^4)$

     8.424×10^7

Unit 5 Performance Tasks

1. **CAREERS IN MATH** Astronomer An astronomer is studying Proxima Centauri, which is the closest star to our Sun. Proxima Centauri is 39,900,000,000,000,000 meters away.

   a. Write this distance in scientific notation.

   3.99×10^{16} m

   b. Light travels at a speed of 3.0×10^8 m/s (meters per second). How can you use this information to calculate the time in seconds it takes for light from Proxima Centauri to reach Earth? How many seconds does it take? Write your answer in scientific notation.

   Divide the distance Proxima Centauri is from Earth by the speed of light; 1.33×10^8 s

   c. Knowing that 1 year $= 3.1536 \times 10^7$ seconds, how many years does it take for light to travel from Proxima Centauri to Earth? Write your answer in standard notation. Round your answer to two decimal places.

   4.22 years

2. Cory is making a poster of common geometric shapes. He draws a square with a side of length 4^3 cm, an equilateral triangle with a height of $\sqrt{200}$ cm, a circle with a circumference of 8π cm, a rectangle with length $\frac{122}{5}$ cm, and a parallelogram with base 3.14 cm.

   a. Which of these numbers are irrational?

   $\sqrt{200}$ and 8π

   b. Write the numbers in this problem in order from least to greatest. Approximate π as 3.14.

   $3.14, \sqrt{200}, \frac{122}{5}, 8\pi, 4^3$

   c. Explain why 3.14 is rational, but π is not.

   3.14 is a terminating decimal that can be written in the form $\frac{a}{b}$: $\frac{314}{1000}$ or $\frac{157}{500}$. π is a nonrepeating, nonterminating decimal that cannot be written in the form $\frac{a}{b}$.

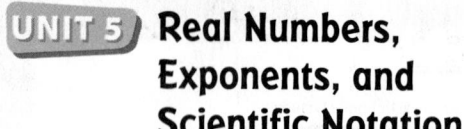

PARCC Assessment Readiness

Additional Resources

Personal Math Trainer

Online Assessment and Intervention

my.hrw.com

Assessment Resources
- Leveled Unit Tests: A, B, C, D
- Performance Assessment

Assessment Readiness Tip Students can work backwards to find solutions for more difficult questions.

Item 1 Students are asked to estimate the square root of 4220. Rather than having to go through with guessing and checking, the students can check each multiple choice solution, squaring the numbers and seeing which pair gives numbers on either side of 4220.

Avoid Common Errors

Item 3 Many students automatically look for what is true, even when the question asks for what is false, because that is a natural instinct when dealing with multiple choice. Suggest that students highlight the word "false," reminding them that they are looking for the statement that is *incorrect*.

Item 10 Students may automatically choose the positive exponent of 2 because they moved the decimal two places. Remind them that a large number will have a positive exponent once placed in scientific notation, but a small number, like 0.025, will have a negative exponent.

 Florida Common Core Standards

Items	Grade 8 Standards	Mathematical Practices
1*	7.G.2.6, 8.EE.1.2	MP.4.1
2	8.NS.1.1	MP.7.1
3	8.NS.1.1	MP.7.1
4	8.EE.1.4	MP.4.1
5	8.EE.1.2, 8.NS.1.1, 8.NS.1.2	MP.7.1
6	8.EE.1.2, 8.NS.1.1, 8.NS.1.2	MP.7.1
7	8.NS.1.1, 8.NS.1.2	MP.2.1
8	8.EE.1.4	MP.2.1
9*	7.G.2.5	MP.6.1
10	8.EE.1.4	MP.4.1
11*	7.NS.1.2d, 8.NS.1.1	MP.5.1
12	8.EE.1.2	MP.5.1
13	8.EE.1.1	MP.2.1
14	8.EE.1.3	MP.1.1
15*	7.SP.3.7a	MP.4.1
16	8.EE.1.4	MP.5.1
17	8.EE.1.2	MP.2.1
18	8.EE.1.4	MP.1.1

* Item integrates mixed review concepts from previous modules or a previous course.

UNIT 5 MIXED REVIEW
PARCC Assessment Readiness

Personal Math Trainer

my.hrw.com
Online Assessment and Intervention

Selected Response

1. A square on a large calendar has an area of 4,220 square millimeters. Between which two integers is the length of one side of the square?

Ⓐ between 20 and 21 millimeters

Ⓑ between 64 and 65 millimeters

Ⓒ between 204 and 205 millimeters

Ⓓ between 649 and 650 millimeters

2. Which of the following numbers is rational but **not** an integer?

Ⓐ −9   Ⓒ 0

Ⓑ −4.3   Ⓓ 3

3. Which statement is false?

Ⓐ No integers are irrational numbers.

Ⓑ All whole numbers are integers.

Ⓒ All rational numbers are real numbers.

Ⓓ All integers are whole numbers.

4. In 2011, the population of Laos was about 6.586×10^6 people. What is this number written in standard notation?

Ⓐ 6,586 people

Ⓑ 658,600 people

Ⓒ 6,586,000 people

Ⓓ 65,860,000 people

5. Which of the following is **not** true?

Ⓐ $\sqrt{16} + 4 > \sqrt{4} + 5$

Ⓑ $4\pi > 12$

Ⓒ $\sqrt{18} + 2 < \frac{15}{2}$

Ⓓ $6 - \sqrt{35} < 0$

6. Which number is between $\sqrt{50}$ and $\frac{5\pi}{2}$?

Ⓐ $\frac{22}{3}$ Ⓒ 6

Ⓑ $2\sqrt{8}$ Ⓓ $\pi + 3$

7. Which number is indicated on the number line?

```
+--+--+--+--+--●--+--+
7  7.2 7.4 7.6 7.8  8
```

Ⓐ $\pi + 4$ Ⓒ $\sqrt{14} + 4$

Ⓑ $\frac{152}{20}$ Ⓓ $7.\overline{8}$

8. Which of the following is the number 5.03×10^{-5} written in standard form?

Ⓐ 503,000

Ⓑ 50,300,000

Ⓒ 0.00503

Ⓓ 0.0000503

9. Which correctly describes the relationship between supplementary angles?

Ⓐ They have the same angle measure.

Ⓑ The sum of their angle measures is 90 degrees.

Ⓒ The sum of their angle measures is 180 degrees.

Ⓓ The sum of their angle measures is 360 degrees.

10. A quarter weighs about 0.025 pounds. What is this weight written in scientific notation?

Ⓐ 2.5×10^{-2} pounds

Ⓑ 2.5×10^{1} pounds

Ⓒ 2.5×10^{-1} pounds

Ⓓ 2.5×10^{2} pounds

11. Which fraction is equivalent to $0.\overline{45}$?

Ⓐ $\frac{4}{9}$ Ⓒ $\frac{4}{5}$

Ⓑ $\frac{5}{9}$ Ⓓ $\frac{5}{11}$

12. What is the value of x if $x^2 = \frac{36}{81}$?

Ⓐ $\frac{2}{3}$ Ⓒ $\frac{4}{9}$

Ⓑ $\pm\frac{2}{3}$ Ⓓ $\pm\frac{4}{9}$

13. What is $\frac{[(9-2)^2]^4}{(4+3)^5}$ written in simplest form?

Ⓐ 7

Ⓑ 21

Ⓒ 49

Ⓓ 343

14. The total land area on Earth is about 6×10^7 square miles. The land area of Australia is about 3×10^6 square miles. About how many times larger is the land area on Earth than the land area of Australia?

Ⓐ 2

Ⓑ 10

Ⓒ 20

Ⓓ 60

15. Ricardo rolls a standard number cube 48 times. What is the best prediction for the number of times he will roll an even number that is greater than 2?

Ⓐ 4   Ⓒ 24

Ⓑ 16   Ⓓ 32

16. What is the value of the expression $(2.3 \times 10^7)(1.4 \times 10^{-2})$ written in scientific notation?

Ⓐ 3.7×10^{-14}

Ⓑ 3.7×10^5

Ⓒ 0.322×10^6

Ⓓ 3.22×10^5

17. What is the value of $\sqrt[3]{64}$?

Ⓐ 2

Ⓑ 4

Ⓒ 8

Ⓓ 16

Mini-Task

18. Amanda says that a human fingernail has a thickness of about 4.2×10^{-4} meter. Justin says that a human fingernail has a thickness of about 0.42 millimeter.

a. What is the width in meters written in standard notation?

0.00042 m

b. Do Justin's and Amanda's measurements agree? Explain.

Yes; 0.00042 m × 1,000 mm/m = 0.42 mm

c. Explain why Justin's estimate of the thickness of a human fingernail is more appropriate than Amanda's estimate.

Sample answer: Since the thickness of a fingernail is a very small number, it is more appropriate to measure the thickness in millimeters than in meters.

UNIT 6

COMMON CORE

Proportional and Nonproportional Relationships and Functions

Contents

Unit Pacing Guide

45-Minute Classes

Module 11

DAY 1	DAY 2	DAY 3	DAY 4	
Lesson 11.1	Lesson 11.2	Lesson 11.3	Ready to Go On? PARCC Assessment Readiness	

Module 12

DAY 1	DAY 2	DAY 3	DAY 4	DAY 5
Lesson 12.1	Lesson 12.2	Lesson 12.3	Lesson 12.4	Ready to Go On? PARCC Assessment Readiness

Module 13

DAY 1	DAY 2	DAY 3	DAY 4	DAY 5
Lesson 13.1	Lesson 13.2	Lesson 13.3	Lesson 13.3	Ready to Go On? PARCC Assessment Readiness

Module 14

DAY 1	DAY 2	DAY 3	DAY 4	DAY 5
Lesson 14.1	Lesson 14.1	Lesson 14.2	Lesson 14.3	Lesson 14.3

DAY 6	DAY 7	DAY 8
Lesson 14.4	Ready to Go On? PARCC Assessment Readiness	Study Guide PARCC Assessment Readiness

90-Minute Classes

Module 11

DAY 1	DAY 2
Lesson 11.1 Lesson 11.2	Lesson 11.3 Ready to Go On? PARCC Assessment Readiness

Module 12

DAY 1	DAY 2	DAY 3
Lesson 12.1 Lesson 12.2	Lesson 12.3 Lesson 12.4	Lesson 12.4 Ready to Go On? PARCC Assessment Readiness

Module 13

DAY 1	DAY 2	DAY 3
Lesson 13.1 Lesson 13.2	Lesson 13.2 Lesson 13.3	Lesson 13.3 Ready to Go On? PARCC Assessment Readiness

Module 14

DAY 1	DAY 2	DAY 3	DAY 4	
Lesson 14.1	Lesson 14.2 Lesson 14.3	Lesson 14.3 Lesson 14.4	Ready to Go On? PARCC Assessment Readiness	Study Guide PARCC Assessment Readiness

Program Resources

⏻ Plan

Online Teacher Edition

Access a full suite of teaching resources online—plan, present, and manage classes, assignments, and activities.

ePlanner Easily plan your classes, create and view assignments, and access all program resources with your online, customizable planning tool.

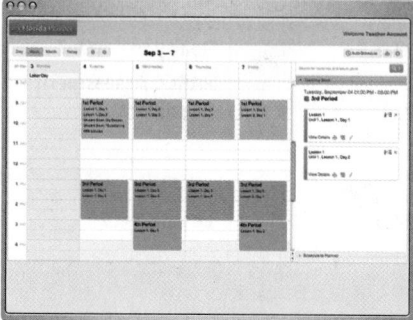

Professional Development Videos

Author Juli Dixon models successful teaching practices and strategies in actual classroom settings.

QR Codes Scan with your smart phone to jump directly from your print book to online videos and other resources.

Teacher's Edition

Support students with point-of-use Questioning Strategies, teaching tips, resources for differentiated instruction, additional activities, and more.

⏻ Engage and Explore

Real-World Videos Engage students with interesting and relevant applications of the mathematical content of each module.

Animated Math Online interactive simulations, tools, and games help students actively learn and practice key concepts.

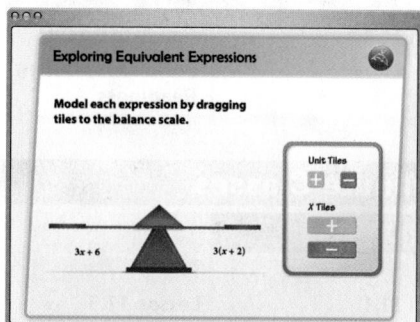

Explore Activities

Students interactively explore new concepts using a variety of tools and approaches.

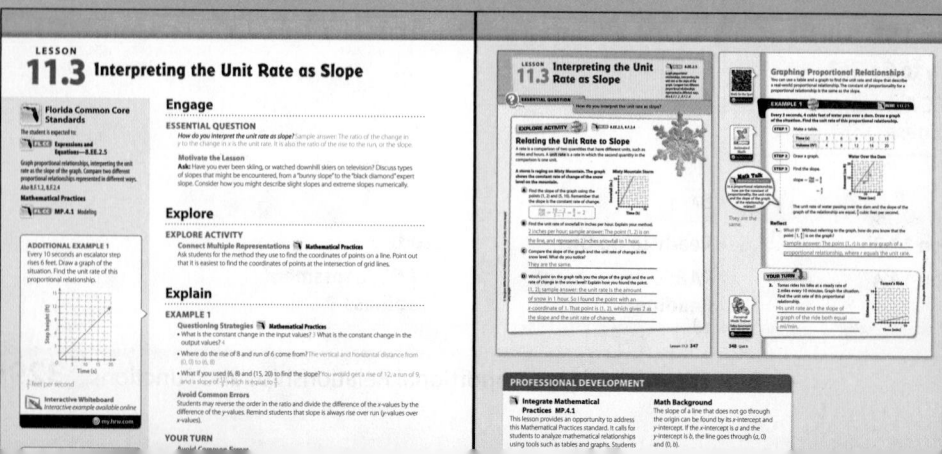

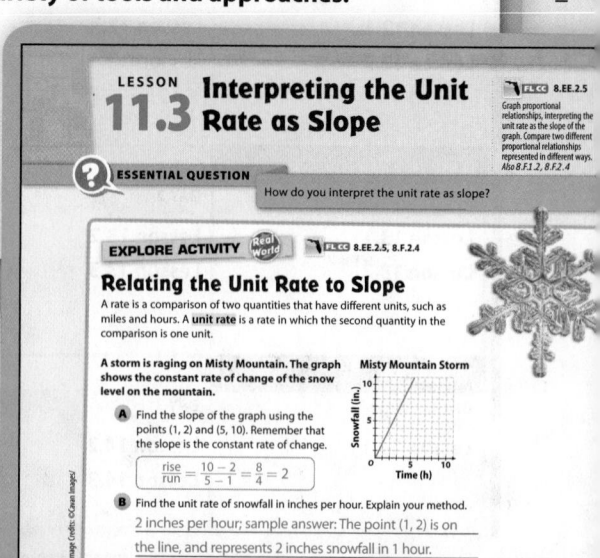

LESSON
11.3 Interpreting the Unit Rate as Slope

FL CC 8.EE.2.5

Graph proportional relationships, interpreting the unit rate as the slope of the graph. Compare two different proportional relationships represented in different ways. Also 8.F.1.2, 8.F.2.4

ESSENTIAL QUESTION

How do you interpret the unit rate as slope?

EXPLORE ACTIVITY Real World   FL CC 8.EE.2.5, 8.F.2.4

Relating the Unit Rate to Slope

A rate is a comparison of two quantities that have different units, such as miles and hours. A **unit rate** is a rate in which the second quantity in the comparison is one unit.

A storm is raging on Misty Mountain. The graph shows the constant rate of change of the snow level on the mountain.

Misty Mountain Storm

A Find the slope of the graph using the points (1, 2) and (5, 10). Remember that the slope is the constant rate of change.

$$\frac{\text{rise}}{\text{run}} = \frac{10 - 2}{5 - 1} = \frac{8}{4} = 2$$

B Find the unit rate of snowfall in inches per hour. Explain your method.

2 inches per hour; sample answer: The point (1, 2) is on the line, and represents 2 inches snowfall in 1 hour.

C Compare the slope of the graph and the unit rate of change in the snow level. What do you notice?

They are the same.

D Which point on the graph tells you the slope of the graph and the unit

⏻ Teach

Math On the Spot video tutorials, featuring program authors Dr. Edward Burger and Martha Sandoval-Martinez, accompany every example in the textbook and give students step-by-step instructions and explanations of key math concepts.

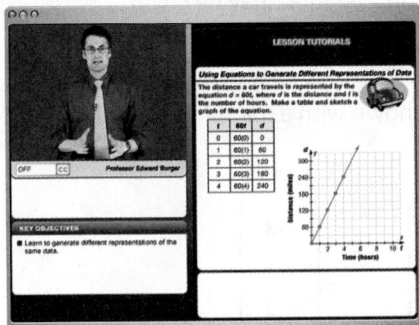

Present engaging content on a multitude of devices, including tablets and interactive whiteboards.

 Math Talk Continually monitor and assess student progress with integrated formative assessment.

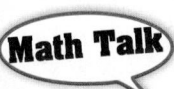 **CLUSTER CONNECTION** Look for exercises indicated with this icon to build connections among standards within Florida Common Core clusters.

Differentiated Instruction Print Resources

Support all learners with Differentiated Instruction Resources, including

- **Leveled Practice and Problem Solving**
- **Reteach**
- **Reading Strategies**
- **Success for English Learners**
- **Challenge**

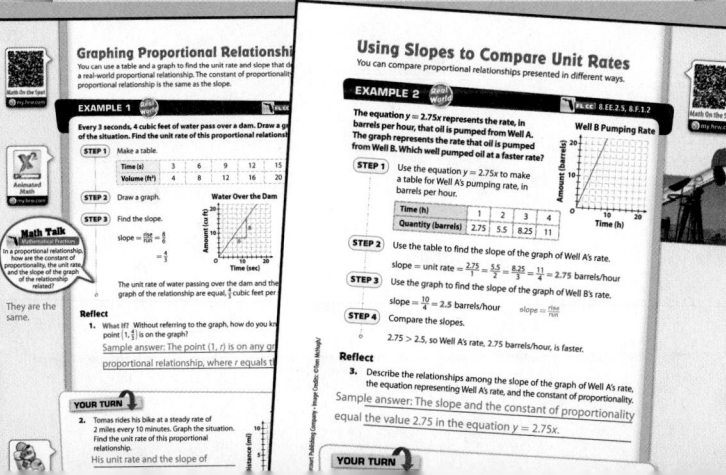

⏻ Assessment and Intervention

The **Personal Math Trainer** provides online practice, homework, assessments, and intervention. Monitor student progress through reports and alerts. Create and customize assignments aligned to specific lessons or standards.

- **Practice** – With dynamic items and assignments, students get unlimited practice on key concepts supported by guided examples, step-by-step solutions, and video tutorials.
- **Assessments** – Choose from course assignments or customize your own based on course content, standards, difficulty levels, and more.
- **Homework** – Students can complete online homework with a wide variety of problem types, including the ability to enter expressions, equations, and graphs. Let the system automatically grade homework, so you can focus where your students need help the most!
- **Intervention** – Let the Personal Math Trainer automatically prescribe a targeted, personalized intervention path for your students.

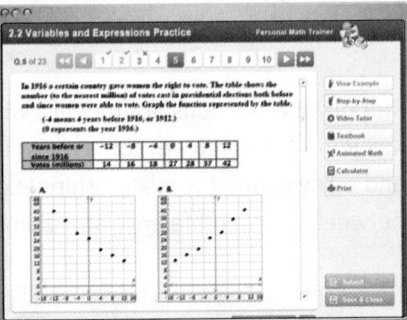

 Raise the bar with homework and practice that incorporates higher-order thinking and mathematical processes in every lesson.

 **PARCC Assessment Readiness**
Prepare students for success on the PARCC math test with practice at every module and unit.

Assessment Resources

Tailor assessments to meet the needs of all your classes and students, including

- **Leveled Module Quizzes**
- **Leveled Unit Tests**
- **Unit Performance Tasks**
- **Placement, Diagnostic, and Quarterly Benchmark Tests**

Math Background

Representing Proportional Relationships
8.EE.2.6, 8.F.2.4
LESSON 11.1

A *proportional relationship* is a special type of linear function that can be written in the form $y = kx$, where k is a nonzero constant. Equivalently, the phrase "y is proportional to x" means that there exists a nonzero k such that $y = kx$. The constant k is called the *constant of proportionality*.

The graph of a proportional relationship is a straight line through the origin. The line passes through the origin because $(0, 0)$ is a solution of the equation $y = kx$ for all values of k. The slope of the line is k. This can be shown as follows: Suppose the points (x_1, y_1) and (x_2, y_2) lie on the line. Then $y_1 = kx_1$ and $y_2 = kx_2$. The slope is

$$\frac{y_2 - y_1}{x_2 - x_1} = \frac{kx_1 - kx_2}{x_2 - x_1} = \frac{k(x_2 - x_1)}{x_2 - x_1} = k.$$

Proportional relationships model a wide range of situations, including measurement conversions (e.g., feet to inches) and many geometric relationships (e.g., the relationship between the circumference and diameter of a circle).

Linear Relationships in Tables **8.F.1.3**
LESSON 12.1

If an equation is linear, then a constant change in the x-value corresponds to a constant change in the y-value. This is reflected in any table of values for the equation, as long as the table contains equally spaced x-values. In this case, the differences in the y-values are called *first differences*.

The ordered pairs in a table satisfy a linear equation if and only if the first differences are constant. For example, in the table below, the x-values are equally spaced and the first differences are all 2, so the ordered pairs satisfy a linear equation.

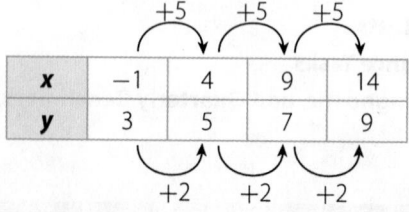

Identifying and Describing Functions **8.F.1.1, 8.F.1.3**
LESSONS 14.1 and 14.2

A *relation* is simply a set of ordered pairs. In each ordered pair, the first value (or x-value) is the domain value or input, and the second value (or y-value) is the range value or output. The ordered pairs in a relation may be given as a set. For example, the relation described by the set $\{(-2, 3), (4, 1), (4, 5), (5, -3)\}$ consists of four ordered pairs. This relation can also be shown with a mapping diagram.

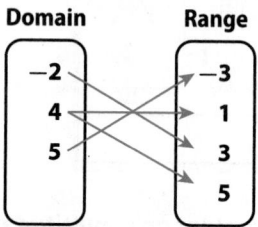

A *function* is a relation in which each domain value is paired with exactly one range value. The relation shown above is not a function, since the domain value 4 is paired with two different range values, 1 and 5.

The relation described by the set $\{(-3, -4), (1, 1), (3, 1), (7, -2)\}$ is a function. Each domain value is paired with exactly one range value. This can be seen in the mapping diagram below. Note that each domain value has only one arrow emanating from it.

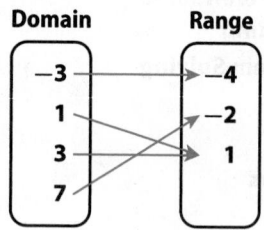

Students may wonder why functions are so important in mathematics. The restriction that each domain value be paired with only one range value may seem unmotivated. By looking at a variety of real-world problems, students should come to see that functions are a natural way to model a wide range of phenomena. For example, a scientist might record the population of bacteria in a Petri dish at various times. For each time (domain value) there is only one population (range value). Therefore, this relation is an example of a function.

Because many students have the mistaken belief that functions must be described by equations, it is helpful to introduce functions by defining them as a set of ordered pairs with the property that each domain value is paired with exactly one range value. It is also useful to give examples of functions for which no formula is known, such as the temperature at noon at an airport as a function of the date.

With experience, students should be able to generate their own examples of relations that are functions and relations that are not functions. This helps them internalize the idea that every function is a relation, but not every relation is a function.

Representing and Comparing Functions 8.F.1.1, 8.F.1.2, 8.F.1.3
LESSONS 14.2 and 14.3

Functions can be represented in many ways:

Ordered pairs: (0, 0), (1, 3), (2, 6)
Mapping diagram:

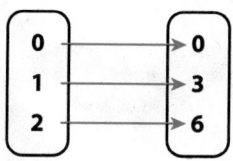

Words: Apples are $3 per pound.
Table:

x	0	1	2
y	0	3	6

Equation: $y = 3x$
Graph:

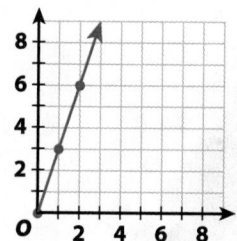

An equation usually conveys more information than a table. A table can present only a limited number of ordered pairs, whereas an infinite number of ordered pairs can be generated from an equation. An equation is also more compact than a table. A table may make it easier to recognize patterns compared to a list of ordered pairs. It can also be easier to create a graph from a table than from an equation.

Proportional and Nonproportional Relationships and Functions

CAREERS IN MATH

Cost Estimator A cost estimator determines the cost of a product or project, which helps businesses decide whether or not to manufacture a product or build a structure. Cost estimators analyze the costs of labor, materials, and use of equipment, among other things. Cost estimators use math when they assemble and analyze data. If you are interested in a career as a cost estimator, you should study these mathematical subjects:
- Algebra
- Trigonometry
- Calculus

Research other careers that require analyzing costs.

Unit 6 Performance Task

At the end of the unit, check out how **cost estimators** use math.

Careers in Math

Cost Estimator

Cost estimators need to accurately estimate the cost of projects such as manufacturing a product or constructing a building, taking into account prices of materials, labor costs, and all other factors that might influence the cost of a project. You will learn more about this in the Performance Tasks at the end of the unit.

For more information about careers in mathematics as well as various mathematics appreciation topics, visit the American Mathematical Society at www.ams.org

Vocabulary Preview

Use the puzzle to give students a preview of important concepts in this unit. Students may work individually, in pairs, or in groups.

Unit Resources

Go online to access all your unit resources.

my.hrw.com

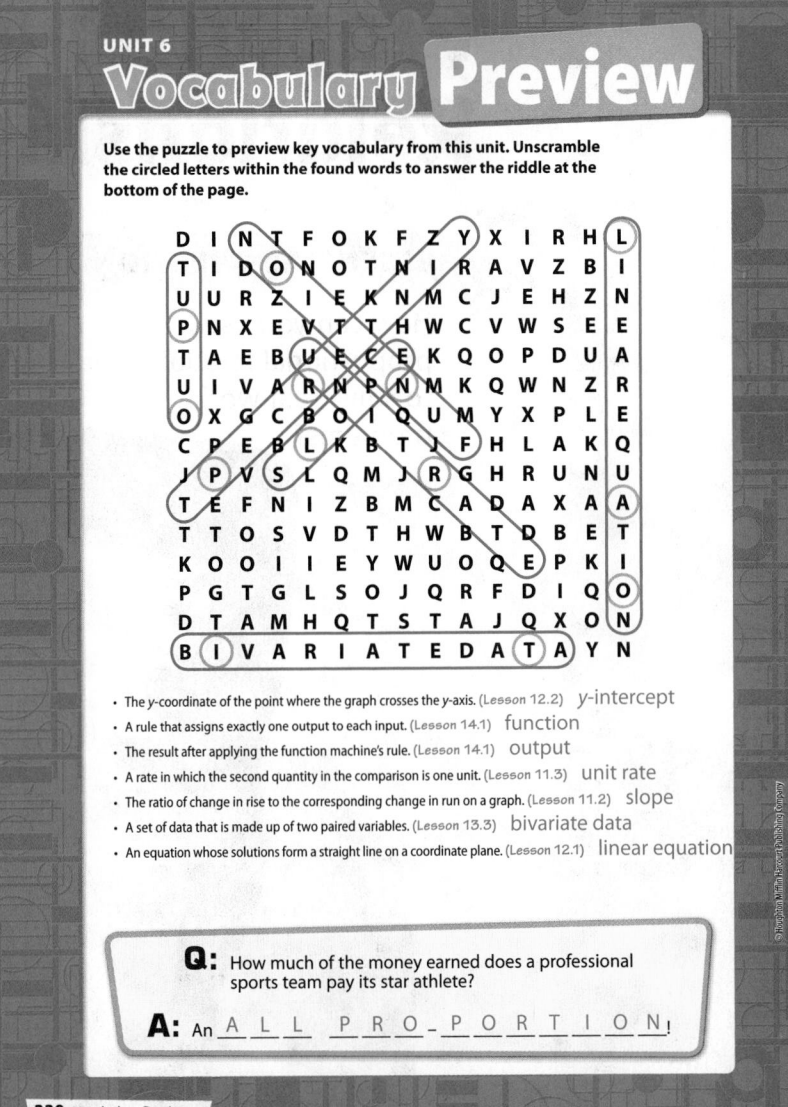

Vocabulary Preview

Use the puzzle to preview key vocabulary from this unit. Unscramble the circled letters within the found words to answer the riddle at the bottom of the page.

```
D  I  N  T  F  O  K  F  Z  Y  X  I  R  H  L
T  I  D  O  N  O  T  N  I  R  A  V  Z  B  I
U  U  R  Z  I  E  K  N  M  C  J  E  H  Z  N
P  N  X  E  V  T  T  H  W  C  V  W  S  E  E
T  A  E  B  U  E  C  E  K  Q  O  P  D  U  A
U  I  V  A  R  N  P  N  M  K  Q  W  N  Z  R
O  X  G  C  B  O  I  Q  U  M  Y  X  P  L  E
C  P  E  B  L  K  B  T  J  F  H  L  A  K  Q
J  P  V  S  L  Q  M  J  R  G  H  R  U  N  U
T  E  F  N  I  Z  B  M  C  A  D  A  X  A  A
T  T  O  S  V  D  T  H  W  B  T  D  B  E  T
K  O  O  I  I  E  Y  W  U  O  Q  E  P  K  I
P  G  T  G  L  S  O  J  Q  R  F  D  I  Q  O
D  T  A  M  H  Q  T  S  T  A  J  Q  X  O  N
B  I  V  A  R  I  A  T  E  D  A  T  A  Y  N
```

- The *y*-coordinate of the point where the graph crosses the *y*-axis. (Lesson 12.2) *y*-intercept
- A rule that assigns exactly one output to each input. (Lesson 14.1) function
- The result after applying the function machine's rule. (Lesson 14.1) output
- A rate in which the second quantity in the comparison is one unit. (Lesson 11.3) unit rate
- The ratio of change in rise to the corresponding change in run on a graph. (Lesson 11.2) slope
- A set of data that is made up of two paired variables. (Lesson 13.3) bivariate data
- An equation whose solutions form a straight line on a coordinate plane. (Lesson 12.1) linear equation

Q: How much of the money earned does a professional sports team pay its star athlete?

A: An A L L P R O _ _ P O R T I O N !

Before

Students understand proportional relationships:

- rates and proportionality
- linear relationships represented by tables, graphs, or equations
- constant rates of change represented by tables, descriptions, equations, or graphs

In this Unit

Students will learn about:

- linear proportional and nonproportional relationships
- unit rate and slope
- constant of proportionality
- direct variation
- equations in the form $y = mx + b$
- systems of equations
- functions

After

Students will connect:

- proportional relationships and constant rate of change
- proportionality and direct variation
- linear relationships and their graphs and equations in the form $y = mx + b$

Proportional Relationships

MODULE 11

ESSENTIAL QUESTION

How can you use proportional relationships to solve real-world problems?

You can solve problems about real-world proportional relationships by analyzing tables, equations, and graphs that represent them.

Real-World Video

Speedboats can travel at fast rates while sailboats travel more slowly. If you graphed distance versus time for both types of boats, you could tell by the steepness of the graph which boat was faster.

⏻ my.hrw.com

© Houghton Mifflin Harcourt Publishing Company • Image Credits: ©Angelo Giampiccolo/Shutterstock

GO DIGITAL

my.hrw.com

my.hrw.com

Go digital with your write-in student edition, accessible on any device.

Math On the Spot

Scan with your smart phone to jump directly to the online edition, video tutor, and more.

Animated Math

Interactively explore key concepts to see how math works.

Personal Math Trainer

Get immediate feedback and help as you work through practice sets.

Are You Ready?

Assess Readiness

Use the assessment on this page to determine if students need intensive or strategic intervention for the module's prerequisite skills.

 **Response to Intervention**

Intervention	Enrichment

Access Are You Ready? assessment online, and receive instant scoring, feedback, and customized intervention or enrichment.

Personal Math Trainer
Online Assessment and Intervention
⏻ my.hrw.com

Online and Print Resources

Skills Intervention worksheets
- Skill 26 Write Fractions as Decimals
- Skill 65 Solve Proportions

Differentiated Instruction
- Challenge worksheets **PRE-AP**
- Extend the Math **PRE-AP** Lesson Activities in TE

Are YOU Ready?

Complete these exercises to review skills you will need for this module.

Personal Math Trainer
Online Assessment and Intervention
my.hrw.com

Write Fractions as Decimals

EXAMPLE $\frac{1.7}{2.5} = ?$

Multiply the numerator and the denominator by a power of 10 so that the denominator is a whole number.

$$\frac{1.7 \times 10}{2.5 \times 10} = \frac{17}{25}$$

Write the fraction as a division problem. Write a decimal point and zeros in the dividend. Place a decimal point in the quotient. Divide as with whole numbers.

$$\begin{array}{r} 0.68 \\ 25\overline{)17.00} \\ -15\,0 \\ \hline 2\,00 \\ -2\,00 \\ \hline 0 \end{array}$$

Write each fraction as a decimal.

1. $\frac{3}{8}$ __0.375__
2. $\frac{0.3}{0.4}$ __0.75__
3. $\frac{0.13}{0.2}$ __0.65__
4. $\frac{0.39}{0.75}$ __0.52__
5. $\frac{4}{5}$ __0.8__
6. $\frac{0.1}{2}$ __0.05__
7. $\frac{3.5}{14}$ __0.25__
8. $\frac{7}{14}$ __0.5__
9. $\frac{0.3}{10}$ __0.03__

Solve Proportions

EXAMPLE $\frac{5}{7} = \frac{x}{14}$

$$\frac{5 \times 2}{7 \times 2} = \frac{x}{14}$$

$7 \times 2 = 14$, so multiply the numerator and denominator by 2.

$$\frac{10}{14} = \frac{x}{14}$$

$5 \times 2 = 10$

$$x = 10$$

Solve each proportion for x.

10. $\frac{20}{18} = \frac{10}{x}$ __$x = 9$__
11. $\frac{x}{12} = \frac{30}{72}$ __$x = 5$__
12. $\frac{x}{4} = \frac{4}{16}$ __$x = 1$__
13. $\frac{11}{x} = \frac{132}{120}$ __$x = 10$__
14. $\frac{36}{48} = \frac{x}{4}$ __$x = 3$__
15. $\frac{x}{9} = \frac{21}{27}$ __$x = 7$__
16. $\frac{24}{16} = \frac{x}{2}$ __$x = 3$__
17. $\frac{30}{15} = \frac{6}{x}$ __$x = 3$__
18. $\frac{3}{x} = \frac{18}{36}$ __$x = 6$__

© Houghton Mifflin Harcourt Publishing Company

PROFESSIONAL DEVELOPMENT VIDEO

 Author Juli Dixon models successful teaching practices as she explores the concept of proportional relationships in an actual eighth-grade classroom.

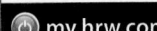

Professional Development
⏻ my.hrw.com

GO DIGITAL
my.hrw.com

 Online Teacher Edition
Access a full suite of teaching resources online—plan, present, and manage classes and assignments.

 ePlanner
Easily plan your classes and access all your resources online.

 Interactive Answers and Solutions
Customize answer keys to print or display in the classroom. Choose to include answers only or full solutions to all lesson exercises.

 Interactive Whiteboards
Engage students with interactive whiteboard-ready lessons and activities.

 Personal Math Trainer: Online Assessment and Intervention
Assign automatically graded homework, quizzes, tests, and intervention activities. Prepare your students with updated practice tests aligned with Common Core.

Reading Start-Up

Have students complete the activities on this page by working alone or with others.

Visualize Vocabulary

The case diagram will help students to review concepts related to proportions. Students should write one review word in each bubble.

Understand Vocabulary

Use the following explanation to help students learn the preview words.

Proportional relationships can be used in many everyday situations. For example, if you need 1.5 hours to study 2 math lessons, you can figure out how much time you need to study 6 math lessons. If you know that 2 math lessons requires 1.5 hours, then 4 math lessons requires 3 hours, and 6 math lesson requires 4.5 hours.

In this lesson, you will learn how to use the **constant of proportionality** to find proportional relationships.

Active Reading

Integrating Language Arts

Students can use these reading and note-taking strategies to help them organize and understand new concepts and vocabulary.

FL CC **LACC.68.RST.3.7** Integrate quantitative or technical information expressed in words in a text with a version of that information expressed visually (e.g., in a flowchart, diagram, model, graph, or table).

Additional Resources

Differentiated Instruction

• Reading Strategies **ELL**

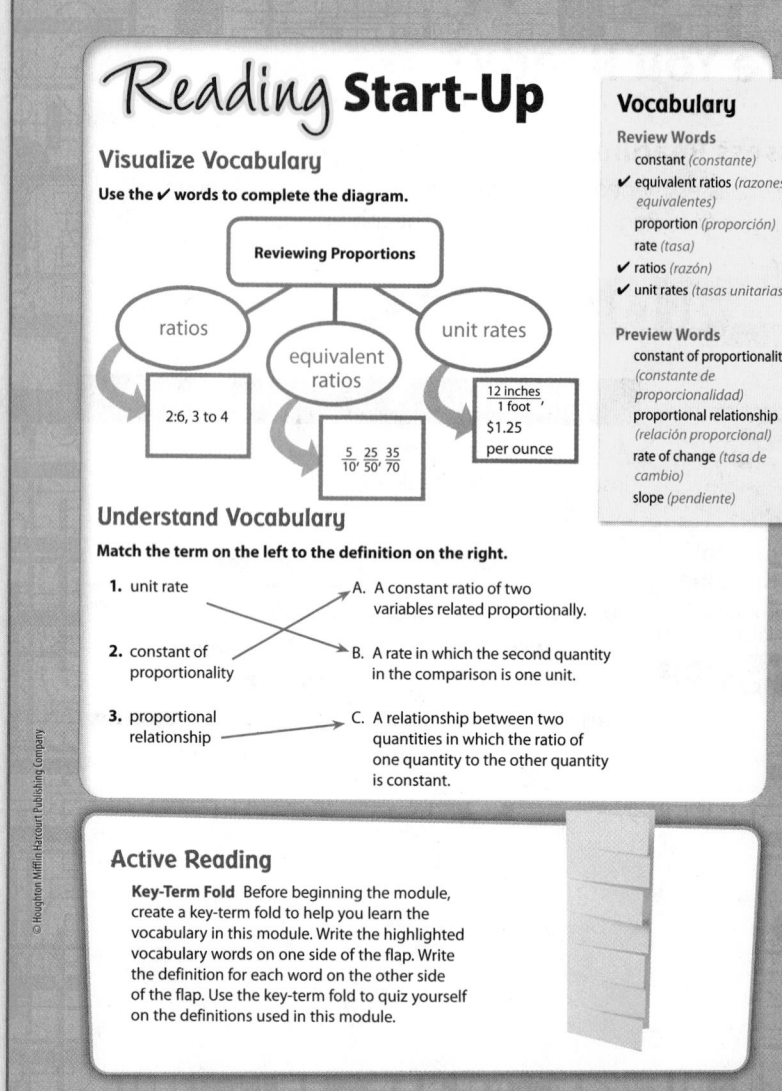

Before	In this module	After
Students understand rates and proportional relationships: • find unit rate • use tables and verbal descriptions to represent two-variable relationships • write and graph a linear relationship	Students represent and solve problems involving proportional relationships: • represent linear proportional situations with tables, graphs, and equations • use data from a table or graph to determine the rate of change or slope and *y*-intercept in mathematical and real-world problems • graph proportional relationships, interpreting the unit rate as the slope of the line that models the relationship	Students will connect: • proportional relationships with constant rate of change • proportionality and direct variation

Unpacking the Standards

Use the examples on this page to help students know exactly what they are expected to learn in this module.

Florida Common Core Standards

Content Areas

 **FL CC** **Expressions and Equations—8.EE.2**

Understand the connections between proportional relationships, lines, and linear equations.

Go online to see a complete unpacking of the Florida Common Core Standards.

my.hrw.com

MODULE 11

Unpacking the Standards

Understanding the standards and the vocabulary terms in the standards will help you know exactly what you are expected to learn in this module.

FL CC **8.EE.2.5**

Graph proportional relationships, interpreting the unit rate as the slope of the graph. Compare two different proportional relationships represented in different ways.

Key Vocabulary

proportional relationship *(relación proporcional)*
A relationship between two quantities in which the ratio of one quantity to the other quantity is constant.

slope *(pendiente)*
A measure of the steepness of a line on a graph; the rise divided by the run.

unit rate *(tasa unitaria)*
A rate in which the second quantity in the comparison is one unit.

What It Means to You

You will use data from a table and a graph to apply your understanding of rates to analyzing real-world situations.

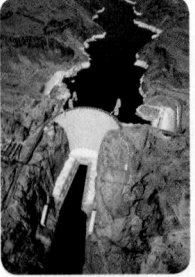

UNPACKING EXAMPLE 8.EE.2.5

The table shows the volume of water released by Hoover Dam over a certain period of time. Use the data to make a graph. Find the slope of the line and explain what it shows.

Water Released from Hoover Dam

Time (s)	Volume of water (m³)
5	75,000
10	150,000
15	225,000
20	300,000

Water Released from Hoover Dam

The slope of the line is 15,000. This means that for every second that passed, 15,000 m³ of water was released from Hoover Dam.

Suppose another dam releases water over the same period of time at a rate of 50 m³ per minute. How do the two rates compare?

50 m³ per minute is equal to 3,000 m³ per second. This rate is one fifth the rate released by the Hoover Dam over the same time period.

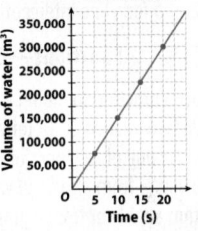

Visit my.hrw.com to see all Florida Common Core Standards unpacked.

my.hrw.com

Florida Common Core Standards	Lesson 11.1	Lesson 11.2	Lesson 11.3
FL CC **8.EE.2.5** Graph proportional relationships, interpreting the unit rate as the slope of the graph. Compare two different proportional relationships represented in different ways.			
FL CC **8.EE.2.6** ... derive the equation $y = mx$ for a line through the origin and the equation $y = mx + b$ for a line intercepting the vertical axis at b.	✦		
FL CC **8.F.1.2** Compare properties of two functions each represented in a different way (algebraically, graphically, numerically in tables, or by verbal descriptions).			✦
FL CC **8.F.2.4** ... Determine the rate of change and initial value of the function from a description of a relationship or from two (x, y) values, including reading these from a table or from a graph. Interpret the rate of change and initial value of a linear function in terms of the situation it models, and in terms of its graph or a table of values.	✦	✦	✦

LESSON
11.1 Representing Proportional Relationships

Florida Common Core Standards

The student is expected to:

 **Expressions and Equations—8.EE.2.6**

Use similar triangles to explain why the slope m is the same between any two distinct points on a non-vertical line in the coordinate plane; derive the equation $y = mx$ for a line through the origin and the equation $y = mx + b$ for a line intercepting the vertical axis at b.

 Functions—8.F.2.4

Construct a function to model a linear relationship between two quantities. Determine the rate of change and initial value of the function from a description of a relationship or from two (x, y) values, including reading these from a table or from a graph. Interpret the rate of change and initial value of a linear function in terms of the situation it models, and in terms of its graph or a table of values.

Mathematical Practices

 MP.4.1 Modeling

ADDITIONAL EXAMPLE 1
Marco earns $36.50 per hour as an accountant. Show that the relationship between the amount he earns and the number of hours he works is a proportional relationship. Then write an equation for the relationship.

$$\frac{\text{amount earned}}{\text{number of hours}} =$$

$$\frac{36.5}{1} = \frac{73}{2} = \frac{146}{4} = \frac{292}{8} = 36.5;$$

$y = 36.5x$, where x is the number of hours, and y is the amount earned.

 Interactive Whiteboard
Interactive example available online

 my.hrw.com

Engage

ESSENTIAL QUESTION
How can you use tables, graphs, and equations to represent proportional situations?
Sample answer: If the ratio between one quantity and another is constant, you can use tables, graphs, and equations of the form $y = kx$ to represent a proportional relationship between the quantities.

Motivate the Lesson
Ask: The circumference of Earth is about 25,000 miles. How many miles did the Nautilus travel in *20,000 Leagues Under the Sea*? Take a guess. Begin the Explore Activity to find out.

Explore

EXPLORE ACTIVITY
Focus on Patterns Mathematical Practices
Point out to students that they can use a pattern to complete the table relating the distance in leagues to the distance in miles. The pattern is multiply the distance in leagues by 3 to get the number of miles (or divide by 3 to find leagues from miles).

Explain

EXAMPLE 1
Connect Vocabulary ELL
Remind students that a proportional relationship is a relationship between two quantities in which the ratio of one quantity to the other quantity is constant.

Questioning Strategies Mathematical Practices
- In Step 2, which row of the table is the numerator of each ratio? the bottom row Which row is the denominator? the top row
- What do you look for in the table in order to decide whether the relationship is proportional? The amount earned divided by the hours is the same for each pair of values.

YOUR TURN
Avoid Common Errors
Make sure that students divide the number of bicycles by the number of hours, not the number of hours by the number of bicycles.

Talk About It
Check for Understanding
Ask: Bicycles are produced at a constant rate of 15 per hour. Why can the relationship be described by the equation $y = 15x$? Since bicycles are produced at a constant rate, 15 is the constant of proportionality, k. An equation describing a proportional relationship is of the form $y = kx$. Substitute 15 for k to get $y = 15x$.

Representing Proportional Relationships

FL CC 8.EE.2.6

...derive the equation $y = mx$ for a line through the origin... Also 8.F.2.4

? **ESSENTIAL QUESTION**
How can you use tables, graphs, and equations to represent proportional situations?

EXPLORE ACTIVITY Real World
FL CC Prep for 8.EE.2.6

Representing Proportional Relationships with Tables

In 1870, the French writer Jules Verne published *20,000 Leagues Under the Sea*, one of the most popular science fiction novels ever written. One definition of a *league* is a unit of measure equaling 3 miles.

A Complete the table.

Distance (leagues)	1	2	6	12	20,000
Distance (miles)	3	6	18	36	60,000

B What relationships do you see among the numbers in the table?
Every number in the bottom row is 3 times the number in the top row.

C For each column of the table, find the ratio of the distance in miles to the distance in leagues. Write each ratio in simplest form.

$$\frac{3}{1} = \boxed{3} \qquad \frac{6}{2} = \boxed{3} \qquad \frac{18}{6} = \boxed{3} \qquad \frac{36}{12} = \boxed{3} \qquad \frac{60,000}{20,000} = \boxed{3}$$

D What do you notice about the ratios? They are all equal to 3.

Reflect

1. If you know the distance between two points in leagues, how can you find the distance in miles? Multiply the distance in leagues by 3.

2. If you know the distance between two points in miles, how can you find the distance in leagues? Divide the distance in miles by 3.

Math On the Spot
my.hrw.com

Representing Proportional Relationships with Equations

The ratio of the distance in miles to the distance in leagues is constant. This relationship is said to be *proportional*. A **proportional relationship** is a relationship between two quantities in which the ratio of one quantity to the other quantity is constant.

A proportional relationship can be described by an equation of the form $y = kx$, where k is a number called the **constant of proportionality**.

Sometimes it is useful to use another form of the equation, $k = \frac{y}{x}$.

EXAMPLE 1 Real World
FL CC 8.EE.2.6

Meghan earns $12 an hour at her part-time job. Show that the relationship between the amount she earned and the number of hours she worked is a proportional relationship. Then write an equation for the relationship.

STEP 1 Make a table relating amount earned to number of hours.

> For every hour Meghan works, she earns $12. So, for 8 hours of work, she earns $8 \times \$12 = \$96$.

Number of hours	1	2	4	8
Amount earned ($)	12	24	48	96

STEP 2 For each number of hours, write the relationship of the amount earned and the number of hours as a ratio in simplest form.

$$\frac{\text{amount earned}}{\text{number of hours}} \qquad \frac{12}{1} = 12 \qquad \frac{24}{2} = 12 \qquad \frac{48}{4} = 12 \qquad \frac{96}{8} = 12$$

Since the ratios between the two quantities are all equal to 12, the relationship is proportional.

STEP 3 Write an equation.

> First tell what the variables represent.

Let x represent the number of hours.
Let y represent the amount earned.

Use the ratio as the constant of proportionality in the equation $y = kx$.

The equation is $y = 12x$.

Sample answer: The relationship between x, an amount of money in quarters, and y, the same amount in cents.

Math Talk
Mathematical Practices

Describe two real-world quantities with a proportional relationship that can be described by the equation $y = 25x$.

Personal Math Trainer
Online Assessment and Intervention
my.hrw.com

YOUR TURN

3. Fifteen bicycles are produced each hour at the Speedy Bike Works. Show that the relationship between the number of bikes produced and the number of hours is a proportional relationship. Then write an equation for the relationship.
$y = 15x$

PROFESSIONAL DEVELOPMENT

Integrate Mathematical Practices MP.4.1

This lesson provides an opportunity to address this Mathematical Practices standard. It calls for students to use tables and equations to model a relationship between corresponding real-world proportional values. Then students use graphs to visualize the proportional relationship and to create tables to model the relationship. In this way, students are able to use multiple representations to model real-world situations.

Math Background

A proportional relationship is sometimes called a direct variation. You can say that the value of y varies directly with the value of x or that y is directly proportional to x. As the value of x increases or decreases, the respective value of y increases or decreases. These equations are usually written in the form $y = kx$, where k is called the constant of variation.

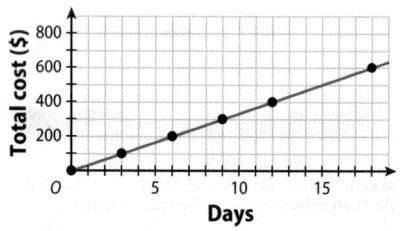
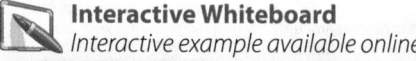
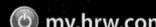
EXAMPLE 2

Questioning Strategies 🏴 Mathematical Practices

- What happens to the weight of an object on the Moon as the weight of an object on Earth increases? As it decreases? The weight increases; the weight decreases.

- How do you know whether the constant of proportionality is $\frac{1}{6}$ or 6? The equation is $y = kx$, where k is the constant of proportionality; so k is multiplied by x to get y. You can use the coordinates of a given point to find k: $y = kx$; $2 = k \cdot 12$, so $k = \frac{1}{6}$.

Focus on Modeling 🏴 Mathematical Practices

In Example 2, students use data from a graph to create a table and an equation that models a real-world situation. Ensure that students understand the concept of using variables to represent real-world quantities.

YOUR TURN

Focus on Math Connections 🏴 Mathematical Practices

Make sure that students understand the connections between the rate 6 miles in 5 hours, the point (5, 6), the constant of proportionality $\frac{6}{5}$, and the equation $y = \frac{6}{5}x$.

Engage with the Whiteboard

Have students use the grid on the student page to draw a new line that contains the origin. They should draw the line so that it passes through the intersections of the vertical and horizontal grid lines. Have them make tables for both lines by picking points and recording the x- and y-values. Next they should find the rates of change by dividing the y-coordinate by the x-coordinate. This will help them visualize the constant rate of change as the ratio of the y-value to the x-value.

Elaborate

Talk About It
Summarize the Lesson

Ask: When you know a relationship between variables is a proportional relationship, like the weight of an object on the Moon and on Earth from Example 2, how do you express the relationship in an equation? Express the equation in the form $y = kx$, where k is the constant of proportionality. In Example 2, the equation relating the weight on the Moon, y, with its weight on Earth, x, is $y = \frac{1}{6}x$.

GUIDED PRACTICE

Engage with the Whiteboard

Have students plot each point in the table for Exercise 3 on the grid in Exercise 5, plotting weeks on the x-axis and days on the y-axis. They will have to extend the x-axis or change the scale so that each tic mark is 1 week. Then have them draw a line through the points to show that the table is a proportional relationship containing the point (0, 0).

Avoid Common Errors

Exercises 1–2 Remind students that the equations describing these proportional relationships have a constant of proportionality equal to the y-value divided by the x-value, not the x-value divided by the y-value.

Exercise 5 Remind students that the relationship shown in the graph is a proportional relationship because the line contains (0, 0).

Representing Proportional Relationships with Graphs

You can represent a proportional relationship with a graph. The graph will be a line that passes through the origin (0, 0). The graph shows the relationship between distance measured in miles to distance measured in leagues.

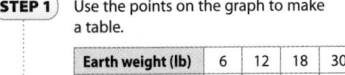

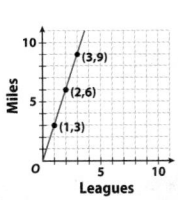

EXAMPLE 2

FL CC 8.EE.2.6

The graph shows the relationship between the weight of an object on the Moon and its weight on Earth. Write an equation for this relationship.

STEP 1 Use the points on the graph to make a table.

Earth weight (lb)	6	12	18	30
Moon weight (lb)	1	2	3	5

STEP 2 Find the constant of proportionality.

$$\frac{\text{Moon weight}}{\text{Earth weight}} \qquad \frac{1}{6} = \frac{1}{6} \qquad \frac{2}{12} = \frac{1}{6} \qquad \frac{3}{18} = \frac{1}{6} \qquad \frac{5}{30} = \frac{1}{6}$$

The constant of proportionality is $\frac{1}{6}$.

STEP 3 Write an equation.

Let x represent weight on Earth.

Let y represent weight on the Moon.

The equation is $y = \frac{1}{6}x$.   Replace k with $\frac{1}{6}$ in $y = kx$.

YOUR TURN

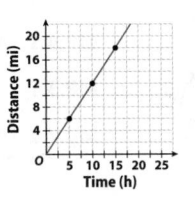

The graph shows the relationship between the amount of time that a backpacker hikes and the distance traveled.

4. What does the point (5, 6) represent?
    6 miles hiked in 5 hours

5. What is the equation of the relationship?
    $y = \frac{6}{5}x$

Math On the Spot
@ my.hrw.com

Personal Math Trainer
Online Assessment and Intervention
@ my.hrw.com

Lesson 11.1 **337**

Guided Practice

1. Vocabulary A proportional relationship is a relationship between two quantities in which the ratio of one quantity to the other quantity [is] / is not constant.

2. Vocabulary When writing an equation of a proportional relationship in the form $y = kx$, k is replaced with the __constant of proportionality__.

3. Write an equation that describes the proportional relationship between the number of days and the number of weeks in a given length of time. (Explore Activity and Example 1)

a. Complete the table.

Time (weeks)	1	2	4	8	10
Time (days)	7	14	28	56	70

b. Let x represent ____the time in weeks____.

Let y represent ____the time in days____

The equation that describes the relationship is ____$y = 7x$____.

Each table or graph represents a proportional relationship. Write an equation that describes the relationship. (Example 1 and Example 2)

4. Physical Science The relationship between the numbers of oxygen atoms and hydrogen atoms in water

Oxygen atoms	2	5	17	120
Hydrogen atoms	4	10	34	240

____$y = 2x$____

5. Map of Iowa

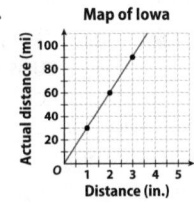

____$y = 30x$____

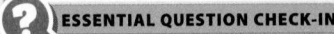

ESSENTIAL QUESTION CHECK-IN

6. If you know the equation of a proportional relationship, how can you draw the graph of the equation?

Sample answer: Use the equation to make a table with x-values and y-values. Then graph the points (x, y) and draw a line through the points.

338 Unit 6

DIFFERENTIATE INSTRUCTION

Cooperative Learning
Have students discuss different ways to use tables, equations, and graphs to represent proportional relationships.

Student 1: I used the constant ratio of y to x in each table column to write an equation of the form $y = kx$ for the proportional relationship.

Student 2: I just take the x- and y-values from a point on the graph, divide y by x to get k, and then write an equation of the form $y = kx$.

Critical Thinking
Point out to students that on the graph of a proportional relationship, the ratio of the y-coordinate of a point to the x-coordinate of that point gives the constant of proportionality. Ask students to examine this claim, discuss why it is true, and justify it with a logical argument.

The equation of the graph of a proportional relationship can be expressed as $y = kx$, where k is the constant of proportionality. The ratio of the y-coordinate to the x-coordinate of a point on the graph is $\frac{y}{x}$. Since $\frac{y}{x} = k$ is an equivalent form of the equation $y = kx$, $\frac{y}{x}$ gives the constant of proportionality k.

Additional Resources
Differentiated Instruction includes:
- Reading Strategies
- Success for English Learners **ELL**
- Reteach
- Challenge **PRE-AP**

Representing Proportional Relationships **338**

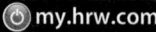
11.1 LESSON QUIZ

 **FL CC** 8.EE.2.6, 8.F.2.4

1. Nico earns $12.50 per hour as a math tutor. Show that the relationship between the amount he earns and the number of hours he tutors is a proportional relationship. Then write the equation for the relationship.

2. The graph shows the relationship between the number of cups of flour and the number of cookies made. Write an equation for the proportional relationship.

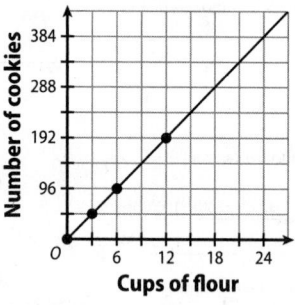

3. The table shows a proportional relationship. Write an equation that describes the relationship.

Acres	5	8	15
Bushels of wheat	140	224	420

Lesson Quiz available online

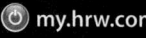
 my.hrw.com

Answers

1. $\frac{\text{amount earned}}{\text{number of hours}} =$
$\frac{12.5}{1} = \frac{25}{2} = \frac{50}{4} = \frac{100}{8} = 12.5$;
$y = 12.5x$, where x is the number of hours and y is the amount earned.

2. $y = 16x$

3. $y = 28x$

Evaluate

GUIDED AND INDEPENDENT PRACTICE

 **FL CC** 8.EE.2.6, 8.F.2.4

Concepts & Skills	Practice
Explore Activity Representing Proportional Relationships with Tables	Exercises 3, 7, 13
Example 1 Representing Proportional Relationships with Equations	Exercises 3–4, 10, 13
Example 2 Representing Proportional Relationships with Graphs	Exercises 5, 8, 13

Exercise	Depth of Knowledge (D.O.K.)	**FL CC** Mathematical Practices
7–8	**2** Skills/Concepts	**MP.4.1** Modeling
9–10	**2** Skills/Concepts	**MP.6.1** Precision
11–12	**2** Skills/Concepts	**MP.5.1** Using Tools
13	**2** Skills/Concepts	**MP.4.1** Modeling
14	**3** Strategic Thinking H.O.T.	**MP.3.1** Logic
15–16	**3** Strategic Thinking H.O.T.	**MP.7.1** Using Structure

Additional Resources

Differentiated Instruction includes:

• Leveled Practice worksheets

11.1 Independent Practice

FL CC 8.EE.2.6, 8.F.2.4

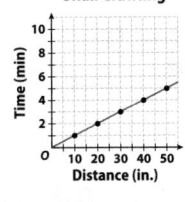

Personal
Math Trainer
Online
Assessment and
Intervention
my.hrw.com

The table shows the relationship between temperatures measured on the Celsius and Fahrenheit scales.

Celsius temperature	0	10	20	30	40	50
Fahrenheit temperature	32	50	68	86	104	122

7. Is the relationship between the temperature scales proportional? Why or why not?

No; the ratios of the numbers in each column are not equal.

8. Describe the graph of the Celsius-Fahrenheit relationship.

Sample answer: a line starting at (0, 32) and slanting upward to the right

9. Analyze Relationships Ralph opened a savings account with a deposit of $100. Every month after that, he deposited $20 more.

a. Why is the relationship described not proportional?

Sample answer: The account had a balance of $100 to begin with.

b. How could the situation be changed to make the situation proportional?

Sample answer: Have Ralph open the account with no money to begin with and then put $20 in every month.

10. Represent Real-World Problems Describe a real-world situation that can be modeled by the equation $y = \frac{1}{20}x$. Be sure to describe what each variable represents.

Sample answer: If x is the number of nickels you have, $y = \frac{1}{20}x$ is the amount of money you have in dollars.

Look for a Pattern The variables x and y are related proportionally.

11. When $x = 8$, $y = 20$. Find y when $x = 42$. _____ $y = 105$

12. When $x = 12$, $y = 8$. Find x when $y = 12$. _____ $x = 18$

13. The graph shows the relationship between the distance that a snail crawls and the time that it crawls.

a. Use the points on the graph to make a table.

Distance (in.)	10	20	30	40	50
Time (min)	1	2	3	4	5

b. Write the equation for the relationship and tell what each variable represents.

$y = \frac{1}{10}x$, where y is the time in minutes and x is the distance in inches

c. How long does it take the snail to crawl 85 inches? __8.5 minutes__

Snail Crawling

(graph: Time (min) vs Distance (in.))

H.O.T. FOCUS ON HIGHER ORDER THINKING

Work Area

14. Communicate Mathematical Ideas Explain why all of the graphs in this lesson show the first quadrant but omit the other three quadrants.

Sample answer: All of the graphs represent real-world data for which both x and y take on only positive values, which graph in the first quadrant. If either x or y or both could be negative, then other quadrants would be needed.

15. Analyze Relationships Complete the table.

Length of side of square	1	2	3	4	5
Perimeter of square	4	8	12	16	20
Area of square	1	4	9	16	25

a. Are the length of the side of a square and the perimeter of the square related proportionally? Why or why not?

Yes. The ratio of the perimeter of a square to its side length is always 4.

b. Are the length of the side of a square and the area of the square related proportionally? Why or why not?

No. The ratio of the area of a square to its side length is not constant.

16. Make a Conjecture A table shows a proportional relationship where k is the constant of proportionality. The rows are then switched. How does the new constant of proportionality relate to the original one?

It is the reciprocal of the original constant of proportionality.

EXTEND THE MATH PRE-AP

Activity available online my.hrw.com

Activity The table and graph show values representing a proportional relationship. Use the graph labels to describe the proportional relationship. Complete the table and graph the points from the table. Then write an algebraic equation for the proportional relationship.

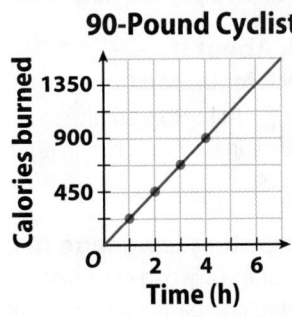

90-Pound Cyclist

(graph: Calories burned vs Time (h))

Hours	1	2	3	4
Calories burned	225	450	675	900

The number of calories burned by a 90-pound cyclist is proportional to the number of hours the cyclist rode. The constant of proportionality is 225, and an equation for the proportional relationship is $y = 225x$.

11.2 Rate of Change and Slope

Florida Common Core Standards

The student is expected to:

 **FL CC** Functions—8.F.2.4

Construct a function to model a linear relationship between two quantities. Determine the rate of change and initial value of the function from a description of a relationship or from two (x, y) values, including reading these from a table or from a graph. Interpret the rate of change and initial value of a linear function in terms of the situation it models, and in terms of its graph or a table of values.

Mathematical Practices

 **FL CC** MP.7.1 Structure

---

ADDITIONAL EXAMPLE 1

Hector keeps a record of the total number of clients he has and the amount he earns as a personal trainer. Tell whether the rates of change are constant or variable.

	Day 1	Day 2	Day 3	Day 4
Number of clients	1	3	4	7
Amount earned ($)	45	135	180	315

constant

 Interactive Whiteboard
Interactive example available online

⏻ my.hrw.com

Engage

ESSENTIAL QUESTION

How do you find a rate of change or a slope? Sample answer: Find the ratio of the change in output values to the change in input values in tables or graphs.

Motivate the Lesson

Ask: All cars have a speedometer and an odometer. Which one measures a rate of change? What are the two variables in this rate of change?

Explore

Have students consider speed as a rate of change. Have them describe how the rate of change may differ for a bicycle, a car, and a plane. See also Explore Activity in student text.

Explain

EXAMPLE 1

Questioning Strategies 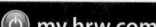 Mathematical Practices

- How can you tell which row in the table represents the input values? The number of lawns; as the number of lawns increases, the amount earned increases.
- How do you find the change in the input values? In the output values? Find the difference in consecutive values in the input row; find the differences in the output row.

YOUR TURN

Avoid Common Errors

Students may see that an input value of 0 results in an output value of 0 and assume that the table represents a proportional relationship. Caution them to find the rate of change for all pairs of input and output values before they decide if the rate of change is constant.

Talk About It
Check for Understanding

 Ask: How are the rates of change for the table in Your Turn different from the table in Example 1? The rates of change for the table in Your Turn are variable, while the rates of change for the table in Example 1 are constant.

Integrating Language Arts **ELL**

Encourage a broad class discussion on the Math Talk. English learners will benefit from hearing and participating in classroom discussions.

EXPLORE ACTIVITY

Focus on Reasoning 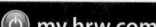 Mathematical Practices

Discuss with students how the graph and the rate of change would be affected if Nathan rode 15 miles in the first hour, but only 12 miles in the second hour and 10 miles in the third. Students should realize that the rates of change would be variable, not constant, and they should reason that the values when graphed could not lie on a single line.

Rate of Change and Slope

FL CC 8.F.2.4
...Determine the rate of change...of the function from...two (x, y) values, including reading these from a table or from a graph....

? ESSENTIAL QUESTION

How do you find a rate of change or a slope?

Investigating Rates of Change

A **rate of change** is a ratio of the amount of change in the output to the amount of change in the input.

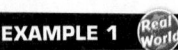

EXAMPLE 1 · Real World

FL CC 8.F.2.4

Eve keeps a record of the number of lawns she has mowed and the money she has earned. Tell whether the rates of change are constant or variable.

	Day 1	Day 2	Day 3	Day 4
Number of lawns	1	3	6	8
Amount earned ($)	15	45	90	120

STEP 1 Identify the input and output variables.

Input variable: number of lawns   Output variable: amount earned

STEP 2 Find the rates of change.

Day 1 to Day 2: $\dfrac{\text{change in \$}}{\text{change in lawns}} = \dfrac{45-15}{3-1} = \dfrac{30}{2} = 15$

Day 2 to Day 3: $\dfrac{\text{change in \$}}{\text{change in lawns}} = \dfrac{90-45}{6-3} = \dfrac{45}{3} = 15$

Day 3 to Day 4: $\dfrac{\text{change in \$}}{\text{change in lawns}} = \dfrac{120-90}{8-6} = \dfrac{30}{2} = 15$

The rates of change are constant: $15 per lawn.

Math Talk
Mathematical Practices

Would you expect the rates of change of a car's speed during a drive through a city to be constant or variable? Explain.

Variable; sample answer: It would be difficult to maintain a constant rate of speed because of such factors as traffic slowing down and speeding up, traffic lights, stop signs, and turns.

Math On the Spot
my.hrw.com

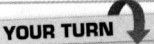

1. The table shows the approximate height of a football after it is kicked. Tell whether the rates of change are constant or variable.

Time (s)	Height (ft)
0	0
0.5	18
1.5	31
2	26

Find the rates of change:

36, 13, −10

The rates of change are **constant / variable**.

Personal Math Trainer
Online Assessment and Intervention
my.hrw.com

EXPLORE ACTIVITY · Real World

FL CC 8.F.2.4

Using Graphs to Find Rates of Change

You can also use a graph to find rates of change.

The graph shows the distance Nathan bicycled over time. What is Nathan's rate of change?

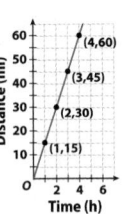

A Find the rate of change from 1 hour to 2 hours.

$\dfrac{\text{change in distance}}{\text{change in time}} = \dfrac{30 - \boxed{15}}{2 - 1} = \dfrac{\boxed{15}}{1} = \boxed{15}$ miles per hour

B Find the rate of change from 1 hour to 4 hours.

$\dfrac{\text{change in distance}}{\text{change in time}} = \dfrac{60 - \boxed{15}}{4 - \boxed{1}} = \dfrac{\boxed{45}}{\boxed{3}} = \boxed{15}$ miles per hour

C Find the rate of change from 2 hour to 4 hours.

$\dfrac{\text{change in distance}}{\text{change in time}} = \dfrac{60 - \boxed{30}}{4 - \boxed{2}} = \dfrac{\boxed{30}}{\boxed{2}} = \boxed{15}$ miles per hour

D Recall that the graph of a proportional relationship is a line through the origin. Explain whether the relationship between Nathan's time and distance is a proportional relationship.

Yes; the graph is a line through the origin.

Reflect

2. **Make a Conjecture** Does a proportional relationship have a constant rate of change?

Yes

3. Does it matter what interval you use when you find the rate of change of a proportional relationship? Explain.

No; in a proportional relationship, the rate of change is constant.

PROFESSIONAL DEVELOPMENT

Integrate Mathematical Practices MP.7.1

This lesson provides an opportunity to address this Mathematical Practices standard. It calls for students to discern a structure. Students find and analyze the rates of changes in input and output tables. Then students use graphs to visualize constant rates of change and to describe a constant rate of change as the slope of a line. In this way, students analyze input-output tables and graphs to make the connection between rate of change and slope.

Math Background

A linear relationship expresses a constant rate of change, called the slope. The algebraic formula to find the slope m of a line containing the points (x_1, y_1) and (x_2, y_2) is given by the equation $m = \dfrac{y_2 - y_1}{x_2 - x_1}$.

The rate of change can also be described as

$\dfrac{\text{change in dependent variable}}{\text{change in independent variable}}$, where x represents the independent variable, and y represents the dependent variable.

ADDITIONAL EXAMPLE 2
Find the slope of the line.

$-\dfrac{3}{4}$

Interactive Whiteboard
Interactive example available online

⏻ my.hrw.com

EXAMPLE 2

Questioning Strategies   🏴 Mathematical Practices

• How do you know from the signs of the rise and run if a slope is positive or negative? The rise is positive and the run is negative so their quotient and, therefore, the slope is negative.

• If you chose the same two points as shown in the example, but found the changes in values moving from the left-most point to the right-most point, how would that alter the change in rise and run and the sign of the slope? The rise is -2 and the run is 3; the sign and value of the slope is unchanged.

Engage with the Whiteboard

Have a student draw a vertical line at $x = 4$ and place two points on it. Have another student draw a horizontal line at $y = -5$ and place two points on it. Ask students to find the slopes of the horizontal (slope is equal to 0) and vertical lines (slope is undefined).

Focus on Communication   🏴 Mathematical Practices

Emphasize the relationship between the slope and graph of the line. A graph that rises from left to right has a positive slope; a graph that falls from left to right has a negative slope. A horizontal line has a slope of 0. A vertical line has an undefined slope.

YOUR TURN

Focus on Math Connections   🏴 Mathematical Practices

Make sure that students understand the connections between the rate of leaking, the slope of the line, and the proportional relationship shown in the graph. Students may see that the graph is increasing and think that the amount of water is increasing. Make sure they understand that the graph shows the amount of water that has leaked out of the tank.

Elaborate

Talk About It
Summarize the Lesson

💬 Complete the graphic organizer with the students while discussing constant and variable rates of change.

	Gallons	3	6	12	Items	10	20	30
	Quarts	12	24	48	Cost ($)	25	50	90
Rates of change	4, 4, 4				2.5, 2.5, 3			
Constant or variable	constant				variable			

GUIDED PRACTICE

Engage with the Whiteboard

In Exercises 5 and 6, have students plot the points on the graph that are indicated by the words in the exercise. For Exercise 5, students should plot points (1, 200) and (2, 400), which represent the distances after 1 minute and 2 minutes, respectively.

Avoid Common Errors

Exercise 2 Remind students to check all pairs of values in the table before deciding if the rates of change are constant or variable.

Calculating Slope

When the rate of change of a relationship is constant, every segment of its graph has the same steepness, and the segments together form a line. The constant rate of change is called the *slope* of the line.

The **slope** of a line is the ratio of the change in y-values (rise) for a segment of the graph to the corresponding change in x-values (run).

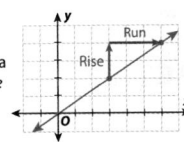

Math On the Spot
@ my.hrw.com

EXAMPLE 2
FL CC 8.F.2.4

Find the slope of the line.

STEP 1 Choose two points on the line.

STEP 2 Find the change in y-values (rise) and the change in x-values (run) as you move from one point to the other.

> If you move up or right, the change is positive. If you move down or left, the change is negative.

rise $= +2$ run $= -3$

STEP 3 Slope $= \dfrac{rise}{run}$

$= \dfrac{2}{-3}$

$= -\dfrac{2}{3}$

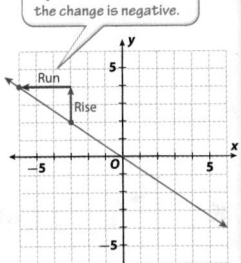

YOUR TURN

4. The graph shows the rate at which water is leaking from a tank. The slope of the line gives the leaking rate in gallons per minute.

Rise $= \underline{\hspace{1cm} +3 \hspace{1cm}}$

Run $= \underline{\hspace{1cm} +4 \hspace{1cm}}$

Rate of leaking $= \underline{\dfrac{3}{4}}$ gallon(s) per minute

Leaking tank

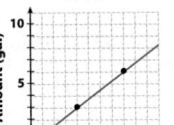

Personal Math Trainer
Online Assessment and Intervention
@ my.hrw.com

Tell whether the rates of change are constant or variable. (Example 1)

1. building measurements ___constant___

Feet	3	12	27	75
Yards	1	4	9	25

2. computers sold ___variable___

Week	2	4	9	20
Number Sold	6	12	25	60

3. distance an object falls ___variable___

Distance (ft)	16	64	144	256
Time (s)	1	2	3	4

4. cost of sweaters ___constant___

Number	2	4	7	9
Cost ($)	38	76	133	171

Erica walks to her friend Philip's house. The graph shows Erica's distance from home over time. (Explore Activity)

5. Find the rate of change from 1 minute to 2 minutes.

$$\dfrac{\text{change in distance}}{\text{change in time}} = \dfrac{400 - \boxed{200}}{2 - \boxed{1}} = \dfrac{\boxed{200}}{\boxed{1}} = \boxed{200} \text{ ft per min}$$

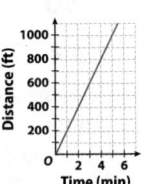

6. Find the rate of change from 1 minute to 4 minutes. ___200 ft per min___

Find the slope of each line. (Example 2)

7.

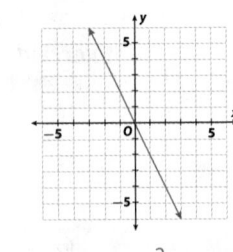

slope = ___−2___

8.

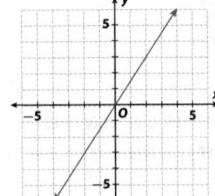

slope = ___$\dfrac{3}{2}$___

? ESSENTIAL QUESTION CHECK-IN

9. If you know two points on a line, how can you find the rate of change of the variables being graphed?

Sample answer: Find the coordinates of two points on the line. Then divide the change in y-values from one point to the next by the change in x-values.

DIFFERENTIATE INSTRUCTION

Communicating Math
Have students summarize the slopes of the lines in the graphs below in terms of rates of change. Ask them to explain how they would calculate the slopes. positive, negative, zero, undefined

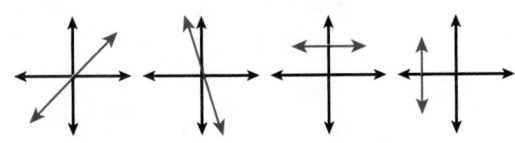

Cognitive Strategies
Point out to students that moving from left to right on the diagrams below, "going up the stairs" has a positive slope, and "going down the stairs" has a negative slope.

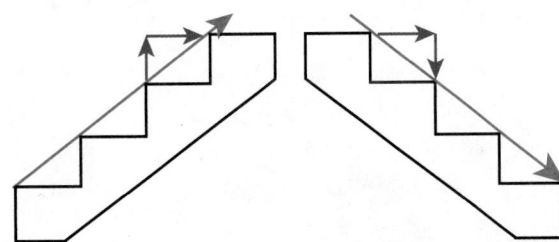

Additional Resources
Differentiated Instruction includes:
- Reading Strategies
- Success for English Learners **ELL**
- Reteach
- Challenge **PRE-AP**

Personal Math Trainer

Online Assessment and Intervention

Online homework assignment available

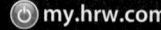
my.hrw.com

11.2 LESSON QUIZ

 8.F.2.4

1. The table represents the number of computer tablets sold. Tell whether the rates of change are constant or variable.

Week	1	3	4	8
Number sold	32	96	128	224

Dev keeps a record in graph form of how far his car travels and the number of gallons of gasoline it uses.

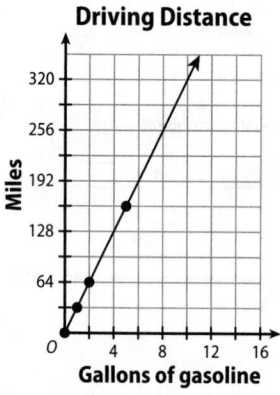

Driving Distance

2. How many miles per gallon does Dev get with his car?

3. What is the slope of the graph?

4. How far can Dev travel on 4 gallons of gasoline?

5. Dev knows he only has 8 gallons of gasoline in the tank. He wants to go on a 300-mile trip. Will he have to buy more gasoline? Explain.

Lesson Quiz available online

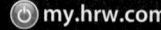
my.hrw.com

Answers
1. variable   **2.** 32 mi/gal

3. 32   **4.** 128 mi

5. Yes; he can only travel 256 miles on 8 gallons of gas. So he has to buy more gasoline.

Evaluate

GUIDED AND INDEPENDENT PRACTICE

 8.F.2.4

Concepts & Skills	Practice
Example 1 Investigating Rates of Change	Exercises 1–4
Explore Activity Using Graphs to Find Rates of Change	Exercises 5–6
Example 2 Calculating Slope	Exercises 7–8, 10, 14–15

Exercise	Depth of Knowledge (D.O.K.)	Mathematical Practices
10	**3** Strategic Thinking H.O.T.	**MP.7.1** Using Structure
11	**2** Skills/Concepts	**MP.4.1** Modeling
12	**2** Skills/Concepts	**MP.5.1** Using Tools
13	**2** Skills/Concepts	**MP.4.1** Modeling
14	**2** Skills/Concepts	**MP.3.1** Logic
15	**2** Skills/Concepts	**MP.2.1** Reasoning
16–17	**3** Strategic Thinking H.O.T.	**MP.7.1** Using Structure
18	**3** Strategic Thinking H.O.T.	**MP.3.1** Logic

Additional Resources
Differentiated Instruction includes:
• Leveled Practice worksheets

11.2 Independent Practice

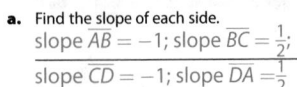

Personal
Math Trainer

Online
Assessment and
Intervention

my.hrw.com

FL CC 8.F.2.4

10. Rectangle *EFGH* is graphed on a coordinate plane with vertices at
$E(-3, 5)$, $F(6, 2)$, $G(4, -4)$, and $H(-5, -1)$.

   a. Find the slopes of each side.
   slope $\overline{EF} = -\frac{1}{3}$; slope $\overline{FG} = 3$; slope $\overline{GH} = -\frac{1}{3}$; slope $\overline{HE} = 3$

   b. What do you notice about the slopes of opposite sides?
   They are the same.

   c. What do you notice about the slopes of adjacent sides?
   They are negative reciprocals of one another.

11. A bicyclist started riding at 8:00 A.M. The diagram below shows the
distance the bicyclist had traveled at different times. What was
the bicyclist's average rate of speed in miles per hour?

8:00 A.M. ◄— 4.5 miles —► 8:18 A.M. ◄———— 7.5 miles ————► 8:48 A.M.

   15 miles per hour

12. **Multistep** A line passes through (6, 3), (8, 4), and $(n, -2)$. Find the value of *n*.
   $n = -4$

13. A large container holds 5 gallons of water. It begins leaking at a constant
rate. After 10 minutes, the container has 3 gallons of water left.

   a. At what rate is the water leaking?
   1 gallon every 5 minutes, or 0.2 gal/min

   b. After how many minutes will the container be empty?
   25 minutes

14. **Critique Reasoning** Billy found the slope of the line through the
points (2, 5) and $(-2, -5)$ using the equation $\frac{2 - (-2)}{5 - (-5)} = \frac{2}{5}$. What mistake
did he make?

   He used the change in *x* over the change in *y* instead of
   the change in *y* over the change in *x*.

15. **Multiple Representations** Graph parallelogram
ABCD on a coordinate plane with vertices at $A(3, 4)$,
$B(6, 1)$, $C(0, -2)$, and $D(-3, 1)$.

   a. Find the slope of each side.
   slope $\overline{AB} = -1$; slope $\overline{BC} = \frac{1}{2}$;
   slope $\overline{CD} = -1$; slope $\overline{DA} = \frac{1}{2}$

   b. What do you notice about the slopes?
   The slopes of the opposite

   sides are the same.

   c. Draw another parallelogram on the coordinate
   plane. Do the slopes have the same characteristics?
   Yes; opposite sides still have the same slope.

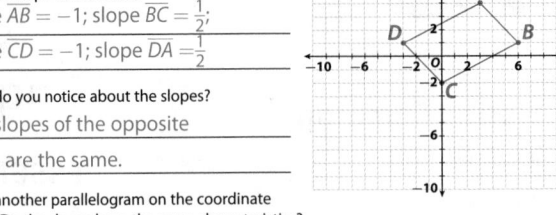

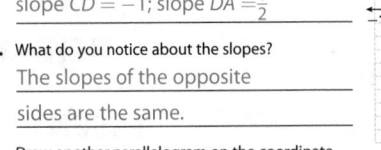

H.O.T. FOCUS ON HIGHER ORDER THINKING

16. **Communicate Mathematical Ideas** Ben and Phoebe are finding the
slope of a line. Ben chose two points on the line and used them to find
the slope. Phoebe used two different points to find the slope. Did they
get the same answer? Explain.

   Yes; the slope of a line is constant. Therefore, the slope

   that you calculate will be the same no matter which two

   points you choose.

17. **Analyze Relationships** Two lines pass through the origin. The lines have
slopes that are opposites. Compare and contrast the lines.

   Sample answer: One line has a positive slope and one

   has a negative slope. The lines are equally steep, but

   one slants upward left to right while the other slants

   downward left to right. The lines cross at the origin.

18. **Reason Abstractly** What is the slope of the *x*-axis? Explain.

   Zero; sample answer: Every point on the *x*-axis has a

   y-coordinate of 0. Therefore, the numerator in the slope

   formula will always be 0.

Work Area

EXTEND THE MATH PRE-AP

Activity available online my.hrw.com

Activity The table shows the prices for various electronics during a storewide sale.
Each item has the same percent discount. Complete the table and graph the points
from the table. Then find the slope of the line connecting the points and give the
percent discount.

Item	Tablet Computer	Disk Player	32-inch TV	Smart-phone
Original price ($)	350	375	400	200
Sale price ($)	280	300	320	160

The slope is 0.8; the percent discount is 20%.

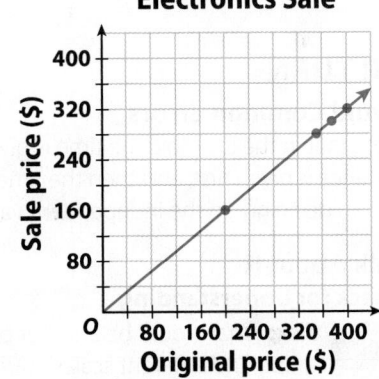

Electronics Sale

Florida Common Core Standards

The student is expected to:

 **Expressions and Equations—8.EE.2.5**

Graph proportional relationships, interpreting the unit rate as the slope of the graph. Compare two different proportional relationships represented in different ways. *Also* 8.F.1.2, 8.F.2.4

Mathematical Practices

 **MP.4.1** Modeling

---

ADDITIONAL EXAMPLE 1
Every 10 seconds an escalator step rises 6 feet. Draw a graph of the situation. Find the unit rate of this proportional relationship.

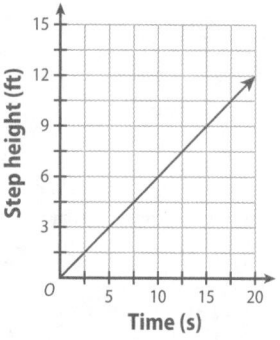

$\frac{3}{5}$ feet per second

 Interactive Whiteboard
Interactive example available online

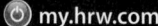 my.hrw.com

---

 Animated Math
Proportional Relationships

Students explore how changing the parameters of a real-world proportional relationship affects tables and graphs.

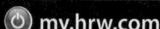 my.hrw.com

Engage

ESSENTIAL QUESTION

How do you interpret the unit rate as slope? Sample answer: The ratio of the change in *y* to the change in *x* is the unit rate. It is also the ratio of the rise to the run, or the slope.

Motivate the Lesson
Ask: Have you ever been skiing, or watched downhill skiers on television? Discuss types of slopes that might be encountered, from a "bunny slope" to the "black diamond" expert slope. Consider how you might describe slight slopes and extreme slopes numerically.

Explore

EXPLORE ACTIVITY

Connect Multiple Representations **Mathematical Practices**
Ask students for the method they use to find the coordinates of points on a line. Point out that it is easiest to find the coordinates of points at the intersection of grid lines.

Explain

EXAMPLE 1

Questioning Strategies **Mathematical Practices**
- What is the constant change in the input values? 3 What is the constant change in the output values? 4

- Where do the rise of 8 and run of 6 come from? The vertical and horizontal distance from (0, 0) to (6, 8)

- What if you used (6, 8) and (15, 20) to find the slope? You would get a rise of 12, a run of 9, and a slope of $\frac{12}{9}$ which is equal to $\frac{4}{3}$.

Avoid Common Errors
Students may reverse the order in the ratio and divide the difference of the *x*-values by the difference of the *y*-values. Remind students that slope is always rise over run (*y*-values over *x*-values).

YOUR TURN

Avoid Common Errors
Note that in the Example the time is given first, and then the volume. In Exercise 2, the distance is given first, and then the time. Caution students to read the information carefully before deciding on the independent variable.

Talk About It
Check for Understanding
Ask: What would be another point on the line that could be shown with a larger graph and different scales? Sample answer: (15, 3)

11.3 Interpreting the Unit Rate as Slope

 8.EE.2.5

Graph proportional relationships, interpreting the unit rate as the slope of the graph. Compare two different proportional relationships represented in different ways. *Also 8.F.1.2, 8.F.2.4*

? ESSENTIAL QUESTION
How do you interpret the unit rate as slope?

EXPLORE ACTIVITY  8.EE.2.5, 8.F.2.4

Relating the Unit Rate to Slope

A rate is a comparison of two quantities that have different units, such as miles and hours. A **unit rate** is a rate in which the second quantity in the comparison is one unit.

A storm is raging on Misty Mountain. The graph shows the constant rate of change of the snow level on the mountain.

Misty Mountain Storm

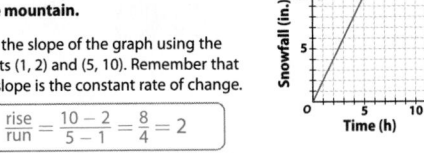

A Find the slope of the graph using the points (1, 2) and (5, 10). Remember that the slope is the constant rate of change.

$$\frac{rise}{run} = \frac{10 - 2}{5 - 1} = \frac{8}{4} = 2$$

B Find the unit rate of snowfall in inches per hour. Explain your method.

2 inches per hour; sample answer: The point (1, 2) is on the line, and represents 2 inches snowfall in 1 hour.

C Compare the slope of the graph and the unit rate of change in the snow level. What do you notice?

They are the same.

D Which point on the graph tells you the slope of the graph and the unit rate of change in the snow level? Explain how you found the point.

(1, 2); sample answer: the unit rate is the amount of snow in 1 hour. So I found the point with an x-coordinate of 1. That point is (1, 2), which gives 2 as the slope and the unit rate of change.

Graphing Proportional Relationships

You can use a table and a graph to find the unit rate and slope that describe a real-world proportional relationship. The constant of proportionality for a proportional relationship is the same as the slope.

 Math On the Spot
my.hrw.com

EXAMPLE 1  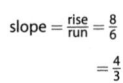 FL CC 8.EE.2.5

Every 3 seconds, 4 cubic feet of water pass over a dam. Draw a graph of the situation. Find the unit rate of this proportional relationship.

STEP 1 Make a table.

Time (s)	3	6	9	12	15
Volume (ft³)	4	8	12	16	20

STEP 2 Draw a graph.

Water Over the Dam

STEP 3 Find the slope.

$$slope = \frac{rise}{run} = \frac{8}{6}$$
$$= \frac{4}{3}$$

The unit rate of water passing over the dam and the slope of the graph of the relationship are equal, $\frac{4}{3}$ cubic feet per second.

Math Talk
Mathematical Practices

In a proportional relationship, how are the constant of proportionality, the unit rate, and the slope of the graph of the relationship related?

They are the same.

Reflect

1. **What If?** Without referring to the graph, how do you know that the point $\left(1, \frac{4}{3}\right)$ is on the graph?

Sample answer: The point (1, r) is on any graph of a proportional relationship, where r equals the unit rate.

YOUR TURN

2. Tomas rides his bike at a steady rate of 2 miles every 10 minutes. Graph the situation. Find the unit rate of this proportional relationship.

His unit rate and the slope of a graph of the ride both equal $\frac{1}{5}$ mi/min.

Tomas's Ride

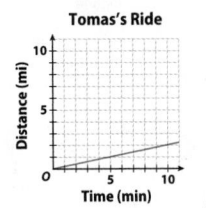

Personal Math Trainer
Online Assessment and Intervention
my.hrw.com

PROFESSIONAL DEVELOPMENT

Integrate Mathematical Practices MP.4.1

This lesson provides an opportunity to address this Mathematical Practices standard. It calls for students to analyze mathematical relationships using tools such as tables and graphs. Students find and analyze the unit rate in input and output tables. Then students use graphs to find the slope of a line. In this way, students are led to make the connection between unit rate and slope.

Math Background

The slope of a line that does not go through the origin can be found by its x-intercept and y-intercept. If the x-intercept is a and the y-intercept is b, the line goes through $(a, 0)$ and $(0, b)$.

The slope m of the line containing the points is $m = \frac{b - 0}{0 - a} = -\frac{b}{a}$.

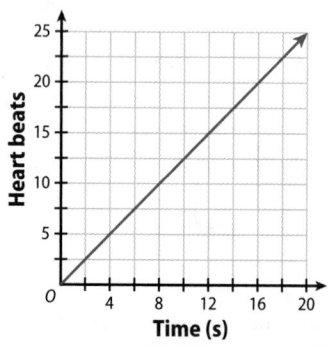

EXAMPLE 2

Questioning Strategies — Mathematical Practices

- What does the point (2, 5) represent in the graph? Well B pumps 5 barrels of oil in 2 hours.

- In the equation $y = 2.75x$, what does 2.75 represent in the graph of the equation? The slope of the graph

Focus on Modeling — Mathematical Practices

Have students reproduce the graph on their own sheet of graph paper. Ask them to describe how they can make sure that the graph they draw accurately matches the graph in the book. Encourage the use of a ruler and sharpened pencil.

Engage with the Whiteboard

Have a student plot the points for Well A from the table on the graph and connect them. Ask students to compare the rise and run for each graph. This will help them confirm that the slope is greater for Well A than Well B.

YOUR TURN

Connect Multiple Representations — Mathematical Practices

Students find the greater rate from an equation and a table. In Example 2, students found the greater rate from an equation and a graph. Students should feel confident they can find the greater rate using any two representations.

Elaborate

Talk About It
Summarize the Lesson

Ask: How do you find the slope when you are only given an equation or a table? Sample answer: For an equation such as $y = 2.6x$, the slope is the unit rate, which is the coefficient of x. For a table, the change in y divided by the change in x is the unit rate, or slope.

GUIDED PRACTICE

Engage with the Whiteboard

For Exercises 1–2, after students complete each exercise, have them copy the graph for Akiko onto the graph for Jorge. Have them determine whether Jorge or Akiko is the faster hiker and use the graph to explain their answer. In Exercise 3, students should graph the equation for Henry on the graph for Clark.

Avoid Common Errors

Exercise 3 Help students understand that comparing rates, or slopes, is the same as comparing rational numbers. Students can write each unit rate as a decimal, if necessary.

Integrating Language Arts ELL

Encourage English learners to use the text and table in Exercises 1–2 to help them understand the content of the graphs.

Using Slopes to Compare Unit Rates

You can compare proportional relationships presented in different ways.

© Houghton Mifflin Harcourt Publishing Company • Image Credits: ©Tom McHugh/ Photo Researchers, Inc.

EXAMPLE 2

FL CC 8.EE.2.5, 8.F.1.2

The equation $y = 2.75x$ represents the rate, in barrels per hour, that oil is pumped from Well A. The graph represents the rate that oil is pumped from Well B. Which well pumped oil at a faster rate?

Well B Pumping Rate

STEP 1 Use the equation $y = 2.75x$ to make a table for Well A's pumping rate, in barrels per hour.

Time (h)	1	2	3	4
Quantity (barrels)	2.75	5.5	8.25	11

STEP 2 Use the table to find the slope of the graph of Well A's rate.

slope = unit rate = $\frac{2.75}{1} = \frac{5.5}{2} = \frac{8.25}{3} = \frac{11}{4} = $ **2.75** barrels/hour

STEP 3 Use the graph to find the slope of the graph of Well B's rate.

slope = $\frac{10}{4} = $ **2.5** barrels/hour   slope = $\frac{rise}{run}$

STEP 4 Compare the slopes.

2.75 > 2.5, so Well A's rate, 2.75 barrels/hour, is faster.

Reflect

3. Describe the relationships among the slope of the graph of Well A's rate, the equation representing Well A's rate, and the constant of proportionality.

Sample answer: The slope and the constant of proportionality equal the value 2.75 in the equation $y = 2.75x$.

YOUR TURN

4. The equation $y = 375x$ represents the relationship between x, the time that a plane flies in hours, and y, the distance the plane flies in miles for Plane A. The table represents the relationship for Plane B. Find the slope of the graph for each plane and the plane's rate of speed. Determine which plane is flying at a faster rate of speed.

Time (h)	1	2	3	4
Distance (mi)	425	850	1275	1700

A: 375, 375 mi/h; B: 425, 425 mi/h; B is flying faster.

Personal Math Trainer
Online Assessment and Intervention
my.hrw.com

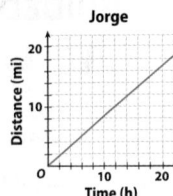

Math On the Spot
my.hrw.com

Give the slope of the graph and the unit rate. (Explore Activity and Example 1)

1. Jorge: 5 miles every 6 hours

Jorge

slope = unit rate = $\frac{5}{6}$ mi/h

2. Akiko

Time (h)	4	8	12	16
Distance (mi)	5	10	15	20

Akiko

slope = unit rate = $\frac{5}{4}$ mi/h

3. The equation $y = 0.5x$ represents the distance Henry hikes in miles over time in hours. The graph represents the rate that Clark hikes. Determine which hiker is faster. Explain. (Example 2)

Clark is faster. From the equation, Henry's rate is equal to 0.5, or $\frac{1}{2}$ mile per hour. Clark's rate is the slope of the line, which is $\frac{3}{2}$, or 1.5 miles per hour.

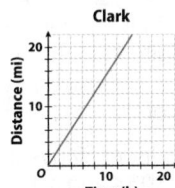

Clark

Write an equation relating the variables in each table. (Example 2)

4.
Time (x)	1	2	4	6
Distance (y)	15	30	60	80

$y = 15x$

5.
Time (x)	16	32	48	64
Distance (y)	6	12	18	24

$y = \frac{3}{8}x$

? ESSENTIAL QUESTION CHECK-IN

6. Describe methods you can use to show a proportional relationship between two variables, x and y. For each method, explain how you can find the unit rate and the slope.

Table of values: The ratio of y to x gives the unit rate and slope. Equation: Make a table of values. The ratio of y to x gives the unit rate and slope. Graph: The slope of the graph gives the unit rate and the slope.

© Houghton Mifflin Harcourt Publishing Company

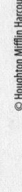

DIFFERENTIATE INSTRUCTION

Technology

Have students use a graphing calculator to examine slopes and rate of change. For example, have them graph $y = 1.5x$ and use the TRACE function to find points on the line.

Lead them through the process of finding a "friendly" graphing window by first using the ZOOM ZDecimal function. A good first quadrant window is $X_{Min} = 0$, $X_{Max} = 9.4$, $Y_{Min} = 0$, $Y_{Max} = 6.2$. You can multiply these numbers by whole numbers to use larger windows.

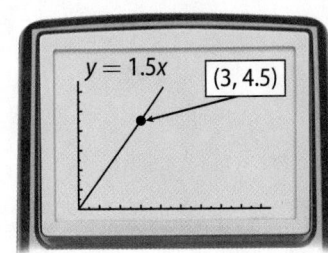

$y = 1.5x$ (3, 4.5)

Additional Resources

Differentiated Instruction includes:

- Reading Strategies
- Success for English Learners **ELL**
- Reteach
- Challenge **PRE-AP**

Personal Math Trainer

Online Assessment and Intervention

Online homework assignment available

⏻ my.hrw.com

11.3 LESSON QUIZ

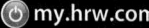 **FL CC** 8.EE.2.5, 8.F.1.2, 8.F.2.4

1. Every 4 seconds, a ski lift chair rises 14 feet. Draw a graph of the situation. Then describe the relationship between the height of the chair and the time.

2. Under Plan A, a 2-minute call costs $0.54 and a 4-minute call costs $1.08. Under Plan B, the cost for x minutes is given by $y = 0.289x$. Which plan is cheaper? Why?

3. The equation $y = 13x$ represents the rate, in gallons per minute, that Tank A at an aquarium fills with water. The table represents the rate that Tank B fills with water. Determine which tank fills faster.

Time (min)	4	12	15	20
Amount (gal)	44	132	165	220

Lesson Quiz available online

⏻ my.hrw.com

Answers
1.

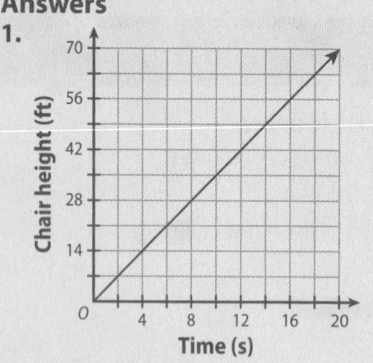

The unit rate of the height of the chair is $\frac{7}{2}$ feet per second.

2. Plan A; $0.27/min < $0.289/min

3. Tank A; 13 gal/min > 11 gal/min

Evaluate

GUIDED AND INDEPENDENT PRACTICE

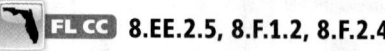 **FL CC** 8.EE.2.5, 8.F.1.2, 8.F.2.4

Concepts & Skills	Practice
Explore Activity Relating the Unit Rate to Slope	Exercises 1–2
Example 1 Graphing Proportional Relationships	Exercises 1–2, 7
Example 2 Using Slopes to Compare Unit Rates	Exercises 3–5, 9–10, 12

Exercise	Depth of Knowledge (D.O.K.)	**FL CC** Mathematical Practices
7	**2** Skills/Concepts	**MP.4.1** Modeling
8	**1** Recall	
9–10	**2** Skills/Concepts	**MP.4.1** Modeling
11–12	**3** Strategic Thinking **H.O.T.**	**MP.3.1** Logic
13	**3** Strategic Thinking **H.O.T.**	**MP.2.1** Reasoning

Additional Resources
Differentiated Instruction includes:
• Leveled Practice worksheets

CLUSTER CONNECTION   **Exercise 12** combines concepts from the Florida Common Core cluster "Understand the connections between proportional relationships, lines, and linear equations."

11.3 Independent Practice

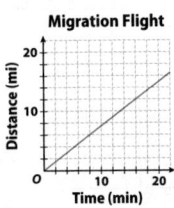

FL CC 8.EE.2.5, 8.F.1.2, 8.F.2.4

Personal Math Trainer

Online Assessment and Intervention

my.hrw.com

7. A Canadian goose migrated at a steady rate of 3 miles every 4 minutes.

a. Fill in the table to describe the relationship.

Time (min)	4	8	12	16	20
Distance (mi)	3	6	9	12	15

b. Graph the relationship.

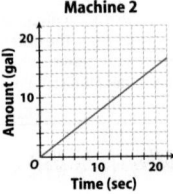

Migration Flight

c. Find the slope of the graph and describe what it means in the context of this problem.

$\frac{3}{4}$; The unit rate of migration of the goose and the slope of the graph both equal $\frac{3}{4}$ mi/min.

8. **Vocabulary** A unit rate is a rate in which the

(first quantity / **second quantity**) in the comparison is one unit.

9. The table and the graph represent the rate at which two machines are bottling milk in gallons per second.

Machine 1

Time (s)	1	2	3	4
Amount (gal)	0.6	1.2	1.8	2.4

Machine 2

a. Determine the slope and unit rate of each machine.

Machine 1: slope = unit rate = $\frac{0.6}{1}$ = 0.6 gal/s;

Machine 2: slope = unit rate = $\frac{3}{4}$ = 0.75 gal/s

b. Determine which machine is working at a faster rate.

Machine 2 is working at a faster rate since 0.75 > 0.6.

10. **Cycling** The equation $y = \frac{1}{9}x$ represents the distance y, in kilometers, that Patrick traveled in x minutes while training for the cycling portion of a triathlon. The table shows the distance y Jennifer traveled in x minutes in her training. Who has the faster training rate?

Time (min)	40	64	80	96
Distance (km)	5	8	10	12

Patrick's rate is $\frac{1}{9}$ kilometer per minute. Jennifer's rate is $\frac{1}{8}$ kilometer per minute. $\frac{1}{9} < \frac{1}{8}$, so Jennifer has the faster training rate.

H.O.T. FOCUS ON HIGHER ORDER THINKING

Work Area

11. **Analyze Relationships** There is a proportional relationship between minutes and cost per minute in dollars. The graph passes through the point (1, 4.75). What is the slope of the graph? What is the unit rate? Explain.

slope = unit rate = 4.75. If the graph of a proportional relationship passes through the point (1, r), then r equals the slope and the unit rate, which is $4.75/min.

12. **Draw Conclusions** Two cars start at the same time and travel at different constant rates. The graph of the distance in miles given the time in hours for Car A passes through the point (0.5, 27.5), and the graph for Car B passes through the point (4, 240). Which car is traveling faster? Explain.

Car B; the slope and unit rate of speed of Car A is $\frac{27.5 - 0}{0.5 - 0} = \frac{27.5}{0.5} = 55$ mi/h. The slope and unit rate of speed of Car B is $\frac{240 - 0}{4 - 0} = \frac{240}{4} = 60$ mi/h. 60 > 55, so Car B is traveling faster.

13. **Critical Thinking** The table shows the rate at which water is being pumped into a swimming pool.

Time (min)	2	5	7	12
Amount (gal)	36	90	126	216

Use the unit rate and the amount of water pumped after 12 minutes to find how much water will have been pumped into the pool after $13\frac{1}{2}$ minutes. Explain your reasoning.

243 gallons; sample answer: The unit rate is $\frac{36}{2} = 18$ gal/min. So $1\frac{1}{2}$ minutes after 12 minutes, an additional $18 \times 1\frac{1}{2} = 27$ gallons will be pumped in, so the total is 216 + 27 = 243 gal.

EXTEND THE MATH PRE-AP

Activity available online my.hrw.com

Activity Have students select any of the proportional relationships in the lesson, given as an equation, table, or graph. Then have them consider whether there is still a proportional relationship if each of these operations is performed on the *y*-values.

- double the *y*-values yes
- divide the *y*-values by 10 yes
- add 5 to the *y*-values no
- subtract 5 from the *y*-values no

Then have them classify which operations kept the proportional relationship and which did not. Multiplication and division preserve the proportional relationship; addition and subtraction do not.

Ready to Go On?

Assess Mastery

Use the assessment on this page to determine if students have mastered the concepts and standards covered in this module.

 **RtI** Response to Intervention

Personal Math Trainer

Online Assessment and Intervention

⏻ my.hrw.com

Intervention	Enrichment
Access Ready to Go On? assessment online, and receive instant scoring, feedback, and customized intervention or enrichment.	

Online and Print Resources

Differentiated Instruction
- Reteach worksheets
- Reading Strategies **ELL**
- Success for English Learners **ELL**

Differentiated Instruction
- Challenge worksheets **PRE-AP**
- Extend the Math **PRE-AP** Lesson Activities in TE

Additional Resources

Assessment Resources includes
- Leveled Module Quizzes

Ready to Go On?

Personal Math Trainer

Online Assessment and Intervention

ⓜ my.hrw.com

11.1 Representing Proportional Relationships

1. Find the constant of proportionality for the table of values.

$k = 1.5$

x	2	3	4	5
y	3	4.5	6	7.5

2. Phil is riding his bike. He rides 25 miles in 2 hours, 37.5 miles in 3 hours, and 50 miles in 4 hours. Find the constant of proportionality and write an equation to describe the situation.

$k = 12.5; y = 12.5x$

11.2 Rate of Change and Slope

Find the slope of each line.

3.

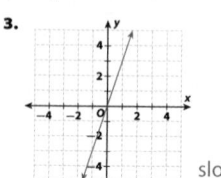

slope = 3

4.

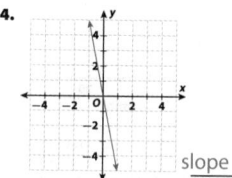

slope = −5

11.3 Interpreting the Unit Rate as Slope

5. The distance Train A travels is represented by $d = 70t$, where d is the distance in kilometers and t is the time in hours. The distance Train B travels at various times is shown in the table. What is the rate of each train? Which train is going faster?

Time (hours)	Distance (km)
2	150
4	300
5	375

Train A: 70 km per hour; Train B: 75 km per hour; Train B is faster.

? ESSENTIAL QUESTION

6. What is the relationship among proportional relationships, lines, rates of change, and slope?

Sample answer: The graph of a proportional relationship is a line through the origin whose slope is the unit rate of change.

© Houghton Mifflin Harcourt Publishing Company

 ## Florida Common Core Standards

Lesson	Exercises	🏴 Common Core Standards
11.1	1–2	**8.EE.2.6, 8.F.2.4**
11.2	3–4	**8.F.2.4**
11.3	5	**8.EE.2.5, 8.F.1.2, 8.F.2.4**

PARCC Assessment Readiness

Assessment Readiness Tip Students can use estimation to eliminate some or all of the incorrect answer choices.

Item 3 About 3,000 widgets are produced in 4 hours, so about 750 widgets are produced per hour. This allows students to eliminate choices A and D.

Item 4 If the lake has dropped 3 feet after 4 weeks, it is dropping at a rate a little slower than −1 feet per week. Only answer choice C fits the situation.

Avoid Common Errors

Item 2 Remind students to examine the relationship between both rows of a table before answering. The pattern 9, 18, 27 in choice C may appear correct but does not match the relationship given in the problem.

Item 5 Remind students how a negative sign affects the slope of a line and that slope is rise over run.

Additional Resources

Personal Math Trainer

Online Assessment and Intervention

my.hrw.com

MODULE 11 MIXED REVIEW

PARCC Assessment Readiness

Personal Math Trainer

Online Assessment and Intervention

my.hrw.com

Selected Response

1. Which of the following is equivalent to 5^{-1}?

Ⓐ 4   Ⓒ $-\frac{1}{5}$

Ⓑ $\frac{1}{5}$ Ⓓ -5

2. Prasert earns $9 an hour. Which table represents this proportional relationship?

Ⓐ
Hours	4	6	8
Earnings ($)	36	54	72

Ⓑ
Hours	4	6	8
Earnings ($)	36	45	54

Ⓒ
Hours	2	3	4
Earnings ($)	9	18	27

Ⓓ
Hours	2	3	4
Earnings ($)	18	27	54

3. A factory produces widgets at a constant rate. After 4 hours, 3,120 widgets have been produced. At what rate are the widgets being produced?

Ⓐ 630 widgets per hour

Ⓑ 708 widgets per hour

Ⓒ 780 widgets per hour

Ⓓ 1,365 widgets per hour

4. A full lake begins dropping at a constant rate. After 4 weeks it has dropped 3 feet. What is the unit rate of change in the lake's level compared to its full level?

Ⓐ 0.75 feet per week

Ⓑ 1.33 feet per week

Ⓒ −0.75 feet per week

Ⓓ −1.33 feet per week

5. What is the slope of the line below?

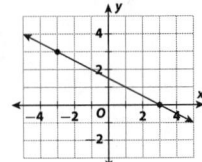

Ⓐ −2   Ⓒ $\frac{1}{2}$

Ⓑ $-\frac{1}{2}$ Ⓓ 2

6. Jim earns $41.25 in 5 hours. Susan earns $30.00 in 4 hours. Pierre's hourly rate is less than Jim's, but more than Susan's. What is his hourly rate?

Ⓐ $6.50   Ⓒ $7.35

Ⓑ $7.75   Ⓓ $8.25

Mini-Task

7. Joelle can read 3 pages in 4 minutes, 4.5 pages in 6 minutes, and 6 pages in 9 minutes.

a. Make a table of the data.

Minutes	4	6	9
Pages	3	4.5	6

b. Use the values in the table to find the unit rate.

0.75 page per minute

c. Graph the relationship between minutes and pages read.

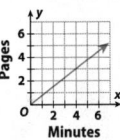

© Houghton Mifflin Harcourt Publishing Company

Florida Common Core Standards

Items	Grade 8 Standards	Mathematical Practices
1*	8.EE.1.1	
2	8.F.2.4	MP.4.1
3	8.F.2.4	MP.4.1
4	8.F.2.4	MP.4.1
5	8.F.2.4	
6	8.F.2.4	MP.4.1
7	8.F.2.4, 8.EE.2.5	MP.4.1

* Item integrates mixed review concepts from previous modules or a previous course.

Nonproportional Relationships

MODULE

12

? **ESSENTIAL QUESTION**

How can you use non-proportional relationships to solve real-world problems?

You can make tables, write equations, and draw graphs to model real-world non-proportional relationships.

Real-World Video

The distance a car can travel on a tank of gas or a full battery charge in an electric car depends on factors such as fuel capacity and the car's efficiency. This is described by a nonproportional relationship.

my.hrw.com

© Houghton Mifflin Harcourt Publishing Company • Image Credits: ©viappy/Shutterstock

GO DIGITAL

my.hrw.com

my.hrw.com

Go digital with your write-in student edition, accessible on any device.

Math On the Spot

Scan with your smart phone to jump directly to the online edition, video tutor, and more.

Animated Math

Interactively explore key concepts to see how math works.

Personal Math Trainer

Get immediate feedback and help as you work through practice sets.

Are You Ready?

Assess Readiness

Use the assessment on this page to determine if students need intensive or strategic intervention for the module's prerequisite skills.

 **RtI** **Response to Intervention**

 **Personal Math Trainer**

Online Assessment and Intervention

my.hrw.com

Intervention	Enrichment

Access Are You Ready? assessment online, and receive instant scoring, feedback, and customized intervention or enrichment.

Online and Print Resources

Skills Intervention worksheets
- Skill 47 Integer Operations
- Skill 69 Graph Ordered Pairs (First Quadrant)

Differentiated Instruction
- Challenge worksheets **PRE-AP**
- Extend the Math **PRE-AP** Lesson Activities in TE

Are YOU Ready?

Complete these exercises to review skills you will need for this module.

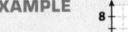 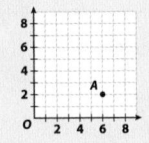 **Personal Math Trainer**
Online Assessment and Intervention
my.hrw.com

Integer Operations

EXAMPLE $-7-(-4) = -7+4$
$|-7| - |4|$
$7 - 4,$ or 3
$= -3$

To subtract an integer, add its opposite. The signs are different, so find the difference of the absolute values. Use the sign of the number with the greater absolute value.

Find each difference.

1. $3 - (-5)$ ___8___
2. $-4 - 5$ ___−9___
3. $6 - 10$ ___−4___
4. $-5 - (-3)$ ___−2___
5. $8 - (-8)$ ___16___
6. $9 - 5$ ___4___
7. $-3 - 9$ ___−12___
8. $0 - (-6)$ ___6___
9. $12 - (-9)$ ___21___
10. $-6 - (-4)$ ___−2___
11. $-7 - 10$ ___−17___
12. $5 - 14$ ___−9___

Graph Ordered Pairs (First Quadrant)

EXAMPLE

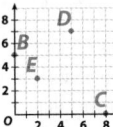

To graph a point at (6, 2), start at the origin.
Move 6 units right.
Then move 2 units up.
Graph point A(6, 2).

Graph each point on the coordinate grid.

13. B (0, 5)
14. C (8, 0)
15. D (5, 7)
16. E (2, 3)

 **GO DIGITAL** my.hrw.com

PROFESSIONAL DEVELOPMENT VIDEO

 Author Juli Dixon models successful teaching practices as she explores the concept of nonproportional relationships in an actual eighth-grade classroom.

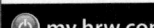 **Professional Development**
my.hrw.com

 Online Teacher Edition
Access a full suite of teaching resources online—plan, present, and manage classes and assignments.

 ePlanner
Easily plan your classes and access all your resources online.

 Interactive Answers and Solutions
Customize answer keys to print or display in the classroom. Choose to include answers only or full solutions to all lesson exercises.

 Interactive Whiteboards
Engage students with interactive whiteboard-ready lessons and activities.

 Personal Math Trainer: Online Assessment and Intervention
Assign automatically graded homework, quizzes, tests, and intervention activities. Prepare your students with updated practice tests aligned with Common Core.

Nonproportional Relationships **356**

Reading Start-Up

Have students complete the activities on this page by working alone or with others.

Visualize Vocabulary

The diagram helps students review the concept of slope that is fundamental to linear relationships. Students should write one or more review words in each box to complete the definition.

Understand Vocabulary

Use the following explanation to help students learn the preview words.

> The word *linear* means "in the shape of a line." A **linear equation** is an equation whose solution forms a line. Linear relationships can represent either proportional or nonproportional relationships. When you graph linear equations, remember that the graph may be a line, but that does not mean the relationship is proportional.

Active Reading

Integrating Language Arts

Students can use these reading and note-taking strategies to help them organize and understand new concepts and vocabulary.

FL CC **LACC.68.RST.3.7** Integrate quantitative or technical information expressed in words in a text with a version of that information expressed visually (e.g., in a flowchart, diagram, model, graph, or table).

Additional Resources

Differentiated Instruction

• Reading Strategies **ELL**

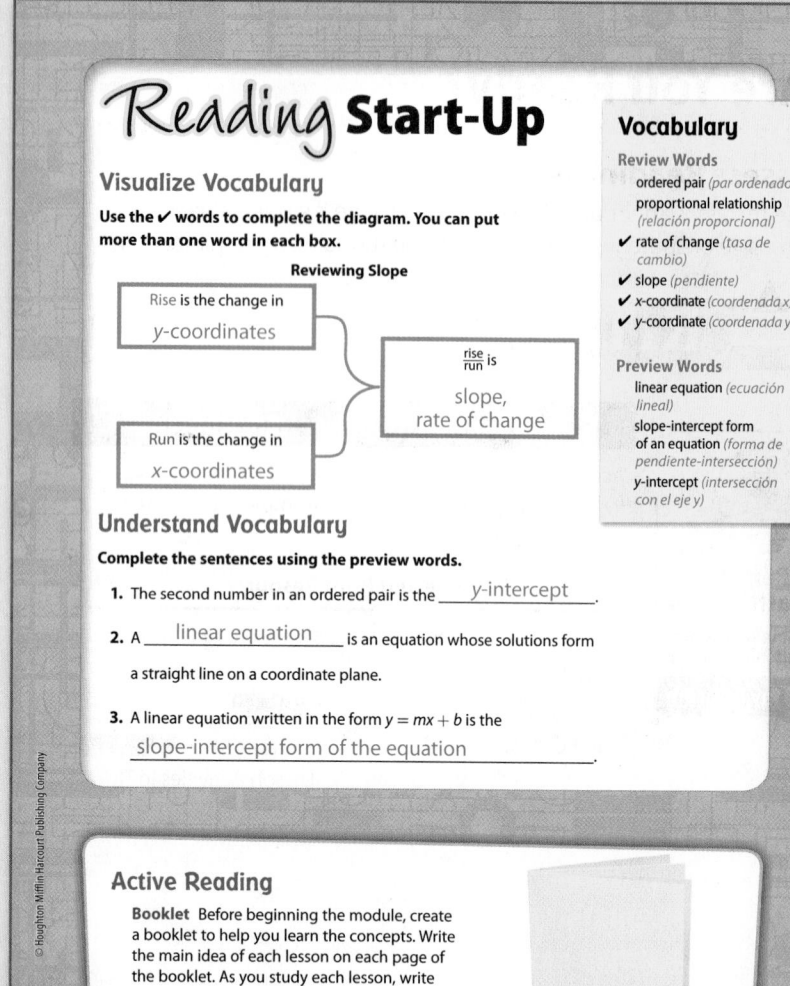

Reading Start-Up

Reading Start-Up

Visualize Vocabulary

Use the ✔ words to complete the diagram. You can put more than one word in each box.

Reviewing Slope

Rise is the change in **y-coordinates**

Run is the change in **x-coordinates**

$\frac{rise}{run}$ is **slope, rate of change**

Vocabulary

Review Words
- ordered pair *(par ordenado)*
- proportional relationship *(relación proporcional)*
- ✔ rate of change *(tasa de cambio)*
- ✔ slope *(pendiente)*
- ✔ x-coordinate *(coordenada x)*
- ✔ y-coordinate *(coordenada y)*

Preview Words
- linear equation *(ecuación lineal)*
- slope-intercept form of an equation *(forma de pendiente-intersección)*
- y-intercept *(intersección con el eje y)*

Understand Vocabulary

Complete the sentences using the preview words.

1. The second number in an ordered pair is the _____ *y-intercept* _____.

2. A _____ *linear equation* _____ is an equation whose solutions form a straight line on a coordinate plane.

3. A linear equation written in the form $y = mx + b$ is the _____ *slope-intercept form of the equation* _____.

Active Reading

Booklet Before beginning the module, create a booklet to help you learn the concepts. Write the main idea of each lesson on each page of the booklet. As you study each lesson, write important details that support the main idea, such as vocabulary and formulas. Refer to your finished booklet as you work on assignments and study for tests.

Module 12 **357**

Before	In this module	After
Students understand proportional and linear relationships: • use tables and verbal descriptions to describe a linear relationship • write and graph a linear relationship • represent constant rates of change given a table, verbal description, equation, or graph • determine constant of proportionality in real-world situations	Students represent and solve problems involving proportional and nonproportional relationships: • represent linear nonproportional situations with tables, graphs, and equations in the form of $y = mx + b, b \neq 0$. • use data from a table or graph to determine the rate of change or slope and y-intercept in real-world problems • distinguish between proportional and nonproportional situations using tables, graphs, and equations in the form $y = kx$ and $y = mx + b$, where $b \neq 0$	Students will connect that: • proportional relationships are in the form $y = kx$ and their graphs will pass through the origin • nonproportional relationships are in the form $y = mx + b$, where $b \neq 0$ and their graphs do not pass through the origin

Unpacking the Standards

Use the examples on this page to help students know exactly what they are expected to learn in this module.

 Florida Common Core Standards

Content Areas

 **Functions—8.F.1**

Define, evaluate, and compare functions.

Go online to see a complete unpacking of the Florida Common Core Standards.

⏻ my.hrw.com

MODULE 12
Unpacking the Standards

Understanding the standards and the vocabulary terms in the standards will help you know exactly what you are expected to learn in this module.

FL CC 8.F.1.3

Interpret the equation $y = mx + b$ as defining a linear function whose graph is a straight line.

Key Vocabulary

slope *(pendiente)*
A measure of the steepness of a line on a graph; the rise divided by the run.

y-intercept *(intersección con el eje y)*
The y-coordinate of the point where the graph of a line crosses the y-axis.

What It Means to You

You will identify the slope and the y-intercept of a line by looking at its equation and use them to graph the line.

UNPACKING EXAMPLE 8.F.1.3

Graph $y = 3x - 2$ using the slope and the y-intercept.

$$y = mx + b$$

slope   y-intercept

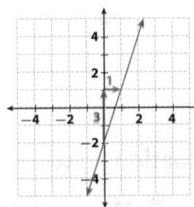

The slope m is 3, and the y-intercept is -2.

Plot the point $(0, -2)$. Use the slope $3 = \frac{3}{1}$ to find another point by moving *up* 3 and to the *right* 1. Connect the points.

FL CC 8.F.1.3

Give examples of functions that are not linear.

Key Vocabulary

function *(función)*
An input-output relationship that has exactly one output for each input.

linear function *(función lineal)*
A function whose graph is a straight line.

What It Means to You

You will distinguish linear relationships from nonlinear relationships by looking at graphs.

UNPACKING EXAMPLE 8.F.1.3

Which relationship is linear and which is nonlinear?

$P = 4s$

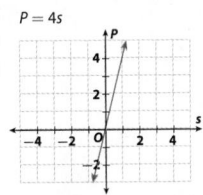

$A = s^2$

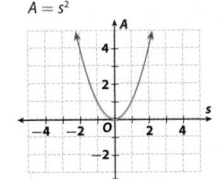

$P = 4s$ is linear because its graph is a line.

$A = s^2$ is not linear because its graph is not a line.

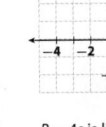 Visit my.hrw.com to see all Florida Common Core Standards unpacked.

⏻ my.hrw.com

358 Unit 6

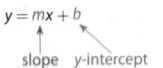 Florida Common Core Standards	Lesson 12.1	Lesson 12.2	Lesson 12.3	Lesson 12.4
FL CC 8.EE.2.6 ... derive the equation $y = mx$ for a line through the origin and the equation $y = mx + b$ for a line intercepting the vertical axis at b.		✦		
FL CC 8.F.1.2 Compare properties of two functions each represented in a different way (algebraically, graphically, numerically in tables, or by verbal descriptions).				✦
FL CC 8.F.1.3 Interpret the equation $y = mx + b$ as defining a linear function, whose graph is a straight line; give examples of functions that are not linear.	✦		✦	✦
FL CC 8.F.2.4 ... Determine the rate of change and initial value of the function from a description of a relationship or from two (x, y) values, including reading these from a table or from a graph. Interpret the rate of change and initial value of a linear function in terms of the situation it models, and in terms of its graph or a table of values.		✦	✦	✦

LESSON
12.1 Representing Linear Nonproportional Relationships

 Florida Common Core Standards

The student is expected to:

 **Functions—8.F.1.3**

Interpret the equation $y = mx + b$ as defining a linear function, whose graph is a straight line; give examples of functions that are not linear.

Mathematical Practices

 **MP.4.1** Modeling

---

ADDITIONAL EXAMPLE 1
The equation $y = 2x + 5$ gives the total height, y, of a plant in an experiment that was 5 cm tall at the beginning of the experiment and grew 2 cm each day. Make a table of values for this situation.

x (number of days)	1	2	3	4
y (height in cm)	7	9	11	13

 Interactive Whiteboard
Interactive example available online

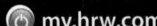 my.hrw.com

Engage

ESSENTIAL QUESTION
How can you use tables, graphs, and equations to represent linear nonproportional situations? Sample answer: Make a table from an equation by calculating corresponding y-values for different x-values. A table of values generates ordered pairs that you can graph.

Motivate the Lesson
Ask: Do you have to pay a monthly amount to your cell phone carrier even if you don't use it? In some cases you may only have to pay an amount that depends on the minutes you use. In other cases you have to pay a monthly fee in addition to charges for minutes.

Explore

Help students make a list of purchases for which the amount they pay reflects only the amount they use. This may include buying shirts, going to the movies, pay-as-you-go cell phone plans, or bus fares. Have them make a list of services or activities where they pay a base amount plus a fee for the amount they use. This may include home electricity or water, some cell phone contracts, and taxi fares. See also Explore Activity in student text.

Explain

EXAMPLE 1
Questioning Strategies Mathematical Practices
• In $y = 3x + 2$, what could 2 represent? Sample answer: the cost of renting bowling shoes
• Would it make sense to choose x-values that are negative? Why? No. You cannot bowl a negative number of games.

Focus on Patterns
Point out to students that y-values increase by 3 as the x-values increase by 1.

YOUR TURN
Talk About It
Check for Understanding
Ask: Francisco spends $4 on transportation. Why isn't the equation $y = 12x + 4$ instead of $y = 12x - 4$? Finding earnings after transportation costs requires subtracting transportation costs from earnings.

EXPLORE ACTIVITY
Avoid Common Errors
Be sure students understand the context of a problem to determine whether the graph of a linear relationship is a solid line or a set of unconnected points.

LESSON 12.1 Representing Linear Nonproportional Relationships

FL CC 8.F.1.3
Interpret the equation $y = mx + b$ as defining a linear function, whose graph is a straight line; …

ESSENTIAL QUESTION

How can you use tables, graphs, and equations to represent linear nonproportional situations?

Representing Linear Relationships Using Tables

You can use an equation to describe the relationship between two quantities in a real-world situation. You can use a table to show some values that make the equation true.

EXAMPLE 1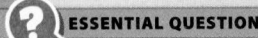

FL CC Prep for 8.F.1.3

The equation $y = 3x + 2$ gives the total charge, y, for bowling x games at Baxter Bowling Lanes based on the prices shown. Make a table of values for this situation.

STEP 1 Choose several values for x that make sense in context.

x (number of games)	1	2	3	4
y (total cost in dollars)				

STEP 2 Use the equation $y = 3x + 2$ to find y for each value of x.

x (number of games)	1	2	3	4
y (total cost in dollars)	5	8	11	14

Substitute 1 for x:
$y = 3(1) + 2 = 5$.

BAXTER bowling lanes
$3 per game
$2 shoe rental

YOUR TURN

1. Francisco makes $12 per hour doing part-time work on Saturdays. He spends $4 on transportation to and from work. The equation $y = 12x - 4$ gives his earnings y, after transportation costs, for working x hours. Make a table of values for this situation. Sample answer:

x (number of hours)	2	3	4	5
y (earnings in dollars)	20	32	44	56

Math On the Spot
my.hrw.com

Personal Math Trainer
Online Assessment and Intervention
my.hrw.com

Lesson 12.1 **359**

EXPLORE ACTIVITY Real World

FL CC 8.F.1.3

Examining Linear Relationships

Recall that a proportional relationship is a relationship between two quantities in which the ratio of one quantity to the other quantity is constant. The graph of a proportional relationship is a line through the origin. Relationships can have a constant rate of change but not be proportional.

The entrance fee for Mountain World theme park is $20. Visitors purchase additional $2 tickets for rides, games, and food. The equation $y = 2x + 20$ gives the total cost, y, to visit the park, including purchasing x tickets.

STEP 1 Complete the table.

x (number of tickets)	0	2	4	6	8
y (total cost in dollars)	20	24	28	32	36

STEP 2 Plot the ordered pairs from the table. Describe the shape of the graph.

The points lie on a line.

STEP 3 Find the rate of change between each point and the next. Is the rate constant?

$2 per ticket; yes

STEP 4 Calculate $\frac{y}{x}$ for the values in the table. Explain why the relationship between number of tickets and total cost is not proportional.

Undefined, 12, 7, about 5.3, 4.5; The ratio of the total cost and the number of tickets sold is not constant, and the graph doesn't pass through the origin.

Theme Park Costs

Reflect

2. **Analyze Relationships** Would it make sense to add more points to the graph from $x = 0$ to $x = 10$? Would it make sense to connect the points with a line? Explain.

Yes; you could add the points (1, 22), (3, 26), (5, 30), (7, 34), (9, 38), and (10, 40). No; Sample answer: The number of tickets can only be a whole number.

360 Unit 6

PROFESSIONAL DEVELOPMENT

Integrate Mathematical Practices MP.4.1

This lesson provides an opportunity to address this Mathematical Practices standard. It calls for students to use equations, tables, and graphs to represent relationships. Students use equations to represent a relationship between corresponding values. Then students make tables to represent some values in the relationship. Finally, students use graphs to visualize the relationship.

Math Background

An equation, table, and graph can all represent the same linear relationship. Given an equation, one can generate a table and a graph by substituting for one variable and finding ordered pair solutions. However, a table can only present a finite number of ordered pairs, and a graph can only represent a relationship over a limited range. Despite the visual appeal of a table or graph, only an equation can fully represent a relationship and conclusively demonstrate that a relationship is proportional or linear for all input values.

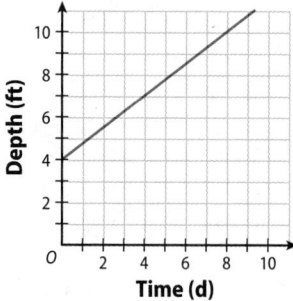

EXAMPLE 2

Questioning Strategies Mathematical Practices

• Why is there no point for the *x*-coordinate of 40 on the graph? The *x*-value of 40 is not in the table.

• Why do you think only multiples of 10 are chosen for the *x*-values? It is easier to find $\frac{2}{5}$ of a multiple of 10.

Engage with the Whiteboard

Have students consider how the graph would change if the beginning diameter of the tree is 4 inches. Have students write the new diameter values after *x* years below the table and plot the new ordered pairs on the graph. Connect the points with a line, and visually compare the slopes of the lines.

Focus on Modeling Mathematical Practices

In Example 2, students use an equation that models a real-world situation to make a table of values and a graph. Ensure that students understand the real-world quantities involved in the problem.

Integrating Language Arts ELL

Encourage English learners to take notes on new terms or concepts and to write them in familiar language.

YOUR TURN

Avoid Common Errors Mathematical Practices

Remind students of the rules for multiplying by a negative number. If the signs are the same, the product is positive. If the signs are different, the product is negative.

Elaborate

Talk About It
Summarize the Lesson

Have students complete the graphic organizer showing at least one similarity and one difference between proportional and nonproportional linear relationships.

Similarities	Differences
Sample answer: Both graph as lines. Both have a constant rate of change.	Sample answer: Proportional linear relationship: The line passes through the origin. Nonproportional linear relationship: The line does not pass through the origin.

GUIDED PRACTICE

Engage with the Whiteboard

 Have students label the coordinates of several points in Exercise 4. Then have them demonstrate that the *x*- and *y*-values do not form a proportion.

Avoid Common Errors

Exercise 3 Remind students that the value of $\frac{y}{x}$ when *y* is 3 and *x* is 0 is undefined because the denominator of the fraction is 0.

Exercise 4 Remind students that the graph of a nonproportional linear relationship is a line that does not pass through the origin.

Representing Linear Relationships Using Graphs

A **linear equation** is an equation whose solutions are ordered pairs that form a line when graphed on a coordinate plane. Linear equations can be written in the form $y = mx + b$. When $b \neq 0$, the relationship between x and y is *nonproportional*.

Math On the Spot
my.hrw.com

EXAMPLE 2 (Real World)

FL CC 8.F.1.3

The diameter of a Douglas fir tree is currently 10 inches when measured at chest height. Over the next 50 years, the diameter is expected to increase by an average growth rate of $\frac{2}{5}$ inch per year. The equation $y = \frac{2}{5}x + 10$ gives y, the diameter of the tree in inches, after x years. Draw a graph of the equation. Describe the relationship.

STEP 1 Make a table. Choose several values for x that make sense in context. To make calculations easier, choose multiples of 5.

x (years)	0	10	20	30	50
y (diameter in inches)	10	14	18	22	30

STEP 2 Plot the ordered pairs from the table. Then draw a line connecting the points to represent all the possible solutions.

STEP 3 The relationship is linear but nonproportional. The graph is a line but it does not go through the origin.

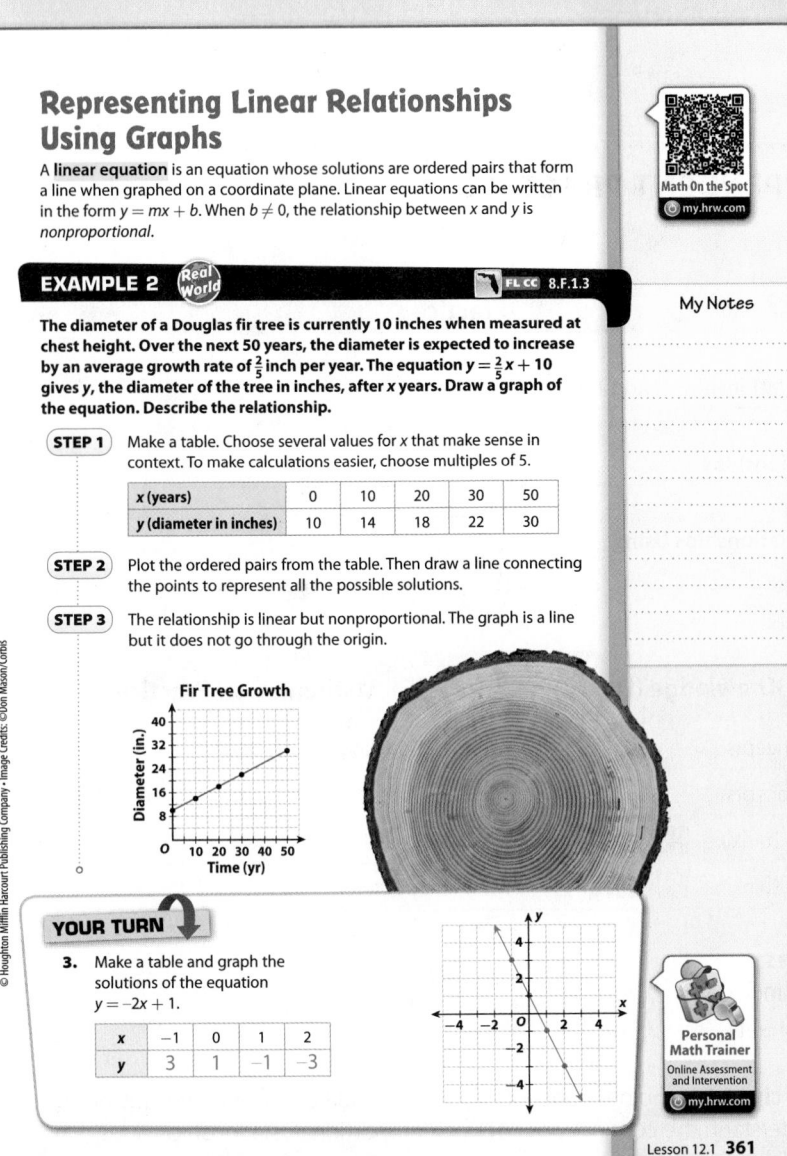

Fir Tree Growth

YOUR TURN

3. Make a table and graph the solutions of the equation $y = -2x + 1$.

x	−1	0	1	2
y	3	1	−1	−3

Personal Math Trainer
Online Assessment and Intervention
my.hrw.com

My Notes

Guided Practice

Make a table of values for each equation. (Example 1)

1. $y = 2x + 5$

x	−2	−1	0	1	2
y	1	3	5	7	9

2. $y = \frac{3}{8}x - 5$

x	−8	0	8	16	24
y	−8	−5	−2	1	4

Explain why each relationship is not proportional. (Explore Activity)

3.

x	0	2	4	6	8
y	3	7	11	15	19

First calculate $\frac{y}{x}$ for the values in the table.

Undefined, 3.5, 2.75, 2.5, 2.375;

The ratio $\frac{y}{x}$ is not constant.

4.

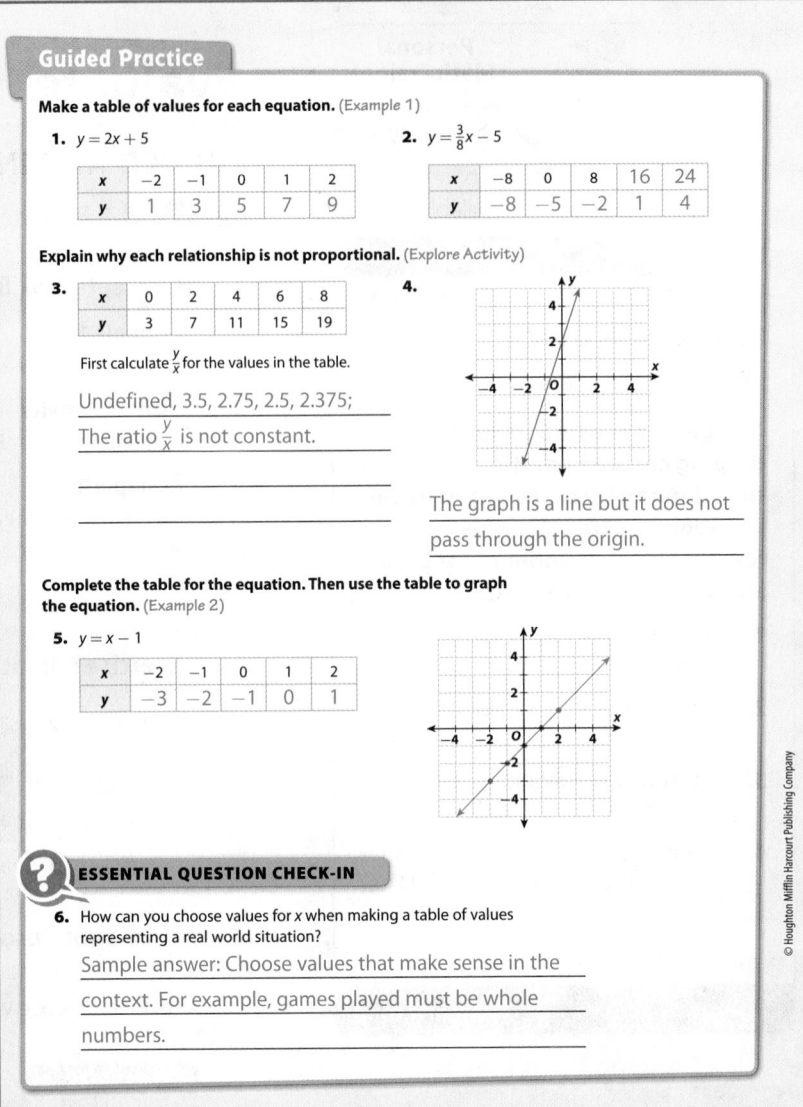

The graph is a line but it does not pass through the origin.

Complete the table for the equation. Then use the table to graph the equation. (Example 2)

5. $y = x - 1$

x	−2	−1	0	1	2
y	−3	−2	−1	0	1

ESSENTIAL QUESTION CHECK-IN

6. How can you choose values for x when making a table of values representing a real world situation?

Sample answer: Choose values that make sense in the context. For example, games played must be whole numbers.

DIFFERENTIATE INSTRUCTION

Cooperative Learning

Divide the class into groups of three. Have each student write the equation of a nonproportional linear relationship such as $y = 2x + 5$ on a piece of paper. Students should then pass their papers to the next person in the group. Each student should create a table of values with five ordered pairs using the equation handed to him or her. After they have completed the tables, have them pass their papers again. Each student should then plot the ordered pairs from the table handed to him or her and draw a line connecting the points.

Curriculum Integration

The relationship between temperature in degrees Fahrenheit °F, and temperature in degrees Celsius °C, is given by the equation $F = \frac{9}{5}C + 32$. Ask students to show that this equation represents a nonproportional linear relationship. Students should make a table of values and graph the ordered pairs.

Additional Resources

Differentiated Instruction includes

• Reading Strategies
• Success for English Learners **ELL**
• Reteach
• Challenge **PRE-AP**

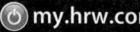

12.1 LESSON QUIZ

FL CC 8.F.1.3

A large pizza costs \$10. Each topping costs an additional \$2. This situation can be represented by the equation $y = 10 + 2x$, where x represents the number of toppings and y represents the total cost.

1. Make a table of values for this situation.

2. Draw a graph to represent this situation.

3. Explain why this relationship is not proportional.

4. Does it make sense to connect the points on the graph with a solid line? Explain.

Lesson Quiz available online

my.hrw.com

Answers

1.

x	1	2	3	4
y	12	14	16	18

2.

Pizza with Toppings

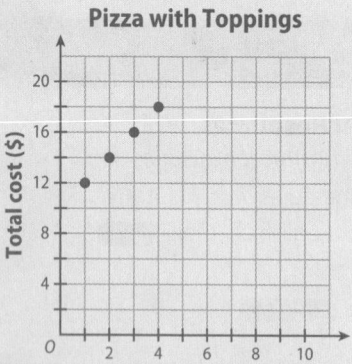

3. Sample answer: The graph does not go through the origin.

4. No. The number of toppings must be a whole number, so the total cost goes up \$2 for each additional topping.

Evaluate

GUIDED AND INDEPENDENT PRACTICE

 FL CC 8.F.1.3

Concepts & Skills	Practice
Example 1 Representing Linear Relationships Using Tables	Exercises 1–2, 5, 9
Explore Activity Examining Linear Relationships	Exercises 3–4, 7–8
Example 2 Representing Linear Relationships Using Graphs	Exercises 5, 9

Exercise	Depth of Knowledge (D.O.K.)	 **Mathematical Practices**
7–9	**2** Skills/Concepts	**MP.4.1** Modeling
10–11	**2** Skills/Concepts	**MP.3.1** Logic
12	**3** Strategic Thinking H.O.T.	**MP.3.1** Logic
13	**3** Strategic Thinking H.O.T.	**MP.7.1** Structure

Additional Resources

Differentiated Instruction includes:

• Leveled Practice worksheets

 CLUSTER CONNECTION   **Exercise 11** combines concepts from the Florida Common Core cluster "Understand the connections between proportional relationships, lines, and linear equations."

Name_____ Class_____ Date_____

Personal
Math Trainer
Online
Assessment and
Intervention
my.hrw.com

State whether the graph of each linear relationship is a solid line or a set of unconnected points. Explain your reasoning.

7. The relationship between the number of $4 lunches you buy with a $100 school lunch card and the money remaining on the card

Set of unconnected points;

Sample answer: You cannot buy

a fractional part of a lunch.

8. The relationship between time and the distance remaining on a 3-mile walk for someone walking at a steady rate of 2 miles per hour

Solid line; Sample answer:

The distance remaining can be

measured at any moment in

time.

9. Analyze Relationships Simone paid $12 for an initial year's subscription to a magazine. The renewal rate is $8 per year. This situation can be represented by the equation $y = 8x + 12$, where x represents the number of years the subscription is renewed and y represents the total cost.

a. Make a table of values for this situation. Sample answer:

x (number of years renewed)	0	1	2	3	4
y (total cost in dollars)	12	20	28	36	44

b. Draw a graph to represent the situation. Include a title and axis labels.

c. Explain why this relationship is not proportional.

Sample answer: The graph does not

include the origin. Also, the ratio of the

total cost and number of years is not

constant.

d. Does it make sense to connect the points on the graph with a solid line? Explain.

No; the number of years must be a whole

number, so total cost goes up in $8

increments.

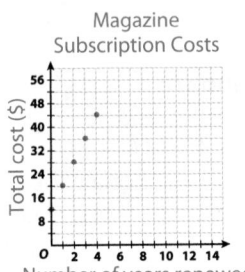

Magazine
Subscription Costs

Total cost ($)

Number of years renewed

10. Analyze Relationships A direct variation is a linear relationship because the rate of change is constant (and equal to the constant of variation). What is required of a direct variation relationship that is *not* required of a general linear relationship?

The graph must pass through the origin.

11. Communicate Mathematical Ideas Explain how you can identify a linear non-proportional relationship from a table, a graph, and an equation.

Sample answer: In a table, the ratios $\frac{y}{x}$ will not be equal;

a graph will not pass through the origin; an equation

will be in the form $y = mx + b$, where $b \neq 0$.

H.O.T. FOCUS ON HIGHER ORDER THINKING

12. Critique Reasoning George observes that for every increase of 1 in the value of x, there is an increase of 60 in the corresponding value of y. He claims that the relationship represented by the table is proportional. Critique George's reasoning.

x	1	2	3	4	5
y	90	150	210	270	330

Sample answer: George's observation is true, but

his claim is false. There is a constant rate of change.

However, the relationship is not proportional because

the ratio of y to x (90, 75, 70, 67.5, 66) is not constant.

13. Make a Conjecture Two parallel lines are graphed on a coordinate plane. How many of the lines could represent proportional relationships? Explain.

At most one; sample answer: A line representing a

proportional relationship must pass through the origin.

A line parallel to it cannot also pass through the origin,

so at most one of the lines can represent a proportional

relationship.

Work Area

EXTEND THE MATH PRE-AP *Activity available online* my.hrw.com

Activity The equation $y = 2.5x - 1500$ represents the profit made by a manufacturer that sells a product for $2.50 each, where y is the profit and x is the number of units sold. Construct a table to find the number of units that must be sold for the manufacturer to break even. The break-even point is where profit is equal to 0. Explain the data in the table.

x	100	200	300	400	500	600
y	−1250	−1000	−750	−500	−250	0

Sample answer: When the y-values are negative, it means that that manufacturer has lost money. When x is 600, the y-value is 0, so the break-even point is when 600 units are sold.

LESSON
12.2 Determining Slope and *y*-intercept

ADDITIONAL EXAMPLE 1
Gregg deposits the money he makes from mowing lawns into his savings account, adding it to the money his father gave him to open the account. Confirm the relationship is linear and give the constant rate of change and the initial value.

Lawns mowed	5	10	15	20
Money saved ($)	110	170	230	290

The constant rate of change is 12. The initial value is $50.

 Interactive Whiteboard
Interactive example available online

 my.hrw.com

Engage

ESSENTIAL QUESTION
How can you determine the slope and the y-intercept of a line? Sample answer: Find the slope of the line using the coordinates of two points found on the graph. Then find the *y*-coordinate of the point where the graph crosses the *y*-axis.

Motivate the Lesson
Ask: What can the equation for a line tell you about the slope and *y*-intercept of the line? Begin Explore Activity 1 to find out.

Explore

EXPLORE ACTIVITY 1
Engage with the Whiteboard
Have students draw vertical and horizontal arrows to represent the rise and the run between the points (0, 4) and (−3, 6) on the graph. Then have them do the same for two other points on the line. Next, calculate the slope using the new pair of points. Point out the slope is the same for both pairs of points.

Explain

EXAMPLE 1
Questioning Strategies Mathematical Practices
• What are the slope and *y*-intercept for the graph of this relationship? Explain your answer. The slope is 15 or $\frac{15}{1}$ and the *y*-intercept is 330. The slope is the rate of change and the initial value is the *y*-intercept.

• What if the salesperson only sold 5 phones in a week? Explain how to find the weekly income. Since the salesperson receives $15 for each phone sold, the commission would be 5 × $15, or $75. The minimum weekly salary is $330, so the salary with commission would be $405 for the week.

Focus on Patterns
Point out to students that the change in phones sold is always 10 and the change in income is always 150. In Step 2, in order to find the initial value, they need to subtract 10 from the number of phones sold and 150 from the weekly income.

YOUR TURN
Avoid Common Errors
Remind students to find the ratio of the change in *y* over the change in *x* to find the slope, *m*. They cannot just divide the first value of *y* by the corresponding value of *x* to find the slope.

Focus on Communication
Be sure that students can explain that in order to find the *y*-intercept, they need to work backward to find the *y*-value when *x* is 0.

12.2 Determining Slope and *y*-intercept

FL CC 8.EE.2.6
...; derive the equation $y = mx$ for a line through the origin and the equation $y = mx + b$ for a line intercepting the vertical axis at *b*. Also 8.F.2.4

? ESSENTIAL QUESTION

How can you determine the slope and the *y*-intercept of a line?

EXPLORE ACTIVITY 1 FL CC 8.EE.2.6

Investigating Slope and *y*-intercept

The graph of every nonvertical line crosses the *y*-axis. The **y-intercept** is the *y*-coordinate of the point where the graph intersects the *y*-axis. The *x*-coordinate of this point is always 0.

The graph represents the linear equation $y = -\frac{2}{3}x + 4$.

STEP 1 Find the slope of the line using the points (0, 4) and (−3, 6).

$$m = \frac{6 - \boxed{4}}{\boxed{-3} - 0} = \frac{\boxed{2}}{\boxed{-3}} = \boxed{-\frac{2}{3}}$$

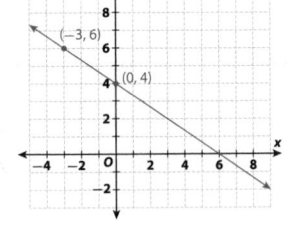
(−3, 6)
(0, 4)

STEP 2 The line also contains the point (6, 0). What is the slope using (0, 4) and (6, 0)? Using (−3, 6) and (6, 0)? What do you notice?

$-\frac{2}{3}; -\frac{2}{3};$ it is the same as in Step 1

STEP 3 Compare your answers in Steps 1 and 2 with the equation of the graphed line.

The slope $m = -\frac{2}{3}$ is the coefficient of the variable *x* in $y = -\frac{2}{3}x + 4$.

STEP 3 Find the value of *y* when *x* = 0 using the equation $y = -\frac{2}{3}x + 4$. Describe the point on the graph that corresponds to this solution.

4; (0, 4) is where the line intersects the *y*-axis.

STEP 5 Compare your answer in Step 3 with the equation of the line.

The number 4 is the same as the number that is added to the *x*-term in the equation $y = -\frac{2}{3}x + 4$.

© Houghton Mifflin Harcourt Publishing Company

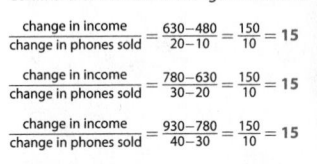
Math On the Spot
my.hrw.com

Determining Rate of Change and Initial Value

The linear equation shown is written in the **slope-intercept form of an equation.** Its graph is a line with **slope** *m* and **y-intercept** *b*.

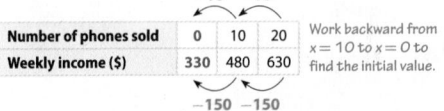
$$y = mx + b$$
slope   y-intercept

A linear relationship has a constant rate of change. You can find the **rate of change *m*** and the **initial value *b*** for a linear situation from a table of values.

EXAMPLE 1 Real World   FL CC 8.F.2.4

A phone salesperson is paid a minimum weekly salary and a commission for each phone sold, as shown in the table. Confirm that the relationship is linear and give the constant rate of change and the initial value.

STEP 1 Confirm that the rate of change is constant.

$$\frac{\text{change in income}}{\text{change in phones sold}} = \frac{630 - 480}{20 - 10} = \frac{150}{10} = 15$$

$$\frac{\text{change in income}}{\text{change in phones sold}} = \frac{780 - 630}{30 - 20} = \frac{150}{10} = 15$$

$$\frac{\text{change in income}}{\text{change in phones sold}} = \frac{930 - 780}{40 - 30} = \frac{150}{10} = 15$$

Number of Phones Sold	Weekly Income ($)
10	$480
20	$630
30	$780
40	$930

The rate of change is a constant, 15.

The salesperson receives a $15 commission for each phone sold.

STEP 2 Find the initial value when the number of phones sold is 0.

Number of phones sold	0	10	20
Weekly income ($)	330	480	630

−10   −10
−150   −150

Work backward from *x* = 10 to *x* = 0 to find the initial value.

The initial value is $330. The salesperson receives a salary of $330 each week before commissions.

Math Talk
Mathematical Practices

How do you use the rate of change to work backward to find the initial value?

Sample answer: Work backward from the greatest number of phones to 0. Then work the weekly income back proportionally.

YOUR TURN

Personal Math Trainer
Online Assessment and Intervention
my.hrw.com

Find the slope and *y*-intercept of the line represented by each table.

1.

x	2	4	6	8
y	22	32	42	52

$m = 5; b = 12$

2.

x	1	2	3	4
y	8	15	22	29

$m = 7; b = 1$

© Houghton Mifflin Harcourt Publishing Company

PROFESSIONAL DEVELOPMENT

Integrate Mathematical Practices MP.7.1

This lesson provides an opportunity to address this Mathematical Practices standard. It calls for students to discern structure. In this lesson, students discern the relationship between slope and rate of change. In Example 1, students use a table to find the constant rate of change and the initial value and relate these to a salesperson's commission and minimum weekly salary.

Math Background

Horizontal lines have a slope of 0 since the rise is 0 for any run, and 0 divided by a nonzero number is 0. Therefore, an equation for a horizontal line takes the form $y = b$, where *b* is the *y*-intercept. The slope of a vertical line is undefined because any two points on the line will have a run of 0, and division by 0 is undefined. A vertical line also has no *y*-intercept, unless it passes through the origin, in which case the line contains all points on the *y*-axis.

EXPLORE ACTIVITY 2

Questioning Strategies ⬛ Mathematical Practices

- When you find the change in x-values and y-values in Step 2, does it make a difference in which order you subtract? Explain. Sample answer: Yes. You must subtract the x-values in the same order that you subtract the y-values.

- Compare the slopes and y-intercepts of two lines with the equations $y = 2x + 3$ and $y = 2x + 5$. The slopes are the same; the y-intercepts are different (the lines are parallel).

Focus on Math Connections

Point out that in Step 3, students are following the same steps they would use to solve a linear equation. The only difference is that there are variables instead of numbers.

Elaborate

. . . .

Talk About It
Summarize the Lesson

Ask: How can you determine the slope and y-intercept of a line represented by a table? Find the constant rate of change, which is the slope. Find the initial value, y when $x = 0$ from the table, or work backward to find it. This value will be the y-intercept.

GUIDED PRACTICE

Engage with the Whiteboard

In Exercises 3–4, have students plot the two points they use to find the slope. In Exercises 1–4 have them draw vertical and horizontal arrows to represent the rise and run between the two plotted points.

Avoid Common Errors

Exercises 1, 4 Students must assign a negative number to the rise or the run. Remind students that since the line slants down from left to right, the slope will be negative.

Deriving the Slope-intercept Form of an Equation

In the following Explore Activity, you will derive the slope-intercept form of an equation.

STEP 1 Let L be a line with slope m and y-intercept b. Circle the point that must be on the line. Justify your choice.

$(b, 0)$ $(0, b)$ $(0, m)$ $(m, 0)$

The coordinate of x is 0 in the point that includes

the y-intercept.

STEP 2 Recall that slope is the ratio of change in y to change in x. Complete the equation for the slope m of the line using the y-intercept $(0, b)$ and another point (x, y) on the line.

$$m = \frac{y - \boxed{b}}{\boxed{x} - 0}$$

STEP 3 In an equation of a line, we often want y by itself on one side of the equation. Solve the equation from Step 2 for y.

$m = \dfrac{y - b}{x}$ Simplify the denominator.

$m \cdot \boxed{x} = \dfrac{y - b}{x} \cdot \boxed{x}$ Multiply both sides of the equation by $\underline{x}$.

$m\boxed{x} = y - b$

$mx + \boxed{b} = y - b + \boxed{b}$ Add $\underline{b}$ to both sides of the equation.

$mx + \boxed{b} = y$

$y = mx + \boxed{b}$ Write the equation with y on the left side.

Reflect

3. Critical Thinking Write the equation of a line with slope m that passes through the origin. Explain your reasoning.

$y = mx$; Sample answer: Because the origin is on the y-axis, the graph crosses the y-axis at $(0, 0)$. So, the y-intercept b is 0, and $y = mx + b$ becomes $y = mx$.

Guided Practice

Find the slope and y-intercept of the line in each graph. (Explore Activity 1)

1.

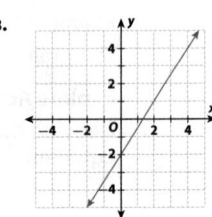

(0, 1), (2, −3)

slope $m = \underline{-2}$ y-intercept $b = \underline{1}$

2.

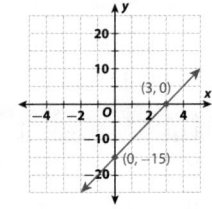

(3, 0), (0, −15)

slope $m = \underline{5}$ y-intercept $b = \underline{-15}$

3.

slope $m = \underline{\dfrac{3}{2}}$ y-intercept $b = \underline{-2}$

4.

slope $m = \underline{-3}$ y-intercept $b = \underline{9}$

Find the slope and y-intercept of the line represented by each table. (Example 1)

5.

x	0	2	4	6	8
y	1	7	13	19	25

slope $m = \underline{3}$ y-intercept $b = \underline{1}$

6.

x	0	5	10	15	20
y	140	120	100	80	60

slope $m = \underline{-4}$ y-intercept $b = \underline{140}$

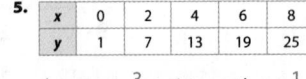

ESSENTIAL QUESTION CHECK-IN

7. How can you determine the slope and the y-intercept of a line from a graph?

Find the slope of the line using the coordinates of two points found on the graph. Then find the y-coordinate of the point where the graph crosses the y-axis.

DIFFERENTIATE INSTRUCTION

Multiple Representations

Have students sketch graphs on a grid. Have them calculate the slope and y-intercept of the graph. Next have students exchange graphs with another student. Have the students create a table of values from the graph and calculate the slope and y-intercept from the table. Have them check to see if the slopes and intercepts calculated from the graphs and the table match. If they don't match, have them check for errors.

Visual Cues

When finding the slope of a line from a graph, have students draw in the right triangle indicating the rise and the run between two points on the line. When finding the y-intercept of a line from a graph, have students put a dot at the point where the line crosses the y-axis.

Additional Resources

Differentiated Instruction includes

- Reading Strategies
- Success for English Learners **ELL**
- Reteach
- Challenge **PRE-AP**

12.2 LESSON QUIZ

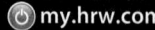 **FL CC** 8.EE.2.6, 8.F.2.4

1. Find the slope and y-intercept of the line represented by the table.

x	3	6	9	12
y	10	19	28	37

A large barrel that holds water is leaking. The table shows how much water is left after a specific number of minutes.

Minutes	5	10	15	20
Water (gal)	16	14	12	10

2. Find and interpret the rate of change.

3. Find and interpret the initial value.

4. After how many minutes will the barrel be empty? Explain.

Lesson Quiz available online

⏻ my.hrw.com

Answers

1. $m = 3, b = 1$

2. The rate of change is $-\frac{2}{5}$. This means that the water is leaking out at a rate of 2 gallons every 5 minutes.

3. The initial value is 18 gallons. This means that the barrel originally had 18 gallons of water in it.

4. The barrel will be empty after 45 minutes. Sample answer: I extended the table until the y-value was 0.

Evaluate

GUIDED AND INDEPENDENT PRACTICE

 **FL CC** 8.EE.2.6, 8.F.2.4

Concepts & Skills	Practice
Explore Activity 1 Investigating Slope and y-intercept	Exercises 1–4
Example 1 Determining Rate of Change and Initial Value	Exercises 5–6, 8–10
Explore Activity 2 Deriving the Slope-intercept Form of an Equation	Exercise 13

Exercise	Depth of Knowledge (D.O.K.)	**FL CC** Mathematical Practices
8	**2** Skills/Concepts	**MP.6.1** Precision
9–10	**2** Skills/Concepts	**MP.1.1** Problem Solving
11–12	**2** Skills/Concepts	**MP.6.1** Precision
13	**2** Skills/Concepts	**MP.3.1** Logic
14–15	**3** Strategic Thinking	**MP.3.1** Logic

Additional Resources

Differentiated Instruction includes:

• Leveled Practice worksheets

12.2 Independent Practice

FL CC 8.EE.2.6, 8.F.2.4

8. Some carpet cleaning costs are shown in the table. The relationship is linear. Find and interpret the rate of change and the initial value for this situation.

Rooms cleaned	1	2	3	4
Cost ($)	125	175	225	275

The rate of change is $50 per room. The initial value is $75, which is a flat fee no matter how many rooms are cleaned.

9. Make Predictions The total cost to pay for parking at a state park for the day and rent a paddleboat are shown.

Number of Hours	Cost ($)
1	$17
2	$29
3	$41
4	$53

  a. Find the cost to park for a day and the hourly rate to rent a paddleboat.

  $5 to park; $12 per hour

  b. What will Lin pay if she rents a paddleboat for 3.5 hours and splits the total cost with a friend? Explain.

  $23.50; (3.5 hours × $12 per hour + $5) ÷ 2 = $23.50

10. Multi-Step Raymond's parents will pay for him to take sailboard lessons during the summer. He can take half-hour group lessons or half-hour private lessons. The relationship between cost and number of lessons is linear.

Lessons	1	2	3	4
Group ($)	55	85	115	145
Private ($)	75	125	175	225

  a. Find the rate of change and the initial value for the group lessons.

  The rate of change is $30 per lesson. The initial value is $25.

  b. Find the rate of change and the initial value for the private lessons.

  The rate of change is $50 per lesson. The initial value is $25.

  c. Compare and contrast the rates of change and the initial values.

  Both rates of change are constant, but the private lessons cost more. There is a flat fee of $25 no matter which type of lessons Raymond takes.

Vocabulary Explain why each relationship is not linear.

11.

x	1	2	3	4
y	4.5	6.5	8.5	11.5

Rate of change is constant from 1 to 2 to 3, but not from 3 to 4.

12.

x	3	5	7	9
y	140	126	110	92

Rate of change is not constant. It goes from −7 to −8 to −9.

13. Communicate Mathematical Ideas Describe the procedure you performed to derive the slope-intercept form of a linear equation.

Express the slope m between a random point (x, y) on the line and the point $(0, b)$ where the line crosses the y-axis. Then solve the equation for y.

H.O.T. FOCUS ON HIGHER ORDER THINKING

Work Area

14. Critique Reasoning Your teacher asked your class to describe a real-world situation in which a y-intercept is 100 and the slope is 5. Your partner gave the following description: *My younger brother originally had 100 small building blocks, but he has lost 5 of them every month since.*

  a. What mistake did your partner make?

  The slope is positive, so the amount should be increasing, not decreasing.

  b. Describe a real-world situation that does match the situation.

  Sample answer: I opened a savings account with $100 of birthday money and I add $5 from my allowance every month.

15. Justify Reasoning John has a job parking cars. He earns a fixed weekly salary of $300 plus a fee of $5 for each car he parks. His potential earnings for a week are shown in the graph. At what point does John begin to earn more from fees than his fixed salary? Justify your answer.

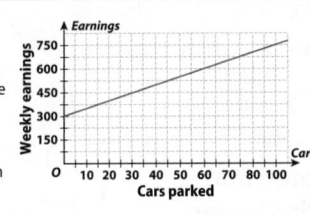

After parking 61 cars; John earns a fixed weekly salary of $300 plus $5 for each car he parks. He earns the same in fees as his fixed salary for parking 300 ÷ 5 = 60 cars.

EXTEND THE MATH PRE-AP

Activity available online my.hrw.com

Activity Points that lie on the same line are called *collinear* points. Without graphing the ordered pairs, determine if each set of points is collinear. Explain your answer.

1. (3, 5), (5, 9), (9, 13)

2. (−1, −4), (2, 5), (6, 17)

These three points are collinear. Find the missing coordinate.

3. (2, −3), (4, 3), (7, y)

4. (−5, 1), (−1, 9), (x, 15)

1. No. The rate of change is not constant.

2. Yes. The rate of change is constant.

3. 12

4. 2

Florida Common Core Standards

The student is expected to:

 **Functions—8.F.2.4**

Construct a function to model a linear relationship between two quantities. Determine the rate of change and initial value of the function from a description of a relationship or from two (x, y) values, including reading these from a table or from a graph. Interpret the rate of change and initial value of a linear function in terms of the situation it models, and in terms of its graph or a table of values.

 **Functions—8.F.1.3**

Interpret the equation $y = mx + b$ as defining a linear function, whose graph is a straight line; give examples of functions that are not linear.

Mathematical Practices

 **MP.6.1** Precision

 **Animated Math
Exploring Linear
Graphs**

Students explore graphs of linear relationships by changing the values of m and b using interactive sliders.

 **my.hrw.com**

ADDITIONAL EXAMPLE 1
Graph each equation.

A $y = 3x + 2$

B $y = -\frac{3}{4}x - 2$

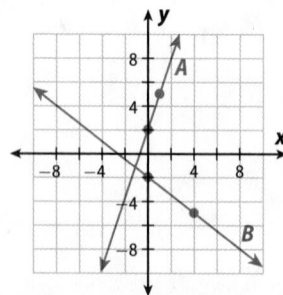

 Interactive Whiteboard
Interactive example available online

 **my.hrw.com**

Engage

ESSENTIAL QUESTION

How can you graph a line using the slope and y-intercept? Sample answer: First, plot the point that contains the *y*-intercept. Then use the slope to find another point on the line and draw a line through the points.

Motivate the Lesson
Ask: In the equation $y = 2x + 1$, what is the slope? What is the *y*-intercept?

Explore

Discuss with students what it means for a line to have a slope of 2. If the line passes through the origin ($b = 0$), what would be another point on the line?

Explain

EXAMPLE 1

Questioning Strategies **Mathematical Practices**

• In Step 2 of part A, why do you count up 2 and right 3? Sample answer: The numerator and denominator of the slope are both positive, so you count up and to the right.

• In Step 2 of part B, why do you count down 5 and right 2 or up 5 and left 2? Sample answer: The slope of the line is negative, so you count down and to the right or up and to the left.

Focus on Math Connections
Help students make the connection between the slopes of the graphed lines and the coefficient of x in the equations in parts A and B of this example. If slope is $\frac{rise}{run}$ and the slope is $\frac{2}{3}$, then the rise is 2 and the run is 3.

YOUR TURN

Engage with the Whiteboard
Have students select a point on the line and locate a second point using the slope of the line.

Avoid Common Errors
Make sure students correctly distinguish the slope and the *y*-intercept. They could write out the slope and *y*-intercept for each equation, or underline the slope and circle the *y*-intercept.

EXAMPLE 2

Questioning Strategies **Mathematical Practices**

• How many calories does Ken burn each hour by walking briskly? Explain how you know. 300 calories; calories left to burn decreases by 300 with each hour of walking.

• What does the point (3, 1500) represent on the graphed line? After walking briskly for 3 hours, Ken still needs to burn 1500 calories.

Graphing Linear Nonproportional Relationships Using Slope and *y*-intercept

FL CC 8.F.2.4
... Interpret the rate of change and initial value of a linear function in terms of the situation it models, and in terms of its graph.... *Also 8.F.1.3*

? ESSENTIAL QUESTION

How can you graph a line using the slope and *y*-intercept?

Using Slope-intercept Form to Graph a Line

Recall that $y = mx + b$ is the slope-intercept form of the equation of a line. In this form, it is easy to see the slope m and the *y*-intercept b. So you can use this form to quickly graph a line by plotting the point $(0, b)$ and using the slope to find a second point.

EXAMPLE 1
FL CC 8.F.1.3

A Graph $y = \frac{2}{3}x - 1$.

STEP 1 The *y*-intercept is $b = -1$. Plot the point that contains the *y*-intercept: $(0, -1)$.

STEP 2 The slope is $m = \frac{2}{3}$. Use the slope to find a second point. From $(0, -1)$, count *up* 2 and *right* 3. The new point is $(3, 1)$.

STEP 3 Draw a line through the points.

B Graph $y = -\frac{5}{2}x + 3$.

STEP 1 The *y*-intercept is $b = 3$. Plot the point that contains the *y*-intercept: $(0, 3)$.

STEP 2 The slope is $m = -\frac{5}{2}$. Use the slope to find a second point. From $(0, 3)$, count *down* 5 and *right* 2, or *up* 5 and *left* 2. The new point is $(2, -2)$ or $(-2, 8)$.

STEP 3 Draw a line through the points.

Note that the line passes through all three points: $(-2, 8)$, $(0, 3)$, and $(2, -2)$.

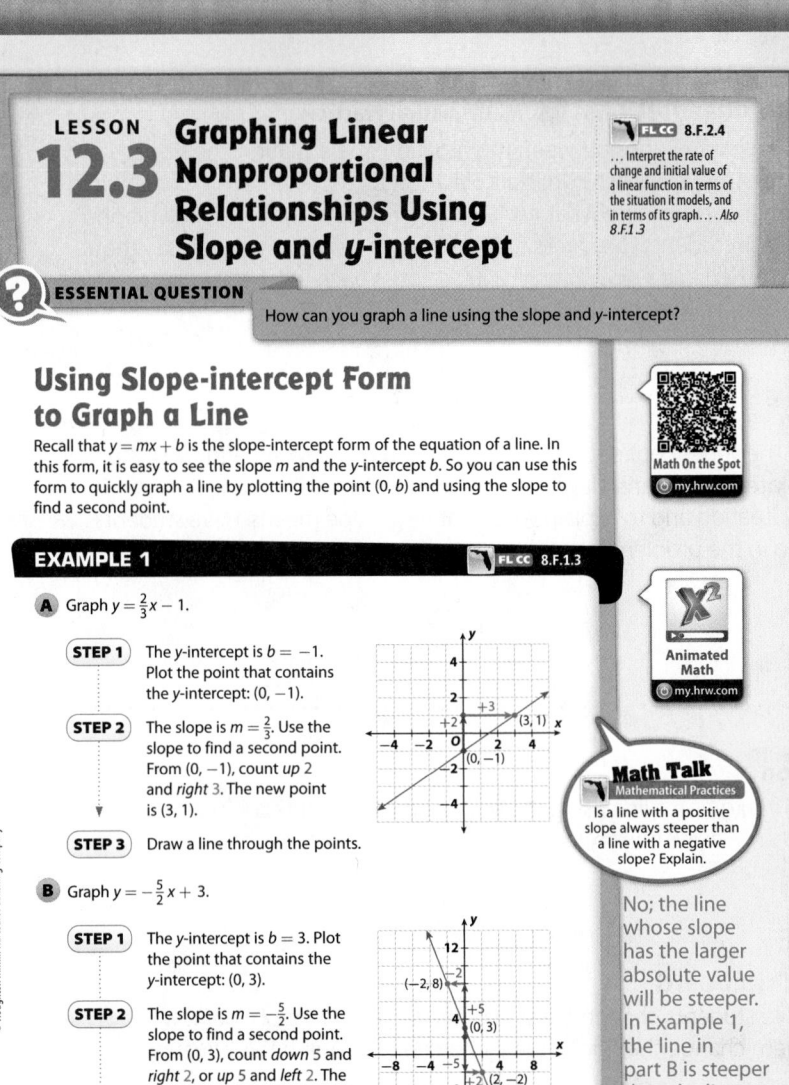

Math On the Spot my.hrw.com

X² **Animated Math** my.hrw.com

Math Talk
Mathematical Practices

Is a line with a positive slope always steeper than a line with a negative slope? Explain.

No; the line whose slope has the larger absolute value will be steeper. In Example 1, the line in part B is steeper than the line in part A even though its slope is negative.

Lesson 12.3 **371**

Reflect

1. **Draw Conclusions** How can you use the slope of a line to predict the way the line will be slanted? Explain.

A line with positive slope will rise from left to right.

A line with a negative slope will fall from left to right.

Personal Math Trainer Online Assessment and Intervention my.hrw.com

YOUR TURN

Graph each equation.

2. $y = \frac{1}{2}x + 1$

3. $y = -3x + 4$

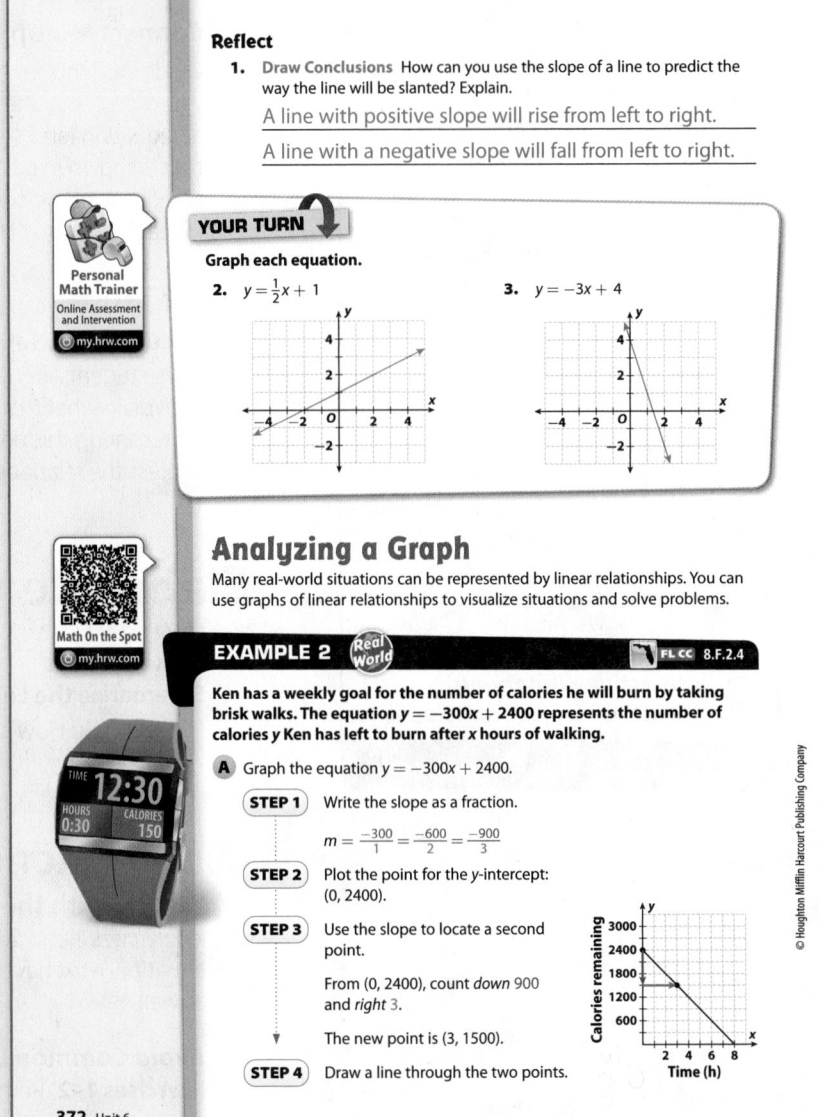

Analyzing a Graph

Many real-world situations can be represented by linear relationships. You can use graphs of linear relationships to visualize situations and solve problems.

Math On the Spot my.hrw.com

EXAMPLE 2 Real World
FL CC 8.F.2.4

Ken has a weekly goal for the number of calories he will burn by taking brisk walks. The equation $y = -300x + 2400$ represents the number of calories y Ken has left to burn after x hours of walking.

A Graph the equation $y = -300x + 2400$.

STEP 1 Write the slope as a fraction.

$m = \frac{-300}{1} = \frac{-600}{2} = \frac{-900}{3}$

STEP 2 Plot the point for the *y*-intercept: $(0, 2400)$.

STEP 3 Use the slope to locate a second point.

From $(0, 2400)$, count *down* 900 and *right* 3.

The new point is $(3, 1500)$.

STEP 4 Draw a line through the two points.

372 Unit 6

PROFESSIONAL DEVELOPMENT

Integrate Mathematical Practices MP.6.1

This lesson provides an opportunity to address this Mathematical Practices standard. It calls for students to communicate precisely, including communicating through the use of symbols and graphs. In Example 2, students begin with a real-world situation represented by a linear equation, they find the *y*-intercept and slope, and then represent the equation with a graph.

Math Background

This lesson shows how to graph equations of lines that are not horizontal or vertical. For horizontal lines, there is a *y*-intercept, but no *x*-intercept (unless the horizontal line is the *x*-axis), and the slope is zero. The equation for a horizontal line is of the form $y = b$, where b is a fixed real number. For vertical lines, there is an *x*-intercept, but no *y*-intercept (unless the vertical line is the *y*-axis), and the slope is undefined. The equation for a vertical line is of the form $x = a$, where a is a fixed real number.

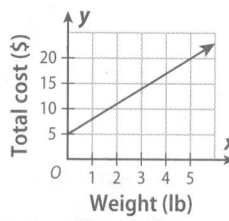

Connect Multiple Representations **Mathematical Practices**

Guide students in making connections between the situation, the equation, the slope, the
y-intercept, and the graph. The relationship in Example 2 can be represented in words, with
an equation (and statements explaining what each variable represents), and by the graph
that is shown in part A. Ask students to express the relationship in their own words without
an equation. For example: Ken has a goal to burn 2400 calories each week by walking fast;
for each hour that he walks, he burns 300 calories.

YOUR TURN

Focus on Modeling

Have students identify the *y*-intercept of the line representing this new situation. Ask them
to explain what that *y*-intercept means. Have students identify the slope of the line
representing this new situation and to explain what that new slope means. Have students
express the relationship in the problem in words without an equation.

Elaborate

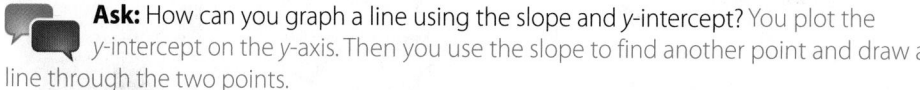

Talk About It
Summarize the Lesson

Ask: How can you graph a line using the slope and *y*-intercept? You plot the
y-intercept on the *y*-axis. Then you use the slope to find another point and draw a
line through the two points.

GUIDED PRACTICE

Engage with the Whiteboard

In Exercises 1 and 2, have students change the sign of the slope and graph the new
equation. Next have them change the sign of the *y*-intercept and graph this equation
as well.

Avoid Common Errors

Exercises 1–2 Remind students that the *y*-intercept of a line is the number on the *y*-axis
where the line intersects the *y*-axis.

Exercise 3 Students may think that any point with a whole number *y*-coordinate makes
sense. Have students find the *x*-coordinate when $y = 12$. Explain that after 2 weeks you have
10 cards and after 3 weeks you have 14 cards. Since the cards are only bought once a week
and you buy 4 at a time, there is no point at which you will have 12 cards.

B After how many hours of walking will Ken have 600 calories left to burn? After how many hours will he reach his weekly goal?

STEP 1 Locate 600 calories on the y-axis. Read across and down to the x-axis.

Ken will have 600 calories left to burn after 6 hours.

STEP 2 Ken will reach his weekly goal when the number of calories left to burn is 0. Because every point on the x-axis has a y-value of 0, find the point where the line crosses the x-axis.

○ Ken will reach his goal after 8 hours of brisk walking.

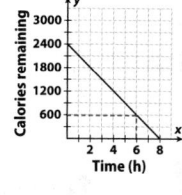

YOUR TURN

What If? Ken decides to modify his exercise plans from Example 2 by slowing the speed at which he walks. The equation for the modified plan is $y = -200x + 2400$.

4. Graph the equation.

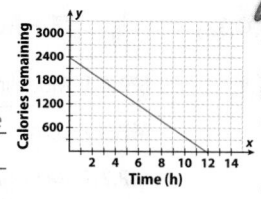

5. How does the graph of the new equation compare with the graph in Example 2?

The new graph has the same y-intercept but a slope of -200 instead of -300.

6. Will Ken have to exercise more or less to meet his goal? Explain.

The calories left to burn will decrease more slowly with each hour of exercise, so it will take longer for Ken to meet his goal.

7. Suppose that Ken decides that instead of walking, he will jog, and that jogging burns 600 calories per hour. How do you think that this would change the graph?

Sample answer: The y-intercept would not change, but the slope would become -600, which is much steeper. The line would intersect the x-axis when $x = 4$ hours.

Math Talk
Mathematical Practices
What do the slope and the y-intercept of the line represent in this situation?

The slope is -200, which means the number of calories left to burn decreases by 200 calories for every hour of walking. The y-intercept is 2400, which means Ken's weekly goal is to burn 2400 calories by walking.

Personal Math Trainer
Online Assessment and Intervention
my.hrw.com

Graph each equation using the slope and the y-intercept. (Example 1)

1. $y = \frac{1}{2}x - 3$

slope = $\underline{\frac{1}{2}}$ y-intercept = $\underline{-3}$

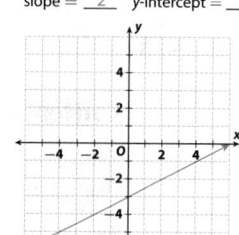

2. $y = -3x + 2$

slope = $\underline{-3}$ y-intercept = $\underline{2}$

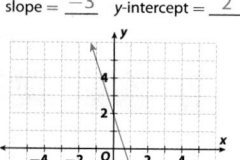

3. A friend gives you two baseball cards for your birthday. Afterward, you begin collecting them. You buy the same number of cards once each week. The equation $y = 4x + 2$ describes the number of cards, y, you have after x weeks. (Example 2)

a. Find and interpret the slope and the y-intercept of the line that represents this situation. Graph $y = 4x + 2$. Include axis labels.

Slope = 4; y-intercept = 2; you start with 2 cards and add 4 cards each week.

b. Discuss which points on the line do not make sense in this situation. Then plot three more points on the line that do make sense.

The points with coordinates that are not whole numbers; You will not buy part of a baseball card and you are buying only once a week.

Weeks

ESSENTIAL QUESTION CHECK-IN

4. Why might someone choose to use the y-intercept and the slope to graph a line?

Sample answer: You can easily identify the slope m and y-intercept b from the slope-intercept form $y = mx + b$ and quickly use them to locate two points that determine the line.

DIFFERENTIATE INSTRUCTION

Kinesthetic Experience

Some students may still be having difficulty remembering that lines with positive slopes go up as one moves from left to right and lines with negative slopes go down as one moves from left to right. Draw a line on the board that has a positive or negative slope. Have students extend their right arms to model the slope of the line. Have students say whether the slope of their arms is positive or negative and then explain why. Repeat with other lines. Then say the words "positive" or "negative" and have students use their arms to model a line with such a slope.

Cooperative Learning

Have students work in pairs. Have each pair choose one student to be the Equation Creator and the other student to be the Equation Grapher. The Equation Creator should create a linear equation in slope-intercept form with integer coefficients that are between -5 and 5. The Equation Grapher should check that the equation is in that form. The Equation Grapher should then graph the equation and the Equation Creator should check that the graph is correct. Encourage students to use the y-intercept and the slope to graph the equations. After the Equation Grapher has graphed one or two equations, have students switch roles.

Additional Resources

Differentiated Instruction includes

- Reading Strategies
- Success for English Learners **ELL**
- Reteach
- Challenge **PRE-AP**

Graphing Linear Nonproportional Relationships Using Slope and y-intercept **374**

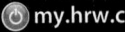
12.3 LESSON QUIZ

FL CC 8.F.1.3, 8.F.2.4

1. Graph the equation $y = -\frac{3}{2}x - 2$.

2. Maria is ordering comic books online. The equation $y = 8x + 4$ represents the total cost in dollars, y, including shipping, for ordering x number of comic books.

   a. Graph the equation.

   b. If the total cost including shipping is $60, how many comic books is Maria ordering?

3. Mr. Goldstein is driving to Houston. The equation $y = -45x + 270$ represents the numbers of miles that he still has to travel after driving for x hours. Find and interpret the slope and y-intercept of the line that represents this situation.

Lesson Quiz available online

my.hrw.com

Answers

1.

2. a.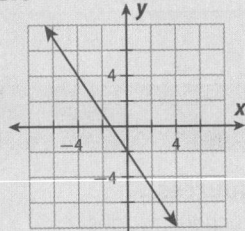

   b. 7 comic books

3. Slope $= -45$; y-intercept $= 270$; he is driving 45 miles per hour and at the beginning, had 270 miles to drive.

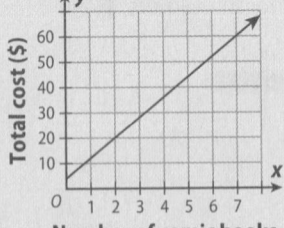

Evaluate

GUIDED AND INDEPENDENT PRACTICE

 **FL CC** 8.F.1.3, 8.F.2.4

Concepts & Skills	Practice
Example 1 Using Slope-Intercept Form to Graph a Line	Exercises 1–2, 5, 13, 16
Example 2 Analyzing a Graph	Exercises 3, 5, 13

Exercise	Depth of Knowledge (D.O.K.)	**FL CC** Mathematical Practices
5	**3** Strategic Thinking **H.O.T.**	**MP.4.1** Modeling
6–11	**2** Skills/Concepts	**MP.5.1** Using Tools
12	**2** Skills/Concepts	**MP.2.1** Reasoning
13–14	**3** Strategic Thinking **H.O.T.**	**MP.3.1** Logic
15–16	**3** Strategic Thinking **H.O.T.**	**MP.2.1** Reasoning

Additional Resources

Differentiated Instruction includes:

• Leveled Practice worksheets

12.3 Independent Practice

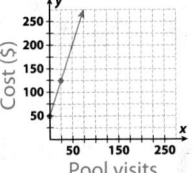

FL CC 8.F.1.3, 8.F.2.4

Personal Math Trainer

Online Assessment and Intervention

my.hrw.com

5. **Science** A spring stretches in relation to the weight hanging from it according to the equation $y = 0.75x + 0.25$ where x is the weight in pounds and y is the length of the spring in inches.

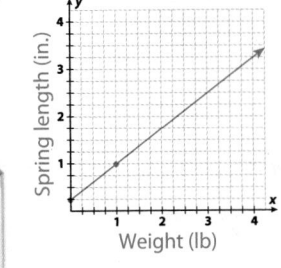

   a. Graph the equation. Include axis labels.

   b. Interpret the slope and the y-intercept of the line.

   The slope, 0.75, means that the spring stretches by 0.75 inch with each additional pound of weight. The y-intercept, 0.25, is the unstretched length of the spring in inches.

   c. How long will the spring be if a 2-pound weight is hung on it? Will the length double if you double the weight? Explain

   1.75 inches; no; the length with a 4-pound weight is 3.25 in., not 3.5 in.

Look for a Pattern Identify the coordinates of four points on the line with each given slope and y-intercept. Sample answers are given.

6. slope $= 5$, y-intercept $= -1$
   (0, −1), (1, 4), (2, 9), (3, 14)

7. slope $= -1$, y-intercept $= 8$
   (0, 8), (1, 7), (2, 6), (3, 5)

8. slope $= 0.2$, y-intercept $= 0.3$
   (0, 0.3), (1, 0.5), (2, 0.7), (3, 0.9)

9. slope $= 1.5$, y-intercept $= -3$
   (0, −3), (1, −1.5), (2, 0), (3, 1.5)

10. slope $= -\frac{1}{2}$, y-intercept $= 4$
    (0, 4), (2, 3), (4, 2), (6, 1)

11. slope $= \frac{2}{3}$, y-intercept $= -5$
    (0, −5), (3, −3), (6, −1), (9, 1)

12. A music school charges a registration fee in addition to a fee per lesson. Music lessons last 0.5 hour. The equation $y = 40x + 30$ represents the total cost y of x lessons. Find and interpret the slope and y-intercept of the line that represents this situation. Then find four points on the line.

    Slope = 40, so the cost per lesson is $40; y-intercept = 30, so the registration fee is $30; sample answers: (0, 30), (1, 70), (2, 110), (3, 150).

13. A public pool charges a membership fee and a fee for each visit. The equation $y = 3x + 50$ represents the cost y for x visits.

    a. After locating the y-intercept on the coordinate plane shown, can you move up three gridlines and right one gridline to find a second point? Explain.

    Yes.; Since the horizontal and vertical gridlines each represent 25 units, moving up 3 gridlines and right 1 gridline represents a slope of $\frac{75}{25}$, or 3.

    b. Graph the equation $y = 3x + 50$. Include axis labels. Then interpret the slope and y-intercept.

    $m = 3$ so $3 is the charge per visit; $b = 50$ so the membership fee is $50.

    c. How many visits to the pool can a member get for $200?

    50 visits

H.O.T. FOCUS ON HIGHER ORDER THINKING

14. **Explain the Error** A student says that the slope of the line for the equation $y = 20 - 15x$ is 20 and the y-intercept is 15. Find and correct the error.

    The coefficient of x, −15, is the slope, not the constant term. The constant term is the y-intercept, 20.

15. **Critical Thinking** Suppose you know the slope of a linear relationship and a point that its graph passes through. Can you graph the line even if the point provided does *not* represent the y-intercept? Explain.

    Yes; you can plot the point and use the slope to find a second point. Then draw a line through the two points.

16. **Make a Conjecture** Graph the lines $y = 3x$, $y = 3x - 3$, and $y = 3x + 3$. What do you notice about the lines? Make a conjecture based on your observation.

    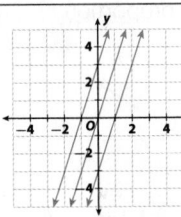

    The lines appear to be parallel. Parallel lines have the same slope but different y-intercepts.

Work Area

EXTEND THE MATH PRE-AP

Activity available online my.hrw.com

Activity Have students use graphing calculators to graph on the same set of axes three linear equations whose graphs have the same slope. For example, have them graph $y = 2x$, $y = 2x + 3$, and $y = 2x - 4$. Then have them graph, on a new pair of axes, another set of linear equations whose graphs have the same slope, but different from the slope of the first set of lines. For example, have them graph $y = -3x$, $y = -3x + 2$, and $y = -3x - 1$. Ask students to make a conjecture about lines with the same slopes (they are parallel). Have them try out other sets of linear equations to test their conjectures.

LESSON 12.4 Proportional and Nonproportional Situations

Florida Common Core Standards

The student is expected to:

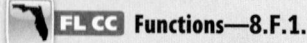 **Functions—8.F.1.2**

Compare properties of two functions each represented in a different way (algebraically, graphically, numerically in tables, or by verbal descriptions).
Also 8.F.1.3, 8.F.2.4

Mathematical Practices

 **MP.6.1** Precision

---

ADDITIONAL EXAMPLE 1

The graph shows the water level as a bathtub fills. Does the graph show a linear relationship? Is the relationship proportional or nonproportional?

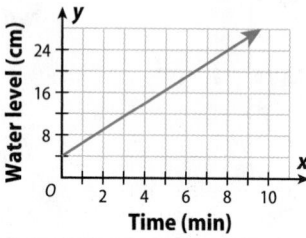

yes; nonproportional

 Interactive Whiteboard
Interactive example available online

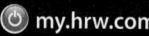 my.hrw.com

---

ADDITIONAL EXAMPLE 2

The change in a test score for each incorrect answer is represented by the equation $y = -\frac{x}{2}$, where x is the number of incorrect answers. Is the relationship between the number of incorrect answers and the change in score proportional or nonproportional?
proportional

 Interactive Whiteboard
Interactive example available online

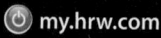 my.hrw.com

---

Engage

....

ESSENTIAL QUESTION

How can you distinguish between proportional and nonproportional situations?
Sample answer: Determine whether the relationship is linear and the *y*-intercept is 0.

Motivate the Lesson

Ask: What are some things where the unit price changes as you buy more of them? Is the price proportional to the number of items you buy?

Explore

....

EXPLORE ACTIVITY

Two batteries cost $3.00. A twelve-pack of the same batteries costs $15. Is the relationship between the number of batteries and the price proportional?

Explain

....

EXAMPLE 1

Questioning Strategies Mathematical Practices

• Is a *y*-intercept of 0 enough to conclude that the relationship is proportional? Explain.
No; the relationship must also be linear.

Engage with the Whiteboard

Have students add a line to the graph that would show a nonproportional linear relationship.

YOUR TURN

Connect Vocabulary **ELL**

Saying that an equation is "nonproportional" or "nonlinear" is the same as saying that an equation is "not proportional" or "not linear". The prefix *non-* means not.

EXAMPLE 2

Questioning Strategies Mathematical Practices

• How old was Keith when he graduated from middle school? 14 years old

Focus on Modeling Mathematical Practices

In the linear equation $y = mx + b$, just as *m* and *b* both represent any constant, *x* and *y* represent any two variables. Therefore, $y = 1x - 14$ is equivalent to $y = a - 14$.

YOUR TURN

Avoid Common Errors

Tell students that two different variables are needed for a proportional relationship. In Exercise 8, they may see that there is only one term on each side of the equation and assume that it is proportional.

LESSON 12.4 Proportional and Nonproportional Situations

FL CC 8.F.1.2
Compare properties of two functions each represented in a different way (algebraically, graphically, numerically in tables, or by verbal descriptions). Also 8.F.1.3, 8.F.2.4

? **ESSENTIAL QUESTION** How can you distinguish between proportional and nonproportional situations?

Distinguish Between Proportional and Nonproportional Situations Using a Graph

If a relationship is nonlinear, it is nonproportional. If it is linear, it may be either proportional or nonproportional. When the graph of the linear relationship contains the origin, the relationship is proportional.

Math On the Spot
my.hrw.com

EXAMPLE 1 Real World   FL CC 8.F.1.3

The graph shows the sales tax charged based on the amount spent at a video game store in a particular city. Does the graph show a linear relationship? Is the relationship proportional or nonproportional?

The graph shows a linear proportional relationship because it is a line that contains the origin.

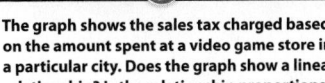
Sales tax ($) vs Amount spent ($)

The slope is $0.06. It is the change in the amount of sales tax paid for each dollar spent. The y-intercept is 0, meaning you pay no sales tax if you don't buy anything.

YOUR TURN

Determine if each of the following graphs represents a proportional or nonproportional relationship.

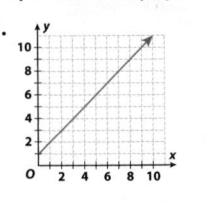

1. nonproportional

2. proportional

Math Talk
Mathematical Practices
What do the slope and the y-intercept of the graph represent in this situation?

Personal Math Trainer
Online Assessment and Intervention
my.hrw.com

Math On the Spot
my.hrw.com

Animated Math
my.hrw.com

Distinguish Between Proportional and Nonproportional Situations Using an Equation

If an equation is not a linear equation, it represents a nonproportional relationship. A linear equation of the form $y = mx + b$ may represent either a proportional ($b = 0$) or nonproportional ($b \neq 0$) relationship.

EXAMPLE 2 Real World   FL CC 8.F.2.4

The number of years since Keith graduated from middle school can be represented by the equation $y = a - 14$, where y is the number of years and a is his age. Is the relationship between the number of years since Keith graduated and his age proportional or nonproportional?

$$y = a - 14$$

The equation is in the form $y = mx + b$, with a being used as the variable instead of x. The value of m is 1, and the value of b is -14. Since b is not 0, the relationship between the number of years since Keith graduated and his age is nonproportional.

Reflect

3. **Communicate Mathematical Ideas** In a proportional relationship, the ratio $\frac{y}{x}$ is constant. Show that this ratio is not constant for the equation $y = a - 14$.

   Sample answer: (16, 2) and (21, 7) are solutions, but $\frac{y}{x} = \frac{2}{16} = \frac{1}{8}$ and $\frac{y}{x} = \frac{7}{21} = \frac{1}{3}$

4. **What If?** Suppose another equation represents Keith's age in months y given his age in years a. Is this relationship proportional? Explain.

   Yes; the ratio of age in months to age in years is constant.

YOUR TURN

Determine if each of the following equations represents a proportional or nonproportional relationship.

5. $d = 65t$
   proportional

6. $p = 0.1s + 2000$
   nonproportional

7. $n = 450 - 3p$
   nonproportional

8. $36 = 12d$
   nonproportional

Personal Math Trainer
Online Assessment and Intervention
my.hrw.com

PROFESSIONAL DEVELOPMENT

Integrate Mathematical Practices MP.6.1

This lesson provides an opportunity to address this Mathematical Practices standard. It calls for students to communicate mathematical ideas and arguments using precise mathematical language. Students analyze relationships represented by words, tables, equations, and graphs and must describe the relationships with terms such as proportional, nonproportional, linear, and nonlinear.

Math Background

A function with a restricted domain may also be a linear, proportional relationship. For example, the line segment from (2, 6) to (4, 12) is a linear, proportional relationship with a domain of $\{2 \leq x \leq 4\}$.

Similarly, a portion of a *piecewise function* may be a linear, proportional relationship. For $x \geq 2$, the piecewise function has a linear, proportional relationship.

$$f(x) = \begin{cases} 4 & x < 2 \\ 2x & x \geq 2 \end{cases}$$

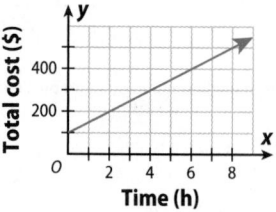

EXAMPLE 3

Questioning Strategies 🔲 Mathematical Practices

• What number could you multiply the number in the first column by to get the number in the second column? 13

• What would a graph of this data look like? The points (130, 1690), (255, 3315), and (505, 6565) would lie along a straight line.

Focus on Critical Thinking 🔲 Mathematical Practices

Suppose a fourth tourist traded 50 U.S. dollars and received 630 Mexican pesos in return, and this data were added to the table. Would this change your answer? Explain. Students should realize this would make the relationship nonlinear as the ratio is no longer 13.

Integrating Language Arts ELL

Encourage a broad class discussion on the Math Talk. English learners will benefit from hearing and participating in classroom discussions.

YOUR TURN

Focus on Math Connections 🔲 Mathematical Practices

Point out to students that in Exercise 10, y is less than x so they will find ratios that are less than 1. Assure them that they can compare fractions or decimal equivalents.

EXAMPLE 4

Questioning Strategies 🔲 Mathematical Practices

• How could you write the total charge for Arena B in $y = mx + b$ form? $y = 200x + 50$

• How could you write the total charge for Painter B in $y = mx + b$ form? $y = 35x + 20$

Engage with the Whiteboard

Have a student add the line representing the total charge for Arena A to the graph for Arena B. Ask students for a range of hours when each arena appears to be less costly.

Distinguish Between Proportional and Nonproportional Situations Using a Table

If there is not a constant rate of change in the data displayed in a table, then the table represents a nonlinear nonproportional relationship.

A linear relationship represented by a table is a proportional relationship when the quotient of each pair of numbers is constant. Otherwise, the linear relationship is nonproportional.

EXAMPLE 3 — Real World
FL CC 8.F.2.4

The values in the table represent the numbers of U.S. dollars three tourists traded for Mexican pesos. The relationship is linear. Is the relationship proportional or nonproportional?

U.S. Dollars Traded	Mexican Pesos Received
130	1,690
255	3,315
505	6,565

$$\frac{1,690}{130} = \frac{169}{13} = 13$$

$$\frac{3,315}{255} = \frac{221}{17} = 13$$

$$\frac{6,565}{505} = \frac{1313}{101} = 13$$

Simplify the ratios to compare the pesos received to the dollars traded.

The ratio of pesos received to dollars traded is constant at 13 Mexican pesos per U.S. dollar. This is a proportional relationship.

YOUR TURN

Determine if the linear relationship represented by each table is a proportional or nonproportional relationship.

9.

x	y
2	30
8	90
14	150

nonproportional

10.

x	y
5	1
40	8
65	13

proportional

Math On the Spot
my.hrw.com

Animated Math
my.hrw.com

Math Talk
Mathematical Practices

How could you confirm that the values in the table have a linear relationship?

Compare the change in Mexican pesos to the change in U.S. dollars from each pair of numbers to the next. The results should all be the same.

Personal Math Trainer
Online Assessment and Intervention
my.hrw.com

Comparing Proportional and Nonproportional Situations

You can use what you have learned about proportional and nonproportional relationships to compare similar real-world situations that are given using different representations.

EXAMPLE 4 — Real World
FL CC 8.F.1.2

A A laser tag league has the choice of two arenas for a tournament. In both cases, x is the number of hours and y is the total charge. Compare and contrast these two situations.

Arena A

$y = 225x$

Arena B

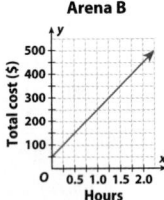

- **Arena A's** equation has the form $y = mx + b$, where $b = 0$. So, Arena A's charges are a proportional relationship. The hourly rate, $225, is greater than Arena B's, but there is no additional fee.

- **Arena B's** graph is a line that does not include the origin. So, Arena B's charges are a nonproportional relationship. Arena B has a $50 initial fee but its hourly rate, $200, is lower.

B Jessika is remodeling and has the choice of two painters. In both cases, x is the number of hours and y is the total charge. Compare and contrast these two situations.

Painter A

$y = \$45x$

Painter B

x	0	1	3	4
y	20	55	90	125

Painter A's equation has the form $y = mx + b$, where $b = 0$. So, Painter A's charges are proportional. The hourly rate, $45, is greater than Painter B's, but there is no additional fee.

Painter B's table is a nonproportional relationship because the ratio of y to x is not constant. Because the table contains the ordered pair (0, 20), Painter B charges an initial fee of $20, but the hourly rate, $35, is less than Painter A's.

Math Talk
Mathematical Practices

How might graphing the equation for Arena A help you to compare the situations?

Sample answer: By graphing the two situations together, you can more easily see when one option is better than another.

DIFFERENTIATE INSTRUCTION

Auditory Cues

Proportional relationships generally have one condition, while nonproportional ones have an additional condition. Emphasize connecting words like *and* and *but* for nonproportional situations that indicate a second condition, and teach students to do the same.

Examples might be "boats rent for $12 an hour *and* a daily fee of $10" or "the cost is $25 an hour *but* she has a coupon for $50 off."

Critical Thinking

Rounding or taking the integer part of an otherwise proportional relationship can make the relationship nonproportional. Students might consider a situation where the price is rounded up to the next cent. An item that sells for 3 for $1 will cost $0.34 for one item, for example.

Have students determine whether these situations might still be considered proportional for specific purposes, even though they technically are not.

Additional Resources

Differentiated Instruction includes

- Reading Strategies
- Success for English Learners **ELL**
- Reteach
- Challenge **PRE-AP**

Connect to Daily Life **Mathematical Practices**

Have students consider the coupon for Test-Prep Center B and create a table or graph for this situation. Students should see that for less than 4 hours, the cost is negative. Encourage students to provide some likely restrictions on the use of the coupon.

Elaborate

Talk About It
Summarize the Lesson

Ask: How do you know that a linear relationship given by a graph, a table, or an equation represents a nonproportional relationship? Sample answer: The y-intercept, the value of the dependent variable when $x = 0$, is not 0.

GUIDED PRACTICE

Engage with the Whiteboard

Have students write the ratio of y to x for each row of the table in Exercises 5 and 6.

Avoid Common Errors

Exercise 4 Remind students that in $y = mx + b$ form, the value of m does not need to be an integer in order for a relationship to be proportional.

Exercise 7 Students should take care in dividing, due to the size of the numbers. Even using a calculator, they may find that two quotients differ by a power of ten, although they should all be the same.

Personal
Math Trainer
Online Assessment
and Intervention
my.hrw.com

11. Compare and contrast the following two situations.

Test-Prep Center A	Test-Prep Center B
The cost for Test-Prep Center A is given by $c = 20h$, where c is the cost in dollars and h is the number of hours you attend.	Test-Prep Center B charges $25 per hour to attend, but you have a $100 coupon that you can use to reduce the cost.

Test-Prep Center A's charges are a proportional
relationship, but B's charges are not. Center B offers a
coupon that gives you an initial credit, but its hourly
rate, $25, is higher than Center A's hourly rate of $20.
So, Center B will cost more in the long run.

Guided Practice

Determine if each relationship is a proportional or nonproportional
situation. Explain your reasoning. (Example 1, Example 2, Example 4)

1.
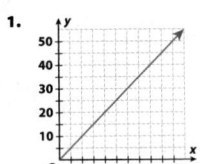

Look at the origin.
Proportional; the line includes the
origin.

2.

Nonproportional; the line does
not include the origin.

3. $q = 2p + \frac{1}{2}$

Compare the equation with $y = mx + b$.
Nonproportional; when the
equation is written in the form
$y = mx + b$, the value of b is not 0.

4. $v = \frac{1}{10}u$

Proportional; when the equation
is written in the form $y = mx + b$,
the value of b is 0.

The tables represent linear relationships. Determine if each relationship is a
proportional or nonproportional situation. (Example 3, Example 4)

5.

x	y
3	12
9	36
21	84

6.

x	y
22	4
46	8
58	10

Find the quotient of y and x.

Proportional; the quotient of y and
x is constant, 4, for every number
pair.

No, because when the equation
$y = mx + b$ is written for the
values, the value of b is not 0.

7. The values in the table represent the numbers of households that
watched three TV shows and the ratings of the shows. The relationship
is linear. Describe the relationship in other ways. (Example 4)

Number of Households that Watched TV Show	TV Show Rating
15,000,000	12
20,000,000	16
25,000,000	20

Sample answer: The TV show rating is proportional to
the number of households that watched, because the
quotient when you divide the rating by the number of
households is always 0.0000008.

ESSENTIAL QUESTION CHECK-IN

8. How are using graphs, equations, and tables similar when distinguishing
between proportional and nonproportional situations?
Sample answer: You look to see whether the y-intercept
of a linear relationship is 0 to identify proportional
relationships for both graphs and equations.

© Houghton Mifflin Harcourt Publishing Company

Personal
Math Trainer

Online Assessment
and Intervention

Online homework
assignment available

⏻ my.hrw.com

12.4 LESSON QUIZ

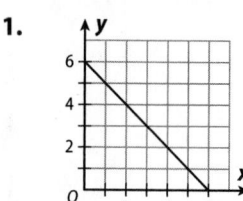 **FL CC** 8.F.1.2, 8.F.1.3, 8.F.2.4

**Explain whether each shows a
proportional relationship.**

1.

2.

x	9	36	63
y	7	28	49

3. $12x = 5y$

4. Compare and contrast.

Without Discount Card	With Discount Card
The cost for cat food is	The cost is given by $c = 9.5n + 5$ where n is the number of cases.

Cases	2	3
Cost ($)	21	31.50

Lesson Quiz available online

⏻ my.hrw.com

Answers
1. No; the graph does not go through the origin.

2. Yes; the ratio of y to x is constant.

3. Yes; the equation can be written in the form $y = mx + b$, and $b = 0$.

4. The cost without a discount card is proportional, with a discount card it is not. The cost is more expensive with the discount card initially, but the per-case rate without it is more expensive.

Evaluate

GUIDED AND INDEPENDENT PRACTICE

 **FL CC** 8.F.1.2, 8.F.1.3, 8.F.2.4

Concepts & Skills	Practice
Example 1 Distinguish Between Proportional and Nonproportional Situations Using a Graph	Exercises 1–2, 9
Example 2 Distinguish Between Proportional and Nonproportional Situations Using an Equation	Exercises 3–4, 11
Example 3 Distinguish Between Proportional and Nonproportional Situations Using a Table	Exercises 5–7, 15
Example 4 Comparing Proportional and Nonproportional Situations	Exercise 12

Exercise	Depth of Knowledge (D.O.K.)	**FL CC** Mathematical Practices
9	**2** Skills/Concepts	**MP.2.1** Reasoning
10–11	**2** Skills/Concepts	**MP.4.1** Modeling
12–13	**2** Skills/Concepts	**MP.6.1** Precision
14	**3** Strategic Thinking H.O.T.	**MP.2.1** Reasoning
15	**3** Strategic Thinking H.O.T.	**MP.3.1** Logic

Additional Resources
Differentiated Instruction includes:
• Leveled Practice worksheets

CLUSTER CONNECTION **Exercises 10–11** combine concepts from the Florida Common Core cluster "Define, evaluate, and compare functions."

12.4 Independent Practice

FL CC 8.F.1.2, 8.F.1.3, 8.F.2.4

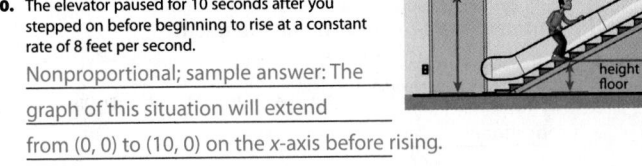

Personal
Math Trainer
Online
Assessment and
Intervention
my.hrw.com

9. The graph shows the weight of a cross-country team's beverage cooler based on how much sports drink it contains.

a. Is the relationship proportional or nonproportional? Explain.

Nonproportional; the graph does not pass through

the origin, so $b \neq 0$.

b. Identify and interpret the slope and the y-intercept.

$m = 0.5$, $b = 10$; each cup sports drink weighs a half

pound. The empty cooler weighs 10 pounds.

In 10–11, tell if the relationship between a rider's height above the first floor and the time since the rider stepped on the elevator or escalator is proportional or nonproportional. Explain your reasoning.

10. The elevator paused for 10 seconds after you stepped on before beginning to rise at a constant rate of 8 feet per second.

Nonproportional; sample answer: The

graph of this situation will extend

from (0, 0) to (10, 0) on the x-axis before rising.

height above floor

height above floor

11. Your height, h, in feet above the first floor on the escalator is given by $h = 0.75t$, where t is the time in seconds.

Proportional; this equation has the form $y = mx + b$ where $b = 0$.

12. **Analyze Relationships** Compare and contrast the two graphs.

Graph A
$y = \frac{1}{3}x$
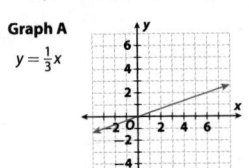

Graph B
$y = \sqrt{x}$
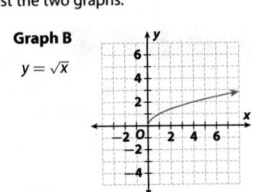

Both include the origin, but only A is a line, making it linear

and proportional. B is nonlinear and nonproportional.

13. **Represent Real-World Problems** Describe a real-world situation where the relationship is linear and nonproportional.

Sample answer: Amanda buys a flute for $500 and then

pays $35 per week for lessons.

H.O.T. FOCUS ON HIGHER ORDER THINKING

Work Area

14. **Mathematical Reasoning** Suppose you know the slope of a linear relationship and one of the points that its graph passes through. How can you determine if the relationship is proportional or nonproportional?

You can plot the point, use the slope to find another

point, and draw a line through the points to see if it

passes through the origin.

15. **Multiple Representations** An entrant at a science fair has included information about temperature conversion in various forms, as shown. The variables F, C, and K represent temperatures in degrees Fahrenheit, degrees Celsius, and Kelvin, respectively.

Equation A	Table C	
$F = \frac{9}{5}C + 32$	Degrees Celsius	kelvins
	8	281.15
Equation B	15	288.15
$K = C + 273.15$	36	309.15

a. Is the relationship between kelvins and degrees Celsius proportional? Justify your answer in two different ways.

No; using Equation B you see that the y-intercept

is 273.15, not 0, so the graph does not include the

origin. Using Table C you see that the quotient of K

and C is not constant: about 35.1, 19.21, and 8.5875.

b. Is the relationship between degrees Celsius and degrees Fahrenheit proportional? Why or why not?

No; Equation A is in the form $y = mx + b$, with F

being used instead of y and C being used instead

of x. The value of b is 32. Since b is not 0, the

relationship is not proportional.

EXTEND THE MATH PRE-AP

Activity available online my.hrw.com

Activity A *geometric progression* is a *sequence* or list of numbers with a common ratio r between the terms. One geometric progression is a sequence with a common ratio of 2:

1, 2, 4, 8, 16, 32 ...

Have students make a geometric progression using the following rule:

Choose a number between 1 and 5 for the first value of x and choose another number between 2 and 5 for r. Multiply x by r to get the first value of y. Use this value of y as the next value of x. Multiply by r again to get the next value of y.

Have them write the geometric expression and determine if it is a linear relationship.

Sample answer: 2, 6, 18, 54, 162, 486....; yes, it is linear.

Proportional and Nonproportional Situations **384**

Ready to Go On?

Assess Mastery

Use the assessment on this page to determine if students have mastered the concepts and standards covered in this module.

 **RtI** Response to Intervention

Personal Math Trainer
Online Assessment and Intervention
🕐 my.hrw.com

Access *Ready to Go On?* assessment online, and receive instant scoring, feedback, and customized intervention or enrichment.

Intervention	Enrichment

Online and Print Resources

Differentiated Instruction
• Reteach worksheets
• Reading Strategies **ELL**
• Success for English Learners **ELL**

Differentiated Instruction
• Challenge worksheets **PRE-AP**
• Extend the Math **PRE-AP** Lesson Activities in TE

Additional Resources

Assessment Resources includes:
• Leveled Module Quizzes

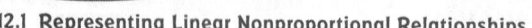

Ready to Go On?

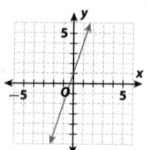
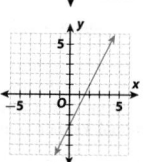

Personal Math Trainer
Online Assessment and Intervention
🕐 my.hrw.com

12.1 Representing Linear Nonproportional Relationships

1. Complete the table using the equation $y = 3x + 2$.

x	−1	0	1	2	3
y	−1	2	5	8	11

12.2 Determining Slope and *y*-intercept

2. Find the slope and *y*-intercept of the line in the graph.

slope: 3; *y*-intercept: 1

12.3 Graphing Linear Nonproportional Relationships

3. Graph the equation $y = 2x - 3$ using slope and *y*-intercept.

12.4 Proportional and Nonproportional Situations

4. Does the table represent a proportional or a nonproportional linear relationship?

x	1	2	3	4	5
y	4	8	12	16	20

proportional

5. Does the graph in Exercise 2 represent a proportional or a nonproportional linear relationship?

nonproportional

6. Does the graph in Exercise 3 represent a proportional or a nonproportional relationship?

nonproportional

 **ESSENTIAL QUESTION**

7. How can you identify a linear nonproportional relationship from a table, a graph, and an equation?

Table: for an ordered pair (0, *y*), *y* will not be 0; graph: the *y*-intercept will not be 0; equation: it will have the form $y = mx + b$ where $b \neq 0$.

Module 12 **385**

 ## Florida Common Core Standards

Lesson	Exercises	🏴 Common Core Standards
12.1	1	**8.F.1.3**
12.2	2	**8.EE.2.6, 8.F.2.4**
12.3	3	**8.F.1.3, 8.F.2.4**
12.4	4–6	**8.F.1.2**

PARCC Assessment Readiness

Assessment Readiness Tip Point out that students can create a different representation of a linear relationship if it makes them more comfortable or if it could help in solving the problem.

Item 1 If students plot the points given in the table and sketch the graph, it will be clear that the slope is positive. With this information, the only possible answer is C.

Item 2 If students are more comfortable finding an equation from a table than from a graph, encourage them to create a table using three or four points from the graph.

Avoid Common Errors

Item 4 Note that even though answer A is in $y = mx + b$ form, $b = 0$ and the point $(0, 0)$ satisfies the equation, so the relationship must be proportional. Point out that $y = 3x$ is an equivalent form of this equation.

Item 6 Remind students that the exponent reflects the number of decimal places that the decimal point must move to be to the right of the first nonzero digit. The exponent is not equal to the number of zeros to the right of the decimal point in the standard notation form.

Additional Resources

Personal Math Trainer

Online Assessment and Intervention

my.hrw.com

MODULE 12 MIXED REVIEW

PARCC Assessment Readiness

Personal Math Trainer

Online Assessment and Intervention

my.hrw.com

Selected Response

1. The table below represents which equation?

x	−1	0	1	2
y	−10	−6	−2	2

Ⓐ $y = -x - 10$ Ⓒ $y = 4x - 6$
Ⓑ $y = -6x$ Ⓓ $y = -4x + 2$

2. The graph of which equation is shown below?

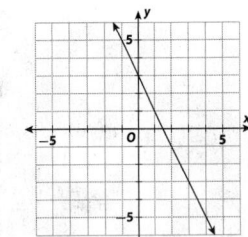

Ⓐ $y = -2x + 3$ Ⓒ $y = 2x + 3$
Ⓑ $y = -2x + 1.5$ Ⓓ $y = 2x + 1.5$

3. The table below represents a linear relationship.

x	2	3	4	5
y	4	7	10	13

What is the y-intercept?

Ⓐ −4 Ⓒ 2
Ⓑ −2 Ⓓ 3

4. Which equation represents a nonproportional relationship?

Ⓐ $y = 3x + 0$ Ⓒ $y = 3x + 5$
Ⓑ $y = -3x$ Ⓓ $y = \frac{1}{3}x$

5. The table shows a proportional relationship. What is the missing y-value?

x	4	10	12
y	6	15	?

Ⓐ 16 Ⓒ 18
Ⓑ 20 Ⓓ 24

6. What is 0.00000598 written in scientific notation?

Ⓐ 5.98×10^{-6} Ⓒ 59.8×10^{-6}
Ⓑ 5.98×10^{-5} Ⓓ 59.8×10^{-7}

Mini-Task

7. The graph shows a linear relationship.

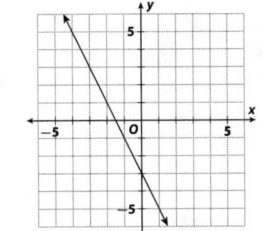

a. Is the relationship proportional or nonproportional?

nonproportional

b. What is the slope of the line?

−2

c. What is the y-intercept of the line?

−3

d. What is the equation of the line?

$y = -2x - 3$

 Florida Common Core Standards

Items	Grade 8 Standards	Mathematical Practices
1	8.F.2.4	MP.4.1
2	8.F.2.4	MP.4.1
3	8.F.2.4	MP.2.1
4	8.EE.2.6	MP.7.1
5	8.F.2.4	MP.2.1
6*	8.EE.1.4	
7	8.EE.2.6, 8.F.2.4	MP.2.1, MP.4.1

* Item integrates mixed review concepts from previous modules or a previous course.

Writing Linear Equations

**ESSENTIAL QUESTION**

How can you use linear equations to solve real-world problems?

You can use linear equations and their graphs to model real-world relationships involving constant rates of change.

LESSON 13.1

Writing Linear Equations from Situations and Graphs

FL CC 8.F.2.4

LESSON 13.2

Writing Linear Equations from a Table

FL CC 8.F.2.4

LESSON 13.3

Linear Relationships and Bivariate Data

FL CC 8.SP.1.1, 8.SP.1.2, 8.SP.1.3

Real-World Video

Linear equations can be used to describe many situations related to shopping. If a store advertised four books for $32.00, you could write and solve a linear equation to find the price of each book.

my.hrw.com

GO DIGITAL

my.hrw.com

my.hrw.com

Go digital with your write-in student edition, accessible on any device.

Math On the Spot

Scan with your smart phone to jump directly to the online edition, video tutor, and more.

Animated Math

Interactively explore key concepts to see how math works.

Personal Math Trainer

Get immediate feedback and help as you work through practice sets.

© Houghton Mifflin Harcourt Publishing Company • Image Credits: ©Yellow Dog Productions/Getty Images

Are You Ready?

Assess Readiness

Use the assessment on this page to determine if students need intensive or strategic intervention for the module's prerequisite skills.

 **RtI** **Response to Intervention**

Intervention	Enrichment

Access Are You Ready? assessment online, and receive instant scoring, feedback, and customized intervention or enrichment.

Personal Math Trainer
Online Assessment and Intervention
⏻ my.hrw.com

Online and Print Resources

Skills Intervention worksheets
- Skill 26 Write Fractions as Decimals
- Skill 57 Inverse Operations

Differentiated Instruction
- Challenge worksheets **PRE-AP**
- Extend the Math **PRE-AP** Lesson Activities in TE

Are YOU Ready?

Complete these exercises to review skills you will need for this module.

 Personal Math Trainer Online Assessment and Intervention — ⏻ my.hrw.com

Write Fractions as Decimals

EXAMPLE $\frac{0.5}{0.8} = ?$

Multiply the numerator and the denominator by a power of 10 so that the denominator is a whole number.

$\frac{0.5 \times 10}{0.8 \times 10} = \frac{5}{8}$

Write the fraction as a division problem.
Write a decimal point and zeros in the dividend.
Place a decimal point in the quotient.
Divide as with whole numbers.

```
    0.625
8 ) 5.000
   -48
     20
    -16
     40
    -40
      0
```

Write each fraction as a decimal.

1. $\frac{3}{8}$ ___0.375___
2. $\frac{0.3}{0.4}$ ___0.75___
3. $\frac{0.13}{0.2}$ ___0.65___
4. $\frac{0.39}{0.75}$ ___0.52___

Inverse Operations

EXAMPLE

$5n = 20$
$\frac{5n}{5} = \frac{20}{5}$
$n = 4$

n is multiplied by 5.
To solve the equation, use the inverse operation, division.

$k + 7 = 9$
$k + 7 - 7 = 9 - 7$
$k = 2$

7 is added to k.
To solve the equation, use the inverse operation, subtraction.

Solve each equation using the inverse operation.

5. $7p = 28$ ___$p = 4$___
6. $h - 13 = 5$ ___$h = 18$___
7. $\frac{y}{3} = -6$ ___$y = -18$___
8. $b + 9 = 21$ ___$b = 12$___
9. $c - 8 = -8$ ___$c = 0$___
10. $3n = -12$ ___$n = -4$___
11. $-16 = m + 7$ ___$m = -23$___
12. $\frac{t}{-5} = -5$ ___$t = 25$___

© Houghton Mifflin Harcourt Publishing Company

PROFESSIONAL DEVELOPMENT VIDEO

 Author Juli Dixon models successful teaching practices as she explores the concept of writing linear equations in an actual eighth-grade classroom.

 **Professional Development** — ⏻ my.hrw.com

GO DIGITAL
my.hrw.com

 Online Teacher Edition
Access a full suite of teaching resources online—plan, present, and manage classes and assignments.

 ePlanner
Easily plan your classes and access all your resources online.

Interactive Answers and Solutions
Customize answer keys to print or display in the classroom. Choose to include answers only or full solutions to all lesson exercises.

Interactive Whiteboards
Engage students with interactive whiteboard-ready lessons and activities.

Personal Math Trainer: Online Assessment and Intervention
Assign automatically graded homework, quizzes, tests, and intervention activities. Prepare your students with updated practice tests aligned with Common Core.

Writing Linear Equations **388**

Reading Start-Up

Have students complete the activities on this page by working alone or with others.

Visualize Vocabulary

The concept web helps students review vocabulary associated with linear relationships. In each bubble, students should write one or more words associated with the linear equation $y = mx + b$.

Understand Vocabulary

Use the following explanations to help students learn the preview words.

Some relationships are **nonlinear relationships.** *Nonlinear* means "not in the shape of a line." In nonlinear relationships, the rate of change is not constant. Graphs that represent nonlinear relationships will not be lines.

Many real-world situations have nonlinear relationships. For example, the growth of a plant is usually not a linear relationship because plants do not grow the same amount every day.

Active Reading

Integrating Language Arts

Students can use these reading and note-taking strategies to help them organize and understand new concepts and vocabulary.

FL CC LACC.68.RST.3.7 Integrate quantitative or technical information expressed in words in a text with a version of that information expressed visually (e.g., in a flowchart, diagram, model, graph, or table).

Additional Resources

Differentiated Instruction

• Reading Strategies **ELL**

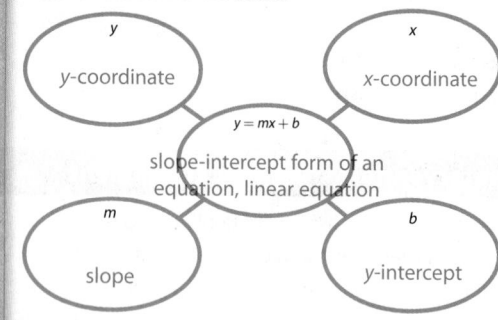

Reading Start-Up

Visualize Vocabulary

Use the ✔ words to complete the diagram. You can put more than one word in each bubble.

- y — *y-coordinate*
- x — *x-coordinate*
- $y = mx + b$ — slope-intercept form of an equation, linear equation
- m — slope
- b — y-intercept

Vocabulary

Review Words
✔ linear equation *(ecuación lineal)*
  ordered pair *(par ordenado)*
  proportional relationship *(relación proporcional)*
  rate of change *(tasa de cambio)*
✔ slope *(pendiente)*
✔ slope-intercept form of an equation *(forma de pendiente-intersección)*
✔ x-coordinate *(coordenada x)*
✔ y-coordinate *(coordenada y)*
✔ y-intercept *(intersección con el eje y)*

Preview Words
  bivariate data *(datos bivariados)*
  nonlinear relationship *(relación no lineal)*

Understand Vocabulary

Complete the sentences using the preview words.

1. A set of data that is made up of two paired variables is ____bivariate data____.

2. When the rate of change varies from point to point, the relationship is a ____nonlinear relationship____.

Active Reading

Tri-Fold Before beginning the module, create a tri-fold to help you learn the concepts and vocabulary in this module. Fold the paper into three sections. Label the columns "What I Know," "What I Need to Know," and "What I Learned." Complete the first two columns before you read. After studying the module, complete the third column.

Before	In this module	After
Students understand proportional and linear relationships: • use tables and verbal descriptions to describe a linear relationship • write and graph a linear relationship	Students represent and use linear relationships: • write an equation in the form $y = mx + b$ to model a linear relationship between two quantities using verbal, numerical, tabular, and graphical representations • contrast bivariate sets of data that suggest a linear relationship with bivariate sets of data that do not suggest a linear relationship from a graphical representation	Students will connect that: • there are various forms of linear equations • in nonlinear relationships, the rate of change can vary from point to point

Unpacking the Standards

Use the examples on this page to help students know exactly what they are expected to learn in this module.

 Florida Common Core Standards

Content Areas

 **FL CC** Functions—8.F.2

Use functions to model relationships between quantities.

 FL CC Statistics and Probability—8.SP.1

Investigate patterns of association in bivariate data.

Go online to see a complete unpacking of the Florida Common Core Standards.

⏻ my.hrw.com

MODULE 13

Unpacking the Standards

Understanding the standards and the vocabulary terms in the standards will help you know exactly what you are expected to learn in this module.

FL CC 8.F.2.4

Construct a function to model a linear relationship between two quantities. Determine the rate of change and initial value of the function from a description of a relationship.... Interpret the rate of change and initial value of a linear function in terms of the situation it models, and in terms of its graph or a table of values.

Key Vocabulary
rate of change *(tasa de cambio)*
A ratio that compares the amount of change in a dependent variable to the amount of change in an independent variable.

What It Means to You

You will learn how to write an equation based on a situation that models a linear relationship.

UNPACKING EXAMPLE 8.F.2.4

In 2006 the fare for a taxicab was an initial charge of $2.50 plus $0.30 per mile. Write an equation in slope-intercept form that can be used to calculate the total fare.

The constant charge is $2.50.
The rate of change is $0.30 per mile.

The input variable, x, is the number of miles driven.
So $0.3x$ is the cost for the miles driven.

The equation for the total fare, y, is as follows:

$y = 0.3x + 2.5$

FL CC 8.SP.1.3

Use the equation of a linear model to solve problems in the context of bivariate measurement data, interpreting the slope and intercept.

Key Vocabulary
bivariate data *(datos bivariados)*
A set of data that is made up of two paired variables.

Visit my.hrw.com to see all Florida Common Core Standards unpacked.

⏻ my.hrw.com

What It Means to You

You will see how to use a linear relationship between sets of data to make predictions.

UNPACKING EXAMPLE 8.SP.1.3

The graph shows the temperatures in degrees Celsius inside the earth at certain depths in kilometers. Use the graph to write an equation and find the temperature at a depth of 12 km.

The initial temperature is 20°C.
It increases at a rate of 10°C/km.

The equation is $t = 10d + 20$.
At a depth of 12 km, the temperature is 140°C.

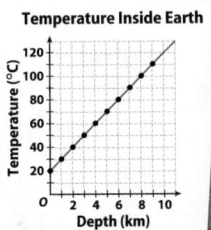
Temperature Inside Earth

390 Unit 6

Florida Common Core Standards	Lesson 13.1	Lesson 13.2	Lesson 13.3
FL CC 8.F.2.4 Construct a function to model a linear relationship between two quantities. Determine the rate of change and initial value of the function from a description of a relationship or from two (x, y) values, including reading these from a table or from a graph. Interpret the rate of change and initial value	🏴	🏴	
FL CC 8.SP.1.1 Construct and interpret scatter plots for bivariate measurement data to investigate patterns of association between two quantities. Describe patterns such as clustering, outliers, positive or negative association, linear association, and nonlinear association.			🏴
FL CC 8.SP.1.2 ... For scatter plots that suggest a linear association, informally fit a straight line, ...			🏴
FL CC 8.SP.1.3 Use the equation of a linear model to solve problems in the context of bivariate measurement data, interpreting the slope and intercept.			🏴

LESSON 13.1
Writing Linear Equations from Situations and Graphs

Florida Common Core Standards

The student is expected to:

 **Functions—8.F.2.4**

Construct a function to model a linear relationship between two quantities. Determine the rate of change and initial value of the function from a description of a relationship or from two (x, y) values, including reading these from a table or from a graph. Interpret the rate of change and initial value of a linear function in terms of the situation it models, and in terms of its graph or a table of values.

Mathematical Practices

 **MP.2.1** Reasoning

ADDITIONAL EXAMPLE 1
A DJ charges a setup fee plus an hourly fee to provide music for a dance party. Use the graph to write an equation in slope-intercept form to represent the amount spent, y, on x hours of music.

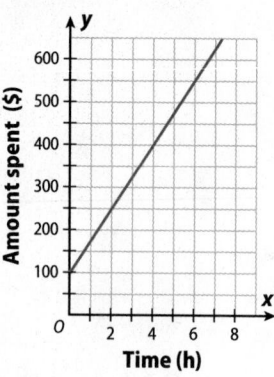

$y = 75x + 100$

 **Interactive Whiteboard**
Interactive example available online

my.hrw.com

Engage

ESSENTIAL QUESTION
How do you write an equation to model a linear relationship given a graph or a description? Use pairs of values for input and output to determine the values for the slope m and the y-intercept b in the equation $y = mx + b$.

Motivate the Lesson
Ask: How can you figure out the total cost for different plans for your cell phone when the fees and charges are not the same? What choices have you made that involved comparing memberships or rentals? The Explore Activity shows how to write an equation to help you evaluate and compare costs.

Explore

EXPLORE ACTIVITY
Connect Vocabulary [ELL]
Explain the terms *potter's wheel* (a rotating disk used for shaping clay) and *kiln* (an oven for baking or drying clay or pottery). Ask if any students have worked with clay. Any such students may be able to explain these terms to the class.

Explain

EXAMPLE 1
Questioning Strategies ⬥ Mathematical Practices
• Why do you think that the points (0, 8) and (8, 18) were used to find the slope? Sample answer: These two points clearly lie at the intersection of vertical and horizontal grid lines. You can't be sure of the values of y for the other points on the line.

• Describe the new graph if the membership fee were changed to $10. The y-intercept moves up to (0, 10); the slope stays the same.

Engage with the Whiteboard
Draw arrows showing the rise and run between the two points (0, 8) and (8, 18) on the graph. Ask students what the y-intercept, rise, and run represent in terms of the membership fee and rental fee.

YOUR TURN
Avoid Common Errors
Students may be confused about which axis is which and about the meaning of the y-intercept. Verify that they understand that the x-value is zero at the y-intercept, and that the y-intercept is the y-value of the point where the graph crosses the y-axis.

Writing Linear Equations from Situations and Graphs

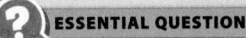 FL CC 8.F.2.4

Construct a function to model a linear relationship between two quantities. Determine the rate of change and initial value.... Interpret the rate of change and initial value....

? ESSENTIAL QUESTION

How do you write an equation to model a linear relationship given a graph or a description?

EXPLORE ACTIVITY Real World

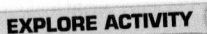  FL CC 8.F.2.4

Writing an Equation in Slope-Intercept Form

Greta makes clay mugs and bowls as gifts at the Crafty Studio. She pays a membership fee of $15 a month and an equipment fee of $3.00 an hour to use the potter's wheel, table, and kiln. Write an equation in the form $y = mx + b$ that Greta can use to calculate her monthly costs.

A What is the input variable, x, for this situation?
the number of hours Greta uses the studio

What is the output variable, y, for this situation?
the money Greta pays the studio each month

Math Talk
Mathematical Practices
What change could the studio make that would make a difference to the y-intercept of the equation?

B During April, Greta does not use the equipment at all. What will be her number of hours (x) for April? ____0____

What will be her cost (y) for April? ____$15____

What will be the y-intercept, b, in the equation? ____15____

Changing the membership fee changes the y-intercept.

C Greta spends 8 hours in May for a cost of $15 + 8($3) = ____$39____.

In June, she spends 11 hours for a cost of ____$48____.

From May to June, the change in x-values is ____+3____.

From May to June, the change in y-values is ____+9____.

What will be the slope, m, in the equation? ____3____

D Use the values for m and b to write an equation for Greta's costs in the form $y = mx + b$: ____$y = 3x + 15$____

Writing an Equation from a Graph

You can use information presented in a graph to write an equation in slope-intercept form.

Math On the Spot
my.hrw.com

EXAMPLE 1 Real World

 FL CC 8.F.2.4

A video club charges a one-time membership fee plus a rental fee for each DVD borrowed. Use the graph to write an equation in slope-intercept form to represent the amount spent, y, on x DVD rentals.

STEP 1 Choose two points on the graph to find the slope.

$m = \dfrac{y_2 - y_1}{x_2 - x_1}$ Use the slope formula.

$m = \dfrac{18 - 8}{8 - 0}$ Substitute (0, 8) for (x_1, y_1) and (8,18) for (x_2, y_2).

$m = \dfrac{10}{8} = 1.25$ Simplify.

Math Talk
Mathematical Practices
If the graph of an equation is a line that goes through the origin, what is the value of the y-intercept?

The value of the y-intercept is zero.

STEP 2 Read the y-intercept from the graph.

The y-intercept is 8.

STEP 3 Use your slope and y-intercept values to write an equation in slope-intercept form.

$y = mx + b$ Slope-intercept form

$y = 1.25x + 8$ Substitute 1.25 for m and 8 for y.

Reflect

1. What does the value of the slope represent in this context?
cost per DVD rental

2. Describe the meaning of the y-intercept.
amount spent for 0 rentals, or the membership fee of $8

YOUR TURN

Personal Math Trainer
Online Assessment and Intervention
my.hrw.com

3. The cash register subtracts $2.50 from a $25 Coffee Café gift card for every medium coffee the customer buys. Use the graph to write an equation in slope-intercept form to represent this situation.
$y = -2.5x + 25$

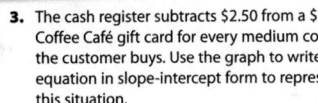
Amount on Gift Card

PROFESSIONAL DEVELOPMENT

Integrate Mathematical Practices MP.2.1

This lesson provides an opportunity to address this Mathematical Practices standard. It calls for students to represent a situation symbolically. Students read values from a graph and create a new representation of the linear relationship in the form of an equation.

Math Background

A constant rate of change can be shown by a linear graph. The rate of change is the slope of the line. Lines with positive slopes rise from left to right; lines with negative slopes go down.

The *magnitude* of the slope describes the steepness. The line $y = x$ makes a 45° angle with the x-axis and has a slope of 1. A line with a slope whose absolute value is between 0 and 1 is less steep than a 45° line. A line whose absolute value of the slope is greater than 1 is steeper than a 45° line.

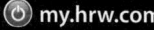
EXAMPLE 2

Questioning Strategies ⬏ Mathematical Practices

- What does the rise over the run, or the slope, represent in the problem situation? change in rent over change in square feet, or rent per square foot
- If the equation for the rent were $y = \frac{4}{3}x + 25$, how would this change the rent? The rent would be $75 more for any number of square feet.

Focus on Critical Thinking

In Example 2, one student wrote this equation for the slope: $m = \frac{1150 - 750}{600 - 900}$. Explain what error was made in this equation. The coordinates for the points must be in the same order in the numerator and in the denominator.

YOUR TURN

Focus on Modeling ⬏ Mathematical Practices

Make sure that students understand that the number of chores Hari chooses to do is the independent, or input, variable, and the allowance he receives is the dependent, or output, variable.

Integrating Language Arts ⬛ELL

Encourage English learners to take notes on new terms or concepts and to write them in familiar language.

Elaborate

. . . .

Talk About It
Summarize the Lesson

💬 **Ask:** In a linear relationship represented by $y = mx + b$, how do you find m, the value for the constant rate of change, and the y-intercept, b? Use two sets of x- and y-values to find m, the change in y over the change in x. Then substitute m, x, and y in $y = mx + b$ and solve to find b.

GUIDED PRACTICE

Engage with the Whiteboard

🖊 For Exercise 2, have two students label the graph with the coordinates of the two different points they choose to find the slope. Emphasize that using *any* two points on the line will result in the same slope.

Avoid Common Errors

Exercise 2 Ask students to predict whether the slope will be positive or negative before they do any calculations, and to explain their answer before finding the slope. Students may enter y_1 and y_2 in a different order than x_1 and x_2 and get the opposite slope.

Exercise 3 Students may use the wrong independent variable. Have them consider whether temperature is dependent upon chirps or chirps dependent upon temperature.

Writing an Equation from a Description

You can use information from a description of a linear relationship to find the slope and y-intercept and to write an equation.

EXAMPLE 2 **FL CC 8.F.2.4**

The rent charged for space in an office building is a linear relationship related to the size of the space rented. Write an equation in slope-intercept form for the rent at West Main Street Office Rentals.

West Main St. Office Rentals
Offices for rent at convenient locations.
Monthly Rates:
600 square feet for **$750**
900 square feet for **$1150**

STEP 1 Identify the input and output variables.

The input variable is the square footage of floor space.

The output variable is the monthly rent.

STEP 2 Write the information given in the problem as ordered pairs.

The rent for 600 square feet of floor space is $750: (600, 750)

The rent for 900 square feet of floor space is $1150: (900, 1150)

STEP 3 Find the slope.

$$m = \frac{y_2 - y_1}{x_2 - x_1} = \frac{1150 - 750}{900 - 600} = \frac{400}{300} = \frac{4}{3}$$

STEP 4 Find the y-intercept. Use the slope and one of the ordered pairs.

$y = mx + b$	Slope-intercept form
$750 = \frac{4}{3} \cdot 600 + b$	Substitute for y, m, and x.
$750 = 800 + b$	Multiply.
$-50 = b$	Subtract 800 from both sides.

STEP 5 Substitute the slope and y-intercept.

$y = mx + b$	Slope-intercept form
$y = \frac{4}{3}x - 50$	Substitute $\frac{4}{3}$ for m and −50 for b.

Reflect

4. Without graphing, tell whether the graph of this equation rises or falls from left to right. What does the sign of the slope mean in this context?

Slope is positive, so the graph rises from left to right.

This means that the rent increases as the square

footage increases.

Math On the Spot
 my.hrw.com

My Notes

Personal Math Trainer
Online Assessment and Intervention
my.hrw.com

YOUR TURN

5. Hari's weekly allowance varies depending on the number of chores he does. He received $16 in allowance the week he did 12 chores, and $14 in allowance the week he did 8 chores. Write an equation for his allowance in slope-intercept form. $y = 0.5x + 10$

Guided Practice

1. Li is making beaded necklaces. For each necklace, she uses 27 spacers, plus 5 beads per inch of necklace length. Write an equation to find how many beads Li needs for each necklace. (Explore Activity)

   a. input variable: the length of the necklace in inches

   b. output variable: the total number of beads in the necklace

   c. equation: $y = 5x + 27$

2. Kate is planning a trip to the beach. She estimates her average speed to graph her expected progress on the trip. Write an equation in slope-intercept form that represents the situation. (Example 1)

Choose two points on the graph to find the slope.

$$m = \frac{y_2 - y_1}{x_2 - x_1} = \frac{0 - 300}{5 - 0} = \frac{-300}{5} = -60$$

Read the y-intercept from the graph: $b = 300$

Use your slope and y-intercept values to write an equation in slope-intercept form. $y = -60x + 300$

3. At 59 °F, crickets chirp at a rate of 76 times per minute, and at 65 °F, they chirp 100 times per minute. Write an equation in slope-intercept form that represents the situation. (Example 2)

Input variable: temperature   Output variable: chirps per minute

$$m = \frac{y_2 - y_1}{x_2 - x_1} = \frac{100 - 76}{65 - 59} = \frac{24}{6} = 4$$

Substitute in $y = mx + b$: $100 = 4 \cdot 65 + b$; $-160 = b$

Write an equation in slope-intercept form. $y = 4x - 160$

? ESSENTIAL QUESTION CHECK-IN

4. Explain what m and b in the equation $y = mx + b$ tell you about the graph of the line with that equation.

The slope of the graphed line is m, and the y-intercept is b.

DIFFERENTIATE INSTRUCTION

Multiple Representations

Have students discuss the different ways they know to describe the slope of a line. Have them write a list, such as this: rise over run, change in y over change in x, $\frac{y_2 - y_1}{x_2 - x_1}$, slope, constant rate of change. Have them sketch a line that has a positive slope, another with a negative slope, and a line with a slope of zero (horizontal), and a line with an undefined slope (vertical).

Visual Cues

Draw a linear graph and mark two points on it in red. Then, on the same graph, mark two different points on it in blue. Ask students to discuss whether the slope of the line will be greater between the two red points or between the two blue points. Lead them to see that the slope of a given linear graph is always the same between any two points on the line.

Additional Resources

Differentiated Instruction includes:
- Reading Strategies
- Success for English Learners **ELL**
- Reteach
- Challenge **PRE-AP**

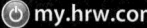

13.1 LESSON QUIZ

FL CC 8.F.2.4

1. Lee charges $3 for a basket and $2.50 for each pound of fruit picked at the orchard. Write an equation in $y = mx + b$ form for the total cost of x pounds of fruit from the orchard.

2. A camp charges families a fee of $625 per month for one child and a certain amount more per month for each additional child. Use the graph to write an equation in slope-intercept form to represent the amount a family with x additional children would pay.

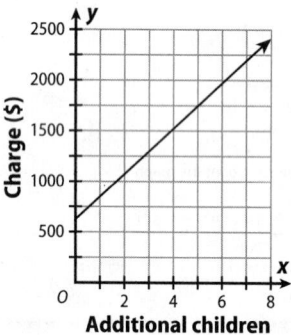

3. Identify the y-intercept in question **2** above. Tell what the y-intercept means in this context.

4. A driving range charges $4 to rent a golf club plus $2.75 for every bucket of golf balls you hit. Write an equation that shows the total cost c of hitting b buckets of golf balls.

Lesson Quiz available online

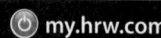 my.hrw.com

Answers

1. $y = 2.50x + 3$

2. $y = 225x + 625$

3. $b = 625$, the fixed fee for one child

4. $c = 2.75b + 4$

Evaluate

GUIDED AND INDEPENDENT PRACTICE

 **FL CC** 8.F.2.4

Concepts & Skills	Practice
Explore Activity Writing an Equation in Slope-Intercept Form	Exercise 1
Example 1 Writing an Equation from a Graph	Exercises 2, 7–9, 12–15
Example 2 Writing an Equation from a Description	Exercises 3, 5–6, 10–11

Exercise	Depth of Knowledge (D.O.K.)	**FL CC** Mathematical Practices
5–6	**2** Skills/Concepts	**MP.4.1** Modeling
7–9	**2** Skills/Concepts	**MP.6.1** Precision
10–11	**2** Skills/Concepts	**MP.4.1** Modeling
12–15	**2** Skills/Concepts	**MP.2.1** Reasoning
16–18	**3** Strategic Thinking **H.O.T.**	**MP.3.1** Logic

Additional Resources

Differentiated Instruction includes:

• Leveled Practice worksheets

13.1 Independent Practice

FL CC 8.F.2.4

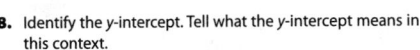

5. A dragonfly can beat its wings 30 times per second. Write an equation in slope-intercept form that shows the relationship between flying time in seconds and the number of times the dragonfly beats its wings.

$$y = 30x$$

6. A balloon is released from the top of a platform that is 50 meters tall. The balloon rises at the rate of 4 meters per second. Write an equation in slope-intercept form that tells the height of the balloon above the ground after a given number of seconds.

$$y = 4x + 50$$

The graph shows a scuba diver's ascent over time.

Scuba Diver's Ascent

7. Use the graph to find the slope of the line. Tell what the slope means in this context.

$m = 0.125$; the diver ascends at a rate of 0.125 m/s

8. Identify the y-intercept. Tell what the y-intercept means in this context.

-10; the diver starts 10 meters below the water's surface.

9. Write an equation in slope-intercept form that represents the diver's depth over time.

$$y = 0.125x - 10$$

10. The formula for converting Celsius temperatures to Fahrenheit temperatures is a linear equation. Water freezes at 0 °C, or 32 °F, and it boils at 100 °C, or 212 °F. Find the slope and y-intercept for a graph that gives degrees Celsius on the horizontal axis and degrees Fahrenheit on the vertical axis. Then write an equation in slope-intercept form that converts degrees Celsius into degrees Fahrenheit.

$m = \frac{9}{5}$; $b = 32$; $y = \frac{9}{5}x + 32$ where $y =$ °F and $x =$ °C

11. The cost of renting a sailboat at a lake is $20 per hour plus $12 for lifejackets. Write an equation in slope-intercept form that can be used to calculate the total amount you would pay for using this sailboat.

$$y = 20x + 12$$

The graph shows the activity in a savings account.

12. What was the amount of the initial deposit that started this savings account?

$1000

13. Find the slope and y-intercept of the graphed line.

$m = 500$; $b = 1000$

14. Write an equation in slope-intercept form for the activity in this savings account.

$$y = 500x + 1000$$

15. Explain the meaning of the slope in this graph.

The amount of money in the savings account increases by $500 each month.

H.O.T. FOCUS ON HIGHER ORDER THINKING

Work Area

16. Communicate Mathematical Ideas Explain how you decide which part of a problem will be represented by the variable x, and which part will be represented by the variable y in a graph of the situation.

Examine the problem and decide what quantity you start with, or the input, and what quantity you are trying to find, or the output. Use the input quantity for x and the output quantity for y.

17. Represent Real-World Problems Describe what would be true about the rate of change in a situation that could *not* be represented by a graphed line and an equation in the form $y = mx + b$.

The rate of change would not be constant. Using different pairs of points in the slope formula would give you different results.

18. Draw Conclusions Must m, in the equation $y = mx + b$, always be a positive number? Explain.

No. A negative number for m means the dependent variable is decreasing as the independent variable increases, so the graph falls from left to right.

EXTEND THE MATH PRE-AP

Activity available online my.hrw.com

Activity Give each pair of students a sheet of graph paper marked with the x- and y-axes, and pencils or pieces of wire or spaghetti to use for the lines to make quick graphs. One student calls out a slope (for example, $m = 0$ or 1, or 0.5, or 5, or -1) and the other places the line on the graph in the approximate position going through the origin, (for example: horizontal, bisecting QI, less steep than $y = x$, steeper than $y = x$, or bisecting QII).

Then have one student call out a slope and a y-intercept and the other place the line. If students have trouble, have them place a line with the same slope through the origin and then move it to go through the y-intercept.

13.2 Writing Linear Equations from a Table

 Florida Common Core Standards

The student is expected to:

 **Functions—8.F.2.4**

Construct a function to model a linear relationship between two quantities. Determine the rate of change and initial value of the function from a description of a relationship or from two (x, y) values, including reading these from a table or from a graph. Interpret the rate of change and initial value of a linear function in terms of the situation it models, and in terms of its graph or a table of values.

Mathematical Practices

 **MP.4.1** Modeling

---

ADDITIONAL EXAMPLE 1
The Dailey family uses maple sap to make syrup. The table shows the temperature of the sap as it heats. Graph the data, and find the slope and y-intercept from the graph. Then write the equation for the graph in slope-intercept form.

Time (h)	0	1	2	3	4
Temp (°F)	38	83	128	173	218

Syrup Temperature

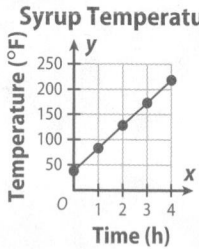

$$°F = 45h + 38$$

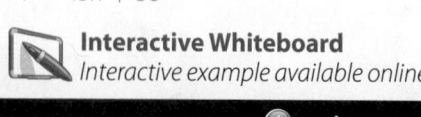 **Interactive Whiteboard**
Interactive example available online

⊙ my.hrw.com

Engage

ESSENTIAL QUESTION

How do you write an equation to model a linear relationship given a table? Use pairs of input and output values to determine the slope m and the y-intercept b in the equation $y = mx + b$.

Motivate the Lesson
Ask: Have you ever recorded measurements in a table? Tables are often used in science labs to record temperatures, weights, and other measures. Graphing the information in a table provides another way to look at the data.

Explore

Have a student provide a number between 10 and 20. Then have students make a table with integer x-values from 1 through 10. Fill in the y-values so that x and y for each column add to the selected number. Ask students to write an equation for the relationship.

Explain

EXAMPLE 1

Questioning Strategies 🏳 Mathematical Practices

• Describe informally what is happening in this experiment. The temperature of a fish tank is measured at the beginning as 82 degrees Fahrenheit. This temperature gradually falls over 5 hours at a steady rate until it reaches 72 degrees Fahrenheit.

• Could you find the equation from the table without drawing a graph? Explain. Yes; choose two points from the table to find the slope, and use (0, 82) to find the y-intercept.

Engage with the Whiteboard

Have students draw lines to extend the x-axis and the graphed line. Where will the line meet the x-axis if the rate of cooling stays the same? Students should check their prediction by substituting 0 for y in the equation and solving for x (41 h).

YOUR TURN

Avoid Common Errors
Remind students to refer to the slope formula on the previous page when calculating the slope. They should write out the formula and substitute the coordinates of two points.

EXAMPLE 2

Questioning Strategies 🏳 Mathematical Practices

• How can you find the y-intercept when it is not given as one of the points in the table? Substitute m and any point in the table as (x, y) to solve for b in $y = mx + b$.

• What does the y-intercept represent in this situation? the base price without minutes

Writing Linear Equations from a Table

FL CC 8.F.2.4
Construct a function to model a linear relationship between two quantities. Determine the rate of change and initial value.... Interpret the rate of change and initial value....

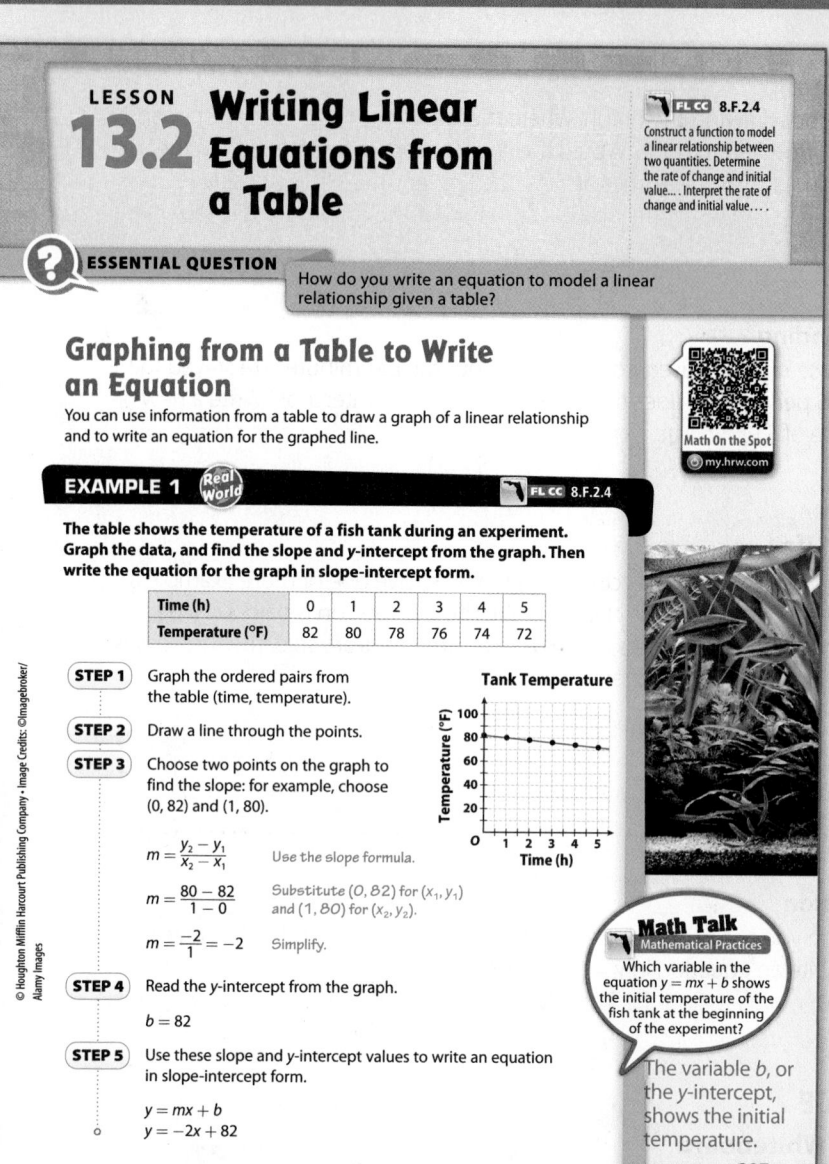

? ESSENTIAL QUESTION
How do you write an equation to model a linear relationship given a table?

Graphing from a Table to Write an Equation

You can use information from a table to draw a graph of a linear relationship and to write an equation for the graphed line.

Math On the Spot
my.hrw.com

EXAMPLE 1 Real World
FL CC 8.F.2.4

The table shows the temperature of a fish tank during an experiment. Graph the data, and find the slope and y-intercept from the graph. Then write the equation for the graph in slope-intercept form.

Time (h)	0	1	2	3	4	5
Temperature (°F)	82	80	78	76	74	72

STEP 1 Graph the ordered pairs from the table (time, temperature).

STEP 2 Draw a line through the points.

STEP 3 Choose two points on the graph to find the slope: for example, choose (0, 82) and (1, 80).

$m = \dfrac{y_2 - y_1}{x_2 - x_1}$ Use the slope formula.

$m = \dfrac{80 - 82}{1 - 0}$ Substitute (0, 82) for (x_1, y_1) and (1, 80) for (x_2, y_2).

$m = \dfrac{-2}{1} = -2$ Simplify.

STEP 4 Read the y-intercept from the graph.

$b = 82$

STEP 5 Use these slope and y-intercept values to write an equation in slope-intercept form.

$y = mx + b$
$y = -2x + 82$

Math Talk
Mathematical Practices
Which variable in the equation $y = mx + b$ shows the initial temperature of the fish tank at the beginning of the experiment?

The variable b, or the y-intercept, shows the initial temperature.

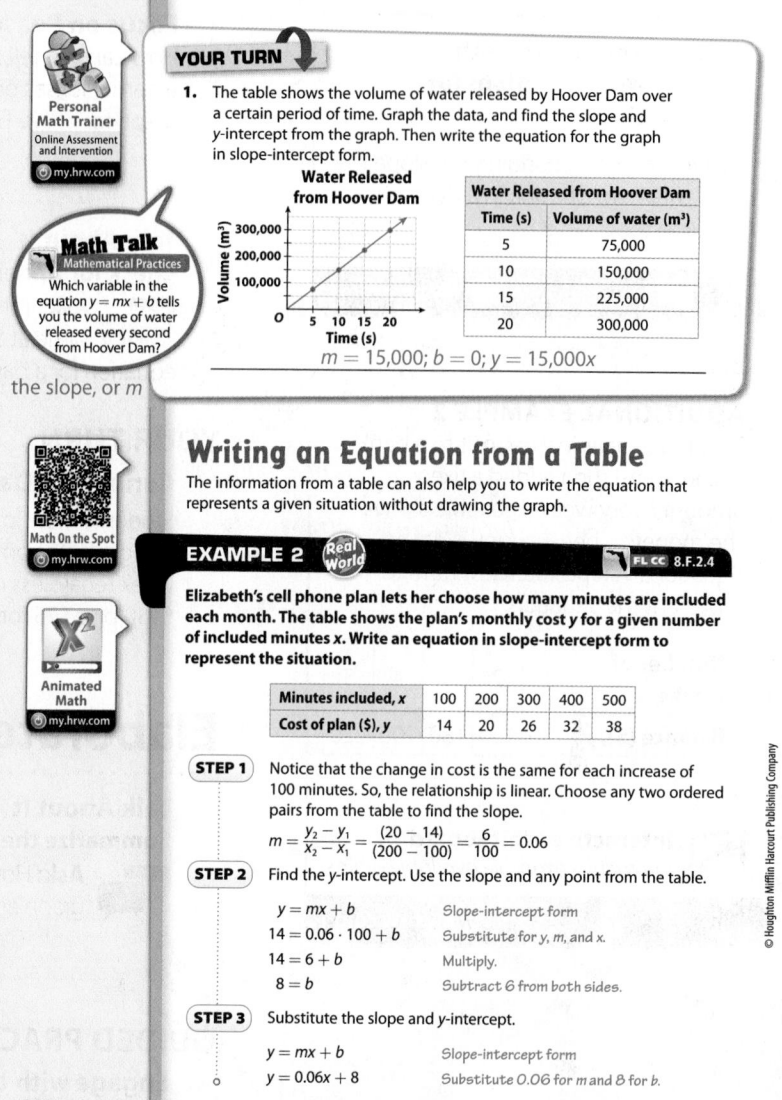

Personal Math Trainer
Online Assessment and Intervention
my.hrw.com

YOUR TURN

1. The table shows the volume of water released by Hoover Dam over a certain period of time. Graph the data, and find the slope and y-intercept from the graph. Then write the equation for the graph in slope-intercept form.

Water Released from Hoover Dam

Time (s)	Volume of water (m³)
5	75,000
10	150,000
15	225,000
20	300,000

Math Talk
Mathematical Practices
Which variable in the equation $y = mx + b$ tells you the volume of water released every second from Hoover Dam?

the slope, or m

$m = 15,000; b = 0; y = 15,000x$

Writing an Equation from a Table

The information from a table can also help you to write the equation that represents a given situation without drawing the graph.

Math On the Spot
my.hrw.com

Animated Math
my.hrw.com

EXAMPLE 2 Real World
FL CC 8.F.2.4

Elizabeth's cell phone plan lets her choose how many minutes are included each month. The table shows the plan's monthly cost y for a given number of included minutes x. Write an equation in slope-intercept form to represent the situation.

Minutes included, x	100	200	300	400	500
Cost of plan ($), y	14	20	26	32	38

STEP 1 Notice that the change in cost is the same for each increase of 100 minutes. So, the relationship is linear. Choose any two ordered pairs from the table to find the slope.

$m = \dfrac{y_2 - y_1}{x_2 - x_1} = \dfrac{(20 - 14)}{(200 - 100)} = \dfrac{6}{100} = 0.06$

STEP 2 Find the y-intercept. Use the slope and any point from the table.

$y = mx + b$ Slope-intercept form
$14 = 0.06 \cdot 100 + b$ Substitute for y, m, and x.
$14 = 6 + b$ Multiply.
$8 = b$ Subtract 6 from both sides.

STEP 3 Substitute the slope and y-intercept.

$y = mx + b$ Slope-intercept form
$y = 0.06x + 8$ Substitute 0.06 for m and 8 for b.

PROFESSIONAL DEVELOPMENT

Integrate Mathematical Practices MP.4.1

This lesson provides an opportunity to address this Mathematical Practices standard. It calls for students to apply mathematics to problems arising in everyday life, society, and the workplace. Students apply what they know about linear relationships to problems arising from an experiment measuring changes in temperature, measuring the flow of water, and examining the cost of a cell-phone plan. They relate details of everyday relationships to the formal summary of a linear equation in mathematical terms.

Math Background

A table of values generated from measurements such as temperature will often not have a constant rate of change and cannot be precisely described by a linear relationship. In many cases, however, the ordered pairs can be plotted and a line of best fit can be drawn through them. The slope and y-intercept of the line of best fit can be determined and used to write an equation that describes the relationship.

Focus on Reasoning
How can you tell, without drawing the graph, where the line of the graph would start and whether it rises or falls from left to right? Would the line be more or less steep than the graph for $y = x$? Explain. The *y*-intercept tells where the line starts (0, 8); the positive slope of 0.06 tells that the line rises. Since the slope is less than one, the graph is less steep than $y = x$.

Talk About It
Check for Understanding
 Ask: If the base rate increased from $8 to $12 but the per minute rate stayed the same at $0.06 per minute, does the slope change? The *y*-intercept? Write a new equation for a base fee of $12. no; yes; $y = 0.06x + 12$

YOUR TURN

Connect to Daily Life
Students may not understand how sales commission works. Give one or more examples, using points from the table to make this clear, explain: The salesperson is paid $250 per week regardless of how many computers are sold. If 10 computers are sold, the total pay is $250 plus $75 for each of the 10 computers.

Elaborate

Talk About It
Summarize the Lesson
Ask: How can you use values given in a table of a linear relationship to draw a graph and write an equation in $y = mx + b$ form? Use values from the table to draw a graph. Use two points to find the slope. To find the *y*-intercept, either read it from the graph or substitute *m* and any point in the table as (x, y) to solve for *b* in $y = mx + b$.

GUIDED PRACTICE

Engage with the Whiteboard
For Exercise 1, have students mark on the graph several points that are not in the table, such as the points that tell how much is left on the pass after 3 rides and after 14 rides. Label the points with their coordinates.

Focus on Communication
Have students informally describe the information that is shown in the table for Exercises 2–5, and what it might mean for someone who is climbing mountains. It gets colder the higher you climb.

Avoid Common Errors
Exercise 5 To avoid calculating an incorrect value, remind students that they can use the table to predict, or check, the reasonableness of the temperature. They should see that the temperature must be between 35 °F and 43 °F.

Reflect

2. What is the base price for the cell phone plan, regardless of how many minutes are included? What is the cost per minute? Explain.

$8; $0.06; in the equation for the table, $y = 0.06 + 8$, the y-intercept, 8, is an initial amount that does not depend on the rate of change. The slope, 0.06, represents the rate of change, which is the per-minute cost.

3. **What If?** Elizabeth's cell phone company changes the cost of her plan as shown below. Write an equation in slope-intercept form to represent the situation. How did the plan change?

Minutes included, x	100	200	300	400	500
Cost of plan ($), y	30	35	40	45	50

$y = 0.05x + 25$; The fee was increased by $17, and the per-minute rate was decreased by 1 cent.

YOUR TURN

4. A salesperson receives a weekly salary plus a commission for each computer sold. The table shows the total pay, p, and the number of computers sold, n. Write an equation in slope-intercept form to represent this situation.

Number of computers sold, n	4	6	8	10	12
Total pay ($), p	550	700	850	1000	1150

$p = 75n + 250$

5. To rent a van, a moving company charges $40.00 plus $0.50 per mile. The table shows the total cost, c, and the number of miles driven, d. Write an equation in slope-intercept form to represent this situation.

Number of miles driven, d	10	20	30	40	50
Total cost ($), c	45	50	55	60	65

$c = 0.50d + 40$

The slope, or m, is the commission of $75 for each computer sold and the y-intercept, or b, is the base salary of $250.

Math Talk
Mathematical Practices
Explain the meaning of the slope and y-intercept of the equation.

Personal Math Trainer
Online Assessment and Intervention
my.hrw.com

1. Jaime purchased a $20 bus pass. Each time she rides the bus, a certain amount is deducted from the pass. The table shows the amount, y, left on her pass after x rides. Graph the data, and find the slope and y-intercept from the graph. Then write the equation for the graph in slope-intercept form. (Example 1)

Number of rides, x	0	4	8	12	16
Amount left on pass ($), y	20	15	10	5	0

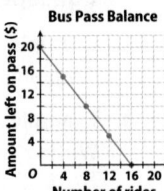

Bus Pass Balance

$m = -1.25; b = 20; y = -1.25x + 20$

The table shows the temperature (y) at different altitudes (x). This is a linear relationship. (Example 2)

Altitude (ft), x	0	2000	4000	6000	8000	10000	12000
Temperature (°F), y	59	51	43	35	27	19	11

2. Find the slope for this relationship.

$m = \dfrac{51 - 59}{2000 - 0} = \dfrac{-8}{2000} = -0.004$

3. Find the y-intercept for this relationship.

$b = 59$

4. Write an equation in slope-intercept form that represents this relationship.

$y = -0.004x + 59$

5. Use your equation to determine the temperature at an altitude of 5000 feet.

$y = -0.004(5000) + 59 = 39\ °F$

? ESSENTIAL QUESTION CHECK-IN

6. Describe how you can use the information in a table showing a linear relationship to find the slope and y-intercept for the equation.

Use two points from the table to find the slope, and then use a point and the slope to solve for the y-intercept.

DIFFERENTIATE INSTRUCTION

Technology
Students can see the effect of increasing the absolute value of m, the slope, by graphing these equations on the same screen of a graphing calculator: $y = 0.5x, y = 1x, y = 1.5x, y = 2x, y = 5x$. They can also see the effect of increasing the value of b, the y-intercept, by graphing these equations on the same screen of a graphing calculator: $y = x - 2, y = x + 1, y = x + 3, y = x + 5$. All of these equations have a positive slope. Ask students to conjecture how the graph would change if they had a negative slope. They can verify their conjectures by graphing $y = x + 3$ and $y = -x + 3$.

Communicating Math
Help students be precise in their use of mathematics language by discussing the difference between "What is the y-intercept?" and "At what point on the graph does the line cross the y-axis?" The y-intercept is a single value, b, the y-coordinate of the point, which is $(0, b)$.

Students often ask why m is used to represent the slope. Mathematicians do not know a definite answer to this, although m has been used for slope for centuries. Some students like to remember the meaning of m by relating it to mountain slope.

Additional Resources
Differentiated Instruction includes:
- Reading Strategies
- Success for English Learners **ELL**
- Reteach
- Challenge **PRE-AP**

Personal Math Trainer

Online Assessment and Intervention

Online homework assignment available

ⓢ my.hrw.com

13.2 LESSON QUIZ

FL CC 8.F.2.4

The table shows Eli's distance from home as he rides his bike at a steady rate after meeting a friend.

Time (h)	1	2	3	4	5
Distance (mi)	14	26	38	50	62

1. Graph the data.

2. Find the slope and y-intercept.

3. How fast does Eli ride his bike, in miles per hour?

4. Write an equation in $y = mx + b$ form that represents the miles, y, that Eli goes in x hours.

5. If each distance were halved, what would the equation be? What would it mean in terms of the problem? Explain.

Lesson Quiz available online

ⓢ my.hrw.com

Answers

1.

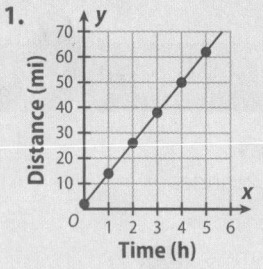

2. $m = 12; b = 2$

3. 12 mi/h

4. $y = 12x + 2$

5. $y = 6x + 1$; Eli starts 1 mile from home and goes 6 mi/h.

Evaluate

GUIDED AND INDEPENDENT PRACTICE

 **FL CC** 8.F.2.4

Concepts & Skills	Practice
Example 1 Graphing from a Table to Write an Equation	Exercises 1, 7–8
Example 2 Writing an Equation from a Table	Exercises 2–5, 9–13

Exercise	Depth of Knowledge (D.O.K.)	**FL CC** Mathematical Practices
7–9	**2** Skills/Concepts	**MP.4.1** Modeling
10–11	**2** Skills/Concepts	**MP.2.1** Reasoning
12	**2** Skills/Concepts	**MP.4.1** Modeling
13	**2** Skills/Concepts	**MP.3.1** Logic
14–15	**3** Strategic Thinking **H.O.T.**	**MP.3.1** Logic

Additional Resources

Differentiated Instruction includes:

• Leveled Practice worksheets

CLUSTER CONNECTION **Exercise 9** combines concepts from the Florida Common Core cluster "Use functions to model relationships between quantities."

Name_____ Class_____ Date_____

13.2 Independent Practice

FL CC 8.F.2.4

7. The table shows the costs of a large cheese pizza with toppings at a local pizzeria. Graph the data, and find the slope and y-intercept from the graph. Then write the equation for the graph in slope-intercept form.

Number of toppings, t	0	1	2	3	4	5
Total cost ($), C	8	10	12	14	16	18

$$m = 2; b = 8; C = 2t + 8$$

Cost of Large Pizza

8. The table shows how much an air-conditioning repair company charges for different numbers of hours of work. Graph the data, and find the slope and y-intercept from the graph. Then write the equation for the graph in slope-intercept form.

Number of hours (h), t	0	1	2	3	4	5
Amount charged ($), A	50	100	150	200	250	300

$$m = 50; b = 50; A = 50t + 50$$

9. A friend gave Ms. Morris a gift card for a local car wash. The table shows the linear relationship of how the value left on the card relates to the number of car washes.

Number of car washes, x	0	8	12
Amount left on card ($), y	30	18	12

a. Write an equation that shows the number of dollars left on the card.

$$y = -1.5x + 30$$

b. Explain the meaning of the negative slope in this situation.

The amount of dollars left decreases as the number of car washes increases.

c. What is the maximum value of x that makes sense in this context? Explain.

20; after 20 washes there is no money left on the card

The tables show linear relationships between x and y. Write an equation in slope-intercept form for each relationship.

10.

x	−2	−1	0	2
y	−1	0	1	3

$$y = x + 1$$

11.

x	−4	1	0	6
y	14	4	6	−6

$$y = -2x + 6$$

12. **Finance** Desiree starts a savings account with $125.00. Every month, she deposits $53.50.

a. Complete the table to model the situation.

Month, x	0	1	2	3	4
Amount in Savings ($), y	125.00	178.50	232.00	285.50	339.00

b. Write an equation in slope-intercept form that shows how much money Desiree has in her savings account after x months.

$$y = 53.50x + 125.00$$

c. Use the equation to find how much money Desiree will have in savings after 11 months.

$713.50

13. Monty documented the amount of rain his farm received on a monthly basis, as shown in the table.

Month, x	1	2	3	4	5
Rainfall (in.), y	5	3	4.5	1	7

a. Is the relationship linear? Why or why not?

No, the change between weeks is constant, but the change in the amount of rain is not constant.

b. Can an equation be written to describe the amount of rain? Explain.

No; there is no apparent pattern in the table.

 **FOCUS ON HIGHER ORDER THINKING**

Work Area

14. **Analyze Relationships** If you have a table that shows a linear relationship, when can you read the value for b, in $y = mx + b$, directly from the table without drawing a graph or doing any calculations? Explain.

If there is a point $(0, y)$ in the table, then $y = b$ because at the y-intercept the value of x is zero.

15. **What If?** Jaíme graphed linear data given in the form (cost, number). The y-intercept was 0. Jayla graphed the same data given in the form (number, cost). What was the y-intercept of her graph? Explain.

0; Jaíme's graph contained (0, 0). Since Jayla's data were the same, but with x and y switched, her graph also contained (0, 0).

EXTEND THE MATH PRE-AP

Activity available online my.hrw.com

Activity To extend the relationships between values in a table, points on a graphed line, and ordered pairs that satisfy a linear equation, have students draw graphs that use the other three quadrants. For example, ask them to create a table of ordered pairs for the equations $y = x + 3$ and $y = -x - 2$ using both negative and positive values of x. Have them graph the points in the table and draw a line through the points. Discuss situations that might be represented by such equations, for example, charging purchases, debt, temperatures below zero, diving below sea level.

LESSON
13.3 Linear Relationships and Bivariate Data

Florida Common Core Standards

The student is expected to:

 FL CC **Statistics and Probability—8.SP.1.1**

Construct and interpret scatter plots for bivariate measurement data to investigate patterns of association between two quantities. Describe patterns such as clustering, outliers, positive or negative association, linear association, and nonlinear association.

 FL CC **Statistics and Probability—8.SP.1.2**

Know that straight lines are widely used to model relationships between two quantitative variables. For scatter plots that suggest a linear association, informally fit a straight line, and informally assess the model fit by judging the closeness of the data points to the line.

 FL CC **Statistics and Probability—8.SP.1.3**

Use the equation of a linear model to solve problems in the context of bivariate measurement data, interpreting the slope and intercept.

Mathematical Practices

 FL CC **MP.6.1** Precision

ADDITIONAL EXAMPLE 1
The charge for a cheese pizza changes as the number of toppings changes. Show that the relationship is linear, and then find the equation for the relationship.

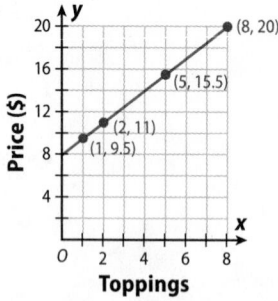

A line passes through all the graphed points so the relationship is linear.
$y = 1.5x + 8$

Interactive Whiteboard

Interactive example available online

 my.hrw.com

Engage

ESSENTIAL QUESTION
How can you contrast linear and nonlinear sets of bivariate data? The graph of a linear set of data is a single line; the graph of a nonlinear set of data is not a single line.

Motivate the Lesson
Ask: Does a table of paired values always graph as a single line?

Explore

If you made a table showing the side length of a square and its area and then graphed those points, would the relationship be linear?

Explain

EXAMPLE 1
Questioning Strategies Mathematical Practices

• According to the line on the graph, what is the height of the handrail from the floor where the stairway starts? Does that height satisfy the equation? Explain. 3 ft; yes, (0, 3) satisfies the equation because $3 = 0.8(0) + 3$.

• Would you get a different value for the rate of change, or slope, if you chose two other points? Explain. No; the slope is constant for a linear relationship.

Engage with the Whiteboard
On the graph in Step 1, have students plot the point where the graph crosses the *y*-axis and label the point with its coordinates.

YOUR TURN
Avoid Common Errors
In Exercise 1, students may misread the second point on the graph as (10, 50). Remind students to determine unlabeled values on an axis by looking at both the closest lesser axis label and the closest greater axis label.

Talk About It
Check for Understanding
Ask: In Exercise 1, why does the line not go through the origin? There is an initial fee at the beginning, regardless of the number of minutes.

EXAMPLE 2
Questioning Strategies Mathematical Practices
• Why does the graph of the line not go through the origin? there is an initial cost of $3

• How would you describe in words the cost of taxi rides shown in the graph? The cost is $3 plus $2 for every mile traveled.

LESSON 13.3 Linear Relationships and Bivariate Data

FL CC 8.SP.1.1
Construct and interpret scatter plots for bivariate measurement data.... Describe patterns such as... linear association, and nonlinear association. *Also 8.SP.1.2, 8.SP.1.3*

? ESSENTIAL QUESTION

How can you contrast linear and nonlinear sets of bivariate data?

Finding the Equation of a Linear Relationship

You can use the points on a graph of a linear relationship to write an equation for the relationship. The equation of a linear relationship is $y = mx + b$, where m is the rate of change, or slope, and b is the value of y when x is 0.

Math On the Spot my.hrw.com

EXAMPLE 1 Real World

FL CC 8.SP.1.2

A handrail runs alongside a stairway. As the horizontal distance from the bottom of the stairway changes, the height of the handrail changes. Show that the relationship is linear, and then find the equation for the relationship.

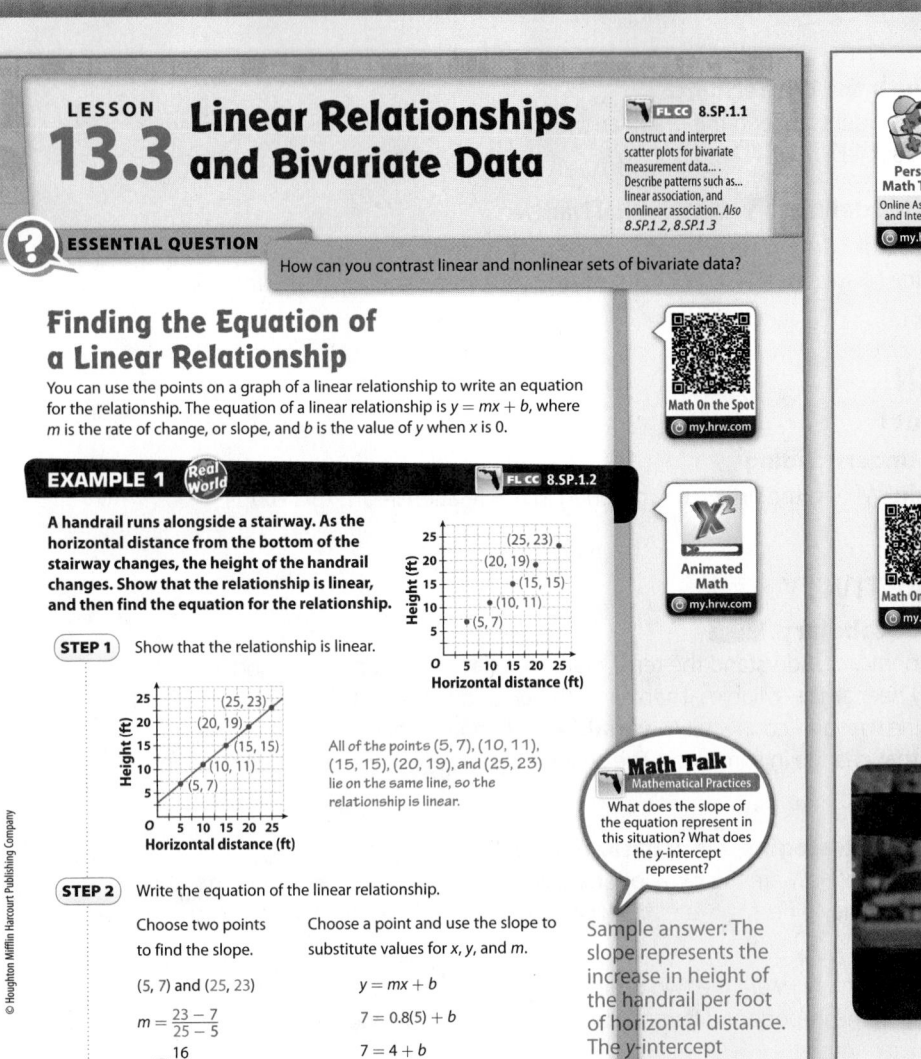

(25, 23)
(20, 19)
(15, 15)
(10, 11)
(5, 7)

Height (ft) / Horizontal distance (ft)

STEP 1 Show that the relationship is linear.

All of the points (5, 7), (10, 11), (15, 15), (20, 19), and (25, 23) lie on the same line, so the relationship is linear.

STEP 2 Write the equation of the linear relationship.

Choose two points to find the slope.

(5, 7) and (25, 23)

$m = \dfrac{23 - 7}{25 - 5}$

$= \dfrac{16}{20}$

$= 0.8$

Choose a point and use the slope to substitute values for x, y, and m.

$y = mx + b$

$7 = 0.8(5) + b$

$7 = 4 + b$

$3 = b$

The equation of the linear relationship is $y = 0.8x + 3$.

Animated Math my.hrw.com

Math Talk Mathematical Practices

What does the slope of the equation represent in this situation? What does the y-intercept represent?

Sample answer: The slope represents the increase in height of the handrail per foot of horizontal distance. The y-intercept represents the height of the handrail at the bottom of the stairway.

Lesson 13.3 **403**

Personal Math Trainer
Online Assessment and Intervention
my.hrw.com

YOUR TURN

Find the equation of each linear relationship.

1.

Cost ($) / Time (min)

$y = 4x + 20$

2.

Hours (x)	Number of units (y)
2	480
15	3,600
24	5,760
30	7,200
48	11,520
55	13,200

$y = 240x$

Making Predictions

You can use an equation of a linear relationship to predict a value between data points that you already know.

Math On the Spot my.hrw.com

EXAMPLE 2 Real World

FL CC 8.SP.1.3

The graph shows the cost for taxi rides of different distances. Predict the cost of a taxi ride that covers a distance of 6.5 miles.

STEP 1 Write the equation of the linear relationship.

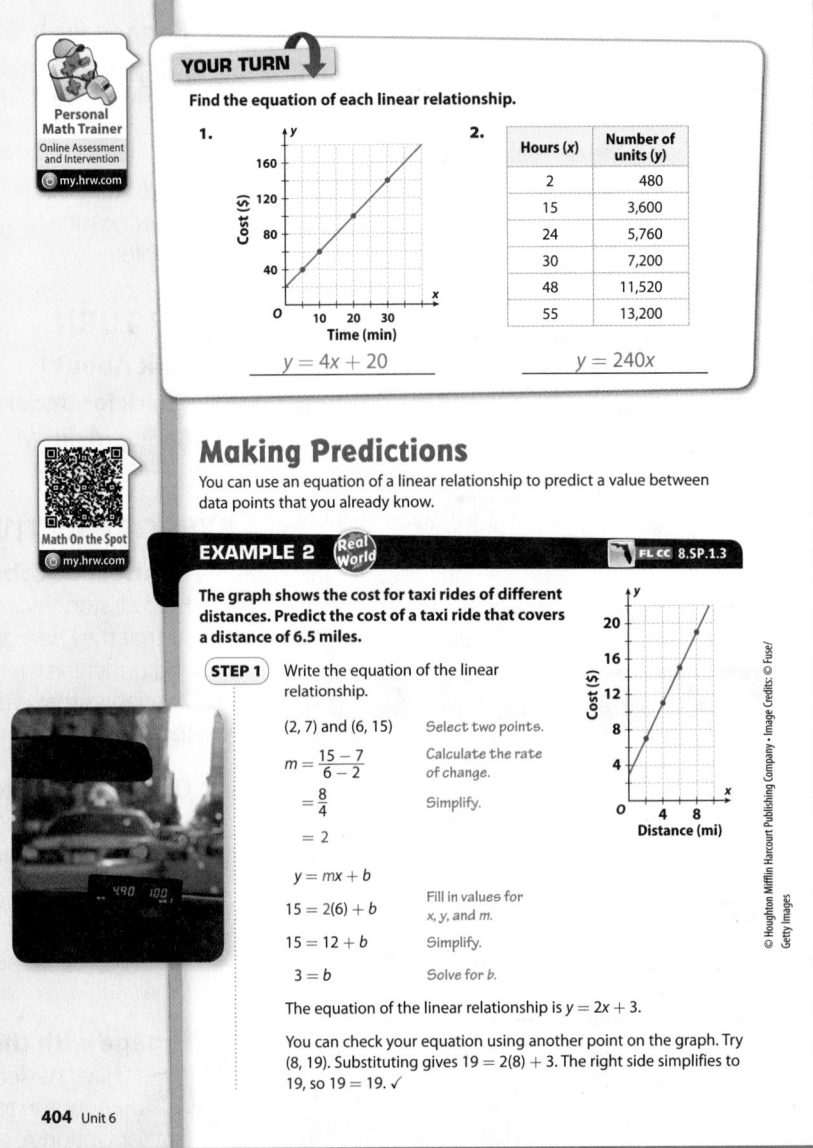

Cost ($) / Distance (mi)

(2, 7) and (6, 15)   Select two points.

$m = \dfrac{15 - 7}{6 - 2}$ Calculate the rate of change.

$= \dfrac{8}{4}$ Simplify.

$= 2$

$y = mx + b$

$15 = 2(6) + b$ Fill in values for x, y, and m.

$15 = 12 + b$ Simplify.

$3 = b$ Solve for b.

The equation of the linear relationship is $y = 2x + 3$.

You can check your equation using another point on the graph. Try (8, 19). Substituting gives $19 = 2(8) + 3$. The right side simplifies to 19, so $19 = 19$. ✓

404 Unit 6

PROFESSIONAL DEVELOPMENT

Integrate Mathematical Practices MP.6.1

This lesson provides an opportunity to address this Mathematical Practices standard. It calls for students to precisely communicate mathematical ideas and reasoning. Students use tables and graphs and equations to represent linear and nonlinear relationships. Students use these multiple representations to compare and contrast linear and nonlinear relationships and to communicate their understanding.

Math Background

Simple interest is paid on the amount of an investment or loan. The amount of interest does not change if the interest earned is added to the original amount or if interest charges increase the amount of a debt. With compound interest, interest is paid on the accumulated interest as well as the original amount. In the case of an investment, that means the interest is also earning interest (unless it is withdrawn from the investment), and in the case of a loan, the debtor pays interest on the interest unless loan payments are large enough to offset the interest charges.

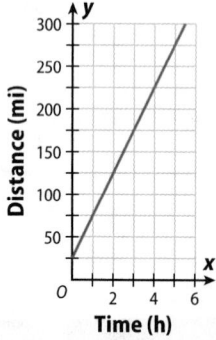
 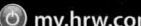
Engage with the Whiteboard

 Have students extend the graph and predict the cost of various rides greater than 8 miles.

Focus on Modeling   Mathematical Practices

Have students discuss why extending the line to the left by graphing this relationship in other quadrants, such as II or III, does not make sense in the context of the real-world problem.

YOUR TURN

Talk About It

Check for Understanding

💬 **Ask:** What is the hourly pay graphed in this relationship? $15

EXPLORE ACTIVITY

Connect Vocabulary ELL

Help all students to understand the term **bivariate data** by first pronouncing it slowly so that they hear all the syllables. Then circle the *bi-* and connect it to a *bi-cycle* (2 wheels), and underline *vari-* and connect it to **variable** or *change*. So bivariate data is data in pairs of 2 variables that change in some way. The change is constant (linear) or is not constant (nonlinear).

Questioning Strategies Mathematical Practices

• Look at the table. How are the two options alike? The amount at the beginning is the same. How do they differ? The rate at which they increase is not the same; Option B grows faster than Option A.

• Read the problem. How are the two options alike? Both have interest rates of 5%. Which words tell you the important difference between these two options? *simple interest* and *compounded annually*

Engage with the Whiteboard

Have students extend the coordinate plane and the two lines, and make conjectures about the total amounts after 25 and 30 years. Students should be able to determine that for Option A, simple interest, there will be $450 after 25 years and $500 after 30 years. Students will only be able to estimate the values for Option B; the exact values are $677.27 after 25 years and $864.39 after 30 years.

STEP 2 Use your equation from Step 1 to predict the cost of a 6.5-mile taxi ride.

$y = 2x + 3$

Substitute x = 6.5.

$y = 2(6.5) + 3$

Solve for y.

$y = 16$

A taxi ride that covers a distance of 6.5 miles will cost $16.

Reflect

3. What If? Suppose a regulation changes the cost of the taxi ride to $1.80 per mile, plus a fee of $4.30. How does the price of the 6.5 mile ride compare to the original price?

It is the same. The new equation is $y = 1.8x + 4.3$,
so $y = 1.8(6.5) + 4.3 = 11.7 + 4.3 = 16$.

4. How can you use a graph of a linear relationship to predict a value for a new input?

Sample answer: Use the graph to write an equation,
and then substitute the new input into the equation
to make the prediction.

5. How can you use a table of linear data to predict a value?

Sample answer: Use the table of values to write
an equation and then use the equation to make
the prediction.

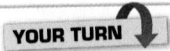

YOUR TURN

Paulina's income from a job that pays her a fixed amount per hour is shown in the graph. Use the graph to find the predicted value.

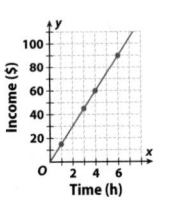

6. Income earned for working 2 hours

$30

7. Income earned for working 3.25 hours

$48.75

8. Total income earned for working for five 8-hour days all at the standard rate $600

Personal Math Trainer

Online Assessment and Intervention

my.hrw.com

My Notes

EXPLORE ACTIVITY *Real World*

Contrasting Linear and Nonlinear Data

Bivariate data is a set of data that is made up of two paired variables. If the relationship between the variables is linear, then the rate of change (slope) is constant. If the graph shows a **nonlinear relationship**, then the rate of change varies between pairs of points.

Andrew has two options in which to invest $200. Option A earns simple interest of 5%, while Option B earns interest of 5% compounded annually. The table shows the amount of the investment for both options over 20 years. Graph the data and describe the differences between the two graphs.

Year, x	Option A Total ($)	Option B Total ($)
0	200.00	200.00
5	250.00	255.26
10	300.00	325.78
15	350.00	415.79
20	400.00	530.66

STEP 1 Graph the data from the table for Options A and B on the same coordinate grid.

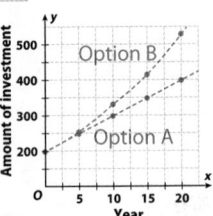

STEP 2 Find the rate of change between pairs of points for Option A and classify the relationship.

Option A	Rate of Change
(0, 200) and (5, 250)	$m = \dfrac{250 - 200}{5 - 0} = 10$
(5, 250) and (10, 300)	$m = \dfrac{300 - 250}{10 - 5} = 10$
(10, 300) and (15, 350)	$m = \dfrac{350 - 300}{15 - 10} = 10$

The rate of change between the data values is ___constant___, so the graph of Option A shows a ___linear___ relationship.

DIFFERENTIATE INSTRUCTION

Modeling

To help students understand the difference between amount of change and rate of change, have them make a table (similar to the one in the Explore Activity) showing the side of a square, its perimeter, and its area. Then have them graph these two sets of points for *P* and *A*. Ask students to compare the resulting graphs. Help them realize that, beyond a side of 4, the area increases much faster than the perimeter.

Technology

Have students make the comparison described in Modeling by using a graphing calculator to graph and compare $y = 4x$ and $y = x^2$ (for the perimeter and area of a square with side *x*). Use a window that shows the first quadrant only and lead students to see that when *x* has a value greater than 4, the *y*-value of the curve is increasing much faster than that of the straight line.

Additional Resources

Differentiated Instruction includes:

- Reading Strategies
- Success for English Learners **ELL**
- Reteach
- Challenge **PRE-AP**

Elaborate

. . . .

Talk About It
Summarize the Lesson

Ask: If you were given two graphed lines, one of a linear set of data and the other of a nonlinear set of data, how could you tell which line goes with which set of data? The graph of the linear set of data will be a single line.

GUIDED PRACTICE

Engage with the Whiteboard

In Exercises 1–2, have students draw a line through the points and the *y*-axis. Have them label the *y*-intercept. In Exercises 4–5, have students attempt to draw a line through all the points.

Avoid Common Errors

Exercise 2 Some students may attempt to draw a line through all of the points and the origin and decide that the relationship is not linear. Remind students that the origin is not necessarily part of the graph unless it is marked as such.

Exercises 4–5 Remind students that the line must contain *all* of the points and that a line is always straight.

STEP 3 Find the rate of change between pairs of points for Option B and classify the relationship.

Option B	Rate of Change
(0, 200) and (5, 255.26)	$m = \frac{252.26 - 200}{5 - 0} \approx 10.5$
(5, 255.26) and (10, 325.78)	$m = \frac{325.78 - 252.26}{10 - 5} \approx 14.7$
(10, 325.78) and (15, 415.79)	$m = \frac{415.79 - 325.78}{15 - 10} \approx 18.0$

The rate of change between the data values is __not constant__, so the graph of Option B shows a __nonlinear__ relationship.

Reflect

9. Why are the graphs drawn as lines or curves and not discrete points?

Sample answer: You can calculate the value of the account at any time as the money grows. All points along the line or curve are reasonable and possible.

10. Can you determine by viewing the graph if the data have a linear or nonlinear relationship? Explain.

Sample answer: Yes. If all of the data lie on a line, then the data have a linear relationship. If the graph is a curve (or not a line), then the data have a nonlinear relationship.

11. **Draw Conclusions** Find the differences in the account balances to the nearest dollar at 5 year intervals for Option B. How does the length of time that money is in an account affect the advantage that compound interest has over simple interest?

$55, $71, $90, $115; the longer that the money is in the account, the greater the relative advantage of it earning compound interest will be.

Use the following graphs to find the equation of the linear relationship. (Example 1)

1.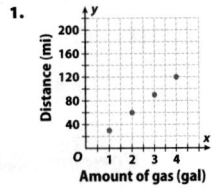

Distance (mi) / Amount of gas (gal)

$y = 30x$

2.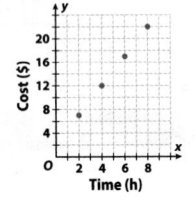

Cost ($) / Time (h)

$y = 2.5x + 2$

3. The graph shows the relationship between the number of hours a kayak is rented and the total cost of the rental. Write an equation of the relationship. Then use the equation to predict the cost of a rental that lasts 5.5 hours. (Example 2)

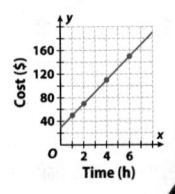

Cost ($) / Time (h)

$y = 20x + 30; \$140$

Does each of the following graphs represent a linear relationship? Why or why not? (Explore Activity)

4.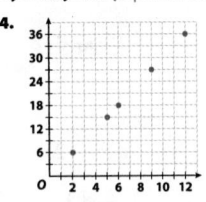

Yes, because the graph has a constant rate of change.

5.

No, because the graph does not have a constant rate of change.

? ESSENTIAL QUESTION CHECK-IN

6. How can you tell if a set of bivariate data shows a linear relationship?

Sample answer: Graph the data points. If the points lie along a straight line, the data is linear.

13.3 LESSON QUIZ

FL CC 8.SP.1.1, 8.SP.1.2, 8.SP.1.3

x	1	2	3	4	5
y	5	8	12	14	17

1. Does this table represent a linear relationship? Why or why not?

2. Change one value in this table so that this table does represent a linear relationship.

Explain whether or not each relationship is linear.

3. The number of inches in a student's height and the height in feet

4. The radius of a circle and its area

5. An amusement park charges a price for admission and a price for each ride. Joe spent $10.50 and went on 4 rides. Janie spent $14.25 and went on 9 rides. Write a linear equation for the amount spent and predict the amount you would spend to go on 17 rides.

Lesson Quiz available online

⏻ my.hrw.com

Answers

1. No, the slope is not the same between 2 and 3 and between 3 and 4.

2. Change y to 11 for $x = 3$.

3. Yes, the rate of change is a constant 12 inches per foot.

4. No; the rate of change is not constant.

5. $a = 0.75r + 7.5$; $20.25

Evaluate

GUIDED AND INDEPENDENT PRACTICE

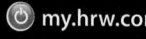 **FL CC** 8.SP.1.1, 8.SP.1.2, 8.SP.1.3

Concepts & Skills	Practice
Example 1 Finding the Equation of a Linear Relationship	Exercises 1–2, 13
Example 2 Making Predictions	Exercises 3, 13
Explore Activity Contrasting Linear and Nonlinear Data	Exercises 4–5, 7–13

Exercise	Depth of Knowledge (D.O.K.)	FL CC Mathematical Practices
7–8	**2** Skills/Concepts	**MP.3.1** Logic
9–12	**2** Skills/Concepts	**MP.2.1** Reasoning
13	**2** Skills/Concepts	**MP.4.1** Modeling
14	**3** Strategic Thinking H.O.T.	**MP.3.1** Logic
15	**3** Strategic Thinking H.O.T.	**MP.2.1** Using Structure
16–18	**3** Strategic Thinking H.O.T.	**MP.3.1** Logic

Additional Resources

Differentiated Instruction includes:

• Leveled Practice worksheets

13.3 Independent Practice

FL CC 8.SP.1.1, 8.SP.1.2, 8.SP.1.3

Personal Math Trainer

Online Assessment and Intervention

my.hrw.com

Does each of the following tables represent a linear relationship? Why or why not?

7.

Number of boxes	Weight (kg)
3	15
9	45
21	105

Yes, because the rate of change is constant.

8.

Day	Height (cm)
5	30
8	76.8
14	235.2

No, because the rate of change is not constant.

Explain whether or not you think each relationship is linear.

9. the cost of equal-priced DVDs and the number purchased

Linear; the rate of change is the cost of a DVD, which is constant.

10. the height of a person and the person's age

Not linear; the rate of growth is less as a person gets older.

11. the area of a square quilt and its side length

Not linear; the rate of change in the area of a square increases as the side length increases.

12. the number of miles to the next service station and the number of kilometers

Linear; the rate of change between units is the conversion factor, which is constant.

13. **Multistep** The Mars Rover travels 0.75 feet in 6 seconds. Add the point to the graph. Then determine whether the relationship between distance and time is linear, and if so, predict the distance that the Mars Rover would travel in 1 minute.

The relationship is linear; the equation of the linear relationship is $y = 0.125x$, so the Mars Rover would travel 7.5 feet in 60 seconds.

Mars Rover

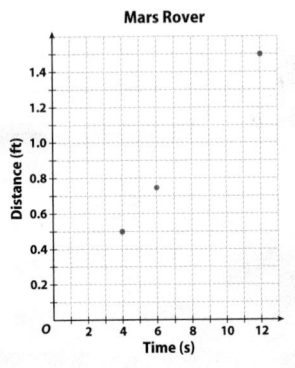

14. **Make a Conjecture** Zefram analyzed a linear relationship, found that the slope-intercept equation was $y = 3.5x + 16$, and made a prediction for the value of y for a given value of x. He realized that he made an error calculating the y-intercept and that it was actually 12. Can he just subtract 4 from his prediction if he knows that the slope is correct? Explain.

Yes; decreasing the value of b by 4 decreases the value of $mx + b$ by 4 because the value of mx stays the same.

H.O.T. FOCUS ON HIGHER ORDER THINKING

15. **Communicate Mathematical Ideas** The table shows a linear relationship. How can you predict the value of y when $x = 6$ without finding the equation of the relationship?

x	y
4	38
8	76
12	114

Sample answer: Because $x = 6$ lies halfway between $x = 4$ and $x = 8$, the y-value should lie halfway between the corresponding y-values.

16. **Critique Reasoning** Louis says that if the differences between the values of x are constant between all the points on a graph, then the relationship is linear. Do you agree? Explain.

No; the rate of change must be constant, and the rate of change is the difference in y-values divided by the difference in x-values.

17. **Make a Conjecture** Suppose you know the slope of a linear relationship and one of the points that its graph passes through. How could you predict another point that falls on the graph of the line?

Find the equation of the linear relationship using the slope and given point, and then insert any x-value to find a y-value on the graph of the line.

18. **Explain the Error** Thomas used (7, 17.5) and (18, 45) from a graph to find the equation of a linear relationship as shown. What was his mistake?

$$m = \frac{45 - 7}{18 - 17.5} = \frac{38}{0.5} = 79$$

$$y = 79x + b$$

$$45 = 79 \cdot 18 + b$$

$$45 = 1422 + b, \text{ so } b = -1377$$

The equation is $y = 79x - 1377$.

He substituted into the slope formula incorrectly.

Work Area

EXTEND THE MATH PRE-AP

Activity available online ⏻ my.hrw.com

Activity The formula for compound interest is $A = P\left(1 + \frac{r}{n}\right)^{nt}$, where A is the total amount of money after n years, including interest, and P is the principal, or initial investment. The annual rate of interest as a decimal is r. If the interest is compounded annually, $n = 1$, since n is the number of times the interest is compounded per year. The total number of years is t. Use a calculator or an online compound interest calculator to find the amount after 4 years for Option B of the Explore Activity. $243.10

Ready to Go On?

Assess Mastery

Use the assessment on this page to determine if students have mastered the concepts and standards covered in this module.

 **Response to Intervention**

Intervention	Enrichment

Personal Math Trainer

Online Assessment and Intervention

⏻ my.hrw.com

Access Ready to Go On? assessment online, and receive instant scoring, feedback, and customized intervention or enrichment.

Online and Print Resources

Differentiated Instruction	*Differentiated Instruction*
• Reteach worksheets	• Challenge worksheets **PRE-AP**
• Reading Strategies **ELL**	
• Success for English Learners **ELL**	Extend the Math **PRE-AP** Lesson Activities in TE

Additional Resources

Assessment Resources includes

• Leveled Module Quizzes

Ready to Go On?

Personal Math Trainer
Online Assessment and Intervention
⏻ my.hrw.com

13.1 Writing Linear Equations from Situations and Graphs

Write the equation of each line in slope-intercept form.

1.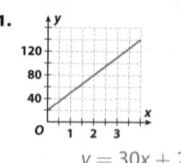

$y = 30x + 20$

2.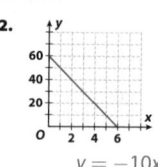

$y = -10x + 60$

13.2 Writing Linear Equations from a Table

Write the equation of each linear relationship in slope-intercept form.

3.

x	0	100	200	300
y	1.5	36.5	71.5	106.5

$y = 0.35x + 1.5$

4.

x	25	35	45	55
y	94	88	82	76

$y = -0.6x + 109$

13.3 Linear Relationships and Bivariate Data

Write the equation of the line that connects each set of data points.

5.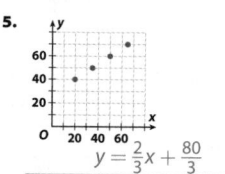

$y = \frac{2}{3}x + \frac{80}{3}$

6.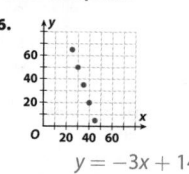

$y = -3x + 140$

? ESSENTIAL QUESTION

7. Write a real-world situation that can be represented by a linear relationship.

Sample answer: A video game rental store charges $3 per game and a membership fee of $10.

 ## Florida Common Core Standards

Lesson	Exercises	🏴 Common Core Standards
13.1	1–2	**8.F.2.4**
13.2	3–4	**8.F.2.4**
13.3	5–6	**8.SP.1.1, 8.SP.1.2**

PARCC Assessment Readiness

Assessment Readiness Tip Encourage students to highlight or underline important information to help them solve problems.

Item 1 Students need to focus on the information they will need to find the slope and *y*-intercept of the equation. They should highlight "3 minutes" and "855 mm of sand" and then "10 minutes" and "750 mm of sand" to isolate what they need.

Item 5 Students, after reading the entire problem, should realize that they only need the information in the table. They should highlight the table and then use that information to answer the questions.

Avoid Common Errors

Item 2 Remind students that a linear relationship has every single point in the graph on a line. Some students may incorrectly think that a relationship that is mostly linear, as in answer choice C, is acceptable.

Item 3 Some students might invert the slope since the *x*-values are written in the top row of the table and the *y*-values are in the bottom row. Remind the students to write out the formula for finding the slope, and check that they are substituting from the correct cells of the table.

Additional Resources

Personal Math Trainer
Online Assessment and Intervention
my.hrw.com

Selected Response

1. An hourglass is turned over with the top part filled with sand. After 3 minutes, there are 855 mL of sand in the top half. After 10 minutes, there are 750 mL of sand in the top half. Which equation represents this situation?

- (A) $y = 285x$
- (B) $y = -10.5x + 900$
- (C) $y = -15x + 900$
- (D) $y = 75x$

2. Which graph shows a linear relationship?

(A)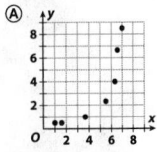

(B)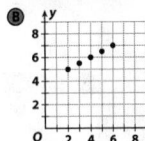

(C)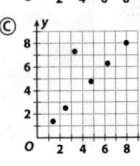

(D)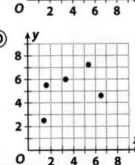

3. What are the slope and *y*-intercept of the relationship shown in the table?

x	10,000	20,000	30,000
y	2,500	3,000	3,500

- (A) slope = 0.05, *y*-intercept = 1,500
- (B) slope = 0.5, *y*-intercept = 1,500
- (C) slope = 0.05, *y*-intercept = 2,000
- (D) slope = 0.5, *y*-intercept = 2,000

4. Which is the sum of $3.15 \times 10^7 + 9.3 \times 10^6$? Write your answer in scientific notation.

- (A) 4.08×10^7
- (B) 4.08×10^6
- (C) 0.408×10^8
- (D) 40.8×10^6

Mini-Task

5. Franklin's faucet was leaking, so he put a bucket underneath to catch the water. After a while, Franklin started keeping track of how much water was in the bucket. His data is in the table below.

Hours	2	3	4	5
Quarts	5	6.5	8	9.5

a. Is the relationship linear or nonlinear?

linear

b. Write the equation for the relationship.

$y = 1.5x + 2$

c. Predict how much water will be in the bucket after 14 hours if Franklin doesn't stop the leak.

23 quarts

© Houghton Mifflin Harcourt Publishing Company

Florida Common Core Standards

Items	Grade 8 Standards	Mathematical Practices
1	8.F.2.4	MP.4.1
2	8.SP.1.1	MP.4.1
3	8.F.2.4	MP.2.1
4*	8.EE.1.4	
5	8.F.2.4	MP.4.1

* Item integrates mixed review concepts from previous modules or a previous course.

Functions

MODULE 14

ESSENTIAL QUESTION

How can you use functions to solve real-world problems?

You can draw tables and graphs and evaluate functions for values of the variables that represent real-world situations.

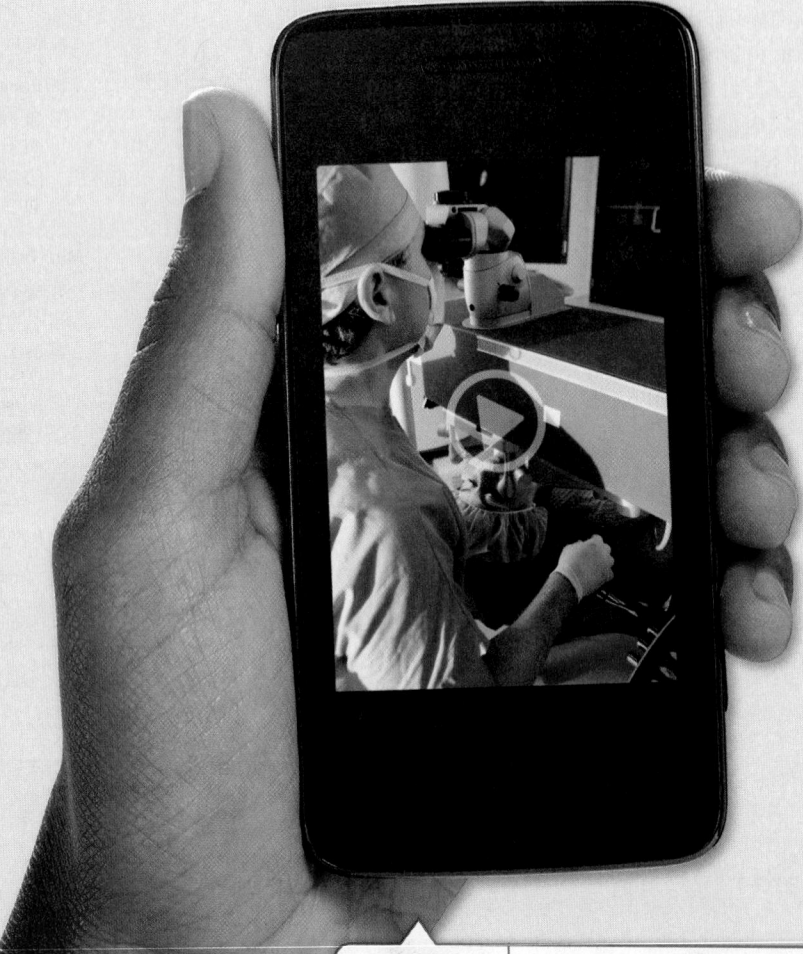

my.hrw.com

Real-World Video

Computerized machines can assist doctors in surgeries such as laser vision correction. Each action the surgeon takes results in one end action by the machine. In math, functions also have a one-in-one-out relationship.

© Houghton Mifflin Harcourt Publishing Company • Image Credits: ©Huntstock/Getty Images

GO DIGITAL
my.hrw.com

 **my.hrw.com**	 **Math On the Spot**	 **Animated Math**	 **Personal Math Trainer**
Go digital with your write-in student edition, accessible on any device.	Scan with your smart phone to jump directly to the online edition, video tutor, and more.	Interactively explore key concepts to see how math works.	Get immediate feedback and help as you work through practice sets.

Are You Ready?

Assess Readiness

Use the assessment on this page to determine if students need intensive or strategic intervention for the module's prerequisite skills.

 **Response to Intervention**

Personal Math Trainer
Online Assessment and Intervention
my.hrw.com

Intervention	Enrichment

Access Are You Ready? assessment online, and receive instant scoring, feedback, and customized intervention or enrichment.

Online and Print Resources

Skills Intervention worksheets
- Skill 54 Evaluate Expressions
- Skill 56 Connect Words and Equations

Differentiated Instruction
- Challenge worksheets **PRE-AP**
- Extend the Math **PRE-AP** Lesson Activities in TE

Are YOU Ready?

Complete these exercises to review skills you will need for this module.

Personal Math Trainer
Online Assessment and Intervention
my.hrw.com

Evaluate Expressions

EXAMPLE	Evaluate $3x - 5$ for $x = -2$.	
	$3x - 5 = 3(-2) - 5$	Substitute the given value of x for x.
	$= -6 - 5$	Multiply.
	$= -11$	Subtract.

Evaluate each expression for the given value of *x*.

1. $2x + 3$ for $x = 3$ ___9___

2. $-4x + 7$ for $x = -1$ ___11___

3. $1.5x - 2.5$ for $x = 3$ ___2___

4. $0.4x + 6.1$ for $x = -5$ ___4.1___

5. $\frac{2}{3}x - 12$ for $x = 18$ ___0___

6. $-\frac{5}{8}x + 10$ for $x = -8$ ___15___

Connect Words and Equations

EXAMPLE	Erik's earnings equal 9 dollars per hour.	Define the variables used in the situation.
	e = earnings; h = hours multiplication	Identify the operation involved. "Per" indicates multiplication.
	$e = 9 \times h$	Write the equation.

Define the variables for each situation. Then write an equation.

7. Jana's age plus 5 equals her sister's age.
   j = Jana's age; s = sister's age; $j + 5 = s$

8. Andrew's class has 3 more students than Lauren's class.
   a = Andrew's class; l = Lauren's class; $a = 3 + l$

9. The bank is 50 feet shorter than the firehouse.
   b = bank's height; f = firehouse's height; $b = f - 50$

10. The pencils were divided into 6 groups of 2.
    p = pencils; $\frac{p}{6} = 2$

PROFESSIONAL DEVELOPMENT VIDEO

Author Juli Dixon models successful teaching practices as she explores the concept of functions in an actual eighth-grade classroom.

Professional Development
my.hrw.com

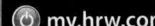
GO DIGITAL
my.hrw.com

Online Teacher Edition
Access a full suite of teaching resources online—plan, present, and manage classes and assignments.

ePlanner
Easily plan your classes and access all your resources online.

Interactive Answers and Solutions
Customize answer keys to print or display in the classroom. Choose to include answers only or full solutions to all lesson exercises.

Interactive Whiteboards
Engage students with interactive whiteboard-ready lessons and activities.

Personal Math Trainer: Online Assessment and Intervention
Assign automatically graded homework, quizzes, tests, and intervention activities. Prepare your students with updated practice tests aligned with Common Core.

Reading Start-Up

Have students complete the activities on this page by working alone or with others.

Visualize Vocabulary

The four-square graphic helps students review vocabulary associated with linear relationships. Students should write one or more review words that apply to the given information in each square.

Understand Vocabulary

Use the following explanations to help students learn the preview words.

> A **function** is a special rule. You can think of a function as a machine. What you put into the machine is called the **input**. The input is altered according to the rule to produce the **output** of the machine.

Active Reading

Integrating Language Arts

Students can use these reading and note-taking strategies to help them organize and understand new concepts and vocabulary.

FL CC **LACC.68.RST.3.7** Integrate quantitative or technical information expressed in words in a text with a version of that information expressed visually (e.g., in a flowchart, diagram, model, graph, or table).

Additional Resources

Differentiated Instruction
- Reading Strategies **ELL**

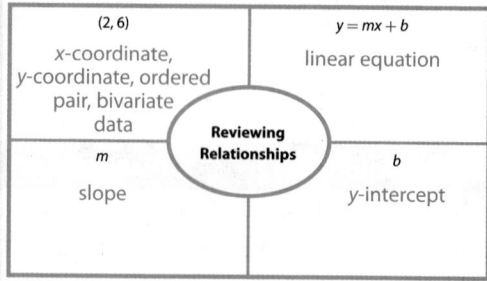

Reading Start-Up

Visualize Vocabulary

Use the ✔ words to complete the diagram. You can put more than one word in each section of the diagram.

(2, 6)	$y = mx + b$
x-coordinate, y-coordinate, ordered pair, bivariate data	linear equation
m	*b*
slope	y-intercept

Center: **Reviewing Relationships**

Understand Vocabulary

Complete the sentences using the preview words.

1. A rule that assigns exactly one output to each input is a ___function___.

2. The value that is put into a function is the ___input___.

3. The result after applying the function machine's rule is the ___output___.

Vocabulary

Review Words
- ✔ bivariate data *(datos bivariados)*
- ✔ linear equation *(ecuación lineal)*
- nonlinear relationship *(relación no lineal)*
- ✔ ordered pair *(par ordenado)*
- proportional relationship *(relación proporcional)*
- ✔ slope *(pendiente)*
- ✔ x-coordinate *(coordenada x)*
- ✔ y-coordinate *(coordenada y)*
- ✔ y-intercept *(intersección con el eje y)*

Preview Words
- function *(función)*
- input *(valor de entrada)*
- linear function *(función lineal)*
- output *(valor de salida)*

Active Reading

Double-Door Fold Create a double-door fold to help you understand the concepts in this module. Label one flap "Proportional Functions" and the other flap "Non-proportional Functions." As you study each lesson, write important ideas under the appropriate flap. Include any sample problems that will help you remember the concepts when you look back at your notes.

Before	**In this module**	**After**
Students understand proportional and linear relationships: • use tables and verbal descriptions to describe a linear relationship • write and graph a linear relationship	Students represent and use functions: • identify functions using sets of ordered pairs, tables, mappings, and graphs • identify examples of proportional and nonproportional functions that arise from mathematical and real-world problems • distinguish between proportional and nonproportional situations using tables, graphs, and equations in the form $y = kx$ or $y = mx + b$, where $b \neq 0$ • analyze and interpret graphs	Students will connect relationships and functions: • linear functions • relations • quadratic functions • exponential functions

© Houghton Mifflin Harcourt Publishing Company

Unpacking the Standards

Use the examples on this page to help students know exactly what they are expected to learn in this module.

Florida Common Core Standards

Content Areas

 **Functions—8.F.1**

Define, evaluate, and compare functions.

Go online to see a complete unpacking of the Florida Common Core Standards.

my.hrw.com

MODULE 14

Unpacking the Standards

Understanding the standards and the vocabulary terms in the standards will help you know exactly what you are expected to learn in this module.

FL CC 8.F.1.1

Understand that a function is a rule that assigns to each input exactly one output. The graph of a function is the set of ordered pairs consisting of an input and the corresponding output.

Key Vocabulary

function *(función)*
An input-output relationship that has exactly one output for each input.

What It Means to You

You will identify sets of ordered pairs that are functions. A function is a rule that assigns exactly one output to each input.

UNPACKING EXAMPLE 8.F.1.1

Does the following table of inputs and outputs represent a function?

Input	Output
14	110
20	130
22	120
30	110

Yes, it is a function because each number in the input column is assigned to only one number in the output column.

FL CC 8.F.1.2

Compare properties of two functions each represented in a different way (algebraically, graphically, numerically in tables, or by verbal descriptions).

What It Means to You

You will learn to identify and compare functions expressed as equations and tables.

UNPACKING EXAMPLE 8.F.1.2

A spider descends a 20-foot drainpipe at a rate of 2.5 feet per minute. Another spider descends a drainpipe as shown in the table. Find and compare the rates of change and initial values of the linear functions in terms of the situations they model.

Spider #1: $f(x) = -2.5x + 20$

Spider #2:

Time (min)	0	1	2
Height (ft)	32	29	26

For Spider #1, the rate of change is −2.5, and the initial value is 20. For Spider #2, the rate of change is −3, and the initial value is 32.

Spider #2 started at 32 feet, which is 12 feet higher than Spider #1. Spider #1 is descending at 2.5 feet per minute, which is 0.5 feet per minute slower than Spider #2.

Visit **my.hrw.com** to see all Florida Common Core Standards unpacked.

my.hrw.com

Florida Common Core Standards	Lesson 14.1	Lesson 14.2	Lesson 14.3	Lesson 14.4
FL CC 8.EE.2.5 … Compare two different proportional relationships represented in different ways.				
FL CC 8.F.1.1 Understand that a function is a rule that assigns to each input exactly one output. The graph of a function is the set of ordered pairs consisting of an input and the corresponding output.		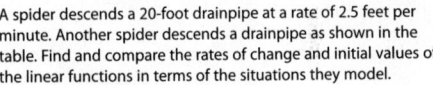		
FL CC 8.F.1.2 Compare properties of two functions each represented in a different way (algebraically, graphically, numerically in tables, or by verbal descriptions).				
FL CC 8.F.1.3 Interpret the equation $y = mx + b$ as defining a linear function, whose graph is a straight line; give examples of functions that are not linear.				
FL CC 8.F.2.4 … Interpret the rate of change and initial value of a linear function in terms of the situation it models, and in terms of its graph or a table of values.				
FL CC 8.F.2.5 Describe qualitatively the functional relationship between two quantities by analyzing a graph …. Sketch a graph that exhibits the qualitative features of a function that has been described verbally.				

LESSON
14.1 Identifying and Representing Functions

Florida Common Core Standards

The student is expected to:

 **Functions—8.F.1.1**

Understand that a function is a rule that assigns to each input exactly one output. The graph of a function is the set of ordered pairs consisting of an input and the corresponding output.

Mathematical Practices

 **MP.4.1** Modeling

Engage

ESSENTIAL QUESTION

How can you identify and represent functions? Sample answer: Some ways to represent a function are a mapping diagram, a table, a graph, and ordered pairs. To determine whether a relationship is a function, check that each input value is matched with only one output value.

Motivate the Lesson

Ask: Suppose students are buying pencils and all of the pencils cost the same amount. Can you create a rule to describe the relationship between the number of pencils a student buys and their cost? Begin the Explore Activity to find out.

Explore

EXPLORE ACTIVITY

Focus on Patterns

After students have filled in the first three rows of the table, guide them to find more than one pattern in the table.

Explain

EXAMPLE 1

Connect Vocabulary **ELL**

Remind students that a function is a rule that explains what to do with the input value to get the output value. The rule may involve one or more operations but each input value results in *exactly* one output.

Questioning Strategies Mathematical Practices

• How do you know which oval shows the input values? The oval on the left shows the input values because the arrows go from that oval to the one on the right.

• What do you look for in a mapping diagram to determine whether the relationship is a function? Each value in the input is paired with only one of the output values.

Engage with the Whiteboard

In Example 1B, have a student change the input data and arrows so that the relationship is a function.

ADDITIONAL EXAMPLE 1
Determine whether each relationship is a function.

A
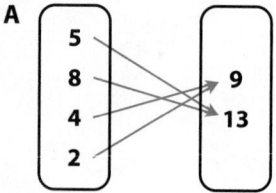
function

B
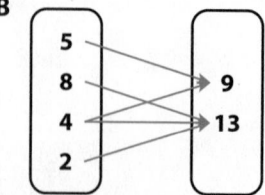
not a function

 Interactive Whiteboard
Interactive example available online

 my.hrw.com

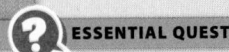
Identifying and Representing Functions

FL CC 8.F.1.1

Understand that a function is a rule that assigns to each input exactly one output. The graph of a function is the set of ordered pairs consisting of an input and the corresponding output.

 ESSENTIAL QUESTION

How can you identify and represent functions?

 EXPLORE ACTIVITY  **FL CC 8.F.1.1**

Understanding Relationships

Carlos needs to buy some new pencils from the school supply store at his school. Carlos asks his classmates if they know how much pencils cost. Angela says she bought 2 pencils for $0.50. Paige bought 3 pencils for $0.75, and Spencer bought 4 pencils for $1.00.

Carlos thinks about the rule for the price of a pencil as a machine. When he puts the number of pencils he wants to buy into the machine, the machine applies a rule and tells him the total cost of that number of pencils.

Input → [machine] → Output

	Number of Pencils	Rule	Total Cost
i.	2	?	$0.50
ii.	3	?	$0.75
iii.	4	?	$1.00
iv.	x	$0.25x$	
v.	12	0.25×12	$3.00

A Use the prices in the problem to fill in total cost in rows **i–iii** of the table.

B Describe any patterns you see. Use your pattern to determine the cost of 1 pencil.

When the number of pencils increases by 1, the cost of the pencils increases by $0.25; 1 pencil must cost $0.25.

EXPLORE ACTIVITY *(cont'd)*

C Use the pattern you identified to write the rule applied by the machine. Write the rule as an algebraic expression and fill in rule column row **iv** of the table.

D Carlos wants to buy 12 pencils. Use your rule to fill in row **v** of the table to show how much Carlos will pay for 12 pencils.

Reflect

1. How did you decide what operation to use in your rule?

   Since one pencil costs $0.25, the cost of any number of pencils is a multiple of $0.25. This means I have to use multiplication.

2. **What If?** Carlos decides to buy erasers in a package. There are 6 pencil-top erasers in 2 packages of erasers.

   a. Write a rule in words for the number of packages Carlos needs to buy to get x erasers. Then write the rule as an algebraic expression.

   divide the number of erasers by 3; $\frac{x}{3}$

   b. How many packages does Carlos need to buy to get 18 erasers?

   $\frac{18}{3} = 6$ packages

 Math On the Spot
my.hrw.com

Identifying Functions from Mapping Diagrams

A **function** assigns exactly one output to each input. The value that is put into a function is the **input**. The result is the **output**.

A mapping diagram can be used to represent a relationship between input values and output values. A mapping diagram represents a function if each input value is paired with only one output value.

EXAMPLE 1 **FL CC 8.F.1.1**

Determine whether each relationship is a function.

A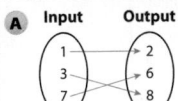
Input   Output

1 → 2
3 → 6
7 → 8

Since each input value is paired with only one output value, the relationship is a function.

PROFESSIONAL DEVELOPMENT

Integrate Mathematical Practices MP.4.1

This lesson provides an opportunity to address this Mathematical Practices standard. It calls for students to represent relationships using diagrams, tables, graphs, and symbols. Students learn to identify and represent a function using a set of ordered pairs, a mapping diagram, words, a table, an equation, and a graph. These multiple representations are used to communicate the idea of a function.

Math Background

The set of all inputs for a function is called the domain. The set of all possible outputs of a function is called the range. For many functions the domain is the set of real numbers. However, the domain is frequently restricted. For example, the domain may be restricted to all positive real numbers and zero if negative numbers do not make sense. For some functions, the domain may be restricted to the positive integers and zero. For example, a function describing the total costs of tickets to a concert would be restricted to the positive integers and zero since you cannot buy a fraction of a ticket or a negative number of tickets.

Focus on Modeling

In Exercise 4, the input values 8 and 9 are both connected to the output value 1. Explain that as long as each input value is connected to only one output, the relationship is still a function.

Talk About It
Check for Understanding

Ask: Seth has exactly three input values in a mapping diagram that he drew. He draws five arrows from the input values to the output values. Why is the relationship shown in Seth's diagram not a function? Three input values should have exactly three arrows drawn (one from each) to the output values. In Seth's diagram, at least one input value must be paired with more than one output value.

EXAMPLE 2

Questioning Strategies Mathematical Practices

- In part A, for the relationship to be a function, does it matter how many times a number is repeated in the output column? No.

- In part B, what is one way the table could be changed so it would represent a function? Sample answer: Change one of the 1s in the input column to a 2.

Avoid Common Errors

Some students think that if there is an output value that corresponds to more than one input value, the relationship is not a function. Remind students that a function is a rule that assigns exactly one output to each input, but two or more input values can give the same output value.

Engage with the Whiteboard

In the margin next to part A invite a student to draw a mapping diagram for the input and output values. Then have another student do the same for part B. This will help students make a connection to these two ways of representing a function.

Talk About It
Check for Understanding

Ask: Angie has four different numbers in the left column of her input/output table. She writes the number 8 in the output column in each row of her table. Why is the relationship shown in Angie's table a function? Since each input value is paired with only one output value, the relationship is a function.

YOUR TURN

Focus on Math Connections Mathematical Practices

Suggest that students draw a mapping diagram for each table to help them determine which of the relationships are functions.

ADDITIONAL EXAMPLE 2
Determine whether each relationship is a function.

A

Input	Output
2	10
4	12
6	24
4	8

not a function

B

Input	Output
2	10
4	10
6	6
8	8

function

 Interactive Whiteboard
Interactive example available online

 ⏻ my.hrw.com

---

Determine whether each relationship is a function.

B Since 2 is paired with more than one output value (both 4 and 5), the relationship is not a function.

0 → 1
0 → 4
2 → 5

Reflect

3. Is it possible for a function to have more than one input value but only one output value? Provide an illustration to support your answer.

1, 2, 3 → 4

Yes

Math Talk
Anno: Sample answer: There is never more than one arrow coming from each input value.

YOUR TURN

Determine whether each relationship is a function. Explain.

4.
7, 8, 9, 10 → 1, 2, 3

function; each input value is paired with only one output value

5.
3 → 0, 2, 4, 6

not a function; the input value is paired with more than one output value

Personal Math Trainer
Online Assessment and Intervention
● my.hrw.com

Math Talk
Mathematical Practices
What is always true about a mapping diagram that represents a function?

Identifying Functions from Tables

Relationships between input values and output values can also be represented using tables. The values in the first column are the input values. The values in the second column are the output values. The relationship represents a function if each input value is paired with only one output value.

Math On the Spot
● my.hrw.com

EXAMPLE 2
FL CC 8.F.1.1

Determine whether each relationship is a function.

A

Input	Output
5	7
10	6
15	15
20	2
25	15

Since 15 is a repeated output value, one output value is paired with two input values. If this occurs in a relationship, the relationship can still be a function.

Since each input value is paired with only one output value, the relationship is a function.

My Notes

Determine whether each relationship is a function.

B

Input	Output
1	10
5	8
4	6
1	4
7	2

Since 1 is a repeated input value, one input value is paired with two output values. Look back at the rule for functions. Is this relationship a function?

Since the input value 1 is paired with more than one output value (both 10 and 4), the relationship is not a function.

Reflect

6. What is always true about the numbers in the first column of a table that represents a function? Why must this be true?

They must all be different numbers, because if a number is repeated, then that input value is paired with more than one output value and the relationship is not a function.

YOUR TURN

Determine whether each relationship is a function. Explain

7.

Input	Output
53	53
24	24
32	32
17	17
45	45

function; each input value is paired with only one output value

8.

Input	Output
14	52
8	21
27	16
36	25
8	34

not a function; the input value 8 is paired with more than one output value

Personal Math Trainer
Online Assessment and Intervention
● my.hrw.com

DIFFERENTIATE INSTRUCTION

World History
Explain to students that almost 4000 years ago, the Babylonians had a working idea of functions: some of the clay tablets they made show tables representing functions. The mathematician and philosopher Leibniz was the first to use the term *function* to mean what it means in this lesson. Discuss some different uses of the term *function* in our modern society.

Kinesthetic Experience
Give each student an index card. On each side of the card have them draw two ovals to make a mapping diagram. On one side, have students create a mapping that represents a relationship of a real-word situation that is a function. On the other side, have students create a mapping that represents a relationship of a real-word situation that is not a function. (Example 3 and its corresponding Your Turn are examples of real-world relationships that are not functions.) Use pipe cleaners to connect each input value to its output value(s). Have students label each diagram with the words *function* and *not a function*.

Additional Resources
Differentiated Instruction includes
• Reading Strategies
• Success for English Learners **ELL**
• Reteach
• Challenge **PRE-AP**

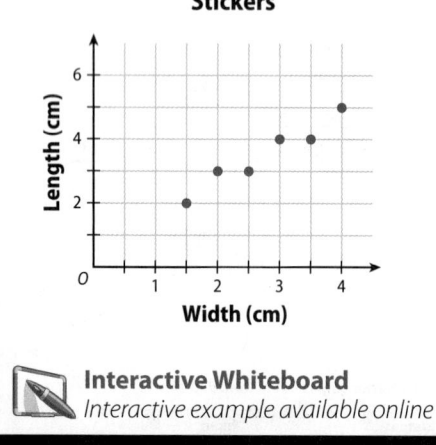

EXAMPLE 3

Questioning Strategies Mathematical Practices

- Without knowing any values, how can you look at the graph and know the relationship is not a function? There is at least one dot that is right above another dot. For example the dot at (2, 85) is right above the dot for (2, 70).

- If you drew a mapping diagram for the situation in Example 3, how many arrows would be coming from the number 1? The number 2? The number 3? Why? 1; 2; 1; because the number 1 is paired with one number (70), the number 2 is paired with two numbers (70 and 85), and the number 3 is paired with one number (75).

Engage with the Whiteboard

Have students draw a vertical line through the points at (2, 70) and (2, 85) and another through the points at (9, 90) and (9, 95). This will help them see that 2 hours of study and 9 hours of study are paired with more than one exam grade.

Focus on Critical Thinking Mathematical Practices

Introduce the vertical line test: If each vertical line passes through at most one point on a graph of a relationship; the relationship is a function. If there is at least one vertical line that passes through more than one point, the relationship is not a function. Have students explain why the vertical line test works.

YOUR TURN

Focus on Patterns Mathematical Practices

Point out to students that the graph of a function can be isolated points rather than a line. Remind them that what matters is whether the graph passes the vertical line test.

Integrating Language Arts ELL

Encourage English learners to use surrounding visuals to help them understand the problem.

Elaborate

Talk About It
Summarize the Lesson

Ask: How do you know that a relationship represented by a mapping diagram, a table of values, or a graph is a function? In a mapping diagram there will be only one arrow drawn from each input value. In a table of values, each input value (*x*-value) will correspond to only one output value (*y*-value). The graph of a function will pass the vertical line test.

GUIDED PRACTICE

Avoid Common Errors

Exercises 1–3 Remind students that the rule they write must work for each and every input and output pair.

Exercise 4 Remind students that for the relationship to be a function, each input value can only be connected with one output value.

Exercise 5 Remind students that the relationship is not a function if there is at least one input value that corresponds to more than one output value.

Engage with the Whiteboard

For Exercise 6, invite a student to draw a mapping diagram using the ordered pairs from the graph. This should help students confirm that the relationship is a function.

Identifying Functions from Graphs

Graphs can be used to display relationships between two sets of numbers. Each point on a graph represents an ordered pair. The first coordinate in each ordered pair is the input value. The second coordinate is the output value. The graph represents a function if each input value is paired with only one output value.

Math On the Spot
my.hrw.com

EXAMPLE 3 Real World
FL CC 8.F.1.1

The graph shows the relationship between the number of hours students spent studying for an exam and the exam grades. Is the relationship represented by the graph a function?

The input values are the number of hours spent studying by each student. The output values are the exam grades. The points represent the following ordered pairs:

(1, 70)   (2, 70)   (2, 85)   (3, 75)   (5, 80)
(6, 82)   (7, 88)   (9, 90)   (9, 95)   (12, 98)

Hours Studied and Exam Grade

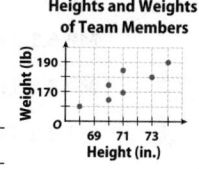

Notice that 2 is paired with both 70 and 85, and 9 is paired with both 90 and 95. Therefore, since these input values are paired with more than one output value, the relationship is not a function.

Reflect

9. Many real-world relationships are functions. For example, the amount of money made at a car wash is a function of the number of cars washed. Give another example of a real-world function.

Sample answer: The amount earned at an hourly-wage is a function of the number of hours worked.

YOUR TURN

10. The graph shows the relationship between the heights and weights of the members of a basketball team. Is the relationship represented by the graph a function? Explain.

not a function; input values are paired with more than one output values; (70,165) and (70, 178)

Heights and Weights of Team Members

Personal Math Trainer
Online Assessment and Intervention
my.hrw.com

Guided Practice

Complete each table. In the row with *x* as the input, write a rule as an algebraic expression for the output. Then complete the last row of the table using the rule. (Explore Activity)

1.

Input	Output
Tickets	Cost ($)
2	40
5	100
7	140
x	20x
10	200

2.

Input	Output
Minutes	Pages
2	1
10	5
20	10
x	$\frac{x}{2}$
30	15

3.

Input	Output
Muffins	Cost ($)
1	2.25
3	6.75
6	13.50
x	2.25x
12	27.00

Determine whether each relationship is a function. (Examples 1 and 2)

4.

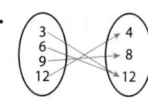

function; each input value is paired with only one output value

5.

Input	Output
3	20
4	25
5	30
4	35
6	40

not a function; the input value 4 is paired with more than one output value

6. The graph shows the relationship between the weights of 5 packages and the shipping charge for each package. Is the relationship represented by the graph a function? Explain.

Yes; each input value is paired with only one output value.

Weights and Shipping Costs

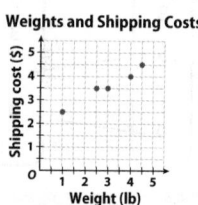

ESSENTIAL QUESTION CHECK-IN

7. What are four different ways of representing functions? How can you tell if a relationship is a function?

Mapping diagrams, tables, graphs, ordered pairs; a relationship is a function if each input value is paired with only one output value.

Personal Math Trainer

Online Assessment and Intervention

Online homework assignment available

my.hrw.com

14.1 LESSON QUIZ

 **FL CC** 8.F.1.1

1. There are 12 iron-on patches in 4 packages. Each package has the same number of patches. Write a rule in words for the number of packages Leah needs to buy to get x patches. Then write the rule as an algebraic expression.

Determine whether each relationship is a function.

2.

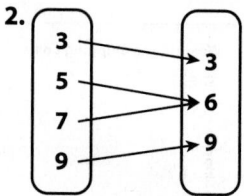

3.

Input	Output
2	7
5	10
8	13
5	7

4. The graph shows the relationship between the number of texts a person sends and the number of hours the person spends outside during the summer. Is the relationship represented by the graph a function? Explain.

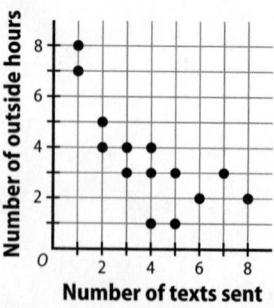

Lesson Quiz available online

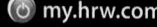 my.hrw.com

Evaluate

GUIDED AND INDEPENDENT PRACTICE

FL CC 8.F.1.1

Concepts & Skills	Practice
Explore Activity Understanding Relationships	Exercises 1–3, 10, 12
Example 1 Identifying Functions from Mapping Diagrams	Exercises 4, 15
Example 2 Identifying Functions from Tables	Exercise 5
Example 3 Identifying Functions from Graphs	Exercises 6, 11, 13–14

Exercise	Depth of Knowledge (D.O.K.)		**FL CC** Mathematical Practices
8–10	**1** Recall of Information		**MP.6.1** Precision
11	**3** Strategic Thinking	H.O.T.	**MP.3.1** Logic
12	**3** Strategic Thinking	H.O.T.	**MP.4.1** Modeling
13	**2** Skills/Concepts		**MP.6.1** Precision
14	**3** Strategic Thinking	H.O.T.	**MP.3.1** Logic
15	**3** Strategic Thinking	H.O.T.	**MP.2.1** Reasoning
16	**3** Strategic Thinking	H.O.T.	**MP.3.1** Logic

Additional Resources

Differentiated Instruction includes:

• Leveled Practice worksheets

Answers

1. Divide the number of patches by 3; $\frac{x}{3}$

2. function

3. not a function

4. No; at least one of the input values is paired with more than one output value; in fact, many of the input values are paired with more than one output value.

14.1 Independent Practice

FL CC 8.F.1.1

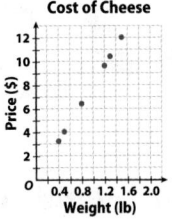

Personal Math Trainer
Online Assessment and Intervention
my.hrw.com

Determine whether each relationship represented by the ordered pairs is a function. Explain.

8. (2, 2), (3, 1), (5, 7), (8, 0), (9, 1)

function; each input value is paired with only one output value
_____

9. (0, 4), (5, 1), (2, 8), (6, 3), (5, 9)

not a function; the input value 5 is paired with more than one output value

10. Draw Conclusions Joaquin receives $0.40 per pound for 1 to 99 pounds of aluminum cans he recycles. He receives $0.50 per pound if he recycles more than 100 pounds. Is the amount of money Joaquin receives a function of the weight of the cans he recycles? Explain your reasoning.

Yes. For each pound of aluminum he recycles (input), there can only be one dollar amount representing the amount of money he receives (outcome).

11. A biologist tracked the growth of a strain of bacteria, as shown in the graph.

a. Explain why the relationship represented by the graph is a function.

There is only one number of bacteria for each number of hours, so each input is paired with only one output.

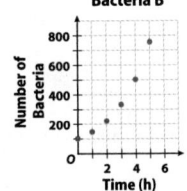

Bacteria B

b. What If? Suppose there was the same number of bacteria for two consecutive hours. Would the graph still represent a function? Explain.

Yes. Each input value would still be paired with only one output value.

12. Multiple Representations Give an example of a function in everyday life, and represent it as a graph, a table, and a set of ordered pairs. Describe how you know it is a function.

Check students' work

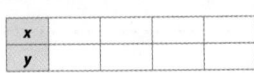

x				
y				

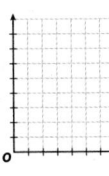

The graph shows the relationship between the weights of six wedges of cheese and the price of each wedge.

Cost of Cheese

13. Is the relationship represented by the graph a function? Justify your reasoning. Use the words "input" and "output" in your explanation, and connect them to the context represented by the graph.

Yes. Each input value (the weight) is paired with only one output value (the price).

14. Analyze Relationships Suppose the weights and prices of additional wedges of cheese were plotted on the graph. Might that change your answer to question 13? Explain your reasoning.

Sample answer: No. The points appear to lie along a straight line. Any additional wedge of cheese will probably also lie along this line, and the relationship will remain a function.

H.O.T. FOCUS ON HIGHER ORDER THINKING

15. Justify Reasoning A mapping diagram represents a relationship that contains three different input values and four different output values. Is the relationship a function? Explain your reasoning.

It does not represent a function. For the input values to be paired with all four output values, at least one of the input values would be paired with more than one output value.

16. Communicate Mathematical Ideas An onion farmer is hiring workers to help harvest the onions. He knows that the number of days it will take to harvest the onions is a function of the number of workers he hires. Explain the use of the word "function" in this context.

The number of days it will take to harvest the onions depends on the number of workers he hires. The input values of the function are the number of workers. The output values are the number of days. For any particular number of workers, the job will take a certain number of days.

Work Area

EXTEND THE MATH PRE-AP

Activity available online my.hrw.com

Activity The inverse of a relationship is found by switching the coordinates in each ordered pair of the relationship. So, for each ordered pair (x, y) in the relationship, the ordered pair (y, x) will appear in its inverse. Graph the function {(1, 3), (2, 4), (3, 5), (−1, 1), (−3, −1)}, find its inverse, and graph the inverse. Is the inverse of this function a function? Try to find a counterexample to determine whether the inverse of a function is always a function.

Inverse of the function: {(3, 1), (4, 2), (5, 3), (1, −1), (−3, −1)}; yes, the inverse of the function is a function. Sample answer (counterexample): function: {(5, 2), (7, 2), (−3, 1), (−5, 0)}; inverse of the function: {(2, 5), (2, 7), (−3, 1), (0, −5)}; the inverse is not a function. So, the inverse of a function is not always a function.

LESSON 14.2 Describing Functions

Engage

ESSENTIAL QUESTION

What are some characteristics that you can use to describe functions? Sample answer: A function can be linear or nonlinear. A linear function can be proportional or nonproportional.

Motivate the Lesson

Ask: Suppose that it started raining today at a constant rate and you make a table showing the amount of rain that has fallen after 1 hour, 2 hours, 3 hours, and so on. What kind of function would that table represent?

Explore

EXPLORE ACTIVITY

Focus on Patterns

After students complete parts A and B, have them describe the patterns that they see in the table and graph. Is the relationship linear? Is it proportional?

Explain

EXAMPLE 1

Questioning Strategies **Mathematical Practices**

- How do you find the values for the table? Select several integers for the x values (the number of hours). Multiply the number of hours by 2 and then add 8 to get the y values.

- How do you know whether or not to connect the points in the graph with a line? Because the time and temperature are not just integer amounts, there are an infinite number of values for time and temperature between each of the given values. A line is appropriate.

Focus on Technology

In Example 1, students could enter the equation $y = 2x + 8$ into the Y = editor on a graphing calculator. If a standard viewing window is chosen, students will see the graph in a four-quadrant coordinate system. Discuss why the graph only involves the first quadrant.

Engage with the Whiteboard

Cover up the text shown under the headings in columns 2–4. Have students take turns showing how to complete the table to find the ordered pairs.

YOUR TURN

Avoid Common Errors

Students may graph the equation incorrectly. Suggest that students determine and graph at least three ordered pairs.

ADDITIONAL EXAMPLE 1

Vance charges $20 an hour to plow the snow off of driveways. The equation $y = 20x$ gives the cost y in dollars for x hours. State whether the relationship between the time and the cost is proportional or nonproportional. Then graph the function. Since $b = 0$, the graph is proportional.

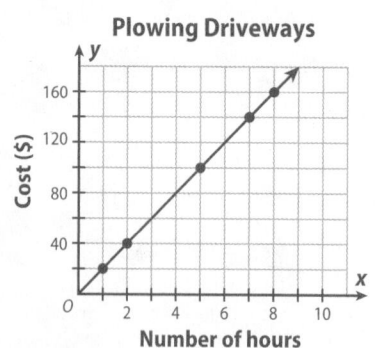

Plowing Driveways

Interactive Whiteboard
Interactive example available online

 my.hrw.com

LESSON 14.2 Describing Functions

FL CC 8.F.1.3
Interpret the equation $y = mx + b$ as defining a linear function, whose graph is a straight line; give examples of functions that are not linear.
Also 8.F.1.1

? ESSENTIAL QUESTION

What are some characteristics that you can use to describe functions?

EXPLORE ACTIVITY FL CC 8.F.1.1

Investigating a Constant Rate of Change

The U.S. Department of Agriculture defines heavy rain as rain that falls at a rate of 1.5 centimeters per hour.

A The table shows the total amount of rain that falls in various amounts of time during a heavy rain. Complete the table.

Time (h)	0	1	2	3	4	5
Total Amount of Rain (cm)	0	1.5	3	4.5	6	7.5

B Plot the ordered pairs from the table on the coordinate plane at the right.

C How much rain falls in 3.5 hours? __5.25 cm__

D Plot the point corresponding to 3.5 hours of heavy rain.

E What do you notice about all of the points you plotted?

All of the points lie along a line.

Heavy Rainfall

(graph: Total Amount of Rain (cm) vs Time (h))

F Is the total amount of rain that falls a function of the number of hours that rain has been falling? Why or why not?

Yes. For any given input of time, there can be one and only one output of total amount of rain.

Reflect

1. Suppose you continued to plot points for times between those in the table, such as 1.2 hours or 4.5 hours. What can you say about the locations of these points?

The points would fill in the gaps along the line determined by the existing points of the graph.

Lesson 14.2 **425**

Math On the Spot
my.hrw.com

Graphing Linear Functions

The relationship you investigated in the previous activity can be represented by the equation $y = 1.5x$, where x is the time and y is the total amount of rain. The graph of the relationship is a line, so the equation is a **linear equation**. Since there is exactly one value of y for each value of x, the relationship is a function. It is a **linear function** because its graph is a nonvertical line.

EXAMPLE 1 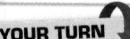 FL CC 8.F.1.3

The temperature at dawn was 8°F and increased steadily 2°F every hour. The equation $y = 2x + 8$ gives the temperature y after x hours. State whether the relationship between the time and the temperature is proportional or nonproportional. Then graph the function.

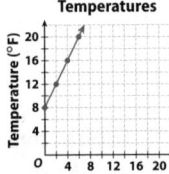

Math Talk
Mathematical Practices

Carrie said that for a function to be a linear function, the relationship it represents must be proportional. Do you agree or disagree? Explain.

Disagree; sample answer: the only requirement is that the graph of the function be a nonvertical line. Whether the graph passes through the origin (proportional) or not (nonproportional) does not matter.

STEP 1 Compare the equation with the general linear equation $y = mx + b$. $y = 2x + 8$ is in the form $y = mx + b$, with $m = 2$ and $b = 8$. Therefore, the equation is a linear equation. Since $b \neq 0$, the relationship is nonproportional.

STEP 2 Choose several values for the input x. Substitute these values for x in the equation to find the output y.

x	$2x + 8$	y	(x, y)
0	$2(0) + 8$	8	(0, 8)
2	$2(2) + 8$	12	(2, 12)
4	$2(4) + 8$	16	(4, 16)
6	$2(6) + 8$	20	(6, 20)

STEP 3 Graph the ordered pairs. Then draw a line through the points to represent the solutions of the function.

Temperatures

(graph: Temperature (°F) vs Time (h))

Personal Math Trainer
Online Assessment and Intervention
my.hrw.com

YOUR TURN

2. State whether the relationship between x and y in $y = 0.5x$ is proportional or nonproportional. Then graph the function.

__proportional__

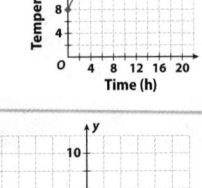

426 Unit 6

PROFESSIONAL DEVELOPMENT

Integrate Mathematical Practices MP.6.1

This lesson provides an opportunity to address this Mathematical Practices standard. It calls for students to precisely communicate mathematical ideas and reasoning. Students model real-world and mathematical functions by creating a table of values and then graphing the ordered pairs on a coordinate grid. They determine whether the functions are proportional or nonproportional, and linear or nonlinear.

Math Background

Linear equations (e.g., $y = x$ and $y = 4x + 5$) are called *first degree equations* because the greatest power of the variable x is 1. Quadratic equations (e.g., $y = x^2$ and $y = 4x^2 + 2x + 5$) are called *second degree equations* because the greatest power of x is 2. Cubic equations (e.g., $y = x^3$ and $y = 4x^3 + x^2 + 3x + 5$) are called *third degree equations* because the greatest power of x is 3.

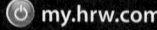

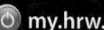
EXAMPLE 2

Questioning Strategies Mathematical Practices

• How do you decide which values of x to use? The values of x must all be positive in order to work for the real-world situation described.

• How are the values of y related to the values of x? Each y value is the square of the corresponding x value.

Focus on Modeling Mathematical Practices

In Example 2, students use data from a table to create a graph that models a real-world situation. Ensure that students understand the real-world quantities involved in the problem.

YOUR TURN

Focus on Math Connections Mathematical Practices

Make sure that students understand the connection between the numbers in the table having a constant rate of change and the relationship being linear.

Elaborate

Talk About It
Summarize the Lesson

Ask: How can you show that the relationship between x and y given in the form of an equation is a linear relationship and also a proportional relationship? Sample answer: First make a table of values for the equation and graph the ordered pairs; if the rate of change in the table is constant and the graph is a line through (0, 0), then the relationship is a proportional linear relationship.

GUIDED PRACTICE

Engage with the Whiteboard

Have students verify their answers to Exercises 3 and 4 by graphing the equations on the coordinate grids shown in Exercises 1 and 2.

Avoid Common Errors
Exercise 1 Remind students that $y = 5 - 2x$ is the same as $y = -2x + 5$.

Exercise 5 Remind students that the graph of a proportional relationship is a line that goes through the origin.

Determining Whether a Function is Linear

The linear equation in Example 1 has the form $y = mx + b$, where m and b are real numbers. Every equation in the form $y = mx + b$ is a linear equation. The linear equations represent linear functions. Equations that cannot be written in this form are not linear equations, and therefore are not linear functions.

Math On the Spot
my.hrw.com

EXAMPLE 2

   **FL CC** 8.F.1.3

A square tile has a side length of x inches. The equation $y = x^2$ gives the area of the tile in square inches. Determine whether the relationship between x and y is linear and, if so, if it is proportional.

STEP 1 Choose several values for the input x. Substitute these values for x in the equation to find the output y.

x	x^2	y	(x, y)
1	1^2	1	(1, 1)
2	2^2	4	(2, 4)
3	3^2	9	(3, 9)
4	4^2	16	(4, 16)

STEP 2 Graph the ordered pairs.

STEP 3 Identify the shape of the graph. The points suggest a curve, not a line. Draw a curve through the points to represent the solutions of the function.

STEP 4 Describe the relationship between x and y.

The graph is not a line so the relationship is not linear.

Only a linear relationship can be proportional, so the relationship is not proportional.

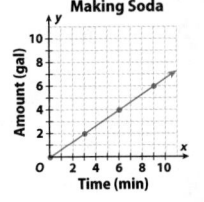

Math Talk
Mathematical Practices

How can you use the numbers in the table to decide whether or not the relationship between x and y is linear?

Sample answer: I can check to see whether the rate of change is constant. Since it is not constant, the relationship is not linear.

YOUR TURN

3. A soda machine makes $\frac{2}{3}$ gallon of soda every minute. The total amount y that the machine makes in x minutes is given by the equation $y = \frac{2}{3}x$. Determine whether the relationship between x and y is linear and, if so, if it is proportional.

Making Soda

Time (min), x	0	3	6	9
Amount (gal), y	0	2	4	6

linear; proportional

Animated Math
my.hrw.com

Personal Math Trainer
Online Assessment and Intervention
my.hrw.com

Plot the ordered pairs from the table. Then graph the function represented by the ordered pairs and tell whether the function is linear or nonlinear. (Examples 1 and 2)

1. $y = 5 - 2x$

Input, x	−1	1	3	5
Output, y	7	3	−1	−5

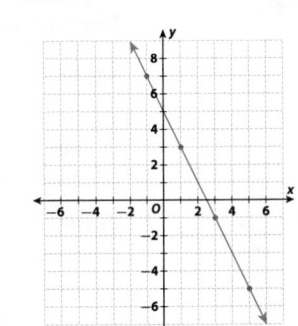

linear

2. $y = 2 - x^2$

Input, x	−2	−1	0	1	2
Output, y	−2	1	2	1	−2

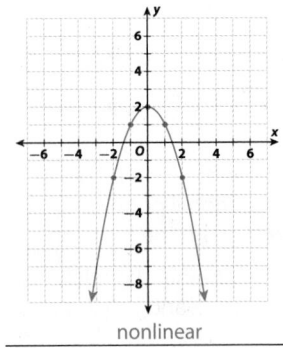

nonlinear

Explain whether each equation is a linear equation. (Example 2)

3. $y = x^2 - 1$

No; the equation cannot be written in the form $y = mx + b$, and the graph of the solutions is not a line.

4. $y = 1 - x$

Yes; the equation can be written in the form $y = mx + b$, and the graph of the solutions is a line.

 **ESSENTIAL QUESTION CHECK-IN**

5. Explain how you can use a table of values, an equation, and a graph to determine whether a function represents a proportional relationship.

A table of values will include (0, 0) and show a constant rate of change. An equation will be of the form $y = mx$. A graph will be a line passing through the origin.

DIFFERENTIATE INSTRUCTION

Cognitive Strategies

Explain that temperatures in most other countries are given in degrees Celsius rather than in degrees Fahrenheit. Ask students how they would decide what to wear to go outside in such a country. Students may take several approaches. Some students may have a sense of the meaning of Celsius temperatures. Some may use the formula $F = 1.8C + 32$ to convert the Celsius temperatures (C) to Fahrenheit temperatures (F). For a quick approximation, students can double the Celsius temperature and add 30 to get a rough estimate of the Fahrenheit temperatures. Have students write an equation for that relationship ($F = 2C + 30$).

Critical Thinking

Ask students to explain why the relationship given by the equation $y = 2x + 6$ is a linear function. Then ask them to determine whether all lines represent functions. Students should justify their answer with a logical argument. (The relationship given by the equation $y = 2x + 6$ is a function because each x value is paired with a unique y value. The function is linear because it is of the form $y = mx + b$. Vertical lines are not functions. For example, the vertical line through the point 3 on the x-axis does not represent a function because there is only one x value and it is paired with an infinite number of y values.)

Additional Resources

Differentiated Instruction includes

- Reading Strategies
- Success for English Learners **ELL**
- Reteach
- Challenge **PRE-AP**

Describing Functions **428**

Personal Math Trainer

Online Assessment and Intervention

Online homework assignment available

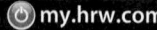
⏻ my.hrw.com

14.2 LESSON QUIZ

FL CC 8.F.1.1, 8.F.1.3

1. State whether the relationship between x and y in $y = 2x - 3$ is proportional or nonproportional. Then graph the function.

2. State whether the relationship between x and y in $y = x^2 - 1$ is linear and, if so, if it is proportional or nonproportional. Then graph the function.

3. Lenora is making rice at a women's shelter. The table shows y, the total number of cups of water she needs to use for x cups of rice.

x	1	3	5	7
y	2.5	7.5	12.5	17.5

   a. Use the data to draw a graph. Is the relationship between x and y linear? Explain.

   b. Use your graph to predict the number of cups of water to use when using 10 cups of rice.

Lesson Quiz available online

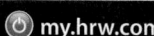
⏻ my.hrw.com

Evaluate

GUIDED AND INDEPENDENT PRACTICE

FL CC 8.F.1.1, 8.F.1.3

Concepts & Skills	Practice
Explore Activity Investigating a Constant Rate of Change	Exercises 1, 8–9
Example 1 Graphing Linear Functions	Exercises 1, 6, 9
Example 2 Determining Whether a Function is Linear	Exercises 1–4, 7–11

Exercise	Depth of Knowledge (D.O.K.)		**FL CC** Mathematical Practices
6	2 Skills/Concepts		**MP.2.1** Reasoning
7–10	2 Skills/Concepts		**MP.3.1** Logic
11–13	3 Strategic Thinking	H.O.T.	**MP.2.1** Reasoning
14	3 Strategic Thinking	H.O.T.	**MP.3.1** Logic
15	3 Strategic Thinking	H.O.T.	**MP.5.1** Using Tools

Additional Resources

Differentiated Instruction includes:

• Leveled Practice worksheets

Answers

1. nonproportional

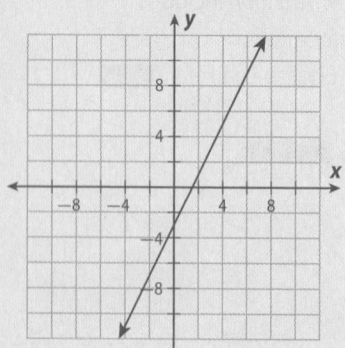

2. not linear, nonproportional

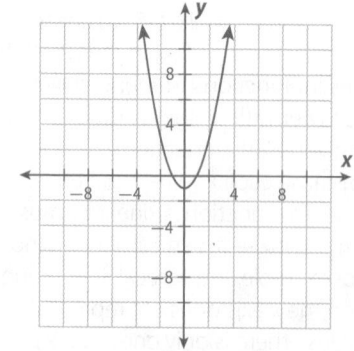

3a. Yes, it is linear; the graph of the solutions lie in a straight line.

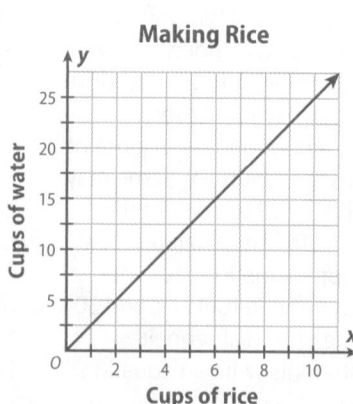

Making Rice

3b. 25 cups of water

14.2 Independent Practice

FL CC 8.F.1.1, 8.F.1.3

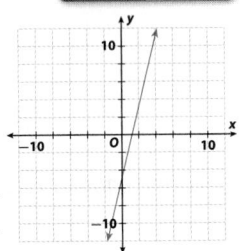

Personal Math Trainer

Online Assessment and Intervention

my.hrw.com

6. State whether the relationship between x and y in $y = 4x - 5$ is proportional or nonproportional. Then graph the function.

nonproportional

7. The Fortaleza telescope in Brazil is a radio telescope. Its shape can be approximated with the equation $y = 0.013x^2$. Is the relationship between x and y linear? Is it proportional? Explain.

No. The relationship is not linear because x is squared, so it will not be proportional.

8. Kiley spent $20 on rides and snacks at the state fair. If x is the amount she spent on rides, and y is the amount she spent on snacks, the total amount she spent can be represented by the equation $x + y = 20$. Is the relationship between x and y linear? Is it proportional? Explain.

If you solve for y, the relationship is $y = -x + 20$. Since the equation is in the form $y = mx + b$ with $m = -1$ and $b = 20$, the equation is linear. It is not proportional because $b \neq 0$.

9. **Represent Real-World Problems** The drill team is buying new uniforms. The table shows y, the total cost in dollars, and x, the number of uniforms purchased.

Number of uniforms, x	1	3	5	9
Total cost ($), y	60	180	300	540

a. Use the data to draw a graph. Is the relationship between x and y linear? Explain.

Yes. The graph of the solutions lie in a line.

b. Use your graph to predict the cost of purchasing 12 uniforms.

$720

Drill Team Uniforms

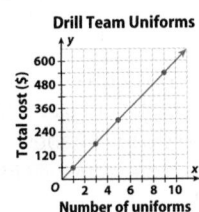

10. Marta, a whale calf in an aquarium, is fed a special milk formula. Her handler uses a graph to track the number of gallons of formula y the calf drinks in x hours. Is the relationship between x and y linear? Is it proportional? Explain.

Yes, it is linear; all of the points lie along a line. Yes, it is proportional; the graph contains the point (0, 0).

Marta's Feedings

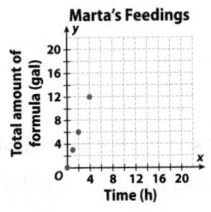

11. **Critique Reasoning** A student claims that the equation $y = 7$ is not a linear equation because it does not have the form $y = mx + b$. Do you agree or disagree? Why?

Disagree; the equation can be written in the form $y = mx + b$ where m is 0, and the graph of the solutions is a horizontal line.

12. **Make a Prediction** Let x represent the number of hours you read a book and y represent the total number of pages you have read. You have already read 70 pages and can read 30 pages per hour. Write an equation relating x hours and y pages you read. Then predict the total number of pages you will have read after another 3 hours.

$y = 30x + 70$; 160 pages

H.O.T. FOCUS ON HIGHER ORDER THINKING

13. **Draw Conclusions** Rebecca draws a graph of a real-world relationship that turns out to be a set of unconnected points. Can the relationship be linear? Can it be proportional? Explain your reasoning.

The relationship will be linear if the points all lie on the same line. The relationship will be proportional if it is linear and if a line through the points passes through the origin.

14. **Communicate Mathematical Ideas** Write a real-world problem involving a proportional relationship. Explain how you know the relationship is proportional.

Sample answer: Jacob charges $30 to mow a lawn. How much does he earn mowing lawns?

The relationship is proportional because the equation of the relationship is $y = 30x$ and is in the form $y = mx$.

15. **Justify Reasoning** Show that the equation $y + 3 = 3(2x + 1)$ is linear and that it represents a proportional relationship between x and y.

$y + 3 = 3(2x + 1)$

$y + 3 = 6x + 3$ Use the Distributive Property.

$\quad y = 6x$ Subtract 3 from both sides.

The equation is in the form $y = mx + b$, so it is linear. Since $b = 0$, it represents a proportional relationship.

Work Area

EXTEND THE MATH PRE-AP

Activity available online my.hrw.com

Activity The inverse of a function is found by switching the coordinates in each ordered pair of the function. Given the nonlinear function $y = x^2 - 2$, find the equation for its inverse. Graph both relations on the same graph. Tell whether the inverse of the function is a function. Explain how you know.

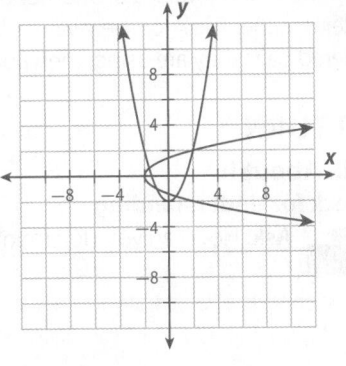

The inverse of $y = x^2 - 2$ is $x = y^2 - 2$. The graph shows that the inverse is not a function because each value of x, except for $x = -2$, results in two different values of y; for example (2, 2) and (2, -2).

LESSON
14.3 Comparing Functions

 Florida Common Core Standards

The student is expected to:

 **FL CC** Functions—8.F.1.2

Compare properties of two functions each represented in a different way (algebraically, graphically, numerically in tables, or by verbal descriptions).

 **FL CC** Expressions and Equations—8.EE.2.5

Graph proportional relationships, interpreting the unit rate as the slope of the graph. Compare two different proportional relationships represented in different ways.

 FL CC Functions—8.F.2.4

Construct a function to model a linear relationship between two quantities. Determine [and] ... Interpret the rate of change and initial value of a linear function ...

Mathematical Practices

 **FL CC** MP.3.1 Logic

---

ADDITIONAL EXAMPLE 1

Melanie and Patrick have different phone services. The relationship of the monthly cost, y dollars, to send or receive x text messages, is a linear function. The cost of Patrick's texting is described by $y = 0.03x + 5$. The cost of Melanie's texting is shown in the table.

Melanie's Monthly Texting Cost

x	5	10	15	20	25
y	1.25	2.50	3.75	5.00	6.25

A Write an equation to represent Melanie's monthly texting cost.
$y = 0.25x$

B Which service is cheaper when 50 texts are sent or received in one month? Patrick's service would cost $6.50. Melanie's would cost $12.50. Patrick's is cheaper.

 Interactive Whiteboard
Interactive example available online

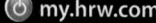 my.hrw.com

---

Engage

ESSENTIAL QUESTION

How can you use tables, graphs, and equations to compare functions? Sample answer: You can compare functions by graphing each function and comparing the graphs, or by writing each function as an equation and comparing the equations.

Motivate the Lesson
Ask: If you are given the graph of two linear functions, how can you compare the slopes of the lines representing the functions?

Explore

Review the different ways to represent a function. If you want to compare two functions, what are the advantages and disadvantages of using a graph, an equation, or a table? See also Explore Activity 1 and Explore Activity 2 in student text.

Explain

EXAMPLE 1

Questioning Strategies  **Mathematical Practices**

• When you use the slope and a point to find the y-intercept, how do you know what values to use for x and y? You can use the x- and y-values of any point in the table.

• How can you use the values in the table to decide whether the relationship is proportional? Write an equation in the form $y = mx + b$. If $b = 0$ the relationship is proportional.

Avoid Common Errors
Remind students that to find the slope, they must subtract the x- and y-values of one point from the x- and y-values of another point. Students sometimes inadvertently change the order of either the x- or the y-values before subtraction. Suggest they write out the two ordered pairs they are using, then above each write (x_1, y_1) and (x_2, y_2).

YOUR TURN
Talk About It
Check for Understanding

Ask: How can you determine that ordering online is not always less expensive? Make a table with $x = 1, 2, 3, 4,$ and 5, and find $y = 6.95x + 1.50$ for each x-value. Comparing the values of y in the new table to the table for the bookstore will show that the bookstore's cost is sometimes less.

EXPLORE ACTIVITY 1

Questioning Strategies  **Mathematical Practices**

• How can you find the unit rates for the functions? Write the slope as a fraction with a denominator of 1.

• Which relationship has the greater rate of change? Compare unit rates: 15 wpm < 20 wpm.

14.3 Comparing Functions

FL CC 8.F.1.2

Compare properties of two functions each represented in a different way (algebraically, graphically, numerically in tables, or by verbal descriptions). *Also 8.EE.2.5, 8.F.2.4*

ESSENTIAL QUESTION How can you use tables, graphs, and equations to compare functions?

Comparing a Table and an Equation

To compare a function written as an equation and another function represented by a table, find the equation for the function in the table.

 Math On the Spot
my.hrw.com

EXAMPLE 1 *Real World* **FL CC** 8.F.1.2, 8.F.2.4

Josh and Maggie buy MP3 files from different music services. The monthly cost, *y* dollars, for *x* songs is linear. The cost of Josh's service is $y = 0.50x + 10$. The cost of Maggie's service is shown below.

Monthly Cost of MP3s at Maggie's Music Service					
Songs, *x*	5	10	15	20	25
Cost ($), *y*	4.95	9.90	14.85	19.80	24.75

A Write an equation to represent the monthly cost of Maggie's service.

STEP 1 Choose any two ordered pairs from the table to find the slope.

$$m = \frac{y_2 - y_1}{x_2 - x_1} = \frac{9.90 - 4.95}{10 - 5} = \frac{4.95}{5} = 0.99$$

The points (5, 4.95) and (10, 9.90) were used.

STEP 2 Find the *y*-intercept. Use the slope and any point.

$y = mx + b$ Slope-intercept form.

$4.95 = 0.99 \cdot 5 + b$ Substitute for *y*, *m*, and *x*.

$0 = b$

STEP 3 Substitute the slope and *y*-intercept.

$y = 0.99x + 0$ or $y = 0.99x$ Substitute 0.99 for *m* and 0 for *y*.

Math Talk
Mathematical Practices

Describe each service's cost in words using the meanings of the slopes and *y*-intercepts.

B Which service is cheaper when 30 songs are downloaded?

Josh's service: Maggie's service:

$y = 0.50 \times 30 + 10$ $y = 0.99 \times 30$

$y = 25$ $y = 29.7$

Josh's service is cheaper.

Josh pays a $10/month fee but only pays $0.50 per song. Maggie has no monthly fee but pays $0.99 per song.

 Personal Math Trainer
Online Assessment and Intervention
my.hrw.com

YOUR TURN

1. Quentin is choosing between buying books at the bookstore or buying online versions of the books for his tablet. The cost, *y* dollars, of ordering books online for *x* books is $y = 6.95x + 1.50$. The cost of buying the books at the bookstore is shown in the table. Which method of buying books is more expensive if Quentin wants to buy 6 books?

Cost of Books at the Bookstore					
Books, *x*	1	2	3	4	5
Cost ($), *y*	7.50	15.00	22.50	30.00	37.50

Buying at the bookstore is more expensive.

EXPLORE ACTIVITY 1 *Real World* **FL CC** 8.F.1.2, 8.EE.2.5

Comparing a Table and a Graph

The table and graph show how many words Morgan and Brian typed correctly on a typing test. For both students, the relationship between words typed correctly and time is linear.

Brian's Typing Test

(graph with x-axis "Time (min)" 0–10 and y-axis "Words" 0–180)

Morgan's Typing Test					
Time (min)	2	4	6	8	10
Words	30	60	90	120	150

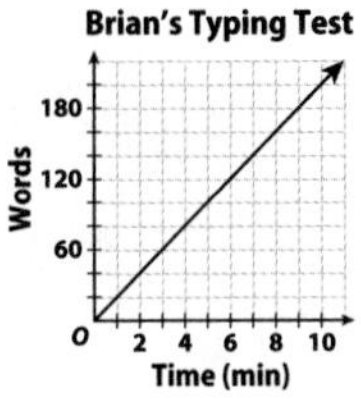

A Find Morgan's unit rate.

$m = \frac{60 - 30}{4 - 2} = \frac{30}{2} = 15$; 15 words per minute

B Find Brian's unit rate.

$m = \frac{80 - 40}{4 - 2} = \frac{40}{2} = 20$; 20 words per minute

C Which student types more correct words per minute?

Brian types 5 more correct words per minute.

Reflect

2. Katie types 17 correct words per minute. Explain how a graph of Katie's test results would compare to Morgan's and Brian's.

Katie's graph would go through the origin. Katie's graph would be less steep than Brian's but steeper than Morgan's.

PROFESSIONAL DEVELOPMENT

Integrate Mathematical Practices MP.3.1

This lesson provides an opportunity to address this Mathematical Practices standard. It calls for students to analyze mathematical relationships to connect and communicate mathematical ideas. Students compare linear relationships whether they are modeled with a verbal description, tables, equations, or graphs. By comparing linear relationships students analyze the mathematical relationships of different real-world settings.

Math Background

Comparing the graph of two functions is similar to working with a system of two equations. Two functions that have the same graph represent the same function and have an infinite number of common solutions. Two linear functions that never intersect are parallel lines, have the same slope but different *y*-intercepts, and have no solutions in common. Two linear functions can intersect at only one point. The point of intersection is a solution of both equations. If this intersection occurs at the origin, then both functions represent proportional relationships.

EXPLORE ACTIVITY 2

Questioning Strategies 🏴 Mathematical Practices

- Does the *y*-intercept represent the intial payment? No. The *y*-intercept represents the amount owed after the initial payment. For Store A, the initial payment and the amount owed after the initial payment are both $100.

- How can you use the graph of the plan at Store A to write a description of that plan? The point (0, 100) shows that the amount owed after the initial payment is $100; therefore, the initial payment is also $100. The slope of the line, −10, shows that the weekly payments are $10. The point (10, 0) shows that it will take 10 weeks to pay the balance in full.

Focus on Communication
Have students discuss the advantages and disadvantages of the two different plans. The discussion should include the amount of the initial payment, the amounts of the weekly payments, and how fast the balance will be paid off.

Elaborate

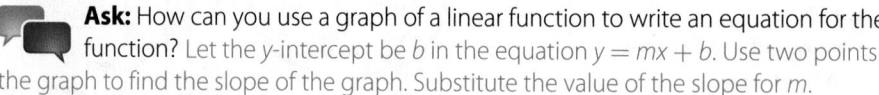

Talk About It
Summarize the Lesson
Ask: How can you use a graph of a linear function to write an equation for the function? Let the *y*-intercept be *b* in the equation $y = mx + b$. Use two points on the graph to find the slope of the graph. Substitute the value of the slope for *m*.

GUIDED PRACTICE

Engage with the Whiteboard
 Have students draw the graph in Exercise 4. Then for Exercise 5 have a student label the coordinates of the intersection of the two graphs. Before going on to Exercise 6, have students draw a box around the range of hours for which Plan 1 is cheaper (up to 4 hours), and in a different color draw a box around the hours that Plan 2 is cheaper.

Avoid Common Errors
Exercises 1–2 Remind students that the equation $y = 220 - x$ can be also be written as $y = -1x + 220$ so that it is in the familiar $y = mx + b$ form.

Exercise 7 Remind students that the graph of a proportional relationship is a line that goes through the origin, (0, 0). Two different lines cannot both represent proportional relationships unless they intersect at the origin.

EXPLORE ACTIVITY 2 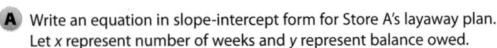 FL CC 8.F.1.2, 8.F.2.4

Comparing a Graph and a Description

Jamal wants to buy a new game system that costs $200. He does not have enough money to buy it today, so he compares layaway plans at different stores.

The plan at Store A is shown on the graph.

Store B requires an initial payment of $60 and weekly payments of $20 until the balance is paid in full.

A Write an equation in slope-intercept form for Store A's layaway plan. Let x represent number of weeks and y represent balance owed.

$$y = -10x + 100$$

B Write an equation in slope-intercept form for Store B's layaway plan. Let x represent number of weeks and y represent balance owed.

$$y = -20x + 140$$

C Sketch a graph of the plan at Store B on the same grid as Store A.

D How can you use the graphs to tell which plan requires the greater down payment? How can you use the equations?

The y-intercept (balance owed at week 0) for Store A is less than Store B, so Store A requires a greater down payment. Compare the values of b in the equations.

E How can you use the graphs to tell which plan requires the greater weekly payment? How can you use the equations?

The slope (rate of change) for Store B is greater, so Store B requires a greater weekly payment. Compare the values of m in the equations.

F Which plan allows Jamal to pay for the game system faster? Explain.

Store B; the balance owed at Store B is $0 after only 7 weeks.

© Houghton Mifflin Harcourt Publishing Company

Guided Practice

Doctors have two methods of calculating maximum heart rate. With the first method, maximum heart rate, y, in beats per minute is $y = 220 - x$, where x is the person's age. Maximum heart rate with the second method is shown in the table. (Example 1)

Age, x	20	30	40	50	60
Heart rate (bpm), y	194	187	180	173	166

1. Which method gives the greater maximum heart rate for a 70-year-old?

The second method (159 bpm vs. 150 bpm) gives the greater heart rate.

2. Are heart rate and age proportional or nonproportional for each method?

Heart rate and age are nonproportional for each method.

Aisha runs a tutoring business. With Plan 1, students may choose to pay $15 per hour. With Plan 2, they may follow the plan shown on the graph. (Explore Activity 1 and 2)

3. Describe the plan shown on the graph.

Students pay a $40 fee and $5 per hour.

4. Sketch a graph showing the $15 per hour option.

5. What does the intersection of the two graphs mean?

With both plans, it costs $60 for 4 hours of tutoring.

6. Which plan is cheaper for 10 hours of tutoring?

Plan 2 ($90 vs. $150) is cheaper for 10 hours of tutoring.

7. Are cost and time proportional or nonproportional for each plan?

Cost and time are proportional for Plan 1 and nonproportional for Plan 2.

? ESSENTIAL QUESTION CHECK-IN

8. When using tables, graphs, and equations to compare functions, why do you find the equations for tables and graphs?

You find the equations so that you can substitute numbers into them and compare results.

© Houghton Mifflin Harcourt Publishing Company • Image Credits: ©PhotoAlto/Getty Images

---

DIFFERENTIATE INSTRUCTION

Modeling

Provide students with toothpicks. Have students create a sequence of 3 or 4 figures (labeled figure 1, figure 2, etc.) using a quantity of toothpicks that increases by a constant amount. Students should let the figure number be x and the number of toothpicks used in the figure be y. Have students identify the constant ratio, write an equation for their function, make a table of values, and then graph the equation. Finally, have pairs of students compare their tables, equations, and graphs.

Sample answer:

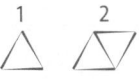   

constant ratio: 2; equation: $y = 2x + 1$

x	1	2	3	4
y	3	5	7	9

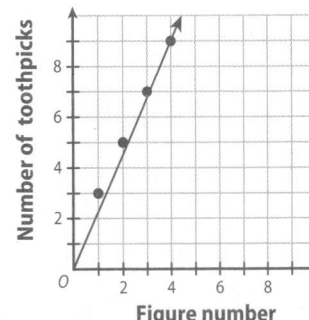

Additional Resources

Differentiated Instruction includes

• Reading Strategies
• Success for English Learners **ELL**
• Reteach
• Challenge **PRE-AP**

Comparing Functions **434**

Personal Math Trainer

Online Assessment and Intervention

Online homework assignment available

⏲ my.hrw.com

14.3 LESSON QUIZ

FL CC 8.F.1.2, 8.EE.2.5, 8.F.2.4

The table and graph show the relationships between the number of miles driven and amount of gas used for two different cars.

Car A

Miles, x	25	50	75	100
Gas (gal), y	1	2	3	4

Car B

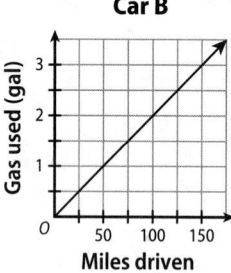

1. Which car uses fewer gallons of gas when 200 miles are driven?

2. Are the relationships proportional or nonproportional?

3. Write equations in slope-intercept form for Car A and Car B. Let x represent miles driven and y represent gallons of gas used.

The monthly cost, in y dollars, to download x movies is a linear function. The cost of Nate's service is described by $y = 4x + 6$. The table shows the cost of Beth's service.

Movies, x	2	4	6	8
Cost ($), y	10	20	30	40

4. Write an equation to represent the monthly cost of Beth's service.

5. Which service is cheaper for 8 movies in one month?

Lesson Quiz available online

⏲ my.hrw.com

Evaluate

GUIDED AND INDEPENDENT PRACTICE

 **FL CC** 8.F.1.2, 8.EE.2.5, 8.F.2.4

Concepts & Skills	Practice
Example 1 Comparing a Table and an Equation	Exercises 1–2, 11–12
Explore Activity 1 Comparing a Table and a Graph	Exercises 3–7, 9–10, 14
Explore Activity 2 Comparing a Graph and a Description	Exercises 3–7

Exercise	Depth of Knowledge (D.O.K.)	**FL CC** Mathematical Practices
9–12	**2** Skills/Concepts	**MP.4.1** Modeling
13	**2** Skills/Concepts	**MP.3.1** Logic
14	**2** Skills/Concepts	**MP.4.1** Modeling
15	**3** Strategic Thinking **H.O.T.**	**MP.3.1** Logic
16	**3** Strategic Thinking **H.O.T.**	**MP.2.1** Reasoning
17	**3** Strategic Thinking **H.O.T.**	**MP.3.1** Logic

Additional Resources

Differentiated Instruction includes:

• Leveled Practice worksheets

CLUSTER CONNECTION

Exercises 11–12 combine concepts from the Florida Common Core cluster "Define, evaluate, and compare functions."

Answers

1. Car B

2. proportional for both cars

3. Car A: $y = 0.04x$; Car B: $y = 0.02x$

4. $y = 5x$

5. Nate's service ($38 vs. $40) is cheaper for 8 movies.

14.3 Independent Practice

FL CC 8.EE.2.5, 8.F.1.2, 8.F.2.4

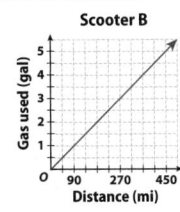

Personal Math Trainer
Online Assessment and Intervention
my.hrw.com

The table and graph show the miles driven and gas used for two scooters.

Scooter A

Distance (mi), x	Gas used (gal), y
150	2
300	4
450	6
600	8
750	10

Scooter B

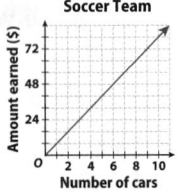

9. Which scooter uses fewer gallons of gas when 1350 miles are driven?
Scooter B (15 gallons vs. 18 gallons) uses fewer gallons of gas.

10. Are gas used and miles proportional or nonproportional for each scooter?
Gas used and miles are proportional for each scooter.

A cell phone company offers two texting plans to its customers. The monthly cost, y dollars, of one plan is $y = 0.10x + 5$, where x is the number of texts. The cost of the other plan is shown in the table.

Number of texts, x	100	200	300	400	500
Cost ($), y	25	25	30	35	40

11. Which plan is cheaper for under 200 texts? ____ the first plan

12. The graph of the first plan does not pass through the origin. What does this indicate?
x and y are nonproportional. There is a monthly charge of $5 even if no texting was done.

13. Brianna wants to buy a digital camera for a photography class. One store offers the camera for $50 down and a payment plan of $20 per month. The payment plan for a second store is described by $y = 15x + 80$, where y is the total cost in dollars and x is the number of months. Which camera is cheaper when the camera is paid off in 12 months? Explain.
The camera at the second store; the cost at the first store is $290 and the cost at the second store is $260.

14. The French club and soccer team are washing cars to earn money. The amount earned, y dollars, for washing x cars is a linear function. Which group makes the most money per car? Explain.

French Club

Number of cars, x	Amount earned ($), y
2	10
4	20
6	30
8	40
10	50

Soccer Team

The soccer team; the unit rate, or cost per car, for the French club is $5 per car. The unit rate for the soccer team is $8 per car.

H.O.T. FOCUS ON HIGHER ORDER THINKING

Work Area

15. Draw Conclusions Gym A charges $60 a month plus $5 per visit. The monthly cost at Gym B is represented by $y = 5x + 40$, where x is the number of visits per month. What conclusion can you draw about the monthly costs of the gyms?
Since the rate per visit is the same, the monthly cost of Gym A is always more than Gym B.

16. Justify Reasoning Why will the value of y for the function $y = 5x + 1$ always be greater than that for the function $y = 4x + 2$ when $x > 1$?
Since $y = 5x + 1$ has a steeper slope, once its y-value becomes greater, it will remain greater.

17. Analyze Relationships The equations of two functions are $y = -21x + 9$ and $y = -24x + 8$. Which function is changing more quickly? Explain.
$y = -24x + 8$ is changing more quickly because even though -24 is less than -21, the absolute value of -24 is greater than the absolute value of -21. So, a slope of -24 is steeper.

EXTEND THE MATH PRE-AP

Activity available online my.hrw.com

Activity Introduce function notation. If x represents the input value (domain) of a function and y represents the output value (range), then the function notation for y is $f(x)$, read "f of x", where f names the function. So, for the function represented by the equation $y = 3x + 2$, the function notation is $f(x) = 3x + 2$. $f(x)$ represents the value in the range that corresponds to the value of x in the domain. For example, $f(0)$ is the value in the range that corresponds to the value 0 in the domain, so $f(0) = 3(0) + 2 = 2$. Letters other than f are also used to name functions. For example, if $h(x) = x + 1$, then $h(3) = 3 + 1 = 4$. Have students use these two functions to find $f(3)$, $f(-3)$, $h(3)$, $h(-3)$, and $f(h(2))$.

$f(3) = 11, f(-3) = -7, h(3) = 4, h(-3) = -2,$

$f(h(2)) = f(2 + 1) = f(3) = 11$

LESSON
14.4 Analyzing Graphs

 Florida Common Core Standards

The student is expected to:

 **Functions—8.F.2.5**

Describe qualitatively the functional relationship between two quantities by analyzing a graph (e.g., where the function is increasing or decreasing, linear or nonlinear). Sketch a graph that exhibits the qualitative features of a function that has been described verbally.

Mathematical Practices

 **MP.4.1** Modeling

Engage

ESSENTIAL QUESTION

How can you describe a relationship given a graph and sketch a graph given a description? Sample answer: Determine where the function is increasing, decreasing, or constant. Analyze the rate of change to determine if the function is changing quickly or slowly. Describe what these features mean in the context of the problem. Use the same features to sketch a graph.

Motivate the Lesson
Ask: What can the features of a graph tell you about the attendance at a roller coaster park? Begin the Explore Activity to find out.

Explore

EXPLORE ACTIVITY 1

Focus on Patterns
Point out to students that the graph shows when park attendance stayed constant, increased, and decreased over time. An analysis of the graph would include possible explanations as to why the attendance was constant, increased, or decreased during each particular time segment. See also Explore Activities 2 and 3 in student text.

Explain

EXPLORE ACTIVITY 2

Questioning Strategies Mathematical Practices
• What are two characteristics you look for to decide if a graph is proportional? The graph is linear and goes through (0, 0).

• How can you tell which graph shows a slower memorization rate at the beginning than at the end? The curve will not be as steep at the beginning as it is at the end.

• How would a graph be affected if a student had known some of the words before receiving the list? The graph would start at a higher point on the vertical axis.

Focus on Modeling Mathematical Practices
Make sure students understand that a nearly horizontal line on the graph means that few new words are learned each day, while a nearly vertical line means that the number of words learned is increasing rapidly.

Avoid Common Errors
Students may think that all graphs going through (0, 0) are proportional. Remind them that the graph must also form a straight line.

LESSON

14.4 Analyzing Graphs

 FL CC 8.F.2.5

Describe qualitatively the functional relationship between two quantities by analyzing a graph ... . Sketch a graph that exhibits the qualitative features of a function that has been described verbally.

? ESSENTIAL QUESTION

How can you describe a relationship given a graph and sketch a graph given a description?

EXPLORE ACTIVITY 1 *Real World*   **FL CC** 8.F.2.5

Interpreting Graphs

A roller coaster park is open from May to October each year. The graph shows the number of park visitors over its season.

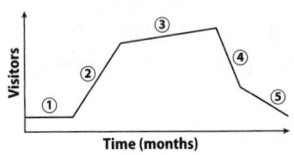

A Segment 1 shows that attendance during the opening weeks of the park's season stayed constant. Describe what Segment 2 shows.

A steep upward slope shows that attendance rises quickly.

B Based on the time frame, give a possible explanation for the change in attendance represented by Segment 2.

The increase might coincide with summer break from school.

C Which segments of the graph show decreasing attendance? Give a possible explanation.

Segments 4 and 5; the decrease might coincide with the end of summer break when school starts again.

Reflect

1. Explain how the slope of each segment of the graph is related to whether attendance increases or decreases.

A positive slope shows that attendance increases.

A negative slope shows that attendance decreases.

Lesson 14.4 **437**

EXPLORE ACTIVITY 2 *Real World*   **FL CC** 8.F.2.5

Matching Graphs to Situations

Grace, Jet, and Mike are studying 100 words for a spelling bee.

- Grace started by learning how to spell many words each day, but then learned fewer and fewer words each day.
- Jet learned how to spell the same number of words each day.
- Mike started by learning how to spell only a few words each day, but then learned a greater number of words each day.

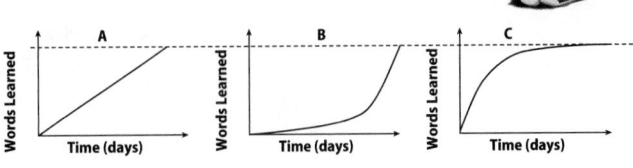

Jet   Mike   Grace

A Describe the progress represented by Graph A.

Graph A shows a constant rate. This means the student learned how to spell the same number of words each day.

B Describe the progress represented by Graph B.

Graph B begins with a shallow curve and gets steeper. This means the student learned a few words at first, and then learned more at the end.

C Describe the progress represented by Graph C.

Graph C begins with a steep curve that gets more shallow. This student learned many words at first, and then learned fewer words at the end.

D Determine which graph represents each student's study progress and write the students' names under the appropriate graphs.

Math Talk
Mathematical Practices

Tell whether each graph is linear or nonlinear and proportional or nonproportional.

(A) linear; proportional
(B) nonlinear; nonproportional
(C) nonlinear; nonproportional

Reflect

2. What would it mean if one of the graphs slanted downward?

A student forgot how to spell words that he or she had already learned.

438 Unit 6

PROFESSIONAL DEVELOPMENT

Integrate Mathematical Practices MP.4.1

This lesson provides an opportunity to address this Mathematical Practice standard. It calls for students to model with mathematics. Students apply mathematics to describe a relationship arising in everyday life. They use a given graph or sketch a graph to model a complicated real-world situation, draw conclusions, and reflect on whether the results make sense. The graph helps them to interpret the situation in ways that the information written in the problem does not permit.

Math Background

A linear function increases or decreases at a constant rate. If the graph of a function is a curve, then its rate of change is variable. You can approximate the rate of change at any point in the domain by sketching a line tangent to the curve. The slope of the tangent line is the rate of change of the function's graph at the tangent point.

EXPLORE ACTIVITY 3

Questioning Strategies Mathematical Practices

- Can the graphs made in Part A vary, or is there just one correct answer? They will vary. The graph will be the same for the first week, and the rate of increase after one week may vary according to each student's interpretation of the words *"gradually increases."*

- Why do you think the horizontal axis has a scale but the vertical axis does not? The information given specifies weeks 1 to 3, so a scale can be used. Since the exact number of students is not provided, no numbers can be used on the vertical axis.

- How does the graph in Part C show that the number of students using the tutoring service declines after the test? The line shows a negative slope, indicating that the number of students decreases over time.

Connect to Daily Life

Have students write other scenarios that would match the graph drawn in Part C. The vertical axis should represent a quantity in their scenario, and the horizontal axis should represent time in any units.

Engage with the Whiteboard

For Parts A and C, have several volunteers sketch graphs that describe the situation. Point out the ways in which the graphs can vary but still be correct.

Elaborate

Talk About It
Summarize the Lesson

 Ask: How do the features of a graph help you interpret a real-world situation? The axis labels and units tell you what quantities are being compared. The slope, height, and length of different sections of the graph describe how the quantities are related.

GUIDED PRACTICE

Engage with the Whiteboard

For Exercise 5, have a volunteer sketch a graph that represents the situation. Have another volunteer sketch a graph that is different but still correct.

Avoid Common Errors

Exercises 1–2 Suggest that students analyze the graph before answering these exercises. They should note that the phases have different widths, meaning the time involved for each phase is different.

Exercises 3–4 There may be confusion interpreting these graphs, as all three graphs begin with a steady increase in speed. Suggest that students examine all three graphs to see what happens after the steady increase before answering these exercises.

EXPLORE ACTIVITY 3 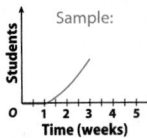 🔲 FL CC 8.F.2.5

Sketching a Graph for a Situation

Mrs. Sutton provides free math tutoring to her students every day after school. No one comes to tutoring sessions during the first week of school. Over the next two weeks, use of the tutoring service gradually increases.

A Sketch a graph showing the number of students who use the tutoring service over the first three weeks of school.

Sample:

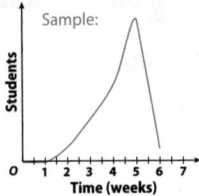

B Mrs. Sutton's students are told that they will have a math test at the end of the fifth week of school. How do you think this will affect the number of students who come to tutoring?

Sample answer: More students might come to tutoring before the test. After the test, the number might decrease.

C Considering your answer to **B**, sketch a graph showing the number of students who might use the tutoring service over the first six weeks of school.

Sample:

Reflect

3. If Mrs. Sutton offers bonus credit to students who come to tutoring, how might this affect the number of students?

Sample answer: More students might come to tutoring.

4. How would your answer to Question 3 affect the graph?

Sample answer: The graph would shift upward because more students would participate. Overall, trends would stay the same.

Lesson 14.4 **439**

Guided Practice

In a lab environment, colonies of bacteria follow a predictable pattern of growth. The graph shows this growth over time. (Explore Activity 1)

1. What is happening to the population during Phase 2?

The graph is increasing quickly. This shows a period of rapid growth.

2. What is happening to the population during Phase 4?

The number of bacteria is decreasing.

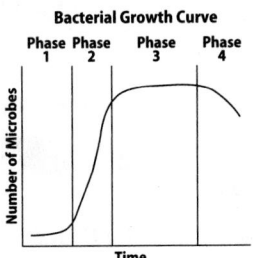

Bacterial Growth Curve

The graphs give the speeds of three people who are riding snowmobiles. Tell which graph corresponds to each situation. (Explore Activity 2)

Graph 1 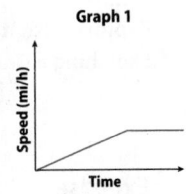 **Graph 2** 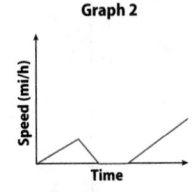 **Graph 3**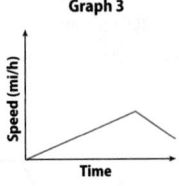

3. Chip begins his ride slowly but then stops to talk with some friends. After a few minutes, he continues his ride, gradually increasing his speed.

Graph 2

4. Linda steadily increases her speed through most of her ride. Then she slows down as she nears some trees.

Graph 3

5. Paulo stood at the top of a diving board. He walked to the end of the board, and then dove forward into the water. He plunged down below the surface, then swam straight forward while underwater. Finally, he swam forward and upward to the surface of the water. Draw a graph to represent Paulo's elevation at different distances from the edge of the pool. (Explore Activity 3)

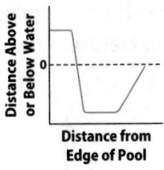 

440 Unit 6

DIFFERENTIATE INSTRUCTION

Curriculum Integration

Have students choose a familiar fairy tale that involves time and at least one other quantity, such as the "Tortoise and the Hare" (time and distance the tortoise or hare traveled in the race) or "Little Red Riding Hood" (time and distance Red traveled to Grandmother's cottage). Next, have students write the relevant information from the story in a short paragraph. Finally, have students draw a graph that represents the relationship between time and one other quantity in the tale.

Kinesthetic Experience

Have students make up a story about a journey to a specific place, such as their travels to the cafeteria for lunch or getting around the bases to home plate after their turn at bat. The journey can cover any distance and any length of time. On poster board, have students create a graph relating the time and the distance of their journey. Have students glue yarn to their graph to represent the different segments of their journey. Under the graph, have students describe their journey.

Additional Resources

Differentiated Instruction includes:

- Reading Strategies
- Success for English Learners **ELL**
- Reteach
- Challenge **PRE-AP**

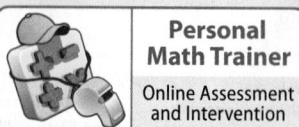
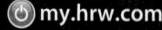
14.4 LESSON QUIZ

 8.F.2.5

1. The graph shows the speed of Denise's car during a trip. Describe what the graph shows.

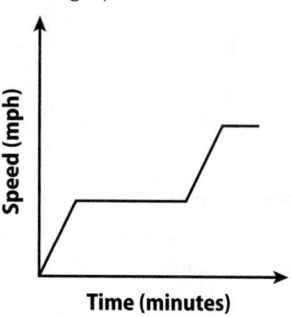

Tell which graph corresponds to each situation below.

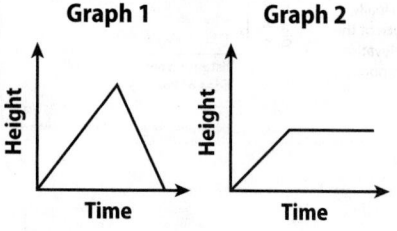

2. A woman climbs up a hill and then runs down the hill.

3. A child climbs the porch steps and sits on a chair on the porch.

4. Sketch a graph that shows the height over time of a man who climbs up a ladder, fixes a roof gutter, and then climbs back down the ladder.

Lesson Quiz available online

Answers

1. Sample answer: The graph shows Denise accelerating to a moderate speed, driving at that speed for a while, then accelerating again to a higher speed.

2. Graph 1

Evaluate

GUIDED AND INDEPENDENT PRACTICE

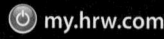 **FL CC** 8.F.2.5

Concepts & Skills	Practice
Explore Activity 1 Interpreting Graphs	Exercises 1–2, 9–10, 12–13
Explore Activity 2 Matching Graphs to Situations	Exercises 3–4, 6–8
Explore Activity 3 Sketching a Graph for a Situation	Exercises 5, 11

Exercise	Depth of Knowledge (D.O.K.)	**FL CC** Mathematical Practices
6–8	**2** Skills/Concepts	**MP.4.1** Modeling
9	**2** Skills/Concepts	**MP.6.1** Precision
10	**2** Skills/Concepts	**MP.2.1** Reasoning
11	**2** Skills/Concepts	**MP.4.1** Modeling
12–13	**2** Skills/Concepts	**MP.2.1** Reasoning
14	**3** Strategic Thinking **H.O.T.**	**MP.3.1** Logic
15–16	**3** Strategic Thinking **H.O.T.**	**MP.4.1** Modeling

Additional Resources

Differentiated Instruction includes:

• Leveled Practice worksheets

3. Graph 2

4. Sample answer:

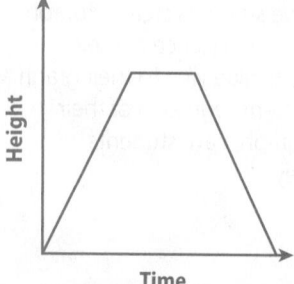

Name _____ Class _____ Date _____

14.4 Independent Practice

FL CC 8.F.2.5

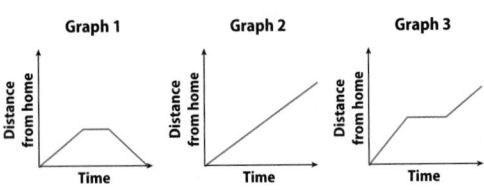

Personal Math Trainer

Online Assessment and Intervention

my.hrw.com

Tell which graph corresponds to each situation below.

Graph 1

Distance from home / Time

Graph 2

Distance from home / Time

Graph 3

Distance from home / Time

6. Arnold started from home and walked to a friend's house. He stayed with his friend for a while and then walked to another friend's house farther from home.

   Graph 3

7. Francisco started from home and walked to the store. After shopping, he walked back home.

   Graph 1

8. Celia walks to the library at a steady pace without stopping.

   Graph 2

Regina rented a motor scooter. The graph shows how far away she is from the rental site after each half hour of riding.

9. **Represent Real-World Problems** Use the graph to describe Regina's trip. You can start the description like this: "Regina left the rental site and rode for an hour…"

   Regina left the rental shop and rode for an hour.
   She took a half-hour rest and then started back.
   She changed her mind and continued for another
   half hour. She took a half-hour break and then
   returned to the rental shop.

10. **Analyze Relationships** Determine during which half hour Regina covered the greatest distance.

    From 0.5 to 1.0 hour.

Distance from Rental Site

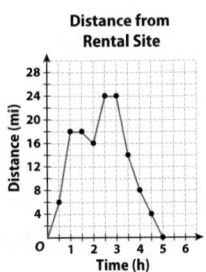

The data in the table shows the speed of a ride at an amusement park at different times one afternoon.

Time	3:20	3:21	3:22	3:23	3:24	3:25
Speed (mi/h)	0	14	41	62	8	0

11. Sketch a graph that shows the speed of the ride over time.

12. Between which times is the ride's speed increasing the fastest?

    3:21 to 3:22

13. Between which times is the ride's speed decreasing the fastest?

    3:23 to 3:24

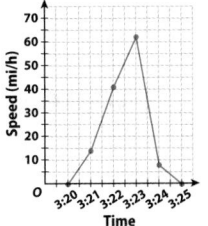

H.O.T. FOCUS ON HIGHER ORDER THINKING

A woodland area on an island contains a population of foxes. The graph describes the changes in the population over time.

14. **Justify Reasoning** What is happening to the fox population before time *t*? Explain your reasoning.

    The population is decreasing
    at first, but begins to increase
    again. The graph declines and
    then begins to rise midway
    through the time period.

Fox Population

15. **What If?** Suppose at time *t*, a conservation organization moves a large group of foxes to the island. Sketch a graph to show how this action might affect the population on the island after time *t*.

16. **Make a Prediction** At some point after time *t*, a forest fire destroys part of the woodland area on the island. Describe how your graph from problem 15 might change.

    The graph would show a steep decline at the point that
    represents the fire. Then as the forest regrows, the gradual
    increasing and decreasing pattern would resume.

Fox Population

Work Area

EXTEND THE MATH   PRE-AP

Activity available online ⊙ my.hrw.com

Activity Determine which of the graphs below, showing time and distance from the starting point, could represent a person taking a walk. Justify your answer.

Graph 1

Distance / Time

Graph 2

Distance / Time

Graph 3

Distance / Time

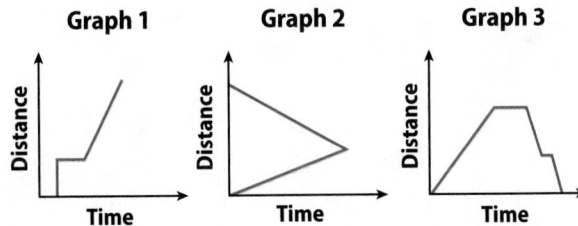

Graph 1 shows a change distance with no change in time (represented by the vertical line), so it cannot be the answer. Graph 2 cannot be the answer as it shows different distances at the same point in time. Graph 3 could be a person walking to a destination, staying there for a period of time, and returning to their starting point with one more brief stop.

Ready to Go On?

Assess Mastery

Use the assessment on this page to determine if students have mastered the concepts and standards covered in this module.

 **Response to Intervention**

Personal Math Trainer
Online Assessment and Intervention
my.hrw.com

Intervention	Enrichment

Access Ready to Go On? assessment online, and receive instant scoring, feedback, and customized intervention or enrichment.

Online and Print Resources

Differentiated Instruction
• Reteach worksheets
• Reading Strategies **ELL**
• Success for English Learners **ELL**

Differentiated Instruction
• Challenge worksheets **PRE-AP**
• Extend the Math **PRE-AP** Lesson Activities in TE

Additional Resources

Assessment Resources includes:
• Leveled Module Quizzes

Ready to Go On?

Personal Math Trainer
Online Assessment and Intervention
my.hrw.com

14.1 Identifying and Representing Functions

Determine whether each relationship is a function.

1.
x → y
2 → 0
5 → 1
8 → 2
→ 3

____no____

2.
Input, x	Output, y
−1	6
3	5
6	5

____yes____

3. (2, 5), (7, 2), (−3, 4), (2, 9), (1, 1)

____no____

14.2 Describing Functions

Determine whether each situation is linear or nonlinear, and proportional or nonproportional.

4. Joanna is paid $14 per hour.

____linear; proportional____

5. Alberto started out bench pressing 50 pounds. He then added 5 pounds every week.

____linear; nonproportional____

14.3 Comparing Functions

6. Which function is changing more quickly? Explain.

Function 2; absolute value of Function 2 slope is greater

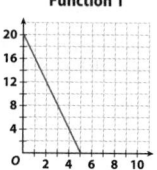
Function 1

Function 2	
Input, x	Output, y
2	11
3	6.5
4	2

14.4 Analyzing Graphs

7. Describe a graph that shows Sam running at a constant rate.

a line that starts at (0, 0) with a constant positive slope

? ESSENTIAL QUESTION

8. How can you use functions to solve real-world problems?

You can use functions written as tables, graphs, or equations.

© Houghton Mifflin Harcourt Publishing Company

Module 14 **443**

 ## Florida Common Core Standards

Lesson	Exercises	Common Core Standards
14.1	1–3	**8.F.1.1**
14.2	4–5	**8.F.1.3**
14.3	6	**8.F.1.2, 8.EE.2.5, 8.F.2.4**
14.4	7	**8.F.2.5**

PARCC Assessment Readiness

Assessment Readiness Tip Students can often eliminate some answer choices of multiple-choice questions using logic.

Item 1 Students should realize that in a proportional relationship, when $x = 0$, $y = 0$. Since all four tables show the value of y when $x = 0$, students can quickly eliminate choices A, B, and D. They should then confirm that the correct choice, C, has a constant rate of change.

Item 2 Students should recognize that y increases as x increases. Therefore, the slope is positive and they can eliminate choices A and B.

Avoid Common Errors

Item 2 Students may have difficulty finding the slope of the function, since the table does not provide the value of y when $x = 0$. Students should find the slope first, and deduce that when x decreases by 1, y decreases by 2.

Item 5 Students should recognize that x in the first function represents the floor area. They should write an equation for the table to compare the two functions, making sure that they use x to represent the floor area, not the price.

Additional Resources

Personal Math Trainer

Online Assessment and Intervention

my.hrw.com

Selected Response

1. Which table shows a proportional function?

Ⓐ
x	0	5	10
y	3	15	30

Ⓑ
x	0	5	10
y	10	20	30

Ⓒ
x	0	5	10
y	0	50	100

Ⓓ
x	0	5	10
y	10	5	0

2. What is the slope and y-intercept of the function shown in the table?

x	1	4	7
y	6	12	18

Ⓐ $m = -2; b = -4$

Ⓑ $m = -2; b = 4$

Ⓒ $m = 2; b = 4$

Ⓓ $m = 4; b = 2$

3. The table below shows some input and output values of a function.

Input	4	5	6	7
Output	14	17.5		24.5

What is the missing output value?

Ⓐ 20

Ⓑ 21

Ⓒ 22

Ⓓ 23

4. Tom walked to school at a steady pace, met his sister, and they walked home at a steady pace. Describe the graph relating Tom's distance from home to time.

Ⓐ V-shaped

Ⓑ upside down V-shaped

Ⓒ Straight line sloping up

Ⓓ Straight line sloping down

Mini-Task

5. Linear functions can be used to find the price of a building based on its floor area. Below are two of these functions.
$y = 40x + 15,000$

Floor Area (ft²)	400	700	1,000
Price ($1,000s)	32	56	80

a. Find and compare the slopes.

slope of 1st function is 40;

slope of 2nd function is 80;

slope of 2nd function is greater.

b. Find and compare the y-intercepts.

y-inter of 1st function is 15,000;

y-inter of 2nd function is 0;

y-inter of 1st function is greater.

c. Describe each function as proportional or nonproportional.

1st function is nonproportional;

2nd function is proportional

Florida Common Core Standards

Items	🏴 Grade 8 Standards	🏴 Mathematical Practices
1	8.EE.2.5, 8.F.2.4	MP.6.1
2*	8.EE.2.6, 8.F.2.4	MP.6.1
3	8.F.1.1	MP.2.1
4	8.F.2.5	MP.4.1
5	8.F.1.2	MP.4.1

* Item integrates mixed review concepts from previous modules or a previous course.

Study Guide Review

Vocabulary Development

Integrating Language Arts

Encourage students to practice using the unit vocabulary as they talk and write about mathematics. Understanding vocabulary will aid their understanding of the concepts.

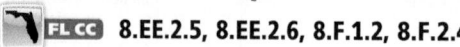 **FL CC** **LACC.68.RST.2.4** Determine the meaning of symbols, key terms, and other domain-specific words and phrases as they are used in a specific scientific or technical context relevant to grades 6–8 texts and topics.

MODULE 11 Proportional Relationships

FL CC **8.EE.2.5, 8.EE.2.6, 8.F.1.2, 8.F.2.4**

Key Concepts

• Proportional relationships can be described by an equation of the form $y = kx$, where k is the constant of proportionality. *(Lesson 11.1)*

• A rate of change is the ratio of the amount of change in the output to the amount of change in the input. *(Lesson 11.2)*

• A relationship with a constant rate of change forms a line, and the rate of change is the slope of the line. *(Lesson 11.2)*

• The unit rate and the constant of proportionality are the same as the slope of a linear relationship. *(Lesson 11.3)*

MODULE 12 Nonproportional Relationships

 **FL CC** **8.EE.2.6, 8.F.1.2, 8.F.1.3, 8.F.2.4**

Key Concepts

• Linear relationships can be written in the slope-intercept form, $y = mx + b$, where m is the slope and b is the y-intercept. When $b \neq 0$, the relationship between the variables is nonproportional. *(Lessons 12.1, 12.2, 12.3)*

• The y-intercept is the y-coordinate of the point where the graph intersects the y-axis. *(Lesson 12.2)*

• In a linear relationship $y = mx + b$, when $b \neq 0$, the relationship between the variables is nonproportional. *(Lessons 12.1, 12.4)*

Study Guide Review

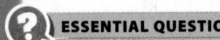

MODULE 11 Proportional Relationships

? ESSENTIAL QUESTION

How can you use proportional relationships to solve real-world problems?

Key Vocabulary

constant of proportionality *(constante de proporcionalidad)*
proportional relationship *(relación proporcional)*
slope *(pendiente)*

EXAMPLE 1

Write an equation that represents the proportional relationship shown in the graph.

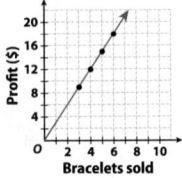

Use the points on the graph to make a table.

Bracelets sold	3	4	5	6
Profit ($)	9	12	15	18

Let x represent the number of bracelets sold.

Let y represent the profit.

The equation is $y = 3x$.

EXAMPLE 2

Find the slope of the line.

$$\text{slope} = \frac{\text{rise}}{\text{run}}$$

$$= \frac{3}{-4}$$

$$= -\frac{3}{4}$$

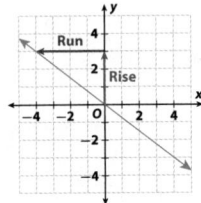

EXERCISES

1. The table represents a proportional relationship. Write an equation that describes the relationship. Then graph the relationship represented by the data. (Lessons 11.1, 11.2, 11.3)

Time (x)	6	8	10	12
Distance (y)	3	4	5	6

$y = \frac{1}{2} x$

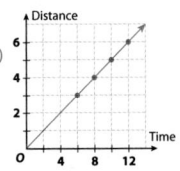

Find the slope and the unit rate represented on each graph. (Lessons 11.2, 11.3)

2.

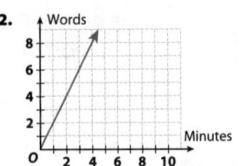

slope = unit rate = 2 words/min

3.

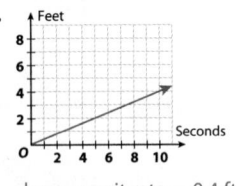

slope = unit rate = 0.4 ft/s

MODULE 12 Nonproportional Relationships

? ESSENTIAL QUESTION

How can you use nonproportional relationships to solve real-world problems?

Key Vocabulary

linear equation *(ecuación lineal)*
slope-intercept form of an equation *(forma de pendiente-intersección)*
y-intercept *(intersección con el eje y)*

EXAMPLE 1

Jai is saving to buy his mother a birthday gift. Each week, he saves $5. He started with $25. The equation $y = 5x + 25$ gives the total Jai has saved, y, after x weeks. Draw a graph of the equation. Then describe the relationship.

Use the equation to make a table. Then, graph the ordered pairs from the table, and draw a line through the points.

x (weeks)	0	1	2	3	4
y (savings in dollars)	25	30	35	40	45

The relationship is linear but nonproportional.

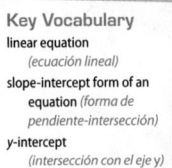

MODULE 13 Writing Linear Equations

 **FL CC** 8.F.2.4, 8.SP.1.1, 8.SP.1.2, 8.SP.1.3

Key Concepts

- The equation of a linear relationship can be written in slope-intercept form if you know the slope and the *y*-intercept. *(Lessons 13.1, 13.2, 13.3)*

- A set of data made up of two paired variables is bivariate data and can have a linear or a nonlinear relationship. *(Lesson 13.3)*

- Bivariate data has a linear relationship if the rate of change is constant. Bivariate data with a nonlinear relationship will not have a constant rate of change. *(Lessons 13.3)*

EXAMPLE 2

Graph $y = -\frac{1}{2}x - 2$.

The slope is $\frac{-1}{2}$, or $-\frac{1}{2}$.

The y-intercept is -2.

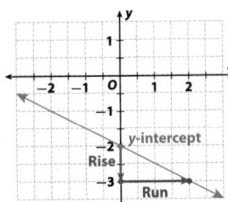

EXERCISES

Complete each table. Explain whether the relationship between x and y is proportional or nonproportional and whether it is linear. (Lesson 12.1)

1. $y = 10x - 4$

x	0	2	4	6
y	−4	16	36	56

nonproportional, linear

2. $y = -\frac{3}{2}x$

x	0	1	2	3
y	0	−1.5	−3	−4.5

proportional, linear

3. Find the slope and y-intercept for the linear relationship shown in the table. Graph the line. Is the relationship proportional or nonproportional? (Lessons 12.2, 12.4)

x	−4	−1	0	1
y	−4	2	4	6

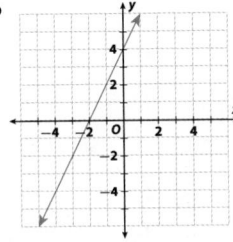

slope ____2____

y-intercept ____4____

The relationship is ____nonproportional____.

4. Tom's Taxis charges a fixed rate of $4 per ride plus $0.50 per mile. Carla's Cabs does not charge a fixed rate but charges $1.00 per mile. (Lessons 12.3)

a. Write an equation that represents the cost of Tom's Taxis. $y = 0.5x + 4$

b. Write an equation that represents the cost of Carla's cabs. $y = x$

c. Steve calculated that for the distance he needs to travel, Tom's Taxis will charge the same amount as Carla's Cabs. Graph both equations. How far is Steve going to travel and how much will he pay?

Steve is going to travel 8 miles and will pay $8.00.

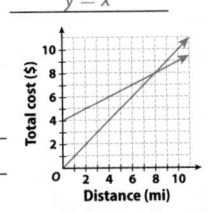

Key Vocabulary
bivariate data (*datos bivariados*)
nonlinear relationship (*relación no lineal*)

? ESSENTIAL QUESTION

How can you use linear equations to solve real-world problems?

EXAMPLE 1

Jose is renting a backhoe for a construction job. The rental charge for a month is based on the number of days in the month and a set charge per month. In September, which has 30 days, Jose paid $700. In August, which has 31 days, he paid $715. Write an equation in slope-intercept form that represents this situation.

$(x_1, y_1), (x_2, y_2) \rightarrow (30, 700), (31, 715)$ Write the information given as ordered pairs.

$m = \frac{y_2 - y_1}{x_2 - x_1} = \frac{715 - 700}{31 - 30} = 15$ Find the slope.

$y = mx + b$ Slope-intercept form

$715 = 15(31) + b$ Substitute for y, m, and x to find b.

$250 = b$ Solve for b.

$y = 15x + 250$ Write the equation.

EXAMPLE 2

Determine if the graph shown represents a linear or nonlinear relationship.

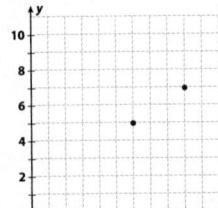

Points	Rate of Change
(0, 0) and (6, 5)	$m = \frac{5 - 0}{6 - 0} = \frac{5}{6}$
(6, 5) and (9, 7)	$m = \frac{7 - 5}{9 - 6} = \frac{2}{3}$
(0, 0) and (9, 7)	$m = \frac{7 - 0}{9 - 0} = \frac{7}{9}$

The rates of change are not constant. The graph represents a nonlinear relationship.

MODULE 14 Functions

FL CC 8.EE.2.5, 8.F.1.1, 8.F.1.2, 8.F.1.3, 8.F.2.4, 8.F.2.5

Key Concepts

- A function is a rule that assigns exactly one output to each input. *(Lesson 14.1)*

- Nonvertical lines are linear functions. All linear equations in the form $y = mx + b$ are linear functions. *(Lesson 14.2)*

- Two functions can be compared by comparing the slopes and y-intercepts. *(Lesson 14.3)*

- Understanding the shape of a graph and its slope are important to interpreting the meaning of a graph. *(Lesson 14.4)*

EXERCISES

1. Ms. Thompson is grading math tests. She is giving everyone that took the test a 10-point bonus. Each correct answer is worth 5 points. Write an equation in slope-intercept form that represents the scores on the tests. (Lesson 13.1)

$y = 5x + 10$

The table shows a pay scale based on years of experience. (Lessons 13.1, 13.2)

Experience (years), x	0	2	4	6	8
Hourly pay ($), y	9	14	19	24	29

2. Find the slope for this relationship. $\frac{5}{2}$

3. Find the y-intercept. 9

4. Write an equation in slope-intercept form that represents this relationship. $y = \frac{5}{2}x + 9$

5. Graph the equation, and use it to predict the hourly pay of someone with 10 years of experience.

Someone with 10 years of experience will be paid $34 an hour.

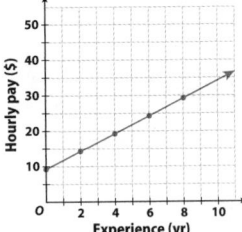

Does each of the following graphs represent a linear relationship? Why or why not? (Lesson 13.3)

6.

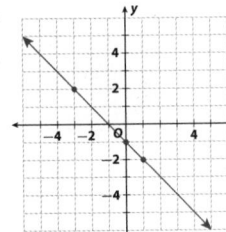

Yes; the rate of change is −1 between every pair of points.

7.

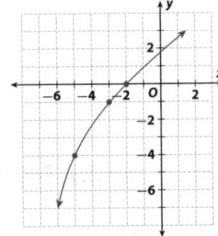

No; the rates of change are different between different pairs of points.

? ESSENTIAL QUESTION

How can you use functions to solve real-world problems?

EXAMPLE 1

Determine whether each relationship is a function.

A

Input	Output
3	10
4	4
5	2
4	0
6	5

The relationship is not a function, because an input, 4, is paired with 2 different outputs, 4 and 0.

B

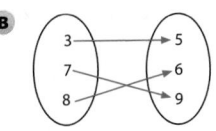

Since each input value is paired with only one output value, the relationship is a function.

EXAMPLE 2

Sally and Louis are on a long-distance bike ride. Sally bikes at a steady rate of 18 miles per hour. The distance y that Sally covers in x hours is given by the equation y = 18x. Louis's speed can be found by using the numbers in the table. Who will travel farther in 4 hours and by how much?

Louis's Biking Speed			
Time (h), x	3	5	7
Distance (mi), y	60	100	140

Each distance in the table is 20 times each number of hours. Louis's speed is 20 miles per hour, and his distance covered is represented by y = 20x.

Sally's ride: Louis's ride:

$y = 18x$ $y = 20x$

$y = 18(4)$ $y = 20(4)$

$y = 72$ $y = 80$

Sally will ride 72 miles in 4 hours. Louis will ride 80 miles in 4 hours. Louis will go 8 miles farther.

Unit 6 Performance Tasks

The Performance Tasks provide students with the opportunity to apply concepts from this unit in real-world problem situations.

CAREERS IN MATH

For more information about careers in mathematics as well as various mathematics appreciation topics, visit the American Mathematical Society at www.ams.org.

CAREERS IN MATH

Cost Estimator In Performance Task Item 1, students can see how a cost estimator uses mathematics on the job.

SCORING GUIDES FOR PERFORMANCE TASKS

1. MATHEMATICAL PRACTICES  **MP.3.1, MP.4.1**

Task	Possible Points (Total: 6)
a	**1 point** for defining a variable, for example, p. **1 point** for writing equation: $c = 1500 + 45p$
b	**1 point** for correct answer and work: $5460 = 1500 + 45p \rightarrow 3960 = 45p \rightarrow p = 88$
c	**2 points** for explanation and **1 point** for correct answer: The cost to make 80 MP3 players in one week is $5100. If they sell the players for $120 each, they will make $9600 that week. Subtracting costs, this gives a profit of $4500.

2. MATHEMATICAL PRACTICES  **MP.2.1, MP.4.1**

Task	Possible Points (Total: 6)
a	**1 point** for the correct Portland equation: $y = 2x + 56$. **1 point** for the correct San Francisco equation: $y = -0.5x + 66$.
b	**1 point** for correct description of slope for both cities: the slope is the hourly change in temperature, which is 2°F for Portland and −0.5°F for San Francisco. **1 point** for correct description of y-intercept for both cities: the y-intercept is the temperature at 9 a.m., which is 56°F for Portland and 66°F for San Francisco.
c	**1 point** for the correct graph: *(graph of Temperature vs. Hours showing Portland and San Francisco lines)*
d	**1 point** for correct explanation: The intersection represents when the temperature is the same in both cities: 64°F at 4 hours after 9 a.m., which is 1 p.m.

EXERCISES

Determine whether each relationship is a function. (Lesson 14.1)

1.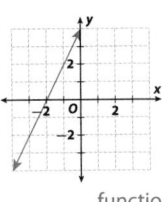

function

2.

Input	Output
−1	8
0	4
1	8
2	16

function

Tell whether the function is linear or nonlinear. (Lesson 14.2)

3. $y = 5x + \frac{1}{2}$ _____linear_____

4. $y = x^2 + 3$ _____nonlinear_____

5. Elaine has a choice of two health club memberships. The first membership option is to pay $500 now and then pay $150 per month. The second option is shown in the table. Elaine plans to go to the club for 12 months. Which option is cheaper? Explain. (Lesson 14.3)

Months, x	1	2	3
Total paid ($), y	215	430	645

The first option is cheaper. $500 + 12($150) = $2300, which is less than 12($215) = $2580.

6. Jenny rode her bike around her neighborhood. Use the graph to describe Jenny's bike ride. (Lesson 14.4)

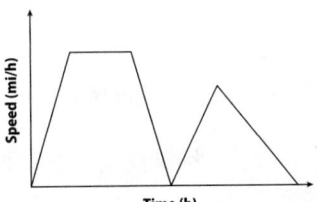

Sample answer: Jenny starts by riding her bike at an increasing speed. Then she rides at a steady rate. She then slows down to a full stop. She starts again riding at an increasing speed until she reaches a maximum speed that was lower than her previous steady rate, then starts slowing down again to a full stop.

Unit 6 Performance Tasks

1. **CAREERS IN MATH** Cost Estimator To make MP3 players, a cost estimator determined it costs a company $1,500 per week for overhead and $45 for each MP3 player made.

a. Define a variable to represent the number of players made. Then write an equation to represent the company's total cost c.

let p = number of players; $c = 1{,}500 + 45p$

b. One week, the company spends $5460 making MP3 players. How many players were made that week? Show your work.

$5{,}460 = 1{,}500 + 45p$, $3{,}960 = 45p$, $p = 88$; the company made 88 players.

c. If the company sells MP3 players for $120, how much profit would it make if it sold 80 players in one week? Explain how you found your answer.

$4,500; I subtracted the cost of making 80 players from the total revenue.

2. The temperature in Portland was 56 °F at 9 a.m. and increased 2° per hour during the day. For the same day in San Francisco, the temperature y in degrees Fahrenheit for x hours after 9 a.m. was recorded in the table shown.

x	0	1	2	3	4	5	6	7
y	66	65.5	65	64.5	64	63.5	63	62.5

a. For each city, write an equation in slope-intercept form for the temperature as a function of hours after 9 a.m.

Portland: $y = 2x + 56$, x is time in hours after 9 a.m. and y is temperature in °F; San Francisco: $y = -0.5x + 66$, x is time in hours after 9 a.m. and y is temperature in °F

b. What does the slope and y-intercept represent in the equation for each city?

slope is the hourly increase in temperature: 2 °F for Portland and 0.5 decrease for San Francisco; the y-intercept is the temperature at 9 a.m.

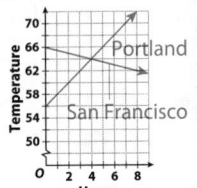

c. Graph the relationships you found in part **a** in the grid provided.

d. Explain what the intersection point represents.

The temperature is the same in Portland and San Francisco at the same time: 64 °F at 4 hours after 9 a.m. or 1 p.m.

PARCC Assessment Readiness

Additional Resources

Personal Math Trainer

Online Assessment and Intervention

my.hrw.com

Assessment Resources

- Leveled Unit Tests: A, B, C, D
- Performance Assessment

Assessment Readiness Tip Students can highlight or underline key terms, important information, or equations in a word problem.

Item 10 With longer word problems, sometimes students can lose track of the information they really need. By highlighting or underlining that information, they can keep better track. If the students highlight Carl's sentence and Jeannine's equation, they can better compare the situations by isolating what they need.

Avoid Common Errors

Item 2 Students may see the repeated y-coordinate of 3 in answer choice C, and eliminate it as a possible correct answer. Remind them that functions written as a set of ordered pairs may have repeated y-coordinates but not repeated x-coordinates.

Item 9 Some students will realize that 2 and 0.5 must appear in the correct equation but may have a hard time deciding which value should be the coefficient of x. Remind them that the coefficient of x is the slope, which is the rate of change.

 Florida Common Core Standards

Items	Grade 8 Standards	Mathematical Practices
1	8.F.2.4	MP.4.1
2	8.F.1.1	MP.2.1
3*	8.NS.1.1	MP.7.1
4	8.EE.2.5	MP.2.1
5	8.EE.2.6, 8.F.2.4	MP.6.1
6	8.EE.2.5	MP.2.1
7*	8.EE.1.4	MP.2.1
8	8.EE.2.5, 8.F.1.1	MP.6.1
9	8.F.1.3, 8.F.2.4	MP.7.1
10	8.F.1.3, 8.F.2.4	MP.7.1
11	8.EE.2.6, 8.F.2.4	MP.1.1
12	8.F.2.4	MP.4.1

* Item integrates mixed review concepts from previous modules or a previous course.

PARCC Assessment Readiness

Personal Math Trainer
Online Assessment and Intervention
my.hrw.com

Selected Response

1. Rickie earns $7 an hour babysitting. Which table represents this proportional relationship?

Ⓐ
Hours	4	6	8
Earnings ($)	28	42	56

Ⓑ
Hours	4	6	8
Earnings ($)	28	35	42

Ⓒ
Hours	2	3	4
Earnings ($)	7	14	21

Ⓓ
Hours	2	3	4
Earnings ($)	14	21	42

2. Which of the relationships below is a function?

Ⓐ (6, 3), (5, 2), (6, 8), (0, 7)

Ⓑ (8, 2), (1, 7), (−1, 2), (1, 9)

Ⓒ (4, 3), (3, 0), (−1, 3), (2, 7)

Ⓓ (7, 1), (0, 0), (6, 2), (0, 4)

3. Which set best describes the numbers used on the scale for a standard thermometer?

Ⓐ whole numbers

Ⓑ rational numbers

Ⓒ real numbers

Ⓓ integers

4. Which term refers to slope?

Ⓐ rate of change

Ⓑ equation

Ⓒ y-intercept

Ⓓ coordinate

5. The graph of which equation is shown below?

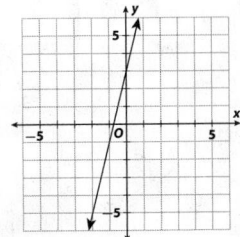

Ⓐ $y = 4x + 3$

Ⓑ $y = -4x - 0.75$

Ⓒ $y = -4x + 3$

Ⓓ $y = 4x - 0.75$

6. Which equation represents a nonproportional relationship?

Ⓐ $y = 5x$

Ⓑ $y = -5x$

Ⓒ $y = 5x + 3$

Ⓓ $y = -\frac{1}{5}x$

7. Which number is 7.0362×10^{-4} written in standard notation?

Ⓐ 0.000070362

Ⓑ 0.00070362

Ⓒ 7.0362

Ⓓ 7,036.2

8. Which term does not correctly describe the relationship shown in the table?

x	0	2	4
y	0	70	140

Ⓐ function

Ⓑ linear

Ⓒ proportional

Ⓓ nonproportional

9. As part of a science experiment, Greta measured the amount of water flowing from Container A to Container B. Container B had half a gallon of water in it to start the experiment. Greta found that the water was flowing at a rate of two gallons per hour. Which equation represents the amount of water in Container B?

Ⓐ $y = 2x$

Ⓑ $y = 0.5x$

Ⓒ $y = 2x + 0.5$

Ⓓ $y = 0.5x + 2$

10. Carl and Jeannine both work at appliance stores. Carl earns a weekly salary of $600 plus $40 for each appliance he sells. The equation $p = 50n + 550$ represents the amount of money Jeannine earns in a week, p ($), as a function of the number of appliances she sells, n. Which of the following statements is true?

Ⓐ Carl has a greater salary and a greater rate per appliance sold.

Ⓑ Jeannine has a greater salary and a greater rate per appliance sold.

Ⓒ Carl will earn more than Jeannine if they each sell 10 appliances in a given week.

Ⓓ Both Carl and Jeannine earn the same amount if they each sell 5 appliances in a given week.

Mini-Tasks

11. The table below represents a linear relationship.

x	2	3	4	5
y	14	17	20	23

a. Find the slope for this relationship.

$$\frac{3}{1}$$

b. Find the y-intercept. Explain how you found it.

8; Sample answer: I graphed the relationship and found the point where the graph crossed the y-axis.

c. Write an equation in slope-intercept form that represents this relationship.

$$y = 3x + 8$$

 Hot Tip! Estimate your answer before solving the problem. Use your estimate to check the reasonableness of your answer.

12. Jacy has a choice of cell phone plans. Plan A is to pay $260 for the phone and then pay $70 per month for service. Plan B is to get the phone for free and pay $82 per month for service.

a. Write an equation to represent the total cost, c, of Plan A for m months.

$$c = 260 + 70m$$

b. Write an equation to represent the total cost, c, of Plan B for m months.

$$c = 82m$$

c. If Jacy plans to keep the phone for 24 months, which plan is cheaper? Explain.

Plan A is cheaper. Plan A will cost $1,940 for 24 months and Plan B will cost $1,968 for 24 months.

UNIT 7

Solving Equations and Systems of Equations

Contents

Unit Pacing Guide

45-Minute Classes

Module 15

DAY 1	DAY 2	DAY 3	DAY 4	DAY 5
Lesson 15.1	Lesson 15.1	Lesson 15.2	Lesson 15.3	Lesson 15.3

DAY 6	DAY 7			
Lesson 15.4	Ready to Go On? PARCC Assessment Readiness			

Module 16

DAY 1	DAY 2	DAY 3	DAY 4	DAY 5
Lesson 16.1	Lesson 16.1	Lesson 16.2	Lesson 16.2	Lesson 16.3

DAY 6	DAY 7	DAY 8	DAY 9	DAY 10
Lesson 16.3	Lesson 16.4	Lesson 16.4	Lesson 16.5	Ready to Go On? PARCC Assessment Readiness

DAY 11				
Study Guide PARCC Assessment Readiness				

90-Minute Classes

Module 15

DAY 1	DAY 2	DAY 3	DAY 4	
Lesson 15.1	Lesson 15.2	Lesson 15.3	Lesson 15.4 Ready to Go On? PARCC Assessment Readiness	

Module 16

DAY 1	DAY 2	DAY 3	DAY 4	DAY 5
Lesson 16.1	Lesson 16.2	Lesson 16.3	Lesson 16.4	Lesson 16.5

DAY 6				
Ready to Go On? PARCC Assessment Readiness	Study Guide PARCC Assessment Readiness			

Program Resources

⏻ Plan

Online Teacher Edition

Access a full suite of teaching resources online—plan, present, and manage classes, assignments, and activities.

ePlanner Easily plan your classes, create and view assignments, and access all program resources with your online, customizable planning tool.

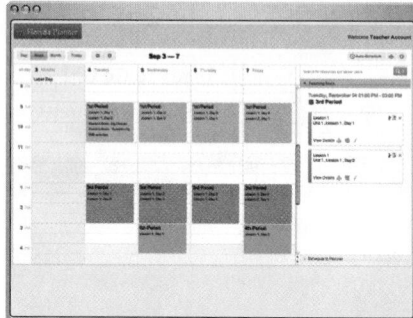

Professional Development Videos

Author Juli Dixon models successful teaching practices and strategies in actual classroom settings.

QR Codes Scan with your smart phone to jump directly from your print book to online videos and other resources.

Teacher's Edition

Support students with point-of-use Questioning Strategies, teaching tips, resources for differentiated instruction, additional activities, and more.

⏻ Engage and Explore

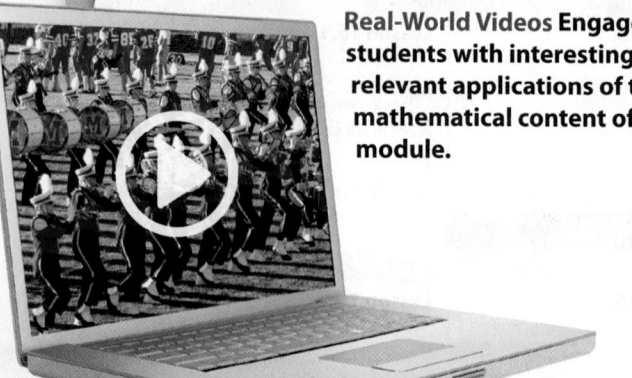

Real-World Videos Engage students with interesting and relevant applications of the mathematical content of each module.

Animated Math Online interactive simulations, tools, and games help students actively learn and practice key concepts.

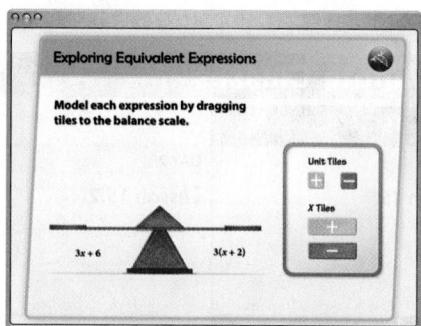

Exploring Equivalent Expressions

Model each expression by dragging tiles to the balance scale.

Unit Tiles
X Tiles

$3x + 6$ $3(x + 2)$

Explore Activities

Students interactively explore new concepts using a variety of tools and approaches.

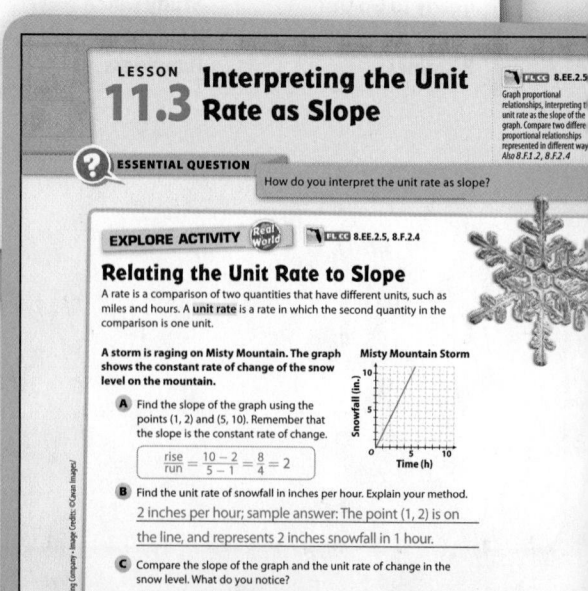

LESSON 11.3 Interpreting the Unit Rate as Slope   FL CC 8.EE.2.5

Graph proportional relationships, interpreting the unit rate as the slope of the graph. Compare two different proportional relationships represented in different ways. Also 8.EE.1.2, 8.F.2.4

ESSENTIAL QUESTION
How do you interpret the unit rate as slope?

EXPLORE ACTIVITY Real World   FL CC 8.EE.2.5, 8.F.2.4

Relating the Unit Rate to Slope

A rate is a comparison of two quantities that have different units, such as miles and hours. A **unit rate** is a rate in which the second quantity in the comparison is one unit.

A storm is raging on Misty Mountain. The graph shows the constant rate of change of the snow level on the mountain.

Misty Mountain Storm

A. Find the slope of the graph using the points (1, 2) and (5, 10). Remember that the slope is the constant rate of change.

$$\frac{rise}{run} = \frac{10 - 2}{5 - 1} = \frac{8}{4} = 2$$

B. Find the unit rate of snowfall in inches per hour. Explain your method.

2 inches per hour; sample answer: The point (1, 2) is on the line, and represents 2 inches snowfall in 1 hour.

C. Compare the slope of the graph and the unit rate of change in the snow level. What do you notice?

They are the same.

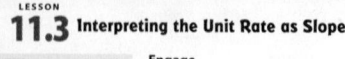

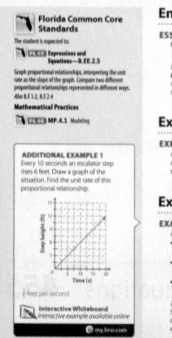

LESSON 11.3 Interpreting the Unit Rate as Slope

Florida Common Core Standards

The student is expected to:

FL CC Expressions and Equations—8.EE.2.5

Graph proportional relationships, interpreting the unit rate as the slope of the graph. Compare two different proportional relationships represented in different ways. Also 8.F.1.2, 8.F.2.4

Mathematical Practices

FL CC MP.4.1 Modeling

ADDITIONAL EXAMPLE 1
Every 10 seconds an escalator step rises 6 feet. Draw a graph of the situation. Find the unit rate of this proportional relationship.

6 feet per second

Interactive Whiteboard
Interactive example available online
my.hrw.com

Engage

ESSENTIAL QUESTION
How do you interpret the unit rate as slope? Sample answer: The ratio of the change in y to the change in x is the unit rate. It is also the ratio of the rise to the run, or the slope.

Motivate the Lesson
Ask: Have you ever been skiing, or watched downhill skiers on television? Discuss types of slopes that might be encountered, from a "bunny slope" to the "black diamond" expert slope. Consider how you might describe slight slopes and extreme slopes numerically.

Explore

EXPLORE ACTIVITY
Connect Multiple Representations Mathematical Practices
Ask students for the method they use to find the coordinates of points on a line. Point out that it is easiest to find the coordinates of points at the intersection of grid lines.

Explain

EXAMPLE 1
Questioning Strategies Mathematical Practices
• What is the constant change in the input values? What is the constant change in the output values?
• Where do the values of 8 and run of 6 come from? The vertical and horizontal distance from (0, 0) to (6, 8).
• What if you used (6, 8) and (15, 20) to find the slope? You would get a rise of 12, a run of 9, and a slope of 12/9 which is equal to 4/3.

Avoid Common Errors
Students may reverse the order in the ratio and divide the difference of the x-values by the difference of the y-values. Remind students that slope is always rise over run (y-values over x-values).

YOUR TURN

PROFESSIONAL DEVELOPMENT

Integrate Mathematical Practices MP.4.1
This lesson provides an opportunity to address this Mathematical Practices standard. It calls for students to analyze mathematical relationships.

Math Background
The slope of a line that does not go through the origin can be found by its x-intercept and y-intercept. If the x-intercept is a and the y-intercept is b, the line goes through (a, 0) and (0, b).

RtI Response to Intervention

⏻ Teach

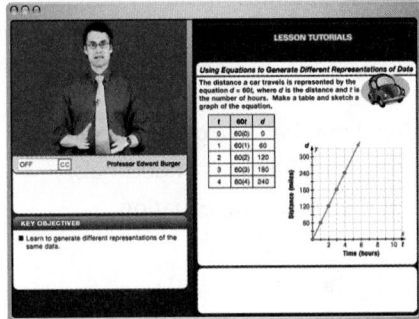

Math On the Spot video tutorials, featuring program authors Dr. Edward Burger and Martha Sandoval-Martinez, accompany every example in the textbook and give students step-by-step instructions and explanations of key math concepts.

 Present engaging content on a multitude of devices, including tablets and interactive whiteboards.

Math Talk Continually monitor and assess student progress with integrated formative assessment.

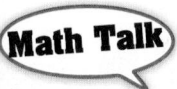 **CLUSTER CONNECTION** Look for exercises indicated with this icon to build connections among standards within Florida Common Core clusters.

Differentiated Instruction Print Resources

Support all learners with Differentiated Instruction Resources, including

- **Leveled Practice and Problem Solving**
- **Reteach**
- **Reading Strategies**
- **Success for English Learners**
- **Challenge**

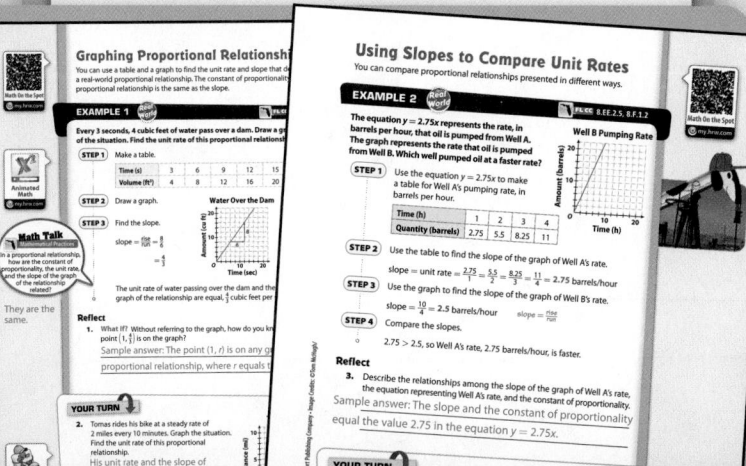

⏻ Assessment and Intervention

The **Personal Math Trainer** provides online practice, homework, assessments, and intervention.
Monitor student progress through reports and alerts. Create and customize assignments aligned to specific lessons or standards.

- **Practice** – With dynamic items and assignments, students get unlimited practice on key concepts supported by guided examples, step-by-step solutions, and video tutorials.

- **Assessments** – Choose from course assignments or customize your own based on course content, standards, difficulty levels, and more.

- **Homework** – Students can complete online homework with a wide variety of problem types, including the ability to enter expressions, equations, and graphs. Let the system automatically grade homework, so you can focus where your students need help the most!

- **Intervention** – Let the Personal Math Trainer automatically prescribe a targeted, personalized intervention path for your students.

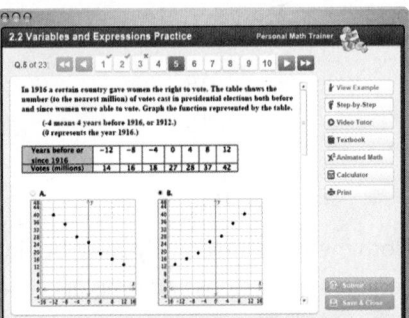

 Raise the bar with homework and practice that incorporates higher-order thinking and mathematical processes in every lesson.

 **PARCC Assessment Readiness**
Prepare students for success on the PARCC math test with practice at every module and unit.

Assessment Resources

Tailor assessments to meet the needs of all your classes and students, including

- **Leveled Module Quizzes**
- **Leveled Unit Tests**
- **Unit Performance Tasks**
- **Placement, Diagnostic, and Quarterly Benchmark Tests**

Math Background

Writing and Solving Equations with Variables on Both Sides
8.EE.3.7, 8.EE.3.7b
LESSON 15.1

When solving equations with variables on both sides, students should remember that the goal is to isolate the terms containing variables on one side of the equation and the constants on the other side. Variable terms may be grouped on either side of the equation. However, grouping the variable terms on the side that results in a positive coefficient may be more efficient and result in fewer calculation errors. Consider the two methods shown below for solving $2x + 8 = 3x - 1$.

$$
\begin{aligned}
2x + 8 &= 3x - 7 \\
-3x & \qquad -3x \\
\hline
-x + 8 &= -7 \\
-8 & \qquad -8 \\
\hline
-x &= -15 \\
\frac{-x}{-1} &= \frac{-15}{-1} \\
x &= 15
\end{aligned}
\qquad
\begin{aligned}
2x + 8 &= 3x - 7 \\
-2x & \qquad -2x \\
\hline
8 &= x - 7 \\
+7 & \qquad +7 \\
\hline
15 &= x
\end{aligned}
$$

Both methods are equally valid, but in this case, one requires fewer steps and simpler calculations than the other.

Encourage students to check their solutions in the original equation. This is important because a mistake might have been made in the solution process, and one of the "transformed" equations may no longer be equivalent to the original equation.

Multiplying both sides of an equation by zero is called an irreversible step because you cannot perform the inverse operation of dividing both sides by zero since division by zero is undefined. Irreversible steps can introduce extraneous solutions—solutions that satisfy the transformed equation but do not satisfy the original equation. This concept will become important in future algebra classes when students will multiply both sides of an equation by an algebraic expression that can sometimes be zero.

Equations with Rational Numbers **8.EE.3.7, 8.EE.3.7b**
LESSON 15.2

René Descartes (1596–1650) was a French mathematician and philosopher. In his work titled *Rules for the Direction of the Mind*, he included this suggestion: break your work up into small steps that you can understand completely and about which you have utter certainty, and check your work often.

Solving equations with rational numbers is a good place to apply Descartes' rule. First, eliminate fractions or decimals, then isolate the variable, and then solve the equation.

Equations with Many Solutions or No Solution **8.EE.3.7a**
LESSON 15.4

A one-variable linear equation may have no solution, one solution, or infinitely many solutions. The equation $x + 4 = x + 2$ has no solution because it is false for every real number. The equation $x + 3 = 3 + x$ has infinitely many solutions because it is true for every real number. Using set notation, no solution is called the *empty set* and written as $\{\,\}$ or $\varnothing$.

Solving Systems of Linear Equations

8.EE.3.8a, 8.EE.3.8b
LESSONS 16.1 to 16.5

A *system of equations* is a set of two or more equations that each involve the same set of two or more variables. In this course, all of the systems that students see are systems of two linear equations in two unknowns. That is, each of the two equations has two variables, x and y. A *solution* of a system of equations is a set of values that are solutions of all of the equations in the system.

Consider the system of equations shown below.

$$y = 3x + 2$$
$$y = 5x - 6$$

The values $x = 4$, $y = 14$ are a solution of the system since these values are solutions of each equation. The solution can be written as an ordered pair, (4, 14).

Systems of equations can be solved either graphically or algebraically. To solve the above system graphically, recall that the graphs of $y = 3x + 2$ and $y = 5x - 6$ are both straight lines. Each line represents all the points that are solutions of the corresponding equation. The point where the lines intersect must be a solution of both equations and therefore a solution of the system.

Solving algebraically can be done using either substitution or elimination (with or without multiplication). The above system can be most easily solved by substitution, which is based on the Substitution Property of Equality (If $a = b$, then b can be substituted for a in any expression.). To use substitution, note that second equation states that $y = 5x - 6$. Therefore, by the Substitution Property of Equality, $5x - 6$ can replace y in any expression, including the expression on the left side of the first equation. This gives $5x - 6 = 3x + 2$. In this way, the substitution method reduces a system of two equations in two variables to a single equation in one variable. This new equation can be solved by using techniques students have already learned. After solving for x, students can substitute that value in either original equation to find the value of y.

The graphical approach makes it clear that a system of linear equations can have no solutions (if the lines do not intersect), infinitely many solutions (if the lines coincide with each other), or a single solution (if the lines intersect at a point). Although most of the systems that students see in this course will have a single solution, students should be aware that there are other possibilities.

Finally, students should realize that it is possible to check a solution of a system of equations, but that this process takes a bit more work than checking the solution of a single linear equation. In particular, the solution must be checked in both equations of the system.

 **UNIT 7**

Solving Equations and Systems of Equations

CAREERS IN MATH

Hydraulic Engineer A hydraulic engineer specializes in the behavior of fluids, mainly water. A hydraulic engineer applies the mathematics of fluid dynamics to the collection, transport, measurement, and regulation of water and other fluids.

If you are interested in a career in hydraulic engineering, you should study the following mathematical subjects:

- Algebra
- Geometry
- Trigonometry
- Probability and Statistics
- Calculus

Research other careers that require the understanding of the mathematics of fluid dynamics.

Unit 7 Performance Task

At the end of the unit, check out how **hydraulic engineers** use math.

© Houghton Mifflin Harcourt Publishing Company • Image Credits: ©David R. Frazier Photolibrary, Inc./Alamy Images

Careers in Math

Hydraulic Engineer

Hydraulic engineering is based on the mathematical understanding of how fluids behave, including pressure at different depths and the nature of fluid flow. You will learn more about how hydraulic engineers calculate the pressure of fluids in the Performance Tasks at the end of the unit.

For more information about careers in mathematics as well as various mathematics appreciation topics, visit the American Mathematical Society at www.ams.org

Vocabulary Preview

Use the puzzle to give students a preview of important concepts in this unit. Students may work individually, in pairs, or in groups.

Unit Resources

Go online to access all your unit resources.

my.hrw.com

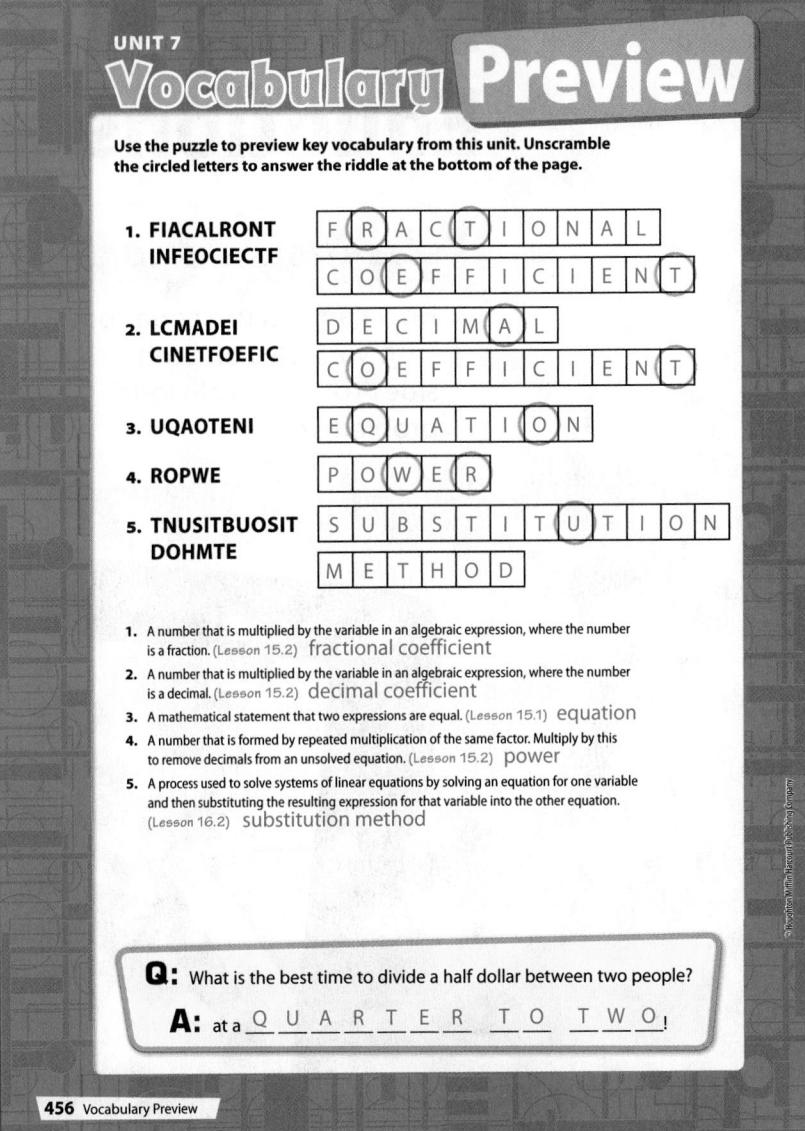

UNIT 7
Vocabulary Preview

Use the puzzle to preview key vocabulary from this unit. Unscramble the circled letters to answer the riddle at the bottom of the page.

1. **FIACALRONT INFEOCIECTF** — F R A C T I O N A L / C O E F F I C I E N T
2. **LCMADEI CINETFOEFIC** — D E C I M A L / C O E F F I C I E N T
3. **UQAOTENI** — E Q U A T I O N
4. **ROPWE** — P O W E R
5. **TNUSITBUOSIT DOHMTE** — S U B S T I T U T I O N / M E T H O D

1. A number that is multiplied by the variable in an algebraic expression, where the number is a fraction. (Lesson 15.2) fractional coefficient
2. A number that is multiplied by the variable in an algebraic expression, where the number is a decimal. (Lesson 15.2) decimal coefficient
3. A mathematical statement that two expressions are equal. (Lesson 15.1) equation
4. A number that is formed by repeated multiplication of the same factor. Multiply by this to remove decimals from an unsolved equation. (Lesson 15.2) power
5. A process used to solve systems of linear equations by solving an equation for one variable and then substituting the resulting expression for that variable into the other equation. (Lesson 16.2) substitution method

Q: What is the best time to divide a half dollar between two people?

A: at a Q U A R T E R T O T W O !

Before	In this Unit	After
Students understand equations: • write and solve two-step equations	Students will learn about: • solving equations with the variable on both sides and with rational number coefficients and constants • solving systems of equations by graphing, substitution, or elimination	Students will connect: • solving multistep equations with the variable on both sides • solving multistep equations with rational number coefficients and constants • real-world situations and systems of equations.

Solving Linear Equations

ESSENTIAL QUESTION

How can you use equations with variables on both sides to solve real-world problems?

You can model real-world problems with equations and use algebraic methods to solve the equations.

Real-World Video

Some employees earn commission plus their salary when they make a sale. There may be options about their pay structure. They can find the best option by solving an equation with variables on both sides.

my.hrw.com

© Houghton Mifflin Harcourt Publishing Company • Image Credits:
© Image Source/Alamy Images

GO DIGITAL

my.hrw.com

my.hrw.com

Go digital with your write-in student edition, accessible on any device.

Math On the Spot

Scan with your smart phone to jump directly to the online edition, video tutor, and more.

Animated Math

Interactively explore key concepts to see how math works.

Personal Math Trainer

Get immediate feedback and help as you work through practice sets.

Are You Ready?

Assess Readiness

Use the assessment on this page to determine if students need intensive or strategic intervention for the module's prerequisite skills.

 **Response to Intervention**

Intervention	Enrichment
Access Are You Ready? assessment online, and receive instant scoring, feedback, and customized intervention or enrichment.	

Personal Math Trainer
Online Assessment and Intervention
my.hrw.com

Online and Print Resources

Skills Intervention worksheets
- Skill 23 Find Common Denominators
- Skill 41 Multiply Decimals by Powers of 10
- Skill 56 Connect Words and Equations

Differentiated Instruction
- Challenge worksheets **PRE-AP**

Extend the Math **PRE-AP**
Lesson Activities in TE

Are YOU Ready?

Complete these exercises to review skills you will need for this module.

Personal Math Trainer
Online Assessment and Intervention
my.hrw.com

Find Common Denominators

EXAMPLE Find the LCD of 3, 5, and 10.

3: 3, 6, 9, 12, 15, 18, 21, 24, 27, 30,...   *List the multiples of each number.*
5: 5, 10, 15, 20, 25, 30, 35,...   *Choose the least multiple the lists have in common.*
10: 10, 20, 30, 40, 50,...   LCD(3, 5, 10) = 30

Find the LCD.

1. 8, 12 ___24___ 2. 9, 12 ___36___ 3. 15, 20 ___60___ 4. 8, 10 ___40___

Multiply Decimals by Powers of 10

EXAMPLE 3.719×100 *Count the zeros in 100: 2 zeros*
$3.719 \times 100 = 371.9$ *Move the decimal point 2 places to the right.*

Find the product.

5. 0.683×100 6. $9.15 \times 1,000$ 7. 0.005×100 8. $1,000 \times 1,000$
   68.3   9,150   0.5   1,000,000

Connect Words and Equations

EXAMPLE Two times a number decreased by 5 is −6.

Two times x decreased by 5 is −6.   *Represent the unknown with a variable.*
$2x - 5$ is −6   *Times means multiplication.*
$2x - 5 = -6$ *Decreased by means subtraction.*
   Place the equal sign.

Write an algebraic equation for the sentence.

9. The difference between three times a number and 7 is 14. $3x - 7 = 14$

10. The quotient of five times a number and 7 is no more than 10. $\frac{5x}{7} \leq 10$

11. 14 less than 3 times a number is 5 more than half of the number. $3x - 14 = \frac{1}{2}x + 5$

PROFESSIONAL DEVELOPMENT VIDEO

Author Juli Dixon models successful teaching practices as she explores the concept of equations and inequalities with the variable on both sides in an actual eighth-grade classroom.

Professional Development
my.hrw.com

GO DIGITAL
my.hrw.com

 Online Teacher Edition
Access a full suite of teaching resources online—plan, present, and manage classes and assignments.

ePlanner
Easily plan your classes and access all your resources online.

Interactive Answers and Solutions
Customize answer keys to print or display in the classroom. Choose to include answers only or full solutions to all lesson exercises.

 Interactive Whiteboards
Engage students with interactive whiteboard-ready lessons and activities.

 Personal Math Trainer: Online Assessment and Intervention
Assign automatically graded homework, quizzes, tests, and intervention activities. Prepare your students with updated practice tests aligned with Common Core.

Solving Linear Equations   **458**

Reading Start-Up

Have students complete the activities on this page by working alone or with others.

Visualize Vocabulary

The concept web helps students review vocabulary associated with equations and inequalities. Students should write one or more review words in each oval. As a class, add additional ovals to the graphic and brainstorm additional terms and definitions related to the content in this module.

Understand Vocabulary

Use the following explanation to help students review the vocabulary words.

An expression includes numbers and operations. An **algebraic expression** includes at least one variable. A **variable** represents an unknown number. The word *variable* means "able to change." A term in an expression that never changes is called a **constant.**

Active Reading

Integrating Language Arts

Students can use these reading and note-taking strategies to help them organize and understand new concepts and vocabulary.

FL CC LACC.68.RST.3.7 Integrate quantitative or technical information expressed in words in a text with a version of that information expressed visually (e.g., in a flowchart, diagram, model, graph, or table).

Additional Resources

Differentiated Instruction
• Reading Strategies **ELL**

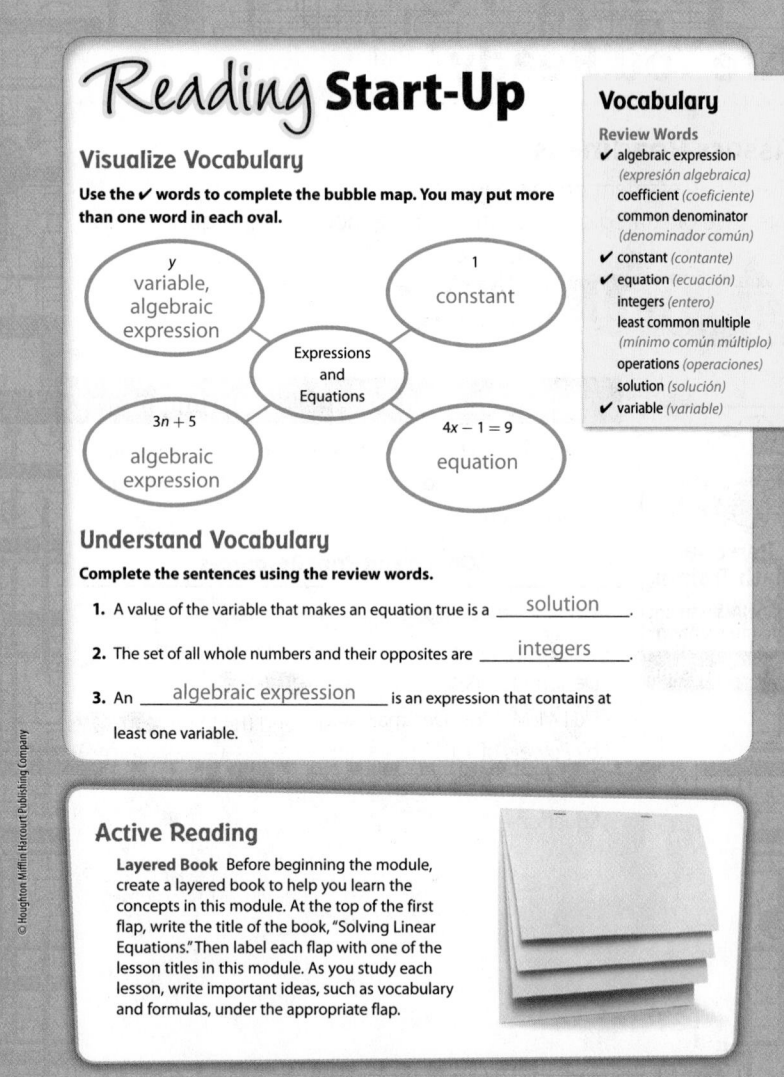

Reading Start-Up

Vocabulary

Review Words
✔ algebraic expression *(expresión algebraica)*
coefficient *(coeficiente)*
common denominator *(denominador común)*
✔ constant *(contante)*
✔ equation *(ecuación)*
integers *(entero)*
least common multiple *(mínimo común múltiplo)*
operations *(operaciones)*
solution *(solución)*
✔ variable *(variable)*

Visualize Vocabulary

Use the ✔ words to complete the bubble map. You may put more than one word in each oval.

- y — variable, algebraic expression
- 1 — constant
- **Expressions and Equations**
- $3n + 5$ — algebraic expression
- $4x - 1 = 9$ — equation

Understand Vocabulary

Complete the sentences using the review words.

1. A value of the variable that makes an equation true is a ___solution___.

2. The set of all whole numbers and their opposites are ___integers___.

3. An ___algebraic expression___ is an expression that contains at least one variable.

Active Reading

Layered Book Before beginning the module, create a layered book to help you learn the concepts in this module. At the top of the first flap, write the title of the book, "Solving Linear Equations." Then label each flap with one of the lesson titles in this module. As you study each lesson, write important ideas, such as vocabulary and formulas, under the appropriate flap.

Module 15 **459**

Before	In this module	After
Students understand equations: • write and solve two-step equations	Students will learn about: • solving equations with the variable on both sides and with rational number coefficients and constants	Students will solve: • multistep equations with the variable on one or both sides • equations with rational number coefficients and constants

Unpacking the Standards

Use the examples on the page to help students know exactly what they are expected to learn in this module.

Florida Common Core Standards

Content Areas

 **FL CC** **Expressions and Equations—8.EE.3**

Analyze and solve linear equations and pairs of simultaneous linear equations.

> Go online to see a complete unpacking of the Florida Common Core Standards.
>
> ⏻ my.hrw.com

MODULE 15

Unpacking the Standards

Understanding the standards and the vocabulary terms in the standards will help you know exactly what you are expected to learn in this module.

FL CC 8.EE.3.7a

Give examples of linear equations in one variable with one solution, infinitely many solutions, or no solutions. Show which of these possibilities is the case by successively transforming the given equation into simpler forms, until an equivalent equation of the form $x = a$, $a = a$, or $a = b$ results (where a and b are different numbers).

Key Vocabulary

linear equation in one variable
(ecuación lineal en una variable)
An equation that can be written in the form $ax = b$ where a and b are constants and $a \neq 0$.

What It Means to You

You will identify the number of solutions an equation has.

UNPACKING EXAMPLE 8.EE.3.7a

Your gym charges $50 per month. Find the number of months for which your costs will equal the cost of membership at each gym shown.

A: $40 per month plus $100 one-time fee
$50x = 40x + 100 \rightarrow x = 10$
Equal in 10 months → one solution

B: $50 per month plus $25 one-time fee
$50x = 50x + 25 \rightarrow 0 = 25$
Never equal → no solution

C: $40 per month plus $10 monthly garage fee
$50x = 40x + 10x \rightarrow x = x$
Equal for any number of months → infinitely many solutions

FL CC 8.EE.3.7b

Solve linear equations with rational number coefficients, including equations whose solutions require expanding expressions using the distributive property and collecting like terms.

Key Vocabulary

solution *(solución)*
In an equation, the value for the variable that makes the equation true.

Visit my.hrw.com to see all Florida Common Core Standards unpacked.

⏻ my.hrw.com

What It Means to You

You can write and solve an equation that has a variable on both sides of the equal sign.

UNPACKING EXAMPLE 8.EE.3.7b

Yellow Taxi has no pickup fee but charges $0.25 per mile. AAA Taxi charges $3 for pickup and $0.15 per mile. Find the number of miles for which the cost of the two taxis is the same.

$$0.25x = 3 + 0.15x$$
$$100(0.25x) = 100(3) + 100(0.15x)$$
$$25x = 300 + 15x$$
$$10x = 300$$
$$x = 30$$

The cost is the same for 30 miles.

Florida Common Core Standards	Lesson 15.1	Lesson 15.2	Lesson 15.3	Lesson 15.4
FL CC **8.EE.3.7** Solve linear equations in one variable.	✓	✓		
FL CC **8.EE.3.7a** Give examples of linear equations in one variable with one solution, infinitely many solutions, or no solutions. Show which of these possibilities is the case by successively transforming the given equation into simpler forms, until an equivalent equation of the form $x = a$, $a = a$, or $a = b$ results (where a and b are different numbers).				✓
FL CC **8.EE.3.7b** Solve linear equations with rational number coefficients, including equations whose solutions require expanding expressions using the distributive property and collecting like terms.	✓	✓	✓	

LESSON
15.1 Equations with the Variable on Both Sides

Florida Common Core Standards

The student is expected to:

 **Expressions and Equations—8.EE.3.7**

Solve linear equations in one variable.

 **Expressions and Equations—8.EE.3.7b**

Solve linear equations with rational number coefficients, including equations whose solutions require expanding expressions using the distributive property and collecting like terms.

Mathematical Practices

 **MP.4.1** Modeling

ADDITIONAL EXAMPLE 1
Peppy Pets charges a flat fee of $15 plus $3 per hour to keep a dog during the day. Happy Hounds charges a flat fee of $21 plus $1 per hour. For how many hours is the total fee charged by the companies the same?

3 hours

 Interactive Whiteboard
Interactive example available online

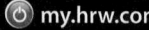 my.hrw.com

 Animated Math
Solving Equations with Variables on Both Sides

Students build fluency in solving equations using an interactive game.

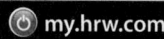 my.hrw.com

Engage

ESSENTIAL QUESTION

How can you represent and solve equations with the variable on both sides? Sample answer: You can use algebra tiles to model and solve equations with the variable on both sides. You can also use inverse operations to get the variable terms on one side of the equal sign and the constant terms on the other side, and then divide both sides by the coefficient of the resulting variable term.

Motivate the Lesson
Ask: How can you use zero pairs to help you solve an equation? Begin the Explore Activity to find out.

Explore

EXPLORE ACTIVITY

Focus on Reasoning Mathematical Practices
Have students model subtracting x from both sides of the equation and then adding 1 to both sides of the equation. Then have students start with the original equation again and model adding 1 to both sides of the equation and then subtracting x from both sides of the equation. Have students compare the solutions that are obtained in both ways.

Explain

EXAMPLE 1

Questioning Strategies Mathematical Practices
• Why can you add or subtract the same term, for example $28x$ or 20, on both sides of the equation? Because the resulting equations are equivalent to the original equation; that is, they have the same solution as the original equation: if $a = b$, then $a + c = b + c$ and $a - c = b - c$.

• How does the method used to get the variable terms on one side of the equation compare to the method used to get the constant terms on one side of the equation? Both use inverse operations.

• Explain why it does not matter which side of the equation you get the variable terms on. The results would either be $x = 4$ or $4 = x$. In either case the value of x is 4.

Engage with the Whiteboard
Have students circle or underscore the information in the question that is needed when writing the equation.

Avoid Common Errors
Students might use two different variables when representing the two expressions. Point out that in both expressions the variable x represents the number of days that a car has been rented and that the variable must be the same for both expressions in order to solve the problem.

Equations with the Variable on Both Sides

FL CC 8.EE.3.7
Solve linear equations in one variable. Also 8.EE.3.7b

? ESSENTIAL QUESTION

How can you represent and solve equations with the variable on both sides?

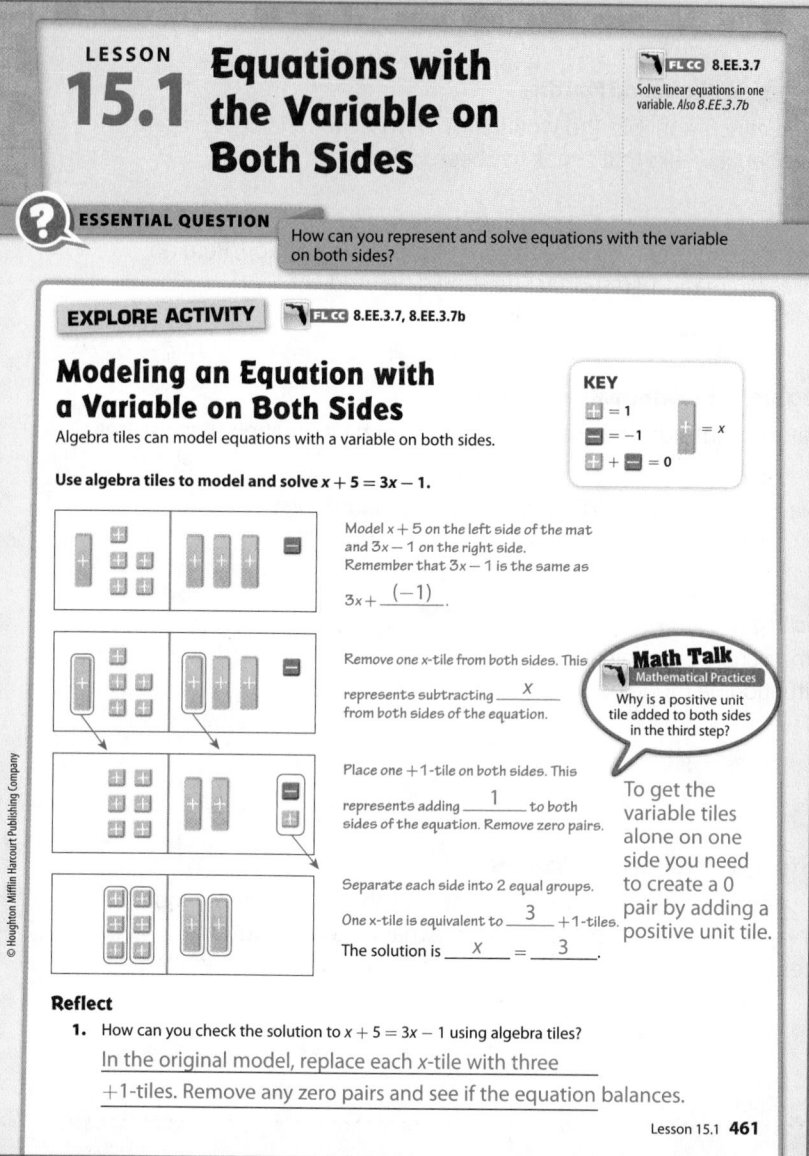

EXPLORE ACTIVITY
FL CC 8.EE.3.7, 8.EE.3.7b

Modeling an Equation with a Variable on Both Sides

Algebra tiles can model equations with a variable on both sides.

KEY

□+ = 1
■- = -1
□+ ■- = 0
▮+ = x

Use algebra tiles to model and solve $x + 5 = 3x - 1$.

Model $x + 5$ on the left side of the mat and $3x - 1$ on the right side.
Remember that $3x - 1$ is the same as

$3x + \underline{(-1)}$.

Remove one x-tile from both sides. This represents subtracting $\underline{x}$ from both sides of the equation.

Math Talk
Mathematical Practices
Why is a positive unit tile added to both sides in the third step?

Place one +1-tile on both sides. This represents adding $\underline{1}$ to both sides of the equation. Remove zero pairs.

Separate each side into 2 equal groups.

One x-tile is equivalent to $\underline{3}$ +1-tiles.

The solution is $\underline{x} = \underline{3}$.

To get the variable tiles alone on one side you need to create a 0 pair by adding a positive unit tile.

Reflect

1. How can you check the solution to $x + 5 = 3x - 1$ using algebra tiles?

In the original model, replace each x-tile with three +1-tiles. Remove any zero pairs and see if the equation balances.

Lesson 15.1 **461**

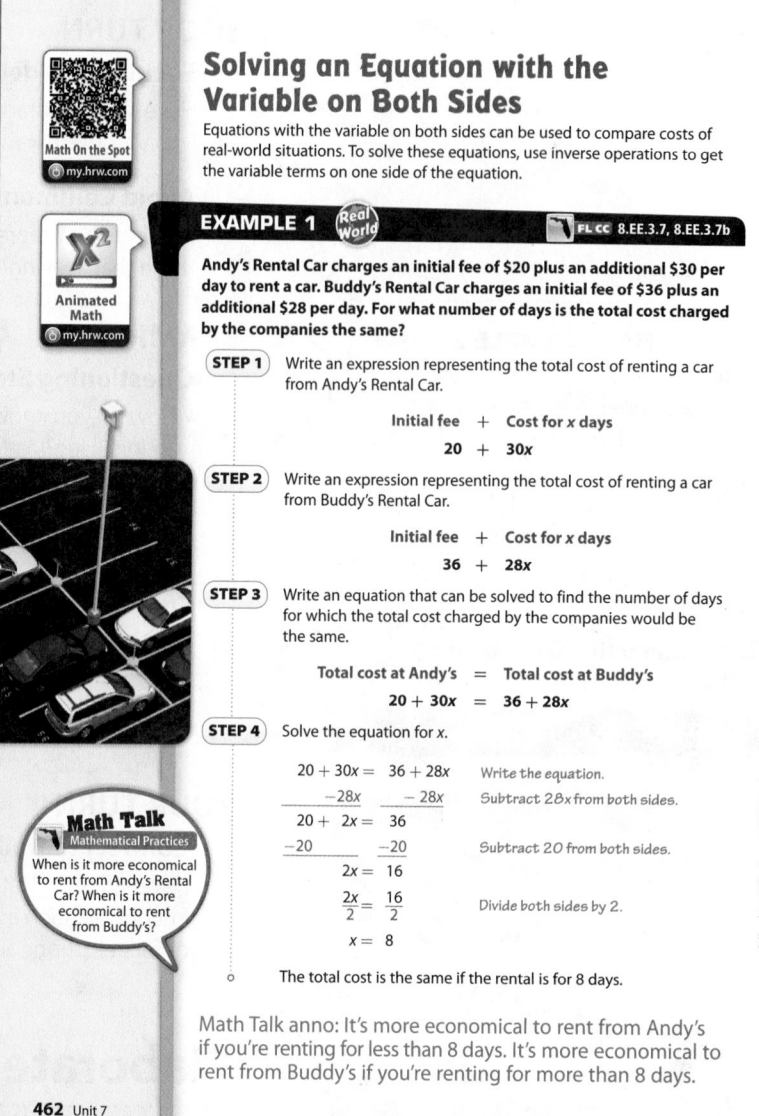

Math On the Spot
my.hrw.com

Animated Math
my.hrw.com

Solving an Equation with the Variable on Both Sides

Equations with the variable on both sides can be used to compare costs of real-world situations. To solve these equations, use inverse operations to get the variable terms on one side of the equation.

EXAMPLE 1 Real World
FL CC 8.EE.3.7, 8.EE.3.7b

Andy's Rental Car charges an initial fee of $20 plus an additional $30 per day to rent a car. Buddy's Rental Car charges an initial fee of $36 plus an additional $28 per day. For what number of days is the total cost charged by the companies the same?

STEP 1 Write an expression representing the total cost of renting a car from Andy's Rental Car.

Initial fee + Cost for x days
20 + 30x

STEP 2 Write an expression representing the total cost of renting a car from Buddy's Rental Car.

Initial fee + Cost for x days
36 + 28x

STEP 3 Write an equation that can be solved to find the number of days for which the total cost charged by the companies would be the same.

Total cost at Andy's = Total cost at Buddy's
20 + 30x = 36 + 28x

Math Talk
Mathematical Practices
When is it more economical to rent from Andy's Rental Car? When is it more economical to rent from Buddy's?

STEP 4 Solve the equation for x.

$$20 + 30x = 36 + 28x \quad \text{Write the equation.}$$
$$\underline{-28x \qquad -28x} \quad \text{Subtract 28x from both sides.}$$
$$20 + 2x = 36$$
$$\underline{-20 \qquad -20} \quad \text{Subtract 20 from both sides.}$$
$$2x = 16$$
$$\frac{2x}{2} = \frac{16}{2} \quad \text{Divide both sides by 2.}$$
$$x = 8$$

The total cost is the same if the rental is for 8 days.

Math Talk anno: It's more economical to rent from Andy's if you're renting for less than 8 days. It's more economical to rent from Buddy's if you're renting for more than 8 days.

462 Unit 7

PROFESSIONAL DEVELOPMENT

Integrate Mathematical Practices MP.4.1

This lesson provides an opportunity to address this Mathematical Practices standard. It calls for students to apply mathematics to problems arising in everyday life, society, and the workplace. Students use information about two related real-world situations to write and solve an equation with the same variable on both sides of the equation. Students must also describe a real-world situation that could be modeled by a given equation.

Math Background

A one-variable equation can have one solution, as seen in this lesson. It is also possible for a one-variable equation to have no solutions or infinitely many solutions. For example, the equation $x + 4 = x + 2$ has no solution. The equation $x + 3 = 3 + x$ is true for every real number x: it has infinitely many solutions.

YOUR TURN

Focus on Modeling Mathematical Practices

Have students start by selecting a variable and writing down what the variable represents. For example, $t =$ the number of weeks that a tank has been leaking.

Avoid Common Errors

Students may represent each expression using addition instead of subtraction. Remind them that "leaking" implies decreasing, so subtraction should be used.

EXAMPLE 2

Questioning Strategies Mathematical Practices

• How do you know that the right side of the equation could not be a situation that charges an initial fee? There is no constant added to the variable term.

• What does the variable x represent in the given real-world situation? the number of hours that it takes to paint the house

Talk About It
Check for Understanding

Ask: A handyman charges an initial fee of $150 and $25 per hour to paint. Why couldn't this situation be modeled by the expression $150 - 25x$? The total cost is the initial fee plus the cost of each hour. If it were minus then the painter would get paid less and less for each hour worked.

YOUR TURN

Connect to Daily Life Mathematical Practices

Have students state a real-world situation for this equation that they themselves might encounter, such as the variety of deals for purchasing yearly passes to an amusement park or for cell phone services.

Elaborate

Talk About It
Summarize the Lesson

Ask: What is the method for solving an equation with the same variable on both sides of the equation? Add or subtract the same terms, for example $3x$ or 7, on both sides of the equation to get the variable term on one side of the equation and the constant term on the other side of the equation. Then solve the resulting equation by dividing both sides by the coefficient of the variable.

GUIDED PRACTICE

Engage with the Whiteboard

For Exercise 3, write an "x" next to the coefficients of the variable. Circle the constants. Explain that x represents the number of personal training sessions that a person buys in one month. Have a student write an expression for the cost of a gym membership at Silver Gym for one month and x personal training sessions. Then have another student write an expression for the cost of a gym membership at Fit Factor for one month and x personal training sessions.

Avoid Common Errors

Exercise 1 Remind students that their model should involve making 0 pairs. An x on one side and a $-x$ on the other is not an example of a 0 pair.

Exercise 5 Remind students that the equation shows expressions that involve subtraction, so their situation should involve some decrease from a total amount.

463 Lesson 15.1

YOUR TURN

2. A water tank holds 256 gallons but is leaking at a rate of 3 gallons per week. A second water tank holds 384 gallons but is leaking at a rate of 5 gallons per week. After how many weeks will the amount of water in the two tanks be the same?

_____ 64 weeks _____

Personal Math Trainer
Online Assessment and Intervention
ⓜ my.hrw.com

Writing a Real-World Situation from an Equation

As shown in Example 1, an equation with the variable on both sides can be used to represent a real-world situation. You can reverse this process by writing a real-world situation for a given equation.

Math On the Spot
ⓜ my.hrw.com

EXAMPLE 2 🌎 Real World

FL CC 8.EE.3.7

Write a real-world situation that could be modeled by the equation $150 + 25x = 55x$.

STEP 1 The left side of the equation consists of a constant plus a variable term. It could represent the total cost for doing a job where there is an initial fee plus an hourly charge.

STEP 2 The right side of the equation consists of a variable term. It could represent the cost for doing the same job based on an hourly charge only.

STEP 3 The equation $150 + 25x = 55x$ could be represented by this situation: A handyman charges $150 plus $25 per hour for house painting. A painter charges $55 per hour. How many hours would a job have to take for the handyman's fee and the painter's fee to be the same?

YOUR TURN

3. Write a real-world situation that could be modeled by the equation $30x = 48 + 22x$.

Sample answer: One tennis club charges $30 per session to play tennis. Another tennis club charges an annual fee of $48 plus $22 per session. After how many sessions is the cost at the two clubs the same?

Personal Math Trainer
Online Assessment and Intervention
ⓜ my.hrw.com

My Notes

Lesson 15.1 **463**

Guided Practice

Use algebra tiles to model and solve each equation (Explore Activity)

1. $x + 4 = -x - 4$ _____ $x = -4$ _____   **2.** $2 - 3x = -x - 8$ _____ $x = 5$ _____

3. At Silver Gym, membership is $25 per month, and personal training sessions are $30 each. At Fit Factor, membership is $65 per month, and personal training sessions are $20 each. In one month, how many personal training sessions would Sarah have to buy to make the total cost at the two gyms equal? (Example 1)

4 personal training sessions

4. Write a real-world situation that could be modeled by the equation $120 + 25x = 45x$. (Example 2)

Sample answer: A DJ charges a flat fee of $120 plus $25 an hour. A second DJ charges $45 an hour. After how many hours is the charge for the two DJs the same?

5. Write a real-world situation that could be modeled by the equation $100 - 6x = 160 - 10x$. (Example 2)

Sample answer: Xavier has $100 in his lunch account. He spends $6 for lunch each day. Zack has $160 in his lunch account. He spends $10 each day. After how many days will the boys have the same amount of money in their accounts?

❓ ESSENTIAL QUESTION CHECK-IN

6. How can you solve an equation with a variable on both sides?

You can solve the equation by using inverse operations to get the variable terms on one side of the equal sign and the constant terms on the other side, and then dividing both sides by the coefficient of the resulting variable term.

464 Unit 7

DIFFERENTIATE INSTRUCTION

Cooperative Learning

Have students work in pairs to use algebra tiles to model and solve equations. Have one student model the left side of the equation and another student model the right side. Then have one student model how to get the variable terms on one side of the equation and the other student model how to get the constant terms on the other side of the equation.

Technology

Using the expressions in Example 1, demonstrate for students how the situation can be represented on a graphing calculator. Have students graph the equations $y = 20 + 30x$ and $y = 36 + 28x$ on one screen. The x-value for the ordered pair at the point (8, 260), where the two lines intersect, is the number of days (8) for which the cost of either rental agency is the same. The y-value is the total cost ($260).

Additional Resources

Differentiated Instruction includes:
- Reading Strategies
- Success for English Learners **ELL**
- Reteach
- Challenge **PRE-AP**

Equations with the Variable on Both Sides   **464**

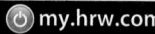
15.1 LESSON QUIZ

 **FL CC** 8.EE.3.7, 8.EE.3.7b

Solve each equation.

1. $3x + 5 = -x - 7$

2. $3 - 5x = -9 + x$

3. Joe's Canoes charges an initial fee of $20 plus $4 an hour. Callie's Canoes charges a flat rate of $14 an hour. Find the number of hours for which the total amount that both places charge would be the same.

4. Write a real-world situation that could be modeled by the equation $500 + 250x = 300x$.

Lesson Quiz available online

 my.hrw.com

Answers

1. $x = -3$

2. $x = 2$

3. 2 hours

4. Sample answer: One car dealer sells a car with a $500 down payment and payments of $250 per month. Another car dealer sells the same type of car with no down payment and monthly payments of $300 per month. After how many months will the buyers have paid the same amount?

Evaluate

GUIDED AND INDEPENDENT PRACTICE

 **FL CC** 8.EE.3.7, 8.EE.3.7b

Concepts & Skills	Practice
Explore Activity Modeling an Equation with a Variable on Both Sides	Exercises 1–2
Example 1 Solving an Equation with the Variable on Both Sides	Exercises 3, 7–8
Example 2 Writing a Real-World Situation from an Equation	Exercises 4–5

Exercise	Depth of Knowledge (D.O.K.)	**FL CC** Mathematical Practices
7	**2** Skills/Concepts	**MP.4.1** Modeling
8	**2** Skills/Concepts	**MP.2.1** Reasoning
9–11	**2** Skills/Concepts	**MP.6.1** Precision
12	**2** Skills/Concepts	**MP.5.1** Using Tools
13	**3** Strategic Thinking **H.O.T.**	**MP.2.1** Reasoning
14	**3** Strategic Thinking **H.O.T.**	**MP.3.1** Logic
15	**3** Strategic Thinking **H.O.T.**	**MP.2.1** Reasoning

Additional Resources

Differentiated Instruction includes:

• Leveled Practice worksheets

15.1 Independent Practice

FL CC 8.EE.3.7, 8.EE.3.7b

Personal Math Trainer
Online Assessment and Intervention
my.hrw.com

7. Derrick' Dog Sitting and Darlene's Dog Sitting are competing for new business. The companies ran the ads shown.

a. Write and solve an equation to find the number of hours for which the total cost will be the same for the two services.

$12 + 5x = 18 + 3x$; $x = 3$; 3 hours

b. **Analyze Relationships** Which dog sitting service is more economical to use if you need 5 hours of service? Explain.

Darlene's Dog Sitting; the cost would be $33, as opposed to $37 at Derrick's Dog Sitting.

Derrick's Dog Sitting
$12 plus
$5 per hour

Darlene's Dog Sitting
$18 plus
$3 per hour

8. Country Carpets charges $22 per square yard for carpeting, and an additional installation fee of $100. City Carpets charges $25 per square yard for the same carpeting, and an additional installation fee of $70.

a. Write and solve an equation to find the number of square yards of carpeting for which the total cost charged by the two companies will be the same.

$22x + 100 = 25x + 70$; $x = 10$; 10 square yards

b. **Justify Reasoning** Mr. Shu wants to hire one of the two carpet companies to install carpeting in his basement. Is he more likely to hire Country Carpets or City Carpets? Explain your reasoning.

Country Carpets; Mr. Shu's basement is probably larger than 10 square yards, and Country Carpets is cheaper than City Carpets for amounts greater than 10 square yards.

Write an equation to represent each relationship. Then solve the equation.

9. Two less than 3 times a number is the same as the number plus 10.

$3x - 2 = x + 10$; $x = 6$

10. A number increased by 4 is the same as 19 minus 2 times the number.

$x + 4 = 19 - 2x$; $x = 5$

11. Twenty less than 8 times a number is the same as 15 more than the number.

$8x - 20 = x + 15$; $x = 5$

12. The charges for an international call made using the calling card for two phone companies are shown in the table.

Phone Company	Charges
Company A	35¢ plus 3¢ per minute
Company B	45¢ plus 2¢ per minute

a. What is the length of a phone call that would cost the same no matter which company is used?

10 minutes

b. **Analyze Relationships** When is it better to use the card from Company B?

Company B is a better choice whenever you expect a phone call will take more than 10 minutes.

H.O.T. FOCUS ON HIGHER ORDER THINKING

13. **Draw Conclusions** Liam is setting up folding chairs for a meeting. If he arranges the chairs in 9 rows of the same length, he has 3 chairs left over. If he arranges the chairs in 7 rows of that same length, he has 19 left over. How many chairs does Liam have?

$9x + 3 = 7x + 19$; $x = 8$; 75 chairs

14. **Explain the Error** Rent-A-Tent rents party tents for a flat fee of $365 plus $125 a day. Capital Rentals rents party tents for a flat fee of $250 plus $175 a day. Delia wrote the following equation to find the number of days for which the total cost charged by the two companies would be the same:

$$365x + 125 = 250x + 175$$

Find and explain the error in Delia's work. Then write the correct equation.

Delia multiplied the flat fee, instead of the daily rate, by the number of days x. The total cost for each company is the flat fee plus the product of the daily rate and the number of days; $365 + 125x = 250 + 175x$.

15. **Persevere in Problem Solving** Lilliana is training for a marathon. She runs the same distance every day for a week. On Monday, Wednesday, and Friday, she runs 3 laps on a running trail and then runs 6 more miles. On Tuesday and Sunday, she runs 5 laps on the trail and then runs 2 more miles. On Saturday, she just runs laps. How many laps does Lilliana run on Saturday?

$3x + 6 = 5x + 2$; $x = 2$; 6 laps

Work Area

EXTEND THE MATH PRE-AP

Activity available online ⊙ my.hrw.com

Activity The numbers 5, 7, and 9 are an example of three consecutive odd integers. Write and solve an equation for the problem below.

Find three consecutive odd integers whose sum is 121 minus twice the first integer.

Let $x =$ the first number, $x + 2 =$ the second number, and $x + 4 =$ the third number. Then $x + (x + 2) + (x + 4) = 121 - 2x$, or $5x = 115$. Therefore, $x = 23$. The consecutive odd integers are 23, 25, and 27.

LESSON
15.2 Equations with Rational Numbers

ADDITIONAL EXAMPLE 1

Solve $\frac{3}{5}x + \frac{1}{4} = \frac{7}{20}x - 4$. $x = -17$

 Interactive Whiteboard
Interactive example available online

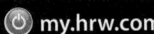 **my.hrw.com**

ADDITIONAL EXAMPLE 2

Sasha walks to school at a constant rate. She meets her friend Hannah 0.6 kilometers along the way, and they continue walking at the same constant rate. When they get to school, Sasha has walked for 0.6 hour and Hannah has walked for 0.45 hour. What is the rate in kilometers per hour at which they walked to school? 4 km/h

 Interactive Whiteboard
Interactive example available online

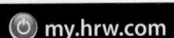 **my.hrw.com**

Engage

ESSENTIAL QUESTION

How can you solve equations with rational number coefficients and constants? Sample answer: Start by eliminating the fractions or decimals from the equation by multiplying both sides of the equation by the same factor. Continue by isolating the variable using the same steps that were used for solving equations with integer coefficients and constants.

Motivate the Lesson

Ask: Fractions can appear in the equations that you will be solving. What are some ways to create a new equation with no fractions and the same solution as the original equation?

Explore

Present a simple equation, such as $\frac{2}{15}x = \frac{4}{10}$. Ask students to suggest ways to create a new equivalent equation with no fractions in it. Students may suggest using cross products, multiplying by the multiplicative inverse, or multiplying by the LCM of the denominators.

Explain

EXAMPLE 1

Questioning Strategies 🖊 Mathematical Practices

- Why must you multiply <u>both</u> sides of the equation by the LCM? The same operations must be carried out on both sides of the equation so that the resulting equation has the same solution as the original equation.

Focus on Communication

Ensure that students understand that the idea is to find the LCM of the denominators and then multiply both sides of the equation by the LCM.

YOUR TURN

Avoid Common Errors

Make sure that students understand that when multiplying by the LCM all terms on the left and on the right of the equal sign get multiplied by the LCM, not just the fractions.

EXAMPLE 2

Questioning Strategies 🖊 Mathematical Practices

- Which brother is represented by the expression $0.2r + 0.75$? Raul By $0.5r$? Javier

- Name and describe the property that is used on the left side of the equation in Step 2. The Distributive Property; each term of $(0.2r + 0.75)$ is multiplied by 100.

Focus on Modeling 🖊 Mathematical Practices

In Example 2, students use information given in the question to create an equation that models a real-world situation. Ensure that students understand the real-world quantities involved in the problem.

LESSON 15.2 Equations with Rational Numbers

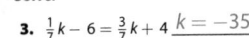
FL CC 8.EE.3.7b
Solve linear equations with rational number coefficients, ... Also 8.EE.3.7

ESSENTIAL QUESTION How can you solve equations with rational number coefficients and constants?

Solving an Equation that Involves Fractions

To solve an equation with the variable on both sides that involves fractions, start by eliminating the fractions from the equation.

EXAMPLE 1
FL CC 8.EE.3.7b, 8.EE.3.7

Solve $\frac{7}{10}n + \frac{3}{2} = \frac{3}{5}n + 2$.

STEP 1 Determine the least common multiple of the denominators: LCM(10, 5, 2) = 10

$$10 = 10 \times 1 = 5 \times 2 = 2 \times 5$$

STEP 2 Multiply both sides of the equation by the LCM.

$$10\left(\frac{7}{10}n + \frac{3}{2}\right) = 10\left(\frac{3}{5}n + 2\right)$$

$${}^{1}\!10\left(\frac{7}{10}n\right) + {}^{5}\!10\left(\frac{3}{2}\right) = {}^{2}\!10\left(\frac{3}{5}n\right) + 10(2)$$

$$7n + 15 = 6n + 20$$

STEP 3 Use inverse operations to solve the equation.

$$
\begin{array}{rcl}
7n + 15 & = & 6n + 20 \\
-15 & & -15 \qquad \text{Subtract 15 from both sides.} \\
\hline
7n & = & 6n + 5 \\
-6n & & -6n \\
\hline
n & = & 5 \qquad \text{Subtract 6n from both sides.}
\end{array}
$$

Reflect

1. What is the advantage of multiplying both sides of the equation by the least common multiple of the denominators in the first step?

   It simplifies the calculations by eliminating all the fractions.

2. **What If?** What happens in the first step if you multiply both sides by a common multiple of the denominators that is not the LCM?

   You would eliminate the fractions, but the result would be an equation with greater integer coefficients.

Math Talk
Mathematical Practices

The constant on the right side, 2, is not a fraction. Why do you still need to multiply it by the LCM, 10?

To create an equation that is equivalent to the original equation, you must multiply all terms by the LCM whether they are fractions or not.

Math On the Spot
© my.hrw.com

Personal Math Trainer
Online Assessment and Intervention
© my.hrw.com

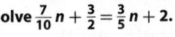

Solve.

3. $\frac{1}{7}k - 6 = \frac{3}{7}k + 4 \quad \underline{k = -35}$

4. $\frac{5}{6}y + 1 = -\frac{1}{2}y + \frac{1}{4} \quad \underline{y = -\frac{9}{16}}$

Solving an Equation that Involves Decimals

Solving an equation with the variable on both sides that involves decimals is similar to solving an equation with fractions. But instead of first multiplying both sides by the LCM, multiply by a power of 10 to eliminate the decimals.

EXAMPLE 2 (Real World)
FL CC 8.EE.3.7, 8.EE.3.7b

Javier walks from his house to the zoo at a constant rate. After walking 0.75 mile, he meets his brother, Raul, and they continue walking at the same constant rate. When they arrive at the zoo, Javier has walked for 0.5 hour and Raul has walked for 0.2 hour. What is the rate in miles per hour at which the brothers walked to the zoo?

STEP 1 Write an equation for the distance from the brothers' house to the zoo, using the fact that distance equals rate times time. Let r = the brothers' walking rate.

$$\underbrace{0.2r + 0.75}_{\text{distance to zoo}} = \underbrace{0.5r}_{\text{distance to zoo}}$$

STEP 2 Multiply both sides of the equation by $10^2 = 100$.

$$100(0.2r) + 100(0.75) = 100(0.5r)$$

$$20r + 75 = 50r$$

> Multiplying by 100 clears the equation of decimals. Multiplying by 10 does not: $10 \times 0.75 = 7.5$.

STEP 3 Use inverse operations to solve the equation.

$$
\begin{array}{rcl}
20r + 75 & = & 50r \qquad \text{Write the equation.} \\
-20r & & -20r \qquad \text{Subtract 20r from both sides.} \\
\hline
75 & = & 30r \\
\frac{75}{30} & = & \frac{30r}{30} \qquad \text{Divide both sides by 30.} \\
2.5 & = & r
\end{array}
$$

So, the brothers' constant rate of speed was 2.5 miles per hour.

PROFESSIONAL DEVELOPMENT

Integrate Mathematical Practices MP.6.1

This lesson provides an opportunity to address this Mathematical Practices standard. It calls for students to communicate precisely. Students write equations involving fractions or decimals to represent real-world situations and solve real-world problems. They also create real-world situations that can be modeled by equations involving fractions or decimals.

Math Background

The Properties of Equality for addition, subtraction, and multiplication state that you can add, subtract, or multiply both sides of an equation by any real number, and the resulting equation has the same solution set as the original equation. The Division Property of Equality states that this is also true for division by any non-zero real number.

YOUR TURN

Avoid Common Errors

Make sure that students understand that the variable represents the weight of a cubic foot of water. Students may be tempted to add 37.44 to $1.9x$. Explain that for the two sides of the equation to be equal, they must subtract 37.44 from $1.9x$ or add 37.44 to $1.3x$.

Engage with the Whiteboard

 Draw a diagram of the two aquariums. Label the smaller aquarium $1.3x + 37.44$ and the other aquarium $1.9x$.

ADDITIONAL EXAMPLE 3

Write a real-world situation that can be modeled by the equation $5.25x + 3.25 = 1.75x + 10.25$. Sample answer: One sandbox has 3.25 pounds of sand. You are filling the sandbox with a bucket that holds 5.25 pounds of sand. Another sandbox has 10.25 pounds of sand. Your brother is filling it with a bucket that holds 1.75 pounds of sand. How many buckets of sand will it take to have the same weight of sand in each sandbox?

 Interactive Whiteboard
Interactive example available online

⏻ my.hrw.com

EXAMPLE 3

Questioning Strategies Mathematical Practices

• If you are creating a situation about rates, which numbers in the equation you are given will represent the rates? The rates will be the coefficients of the variable terms.

• What is the answer to the problem in Example 3? 150 songs

Focus on Modeling 🚩 Mathematical Practices

In Example 3, students are given an equation and asked to create a real-world situation the equation could model. Ensure that students understand that the situation they create should ask when two real-world quantities are equal.

Integrating Language Arts ᴇʟʟ

You may want to pair up English learners with a partner for Example 1 to help them develop their language skills.

YOUR TURN

Talk About It
Check for Understanding

💬 **Ask:** Given the sample answer for Exercise 6, what does x represent in the equation? x represents the weight of rice in the bin when it is full.

Elaborate

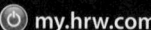

Talk About It
Summarize the Lesson

💬 **Ask:** How do you determine what to multiply an equation by so that you eliminate fractions or decimals from the equation? If the equation has fractions in it, multiply both sides of the equation by the LCM (or any common multiple) of the denominators. If the equation has decimals in it, multiply both sides of the equation by the appropriate power of 10 to eliminate the decimals.

GUIDED PRACTICE

Engage with the Whiteboard

For Exercise 1, have a student write an expression for how much Fast Internet charges. Have another student write an expression for Quick Internet. In Exercises 2–4, have students write the LCM for the fractions in each equation.

Avoid Common Errors

Exercises 2–7 Remind students that the solution of an equation can be a decimal or a fraction, even though they eliminated fractions or decimals from the original equation.

5. Logan has two aquariums. One aquarium contains 1.3 cubic feet of water and the other contains 1.9 cubic feet of water. The water in the larger aquarium weighs 37.44 pounds more than the water in the smaller aquarium. Write an equation with a variable on both sides to represent the situation. Then find the weight of 1 cubic foot of water.

$1.9x = 1.3x + 37.44$; 62.4 lb

Writing a Real-World Situation from an Equation

Real-world situations can often be represented by equations involving fractions and decimals. Fractions and decimals can represent quantities such as weight, volume, capacity, time, and temperature. Decimals can also be used to represent dollars and cents.

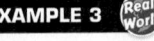

EXAMPLE 3 (Real World)   FL CC 8.EE.3.7

Write a real-world situation that can be modeled by the equation $0.95x = 0.55x + 60$.

The left side of the equation consists of a variable term. It could represent the total cost for x items.

The right side of the equation consists of a variable term plus a constant. It could represent the total cost for x items plus a flat fee.

The equation $0.95x = 0.55x + 60$ could be represented by this situation: Toony Tunes charges $0.95 for each song you download. Up With Downloads charges $0.55 for each song but also charges an annual membership fee of $60. How many songs must a customer download in a year so that the cost will be the same at both websites?

YOUR TURN

6. Write a real-world problem that can be modeled by the equation $\frac{1}{3}x + 10 = \frac{3}{5}x$.

Sample answer: A bin of rice at a store is one third full. After 10 additional pounds of rice is added to the bin, the bin is three fifths full. How much rice does the bin hold when it is full?

Personal Math Trainer
Online Assessment and Intervention
my.hrw.com

Personal Math Trainer
Online Assessment and Intervention
my.hrw.com

Math On the Spot
my.hrw.com

My Notes

© Houghton Mifflin Harcourt Publishing Company

---

1. Sandy is upgrading her Internet service. Fast Internet charges $60 for installation and $50.45 per month. Quick Internet has free installation but charges $57.95 per month. (Example 2)

   a. Write an equation that can be used to find the number of months after which the Internet service would cost the same.

   $$60 + 50.45x = 57.95x$$

   b. Solve the equation.

   $x = 8$; 8 months

Solve. (Examples 1 and 2)

2. $\frac{3}{4}n - 18 = \frac{1}{4}n - 4$
   $n = 28$

3. $6 + \frac{4}{5}b = \frac{9}{10}b$
   $b = 60$

4. $\frac{2}{11}m + 16 = 4 + \frac{6}{11}m$
   $m = 33$

5. $2.25t + 5 = 13.5t + 14$
   $t = -0.8$

6. $3.6w = 1.6w + 24$
   $w = 12$

7. $-0.75p - 2 = 0.25p$
   $p = -2$

8. Write a real-world problem that can be modeled by the equation $1.25x = 0.75x + 50$. (Example 3)

   Sample answer: A store charges $1.25 per bathroom tile and lets you use their installation tools for free. Another store charges $0.75 per tile but charges you $50 to use their tools. How many tiles would you need to buy for the total cost to be the same?

? ESSENTIAL QUESTION CHECK-IN

9. How does the method for solving equations with fractional or decimal coefficients and constants compare with the method for solving equations with integer coefficients and constants?

   The methods are essentially the same. The only extra step is that you begin solving by eliminating the fractions or the decimals from the equation.

© Houghton Mifflin Harcourt Publishing Company

DIFFERENTIATE INSTRUCTION

Number Sense
Students should note that when eliminating decimals from an equation the greatest number of decimal places in the terms will determine the power of 10 they should multiply by. For an equation with terms having decimal numbers in the tenths, hundredths, and thousandths, they would multiply by 10^3 or 1000 since thousandths is the greatest decimal place value. The number of place values to the left of the decimal has no bearing on which power of 10 to use.

World History
René Descartes (1596–1650) was a French mathematician and philosopher. In his work, titled *Rules*, he included this suggestion: break your work up into small steps that you can understand completely and about which you have utter certainty, and check your work often. Solving equations with rational numbers is a good place to apply Descartes' rule. First eliminate fractions or decimals, then isolate the variable, and then solve the equation.

Additional Resources
Differentiated Instruction includes:
- Reading Strategies
- Success for English Learners **ELL**
- Reteach
- Challenge **PRE-AP**

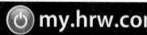
15.2 LESSON QUIZ

 8.EE.3.7b, 8.EE.3.7

1. Solve $\frac{7}{8}x - \frac{1}{2} = \frac{3}{16}x + 5$.

2. Marsha is changing her phone service. One data package charges an initial fee of $50 and $13.25 per month. The other has no initial fee but charges $25.75 per month for the same data package. After how many months would Marsha have paid the same amount for either data package?

3. Write a real-world situation that can be modeled by the equation $8.35x = 4.25x + 36.90$.

4. The perimeter of one square is given as $4x$. Its perimeter is equal to the perimeter of a rectangle given as $2.5x + 3.75$. What is the perimeter of each figure?

Lesson Quiz available online

 my.hrw.com

Answers

1. $x = 8$

2. 4 months

3. Sample answer: Mark paid $8.35 per pound for fish at one market. Then he found another market that charges a member's fee of $36.90 a year plus $4.25 per pound for fish. How many pounds of fish would Mark need to buy for the total cost to be the same?

4. 10 units

Evaluate

GUIDED AND INDEPENDENT PRACTICE

 8.EE.3.7b, 8.EE.3.7

Concepts & Skills	Practice
Example 1 Solving an Equation that Involves Fractions	Exercises 2–4, 18
Example 2 Solving an Equation that Involves Decimals	Exercises 1, 5–7, 10–13, 16–17
Example 3 Writing a Real-World Situation from an Equation	Exercise 8

Exercise	Depth of Knowledge (D.O.K.)	FL CC Mathematical Practices
10–13	**2** Skills/Concepts	**MP.5.1** Using Tools
14–17	**2** Skills/Concepts	**MP.4.1** Modeling
18	**2** Skills/Concepts	**MP.3.1** Logic
19	**3** Strategic Thinking **H.O.T.**	**MP.5.1** Using Tools
20	**3** Strategic Thinking **H.O.T.**	**MP.8.1** Patterns
21	**3** Strategic Thinking **H.O.T.**	**MP.2.1** Reasoning

Additional Resources

Differentiated Instruction includes:

• Leveled Practice worksheets

15.2 Independent Practice

FL CC 8.EE.3.7, 8.EE.3.7b

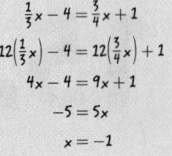
Personal Math Trainer
Online Assessment and Intervention
my.hrw.com

10. Members of the Wide Waters Club pay $105 per summer season, plus $9.50 each time they rent a boat. Nonmembers must pay $14.75 each time they rent a boat. How many times would a member and a non-member have to rent a boat in order to pay the same amount?

__20 times__

11. Margo can purchase tile at a store for $0.79 per tile and rent a tile saw for $24. At another store she can borrow the tile saw for free if she buys tiles there for $1.19 per tile. How many tiles must she buy for the cost to be the same at both stores?

__60 tiles__

12. The charges for two shuttle services are shown in the table. Find the number of miles for which the cost of both shuttles is the same.

	Pickup Charge ($)	Charge per Mile ($)
Easy Ride	10	0.10
Best	0	0.35

__40 miles__

13. **Multistep** Rapid Rental Car charges a $40 rental fee, $15 for gas, and $0.25 per mile driven. For the same car, Capital Cars charges $45 for rental and gas and $0.35 per mile.

a. For how many miles is the rental cost at both companies the same?

__100 mi__

b. What is that cost?

__$80__

14. Write an equation with the solution $x = 20$. The equation should have the variable on both sides, a fractional coefficient on the left side, and a fraction anywhere on the right side.

Sample answer: $\frac{4}{5}x - 3 = \frac{3}{10}x + 7$

15. Write an equation with the solution $x = 25$. The equation should have the variable on both sides, a decimal coefficient on the left side, and a decimal anywhere on the right side. One of the decimals should be written in tenths, the other in hundredths.

Sample answer: $0.4x - 5 = 0.08x + 3$

16. **Geometry** The perimeters of the rectangles shown are equal. What is the perimeter of each rectangle?

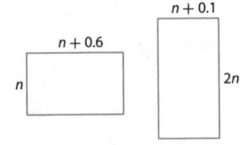

__3.2 units__

17. **Analyze Relationships** The formula $F = 1.8C + 32$ gives the temperature in degrees Fahrenheit (F) for a given temperature in degrees Celsius (C). There is one temperature for which the number of degrees Fahrenheit is equal to the number of degrees Celsius. Write an equation you can solve to find that temperature and then use it to find the temperature.

$C = 1.8C + 32; -40°F = -40°C$

18. **Explain the Error** Agustin solved an equation as shown. What error did Agustin make? What is the correct answer?

Agustin multiplied only the terms with fractional coefficients by the LCD. He should have multiplied all the terms. The correct answer is $x = -12$.

$$\frac{1}{3}x - 4 = \frac{3}{4}x + 1$$
$$12\left(\frac{1}{3}x\right) - 4 = 12\left(\frac{3}{4}x\right) + 1$$
$$4x - 4 = 9x + 1$$
$$-5 = 5x$$
$$x = -1$$

H.O.T. FOCUS ON HIGHER ORDER THINKING

Work Area

19. **Draw Conclusions** Solve the equation $\frac{1}{2}x - 5 + \frac{2}{3}x = \frac{7}{6}x + 4$. Explain your results.

When you attempt to solve the equation, you eliminate the variable from both sides of the equation, leaving a false statement such as $-30 = 24$. Since the statement is false, the equation must not have a solution.

20. **Look for a Pattern** Describe the pattern in the equation. Then solve the equation.

$$0.3x + 0.03x + 0.003x + 0.0003x + \ldots = 3$$

Each term on the left side of the equation is one tenth of the previous term. Since the pattern continues without end, the sum of the terms is $0.3333 \ldots x$, which equals $\frac{1}{3}x$. Since $\frac{1}{3}x = 3$, $x = 9$.

21. **Critique Reasoning** Jared wanted to find three consecutive even integers whose sum was 4 times the first of those integers. He let k represent the first integer, then wrote and solved this equation: $k + (k + 1) + (k + 2) = 4k$. Did he get the correct answer? Explain.

No; the solution to his equation is $k = 3$, giving 3, 4, and 5 as the three integers. However, 3 and 5 are not even integers. He should have used the equation $k + (k + 2) + (k + 4) = 4k$, which gives $k = 6$ and the correct answer 6, 8, 10.

EXTEND THE MATH PRE-AP

Activity available online my.hrw.com

Activity The following equation is nonlinear but becomes linear when the fractions are eliminated from the equation. Solve the equation.

$$\frac{x}{x-2} = 2 + \frac{3}{x-2}$$
$$\frac{x}{x-2} = 2 + \frac{3}{x-2}$$
$$(x-2)\left(\frac{x}{x-2}\right) = \left(2 + \frac{3}{x-2}\right)(x-2)$$
$$x = 2x - 4 + 3$$
$$x = 2x - 1$$
$$x = 1$$

© Houghton Mifflin Harcourt Publishing Company

LESSON
15.3 Equations with the Distributive Property

Florida Common Core Standards

The student is expected to:

 **FL CC** **Expressions and Equations—8.EE.3.7b**

Solve linear equations with rational number coefficients, including equations whose solutions require expanding expressions using the distributive property and collecting like terms.

Mathematical Practices

 **FL CC** **MP.1.1** Problem Solving

---

ADDITIONAL EXAMPLE 1

A Solve: $2(x - 6) + 3 = 4 + x$ $x = 13$

B Solve: $3x - 8 = 10 - 3(x - 4)$
$x = 5$

 Interactive Whiteboard
Interactive example available online

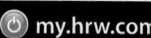 ⏻ my.hrw.com

---

ADDITIONAL EXAMPLE 2

Solve: $-\frac{3}{5}(5 - 2y) = -3(y - 5) - 18$
$y = 0$

 Interactive Whiteboard
Interactive example available online

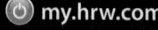 ⏻ my.hrw.com

---

Engage

ESSENTIAL QUESTION

How do you use the Distributive Property to solve equations? Sample answer: Distribute a factor to all terms within parentheses, then solve for the variable.

Motivate the Lesson
Ask: How can the Distributive Property and inverse operations help you simplify equations? Begin the lesson to find out.

Explore

Write the equation in Example 1A on the board. Ask students if they think they can solve an equation with parentheses. What additional steps might be involved?

Explain

EXAMPLE 1

Questioning Strategies Mathematical Practices
• Why is it necessary to apply the Distributive Property before isolating the variable on one side? The order of operations states that expressions in parentheses are simplified first.

Focus on Critical Thinking
Make sure students understand that only the terms within the parentheses are multiplied by the factor outside the parentheses.

YOUR TURN

Avoid Common Errors
To prevent errors with signs, encourage students to distribute -9 instead of 9 in Exercise 1.

EXAMPLE 2

Questioning Strategies Mathematical Practices
• Why are fractions eliminated before applying the Distributive Property? Eliminating the fractions first allows for distributing whole numbers, which are easier to work with.

Focus on Reasoning Mathematical Practices
Discuss with students which terms are multiplied by the LCD. In Example 2, none of the terms in the expressions within the parentheses are directly multiplied by the LCD, but in the equation $\frac{3}{4} + (x - 13) = -2 + (9 + x)$, all terms are multiplied by the LCD.

YOUR TURN

Engage with the Whiteboard
For Exercises 3 and 4, have volunteers demonstrate while they explain how to find the LCD and use the Distributive Property to solve each equation.

LESSON 15.3 Equations with the Distributive Property

FL CC 8.EE.3.7b
Solve linear equations with rational number coefficients, including equations whose solutions require expanding expressions using the distributive property and collecting like terms.

? ESSENTIAL QUESTION
How do you use the Distributive Property to solve equations?

Using the Distributive Property
The Distributive Property can be useful in solving equations.

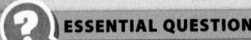
Math On the Spot
my.hrw.com

EXAMPLE 1
FL CC 8.EE.3.7b

A Solve: $3(x - 5) + 1 = 2 + x$

STEP 1 Use the Distributive Property.

$3x - 15 + 1 = 2 + x$ — Distribute 3 to the terms within the parentheses.

$3x - 14 = 2 + x$ — Simplify.

STEP 2 Use inverse operations to solve the equation.

$$3x - 14 = 2 + x$$
$$\underline{-x \qquad\qquad -x}$$ — Subtract x from both sides.
$$2x - 14 = 2$$
$$\underline{+14 \qquad +14}$$ — Add 14 to both sides.
$$2x = 16$$ — Divide both sides by 2.
$$x = 8$$

B Solve: $5 - 7k = -4(k + 1) - 3$

STEP 1 Use the Distributive Property.

$5 - 7k = -4k - 4 - 3$ — Distribute −4 to the terms within the parentheses.

$5 - 7k = -4k - 7$ — Simplify.

STEP 2 Use inverse operations to solve the equation.

$$5 - 7k = -4k - 7$$
$$\underline{+4k \qquad +4k}$$ — Add 4k to both sides.
$$5 - 3k = -7$$
$$\underline{-5 \qquad\quad -5}$$ — Subtract 5 from both sides.
$$-3k = -12$$ — Divide both sides by −3.
$$k = 4$$

Math Talk
Mathematical Practices

How can you rewrite $7 - (2a + 3) = 12$ without parentheses? Explain your answer.

$7 - 2a - 3 = 12$; the minus sign represents multiplying by −1, so $7 - (2a + 3) =$ $7 - 1(2a + 3) =$ $7 + (-1)2a + (-1)3 =$ $7 - 2a - 3$.

Lesson 15.3 **473**

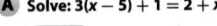
Personal Math Trainer
Online Assessment and Intervention
my.hrw.com

YOUR TURN

Solve each equation.

1. $y - 5 = 3 - 9(y + 2)$ $\quad y = -1$

2. $2(x - 7) - 10 = 12 - 4x$ $\quad x = 6$

Math On the Spot
my.hrw.com

Using the Distributive Property on Both Sides
Some equations require the use of the Distributive Property on both sides.

EXAMPLE 2
FL CC 8.EE.3.7b

Solve: $\frac{3}{4}(x - 13) = -2(9 + x)$

STEP 1 Eliminate the fraction.

$$\frac{3}{4}(x - 13) = -2(9 + x)$$
$$4 \times \frac{3}{4}(x - 13) = 4 \times [-2(9 + x)]$$ — Multiply both sides by 4.
$$3(x - 13) = -8(9 + x)$$

Math Talk
Mathematical Practices

How can you eliminate fractions if there is a fraction being distributed on both sides of an equation?

Multiply both sides of the equation by the LCD of the fractions before applying the Distributive Property.

STEP 2 Use the Distributive Property.

$3x - 39 = -72 - 8x$ — Distribute 3 and −8 to the terms within the parentheses.

STEP 3 Use inverse operations to solve the equation.

$$3x - 39 = -72 - 8x$$
$$\underline{+8x \qquad\qquad +8x}$$ — Add 8x to both sides.
$$11x - 39 = -72$$
$$\underline{+39 \qquad +39}$$ — Add 39 to both sides.
$$11x = -33$$
$$\frac{11x}{11} = \frac{-33}{11}$$ — Divide both sides by 11.
$$x = -3$$

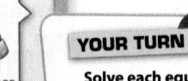
Personal Math Trainer
Online Assessment and Intervention
my.hrw.com

YOUR TURN

Solve each equation.

3. $-4(-5 - b) = \frac{1}{3}(b + 16)$ $\quad b = -4$

4. $\frac{3}{5}(t + 18) = -3(2 - t)$ $\quad t = 7$

474 Unit 7

PROFESSIONAL DEVELOPMENT

Integrate Mathematical Practices MP.1.1

This lesson provides an opportunity to address this Mathematical Practice standard. It calls for students to make sense of problems and persevere in solving them.

Example 3 uses a four-step problem-solving process to determine the amount of a restaurant bill before a discount was applied. Students analyze the information, formulate a plan, solve the problem, and justify and evaluate the solution.

Math Background
The Distributive Property only holds true for multiplication and division over addition or subtraction:

1. Multiplication over addition: $a(b + c) = ab + ac$; Example: $3(b + 5) = 3b + 15$

2. Multiplication over subtraction: $a(b - c) = ab - ac$; Example: $3(b - 5) = 3b - 15$

3. Division over addition: $\frac{(b + c)}{a} = \frac{b}{a} + \frac{c}{a}$

   Example: $\frac{(b + 6)}{2} = \frac{b}{2} + 3$

4. Division over subtraction: $\frac{(b - c)}{a} = \frac{b}{a} - \frac{c}{a}$; $a \neq 0$

   Example: $\frac{(b - 6)}{2} = \frac{b}{2} - 3$

Equations with the Distributive Property **474**

EXAMPLE 3

Questioning Strategies 🏴 Mathematical Practices

• Would multiplying the entire equation by 10 before using the Distributive Property be another way to solve this equation? Justify your answer. Yes, but the decimal 7.5 would not be eliminated as it is within the parentheses. The result would be $2(x - 7.5) = 89$. However, using the Distributive Property as your next step would eliminate the decimal, as $2(7.5) = 15$.

• What can you do to mentally determine whether $52 is a reasonable answer? You could round $8.90 to $9 and then work backward. $52 - $9 = $43; 20% of $43 is $8.60; since $8.60 is close to $8.90, $52 is a reasonable answer.

Focus on Communication

Have students identify the key words in the problem that they would use to write the equation given in Step 1. Discuss why it is important to specify exactly what the variable represents.

YOUR TURN

Engage with the Whiteboard

For Exercise 5, have volunteers underline the information needed to write an equation describing the situation. Have other volunteers write and solve the equation.

Elaborate

Talk About It
Summarize the Lesson

Ask: How can the Distributive Property help you solve equations? When an equation contains an expression in parentheses multiplied by a factor, the Distributive Property allows you to distribute the factor and get rid of the parentheses. This allows the equation to be solved.

GUIDED PRACTICE

Engage with the Whiteboard

For Exercises 1 and 2, have volunteers explain the process of arriving at the correct value as they complete the write-in boxes for each exercise. Have other volunteers show how to check the answers using substitution.

Avoid Common Errors

Exercises 3, 6–10 Students may apply the negative sign to only the first term when distributing. Remind students that negative factors must be distributed to both terms within the parentheses.

Exercises 7–10 Remind students to eliminate the fractions before using inverse operations.

Solving a Real-World Problem Using the Distributive Property

Solving a real-world problem may involve using the Distributive Property.

Math On the Spot
my.hrw.com

EXAMPLE 3 Problem Solving

FL CC 8.EE.3.7b

The Coleman family had their bill at a restaurant reduced by $7.50 because of a special discount. They left a tip of $8.90, which was 20% of the reduced amount. How much was their bill before the discount?

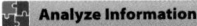
Analyze Information

The answer is the amount before the discount.

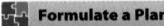
Formulate a Plan

Use an equation to find the amount before the discount.

Solve

STEP 1 Write the equation $0.2(x - 7.5) = 8.9$, where x is the amount of the Coleman family's bill before the discount.

STEP 2 Use the Distributive Property: $0.2x - 1.5 = 8.9$

STEP 3 Use inverse operations to solve the equation.

$$0.2x - 1.5 = 8.9$$
$$\underline{+1.5 \quad +1.5} \qquad \text{Add 1.5 to both sides.}$$
$$0.2x = 10.4$$
$$\frac{0.2x}{0.2} = \frac{10.4}{0.2} \qquad \text{Divide both sides by 0.2.}$$
$$x = 52$$

The Coleman family's bill before the discount was $52.00.

Math Talk
Mathematical Practices

Why do you use 0.2 in Step 1?

0.2 is 20% written as a decimal.

Justify and Evaluate

$52.00 - $7.50 = $44.50 and $0.2($44.50) = 8.90. This is the amount of the tip the Colemans left. The answer is reasonable.

YOUR TURN

5. The Smiths spend 8% of their budget on entertainment. Their total budget this year is $2,000 more than last year, and this year they plan to spend $3,840 on entertainment. What was their total budget last year? $46,000

Personal Math Trainer
Online Assessment and Intervention
my.hrw.com

Lesson 15.3 **475**

Solve each equation.

1. $4(x + 8) - 4 = 34 - 2x$ (Ex. 1)

$$\boxed{4}\,x + \boxed{32} - 4 = 34 - 2x$$
$$\boxed{4}\,x + \boxed{28} = 34 - 2x$$
$$\boxed{6}\,x + \boxed{28} = 34$$
$$\boxed{6}\,x = \boxed{6}$$
$$\frac{\boxed{6}\,x}{\boxed{6}} = \frac{\boxed{6}}{\boxed{6}}$$
$$x = \boxed{1}$$

2. $\frac{2}{3}(9 + x) = -5(4 - x)$ (Ex. 2)

$$\boxed{3} \times \frac{2}{3}(9 + x) = \boxed{3} \times [-5(4 - x)]$$
$$\boxed{2}\,(9 + x) = \boxed{-15}\,(4 - x)$$
$$\boxed{18} + \boxed{2}\,x = \boxed{-60} \; \boxed{+} \; \boxed{15}\,x$$
$$\boxed{-13}\,x = \boxed{-78}$$
$$\frac{\boxed{-13}\,x}{\boxed{-13}} = \frac{\boxed{-78}}{\boxed{-13}}$$
$$x = \boxed{6}$$

3. $-3(x + 4) + 15 = 6 - 4x$ (Ex. 1)
$$x = 3$$

4. $10 + 4x = 5(x - 6) + 33$ (Ex. 1)
$$x = 7$$

5. $x - 9 = 8(2x + 3) - 18$ (Ex. 1)
$$x = -1$$

6. $-6(x - 1) - 7 = -7x + 2$ (Ex. 1)
$$x = 3$$

7. $\frac{1}{10}(x + 11) = -2(8 - x)$ (Ex. 2)
$$x = 9$$

8. $-(4 - x) = \frac{3}{4}(x - 6)$ (Ex. 2)
$$x = -2$$

9. $-8(8 - x) = \frac{4}{5}(x + 10)$ (Ex. 2)
$$x = 10$$

10. $\frac{1}{2}(16 - x) = -12(x + 7)$ (Ex. 2)
$$x = -8$$

11. Sandra saves 12% of her salary for retirement. This year her salary was $3,000 more than in the previous year, and she saved $4,200. What was her salary in the previous year? (Example 3)

Write an equation. $0.12(x + 3,000) = 4,200$

Sandra's salary in the previous year was $32,000 .

ESSENTIAL QUESTION CHECK-IN

12. When solving an equation using the Distributive Property, if the numbers being distributed are fractions, what is your first step? Why?

You eliminate the fractions by using their LCD. The resulting computations will be less complicated without fractions.

DIFFERENTIATE INSTRUCTION

Number Sense
Assign each student a fraction and a simple expression in parentheses, such as $(x - 1)$, $(x - 2)$, or $(2x + 1)$. Pairs of students should work together to determine the LCD of their fractions. Then have each pair use their fractions and expressions to make a single equation. Finally, they should work together to eliminate the fractions and solve for x.

Visual Cues
Have students draw arrows on their equations to show that the number being distributed goes to each term in the parentheses.

$$3(x + 10) + 6 = 12$$
$$3(x) + 3(10) + 6 = 12$$

Additional Resources
Differentiated Instruction includes:
- Reading Strategies
- Success for English Learners **ELL**
- Reteach
- Challenge **PRE-AP**

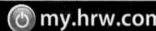
15.3 LESSON QUIZ

 **8.EE.3.7b**

Solve each equation.

1. $5(x + 6) + 11 = 25 - 3x$

2. $-\frac{3}{8}(-6 - 2y) = \frac{1}{2}(2y - 3) - 1$

Solve

3. Kyle saves 8% of his income for a new car. This year his salary was $2,000 less than in the previous year, and he saved $3,000. What was his salary in the previous year?

4. Leslie is currently 8 years older than her neighbor Bill. In 4 years she will be 2 times as old as Bill. Let x equal Bill's current age.

   a. What expression represents Leslie's current age?

   b. What expression represents Bill's age in 4 years? What expression represents Leslie's age in 4 years?

   c. What equation can you write based on the given information?

   d. What is Bill's current age? What is Leslie's current age?

Lesson Quiz available online

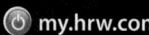 my.hrw.com

Answers

1. $x = -2$

2. $y = 19$

3. $39,500

4. a. $x + 8$

   b. $x + 4$; $x + 12$ or $2(x + 4)$

   c. $x + 12 = 2(x + 4)$

   d. Bill: 4 years old; Leslie: 12 years old

Evaluate

GUIDED AND INDEPENDENT PRACTICE

 8.EE.3.7b

Concepts & Skills	Practice
Example 1 Using the Distributive Property	Exercises 1, 3–6
Example 1 Using the Distributive Property on Both Sides	Exercises 2, 7–10, 15–16
Example 1 Solving a Real-World Problem Using the Distributive Property	Exercises 11, 13–14, 17

Exercise	Depth of Knowledge (D.O.K.)		FL CC Mathematical Practices	
13–14	2	Skills/Concepts	**MP.4.1**	Modeling
15	3	Strategic Thinking **H.O.T.**	**MP.3.1**	Logic
16	2	Skills/Concepts	**MP.2.1**	Reasoning
17	2	Skills/Concepts	**MP.4.1**	Modeling
18	3	Strategic Thinking **H.O.T.**	**MP.3.1**	Logic
19	3	Strategic Thinking **H.O.T.**	**MP.8.1**	Patterns

Additional Resources

Differentiated Instruction includes:

• Leveled Practice worksheets

15.3 Independent Practice

FL CC 8.EE.3.7b

Personal Math Trainer

Online Assessment and Intervention

my.hrw.com

13. Multistep Martina is currently 14 years older than her cousin Joey. In 5 years she will be 3 times as old as Joey. Use this information to answer the following questions.

a. If you let x represent Joey's current age, what expression can you use to represent Martina's current age?

$x + 14$

b. Based on your answer to part a, what expression represents Joey's age in 5 years? What expression represents Martina's age in 5 years?

Joey's age in 5 years: $x + 5$; Martina's age in 5 years: $x + 19$

c. What equation can you write based on the information given?

$3(x + 5) = x + 19$

d. What is Joey's current age? What is Martina's current age?

Joey: 2 years old; Martina: 16 years old

14. As part of a school contest, Sarah and Luis are playing a math game. Sarah must pick a number between 1 and 50 and give Luis clues so he can write an equation to find her number. Sarah says, "If I subtract 5 from my number, multiply that quantity by 4, and then add 7 to the result, I get 35." What equation can Luis write based on Sarah's clues and what is Sarah's number?

$4(x - 5) + 7 = 35$; 12

15. Critical Thinking When solving an equation using the Distributive Property that involves distributing fractions, usually the first step is to multiply by the LCD to eliminate the fractions in order to simplify computation. Is it necessary to do this to solve $\frac{1}{2}(4x + 6) = \frac{1}{3}(9x - 24)$? Why or why not?

It is not necessary. In this case, distributing the fractions directly results in whole number coefficients and constants.

16. Solve the equation given in Exercise 15 with and without using the LCD of the fractions. Are your answers the same?

Yes; using either method gives $x = 11$.

© Houghton Mifflin Harcourt Publishing Company

17. Represent Real-World Problems A chemist mixed x milliliters of 25% acid solution with some 15% acid solution to produce 100 milliliters of a 19% acid solution. Use this information to fill in the missing information in the table and answer the questions that follow.

	ml of Solution	Percent Acid as a Decimal	ml of Acid
25% Solution	x	0.25	$0.25x$
15% Solution	$100 - x$	0.15	$0.15(100 - x)$
Mixture (19% Solution)	100	0.19	19

a. What is the relationship between the milliliters of acid in the 25% solution, the milliliters of acid in the 15% solution, and the milliliters of acid in the mixture? The milliliters of acid in the 25% solution plus the milliliters of acid in the 15% solution equals the milliliters of acid in the mixture.

b. What equation can you use to solve for x based on your answer to part a? $0.25x + 0.15(100 - x) = 19$

c. How many milliliters of the 25% solution and the 15% solution did the chemist use in the mixture? The chemist used 40 ml of the 25% solution and 60 ml of the 15% solution.

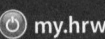 **H.O.T.** FOCUS ON HIGHER ORDER THINKING

18. Explain the Error Anne solved $5(2x) - 3 = 20x + 15$ for x by first distributing 5 on the left side of the equation. She got the answer $x = -3$. However, when she substituted -3 into the original equation for x, she saw that her answer was wrong. What did Anne do wrong, and what is the correct answer? Anne did not need to use the Distributive Property. The parentheses are only around $2x$ and are used to represent $5 \cdot 2x$, not $5(2x - 3)$. The correct answer is $x = -1.8$.

19. Communicate Mathematical Ideas Explain a procedure that can be used to solve $5[3(x + 4) - 2(1 - x)] - x - 15 = 14x + 45$. Then solve the equation. Use the Distributive Property to distribute both 3 and 2 inside the square parentheses on the left side. Combine like terms inside the square parentheses. Then use the Distributive Property again to distribute 5. Combine like terms on the left side and use inverse operations to solve the equation. $x = 1$

Work Area

© Houghton Mifflin Harcourt Publishing Company • Image Credits: ©D. Hurst/Alamy Images

EXTEND THE MATH PRE-AP

Activity available online my.hrw.com

Activity When solving an equation with one variable, it is possible to have one solution, no solutions, or infinitely many solutions. Determine how many solutions each of the following equations has. Justify your answers.

$-x + 3(x - 2) = 2(x - 2) - 3$ no solution; the equation simplifies to $-6 \neq -7$, so no value for x will make the equation true.

$3x - 4 = 2(x - 1)$ one solution; the equation simplifies to $x = 2$.

$3x + 2(4x - 6) = 7x + 4(x - 3)$ infinitely many solutions; the equation simplifies to $-12 = -12$, so any value for x will make the equation true.

15.4 Equations with Many Solutions or No Solution

 Florida Common Core Standards

The student is expected to:

 **FL CC** **Expressions and Equations—8.EE.3.7a**

Give examples of linear equations in one variable with one solution, infinitely many solutions, or no solutions. Show which of these possibilities is the case by successively transforming the given equation into simpler forms, until an equivalent equation of the form $x = a$, $a = a$, or $a = b$ results (where a and b are different numbers).

Mathematical Practices

 **FL CC** **MP.8.1** Patterns

---

ADDITIONAL EXAMPLE 1
Use the properties of equality to simplify each equation. Tell whether the final equation is a true statement.

A $3x - 6 = 4 + 2x$ $x = 10$; true

B $3x - 8 = 3(x - 4) + 1$ $-8 = -11$; false

C $3x - 7 = 3(x - 3) + 2$ $-7 = -7$; true

 Interactive Whiteboard
Interactive example available online

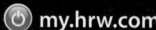 **my.hrw.com**

Engage

ESSENTIAL QUESTION

How can you give examples of equations with a given number of solutions? Sample answer: Equations that simplify to the form $x = a$ have one solution, equations that simplify to $a = a$ have many solutions, and equations that simplify to the form $a = b$, where $a \neq b$, have no solution.

Motivate the Lesson

Ask: What is the greatest number of solutions an equation can have? Take a guess. Begin the lesson to find out.

Explore

Present students with the equation $x = x$. Examine a few possible values of x. Change the equation to $x + 1 = x + 1$. Examine the final equation in the solution process.

Explain

EXAMPLE 1

Questioning Strategies 🏴 Mathematical Practices

• In Part A, is the equation true if any value besides 8 is substituted for x? Explain. No; substituting 8 for x makes the equation true, but any other value makes the equation false.

• In Part B, does the simplified equation mean that -5 is the only solution of the equation? No; substituting any value for x, including -5, will make the equation true.

• In Part C, does the simplified equation mean that 0 or -7 are solutions of the equation? Explain. No; substituting either 0 or -7 or any other value for x will make the equation false.

Focus on Reasoning 🏴 Mathematical Practices

Discuss how the final equation in Part B would change if 5 had been added to each side before subtracting $4x$ from each side.

YOUR TURN

Focus on Critical Thinking

Point out to students that they can sometimes see that an equation is false without finding the final equation. An example of this could be Exercise 4. But for now, suggest that they still complete the steps for simplifying each equation.

Avoid Common Errors

Students may find the final, simplified equation and then stop. Remind them that the directions ask for them to evaluate whether that final equation is true or false.

Equations with Many Solutions or No Solution

 **FL CC** 8.EE.3.7a

Give examples of linear equations … with one solution, infinitely many solutions, or no solutions. Show which of these … is the case by … transforming the given equation into … $x = a$, $a = a$, or $a = b$ ….

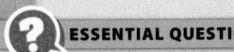 **ESSENTIAL QUESTION**

How can you give examples of equations with a given number of solutions?

Determining the Number of Solutions

So far, when you solved a linear equation in one variable, you found one value of x that makes the equation a true statement. When you simplify some equations, you may find that they do not have one solution.

EXAMPLE 1

FL CC 8.EE.3.7a

Use the properties of equality to simplify each equation. Tell whether the final equation is a true statement.

A $4x - 3 = 2x + 13$

$4x - 3 = 2x + 13$

$+3 = +3$ Add 3 to both sides.

$4x = 2x + 16$

$-2x -2x$ Subtract 2x from both sides.

$2x = 16$

$\dfrac{2x}{2} = \dfrac{16}{2}$ Divide both sides by 2.

$x = 8$

The statement is true. There is one solution.

B $4x - 5 = 2(2x - 1) - 3$

$4x - 5 = 2(2x - 1) - 3$

$4x - 5 = 4x - 2 - 3$ Distributive Property

$4x - 5 = 4x - 5$ Simplify.

$-4x -4x$ Subtract 4x from both sides.

$-5 = -5$

The statement is true. There are many solutions.

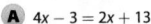

Math On the Spot

my.hrw.com

My Notes

If you make a mistake when you simplify the equation, the check will not be accurate. Using the original equation produces an accurate check.

C $4x + 2 = 4x - 5$

$4x + 2 = 4x - 5$

$-2 -2$ Subtract 2 from both sides.

$4x = 4x - 7$

$-4x -4x$ Subtract 4x from both sides.

$0 = -7$

The statement is false. There is no solution.

Reflect

1. What happens when you substitute any value for x in the original equation in part B? In the original equation in part C?

In part B, any value of x will result in a true statement.

In part C, any value of x will result in a false statement.

Math Talk
Mathematical Practices

Why do you substitute values for x into the *original* equation?

Personal Math Trainer
Online Assessment and Intervention
my.hrw.com

YOUR TURN

Use the properties of equality to simplify each equation. Tell whether the final equation is a true statement.

2. $2x + 1 = 5x - 8$ 3. $3(4x + 3) - 2 = 12x + 7$ 4. $3x - 9 = 5 + 3x$

    True   True   False

Writing Equations with a Given Number of Solutions

When you simplify an equation using the properties of equality, you will find one of three results.

Result	What does this mean?	How many solutions?
$x = a$	When the value of x is a, the equation is a true statement.	1
$a = a$	Any value of x makes the equation a true statement.	Infinitely many
$a = b$	There is no value of x that makes the equation a true statement.	0

You can use these results to write a linear equation that has a given number of solutions.

Math On the Spot

my.hrw.com

PROFESSIONAL DEVELOPMENT

Integrate Mathematical Practices MP.8.1

This lesson provides an opportunity to address this Mathematical Practice standard. It calls for students to look for and express regularity in repeated reasoning. Students should see patterns in the processes of simplifying and building equations. They should notice that linear equations in one variable that have no solutions always result in a false statement after the x term has been eliminated. Using this pattern, students use the work backward strategy to reinstate an x value on both sides of a false statement involving two numbers. The result is a linear equation that has no solutions.

Math Background

Linear equations assume many forms. In this lesson, students work with linear equations in one variable. The standard form of a linear equation in one variable is $ax + b = c$, although not every linear equation is presented in standard form. Every linear equation in one variable can, however, be simplified to one of the three forms: $x = a$, $a = a$, or $a = b$, where $a \neq b$. The values for a and b in these three forms are not necessarily the same values for a and b used in the standard form $ax + b = c$.

ADDITIONAL EXAMPLE 2
Write a linear equation in one variable that has many solutions.

Sample answer: $4x + 17 = 4(x + 3) + 5$

 Interactive Whiteboard
Interactive example available online

⏻ my.hrw.com

EXAMPLE 2

Questioning Strategies Mathematical Practices

• Does multiplying both sides of a false statement by the same number change the fact that the statement is false? Usually the statement remains false when both sides are multiplied by the same number. The only exception is when both sides are multiplied by 0, which creates $0 = 0$, a true statement.

• If you subtracted 10 from both sides in Step 3 would you still get a false statement? Justify your answer. Yes, the result would be $x = 2 + x$, which then simplifies to $0 = 2$, a false statement.

Focus on Patterns Mathematical Practices

Have students examine the table on page 216. Point out that they can use the equations in the Result column of the table as a starting point for writing the three types of equations.

YOUR TURN

Engage with the Whiteboard

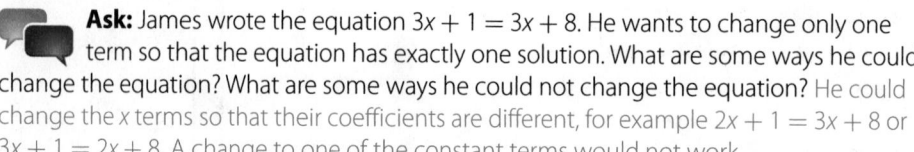 For Exercise 8, have 3 or more volunteers complete the equation with a different value and show why the value they chose creates an equation with no solution.

Elaborate

. . . .

Talk About It
Summarize the Lesson

 Ask: James wrote the equation $3x + 1 = 3x + 8$. He wants to change only one term so that the equation has exactly one solution. What are some ways he could change the equation? What are some ways he could not change the equation? He could change the x terms so that their coefficients are different, for example $2x + 1 = 3x + 8$ or $3x + 1 = 2x + 8$. A change to one of the constant terms would not work.

GUIDED PRACTICE

Engage with the Whiteboard

For Exercises 1, 2, and 5, have volunteers explain the process of arriving at the correct values or words as they complete each of the write-in boxes.

Avoid Common Errors

Exercise 2 In the fourth line, students could subtract 1 from each side, resulting in $2x - 5 = 2x$. In this case, an extra line would be needed to arrive at the correct solution. Point out that although this solution method is correct, subtracting $2x$ allows you to arrive at the correct solution more quickly.

Exercise 5 Students may attempt to fill in the blanks on the left side, then proceed to the right side. Point out that they will need to refer to both sides to be able to fill in the blanks correctly.

EXAMPLE 2 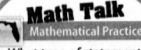 FL CC 8.EE.3.7a

Write a linear equation in one variable that has no solution.

You can use the strategy of working backward:

STEP 1 Start with a false statement such as $3 = 5$. Add the same variable term to both sides.

$3 + x = 5 + x$ *Add x to both sides.*

STEP 2 Next, add the same constant to both sides and combine like terms on each side of the equation.

$10 + x = 12 + x$ *Add 7 to both sides.*

STEP 3 Verify that your equation has no solutions by using properties of equality to simplify your equation.

$$10 + x = 12 + x$$
$$\underline{ - x = - x}$$
$$10 = 12$$

Math Talk
Mathematical Practices

What type of statement do you start with to write an equation with infinitely many solutions? Give an example.

You start with a true statement because when you solve an equation that has infinitely many solutions, you arrive at a true statement; $8 = 8$

Reflect

5. Explain why the result of the process above is an equation with no solution.

You started with a false statement and performed balanced operations on both sides of the equation. This does not change the true or false nature of the original statement.

YOUR TURN   For Ex. 8, any number except 1

Tell whether each equation has one, zero, or infinitely many solutions.

6. $6 + 3x = x - 8$ One solution

7. $8x + 4 = 4(2x + 1)$ Infinitely many solutions

Complete each equation so that it has the indicated number of solutions.

8. No solution: $3x + 1 = 3x +$ _____ Sample answer: 6

9. Infinitely many: $2x - 4 = 2x -$ _____ 4

Personal Math Trainer
Online Assessment and Intervention
my.hrw.com

Guided Practice

Use the properties of equality to simplify each equation. Tell whether the final equation is a true statement. (Example 1)

1. $3x - 2 = 25 - 6x$

$$\underline{+6x +6x}$$
$$\boxed{9x} - 2 = \boxed{25}$$
$$\boxed{+2} = \boxed{+2}$$
$$\boxed{9}x = \boxed{27}$$
$$\frac{\boxed{9}x}{\boxed{9}} = \frac{\boxed{27}}{\boxed{9}}$$
$$x = \boxed{3}$$

The statement is $\boxed{\text{true}}$.

2. $2x - 4 = 2(x - 1) + 3$

$$2x - 4 = \boxed{2x - 2} + 3$$
$$2x - 4 = 2x + \boxed{1}$$
$$\underline{-\boxed{2x} = -\boxed{2x}}$$
$$\boxed{-4} = \boxed{1}$$

The statement is $\boxed{\text{false}}$.

3. How many solutions are there to the equation in Exercise 2? _____ none

4. After simplifying an equation, Juana gets $6 = 6$. Explain what this means.

Any value of x will result in a true statement; infinitely many solutions.

Write a linear equation in one variable that has infinitely many solutions. (Example 2)

5. Start with a _____ true _____ statement. $10 = \boxed{10}$

Add the _____ same variable _____ to both sides. $10 + x = \boxed{10 + x}$

Add the _____ same constant _____ to both sides. $10 + x + 5 = \boxed{10 + x + 5}$

Combine _____ like _____ terms. $\boxed{15 + x} = \boxed{15 + x}$

? ESSENTIAL QUESTION CHECK-IN

6. Give an example of an equation with an infinite number of solutions. Then make one change to the equation so that it has no solution.

Sample answer: infinitely many solutions: $2x + 1 = 2x + 1$; no solution: $2x + 1 = 2x$

DIFFERENTIATE INSTRUCTION

World History

The Rhind Mathematical Papyrus is evidence that complex mathematics was used in ancient Egypt. This document is also known as the Ahmes Papyrus, named for the scribe Ahmes who wrote the papyrus. It contains over 80 different problems, 15 of which are algebra problems that ask the reader to find x and a fraction of x such that their sum equals an integer. Ask students to solve this example and state how many solutions there are:

$$x + \left(\frac{2}{3} + \frac{1}{2} + \frac{1}{7}\right)x = 37$$

Answer: There is one solution to this problem, $x = \frac{1554}{97} = 16\frac{2}{97}$.

Cooperative Learning

Group the students into pairs. Have each student create three equations—one with no solution, one with one solution, and one with many solutions. Have the pairs trade equations, simplify, and identify which equation is which.

Additional Resources

Differentiated Instruction includes:

- Reading Strategies
- Success for English Learners   **ELL**
- Reteach
- Challenge   **PRE-AP**

Personal Math Trainer

Online Assessment and Intervention

Online homework assignment available

ⓞ my.hrw.com

15.4 LESSON QUIZ

 FL CC 8.EE.3.7a

Use the properties of equality to simplify each equation. Tell whether the final equation is a true statement.

1. $5x + 6 = 2 + 3x$

2. $2(6 - 2y) = -1(4y - 9)$

3. $2z - 6 = 2(z + 2) - 10$

Complete each equation so that it has the indicated number of solutions.

4. no solutions: $5x + 1 = 5x +$ ____

5. one solution: $3x - 3 =$ __$x + 11$

6. infinitely many: $8x - 7 = 8x -$ ____

Lesson Quiz available online

ⓞ my.hrw.com

Answers

1. $x = -2$; the statement is true.

2. $12 = 9$; the statement is false.

3. $-6 = -6$; the statement is true.

4. Sample answer: 8

5. Sample answer: 2

6. 7

Evaluate

GUIDED AND INDEPENDENT PRACTICE

 **FL CC** 8.EE.3.7a

Concepts & Skills	Practice
Example 1 Determining the Number of Solutions	Exercises 1–2, 7–8
Example 2 Writing Equations with a Given Number of Solutions	Exercises 3–5, 9–12

Exercise	Depth of Knowledge (D.O.K.)		**FL CC** Mathematical Practices
7–12	**1** Recall of Information		**MP.2.1** Reasoning
13	**3** Strategic Thinking	H.O.T.	**MP.4.1** Modeling
14	**3** Strategic Thinking	H.O.T.	**MP.3.1** Logic
15	**3** Strategic Thinking	H.O.T.	**MP.4.1** Modeling
16–17	**3** Strategic Thinking	H.O.T.	**MP.3.1** Logic

Additional Resources

Differentiated Instruction includes:

• Leveled Practice worksheets

CLUSTER CONNECTION

Exercise 13 combines concepts from the Florida Common Core cluster "Analyze and solve linear equations and pairs of simultaneous linear equations."

Name_____ Class_____ Date_____

15.4 Independent Practice

 FL CC 8.EE.3.7a

Personal Math Trainer

Online Assessment and Intervention
my.hrw.com

Tell whether each equation has one, zero, or infinitely many solutions.

7. $-(2x + 2) - 1 = -x - (x + 3)$

0 = 0; infinitely many solutions

8. $-2(z + 3) - z = -z - 4 (z + 2)$

$z = -1$; one solution

Create an equation with the indicated number of solutions.

9. No solution:

$3\left(x - \dfrac{4}{3}\right) = 3x + \boxed{5}$

Any number except -4.
A sample is given.

10. Infinitely many solutions:

$2(x - 1) + 6x = 4\left(\boxed{2x} - 1\right) + 2$

11. One solution of $x = -1$:

$5x - (x - 2) = 2x - \boxed{(x + 1)}$

12. Infinitely many solutions:

$-(x - 8) + 4x = 2\left(\boxed{x + 4}\right) + x$

13. Persevere in Problem Solving The Dig It Project is designing two gardens that have the same perimeter. One garden is a trapezoid whose nonparallel sides are equal. The other is a quadrilateral. Two possible designs are shown at the right.

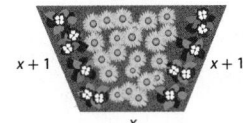
2x − 2
x + 1
x + 1
x

a. Based on these designs, is there more than one value for *x*? Explain how you know this.

Yes; because the perimeters are equal you get the equation $(2x - 2) + (x + 1) + x + (x + 1) = (2x - 9) + (x + 1) + (x + 8) + x$, or $5x = 5x$. Since $5x = 5x$ is a true statement there are an infinite number of values for *x*.

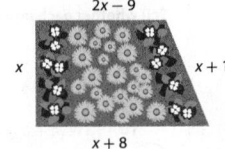
2x − 9
x
x + 1
x + 8

b. Why does your answer to part a make sense in this context?

The condition was that the two perimeters are to be equal. However, a specific number was not given, so there are an infinite number of possible perimeters.

c. Suppose the Dig It Project wants the perimeter of each garden to be 60 meters. What is the value of *x* in this case? How did you find this?

12; Sample answer: I used the trapezoid and wrote the equation $(2x - 2) + (x + 1) + x + (x + 1) = 60$. Solving this gives $x = 12$.

14. Critique Reasoning Lisa says that the indicated angles cannot have the same measure. Marita disagrees and says she can prove that they can have the same measure. Who do you agree with? Justify your answer.

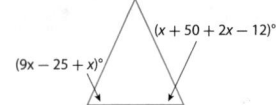
$(x + 50 + 2x - 12)°$
$(9x - 25 + x)°$

Marita; If the angles have the same measure, $9x - 25 + x = x + 50 + 2x - 12$. Solving this equation gives a single solution, $x = 9$. Since $9(9) - 25 + 9 = 81 - 25 + 9 = 65$ and $9 + 50 + 2(9) - 12 = 59 + 18 - 12 = 65$, each angle measures 65°.

15. Represent Real-World Problems Adele opens an account with $100 and deposits $35 a month. Kent opens an account with $50 and also deposits $35 a month. Will they have the same amount in their accounts at any point? If so, in how many months and how much will be in each account? Explain.

No; setting the expressions equal to each other and solving gives $100 + 35x = 50 + 35x$, or $100 = 50$, which is false.

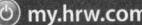
H.O.T. FOCUS ON HIGHER ORDER THINKING

Work Area

16. Communicate Mathematical Ideas Frank solved an equation and got the result $x = x$. Sarah solved the same equation and got $12 = 12$. Frank says that one of them is incorrect because you cannot get different results for the same equation. What would you say to Frank? If both results are indeed correct, explain how this happened.

The results may appear different, but their meaning is the same. Both are true statements, so the equation has infinitely many solutions. Frank solved the equation by eliminating 12, while Sarah eliminated *x*.

17. Critique Reasoning Matt said $2x - 7 = 2(x - 7)$ has infinitely many solutions. Is he correct? Justify Matt's answer or show how he is incorrect.

Matt is incorrect. He applied the Distributive Property to the right side incorrectly. Correctly simplified, the equation is $0 = -7$, which is false, meaning no solution.

EXTEND THE MATH PRE-AP

Activity available online 🔘 my.hrw.com

Activity The larger of two numbers is twice the smaller. Their sum is three times their difference. Find the numbers.

Let y = the smaller number. Let $2y$ = the larger number.
$y + 2y = 3(2y - y)$
$3y = 6y - 3y$
$3y = 3y$
$y = y$
There are infinitely many solutions.

Ready to Go On?

Assess Mastery

Use the assessment on this page to determine if students have mastered the concepts and standards covered in this module.

 **Response to Intervention**

Personal Math Trainer

Online Assessment and Intervention

my.hrw.com

Intervention	Enrichment
Access Ready to Go On? assessment online, and receive instant scoring, feedback, and customized intervention or enrichment.	

Online and Print Resources

Differentiated Instruction
- Reteach worksheets
- Reading Strategies **ELL**
- Success for English Learners **ELL**

Differentiated Instruction
- Challenge worksheets
  PRE-AP
- Extend the Math **PRE-AP**
  Lesson Activities in TE

Additional Resources

Assessment Resources includes:
- Leveled Module Quizzes

© Houghton Mifflin Harcourt Publishing Company

MODULE QUIZ

Ready to Go On?

Personal Math Trainer

Online Assessment and Intervention

my.hrw.com

15.1 Equations with the Variable on Both Sides

Solve.

1. $4a - 4 = 8 + a$ _____ $a = 4$ 2. $4x + 5 = x + 8$ _____ $x = 1$

3. Hue is arranging chairs. She can form 6 rows of a given length with 3 chairs left over, or 8 rows of that same length if she gets 11 more chairs. Write and solve an equation to find how many chairs are in that row length.

   _____ $6c + 3 = 8c - 11$; $c = 7$; 7 chairs _____

15.2 Equations with Rational Numbers

Solve.

4. $\frac{2}{3}n - \frac{2}{3} = \frac{n}{6} + \frac{4}{3}$ _____ $n = 4$ 5. $1.5d + 3.25 = 1 + 2.25d$ _____ $d = 3$

15.3 Equations with the Distributive Property

Solve.

6. $14 + 5x = 3(-x + 3) - 11$ _____ $x = -2$

7. $-5(2x - 9) = 2(x - 8) - 11$ _____ $x = 6$

15.4 Equations with Many Solutions or No Solution

Tell whether each equation has one, zero, or infinitely many solutions.

8. $5(x - 3) + 6 = 5x - 9$ _____ infinitely many solutions

9. $5(x - 3) + 6 = 5x - 10$ _____ zero solutions

10. $5(x - 3) + 6 = 4x + 3$ _____ one solution

 ESSENTIAL QUESTION

11. How can you use equations with the variable on both sides to solve real-world problems?

    Sample answer: You can compare the costs of services that

    charge hourly or weekly rates.

 ## Florida Common Core Standards

Lesson	Exercises	Common Core Standards
15.1	1–3	**8.EE.3.7**
15.2	4–6	**8.EE.3.7b**
15.3	7–10	**8.EE.3.7b**
15.4	11–13	**8.EE.3.7a**

PARCC Assessment Readiness

Assessment Readiness Tip Students can choose between testing the answer choices or writing and solving an equation or inequality.

Item 3 Students can find the two expressions to represent this problem, $27.5x$ and $17 + 23.25x$, set them equal to each other, and then solve. However, they may find it easier and quicker to test the answer choices.

Item 6 Students may initially assume that testing individual answer choices is the only way to find the solution, because the given equation has two unknowns. However, if they simplify the equation, they will find that the x terms cancel out, leaving the correct value of k as the answer.

Avoid Common Errors

Item 5 Remind students that since the tip was applied to the cost of both meals, parentheses must be used to ensure the addition is performed before the multiplication.

Item 8 Students may only sum x and $x + 5$ when finding the perimeter of the rectangle. Remind them that they must sum the lengths of all four sides, so x and $x + 5$ must both be used twice.

Additional Resources

Personal Math Trainer
Online Assessment and Intervention
my.hrw.com

Selected Response

1. Two cars are traveling in the same direction. The first car is going 40 mi/h, and the second car is going 55 mi/h. The first car left 3 hours before the second car. Which equation could you solve to find how many hours it will take for the second car to catch up to the first car?

- Ⓐ $55t + 3 = 40t$
- Ⓑ $55t + 165 = 40t$
- Ⓒ $40t + 3 = 55t$
- Ⓓ $40t + 120 = 55t$

2. Which linear equation is represented by the table?

x	-2	1	3	6
y	7	4	2	-1

- Ⓐ $y = -x + 5$
- Ⓒ $y = x + 3$
- Ⓑ $y = 2x - 1$
- Ⓓ $y = -3x + 11$

3. Shawn's Rentals charges $27.50 per hour to rent a surfboard and a wetsuit. Darla's Surf Shop charges $23.25 per hour to rent a surfboard plus $17 extra for a wetsuit. For what total number of hours are the charges for Shawn's Rentals the same as the charges for Darla's Surf Shop?

- Ⓐ 3
- Ⓒ 5
- Ⓑ 4
- Ⓓ 6

4. Which of the following is irrational?

- Ⓐ -8
- Ⓒ $\sqrt{11}$
- Ⓑ 4.63
- Ⓓ $\frac{1}{3}$

5. Greg and Jane left a 15% tip after dinner. The amount of the tip was $9. Greg's dinner cost $24. Which equation can you use to find x, the cost of Jane's dinner?

- Ⓐ $0.15x + 24 = 9$
- Ⓑ $0.15(x + 24) = 9$
- Ⓒ $15(x + 24) = 9$
- Ⓓ $0.15x = 24 + 9$

6. For the equation $3(2x - 5) = 6x + k$, which value of k will create an equation with infinitely many solutions?

- Ⓐ 15
- Ⓒ 5
- Ⓑ -5
- Ⓓ -15

7. Which of the following is equivalent to 2^{-4}?

- Ⓐ $\frac{1}{16}$
- Ⓒ -2
- Ⓑ $\frac{1}{8}$
- Ⓓ -16

Mini-Task

8. Use the figures below for parts a and b.

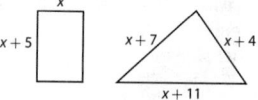

a. Both figures have the same perimeter. Solve for x.

$$x = 12$$

b. What is the perimeter of each figure?

58 units

Florida Common Core Standards

Items	Grade 8 Standards	Mathematical Practices
1	8.EE.3.7	MP.4.1
2*	8.F.2.4	MP.4.1
3	8.EE.3.7b	MP.4.1
4*	8.NS.1.1	MP.6.1
5	8.EE.3.7b	MP.4.1
6	8.EE.3.7a	MP.2.1
7*	8.EE.1.1	
8	8.EE.3.7	MP.4.1

* Item integrates mixed review concepts from previous modules or a previous course.

Solving Systems of Linear Equations

ESSENTIAL QUESTION

How can you use systems of equations to solve real-world problems?

You can use systems of linear equations to find ordered pairs where two quantities are the same, such as costs for services from two different businesses.

Real-World Video

The distance contestants in a race travel over time can be modeled by a system of equations. Solving such a system can tell you when one contestant will overtake another who has a head start, as in a boating race or marathon.

my.hrw.com

© Houghton Mifflin Harcourt Publishing Company • Image Credits: ©Kenny Ferguson/Alamy Images

GO DIGITAL

my.hrw.com

my.hrw.com

Go digital with your write-in student edition, accessible on any device.

Math On the Spot

Scan with your smart phone to jump directly to the online edition, video tutor, and more.

Animated Math

Interactively explore key concepts to see how math works.

Personal Math Trainer

Get immediate feedback and help as you work through practice sets.

Are You Ready?

Assess Readiness

Use the assessment on this page to determine if students need intensive or strategic intervention for the module's prerequisite skills.

 **Response to Intervention**

Personal Math Trainer
Online Assessment and Intervention
my.hrw.com

Intervention	Enrichment

Access Are You Ready? assessment online, and receive instant scoring, feedback, and customized intervention or enrichment.

Online and Print Resources

Skills Intervention worksheets
- Skill 55 Simplify Algebraic Expressions
- Skill 64 Graph Linear Equations

Differentiated Instruction
- Challenge worksheets **PRE-AP**
- Extend the Math **PRE-AP** Lesson Activities in TE

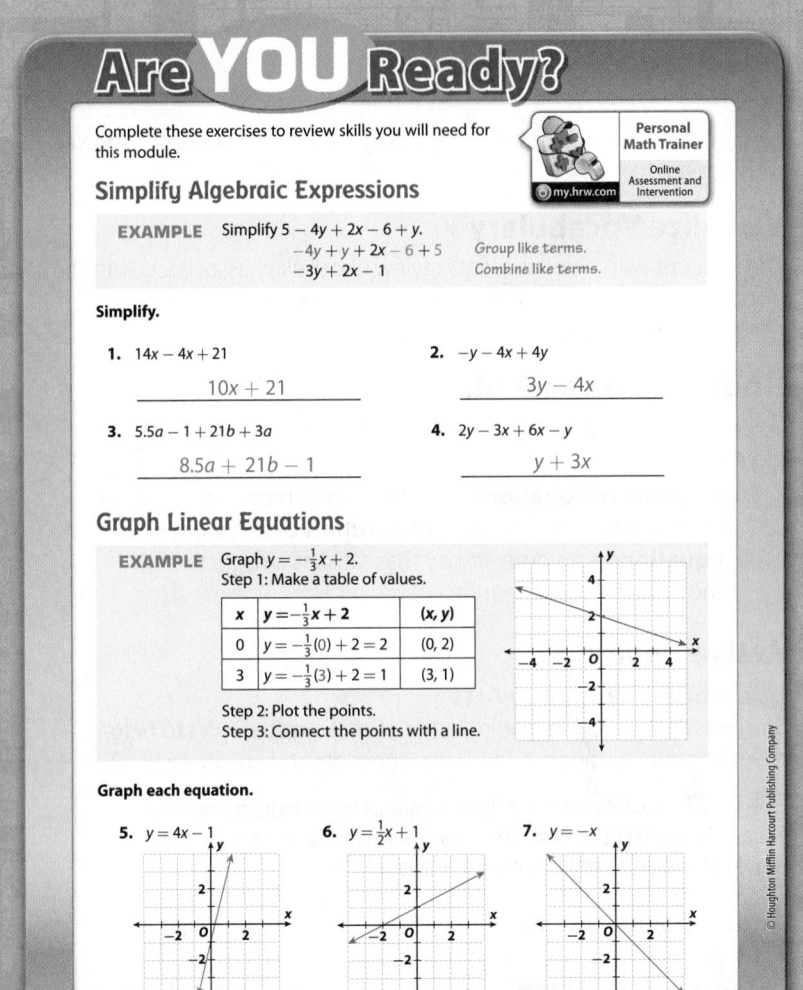

Are YOU Ready?

Complete these exercises to review skills you will need for this module.

Personal Math Trainer
Online Assessment and Intervention
my.hrw.com

Simplify Algebraic Expressions

EXAMPLE

Simplify $5 - 4y + 2x - 6 + y$.
$-4y + y + 2x - 6 + 5$ Group like terms.
$-3y + 2x - 1$ Combine like terms.

Simplify.

1. $14x - 4x + 21$
$$10x + 21$$

2. $-y - 4x + 4y$
$$3y - 4x$$

3. $5.5a - 1 + 21b + 3a$
$$8.5a + 21b - 1$$

4. $2y - 3x + 6x - y$
$$y + 3x$$

Graph Linear Equations

EXAMPLE

Graph $y = -\frac{1}{3}x + 2$.
Step 1: Make a table of values.

x	$y = -\frac{1}{3}x + 2$	(x, y)
0	$y = -\frac{1}{3}(0) + 2 = 2$	$(0, 2)$
3	$y = -\frac{1}{3}(3) + 2 = 1$	$(3, 1)$

Step 2: Plot the points.
Step 3: Connect the points with a line.

Graph each equation.

5. $y = 4x - 1$

6. $y = \frac{1}{2}x + 1$

7. $y = -x$

© Houghton Mifflin Harcourt Publishing Company

PROFESSIONAL DEVELOPMENT VIDEO

Author Juli Dixon models successful teaching practices as she explores the concept of systems of equations in an actual eighth-grade classroom.

Professional Development
my.hrw.com

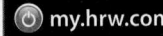
DIGITAL
my.hrw.com

Online Teacher Edition
Access a full suite of teaching resources online—plan, present, and manage classes and assignments.

ePlanner
Easily plan your classes and access all your resources online.

Interactive Answers and Solutions
Customize answer keys to print or display in the classroom. Choose to include answers only or full solutions to all lesson exercises.

Interactive Whiteboards
Engage students with interactive whiteboard-ready lessons and activities.

Personal Math Trainer: Online Assessment and Intervention
Assign automatically graded homework, quizzes, tests, and intervention activities. Prepare your students with updated practice tests aligned with Common Core.

Reading Start-Up

Have students complete the activities on this page by working alone or with others.

Visualize Vocabulary

The concept web helps students review vocabulary associated with the slope-intercept form of a linear equation. Students should write one review word in each oval.

Understand Vocabulary

Use the following explanations to help students learn the preview words.

> A **system of equations** is a set of two or more equations that have the same variables. A **solution of a system of equations** is an ordered pair that satisfies all equations in the system simultaneously.

Active Reading

Integrating Language Arts

Students can use these reading and note-taking strategies to help them organize and understand new concepts and vocabulary.

FL CC LACC.68.RST.3.7 Integrate quantitative or technical information expressed in words in a text with a version of that information expressed visually (e.g., in a flowchart, diagram, model, graph, or table).

Additional Resources

Differentiated Instruction

- Reading Strategies **ELL**

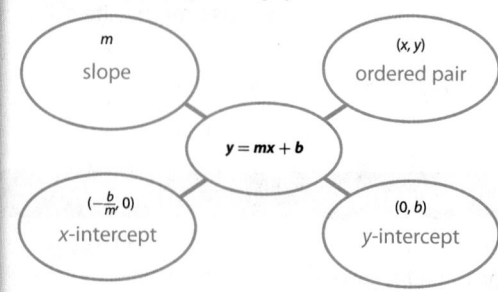

Reading Start-Up

Visualize Vocabulary

Use the ✔ words to complete the graphic.

- m — slope
- (x, y) — ordered pair
- $y = mx + b$
- $(-\frac{b}{m}, 0)$ — x-intercept
- $(0, b)$ — y-intercept

Vocabulary

Review Words
- linear equation *(ecuación lineal)*
- ✔ ordered pair *(par ordenado)*
- ✔ slope *(pendiente)*
- slope-intercept form *(forma pendiente intersección)*
- x-axis *(eje x)*
- ✔ x-intercept *(intersección con el eje x)*
- y-axis *(eje y)*
- ✔ y-intercept *(intersección con el eje y)*

Preview Words
- solution of a system of equations *(solución de un sistema de ecuaciones)*
- system of equations *(sistema de ecuaciones)*

Understand Vocabulary

Complete the sentences using the preview words.

1. A ___solution of a system of equations___ is any ordered pair that satisfies all the equations in a system.

2. A set of two or more equations that contain two or more variables is called a ___system of equations___.

Active Reading

Four-Corner Fold Before beginning the module, create a four-corner fold to help you organize what you learn about solving systems of equations. Use the categories "Solving by Graphing," "Solving by Substitution," "Solving by Elimination," and "Solving by Multiplication." As you study this module, note similarities and differences among the four methods. You can use your four-corner fold later to study for tests and complete assignments.

© Houghton Mifflin Harcourt Publishing Company

Module 16 **489**

Before	In this module	After
Students understand: • how to solve linear equations • how to graph linear equations	Students will learn how to: • solve systems of two linear equations in two variables using graphing, elimination, and substitution • analyze special systems that have no solution or an infinite number of solutions • represent real-world situations using systems of equations	Students will connect: • graphical and algebraic representations of systems of equations and their solutions

Unpacking the Standards

Use the exercises on this page to determine if students need intensive or strategic intervention for the module's prerequisite skills.

 Florida Common Core Standards

Content Areas

 **FL CC Expressions and Equations—8.EE.8**

Analyze and solve linear equations and pairs of simultaneous linear equations.

Go online to see a complete unpacking of the Florida Common Core Standards.

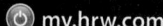 my.hrw.com

---

Unpacking the Standards

Understanding the standards and the vocabulary terms in the standards will help you know exactly what you are expected to learn in this module.

FL CC 8.EE.3.8a

Understand that solutions to a system of two linear equations in two variables correspond to points of intersection of their graphs, because points of intersection satisfy both equations simultaneously.

FL CC 8.EE.3.8b

Solve systems of two linear equations in two variables algebraically, and estimate solutions by graphing the equations. Solve simple cases by inspection.

Key Vocabulary

solution of a system of equations *(solución de un sistema de ecuaciones)* A set of values that make all equations in a system true.

system of equations *(sistema de ecuaciones)* A set of two or more equations that contain two or more variables.

What It Means to You

You will understand that the points of intersection of two or more graphs represent the solution to a system of linear equations.

UNPACKING EXAMPLE 8.EE.3.8a, 8.EE.3.8b

Use the elimination method.

A.
$$-x = -1 + y$$
$$x + y = 4$$
$$\overline{\quad y = y + 3}$$

This is never true, so the system has no solution.

The lines never intersect.

B.
$$2y + x = 1$$
$$y - 2 = x$$

Use the substitution method.

$$2y + (y - 2) = 1$$
$$3y - 2 = 1$$
$$y = 1$$

There is only one solution.

The lines intersect at a single point.

C.
$$3y - 6x = 3$$
$$y - 2x = 1$$

Use the multiplication method.

$$3y - 6x = 3$$
$$\underline{3y - 6x = 3}$$
$$0 = 0$$

This is always true. So the system has infinitely many solutions.

The graphs overlap completely. They represent the same line.

 Visit my.hrw.com to see all Florida Common Core Standards unpacked. my.hrw.com

---

Florida Common Core Standards	Lesson 16.1	Lesson 16.2	Lesson 16.3	Lesson 16.4	Lesson 16.5
FL CC 8.EE.3.8 Analyze and solve pairs of simultaneous linear equations.	■				
FL CC 8.EE.3.8a Understand that solutions to a system of two linear equations in two variables correspond to points of intersection of their graphs, because points of intersection satisfy both equations simultaneously.	■				
FL CC 8.EE.3.8b Solve systems of two linear equations in two variables algebraically, and estimate solutions by graphing the equations. Solve simple cases by inspection. For example, $3x + 2y = 5$ and $3x + 2y = 6$ have no solution because $3x + 2y$ cannot simultaneously be 5 and 6.		■	■	■	■
FL CC 8.EE.3.8c Solve real-world and mathematical problems leading to two linear equations in two variables. For example, given coordinates for two pairs of points, determine whether the line through the first pair of points intersects the line through the second pair.	■	■	■	■	■

Solving Systems of Linear Equations **490**

LESSON 16.1 Solving Systems of Linear Equations by Graphing

 Florida Common Core Standards

The student is expected to:

 **Expressions and Equations—8.EE.3.8a**

Understand that solutions to a system of two linear equations in two variables correspond to points of intersection of their graphs, because points of intersection satisfy both equations simultaneously.
Also 8.EE.3.8, 8.EE.3.8c

Mathematical Practices

 **MP.3.1** Logic

ADDITIONAL EXAMPLE 1
Solve each system by graphing.

A $\begin{cases} y = -2x - 4 \\ y = 3x + 1 \end{cases}$ $(-1, -2)$

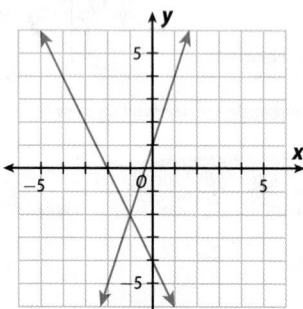

B $\begin{cases} y = 3x - 3 \\ y = 3x + 1 \end{cases}$ no solution

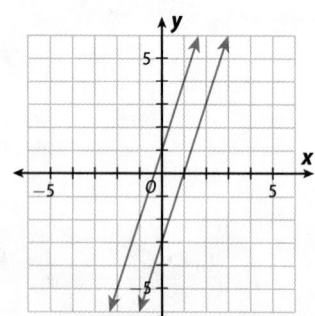

Interactive Whiteboard
Interactive example available online

⏻ my.hrw.com

Engage

ESSENTIAL QUESTION

How can you solve a system of equations by graphing? Sample answer: Find the ordered pair at the point where the graphs of the equations intersect.

Motivate the Lesson
Ask: Do you think you could catch up with your friend before he gets home if you leave school 10 minutes later but travel twice as fast? Begin the Explore Activity to see how you can solve an algebraic version of a problem like this.

Explore

EXPLORE ACTIVITY

Focus on Reasoning
Elicit from students that the solution is the ordered pair represented by the point where the two lines intersect.

Explain

EXAMPLE 1

Connect Vocabulary **ELL**

A *system* is a set of things working together. If any one of the things is not working, then the system does not work. Similarly, an ordered pair is the solution of a system of equations only if it is the solution for each equation.

Questioning Strategies 🌴 **Mathematical Practices**

• Why is the point of intersection a solution? It is the only ordered pair whose *x*- and *y*-values satisfy both equations.

• What is the solution if the two lines are parallel lines? There is no solution because they never intersect.

Integrating Language Arts **ELL**

Encourage English learners to take notes on new terms or concepts and to write them in familiar language.

Solving Systems of Linear Equations by Graphing

FL CC 8.EE.3.8a

Understand that solutions to a system of two linear equations in two variables correspond to points of intersection of their graphs, because points of intersection satisfy both equations simultaneously. *Also* 8.EE.3.8, 8.EE.3.8c

? **ESSENTIAL QUESTION**

How can you solve a system of equations by graphing?

EXPLORE ACTIVITY 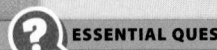 FL CC 8.EE.3.8a

Investigating Systems of Equations

You have learned several ways to graph a linear equation in slope-intercept form. For example, you can use the slope and y-intercept or you can find two points that satisfy the equation and connect them with a line.

> Slope-intercept form is $y = mx + b$, where m is the slope and b is the y-intercept.

A Graph the pair of equations together: $\begin{cases} y = 3x - 2 \\ y = -2x + 3 \end{cases}$.

B Explain how to tell whether $(2, -1)$ is a solution of the equation $y = 3x - 2$ without using the graph.

Substituting $(2, -1)$ into the equation results in a false statement, so it is not a solution.

C Explain how to tell whether $(2, -1)$ is a solution of the equation $y = -2x + 3$ without using the graph.

Substituting $(2, -1)$ into the equation results in a true statement, so it is a solution.

D Explain how to use the graph to tell whether the ordered pair $(2, -1)$ is a solution of either equation.

If $(2, -1)$ is on the line, it is a solution.

E Find the point of intersection of the two lines. Check by substitution to determine if it is a solution to both equations.

Point of intersection ($\boxed{1}$, $\boxed{1}$)

$y = 3x - 2$ $y = -2x + 3$

$\boxed{1} = 3 \boxed{1} - 2$ $\boxed{1} = -2 \boxed{1} + 3$

$1 = \boxed{1}$ $1 = \boxed{1}$

The point of intersection (**is** / is not) the solution of both equations.

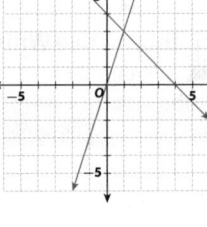

Math On the Spot
my.hrw.com

My Notes

Solving Systems Graphically

An ordered pair (x, y) is a solution of an equation in two variables if substituting the x- and y-values into the equation results in a true statement. A **system of equations** is a set of equations that have the same variables. An ordered pair is a **solution** of a system of equations if it is a solution of every equation in the system.

Since the graph of an equation represents all ordered pairs that are solutions of the equation, if a point lies on the graphs of two equations, the point is a solution of both equations and is, therefore, a **solution of the system**.

EXAMPLE 1 FL CC 8.EE.3.8

Solve each system by graphing.

A $\begin{cases} y = -x + 4 \\ y = 3x \end{cases}$

STEP 1 Start by graphing each equation.

STEP 2 Find the point of intersection of the two lines. It appears to be $(1, 3)$. Check by substitution to determine if it is a solution to both equations.

$y = -x + 4 \quad y = 3x$

$3 \overset{?}{=} -(1) + 4 \quad 3 \overset{?}{=} 3(1)$

$3 = 3 \checkmark \qquad 3 = 3 \checkmark$

The solution of the system is $(1, 3)$.

B $\begin{cases} y = 3x - 3 \\ y = 3(x - 1) \end{cases}$

STEP 1 Start by graphing each equation.

STEP 2 Identify any ordered pairs that are solutions of both equations.

The graphs of the equations are the same line. So, every ordered pair that is a solution of one equation is also a solution of the other equation. The system has infinitely many solutions.

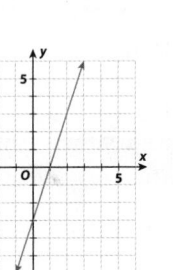

PROFESSIONAL DEVELOPMENT

🏴 Integrate Mathematical Practices MP.3.1

This lesson provides an opportunity to address this Mathematical Practices standard. It calls for students to make conjectures and explore the truth of their conjectures. Students will find the solution of a system of equations working with equations and their graphs. Students will make conjectures about the number of solutions based on algebraic and graphical representations and confirm the truth of their conjectures.

Math Background

Solving a system of equations by graphing has a limitation that algebraic methods do not. Only an algebraic method such as substitution or elimination (which students will learn later) can determine the exact solution to a system. Graphical solutions are considered approximate. This is evident if the solution is not a lattice point where grid lines meet.

YOUR TURN

Focus on Modeling Mathematical Practices

Review methods of graphing lines. Students can either use a table of values or plot the *y*-intercept and use the slope to plot additional points on the line. Explain that if either line is not drawn accurately, the solution point will not be correct.

EXAMPLE 2

Questioning Strategies Mathematical Practices

- Which line represents the amount of money spent? How do you know? The steeper line is the money spent because when $0 is spent on hot dogs, $11 is spent on drinks.

- What would you do if either *x* or *y* appeared to be a number that is not an integer? Recheck my work because you cannot buy part of a soda or part of a hot dog.

Avoid Common Errors

Make sure that students understand that, in order to graph an equation, they must rewrite the equation in slope-intercept form.

Reflect

1. A system of linear equations has infinitely many solutions. Does that mean any ordered pair in the coordinate plane is a solution?

   No, only ordered pairs that lie on the graph are solutions.

2. Can you show algebraically that both equations in part B represent the same line? If so, explain how.

   Yes; by simplifying the second equation, $y = 3(x - 1) = 3x - 3$, you can see that both equations are identical.

YOUR TURN

Solve each system by graphing. Check by substitution.

3. $\begin{cases} y = -x + 2 \\ y = -4x - 1 \end{cases}$ $(-1, 3)$

Check:

$y = -x + 2$	$y = -4x - 1$
$3 = -(-1) + 2$	$3 = -4(-1) - 1$
$3 = 3 ✓$	$3 = 3 ✓$

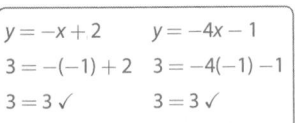

4. $\begin{cases} y = -2x + 5 \\ y = 3x \end{cases}$ $(1, 3)$

Check:

$y = -2x + 5$	$y = 3x$
$3 = -2(1) + 5$	$3 = 3(1)$
$3 = 3 ✓$	$3 = 3 ✓$

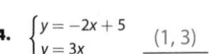

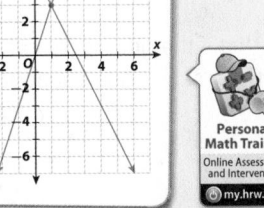
Personal
Math Trainer
Online Assessment
and Intervention
my.hrw.com

Math On the Spot
my.hrw.com

Solving Problems Using Systems of Equations

When using graphs to solve a system of equations, it is best to rewrite both equations in slope-intercept form for ease of graphing.

To write an equation in slope-intercept form starting from $ax + by = c$:

$$ax + by = c$$

$by = c - ax$	Subtract ax from both sides.
$y = \frac{c}{b} - \frac{ax}{b}$	Divide both sides by b.
$y = -\frac{a}{b}x + \frac{c}{b}$	Rearrange the equation.

EXAMPLE 2   Real World   FL CC 8.EE.3.8c, 8.EE.3.8

Keisha and her friends visit the concession stand at a football game. The stand charges $2 for a hot dog and $1 for a drink. The friends buy a total of 8 items for $11. Tell how many hot dogs and how many drinks they bought.

STEP 1   Let x represent the number of hot dogs they bought and let y represent the number of drinks they bought.

Write an equation representing the **number of items they purchased.**

Number of hot dogs	+	Number of drinks	=	Total items
x	+	y	=	8

Write an equation representing the **money spent on the items.**

Cost of 1 hot dog times number of hot dogs	+	Cost of 1 drink times number of drinks	=	Total cost
$2x$	+	$1y$	=	11

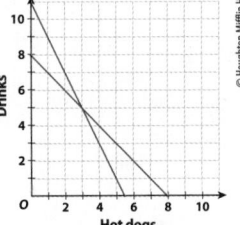
HOT DOG: $2.00
DRINK: $1.00

STEP 2   Write the equations in slope-intercept form. Then graph.

$x + y = 8$

$y = 8 - x$

$y = -x + 8$

$2x + 1y = 11$

$1y = 11 - 2x$

$y = -2x + 11$

Graph the equations $y = -x + 8$ and $y = -2x + 11$.

DIFFERENTIATE INSTRUCTION

Home Connection

Have the whole class plan a party that must stay within a budget. Pairs of students will create a system of linear equations that represents how a certain amount of money will be spent on two items. For example, one pair works with pizza and soda, another with plates and cups.

Kinesthetic Experience

Have students model a problem that involves two objects moving at different speeds. Have two students stand at the same location and have one student walk forward at a slow, steady pace. A few seconds later, have another student walk along the same path at a faster speed until the second student catches up with the first student.

Ask whether the second person could catch up if they walked the same speed or slower. The point at which they catch up is the point at which they intersect.

Additional Resources

Differentiated Instruction includes:

- Reading Strategies
- Success for English Learners **ELL**
- Reteach
- Challenge **PRE-AP**

YOUR TURN

Engage with the Whiteboard

 After graphing both lines, discuss what each line means. Point out that the graph of $2x + 4y = 20$ shows how many of each game can be played for $20 with no restriction on the number of games. Draw graphs of $x + y = 5$ and $x + y = 7$ to see how the solution of the system changes with a different total number of games played.

Elaborate

Talk About It
Summarize the Lesson

Ask: Given a coordinate plane that contains the graph of two linear equations, how can you identify the solution to the system of equations? The solution is the ordered pair at the point of intersection. There is no solution if the lines are parallel. There are infinitely many solutions if the lines are the same line.

GUIDED PRACTICE

Engage with the Whiteboard

For Exercise 2, replace the second equation with $y = \frac{1}{3}x + 2$ and have a student graph this equation. Have students describe the solution to the new system.

Avoid Common Errors

Exercises 1–3 Remind students to check their answers algebraically after finding the solution on the graph.

Exercise 2 Remind students that if the graphs of both lines are the same, the entire line is the intersection and any point that solves one equation also solves the other.

STEP 3 Use the graph to identify the solution of the system of equations. Check your answer by substituting the ordered pair into both equations.

Apparent solution: (3, 5)
Check:

$x + y = 8$	$2x + y = 11$
$3 + 5 \stackrel{?}{=} 8$	$2(3) + 5 \stackrel{?}{=} 11$
$8 = 8 \checkmark$	$11 = 11 \checkmark$

The point (3, 5) is a solution of both equations.

STEP 4 Interpret the solution in the original context.

Keisha and her friends bought 3 hot dogs and 5 drinks.

Reflect

5. **Conjecture** Why do you think the graph is limited to the first quadrant?

It would not make sense to buy a negative number of items or to spend a negative amount of money.

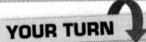
Animated Math
my.hrw.com

YOUR TURN

6. During school vacation, Marquis wants to go bowling and to play laser tag. He wants to play 6 total games but needs to figure out how many of each he can play if he spends exactly $20. Each game of bowling is $2 and each game of laser tag is $4.

   a. Let x represent the number of games Marquis bowls and let y represent the number of games of laser tag Marquis plays. Write a system of equations that describes the situation. Then write the equations in slope-intercept form.

   $x + y = 6$ and $2x + 4y = 20$; $y = -x + 6$ and $y = -0.5x + 5$

   b. Graph the solutions of both equations.

   c. How many games of bowling and how many games of laser tag will Marquis play?

   Marquis will bowl 2 games and play 4 games of laser tag.

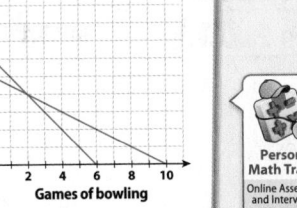

Games of laser tag / Games of bowling

Personal Math Trainer
Online Assessment and Intervention
my.hrw.com

Solve each system by graphing. (Example 1)

1. $\begin{cases} y = 3x - 4 \\ y = x + 2 \end{cases}$ _____(3, 5)_____

2. $\begin{cases} x - 3y = 2 \\ -3x + 9y = -6 \end{cases}$ infinitely many solutions

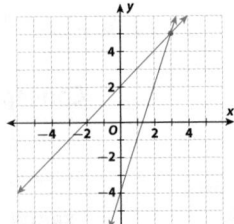
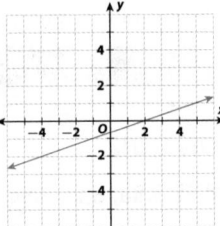

3. Mrs. Morales wrote a test with 15 questions covering spelling and vocabulary. Spelling questions (x) are worth 5 points and vocabulary questions (y) are worth 10 points. The maximum number of points possible on the test is 100. (Example 2)

   a. Write an equation in slope-intercept form to represent the number of questions on the test.

   $y = -x + 15$

   b. Write an equation in slope-intercept form to represent the total number of points on the test.

   $y = -0.5x + 10$

   c. Graph the solutions of both equations.

   d. Use your graph to tell how many of each question type are on the test.

   10 spelling questions and 5 vocabulary questions

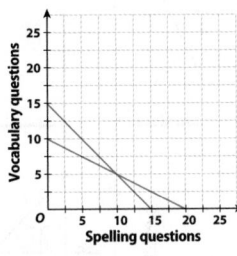

ESSENTIAL QUESTION CHECK-IN

4. When you graph a system of linear equations, why does the intersection of the two lines represent the solution of the system?

   Every point on a line makes a linear equation true. A point that is on both lines (the intersection point) makes both equations true.

Personal Math Trainer

Online Assessment and Intervention

Online homework assignment available

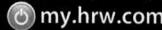

🕐 my.hrw.com

16.1 LESSON QUIZ

FL CC 8.EE.3.8a, 8.EE.3.8c

1. What is the solution to the system of equations shown?

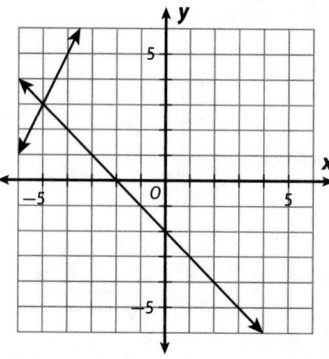

Diego works at a warehouse that ships two types of packages, a red package weighing 4 pounds and a blue package weighing 6 pounds. Diego shipped a total of 40 packages weighing 180 pounds.

2. Graph the system of linear equations.

3. How many red and blue packages were in the shipment?

Lesson Quiz available online

🕐 my.hrw.com

Answers

1. $(-5, 3)$

2.

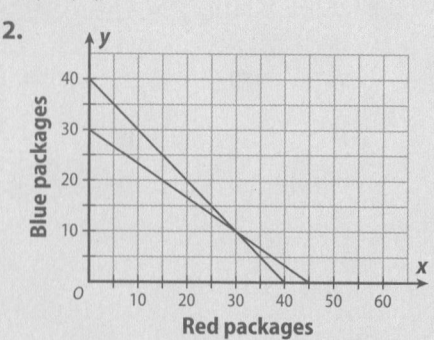

3. 30 red packages and 10 blue packages

Evaluate

GUIDED AND INDEPENDENT PRACTICE

 8.EE.3.8, 8.EE.3.8a, 8.EE.3.8c

Concepts & Skills	Practice
Explore Activity Investigating Systems of Equations	Exercises 1–2
Example 1 Solving Systems Graphically	Exercises 1–3, 6–7
Example 2 Solving Problems Using Systems of Equations	Exercises 3, 6–8

Exercise	Depth of Knowledge (D.O.K.)	**FL CC** Mathematical Practices
5	**1** Recall	**MP.6.1** Precision
6–7	**2** Skills/Concepts	**MP.2.1** Reasoning
8–9	**2** Skills/Concepts	**MP.4.1** Modeling
10	**3** Strategic Thinking **H.O.T.**	**MP.4.1** Modeling
11	**3** Strategic Thinking **H.O.T.**	**MP.3.1** Logic

Additional Resources

Differentiated Instruction includes:

• Leveled Practice worksheets

CLUSTER CONNECTION

Exercise 7 combines concepts from the Florida Common Core cluster "Analyze and solve linear equations and pairs of simultaneous linear equations."

16.1 Independent Practice

FL CC 8.EE.3.8, 8.EE.3.8a, 8.EE.3.8c

Personal Math Trainer

Online Assessment and Intervention

my.hrw.com

5. Vocabulary A _system of equations_ is a set of equations that have the same variables.

6. Eight friends started a business. They will wear either a baseball cap or a shirt imprinted with their logo while working. They want to spend exactly on the shirts and caps. Shirts cost \$6 each and caps cost \$3 each.

a. Write a system of equations to describe the situation. Let x represent the number of shirts and let y represent the number of caps.

$x + y = 8$

$6x + 3y = 36$

b. Graph the system. What is the solution and what does it represent?

Business Logo Wear

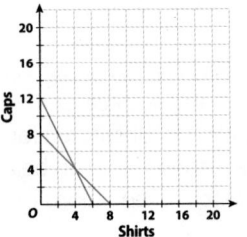

The solution is (4, 4). It represents that 4 people will get shirts and 4 people will get caps.

7. Multistep The table shows the cost for bowling at two bowling alleys.

	Shoe Rental Fee	Cost per Game
Bowl-o-Rama	\$2.00	\$2.50
Bowling Pinz	\$4.00	\$2.00

a. Write a system of equations, with one equation describing the cost to bowl at Bowl-o-Rama and the other describing the cost to bowl at Bowling Pinz. For each equation, let x represent the number of games played and let y represent the total cost.

$y = 2.50x + 2$

$y = 2x + 4$

b. Graph the system. What is the solution and what does it represent?

Cost of Bowling

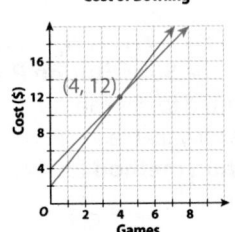

The solution is (4, 12). The cost at both alleys will be the same for 4 games bowled that cost will be \$12.

8. Multi-Step Jeremy runs 7 miles per week and increases his distance by 1 mile each week. Tony runs 3 miles per week and increases his distance by 2 miles each week. In how many weeks will Jeremy and Tony be running the same distance? What will that distance be?

4 weeks; 11 miles

9. Critical Thinking Write a real-world situation that could be represented by the system of equations shown below.

$$\begin{cases} y = 4x + 10 \\ y = 3x + 15 \end{cases}$$

Sample answer: Store A rents carpet cleaners for a fee of \$10, plus \$4 per day. Store B rents carpet cleaners for a fee of \$15, plus \$3 per day.

H.O.T. FOCUS ON HIGHER ORDER THINKING

10. Multistep The table shows two options provided by a high-speed Internet provider.

	Setup Fee (\$)	Cost per Month (\$)
Option 1	50	30
Option 2	No setup fee	\$40

a. In how many months will the total cost of both options be the same? What will that cost be?

5 months; \$200

b. If you plan to cancel your Internet service after 9 months, which is the cheaper option? Explain.

Option 1 is cheaper

Option 1: cost = 30(9) + 50 = \$320

Option 2: cost = 40(9) = \$360

11. Draw Conclusions How many solutions does the system formed by $x - y = 3$ and $ay - ax + 3a = 0$ have for a nonzero number a? Explain.

Infinitely many; sample answer: Rearranging the left side of the 2nd equation and subtracting $3a$ from both sides gives $-ax + ay = -3a$. Dividing both sides by $-a$ gives $x - y = 3$. So, the equations describe the same line.

Work Area

EXTEND THE MATH PRE-AP

Activity available online my.hrw.com

Have students add a third equation with the same variables to a system of two equations in two variables. What is the solution to a system of three equations in two variables? The ordered pair that solves all 3 equations.

How can you add a third line to a graph of a system of two equations with one solution that guarantees that the system of three equations still has one solution?

Any line that includes the intersection point of the first two equations will guarantee that the new system of equations has the same solution.

© Houghton Mifflin Harcourt Publishing Company

LESSON
16.2 Solving Systems by Substitution

 Florida Common Core Standards

The student is expected to:

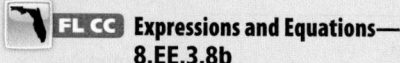 **Expressions and Equations— 8.EE.3.8b**

Solve systems of two linear equations in two variables algebraically, and estimate solutions by graphing the equations. Solve simple cases by inspection.

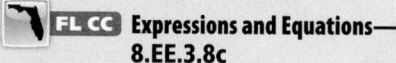 **Expressions and Equations— 8.EE.3.8c**

Solve real-world and mathematical problems leading to two linear equations in two variables.

Mathematical Practices

 **MP.6.1** Precision

ADDITIONAL EXAMPLE 1
Solve the system of linear equations by substitution. Check your answer.

$$\begin{cases} 2x + y = 5 \\ -3x + 2y = 17 \end{cases}$$

$(-1, 7)$

 Interactive Whiteboard
Interactive example available online

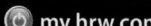 my.hrw.com

Engage

ESSENTIAL QUESTION

How do you use substitution to solve a system of linear equations? Sample answer: Solve for one variable in one of the equations. Substitute the resulting expression for the same variable in the other equation. Substitute the solution into either original equation to find the value of the other variable.

Motivate the Lesson

Ask: How can you turn two equations with two variables into one equation with one variable? Begin the Lesson to find out.

Explore

Lead students in a discussion of the **Substitution Property.** For example, because $5 = 3 + 2$, $3 + 2$ can be substituted for 5 in any expression and 5 can be substituted for $3 + 2$. Note that this also works for variable expressions: if $y = x + 5$, then $x + 5$ can be substituted for y. The **substitution method** for solving a linear system of equations makes use of the Substitution Property.

Explain

EXAMPLE 1

Questioning Strategies 🖋 Mathematical Practices

- Why not solve for x in Step 1? You can solve for x in Step 1, but then you will have fractions in Step 2 of the solution.

- Is (1, 4) the only solution to this system? The graph in Step 4 shows that the graphs of the equations intersect at only one point, so there is only one solution.

Focus on Critical Thinking 🖋 Mathematical Practices

Make sure students understand that in Step 1 either equation could be used and either variable could be solved for. However, it is usually easier to solve for a variable that has a coefficient of 1.

YOUR TURN

Avoid Common Errors

Some students may have difficulty deciding which equation to use in Step 1 of the solution process. Discuss what should be considered when choosing an equation to solve for a variable. For example, in Exercise 4, the most straightforward method would be to solve either equation for y, thereby avoiding fractions in the solution process.

FL CC 8.EE.3.8b
Solve systems of two linear equations in two variables algebraically, and estimate solutions by graphing the equations. ... Also 8.EE.3.8c

? ESSENTIAL QUESTION How do you use substitution to solve a system of linear equations?

Solving a Linear System by Substitution

The **substitution method** is used to solve systems of linear equations by solving an equation for one variable and then substituting the resulting expression for that variable into the other equation. The steps for this method are as follows:

1. Solve one of the equations for one of its variables.

2. Substitute the expression from step 1 into the other equation and solve for the other variable.

3. Substitute the value from step 2 into either original equation and solve to find the value of the variable in step 1.

Math On the Spot
my.hrw.com

EXAMPLE 1
FL CC 8.EE.3.8b

Solve the system of linear equations by substitution. Check your answer.

$$\begin{cases} -3x + y = 1 \\ 4x + y = 8 \end{cases}$$

STEP 1 Solve an equation for one variable.

$-3x + y = 1$ *Select one of the equations.*

$y = 3x + 1$ *Solve for the variable y. Isolate y on one side.*

STEP 2 Substitute the expression for y in the other equation and solve.

$4x + (3x + 1) = 8$ *Substitute the expression for the variable y.*

$7x + 1 = 8$ *Combine like terms.*

$7x = 7$ *Subtract 1 from each side.*

$x = 1$ *Divide each side by 7.*

STEP 3 Substitute the value of x you found into one of the equations and solve for the other variable, y.

$-3(1) + y = 1$ *Substitute the value of x into the first equation.*

$-3 + y = 1$ *Simplify.*

$y = 4$ *Add 3 to each side.*

So, (1, 4) is the solution of the system.

My Notes

Lesson 16.2 **499**

My Notes

STEP 4 Check the solution by graphing.

$-3x + y = 1$ $4x + y = 8$

x-intercept: $-\frac{1}{3}$ x-intercept: 2

y-intercept: 1 y-intercept: 8

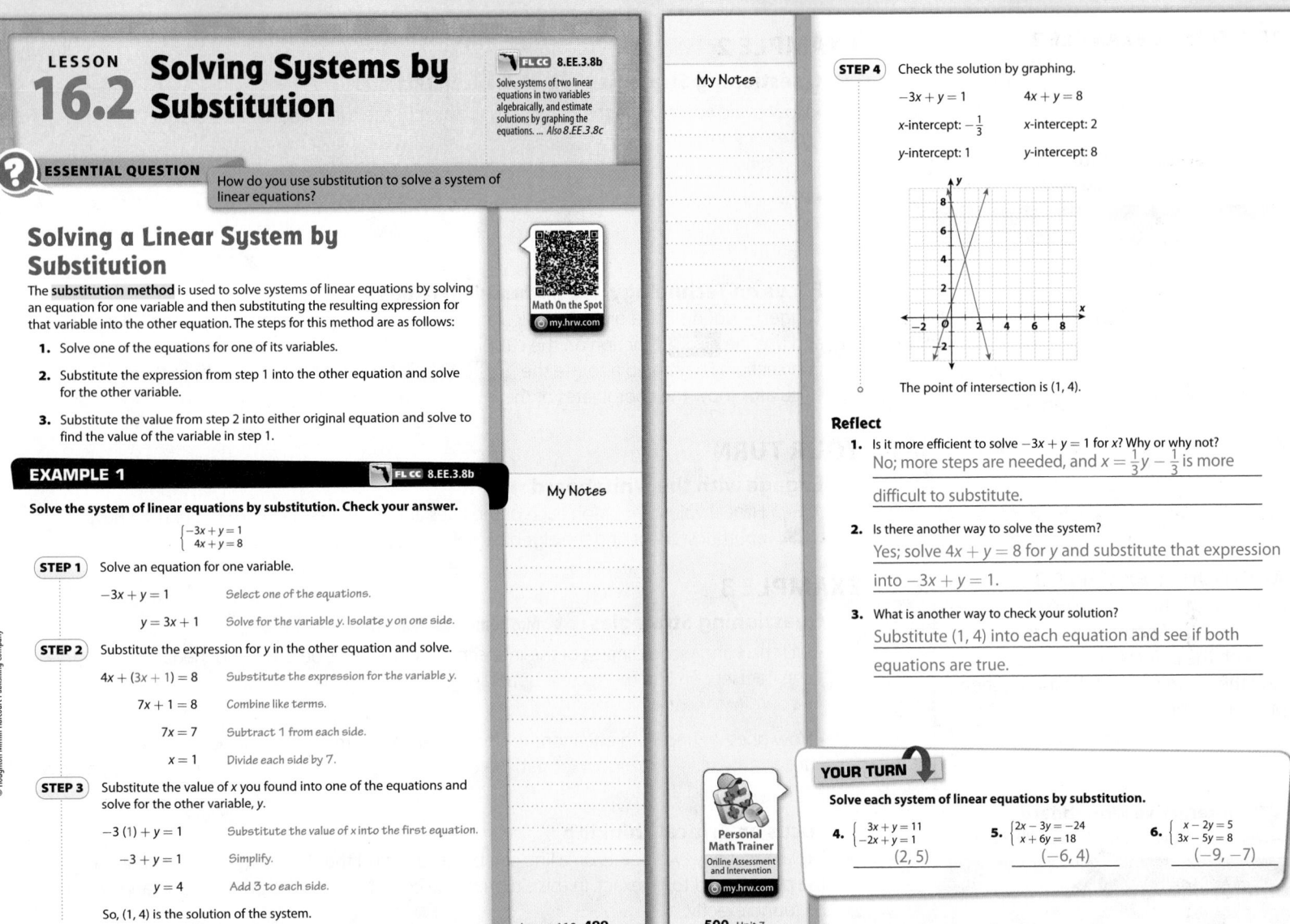

The point of intersection is (1, 4).

Reflect

1. Is it more efficient to solve $-3x + y = 1$ for x? Why or why not?
   No; more steps are needed, and $x = \frac{1}{3}y - \frac{1}{3}$ is more difficult to substitute.

2. Is there another way to solve the system?
   Yes; solve $4x + y = 8$ for y and substitute that expression into $-3x + y = 1$.

3. What is another way to check your solution?
   Substitute (1, 4) into each equation and see if both equations are true.

YOUR TURN

Personal Math Trainer
Online Assessment and Intervention
my.hrw.com

Solve each system of linear equations by substitution.

4. $\begin{cases} 3x + y = 11 \\ -2x + y = 1 \end{cases}$
   (2, 5)

5. $\begin{cases} 2x - 3y = -24 \\ x + 6y = 18 \end{cases}$
   (−6, 4)

6. $\begin{cases} x - 2y = 5 \\ 3x - 5y = 8 \end{cases}$
   (−9, −7)

500 Unit 7

PROFESSIONAL DEVELOPMENT

Integrate Mathematical Practices MP.6.1

This lesson provides an opportunity to address this Mathematical Practice standard. It calls for students to attend to precision. Students examine graphs of systems of equations to understand why the graphical method of solving a system is not always able to provide a precise solution. They learn that a graph of a system of equations can provide an estimate of the coordinates of the solution. Students also learn to use the algebraic method of substitution to find the precise solution to a system of equations.

Math Background

The systems of equations in this lesson are linear equations with one solution. The graphs of these equations are lines that intersect at one point with the coordinates given by the solution of the system. Some systems of linear equations, however, have no solution, and some have an infinite number of solutions. When the equations graphed are parallel lines, there is no solution to the system. Algebraically the result will be a false statement, such as $3 = -2$. When the equations graphed are the same line, then there are an infinite number of solutions. Algebraically the result will be a true statement, such as $0 = 0$.

EXAMPLE 2

Questioning Strategies 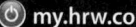 Mathematical Practices

• **How could you change the graph to get closer to the exact coordinates of the intersection?** If the scales of the axes are changed to smaller increments, the estimated coordinates of the point of intersection will be closer to their exact values.

• **How can you check that $\left(-\frac{24}{5}, -\frac{11}{5}\right)$ is the exact solution?** Substitute the values in for x and y in both original equations. If this is the exact solution, both will result in a true statement.

Focus on Technology Mathematical Practices

Suggest students use a graphing calculator to graph both equations in the same window and use the TRACE function on the calculator to find the approximate coordinates of the intersection. They could also use the 2nd CALC **Intersect** function to have their calculator show the coordinates of the intersection.

YOUR TURN

Engage with the Whiteboard

Have a volunteer graph each of the lines and estimate the intersection. Then have another student find the algebraic solution and compare it to the estimate.

EXAMPLE 3

Questioning Strategies 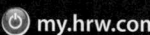 Mathematical Practices

• **Will the x and y-coordinates of the intersection of the lines be positive or negative?** The intersection is in the second quadrant, so the x-coordinate is negative and the y-coordinate is positive.

• **How does writing both equations in slope-intercept form help you solve for x?** When both equations are in $y = mx + b$ format, the expressions for $mx + b$ in each can be set equal to each other and then solved for x.

Focus on Critical Thinking

Explain that any two points on a line can be used to find the slope, but the coordinates of the points need to be exact. In this situation the coordinates of the points A, B, C, and D can be found exactly.

Using a Graph to Estimate the Solution of a System

You can use a graph to estimate the solution of a system of equations before solving the system algebraically.

Math On the Spot
my.hrw.com

EXAMPLE 2

FL CC 8.EE.3.8b

Solve the system $\begin{cases} x - 4y = 4 \\ 2x - 3y = -3 \end{cases}$.

STEP 1 Sketch a graph of each equation by substituting values for x and generating values of y.

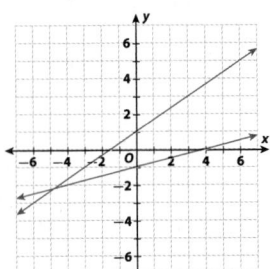

STEP 2 Find the intersection of the lines. The lines appear to intersect near $(-5, -2)$.

STEP 3 Solve the system algebraically.

Solve $x - 4y = 4$ for x.

$x - 4y = 4$
$x = 4 + 4y$

Substitute to find y.

$2(4 + 4y) - 3y = -3$
$8 + 8y - 3y = -3$
$8 + 5y = -3$
$5y = -11$
$y = -\frac{11}{5}$

Substitute to find x.

$x = 4 + 4y$
$= 4 + 4\left(-\frac{11}{5}\right)$
$= \frac{20 - 44}{5}$
$= -\frac{24}{5}$

The solution is $\left(-\frac{24}{5}, -\frac{11}{5}\right)$.

STEP 4 Use the estimate you made using the graph to judge the reasonableness of your solution.

$-\frac{24}{5}$ is close to the estimate of -5, and $-\frac{11}{5}$ is close to the estimate of -2, so the solution seems reasonable.

> **Math Talk**
> Mathematical Practices
> In Step 2, how can you tell that $(-5, -2)$ is not the solution?

The lines intersect near, but not at, $(-5, -2)$. Also, if you substitute $x = -5$ and $y = -2$ into each equation, you get false statements.

Personal Math Trainer
Online Assessment and Intervention
my.hrw.com

YOUR TURN

7. Estimate the solution of the system $\begin{cases} x + y = 4 \\ 2x - y = 6 \end{cases}$ by sketching a graph of each linear function. Then solve the system algebraically. Use your estimate to judge the reasonableness of your solution.

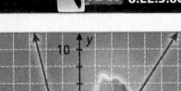

The estimated solution is _____ $(3, 1)$ _____.

The algebraic solution is _____ $\left(\frac{10}{3}, \frac{2}{3}\right)$ _____.

The solution is/is not reasonable because

$\frac{10}{3}$ is close to the estimate of 3,

and $\frac{2}{3}$ is close to the estimate of 1.

Math On the Spot
my.hrw.com

Solving Problems with Systems of Equations

EXAMPLE 3 Real World

FL CC 8.EE.3.8c

As part of Class Day, the eighth grade is doing a treasure hunt. Each team is given the following riddle and map. At what point is the treasure located?

There's pirate treasure to be found. So search on the island, all around. Draw a line through A and B. Then another through C and D. Dance a jig, "X" marks the spot. Where the lines intersect, that's the treasure's plot!

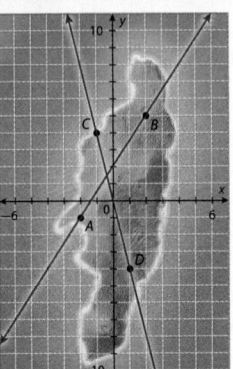

$\left(-\frac{1}{3}, \frac{3}{2}\right)$; This ordered pair can be used as an estimate for the solution.

STEP 1 Give the coordinates of each point and find the slope of the line through each pair of points.

$A: (-2, -1)$ $C: (-1, 4)$
$B: (2, 5)$ $D: (1, -4)$

Slope: Slope:

$\frac{5 - (-1)}{2 - (-2)} = \frac{6}{4}$ $\frac{-4 - 4}{1 - (-1)} = \frac{-8}{2}$

$= \frac{3}{2}$ $= -4$

> **Math Talk**
> Mathematical Practices
> Where do the lines appear to intersect? How is this related to the solution?

DIFFERENTIATE INSTRUCTION

Critical Thinking

Give students two or more systems of equation, such as those below. Have them complete tables that show ordered pair solutions for each of the equations, for all integers from $x = -5$ to $x = 5$. Ask them to find the solution to each system by identifying the ordered pair that appears in both tables for that system.

$\begin{cases} 2x + y = 7 \\ x - 3y = 0 \end{cases}$ $\begin{cases} 2x - 5y = 1 \\ -3x + 4y = 2 \end{cases}$

$(3, 1)$ $(-2, -1)$

Multiple Representations

One way to use substitution to solve a system of equations is to rewrite both equations so that the same variable is isolated and set equal to an expression. Then the Transitive Property can be used to set the expressions equal to each other.

Rewriting the equations in the system found in Example 1 results in $y = 3x + 1$ and $y = -4x + 8$. Using the Transitive Property:

$3x + 1 = -4x + 8$
$7x = 7$ and so $x = 1$

Substitute 1 for x in one of the original equations to find the value of y.

Additional Resources

Differentiated Instruction includes:

- Reading Strategies
- Success for English Learners **ELL**
- Reteach
- Challenge **PRE-AP**

YOUR TURN

Engage with the Whiteboard

 Have volunteers write the two equations that represent the car rentals. Ask another volunteer to demonstrate how to solve the system.

Talk About It
Check for Understanding

Ask: Ronald says that (20, 0.25) is the only combination of cost per day and cost per mile that could have given Carlos his $120 total. Is he right? Justify your answer. No, Ronald is wrong. Any point on the graph of the line that represents Carlos's situation would be a solution. However, (20, 0.25) is the only combination that would work for both Carlos's and Vanessa's situation.

Elaborate

Talk About It
Summarize the Lesson

 Ask: How can a graph of a system of two equations help you determine if your algebraic solution is reasonable? You can see which quadrant the intersection is in and the approximate value of the intersection by looking at the graph. You can compare the algebraic solution to these two pieces of information and confirm that it is reasonable.

GUIDED PRACTICE

Engage with the Whiteboard

For Exercises 5–8, have volunteers graph the equations on the whiteboard and estimate the solution.

Avoid Common Errors

Exercises 5–8 Remind students that to estimate the solution of each system they will first need to graph each system.

Exercise 9 Remind students to first analyze their two equations to determine which has a variable with a coefficient of 1. Then caution students to use the Distributive Property when substituting. So when $y = -3x + 163$ and $2x + 3(-3x + 163) = 174$, the 3 must be distributed to both $-3x$ and 163.

STEP 2 Write equations in slope-intercept form describing the line through points A and B and the line through points C and D.

Line through A and B:

Use the slope and a point to find b.

$5 = \left(\frac{3}{2}\right)2 + b$

$b = 2$

The equation is $y = \frac{3}{2}x + 2$.

Line through C and D:

Use the slope and a point to find b.

$4 = -4(-1) + b$

$b = 0$

The equation is $y = -4x$.

STEP 3 Solve the system algebraically.

Substitute $\frac{3}{2}x + 2$ for y in $y = -4x$ to find x.

$\frac{3}{2}x + 2 = -4x$

$\frac{11}{2}x = -2$

$x = -\frac{4}{11}$

Substitute to find x.

$y = -4\left(-\frac{4}{11}\right) = \frac{16}{11}$

The solution is $\left(-\frac{4}{11}, \frac{16}{11}\right)$.

My Notes

YOUR TURN

8. Ace Car Rental rents cars for x dollars per day plus y dollars for each mile driven. Carlos rented a car for 4 days, drove it 160 miles, and spent $120. Vanessa rented a car for 1 day, drove it 240 miles, and spent $80. Write equations to represent Carlos's expenses and Vanessa's expenses. Then solve the system and tell what each number represents.

Carlos: $4x + 160y = 120$

Vanessa: $x + 240y = 80$

$(20, 0.25)$;

20 represents the cost per day: $20;

0.25 represents the cost per mile: $0.25

Personal
Math Trainer
Online Assessment
and Intervention
© my.hrw.com

Solve each system of linear equations by substitution. (Example 1)

1. $\begin{cases} 3x - 2y = 9 \\ y = 2x - 7 \end{cases}$ ____(5, 3)____

2. $\begin{cases} y = x - 4 \\ 2x + y = 5 \end{cases}$ ____(3, −1)____

3. $\begin{cases} x + 4y = 6 \\ y = -x + 3 \end{cases}$ ____(2, 1)____

4. $\begin{cases} x + 2y = 6 \\ x - y = 3 \end{cases}$ ____(4, 1)____

Solve each system. Estimate the solution first. (Example 2)

5. $\begin{cases} 6x + y = 4 \\ x - 4y = 19 \end{cases}$

   Estimate ____(1, −4)____

   Solution ____$\left(\frac{7}{5}, \frac{22}{5}\right)$____

6. $\begin{cases} x + 2y = 8 \\ 3x + 2y = 6 \end{cases}$

   Estimate ____(−1, 5)____

   Solution ____$\left(-1, \frac{9}{2}\right)$____

7. $\begin{cases} 3x + y = 4 \\ 5x - y = 22 \end{cases}$

   Estimate ____(3, −6)____

   Solution ____$\left(\frac{13}{4}, \frac{23}{4}\right)$____

8. $\begin{cases} 2x + 7y = 2 \\ x + y = -1 \end{cases}$

   Estimate ____(−2, 1)____

   Solution ____$\left(-\frac{9}{5}, \frac{4}{5}\right)$____

9. Adult tickets to Space City amusement park cost x dollars. Children's tickets cost y dollars. The Henson family bought 3 adult and 1 child tickets for $163. The Garcia family bought 2 adult and 3 child tickets for $174. (Example 3)

   a. Write equations to represent the Hensons' cost and the Garcias' cost.

   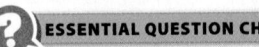

   Hensons' cost: $3x + y = 163$ Garcias' cost: $2x + 3y = 174$

   b. Solve the system.

   adult ticket price: ____$45____   child ticket price: ____$28____

? ESSENTIAL QUESTION CHECK-IN

10. How can you decide which variable to solve for first when you are solving a linear system by substitution?

    Choose the variable whose coefficient is 1. If no

    coefficient is 1, choose the variable with the least

    positive integer coefficient.

16.2 LESSON QUIZ

 **FL CC** 8.EE.3.8b, 8.EE.3.8c

Solve the system of linear equations by substitution. Check your answer.

1. $\begin{cases} x + y = 5 \\ 2x - y = 7 \end{cases}$

2. $\begin{cases} y = -2x + 6 \\ -4x - 6y = 4 \end{cases}$

Solve each system. Estimate the solution first.

3. $\begin{cases} 3x + y = 7 \\ -7x - 5y = 25 \end{cases}$

4. $\begin{cases} x + 3y = 9 \\ 2x + 4y = 7 \end{cases}$

5. Jill bought oranges and bananas. She bought 12 pieces of fruit and spent $5. Oranges cost $0.50 each and bananas cost $0.25 each. Write a system of equations to model the problem. Then solve the system algebraically. How many oranges and how many bananas did Jill buy?

Lesson Quiz available online

 my.hrw.com

Answers

1. $(4, 1)$

2. $(5, -4)$

3. $\left(\frac{15}{2}, -\frac{31}{2} \right)$

4. $\left(-\frac{15}{2}, \frac{11}{2} \right)$

5. $x + y = 12$
$0.50x + 0.25y = 5.00$
$(8, 4)$; 8 oranges and 4 bananas

Evaluate

GUIDED AND INDEPENDENT PRACTICE

 FL CC 8.EE.3.8b, 8.EE.3.8c

Concepts & Skills	Practice
Example 1 Solving a Linear System by Substitution	Exercises 1–4, 14
Example 2 Using a Graph to Estimate the Solution of a System	Exercises 5–8, 11
Example 3 Solving Problems with Systems of Equations	Exercises 9, 12–13, 15

Exercise	Depth of Knowledge (D.O.K.)	**FL CC** Mathematical Practices
11	**3** Strategic Thinking **H.O.T.**	**MP.3.1** Logic
12–13	**2** Skills/Concepts	**MP.4.1** Modeling
14	**2** Skills/Concepts	**MP.1.1** Problem Solving
15	**2** Skills/Concepts	**MP.4.1** Modeling
16	**3** Strategic Thinking **H.O.T.**	**MP.7.1** Using Structure
17	**3** Strategic Thinking **H.O.T.**	**MP.6.1** Precision
18	**3** Strategic Thinking **H.O.T.**	**MP.7.1** Using Structure

Additional Resources

Differentiated Instruction includes:

• Leveled Practice worksheets

16.2 Independent Practice

FL CC 8.EE.3.8b, 8.EE.3.8c

Personal Math Trainer
Online Assessment and Intervention
my.hrw.com

11. Check for Reasonableness Zach solves the system $\begin{cases} x + y = -3 \\ x - y = 1 \end{cases}$ and finds the solution $(1, -2)$. Use a graph to explain whether Zach's solution is reasonable.

The graph shows that the x-coordinate of the solution is negative, so Zach's solution is not reasonable.

12. Represent Real-World Problems Angelo bought apples and bananas at the fruit stand. He bought 20 pieces of fruit and spent $11.50. Apples cost $0.50 and bananas cost $0.75 each.

a. Write a system of equations to model the problem. (Hint: One equation will represent the number of pieces of fruit. A second equation will represent the money spent on the fruit.)

$\begin{cases} x + y = 20 \\ 0.50x + 0.75y = 11.50 \end{cases}$

b. Solve the system algebraically. Tell how many apples and bananas Angelo bought.

14 apples and 6 bananas

Apples $0.50
Bananas $0.75

13. Represent Real-World Problems A jar contains n nickels and d dimes. There is a total of 200 coins in the jar. The value of the coins is $14.00. How many nickels and how many dimes are in the jar?

120 nickels and 80 dimes

14. Multistep The graph shows a triangle formed by the x-axis, the line $3x - 2y = 0$, and the line $x + 2y = 10$. Follow these steps to find the area of the triangle.

a. Find the coordinates of point A by solving the system $\begin{cases} 3x - 2y = 0 \\ x + 2y = 10 \end{cases}$.

Point A: $\left(\dfrac{5}{2}, \dfrac{15}{4}\right)$

b. Use the coordinates of point A to find the height of the triangle.

height: $\dfrac{15}{4}$ units

c. What is the length of the base of the triangle?

base: 10 units

d. What is the area of the triangle? $18\dfrac{3}{4}$ square units

---

15. Jed is graphing the design for a kite on a coordinate grid. The four vertices of the kite are at $A\left(-\dfrac{4}{3}, \dfrac{2}{3}\right)$, $B\left(\dfrac{14}{3}, -\dfrac{4}{3}\right)$, $C\left(\dfrac{14}{3}, -\dfrac{16}{3}\right)$, and $D\left(\dfrac{2}{3}, -\dfrac{16}{3}\right)$. One kite strut will connect points A and C. The other will connect points B and D. Find the point where the struts cross.

$\left(\dfrac{8}{3}, -\dfrac{10}{3}\right)$

H.O.T. FOCUS ON HIGHER ORDER THINKING

Work Area

16. Analyze Relationships Consider the system $\begin{cases} 6x - 3y = 15 \\ x + 3y = -8 \end{cases}$. Describe three different substitution methods that can be used to solve this system. Then solve the system.

Solve the second equation for x ($x = -8 - 3y$) and then substitute that value into the first equation. Solve the first equation for y ($y = 2x - 5$) and then substitute that value into the second equation. Solve either equation for 3y ($3y = -8 - x$ or $3y = 6x - 15$) and then substitute that value into the other equation. Solution: $(1, -3)$

17. Communicate Mathematical Ideas Explain the advantages, if any, that solving a system of linear equations by substitution has over solving the same system by graphing.

The substitution method has the advantage of always giving an exact answer. Graphing produces an exact answer only if the solution is an ordered pair whose coordinates are integers.

18. Persevere in Problem Solving Create a system of equations of the form $\begin{cases} Ax + By = C \\ Dx + Ey = F \end{cases}$ that has $(7, -2)$ as its solution. Explain how you found the system.

Sample answer: $\begin{cases} x + 3y = 1 \\ -2x - 4y = -6 \end{cases}$; I chose random values of A, B, D, and E, substituted them into the equations, and calculated the values of C and F using $x = 7$ and $y = -2$.

EXTEND THE MATH PRE-AP

Activity available online my.hrw.com

Activity Let m represent a real number. Solve the following system of equations. The solution should be in the form (x, y), and x and y will be expressed in terms of m.

$\begin{cases} 8x + y = m \\ 4x + 3y = m \end{cases}$

$\left(\dfrac{1}{10}m, \dfrac{2}{10}m\right)$

LESSON
16.3 Solving Systems by Elimination

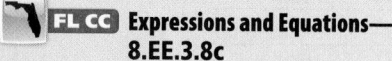
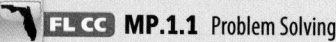
ADDITIONAL EXAMPLE 1
Solve the system of equations by adding. Check your answer.

$$\begin{cases} 2x + y = 8 \\ -2x + 3y = 16 \end{cases}$$

$(1, 6)$

 Interactive Whiteboard
Interactive example available online

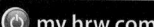 my.hrw.com

Engage

ESSENTIAL QUESTION

How do you solve a system of linear equations by adding or subtracting? Sample answer: Write the equations so that like terms are aligned vertically. Add or subtract the equations to eliminate either the x or y variable. Simplify to solve for the variable that was not eliminated. Then, substitute that value into one of the original equations to solve for the other variable.

Motivate the Lesson
Ask: How can you turn two equations with two variables into one equation with one variable without substituting? Begin the lesson to find out.

Explore

Remind students of the Addition and Subtraction Properties of Equality, where the same quantity can be added or subtracted from both sides of an equation. Ask them to think about adding or subtracting two equations. Have them discuss whether the properties of equality apply in this case.

Explain

EXAMPLE 1

Questioning Strategies **Mathematical Practices**

- What type of equations would have both the x and y values eliminated when combining the two equations? The x and y terms would have to both be the same or both be opposites. The constant terms could be different.

- In Step 2, if 6 is substituted for x in the other equation, $2x - 3y = 12$, what is the value of y? $y = 0$

Focus on Critical Thinking
Make sure students understand that the addition shown in Step 1 is a way to combine the information given in both equations into one equation with one variable.

YOUR TURN

Avoid Common Errors
In Exercise 5, be sure students correctly align the terms in the equations. The constant terms should be aligned by place value, so that $4 + 20$ is correctly found to be 24, not 60.

Solving Systems by Elimination

 **FL CC** 8.EE.3.8b
Solve systems of two linear equations in two variables algebraically, ... *Also* 8.EE.3.8c

ESSENTIAL QUESTION How do you solve a system of linear equations by adding or subtracting?

Solving a Linear System by Adding

The **elimination method** is another method used to solve a system of linear equations. In this method, one variable is *eliminated* by adding or subtracting the two equations of the system to obtain a single equation in one variable. The steps for this method are as follows:

1. Add or subtract the equations to eliminate one variable.

2. Solve the resulting equation for the other variable.

3. Substitute the value into either original equation to find the value of the eliminated variable.

Math On the Spot
my.hrw.com

EXAMPLE 1
FL CC 8.EE.3.8b

Solve the system of equations by adding. Check your answer.

$$\begin{cases} 2x - 3y = 12 \\ x + 3y = 6 \end{cases}$$

My Notes

STEP 1 Add the equations.

$2x - 3y = 12$	Write the equations so that like terms are aligned.
$+\ x + 3y = 6$	Notice that the terms $-3y$ and $3y$ are opposites.
$3x + 0\ = 18$	Add to eliminate the variable y.
$3x = 18$	Simplify and solve for x.
$\frac{3x}{3} = \frac{18}{3}$	Divide each side by 3.
$x = 6$	Simplify.

STEP 2 Substitute the solution into one of the original equations and solve for y.

$x + 3y = 6$	Use the second equation.
$6 + 3y = 6$	Substitute 6 for the variable x.
$3y = 0$	Subtract 6 from each side.
$y = 0$	Divide each side by 3 and simplify.

STEP 3 Write the solution as an ordered pair: (6, 0)

STEP 4 Check the solution by graphing.

$2x - 3y = 12$	$x + 3y = 6$
x-intercept: 6	x-intercept: 6
y-intercept: -4	y-intercept: 2

Substituting; if the x- and y-values of the solution are not integers, graphing will not produce an accurate check.

Math Talk
Mathematical Practices

Is it better to check a solution by graphing or by substituting the values in the original equations?

The point of intersection is (6, 0).

Reflect

1. Can this linear system be solved by subtracting one of the original equations from the other? Why or why not?

   No; if either of the original equations is subtracted from the other, neither variable will be eliminated.

2. What is another way to check your solution?

   Substitute (6, 0) into each equation and see if both equations are true.

YOUR TURN

Personal Math Trainer
Online Assessment and Intervention
my.hrw.com

Solve each system of equations by adding. Check your answers.

3. $\begin{cases} x + y = -1 \\ x - y = 7 \end{cases}$ 4. $\begin{cases} 2x + 2y = -2 \\ 3x - 2y = 12 \end{cases}$ 5. $\begin{cases} 6x + 5y = 4 \\ -6x + 7y = 20 \end{cases}$

     (3, −4)   (2, −3)   (−1, 2)

© Houghton Mifflin Harcourt Publishing Company

PROFESSIONAL DEVELOPMENT

Integrate Mathematical Practices MP.1.1

This lesson provides an opportunity to address this Mathematical Practice standard. It calls for students to make sense of problems and persevere in solving them. Students solve systems of equations using either addition or subtraction to eliminate one of the variables. Then students ask themselves if the solution they found makes sense. They use what they learned about graphing systems of equations to check the accuracy or reasonableness of the solution they found. They also learn to translate real-world problems into systems of equations and solve them.

Math Background

Systems of equations containing more than two equations and/or more than two variables can be solved by representing the equations with matrices. A matrix is a rectangular array of numbers. Matrix methods involve operations performed on the rows of numbers to create 0s in particular areas of the matrix. In part, the matrix method uses elimination. For example, the matrix for a simple two-equation system

$\begin{cases} 3x + 5y = -2 \\ 3x - 5y = 8 \end{cases}$ is $\begin{bmatrix} 3 & 5 & -2 \\ 3 & -5 & 8 \end{bmatrix}$. After adding row 2 to

row 1, the matrix becomes $\begin{bmatrix} 6 & 0 & 6 \\ 3 & -5 & 8 \end{bmatrix}$. From this

matrix you can see that $6x = 6$, so $x = 1$. Using substitution, $y = -1$.

EXAMPLE 2

Questioning Strategies 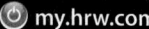 Mathematical Practices

• How can you tell when you should subtract rather than add the equations? One of the variable terms will be identical in both equations.

• In Step 2, if 3 is substituted for y in the other equation, $3x + 3y = 6$, what is the value of x?
  $x = -1$

Focus on Critical Thinking

Discuss with students how subtracting the second equation is the same as adding the opposite of each term, including those terms on the right side of the equal sign.

YOUR TURN

Engage with the Whiteboard

For Exercises 8–10, have volunteers write the subtraction sign in front of the second equation in each and then demonstrate how to subtract each term from the equation on top. Close attention should be paid to subtracting negative terms. Have other volunteers demonstrate subtracting the top equation from the bottom equation.

EXAMPLE 3

Questioning Strategies   Mathematical Practices

• How does organizing the information in a table help you determine the equations to write for this situation? Would another column added to the table be helpful? If so, what would be included in that column? The table is helpful in that it clearly shows the cost for the shoes and stoves at both stores. A column for the amount spent at each store could be included to the right of the camp stoves column. With this column added to the table, the coefficients of the variables and the constant term of each equation are easily seen.

• How do you decide whether to add or subtract the two equations? The goal is to eliminate one of the variable terms. Since the coefficients of the variable y are the same in both equations, you subtract.

• Where should the club buy the equipment? They will save money buying at Top Sport, but since it is farther away, they may choose to save time and transportation costs by buying at Outdoor Explorer.

Focus on Communication

Emphasize the importance of naming the variables being used and what they represent. Any pair of variables can be used, but there must be one to represent the number of pairs of snowshoes and a different one to represent the number of camp stoves.

Solving a Linear System by Subtracting

If both equations contain the same *x*- or *y*-term, you can solve by subtracting.

Math On the Spot
my.hrw.com

EXAMPLE 2   FL CC 8.EE.3.8b

Solve the system of equations by subtracting. Check your answer.

$$\begin{cases} 3x + 3y = 6 \\ 3x - y = -6 \end{cases}$$

STEP 1 Subtract the equations.

$3x + 3y = 6$	Write the equations so that like terms are aligned.
$-(3x - y = -6)$	Notice that both equations contain the term $3x$.
$0 + 4y = 12$	Subtract to eliminate the variable x.
$4y = 12$	Simplify and solve for y.
$y = 3$	Divide each side by 4 and simplify.

STEP 2 Substitute the solution into one of the original equations and solve for *x*.

$3x - y = -6$	Use the second equation.
$3x - 3 = -6$	Substitute 3 for the variable y.
$3x = -3$	Add 3 to each side.
$x = -1$	Divide each side by 3 and simplify.

STEP 3 Write the solution as an ordered pair: $(-1, 3)$

STEP 4 Check the solution by graphing.

$3x + 3y = 6$	$3x - y = -6$
x-intercept: 2	*x*-intercept: -2
y-intercept: 2	*y*-intercept: 6

The point of intersection is $(-1, 3)$.

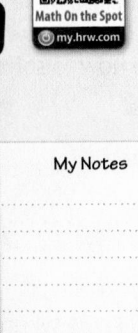

Reflect

6. What would happen if you added the original equations?

You would get $6x + 2y = 0$. This does not help to solve the system. Neither variable would be eliminated.

My Notes

---

7. How can you decide whether to add or subtract to eliminate a variable in a linear system? Explain your reasoning.

If the equations have two terms that are opposites, then you can add to eliminate a variable; if the equations have two terms that are the same, then you can subtract to eliminate a variable.

Personal Math Trainer
Online Assessment and Intervention
my.hrw.com

YOUR TURN

Solve each system of equations by subtracting. Check your answers.

8. $\begin{cases} 6x - 3y = 6 \\ 6x + 8y = -16 \end{cases}$ $(0, -2)$

9. $\begin{cases} 4x + 3y = 19 \\ 6x + 3y = 33 \end{cases}$ $(7, -3)$

10. $\begin{cases} 2x + 6y = 17 \\ 2x - 10y = 9 \end{cases}$ $\left(7, \frac{1}{2}\right)$

Math On the Spot
my.hrw.com

Solving Problems with Systems of Equations

Many real-world situations can be modeled and solved with a system of equations.

EXAMPLE 3   FL CC 8.EE.3.8c

The Polar Bear Club wants to buy snowshoes and camp stoves. The club will spend $554.50 to buy them at Top Sports and $602.00 to buy them at Outdoor Explorer, before taxes, but Top Sports is farther away. How many of each item does the club intend to buy?

	Snowshoes	Camp Stoves
Top Sports	$79.50 per pair	$39.25
Outdoor Explorer	$89.00 per pair	$39.25

DIFFERENTIATE INSTRUCTION

Cooperative Learning

Divide students into groups of three and give each group a system of equations, such as the one below. Have one student solve the system by substitution, another solve by graphing, and the third solve by elimination. Have students discuss which method they think is the quickest and easiest way to solve their system.

$$\begin{cases} 2x + y = 7 \\ 8x - y = 3 \end{cases}$$

$(1, 5)$

Number Sense

Have students switch the order of the equations in Examples 1 and 2. Ask students if switching their order will affect the solution. Then have students solve the systems. Help students understand that switching the order does not affect the solution. Graphing the lines is a good way to establish this fact. The graphs (and the solution) remain the same regardless of the order in which the equations are graphed.

Additional Resources

Differentiated Instruction includes:

- Reading Strategies
- Success for English Learners **ELL**
- Reteach
- Challenge **PRE-AP**

YOUR TURN

Engage with the Whiteboard

 Have a volunteer make a table to organize the information in the problem. Have another volunteer write the two equations for the system of equations. Ask another volunteer to demonstrate how to solve the system.

Elaborate

Talk About It

Summarize the Lesson

Ask: How do you know when to add or subtract when solving a system of equations by elimination? The goal is to eliminate one of the variable terms. If the coefficients of one variable term are the same in both equations, then you subtract. If they are opposites, you add.

GUIDED PRACTICE

Engage with the Whiteboard

 For Exercise 1, have volunteers explain the process of arriving at the correct value as they complete the write-in boxes for each step.

Avoid Common Errors

Exercise 3 Remind students to be cautious with the signs of the terms. Subtracting $-2y$ from y is the same as adding $2y$ to y. Suggest that if they have trouble correctly subtracting each term, they might choose to rewrite the second equation with the opposite of each term and then add the equations.

Exercise 8 Suggest that students organize the information in this situation in a table and identify what their variables represent.

STEP 1 Choose variables and write a system of equations.
Let x represent the number of pairs of snowshoes.
Let y represent the number of camp stoves.

Top Sports cost: $79.50x + 39.25y = 554.50$
Outdoor Explorer cost: $89.00x + 39.25y = 602.00$

STEP 2 Subtract the equations.

$79.50x + 39.25y = 554.50$ Both equations contain the term $39.25y$.

$-(89.00x + 39.25y = 602.00)$

$-9.50x + 0 \quad\quad = -47.50$ Subtract to eliminate the variable y.

$-9.50x = -47.50$ Simplify and solve for x.

$\dfrac{-9.50x}{-9.50} = \dfrac{-47.50}{-9.50}$ Divide each side by -9.50.

$x = 5$ Simplify.

STEP 3 Substitute the solution into one of the original equations and solve for y.

$79.50x + 39.25y = 554.50$ Use the first equation.

$79.50(5) + 39.25y = 554.50$ Substitute 5 for the variable x.

$397.50 + 39.25y = 554.50$ Multiply.

$39.25y = 157.00$ Subtract 397.50 from each side.

$\dfrac{39.25y}{39.25} = \dfrac{157.00}{39.25}$ Divide each side by 39.25.

$y = 4$ Simplify.

STEP 4 Write the solution as an ordered pair: (5, 4)

The club intends to buy 5 pairs of snowshoes and 4 camp stoves.

My Notes

YOUR TURN

11. At the county fair, the Baxter family bought 6 hot dogs and 4 juice drinks for $16.70. The Farley family bought 3 hot dogs and 4 juice drinks for $10.85. Find the price of a hot dog and the price of a juice drink.

hot dog: $1.95; juice drink: $1.25

Personal Math Trainer
Online Assessment and Intervention
@ my.hrw.com

---

1. Solve the system $\begin{cases} 4x + 3y = 1 \\ x - 3y = -11 \end{cases}$ by adding. (Example 1)

STEP 1 Add the equations.

$4x + 3y = 1$ Write the equations so that like terms are aligned.

$+ \quad x - 3y = -11$

$5x + \boxed{0} = \boxed{-10}$ Add to eliminate the variable $\boxed{y}$.

$5x = \boxed{-10}$ Simplify and solve for x.

$x = \boxed{-2}$ Divide both sides by $\boxed{5}$ and simplify.

STEP 2 Substitute into one of the original equations and solve for y.

$y = \boxed{3}$ So, $\boxed{(-2, 3)}$ is the solution of the system.

Solve each system of equations by adding or subtracting. (Examples 1, 2)

2. $\begin{cases} x + 2y = -2 \\ -3x + 2y = -10 \end{cases}$ $(2, -2)$

3. $\begin{cases} 3x + y = 23 \\ 3x - 2y = 8 \end{cases}$ $(6, 5)$

4. $\begin{cases} -4x - 5y = 7 \\ 3x + 5y = -14 \end{cases}$ $(7, -7)$

5. $\begin{cases} x - 2y = -19 \\ 5x + 2y = 1 \end{cases}$ $(-3, 8)$

6. $\begin{cases} 3x + 4y = 18 \\ -2x + 4y = 8 \end{cases}$ $(2, 3)$

7. $\begin{cases} -5x + 7y = 11 \\ -5x + 3y = 19 \end{cases}$ $(-5, -2)$

8. The Green River Freeway has a minimum and a maximum speed limit. Tony drove for 2 hours at the minimum speed limit and 3.5 hours at the maximum limit, a distance of 355 miles. Rae drove 2 hours at the minimum speed limit and 3 hours at the maximum limit, a distance of 320 miles. What are the two speed limits? (Example 3)

   a. Write equations to represent Tony's distance and Rae's distance.

   Tony: $2x + 3.5y = 355$ Rae: $2x + 3y = 320$

   b. Solve the system.

   minimum speed limit: 55 mi/h   maximum speed limit: 70 mi/h

ESSENTIAL QUESTION CHECK-IN

9. Can you use addition or subtraction to solve any system? Explain.

   no; Addition or subtraction can be used only when the coefficients of the x-terms or the y-terms are the same or opposites.

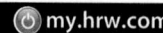
16.3 LESSON QUIZ

 **FL CC** 8.EE.3.8b, 8.EE.3.8c

Solve each system of equations by adding or subtracting.

1. $\begin{cases} x + 5y = 8 \\ 2x - 5y = 1 \end{cases}$

2. $\begin{cases} 2x + y = -1 \\ -2x - 4y = -16 \end{cases}$

3. $\begin{cases} 3x + 7y = 47 \\ -4x + 7y = 19 \end{cases}$

4. $\begin{cases} x + 3y = -23 \\ -x + 4y = -26 \end{cases}$

5. The perimeter of a rectangle is 24 inches. Twice the length decreased by three times the width is 4 inches. What are the dimensions of the rectangle?

Lesson Quiz available online

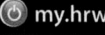 my.hrw.com

Answers

1. (3, 1)

2. (2, 3)

3. (4, 5)

4. (−2, −7)

5. length = 8 inches; width = 4 inches

Evaluate

GUIDED AND INDEPENDENT PRACTICE

 FL CC 8.EE.3.8b, 8.EE.3.8c

Concepts & Skills	Practice
Example 1 Solving a Linear System by Adding	Exercises 1, 4–5
Example 2 Solving a Linear System by Subtracting	Exercises 2–3, 6–7
Example 3 Solving Problems with Systems of Equations	Exercises 8, 10–15

Exercise	Depth of Knowledge (D.O.K.)	**FL CC** Mathematical Practices
10–11	**2** Skills/Concepts	**MP.4.1** Modeling
12	**2** Skills/Concepts	**MP.2.1** Reasoning
13–15	**2** Skills/Concepts	**MP.4.1** Modeling
16	**3** Strategic Thinking **H.O.T.**	**MP.2.1** Reasoning
17	**3** Strategic Thinking **H.O.T.**	**MP.3.1** Logic

Additional Resources

Differentiated Instruction includes:

• Leveled Practice worksheets

16.3 Independent Practice

FL CC 8.EE.3.8b, 8.EE.3.8c

Personal Math Trainer

Online Assessment and Intervention

my.hrw.com

10. **Represent Real-World Problems** Marta bought new fish for her home aquarium. She bought 3 guppies and 2 platies for a total of $13.95. Hank also bought guppies and platies for his aquarium. He bought 3 guppies and 4 platies for a total of $18.33. Find the price of a guppy and the price of a platy.

Guppy: $3.19; platy: $2.19

11. **Represent Real-World Problems** The rule for the number of fish in a home aquarium is 1 gallon of water for each inch of fish length. Marta's aquarium holds 13 gallons and Hank's aquarium holds 17 gallons. Based on the number of fish they bought in Exercise 10, how long is a guppy and how long is a platy?

Guppy: 3 in.; platy: 2 in.

12. Line m passes through the points $(6, 1)$ and $(2, -3)$. Line n passes through the points $(2, 3)$ and $(5, -6)$. Find the point of intersection of these lines.

$\left(\frac{7}{2}, -\frac{3}{2}\right)$

13. **Represent Real-World Problems** Two cars got an oil change at the same auto shop. The shop charges customers for each quart of oil plus a flat fee for labor. The oil change for one car required 5 quarts of oil and cost $22.45. The oil change for the other car required 7 quarts of oil and cost $25.45. How much is the labor fee and how much is each quart of oil?

Labor fee: $14.95; quart of oil: $1.50

14. **Represent Real-World Problems** A sales manager noticed that the number of units sold for two T-shirt styles, style A and style B, was the same during June and July. In June, total sales were $2779 for the two styles, with A selling for $15.95 per shirt and B selling for $22.95 per shirt. In July, total sales for the two styles were $2385.10, with A selling at the same price and B selling at a discount of 22% off the June price. How many T-shirts of each style were sold in June and July combined?

280 T-shirts of style A and style B were sold in June and July.

15. **Represent Real-World Problems** Adult tickets to a basketball game cost $5. Student tickets cost $1. A total of $2,874 was collected on the sale of 1,246 tickets. How many of each type of ticket were sold?

407 adult tickets and 839 student tickets

---

16. **Communicate Mathematical Ideas** Is it possible to solve the system $\begin{cases} 3x - 2y = 10 \\ x + 2y = 6 \end{cases}$ by using substitution? If so, explain how. Which method, substitution or elimination, is more efficient? Why?

Yes; solve the second equation for x to get $x = -2y + 6$. Substitute $-2y + 6$ for x in the first equation to get $3(-2y + 6) - 2y = 10$. Solve this for y to get $y = 1$. Then substitute 1 for y in either original equation to get $x = 4$, for a solution of $(4, 1)$. The elimination method is more efficient because there are fewer calculations and they are simpler to do.

17. Jenny used substitution to solve the system $\begin{cases} 2x + y = 8 \\ x - y = 1 \end{cases}$. Her solution is shown below.

Step 1	$y = -2x + 8$	Solve the first equation for y.
Step 2	$2x + (-2x + 8) = 8$	Substitute the value of y in an original equation.
Step 3	$2x - 2x + 8 = 8$	Use the Distributive Property.
Step 4	$8 = 8$	Simplify.

a. **Explain the Error** Explain the error Jenny made. Describe how to correct it.

She substituted her expression for y in the same equation she used to find y. She should substitute her expression into the other equation.

b. **Communicate Mathematical Ideas** Would adding the equations have been a better method for solving the system? If so, explain why.

Yes; adding the equations would have resulted in $3x = 9$, easily giving $x = 3$ after dividing each side by 3. Substitution requires many more steps.

EXTEND THE MATH PRE-AP

Activity available online my.hrw.com

Activity The solution to a system of three equations in three variables is an ordered triple (x, y, z). You can solve the following system of equations using elimination. Add the first two equations to eliminate z. Add the resulting equation to the third equation to eliminate y. This will give you the value of x, which you can substitute into the third equation to find the value of y. Finally, substitute y in the second equation to find the value of z.

$\begin{cases} 2x + y + z = 12 \\ 3y - z = -10 \\ x - 4y = 7 \end{cases}$

$(3, -1, 7)$

Solving Systems by Elimination with Multiplication

Florida Common Core Standards

The student is expected to:

 **FL CC** **Expressions and Equations—8.EE.3.8b**

Solve systems of two linear equations in two variables algebraically, and estimate solutions by graphing the equations. Solve simple cases by inspection.

 **FL CC** **Expressions and Equations—8.EE.3.8c**

Solve real-world and mathematical problems leading to two linear equations in two variables.

Mathematical Practices

 **FL CC** **MP.1.1** Problem Solving

---

ADDITIONAL EXAMPLE 1
Solve the system of equations by multiplying and adding.

$$\begin{cases} 2x + 5y = 8 \\ -x + 3y = 7 \end{cases}$$

$(-1, 2)$

 Interactive Whiteboard
Interactive example available online

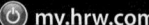 my.hrw.com

---

Engage

ESSENTIAL QUESTION

How do you solve a system of linear equations by multiplying? Sample answer: First, decide which variable to eliminate. Then, multiply one equation by a constant so that adding or subtracting will eliminate that variable. Finally, solve the system using the elimination method.

Motivate the Lesson
Ask: Can you solve a system of equations if adding or subtracting does not eliminate one of the variables? Begin the Lesson to find out how you can rewrite one equation and solve the system of equations.

Explore

Have students compare the equations $3x - 5y = -17$ and $6x - 10y = -34$, using graphs and tables. Also have them rewrite both equations in slope-intercept form. Once they see that the equations are the same line, ask them to identify the operation that must be carried out on one equation to make it equal to the other.

Explain

EXAMPLE 1

Questioning Strategies Mathematical Practices
• What is the purpose of multiplying one of the equations by a constant? When the equations do not have the same (or opposite) coefficient for one of the variables, then one or both of the equations must be multiplied by a constant in order to create a variable that has the same (or opposite) coefficient. Then, one variable can be eliminated by addition or subtraction.

Focus on Reasoning Mathematical Practices
Discuss that the second equation could just as well have been multiplied by -2 and then subtracted, but multiplying by negative numbers and subtracting has a higher chance of leading to errors than multiplying by positive numbers and adding.

YOUR TURN

Avoid Common Errors
Students might not be able to decide which variable to eliminate. Suggest they first check the equations for coefficients that are multiples of each other. If they exist, only one equation need be multiplied before adding or subtracting to eliminate that variable.

Solving Systems by Elimination with Multiplication

FL CC 8.EE.3.8b

Solve systems of two linear equations in two variables algebraically, ... Also 8.EE.3.8c

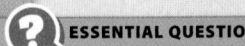 **ESSENTIAL QUESTION**

How do you solve a system of linear equations by multiplying?

Solving a System by Multiplying and Adding

In some linear systems, neither variable can be eliminated by adding or subtracting the equations directly. In systems like these, you need to multiply one of the equations by a constant so that adding or subtracting the equations will eliminate one variable. The steps for this method are as follows:

1. Decide which variable to eliminate.
2. Multiply one equation by a constant so that adding or subtracting will eliminate that variable.
3. Solve the system using the elimination method.

Math On the Spot
my.hrw.com

EXAMPLE 1
FL CC 8.EE.3.8b

Solve the system of equations by multiplying and adding.

$$\begin{cases} 2x + 10y = 2 \\ 3x - 5y = -17 \end{cases}$$

STEP 1 The coefficient of y in the first equation, 10, is 2 times the coefficient of y, 5, in the second equation. Also, the y-term in the first equation is being added, while the y-term in the second equation is being subtracted. To eliminate the y-terms, multiply the second equation by 2 and add this new equation to the first equation.

$2(3x - 5y = -17)$ — Multiply each term in the second equation by 2 to get opposite coefficients for the y-terms.

$6x - 10y = -34$ — Simplify.

$\begin{array}{r} 6x - 10y = -34 \\ + 2x + 10y = 2 \\ \hline 8x + 0y = -32 \end{array}$ — Add the first equation to the new equation.

Add to eliminate the variable y.

$8x = -32$ — Simplify and solve for x.

$\dfrac{8x}{8} = \dfrac{-32}{8}$ — Divide each side by 8.

$x = -4$ — Simplify.

My Notes

STEP 2 Substitute the solution into one of the original equations and solve for y.

$2x + 10y = 2$ — Use the first equation.

$2(-4) + 10y = 2$ — Substitute -4 for the variable x.

$-8 + 10y = 2$ — Simplify.

$10y = 10$ — Add 8 to each side.

$y = 1$ — Divide each side by 10 and simplify.

STEP 3 Write the solution as an ordered pair: $(-4, 1)$

STEP 4 Check your answer algebraically.

Substitute -4 for x and 1 for y in the original system.

$\begin{cases} 2x + 10y = 2 \rightarrow 2(-4) + 10(1) = -8 + 10 = 2 \checkmark \\ 3x - 5y = -17 \rightarrow 3(-4) - 5(1) = -12 - 5 = -17 \checkmark \end{cases}$

The solution is correct.

Math Talk
Mathematical Practices

When you check your answer algebraically, why do you substitute your values for x and y into the original system? Explain.

Reflect

1. How can you solve this linear system by subtracting? Which is more efficient, adding or subtracting? Explain your reasoning.

Multiply the second equation by -2 and then subtract.
Adding is more efficient because the y-terms already have opposite signs.

2. Can this linear system be solved by adding or subtracting without multiplying? Why or why not?

No; without multiplying, neither variable will be eliminated.

3. What would you need to multiply the second equation by to eliminate x by adding? Why might you choose to eliminate y instead of x?

You would need to multiply the second equation by $-\frac{2}{3}$; it is simpler to multiply by the whole number 2.

If there was a multiplication error, the solution might check in the multiplied system even if it were not correct.

Personal Math Trainer
Online Assessment and Intervention
my.hrw.com

YOUR TURN

Solve each system of equations by multiplying and adding.

4. $\begin{cases} 5x + 2y = -10 \\ 3x + 6y = 66 \end{cases}$
$(-8, 15)$

5. $\begin{cases} 4x + 2y = 6 \\ 3x - y = -8 \end{cases}$
$(-1, 5)$

6. $\begin{cases} -6x + 9y = -12 \\ 2x + y = 0 \end{cases}$
$\left(\frac{1}{2}, -1\right)$

PROFESSIONAL DEVELOPMENT

Integrate Mathematical Practices MP.1.1

This lesson provides an opportunity to address this Mathematical Practice standard. It calls for students to make sense of problems and persevere in solving them. Example 3 uses a four-step problem-solving process to determine the number of adult and children tickets purchased. Students analyze the information, formulate a plan, solve the problem, and justify and evaluate the solution.

Math Background

A system of equations can be solved using matrices and row operations. Possible row operations are:

1. Any two rows can be interchanged.
2. Multiply a row by a nonzero constant.
3. Any row can be replaced with the sum of that row and another.

Solve $\begin{cases} 2x + y = 1 \\ 3x - 5y = 8 \end{cases} \rightarrow \begin{bmatrix} 2 & 1 & 1 \\ 3 & -5 & 8 \end{bmatrix}$. Multiply row 1 by 5. $\rightarrow \begin{bmatrix} 10 & 5 & 5 \\ 3 & -5 & 8 \end{bmatrix}$. Add rows 1 and 2. $\rightarrow \begin{bmatrix} 13 & 0 & 13 \\ 3 & -5 & 8 \end{bmatrix}$. So $13x = 13$ and $x = 1$.

Using substitution, $y = -1$.

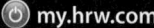

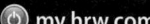
EXAMPLE 2
Questioning Strategies 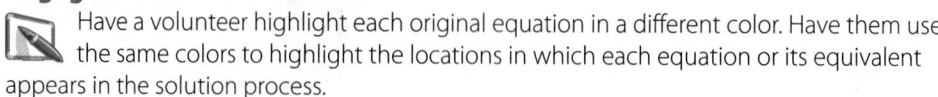 Mathematical Practices

- Why must every term in an equation be multiplied by the same number? It is the only way to obtain an equivalent equation.

- What would be different in the solution had the second equation been multiplied by -3? The new equation in Step 1 would have been $-6x + 12y = 78$. This equation would then have been added to the first equation. The solution $(-3, 5)$ would not have changed.

Engage with the Whiteboard
Have a volunteer highlight each original equation in a different color. Have them use the same colors to highlight the locations in which each equation or its equivalent appears in the solution process.

YOUR TURN
Engage with the Whiteboard
In Exercise 9, have a student volunteer show how to multiply one equation to eliminate x. Have another show how to multiply one equation to eliminate y. Point out that both methods result in the same answer.

EXAMPLE 3
Questioning Strategies 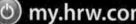 Mathematical Practices

- How many times can you multiply an equation by a number and still get an equivalent equation? an unlimited number of times.

- How many equations in a system can be multiplied by a number when solving a system? Any number of the equations in a system can be multiplied by a number in order to find a way to eliminate one of the variables.

- How do you decide which power of 10 to use to multiply the equations in Step 2? The greatest decimal place in any of the coefficients or constant terms is hundredths. So multiplying by 100 replaces all of the decimal values with whole numbers.

Focus on Communication
Emphasize the importance of naming the variables being used and keeping track of what they represent. Any pair of variables can be used, but there must be one to represent the number of adults and a different one to represent the number of children.

Solving a System by Multiplying and Subtracting

You can solve some systems of equations by multiplying one equation by a constant and then subtracting.

Math On the Spot
my.hrw.com

EXAMPLE 2   FL CC 8.EE.3.8b

Solve the system of equations by multiplying and subtracting.

$$\begin{cases} 6x + 5y = 7 \\ 2x - 4y = -26 \end{cases}$$

STEP 1   Multiply the second equation by 3 and subtract this new equation from the first equation.

$3(2x - 4y) = -26$ Multiply each term in the second equation by 3 to get the same coefficients for the x-terms.

$6x - 12y = -78$ Simplify.

$\begin{aligned} 6x + 5y &= 7 \\ -(6x - 12y &= -78) \end{aligned}$ Subtract the new equation from the first equation.

$0x + 17y = 85$ Subtract to eliminate the variable x.

$17y = 85$ Simplify and solve for y.

$\dfrac{17y}{17} = \dfrac{85}{17}$ Divide each side by 17.

$y = 5$ Simplify.

STEP 2   Substitute the solution into one of the original equations and solve for x.

$6x + 5y = 7$ Use the first equation.

$6x + 5(5) = 7$ Substitute 5 for the variable y.

$6x + 25 = 7$ Simplify.

$6x = -18$ Subtract 25 from each side.

$x = -3$ Divide each side by 6 and simplify.

STEP 3   Write the solution as an ordered pair: $(-3, 5)$

STEP 4   Check your answer algebraically.
Substitute -3 for x and 5 for y in the original system.

$$\begin{cases} 6x + 5y = 7 \rightarrow 6(-3) + 5(5) = -18 + 25 = 7 \checkmark \\ 2x - 4y = -26 \rightarrow 2(-3) - 4(5) = -6 - 20 = -26 \checkmark \end{cases}$$

The solution is correct.

My Notes

Personal Math Trainer
Online Assessment and Intervention
my.hrw.com

YOUR TURN

Solve each system of equations by multiplying and subtracting.

7. $\begin{cases} 3x - 7y = 2 \\ 6x - 9y = 9 \end{cases}$ **8.** $\begin{cases} -3x + y = 11 \\ 2x + 3y = -11 \end{cases}$ **9.** $\begin{cases} 9x + y = 9 \\ 3x - 2y = -11 \end{cases}$

    $(3, 1)$ $(-4, -1)$ $\left(\dfrac{1}{3}, 6\right)$

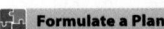

Math On the Spot
my.hrw.com

Solving Problems with Systems of Equations

Many real-world situations can be modeled with a system of equations.

My Notes

EXAMPLE 3   Problem Solving   FL CC 8.EE.3.8c

The Simon family attended a concert and visited an art museum. Concert tickets were $24.75 for adults and $16.00 for children, for a total cost of $138.25. Museum tickets were $8.25 for adults and $4.50 for children, for a total cost of $42.75. How many adults and how many children are in the Simon family?

Analyze Information

The answer is the number of adults and children.

Formulate a Plan

Solve a system to find the number of adults and children.

Solve

STEP 1   Choose variables and write a system of equations. Let x represent the number of adults. Let y represent the number of children.

Concert cost: $24.75x + 16.00y = 138.25$
Museum cost: $8.25x + 4.50y = 42.75$

STEP 2   Multiply both equations by 100 to eliminate the decimals.

$100(24.75x + 16.00y = 138.25) \rightarrow 2,475x + 1,600y = 13,825$

$100(8.25x + 4.50y = 42.75) \rightarrow 825x + 450y = 4,275$

DIFFERENTIATE INSTRUCTION

Cooperative Learning

Divide students into groups of four and give each group a system of equations, such as the one below. Have one student solve the system by substitution, a second by graphing, a third by elimination with addition, and a fourth by elimination by multiplication and subtraction. Have students discuss their results and the method they prefer.

$$\begin{cases} 3x + y = 9 \\ 6x - y = 9 \end{cases}$$

$(2, 3)$

Visual Cues

Many students are not very orderly when using elimination with multiplication and subtraction to solve a system. Suggest they write out the steps they are using, and change subtraction to addition. For example:

$\begin{aligned} 2x + y &= 1 \\ -3x + 5y &= -8 \end{aligned}$

Multiply by 5.	$\begin{aligned} 10x + 5y &= 5 \\ -3x + 5y &= -8 \end{aligned}$
Subtract.	$\begin{aligned} 10x + 5y &= 5 \\ -(-3x + 5y &= -8) \end{aligned}$
Add.	$\begin{aligned} 10x + 5y &= 5 \\ +(3x - 5y &= 8) \\ \hline 13x &= 13 \end{aligned}$

Additional Resources

Differentiated Instruction includes:

• Reading Strategies
• Success for English Learners   **ELL**
• Reteach
• Challenge   **PRE-AP**

YOUR TURN

Engage with the Whiteboard

Have a volunteer write the two equations for the system of equations. Suggest that they make a table to organize the information in the problem. Ask another volunteer to demonstrate how to solve the system.

Talk About It
Check for Understanding

Ask: If nothing else changed, would it have been possible for Seth's average biking speed to be 29.8 mi/h? Justify your answer. It would not be possible. The solution would have been approximately (−1.23, 1), but it is not possible to run for a negative number of hours.

Elaborate

Talk About It
Summarize the Lesson

Ask: How do you know when solving a system of equations that you must multiply before you can add or subtract? If the coefficients of one variable are not the same or are not opposites in the two equations, then you must multiply one or both of the equations until the coefficients of one variable are the same or opposites. Then, you can add or subtract to eliminate one variable.

GUIDED PRACTICE

Engage with the Whiteboard

For Exercise 1, have volunteers explain the process of arriving at the correct values as they complete the write-in boxes for each step.

Avoid Common Errors

Exercise 4 Remind students that either equation can be selected and then multiplied by a number, and either variable can be eliminated. In this exercise the top equation could be multiplied by 3 so x can be eliminated, or the bottom equation could be multiplied by 2 so y can be eliminated.

Exercise 8 Suggest that students organize the information in this situation in a table and identify what the variables represent. Remind them that eliminating the decimals will make the solution process easier.

STEP 3 Multiply the second equation by 3 and subtract this new equation from the first equation.

$3(825x + 450y = 4{,}275)$ — Multiply each term in the second equation by 3 to get the same coefficients for the x-terms.

$2{,}475x + 1{,}350y = 12{,}825$ — Simplify.

$2{,}475x + 1{,}600y = 13{,}825$
$-(2{,}475x + 1{,}350y = 12{,}825)$ — Subtract the new equation from the first equation.

$0x + 250y = 1{,}000$ — Subtract to eliminate the variable x.

$250y = 1{,}000$ — Simplify and solve for y.

$\dfrac{250y}{250} = \dfrac{1{,}000}{250}$ — Divide each side by 250.

$y = 4$ — Simplify.

STEP 4 Substitute the solution into one of the original equations and solve for x.

$8.25x + 4.50y = 42.75$ — Use the second equation.

$8.25x + 4.50(4) = 42.75$ — Substitute 4 for the variable y.

$8.25x + 18 = 42.75$ — Simplify.

$8.25x = 24.75$ — Subtract 18 from each side.

$x = 3$ — Divide each side by 8.25 and simplify.

STEP 5 Write the solution as an ordered pair: (3, 4). There are 3 adults and 4 children in the family.

Justify and Evaluate

Substituting $x = 3$ and $y = 4$ into the original equations results in true statements. The answer is correct.

YOUR TURN

10. Contestants in the Run-and-Bike-a-thon run for a specified length of time, then bike for a specified length of time. Jason ran at an average speed of 5.2 mi/h and biked at an average speed of 20.6 mi/h, going a total of 14.2 miles. Seth ran at an average speed of 10.4 mi/h and biked at an average speed of 18.4 mi/h, going a total of 17 miles. For how long do contestants run and for how long do they bike?

Contestants run 0.75 hour and bike 0.5 hour.

Personal Math Trainer

Online Assessment and Intervention

my.hrw.com

---

1. Solve the system $\begin{cases} 3x - y = 8 \\ -2x + 4y = -12 \end{cases}$ by multiplying and adding. (Example 1)

STEP 1 Multiply the first equation by 4. Add to the second equation.

$4(3x - y = 8)$ — Multiply each term in the first equation by 4 to get opposite coefficients for the y-terms.

$\boxed{12}\,x - \boxed{4}\,y = \boxed{32}$ — Simplify.

$+ \quad (-2x) + \quad 4y \ = -12$ — Add the second equation to the new equation.

$10x = \boxed{20}$ — Add to eliminate the variable $\boxed{y}$.

$x = \boxed{2}$ — Divide both sides by $\boxed{10}$ and simplify.

STEP 2 Substitute into one of the original equations and solve for y.

$y = \boxed{-2}$ So, $\boxed{(2, -2)}$ is the solution of the system.

Solve each system of equations by multiplying first. (Examples 1, 2)

2. $\begin{cases} x + 4y = 2 \\ 2x + 5y = 7 \end{cases}$ $(6, -1)$

3. $\begin{cases} 3x + y = -1 \\ 2x + 3y = 18 \end{cases}$ $(-3, 8)$

4. $\begin{cases} 2x + 8y = 21 \\ 6x - 4y = 14 \end{cases}$ $\left(\dfrac{7}{2}, \dfrac{7}{4}\right)$

5. $\begin{cases} 2x + y = 3 \\ -x + 3y = -12 \end{cases}$ $(3, -3)$

6. $\begin{cases} 6x + 5y = 19 \\ 2x + 3y = 5 \end{cases}$ $(4, -1)$

7. $\begin{cases} 2x + 5y = 16 \\ -4x + 3y = 20 \end{cases}$ $(-2, 4)$

8. Bryce spent \$5.26 on some apples priced at \$0.64 each and some pears priced at \$0.45 each. At another store he could have bought the same number of apples at \$0.32 each and the same number of pears at \$0.39 each, for a total cost of \$3.62. How many apples and how many pears did Bryce buy? (Example 3)

   a. Write equations to represent Bryce's expenditures at each store.

   First store: $0.64x + 0.45y = 5.26$ Second store: $0.32x + 0.39y = 3.62$

   b. Solve the system.

   Number of apples: _____ 4 _____   Number of pears: _____ 6 _____

? ESSENTIAL QUESTION CHECK-IN

9. When solving a system by multiplying and then adding or subtracting, how do you decide whether to add or subtract?

   If the coefficients of a variable have opposite signs, you

   add. If the signs are the same, you subtract.

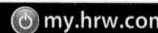
16.4 LESSON QUIZ

 FL CC 8.EE.3.8b, 8.EE.3.8c

Solve the system of linear equations by multiplying first.

1. $\begin{cases} x + 3y = 8 \\ 2x - 5y = -6 \end{cases}$

2. $\begin{cases} 3x + 2y = 2 \\ -2x - 4y = -12 \end{cases}$

3. $\begin{cases} 2x + 15y = 13 \\ -3x + 5y = 8 \end{cases}$

4. $\begin{cases} x + 2y = -8 \\ -8x + 5y = 1 \end{cases}$

5. The perimeter of a rectangle is 42 feet. The length decreased by three times the width is 1 foot. What are the dimensions of the rectangle?

Lesson Quiz available online

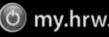 my.hrw.com

Answers

1. $(2, 2)$
2. $(-2, 4)$
3. $(-1, 1)$
4. $(-2, -3)$
5. length = 16 ft; width = 5 ft

Evaluate

GUIDED AND INDEPENDENT PRACTICE

 **FL CC** 8.EE.3.8b, 8.EE.3.8c

Concepts & Skills	Practice
Example 1 Solving a System by Multiplying and Adding	Exercises 1–7, 10
Example 2 Solving a System by Multiplying and Subtracting	Exercises 2–7
Example 3 Solving Problems with Systems of Equations	Exercises 8, 11–13

Exercise	Depth of Knowledge (D.O.K.)	 **FL CC** Mathematical Practices
10	**3** Strategic Thinking **H.O.T.**	**MP.3.1** Logic
11	**3** Strategic Thinking **H.O.T.**	**MP.4.1** Modeling
12	**2** Skills/Concepts	**MP.2.1** Reasoning
13	**2** Skills/Concepts	**MP.4.1** Modeling
14	**3** Strategic Thinking **H.O.T.**	**MP.3.1** Logic
15	**3** Strategic Thinking **H.O.T.**	**MP.7.1** Using Structure

Additional Resources

Differentiated Instruction includes:

• Leveled Practice worksheets

CLUSTER CONNECTION

Exercise 11 combines concepts from the Florida Common Core cluster "Analyze and solve linear equations and pairs of simultaneous linear equations."

16.4 Independent Practice

FL CC 8.EE.3.8b, 8.EE.3.8c

Personal Math Trainer

Online Assessment and Intervention

my.hrw.com

10. Explain the Error Gwen used elimination with multiplication to solve the system $\begin{cases} 2x + 6y = 3 \\ x - 3y = -1 \end{cases}$. Her work to find x is shown. Explain her error. Then solve the system.

$2(x - 3y) = -1$
$2x - 6y = -1$
$+2x + 6y = 3$
$\overline{4x + 0y = 2}$

Gwen forgot to multiply the right side by 2; $\left(\frac{1}{4}, \frac{5}{12}\right)$ $x = \frac{1}{2}$

11. Represent Real-World Problems At Raging River Sports, polyester-fill sleeping bags sell for $79. Down-fill sleeping bags sell for $149. In one week the store sold 14 sleeping bags for $1,456.

Sleeping Bags

a. Let x represent the number of polyester-fill bags sold and let y represent the number of down-fill bags sold. Write a system of equations you can solve to find the number of each type sold.

$\begin{cases} 79x + 149y = 1,456 \\ x + y = 14 \end{cases}$

b. Explain how you can solve the system for y by multiplying and subtracting.

Multiply the second equation by 79. Subtract the new equation from the first one and solve the resulting equation for y.

c. Explain how you can solve the system for y using substitution.

Solve the second equation for x. Substitute the expression for x in the first equation and solve the resulting equation for y.

d. How many of each type of bag were sold?

9 polyester-fill, 5 down-fill

12. Twice a number plus twice a second number is 310. The difference between the numbers is 55. Find the numbers by writing and solving a system of equations. Explain how you solved the system.

105 and 50; Sample answer: I multiplied the second equation in the system $\begin{cases} 2x + 2y = 310 \\ x - y = 55 \end{cases}$ by 2 and then added to eliminate the y-terms.

13. Represent Real-World Problems A farm stand sells apple pies and jars of applesauce. The table shows the number of apples needed to make a pie and a jar of applesauce. Yesterday, the farm picked 169 Granny Smith apples and 95 Golden Delicious apples. How many pies and jars of applesauce can the farm make if every apple is used?

Type of apple	Granny Smith	Golden Delicious
Needed for a pie	5	3
Needed for a jar of applesauce	4	2

21 pies, 16 jars of applesauce

H.O.T. FOCUS ON HIGHER ORDER THINKING

Work Area

14. Make a Conjecture Lena tried to solve a system of linear equations algebraically and in the process found the equation $5 = 9$. Lena thought something was wrong, so she graphed the equations and found that they were parallel lines. Explain what Lena's graph and equation could mean.

Lena's graph shows that the two lines do not intersect. This would seem to mean that the system has no solution. It would seem that solving an equation algebraically and getting a false statement means that the system has no solution.

15. Consider the system $\begin{cases} 2x + 3y = 6 \\ 3x + 7y = -1 \end{cases}$.

a. Communicate Mathematical Ideas Describe how to solve the system by multiplying the first equation by a constant and subtracting. Why would this method be less than ideal?

Multiply the first equation by 1.5 and subtract. This would be less than ideal because you would introduce decimals into the solution process.

b. Draw Conclusions Is it possible to solve the system by multiplying both equations by integer constants? If so, explain how.

Yes; multiply the first equation by 3 and the second equation by 2. Both x-term coefficients would be 6. Solve by eliminating the x-terms using subtraction.

c. Use your answer from part b to solve the system.

$(9, -4)$

EXTEND THE MATH PRE-AP

Activity available online my.hrw.com

Activity The solution to a system of three equations in three variables is (x, y, z). Solve the following system of equations using elimination by multiplication and addition or subtraction. Multiply the first equation by 2. Add the first two equations to eliminate z. Add the resulting equation to the third equation, after multiplying the third equation by 4, to eliminate x. This will give you the value of y, which you can substitute into the third equation to find the value of x. Finally, substitute y in the second equation to find the value of z.

$\begin{cases} 2x + y + 2z = 6 \\ 3y - 4z = -10 \\ x - 4y = 11 \end{cases}$

$(3, -2, 1)$

Florida Common Core Standards

The student is expected to:

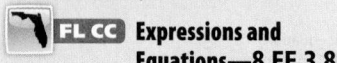 **Expressions and Equations—8.EE.3.8b**

Solve systems of two linear equations in two variables algebraically, and estimate solutions by graphing the equations. Solve simple cases by inspection.

 **Expressions and Equations—8.EE.3.8c**

Solve real-world and mathematical problems leading to two linear equations in two variables.

Mathematical Practices

 **MP.2.1** Reasoning

ADDITIONAL EXAMPLE 1

A Solve the system of linear equations by substitution.

$$\begin{cases} x - y = 8 \\ -x + y = 4 \end{cases}$$

B Solve the system of linear equations by elimination.

$$\begin{cases} 3x + 4y = -7 \\ -9x - 12y = 21 \end{cases}$$

A no solution

B infinitely many solutions

 Interactive Whiteboard
Interactive example available online

 my.hrw.com

Engage

ESSENTIAL QUESTION

How do you solve a system with no solutions or infinitely many solutions? Sample answer: The same methods of graphing, substitution, or elimination are used. If the graph shows parallel lines or if the solution gives a false statement, there is no solution. If the graph shows the lines coincide or if the solution gives a true statement for all ordered pairs, there are infinitely many solutions.

Motivate the Lesson
Ask: Equations whose graphs are intersecting lines have one solution. How many solutions do equations whose graphs are parallel lines have? Take a guess. Begin the Explore Activity to find out.

Explore

EXPLORE ACTIVITY 1

Engage with the Whiteboard
When discussing Step A, have a student highlight each of the equations in different colors and then highlight the corresponding lines in the same colors. When discussing Step B, have a different student highlight the two equations and the corresponding line in the same color.

Explain

EXAMPLE 1

Questioning Strategies Mathematical Practices

• How would the results in Step 2 of Part A change if you were to use addition to solve this system? Would the solution change? The results after adding would be 0 = 2. The solution would still be "no solution."

• How would the results in Step 2 of Part B change if you were to use substitution to solve this system? Would the solution change? The results after substituting would be 0 = 0 or another true statement. The solution would still be "infinitely many solutions."

Engage with the Whiteboard
For Step 4 of Part A in Example 1, have a volunteer graph the equations on the coordinate grid. Discuss ways to check to be sure the two lines are actually parallel, such as finding whether their slopes are equal. Have another volunteer graph the equations in Step 4 of Part B.

Solving Special Systems

FL CC 8.EE.3.8b
Solve systems of two linear
equations in two variables
algebraically, ... Solve
simple cases by inspection.
Also 8.EE.3.8c

? ESSENTIAL QUESTION

How do you solve systems with no solution or infinitely many solutions?

EXPLORE ACTIVITY   FL CC 8.EE.3.8b

Solving Special Systems by Graphing

As with equations, some systems may have no solution or infinitely many solutions. One way to tell how many solutions a system has is by inspecting its graph.

Use the graph to solve each system of linear equations.

A $\begin{cases} x + y = 7 \\ 2x + 2y = 6 \end{cases}$

Is there a point of intersection? Explain.

No, the lines appear to be parallel; they have

no points in common.

Does this linear system have a solution? Use the graph to explain.

This system has no solution; the lines have no points in common, which

means there is no ordered pair that will make both equations true.

B $\begin{cases} 2x + 2y = 6 \\ x + y = 3 \end{cases}$

Is there a point of intersection? Explain.

Yes, the graphs are the same line; all points are points of intersection.

Does this linear system have a solution? Use the graph to explain.

This system has infinitely many solutions; all ordered pairs on the

line will make both equations true.

Reflect

1. Use the graph to identify two lines that represent a linear system with exactly one solution. What are the equations of the lines? Explain your reasoning.

Sample answer : $x + y = 7$ and $3x - y = 1$; the lines intersect at one point.

Lesson 16.5 **523**

---

2. If each equation in a system of two linear equations is represented by a different line when graphed, what is the greatest number of solutions the system can have? Explain your reasoning.

One; because the two lines are different, they are either parallel

and there is no solution, or they intersect at only one point.

3. Identify the three possible numbers of solutions for a system of linear equations. Explain when each type of solution occurs.

one solution when the lines intersect at a single point;

no solution when the lines are parallel; infinitely many

solutions when the lines are the same line

Solving Special Systems Algebraically

As with equations, if you solve a system of equations with no solution, you get a false statement, and if you solve a system with infinitely many solutions, you get a true statement.

Math On the Spot
my.hrw.com

My Notes

EXAMPLE 1   FL CC 8.EE.3.8b

A Solve the system of linear equations by substitution.

$\begin{cases} x - y = -2 \\ -x + y = 4 \end{cases}$

STEP 1   Solve $x - y = -2$ for x:
$x = y - 2$

STEP 2   Substitute the resulting expression into the other equation and solve.

$-(y - 2) + y = 4$ Substitute the expression for the variable x.

$2 = 4$ Simplify.

STEP 3   Interpret the solution. The result is the false statement $2 = 4$, which means there is no solution.

STEP 4   Graph the equations to check your answer. The graphs do not intersect, so there is no solution.

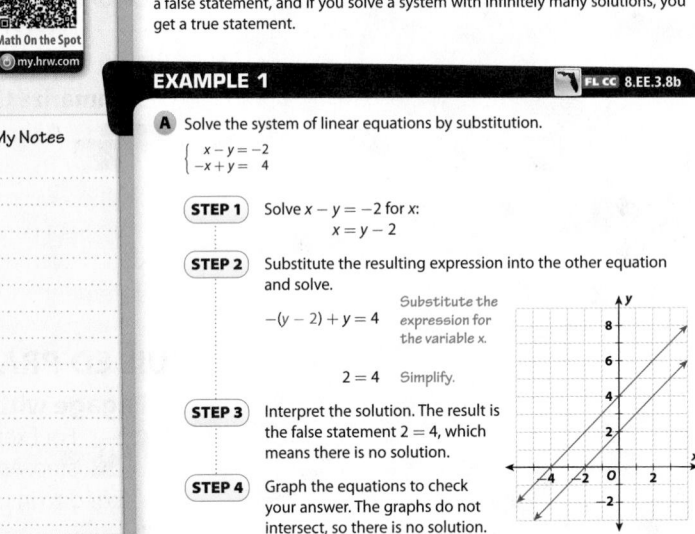

524 Unit 7

PROFESSIONAL DEVELOPMENT

Integrate Mathematical Practices MP.2.1

This lesson provides an opportunity to address this Mathematical Practice standard. It calls for students to reason abstractly and quantitatively. Upon reaching a final algebraic solution of a system of equations, students must reason abstractly to determine whether there is only one solution, no solution, or infinitely many solutions to the system. They must also reason abstractly to analyze the graphs of a system of equations and draw conclusions about the solution(s) of the system.

Math Background

A system of equations is either inconsistent or consistent. An inconsistent system has no solution. A consistent system has at least one solution. A consistent system can be either independent or dependent. An independent system has exactly one solution, and a dependent system has an infinite number of solutions. A dependent consistent system has coefficients and constants that are proportional. For example,

$\begin{cases} 2x + 3y = 8 \\ 4x + 6y = 16 \end{cases}$ is dependent and consistent since

$\frac{2}{4} = \frac{3}{6} = \frac{8}{16}$.

YOUR TURN

Avoid Common Errors

Remind students that when they multiply an equation by a constant, they must multiply each term in the equation by the constant.

Talk About It
Check for Understanding

Ask: If you were to graph the systems in Exercises 7–9, what would you expect each of the graphs to look like? The graph for the system in Exercise 7 would be parallel lines. The graph for the system in Exercise 8 would be lines intersecting at $(10, -2)$. The graph for the system in Exercise 9 would be one line.

Elaborate

Talk About It
Summarize the Lesson

Ask: How can you tell that a system has one, none, or infinitely many solutions? The graph of a system with one solution is a pair of intersecting lines. The algebraic solution will provide a value for x and a value for y. The graph of a system with no solutions is a pair of parallel lines. The algebraic solution will provide a false statement. The graph of a system with infinitely many solutions is one line. The algebraic solution will provide a true statement.

GUIDED PRACTICE

Engage with the Whiteboard

For Exercise 1, have volunteers explain their thinking as they fill in the blanks for each step. Ask volunteers to point out or highlight the equations involved as they are referred to in the steps.

Avoid Common Errors

Exercise 3 If students attempt to solve this exercise by elimination, they may incorrectly identify it as having infinitely many solutions, because they will reach a point where they see that the left sides of both equations are identical. Explain that for there to be infinitely many solutions, the right sides of the equations must also be identical.

Exercises 2–4 Suggest that students graph each system on its own coordinate grid and then use the graph to verify their answers.

B Solve the system of linear equations by elimination.

$$\begin{cases} 2x + y = -2 \\ 4x + 2y = -4 \end{cases}$$

STEP 1 Multiply the first equation by -2.

$$-2(2x + y = -2) \rightarrow -4x + (-2y) = 4$$

STEP 2 Add the new equation from Step 1 to the original second equation.

$$\begin{array}{r} -4x + (-2y) = 4 \\ +\quad 4x + 2y = -4 \\ \hline 0x + 0y = 0 \\ 0 = 0 \end{array}$$

STEP 3 Interpret the solution. The result is the statement $0 = 0$, which is always true. This means that the system has infinitely many solutions.

STEP 4 Graph the equations to check your answer. The graphs are the same line, so there are infinitely many solutions.

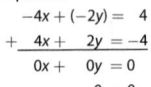

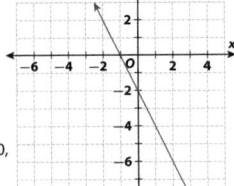

Math Talk
Mathematical Practices

What solution do you get when you solve the system in part B by substitution? Does this result change the number of solutions? Explain.

$-4 = -4$; no, this is still a true statement, so the system still has infinitely many solutions.

Reflect

4. If x represents a variable and a and b represent constants so that $a \neq b$, interpret what each result means when solving a system of equations.

$x = a$ ___The system has one solution.___

$a = b$ ___The system has no solution.___

$a = a$ ___The system has infinitely many solutions.___

5. In part B, can you tell without solving that the system has infinitely many solutions? If so, how?

Yes; the corresponding constants and coefficients of the second equation are twice those of the first equation. Both equations represent the same line, so there are infinitely many solutions.

YOUR TURN

Solve each system. Tell how many solutions each system has.

6. $\begin{cases} 4x - 6y = 9 \\ -2x + 3y = 4 \end{cases}$ ___no solution___

7. $\begin{cases} x + 2y = 6 \\ 2x - 3y = 26 \end{cases}$ ___(10, −2); one solution___

8. $\begin{cases} 12x - 8y = -4 \\ -3x + 2y = 1 \end{cases}$ ___infinitely many solutions___

Personal Math Trainer
Online Assessment and Intervention
my.hrw.com

---

1. Use the graph to solve each system of linear equations. (Explore Activity)

A. $\begin{cases} 4x - 2y = -6 \\ 2x - y = 4 \end{cases}$ **B.** $\begin{cases} 4x - 2y = -6 \\ x + y = 6 \end{cases}$ **C.** $\begin{cases} 2x - y = 4 \\ 6x - 3y = 12 \end{cases}$

STEP 1 Decide if the graphs of the equations in each system intersect, are parallel, or are the same line.

System A: The graphs ___are parallel___.

System B: The graphs ___intersect___.

System C: The graphs ___are the same line___.

STEP 2 Decide how many points the graphs have in common.

Intersecting lines have ___one___ point(s) in common.

Parallel lines have ___no___ point(s) in common.

The same lines have ___an infinite number of___ point(s) in common.

STEP 3 Solve each system.

System A has ___no___ points in common, so it has ___no___ solution.

System B has ___1___ point in common. That point is the solution, ___(1, 5)___.

System C has ___an infinite number of___ points in common. ___All___ ordered pairs on the line will make both equations true.

(graph labels: $x + y = 6$, $4x - 2y = -6$, $2x - y = 4$, $6x - 3y = 12$)

Solve each system. Tell how many solutions each system has. (Example 1)

2. $\begin{cases} x - 3y = 4 \\ -5x + 15y = -20 \end{cases}$ ___infinitely many solutions___

3. $\begin{cases} 6x + 2y = -4 \\ 3x + y = 4 \end{cases}$ ___no solution___

4. $\begin{cases} 6x - 2y = -10 \\ 3x + 4y = -25 \end{cases}$ ___(−3, −4); one solution___

? ESSENTIAL QUESTION CHECK-IN

5. When you solve a system of equations algebraically, how can you tell whether the system has zero, one, or an infinite number of solutions?

If your solution gives specific values for x and y, the system has one solution, (x, y). If it gives a false statement, there is no solution. If it gives a true statement, there are infinitely many solutions.

DIFFERENTIATE INSTRUCTION

Cooperative Learning

Have students work in groups of three. Have each student roll a number cube to determine a value for the variable n in the system below. Have students determine if the systems created have one, none, or an infinite number of solutions.

$$\begin{cases} 4x + 2y = 10 \\ 2x + y = n \end{cases}$$

When $n = 5$, there are an infinite number of solutions; for all other values of n, there are no solutions.

Graphic Organizer

Have students create a concept map to show the connections between different types of systems of two equations. For example:

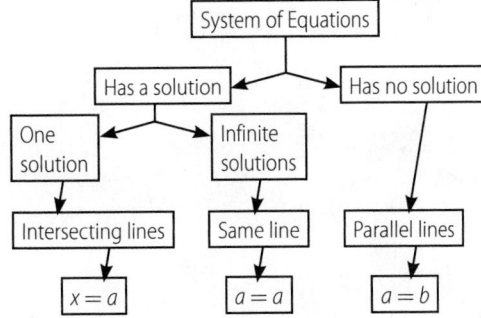

Additional Resources

Differentiated Instruction includes:

- Reading Strategies
- Success for English Learners **ELL**
- Reteach
- Challenge **PRE-AP**

Solving Special Systems **526**

Evaluate

GUIDED AND INDEPENDENT PRACTICE

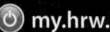 **FL CC** 8.EE.3.8b, 8.EE.3.8c

Concepts & Skills	Practice
Explore Activity Solving Special Systems by Graphing	Exercises 1, 6–7, 14–15
Example 1 Solving Special Systems Algebraically	Exercises 2–4, 8–13, 16–17

Exercise	Depth of Knowledge (D.O.K.)	**FL CC** Mathematical Practices
6–7	**1** Recall	**MP.2.1** Reasoning
8–14	**2** Skills/Concepts	**MP.2.1** Reasoning
15	**3** Strategic Thinking **H.O.T.**	**MP.3.1** Logic
16–17	**3** Strategic Thinking **H.O.T.**	**MP.4.1** Modeling
18–19	**3** Strategic Thinking **H.O.T.**	**MP.3.1** Logic
20	**3** Strategic Thinking **H.O.T.**	**MP.7.1** Using Structure

Additional Resources

Differentiated Instruction includes:

• Leveled Practice worksheets

16.5 Independent Practice

FL CC 8.EE.3.8b, 8.EE.3.8c

Personal Math Trainer

Online Assessment and Intervention

my.hrw.com

Solve each system by graphing. Check your answer algebraically.

6. $\begin{cases} -2x + 6y = 12 \\ x - 3y = 3 \end{cases}$

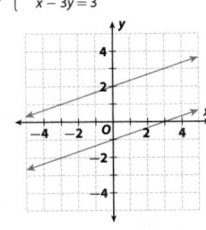

7. $\begin{cases} 15x + 5y = 5 \\ 3x + y = 1 \end{cases}$

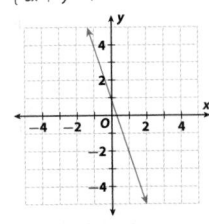

Solution: _____ no solution _____

Solution: _____ infinitely many solutions _____

For Exs. 8–14, state the number of solutions for each system of linear equations.

8. a system whose graphs have the same slope but different y-intercepts
_____ no solution _____

9. a system whose graphs have the same y-intercepts but different slopes
_____ one solution _____

10. a system whose graphs have the same y-intercepts and the same slopes
_____ infinitely many solutions _____

11. a system whose graphs have different y-intercepts and different slopes
_____ one solution _____

12. the system $\begin{cases} y = 2 \\ y = -3 \end{cases}$ _____ no solution _____

13. the system $\begin{cases} x = 2 \\ y = -3 \end{cases}$ _____ one solution _____

14. the system whose graphs were drawn using these tables of values:

Equation 1

x	0	1	2	3
y	1	3	5	7

Equation 2

x	0	1	2	3
y	3	5	7	9

_____ no solution _____

15. **Draw Conclusions** The graph of a linear system appears in a textbook. You can see that the lines do not intersect on the graph, but also they do not appear to be parallel. Can you conclude that the system has no solution? Explain.

No; although the lines do not intersect on the graph, they intersect at a point that is not on the graph. To prove that a system has no solution, you must do so algebraically.

16. **Represent Real-World Problems** Two school groups go to a roller skating rink. One group pays $243 for 36 admissions and 21 skate rentals. The other group pays $81 for 12 admissions and 7 skate rentals. Let x represent the cost of admission and let y represent the cost of a skate rental. Is there enough information to find values for x and y? Explain.

No; there are infinitely many solutions to the system.

17. **Represent Real-World Problems** Juan and Tory are practicing for a track meet. They start their practice runs at the same point, but Tory starts 1 minute after Juan. Both run at a speed of 704 feet per minute. Does Tory catch up to Juan? Explain.

No; both Juan and Tory run at the same rate, so the lines representing the distances each has run are parallel. There is no solution to the system.

H.O.T. FOCUS ON HIGHER ORDER THINKING

Work Area

18. **Justify Reasoning** A linear system with no solution consists of the equation $y = 4x - 3$ and a second equation of the form $y = mx + b$. What can you say about the values of m and b? Explain your reasoning.

$m = 4$ and $b \neq -3$; The graphs of the lines must be parallel and thus must have the same slope, so $m = 4$. The y-intercepts must be different because two equations with the same slope and the same y-intercept are the same line, so $b \neq -3$.

19. **Justify Reasoning** A linear system with infinitely many solutions consists of the equation $3x + 5 = 8$ and a second equation of the form $Ax + By = C$. What can you say about the values of A, B, and C? Explain your reasoning.

A, B, and C must all be the same multiple of 3, 5, and 8, respectively. The two equations represent a single line, so the coefficients and constants of one equation must be a multiple of the other.

20. **Draw Conclusions** Both the points $(2, -2)$ and $(4, -4)$ are solutions of a system of linear equations. What conclusions can you make about the equations and their graphs?

The linear system has more than one solution, so the lines coincide. There are infinitely many solutions.

EXTEND THE MATH PRE-AP

Activity available online ⊙ my.hrw.com

Activity For each of the following systems, find the value or values for a and b that make the system have no solution.

1) $\begin{cases} 3x - y = -4 \\ y = ax + b \end{cases}$
2) $\begin{cases} -x + ay = 0 \\ -2x + 8y = b \end{cases}$
3) $\begin{cases} x = a \\ y = b \end{cases}$

1) a must have a value of 3; b can have any value except 4.

2) a must have a value of 4; b can have any value except 0.

3) This system will have exactly one solution for any possible values of a and b.

Ready to Go On?

Assess Mastery

Use the assessment on this page to determine if students have mastered the concepts and standards covered in this module.

 **Response to Intervention**

Intervention	Enrichment

Access Ready to Go On? assessment online, and receive instant scoring, feedback, and customized intervention or enrichment.

Online and Print Resources

Differentiated Instruction
• Reteach worksheets
• Reading Strategies **ELL**
• Success for English Learners **ELL**

Differentiated Instruction
• Challenge worksheets **PRE-AP**
• Extend the Math **PRE-AP** Lesson Activities in TE

Additional Resources

Assessment Resources includes:
• Leveled Module Quizzes

Ready to Go On?

16.1 Solving Systems of Linear Equations by Graphing

Solve each system by graphing.

1. $\begin{cases} y = x - 1 \\ y = 2x - 3 \end{cases}$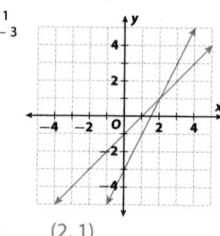

____(2, 1)____

2. $\begin{cases} x + 2y = 1 \\ -x + y = 2 \end{cases}$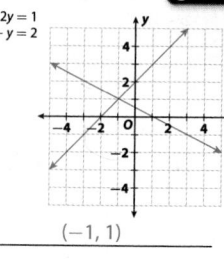

____(−1, 1)____

16.2 Solving Systems by Substitution

Solve each system of equations by substitution.

3. $\begin{cases} y = 2x \\ x + y = -9 \end{cases}$ ____(−3, −6)____

4. $\begin{cases} 3x - 2y = 11 \\ x + 2y = 9 \end{cases}$ ____(5, 2)____

16.3 Solving Systems by Elimination

Solve each system of equations by adding or subtracting.

5. $\begin{cases} 3x + y = 9 \\ 2x + y = 5 \end{cases}$ ____(4, −3)____

6. $\begin{cases} -x - 2y = 4 \\ 3x + 2y = 4 \end{cases}$ ____(4, −4)____

16.4 Solving Systems by Elimination with Multiplication

Solve each system of equations by multiplying first.

7. $\begin{cases} x + 3y = -2 \\ 3x + 4y = -1 \end{cases}$ ____(1, −1)____

8. $\begin{cases} 2x + 8y = 22 \\ 3x - 2y = 5 \end{cases}$ ____(3, 2)____

16.5 Solving Special Systems

Solve each system. Tell how many solutions each system has.

9. $\begin{cases} -2x + 8y = 5 \\ x - 4y = -3 \end{cases}$ ____no solution____

10. $\begin{cases} 6x + 18y = -12 \\ x + 3y = -2 \end{cases}$ ____infinitely many____

 **ESSENTIAL QUESTION**

11. What are the possible solutions to a system of linear equations, and what do they represent graphically?

No solution: parallel lines; one solution: intersecting lines;

infinitely many solutions: same line

 ## Florida Common Core Standards

Lesson	Exercises	Common Core Standards
16.1	1–2	**8.EE.3.8a, 8.EE.3.8c**
16.2	3–4	**8.EE.3.8b, 8.EE.3.8c**
16.3	5–6	**8.EE.3.8b, 8.EE.3.8c**
16.4	7–8	**8.EE.3.8b, 8.EE.3.8c**
16.5	9–10	**8.EE.3.8b, 8.EE.3.8c**

PARCC Assessment Readiness

Assessment Readiness Tip Some items are only solvable by examining the answer choices in turn and eliminating incorrect choices.

Item 5 Several different substitutions are possible. Rather than trying to identify every possible substitution, it is quicker and easier to examine each answer choice and eliminate the choices that are incorrect. Students will be left with answer choice D as the only correct substitution.

Item 7 A variety of first steps are possible—there are several different substitutions as well as a few different ways to set up the equations for elimination. Students should examine the answer choices and use the process of elimination rather than trying to identify all possible first steps.

Avoid Common Errors

Item 2 Students may notice that the coefficients of the variables are different in the two equations, and therefore assume that they represent lines with different slopes that intersect in one place. Remind them that the slope is not equal to either of the coefficients unless the equations are in slope-intercept form.

Item 8 Students are likely to write the equations representing the situation in slope-intercept form, and may be uncertain how to proceed. Point out that with both equations in slope-intercept form, they can immediately substitute for y in one equation without any further manipulation of the equations.

Additional Resources

Personal Math Trainer
Online Assessment and Intervention
my.hrw.com

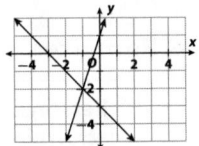
Personal Math Trainer
Online Assessment and Intervention
my.hrw.com

Selected Response

1. The graph of which equation is shown?

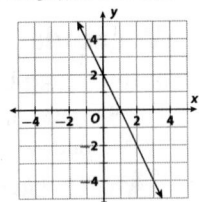

- Ⓐ $y = -2x + 2$ Ⓒ $y = 2x + 2$
- Ⓑ $y = -x + 2$ Ⓓ $y = 2x + 1$

2. Which best describes the solutions to the system $\begin{cases} x + y = -4 \\ -2x - 2y = 0 \end{cases}$?

- Ⓐ one solution   Ⓒ infinitely many
- Ⓑ no solution   Ⓓ (0, 0)

3. Which of the following represents 0.000056023 written in scientific notation?

- Ⓐ 5.6023×10^5 Ⓒ 5.6023×10^{-4}
- Ⓑ 5.6023×10^4 Ⓓ 5.6023×10^{-5}

4. Which is the solution to $\begin{cases} 2x - y = 1 \\ 4x + y = 11 \end{cases}$?

- Ⓐ (2, 3)   Ⓒ (−2, 3)
- Ⓑ (3, 2)   Ⓓ (3, −2)

5. Which expression can you substitute in the indicated equation to solve $\begin{cases} 3x - y = 5 \\ x + 2y = 4 \end{cases}$?

- Ⓐ $2y - 4$ for x in $3x - y = 5$
- Ⓑ $4 - x$ for y in $3x - y = 5$
- Ⓒ $3x - 5$ for y in $3x - y = 5$
- Ⓓ $3x - 5$ for y in $x + 2y = 4$

6. What is the solution to the system of linear equations shown on the graph?

- Ⓐ −1   Ⓒ (−1, −2)
- Ⓑ −2   Ⓓ (−2, −1)

7. Which step could you use to start solving $\begin{cases} x - 6y = 8 \\ 2x - 5y = 3 \end{cases}$?

- Ⓐ Add $2x - 5y = 3$ to $x - 6y = 8$.
- Ⓑ Multiply $x - 6y = 8$ by 2 and add it to $2x - 5y = 3$.
- Ⓒ Multiply $x - 6y = 8$ by 2 and subtract it from $2x - 5y = 3$.
- Ⓓ Substitute $x = 6y - 8$ for x in $2x - 5y = 3$.

Mini-Task

8. A hot-air balloon begins rising from the ground at 4 meters per second at the same time as a parachutist's chute opens at a height of 200 meters. The parachutist descends at 6 meters per second.

a. Define the variables and write a system that represents the situation.

y is the height in meters and x is the time in seconds; $\begin{cases} y = 4x \\ y = 200 - 6x \end{cases}$

b. Find the solution. What does it mean?

20 s, 80 m; the time when the balloon and parachutist are the same height

© Houghton Mifflin Harcourt Publishing Company

Florida Common Core Standards

Items	Grade 8 Standards	Mathematical Practices
1*	8.F.2.4	MP.4.1
2	8.EE.3.8b	MP.2.1
3*	8.EE.1.3	MP.2.1
4	8.EE.3.8b	MP.2.1
5	8.EE.3.8b	MP.2.1
6	8.EE.3.8a	MP.2.1
7	8.EE.3.8b	MP.2.1
8	8.EE.3.8c	MP.4.1

* Item integrates mixed review concepts from previous modules or a previous course.

Study Guide Review

Vocabulary Development

Integrating Language Arts

Encourage students to practice using the unit vocabulary as they talk and write about mathematics. Understanding vocabulary will aid their understanding of the concepts.

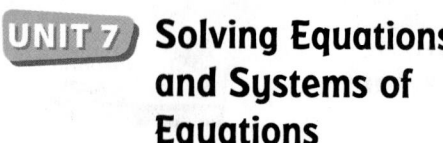 **LACC.68.RST.2.4** Determine the meaning of symbols, key terms, and other domain-specific words and phrases as they are used in a specific scientific or technical context relevant to grades 6–8 texts and topics.

MODULE 15 Solving Linear Equations

FL CC 8.EE.3.7, 8.EE.3.7a, 8.EE.3.7b

Key Concepts

• To solve an equation or inequality with the same variable on both sides of the equal sign, add or subtract to eliminate the variable term from one side of the equation or inequality. *(Lesson 15.1)*

• To eliminate fractions from an equation or inequality, multiply every term by the least common multiple of the denominators to create an equivalent equation or inequality. *(Lesson 15.2)*

• To eliminate decimals from an equation or inequality, multiply every term by a power of 10 to eliminate the decimals and create an equivalent equation or inequality. *(Lesson 15.2)*

• To solve an equation containing an expression in parentheses multiplied by a factor, use the Distributive Property to distribute the factor and eliminate the parentheses. *(Lesson 15.3)*

• Linear equations can have one solution, infinitely many solutions, or, if there is no value of x that makes the equation true, no solution. *(Lesson 15.4)*

Study Guide Review

MODULE 15 Solving Linear Equations

? ESSENTIAL QUESTION

How can you use equations with variables on both sides to solve real-world problems?

EXAMPLE 1

A tutor gives students a choice of how to pay: a base rate of $20 plus $8 per hour, or a set rate of $13 per hour. Find the number of hours of tutoring for which the cost is the same for either choice.

Plan 1 cost: $20 + 8x$ Plan 2 cost: $13x$

$$20 + 8x = 13x \qquad \text{Write the equation.}$$
$$\underline{-8x \quad -8x} \qquad \text{Subtract 8x from both sides.}$$
$$20 = 5x \qquad \text{Divide both sides by 5.}$$
$$x = 4$$

The cost is the same for 4 hours of tutoring.

EXAMPLE 2

Solve $-2.4(3x + 5) = 0.8(x + 3.5)$.

$$-2.4(3x + 5) = 0.8(x + 3.5)$$
$$10(-2.4)(3x + 5) = 10(0.8)(x + 3.5) \qquad \text{Multiply each side by 10 to clear some decimals.}$$
$$-24(3x + 5) = 8(x + 3.5)$$
$$-24(3x) - 24(5) = 8(x) + 8(3.5) \qquad \text{Apply the Distributive Property.}$$
$$-72x - 120 = 8x + 28$$
$$\underline{-8x \qquad -8x} \qquad \text{Subtract 8x from both sides of the equation.}$$
$$-80x - 120 = 28$$
$$\underline{+ 120 \quad + 120} \qquad \text{Add 120 to both sides of the equation.}$$
$$-80x = 148$$
$$\frac{-80x}{-80} = \frac{148}{-80} \qquad \text{Divide both sides of the equation by -80.}$$
$$x = -1.85$$

EXAMPLE 3

Solve $4(3x - 6) = 2(6x - 5)$.

$$4(3x - 6) = 2(6x - 5)$$
$$12x - 24 = 12x - 10 \qquad \text{Apply the Distributive Property.}$$
$$\underline{-12x \qquad -12x} \qquad \text{Subtract 8x from both sides of the equation.}$$
$$-24 = -10 \qquad \text{The statement is false.}$$

There is no value of x that makes a true statement. Therefore, this equation has no solution.

EXERCISES

Solve. (Lessons 15.1, 15.2, 15.3, 15.4)

1. $13 - 6y = 8y$ ___ $y = 0.93$ ___

2. $\frac{1}{5}x + 5 = 19 - \frac{1}{2}x$ ___ $x = 20$ ___

3. $7.3t + 22 = 2.1t - 22.2$ ___ $t = -8.5$ ___

4. $1.4 + \frac{2}{5}e = \frac{3}{15}e - 0.8$ ___ $e = -11$ ___

5. $5(x - 4) = 2(x + 5)$ ___ $x = 10$ ___

6. $-7(3 + t) = 4(2t + 6)$ ___ $t = -3$ ___

7. $\frac{3}{4}(x + 8) = \frac{1}{3}(x + 27)$ ___ $x = 7\frac{1}{5}$ ___

8. $3(4x - 8) = \frac{1}{5}(35x + 30)$ ___ $x = 6$ ___

9. $-1.6(2y + 15) = -1.2(2y - 10)$

10. $9(4a - 2) = 12(3a + 8)$

___ $y = -45$ ___ ___ no solution ___

11. $6(x - \frac{1}{3}) = -2(x + 23)$

12. $8(p - 0.25) = 4(2p - 0.5)$

___ $x = -5\frac{1}{2}$ ___ ___ infinitely many solutions ___

13. Write a real-world situation that could be modeled by the equation $650 + 10m = 60m + 400$. (Lesson 15.1)

Sample answer: Jill and Sam are both putting money in their savings accounts. Jill starts with $650 and puts in $10 a month. Sam starts with $400 and puts in $60 a month. After how many months will Jill and Sam have the same amount in their accounts?

MODULE 16 Solving Systems of Linear Equations

FL CC 8.EE.3.8, 8.EE.3.8a, 8.EE.3.8b, 8.EE.3.8c

Key Concepts

- To solve a system of equations by graphing, find the point of intersection. *(Lesson 16.1)*
- To solve a system of equations by substitution, rewrite one equation as an expression that represents one variable and substitute this expression into the other equation. *(Lesson 16.2)*
- To solve a system of equations by elimination, begin by adding or subtracting the equations in such a way that a variable is eliminated. The equations can first be multiplied by a constant. *(Lessons 16.3, 16.4)*
- Some systems of equations may have no solution or an infinite number of solutions. *(Lesson 16.5)*

Unit 7 Performance Tasks

The Performance Tasks provide students with the opportunity to apply concepts from this unit in real-world problem situations.

CAREERS IN MATH

Hydraulic Engineer In Performance Task Item 1, students can see how a hydraulic engineer uses mathematics on the job.

SCORING GUIDES FOR PERFORMANCE TASKS

1. **MATHEMATICAL PRACTICES**   **FL CC** MP.2.1, MP.3.1, MP.4.1

Task	Possible Points (Total: 6)
a	**1 point** for a correct expression: $101 + 8d_2$
b	**1 point** for the equation $200 = 101 + 8d_1$ and **1 point** for the correct answer $d_1 = 12.375$ m
c	**1 point** for the correct expression: $101 + 9d_2$
d	**1 point** for an explanation, for example, since the pressures are equal, set the two expressions equal to each other; and **1 point** for the answer: $d_1 = \frac{9}{8}d_2$; d_1 is $\frac{9}{8}$ times d_2, or $d_2 = \frac{8}{9}d_1$

CAREERS IN MATH

For more information about careers in mathematics as well as various mathematics appreciation topics, visit the American Mathematical Society at www.ams.org

Solving Systems of Linear Equations

Key Vocabulary
solution of a system of equations *(solución de un sistema de desigualdades)*
system of equations *(sistema de ecuaciones)*

? ESSENTIAL QUESTION

How can you use systems of equations to solve real-world problems?

EXAMPLE 1 Solve the system of equations by substitution.

$$\begin{cases} 3x + y = 7 \\ x + y = 3 \end{cases}$$

Step 1 Solve an equation for one variable.

$$3x + y = 7$$
$$y = -3x + 7$$

Step 2 Substitute the expression for y in the other equation and solve.

$$x + y = 3$$
$$x + (-3x + 7) = 3$$
$$-2x + 7 = 3$$
$$-2x = -4$$
$$x = 2$$

Step 3 Substitute the value of x into one of the equations and solve for the other variable, y.

$$x + y = 3$$
$$2 + y = 3$$
$$y = 1$$

$(2, 1)$ is the solution of the system.

EXAMPLE 2 Solve the system of equations by elimination.

$$\begin{cases} x + y = 8 \\ 2x - 3y = 1 \end{cases}$$

Step 1 Multiply the first equation by 3 and add this new equation to the second equation.

$$3(x + y = 8) = 3x + 3y = 24$$
$$3x + 3y = 24$$
$$\underline{2x - 3y = 1}$$
$$5x + 0y = 25$$
$$5x = 25$$
$$x = 5$$

Step 2 Substitute the solution into one of the original equations and solve for y.

$$x + y = 8$$
$$5 + y = 8$$
$$y = 3$$

$(5, 3)$ is the solution of the system.

EXERCISES

Solve each system of linear equations. (Lessons 16.1, 16.2, 16.3, 16.4, and 16.5)

14. $\begin{cases} x + y = -2 \\ 2x - y = 5 \end{cases}$
$(1, -3)$

15. $\begin{cases} y = 2x + 1 \\ x + 2y = 17 \end{cases}$
$(3, 7)$

16. $\begin{cases} y = -2x - 3 \\ 2x + y = 9 \end{cases}$
no solution

17. $\begin{cases} y = 5 - x \\ 2x + 2y = 10 \end{cases}$
infinitely many solutions

18. $\begin{cases} 2x - y = 26 \\ 3x - 2y = 42 \end{cases}$
$(10, -6)$

19. $\begin{cases} 2x + 3y = 11 \\ 5x - 2y = 18 \end{cases}$
$(4, 1)$

20. Last week Andrew bought 3 pounds of zucchini and 2 pounds of tomatoes for $7.05 at a farm stand. This week he bought 4 pounds of zucchini and 3 pounds of tomatoes, at the same prices, for $9.83. What is the cost of 1 pound of zucchini and 1 pound of tomatoes at the farm stand?

Zucchini: $1.49 per pound, tomatoes: $1.29 per pound

Unit 7 Performance Tasks

1. **CAREERS IN MATH** Hydraulic Engineer A hydraulic engineer is studying the pressure in a particular fluid. The pressure is equal to the atmospheric pressure 101 kN/m plus 8 kN/m for every meter below the surface, where kN/m is kilonewtons per meter, a unit of pressure.

a. Write an expression for the pressure at a depth of d_1 meters below the liquid surface.
$101 + 8d_1$

b. Write and solve an equation to find the depth at which the pressure is 200 kN/m.
$200 = 101 + 8d_1$, $99 = 8d_1$, $d_1 = \frac{99}{8} = 12.375$; $d_1 = 12.375$ m

c. The hydraulic engineer alters the density of the fluid so that the pressure at depth d_2 below the surface is atmospheric pressure 101 kN/m plus 9 kN/m for every meter below the surface. Write an expression for the pressure at depth d_2.
$101 + 9d_2$

d. If the pressure at depth d_1 in the first fluid is equal to the pressure at depth d_2 in the second fluid, what is the relationship between d_1 and d_2? Explain how you found your answer.
Since the pressures are equal, set the two expressions equal to each other: $101 + 8d_1 = 101 + 9d_2$. Then solve for d_1: $d_1 = \frac{9}{8}d_2$. This means that d_1 is $\frac{9}{8}$ times d_2.

MIXED REVIEW

PARCC Assessment Readiness

Assessment Readiness Tip Students can work backwards by using the answer choices to solve problems.

Item 5 After reading the problem, students know that Alana bought a total of 5 rolls of streamers and 3 packages of balloons for a total of $16.25. Using the answer choices, students can multiply the number of streamers by the cost, then the number of balloons by the cost, combining them to see which will give a total of $16.25.

Avoid Common Errors

Item 6 Some students will forget to consider the sides not labeled in the rectangle when finding the perimeter. Remind students that there are two bases and two heights, so the expressions $2x - 1$ and $x + 7$ will each be used twice when writing an expression for the perimeter of the rectangle.

 Florida Common Core Standards

Items	Grade 8 Standards	Mathematical Practices
1*	8.F.2.4	MP.4.1
2	8.EE.3.7, 8.EE.3.7b	MP.4.1
3*	8.EE.2.6, 8.F.2.4	MP.2.1
4	8.EE.3.8, 8.EE.3.8b	MP.4.1
5	8.EE.3.8, 8.EE.3.8b, 8.EE.3.8c	MP.2.1
6	8.EE.3.7, 8.EE.3.7b	MP.7.1
7	8.EE.3.7b	MP.2.1
8*	8.NS.1.1	MP.4.1
9	8.EE.3.8b, 8.EE.3.8c	MP.2.1
10	8.EE.3.8a	MP.3.1
11	8.EE.3.7b	MP.4.1

* Item integrates mixed review concepts from previous modules or a previous course.

PARCC Assessment Readiness

Personal Math Trainer
Online Assessment and Intervention
my.hrw.com

Selected Response

1. Ricardo and John start swimming from the same location. Ricardo starts 15 seconds before John and swims at a rate of 3 feet per second. John swims at a rate of 4 feet per second in the same direction as Ricardo. Which equation could you solve to find how long it will take John to catch up with Ricardo?

Ⓐ $4t + 3 = 3t$

Ⓑ $4t + 60 = 3t$

Ⓒ $3t + 3 = 4t$

Ⓓ $3t + 45 = 4t$

2. Gina and Rhonda work for different real estate agencies. Gina earns a monthly salary of $5,000 plus a 6% commission on her sales. Rhonda earns a monthly salary of $6,500 plus a 4% commission on her sales. How much must each sell to earn the same amount in a month?

Ⓐ $1,500   Ⓒ $75,000

Ⓑ $15,000   Ⓓ $750,000

3. What is the slope of the line?

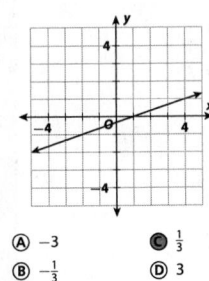

Ⓐ −3   Ⓒ $\frac{1}{3}$

Ⓑ $-\frac{1}{3}$ Ⓓ 3

4. What is the solution of the system of equations?

$$\begin{cases} y = 2x - 3 \\ 5x + y = 11 \end{cases}$$

Ⓐ (2, 1)

Ⓑ (1, 2)

Ⓒ (3, −4)

Ⓓ (1, −1)

5. Alana is having a party. She bought 3 rolls of streamers and 2 packages of balloons for $10.00. She realized she needed more supplies and went back to the store and bought 2 more rolls of streamers and 1 more package of balloons for $6.25. How much did each roll of streamers and each package of balloons cost?

Ⓐ streamers: $3.00, balloons: $2.00

Ⓑ streamers: $2.00, balloons: $1.00

Ⓒ streamers: $1.25, balloons: $2.50

Ⓓ streamers: $2.50, balloons: $1.25

6. The triangle and the rectangle have the same perimeter.

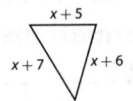 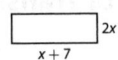

Find the value of x.

Ⓐ 2

Ⓑ 10

Ⓒ 18

Ⓓ 24

7. What is the solution of the equation $8(3x + 4) = 2(12x - 8)$?

Ⓐ $x = -2$

Ⓑ $x = 2$

Ⓒ no solution

Ⓓ infinitely many solutions

8. A square wall tile has an area of 58,800 square millimeters. Between which two measurements is the length of one side?

Ⓐ between 24 and 25 millimeters

Ⓑ between 76 and 77 millimeters

Ⓒ between 242 and 243 millimeters

Ⓓ between 766 and 767 millimeters

Mini-Tasks

9. Lily and Alex went to a Mexican restaurant. Lily paid $9 for 2 tacos and 3 enchiladas, and Alex paid $12.50 for 3 tacos and 4 enchiladas.

a. Write a system of equations that represents this situation.

$2t + 3e = 9$

$3t + 4e = 12.50$

b. Use the system of equations to find how much the restaurant charges for a taco and for an enchilada.

enchilada: $2, taco: $1.50

c. Describe the method you used to solve the system of equations.

Sample answer: Multiply the first equation by 3 and the second by −2, then add. Solve for e, then substitute and solve for t.

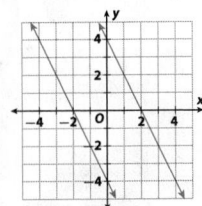
Hot Tip! Solutions of a system of two equations must make both equations true. Check solutions in both equations.

10. Use the system of equations to answer the questions below.

$$\begin{cases} 4x + 2y = -8 \\ 2x + y = 4 \end{cases}$$

a. Graph the equations on the grid.

b. How many solutions does the system of equations have? Explain your answer.

The system of equations has no solution. The lines never intersect.

11. Isaac wants to join a gym. He checked out the membership fees at two gyms.

Gym A charges a new member fee of $65 and $20 per month.

Gym B charges a new member fee of $25 and $35 per month, but Isaac will get a discount of 20% on the monthly fee.

a. Write an equation you can use to find the number of months for which the total costs at the gyms are the same.

$65 + 20m = 25 + (1 - 0.20)35m$

b. Solve the equation to find the number of months for which the total costs of the gyms are the same.

$m = 5$, so after 5 months, the total costs of the two gyms are the same.

UNIT 8

Transformational Geometry

Contents

Unit Pacing Guide

45-Minute Classes

Module 17

DAY 1	DAY 2	DAY 3	DAY 4	DAY 5
Lesson 17.1	Lesson 17.1	Lesson 17.2	Lesson 17.2	Lesson 17.3

DAY 6	DAY 7	DAY 8	DAY 9	DAY 10
Lesson 17.3	Lesson 17.4	Lesson 17.4	Lesson 17.5	Ready to Go On? PARCC Assessment Readiness

Module 18

DAY 1	DAY 2	DAY 3	DAY 4	DAY 5
Lesson 18.1	Lesson 18.1	Lesson 18.2	Lesson 18.2	Lesson 18.3

DAY 6	DAY 7	DAY 8		
Lesson 18.3	Ready to Go On? PARCC Assessment Readiness	Study Guide PARCC Assessment Readiness		

90-Minute Classes

Module 17

DAY 1	DAY 2	DAY 3	DAY 4	DAY 5
Lesson 17.1	Lesson 17.2	Lesson 17.3	Lesson 17.4	Lesson 17.5 Ready to Go On? PARCC Assessment Readiness

Module 18

DAY 1	DAY 2	DAY 3	DAY 4	
Lesson 18.1	Lesson 18.2	Lesson 18.3	Ready to Go On? PARCC Assessment Readiness	Study Guide PARCC Assessment Readiness

Program Resources

⏻ Plan

Online Teacher Edition

Access a full suite of teaching resources online—plan, present, and manage classes, assignments, and activities.

ePlanner Easily plan your classes, create and view assignments, and access all program resources with your online, customizable planning tool.

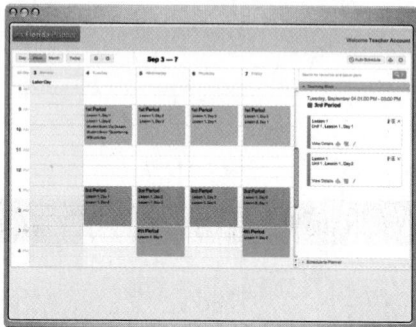

Professional Development Videos

Author Juli Dixon models successful teaching practices and strategies in actual classroom settings.

QR Codes Scan with your smart phone to jump directly from your print book to online videos and other resources.

Teacher's Edition

Support students with point-of-use Questioning Strategies, teaching tips, resources for differentiated instruction, additional activities, and more.

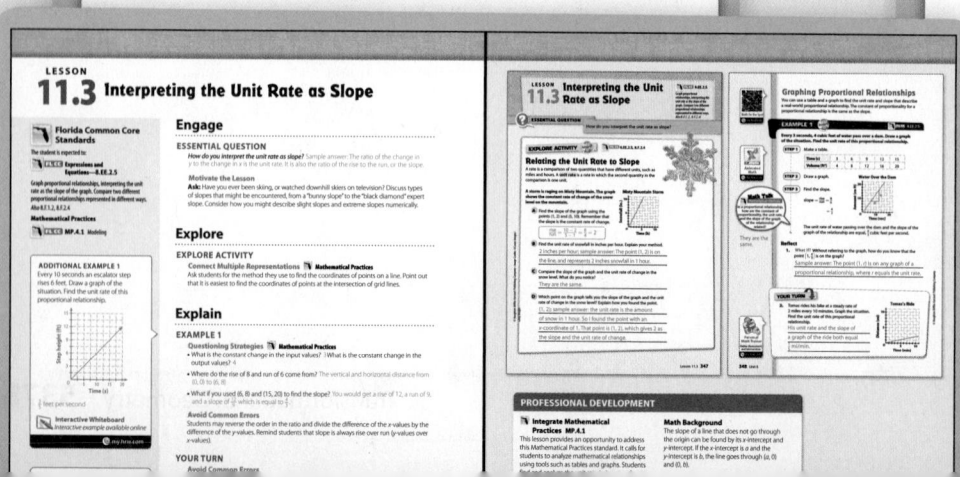

⏻ Engage and Explore

Real-World Videos Engage students with interesting and relevant applications of the mathematical content of each module.

Animated Math Online interactive simulations, tools, and games help students actively learn and practice key concepts.

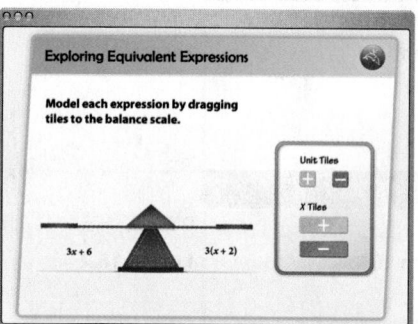

Explore Activities

Students interactively explore new concepts using a variety of tools and approaches.

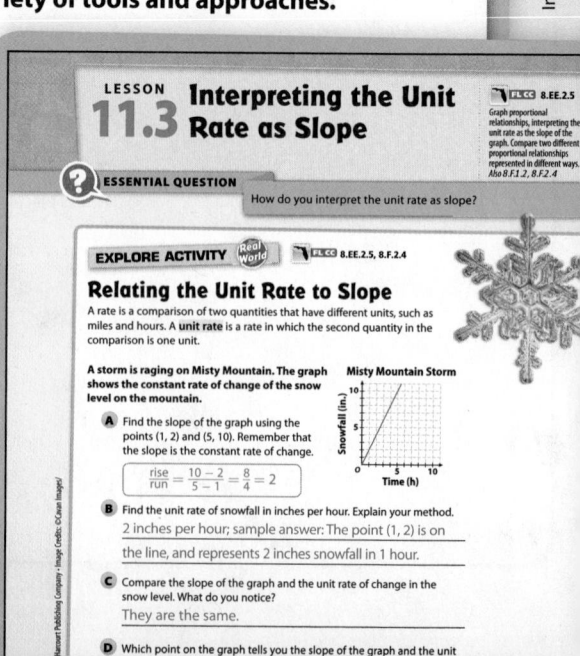

⏻ Teach

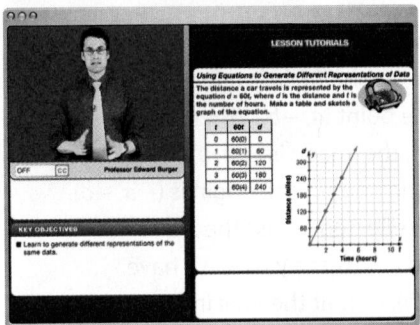

Math On the Spot video tutorials, featuring program authors Dr. Edward Burger and Martha Sandoval-Martinez, accompany every example in the textbook and give students step-by-step instructions and explanations of key math concepts.

Present engaging content on a multitude of devices, including tablets and interactive whiteboards.

 Continually monitor and assess student progress with integrated formative assessment.

 Look for exercises indicated with this icon to build connections among standards within Florida Common Core clusters.

Differentiated Instruction Print Resources

Support all learners with Differentiated Instruction Resources, including

- **Leveled Practice and Problem Solving**
- **Reteach**
- **Reading Strategies**
- **Success for English Learners**
- **Challenge**

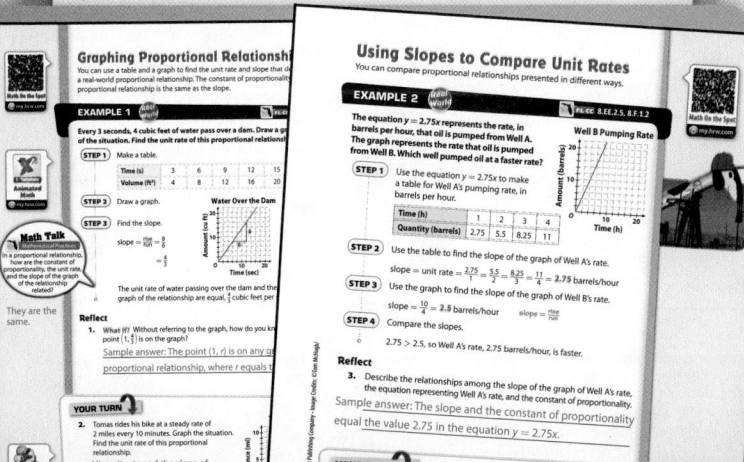

⏻ Assessment and Intervention

The **Personal Math Trainer** provides online practice, homework, assessments, and intervention. Monitor student progress through reports and alerts. Create and customize assignments aligned to specific lessons or standards.

- **Practice** – With dynamic items and assignments, students get unlimited practice on key concepts supported by guided examples, step-by-step solutions, and video tutorials.
- **Assessments** – Choose from course assignments or customize your own based on course content, standards, difficulty levels, and more.
- **Homework** – Students can complete online homework with a wide variety of problem types, including the ability to enter expressions, equations, and graphs. Let the system automatically grade homework, so you can focus where your students need help the most!
- **Intervention** – Let the Personal Math Trainer automatically prescribe a targeted, personalized intervention path for your students.

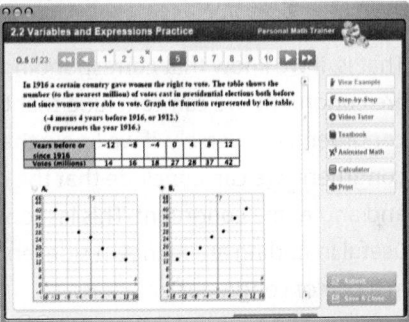

 Raise the bar with homework and practice that incorporates higher-order thinking and mathematical processes in every lesson.

 **PARCC Assessment Readiness**
Prepare students for success on the PARCC math test with practice at every module and unit.

Assessment Resources

Tailor assessments to meet the needs of all your classes and students, including

- **Leveled Module Quizzes**
- **Leveled Unit Tests**
- **Unit Performance Tasks**
- **Placement, Diagnostic, and Quarterly Benchmark Tests**

Math Background

Transformations and Congruence

8.G.1.1, 8.G.1.2, 8.G.1.3
LESSONS 17.1 to 17.5

Loosely speaking, two figures are congruent if they have exactly the same size and shape. Providing a more precise definition of congruence depends on first defining congruence for two of the most basic geometric figures—line segments and angles.

- Two line segments are congruent if they have the same length.
- Two angles are congruent if they have the same measure.

These definitions can be used to build a definition of congruence for polygons. Two polygons are congruent if their sides and angles can be paired so that all of the corresponding pairs of sides and angles are congruent. Note that this definition may be used in two directions. That is, if we know that corresponding sides and angles are congruent, we can conclude that the polygons are congruent. Conversely, if we know that two polygons are congruent, we can conclude that the corresponding sides and angles are congruent. This last observation is often useful in finding an unknown side length or angle measure in a pair of congruent polygons.

Students learn three basic transformations: translations, reflections, and rotations. These transformations are closely connected to the concept of congruence. In particular, the image of any figure under a translation, reflection, or rotation is congruent to the original figure (called the pre-image). These "rigid" transformations preserve the size and shape of figures, and are also known as *isometries*.

Transformations can also be used to define congruence. That is, two figures are congruent if one figure can be transformed into the other through a sequence of translations, reflections, and rotations. This matches our intuitive notion of congruence: given two congruent paper triangles, one triangle may be made to fit exactly on top of the other by sliding, flipping, and turning the paper.

It is instructive to examine transformations on a coordinate plane. For example, when a point (a, b) is reflected across the x-axis, the image is the point $(a, -b)$. When (a, b) is reflected across the y-axis, the image is $(-a, b)$. The image of (a, b) under a $180°$ rotation about the origin is $(-a, -b)$. Notice that when (a, b) is reflected across the x-axis and the image is reflected across the y-axis, we have $(a, b) \rightarrow (a, -b) \rightarrow (-a, -b)$, so that the final image is the same as the image of (a, b) under a $180°$ rotation. In other words, successive reflections across the two axes are equivalent to a single $180°$ rotation about the origin.

Dilations and Similar Figures 8.G.1.3, 8.G.1.4
LESSONS 18.1 to 18.3

Similar figures have the same shape but not necessarily the same size. One way to create similar figures is by performing a sequence of transformations that includes a *dilation* on a figure. A dilation is a transformation in which the lines connecting every point P with its image P' all intersect at a point C known as the center of dilation. In addition, the ratio $\frac{CP'}{CP}$ is the same for all points P. In the figure below, for example, $\triangle D'E'F'$ is a dilation of $\triangle DEF$.

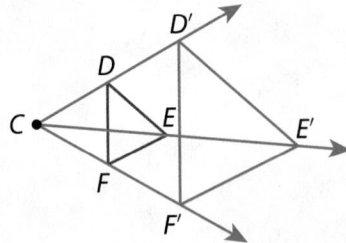

Unlike rigid transformations (translations, reflections, and rotations), dilations may change the size of the pre-image. Dilations are unique among the transformations because they have a scale factor that describes whether the image is a reduction or enlargement of the pre-image.

If the scale factor k is between 0 and 1, the image is a reduction of the pre-image. If the scale factor k is greater than 1, the image is an enlargement of the pre-image. Though uncommon, the scale factor k can be 1. In this case, the image is congruent to the pre-image.

In Grade 8, students study dilations in the coordinate plane with centers located at the origin. This means that for each pre-image point $P(x, y)$, its image after a dilation with scale factor k is $P'(kx, ky)$.

UNIT 8

Transformational Geometry

MODULE 17
Transformations and Congruence

FL CC 8.G.1.1, 8.G.1.2, 8.G.1.3

MODULE 18
Transformations and Similarity

FL CC 8.G.1.3, 8.G.1.4

CAREERS IN MATH

Contractor A contractor is engaged in the construction, repair, and dismantling of structures such as buildings, bridges, and roads. Contractors use math when researching and implementing building codes, making measurements and scaling models, and in financial management.

If you are interested in a career as a contractor, you should study the following mathematical subjects:
- Business Math
- Geometry
- Algebra
- Trigonometry

Research other careers that require the use of business math and scaling.

Unit 8 Performance Task

At the end of the unit, check out how **contractors** use math.

Careers in Math

Contractor

In addition to a hammer and saw, a contractor needs mathematical tools to figure out the amount of materials needed for a job and their cost, to compute areas and volumes, and to determine wages and other expenses. You will learn more about working as a contractor in the Performance Tasks at the end of the unit.

For more information about careers in mathematics as well as various mathematics appreciation topics, visit the American Mathematical Society at www.ams.org

Vocabulary Preview

Use the puzzle to give students a preview of important concepts in this unit. Students may work individually, in pairs, or in groups.

Unit Resources

Go online to access all your unit resources.

my.hrw.com

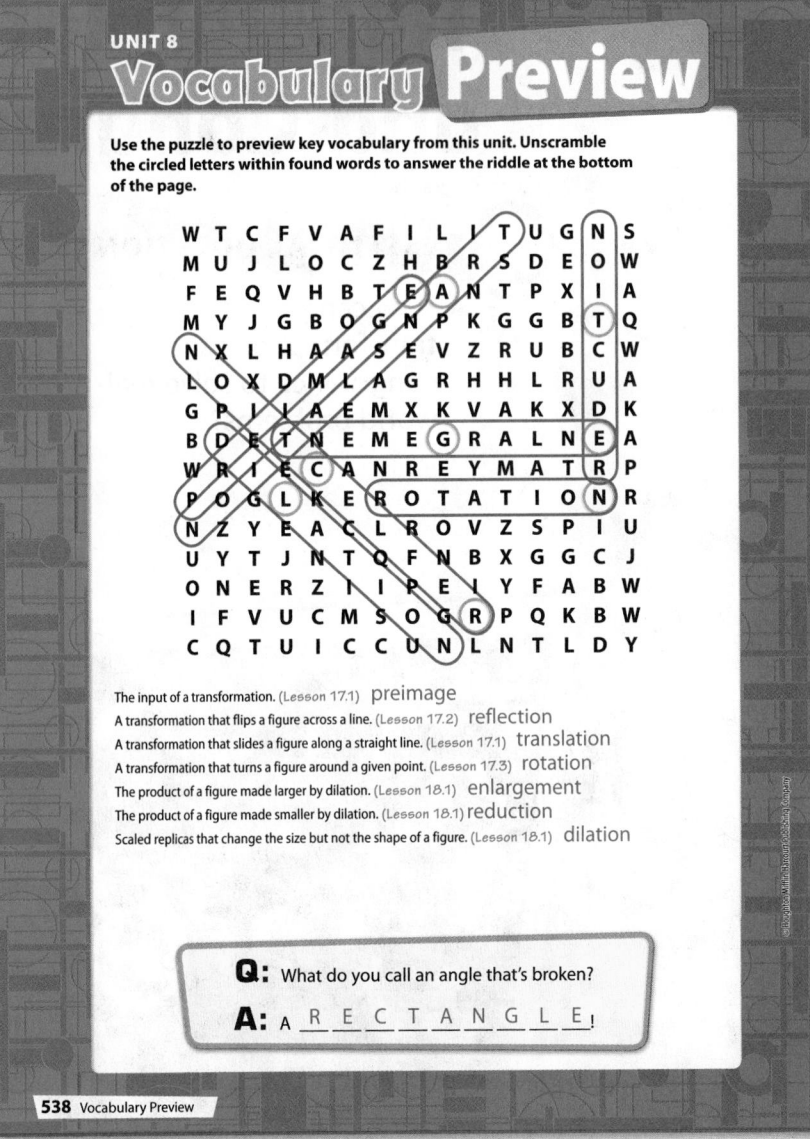

Vocabulary Preview

Use the puzzle to preview key vocabulary from this unit. Unscramble the circled letters within found words to answer the riddle at the bottom of the page.

```
W T C F V A F I L I T U G N S
M U J L O C Z H B R S D E O W
F E Q V H B T E A N T P X I A
M Y J G B O G N P K G G B T Q
N X L H A A S E V Z R U B C W
L O X D M L A G R H H L R U A
G P I I A E M X K V A K X D K
B D E T N E M E G R A L N E A
W R I E C A N R E Y M A T R P
P O G L K E R O T A T I O N R
N Z Y E A C L R O V Z S P I U
U Y T J N T Q F N B X G G C J
O N E R Z I I P E L Y F A B W
I F V U C M S O G R P Q K B W
C Q T U I C C U N L N T L D Y
```

The input of a transformation. (Lesson 17.1) preimage
A transformation that flips a figure across a line. (Lesson 17.2) reflection
A transformation that slides a figure along a straight line. (Lesson 17.1) translation
A transformation that turns a figure around a given point. (Lesson 17.3) rotation
The product of a figure made larger by dilation. (Lesson 18.1) enlargement
The product of a figure made smaller by dilation. (Lesson 18.1) reduction
Scaled replicas that change the size but not the shape of a figure. (Lesson 18.1) dilation

Q: What do you call an angle that's broken?

A: A R E C T A N G L E !

Before	In this Unit	After
Students understand: • how to classify and draw plane figures • how to graph plane figures on the coordinate plane • congruence and similarity	Students will learn about: • effects of transformations • translations • reflections • rotations • dilations • transformations in the coordinate plane	Students will connect: • transformations and dilations with graphic design, art, photography, and scale drawings • transformations and congruence • dilation and similarity

Transformations and Congruence

ESSENTIAL QUESTION

How can you use transformations and congruence to solve real-world problems?

You can analyze how real-world objects are affected when they undergo reflections, translations, rotations, and dilations.

Real-World Video

When a marching band lines up and marches across the field, they are modeling a translation. As they march, they maintain size and orientation. A translation is one type of transformation.

my.hrw.com

GO DIGITAL

my.hrw.com

my.hrw.com

Go digital with your write-in student edition, accessible on any device.

Math On the Spot

Scan with your smart phone to jump directly to the online edition, video tutor, and more.

Animated Math

Interactively explore key concepts to see how math works.

Personal Math Trainer

Get immediate feedback and help as you work through practice sets.

Are You Ready?

Assess Readiness

Use the assessment on this page to determine if students need intensive or strategic intervention for the module's prerequisite skills.

  **Response to Intervention**

Intervention	Enrichment

Access Are You Ready? assessment online, and receive instant scoring, feedback, and customized intervention or enrichment.

Personal Math Trainer
Online Assessment and Intervention
⏻ my.hrw.com

Online and Print Resources

Skills Intervention worksheets
- Skill 47 Integer Operations
- Skill 89 Measure Angles

Differentiated Instruction
- Challenge worksheets **PRE-AP**
- Extend the Math **PRE-AP**
  Lesson Activities in TE

Complete these exercises to review skills you will need for this module.

Personal Math Trainer
Online Assessment and Intervention
⏻ my.hrw.com

Integer Operations

EXAMPLE	$-3 - (-6) = -3 + 6$	To subtract an integer, add its opposite. The signs are different, so find the difference of the absolute values: $6 - 3 = 3$. Use the sign of the number with the greater absolute value.
	$= |-3| - |6|$	
	$= 3$	

Find each difference.

1. $5 - (-9)$
14

2. $-6 - 8$
-14

3. $2 - 9$
-7

4. $-10 - (-6)$
-4

5. $3 - (-11)$
14

6. $12 - 7$
5

7. $-4 - 11$
-15

8. $0 - (-12)$
12

Measure Angles

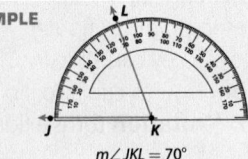

EXAMPLE		Place the center point of the protractor on the angle's vertex. Align one ray with the base of the protractor. Read the angle measure where the other ray intersects the semicircle.

$m\angle JKL = 70°$

Use a protractor to measure each angle.

9.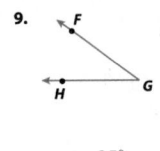
35°

10.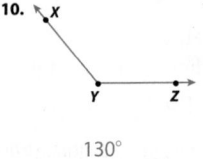
130°

11.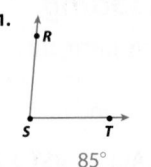
85°

PROFESSIONAL DEVELOPMENT VIDEO

Author Juli Dixon models successful teaching practices as she explores the concept of real numbers in an actual eighth-grade classroom.

 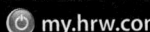

Professional Development
⏻ my.hrw.com

GO DIGITAL
my.hrw.com

 **Online Teacher Edition**
Access a full suite of teaching resources online—plan, present, and manage classes and assignments.

 ePlanner
Easily plan your classes and access all your resources online.

 Interactive Answers and Solutions
Customize answer keys to print or display in the classroom. Choose to include answers only or full solutions to all lesson exercises.

 Interactive Whiteboards
Engage students with interactive whiteboard-ready lessons and activities.

 Personal Math Trainer: Online Assessment and Intervention
Assign automatically graded homework, quizzes, tests, and intervention activities. Prepare your students with updated practice tests aligned with Common Core.

Transformations and Congruence   **540**

Reading Start-Up

Have students complete the activities on this page by working alone or with others.

Visualize Vocabulary

The case diagram helps students review types of quadrilaterals to prepare them to complete the exercises on transformations in this module. Students should write one review word in each oval. If time allows, brainstorm additional shapes and properties as a class and add them to the diagram.

Understand Vocabulary

Use the following explanation to help students learn the preview words.

> The word *transformation* means "change." In math, **transformation** means changes to points or figures. Figures can change in several ways. They can slide in straight lines, called a **translation.** Figures can also flip across a line, called a **reflection.** A **rotation** turns a figure around a point.

Active Reading

Integrating Language Arts

Students can use these reading and note-taking strategies to help them organize and understand new concepts and vocabulary.

🌴 **FL CC** LACC.68.RST.3.7 Integrate quantitative or technical information expressed in words in a text with a version of that information expressed visually (e.g., in a flowchart, diagram, model, graph, or table).

Additional Resources

Differentiated Instruction

• Reading Strategies **ELL**

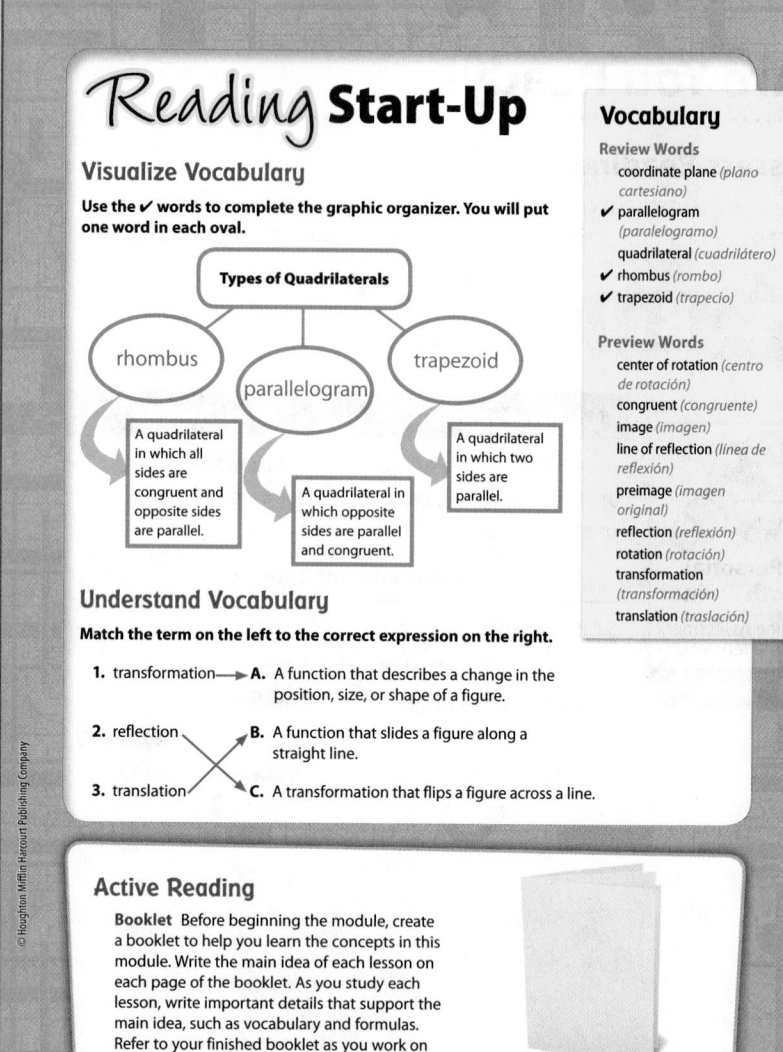

Before	In this module	After
Students understand: • how to classify and draw plane figures • how to graph plane figures on the coordinate plane • congruence	Students use transformational geometry to represent: • properties of orientation and congruence of translations in a coordinate plane • properties of orientation and congruence of reflections in a coordinate plane • properties of orientation and congruence of rotations in a coordinate plane • the effect of translations, reflections, and rotations in a coordinate plane using an algebraic representation	Students will connect: • transformations and congruence • reflections over an axis and symmetry • algebra and coordinate geometry

Unpacking the Standards

Use the examples on the page to help students know exactly what they are expected to learn in this module.

Florida Common Core Standards

Content Areas

 **Geometry—8.G.1**

Understand congruence and similarity using physical models, transparencies, or geometry software.

Go online to see a complete unpacking of the Florida Common Core Standards.

my.hrw.com

MODULE 17

Unpacking the Standards

Understanding the standards and the vocabulary terms in the standards will help you know exactly what you are expected to learn in this module.

FL CC 8.G.1.2

Understand that a two-dimensional figure is congruent to another if the second can be obtained from the first by a sequence of rotations, reflections, and translations; given two congruent figures, describe a sequence that exhibits the congruence between them.

What It Means to You

You will identify a rotation, a reflection, a translation, and a sequence of transformations and understand that the image has the same shape and size as the preimage.

UNPACKING EXAMPLE 8.G.1.2

The figure shows triangle *ABC* and its image after three different transformations. Identify and describe the translation, the reflection, and the rotation of triangle *ABC*.

Figure 1 is a translation 4 units down. Figure 2 is a reflection across the *y*-axis. Figure 3 is a rotation of 180°.

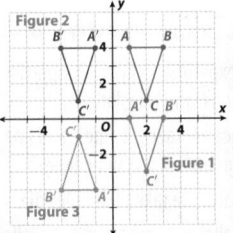

FL CC 8.G.1.3

Describe the effect of dilations, translations, rotations, and reflections on two-dimensional figures using coordinates.

What It Means to You

You can use an algebraic representation to translate, reflect, or rotate a two-dimensional figure.

UNPACKING EXAMPLE 8.G.1.3

Rectangle *RSTU* with vertices $(-4, 1)$, $(-1, 1)$, $(-1, -3)$, and $(-4, -3)$ is reflected across the *y*-axis. Find the coordinates of the image.

The rule to reflect across the *y*-axis is to change the sign of the *x*-coordinate.

Coordinates	Reflect across the *y*-axis $(-x, y)$	Coordinates of image
$(-4, 1)$, $(-1, 1)$, $(-1, -3)$, $(-4, -3)$	$(-(-4), 1)$, $(-(-1), 1)$, $(-(-1), -3)$, $(-(-4), -3)$	$(4, -1)$, $(1, 1)$, $(1, -3)$, $(4, -3)$

The coordinates of the image are $(4, -1)$, $(1, 1)$, $(1, -3)$, and $(4, -3)$.

Visit my.hrw.com to see all Florida Common Core Standards unpacked.

my.hrw.com

© Houghton Mifflin Harcourt Publishing Company

Florida Common Core Standards	Lesson 17.1	Lesson 17.2	Lesson 17.3	Lesson 17.4	Lesson 17.5
FL CC 8.G.1.1 Verify experimentally the properties of rotations, reflections, and translations: **a** Lines are taken to lines, and line segments to line segments of the same length. **b** Angles are taken to angles of the same measure. **c** Parallel lines are taken to parallel lines.	■	■	■		
FL CC 8.G.1.2 Understand that a two-dimensional figure is congruent to another if the second can be obtained from the first by a sequence of rotations, reflections, and translations; given two congruent figures, describe a sequence that exhibits the congruence between them.					■
FL CC 8.G.1.3 Describe the effect of dilations, translations, rotations, and reflections on two-dimensional figures using coordinates.	■	■	■	■	

17.1 Properties of Translations

 Florida Common Core Standards

The student is expected to:

 **Geometry—8.G.1.1**

Verify experimentally the properties of rotations, reflections, and translations.

a. Lines are taken to lines, and line segments to line segments of the same length.

b. Angles are taken to angles of the same measure

c. Parallel lines are taken to parallel lines.

 **Geometry—8.G.1.3**

Describe the effect of dilations, translations, rotations, and reflections on two-dimensional figures using coordinates.

Mathematical Practices

 **MP.6.1** Precision

Engage

ESSENTIAL QUESTION

How do you describe the properties of orientation and congruence of translations?
Sample answer: Translations preserve size, shape, and orientation.

Motivate the Lesson

Ask: What changes when you slide an object, such as a book, from one corner of your desk to different corners of your desk? Does the size or shape of the object change? Begin the Explore Activity to find out how to describe this action mathematically.

Explore

EXPLORE ACTIVITY 1

Focus on Modeling Mathematical Practices

Ask students to move the triangle from the image position back to the preimage position and describe the movement. 7 units left and 5 units up How does the description of the movement change? How does the description stay the same? Students should see that the magnitude of the movement stays the same, but the direction changes.

Explain

EXPLORE ACTIVITY 2

Connect Vocabulary ELL

Emphasize that a *transformation* is a function that describes a change in the position, size, or shape of a figure, and a *translation* is a *type* of transformation in which a shape changes position but not size or orientation. Students often mix up these two terms.

Questioning Strategies Mathematical Practices

• How many different ways could trapezoid *TRAP* be translated? Justify your answer. It can be translated an infinite number of ways. The rule for the translation would be different for each way.

• What characteristics do you look for in an image to know that it has been translated from a preimage? The corresponding sides have the same lengths, and the corresponding angles have the same measures. The shape and size of the image is the same as that of the preimage. The orientation of the image and preimage are the same.

Engage with the Whiteboard

You may wish to have students measure the actual side lengths of the projected image and preimage on the whiteboard, or you can have students count the lengths of the sides in grid units (using the Distance Formula for *PT* and *P'T'*). Point out to students that although the lengths of the sides in centimeters on the projected image will not match the lengths in their books, the angle measurements will be the same.

LESSON
17.1 Properties of Translations

FL CC 8.G.1.1
Verify experimentally the properties of . . . translations.
Also 8.G.1.1a, 8.G.1.1b, 8.G.1.1c, 8.G.1.3

? **ESSENTIAL QUESTION** How do you describe the properties of orientation and congruence of translations?

EXPLORE ACTIVITY 1 FL CC 8.G.1.1

Exploring Translations

You learned that a function is a rule that assigns exactly one output to each input. A **transformation** is a function that describes a change in the position, size, or shape of a figure. The input of a transformation is the **preimage**, and the output of a transformation is the **image**.

A **translation** is a transformation that slides a figure along a straight line.

The triangle shown on the grid is the preimage (input). The arrow shows the motion of a translation and how point A is translated to point A'.

A Trace triangle *ABC* onto a piece of paper. Cut out your traced triangle.

B Slide your triangle along the arrow to model the translation that maps point *A* to point *A'*.

C The image of the translation is the triangle produced by the translation. Sketch the image of the translation.

D The vertices of the image are labeled using prime notation. For example, the image of *A* is *A'*. Label the images of points *B* and *C*.

E Describe the motion modeled by the translation.

Move ____7____ units right and ____5____ units down.

F Check that the motion you described in part **E** is the same motion that maps point *A* onto *A'*, point *B* onto *B'*, and point *C* onto *C'*.

Reflect

1. How is the orientation of the triangle affected by the translation?

It is not affected. The orientation stays the same.

EXPLORE ACTIVITY 2 FL CC 8.G.1.1

Properties of Translations

Use trapezoid *TRAP* to investigate the properties of translations.

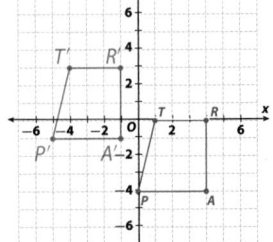

A Trace the trapezoid onto a piece of paper. Cut out your traced trapezoid.

B Place your trapezoid on top of the trapezoid in the figure. Then translate your trapezoid 5 units to the left and 3 units up. Sketch the image of the translation by tracing your trapezoid in this new location. Label the vertices of the image *T'*, *R'*, *A'*, and *P'*.

C Use a ruler to measure the sides of trapezoid *TRAP* in centimeters.

TR = __1.3 cm__ *RA* = __1.7 cm__ *AP* = __1.7 cm__ *TP* = __1.75 cm__

D Use a ruler to measure the sides of trapezoid *T'R'A'P'* in centimeters.

T'R' = __1.3 cm__ *R'A'* = __1.7 cm__ *A'P'* = __1.7 cm__ *T'P'* = __1.75 cm__

E What do you notice about the lengths of corresponding sides of the two figures?

The lengths of corresponding sides are the same.

F Use a protractor to measure the angles of trapezoid *TRAP*.

m∠T = __104°__ m∠R = __90°__ m∠A = __90°__ m∠P = __76°__

G Use a protractor to measure the angles of trapezoid *T'R'A'P'*.

m∠T' = __104°__ m∠R' = __90°__ m∠A' = __90°__ m∠P' = __76°__

H What do you notice about the measures of corresponding angles of the two figures?

The measures of corresponding angles are the same.

I Which sides of trapezoid *TRAP* are parallel? How do you know?

$\overline{TR}$ and $\overline{AP}$; They both lie along horizontal grid lines.

Which sides of trapezoid *T'R'A'P'* are parallel? __$\overline{T'R'}$ and $\overline{A'P'}$__

What do you notice? The sides that were parallel in the preimage remain parallel in the image.

PROFESSIONAL DEVELOPMENT

Integrate Mathematical Practices MP.6.1

This lesson provides an opportunity to address this Mathematical Practices standard. It calls for students to communicate precisely. Students translate a figure on a coordinate grid following a given translation rule. Then, students measure the lengths of the sides and the degrees of the angles to show that the corresponding sides and angles are congruent. Finally, students make a conjecture about the preservation of the size and shape of a figure.

Math Background

In future geometry courses, students will learn special conditions that guarantee that two triangles are congruent. It is not necessary to verify that all three pairs of sides are congruent and all three pairs of angles are congruent. There are numerous "shortcuts," such as the Side-Side-Side (SSS) Congruence Postulate, which states that two triangles are congruent if the corresponding sides of one triangle are congruent to the corresponding sides of the other triangle. In other words, if the corresponding sides are congruent, the angles must also be congruent. However, having all three corresponding angles congruent does not guarantee that the corresponding sides are necessarily congruent.

ADDITIONAL EXAMPLE 1

The figure shows triangle *PQR*. Graph the image of the triangle after a translation of 7 units to the right and 2 units up.

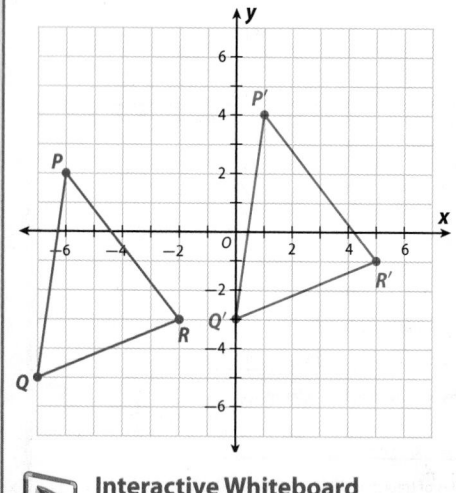

Interactive Whiteboard
Interactive example available online

my.hrw.com

EXAMPLE 1

Questioning Strategies ✍ Mathematical Practices

- What do you notice about the purple lines in the first grid that show the translation of each vertex? They are parallel to each other. They have the same length and slope.

- What do you notice about the corresponding sides of the preimage and the image in Step 4? The corresponding sides are parallel and have the same length and slope.

Engage with the Whiteboard

On the second grid, have a volunteer plot points and draw triangle *X″Y″Z″*, which is the image of *X′Y′Z′* after a translation exactly half as large as the one given in the example.

YOUR TURN

Avoid Common Errors

Students can check that they have not miscounted units in the translation of any one point by checking that the image and preimage have the same size, shape, and orientation.

Talk About It
Check for Understanding

Ask: What translation rule would have moved side *DC* to coincide with the *x*-axis? a translation of 1 unit up and any distance left or right

Elaborate

Talk About It
Summarize the Lesson

Ask: How do you know when a transformation is a translation? The image will have the same size, shape, and orientation as the preimage.

GUIDED PRACTICE

Engage with the Whiteboard

To help students visualize Exercises 3–4, have volunteers sketch the images and preimages on a coordinate grid. In Exercise 3, have the students assign letters to the vertices as well.

Avoid Common Errors

Exercises 3–5 Remind students that a translation is a type of transformation. A translation only causes a change in the position of the figure; everything else remains the same.

Exercise 5 Remind students that the image will have its vertices labeled with the same letters as the corresponding preimage vertices, plus the symbol ′.

Reflect

2. Make a Conjecture Use your results from parts **E**, **H**, and **I** to make a conjecture about translations.

<u>Sample answer: Translations preserve the size and</u>

<u>shape of a figure, as well as its orientation.</u>

3. Two figures that have the same size and shape are called *congruent*. What can you say about translations and congruence?

<u>A translation produces a figure that is congruent to the</u> original figure.

Graphing Translations

To translate a figure in the coordinate plane, translate each of its vertices. Then connect the vertices to form the image.

EXAMPLE 1

FL CC 8.G.1.3

The figure shows triangle *XYZ*. Graph the image of the triangle after a translation of 4 units to the right and 1 unit up.

STEP 1 Translate point *X*.

Count right 4 units and up 1 unit and plot point *X'*.

STEP 2 Translate point *Y*.

Count right 4 units and up 1 unit and plot point *Y'*.

STEP 3 Translate point *Z*.

Count right 4 units and up 1 unit and plot point *Z'*.

STEP 4 Connect *X'*, *Y'*, and *Z'* to form triangle *X'Y'Z'*.

> Each vertex is moved 4 units right and 1 unit up.

Math Talk
Mathematical Practices

Is the image congruent to the preimage? How do you know?

Yes, the figures are congruent. Translations preserve size and shape.

YOUR TURN

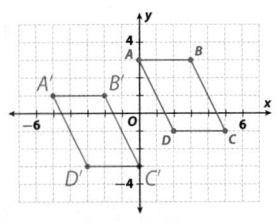

4. The figure shows parallelogram *ABCD*. Graph the image of the parallelogram after a translation of 5 units to the left and 2 units down.

Guided Practice

1. Vocabulary A <u>transformation</u> is a change in the position, size, or shape of a figure.

2. Vocabulary When you perform a transformation of a figure on the coordinate plane, the input of the transformation is called

the <u>preimage</u>, and the output of the transformation is

called the <u>image</u>.

3. Joni translates a right triangle 2 units down and 4 units to the right. How does the orientation of the image of the triangle compare with the orientation of the preimage? (Explore Activity 1)

<u>The orientation will be the same.</u>

4. Rashid drew rectangle *PQRS* on a coordinate plane. He then translated the rectangle 3 units up and 3 units to the left and labeled the image *P'Q'R'S'*. How do rectangle *PQRS* and rectangle *P'Q'R'S'* compare? (Explore Activity 2)

<u>They are congruent.</u>

5. The figure shows trapezoid *WXYZ*. Graph the image of the trapezoid after a translation of 4 units up and 2 units to the left. (Example 1)

? ESSENTIAL QUESTION CHECK-IN

6. What are the properties of translations?

<u>Sample answer: Translations preserve</u>

<u>the size, shape, and orientation of a figure.</u>

DIFFERENTIATE INSTRUCTION

Curriculum Integration

Have groups of students make up a pattern of dance steps formed by translating shapes, which represent dancers' feet, on a grid. Then have students show the class their "dance" using the tiles on the floor as an enlarged grid.

World History

A zoetrope is a device that consists of a cylinder with slits cut vertically around its sides. On the inside of the cylinder is drawn a series of pictures of the same object translated to different positions. When the zoetrope is spun, a person looking through the slits sees what appears to be the object in motion. The earliest known zoetrope was created in China in 180 CE.

Additional Resources

Differentiated Instruction includes:

• Reading Strategies

• Success for English Learners **ELL**

• Reteach

• Challenge **PRE-AP**

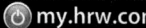
17.1 LESSON QUIZ

 **FL CC** 8.G.1.1, 8.G.1.3

Graph triangle *ABC* with vertices *A*(−3, 4), *B*(0, 2), and *C*(−2, 1) on a coordinate grid.

1. Graph the image of triangle *ABC* after a translation of 4 units right and 3 units down.

2. Which side of the image is congruent to side $\overline{AB}$?

3. Which angle in the image is congruent to angle *B*?

4. Angle *G* in quadrilateral *FGHJ* measures 135°. Brent translates the quadrilateral 3 units right and 1 unit up. What is the measure of the image of angle *G*?

Lesson Quiz available online

Answers

1.
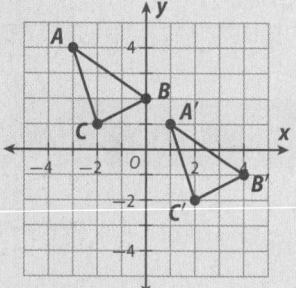

2. $\overline{A'B'}$

3. angle *B'*

4. 135°

Evaluate

GUIDED AND INDEPENDENT PRACTICE

 FL CC 8.G.1.1, 8.G.1.1a, 8.G.1.1b, 8.G.1.1c, 8.G.1.3

Concepts & Skills	Practice
Explore Activity 1 Exploring Translations	Exercises 1–3, 11–12
Explore Activity 2 Properties of Translations	Exercises 4, 7–8
Example 1 Graphing Translations	Exercises 5, 7–10

Exercise	Depth of Knowledge (D.O.K.)	**FL CC** Mathematical Practices
7	**2** Skills/Concepts	**MP.6.1** Precision
8	**2** Skills/Concepts	**MP.7.1** Using Structure
9–10	**2** Skills/Concepts	**MP.8.1** Patterns
11	**2** Skills/Concepts	**MP.4.1** Modeling
12	**2** Skills/Concepts	**MP.3.1** Logic
13	**3** Strategic Thinking H.O.T.	**MP.6.1** Precision
14	**3** Strategic Thinking H.O.T.	**MP.8.1** Patterns
15	**3** Strategic Thinking H.O.T.	**MP.3.1** Logic

Additional Resources

Differentiated Instruction includes:

• Leveled Practice worksheets

17.1 Independent Practice

FL CC 8.G.1.1, 8.G.1.3

Personal Math Trainer
Online Assessment and Intervention
my.hrw.com

7. The figure shows triangle *DEF*.

a. Graph the image of the triangle after the translation that maps point *D* to point *D′*.

b. How would you describe the translation?
The translation moved the triangle
2 units to the left and 4 units down.

c. How does the image of triangle *DEF* compare with the preimage?
They are congruent.

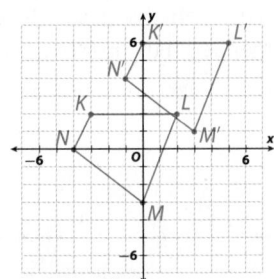

8. a. Graph quadrilateral *KLMN* with vertices *K*(−3, 2), *L*(2, 2), *M*(0, −3), and *N*(−4, 0) on the coordinate grid.

b. On the same coordinate grid, graph the image of quadrilateral *KLMN* after a translation of 3 units to the right and 4 units up.

c. Which side of the image is congruent to side $\overline{LM}$?
$\overline{L′M′}$

Name three other pairs of congruent sides.
$\overline{KL}$ and $\overline{K′L′}$, $\overline{MN}$ and $\overline{M′N′}$, $\overline{KN}$ and $\overline{K′N′}$

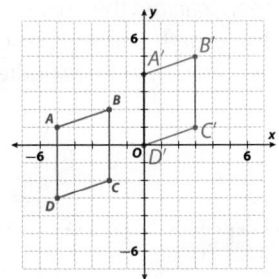

Draw the image of the figure after each translation.

9. 4 units left and 2 units down

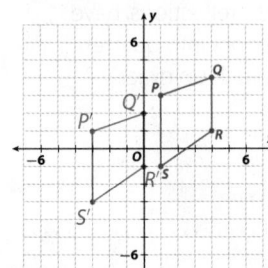

10. 5 units right and 3 units up

11. The figure shows the ascent of a hot air balloon. How would you describe the translation?
The hot air balloon was translated 4 units to the right and 5 units up.

12. Critical Thinking Is it possible that the orientation of a figure could change after it is translated? Explain.
No; when a figure is translated, it is slid to a new location. Since it is not turned or flipped, the orientation will remain the same.

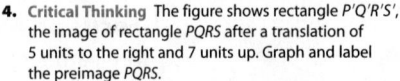
FOCUS ON HIGHER ORDER THINKING

13. a. Multistep Graph triangle *XYZ* with vertices *X*(−2, −5), *Y*(2, −2), and *Z*(4, −4) on the coordinate grid.

b. On the same coordinate grid, graph and label triangle *X′Y′Z′*, the image of triangle *XYZ* after a translation of 3 units to the left and 6 units up.

c. Now graph and label triangle *X″Y″Z″*, the image of triangle *X′Y′Z′* after a translation of 1 unit to the left and 2 units down.

d. Analyze Relationships How would you describe the translation that maps triangle *XYZ* onto triangle *X″Y″Z″*?
Sample answer: The original triangle was translated 4 units up and 4 units to the left.

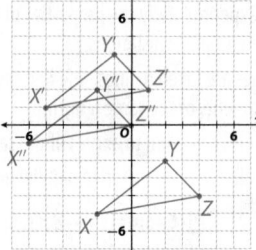

14. Critical Thinking The figure shows rectangle *P′Q′R′S′*, the image of rectangle *PQRS* after a translation of 5 units to the right and 7 units up. Graph and label the preimage *PQRS*.

15. Communicate Mathematical Ideas Explain why the image of a figure after a translation is congruent to its preimage.
Sample answer: Since every point of the original figure is translated the same number of units up/down and left/right, the image is exactly the same size and shape as the preimage. Only the location is different.

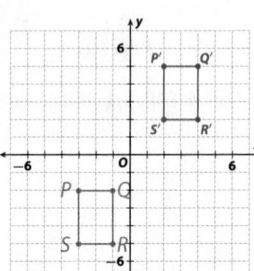

© Houghton Mifflin Harcourt Publishing Company

EXTEND THE MATH PRE-AP

Activity available online my.hrw.com

Activity A strip pattern is a design that repeats itself along a straight line. Some strip patterns, like the one shown, are examples of translations. On a strip of paper, create a design. Then repeat the design by translating it along a straight line to create your own strip pattern.

LESSON
17.2 Properties of Reflections

 Florida Common Core Standards

The student is expected to:

 **Geometry—8.G.1.1**

Verify experimentally the properties of rotations, reflections, and translations.

a. Lines are taken to lines, and line segments to line segments of the same length.

b. Angles are taken to angles of the same measure

c. Parallel lines are taken to parallel lines.

 **Geometry—8.G.1.3**

Describe the effect of dilations, translations, rotations, and reflections on two-dimensional figures using coordinates.

Mathematical Practices

 **MP.5.1** Using Tools

Engage

ESSENTIAL QUESTION
How do you describe the properties of orientation and congruence of reflections?
Sample answer: Reflections preserve size and shape, but not orientation.

Motivate the Lesson
Ask: What changes when you flip an object, such as a book, in any direction? Does the size or shape of the object change? Begin the Explore Activity to find out how to describe this action mathematically.

Explore

EXPLORE ACTIVITY 1

Focus on Modeling **Mathematical Practices**
After students have folded their paper across the axes and drawn both reflections, have them fold their papers over both axes at the same time, folding the paper into quarters. If they have drawn the reflections correctly, all three figures should match up exactly.

Explain

EXPLORE ACTIVITY 2

Connect Vocabulary ELL
Point out that translations and *reflections* are both types of transformations. While a translation does not change the orientation of a figure, a reflection does. Emphasize that a *line of reflection* is often one of the axes, but it can be any line, including lines that are not horizontal or vertical.

Questioning Strategies
• How many different ways could trapezoid *TRAP* be reflected? Justify your answer. It can be reflected an infinite number of ways. Any line can be a line of reflection, and there is an infinite number of lines.

• What characteristics do you look for in an image to know that it has been reflected from a preimage? The corresponding sides have the same lengths, and the corresponding angles have the same measures. The shape and size of the image is the same as that of the preimage. The only difference is the orientation of the image is different from the orientation of the preimage.

Engage with the Whiteboard
Have students draw the reflection of trapezoid *TRAP* across the *x*-axis. Name the new image *T″R″A″P″*. Students can also draw the reflection of *T′R′A′P′* across the *x*-axis and name the new image *T‴R‴A‴P‴*.

LESSON
17.2

Properties of Reflections

FL CC 8.G.1.1
Verify experimentally the properties of … reflections… Also 8.G.1.1a, 8.G.1.1b, 8.G.1.1c, 8.G.1.3

? ESSENTIAL QUESTION How do you describe the properties of orientation and congruence of reflections?

EXPLORE ACTIVITY 1 FL CC 8.G.1.1

Exploring Reflections

A **reflection** is a transformation that flips a figure across a line. The line is called the **line of reflection**. Each point and its image are the same distance from the line of reflection.

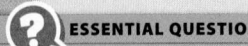

The triangle shown on the grid is the preimage. You will explore reflections across the *x*- and *y*-axes.

A Trace triangle *ABC* and the *x*- and *y*-axes onto a piece of paper.

B Fold your paper along the *x*-axis and trace the image of the triangle on the opposite side of the *x*-axis. Unfold your paper and label the vertices of the image *A'*, *B'*, and *C'*.

C What is the line of reflection for this transformation?

the *x*-axis

D Find the perpendicular distance from each point to the line of reflection.

Point A __5 units__   Point B __2 units__   Point C __2 units__

E Find the perpendicular distance from each point to the line of reflection.

Point A' __5 units__   Point B' __2 units__   Point C' __2 units__

F What do you notice about the distances you found in **D** and **E**?

They are the same for a point and its reflection.

Reflect

1. Fold your paper from **A** along the *y*-axis and trace the image of triangle *ABC* on the opposite side. Label the vertices of the image *A''*, *B''*, and *C''*. What is the line of reflection for this transformation?   the *y*-axis

2. How does each image in your drawings compare with its preimage?

Sample answer: △*A'B'C'* is △*ABC* flipped across the *x*-axis. △*A''B''C''* is △*ABC* flipped across the *y*-axis.

Lesson 17.2 **549**

EXPLORE ACTIVITY 2 FL CC 8.G.1.1

Properties of Reflections

Use trapezoid *TRAP* to investigate the properties of reflections.

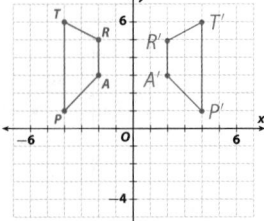

A Trace the trapezoid onto a piece of paper. Cut out your traced trapezoid.

B Place your trapezoid on top of the trapezoid in the figure. Then reflect your trapezoid across the *y*-axis. Sketch the image of the reflection by tracing your trapezoid in this new location. Label the vertices of the image *T'*, *R'*, *A'*, and *P'*.

C Use a ruler to measure the sides of trapezoid *TRAP* in centimeters.

TR = __0.9 cm__   *RA* = __0.8 cm__   *AP* = __1.2 cm__   *TP* = __2.1 cm__

D Use a ruler to measure the sides of trapezoid *T'R'A'P'* in centimeters.

T'R' = __0.9 cm__   *R'A'* = __0.8 cm__   *A'P'* = __1.2 cm__   *T'P'* = __2.1 cm__

E What do you notice about the lengths of corresponding sides of the two figures?

The lengths of corresponding sides are the same.

F Use a protractor to measure the angles of trapezoid *TRAP*.

$m\angle T$ = __63°__ $m\angle R$ = __117°__ $m\angle A$ = __135°__ $m\angle P$ = __45°__

G Use a protractor to measure the angles of trapezoid *T'R'A'P'*.

$m\angle T'$ = __63°__ $m\angle R'$ = __117°__ $m\angle A'$ = __135°__ $m\angle P'$ = __45°__

H What do you notice about the measures of corresponding angles of the two figures?

The measures of corresponding angles are the same.

I Which sides of trapezoid *TRAP* are parallel? $\overline{TP}$ and $\overline{RA}$

Which sides of trapezoid *T'R'A'P'* are parallel? $\overline{T'P'}$ and $\overline{R'A'}$
What do you notice?

The sides that were parallel in the preimage remain

parallel in the image.

550 Unit 8

PROFESSIONAL DEVELOPMENT

Integrate Mathematical Practices MP.5.1

This lesson provides an opportunity to address this Mathematical Practices standard. It calls for students to use tools such as models, rulers, and pencil and paper to analyze relationships. Students use the results of the Explore Activities to make a conjecture that reflections preserve the size and shape of a figure. They find the measures of the angles and side lengths of the image and its preimage and use them to justify their conjecture.

Math Background

Translations, reflections, and rotations are examples of rigid motions. Reflections are sometimes called improper rigid motions as they can cause shapes to flip into a new orientation. However, applying the same reflection twice results in the original orientation. Translations and rotations are sometimes called proper rigid motions as they never cause the shape to flip.

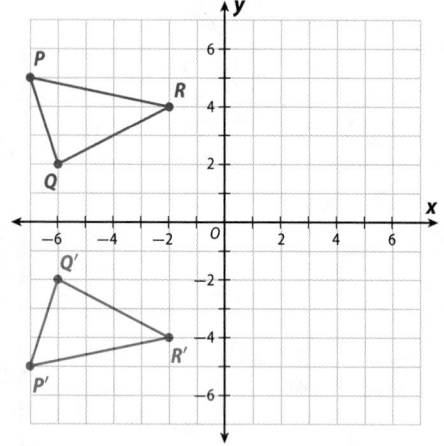
EXAMPLE 1

Questioning Strategies Mathematical Practices

• What do you notice about the purple lines that show the reflection of each vertex? They are parallel to each other. The line of reflection divides each line in half, but all three lines are not the same length.

• Why is triangle *X'Y'Z'* not a translation of triangle *XYZ*? The figures do not have the same orientation.

Engage with the Whiteboard

Have a volunteer plot a new triangle, *X"Y"Z"*, that is a reflection of *X'Y'Z'* across the *y*-axis. Have students compare the orientations of the three triangles.

YOUR TURN

Avoid Common Errors

Students may plot the vertices of the image correctly but label them incorrectly. Suggest that they label each vertex of the image as they plot the point and confirm that each letter matches the letter of the corresponding vertex in the preimage.

Talk About It
Check for Understanding

Ask: How do the coordinates of the image differ from the coordinates of the preimage when a figure is reflected across the *y*-axis? The *x*-values are the opposite of the preimage's *x*-values, but the *y*-values remain the same.

Elaborate

Talk About It
Summarize the Lesson

Ask: How do you know when a transformation is a reflection? The image will have the same size and shape as the preimage, but the orientation will not be the same. There will be a line of reflection such that each image point will be the same distance from that line as its corresponding preimage point.

GUIDED PRACTICE

Engage with the Whiteboard

For Exercise 2 have students graph the reflections of trapezoid *ABCD* across both the *x*-axis and the *y*-axis on the coordinate grid. Label the images *A'B'C'D'* and *A"B"C"D"*.

Avoid Common Errors
Exercise 2a Remind students that the image will have its vertices labeled with the same letters as the corresponding preimage vertices, plus the symbol ʹ.

Reflect

3. **Make a Conjecture** Use your results from , **H**, and **I** to make a conjecture about reflections.

Sample answer: Reflections preserve the size and shape of a figure, but the orientation changes to a mirror image of the original.

Math Talk
Mathematical Practices

What can you say about reflections and congruence?

Math Talk Anno: A reflection produces a figure that is congruent to the original figure.

Graphing Reflections

To reflect a figure across a line of reflection, reflect each of its vertices. Then connect the vertices to form the image. Remember that each point and its image are the same distance from the line of reflection.

EXAMPLE 1   FL CC 8.G.1.3

The figure shows triangle *XYZ*. Graph the image of the triangle after a reflection across the *x*-axis.

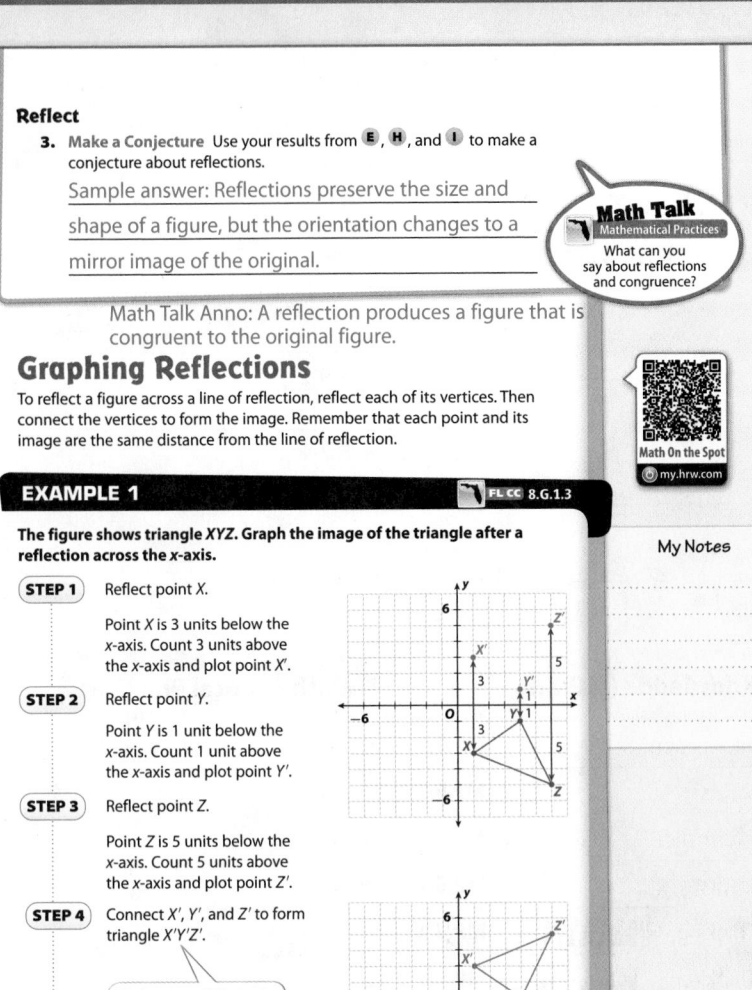

STEP 1   Reflect point *X*.

Point *X* is 3 units below the *x*-axis. Count 3 units above the *x*-axis and plot point *X*′.

STEP 2   Reflect point *Y*.

Point *Y* is 1 unit below the *x*-axis. Count 1 unit above the *x*-axis and plot point *Y*′.

STEP 3   Reflect point *Z*.

Point *Z* is 5 units below the *x*-axis. Count 5 units above the *x*-axis and plot point *Z*′.

STEP 4   Connect *X*′, *Y*′, and *Z*′ to form triangle *X*′*Y*′*Z*′.

Each vertex of the image is the same distance from the *x*-axis as the corresponding vertex in the original figure.

My Notes

Personal Math Trainer
Online Assessment and Intervention

my.hrw.com

YOUR TURN

4. The figure shows pentagon *ABCDE*. Graph the image of the pentagon after a reflection across the *y*-axis.

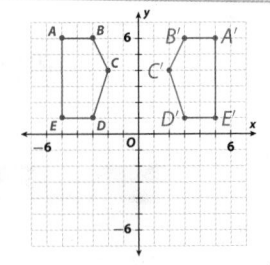

Guided Practice

1. **Vocabulary** A reflection is a transformation that flips a figure across a line called the ___line of reflection___.

2. The figure shows trapezoid *ABCD*. (Explore Activities 1 and 2 and Example 1)

   a. Graph the image of the trapezoid after a reflection across the *x*-axis. Label the vertices of the image.

   b. How do trapezoid *ABCD* and trapezoid *A*′*B*′*C*′*D*′ compare?

   They are congruent.

   c. **What If?** Suppose you reflected trapezoid *ABCD* across the *y*-axis. How would the orientation of the image of the trapezoid compare with the orientation of the preimage?

   The orientation would be reversed horizontally. That is, the figure from left to right in the preimage would match the figure from right to left in the image.

 **ESSENTIAL QUESTION CHECK-IN**

3. What are the properties of reflections?

   Sample answer: Reflections preserve size and shape but not orientation.

DIFFERENTIATE INSTRUCTION

Cooperative Learning

Provide each student with a full sheet of grid paper. Have each student fold their paper into quarters along grid lines. They should mark the fold lines as the *x*- and *y*-axes. Each student should draw half of a face or design to the left of the *y*-axis. The right edge of the face or design should touch the *y*-axis. Students then trade with another student to complete the face or design by drawing a reflection of the drawing across the *y*-axis.

Critical Thinking

Pose this question to your students: If a cat is sitting 8 inches away from the front of a mirror, how far away will the cat's reflection appear to be? The reflection of the cat will appear to be twice the distance the cat is from the mirror, or 16 inches.

Additional Resources

Differentiated Instruction includes:

- Reading Strategies
- Success for English Learners   **ELL**
- Reteach
- Challenge   **PRE-AP**

17.2 LESSON QUIZ

 **FL CC** 8.G.1.1, 8.G.1.3

Graph triangle *ABC* with vertices *A*(−4, 1), *B*(−2, 1), and *C*(−1, −2) on a coordinate grid.

1. Graph the image of triangle *ABC* after a reflection across the *y*-axis.

2. Which side of the image is congruent to side $\overline{AB}$?

3. Which angle in the image is congruent to angle *B*?

4. If a point *M*, 5 units from the *x*-axis, is reflected across the *x*-axis, how far is the image of the point, *M*', from the *x*-axis?

5. Angle *G* in trapezoid *FGHJ* measures 135°. Jasmine reflects the trapezoid over the *x*-axis. What is the measure of the image of angle *G*?

Lesson Quiz available online

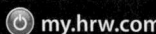 my.hrw.com

Answers

1.

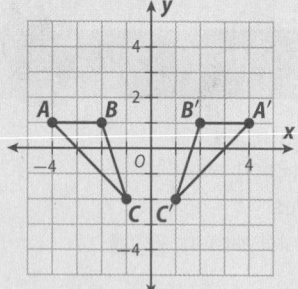

2. $\overline{A'B'}$

3. angle *B'*

4. 5 units

5. 135°

Evaluate

GUIDED AND INDEPENDENT PRACTICE

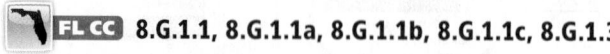 **FL CC** 8.G.1.1, 8.G.1.1a, 8.G.1.1b, 8.G.1.1c, 8.G.1.3

Concepts & Skills	Practice
Explore Activity 1 Exploring Reflections	Exercises 2, 4–5, 9
Explore Activity 2 Properties of Reflections	Exercises 2, 4–5, 7–8
Example 1 Graphing Reflections	Exercises 2, 8

Exercise	Depth of Knowledge (D.O.K.)	**FL CC** Mathematical Practices
4–5	**1** Recall of Information	**MP.2.1** Reasoning
6	**2** Skills/Concepts	**MP.6.1** Precision
7	**1** Recall of Information	**MP.3.1** Logic
8	**2** Skills/Concepts	**MP.6.1** Precision
9	**3** Strategic Thinking H.O.T.	**MP.3.1** Logic
10–11	**3** Strategic Thinking H.O.T.	**MP.6.1** Precision

Additional Resources

Differentiated Instruction includes:

• Leveled Practice worksheets

Name _____ Class _____ Date _____

17.2 Independent Practice

FL CC 8.G.1.1, 8.G.1.3

Personal Math Trainer
Online Assessment and Intervention
my.hrw.com

The graph shows four right triangles. Use the graph for Exercises 4–7.

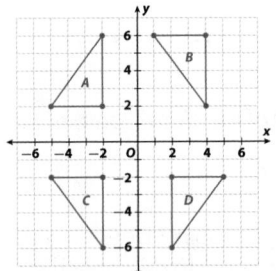

4. Which two triangles are reflections of each other across the *x*-axis?

A and C

5. For which two triangles is the line of reflection the *y*-axis?

C and D

6. Which triangle is a translation of triangle C? How would you describe the translation?

triangle B; a translation of 8 units up and 6 units right

7. Which triangles are congruent? How do you know?

Sample answer: Since each triangle is either a reflection or translation of triangle C, they are all congruent.

8. a. Graph quadrilateral *WXYZ* with vertices *W*(−2, −2), *X*(3, 1), *Y*(5, −1), and *Z*(4, −6) on the coordinate grid.

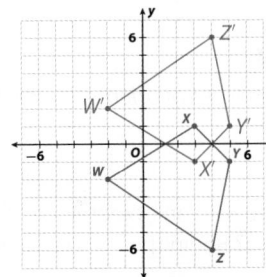

b. On the same coordinate grid, graph quadrilateral *W'X'Y'Z'*, the image of quadrilateral *WXYZ* after a reflection across the *x*-axis.

c. Which side of the image is congruent to side $\overline{YZ}$?

$\overline{Y'Z'}$

Name three other pairs of congruent sides.

$\overline{WX}$ and $\overline{W'X'}$, $\overline{XY}$ and $\overline{X'Y'}$, $\overline{WZ}$ and $\overline{W'Z'}$

d. Which angle of the image is congruent to ∠*X*?

∠*X'*

Name three other pairs of congruent angles.

∠*W* and ∠*W'*, ∠*Y* and ∠*Y'*, ∠*Z* and ∠*Z'*

9. Critical Thinking Is it possible that the image of a point after a reflection could be the same point as the preimage? Explain.

Yes; if the point lies on the line of reflection, then the image and the preimage will be the same point.

H.O.T. FOCUS ON HIGHER ORDER THINKING

10. a. Graph the image of the figure shown after a reflection across the *y*-axis.

b. On the same coordinate grid, graph the image of the figure you drew in part **a** after a reflection across the *x*-axis.

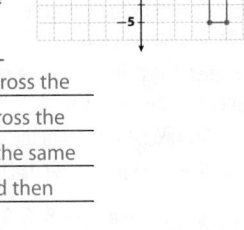

c. Make a Conjecture What other sequence of transformations would produce the same final image from the original preimage? Check your answer by performing the transformations. Then make a conjecture that generalizes your findings.

The same image can be obtained by reflecting first across the *x*-axis and then across the *y*-axis. In general, reflecting a figure first across the *y*-axis and then across the *x*-axis produces the same result as reflecting first across the *x*-axis and then across the *y*-axis.

11. a. Graph triangle *DEF* with vertices *D*(2, 6), *E*(5, 6), and *F*(5, 1) on the coordinate grid.

b. Next graph triangle *D'E'F'*, the image of triangle *DEF* after a reflection across the *y*-axis.

c. On the same coordinate grid, graph triangle *D"E"F"*, the image of triangle *D'E'F'* after a translation of 7 units down and 2 units to the right.

d. Analyze Relationships Find a different sequence of transformations that will transform triangle *DEF* to triangle *D"E"F"*.

Sample answer: Translate triangle *DEF* 7 units down and 2 units to the left. Then reflect the image across the *y*-axis.

EXTEND THE MATH PRE-AP

Activity available online ⏻ my.hrw.com

Activity Reflect triangle *ABC* across line ℓ. Label the image triangle *A'B'C'*. Then reflect triangle *A'B'C'* across line *m*. Label the image triangle *A"B"C"*. What other transformation could you have performed on triangle *ABC* to get triangle *A"B"C"*? Do you think this would be true of any shape that goes through the same process?

Sample answer: A translation of triangle *ABC* could have produced *A"B"C"*. Yes, any shape would be reversed after one reflection, then reversed again to the original figure after the second reflection.

LESSON
17.3 Properties of Rotations

 Florida Common Core Standards

The student is expected to:

 **Geometry—8.G.1.1**

Verify experimentally the properties of rotations, reflections, and translations.

a. Lines are taken to lines, and line segments to line segments of the same length.

b. Angles are taken to angles of the same measure

c. Parallel lines are taken to parallel lines.

 **Geometry—8.G.1.3**

Describe the effect of dilations, translations, rotations, and reflections on two-dimensional figures using coordinates.

Mathematical Practices

 **MP.2.1** Reasoning

Engage

ESSENTIAL QUESTION

How do you describe the properties of orientation and congruence of rotations? Sample answer: Rotations preserve size and shape, but change orientation.

Motivate the Lesson
Ask: What changes when you turn an object, such as a book, around a point? Does the size or shape of the object change? Begin the Explore Activity to find out how to describe this action mathematically.

Explore

EXPLORE ACTIVITY 1

Focus on Modeling 📝 Mathematical Practices
Make sure students understand that point A is the same as point A′ because A lies at the center of rotation. The next Explore Activity shows a rotation where none of the vertices lie at the center of rotation, and therefore all of the vertices change position.

Explain

EXPLORE ACTIVITY 2

Connect Vocabulary ELL

Emphasize that a *transformation* is a function that describes a change in the position, size, or shape of a figure, and a *rotation* is a *type* of transformation. The measures of the figure's sides and angles do not ever change in a rotation. In most rotations, the figure's position and orientation change.

Questioning Strategies 📝 Mathematical Practices
• If you were to draw segments from T to the origin and from T′ to the origin, what angle would the two segments form? They would form a 180° or straight angle.

• How does the distance from the origin to T compare to the distance from the origin to T′? The distance is the same.

• Would you give the same answers to the previous two questions for each of the other vertices and their images? Yes, each pair of vertices (preimage and image) would form a 180° angle with the origin, and their distance from the origin would be the same.

Engage with the Whiteboard
Have students draw semicircular arrows, with the center of the semicircle at the origin, connecting T with T′, A with A′, R with R′ and P with P′. Point out that in this case, counterclockwise and clockwise arrows are equally valid.

Focus on Critical Thinking
Point out to students that a clockwise rotation of 270° results in the same image as a counter-clockwise rotation of 90°. Ask students to examine this claim, discuss why it is true, and justify it with a logical argument. Sample answer: Since 270° + 90° = 360°, and a full rotation is 360°, then rotating 270° in one direction is the same as rotating 90° in the opposite direction.

17.3 Properties of Rotations

🟦 FL CC 8.G.1.1

Verify experimentally the properties of rotations.... Also 8.G.1.1a, 8.G.1.1b, 8.G.1.1c, 8.G.1.3

? ESSENTIAL QUESTION How do you describe the properties of orientation and congruence of rotations?

EXPLORE ACTIVITY 1 🟦 FL CC 8.G.1.1

Exploring Rotations

A **rotation** is a transformation that turns a figure around a given point called the **center of rotation**. The image has the same size and shape as the preimage.

The triangle shown on the grid is the preimage. You will use the origin as the center of rotation.

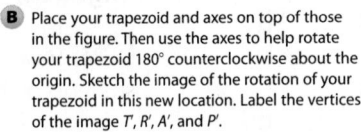

A Trace triangle *ABC* onto a piece of paper. Cut out your traced triangle.

B Rotate your triangle 90° counterclockwise about the origin. The side of the triangle that lies along the *x*-axis should now lie along the *y*-axis.

C Sketch the image of the rotation. Label the images of points *A*, *B*, and *C* as *A′*, *B′*, and *C′*.

D Describe the motion modeled by the rotation.

Rotate ___90___ degrees _counterclockwise_ about the origin.

E Check that the motion you described in **D** is the same motion that maps point *A* onto *A′*, point *B* onto *B′*, and point *C* onto *C′*.

Reflect

1. **Communicate Mathematical Ideas** How are the size and the orientation of the triangle affected by the rotation?

   The size stays the same, but the orientation changes in

   that the triangle is turned or tilted left – what was "up"

   is now "left".

2. Rotate triangle *ABC* 90° clockwise about the origin. Sketch the result on the coordinate grid above. Label the image vertices *A″*, *B″*, and *C″*.

EXPLORE ACTIVITY 2 🟦 FL CC 8.G.1.1

Properties of Rotations

Use trapezoid *TRAP* to investigate the properties of rotations.

A Trace the trapezoid onto a piece of paper. Include the portion of the *x*- and *y*-axes bordering the third quadrant. Cut out your tracing.

B Place your trapezoid and axes on top of those in the figure. Then use the axes to help rotate your trapezoid 180° counterclockwise about the origin. Sketch the image of the rotation of your trapezoid in this new location. Label the vertices of the image *T′*, *R′*, *A′*, and *P′*.

C Use a ruler to measure the sides of trapezoid *TRAP* in centimeters.

TR = __1.3 cm__ *RA* = __1.7 cm__

AP = __1.5 cm__ *TP* = __2.2 cm__

D Use a ruler to measure the sides of trapezoid *T′R′A′P′* in centimeters.

T′R′ = __1.3 cm__ *R′A′* = __1.7 cm__

A′P′ = __1.5 cm__ *T′P′* = __2.2 cm__

E What do you notice about the lengths of corresponding sides of the two figures?

The lengths of corresponding sides are the same.

F Use a protractor to measure the angles of trapezoid *TRAP*.

$m\angle T$ = __90°__ $m\angle R$ = __90°__ $m\angle A$ = __108°__ $m\angle P$ = __72°__

G Use a protractor to measure the angles of trapezoid *T′R′A′P′*.

$m\angle T′$ = __90°__ $m\angle R′$ = __90°__ $m\angle A′$ = __108°__ $m\angle P′$ = __72°__

H What do you notice about the measures of corresponding angles of the two figures?

The measures of corresponding angles are the same.

I Which sides of trapezoid *TRAP* are parallel? __$\overline{TP}$ and $\overline{RA}$__

Which sides of trapezoid *T′R′A′P′* are parallel? __$\overline{T′P′}$ and $\overline{R′A′}$__

What do you notice? The sides that were parallel in the

preimage remain parallel in the image.

PROFESSIONAL DEVELOPMENT

🔲 Integrate Mathematical Practices MP.2.1

This lesson provides an opportunity to address this Mathematical Practices standard. It calls for students to make sense of relationships in a problem. Students use coordinate grids to visualize a relationship between a preimage and a rotation that results in an image. Then students use words to describe the relationship between the preimage and the image following a rotation.

Math Background

A rotation is a mathematical model of the motion of turning. It is a transformation. To rotate a figure you must be given or know three things: the center of rotation, the magnitude (number of degrees), and direction (clockwise or counterclockwise) of the rotation.

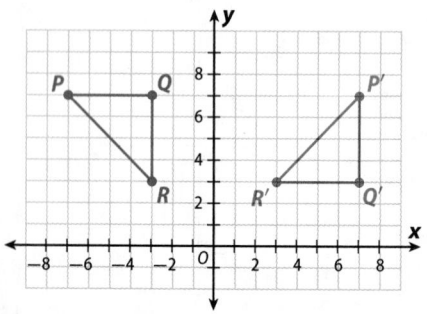
EXAMPLE 1

Questioning Strategies  Mathematical Practices

- About what point do you rotate triangle *ABC*? point *A*.

- Triangle *ABC* is in the first and second quadrants. In which quadrants will the image lie? Quadrants I and IV.

Engage with the Whiteboard

Have a student draw triangle *A″B″C″*, which is *A′B′C′* after a 90° clockwise rotation. Have another student draw *A‴B‴C‴* after another 90° clockwise rotation. Have students predict what another 90° rotation would produce.

YOUR TURN

Avoid Common Errors

Students often confuse clockwise and counterclockwise when performing a rotation. Draw or show the diagram below to show the meanings of the words.

Talk About It
Check for Understanding

Ask: Looking at your answer to Exercise 6, what indicates that quadrilateral *ABCD* was not translated to get quadrilateral *A′B′C′D′*? The size and shape of the figures are the same, but the orientation is different.

Elaborate

Talk About It
Summarize the Lesson

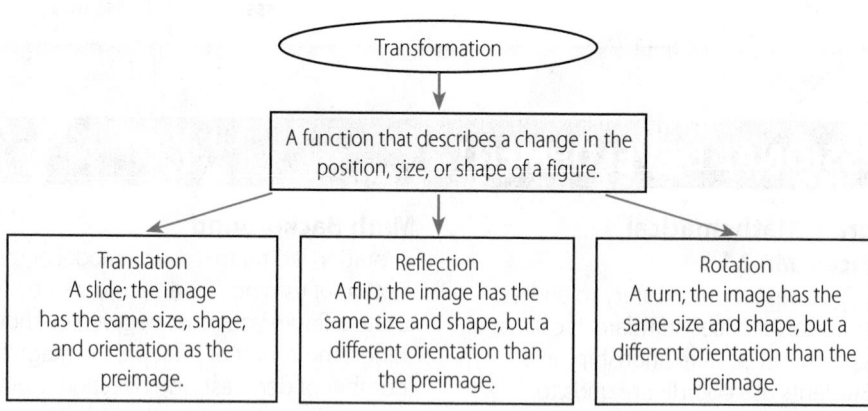

GUIDED PRACTICE

Engage with the Whiteboard

For Exercises 2–5, have volunteers circle the degree, direction, and center of rotation of the figures. In Exercises 4 and 5, draw curved arrows in the direction of rotation.

Avoid Common Errors

Exercise 5 Make sure students label the image correctly. Some students may swap *B′* and *D′* out of carelessness or thinking the order of the labels doesn't matter.

Reflect

3. Make a Conjecture Use your results from **E**, **H**, and **I** to make a conjecture about rotations.

Sample answer: Rotations preserve size and shape, or

congruence, but change a figure's orientation by turning it.

4. Place your tracing back in its original position. Then perform a 180° _clockwise_ rotation about the origin. Compare the result.

A 180° clockwise rotation gives the same image as a

180° counterclockwise rotation.

Graphing Rotations

To rotate a figure in the coordinate plane, rotate each of its vertices. Then connect the vertices to form the image.

EXAMPLE 1   **FL CC** 8.G.1.3

The figure shows triangle _ABC_. Graph the image of triangle _ABC_ after a rotation of 90° clockwise.

STEP 1 Rotate the figure clockwise from the _y_-axis to the _x_-axis. Point _A_ will still be at (0, 0).

Point _B_ is 2 units to the left of the _y_-axis, so point _B'_ is 2 units above the _x_-axis.

Point _C_ is 2 units to the right of the _y_-axis, so point _C'_ is 2 units below the _x_-axis.

STEP 2 Connect _A'_, _B'_, and _C'_ to form the image triangle _A'B'C'_.

Reflect

5. Is the image congruent to the preimage? How do you know?

Sample answer: Yes, you can

see from the grid squares that

the side lengths and angle

measures are the same.

Math Talk
Mathematical Practices
How is the orientation of the triangle affected by the rotation?

Sample answer: The triangle is turned to the right about the origin by the angle of rotation.

Lesson 17.3 **557**

Personal Math Trainer
Online Assessment and Intervention
my.hrw.com

YOUR TURN

Graph the image of quadrilateral _ABCD_ after each rotation.

6. 180°

7. 270° clockwise

8. Find the coordinates of Point _C_ after a 90° counterclockwise rotation followed by a 180° rotation.

_(2, −4)_

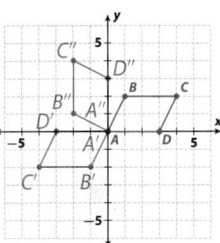

Guided Practice

1. Vocabulary A rotation is a transformation that turns a figure around a given _____point_____ called the center of rotation.

Siobhan rotates a right triangle 90° counterclockwise about the origin.

2. How does the orientation of the image of the triangle compare with the orientation of the preimage? (Explore Activity 1)

The triangle is turned 90° to the left about vertex E.

3. Is the image of the triangle congruent to the preimage? (Explore Activity 2)

Yes, the figures are congruent.

Draw the image of the figure after the given rotation about the origin. (Example 1)

4. 90° counterclockwise

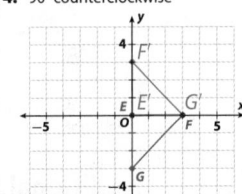

5. 180°

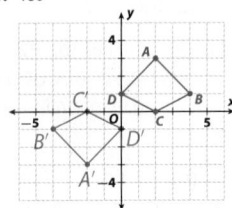

? ESSENTIAL QUESTION CHECK-IN

6. What are the properties of rotations?

Sample answer: Rotations preserve size and shape but change orientation.

558 Unit 8

DIFFERENTIATE INSTRUCTION

Modeling

Students who have trouble finding the location of an image after a rotation may benefit from finding the image of just one point after a rotation. Provide students with examples like the one shown here. The purple lines (which should be drawn by the students) show the angle of rotation and that the image and preimage are the same distance from the point of rotation (the origin).

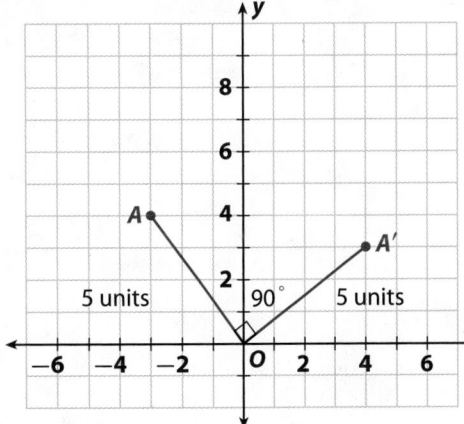

Additional Resources

Differentiated Instruction includes:

• Reading Strategies

• Success for English Learners **ELL**

• Reteach

• Challenge **PRE-AP**

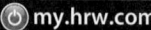
Evaluate

GUIDED AND INDEPENDENT PRACTICE

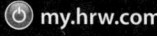 8.G.1.1, 8.G.1.1a, 8.G.1.1b, 8.G.1.1c, 8.G.1.3

Concepts & Skills	Practice
Explore Activity 1 Exploring Rotations	Exercises 2, 9, 16
Explore Activity 2 Properties of Rotations	Exercises 3, 7–9
Example 1 Graphing Rotations	Exercises 4–5, 10–15

Exercise	Depth of Knowledge (D.O.K.)		FL CC Mathematical Practices
7–16	**2** Skills/Concepts		**MP.2.1** Reasoning
17	**3** Strategic Thinking	H.O.T.	**MP.4.1** Modeling
18	**3** Strategic Thinking	H.O.T.	**MP.2.1** Reasoning
19	**3** Strategic Thinking	H.O.T.	**MP.3.1** Logic

Additional Resources

Differentiated Instruction includes:

• Leveled Practice worksheets

Answers

1.

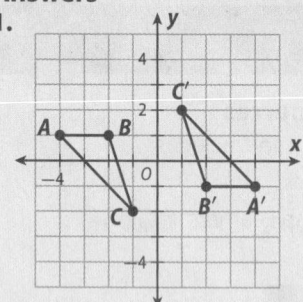

2. $\overline{A'B'}$

3. angle *B*'

4. (−2, −3)

5. 135°

17.3 Independent Practice

FL.CC 8.G.1.1, 8.G.1.3

Personal Math Trainer

Online Assessment and Intervention

my.hrw.com

7. The figure shows triangle *ABC* and a rotation of the triangle about the origin.

a. How would you describe the rotation?

ABC was rotated 90° counterclockwise.

_____

b. What are the coordinates of the image?

A′ (3, 1) , B′ (2, 3) , C′ (−1, 4)

8. The graph shows a figure and its image after a transformation.

a. How would you describe this as a rotation?

The figure was rotated 180° about the

origin.

b. Can you describe this as a transformation other than a rotation? Explain.

Yes, you can also describe it as a reflection

across the y-axis.

9. What type of rotation will preserve the orientation of the H-shaped figure in the grid?

180° rotation

10. A point with coordinates (−2, −3) is rotated 90° clockwise about the origin. What are the coordinates of its image?

(−3, 2)

Complete the table with rotations of 180° or less. Include the direction of rotation for rotations of less than 180°.

	Shape in quadrant	Image in quadrant	Rotation
11.	I	IV	90° clockwise
12.	III	I	180°
13.	IV	III	90° clockwise

Draw the image of the figure after the given rotation about the origin.

14. 180°

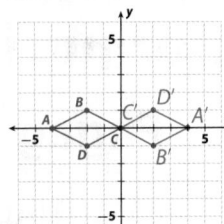

15. 270° counterclockwise

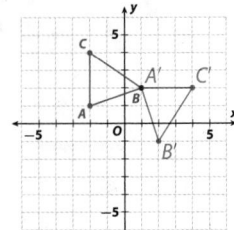

16. Is there a rotation for which the orientation of the image is always the same as that of the preimage? If so, what?

Yes, a 360° rotation

H.O.T. FOCUS ON HIGHER ORDER THINKING

Work Area

17. Problem Solving Lucas is playing a game where he has to rotate a figure for it to fit in an open space. Every time he clicks a button, the figure rotates 90 degrees clockwise. How many times does he need to click the button so that each figure returns to its original orientation?

Figure A 2 times

Figure B 1 time

Figure C 4 times

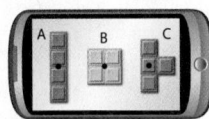

18. Make a Conjecture Triangle *ABC* is reflected across the *y*-axis to form the image *A′B′C′*. Triangle *A′B′C′* is then reflected across the *x*-axis to form the image *A″B″C″*. What type of rotation can be used to describe the relationship between triangle *A″B″C″* and triangle *ABC*?

Triangle *A″B″C″* is a 180° rotation of triangle *ABC*.

19. Communicate Mathematical Ideas Point *A* is on the *y*-axis. Describe all possible locations of image *A′* for rotations of 90°, 180°, and 270°. Include the origin as a possible location for *A*.

Sample answer: If *A* is at the origin, *A′* for any rotation

about the origin is at the origin. Otherwise, *A′* is on the

x-axis for 90° and 270° rotations and on the *y*-axis for a

180° rotation.

EXTEND THE MATH PRE-AP

Activity available online my.hrw.com

Activity The transformed image of point *A* located at (3, 3) is point *A′* located at (−3, −3). Explain how this image could be produced by a translation, a rotation, and by one or more reflections.

By a translation: move 6 units left and 6 units down.

By a rotation: rotate 180° clockwise about the origin.

By a reflection or reflections: the point is reflected across the line y = −x, or is reflected across the x-axis and the y-axis sequentially in either order.

LESSON 17.4 Algebraic Representations of Transformations

Florida Common Core Standards

The student is expected to:

 **Geometry—8.G.1.3**

Describe the effect of dilations, translations, rotations, and reflections on two-dimensional figures using coordinates.

Mathematical Practices

 **MP.3.1** Logic

ADDITIONAL EXAMPLE 1

Triangle *PQR* has vertices *P* (3, 3), *Q* (5, −1), and *R* (1, −2). Find the vertices of triangle *P′Q′R′* after a translation of 3 units to the left and 1 unit up. Then graph the triangle and its image.

P′(0, 4), *Q′*(2, 0), and *R′*(−2, −1)

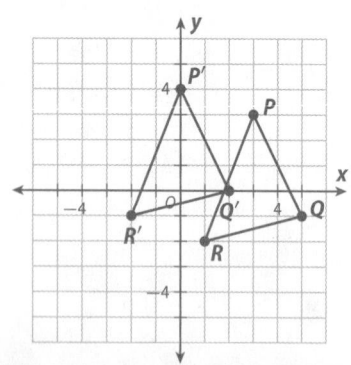

 Interactive Whiteboard
Interactive example available online

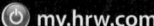 my.hrw.com

Engage

ESSENTIAL QUESTION

How can you describe the effect of a translation, rotation, or reflection on coordinates using an algebraic representation? Sample answer: For a given transformation, the change in the coordinates can be described algebraically following specific rules for that transformation.

Motivate the Lesson

Ask: How can you find the coordinates of the vertices of an image after a translation, rotation, or reflection without graphing?

Explore

What are the signs of the coordinates of a point in each quadrant of the coordinate plane? How do the coordinates change as you move left and right? up and down?

Explain

EXAMPLE 1

Questioning Strategies Mathematical Practices

- Which coordinate changes and how does it change as you translate a vertex right? *x*; increase Left? *x*; decrease Up? *y*; increase Down? *y*; decrease

- How does the distance between vertices of the image change as compared to the distance between vertices in the preimage? The distances stay the same.

Focus on Modeling Mathematical Practices

Explain to students that if you are at a 2 on a horizontal number line and move 3 units to the right, you are now at 2 + 3 or 5. A move left of 3 units moves you to 2 − 3 or −1. On a vertical number line, you add when moving up and subtract when moving down.

YOUR TURN

Avoid Common Errors

Students may make changes to the wrong coordinate. Help them understand that a change to the left or right affects the *x*-coordinate, and a change up or down affects the *y*-coordinate.

EXAMPLE 2

Questioning Strategies

- In a reflection over the *x*- or *y*-axis, what are the only ways in which the coordinates will change? One of the coordinates will be multiplied by −1.

- Would a translation to the right by 5 units produce the same transformation? No; the labels on the vertices would be different if the rectangle was translated.

Engage with the Whiteboard

Extend the table by two columns, and use the coordinate plane to step through and graph a reflection of *RSTU* across the *x*-axis.

Algebraic Representations of Transformations

FL CC 8.G.1.3
Describe the effect of . . . , translations, rotations, and reflections on two-dimensional figures using coordinates.

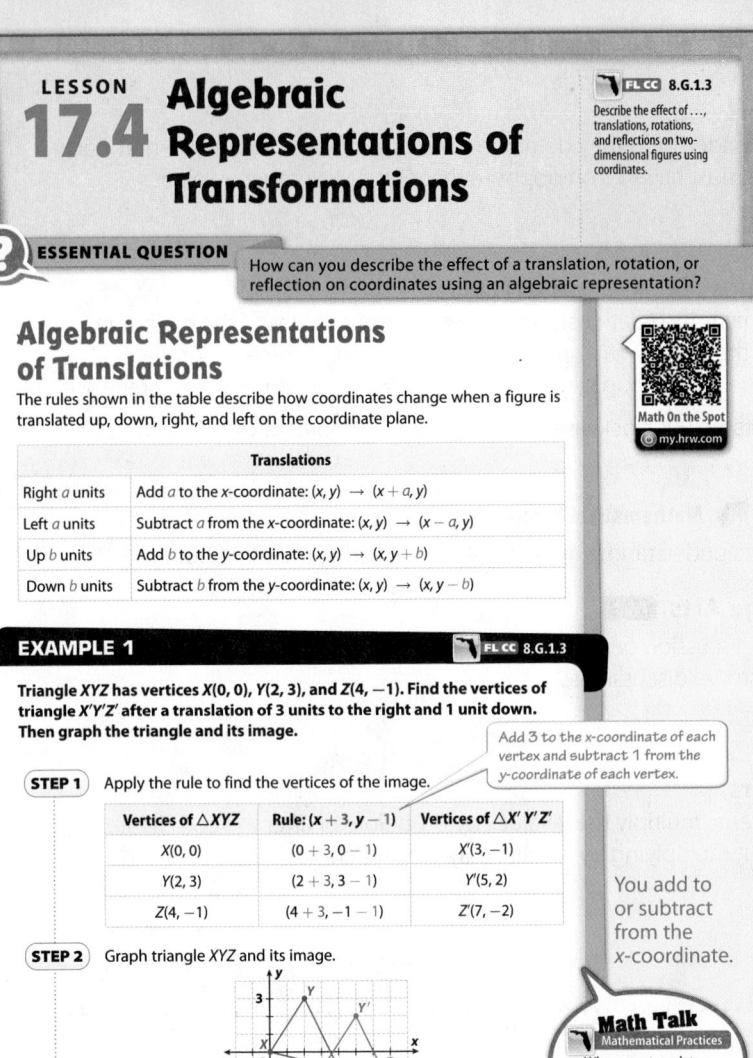

ESSENTIAL QUESTION How can you describe the effect of a translation, rotation, or reflection on coordinates using an algebraic representation?

Algebraic Representations of Translations

The rules shown in the table describe how coordinates change when a figure is translated up, down, right, and left on the coordinate plane.

Translations	
Right a units	Add a to the x-coordinate: $(x, y) \rightarrow (x + a, y)$
Left a units	Subtract a from the x-coordinate: $(x, y) \rightarrow (x - a, y)$
Up b units	Add b to the y-coordinate: $(x, y) \rightarrow (x, y + b)$
Down b units	Subtract b from the y-coordinate: $(x, y) \rightarrow (x, y - b)$

EXAMPLE 1
FL CC 8.G.1.3

Triangle XYZ has vertices $X(0, 0)$, $Y(2, 3)$, and $Z(4, -1)$. Find the vertices of triangle $X'Y'Z'$ after a translation of 3 units to the right and 1 unit down. Then graph the triangle and its image.

Add 3 to the x-coordinate of each vertex and subtract 1 from the y-coordinate of each vertex.

STEP 1 Apply the rule to find the vertices of the image.

Vertices of △XYZ	Rule: $(x + 3, y - 1)$	Vertices of △$X'Y'Z'$
$X(0, 0)$	$(0 + 3, 0 - 1)$	$X'(3, -1)$
$Y(2, 3)$	$(2 + 3, 3 - 1)$	$Y'(5, 2)$
$Z(4, -1)$	$(4 + 3, -1 - 1)$	$Z'(7, -2)$

STEP 2 Graph triangle XYZ and its image.

You add to or subtract from the x-coordinate.

Math Talk
Mathematical Practices

When you translate a figure to the left or right, which coordinate do you change?

My Notes

1. A rectangle has vertices at $(0, -2)$, $(0, 3)$, $(3, -2)$, and $(3, 3)$. What are the coordinates of the vertices of the image after the translation $(x, y) \rightarrow (x - 6, y - 3)$? Describe the translation.

   $(-6, -5)$, $(-6, 0)$, $(-3, -5)$, and $(-3, 0)$; the rectangle is translated 6 units to the left and 3 units down.

Algebraic Representations of Reflections

The signs of the coordinates of a figure change when the figure is reflected across the x-axis and y-axis. The table shows the rules for changing the signs of the coordinates after a reflection.

Reflections	
Across the x-axis	Multiply each y-coordinate by -1: $(x, y) \rightarrow (x, -y)$
Across the y-axis	Multiply each x-coordinate by -1: $(x, y) \rightarrow (-x, y)$

EXAMPLE 2
FL CC 8.G.1.3

Rectangle $RSTU$ has vertices $R(-4, -1)$, $S(-1, -1)$, $T(-1, -3)$, and $U(-4, -3)$. Find the vertices of rectangle $R'S'T'U'$ after a reflection across the y-axis. Then graph the rectangle and its image.

Multiply the x-coordinate of each vertex by -1.

STEP 1 Apply the rule to find the vertices of the image.

Vertices of $RSTU$	Rule: $(-1 \cdot x, y)$	Vertices of $R'S'T'U'$
$R(-4, -1)$	$(-1 \cdot (-4), -1)$	$R'(4, -1)$
$S(-1, -1)$	$(-1 \cdot (-1), -1)$	$S'(1, -1)$
$T(-1, -3)$	$(-1 \cdot (-1), -3)$	$T'(1, -3)$
$U(-4, -3)$	$(-1 \cdot (-4), -3)$	$U'(4, -3)$

STEP 2 Graph rectangle $RSTU$ and its image.

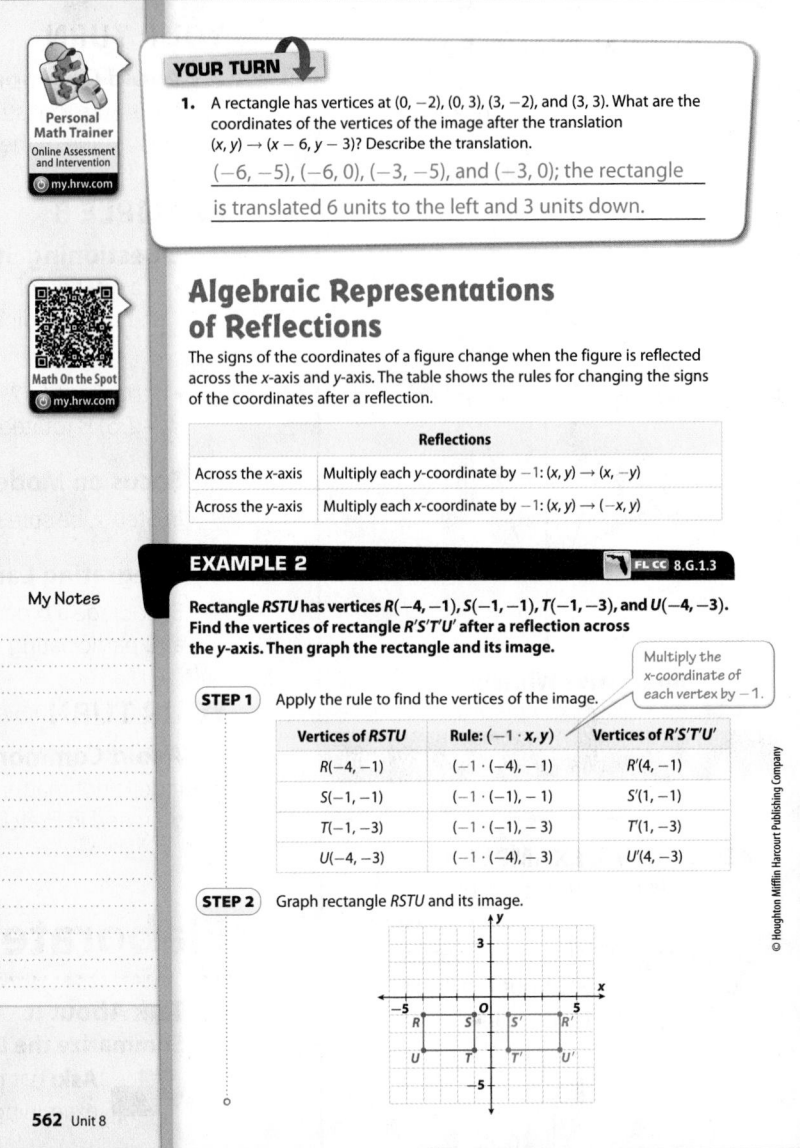

PROFESSIONAL DEVELOPMENT

Integrate Mathematical Practices MP.3.1

This lesson provides an opportunity to address this Mathematical Practices standard. It calls for students to use logic to analyze situations. Students use the rules for translations, reflections, and rotations to find the vertices of the image using an algebraic representation instead of graphs. Also, students use an algebraic rule to create a graph of an image, then use the graph to describe the transformation.

Math Background

Having a good understanding of transformations in both their graphical and algebraic representations will be beneficial for students in more advanced levels of algebra. For example, students will be using a parent parabola that has a vertex at the origin, and then translating it while maintaining its shape. Students will use the equation for the original parabola and the translation rule to write the equation of the translated parabola.

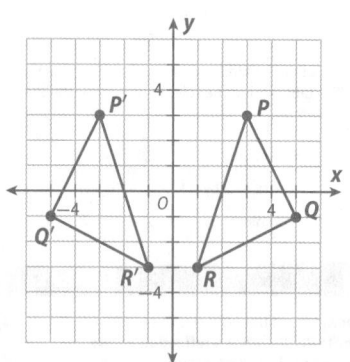

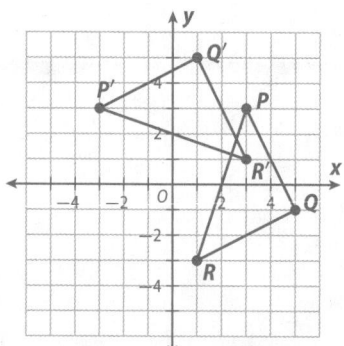

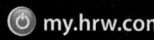
YOUR TURN

Avoid Common Errors

Make sure that students understand they do not just make the *y*-value a negative number. The *y*-value of the image must have a sign opposite that of the preimage's *y*-value.

EXAMPLE 3

Questioning Strategies Mathematical Practices

• In a rotation of 180°, what is the relationship between the coordinates of the preimage and the coordinates of the image? The numbers are the same, but the signs of the coordinates of the image are the opposite of the signs of the coordinates of the preimage.

• If the point (−2, 5) is rotated 90° clockwise, what are the new coordinates? (5, 2) What if (−2, 5) is rotated 180°? (2, −5)

Focus on Modeling Mathematical Practices

In Step 2, be sure students understand why *D* and *D'* are plotted at the same point.

Integrating Language Arts ELL

Encourage a broad class discussion on the Reflect. English learners will benefit from hearing and participating in classroom discussions.

YOUR TURN

Avoid Common Errors

It does not matter if students multiply the *y*-values by −1 before or after the coordinates are switched in Exercise 4, but multiplying by −1 first may prevent errors.

Elaborate

Talk About It
Summarize the Lesson

Ask: Is it possible to determine if a translation, reflection, or rotation occurred by examining the coordinates of the image and preimage? The rules for translations, reflections, and rotations affect coordinates of the ordered pair in distinct ways, so it is often possible to determine which transformation occurred.

GUIDED PRACTICE

Engage with the Whiteboard

For Exercise 2, graph a point such as (2, 2) and reflect it across the *x*-axis on the grid for Exercise 1.

Avoid Common Errors

Exercise 3 Remind students that they must state the number of degrees, point of rotation, and the direction of the rotation.

2. Triangle *ABC* has vertices *A*(−2, 6), *B*(0, 5), and *C*(3, −1). Find the vertices of triangle *A'B'C'* after a reflection across the *x*-axis.

$$A'(-2, -6), B'(0, -5), \text{ and } C'(3, 1)$$

Personal
Math Trainer
Online Assessment
and Intervention
⊙ my.hrw.com

Math On the Spot
⊙ my.hrw.com

Algebraic Representations of Rotations

When points are rotated about the origin, the coordinates of the image can be found using the rules shown in the table.

Rotations	
90° clockwise	Multiply each *x*-coordinate by −1; then switch the *x*- and *y*-coordinates: $(x, y) \rightarrow (y, -x)$
90° counterclockwise	Multiply each *y*-coordinate by −1; then switch the *x*- and *y*-coordinates: $(x, y) \rightarrow (-y, x)$
180°	Multiply both coordinates by −1: $(x, y) \rightarrow (-x, -y)$

EXAMPLE 3   FL CC 8.G.1.3

Quadrilateral *ABCD* has vertices at *A*(−4, 2), *B*(−3, 4), *C*(2, 3), and *D*(0, 0). Find the vertices of quadrilateral *A'B'C'D'* after a 90° clockwise rotation. Then graph the quadrilateral and its image.

STEP 1   Apply the rule to find the vertices of the image.

> Multiply the *x*-coordinate of each vertex by −1, and then switch the *x*- and *y*-coordinates.

Vertices of *ABCD*	Rule: (*y*, −*x*)	Vertices of *A'B'C'D'*
A(−4, 2)	(2, −1 · (−4))	*A'*(2, 4)
B(−3, 4)	(4, −1 · (−3))	*B'*(4, 3)
C(2, 3)	(3, −1 · 2)	*C'*(3, −2)
D(0, 0)	(0, −1 · 0)	*D'*(0, 0)

STEP 2   Graph the quadrilateral and its image.

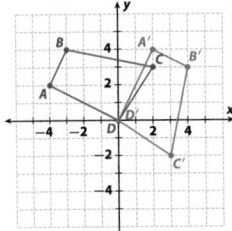

Reflect

3. **Communicate Mathematical Ideas** How would you find the vertices of an image if a figure were rotated 270° clockwise? Explain.

A 270° clockwise rotation is the same as a 90° counterclockwise rotation. Change the sign of the *y*-coordinate and switch the coordinates.

Personal
Math Trainer
Online Assessment
and Intervention
⊙ my.hrw.com

4. A triangle has vertices at *J*(−2, −4), *K*(1, 5), and *L*(2, 2). What are the coordinates of the vertices of the image after the triangle is rotated 90° counterclockwise?

$$J'(4, -2), K'(-5, 1), \text{ and } L'(-2, 2)$$

Guided Practice

1. Triangle *XYZ* has vertices *X*(−3, −2), *Y*(−1, 0), and *Z*(1, −6). Find the vertices of triangle *X'Y'Z'* after a translation of 6 units to the right. Then graph the triangle and its image. (Example 1)

$$X'(3, -2), Y'(5, 0), \text{ and } Z'(7, -6)$$

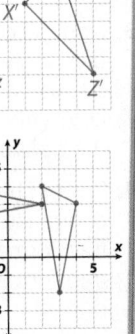

2. Describe what happens to the *x*- and *y*-coordinates after a point is reflected across the *x*-axis. (Example 2)

The *x*-coordinate remains the same, while the *y*-coordinate changes sign.

3. Use the rule $(x, y) \rightarrow (y, -x)$ to graph the image of the triangle at right. Then describe the transformation. (Example 3)

The triangle is rotated 90° clockwise.

? ESSENTIAL QUESTION CHECK-IN

4. How do the *x*- and *y*-coordinates change when a figure is translated right *a* units and down *b* units?

The *x*-coordinates increase by *a*, and the *y*-coordinates decrease by *b*.

DIFFERENTIATE INSTRUCTION

Communicating Math

Have students work in pairs. One student provides a transformation. The other describes how the ordered pairs change using an algebraic representation.

Student 1: Translate right 3 units and up 2 units.

Student 2: Add 3 to the *x*-value, and add 2 to the *y*-value: $(x, y) \rightarrow (x + 3, y + 2)$.

Visual Cues

On three separate index cards, have students write the rules for how to change the coordinates for a figure when it is translated, rotated, and reflected. Have students use colored pencils or markers to emphasize the changes made to the *x*- and *y*-values.

Additional Resources

Differentiated Instruction includes:

- Reading Strategies
- Success for English Learners **ELL**
- Reteach
- Challenge **PRE-AP**

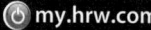
17.4 LESSON QUIZ

 **FL CC** 8.G.1.3

Triangle ABC has vertices A(−4, 1), B(−2, 1), and C(−1, −2).

1. Find the coordinates of the vertices of triangle A′B′C′ after a 90° clockwise rotation about the origin.

2. Find the coordinates of the vertices of triangle A′B′C′ after triangle ABC is reflected across the y-axis.

3. Find the coordinates of the vertices of triangle A′B′C′ after triangle ABC is translated using the rule $(x, y) \rightarrow (x + 5, y − 3)$. Then describe the translation.

4. Point M has coordinates (3, −2). The coordinates of point M′ after a single transformation are (−3, 2). Name a transformation that could have done this.

Lesson Quiz available online

⏻ my.hrw.com

Answers
1. A′(1, 4), B′(1, 2), and C′(−2, 1)

2. A′(4, 1), B′(2, 1), and C′(1, −2)

3. A′(1, −2), B′(3, −2), and C′(4, −5); The triangle is translated 5 units to the right and 3 units down.

4. Sample answers: translation 6 units left and 4 units up; rotation of 180°; reflection across the line $y = x$

Evaluate

GUIDED AND INDEPENDENT PRACTICE

 FL CC 8.G.1.3

Concepts & Skills	Practice
Example 1 Algebraic Representations of Translations	Exercises 1, 5, 7, 9–11
Example 2 Algebraic Representations of Reflections	Exercises 2, 8
Example 3 Algebraic Representations of Rotations	Exercises 3, 6, 12

Exercise	Depth of Knowledge (D.O.K.)	 Mathematical Practices
5–9	**2** Skills/Concepts	**MP.6.1** Precision
10	**2** Skills/Concepts	**MP.7.1** Using Structure
11–12	**2** Skills/Concepts	**MP.6.1** Precision
13	**3** Strategic Thinking **H.O.T.**	**MP.2.1** Reasoning
14	**3** Strategic Thinking **H.O.T.**	**MP.3.1** Logic
15	**3** Strategic Thinking **H.O.T.**	**MP.2.1** Reasoning

Additional Resources
Differentiated Instruction includes:
• Leveled Practice worksheets

CLUSTER CONNECTION

Exercise 13 combines concepts from the Florida Common Core cluster "Understand congruence and similarity using physical models, transparencies, or geometry software."

Name_____ Class_____ Date_____

17.4 Independent Practice

FL CC 8.G.1.3

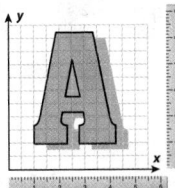

Personal Math Trainer

Online Assessment and Intervention

my.hrw.com

Write an algebraic rule to describe each transformation. Then describe the transformation.

5.

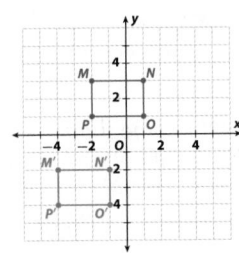

$(x, y) \rightarrow (x - 2, y - 5)$; translation of

2 units to the left and 5 units down

6.

$(x, y) \rightarrow (-x, -y)$; rotation of 180°

7. Triangle XYZ has vertices X(6, −2.3), Y(7.5, 5), and Z(8, 4). When translated, X′ has coordinates (2.8, −1.3). Write a rule to describe this transformation. Then find the coordinates of Y′ and Z′.

$(x, y) \rightarrow (x - 3.2, y + 1)$; Y′(4.3, 6), Z′(4.8, 5)

8. Point L has coordinates (3, −5). The coordinates of point L′ after a reflection are (−3, −5). Without graphing, tell which axis point L was reflected across. Explain your answer.

y-axis; when you reflect a point across the y-axis,

the sign of the x-coordinate changes and the

sign of the y-coordinate remains the same.

9. Use the rule $(x, y) \rightarrow (x - 2, y - 4)$ to graph the image of the rectangle. Then describe the transformation.

The rectangle is translated 2 units to the

left and 4 units down.

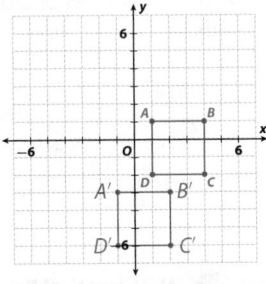

10. Parallelogram ABCD has vertices A(−2, −5½), B(−4, −5½), C(−3, −2), and D(−1, −2). Find the vertices of parallelogram A′B′C′D′ after a translation of 2½ units down.

A′(−2, −8), B′(−4, −8), C′$\left(-3, -4\frac{1}{2}\right)$, and

D′$\left(-1, -4\frac{1}{2}\right)$

Lesson 17.4 **565**

11. Alexandra drew the logo shown on half-inch graph paper. Write a rule that describes the translation Alexandra used to create the shadow on the letter A.

$(x, y) \rightarrow (x + 0.5, y - 0.25)$

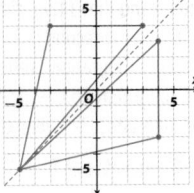

12. Kite KLMN has vertices at K(1, 3), L(2, 4), M(3, 3), and N(2, 0). After the kite is rotated, K′ has coordinates (−3, 1). Describe the rotation, and include a rule in your description. Then find the coordinates of L′, M′, and N′.

90° counterclockwise; $(x, y) \rightarrow (-y, x)$; L′(−4, 2),

M′(−3, 3), and N′(0, 2)

H.O.T. FOCUS ON HIGHER ORDER THINKING

13. Make a Conjecture Graph the triangle with vertices (−3, 4), (3, 4), and (−5, −5). Use the transformation (y, x) to graph its image.

a. Which vertex of the image has the same coordinates as a vertex of the original figure? Explain why this is true.

(−5, −5); x and y are equal, so switching x and y

has no effect on the coordinates.

b. What is the equation of a line through the origin and this point?

$y = x$

c. Describe the transformation of the triangle.

The triangle is reflected across the line $y = x$.

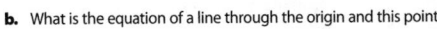

14. Critical Thinking Mitchell says the point (0, 0) does not change when reflected across the x- or y-axis or when rotated about the origin. Do you agree with Mitchell? Explain why or why not.

Yes; reflecting across the x- or y-axis changes the sign of

the y- or x-coordinate; 0 cannot change signs. Rotating

about the origin doesn't change the origin, (0, 0).

Work Area

15. Analyze Relationships Triangle ABC with vertices A(−2, −2), B(−3, 1), and C(1, 1) is translated by $(x, y) \rightarrow (x - 1, y + 3)$. Then the image, triangle A′B′C′, is translated by $(x, y) \rightarrow (x + 4, y - 1)$, resulting in A″B″C″.

a. Find the coordinates for the vertices of triangle A″B″C″.

A″(1, 0), B″(0, 3), and C″(4, 3)

b. Write a rule for one translation that maps triangle ABC to triangle A″B″C″.

$(x, y) \rightarrow (x + 3, y + 2)$

566 Unit 8

EXTEND THE MATH PRE-AP

Activity available online my.hrw.com

Activity Transform the square shown into five smaller, but equal squares, with only four cuts. The sum of the areas of the five smaller squares must total the area of the larger square. Pieces of the larger square, produced when the four cuts are made, can be rotated, reflected, or translated and combined to form the five smaller squares.

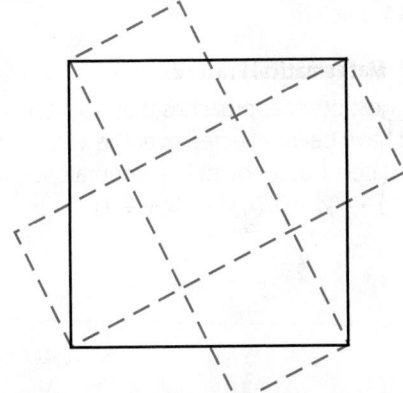

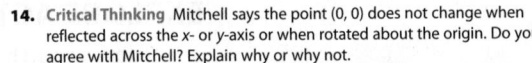
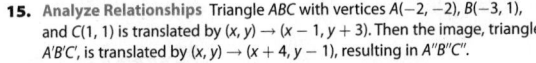

17.5 Congruent Figures

ADDITIONAL EXAMPLE 1

A Identify a sequence of transformations that will transform figure *G* into figure *H*.

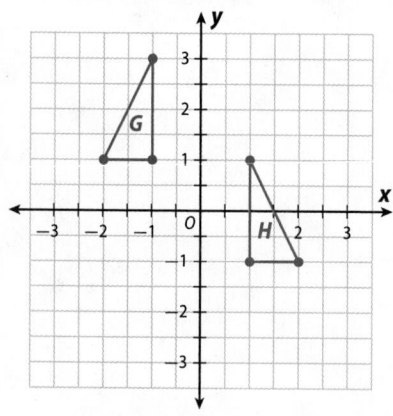

$(x, y) \rightarrow (-x, y), (x, y) \rightarrow (x, y - 2)$

(Continued on page 305)

 Interactive Whiteboard
Interactive example available online

 my.hrw.com

Engage

ESSENTIAL QUESTION

What is the connection between transformations and figures that have the same shape and size? Sample answer: If two figures have the same shape and size, then there exists a sequence of translations, reflections, and/or rotations that transforms one into the other.

Motivate the Lesson

Ask: What effect will a combination of rotations, translations, and/or reflections on a triangle have on its size and shape? Take a guess. Begin the Explore Activity to find out.

Explore

EXPLORE ACTIVITY

Engage with the Whiteboard

Color coding the corresponding sides or labeling the vertices of the triangle and its images will help students better visualize the movement of the triangle.

Explain

EXAMPLE 1

Questioning Strategies Mathematical Practices

• How do you know when a rotation is part of the transformation? The image will be turned when compared to the original figure.

• In Parts B and C, why do you think the rotation is performed before the translation? Sample answer: It can be difficult to see exactly where the figure will end up after a rotation. By rotating first, you can simply translate the figure into the correct place, avoiding this issue.

Engage with the Whiteboard

For each part, have a volunteer graph the intermediate step in producing the final image. For example, in Part A, the volunteer would graph the reflection of figure *A* over the *y*-axis before it is translated 1 unit left.

Focus on Communication Mathematical Practices

In Part C, encourage students to suggest other approaches that might map figure *D* on to figure *E*. For example, figure *D* could have been reflected over the *x*-axis, rotated 90° clockwise about the origin, and translated 1 unit down. The algebraic sequence of transformations is $(x, y) \rightarrow (-x, y), (x, y) \rightarrow (y, -x), (x, y) \rightarrow (x, y - 1)$.

LESSON

17.5 Congruent Figures

FL CC 8.G.1.2

Understand that a two-dimensional figure is congruent to another if the second can be obtained from the first by a sequence of rotations, reflections, and translations; given two congruent figures, describe a sequence that exhibits the congruence between them.

? ESSENTIAL QUESTION What is the connection between transformations and figures that have the same shape and size?

EXPLORE ACTIVITY | FL CC 8.G.1.2

Combining Transformations

Apply the indicated series of transformations to the triangle. Each transformation is applied to the image of the previous transformation, not the original figure. Label each image with the letter of the transformation applied.

A Reflection across the x-axis

B $(x, y) \rightarrow (x - 3, y)$

C Reflection across the y-axis

D $(x, y) \rightarrow (x, y + 4)$

E Rotation 90° clockwise around the origin

F Compare the size and shape of the final image to that of the original figure.

They have the same size and shape, just a different

orientation.

Reflect

1. Which transformation(s) change the orientation of figures? Which do not?

Reflections and rotations; translations

2. **Make a Conjecture** Two figures have the same size and shape. What does this indicate about the figures?

One figure is the image of the other, and there is a

sequence of transformations that will transform one

figure into the other.

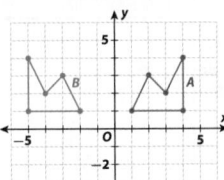

Congruent Figures

Recall that segments and their images have the same length and angles and their images have the same measure under a translation, reflection, or rotation. Two figures are said to be **congruent** if one can be obtained from the other by a sequence of translations, reflections, and rotations. Congruent figures have the same size and shape.

When you are told that two figures are congruent, there must be a sequence of translations, reflections, and/or rotations that transforms one into the other.

EXAMPLE 1 | FL CC 8.G.1.2

A Identify a sequence of transformations that will transform figure A into figure B.

To transform figure A into figure B, you need to reflect it over the y-axis and translate one unit to the left. A sequence of transformations that will accomplish this is $(x, y) \rightarrow (-x, y)$ and $(x, y) \rightarrow (x - 1, y)$.

B Identify a sequence of transformations that will transform figure B into figure C.

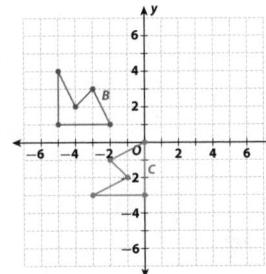

Any sequence of transformations that changes figure B into figure C will need to include a rotation. A 90° counterclockwise rotation around the origin would result in the figure being oriented as figure C.

However, the rotated figure would be 2 units below and 1 unit to the left of where figure C is. You would need to translate the rotated figure up 2 units and right 1 unit.

In both cases, the image is turned sideways from the original figure. Only a rotation will do this.

Math Talk
Mathematical Practices

How do you know that the sequence of transformations in Parts B and C must include a rotation?

© Houghton Mifflin Harcourt Publishing Company

PROFESSIONAL DEVELOPMENT

Integrate Mathematical Practices MP.6.1

This lesson provides an opportunity to address this Mathematical Practice standard. It calls for students to attend to precision. Students pay close attention to the coordinates of the vertices of a figure in order to apply a given sequence of transformations and graph the resulting image. Each transformation must be carefully and precisely applied to obtain the desired outcome. Students also must pay close attention to the coordinates of the vertices of a figure and its images when determining the sequence of transformations that result in a figure being transformed into a particular image.

Math Background

If there exists a sequence of translations, reflections, and/or rotations that will transform one figure into the other, the two figures are congruent. Note that dilations are not included in this list of transformations. The image after a dilation is either an enlargement or reduction of the original figure, making the two figures similar but not congruent. While dilations preserve the shape of a figure, they do not preserve the size. A dilation is often called a similarity transformation.

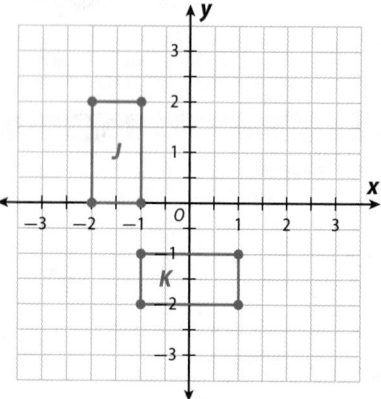
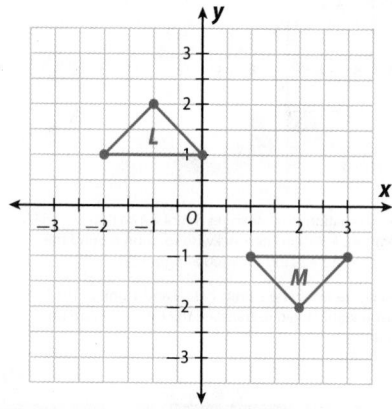

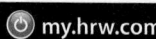
YOUR TURN

Avoid Common Errors

If students cannot visualize the sequence of transformations, suggest they use a cut-out paper triangle the same size and shape as figure *A* that they can rotate and translate on the coordinate grid.

Talk About It
Check for Understanding

 Ask: How do you know if a two-dimensional figure is congruent to another? Two figures are congruent if the second can be obtained from the first by a sequence of rotations, reflections, and translations. The two figures will have the same size and shape.

Elaborate

Talk About It
Summarize the Lesson

Ask: How can seeing a turned image or a mirror image help you decide which transformations were performed in the sequence of transformations? In order to get a turned image, a rotation must have occurred. In order to get a mirror image, a reflection must have occurred.

GUIDED PRACTICE

Engage with the Whiteboard

For Exercise 1, have five volunteers take turns drawing the indicated series of transformations on the coordinate grid provided.

Avoid Common Errors

Exercise 2 Students might think a rotation was used to transform figure *A* into figure *B*. Suggest students use a paper cut-out of triangle *A* and actually rotate it about point (0, 2) to see that the orientation of figure *B* is not right for the transformation to have been a rotation.

Exercise 4 Before trying to write the algebraic sequence of transformations used, suggest that students label figures *A*, *B*, and *C* with the ordered pairs for each of the vertices. Then, analyze the pairs to understand the changes to the *x* and *y* values.

The sequence of transformations is a 90° counterclockwise rotation about the origin, $(x, y) \rightarrow (-y, x)$, followed by $(x, y) \rightarrow (x + 1, y + 2)$.

C Identify a sequence of transformations that will transform figure D into figure E.

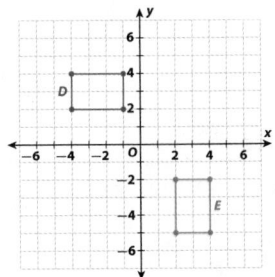

A sequence of transformations that changes figure D to figure E will need to include a rotation. A 90° clockwise rotation around the origin would result in the figure being oriented as figure E.

However, the rotated figure would be 6 units above where figure E is. You would need to translate the rotated figure down 6 units.

The sequence of transformations is a 90° clockwise rotation about the origin, $(x, y) \rightarrow (y, -x)$, followed by $(x, y) \rightarrow (x, y - 6)$.

YOUR TURN

3. Identify a sequence of transformations that will transform figure A into figure B.

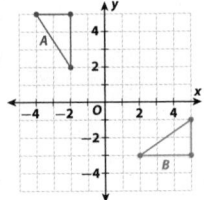

Rotation 90° clockwise about origin, translation 5 units

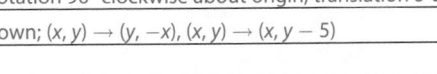

down; $(x, y) \rightarrow (y, -x)$, $(x, y) \rightarrow (x, y - 5)$

Personal Math Trainer
Online Assessment and Intervention
Ⓑ my.hrw.com

Guided Practice

1. Apply the indicated series of transformations to the rectangle. Each transformation is applied to the image of the previous transformation, not the original figure. Label each image with the letter of the transformation applied. (Explore Activity)

   a. Reflection across the y-axis

   b. Rotation 90° clockwise around the origin

   c. $(x, y) \rightarrow (x - 2, y)$

   d. Rotation 90° counterclockwise around the origin

   e. $(x, y) \rightarrow (x - 7, y - 2)$

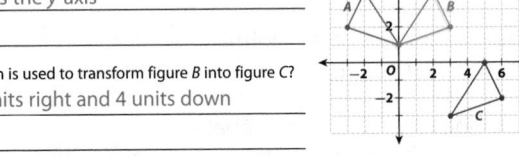

Identify a sequence of transformations that will transform figure A into figure C. (Example 1)

2. What transformation is used to transform figure A into figure B?

   reflection across the y-axis

3. What transformation is used to transform figure B into figure C?

   translation 3 units right and 4 units down

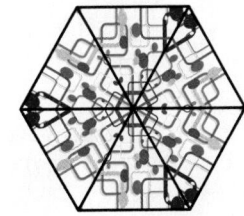

4. What sequence of transformations is used to transform figure A into figure C? Express the transformations algebraically.

   $(x, y) \rightarrow (-x, y)$, $(x, y) \rightarrow (x + 3, y - 4)$

5. **Vocabulary** What does it mean for two figures to be congruent?

   The figures have the same size and the same shape.

? ESSENTIAL QUESTION CHECK-IN

6. After a sequence of translations, reflections, and rotations, what is true about the first figure and the final figure?

   They have the same size and the same shape. (They are congruent.)

DIFFERENTIATE INSTRUCTION

Multiple Representations

Provide students with 6 congruent equilateral triangles. Have students arrange the triangles to form a hexagon. Students should then draw a simple but colorful design on one of the triangles and then reflect that design around the hexagon 5 times onto the other triangles. Explain that their final design will be a kaleidoscope image, as shown here.

Additional Resources

Differentiated Instruction includes:

• Reading Strategies

• Success for English Learners **ELL**

• Reteach

• Challenge **PRE-AP**

Congruent Figures **570**

Personal Math Trainer

Online Assessment and Intervention

Online homework assignment available

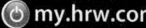

⏻ my.hrw.com

17.5 LESSON QUIZ

FL CC 8.G.1.2

1. On a coordinate grid, graph a triangle with its vertices at (−2, 1), (−4, 1), and (−1, 4). Then apply the indicated series of transformations to the triangle. Each transformation is applied to the image of the previous transformation. Label each image with the letter of the transformation applied.

   A Rotation 90° clockwise around the origin

   B $(x, y) \rightarrow (x, y - 3)$

   C $(x, y) \rightarrow (x - 3, y - 2)$

2. Identify a sequence of transformations that will transform figure A into figure B.

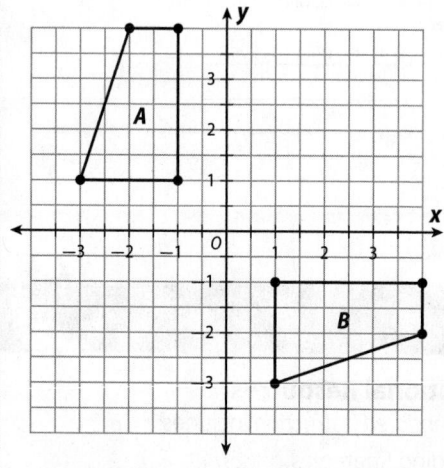

Lesson Quiz available online

⏻ my.hrw.com

Evaluate

GUIDED AND INDEPENDENT PRACTICE

 **FL CC** 8.G.1.2

Concepts & Skills	Practice
Explore Activity Combining Transformations	Exercises 1, 7–10, 12
Example 1 Congruent Figures	Exercises 2–5, 11–12

Exercise	Depth of Knowledge (D.O.K.)		**FL CC** Mathematical Practices
7–10	**1** Recall of Information		**MP.4.1** Modeling
11	**2** Skills/Concepts		**MP.4.1** Modeling
12	**2** Skills/Concepts		**MP.3.1** Logic
13	**3** Strategic Thinking	H.O.T.	**MP.3.1** Logic
14	**3** Strategic Thinking	H.O.T.	**MP.2.1** Reasoning

Additional Resources
Differentiated Instruction includes:
• Leveled Practice worksheets

Answers
1.

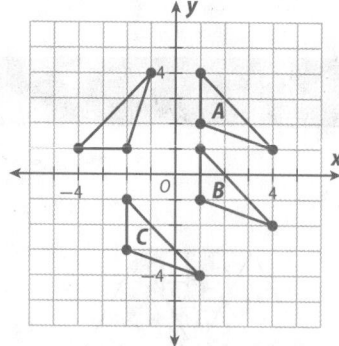

2. Reflection across the *y*-axis, rotation 90° clockwise about the origin; $(x, y) \rightarrow (-x, y)$, $(x, y) \rightarrow (y, -x)$

Name _____ Class _____ Date _____

17.5 Independent Practice

Personal Math Trainer
Online Assessment and Intervention
my.hrw.com

FL CC 8.G.1.2

For each given figure A, graph figures B and C using the given sequence of transformations. State whether figures A and C have the same or different orientation.

7.

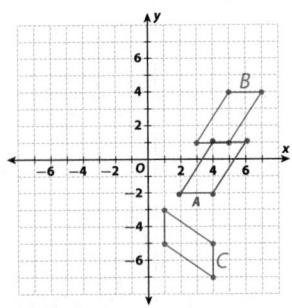

Figure B: a translation of 1 unit to the right and 3 units up

Figure C: a 90° clockwise rotation around the origin

Different orientation

8.

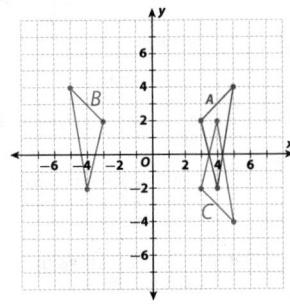

Figure B: a reflection across the y-axis

Figure C: a 180° rotation around the origin

Different orientation

9.

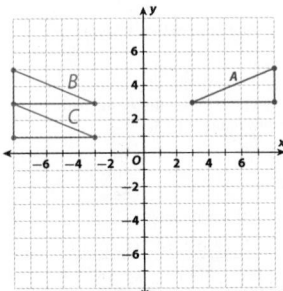

Figure B: a reflection across the y-axis

Figure C: a translation 2 units down

Different orientation

10.

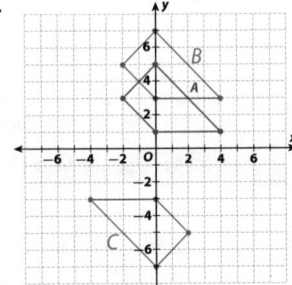

Figure B: a translation 2 units up

Figure C: a rotation of 180° around the origin

Different orientation

Lesson 17.5 **571**

---

11. Represent Real-World Problems A city planner wanted to place the new town library at site A. The mayor thought that it would be better at site B. What transformations were applied to the building at site A to relocate the building to site B? Did the mayor change the size or orientation of the library?

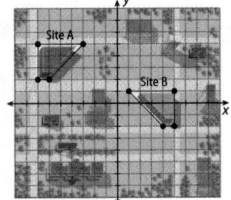

Sample answer: translation 2 units right and

4 units down, reflection across y-axis; size: no;

orientation: yes

12. Persevere in Problem Solving Find a sequence of three transformations that can be used to obtain figure D from figure A. Graph the figures B and C that are created by the transformations.

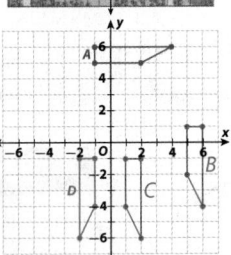

Sample answer: Figure B: rotation 90° clockwise

around origin; figure C: translation 4 units left

and 2 units down; figure D: reflection across

y-axis

H.O.T. FOCUS ON HIGHER ORDER THINKING

Work Area

13. Counterexamples The Commutative Properties for Addition and Multiplication state that the order of two numbers being added or multiplied does not change the sum or product. Are translations and rotations commutative? If not, give a counterexample.

No; the point (1, 2), translated 2 units to the right,

becomes (3, 2), then rotated 90° around the origin it

becomes (2, −3). The point (1, 2) rotated 90° around the

origin becomes (2, −1), then translated 2 units to the

right it becomes (4, −1), which is not the same.

14. Multiple Representations For each representation, describe a possible sequence of transformations.

a. $(x, y) \rightarrow (-x - 2, y + 1)$

Sample answer: translation 2 units right and 1 unit

up, reflection across y-axis

b. $(x, y) \rightarrow (y, -x - 3)$

Sample answer: rotation 90° clockwise around the

origin, translation 3 units down

572 Unit 8

EXTEND THE MATH PRE-AP

Activity available online my.hrw.com

Activity A translation followed by a reflection about a line that is parallel to the line of translation is called a glide reflection. The heart shown below has been glided and reflected twice.

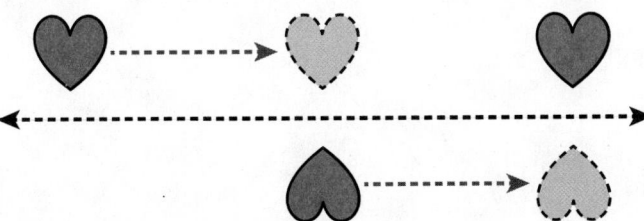

Draw a horizontal line on a piece of paper, choose a shape, and make a glide reflection pattern.

Congruent Figures **572**

Ready to Go On?

Assess Mastery

Use the assessment on this page to determine if students have mastered the concepts and standards covered in this module.

 **Response to Intervention**

Intervention	Enrichment

Personal Math Trainer
Online Assessment and Intervention
⏻ my.hrw.com

Access Ready to Go On? assessment online, and receive instant scoring, feedback, and customized intervention or enrichment.

Online and Print Resources

Differentiated Instruction
• Reteach worksheets
• Reading Strategies **ELL**
• Success for English Learners **ELL**

Differentiated Instruction
• Challenge worksheets
  PRE-AP
• Extend the Math **PRE-AP**
  Lesson Activities in TE

Additional Resources

Assessment Resources includes:
• Leveled Module Quizzes

MODULE QUIZ

Ready to Go On?

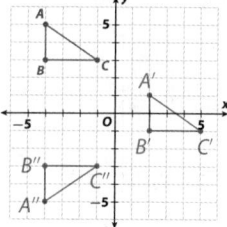
Personal Math Trainer
Online Assessment and Intervention
ⓜ my.hrw.com

17.1–17.3 Properties of Translations, Reflections, and Rotations

1. Graph the image of triangle *ABC* after a translation of 6 units to the right and 4 units down. Label the vertices of the image *A′*, *B′*, and *C′*.

2. On the same coordinate grid, graph the image of triangle *ABC* after a reflection across the *y*-axis. Label the vertices of the image *A″*, *B″*, and *C″*.

3. Graph the image of *HIJK* after it is rotated 180° about the origin. Label the vertices of the image *H′I′J′K′*.

17.4 Algebraic Representations of Transformations

4. A triangle has vertices at (2, 3), (−2, 2), and (−3, 5). What are the coordinates of the vertices of the image after the translation $(x, y) \rightarrow (x + 4, y − 3)$?

   (6, 0), (2, −1), and (1, 2)

17.5 Congruent Figures

5. **Vocabulary** Translations, reflections, and rotations produce a figure that is __congruent__ to the original figure.

6. Use the coordinate grid for Exercise 3. Reflect *H′I′J′K′* over the *y*-axis, then rotate it 180° about the origin. Label the new figure *H″I″J″K″*.

❓ ESSENTIAL QUESTION

7. How can you use transformations to solve real-world problems?
   Sample answer: You can use transformations to determine movement from one location to another.

Module 17 **573**

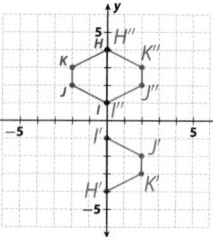

 ## Florida Common Core Standards

Lesson	Exercises	Common Core Standards
17.1	1	**8.G.1.1, 8.G.1.3**
17.2	2	**8.G.1.1, 8.G.1.3**
17.3	3	**8.G.1.1, 8.G.1.3**
17.4	4	**8.G.1.3**
17.5	5–6	**8.G.1.2**

PARCC Assessment Readiness

Assessment Readiness Tip Students can sketch a diagram to help represent information from a problem.

Item 5 Students can sketch a trapezoid with a pair of coordinate axes and then reflect the trapezoid across the *x*-axis to help them visualize the problem.

Item 6 Students can use the coordinate plane from item 3 to plot the points in item 6. It will be slightly off the grid, but it will help them to visualize the initial orientation of the triangle and predict where the image will be located.

Avoid Common Errors

Item 3 Some students have difficulty determining which way is clockwise and which is counterclockwise. Remind the students to glance at a clock, if one is available in the room, to remind them which way is which by following the numbers forward for clockwise, or backward for counterclockwise. They should also label the four quadrants of the coordinate plane before answering the question.

Item 5 Students may miss the word *not* in this question, and instead pick the first thing they see as true instead of looking for the false statement. Remind the students to read carefully, and highlight, underline, or circle key words like *not*, so they can better approach the question.

Additional Resources

Personal Math Trainer

Online Assessment and Intervention

my.hrw.com

Selected Response

1. What would be the orientation of the figure L after a translation of 8 units to the right and 3 units up?

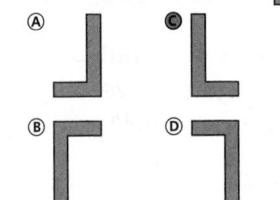

Ⓐ   Ⓒ   Ⓑ   Ⓓ

2. Figure A is reflected over the *y*-axis and then lowered 6 units. Which sequence describes these transformations?

Ⓐ $(x, y) \rightarrow (x, -y)$ and $(x, y) \rightarrow (x, y - 6)$
Ⓑ $(x, y) \rightarrow (-x, y)$ and $(x, y) \rightarrow (x, y - 6)$
Ⓒ $(x, y) \rightarrow (x, -y)$ and $(x, y) \rightarrow (x - 6, y)$
Ⓓ $(x, y) \rightarrow (-x, y)$ and $(x, y) \rightarrow (x - 6, y)$

3. What quadrant would the triangle be in after a rotation of 90° counterclockwise about the origin?

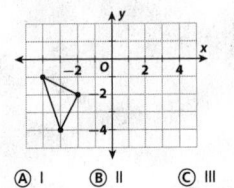

Ⓐ I   Ⓑ II   Ⓒ III   Ⓓ IV

4. Which rational number is greater than $-3\frac{1}{3}$ but less than $-\frac{4}{5}$?

Ⓐ -0.4 Ⓒ -0.19
Ⓑ $-\frac{9}{7}$ Ⓓ $-\frac{22}{5}$

5. Which of the following is **not** true of a trapezoid that has been reflected across the *x*-axis?

Ⓐ The new trapezoid is the same size as the original trapezoid.
Ⓑ The new trapezoid is the same shape as the original trapezoid.
Ⓒ The new trapezoid is in the same orientation as the original trapezoid.
Ⓓ The *x*-coordinates of the new trapezoid are the same as the *x*-coordinates of the original trapezoid.

6. A triangle with coordinates (6, 4), (2, −1), and (−3, 5) is translated 4 units left and rotated 180° about the origin. What are the coordinates of its image?

Ⓐ (2, 4), (−2, −1), (−7, 5)
Ⓑ (4, 6), (−1, 2), (5, −3)
Ⓒ (4, −2), (−1, 2), (5, 7)
Ⓓ (−2, −4), (2, 1), (7, −5)

Mini-Task

7. A rectangle with vertices (3, −2), (3, −4), (7, −2), (7, −4) is reflected across the *x*-axis and then rotated 90° counterclockwise.

a. In what quadrant does the image lie?

II

b. What are the vertices of the image?

(−2, 3), (−4, 3), (−2, 7), (−4, 7)

c. What other transformations produce the same image?

Reflect over *y*-axis, then rotate 90° clockwise about origin

© Houghton Mifflin Harcourt Publishing Company

Florida Common Core Standards

Items	 Grade 8 Standards	 Mathematical Practices
1	8.G.1.1	MP.7.1
2	8.G.1.3	MP.4.1
3	8.G.1.1	MP.4.1
4*	8.NS.1.2	MP.2.1
5	8.G.1.1	MP.7.1
6	8.G.1.3	MP.4.1
7	8.G.1.2, 8.G.1.3	MP.4.1

* Item integrates mixed review concepts from previous modules or a previous course.

Transformations and Similarity

 **ESSENTIAL QUESTION**

How can you use dilations and similarity to solve real-world problems?

You can use similarity to analyze how real-world objects are affected when they undergo dilations.

© Houghton Mifflin Harcourt Publishing Company

Real-World Video

To plan a mural, the artist first makes a smaller drawing showing what the mural will look like. Then the image is enlarged by a scale factor on the mural canvas. This enlargement is called a dilation.

my.hrw.com

GO DIGITAL
my.hrw.com

my.hrw.com
Go digital with your write-in student edition, accessible on any device.

Math On the Spot
Scan with your smart phone to jump directly to the online edition, video tutor, and more.

Animated Math
Interactively explore key concepts to see how math works.

Personal Math Trainer
Get immediate feedback and help as you work through practice sets.

Are You Ready?

Assess Readiness

Use the assessment on this page to determine if students need intensive or strategic intervention for the module's prerequisite skills.

Response to Intervention

Personal Math Trainer

Online Assessment and Intervention

⏻ my.hrw.com

Intervention	Enrichment
Access Are You Ready? assessment online, and receive instant scoring, feedback, and customized intervention or enrichment.	

Online and Print Resources

Skills Intervention worksheets
- Skill 28 Simplify Ratios
- Skill 45 Multiply with Fractions and Decimals
- Skill 69 Graph Ordered Pairs (First Quadrant)

Differentiated Instruction
- Challenge worksheets **PRE-AP**
- Extend the Math **PRE-AP** Lesson Activities in TE

Are YOU Ready?

Complete these exercises to review skills you will need for this module.

Personal Math Trainer
Online Assessment and Intervention
⏻ my.hrw.com

Simplify Ratios

EXAMPLE $\frac{35}{21} = \frac{35 \div 7}{21 \div 7}$ *To write a ratio in simplest form, find the greatest common factor of the numerator and denominator.*

$= \frac{5}{3}$ *Divide the numerator and denominator by the GCF.*

Write each ratio in simplest form.

1. $\frac{6}{15}$ $\frac{2}{5}$ 2. $\frac{8}{20}$ $\frac{2}{5}$ 3. $\frac{30}{18}$ $\frac{5}{3}$ 4. $\frac{36}{30}$ $\frac{6}{5}$

Multiply with Fractions and Decimals

EXAMPLE $2\frac{3}{5} \times 20$ *Write numbers as fractions and multiply.*

$= \frac{13 \times 20}{5 \times 1}$

$= \frac{13 \times \overset{4}{\cancel{20}}}{\underset{1}{\cancel{5}} \times 1}$ *Simplify.*

$= 52$

   68
  $\times 4.5$
  340
$+272$
306.0

Multiply as you would with whole numbers.

Place the decimal point in the answer based on the total number of decimal places in the two factors.

Multiply.

5. $60 \times \frac{25}{100}$ 15   6. 3.5×40 140   7. 4.4×44 193.6   8. $24 \times \frac{8}{9}$ $21\frac{1}{3}$

Graph Ordered Pairs (First Quadrant)

EXAMPLE

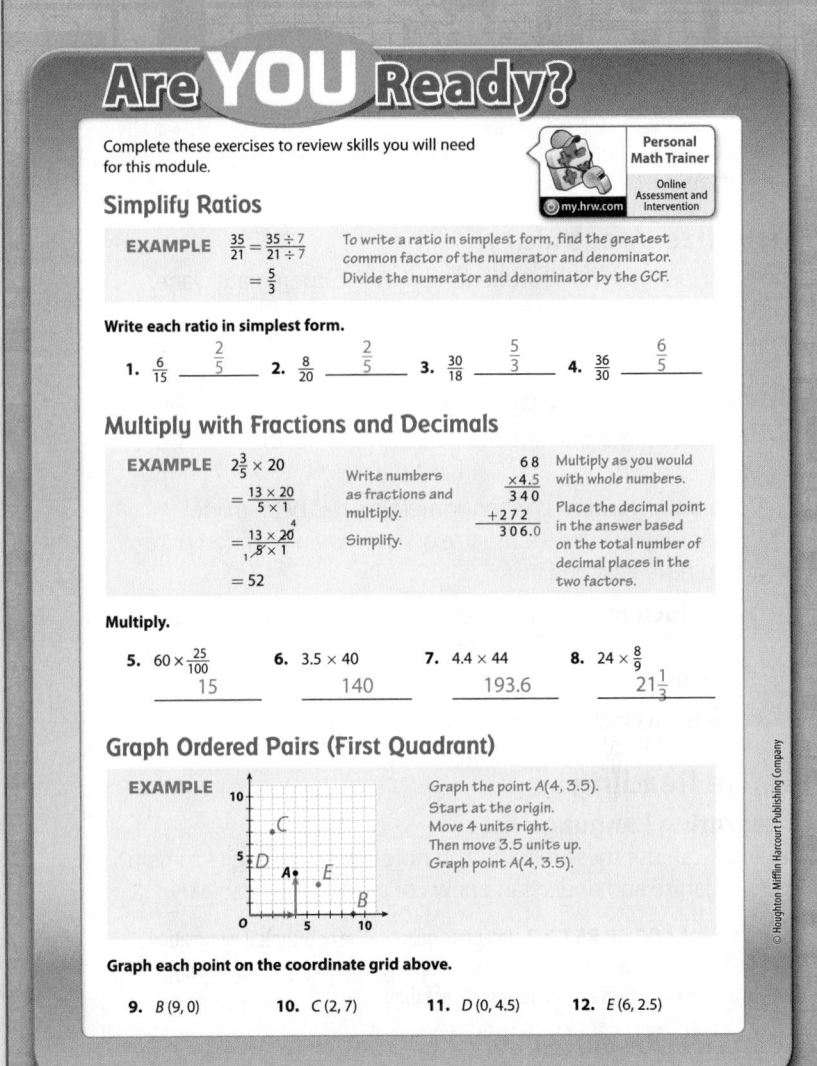

Graph the point A(4, 3.5).
Start at the origin.
Move 4 units right.
Then move 3.5 units up.
Graph point A(4, 3.5).

Graph each point on the coordinate grid above.

9. $B(9, 0)$ 10. $C(2, 7)$ 11. $D(0, 4.5)$ 12. $E(6, 2.5)$

© Houghton Mifflin Harcourt Publishing Company

576 Unit 8

PROFESSIONAL DEVELOPMENT VIDEO

Author Juli Dixon models successful teaching practices as she explores the concept of scientific notation in an actual eighth-grade classroom.

Professional Development

⏻ my.hrw.com

GO DIGITAL
my.hrw.com

Online Teacher Edition
Access a full suite of teaching resources online—plan, present, and manage classes and assignments.

ePlanner
Easily plan your classes and access all your resources online.

Interactive Answers and Solutions
Customize answer keys to print or display in the classroom. Choose to include answers only or full solutions to all lesson exercises.

Interactive Whiteboards
Engage students with interactive whiteboard-ready lessons and activities.

Personal Math Trainer: Online Assessment and Intervention
Assign automatically graded homework, quizzes, tests, and intervention activities. Prepare your students with updated practice tests aligned with Common Core.

Reading Start-Up

Have students complete the activities on this page by working alone or with others.

Visualize Vocabulary

The main idea web helps students review the coordinate plane. Students should write one review word in each rectangle. If time allows, brainstorm additional terms as a class to add to the diagram.

Understand Vocabulary

Use the following explanation to help students learn the preview words.

An **enlargement** is when something has been made larger. If you increase the size of a photo on your computer, you have enlarged it.

A **reduction** is when something has been made smaller. In a dollhouse, the furniture is reduced to scale so that it resembles actual furniture but is small.

Dilations include both enlargements and reductions.

Active Reading

Integrating Language Arts

Students can use these reading and note-taking strategies to help them organize and understand new concepts and vocabulary.

FL CC **LACC.68.RST.3.7** Integrate quantitative or technical information expressed in words in a text with a version of that information expressed visually (e.g., in a flowchart, diagram, model, graph, or table).

Additional Resources

Differentiated Instruction

• Reading Strategies **ELL**

 **Start-Up**

Visualize Vocabulary

Use the ✔ words to complete the graphic organizer. You will put one word in each rectangle.

The four regions on a coordinate plane.	The point where the axes intersect to form the coordinate plane.
quadrants	origin

Reviewing the Coordinate Plane

The horizontal axis of a coordinate plane.	The vertical axis of a coordinate plane.
x-axis	y-axis

Understand Vocabulary

Complete the sentences using the preview words.

1. A figure larger than the original, produced through dilation, is an ___enlargement___.

2. A figure smaller than the original, produced through dilation, is a ___reduction___.

Active Reading

Key-Term Fold Before beginning the module, create a key-term fold to help you learn the vocabulary in this module. Write the highlighted vocabulary words on one side of the flap. Write the definition for each word on the other side of the flap. Use the key-term fold to quiz yourself on the definitions used in this module.

Module 18 **577**

Vocabulary

Review Words
- coordinate plane (*plano cartesiano*)
- image (*imagen*)
- ✔ origin (*origen*)
- preimage (*imagen original*)
- ✔ quadrants (*cuadrante*)
- ratio (*razón*)
- scale (*escala*)
- ✔ x-axis (*eje x*)
- ✔ y-axis (*eje y*)

Preview Words
- center of dilation (*centro de dilatación*)
- dilation (*dilatación*)
- enlargement (*agrandamiento*)
- reduction (*reducción*)
- scale factor (*factor de escala*)
- similar (*similar*)

Before	In this module	After
Students understand: • ratios • similar triangles	Students use transformational geometry to: • compare and contrast the attributes of a shape and its dilation(s) on a coordinate plane • represent algebraically the effect of a scale factor applied to two-dimensional figures on a coordinate plane with the origin as the center of dilation • explore how transformations can be used to obtain similar figures	Students will connect: • dilations and similarity

Unpacking the Standards

Use the examples on the page to help students know exactly what they are expected to learn in this module.

Florida Common Core Standards

Content Areas

 **Geometry—8.G.1**

Understand congruence and similarity using physical models, transparencies, or geometry software.

Go online to see a complete unpacking of the Florida Common Core Standards.

my.hrw.com

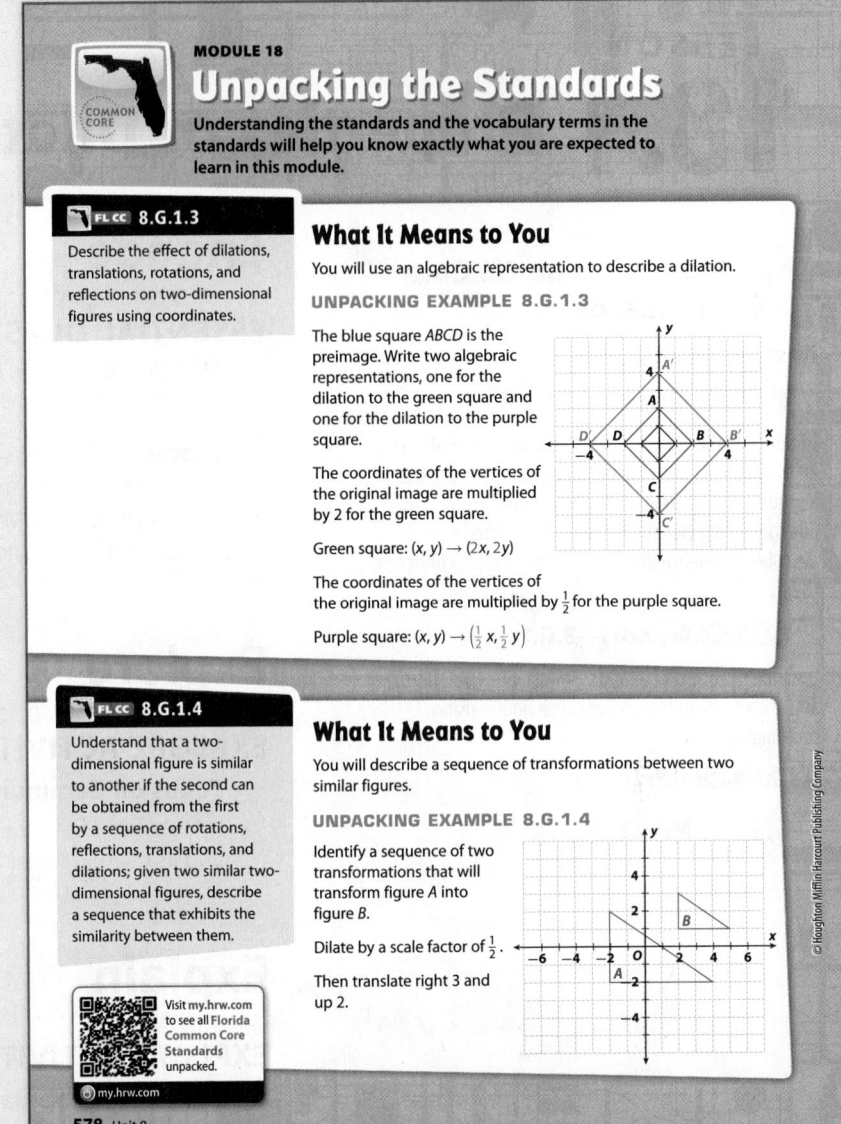

MODULE 18

Unpacking the Standards

Understanding the standards and the vocabulary terms in the standards will help you know exactly what you are expected to learn in this module.

FL CC 8.G.1.3

Describe the effect of dilations, translations, rotations, and reflections on two-dimensional figures using coordinates.

What It Means to You

You will use an algebraic representation to describe a dilation.

UNPACKING EXAMPLE 8.G.1.3

The blue square *ABCD* is the preimage. Write two algebraic representations, one for the dilation to the green square and one for the dilation to the purple square.

The coordinates of the vertices of the original image are multiplied by 2 for the green square.

Green square: $(x, y) \rightarrow (2x, 2y)$

The coordinates of the vertices of the original image are multiplied by $\frac{1}{2}$ for the purple square.

Purple square: $(x, y) \rightarrow \left(\frac{1}{2}x, \frac{1}{2}y\right)$

FL CC 8.G.1.4

Understand that a two-dimensional figure is similar to another if the second can be obtained from the first by a sequence of rotations, reflections, translations, and dilations; given two similar two-dimensional figures, describe a sequence that exhibits the similarity between them.

What It Means to You

You will describe a sequence of transformations between two similar figures.

UNPACKING EXAMPLE 8.G.1.4

Identify a sequence of two transformations that will transform figure *A* into figure *B*.

Dilate by a scale factor of $\frac{1}{2}$.

Then translate right 3 and up 2.

Visit my.hrw.com to see all Florida Common Core Standards unpacked.

my.hrw.com

578 Unit 8

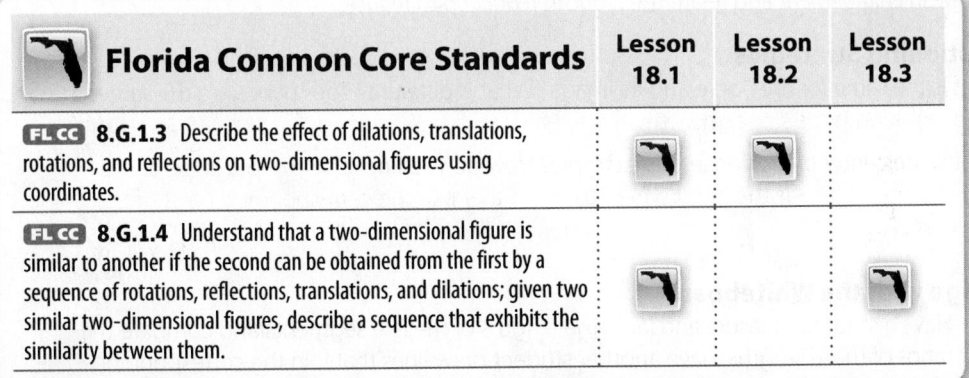

Florida Common Core Standards	Lesson 18.1	Lesson 18.2	Lesson 18.3
FL CC 8.G.1.3 Describe the effect of dilations, translations, rotations, and reflections on two-dimensional figures using coordinates.	🏴	🏴	
FL CC 8.G.1.4 Understand that a two-dimensional figure is similar to another if the second can be obtained from the first by a sequence of rotations, reflections, translations, and dilations; given two similar two-dimensional figures, describe a sequence that exhibits the similarity between them.	🏴		🏴

Transformations and Similarity **578**

LESSON
18.1 Properties of Dilations

 Florida Common Core Standards

The student is expected to:

 **Geometry—8.G.1.4**

Understand that a two-dimensional figure is similar to another if the second can be obtained from the first by a sequence of rotations, reflections, translations, and dilations; given two similar two-dimensional figures, describe a sequence that exhibits the similarity between them.

 **Geometry—8.G.1.3**

Describe the effect of dilations, translations, rotations, and reflections on two-dimensional figures using coordinates.

Mathematical Practices

 **MP.5.1** Using Tools

Engage

ESSENTIAL QUESTION

How do you describe the properties of dilations? Sample answer: Dilations change the size of figures, but not their orientation or shape.

Motivate the Lesson

Ask: Have you ever made an enlarged or reduced copy of a document or photograph on a copying machine? What is the math behind changing the size of an image? Begin the Explore Activity to find out.

Explore

EXPLORE ACTIVITY 1

Focus on Communication Mathematical Practices

In discussing Reflect Exercise 2, you may wish to point out that the orientation of a figure and its dilation remain the same only if the scale factor is positive. See **Extend the Math.**

Explain

EXPLORE ACTIVITY 2

Connect Vocabulary ELL

Help students remember *dilation* by asking if anyone has had an eye exam where their pupils were dilated (made larger) for the exam. Use blocks, models, or pictures to demonstrate the two kinds of dilations: enlargements and reductions. Help students find the *large* in *enlargement* and relate the *reduc* in *reduction* to *reduce*.

Questioning Strategies

• What is the same for the figure and its image? What is different? The shapes are the same; the orientation is the same; the sizes are different.

• What is the center of dilation in this example? How do you know? The origin is the center of dilation because it is the point where the lines that join the corresponding parts of the two figures intersect.

Engage with the Whiteboard

Have a student measure and label the lengths of the line segments and compare the ratios of these lengths. Have another student draw lines that join the corresponding points of the two figures to see where these lines intersect.

LESSON
18.1 Properties of Dilations

FL CC 8.G.1.4

Understand that a two-dimensional figure is similar to another if the second can be obtained from the first by a sequence of ... dilations; ... Also 8.G.1.3

? **ESSENTIAL QUESTION**

How do you describe the properties of dilations?

EXPLORE ACTIVITY 1 (Real World)   FL CC 8.G.1.4

Exploring Dilations

The missions that placed 12 astronauts on the moon were controlled at the Johnson Space Center in Houston. The toy models at the right are scaled-down replicas of the Saturn V rocket that powered the moon flights. Each replica is a transformation called a **dilation**. Unlike the other transformations you have studied—translations, rotations, and reflections—dilations change the size (but not the shape) of a figure.

Every dilation has a fixed point called the **center of dilation** located where the lines connecting corresponding parts of figures intersect.

Triangle R′S′T′ is a dilation of triangle RST. Point C is the center of dilation.

A Use a ruler to measure segments $\overline{CR'}$, $\overline{CR}$, $\overline{CS'}$, $\overline{CS}$, $\overline{CT'}$, and $\overline{CT'}$ to the nearest millimeter. Record the measurements and ratios in the table.

CR′	CR	$\frac{CR'}{CR}$	CS′	CS	$\frac{CS'}{CS}$	CT′	CT	$\frac{CT'}{CT}$
5 cm	2.5 cm	2	4 cm	2 cm	2	6 cm	3 cm	2

B Write a conjecture based on the ratios in the table.

The ratios all equal 2. The distances are proportional.

C Measure and record the corresponding side lengths of the triangles.

R′S′	RS	$\frac{R'S'}{RS}$	S′T′	ST	$\frac{S'T'}{ST}$	R′T′	RT	$\frac{R'T'}{RT}$
2 cm	1 cm	2	2 cm	1 cm	2	2.8 cm	1.4 cm	2

D Write a conjecture based on the ratios in the table.

The ratios all equal 2. The side lengths are proportional.

E Measure the corresponding angles and describe your results.

The corresponding angles are congruent.

EXPLORE ACTIVITY 1 (cont'd)

Reflect

1. Two figures that have the same shape but different sizes are called *similar*. Are triangles RST and R′S′T′ similar? Why or why not?

Yes; their corresponding sides are proportional, and their corresponding angles are congruent.

2. Compare the orientation of a figure with the orientation of its dilation.

A figure and its dilation have the same orientation.

EXPLORE ACTIVITY 2   FL CC 8.G.1.3

Exploring Dilations on a Coordinate Plane

In this activity you will explore how the coordinates of a figure on a coordinate plane are affected by a dilation.

A Complete the table. Record the x- and y-coordinates of the points in the two figures and the ratios of the x-coordinates and the y-coordinates.

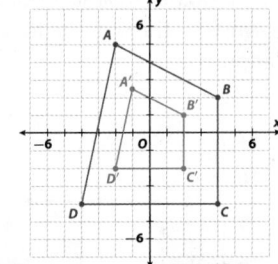

Vertex	x	y	Vertex	x	y	Ratio of x-coordinates (A′B′C′D′ ÷ ABCD)	Ratio of y-coordinates (A′B′C′D′ ÷ ABCD)
A′	−1	2.5	A	−2	5	0.5	0.5
B′	2	1	B	4	2	0.5	0.5
C′	2	−2	C	4	−4	0.5	0.5
D′	−2	−2	D	−4	−4	0.5	0.5

B Write a conjecture about the ratios of the coordinates of a dilation image to the coordinates of the original figure.

Sample answer: The ratios all equal 0.5.

The ratios are in proportion.

PROFESSIONAL DEVELOPMENT

Integrate Mathematical Practices MP.5.1

This lesson provides an opportunity to address this Mathematical Practices standard. It calls for students to consider available tools when solving a problem. Students use tables and a diagram to model a relationship between a figure and its dilation. Then students use graphs on a coordinate plane to generalize the language of dilations and the scale factor. Finally, students use mathematical language to describe, contrast, and compare dilations with other transformations.

Math Background

To make a dilation, you need to know the point that is the center of dilation. If no center of dilation is given, it is usually assumed that the center of dilation is the origin of the coordinate plane. The scale factor is sometimes called the *magnitude* of the dilation.

One notation that is used to specify a dilation is $D_{o,k}$ which means a dilation with center O (at the origin) and a scale factor (or magnitude) of k.

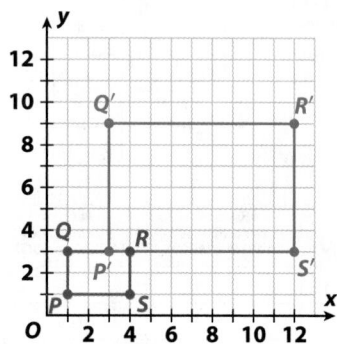

EXAMPLE 1
Questioning Strategies Mathematical Practices
- How can you tell which figure is the original and which is the result of the dilation? The dilated image is labeled with letters that have prime marks; *A'* is the image of *A*.

- How could you find the length of the hypotenuse for each triangle? Use the Pythagorean Theorem.

Avoid Common Errors
Students may sometimes invert the ratio when finding the scale factor. Remind students that the scale factor is always new over original, or image over preimage.

YOUR TURN
Focus on Critical Thinking Mathematical Practices
Have students discuss whether the dilated image can overlap, or be inside, the original figure. Refer them to all the illustrations in the lesson as they decide on their answer.

Integrating Language Arts ELL
Encourage a broad class discussion on the Math Talk. English learners will benefit from hearing and participating in classroom discussions.

Elaborate
. . . .

Talk About It
Summarize the Lesson

Ask: You are given a graph of a dilation and asked to identify its scale factor and whether it is an enlargement or a reduction. What do you look for? Look for the prime marks to indicate the image; if the image is larger than the original, it is an enlargement and the scale factor will be greater than one. Find the ratio of the new side lengths to the original to find the scale factor.

GUIDED PRACTICE
Engage with the Whiteboard
Have a student label each of the six points of the image and preimage with its ordered pair. Have another student measure the side lengths and confirm that corresponding sides are proportional.

Avoid Common Errors
Exercises 1, 3 Remind students that there will be three ratios in each case and that all three must be equal.

Exercise 4 Remind students that the angles, not the sides, of similar figures are congruent.

Reflect

3. In Explore Activity 1, triangle *R'S'T'* was larger than triangle *RST*. How is the relationship between quadrilateral *A'B'C'D'* and quadrilateral *ABCD* different?

Quad. *A'B'C'D'* is smaller than quad. *ABCD*.

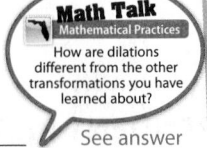
Math Talk
Mathematical Practices

How are dilations different from the other transformations you have learned about?

See answer below.

Math On the Spot
my.hrw.com

Finding a Scale Factor

As you have seen in the two activities, a dilation can produce a larger figure (an **enlargement**) or a smaller figure (a **reduction**). The **scale factor** describes how much the figure is enlarged or reduced. The scale factor is the ratio of a length of the image to the corresponding length on the original figure.

In Explore Activity 1, the side lengths of triangle *R'S'T'* were twice the length of those of triangle *RST*, so the scale factor was 2. In Explore Activity 2, the side lengths of quadrilateral *A'B'C'D'* were half those of quadrilateral *ABCD*, so the scale factor was 0.5.

EXAMPLE 1

FL CC 8.G.1.4

An art supply store sells several sizes of drawing triangles. All are dilations of a single basic triangle. The basic triangle and one of its dilations are shown on the grid. Find the scale factor of the dilation.

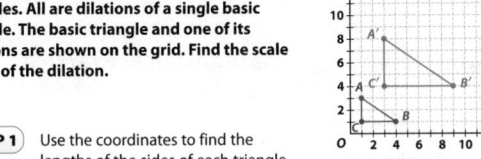

STEP 1 Use the coordinates to find the lengths of the sides of each triangle.

Triangle *ABC*:   *AC* = 2   *CB* = 3

Triangle *A'B'C'*:   *A'C'* = 4   *C'B'* = 6

STEP 2 Find the ratios of the corresponding sides.

$$\frac{A'C'}{AC} = \frac{4}{2} = 2 \qquad \frac{C'B'}{CB} = \frac{6}{3} = 2$$

The scale factor of the dilation is 2.

Reflect

4. Is the dilation an enlargement or a reduction? How can you tell?

An enlargement; sample answer: Triangle *A'B'C'* is larger than triangle *ABC*, and the scale factor is greater than 1.

Since the scale factor is the same for all corresponding sides, you can record just two pairs of side lengths. Use one pair as a check on the other.

Math Talk Anno: A reflection, a translation, and a rotation maintain both the size and the shape of the figure being transformed. A dilation produces a figure that is a different size but the same shape as the figure being transformed.

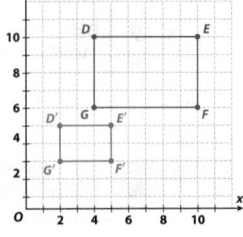
Personal Math Trainer
Online Assessment and Intervention
my.hrw.com

YOUR TURN

5. Find the scale factor of the dilation.

The scale factor is 0.5.

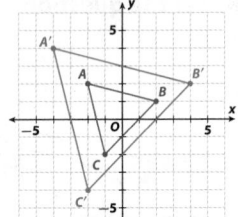

Math Talk
Mathematical Practices

Which scale factors lead to enlargements? Which scale factors lead to reductions?

If the scale factor is greater than 1, the dilation is an enlargement. If it is between 0 and 1, the dilation is a reduction.

Guided Practice

Use triangles *ABC* and *A'B'C'* for 1–5. (Explore Activities 1 and 2, Example 1)

1. For each pair of corresponding vertices, find the ratio of the *x*-coordinates and the ratio of the *y*-coordinates.

ratio of *x*-coordinates = ___2___

ratio of *y*-coordinates = ___2___

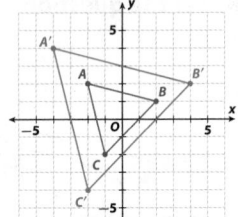

2. I know that triangle *A'B'C'* is a dilation of triangle *ABC* because the ratios of the corresponding

x-coordinates are ___equal___ and the ratios of the corresponding *y*-coordinates are ___equal___.

3. The ratio of the lengths of the corresponding sides of triangle *A'B'C'* and triangle *ABC* equals ___2___.

4. The corresponding angles of triangle *ABC* and triangle *A'B'C'* are ___congruent___.

5. The scale factor of the dilation is ___2___.

? ESSENTIAL QUESTION CHECK-IN

6. How can you find the scale factor of a dilation?

Sample answer: Divide a side length of the dilated figure by the corresponding side length of the original figure.

DIFFERENTIATE INSTRUCTION

Technology

Students can dilate triangles using a graphing calculator. Press **STAT** and select "1:Edit". Enter the *x*-coordinates into L1 and the *y*-coordinates into L2 using the points (2, 4), (2, 2), (4, 2), and repeating the first point (2, 4) to complete the graph so that each list contains four entries.

Press **2nd** **Y=** STAT PLOT, turn on Plot 1, and choose the line graph, L1, and L2. Choose a window that shows just Quadrant I (Xmin and Ymin are both 0, and Xmax and Ymax are both 20). Graph the triangle.

To graph a dilation by a factor of 3 of this triangle, return to **STAT** Edit and, with the cursor highlighting the column head L3, press L1*3, and similarly, put L2*3 in L4.

Press **2nd** **Y=** STAT PLOT, turn on Plot 2, and choose the line graph, L3, and L4. Graph the dilated triangle.

Ask students to name the center of dilation for this dilation. the origin

Additional Resources

Differentiated Instruction includes:
- Reading Strategies
- Success for English Learners **ELL**
- Reteach
- Challenge **PRE-AP**

Personal Math Trainer

Online Assessment and Intervention

Online homework assignment available

 my.hrw.com

---

18.1 LESSON QUIZ

 8.G.1.3, 8.G.1.4

Use triangles *RST* and *R'S'T'* to answer the questions.

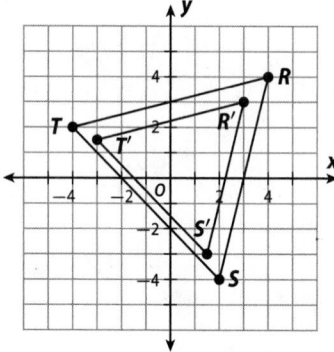

1. For each pair of corresponding vertices, find the ratio of the *x*-coordinates.

2. For each pair of corresponding vertices, find the ratio of the *y*-coordinates.

3. What is the ratio of the lengths of the corresponding sides of triangle *RST* and *R'S'T'*? Explain how you know.

4. What is the scale factor of the dilation? Is it an enlargement or a reduction?

Lesson Quiz available online

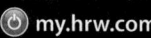 my.hrw.com

Answers
1. $\frac{3}{4} = \frac{1.5}{2} = \frac{-3}{-4} = 0.75$
2. $\frac{3}{4} = \frac{-3}{-4} = \frac{1.5}{2} = 0.75$
3. 0.75; Sample answer: Because the corresponding *x*- and *y*-coordinates are in the same ratio, the figure shows a dilation. Therefore, the side lengths must be in the same ratio as the coordinates.
4. 0.75; reduction

Evaluate

GUIDED AND INDEPENDENT PRACTICE

 8.G.1.3, 8.G.1.4

Concepts & Skills	Practice
Explore Activity 1 Exploring Dilations	Exercises 3–4, 7–10, 15
Explore Activity 2 Exploring Dilations on a Coordinate Plane	Exercises 1–2, 11
Example 1 Finding a Scale Factor	Exercises 5, 16–18

Exercise	Depth of Knowledge (D.O.K.)		Mathematical Practices
7–11	**2** Skills/Concepts		**MP.3.1** Logic
12–15	**1** Recall of Information		**MP.2.1** Reasoning
16	**2** Skills/Concepts		**MP.6.1** Precision
17–18	**2** Skills/Concepts		**MP.5.1** Using Tools
19	**3** Strategic Thinking	H.O.T.	**MP.3.1** Logic
20	**3** Strategic Thinking	H.O.T.	**MP.2.1** Reasoning

Additional Resources
Differentiated Instruction includes:
• Leveled Practice worksheets

18.1 Independent Practice

FL CC 8.G.1.3, 8.G.1.4

Personal Math Trainer
Online Assessment and Intervention
my.hrw.com

For 7–11, tell whether one figure is a dilation of the other or not. Explain your reasoning.

7. Quadrilateral *MNPQ* has side lengths of 15 mm, 24 mm, 21 mm, and 18 mm. Quadrilateral *M'N'P'Q'* has side lengths of 5 mm, 8 mm, 7 mm, and 4 mm.

No; the ratios of the lengths of

the corresponding sides are not

equal.

8. Triangle *RST* has angles measuring 38° and 75°. Triangle *R'S'T'* has angles measuring 67° and 38°. The sides are proportional.

Yes; both triangles have angles

of measure 38°, 75°, and 67°, so

the corresponding angles are

congruent.

9. Two triangles, Triangle 1 and Triangle 2, are similar.

Yes; a dilation produces an image

similar to the original figure.

10. Quadrilateral *MNPQ* is the same shape but a different size than quadrilateral *M'N'P'Q*.

Yes; if figures are the same

shape but a different size, they

are similar. Therefore, one is a

dilation of the other.

11. On a coordinate plane, triangle *UVW* has coordinates *U*(20, −12), *V*(8, 6), and *W*(−24, −4). Triangle *U'V'W'* has coordinates *U'*(15, −9), *V'*(6, 4.5), and *W'*(−18, −3).

Yes; each coordinate of

triangle *U'V'W'* is $\frac{3}{4}$ times the

corresponding coordinate of

triangle *UVW*. So, the scale factor

of the dilation is $\frac{3}{4}$.

Complete the table by writing "same" or "changed" to compare the image with the original figure in the given transformation.

		Image Compared to Original Figure		
		Orientation	Size	Shape
12.	Translation	same	same	same
13.	Reflection	changed	same	same
14.	Rotation	changed	same	same
15.	Dilation	same	changed	same

16. Describe the image of a dilation with a scale factor of 1.

The image is congruent to the original figure.

_____

_____

Identify the scale factor used in each dilation.

17.

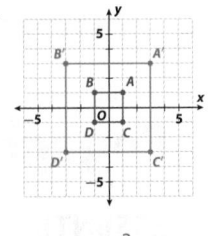

3

18.

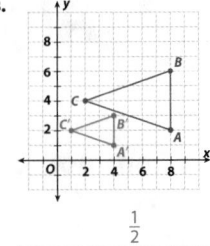

$\frac{1}{2}$

H.O.T. FOCUS ON HIGHER ORDER THINKING

Work Area

19. Critical Thinking Explain how you can find the center of dilation of a triangle and its dilation.

Sample answer: Locate the corresponding vertices of the

triangles and draw lines connecting each pair. The lines

will intersect at the center of dilation.

20. Make a Conjecture

a. A square on the coordinate plane has vertices at (−2, 2), (2, 2), (2, −2), and (−2, −2). A dilation of the square has vertices at (−4, 4), (4, 4), (4, −4), and (−4, −4). Find the scale factor and the perimeter of each square.

scale factor: 2; perimeter of original square: 16;

perimeter of image: 32

b. A square on the coordinate plane has vertices at (−3, 3), (3, 3), (3, −3), and (−3, −3). A dilation of the square has vertices at (−6, 6), (6, 6), (6, −6), and (−6, −6). Find the scale factor and the perimeter of each square.

scale factor: 2; perimeter of original square: 24;

perimeter of image: 48

c. Make a conjecture about the relationship of the scale factor to the perimeter of a square and its image.

Sample answer: The perimeter of the image is the

perimeter of the original figure times the scale factor.

EXTEND THE MATH PRE-AP

Activity available online ⏻ my.hrw.com

Activity Have students graph a dilation with the origin as the center of dilation but with a negative scale factor. For example, have them graph the triangle with vertices at *A*(1, 5), *B*(2, 1), and *C*(2, 4), using a scale factor of −2. Ask them to describe the location and orientation of the original (in QI with the shortest side at the top) and the image (in QIII with the shortest side at the bottom).

Then have them graph the triangle with vertices at *A*(10, 4), *B*(2, 6), and *C*(6, 2), using a scale factor of $-\frac{1}{2}$. Have them compare the orientation of the figure with that of the dilation. Lead students to conclude that the orientation is opposite when the scale factor is less than zero. Point out that this is similar to a dilation with a positive scale factor followed by a reflection in which both coordinates are multiplied by −1.

LESSON
18.2 Algebraic Representations of Dilations

Florida Common Core Standards

The student is expected to:

 **Geometry—8.G.1.3**

Describe the effect of dilations, translations, rotations, and reflections on two-dimensional figures using coordinates.

Mathematical Practices

 **MP.4.1** Modeling

Engage

ESSENTIAL QUESTION

How can you describe the effect of a dilation on coordinates using an algebraic representation? Sample answer: For scale factor *k*, the algebraic representation of the dilation, with center at the origin, is $(x, y) \rightarrow (kx, ky)$.

Motivate the Lesson

Ask: Have you ever drawn a picture or diagram, and then enlarged it to, for example, paint a mural or make a poster? How could you describe and specify such an enlargement using the language of mathematics? Begin the Explore Activity to find out.

Explore

EXPLORE ACTIVITY 1

Connect Vocabulary **ELL**

Have a student read the opening paragraph aloud. Have students practice and discuss the pronunciation and meaning of the math terms. Make sure students understand the meaning of the arrow, and that they read it as "becomes" or "is transformed into."

Explain

EXPLORE ACTIVITY 2

Questioning Strategies **Mathematical Practices**
• What do you do to the *x*-value of the preimage to find the *x*-value of the image? Multiply it by one-half.

• Why doesn't the *x*-value for (0, 5) change in the image? Any number times zero is still zero.

Engage with the Whiteboard
Have a student write the coordinates for the vertices on both figures. Ask a student to label the lengths of the vertical and horizontal segments and then to compare the ratios of these lengths. Have a student draw lines to join the corresponding vertices of the two figures to demonstrate these lines intersect at the origin, or center of dilation.

LESSON 18.2 Algebraic Representations of Dilations

FL CC 8.G.1.3
Describe the effect of dilations, ... on two-dimensional figures using coordinates.

ESSENTIAL QUESTION How can you describe the effect of a dilation on coordinates using an algebraic representation?

EXPLORE ACTIVITY 1 FL CC 8.G.1.3

Graphing Enlargements

When a dilation in the coordinate plane has the origin as the center of dilation, you can find points on the dilated image by multiplying the x- and y-coordinates of the original figure by the scale factor. For scale factor k, the algebraic representation of the dilation is $(x, y) \rightarrow (kx, ky)$. For enlargements, $k > 1$.

The figure shown on the grid is the preimage. The center of dilation is the origin.

A List the coordinates of the vertices of the preimage in the first column of the table.

Preimage (x, y)	Image (3x, 3y)
(2, 2)	(6, 6)
(2, −1)	(6, −3)
(1, −1)	(3, −3)
(1, −2)	(3, −6)
(−2, −2)	(−6, −6)
(−2, 1)	(−6, 3)
(−1, 1)	(−3, 3)
(−1, 2)	(−3, 6)

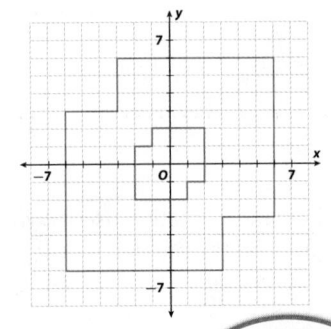

B What is the scale factor for the dilation? __3__

C Apply the dilation to the preimage and write the coordinates of the vertices of the image in the second column of the table.

D Sketch the image after the dilation on the coordinate grid.

Math Talk
Mathematical Practices
What effect would the dilation $(x, y) \rightarrow (4x, 4y)$ have on the radius of a circle?

The radius of the dilated circle will be 4 times as long as the radius of the original circle.

Lesson 18.2 **585**

EXPLORE ACTIVITY 1 (cont'd)

Reflect

1. How does the dilation affect the length of line segments?
Each line segment in the image is three times longer than the corresponding line segment in the preimage.

2. How does the dilation affect angle measures?
The dilation does not change the angle measures.

EXPLORE ACTIVITY 2 FL CC 8.G.1.3

Graphing Reductions

For scale factors between 0 and 1, the image is smaller than the preimage. This is called a reduction.

The arrow shown is the preimage. The center of dilation is the origin.

A List the coordinates of the vertices of the preimage in the first column of the table.

B What is the scale factor for the dilation? $\frac{1}{2}$

C Apply the dilation to the preimage and write the coordinates of the vertices of the image in the second column of the table.

Preimage (x, y)	Image ($\frac{1}{2}x, \frac{1}{2}y$)
(4, 2)	(2, 1)
(0, 5)	(0, 2.5)
(−4, 2)	(−2, 1)
(−2, 2)	(−1, 1)
(−2, −4)	(−1, −2)
(2, −4)	(1, −2)
(2, 2)	(1, 1)

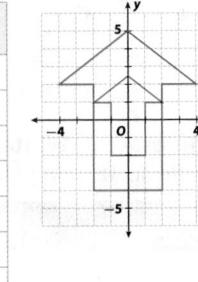

D Sketch the image after the dilation on the coordinate grid.

Reflect

3. How does the dilation affect the length of line segments?
The image length is $\frac{1}{2}$ that of the preimage.

4. How would a dilation with scale factor 1 affect the preimage?
The image and preimage would be the same.

586 Unit 8

PROFESSIONAL DEVELOPMENT

Integrate Mathematical Practices MP.4.1

This lesson provides an opportunity to address this Mathematical Practices standard. It calls for students to use tools such as diagrams, tables, graphs, and formulas. Students change graphic representations into tables, back into a graph of a dilation, and then use words to describe the image. They use algebraic methods to find the new coordinates for a dilation, and graph it. They then use these representations to solve problems involving blueprints. Finally, they generalize the effect of transformations in words.

Math Background

Algebraic transformations specify changes to the coordinates to define a transformation. Multiplying by a scale factor is used only for dilations (and rotations) with the center at the origin.

$(x, y) \rightarrow (y, -x)$ rotates the figure 90° clockwise
$(x, y) \rightarrow (-x, -y)$ rotates the figure 180°
$(x, y) \rightarrow (x, ay)$ stretches or shrinks the figure vertically by a factor of a
$(x, y) \rightarrow (ax, y)$ stretches or shrinks the figure horizontally by a factor of a

In general, multiplying by a stretches if $|a| > 1$, shrinks if $|a| < 1$, and reflects across the axis if $a < 0$.

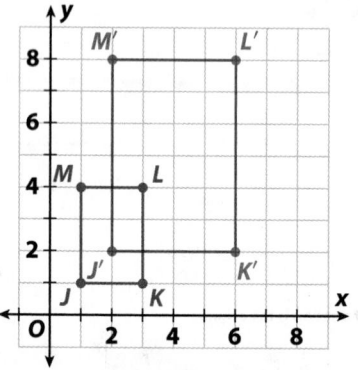

EXAMPLE 1

Questioning Strategies 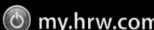 Mathematical Practices

- Before you do any calculation, how can you predict the size of the dilated image? Since the scale factor is 3, the image will be larger than the preimage, and the lengths of the sides will be 3 times the lengths of the sides for the preimage.

- What is the center of dilation for this dilation? Explain. It is the origin, because lines joining the corresponding vertices intersect at that point.

Focus on Critical Thinking ⚑ Mathematical Practices

Have students begin by predicting whether the dilation is an enlargement or a reduction, and explaining how they know.

YOUR TURN

Avoid Common Errors

Have students check their images by confirming that they are the same shape as the preimage.

Elaborate
....

Talk About It
Summarize the Lesson

Ask: Describe the mathematical notation used to write the algebraic representation of a dilation. It begins with the ordered pair (*x*, *y*) and then has an arrow pointing right to another ordered pair that shows both *x* and *y* multiplied by the scale factor.

GUIDED PRACTICE

Engage with the Whiteboard

Have a student label each of the vertices with the ordered pair that names the point. Have a student draw lines to join the corresponding vertices of the two figures to demonstrate these lines intersect at the origin, or center of dilation.

Avoid Common Errors

Exercise 1 Point out that when the center of dilation is not explicitly mentioned, students should assume that it is the origin.

Exercises 2–3 Students may try to draw enlargements so that they enclose the original figure and reductions so that they are enclosed within the original figure. Remind students that this will occur only in certain cases, such as Exercise 1, when the original figure is centered on the origin.

Center of Dilation Outside the Image

The center of dilation can be inside *or* outside the original image and the dilated image. The center of dilation can be anywhere on the coordinate plane as long as the lines that connect each pair of corresponding vertices between the original and dilated image intersect at the center of dilation.

Math On the Spot
my.hrw.com

EXAMPLE 1

FL CC 8.G.1.3

Graph the image of △ABC after a dilation with the origin as its center and a scale factor of 3. What are the vertices of the image?

STEP 1 Multiply each coordinate of the vertices of △ABC by 3 to find the vertices of the dilated image.

$$\triangle ABC\ (x, y) \rightarrow (3x, 3y)\ \triangle A'B'C'$$

$$A(1, 1) \rightarrow A'(1 \cdot 3, 1 \cdot 3) \rightarrow A'(3, 3)$$

$$B(3, 1) \rightarrow B'(3 \cdot 3, 1 \cdot 3) \rightarrow B'(9, 3)$$

$$C(1, 3) \rightarrow C'(1 \cdot 3, 3 \cdot 3) \rightarrow C'(3, 9)$$

The vertices of the dilated image are A'(3, 3), B'(9, 3), and C'(3, 9).

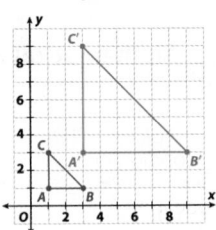

STEP 2 Graph the dilated image.

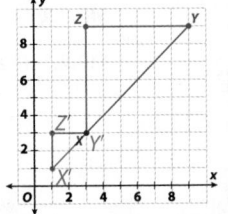

Math Talk
Mathematical Practices

Describe how you can check graphically that you have drawn the image triangle correctly.

Draw segments from the center of dilation through the vertices of the preimage to make sure they pass through the image vertices. Then check the length of 1 side of the image.

YOUR TURN

5. Graph the image of △XYZ after a dilation with a scale factor of $\frac{1}{3}$ and the origin as its center. Then write an algebraic rule to describe the dilation.

$$(x, y) \rightarrow \left(\frac{1}{3}x, \frac{1}{3}y\right)$$

Personal Math Trainer
Online Assessment and Intervention
my.hrw.com

---

1. The grid shows a diamond-shaped preimage. Write the coordinates of the vertices of the preimage in the first column of the table. Then apply the dilation $(x, y) \rightarrow \left(\frac{3}{2}x, \frac{3}{2}y\right)$ and write the coordinates of the vertices of the image in the second column. Sketch the image of the figure after the dilation. (Explore Activities 1 and 2)

Preimage	Image
(2, 0)	(3, 0)
(0, 2)	(0, 3)
(−2, 0)	(−3, 0)
(0, −2)	(0, −3)

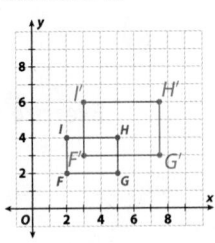

Graph the image of each figure after a dilation with the origin as its center and the given scale factor. Then write an algebraic rule to describe the dilation. (Example 1)

2. scale factor of 1.5

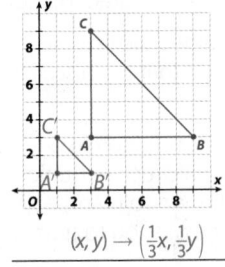

$$(x, y) \rightarrow (1.5x, 1.5y)$$

3. scale factor of $\frac{1}{3}$

$$(x, y) \rightarrow \left(\frac{1}{3}x, \frac{1}{3}y\right)$$

ESSENTIAL QUESTION CHECK-IN

4. A dilation of $(x, y) \rightarrow (kx, ky)$ when $0 < k < 1$ has what effect on the figure? What is the effect on the figure when $k > 1$?

When *k* is between 0 and 1, the dilation is a reduction by the scale factor *k*. When *k* is greater than 1, the dilation is an enlargement by the scale factor *k*.

DIFFERENTIATE INSTRUCTION

Modeling and Cooperative Learning

Have students work in pairs with geoboards to demonstrate various dilations. Rubber bands make effective models for stretching and shrinking.

Have students create the figures in Example 1 as well as Your Turn Exercise 5.

Have one partner call out the coordinates of a figure and the other construct the figure on the geoboard. Then give them a scale factor for a dilation of the figure, and ask them to demonstrate it on the geoboard.

Graphic Organizers

Ask students to create a table or diagram in their notebooks listing the various transformations that they have learned about (translations, reflections, rotations, and dilations).

For each transformation, have them write an ordered pair and then rewrite the ordered pair after the transformation. Next, have them write an algebraic representation of the transformation, and finally have them write a sentence describing the transformation.

Additional Resources

Differentiated Instruction includes:
- Reading Strategies
- Success for English Learners **ELL**
- Reteach
- Challenge **PRE-AP**

Personal Math Trainer

Online Assessment and Intervention

Online homework assignment available

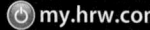 my.hrw.com

18.2 LESSON QUIZ

 **FL CC** 8.G.1.3

1. A rectangle has vertices at $P(6, 6)$, $Q(6, -6)$, $R(-6, -6)$, and $S(-6, 6)$. The origin is the center of dilation, and $(x, y) \rightarrow (\frac{1}{3}x, \frac{1}{3}y)$. What are the vertices of the dilated image?

2. Write an algebraic representation of a dilation that has a scale factor of 0.45.

3. Triangle JKL is the preimage. Write two algebraic representations, one for the dilation to triangle $J'K'L'$ and one for the dilation to triangle $J''K''L''$.

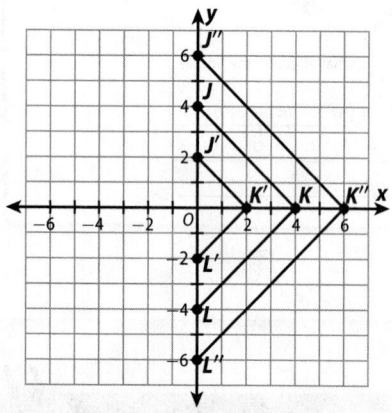

Lesson Quiz available online

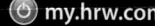 my.hrw.com

Evaluate

GUIDED AND INDEPENDENT PRACTICE

 **FL CC** 8.G.1.3

Concepts & Skills	Practice
Explore Activity 1 Graphing Enlargements	Exercises 1–2, 5–6
Explore Activity 2 Graphing Reductions	Exercises 3, 5, 7–10
Example 1 Center of Dilation Outside the Image	Exercises 2–3, 10

Exercise	Depth of Knowledge (D.O.K.)	**FL CC** Mathematical Practices
5–7	**2** Skills/Concepts	**MP.2.1** Reasoning
8	**3** Strategic Thinking **H.O.T.**	**MP.2.1** Reasoning
9	**3** Strategic Thinking **H.O.T.**	**MP.4.1** Modeling
10	**2** Skills/Concepts	**MP.5.1** Using Tools
11	**3** Strategic Thinking **H.O.T.**	**MP.3.1** Logic
12–13	**3** Strategic Thinking **H.O.T.**	**MP.2.1** Reasoning

Additional Resources

Differentiated Instruction includes:

• Leveled Practice worksheets

Answers

1. $P'(2, 2)$, $Q'(2, -2)$, $R'(-2, -2)$, $S'(-2, 2)$

2. $(x, y) \rightarrow (0.45x, 0.45y)$

3. Triangle $J'K'L'$: $(x, y) \rightarrow (0.5x, 0.5y)$
Triangle $J''K''L''$: $(x, y) \rightarrow (1.5x, 1.5y)$

18.2 Independent Practice

FL CC 8.G.1.3

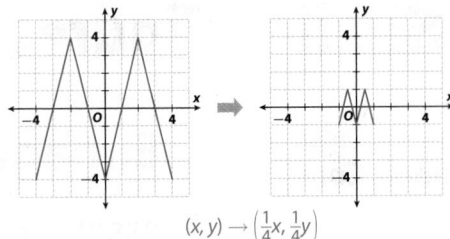

Personal Math Trainer

my.hrw.com

Online Assessment and Intervention

5. The blue square is the preimage. Write two algebraic representations, one for the dilation to the green square and one for the dilation to the purple square.

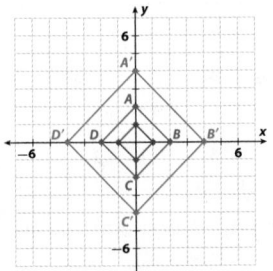

Green square: $(x, y) \rightarrow (2x, 2y)$

Purple square: $(x, y) \rightarrow \left(\frac{1}{2}x, \frac{1}{2}y\right)$

6. Critical Thinking A triangle has vertices $A(-5, -4)$, $B(2, 6)$, and $C(4, -3)$. The center of dilation is the origin and $(x, y) \rightarrow (3x, 3y)$. What are the vertices of the dilated image?

$A'(-15, -12)$, $B'(6, 18)$,

and $C'(12, -9)$

7. Critical Thinking $M'N'O'P'$ has vertices at $M'(3, 4)$, $N'(6, 4)$, $O'(6, 7)$, and $P'(3, 7)$. The center of dilation is the origin. $MNOP$ has vertices at $M(4.5, 6)$, $N(9, 6)$, $O(9, 10.5)$, and $P'(4.5, 10.5)$. What is the algebraic representation of this dilation?

$(x, y) \rightarrow \left(\frac{2}{3}x, \frac{2}{3}y\right)$

8. Critical Thinking A dilation with center $(0,0)$ and scale factor k is applied to a polygon. What dilation can you apply to the image to return it to the original preimage?

a dilation with scale factor $\frac{1}{k}$

9. Represent Real-World Problems The blueprints for a new house are scaled so that $\frac{1}{4}$ inch equals 1 foot. The blueprint is the preimage and the house is the dilated image. The blueprints are plotted on a coordinate plane.

a. What is the scale factor in terms of inches to inches?

The scale factor is 48.

b. One inch on the blueprint represents how many inches in the actual house? How many feet?

48 inches or 4 feet

c. Write the algebraic representation of the dilation from the blueprint to the house.

$(x, y) \rightarrow (48x, 48y)$

d. A rectangular room has coordinates $Q(2, 2)$, $R(7, 2)$, $S(7, 5)$, and $T(2, 5)$ on the blueprint. The homeowner wants this room to be 25% larger. What are the coordinates of the new room?

$Q'(2.5, 2.5)$, $R'(8.75, 2.5)$,

$S'(8.75, 6.25)$, and $T'(2.5, 6.25)$

e. What are the dimensions of the new room, in inches, on the blueprint? What will the dimensions of the new room be, in feet, in the new house?

Dimensions on blueprint:

6.25 in. by 3.75 in.

Dimensions in house: 25 ft

by 15 ft

10. Write the algebraic representation of the dilation shown.

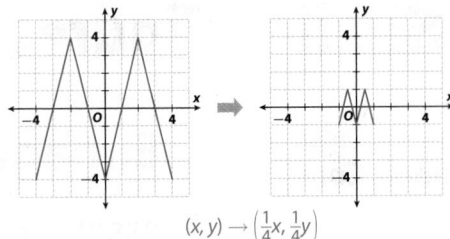

$(x, y) \rightarrow \left(\frac{1}{4}x, \frac{1}{4}y\right)$

H.O.T. FOCUS ON HIGHER ORDER THINKING

Work Area

11. Critique Reasoning The set for a school play needs a replica of a historic building painted on a backdrop that is 20 feet long and 16 feet high. The actual building measures 400 feet long and 320 feet high. A stage crewmember writes $(x, y) \rightarrow \left(\frac{1}{12}x, \frac{1}{12}y\right)$ to represent the dilation. Is the crewmember's calculation correct if the painted replica is to cover the entire backdrop? Explain.

The stage crewmember's calculation is incorrect.

The scale factor for the backdrop is $\frac{1}{20}$, not $\frac{1}{12}$.

12. Communicate Mathematical Ideas Explain what each of these algebraic transformations does to a figure.

a. $(x, y) \rightarrow (y, -x)$ rotates the figure 90° clockwise

b. $(x, y) \rightarrow (-x, -y)$ rotates the figure 180°

c. $(x, y) \rightarrow (x, 2y)$ stretches the figure vertically by a factor of 2

d. $(x, y) \rightarrow \left(\frac{2}{3}x, y\right)$ shrinks the figure horizontally by a factor of $\frac{2}{3}$

e. $(x, y) \rightarrow (0.5x, 1.5y)$ shrinks the figure horizontally by a factor of 0.5 and stretches it vertically by a factor of 1.5

13. Communicate Mathematical Ideas Triangle ABC has coordinates $A(1, 5)$, $B(-2, 1)$, and $C(-2, 4)$. Sketch triangle ABC and $A'B'C'$ for the dilation $(x, y) \rightarrow (-2x, -2y)$. What is the effect of a negative scale factor?

The figure is dilated by a factor of 2, but the orientation of the figure in the coordinate plane is rotated 180°.

EXTEND THE MATH PRE-AP

Activity available online my.hrw.com

Activity Have students discuss various ways they have seen shrinking and stretching in their daily lives. Remind them that they may have seen movies, cartoons, or other entertainment that used this basic principle, as well as books such as *Gulliver's Travels*. Ask them what models they have seen, such as toy cars, action figures, and dolls. Then show them a figure, such as a model car or doll (or have them bring one in), and ask them to calculate (or estimate) the scale compared to the real thing. For example, they can compare their own heights to that of the action figure, and measure other dimensions of the figure to see if they are realistic or exaggerated.

Ask them to make a conjecture whether the model could realistically exist as an actual person or car, given the dimensions of the toy, and what those measurements would be if enlarged.

LESSON
18.3 Similar Figures

ADDITIONAL EXAMPLE 1
A Identify a sequence of transformations that will transform figure *A* into figure *B*.

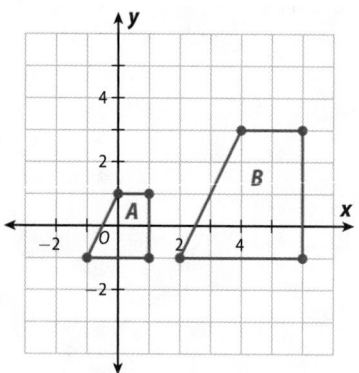

$(x, y) \rightarrow (2x, 2y)$, $(x, y) \rightarrow (x + 4, y + 1)$

(Continued on page 329)

 Interactive Whiteboard
Interactive example available online

 **my.hrw.com**

Engage

ESSENTIAL QUESTION

What is the connection between transformations and similar figures? Sample answer: If two figures are similar, then there exists a sequence of translations, reflections, rotations, and/or dilations that transforms one figure into the other.

Motivate the Lesson
Ask: What kinds of changes can be made to a shape while keeping the new shape similar to the original? Begin the Explore Activity to find out.

Explore

EXPLORE ACTIVITY

Engage with the Whiteboard

Invite a volunteer to label the coordinates of the vertices of the green figure and of figure *A*. Compare those values to the rule given in part A. Repeat for parts B–E.

Explain

EXAMPLE 1

Questioning Strategies Mathematical Practices

• Why is it important to know which figure is the original figure and which is the image? Knowing which is the original figure allows you to find the correct order of the transformations and the scale factor of the dilation.

• How are similar squares different from congruent squares? Congruent squares have the same shape and size. Similar squares have the same shape but are not necessarily the same size.

Engage with the Whiteboard

For each part of the Example, have a volunteer graph the intermediate step or steps in the transformation of the figure. For example, for part A, have a volunteer graph the dilation of figure *A* at the origin, and then explain how the algebraic rule translates the square to figure *B*.

LESSON
18.3 Similar Figures

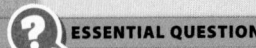
FL CC 8.G.1.4
Understand that a . . . figure is similar to another if the second can be obtained . . . by a sequence of rotations, reflections, translations, and dilations; given two similar . . . figures, describe a sequence that exhibits the similarity between them.

? ESSENTIAL QUESTION What is the connection between transformations and similar figures?

 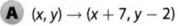
Combining Transformations with Dilations

When creating an animation, figures need to be translated, reflected, rotated, and sometimes dilated. As an example of this, apply the indicated sequence of transformations to the rectangle. Each transformation is applied to the image of the previous transformation, not to the original figure. Label each image with the letter of the transformation applied.

A $(x, y) \rightarrow (x + 7, y - 2)$

B $(x, y) \rightarrow (x, -y)$

C rotation 90° clockwise around the origin

D $(x, y) \rightarrow (x + 5, y + 3)$

E $(x, y) \rightarrow (3x, 3y)$

F List the coordinates of the vertices of rectangle E.
$(3, 6), (3, -6), (-3, -6), (-3, 6)$

G Compare the following attributes of rectangle E to those of the original figure.

Shape	Same shape
Size	The sides of rectangle E are three times the lengths of the sides of the original figure.
Angle Measures	Same angle measures

Lesson 18.3 **591**

Reflect

1. Which transformation represents the dilation? How can you tell?
$(x, y) \rightarrow (3x, 3y)$; the algebraic form of a dilation is
$(x, y) \rightarrow (kx, ky)$; in this case, $k = 3$.

2. A sequence of transformations containing a single dilation is applied to a figure. Are the original figure and its final image congruent? Explain.
No; the dilation would shrink or expand the figure so that it and its final image would not be the same size.

Math On the Spot
© my.hrw.com

My Notes

Similar Figures

Two figures are **similar** if one can be obtained from the other by a sequence of translations, reflections, rotations, and dilations. Similar figures have the same shape but may be different sizes.

When you are told that two figures are similar, there must be a sequence of translations, reflections, rotations, and/or dilations that can transform one to the other.

EXAMPLE 1
FL CC 8.G.1.4

A Identify a sequence of transformations that will transform figure A into figure B. Tell whether the figures are congruent. Tell whether they are similar.

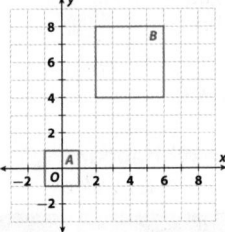

Both figures are squares whose orientations are the same, so no reflection or rotation is needed. Figure B has sides twice as long as figure A, so a dilation with a scale factor of 2 is needed. Figure B is moved to the right and above figure A, so a translation is needed. A sequence of transformations that will accomplish this is a dilation by a scale factor of 2 centered at the origin followed by the translation $(x, y) \rightarrow (x + 4, y + 6)$. The figures are not congruent, but they are similar.

592 Unit 8

PROFESSIONAL DEVELOPMENT

Integrate Mathematical Practices MP.6.1

This lesson provides an opportunity to address this Mathematical Practice standard that calls for students to attend to precision. It is important that students pay close attention to the coordinates of the vertices as they apply transformations and graph the results. Each transformation must be applied carefully and precisely to obtain the desired outcome. For example, the magnitude, direction, and center of a rotation must be stated precisely. The scale factor of a dilation must be calculated precisely to have the algebraic rule be accurate.

Math Background

Every dilation must be described by two pieces of information: the scale factor and the center of dilation. The distance from the center of dilation to each point of the image is equal to the distance from the center of dilation to each corresponding point of the original figure times the scale factor. If the center of dilation is at vertex A of the original figure, the corresponding vertex on the dilation image has the same coordinates as vertex A.

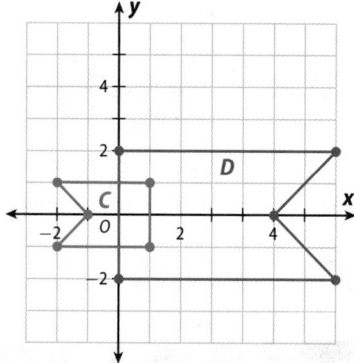

YOUR TURN

Avoid Common Errors

If students cannot visualize the sequence of transformations, suggest they use a paper cut-out rectangle the same size and shape as the green rectangle that they can rotate and translate on a coordinate grid. Once the rectangle is centered on the origin in the proper orientation, it is ready for the dilation into figure E.

Talk About It
Check for Understanding

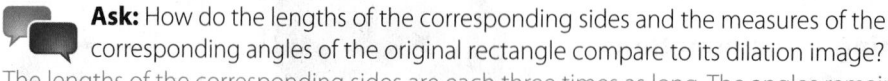 **Ask:** How do the lengths of the corresponding sides and the measures of the corresponding angles of the original rectangle compare to its dilation image? The lengths of the corresponding sides are each three times as long. The angles remain congruent.

Elaborate

. . . .

Talk About It
Summarize the Lesson

 Ask: How do you know when a dilation has occurred? The image is either larger or smaller than the original figure, and the original figure and image are similar.

GUIDED PRACTICE

Engage with the Whiteboard

 For Exercise 1, have four volunteers take turns drawing the indicated series of transformations (A–D) to the blue square on the coordinate grid provided.

Avoid Common Errors

Exercises 2–3 Suggest students use a paper cut-out of trapezoid A and actually slide, turn, and flip it around until they can see the same orientation that figures B and C have.

Exercise 4 Suggest students use the length of the top base or the length of the height to determine the scale factor. The vertices of the bottom base of the enlarged trapezoid do not have whole number x-coordinate values.

B Identify a sequence of transformations that will transform figure C into figure D. Include a reflection. Tell whether the figures are congruent. Tell whether they are similar.

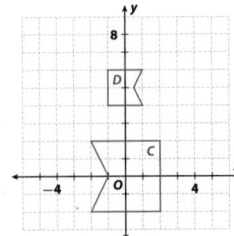

The orientation of figure D is reversed from that of figure C, so a reflection over the y-axis is needed. Figure D has sides that are half as long as figure C, so a dilation with a scale factor of $\frac{1}{2}$ is needed. Figure D is moved above figure C, so a translation is needed. A sequence of transformations that will accomplish this is a dilation by a scale factor of $\frac{1}{2}$ centered at the origin, followed by the reflection $(x, y) \rightarrow (-x, y)$, followed by the translation $(x, y) \rightarrow (x, y + 5)$. The figures are not congruent, but they are similar.

C Identify a sequence of transformations that will transform figure C into figure D. Include a rotation.

The orientation of figure D is reversed from that of figure C, so a rotation of 180° is needed. Figure D has sides that are half as long as figure C, so a dilation with a scale factor of $\frac{1}{2}$ is needed. Figure D is moved above figure C, so a translation is needed. A sequence of transformations that will accomplish this is a rotation of 180° about the origin, followed by a dilation by a scale factor of $\frac{1}{2}$ centered at the origin, followed by the translation $(x, y) \rightarrow (x, y + 5)$.

Math Talk
Mathematical Practices

A figure and its image have different sizes and orientations. What do you know about the sequence of transformations that generated the image?

The sequence must contain a dilation and at least one reflection or rotation.

YOUR TURN

3. Look again at the Explore Activity. Start with the original figure. Create a new sequence of transformations that will yield figure E, the final image. Your transformations do not need to produce the images in the same order in which they originally appeared.

Sample answer: $(x, y) \rightarrow (x + 7, y - 12)$; rotation 90° counterclockwise about the origin; $(x, y) \rightarrow (x + 5, y + 3)$; $(x, y) \rightarrow (3x, 3y)$

Personal Math Trainer
Online Assessment and Intervention
my.hrw.com

---

1. Apply the indicated sequence of transformations to the square. Apply each transformation to the image of the previous transformation. Label each image with the letter of the transformation applied.
(Explore Activity)

A $(x, y) \rightarrow (-x, y)$

B Rotate the square 180° around the origin.

C $(x, y) \rightarrow (x - 5, y - 6)$

D $(x, y) \rightarrow (\frac{1}{2}x, \frac{1}{2}y)$

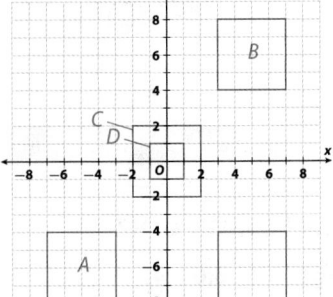

Identify a sequence of two transformations that will transform figure A into the given figure. (Example 1) Sample answers are given.

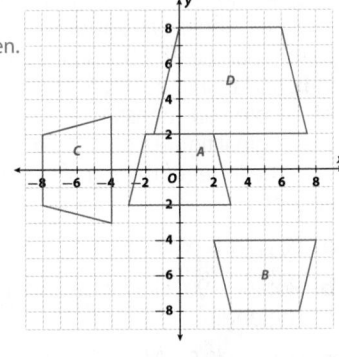

2. figure B

   $(x, y) \rightarrow (x, -y)$

   $(x, y) \rightarrow (x + 5, y - 6)$

3. figure C

   $(x, y) \rightarrow (x, y + 6)$

   rotate 90° counterclockwise

4. figure D

   $(x, y) \rightarrow (1.5x, 1.5y)$

   $(x, y) \rightarrow (x + 3, y + 5)$

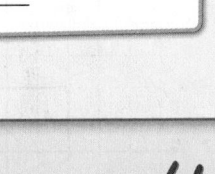
ESSENTIAL QUESTION CHECK-IN

5. If two figures are similar but not congruent, what do you know about the sequence of transformations used to create one from the other?

   At least one transformation must be a dilation with a

   scale factor other than 1.

DIFFERENTIATE INSTRUCTION

Curriculum Integration

A flipbook is a book with a series of pictures that vary very slightly from one page to the next. When the pages are flipped rapidly, the image on the pages appears to be animated. Have students use about 20 index cards and a ruler to draw a series of similar two-dimensional shapes that slowly move across the cards and gradually increase or decrease in size.

Cooperative Learning

Have students work in groups of four. Have one student draw a simple shape on a coordinate grid. Have two of the students come up with an algebraic sequence that includes a dilation and at least two other transformations that the fourth student will apply to the shape. Students should change roles and repeat this activity as time permits.

Additional Resources

Differentiated Instruction includes:

- Reading Strategies
- Success for English Learners **ELL**
- Reteach
- Challenge **PRE-AP**

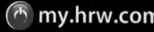
18.3 LESSON QUIZ

 **FL CC** 8.G.1.4

1. On a coordinate grid, graph a triangle with its vertices at $(-2, 0)$, $(-2, 6)$, and $(-8, 0)$. Then apply the indicated series of transformations to the triangle. The transformations in **b**. and **c**. are applied to the image of the previous transformation, not the original figure. Label each image with the letter of the transformation applied.

   a. $(x, y) \rightarrow (-x, y)$

   b. Rotation 90° clockwise about the origin

   c. $(x, y) \rightarrow (0.5x, 0.5y)$

2. Identify a sequence of transformations that will transform figure A into figure B.

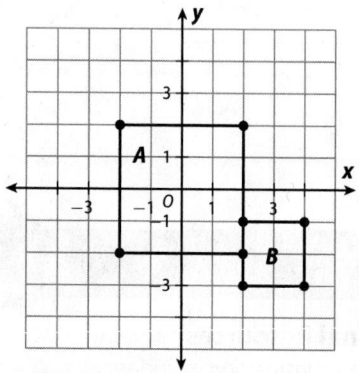

Lesson Quiz available online

Evaluate

GUIDED AND INDEPENDENT PRACTICE

 **FL CC** 8.G.1.4

Concepts & Skills	Practice
Explore Activity Combining Transformations with Dilations	Exercises 1, 6
Example 1 Similar Figures	Exercises 2–4, 7–10

Exercise	Depth of Knowledge (D.O.K.)	**FL CC** Mathematical Practices
6–10	**2** Skills/Concepts	**MP.4.1** Modeling
11	**3** Strategic Thinking **H.O.T.**	**MP.3.1** Logic
12	**3** Strategic Thinking **H.O.T.**	**MP.4.1** Modeling
13	**3** Strategic Thinking **H.O.T.**	**MP.2.1** Reasoning

Additional Resources

Differentiated Instruction includes:

• Leveled Practice worksheets

CLUSTER CONNECTION **Exercise 6** combines concepts from the Florida Common Core cluster "Understand congruence and similarity using physical models, transparencies, or geometry software."

Answers

1.

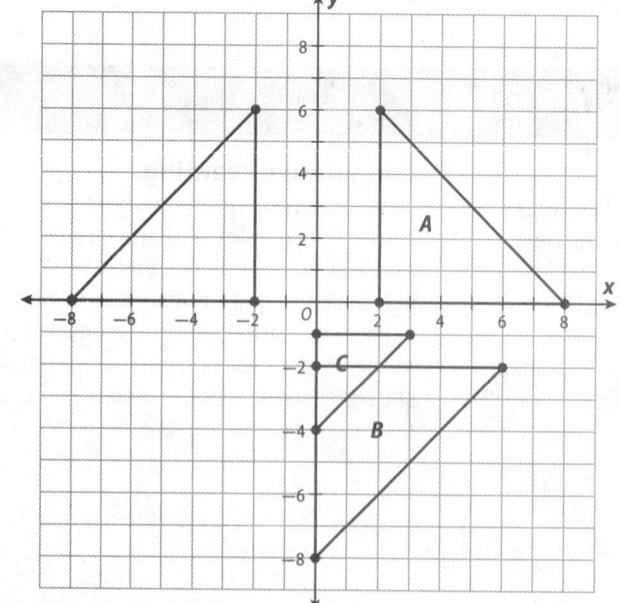

2. $(x, y) \rightarrow (0.5x, 0.5y)$, $(x, y) \rightarrow (x + 3, y - 2)$

18.3 Independent Practice

FL CC 8.G.1.4

Personal Math Trainer

Online Assessment and Intervention
my.hrw.com

6. A designer creates a drawing of a triangular sign on centimeter grid paper for a new business. The drawing has sides measuring 6 cm, 8 cm, and 10 cm, and angles measuring 37°, 53°, and 90°. To create the actual sign shown, the drawing must be dilated using a scale factor of 40.

Jan's Café

a. Find the lengths of the sides of the actual sign.

240 cm, 320 cm, 400 cm

b. Find the angle measures of the actual sign.

37°, 53°, 90°

c. The drawing has the hypotenuse on the bottom. The business owner would like it on the top. Describe two transformations that will do this.

Reflect the drawing over the x-axis; rotate the

drawing 180° around the origin.

d. The shorter leg of the drawing is currently on the left. The business owner wants it to remain on the left after the hypotenuse goes to the top. Which transformation in part c will accomplish this?

Reflecting over the x-axis

In Exercises 7–10, the transformation of a figure into its image is described. Describe the transformations that will transform the image back into the original figure. Then write them algebraically.

7. The figure is reflected across the x-axis and dilated by a scale factor of 3.

Dilate the image by a scale factor of $\frac{1}{3}$ and reflect it back

across the x-axis; $(x, y) \rightarrow (\frac{1}{3}x, \frac{1}{3}y), (x, y) \rightarrow (x, -y)$.

8. The figure is dilated by a scale factor of 0.5 and translated 6 units left and 3 units up.

Translate the image 3 units down and 6 units right and dilate

it by a factor of 2; $(x, y) \rightarrow (x + 6, y - 3), (x, y) \rightarrow (2x, 2y)$.

9. The figure is dilated by a scale factor of 5 and rotated 90° clockwise.

Rotate the image 90° counterclockwise and dilate it by a

factor of $\frac{1}{5}$; $(x, y) \rightarrow (-y, x), (x, y) \rightarrow (\frac{1}{5}x, \frac{1}{5}y)$.

10. The figure is reflected across the y-axis and dilated by a scale factor of 4.

Dilate the image by a factor of $\frac{1}{4}$ and reflect it back

across the y-axis; $(x, y) \rightarrow (\frac{1}{4}x, \frac{1}{4}y), (x, y) \rightarrow (-x, y)$.

H.O.T. FOCUS ON HIGHER ORDER THINKING

Work Area

11. Draw Conclusions A figure undergoes a sequence of transformations that include dilations. The figure and its final image are congruent. Explain how this can happen.

There must be an even number of dilations and for

each dilation applied to the figure, a dilation that has

the opposite effect must be applied as well.

12. Multistep As with geometric figures, graphs can be transformed through translations, reflections, rotations, and dilations. The equation $y = x$ is graphed at the right. Describe how the graph is changed through each of the following transformations.

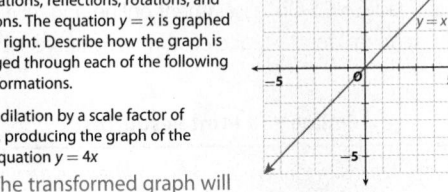

a. a dilation by a scale factor of 4, producing the graph of the equation $y = 4x$

The transformed graph will

be a line with a slope of 4 that passes through

the origin.

b. a translation producing the graph of the equation $y = x - 3$.

The transformed graph will be shifted downward 3

units. The slope will not change.

c. a reflection across the y-axis

The transformed graph will be a line with the

equation $y = -x$.

13. Justify Reasoning The graph of the line $y = x$ is dilated by a scale factor of 3 and then translated up 5 units. Is this the same as translating the graph up 5 units and then dilating by a scale factor of 3? Explain. How are the new graphs related?

No; the first sequence results in $y = 3x + 5$, the

second in $y = 3x + 15$. They are parallel lines.

EXTEND THE MATH PRE-AP

Activity available online my.hrw.com

Activity Similar figures can be created by using a flashlight and a cardboard figure. The projection point (center of dilation) is the flashlight, and each point on the cardboard figure is mapped to exactly one point on the shadow created. The scale factor of the dilation is the distance a point on the shadow is from the projection point divided by the distance the corresponding point on the rectangle is from the projection point. Have one person hold a cardboard rectangle 36 inches from a wall and another person hold the flashlight 12 inches from the cardboard rectangle. Measure the lengths of the sides of the shadow and the cardboard rectangle. What is the scale factor of the dilation? 4

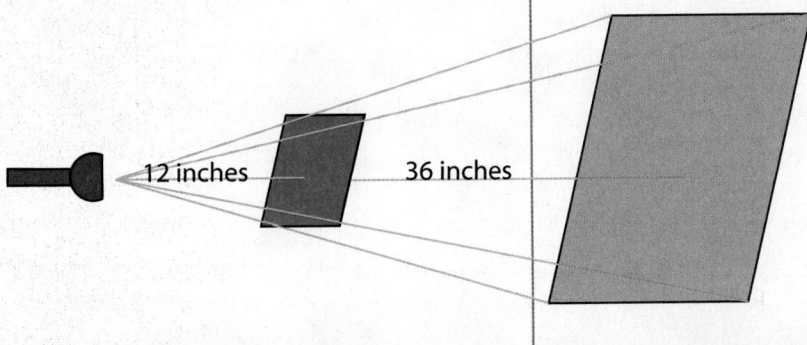

12 inches   36 inches

Ready to Go On?

Assess Mastery

Use the assessment on this page to determine if students have mastered the concepts and standards covered in this module.

Response to Intervention

Intervention	Enrichment

Personal Math Trainer
Online Assessment and Intervention
⏻ my.hrw.com

Access Ready to Go On? assessment online, and receive instant scoring, feedback, and customized intervention or enrichment.

Online and Print Resources

Differentiated Instruction	Differentiated Instruction
• Reteach worksheets	• Challenge worksheets
• Reading Strategies **ELL**	**PRE-AP**
• Success for English Learners **ELL**	Extend the Math **PRE-AP** Lesson Activities in TE

Additional Resources

Assessment Resources includes:
• Leveled Module Quizzes

MODULE QUIZ

Ready to Go On?

Personal Math Trainer
Online Assessment and Intervention
my.hrw.com

18.1 Properties of Dilations

Determine whether one figure is a dilation of the other. Justify your answer.

1. Triangle *XYZ* has angles measuring 54° and 29°. Triangle *X'Y'Z'* has angles measuring 29° and 92°.

   No; the triangles have only one pair of congruent angles.

2. Quadrilateral *DEFG* has sides measuring 16 m, 28 m, 24 m, and 20 m. Quadrilateral *D'E'F'G'* has sides measuring 20 m, 35 m, 30 m, and 25 m.

   Yes; each side of the second figure is 1.25 times the corresponding side of the original figure.

18.2 Algebraic Representations of Dilations

Dilate each figure with the origin as the center of dilation.

3. $(x, y) \rightarrow (0.8x, 0.8y)$

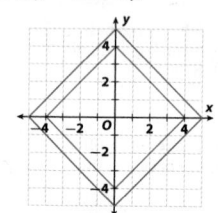

4. $(x, y) \rightarrow (2.5x, 2.5y)$

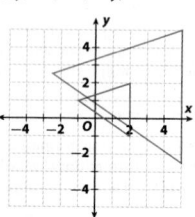

18.3 Similar Figures

5. Describe what happens to a figure when the given sequence of transformations is applied to it: $(x, y) \rightarrow (-x, y)$; $(x, y) \rightarrow (0.5x, 0.5y)$; $(x, y) \rightarrow (x - 2, y + 2)$

   reflection over the *y*-axis; dilation with a scale factor of 0.5; translation 2 units left and 2 units up

? ESSENTIAL QUESTION

6. How can you use dilations to solve real-world problems?
   You can use dilations when drawing blueprints.

©Houghton Mifflin Harcourt Publishing Company

 ## Florida Common Core Standards

Lesson	Exercises	Common Core Standards
18.1	1–2	**8.G.1.3, 8.G.1.4**
18.2	3–4	**8.G.1.3**
18.3	5	**8.G.1.4**

PARCC Assessment Readiness

Assessment Readiness Tip Students should distinguish problems where they can quickly solve the problem and match their answer to the correct answer choice from context-based items where it is impossible to find the answer by reading the stem in isolation.

 Item 1 Students should multiply the given coordinates by 1.5 and find the corresponding answer choice. There is no need to determine the scale factor of each answer choice.

 Item 5 Here, it is impossible to find the correct answer without examining the answer choices, but straightforward if the answer choices are looked at in turn, substituting 0 for y and solving for x.

Avoid Common Errors

 Item 2 Encourage students to actually calculate the ratio between the coordinates of one pair of corresponding vertices rather than trying to identify the ratio by estimating the relative sizes of the figures. Answer choices A, B, and C are all reasonable estimates, but only B is correct.

 Item 3 Encourage students to test their answer with sample coordinates, especially for the first step. They may be confused about which coordinate has the sign change when reflected over the x-axis.

Additional Resources

Personal Math Trainer

Online Assessment and Intervention

my.hrw.com

Selected Response

1. A rectangle has vertices $(6, 4)$, $(2, 4)$, $(6, -2)$, and $(2, -2)$. What are the coordinates of the vertices of the image after a dilation with the origin as its center and a scale factor of 1.5?

 Ⓐ $(9, 6)$, $(3, 6)$, $(9, -3)$, $(3, -3)$

 Ⓑ $(3, 2)$, $(1, 2)$, $(3, -1)$, $(1, -1)$

 Ⓒ $(12, 8)$, $(4, 8)$, $(12, -4)$, $(4, -4)$

 Ⓓ $(15, 10)$, $(5, 10)$, $(15, -5)$, $(5, -5)$

2. Which represents the dilation shown where the black figure is the preimage?

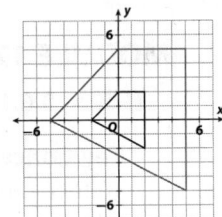

 Ⓐ $(x, y) \rightarrow (1.5x, 1.5y)$

 Ⓑ $(x, y) \rightarrow (2.5x, 2.5y)$

 Ⓒ $(x, y) \rightarrow (3x, 3y)$

 Ⓓ $(x, y) \rightarrow (6x, 6y)$

3. Identify the sequence of transformations that will reflect a figure over the x-axis and then dilate it by a scale factor of 3.

 Ⓐ $(x, y) \rightarrow (-x, y)$; $(x, y) \rightarrow (3x, 3y)$

 Ⓑ $(x, y) \rightarrow (-x, y)$; $(x, y) \rightarrow (x, 3y)$

 Ⓒ $(x, y) \rightarrow (x, -y)$; $(x, y) \rightarrow (3x, y)$

 Ⓓ $(x, y) \rightarrow (x, -y)$; $(x, y) \rightarrow (3x, 3y)$

4. Solve $-a + 7 = 2a - 8$.

 Ⓐ $a = -3$ Ⓒ $a = 5$

 Ⓑ $a = -\frac{1}{3}$ Ⓓ $a = 15$

5. Which equation does **not** represent a line with an x-intercept of 3?

 Ⓐ $y = -2x + 6$ Ⓒ $y = \frac{2}{3}x - 2$

 Ⓑ $y = -\frac{1}{3}x + 1$ Ⓓ $y = 3x - 1$

Mini-Task

6. The square is dilated under the dilation $(x, y) \rightarrow (0.25x, 0.25y)$.

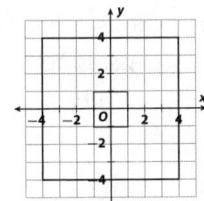

 a. Graph the image. What are the coordinates?

  $(-1, 1)$, $(1, 1)$, $(1, -1)$, $(-1, -1)$

 b. What is the length of a side of the image?

  2 units

 c. What are the perimeter and area of the preimage?

  32 units; 64 square units

 d. What are the perimeter and area of the image?

  8 units; 4 square units

 Florida Common Core Standards

Items	Grade 8 Standards	Mathematical Practices
1	8.G.1.3	MP.4.1
2	8.G.1.3, 8.G.1.4	MP.4.1
3	8.G.1.4	MP.4.1
4*	8.EE.3.7	MP.2.1
5*	8.F.2.4	MP.2.1
6	8.G.1.3, 8.G.1.4	MP.4.1

* Item integrates mixed review concepts from previous modules or a previous course.

Study Guide Review

Vocabulary Development

Integrating Language Arts

Encourage students to practice using the unit vocabulary as they talk and write about mathematics. Understanding vocabulary will aid their understanding of the concepts.

FL CC **LACC.68.RST.2.4** Determine the meaning of symbols, key terms, and other domain-specific words and phrases as they are used in a specific scientific or technical context relevant to grades 6–8 texts and topics.

MODULE 17 Transformations and Congruence

FL CC **8.G.1.1, 8.G.1.2, 8.G.1.3**

Key Concepts
- A transformation is a function that changes the position, size, or shape of a figure. *(Lesson 17.1)*
- Translations, reflections, and rotations are transformations that preserve the size and shape of the preimage. *(Lessons 17.1, 17.2, 17.3)*
- A translation is a transformation that slides a figure along a straight line. *(Lesson 17.1)*
- A reflection is a transformation that flips a figure across a line. Each point and its image are the same distance from the line of refection. *(Lesson 17.2)*
- A rotation is a transformation that turns a figure around a point called the center of rotation. *(Lesson 17.3)*
- To reflect an image over the x-axis, change the sign of the y-coordinates, and to reflect an image over the y-axis, change the sign of the x-coordinates. *(Lesson 17.4)*

Study Guide Review

MODULE 17 Transformations and Congruence

Key Vocabulary
center of rotation *(centro de rotación)*
congruent *(congruente)*
image *(imagen)*
line of reflection *(línea de reflexión)*
preimage *(imagen original)*
reflection *(reflexión)*
rotation *(rotación)*
transformation *(transformación)*
translation *(traslación)*

? ESSENTIAL QUESTION

How can you use transformations and congruence to solve real-world problems?

EXAMPLE

Translate triangle *XYZ* left 4 units and down 2 units. Graph the image and label the vertices.

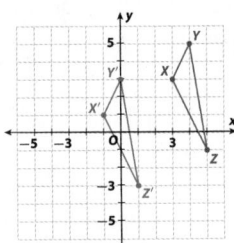

Translate the vertices by subtracting 4 from each *x*-coordinate and 2 from each *y*-coordinate. The new vertices are $X'(-1, 1)$, $Y'(0, 3)$, and $Z'(1, -3)$.

Connect the vertices to draw triangle $X'Y'Z'$.

EXERCISES

Perform the transformation shown. (Lessons 17.1, 17.2, 17.3)

1. Reflection over the *x*-axis

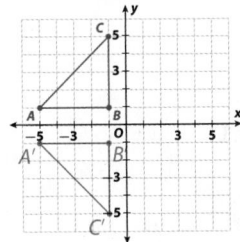

2. Translation 5 units right

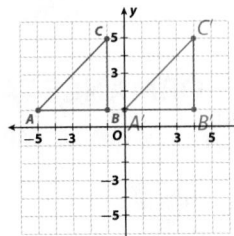

3. Rotation 90° counterclockwise about the origin

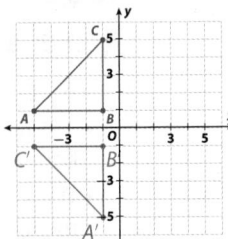

4. Translation 4 units right and 4 units down

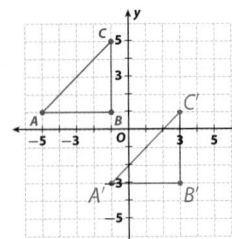

5. Quadrilateral *ABCD* with vertices $A(4, 4)$, $B(5, 1)$, $C(5, -1)$ and $D(4, -2)$ is translated left 2 units and down 3 units. Graph the preimage and the image. (Lesson 17.4)

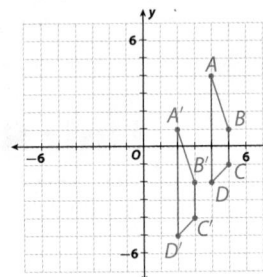

6. Triangle *ABC* with vertices $A(1, 2)$, $B(1, 4)$, and $C(3, 3)$ is translated by $(x, y) \rightarrow (x - 4, y)$, and the result is reflected by $(x, y) \rightarrow (x, -y)$. Graph the preimage and the image. (Lesson 17.5)

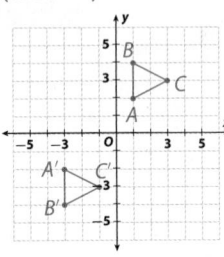

7. Triangle *RST* has vertices at $(-8, 2)$, $(-4, 0)$, and $(-12, 8)$. Find the vertices after the triangle has been reflected over the *y*-axis. (Lesson 17.4)

$(8, 2), (4, 0), (12, 8)$

8. Triangle *XYZ* has vertices at $(3, 7)$, $(9, 14)$, and $(12, -1)$. Find the vertices after the triangle has been rotated 180° about the origin. (Lesson 17.4)

$(-3, -7), (-9, -14), (-12, 1)$

9. Triangle *MNP* has its vertices located at $(-1, -4)$, $(-2, -5)$, and $(-3, -3)$. Find the vertices after the triangle has been reflected by $(x, y) \rightarrow (x, -y)$ and translated by $(x, y) \rightarrow (x + 6, y)$. (Lesson 17.5)

$(5, 4), (4, 5), (3, 3)$

MODULE 18 Transformations and Similarity

FL CC 8.G.1.3, 8.G.1.4

Key Concepts

- A dilation is a transformation that changes the position and size but not the shape of a figure. *(Lesson 18.1)*
- The scale factor of a dilation describes how much the figure is enlarged or reduced and is the ratio of a length of the image to the corresponding length of the preimage. *(Lesson 18.1)*
- To find the coordinates of a dilated image with the origin as the center, multiply the *x*- and *y*-coordinates of the vertices by the scale factor. *(Lesson 18.2)*
- If two figures are similar, then there exists a sequence of translations, reflections, rotations, and/or dilations that transforms one figure into the other. *(Lesson 18.3)*

Unit 8 Performance Tasks

The Performance Tasks provide students with the opportunity to apply concepts from this unit in real-world problem situations.

CAREERS IN MATH

Contractor In Performance Task Item 1, students can see how a contractor uses mathematics on the job.

SCORING GUIDES FOR PERFORMANCE TASKS

1. MATHEMATICAL PRACTICES **FL CC** MP.3.1, MP.4.1, MP.6.1

Task	Possible Points (Total: 6)
a	**1 point** for the correct answer yes, and **2 points** for correctly explaining that the area increased by a factor of 6, from 6 square units to 36 square units.
b	**1 point** for the correct answer no, and **2 points** for a correct explanation, for example: One side length increased by a factor of 2 and the other side length increased by a factor of 3.

2. MATHEMATICAL PRACTICES **FL CC** MP.3.1, MP.4.1, MP.7.1

Possible Points (Total: 6)
2 points for the correct points (0, 0), (7.5, 0), and (7.5, 6)   **2 points** for the correct answer yes, and **2 points** for correctly explaining that the angle measures are the same in both triangles, and the ratio of corresponding side lengths increase by the scale factor.

Transformations and Similarity

Key Vocabulary

center of dilation *(centro de dilatación)*

dilation *(dilatación)*

enlargement *(agrandamiento)*

reduction *(reducción)*

scale factor *(factor de escala)*

similar *(semejantes)*

❓ ESSENTIAL QUESTION

How can you use dilations, similarity, and proportionality to solve real-world problems?

EXAMPLE

Dilate triangle *ABC* with the origin as the center of dilation and scale factor $\frac{1}{2}$. Graph the dilated image.

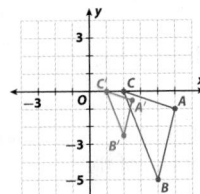

Multiply each coordinate of the vertices of *ABC* by $\frac{1}{2}$ to find the vertices of the dilated image.

$A(5, -1) \rightarrow A'\left(5 \cdot \frac{1}{2}, -1 \cdot \frac{1}{2}\right) \rightarrow A'\left(2\frac{1}{2}, -\frac{1}{2}\right)$

$B(4, -5) \rightarrow B'\left(4 \cdot \frac{1}{2}, -5 \cdot \frac{1}{2}\right) \rightarrow B'\left(2, -2\frac{1}{2}\right)$

$C(2, 0) \rightarrow C'\left(2 \cdot \frac{1}{2}, 0 \cdot \frac{1}{2}\right) \rightarrow C'(1, 0)$

EXERCISES

1. For each pair of corresponding vertices, find the ratio of the *x*-coordinates and the ratio of the *y*-coordinates. (Lesson 18.1)

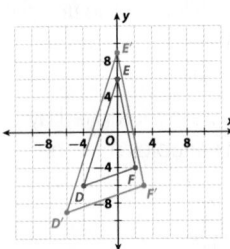

Ratio of *x*-coordinates: ___1.5___

Ratio of *y*-coordinates: ___1.5___

What is the scale factor of the dilation? ___1.5___

2. Rectangle *WXYZ* has vertices at (−2, −1), (−2, 1), (2, −1), and (2, 1). It is first dilated by (x, y) → (2x, 2y), and then translated by (x, y) → (x, y + 3). (Lesson 18.3)

a. What are the vertices of the image? ___(−4, 1), (−4, 5), (4, 1), (4, 5)___

b. Are the preimage and image congruent? Are they similar? Explain.

They are not congruent because the lengths of the corresponding sides of the image and preimage are not equal; they are similar because they have the same shape.

Dilate each figure with the origin as the center of the dilation. List the vertices of the dilated figure then graph the figure. (Lesson 18.2)

3. $(x, y) \rightarrow \left(\frac{1}{4}x, \frac{1}{4}y\right)$

___X'(−2, 1); Y'(−1, 1); Z'(1, 2)___

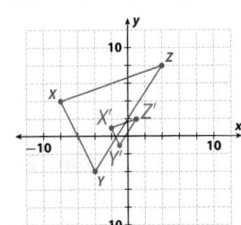

4. $(x, y) \rightarrow (2x, 2y)$

___A'(−2, 4); B'(4, 4); C'(6, −2); D'(0, −2)___

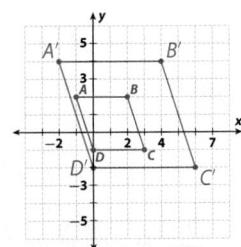

Unit 8 Performance Tasks

1. **CAREERS IN MATH** Contractor Fernando is expanding his dog's play yard. The original yard has a fence represented by rectangle *LMNO* on the coordinate plane. Fernando hires a contractor to construct a new fence that should enclose 6 times as much area as the current fence. The shape of the fence must remain the same. The contractor constructs the fence shown by rectangle *L'M'N'O'*.

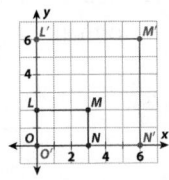

a. Did the contractor increase the area by the amount Fernando wanted? Explain.

Yes; the original area was 2 · 3 = 6 square units, and the new area is 6 · 6 = 36 square units, and 6 · 6 = 36.

b. Does the new fence maintain the shape of the old fence? How do you know?

No; the corresponding side lengths are not in proportion. The ratio of the width is 2, and the ratio of the height is 3.

2. A sail for a sailboat is represented by a triangle on the coordinate plane with vertices (0, 0), (5, 0), and (5, 4). The triangle is dilated by a scale factor of 1.5 with the origin as the center of dilation. Find the coordinates of the dilated triangle. Are the triangles similar? Explain.

(0, 0), (7.5, 0), and (7.5, 6); Yes; the angle measures are the same in both, and the ratio of corresponding side lengths is 1.5 (the scale factor).

MIXED REVIEW

PARCC Assessment Readiness

Assessment Readiness Tip Students can make a graph to help them understand questions for which graphs are not given.

Items 2 and 8 Students can make a graph, plot the points of the original image, then perform the transformations on the figure. They can find the answer by looking at the coordinates of the vertices of the image they create.

Item 5 Students can quickly sketch a graph of a trapezoid and then translate it 8 units down. This allows them to check each statement using a concrete model of the situation.

Avoid Common Errors

Item 4 Some students will only check the first pair of values in the table to see if they work in the equations. In this case, three of the given equations are fulfilled by the first pair of values in the table. Remind them that they need to check multiple pairs of values to make sure the table and equation match each other.

Item 6 Some students will choose answer choice C because *x* and *y* are multiplied by coefficients less than one. Remind students that in a reduction, both variables must be multiplied by the same value.

 Florida Common Core Standards

Items	🏴 Grade 8 Standards	🏴 Mathematical Practices
1	8.G.1.1	MP.2.1
2	8.G.1.3	MP.2.1
3	8.G.1.4	MP.1.1
4*	8.F.2.4	MP.2.1
5	8.G.1.1	MP.6.1
6	8.G.1.3	MP.2.1
7*	8.EE.3.7b	MP.2.1
8	8.G.1.3	MP.2.1
9*	8.EE.3.8b; 8.EE.3.8c	MP.1.1
10*	8.NS.1.1	MP.7.1
11*	8.EE.3.8b	MP.2.1
12	8.G.1.2	MP.4.1
13	8.G.1.3	MP.1.1

* Item integrates mixed review concepts from previous modules or a previous course.

PARCC Assessment Readiness

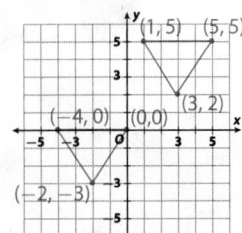

Personal Math Trainer

my.hrw.com

Online Assessment and Intervention

Selected Response

1. What would be the orientation of the figure below after a reflection over the *x*-axis?

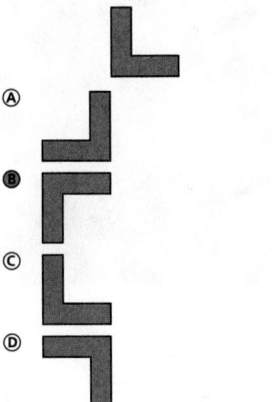

(A)

(B)

(C)

(D)

2. A triangle with coordinates (4, 2), (0, −3), and (−5, 3) is translated 5 units right and rotated 180° about the origin. What are the coordinates of its image?

(A) (9, 2), (−1, −2), (5, −7)

(B) (−10, 3), (−1, 2), (−5, −3)

(C) (2, −1), (−3, −5), (3, −10)

(D) (−9, −2), (−5, 3), (0, −3)

3. Quadrilateral *LMNP* has sides measuring 16, 28, 12, and 32. Which could be the side lengths of a dilation of *LMNP*?

(A) 24, 40, 18, 90

(B) 32, 60, 24, 65

(C) 20, 35, 15, 40

(D) 40, 70, 30, 75

4. The table below represents which equation?

x	−1	0	1	2
y	1	−2	−5	−8

(A) $y = x + 2$

(B) $y = -x$

(C) $y = 3x + 6$

(D) $y = -3x - 2$

5. Which of the following is **not** true of a trapezoid that has been translated 8 units down?

(A) The new trapezoid is the same size as the original trapezoid.

(B) The new trapezoid is the same shape as the original trapezoid.

(C) The new trapezoid is in the same orientation as the original trapezoid.

(D) The *y*-coordinates of the new trapezoid are the same as the *y*-coordinates of the original trapezoid.

6. Which represents a reduction?

(A) $(x, y) \rightarrow (0.9x, 0.9y)$

(B) $(x, y) \rightarrow (1.4x, 1.4y)$

(C) $(x, y) \rightarrow (0.7x, 0.3y)$

(D) $(x, y) \rightarrow (2.5x, 2.5y)$

7. Which is the solution for $4(x + 1) = 2(3x - 2)$?

(A) $x = -4$

(B) $x = -1$

(C) $x = 0$

(D) $x = 4$

8. A rectangle has vertices (8, 6), (4, 6), (8, −4), and (4, −4). What are the coordinates after dilating from the origin by a scale factor of 1.5?

(A) (9, 6), (3, 6), (9, −3), (3, −3)

(B) (10, 8), (5, 8), (10, −5), (5, −5)

(C) (16, 12), (8, 12), (16, −8), (8, −8)

(D) (12, 9), (6, 9), (12, −6), (6, −6)

> **Make sure you look at all answer choices before making your decision. Try substituting each answer choice into the problem if you are unsure of the answer.**

9. Two apples plus four bananas cost $2.00. An apple costs twice as much as a banana. Using the equations $2a + 4b = 2.00$ and $a = 2b$, where *a* is the cost of one apple and *b* is the cost of one banana, what are *a* and *b*?

(A) $a = \$0.25; b = \$0.25$

(B) $a = \$0.25; b = \$0.50$

(C) $a = \$0.50; b = \$0.25$

(D) $a = \$0.50; b = \$0.50$

10. Which statement is false?

(A) No integers are irrational numbers.

(B) All whole numbers are integers.

(C) No real numbers are rational numbers.

(D) All integers greater than or equal to 0 are whole numbers.

11. Consider the system of equations $3x + 4y = 2$ and $2x - 4y = 8$. Which is its solution?

(A) $x = -1, y = -2$

(B) $x = 1, y = 2$

(C) $x = -2, y = 1$

(D) $x = 2, y = -1$

Mini-Tasks

12. A triangle with vertices (−2, −3), (−4, 0), and (0, 0) is congruent to a second triangle located in quadrant I with two of its vertices at (3, 2) and (1, 5).

a. Graph the two triangles on the same coordinate grid.

(1, 5) (5, 5)

(−4, 0) (0,0) (3, 2)

(−2, −3)

b. What are the coordinates of the third vertex of the second triangle?

(5, 5)

13. Tamiko is planning a stone wall shaped like a triangle, with vertices at (−1, −2), (2, 2), and (−2, 2) on a coordinate grid. She plans to add a second wall, in the same shape, enclosing the first wall, with the origin as the center of dilation. The vertices of the second wall are (−3, −6), (6, 6), and (−6, 6).

a. What scale factor did Tamiko use for the second wall?

3

b. Are the two walls similar? Explain.

Yes. Two figures are similar if one can be obtained from the other by dilation.

UNIT 9

Measurement Geometry

Contents

Unit Pacing Guide

45-Minute Classes

Module 19

DAY 1	DAY 2	DAY 3	DAY 4	DAY 5
Lesson 19.1	Lesson 19.1	Lesson 19.2	Lesson 19.3	Lesson 19.3

DAY 6				
Ready to Go On? PARCC Assessment Readiness				

Module 20

DAY 1	DAY 2	DAY 3	DAY 4	DAY 5
Lesson 20.1	Lesson 20.1	Lesson 20.2	Lesson 20.2	Lesson 20.3

DAY 6	DAY 7			
Lesson 20.3	Ready to Go On? PARCC Assessment Readiness			

Module 21

DAY 1	DAY 2	DAY 3	DAY 4	DAY 5
Lesson 21.1	Lesson 21.2	Lesson 21.3	Ready to Go On? PARCC Assessment Readiness	Study Guide PARCC Assessment Readiness

90-Minute Classes

Module 19

DAY 1	DAY 2	DAY 3
Lesson 19.1	Lesson 19.2 Lesson 19.3	Lesson 19.3 Ready to Go On? PARCC Assessment Readiness

Module 20

DAY 1	DAY 2	DAY 3
Lesson 20.1	Lesson 20.2 Lesson 20.3	Lesson 20.3 Ready to Go On? PARCC Assessment Readiness

Module 21

DAY 1	DAY 2	DAY 3	
Lesson 21.1	Lesson 21.2 Lesson 21.3	Ready to Go On? PARCC Assessment Readiness	Study Guide PARCC Assessment Readiness

Program Resources

⏻ Plan

Online Teacher Edition

Access a full suite of teaching resources online—plan, present, and manage classes, assignments, and activities.

 **ePlanner** Easily plan your classes, create and view assignments, and access all program resources with your online, customizable planning tool.

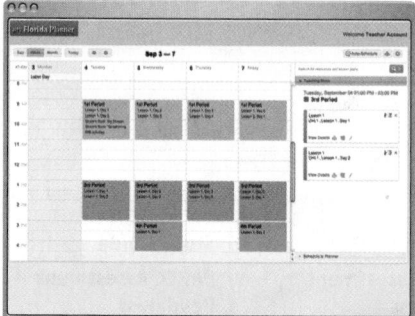

Professional Development Videos

Author Juli Dixon models successful teaching practices and strategies in actual classroom settings.

 **QR Codes** Scan with your smart phone to jump directly from your print book to online videos and other resources.

Teacher's Edition

Support students with point-of-use Questioning Strategies, teaching tips, resources for differentiated instruction, additional activities, and more.

⏻ Engage and Explore

Real-World Videos Engage students with interesting and relevant applications of the mathematical content of each module.

 **Animated Math** Online interactive simulations, tools, and games help students actively learn and practice key concepts.

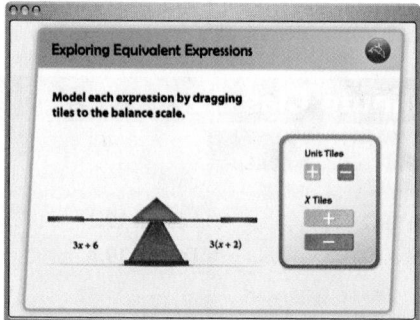

Explore Activities

Students interactively explore new concepts using a variety of tools and approaches.

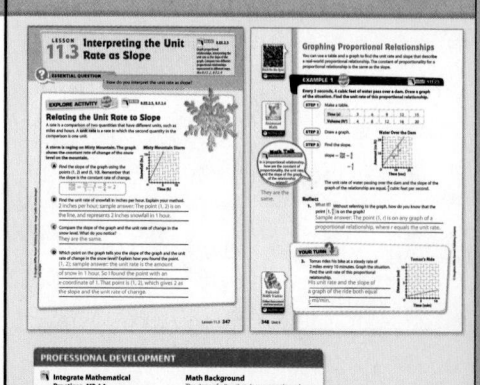

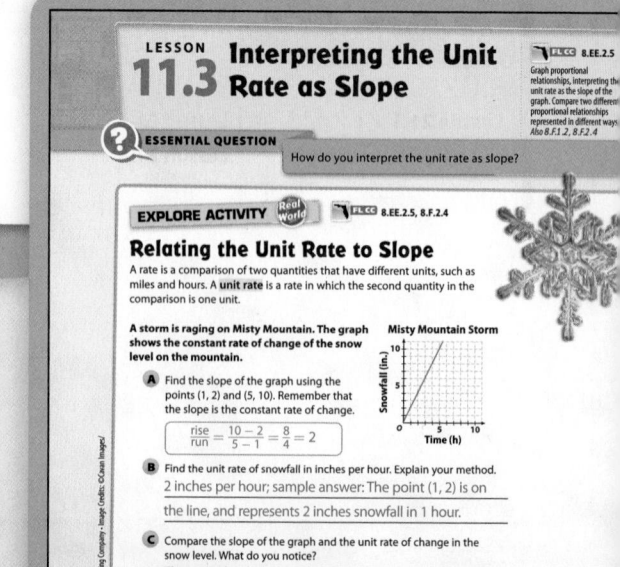

Image Credits: ©wusuowei/Fotolia; (c) ©Juli Dixon

Teach

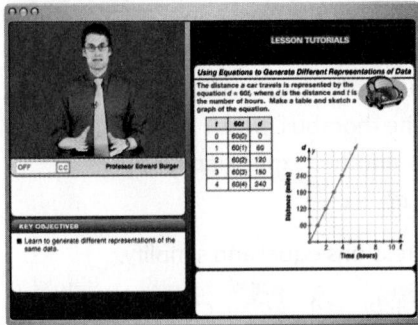

Math On the Spot video tutorials, featuring program authors Dr. Edward Burger and Martha Sandoval-Martinez, accompany every example in the textbook and give students step-by-step instructions and explanations of key math concepts.

Present engaging content on a multitude of devices, including tablets and interactive whiteboards.

Math Talk Continually monitor and assess student progress with integrated formative assessment.

CLUSTER CONNECTION Look for exercises indicated with this icon to build connections among standards within Florida Common Core clusters.

Differentiated Instruction Print Resources

Support all learners with Differentiated Instruction Resources, including

- **Leveled Practice and Problem Solving**
- **Reteach**
- **Reading Strategies**
- **Success for English Learners**
- **Challenge**

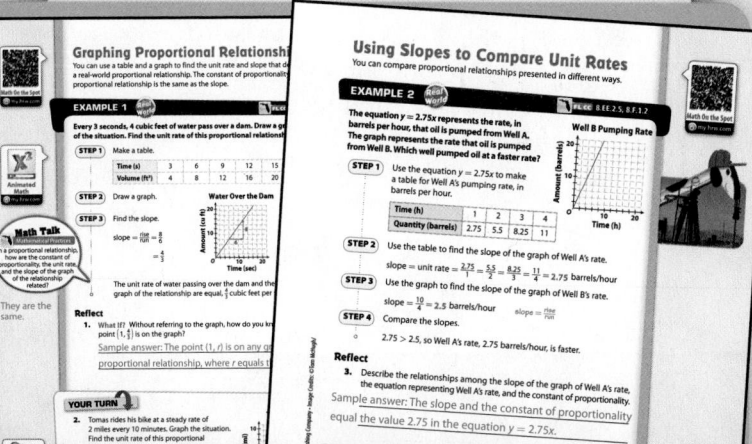

Assessment and Intervention

The **Personal Math Trainer** provides online practice, homework, assessments, and intervention. Monitor student progress through reports and alerts. Create and customize assignments aligned to specific lessons or standards.

- **Practice** – With dynamic items and assignments, students get unlimited practice on key concepts supported by guided examples, step-by-step solutions, and video tutorials.

- **Assessments** – Choose from course assignments or customize your own based on course content, standards, difficulty levels, and more.

- **Homework** – Students can complete online homework with a wide variety of problem types, including the ability to enter expressions, equations, and graphs. Let the system automatically grade homework, so you can focus where your students need help the most!

- **Intervention** – Let the Personal Math Trainer automatically prescribe a targeted, personalized intervention path for your students.

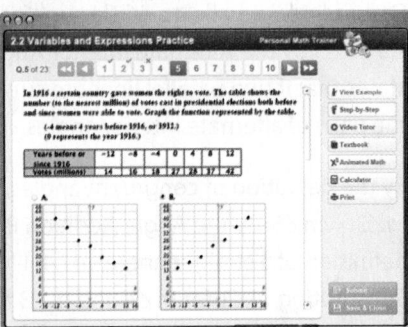

Raise the bar with homework and practice that incorporates higher-order thinking and mathematical processes in every lesson.

PARCC Assessment Readiness
Prepare students for success on the PARCC math test with practice at every module and unit.

Assessment Resources

Tailor assessments to meet the needs of all your classes and students, including

- **Leveled Module Quizzes**
- **Leveled Unit Tests**
- **Unit Performance Tasks**
- **Placement, Diagnostic, and Quarterly Benchmark Tests**

Math Background

Angles Theorems for Triangles 8.G.1.5
LESSON 19.2

The Triangle Sum Theorem states that the sum of the angle measures of a triangle is 180°. The theorem is presented and justified informally to students at this level, but a more formal proof of the theorem is shown below.

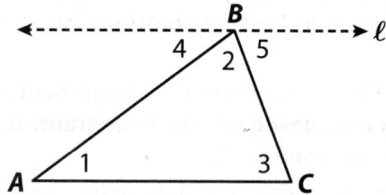

Given: △ABC
Prove: m∠1 + m∠2 + m∠3 = 180°

Draw a line ℓ parallel to $\overline{AC}$ through point B. ∠1 ≅ ∠4 and ∠3 ≅ ∠5 by the Alternate Interior Angles Theorem, which states that if two parallel lines are cut by a transversal, then the pairs of alternate interior angles are congruent.

By the definition of congruent angles, m∠1 = m∠4 and m∠3 = m∠5. By the Angle Addition Postulate and the definition of a straight angle, m∠4 + m∠2 + m∠5 = 180°. Substituting m∠1 for m∠4 and m∠3 for m∠5 gives m∠1 + m∠2 + m∠3 = 180°.

The Pythagorean Theorem 8.G.2.6, 8.G.2.7
LESSONS 20.1 and 20.2

The proof of the Pythagorean Theorem given in the Explore Activity involves using physical objects to demonstrate that the theorem is true. The mathematics behind this physical proof may be of interest to advanced students.

Given a right triangle with legs of length a and b and hypotenuse c, draw a square with sides of length $a + b$ as shown.

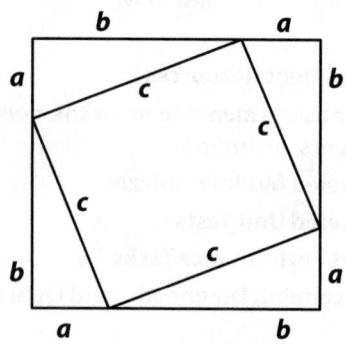

The area of the large square is $(a + b)^2$. The Area Addition Postulate states that the area of a region is equal to the sum of the areas of its nonoverlapping parts, so the area of the large square is also equal to the area of the four triangles plus the area of the interior rhombus. This rhombus can be shown to be a square by noting that along each side of the larger square, the measures of the three angles formed with the vertex of the rhombus must have a sum of 180°. The measures of the other two angles must have a sum of 90° since they are the two acute angles in a right triangle. Therefore, each angle of the rhombus measures 90° and the rhombus is a square. Thus, another expression for the area of the large square is $4 \cdot \frac{1}{2}ab + c^2$.

Now set the two area expressions equal and simplify.

$$(a + b)^2 = 4 \cdot \frac{1}{2}ab + c^2$$
$$a^2 + 2ab + b^2 = 2ab + c^2$$
$$a^2 + b^2 = c^2$$

Given a mathematical statement in the form *If p, then q*, the *converse* of the statement is *If q, then p*. In general, a true statement need not have a true converse. Consider this statement: if a natural number is divisible by 10, then it is even. The statement is true, but its converse—if a natural number is even, then it is divisible by 10—is false.

The converse of the Pythagorean Theorem *is* true: If a triangle has sides of length a, b, and c such that $a^2 + b^2 = c^2$, then the triangle is a right triangle. The Explore Activity that tests the converse of the theorem demonstrates to students that the Pythagorean Theorem works in both directions. Students should recognize when they are using the theorem and when they are using the converse.

Volume of Cylinders, Cones, and Spheres 8.G.3.9
LESSONS 21.1 to 21.3

The study of cylinder volume in this course is limited to *right cylinders*. This is a cylinder that has an axis perpendicular to its bases. An *oblique cylinder* has an axis that is not perpendicular to the cylinder's bases.

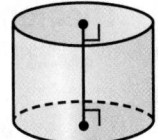 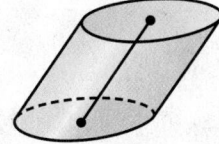

Right cylinder   Oblique cylinder

Interestingly, the volume formula $V = Bh$ works for oblique cylinders as well as right cylinders. This fact is based on Cavalieri's Principle: If two three-dimensional figures have the same height and the same cross-sectional area at every level, then they have the same volume.

An understanding of cylinder and cone volumes gives interested students an opportunity to explore Archimedes' formula for the volume of a sphere. Archimedes viewed his derivation of the formula for the volume of a sphere as his crowning mathematical achievement. He phrased this result as *the volume of a sphere is $\frac{2}{3}$ the volume of the circumscribed cylinder*. This is to be interpreted as in the picture below.

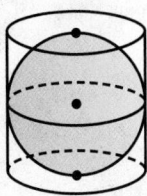

Volume of sphere $= \frac{2}{3} \times$ Volume of cylinder

Note that if the radius of the sphere is r, then the cylinder has height $2r$ and base area πr^2. Therefore, the cylinder has volume $\pi r^2 \cdot 2r = 2\pi r^3$. The volume of the sphere is therefore

$$V = \frac{2}{3}(2\pi r^3) = \frac{4}{3}\pi r^3$$

The method used by Archimedes corresponds to applying Cavalieri's principle to a hemisphere of radius r and the solid obtained by removing a cone from the cylinder in the figure below.

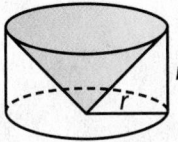 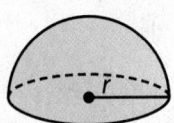

Archimedes showed that horizontal planes intersect these two solids in plane regions of equal area. (If the horizontal plane is at a distance of x from the base of the hemisphere, the region on the left is an annulus with area $\pi r^2 - \pi x^2$. The region on the right is a circle with area $\pi\left(\sqrt{r^2 - x^2}\right)^2$.) Therefore, by Cavalieri's principle, the two solids have equal volumes.

But the volume of the figure on the left is

Volume of cylinder − Volume of cone =
$(\pi r^2)r - \frac{1}{3}(\pi r^2)r = \frac{2}{3}\pi r^3$

Since the volume of a sphere is twice the volume of its related hemisphere, it follows that the volume of a sphere is

$$2\left(\tfrac{2}{3}\right)\pi r^3 = \tfrac{4}{3}\pi r^3.$$

Measurement Geometry

CAREERS IN MATH

Hydrologist A hydrologist is a scientist who studies and solves water-related issues. A hydrologist might work to prevent or clean up polluted water sources, locate water supplies for urban or rural needs, or control flooding and erosion. A hydrologist uses math to assess water resources and mathematical models to understand water systems, as well as statistics to analyze phenomena such as rainfall patterns. If you are interested in a career as a cost estimator, you should study the following mathematical subjects:

- Algebra
- Trigonometry
- Calculus
- Statistics

Research other careers that require creating and using mathematical models to understand physical phenomena.

Unit 9 Performance Task

At the end of the unit, check out how **hydrologists** use math.

Careers in Math

Hydrologist

A hydrologist uses math to to determine the availability of water for urban and rural use and to understand and predict processes in the water cycle. You will learn more about this in the Performance Tasks at the end of the unit.

For more information about careers in mathematics as well as various mathematics appreciation topics, visit the American Mathematical Society at www.ams.org

Vocabulary Preview

Use the puzzle to give students a preview of important concepts in this unit. Students may work individually, in pairs, or in groups.

Unit Resources

Go online to access all your unit resources.

my.hrw.com

Vocabulary Preview

Use the puzzle to preview key vocabulary from this unit. Unscramble the circled letters to answer the riddle at the bottom of the page.

Across

1. The angle formed by two sides of a triangle (2 words) (Lesson 19.2)
5. A three-dimensional figure that has two congruent circular bases. (Lesson 21.1)
6. A three-dimensional figure with all points the same distance from the center. (Lesson 21.3)

Down

2. The line that intersects two or more lines. (Lesson 19.1)
3. The side opposite the right angle in a right triangle. (Lesson 20.1)
4. Figures with the same shape but not necessarily the same size. (Lesson 19.3)
5. A three-dimensional figure that has one vertex and one circular base. (Lesson 21.2)

Q: What do you call an angle that is adorable?

A: A CUTE ANGLE !

Before	In this Unit	After
Students understand: • angle pair relationships • volume of prisms	Students will learn about: • angle relationships of parallel lines and transversals • sum of the measures of the angles of a triangle • exterior angles of a triangle • similarity of triangles • the Pythagorean Theorem and its converse • the Distance Formula • volume of cylinders, cones, and spheres	Students will connect: • angle relationships and transversals of parallel lines • interior and exterior angles of a triangle • similar and congruent triangles • volume of a cylinder, a cone, and a sphere

Angle Relationships in Parallel Lines and Triangles

ESSENTIAL QUESTION

How can you use angle relationships in parallel lines and triangles to solve real-world problems?

You can use the relationships to find the measures of unknown angles in real-world situations.

my.hrw.com

Real-World Video

Many cities are designed on a grid with parallel streets. If another street runs across the parallel lines, it is a transversal. Special relationships exist between parallel lines and transversals.

© Houghton Mifflin Harcourt Publishing Company • Image Credits: ©Nifro Travel Images/Alamy Images

GO DIGITAL

my.hrw.com

my.hrw.com

Go digital with your write-in student edition, accessible on any device.

Math On the Spot

Scan with your smart phone to jump directly to the online edition, video tutor, and more.

Animated Math

Interactively explore key concepts to see how math works.

Personal Math Trainer

Get immediate feedback and help as you work through practice sets.

Are You Ready?

Assess Readiness

Use the assessment on this page to determine if students need intensive or strategic intervention for the module's prerequisite skills.

 **RtI** **Response to Intervention**

Intervention	Enrichment

Personal Math Trainer

Online Assessment and Intervention

my.hrw.com

Access Are You Ready? assessment online, and receive instant scoring, feedback, and customized intervention or enrichment.

Online and Print Resources

Skills Intervention worksheets
- Skill 60 Solve Two-Step Equations
- Skill 75 Name Angles

Differentiated Instruction
- Challenge worksheets **PRE-AP**
- Extend the Math **PRE-AP** Lesson Activities in TE

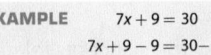 **Are YOU Ready?**

Complete these exercises to review skills you will need for this module.

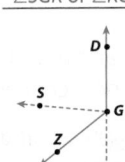 Personal Math Trainer

Online Assessment and Intervention

my.hrw.com

Solve Two-Step Equations

EXAMPLE	$7x + 9 = 30$	Write the equation.
	$7x + 9 - 9 = 30 - 9$	Subtract 9 from both sides.
	$7x = 21$	Simplify.
	$\frac{7x}{7} = \frac{21}{7}$	Divide both sides by 7.
	$x = 3$	Simplify.

Solve for x.

1. $6x + 10 = 46$ 6
2. $7x - 6 = 36$ 6
3. $3x + 26 = 59$ 11
4. $2x + 5 = -25$ -15

5. $6x - 7 = 41$ 8
6. $\frac{1}{2}x + 9 = 30$ 42
7. $\frac{1}{3}x - 7 = 15$ 66
8. $0.5x - 0.6 = 8.4$ 18

Name Angles

EXAMPLE

Use three points of an angle, including the vertex, to name the angle. Write the vertex between the other two points: $\angle JKL$ or $\angle LKJ$. You can also use just the vertex letter to name the angle if there is no danger of confusing the angle with another. This is also $\angle K$.

Give two names for the angle formed by the dashed rays.

9. $\angle MHR$ or $\angle RHM$
10. $\angle SGK$ or $\angle KGS$
11. $\angle BTF$ or $\angle FTB$

PROFESSIONAL DEVELOPMENT VIDEO

Author Juli Dixon models successful teaching practices as she explores the concept of angle relationships in intersecting lines and triangles in an actual eighth-grade classroom.

 **Professional Development** 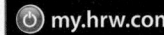 my.hrw.com

GO DIGITAL
my.hrw.com

Online Teacher Edition
Access a full suite of teaching resources online—plan, present, and manage classes and assignments.

ePlanner
Easily plan your classes and access all your resources online.

Interactive Answers and Solutions
Customize answer keys to print or display in the classroom. Choose to include answers only or full solutions to all lesson exercises.

Interactive Whiteboards
Engage students with interactive whiteboard-ready lessons and activities.

Personal Math Trainer: Online Assessment and Intervention
Assign automatically graded homework, quizzes, tests, and intervention activities. Prepare your students with updated practice tests aligned with Common Core.

Reading Start-Up

Have students complete the activities on this page by working alone or with others.

Visualize Vocabulary

The summary triangle helps students review the concepts related to angles and will help prepare them for the exercises in this module. Students should write one or more review words in each section of the triangle.

Understand Vocabulary

Use the following explanation to help students learn the preview words.

> Angles are all around us. For example, streets that intersect form different angles. If one street crosses two parallel streets, it is a **transversal** and creates special angles. **Corresponding angles** and **same-side interior angles** are formed on the same side of the transversal. Across the transversal from each other are the **alternate interior** and **alternate exterior angles.**

Active Reading

Integrating Language Arts

Students can use these reading and note-taking strategies to help them organize and understand new concepts and vocabulary.

🏴 **FL CC** **LACC.68.RST.3.7** Integrate quantitative or technical information expressed in words in a text with a version of that information expressed visually (e.g., in a flowchart, diagram, model, graph, or table).

Additional Resources

Differentiated Instruction
- Reading Strategies **ELL**

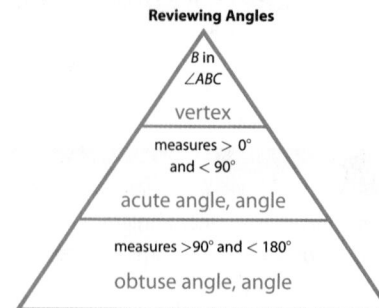

Reading Start-Up

Visualize Vocabulary

Use the ✔ words to complete the graphic. You can put more than one word in each section of the triangle.

Reviewing Angles

- *B* in ∠*ABC*
- vertex
- measures > 0° and < 90°
- acute angle, angle
- measures >90° and < 180°
- obtuse angle, angle

Understand Vocabulary

Complete the sentences using preview words.

1. A line that intersects two or more lines is a ___transversal___.

2. Figures with the same shape but not necessarily the same size are ___similar___.

3. An ___exterior angle___ is an angle formed by one side of the triangle and the extension of an adjacent side.

Vocabulary

Review Words
- ✔ acute angle *(ángulo agudo)*
- ✔ angle *(ángulo)*
- congruent *(congruente)*
- ✔ obtuse angle *(ángulo obtuso)*
- parallel lines *(líneas paralelas)*
- ✔ vertex *(vértice)*

Preview Words
- alternate exterior angles *(ángulos alternos externos)*
- alternate interior angles *(ángulos alternos internos)*
- corresponding angles *(ángulos correspondientes (para líneas))*
- exterior angle *(ángulo externo de un polígono)*
- interior angle *(ángulos internos)*
- remote interior angle *(ángulo interno remoto)*
- same-side interior angles *(ángulos internos del mismo lado)*
- similar *(semejantes)*
- transversal *(transversal)*

Active Reading

Pyramid Before beginning the module, create a pyramid to help you organize what you learn. Label each side with one of the lesson titles from this module. As you study each lesson, write important ideas like vocabulary, properties, and formulas on the appropriate side.

Module 19 **609**

Before	In this module	After
Students understand:	Students represent and determine angle relationships:	Students will connect:
• angle pair relationships • the sum of the angles of a triangle • similar shapes	• angles formed by parallel lines that are cut by a transversal • the sum of the measures of the angles of a triangle • similarity of triangles	• classifying triangles by their angles and their sides • similar and congruent triangles

Unpacking the Standards

Use the examples on this page to help students know exactly what they are expected to learn in this module.

Florida Common Core Standards

Content Areas

 FL CC Geometry—8.G.1

Understand congruence and similarity using physical models, transparencies, or geometry software.

Go online to see a complete unpacking of the Florida Common Core Standards.

my.hrw.com

MODULE 19
Unpacking the Standards

Understanding the standards and the vocabulary terms in the standards will help you know exactly what you are expected to learn in this module.

FL CC 8.G.1.5

Use informal arguments to establish facts about the angle sum and exterior angle of triangles, about the angles created when parallel lines are cut by a transversal, and the angle-angle criterion for similarity of triangles.

Key Vocabulary
transversal *(transversal)*
A line that intersects two or more lines.

What It Means to You

You will learn about the special angle relationships formed when parallel lines are intersected by a third line called a transversal.

UNPACKING EXAMPLE 8.G.1.5

Which angles formed by the transversal and the parallel lines seem to be congruent?

It appears that the angles below are congruent.

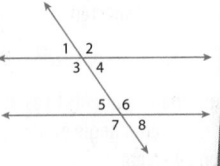

$\angle 1 \cong \angle 4 \cong \angle 5 \cong \angle 8$

$\angle 2 \cong \angle 3 \cong \angle 6 \cong \angle 7$

FL CC 8.G.1.5

Use informal arguments to establish facts about the angle sum and exterior angle of triangles, about the angles created when parallel lines are cut by a transversal, and the angle-angle criterion for similarity of triangles.

What It Means to You

You will use the angle-angle criterion to determine similarity of two triangles.

UNPACKING EXAMPLE 8.G.1.5

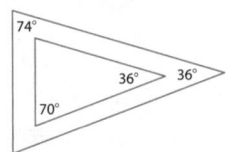

Explain whether the triangles are similar.

$74° + 36° + m\angle 3 = 180°$ $70° + 36° + m\angle 3 = 180°$

$m\angle 3 = 70°$ $m\angle 3 = 74°$

The three angles in the large triangle are congruent to the three angles in the smaller triangle, so the triangles are similar.

 Visit my.hrw.com to see all Florida Common Core Standards unpacked.

my.hrw.com

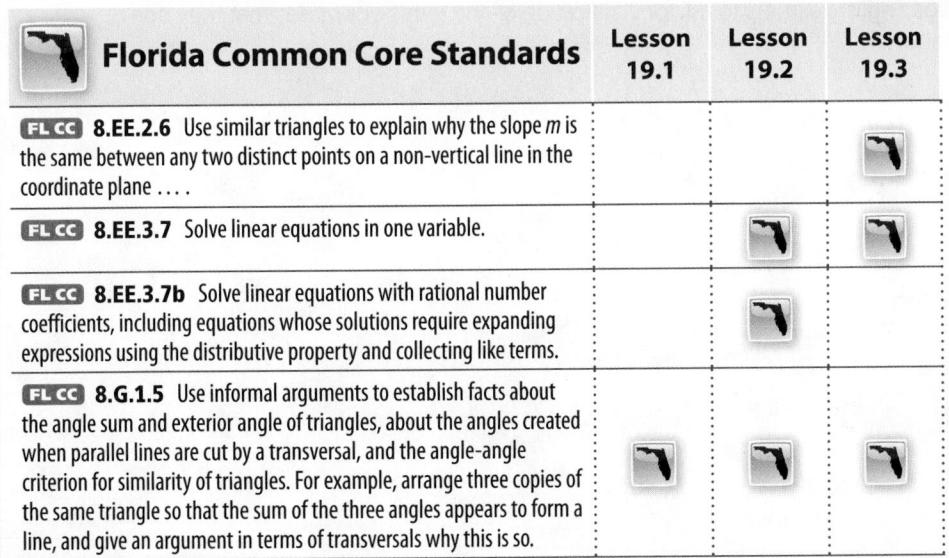

Florida Common Core Standards	Lesson 19.1	Lesson 19.2	Lesson 19.3
FL CC **8.EE.2.6** Use similar triangles to explain why the slope *m* is the same between any two distinct points on a non-vertical line in the coordinate plane			●
FL CC **8.EE.3.7** Solve linear equations in one variable.		●	●
FL CC **8.EE.3.7b** Solve linear equations with rational number coefficients, including equations whose solutions require expanding expressions using the distributive property and collecting like terms.		●	
FL CC **8.G.1.5** Use informal arguments to establish facts about the angle sum and exterior angle of triangles, about the angles created when parallel lines are cut by a transversal, and the angle-angle criterion for similarity of triangles. For example, arrange three copies of the same triangle so that the sum of the three angles appears to form a line, and give an argument in terms of transversals why this is so.	●	●	●

19.1 Parallel Lines Cut by a Transversal

Engage

ESSENTIAL QUESTION

What can you conclude about the angles formed by parallel lines that are cut by a transversal? Sample answer: Eight angles are created by the intersection of two parallel lines and a transversal. Corresponding angles are congruent, alternate interior angles are congruent, alternate exterior angles are congruent, and same-side interior angles are supplementary.

Motivate the Lesson

Ask: Which angles are congruent when you draw two parallel lines and a third line that intersects both of the parallel lines? Begin Explore Activity 1 to find out.

Explore

EXPLORE ACTIVITY 1

Connect Vocabulary `ELL`

Explain that even though *corresponding angles* and *same-side interior angles* are both found on the same side of the transversal, they are not the same pair of angles. Corresponding angles have one angle on the exterior and one on the interior and are congruent, while same-side interior angles are both on the interior and are supplementary.

Focus on Critical Thinking

Discuss with students the number of angles formed and their relationships when two parallel lines are intersected by two parallel transversals. Have students compare the number of each type of angle pair in this situation with the number of angle pairs of the same type when two parallel lines are cut by a transversal.

Integrating Language Arts `ELL`

Encourage English learners to ask for clarification of any terms or phrases that they don't understand.

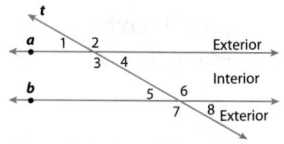
FL CC 8.G.1.5
Use informal arguments to establish facts about... the angles created when parallel lines are cut by a transversal....

? ESSENTIAL QUESTION What can you conclude about the angles formed by parallel lines that are cut by a transversal?

EXPLORE ACTIVITY 1 FL CC 8.G.1.5

Parallel Lines and Transversals

A **transversal** is a line that intersects two lines in the same plane at two different points. Transversal *t* and lines *a* and *b* form eight angles.

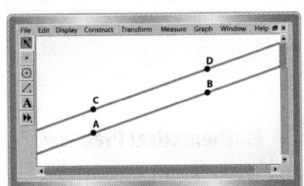

Angle Pairs Formed by a Transversal

Term	Example
Corresponding angles lie on the same side of the transversal *t*, on the same side of lines *a* and *b*.	∠1 and ∠5
Alternate interior angles are nonadjacent angles that lie on opposite sides of the transversal *t*, between lines *a* and *b*.	∠3 and ∠6
Alternate exterior angles lie on opposite sides of the transversal *t*, outside lines *a* and *b*.	∠1 and ∠8
Same-side interior angles lie on the same side of the transversal *t*, between lines *a* and *b*.	∠3 and ∠5

Use geometry software to explore the angles formed when a transversal intersects parallel lines.

A Construct a line and label two points on the line A and B.

B Create point C not on $\overleftrightarrow{AB}$. Then construct a line parallel to $\overleftrightarrow{AB}$ through point C. Create another point on this line and label it D.

EXPLORE ACTIVITY 1 *(cont'd)*

C Create two points outside the two parallel lines and label them E and F. Construct transversal $\overleftrightarrow{EF}$. Label the points of intersection G and H.

D Measure the angles formed by the parallel lines and the transversal. Write the angle measures in the table below.

E Drag point E or point F to a different position. Record the new angle measures in the table.

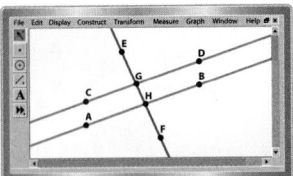

Answers will vary.

Angle	∠CGE	∠DGE	∠CGH	∠DGH	∠AHG	∠BHG	∠AHF	∠BHF
Measure								
Measure								

Reflect

Make a Conjecture Identify the pairs of angles in the diagram. Then make a conjecture about their angle measures. Drag a point in the diagram to confirm your conjecture.

1. corresponding angles

∠CGE and ∠AHG, ∠DGE and ∠BHG, ∠CGH and ∠AHF, ∠DGH and ∠BHF; congruent.

2. alternate interior angles

∠CGH and ∠BHG, ∠DGH and ∠AHG; congruent.

3. alternate exterior angles

∠CGE and ∠BHF, ∠DGE and ∠AHF; congruent.

4. same-side interior angles

∠CGH and ∠AHG, ∠DGH and ∠BHG; supplementary.

PROFESSIONAL DEVELOPMENT

Integrate Mathematical Practices MP.6.1

This lesson provides an opportunity to address this Mathematical Practices standard. It calls for students to communicate mathematical ideas and arguments using precise mathematical language. Students learn to recognize the relationships among the angles formed when two parallel lines intersect a transversal. Students learn the precise terms used to characterize these angles and describe their mathematical relationship.

Math Background

It is important that for this lesson a transversal is defined as a line that intersects two lines in the *same plane*. Two nonintersecting lines that are not in the same plane are called skew lines. Any pair of lines must be intersecting, parallel, or skew. In the figure below, $\overleftrightarrow{AB}$ and $\overleftrightarrow{CD}$ are skew lines.

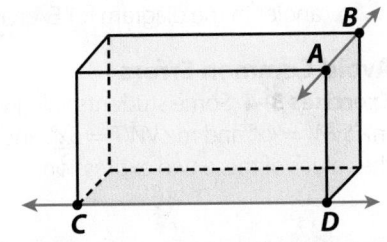

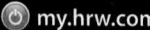
ADDITIONAL EXAMPLE 1
A Find m∠1 when m∠5 = 65°.

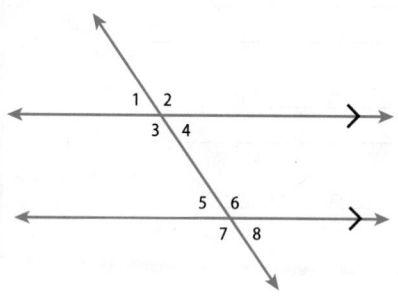

m∠1 = 65°

B Find m∠ADE.

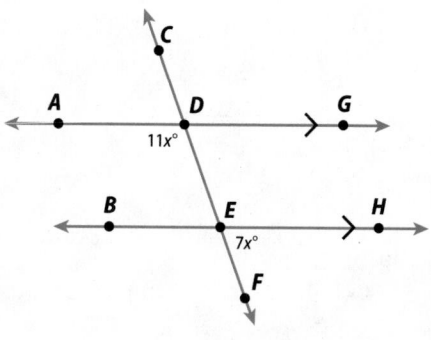

m∠ADE = 110°

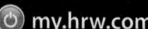
Explain

EXPLORE ACTIVITY 2

Questioning Strategies Mathematical Practices

• Is it possible to draw line *t* so that angles 1 through 4 do not coincide with angles 5 through 8? Justify your answer. no; not possible if lines *a* and *b* are parallel

• What can you say about the eight angles formed if line *t* had been drawn perpendicular to line *a*? Line *t* would be perpendicular to both lines *a* and *b*, so all eight angles would be right angles and therefore congruent to each other.

Engage with the Whiteboard

Have a student circle the number of an angle on the diagram. Then have another student circle the numbers of the angles that are congruent to that first angle.

EXAMPLE 1

Questioning Strategies Mathematical Practices

• After solving part B, how can you find m∠YVW without substituting for *x*? m∠YVW = 180° − m∠VWZ = 180° − 60° = 120°

• Is 20 the only possible value for *x* in part B? Justify your answer. Yes; a linear equation in one variable will have either one solution, no solution, or an infinite number of solutions. The equation in this example has only one solution.

Avoid Common Errors

In part B, stress that ∠YVW and ∠VWZ are a pair of same-side interior angles and are supplementary, not congruent. Remind students that supplementary angles have measures whose sum is 180°.

YOUR TURN

Focus on Reasoning Mathematical Practices

Make sure students know that they should not make any assumptions about the measures of the angles in a diagram based on their appearance.

Elaborate

Talk About It
Summarize the Lesson

Ask: How many *different* angle measures can be found among the eight angles formed when two parallel lines are cut by a transversal? Two; the intersection of the transversal and the parallel lines forms angles with two different measures.

GUIDED PRACTICE

Engage with the Whiteboard

After completing Exercise 5, invite a student to circle each pair of same-side interior angles in the diagram for Exercises 1–4.

Avoid Common Errors

Exercises 3–4 Some students will give the value of *x* as the angle measure. Stress that m∠SVW = 4*x*° and m∠VWT = 5*x*°, and that once the value of *x* is known students must find the values of these two expressions.

EXPLORE ACTIVITY 2   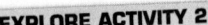 FL CC 8.G.1.5

Justifying Angle Relationships

You can use tracing paper to informally justify your conclusions from the first Explore Activity.

Lines *a* and *b* are parallel. (The black arrows on the diagram indicate parallel lines.)

> Recall that vertical angles are the opposite angles formed by two intersecting lines. ∠1 and ∠4 are vertical angles.

A Trace the diagram onto tracing paper.

B Position the tracing paper over the original diagram so that ∠1 on the tracing is over ∠5 on the original diagram. Compare the two angles. Do they appear to be congruent?

∠1 of the traced diagram coincides with ∠5 of the

original diagram; yes, they appear to be congruent.

C Use the tracing paper to compare all eight angles in the diagram to each other. List all of the congruent angle pairs.

∠1 and ∠5, ∠1 and ∠8, ∠1 and ∠4, ∠2 and ∠6, ∠2 and

∠7, ∠2 and ∠3, ∠3 and ∠6, ∠3 and ∠7, ∠4 and ∠5, ∠4

and ∠8, ∠5 and ∠8, ∠6 and ∠7

Finding Unknown Angle Measures

You can find any unknown angle measure when two parallel lines are cut by a transversal if you are given at least one other angle measure.

> **Math On the Spot**
> my.hrw.com

EXAMPLE 1   FL CC 8.G.1.5

A Find m∠2 when m∠7 = 125°.

∠2 is congruent to ∠7 because they are alternate exterior angles.

Therefore, m∠2 = 125°.

B Find m∠VWZ.

∠VWZ is supplementary to ∠YVW because they are same-side interior angles.

m∠VWZ + m∠YVW = 180°

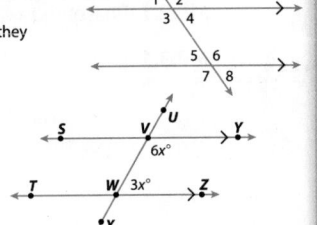

> **Animated Math**
> my.hrw.com

Lesson 19.1 **613**

From the previous page, m∠VWZ + m∠YVW = 180°, m∠VWZ = 3x°, and m∠YVW = 6x°.

$$m\angle VWZ + m\angle YVW = 180°$$
$$3x° + 6x° = 180° \quad \text{Replace } m\angle VWZ \text{ with } 3x° \text{ and } m\angle YVW \text{ with } 6x°.$$
$$9x = 180 \quad \text{Combine like terms.}$$
$$\frac{9x}{9} = \frac{180}{9} \quad \text{Divide both sides by 9.}$$
$$x = 20 \quad \text{Simplify.}$$
$$m\angle VWZ = 3x° = (3 \cdot 20)° = 60°$$

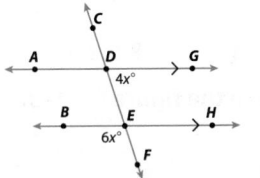

> **Personal Math Trainer**
> Online Assessment and Intervention
> my.hrw.com

YOUR TURN

Find each angle measure.

5. m∠GDE = ___72°___

6. m∠BEF = ___108°___

7. m∠CDG = ___108°___

Guided Practice

Use the figure for Exercises 1–4. (Explore Activity 1 and Example 1)

1. ∠UVY and ___∠VWZ___ are a pair of corresponding angles.

2. ∠WVY and ∠VWT are ___alternate interior___ angles.

3. Find m∠SVW. ___80°___

4. Find m∠VWT. ___100°___

5. **Vocabulary** When two parallel lines are cut by a transversal,
   ___same-side interior___ angles are supplementary. (Explore Activity 1)

 ### ESSENTIAL QUESTION CHECK-IN

6. What can you conclude about the interior angles formed when two parallel lines are cut by a transversal?

Each pair of alternate interior angles is congruent.

Each pair of same-side interior angles is supplementary.

614 Unit 9

DIFFERENTIATE INSTRUCTION

Kinesthetic Experience

Have students look around the classroom to find structures or drawings that show parallel lines cut by a transversal. Have them identify the corresponding angles, alternate interior angles, alternate exterior angles, and same-side interior angles in each example they discover. Examples may appear on bookcases, window panes, floor patterns, desks, bookbags, photos on book covers, posters on the wall, and so on. In many of the examples, the transversal will form right angles with the parallel lines.

Visual Cues

Have students create models of corresponding angles, alternate interior angles, alternate exterior angles, and same-side interior angles on index cards using color-coding. Two examples are shown in the figures below.

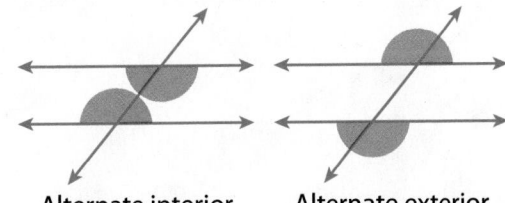

Alternate interior   Alternate exterior

Additional Resources

Differentiated Instruction includes:

- Reading Strategies
- Success for English Learners **ELL**
- Reteach
- Challenge **PRE-AP**

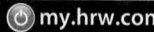
19.1 LESSON QUIZ

FL CC 8.G.1.5

Use the figure for 1–3.

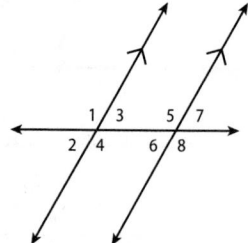

1. Name both pairs of alternate interior angles.

2. Name all pairs of corresponding angles.

3. Name the relationship between ∠2 and ∠7.

Find each angle measure.

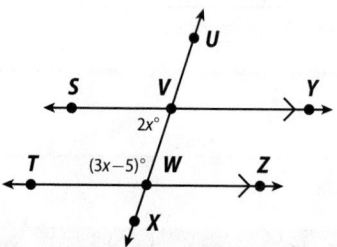

4. m∠UVY if m∠TWX = 84°

5. m∠SVW

6. m∠TWV

Lesson Quiz available online

Answers
1. ∠3 and ∠6, ∠4 and ∠5

2. ∠1 and ∠5, ∠2 and ∠6, ∠3 and ∠7, ∠4 and ∠8

3. alternate exterior angles

4. 84°

5. 74°

6. 106°

Evaluate

GUIDED AND INDEPENDENT PRACTICE

 FL CC 8.G.1.5

Concepts & Skills	Practice
Explore Activity 1 Parallel Lines and Transversals	Exercises 1–2, 5, 7–10, 18
Explore Activity 2 Justifying Angle Relationships	Exercise 18
Example 1 Finding Unknown Angle Measures	Exercises 3–4, 11–17, 19

Exercise	Depth of Knowledge (D.O.K.)	FL CC Mathematical Practices
7–14	**1** Recall of Information	**MP.6.1** Precision
15–16	**2** Skills/Concepts	**MP.2.1** Reasoning
17	**2** Skills/Concepts	**MP.3.1** Logic
18	**3** Strategic Thinking H.O.T.	**MP.2.1** Reasoning
19	**2** Skills/Concepts	**MP.2.1** Reasoning
20–22	**3** Strategic Thinking H.O.T.	**MP.3.1** Logic

Additional Resources
Differentiated Instruction includes:
• Leveled Practice worksheets

Name _____ Class _____ Date _____

19.1 Independent Practice

FL CC 8.G.1.5

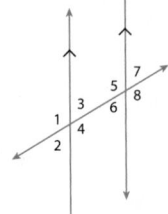

Personal Math Trainer
Online Assessment and Intervention
my.hrw.com

Vocabulary Use the figure for Exercises 7–10.

7. Name all pairs of corresponding angles.
∠1 and ∠5, ∠2 and ∠6, ∠3 and ∠7, ∠4 and ∠8

8. Name both pairs of alternate exterior angles.
∠1 and ∠8, ∠2 and ∠7

9. Name the relationship between ∠3 and ∠6.
alternate interior angles

10. Name the relationship between ∠4 and ∠6.
same-side interior angles

Find each angle measure.

11. m∠AGE when m∠FHD = 30° 30°

12. m∠AGH when m∠CHF = 150° 150°

13. m∠CHF when m∠BGE = 110° 110°

14. m∠CHG when m∠HGA = 120° 60°

15. m∠BGH = 78°

16. m∠GHD = 102°

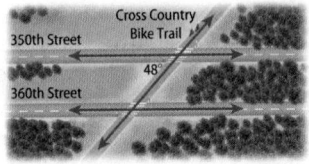

17. The Cross Country Bike Trail follows a straight line where it crosses 350th and 360th Streets. The two streets are parallel to each other. What is the measure of the larger angle formed at the intersection of the bike trail and 360th Street? Explain.

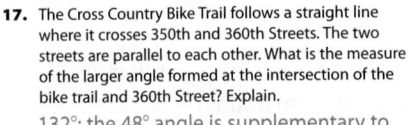

132°; the 48° angle is supplementary to the larger angle because the two angles are same-side interior angles.

18. **Critical Thinking** How many different angles would be formed by a transversal intersecting three parallel lines? How many different angle measures would there be?

12 angles; at most two different angle measures (one if the transversal is perpendicular)

Lesson 19.1 615

19. **Communicate Mathematical Ideas** In the diagram at the right, suppose m∠6 = 125°. Explain how to find the measures of each of the other seven numbered angles.

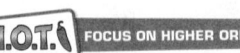

∠6 and ∠2 are corr., so m∠2 = 125°. ∠6 and ∠3 are alt. int., so m∠3 = 125°. ∠3 and ∠7 are corr., so m∠7 = 125°. ∠6 and ∠4 are same-side int., so m∠4 = 180° − 125°, or 55°. ∠4 and ∠8 are corr., so m∠8 = 55°. ∠4 and ∠5 are alt. int., so m∠5 = 55°. ∠1 and ∠5 are corr., so m∠1 = 55°.

H.O.T. FOCUS ON HIGHER ORDER THINKING

Work Area

20. **Draw Conclusions** In a diagram showing two parallel lines cut by a transversal, the measures of two same-side interior angles are both given as 3x°. Without writing and solving an equation, can you determine the measures of both angles? Explain. Then write and solve an equation to find the measures.

Yes. Since the angles are supplementary and have the same measure, each angle measure is one-half of 180°, or 90°; 3x° + 3x° = 180°, 6x = 180, x = 30, so 3x° = (3 · 30)° = 90°.

21. **Make a Conjecture** Draw two parallel lines and a transversal. Choose one of the eight angles that are formed. How many of the other seven angles are congruent to the angle you selected? How many of the other seven angles are supplementary to your angle? Will your answer change if you select a different angle?

3 angles; 4 angles; no

22. **Critique Reasoning** In the diagram at the right, ∠2, ∠3, ∠5, and ∠8 are all congruent, and ∠1, ∠4, ∠6, and ∠7 are all congruent. Aiden says that this is enough information to conclude that the diagram shows two parallel lines cut by a transversal. Is he correct? Justify your answer.

No. For the lines to be parallel, ∠2 must be supplementary to ∠3. Since it is only known that these angles are congruent, the only possibility for them to also be supplementary is if they both measure 90°.

616 Unit 9

EXTEND THE MATH PRE-AP

Activity available online my.hrw.com

Activity The figure shows parallelogram ABCD with its diagonal AC drawn. If m∠1 = 80° and m∠2 = 40°, what are the measures of ∠DAB, ∠B, ∠BCD, and ∠D? Explain how you found your answers.

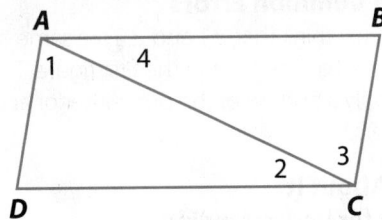

By definition, each pair of opposite sides of the parallelogram is parallel. The diagonal is a transversal to both pairs of parallel sides. If m∠1 = 80°, then m∠3 = 80° since they are alternate interior angles. If m∠2 = 40°, then m∠4 = 40° since they are alternate interior angles. So, m∠DAB = 80° + 40° = 120°. Also, m∠B = 180° − 120° = 60° since m∠DAB and m∠B are supplementary same-side interior angles. So, m∠BCD = 80° + 40° = 120°. Finally, m∠D = 180° − 120° = 60° since m∠BCD and m∠D are supplementary same-side interior angles.

Parallel Lines Cut by a Transversal **616**

19.2 Angle Theorems for Triangles

 Florida Common Core Standards

The student is expected to:

 **Geometry—8.G.1.5**

Use informal arguments to establish facts about the angle sum and exterior angle of triangles, about the angles created when parallel lines are cut by a transversal, and the angle-angle criterion for similarity of triangles.

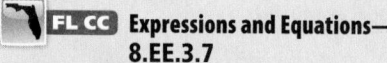 **Expressions and Equations— 8.EE.3.7**

Solve linear equations in one variable.

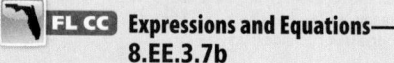 **Expressions and Equations— 8.EE.3.7b**

Solve linear equations with rational number coefficients, including equations whose solutions require expanding expressions using the distributive property and collecting like terms.

Mathematical Practices

 **MP.5.1** Using Tools

Engage

ESSENTIAL QUESTION

What can you conclude about the measures of the angles of a triangle? Sample answer: The sum of the measures of the interior angles of a triangle is always 180°. The measure of an exterior angle is equal to the sum of its remote interior angles.

Motivate the Lesson
Ask: How can tearing a triangle apart help you illustrate the Triangle Sum Theorem? Take a guess, then begin Explore Activity 1 to find out.

Explore

EXPLORE ACTIVITY 1

Focus on Modeling
Students will use a paper triangle to model the Triangle Sum Theorem. Point out that no matter what type of triangle is used, the three torn "corners" will form a straight angle. Have students try the activity using a variety of triangle types.

Explain

EXPLORE ACTIVITY 2

Questioning Strategies  Mathematical Practices

• In the second figure, how do you know that ∠4 and ∠2 are alternate interior angles? Line *t* is a transversal for parallel lines *a* and *b*, and ∠4 and ∠2 are nonadjacent angles on opposite sides of line *t* between lines *a* and *b*.

• If line *t* were perpendicular to lines *a* and *b*, what would be m∠2? 90°

Avoid Common Errors
If students think that ∠1 and ∠2 are same-side interior angles, have them cover the transversal on the right in the first figure. Then point out that while ∠2 is an interior angle, ∠1 is only a portion of the other interior angle on the same side of the remaining transversal.

Talk About It
Check for Understanding
Ask: Why is it important that line *b* be drawn parallel to line *a* in Step C of the activity? In order for the angle pairs in steps F (∠2 and ∠4) and G (∠3 and ∠5) to be congruent, lines *a* and *b* must be parallel.

Angle Theorems for Triangles

FL CC 8.G.1.5
Use informal arguments to establish facts about the angle sum and exterior angle of triangles.... *Also* 8.EE.3.7, 8.EE.3.7b

ESSENTIAL QUESTION What can you conclude about the measures of the angles of a triangle?

EXPLORE ACTIVITY 1 FL CC 8.G.1.5

Sum of the Angle Measures in a Triangle

There is a special relationship between the measures of the interior angles of a triangle.

A Draw a triangle and cut it out. Label the angles A, B, and C.

B Tear off each "corner" of the triangle. Each corner includes the vertex of one angle of the triangle.

C Arrange the vertices of the triangle around a point so that none of your corners overlap and there are no gaps between them.

D What do you notice about how the angles fit together around a point?

Sample answer: The angles form a straight angle.

E What is the measure of a straight angle? __180°__

F Describe the relationship among the measures of the angles of △ABC.

The sum of the angle measures is 180°.

The Triangle Sum Theorem states that for △ABC, m∠A + m∠B + m∠C = __180°__.

Reflect

1. **Justify Reasoning** Can a triangle have two right angles? Explain.

No; the sum of the measures of two right angles is 180°. That means the measure of the third angle would be 180° − 180° = 0°, which is impossible.

2. **Analyze Relationships** Describe the relationship between the two acute angles in a right triangle. Explain your reasoning.

They are complementary; sample answer: the sum of their measures must be 180° − (measure of the right angle) = 180° − 90° = 90°.

EXPLORE ACTIVITY 2 FL CC 8.G.1.5

Justifying the Triangle Sum Theorem

You can use your knowledge of parallel lines intersected by a transversal to informally justify the Triangle Sum Theorem.

Follow the steps to informally prove the Triangle Sum Theorem. You should draw each step on your own paper. The figures below are provided for you to check your work.

A Draw a triangle and label the angles as ∠1, ∠2, and ∠3 as shown.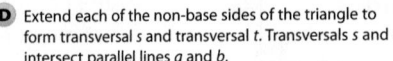

B Draw line *a* through the base of the triangle.

C The Parallel Postulate states that through a point not on a line ℓ, there is exactly one line parallel to line ℓ. Draw line *b* parallel to line *a*, through the vertex opposite the base of the triangle.

D Extend each of the non-base sides of the triangle to form transversal *s* and transversal *t*. Transversals *s* and *t* intersect parallel lines *a* and *b*.

E Label the angles formed by line *b* and the transversals as ∠4 and ∠5.

F Because ∠4 and ____∠2____ are alternate interior angles, they are ____congruent____.

Label ∠4 with the number of the angle to which it is congruent.

G Because ∠5 and ____∠3____ are alternate interior angles, they are ____congruent____.

Label ∠5 with the number of the angle to which it is congruent.

H The three angles that lie along line *b* at the vertex of the triangle are ∠1, ∠4, and ∠5. Notice that these three angles lie along a line.

So, m∠1 + m∠2 + m∠5 = ____180°____.

Because angles 2 and 4 are congruent and angles 3 and 5 are congruent, you can substitute m∠2 for m∠4 and m∠3 for m∠5 in the equation above.

So, m∠1 + m∠2 + m∠3 = ____180°____.

This shows that the sum of the angle measures in a triangle is always ____180°____.

PROFESSIONAL DEVELOPMENT

Integrate Mathematical Practices MP.5.1

This lesson provides an opportunity to address this Mathematical Practices standard. It calls for students to use appropriate tools strategically to solve problems. Students use a paper triangle to model the relationship between the measures of the interior angles of a triangle. They can then use paper and pencil to solve equations to find the measures of the interior angles of a triangle or the measure of an exterior angle of a triangle.

Math Background

The sum of the measures of the interior angles of a triangle is always 180°. This is true for any triangle. In polygons with more than 3 sides, the sum of the interior angles can be determined by drawing diagonals to divide the polygon into triangles. The number of triangles multiplied by 180° gives the sum of the interior angles. This leads to the general formula for the sum of the measures of the interior angles of any convex polygon with *n* sides: (*n* − 2)180°.

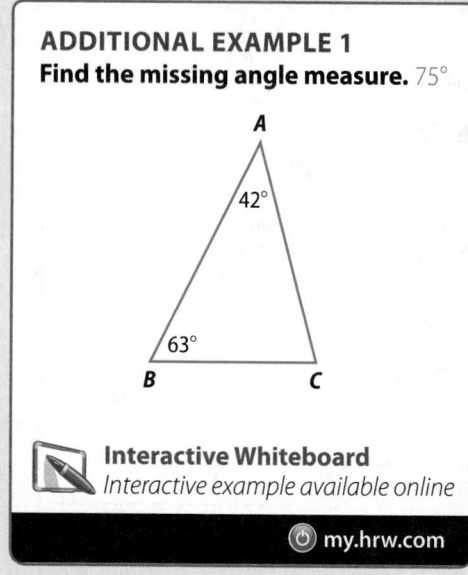

EXAMPLE 1

Questioning Strategies 🏴 Mathematical Practices

- To find the measures of the angles in a triangle, would it be enough to know the measure of just one angle? Justify your answer. No, it would not be enough. You need to know the measure of one other angle, or how the other two angles are related algebraically. The measure of another angle could be determined if you know that the triangle is a right triangle and you know the measure of one of the acute angles, or if the triangle is an equilateral or equiangular triangle, or an isosceles triangle.

- If you know that m∠D is 100° and that the other two angles are congruent, what is the measure of the other two angles? 40°

Focus on Modeling 🏴 Mathematical Practices

After completing Example 1, have students use a compass to draw triangle *DEF* with angles that measure 100° and 55°. Then have students measure the third angle.

YOUR TURN

Engage with the Whiteboard

Under the triangles given in Exercises 4 and 5, have students write the equations that can be used to find the missing angle measures.

Focus on Reasoning 🏴 Mathematical Practices

The triangles in Example 1 and Exercises 4 and 5 should lead students to see that if a triangle has two acute angles, then the third angle could be acute, right, or obtuse. Ask students if a triangle can have two obtuse angles or two right angles.

EXPLORE ACTIVITY 3

Questioning Strategies 🏴 Mathematical Practices

- For the figure in Explore Activity 3, how do you know which angles are remote interior angles to ∠4? The remote interior angles to an exterior angle of a triangle are always the two angles of the triangle that do not share a common vertex with the exterior angle.

- Why is it that you can extend the sides of the triangle? While the line segments that make up the sides of a triangle have definite lengths, they are segments of lines that continue infinitely. The length of the segment does not change if the drawing of the line it lies on is extended.

Avoid Common Errors

If students think ∠1 and ∠2 are same-side interior angles and therefore supplementary, remind them that there are no parallel lines intersected by a transversal in this figure.

Talk About It
Check for Understanding

Ask: How can you find the measure of an exterior angle if its two remote interior angles have measures 75° and 50°? The measure of an exterior angle is equal to the sum of the measures of its remote interior angles. So this exterior angle would have a measure of 75° + 50° = 125°.

Reflect

3. Analyze Relationships How can you use the fact that m∠4 + m∠1 + m∠5 = 180° to show that m∠2 + m∠1 + m∠3 = 180°?

<u>m∠2 = m∠4 and m∠3 = m∠5. Substituting m∠2 for</u>
<u>m∠4 and m∠3 for m∠5 in the equation m∠4 + m∠1</u>
<u>+ m∠5 = 180° gives m∠2 + m∠1 + m∠3 = 180°.</u>

Finding Missing Angle Measures in Triangles

If you know the measures of two angles in a triangle, you can use the Triangle Sum Theorem to find the measure of the third angle.

Math On the Spot
my.hrw.com

EXAMPLE 1
FL CC 8.EE.3.7

Find the missing angle measure.

STEP 1 Write the Triangle Sum Theorem for this triangle.

m∠D + m∠E + m∠F = 180°

STEP 2 Substitute the given angle measures.

55° + m∠E + 100° = 180°

STEP 3 Solve the equation for m∠E.

$$55° + m∠E + 100° = 180°$$
$$155° + m∠E = 180°$$
$$\underline{-155° \qquad\qquad -155°} \qquad \text{Simplify.}$$
$$m∠E = \quad 25° \qquad \text{Subtract 155° from both sides.}$$

So, m∠E = 25°.

My Notes

YOUR TURN

Find the missing angle measure.

4.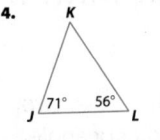

m∠K = _____ <u>53</u>

5.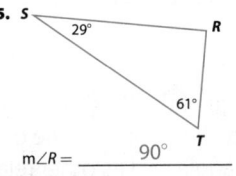

m∠R = _____ <u>90°</u>

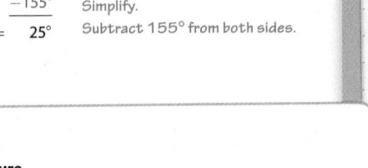
Personal Math Trainer
Online Assessment and Intervention
my.hrw.com

EXPLORE ACTIVITY 3
FL CC 8.G.1.5

Exterior Angles and Remote Interior Angles

An **interior angle** of a triangle is formed by two sides of the triangle. An **exterior angle** is formed by one side of the triangle and the extension of an adjacent side. Each exterior angle has two remote interior angles. A **remote interior angle** is an interior angle that is not adjacent to the exterior angle.

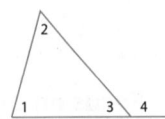

- ∠1, ∠2, and ∠3 are interior angles.
- ∠4 is an exterior angle.
- ∠1 and ∠2 are remote interior angles to ∠4.

There is a special relationship between the measure of an exterior angle and the measures of its remote interior angles.

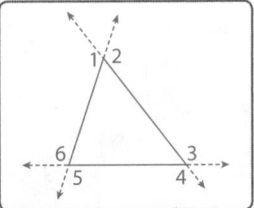

A Extend the base of the triangle and label the exterior angle as ∠4.

B The Triangle Sum Theorem states:

m∠1 + m∠2 + m∠3 = <u>180°</u>.

C ∠3 and ∠4 form a <u>linear pair or straight angle</u>,

so m∠3 + m∠4 = <u>180°</u>.

D Use the equations in **B** and **C** to complete the following equation:

m∠1 + m∠2 + <u>m∠3</u> = <u>m∠3</u> + m∠4

E Use properties of equality to simplify the equation in **D**:

<u>m∠1 + m∠2 = m∠4</u>

The Exterior Angle Theorem states that the measure of an <u>exterior</u> angle is equal to the sum of its <u>remote interior</u> angles.

Reflect

6. Sketch a triangle and draw all of its exterior angles. How many exterior angles does a triangle have at each vertex?

<u>2</u>

7. How many total exterior angles does a triangle have?

<u>6</u>

DIFFERENTIATE INSTRUCTION

Manipulatives

Have students draw a large scalene triangle *ABC* on a piece of construction paper and label the interior angles 1, 2, and 3. Then have them draw all six of the exterior angles and label them angles 4–9. Have students trace triangle *ABC* on another sheet of paper and label its angles 1–3. Now have students cut out the triangle they traced and tear off the three corners (including the numbers). Ask them to place two of the torn corners over the exterior angle for which they are the remote interior angles. A sample is shown at right.

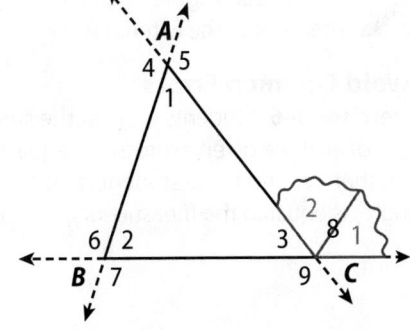

Additional Resources

Differentiated Instruction includes:
- Reading Strategies
- Success for English Learners **ELL**
- Reteach
- Challenge **PRE-AP**

Angle Theorems for Triangles **620**

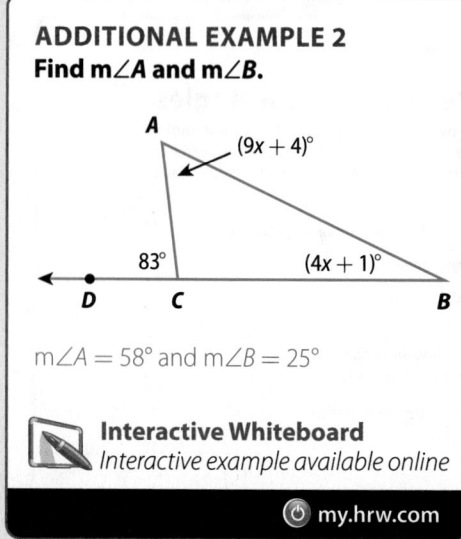
EXAMPLE 2

Questioning Strategies Mathematical Practices

• Why must the value of *y* be greater than 1? If *y* = 1, then m∠A would be 4(1) − 4 = 0°, and if the value of *y* is less than 1, m∠A would be less than 0°.

• Why must the value of *y* be less than 14? The sum of m∠A and m∠B must be 52°. If *y* = 14, then the measure of ∠A would be 4(14) − 4 = 52°, making m∠B = 0°. If the value of *y* were greater than 14, then the measure of ∠B would be less than 0°.

Focus on Critical Thinking Mathematical Practices

Help students reason from the figure that the measures of ∠A and ∠B must each be less than 52°, since the sum of their measures must equal 52°. Point out that making this determination prior to solving the equation in step 3 can help them catch any miscalculations they might make.

YOUR TURN

Talk About It
Check for Understanding

 Ask: To check that your answers are correct, is it enough to check that the sum of the angle measures equals the measure of the exterior angle? Explain how you know. No, the answers must also satisfy the expressions given for the unknown angle measures.

Elaborate

Talk About It
Summarize the Lesson

 Ask: How can you find the measure of the third angle of a triangle if the other two measures are known? How can you find the measure of one remote interior angle of a triangle if the measures of an exterior angle and its other related remote interior angle are known? The sum of the measures of the angles of a triangle is 180°, so subtract the sum of the two known measures from 180°. The sum of the measures of the remote interior angles is equal to the measure of the related exterior angle, so subtract the known measure of one interior angle from the measure of the related exterior angle.

GUIDED PRACTICE

Engage with the Whiteboard

Next to each figure in Exercises 1–6, write an equation using either the Triangle Sum Theorem or the Exterior Angle Theorem to find the angle measure.

Avoid Common Errors

Exercises 5–6 Students may set the sum of the expressions for the interior angles or the sum of all three given expressions equal to 180°. Reteach the definition of an exterior angle and then remind these students that the sum of the measures of the two remote interior angles is equal to the measure of the related exterior angle.

Using the Exterior Angle Theorem

You can use the Exterior Angle Theorem to find the measures of the interior angles of a triangle.

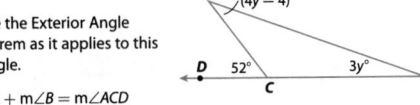
Math On the Spot
my.hrw.com

EXAMPLE 2 FL CC 8.EE.3.7b

Find m∠A and m∠B.

STEP 1 Write the Exterior Angle Theorem as it applies to this triangle.

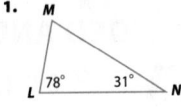

$$m\angle A + m\angle B = m\angle ACD$$

STEP 2 Substitute the given angle measures.

$$(4y - 4)° + 3y° = 52°$$

STEP 3 Solve the equation for y.

$(4y - 4)° + 3y° = 52°$

$4y° - 4° + 3y° = 52°$ Remove parentheses.

$7y° - 4° = 52°$ Simplify.

$\underline{+4° \quad +4°}$ Add 4° to both sides.

$7y° = 56°$ Simplify.

$\dfrac{7y°}{7} = \dfrac{56°}{7}$ Divide both sides by 7.

$y = 8$ Simplify.

STEP 4 Use the value of y to find m∠A and m∠B.

$m\angle A = 4y - 4$ $m\angle B = 3y$

$= 4(8) - 4$ $= 3(8)$

$= 32 - 4$ $= 24$

$= 28$

So, m∠A = 28° and m∠B = 24°.

Math Talk
Mathematical Practices

Describe two ways to find m∠ACB.

Use the Triangle Sum Theorem and subtract the sum of the measures of angles A and B from 180°. Use the fact that an exterior angle and its adjacent interior angle are supplementary and subtract 52° from 180°.

YOUR TURN

8. Find m∠M and m∠N.

m∠M = ___78°___

m∠N = ___68°___

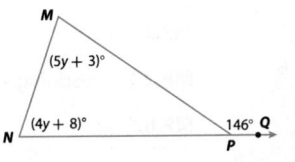

Personal Math Trainer
Online Assessment and Intervention
my.hrw.com

Guided Practice

Find each missing angle measure. (Explore Activity 1 and Example 1)

1.
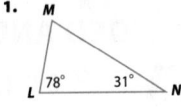

m∠M = ___71°___

2.
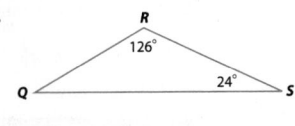

m∠Q = ___30°___

Use the Triangle Sum Theorem to find the measure of each angle in degrees. (Explore Activity 2 and Example 1)

3.
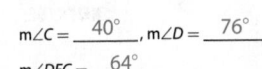

m∠T = ___88°___, m∠U = ___29°___,

m∠V = ___63°___

4.
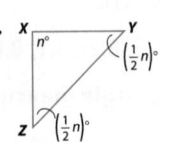

m∠X = ___90°___, m∠Y = ___45°___,

m∠Z = ___45°___

Use the Exterior Angle Theorem to find the measure of each angle in degrees. (Explore Activity 3 and Example 2)

5.
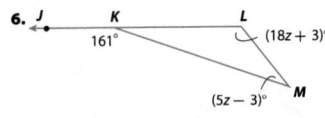

m∠C = ___40°___, m∠D = ___76°___,

m∠DEC = ___64°___

6.

m∠L = ___129°___, m∠M = ___32°___,

m∠LKM = ___19°___

❓ ESSENTIAL QUESTION CHECK-IN

7. Describe the relationships among the measures of the angles of a triangle.

The sum of the interior angles is 180°. The measure of an exterior angle equals the sum of the measures of its two remote interior angles.

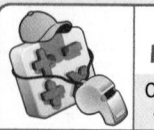

Personal Math Trainer

Online Assessment and Intervention

Online homework assignment available

⏻ my.hrw.com

19.2 LESSON QUIZ

FL CC 8.G.1.5, 8.EE.3.7, 8.EE.3.7b

Find the missing angle measure.

1.

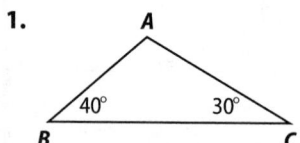

2.

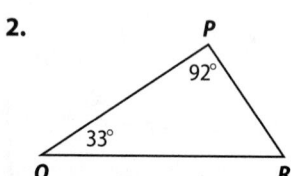

Use the Triangle Sum Theorem to find the measure of each angle in degrees.

3.

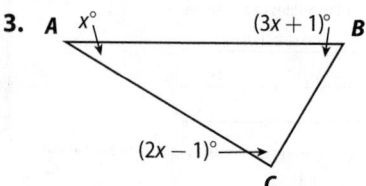

4.

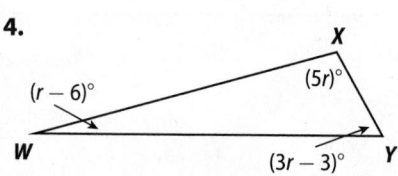

5. Use the Exterior Angle Theorem to find the measures of ∠A, ∠B, and ∠ACB.

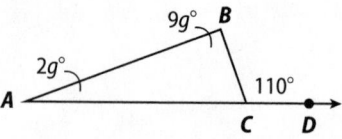

Lesson Quiz available online

⏻ my.hrw.com

Evaluate

GUIDED AND INDEPENDENT PRACTICE

FL CC 8.G.1.5, 8.EE.3.7, 8.EE.3.7b

Concepts & Skills	Practice
Explore Activity 1 Sum of the Angle Measures in a Triangle	Exercises 1–2, 8–10, 14
Explore Activity 2 Justifying the Triangle Sum Theorem	Exercises 3–4
Example 1 Finding Missing Angle Measures in Triangles	Exercises 1–4, 8–10, 14
Explore Activity 3 Exterior Angles and Remote Interior Angles	Exercises 5–6, 11–13
Example 2 Using the Exterior Angle Theorem	Exercises 5–6, 11–13

Exercise	Depth of Knowledge (D.O.K.)	**FL CC** Mathematical Practices
8–14	**2** Skills/Concepts	**MP.5.1** Using Tools
15	**2** Skills/Concepts	**MP.2.1** Reasoning
16	**3** Strategic Thinking **H.O.T.**	**MP.3.1** Logic
17	**3** Strategic Thinking **H.O.T.**	**MP.2.1** Reasoning
18	**3** Strategic Thinking **H.O.T.**	**MP.6.1** Precision

Additional Resources

Differentiated Instruction includes:

• Leveled Practice worksheets

Answers

1. $m\angle A = 110°$

2. $m\angle R = 55°$

3. $m\angle A = 30°$, $m\angle B = 91°$, $m\angle C = 59°$

4. $m\angle W = 15°$, $m\angle X = 105°$, $m\angle Y = 60°$

5. $m\angle A = 20°$, $m\angle B = 90°$, $m\angle ACB = 70°$

623 Lesson 19.2

19.2 Independent Practice

FL CC 8.EE.3.7, 8.EE.3.7b, 8.G.1.5

Personal Math Trainer
Online Assessment and Intervention
my.hrw.com

Find the measure of each angle.

8.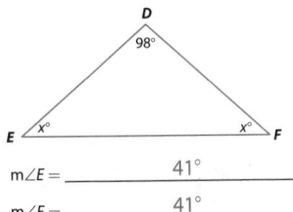

m∠E = _____ 41° _____

m∠F = _____ 41° _____

9.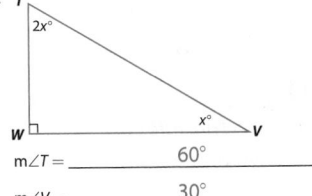

m∠T = _____ 60° _____

m∠V = _____ 30° _____

10.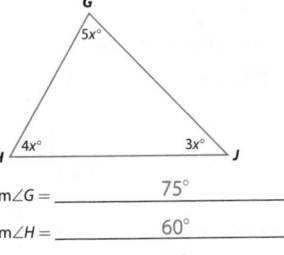

m∠G = _____ 75° _____

m∠H = _____ 60° _____

m∠J = _____ 45° _____

11.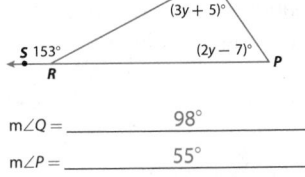

m∠Q = _____ 98° _____

m∠P = _____ 55° _____

m∠QRP = _____ 27° _____

12.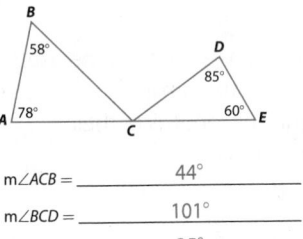

m∠ACB = _____ 44° _____

m∠BCD = _____ 101° _____

m∠DCE = _____ 35° _____

13.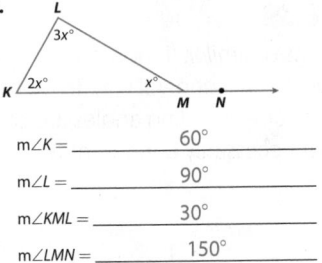

m∠K = _____ 60° _____

m∠L = _____ 90° _____

m∠KML = _____ 30° _____

m∠LMN = _____ 150° _____

14. Multistep The second angle in a triangle is five times as large as the first. The third angle is two-thirds as large as the first. Find the angle measures. _____ 27°, 135°, 18° _____

15. Analyze Relationships Can a triangle have two obtuse angles? Explain.

No; the measure of an obtuse angle is greater than 90°. If a triangle had two obtuse angles, the sum of their measures would be greater than 180°, the sum of the angle measures of a triangle.

H.O.T. FOCUS ON HIGHER ORDER THINKING

16. Critical Thinking Explain how you can use the Triangle Sum Theorem to find the measures of the angles of an equilateral triangle.

The angles of an equilateral triangle are congruent. Let the measure of each angle equal x. Then, by the Triangle Sum Theorem, $x + x + x = 180$. So, $3x = 180$. Solving for x gives $x = 60$. So the measure of each angle is 60°.

17. a. Draw Conclusions Find the sum of the measures of the angles in quadrilateral $ABCD$. (Hint: Draw diagonal $\overline{AC}$. How can you use the figures you have formed to find the sum?)

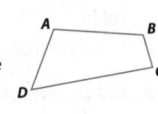

Sum = _____ 360° _____

b. Make a Conjecture Write a "Quadrilateral Sum Theorem." Explain why you think it is true.

The sum of the angle measures of a quadrilateral is 360°. Sample answer: Any quadrilateral can be divided into two triangles. So, the sum of the angle measures of a quadrilateral is twice the sum of the angle measures of a triangle; $2 \times 180° = 360°$

18. Communicate Mathematical Ideas Describe two ways that an exterior angle of a triangle is related to one or more of the interior angles.

(1) The measure of an exterior angle is equal to the sum of the measures of its two remote interior angles. (2) An exterior angle is supplementary to the interior angle adjacent to it.

Work Area

EXTEND THE MATH (PRE-AP)

Activity available online ⏻ my.hrw.com

Activity Use inductive reasoning to make a conjecture about the sum of the measures of the exterior angles of any triangle, one at each vertex. Draw three different large triangles and extend each side in one direction to create one exterior angle at each vertex. For each triangle, measure and label the three exterior angles, and then find the sum of these measures.

Next, following the same method as you did for triangles, find the sum of the measures of the exterior angles of any convex quadrilateral, pentagon, and hexagon. Make a conjecture about the sum of the measures of the exterior angles of any convex polygon. Compare your results with those of other students.

The sum of the exterior angles of any triangle is 360°. The sum of the exterior angles (one at each vertex) of any convex polygon is 360°.

19.3 Angle-Angle Similarity

Florida Common Core Standards

The student is expected to:

 **Geometry—8.G.1.5**

Use informal arguments to establish facts about the angle sum and exterior angle of triangles, about the angles created when parallel lines are cut by a transversal, and the angle-angle criterion for similarity of triangles.

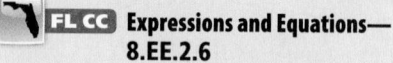 **Expressions and Equations— 8.EE.2.6**

Use similar triangles to explain why the slope m is the same between any two distinct points on a non-vertical line in the coordinate plane; derive the equation $y = mx$ for a line through the origin and the equation $y = mx + b$ for a line intercepting the vertical axis at b.

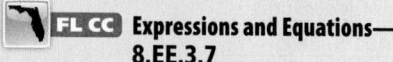 **Expressions and Equations— 8.EE.3.7**

Solve linear equations in one variable.

Mathematical Practices

 **MP.4.1** Modeling

ADDITIONAL EXAMPLE 1
Explain whether the triangles are similar.

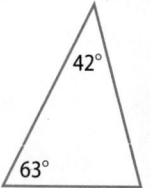 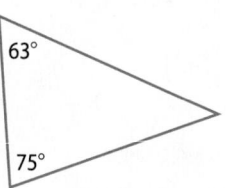

The triangles are similar by the AA Similarity Postulate. The missing angles are 42° in one triangle and 75° in the other. All corresponding angle pairs are congruent.

 Interactive Whiteboard
Interactive example available online

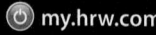 my.hrw.com

Engage

ESSENTIAL QUESTION

How can you determine when two triangles are similar? Sample answer: Two triangles are similar if it can be shown that two angles of one triangle are congruent to two angles of the other triangle.

Motivate the Lesson
Ask: How many different triangles can be drawn that have one angle measuring 45° and another measuring 60°? Take a guess. Begin Explore Activity 1 to find out.

Explore

EXPLORE ACTIVITY 1

Connect Vocabulary ELL

Discuss the various meanings of *similar*. In nonmathematical situations, *similar* can be used to mean *likeness* or *resemblance* in a general way. In mathematical terms, *similar figures* are similar in a specific way: the corresponding angles are congruent. The lengths of their corresponding sides are not necessarily congruent but are proportional.

Explain

EXAMPLE 1

Questioning Strategies
• Why is it not enough to just look at the triangles to say that they are similar?
In mathematics, similarity has a specific meaning and deductive reasoning must show that the triangles meet the definition of similarity.

• Why is it important to find the measure of the third angle? Before determining the measure of the third angle, there is only one pair of angles that is known to be congruent. There must be two pairs of congruent angles for the triangles to be similar. A second pair of congruent angles can be demonstrated by finding the measure of the third angle in either triangle.

Talk About It
Check for Understanding

 Ask: Are all equilateral triangles similar? All equilateral triangles have three 60° angles. So, the AA Similarity Postulate holds for all equilateral triangles.

YOUR TURN

Avoid Common Errors
In Exercise 3, students may assume the triangles are not similar because the triangles are rotated with respect to each other. Remind students that visual inspection is not sufficient to prove or disprove similarity.

19.3 Angle-Angle Similarity

FL CC 8.G.1.5
Use informal arguments to establish facts about . . . the angle-angle criterion for similarity of triangles. Also 8.EE.2.6, 8.EE.3.7

? ESSENTIAL QUESTION

How can you determine when two triangles are similar?

EXPLORE ACTIVITY 1 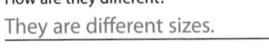 FL CC 8.G.1.5

Discovering Angle-Angle Similarity

Similar figures have the same shape but may have different sizes. Two triangles are **similar** if their corresponding angles are congruent and the lengths of their corresponding sides are proportional.

A Use your protractor and a straightedge to draw a triangle. Make one angle measure 45° and another angle measure 60°.

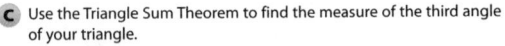

B Compare your triangle to those drawn by your classmates. How are the triangles the same?

They all have the same shape.

How are they different?

They are different sizes.

C Use the Triangle Sum Theorem to find the measure of the third angle of your triangle.

$180° - (45° + 60°) = 180° - 105° = 75°$

Reflect

1. If two angles in one triangle are congruent to two angles in another triangle, what do you know about the third pair of angles?

They must also be congruent.

2. **Make a Conjecture** Are two pairs of congruent angles enough information to conclude that two triangles are similar? Explain.

Yes; by the Triangle Sum Theorem, the third pair of angles must have the same angle measure and thus are congruent, so the triangles must be similar.

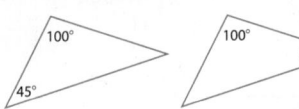
Math On the Spot
my.hrw.com

No; a right triangle has one right angle and two acute angles. The measures of the acute angles can be any number of degrees that add to 90°.

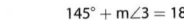
Math Talk
Mathematical Practices

Are all right triangles similar? Why or why not?

Using the AA Similarity Postulate

Angle-Angle (AA) Similarity Postulate

If two angles of one triangle are congruent to two angles of another triangle, then the triangles are similar.

EXAMPLE 1 FL CC 8.G.1.5

Explain whether the triangles are similar.

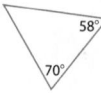 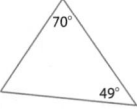

The figure shows only one pair of congruent angles. Find the measure of the third angle in each triangle.

$45° + 100° + m\angle 3 = 180°$ $100° + 35° + m\angle 3 = 180°$

$145° + m\angle 3 = 180°$ $135° + m\angle 3 = 180°$

$145° + m\angle 3 - 145° = 180° - 145°$ $135° + m\angle 3 - 135° = 180° - 135°$

$m\angle 3 = 35°$ $m\angle 3 = 45°$

Because two angles in one triangle are congruent to two angles in the other triangle, the triangles are similar.

YOUR TURN

3. Explain whether the triangles are similar.

The triangles are not similar, because only one angle is congruent. The angle measures of the triangles are 70°, 58°, and 52° and 70°, 61°, and 49°.

Personal Math Trainer

Online Assessment and Intervention

my.hrw.com

PROFESSIONAL DEVELOPMENT

Integrate Mathematical Practices MP.4.1

This lesson provides an opportunity to address this Mathematical Practices standard. It calls for students to apply mathematics to problems arising in everyday life, society, and the workplace. Students use the properties of similar triangles to write proportions and determine the height of a real-world object that would be difficult to measure directly.

Math Background

The AA Similarity Postulate is one way of proving that triangles are similar. The SSS Similarity Postulate is another way. It states that if the ratios of the measures of the corresponding sides are equal, then the triangles are similar. The SAS Similarity Postulate is yet another way. It states that if the ratios of the measures of two pairs of corresponding sides are equal, and the angles formed by those two sides in each triangle are congruent, then the triangles are similar.

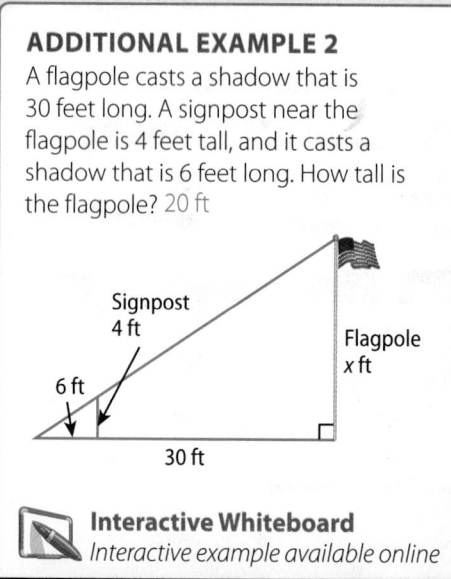
EXAMPLE 2

Questioning Strategies

• What does point *A* in the diagram represent? the point where the ball lands Point *E*? the point where the ball is hit

• What does *AE* represent? the distance the ball travels Do you need to know *AE*? Why or why not? No, you only need to use two pairs of corresponding sides to write the corresponding parts proportion.

• Why do you use *AB* and *AD* in the proportion instead of *AB* and *BD*? *AB* and *AD* are the lengths of the longer sides of the two triangles; *BD* is only part of the length of a side.

Focus on Modeling Mathematical Practices

In Example 2, a diagram of similar triangles is used to write a proportion that models a real-world situation. Ensure that students understand how the real-world quantities mentioned in the problem are portrayed in the diagram.

Engage with the Whiteboard

Use markers of two different colors to outline the two similar triangles. Identify the corresponding angles.

YOUR TURN

Focus on Math Connections Mathematical Practices

Tell students to think of the wheelchair ramp as the graph of a line with the origin at the left end of the ramp. Label the right end of the ramp with the coordinates (24, 2). Ask students what the rise and run are between the origin and the point (24, 2), and what the slope of the line is (rise = 2, run = 24, slope = $\frac{1}{12}$). Label the point (8, *h*). Ask what the rise and run are between the origin and the point (8, *h*) (rise = *h*, run = 8). Ask students if they can find *h* when they know the slope and the run. This will prepare students for the next Explore Activity.

EXPLORE ACTIVITY 2

Questioning Strategies

• Name another pair of parallel lines besides $\overleftrightarrow{AE}$ and $\overleftrightarrow{CF}$. $\overleftrightarrow{BE}$ and $\overleftrightarrow{DF}$

• If the origin lies on line ℓ between points *B* and *C*, such that points *A* and *B* lie in Quadrant III, is the slope between *A* and *B* still the same as the slope between points *C* and *D*? Explain. Yes, the slope is still the same. If points *A* and *B* have negative coordinates instead of positive coordinates, this does not affect the slope.

Focus on Modeling Mathematical Practices

In Explore Activity 2, be sure students are clear on what the diagram looks like after steps A and B. If necessary, consider adding an *x*-axis and *y*-axis to the diagram or drawing the diagram on a grid to help students understand the diagram.

Finding Missing Measures in Similar Triangles

Because corresponding angles are congruent and corresponding sides are proportional in similar triangles, you can use similar triangles to solve real-world problems.

Math On the Spot
my.hrw.com

EXAMPLE 2 Real World
FL CC 8.EE.3.7

While playing tennis, Matt is 12 meters from the net, which is 0.9 meter high. He needs to hit the ball so that it just clears the net and lands 6 meters beyond the base of the net. At what height should Matt hit the tennis ball?

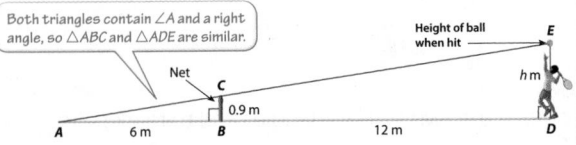

Both triangles contain ∠A and a right angle, so △ABC and △ADE are similar.

In similar triangles, corresponding side lengths are proportional.

$$\frac{AD}{AB} = \frac{DE}{BC} \longrightarrow \frac{6+12}{6} = \frac{h}{0.9}$$

Substitute the lengths from the figure.

$$0.9 \times \frac{18}{6} = \frac{h}{0.9} \times 0.9$$

Use properties of equality to get h by itself.

$$0.9 \times 3 = h$$

Simplify.

$$2.7 = h$$

Multiply.

Matt should hit the ball at a height of 2.7 meters.

Reflect

4. **What If?** Suppose you set up a proportion so that each ratio compares parts of one triangle, as shown below.

height of △ABC ⟶ $\frac{BC}{AB} = \frac{DE}{AD}$ ⟵ height of △ADE
base of △ABC ⟶ ⟵ base of △ADE

Show that this proportion leads to the same value for h as in Example 2.

$$\frac{0.9}{6} = \frac{h}{18}$$
$$18 \times 0.15 = h$$
$$2.7 = h$$

Lesson 19.3 **627**

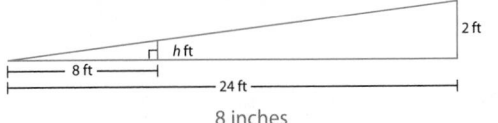
Personal Math Trainer
Online Assessment and Intervention
my.hrw.com

YOUR TURN

5. Rosie is building a wheelchair ramp that is 24 feet long and 2 feet high. She needs to install a vertical support piece 8 feet from the end of the ramp. What is the length of the support piece in inches?

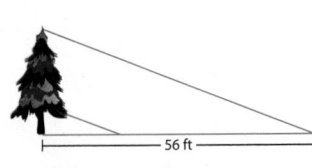

8 inches

6. The lower cable meets the tree at a height of 6 feet and extends out 16 feet from the base of the tree. If the triangles are similar, how tall is the tree?

21 ft

EXPLORE ACTIVITY 2
FL CC 8.EE.2.6

Using Similar Triangles to Explain Slope

You can use similar triangles to show that the slope of a line is constant.

A Draw a line ℓ that is not a horizontal line. Label four points on the line as A, B, C, and D.

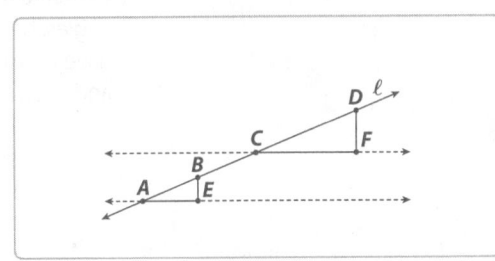

You need to show that the slope between points A and B is the same as the slope between points C and D.

628 Unit 9

DIFFERENTIATE INSTRUCTION

World History

Shadow reckoning is a technique of applying similar triangles to find indirect measurements that dates back to ancient Greece. The Greek mathematician Thales visited Egypt and used this method to find the height of The Great Pyramid. The height of a stick held perpendicular to the ground and the length of its shadow are proportional to the height of the pyramid and the length of its shadow. The heights and their shadows form two sides of similar right triangles.

Modeling

Sierpinski's Triangle is a *fractal* made from similar triangles. To make this fractal, begin with a large equilateral triangle. Connect the midpoints of each side to create four smaller triangles similar to the original. Inside each of the four smaller triangles, connect the midpoints of each side to form four more even smaller equilateral triangles. Repeat to make more and more smaller similar triangles.

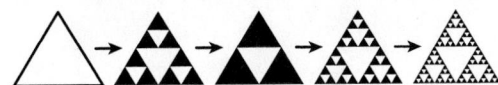

Additional Resources

Differentiated Instruction includes:

• Reading Strategies
• Success for English Learners **ELL**
• Reteach
• Challenge **PRE-AP**

Elaborate

Talk About It

Summarize the Lesson

Ask: What do you need to show in order to prove that two triangles are similar? To prove two triangles are similar, you need to prove that at least two angles in one triangle are congruent to two angles in the other triangle. Or, you can show that the lengths of all three of their corresponding sides are proportional.

GUIDED PRACTICE

Engage with the Whiteboard

For Exercise 2, use color markers to outline the two similar triangles and to mark pairs of corresponding angles.

Avoid Common Errors

Exercise 2 Some students may forget to add the two measures along the bottom of the figure and simply use the three values in the diagram in their proportion. Have students draw separate sketches of the two triangles shown in the figure, one large and one small. This should help students see that the length of the horizontal leg of the large triangle is $16 + 7.5$, or 23.5 feet.

Exercise 3 If students have difficulty identifying that $\angle BAC$ and $\angle CDE$ are alternate interior angles, have students cover $\overleftrightarrow{EB}$ to help them identify this angle relationship. Likewise, have them cover $\overleftrightarrow{AD}$ to help them identify the angle relationship between angles $\angle ABC$ and $\angle CED$.

B Draw the rise and run for the slope between points *A* and *B*. Label the intersection as point *E*. Draw the rise and run for the slope between points *C* and *D*. Label the intersection as point *F*.

C Write expressions for the slope between *A* and *B* and between *C* and *D*.

Slope between *A* and *B*: $\dfrac{BE}{\boxed{AE}}$ Slope between *C* and *D*: $\dfrac{\boxed{DF}}{CF}$

D Extend $\overleftrightarrow{AE}$ and $\overleftrightarrow{CF}$ across your drawing. $\overleftrightarrow{AE}$ and $\overleftrightarrow{CF}$ are both horizontal lines, so they are parallel.

Line ℓ is a __transversal__ that intersects parallel lines.

E Complete the following statements:

∠*BAE* and __∠DCF__ are corresponding angles and are __congruent__.

∠*BEA* and __∠DFC__ are right angles and are __congruent__.

F By Angle–Angle Similarity, △*ABE* and __△CDF__ are similar triangles.

G Use the fact that the lengths of corresponding sides of similar triangles are proportional to complete the following ratios: $\dfrac{BE}{DF} = \dfrac{\boxed{AE}}{CF}$

H Recall that you can also write the proportion so that the ratios compare parts of the same triangle: $\dfrac{\boxed{BE}}{AE} = \dfrac{DF}{\boxed{CF}}$.

I The proportion you wrote in step **H** shows that the ratios you wrote in **C** are equal. So, the slope of line ℓ is constant.

Reflect

7. **What If?** Suppose that you label two other points on line ℓ as *G* and *H*. Would the slope between these two points be different than the slope you found in the Explore Activity? Explain.

No; the slope of the line is constant, so the slope
between the points would be the same.

---

1. Explain whether the triangles are similar. Label the angle measures in the figure. (Explore Activity 1 and Example 1)

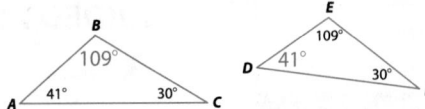

△*ABC* has angle measures __41°, 109°, and 30°__ and △*DEF* has angle measures __41°, 109°, and 30°__. Because __two angles__ in one triangle are congruent to __two angles__ in the other triangle, the triangles are __similar__.

2. A flagpole casts a shadow 23.5 feet long. At the same time of day, Mrs. Gilbert, who is 5.5 feet tall, casts a shadow that is 7.5 feet long. How tall in feet is the flagpole? Round your answer to the nearest tenth. (Example 2)

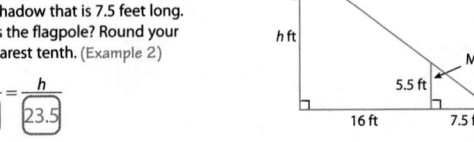

$\dfrac{5.5}{\boxed{7.5}} = \dfrac{h}{\boxed{23.5}}$

$h = $ __17.2__ feet

3. Two transversals intersect two parallel lines as shown. Explain whether △*ABC* and △*DEC* are similar. (Example 1)

∠*BAC* and ∠*EDC* are __congruent__ since they are __alternate interior angles__.

∠*ABC* and ∠*DEC* are __congruent__ since they are __alternate interior angles__.

By __AA Similarity__, △*ABC* and △*DEC* are __similar__.

? ESSENTIAL QUESTION CHECK-IN

4. How can you determine when two triangles are similar?

If two angles of one triangle are congruent to two
angles of the other triangle, the triangles are similar by
the angle–angle similarity postulate.

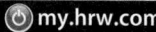
19.3 LESSON QUIZ

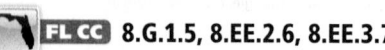 **FL CC** 8.G.1.5, 8.EE.2.6, 8.EE.3.7

1. Explain whether the triangles are similar.

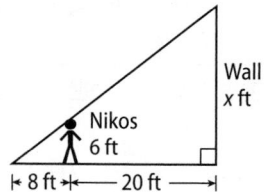

110°   110°
37°   33°

2. Nikos is 6 ft tall and his shadow is 8 ft long. A wall casts a shadow that is 28 ft long. How tall in feet is the wall?

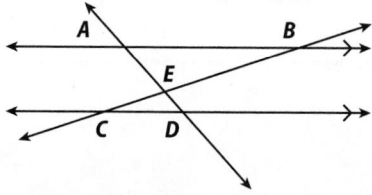

Wall
x ft

Nikos
6 ft

⊢ 8 ft ⊣⊢ 20 ft ⊣

3. Two transversals intersect two parallel lines as shown. Explain whether △ABE and △DCE are similar and list the corresponding pairs of angles.

A   B

E

C   D

Lesson Quiz available online

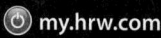
Answers

1. The triangles are similar by the AA Similarity Postulate. The missing angle measure in the triangle on the left is 33°. The missing angle measure in the triangle on the right is 37°. All pairs of corresponding angles are congruent.

2. 21 ft

Evaluate

GUIDED AND INDEPENDENT PRACTICE

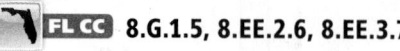 **FL CC** 8.G.1.5, 8.EE.2.6, 8.EE.3.7

Concepts & Skills	Practice
Explore Activity 1 Discovering Angle-Angle Similarity	Exercises 1, 6–7
Example 1 Using the AA Similarity Postulate	Exercises 1, 3, 5–7, 10
Example 2 Finding Missing Measures in Similar Triangles	Exercises 2, 8–9, 11
Explore Activity 2 Using Similar Triangles to Explain Slope	Exercise 3

Exercise	Depth of Knowledge (D.O.K.)		**FL CC** Mathematical Practices
5–7	**1** Recall of Information		**MP.2.1** Reasoning
8–9	**2** Skills/Concepts		**MP.1.1** Problem Solving
10	**2** Skills/Concepts		**MP.2.1** Reasoning
11	**3** Strategic Thinking	H.O.T.!	**MP.3.1** Logic
12	**3** Strategic Thinking	H.O.T.!	**MP.6.1** Precision
13	**3** Strategic Thinking	H.O.T.!	**MP.2.1** Reasoning
14	**3** Strategic Thinking	H.O.T.!	**MP.3.1** Logic

Additional Resources

Differentiated Instruction includes:

• Leveled Practice worksheets

 **Exercise 12** combines concepts from the Florida Common Core cluster "Understand congruence and similarity using physical models, transparencies, or geometry software."

3. ∠EAB and ∠EDC are corresponding and congruent since they are alternate interior angles. ∠ABE and ∠DCE are corresponding and congruent since they are also alternate interior angles. By the AA Similarity Postulate, △ABE and △DCE are similar. ∠AEB and ∠DEC form the third pair of corresponding angles.

19.3 Independent Practice

FL CC 8.EE.2.6, 8.EE.3.7, 8.G.1.5

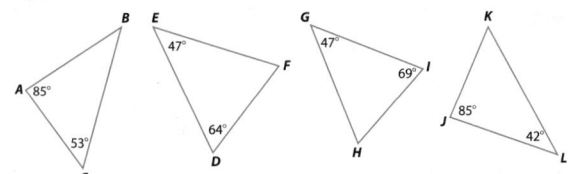
Personal Math Trainer
Online Assessment and Intervention
my.hrw.com

Use the diagrams for Exercises 5–7.

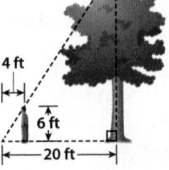

5. Find the missing angle measures in the triangles.

$m\angle B = 42°$, $m\angle F = 69°$, $m\angle H = 64°$, $m\angle K = 53°$

6. Which triangles are similar?

△ABC and △JLK are similar. △DEF and △HGI are similar.

7. **Analyze Relationships** Determine which angles are congruent to the angles in △ABC.

$\angle J \cong \angle A$, $\angle L \cong \angle B$, and $\angle K \cong \angle C$

8. **Multistep** A tree casts a shadow that is 20 feet long. Frank is 6 feet tall, and while standing next to the tree he casts a shadow that is 4 feet long.

  a. How tall is the tree? ____30 ft____

  b. How much taller is the tree than Frank? ____24 ft____

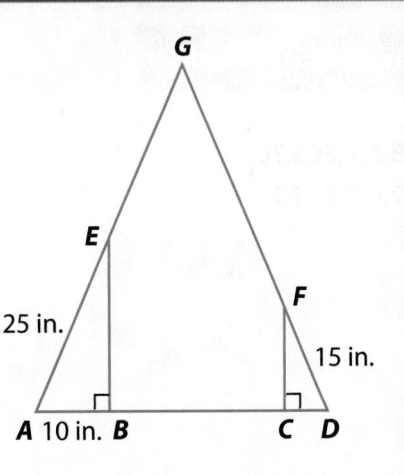

9. **Represent Real-World Problems** Sheila is climbing on a ladder that is attached against the side of a jungle gym wall. She is 5 feet off the ground and 3 feet from the base of the ladder, which is 15 feet from the wall. Draw a diagram to help you solve the problem. How high up the wall is the top of the ladder?

____25 feet____

10. **Justify Reasoning** Are two equilateral triangles always similar? Explain.

Yes; each angle of an equilateral triangle measures 60°, so all three angles of one equilateral triangle are congruent to all three angles of any other equilateral triangle.

---

11. **Critique Reasoning** Ryan calculated the missing measure in the diagram shown. What was his mistake?

$$\frac{3.4}{6.5} = \frac{h}{19.5}$$

$$19.5 \times \frac{3.4}{6.5} = \frac{h}{19.5} \times 19.5$$

$$\frac{66.3}{6.5} = h$$

$$10.2 \text{ cm} = h$$

In the first line, Ryan should have added 19.5 and 6.5 to get a denominator of 26 for the expression on the right side. Doing so gives the correct value of 13.6 cm for h.

H.O.T. FOCUS ON HIGHER ORDER THINKING

Work Area

12. **Communicate Mathematical Ideas** For a pair of triangular earrings, how can you tell if they are similar? How can you tell if they are congruent?

The earrings are similar if two angle measures of one are equal to two angle measures of the other. They are congruent if they are similar and if the side lengths of one are equal to the side lengths of the other.

13. **Critical Thinking** When does it make sense to use similar triangles to measure the height and length of objects in real life?

Sample answer: If the item is too tall or too large to measure with a tape measure or other measuring device, or if a straight–line path is not accessible

14. **Justify Reasoning** Two right triangles on a coordinate plane are similar but not congruent. Each of the legs of both triangles are extended by 1 unit, creating two new right triangles. Are the resulting triangles similar? Explain using an example.

No, the side lengths will no longer be proportional. A right triangle with side lengths 3, 4, and 5 is similar to a right triangle with side lengths 6, 8, and 10. If the legs of both triangles are extended by 1 unit, the leg lengths become 4 and 5 and 7 and 9, and $\frac{7}{4} \neq \frac{9}{5}$.

EXTEND THE MATH PRE-AP

Activity available online ⏻ my.hrw.com

Activity Triangle *AGD*, shown here, is an isosceles triangle with sides *AG* and *DG* congruent. Two line segments, segments *EB* and *FC*, have been drawn perpendicular to side *AD*. Use what you have learned about the AA Similarity Postulate and finding missing measures in similar triangles to describe how you would find the length of line segment *CD*.

Perpendicular segments form right angles, so angle *ABE* and angle *DCF* are congruent. Angles *A* and *D* are congruent because the base angles of an isosceles triangle are congruent. Therefore, triangles *AEB* and *DFC* are similar triangles by the AA Similarity Postulate. This means that their corresponding sides are proportional. So, $\frac{25 \text{ in.}}{15 \text{ in.}} = \frac{10 \text{ in.}}{x \text{ in.}}$ and $x = 6$. Therefore, segment *CD* is 6 inches long.

Ready to Go On?

Assess Mastery

Use the assessment on this page to determine if students have mastered the concepts and standards covered in this module.

 **RtI** Response to Intervention

Personal Math Trainer
Online Assessment and Intervention
⏻ my.hrw.com

Intervention	Enrichment

Access Ready to Go On? assessment online, and receive instant scoring, feedback, and customized intervention or enrichment.

Online and Print Resources

Differentiated Instruction
• Reteach worksheets
• Reading Strategies **ELL**
• Success for English Learners **ELL**

Differentiated Instruction
• Challenge worksheets
  PRE-AP
• Extend the Math **PRE-AP** Lesson Activities in TE

Additional Resources

Assessment Resources include:
• Leveled Module Quizzes

Ready to Go On?

Personal Math Trainer
Online Assessment and Intervention
⏻ my.hrw.com

19.1 Parallel Lines Cut by a Transversal

In the figure, line $p \parallel$ line q. Find the measure of each angle if $m\angle 8 = 115°$.

1. $m\angle 7 =$ _____65°_____

2. $m\angle 6 =$ _____115°_____

3. $m\angle 1 =$ _____115°_____

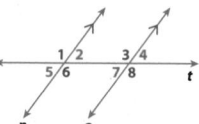

19.2 Angle Theorems for Triangles

Find the measure of each angle.

4. $m\angle A =$ _____48°_____

5. $m\angle B =$ _____58°_____

6. $m\angle BCA =$ _____74°_____

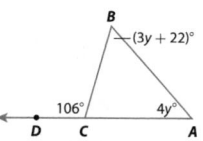

19.3 Angle-Angle Similarity

Triangle *FEG* is similar to triangle *IHJ*. Find the missing values.

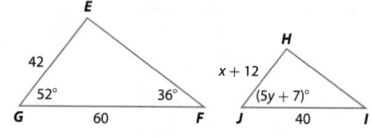

7. $x =$ ____16____ **8.** $y =$ ____9____ **9.** $m\angle H =$ ____92°____

? ESSENTIAL QUESTION

10. How can you use similar triangles to solve real-world problems?
Sample answer: You can find lengths that you can't measure directly.

© Houghton Mifflin Harcourt Publishing Company

 Florida Common Core Standards

Lesson	Exercises	🏴 Common Core Standards
19.1	1–3	**8.G.1.5**
19.2	4–6	**8.G.1.5, 8.EE.3.7, 8.EE.3.7b**
19.3	7–9	**8.G.1.5, 8.EE.2.6, 8.EE.3.7**

PARCC Assessment Readiness

Assessment Readiness Tip Students should underline or highlight the final sentence of the word problem to make sure they have finished the problem, especially in problems with multiple steps.

Item 3 Students might stop after solving for *x*, which would give them answer choice A. If they underline the last sentence in the problem, they will realize that while they have found *x*, they have not yet found the measure of the smallest angle.

Avoid Common Errors

Item 2 Some students may miss the word *not* in the question and instead select an angle that is congruent. Remind students to look diligently for words that indicate opposites, like *not*.

Item 4 Students should remember that the exterior angle must be larger than either of the remote interior angles.

Additional Resources

Personal Math Trainer
Online Assessment and Intervention
my.hrw.com

MODULE 19 MIXED REVIEW
PARCC Assessment Readiness

Personal Math Trainer
Online Assessment and Intervention
my.hrw.com

Selected Response

Use the figure for Exercises 1 and 2.

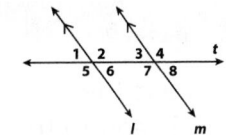

1. Which angle pair is a pair of alternate exterior angles?

- Ⓐ ∠5 and ∠6
- Ⓑ ∠6 and ∠7
- Ⓒ ∠5 and ∠4
- Ⓓ ∠5 and ∠2

2. Which of the following angles is **not** congruent to ∠3?

- Ⓐ ∠1
- Ⓑ ∠2
- Ⓒ ∠6
- Ⓓ ∠8

3. The measures, in degrees, of the three angles of a triangle are given by $2x + 1$, $3x - 3$, and $9x$. What is the measure of the smallest angle?

- Ⓐ 13°
- Ⓑ 27°
- Ⓒ 36°
- Ⓓ 117°

4. Which is a possible measure of ∠DCA in the triangle below?

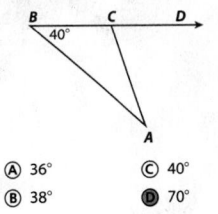

- Ⓐ 36°
- Ⓑ 38°
- Ⓒ 40°
- Ⓓ 70°

5. Kaylee wrote in her dinosaur report that the Jurassic period was 1.75×10^8 years ago. What is this number written in standard form?

- Ⓐ 1,750,000
- Ⓑ 17,500,000
- Ⓒ 175,000,000
- Ⓓ 17,500,000,000

6. Given that *y* is proportional to *x*, what linear equation can you write if *y* is 16 when *x* is 20?

- Ⓐ $y = 20x$
- Ⓑ $y = \frac{5}{4}x$
- Ⓒ $y = \frac{4}{5}x$
- Ⓓ $y = 0.6x$

Mini-Task

7. Two transversals intersect two parallel lines as shown.

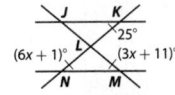

a. What is the value of *x*?

$\underline{\qquad 4 \qquad}$

b. What is the measure of ∠LMN?

$\underline{\qquad 23° \qquad}$

c. What is the measure of ∠KLM?

$\underline{\qquad 48° \qquad}$

d. Which two triangles are similar? How do you know?

Triangle *KLJ* is similar to triangle *NLM* because they have two congruent angles.

© Houghton Mifflin Harcourt Publishing Company

Florida Common Core Standards

Items	Grade 8 Standards	Mathematical Practices
1	8.G.1.5	MP.6.1
2	8.G.1.5	MP.7.1
3	8.EE.3.7	MP.2.1
4	8.G.1.5	MP.4.1
5*	8.EE.1.3	MP.4.1
6*	8.F.2.4	MP.4.1
7	8.EE.3.7, 8.G.1.5	MP.4.1, MP.7.1

* Item integrates mixed review concepts from previous modules or a previous course.

The Pythagorean Theorem

ESSENTIAL QUESTION

How can you use the Pythagorean Theorem to solve real-world problems?

You can use the Pythagorean Theorem to find the length of any side of a right triangle if you know the lengths of the other two sides.

LESSON 20.1

The Pythagorean Theorem

FL CC 8.G.2.6, 8.G.2.7

LESSON 20.2

Converse of the Pythagorean Theorem

FL CC 8.G.2.6

LESSON 20.3

Distance Between Two Points

FL CC 8.G.2.8

Real-World Video

The sizes of televisions are usually described by the length of the diagonal of the screen. To find this length of the diagonal of a rectangle, you can use the Pythagorean Theorem.

my.hrw.com

© Houghton Mifflin Harcourt Publishing Company • Image Credits: ©Yuri Arcurs/ Shutterstock

GO DIGITAL

my.hrw.com

my.hrw.com

Go digital with your write-in student edition, accessible on any device.

Math On the Spot

Scan with your smart phone to jump directly to the online edition, video tutor, and more.

Animated Math

Interactively explore key concepts to see how math works.

Personal Math Trainer

Get immediate feedback and help as you work through practice sets.

Are You Ready?

Assess Readiness

Use the assessment on this page to determine if students need intensive or strategic intervention for the module's prerequisite skills.

Response to Intervention

Personal Math Trainer
Online Assessment and Intervention
my.hrw.com

Intervention	Enrichment
Access Are You Ready? assessment online, and receive instant scoring, feedback, and customized intervention or enrichment.	

Online and Print Resources

Skills Intervention worksheets
- Skill 11 Find the Square of a Number
- Skill 51 Order of Operations
- Skill 52 Simplify Numerical Expressions

Differentiated Instruction
- Challenge worksheets **PRE-AP**
- Extend the Math **PRE-AP** Lesson Activities in TE

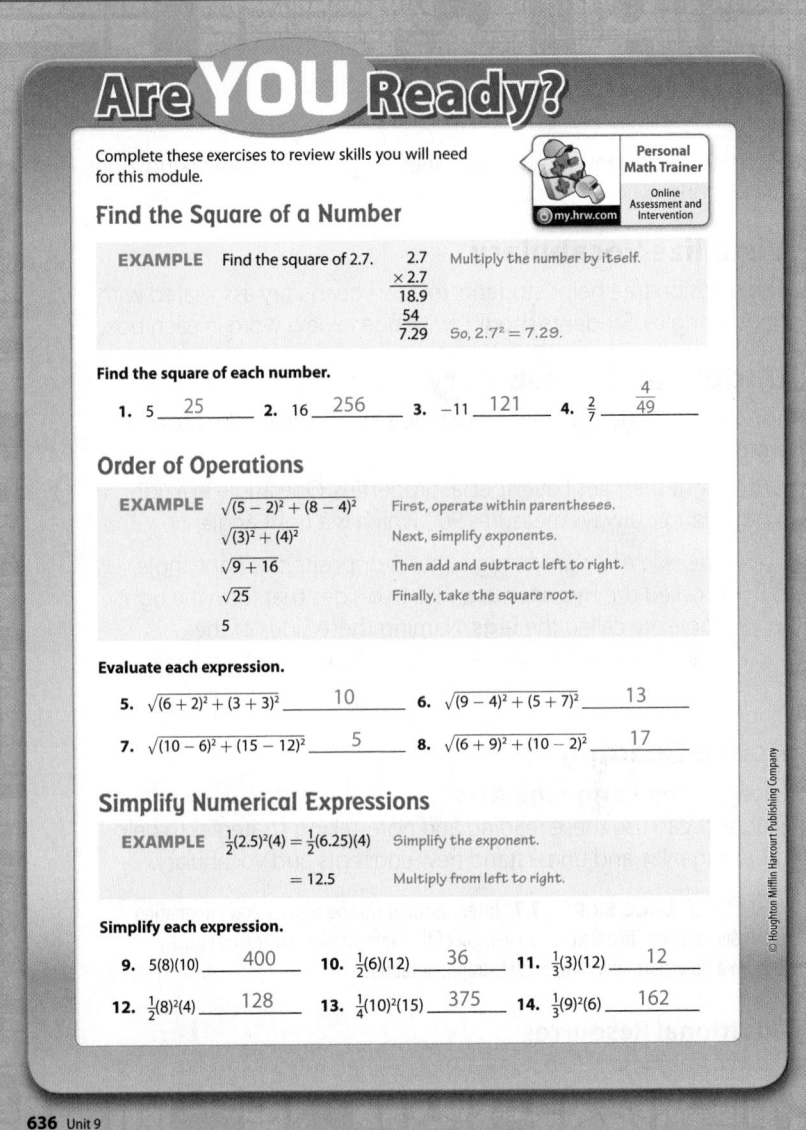

Are YOU Ready?

Complete these exercises to review skills you will need for this module.

Personal Math Trainer
Online Assessment and Intervention
my.hrw.com

Find the Square of a Number

EXAMPLE Find the square of 2.7.

$$\begin{array}{r} 2.7 \\ \times 2.7 \\ \hline 18.9 \\ 54 \\ \hline 7.29 \end{array}$$

Multiply the number by itself.

So, $2.7^2 = 7.29$.

Find the square of each number.

1. 5 ___25___ 2. 16 ___256___ 3. −11 ___121___ 4. $\frac{2}{7}$ ___$\frac{4}{49}$___

Order of Operations

EXAMPLE $\sqrt{(5-2)^2 + (8-4)^2}$ First, operate within parentheses.

$\sqrt{(3)^2 + (4)^2}$ Next, simplify exponents.

$\sqrt{9+16}$ Then add and subtract left to right.

$\sqrt{25}$ Finally, take the square root.

5

Evaluate each expression.

5. $\sqrt{(6+2)^2 + (3+3)^2}$ ___10___ 6. $\sqrt{(9-4)^2 + (5+7)^2}$ ___13___

7. $\sqrt{(10-6)^2 + (15-12)^2}$ ___5___ 8. $\sqrt{(6+9)^2 + (10-2)^2}$ ___17___

Simplify Numerical Expressions

EXAMPLE $\frac{1}{2}(2.5)^2(4) = \frac{1}{2}(6.25)(4)$ Simplify the exponent.

$= 12.5$ Multiply from left to right.

Simplify each expression.

9. $5(8)(10)$ ___400___ 10. $\frac{1}{2}(6)(12)$ ___36___ 11. $\frac{1}{3}(3)(12)$ ___12___

12. $\frac{1}{2}(8)^2(4)$ ___128___ 13. $\frac{1}{4}(10)^2(15)$ ___375___ 14. $\frac{1}{3}(9)^2(6)$ ___162___

PROFESSIONAL DEVELOPMENT VIDEO

Author Juli Dixon models successful teaching practices as she explores the Pythagorean Theorem in an actual eighth-grade classroom.

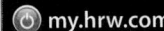

Professional Development
my.hrw.com

GO DIGITAL
my.hrw.com

 Online Teacher Edition
Access a full suite of teaching resources online—plan, present, and manage classes and assignments.

 ePlanner
Easily plan your classes and access all your resources online.

 Interactive Answers and Solutions
Customize answer keys to print or display in the classroom. Choose to include answers only or full solutions to all lesson exercises.

 Interactive Whiteboards
Engage students with interactive whiteboard-ready lessons and activities.

 Personal Math Trainer: Online Assessment and Intervention
Assign automatically graded homework, quizzes, tests, and intervention activities. Prepare your students with updated practice tests aligned with Common Core.

Reading Start-Up

Have students complete the activities on this page by working alone or with others.

Visualize Vocabulary

The decision tree helps students review vocabulary associated with right triangles. Students should write one review word in each box.

Understand Vocabulary

Use the following explanation to help students learn the preview words.

> Right triangles have special properties. One angle in a right triangle always measures 90°, which is a right angle.
>
> The side of a right triangle that is opposite the right angle, is called the **hypotenuse**. The two sides that form the right angle are called the **legs**. Naming these sides of the triangle can help us understand and talk about a triangle and its properties.

Active Reading

Integrating Language Arts

Students can use these reading and note-taking strategies to help them organize and understand new concepts and vocabulary.

FLCC **LACC.68.RST.3.7** Integrate quantitative or technical information expressed in words in a text with a version of that information expressed visually (e.g., in a flowchart, diagram, model, graph, or table).

Additional Resources

Differentiated Instruction

• Reading Strategies **ELL**

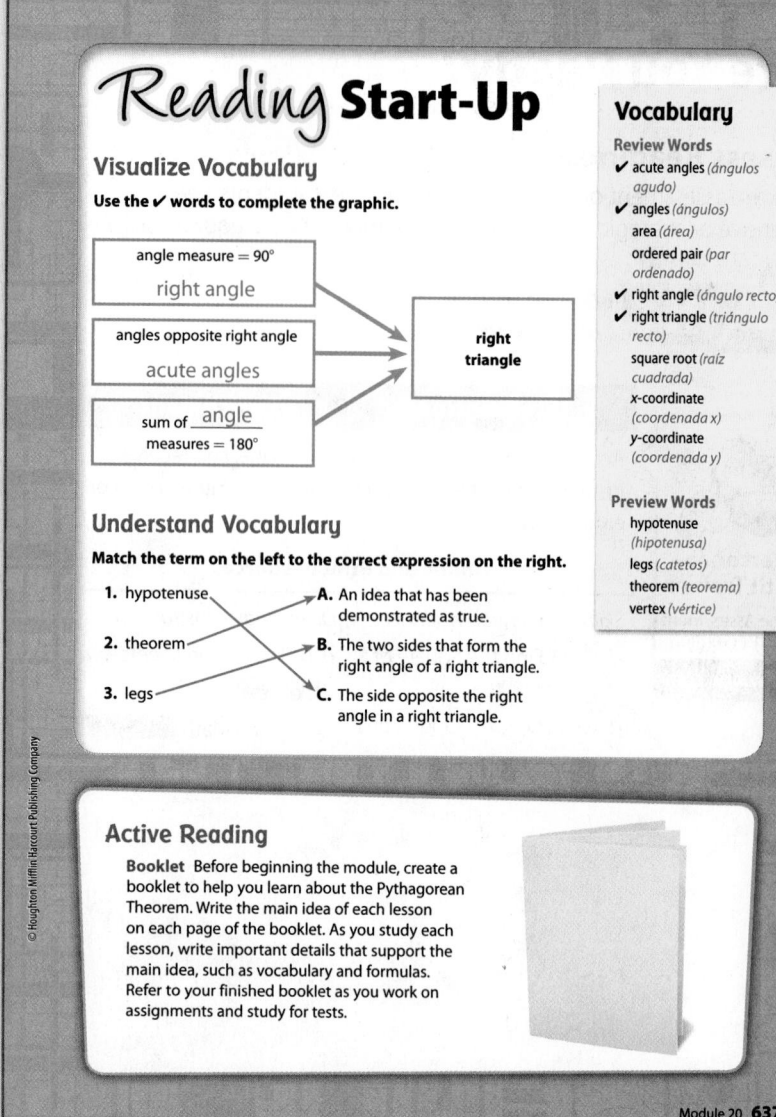

Reading Start-Up

Visualize Vocabulary

Use the ✔ words to complete the graphic.

angle measure = 90°
right angle

angles opposite right angle
acute angles

sum of **angle** measures = 180°

right triangle

Vocabulary

Review Words
✔ acute angles (ángulos agudo)
✔ angles (ángulos)
  area (área)
  ordered pair (par ordenado)
✔ right angle (ángulo recto)
✔ right triangle (triángulo recto)
  square root (raíz cuadrada)
  x-coordinate (coordenada x)
  y-coordinate (coordenada y)

Preview Words
  hypotenuse (hipotenusa)
  legs (catetos)
  theorem (teorema)
  vertex (vértice)

Understand Vocabulary

Match the term on the left to the correct expression on the right.

1. hypotenuse
2. theorem
3. legs

A. An idea that has been demonstrated as true.
B. The two sides that form the right angle of a right triangle.
C. The side opposite the right angle in a right triangle.

Active Reading

Booklet Before beginning the module, create a booklet to help you learn about the Pythagorean Theorem. Write the main idea of each lesson on each page of the booklet. As you study each lesson, write important details that support the main idea, such as vocabulary and formulas. Refer to your finished booklet as you work on assignments and study for tests.

Module 20 **637**

© Houghton Mifflin Harcourt Publishing Company

Before	**In this module**	**After**
Students understand: • how to write and solve an equation • how to use exponents and the order of operations • how to graph points on the coordinate plane	Students represent and solve right triangles using the Pythagorean Theorem: • use models and diagrams to explain the Pythagorean Theorem • use the Pythagorean Theorem and its converse to solve problems • determine the distance between two points on a coordinate plane using the Pythagorean Theorem	Students will connect: • right triangles and the Pythagorean triples • sum of the interior angles of a triangle and sum of the interior angles of a polygon

Unpacking the Standards

Use the examples on this page to help students know exactly what they are expected to learn in this module.

 Florida Common Core Standards

Content Areas

 FL CC **Geometry—8.G.2**

Understand and apply the Pythagorean Theorem.

Go online to see a complete unpacking of the Florida Common Core Standards.

⏻ my.hrw.com

MODULE 20

Unpacking the Standards

Understanding the standards and the vocabulary terms in the standards will help you know exactly what you are expected to learn in this module.

FL CC **8.G.2.7**

Apply the Pythagorean Theorem to determine unknown side lengths in right triangles in real-world and mathematical problems in two and three dimensions.

Key Vocabulary

Pythagorean Theorem
(Teorema de Pitágoras)
In a right triangle, the square of the length of the hypotenuse is equal to the sum of the squares of the lengths of the legs.

What It Means to You

You will find a missing length in a right triangle, or use side lengths to see whether a triangle is a right triangle.

UNPACKING EXAMPLE 8.G.2.7

Mark and Sarah start walking at the same point, but Mark walks 50 feet north while Sarah walks 75 feet east. How far apart are Mark and Sarah when they stop?

$$a^2 + b^2 = c^2$$
$$50^2 + 75^2 = c^2 \quad \text{Pythagorean Theorem}$$
$$2500 + 5625 = c^2 \quad \text{Substitute.}$$
$$8125 = c^2$$
$$90.1 \approx c$$

Mark and Sarah are approximately 90.1 feet apart.

FL CC **8.G.2.8**

Apply the Pythagorean Theorem to find the distance between two points in a coordinate system.

Key Vocabulary

coordinate plane
(plano cartesiano)
A plane formed by the intersection of a horizontal number line called the x-axis and a vertical number line called the y-axis.

Visit my.hrw.com to see all Florida Common Core Standards unpacked.

⏻ my.hrw.com

What It Means to You

You can use the Pythagorean Theorem to find the distance between two points.

UNPACKING EXAMPLE 8.G.2.8

Find the distance between points A and B.

$$(AC)^2 + (BC)^2 = (AB)^2$$
$$(4 - 1)^2 + (6 - 2)^2 = (AB)^2$$
$$3^2 + 4^2 = (AB)^2$$
$$9 + 16 = (AB)^2$$
$$25 = (AB)^2$$
$$5 = AB$$

The distance is 5 units.

Florida Common Core Standards	Lesson 20.1	Lesson 20.2	Lesson 20.3
FL CC **8.G.2.6** Explain a proof of the Pythagorean Theorem and its converse.	✓	✓	
FL CC **8.G.2.7** Apply the Pythagorean Theorem to determine unknown side lengths in right triangles in real-world and mathematical problems in two and three dimensions.	✓		
FL CC **8.G.2.8** Apply the Pythagorean Theorem to find the distance between two points in a coordinate system.			✓

LESSON
20.1 The Pythagorean Theorem

 Florida Common Core Standards

The student is expected to:

 **Geometry—8.G.2.7**

Apply the Pythagorean Theorem to determine unknown side lengths in right triangles in real-world and mathematical problems in two and three dimensions.

 **Geometry—8.G.2.6**

Explain a proof of the Pythagorean Theorem and its converse.

Mathematical Practices

 **MP.5.1** Using Tools

ADDITIONAL EXAMPLE 1
Find the length of the missing side.

A

5 cm

13 cm   12 cm

B   50 in.

                    14 in.

48 in.

 **Interactive Whiteboard**
Interactive example available online

⏻ my.hrw.com

Animated Math
The Pythagorean Theorem

Students explore an interactive model of a dynamic proof of the Pythagorean Theorem.

⏻ my.hrw.com

Engage

ESSENTIAL QUESTION

How can you prove the Pythagorean Theorem and use it to solve problems? Sample answer: You can use the formulas for the area of squares and triangles to prove the Pythagorean Theorem. You can use the Pythagorean Theorem to find the missing lengths of sides of right triangles and to solve real-world problems.

Motivate the Lesson
Ask: If you draw a triangle on a coordinate grid with horizontal and vertical legs and with the vertices at the intersection of grid lines, it is easy to count grid lines to find the length of the legs. How do you find the length of the hypotenuse? Begin the Explore Activity to find out.

Explore

EXPLORE ACTIVITY

Focus on Reasoning
Guide students through the reasoning to see why the unshaded regions of the two congruent squares have the same area. Then guide them to see why $a^2 + b^2 = c^2$.

Explain

EXAMPLE 1

Questioning Strategies 🖊 Mathematical Practices
• How can you identify the hypotenuse of a right triangle? The hypotenuse is the side opposite the right angle.

• In part B, how do you get from $a^2 + 144 = 225$ to $a^2 = 81$? What is the justification for that? You subtract 144 from both sides of the equation. If $a = b$, then $a - c = b - c$.

Focus on Technology 🖊 Mathematical Practices
Support students in using calculators to do the calculations in Example 1, including squaring numbers and taking the square roots of numbers.

Avoid Common Errors
Make sure that students square the side lengths before adding (in part A) or subtracting (in part B). Students may sometimes add or subtract the side lengths and then square the result.

Engage with the Whiteboard
🖊 Label the sides of the triangles a, b, and c to help students substitute the values of the side lengths into the formula. Emphasize that it does not matter which leg is a and which leg is b. After completing the problem, write the missing side length on the triangle and point out that the hypotenuse is always the longest side.

📷 **FL CC** 8.G.2.7

Apply the Pythagorean Theorem to determine unknown side lengths in right triangles in real-world and mathematical problems in two and three dimensions. *Also 8.G.2.6*

? ESSENTIAL QUESTION

How can you prove the Pythagorean Theorem and use it to solve problems?

EXPLORE ACTIVITY 📷 **FL CC** 8.G.2.6

Proving the Pythagorean Theorem

In a right triangle, the two sides that form the right angle are the **legs**. The side opposite the right angle is the **hypotenuse**.

The Pythagorean Theorem

In a right triangle, the sum of the squares of the lengths of the legs is equal to the square of the length of the hypotenuse.

If a and b are legs and c is the hypotenuse, $a^2 + b^2 = c^2$.

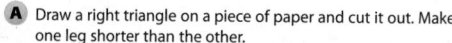
Leg   Hypotenuse
Leg

A Draw a right triangle on a piece of paper and cut it out. Make one leg shorter than the other.

B Trace your triangle onto another piece of paper four times, arranging them as shown. For each triangle, label the shorter leg a, the longer leg b, and the hypotenuse c.

C What is the area of the unshaded square?

c^2 square units

Label the unshaded square with its area.

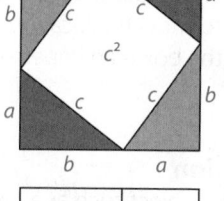

D Trace your original triangle onto a piece of paper four times again, arranging them as shown. Draw a line outlining a larger square that is the same size as the figure you made in **B**.

E What is the area of the unshaded square at the top right of the figure in **D**? at the top left?

a^2 square units; b^2 square units

Label the unshaded squares with their areas.

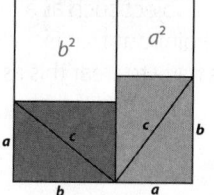

F What is the total area of the unshaded regions in **D**?

$a^2 + b^2$ square units

Lesson 20.1 **639**

EXPLORE ACTIVITY (cont'd)

Reflect

1. Explain whether the figures in **B** and **D** have the same area.

   Yes, the outlines of the figures are the same size.

2. Explain whether the unshaded regions of the figures in **B** and **D** have the same area.

   Yes, the shaded regions have the same area. Subtracting the area of the shaded region from the total area gives the same area for the unshaded region in each figure.

3. **Analyze Relationships** Write an equation relating the area of the unshaded region in step **B** to the unshaded region in **D**.

   $a^2 + b^2 = c^2$

Using the Pythagorean Theorem

You can use the Pythagorean Theorem to find the length of a side of a right triangle when you know the lengths of the other two sides.

Math On the Spot
ⓜ my.hrw.com

Animated Math
ⓜ my.hrw.com

EXAMPLE 1   📷 **FL CC** 8.G.2.7

Find the length of the missing side.

A
7 in.
24 in.

$a^2 + b^2 = c^2$	
$24^2 + 7^2 = c^2$	Substitute into the formula.
$576 + 49 = c^2$	Simplify.
$625 = c^2$	Add.
$25 = c$	Take the square root of both sides.

The length of the hypotenuse is 25 inches.

Math Talk
Mathematical Practices

If you are given the length of the hypotenuse and one leg, does it matter whether you solve for a or b? Explain.

No, the length of the leg can be substituted for either a or b since both a and b represent the lengths of legs.

B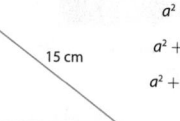
15 cm
12 cm

$a^2 + b^2 = c^2$	
$a^2 + 12^2 = 15^2$	Substitute into the formula.
$a^2 + 144 = 225$	Simplify.
$a^2 = 81$	Use properties of equality to get a^2 by itself.
$a = 9$	Take the square root of both sides.

The length of the leg is 9 centimeters.

640 Unit 9

PROFESSIONAL DEVELOPMENT

📷 **Integrate Mathematical Practices MP.5.1**

This lesson provides an opportunity to address this Mathematical Practices standard. It calls for students to use appropriate tools strategically to solve problems. Students use paper and pencil to create models to prove the Pythagorean Theorem. They go on to solve problems using the Pythagorean Theorem with the aid of number sense to recognize reasonable answers and calculators to determine squares and square roots. They then find the diagonal of a box, an exercise which will be aided by examining a real box.

Math Background

The Pythagorean Theorem can also be proved algebraically as follows:

The area of the largest square in part B of the Explore Activity is $(a + b)^2$. The area of each triangle is $\frac{1}{2}ab$.

To find the area of the inner white square in terms of a and b, subtract the area of the four triangles from the area of the larger square.

$$c^2 = (a + b)^2 - 4\left(\frac{1}{2}ab\right)$$
$$= a^2 + 2ab + b^2 - 2ab$$
$$= a^2 + b^2$$

Therefore, $c^2 = a^2 + b^2$.

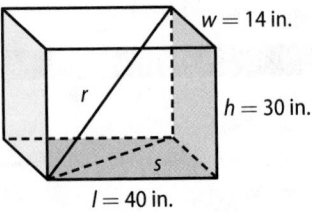
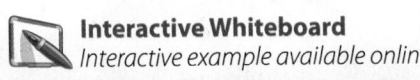
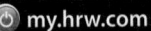
YOUR TURN

Avoid Common Errors
Make sure students correctly identify the hypotenuse before applying the Pythagorean Theorem. Students may assume that the two given side lengths are the legs. In Exercise 5, make sure that students substitute 41 for c in $a^2 + b^2 = c^2$ and then solve the equation correctly to find the length of the vertical leg.

EXAMPLE 2

Questioning Strategies ⬩ Mathematical Practices
- How can a box hold an object that is longer than the length of the box? By positioning the object along a diagonal of the box

- Why is it necessary to find the length of the diagonal across the bottom before finding the diagonal from a bottom corner to the opposite top corner? The diagonal from the bottom corner to the opposite top corner is the hypotenuse of a right triangle with only one known side length, the shorter leg. The length of the other leg is the length of the diagonal across the bottom of the box.

Focus on Modeling
Use a box and a yardstick to illustrate to students the locations of the diagonals and their relative lengths. It is easier to show the location of the internal diagonal with a clear plastic box or storage bin, even if the box is an imperfect rectangular prism with rounded edges.

YOUR TURN

Focus on Communication
Students may object that an object such as a part for a desk may be too thick to be able to fit into the corner of a box. Point out that Exercise 6 asks what is the greatest length the part could be and that students have to treat this as a theoretical maximum.

Elaborate

Talk About It
Summarize the Lesson
💬 Have students complete the graphic organizer below.
Let a, b, and c be the side lengths of a right triangle, with c the length of its hypotenuse.

a	b	c
3	4	5
5	12	13
7	24	25
8	15	17
9	40	41

GUIDED PRACTICE

Engage with the Whiteboard
In Exercise 1, label the sides of the triangle a, b, and c. Either leg can be labeled a or b. After completing the problem, write the missing side length on the triangle.

Avoid Common Errors
Exercise 1 Students may forget to find the square root of c^2. Remind them that the hypotenuse is the longest side of the triangle and that $a + b$ must be greater than c.

YOUR TURN

Find the length of the missing side.

4.

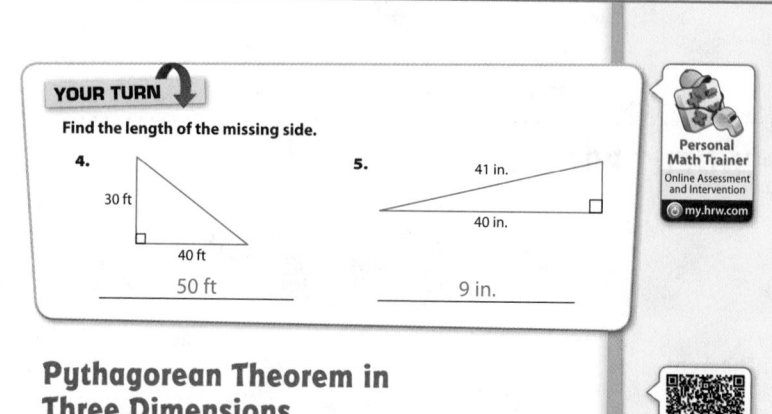

30 ft
40 ft

50 ft

5.

41 in.
40 in.

9 in.

Pythagorean Theorem in Three Dimensions

You can use the Pythagorean Theorem to solve problems in three dimensions.

EXAMPLE 2 (Real World)

FL CC 8.G.2.7

A box used for shipping narrow copper tubes measures 6 inches by 6 inches by 20 inches. What is the length of the longest tube that will fit in the box, given that the length of the tube must be a whole number of inches?

$h = 6$ in.
r
s
$w = 6$ in.
$l = 20$ in.

STEP 1 You want to find r, the length from a bottom corner to the opposite top corner. First, find s, the length of the diagonal across the bottom of the box.

$w^2 + l^2 = s^2$

$6^2 + 20^2 = s^2$ Substitute into the formula.

$36 + 400 = s^2$ Simplify.

$436 = s^2$ Add.

STEP 2 Use your expression for s to find r.

$h^2 + s^2 = r^2$

$6^2 + 436 = r^2$ Substitute into the formula.

$472 = r^2$ Add.

$\sqrt{472} = r$ Take the square root of both sides.

$21.7 \approx r$ Use a calculator to round to the nearest tenth.

The length of the longest tube that will fit in the box is 21 inches.

Math Talk
Mathematical Practices

Looking at Step 2, why did the calculations in Step 1 stop before taking the square root of both sides of the final equation?

By stopping with an expression for s^2, it could be substituted directly into the formula for r^2.

YOUR TURN

6. Tina ordered a replacement part for her desk. It was shipped in a box that measures 4 in. by 4 in. by 14 in. What is the greatest length in whole inches that the part could have been?

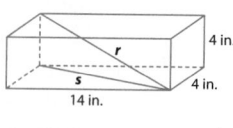

r
4 in.
s
4 in.
14 in.

$4^2 + 14^2 = s^2$	$4^2 + 212 = r^2$
$16 + 196 = s^2$	$228 = r^2$
$212 = s^2$	$\sqrt{228} = r$
	$15.1 \approx r$

The greatest length is 15 in.

Guided Practice

1. Find the length of the missing side of the triangle. (Explore Activity 1 and Example 1)

$a^2 + b^2 = c^2 \rightarrow 24^2 + \boxed{10^2} = c^2 \rightarrow \boxed{676} = c^2$

The length of the hypotenuse is $\boxed{26}$ feet.

10 ft
24 ft

2. Mr. Woo wants to ship a fishing rod that is 42 inches long to his son. He has a box with the dimensions shown. (Example 2)

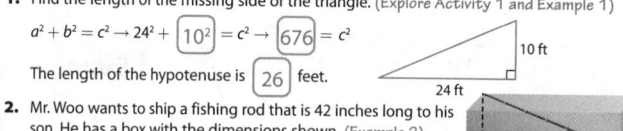

$h = 10$ in.
$l = 40$ in.
$w = 10$ in.

a. Find the square of the length of the diagonal across the bottom of the box.

1700

b. Find the length from a bottom corner to the opposite top corner to the nearest tenth. Will the fishing rod fit?

42.4 in.; yes

❓ ESSENTIAL QUESTION CHECK-IN

3. State the Pythagorean Theorem and tell how you can use it to solve problems.

Sample answer: For a right triangle with legs of lengths a and b and hypotenuse of length c, $a^2 + b^2 = c^2$. You can use it to find the length of a side of a right triangle when the lengths of the other two sides are known.

DIFFERENTIATE INSTRUCTION

Communicating Math

Have students write out a summary of the steps they would use to find (or approximate) the missing length of 39 cm for the triangle below.

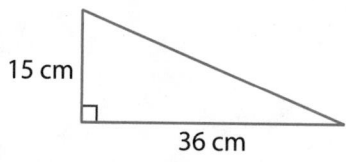

15 cm
36 cm

Manipulatives

Have groups of students carefully draw several right triangles, using a protractor or angle template to draw the right angles. Then have them swap triangles and measure the lengths of the sides to the nearest millimeter. Have them verify the Pythagorean relationship between the side lengths of the right triangles. (Because the measurements are approximate, $a^2 + b^2$ may be close to but not exactly c^2 in some cases.)

Additional Resources

Differentiated Instruction includes:
- Reading Strategies
- Success for English Learners **ELL**
- Reteach
- Challenge **PRE-AP**

The Pythagorean Theorem **642**

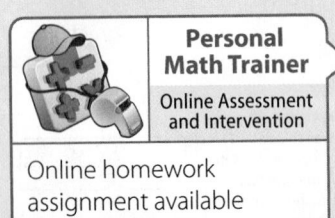

Personal Math Trainer

Online Assessment and Intervention

Online homework assignment available

 my.hrw.com

---

20.1 LESSON QUIZ

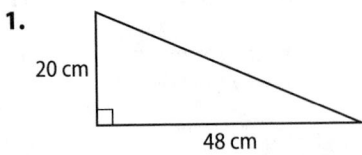 **FL CC** 8.G.2.6, 8.G.2.7

Find the length of the missing side of each triangle.

1.

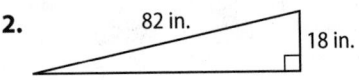

20 cm

48 cm

2.

82 in.

18 in.

3. A box used for shipping a volleyball set measures 10 inches by 20 inches by 40 inches. What is the longest length of support pole that will fit into the box, rounded to a tenth of an inch?

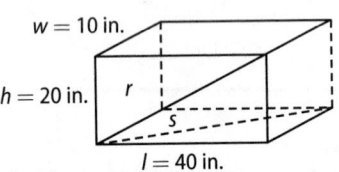

$w = 10$ in.

$h = 20$ in.

r

s

$l = 40$ in.

Lesson Quiz available online

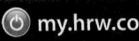 my.hrw.com

Answers

1. 52 cm

2. 80 in.

3. 45.8 in.

Evaluate

GUIDED AND INDEPENDENT PRACTICE

FL CC 8.G.2.6, 8.G.2.7

Concepts & Skills	Practice
Explore Activity Proving the Pythagorean Theorem	Exercise 1
Example 1 Using the Pythagorean Theorem	Exercises 1, 4–8, 10–11
Example 2 Pythagorean Theorem in Three Dimensions	Exercises 2, 9

Exercise	Depth of Knowledge (D.O.K.)		**FL CC** Mathematical Practices
4–5	**2** Skills/Concepts		**MP.5.1** Using Tools
6–10	**2** Skills/Concepts		**MP.4.1** Modeling
11–12	**3** Strategic Thinking	H.O.T.	**MP.4.1** Modeling
13	**3** Strategic Thinking	H.O.T.	**MP.3.1** Logic
14	**3** Strategic Thinking	H.O.T.	**MP.1.1** Problem Solving

Additional Resources

Differentiated Instruction includes:

• Leveled Practice worksheets

20.1 Independent Practice

🔲 FL CC 8.G.2.6, 8.G.2.7

Personal Math Trainer

my.hrw.com

Online Assessment and Intervention

Find the length of the missing side of each triangle. Round your answers to the nearest tenth.

4.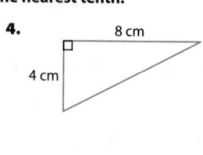

8 cm

4 cm

8.9 cm

5.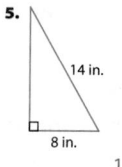

14 in.

8 in.

11.5 in.

6. The diagonal of a rectangular big-screen TV screen measures 152 cm. The length measures 132 cm. What is the height of the screen? _____ 75.4 cm

7. Dylan has a square piece of metal that measures 10 inches on each side. He cuts the metal along the diagonal, forming two right triangles. What is the length of the hypotenuse of each right triangle to the nearest tenth of an inch? _____ 14.1 in.

8. **Represent Real-World Problems** A painter has a 24-foot ladder that he is using to paint a house. For safety reasons, the ladder must be placed at least 8 feet from the base of the side of the house. To the nearest tenth of a foot, how high can the ladder safely reach? _____ 22.6 ft

9. What is the longest flagpole (in whole feet) that could be shipped in a box that measures 2 ft by 2 ft by 12 ft? 12 feet

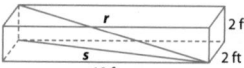

r

s

12 ft

2 ft

2 ft

10. **Sports** American football fields measure 100 yards long between the end zones, and are $53\frac{1}{3}$ yards wide. Is the length of the diagonal across this field more or less than 120 yards? Explain.

Less than; $\sqrt{12844} \cong 113$

11. **Justify Reasoning** A tree struck by lightning broke at a point 12 ft above the ground as shown. What was the height of the tree to the nearest tenth of a foot? Explain your reasoning.

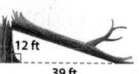

12 ft

39 ft

52.8 ft; $12^2 + 39^2 = c^2$, so $144 + 1521 = c^2$, $1665 = c^2$, and $40.8 \approx c$. Add this length to the height of the bottom of the tree: $40.8 + 12 = 52.8$ ft.

© Houghton Mifflin Harcourt Publishing Company

H.O.T. FOCUS ON HIGHER ORDER THINKING

Work Area

12. **Multistep** Main Street and Washington Avenue meet at a right angle. A large park begins at this corner. Joe's school lies at the opposite corner of the park. Usually Joe walks 1.2 miles along Main Street and then 0.9 miles up Washington Avenue to get to school. Today he walked in a straight path across the park and returned home along the same path. What is the difference in distance between the two round trips? Explain.

1.2 mi; today Joe walked $\sqrt{1.2^2 + 0.9^2} = 1.5$ mi each way.

He usually walks $1.2 + 0.9 = 2.1$ mi each way. So the difference is $2.1 - 1.5 = 0.6$ mi each way, or 1.2 mi.

13. **Analyze Relationships** An isosceles right triangle is a right triangle with congruent legs. If the length of each leg is represented by x, what algebraic expression can be used to represent the length of the hypotenuse? Explain your reasoning.

$\sqrt{x^2 + x^2}$ (or $\sqrt{2x^2}$ or $x\sqrt{2}$); if $a = x$ and $b = x$, then $x^2 + x^2 = c^2$. Thus, $c = \sqrt{x^2 + x^2}$.

14. **Persevere in Problem Solving** A square hamburger is centered on a circular bun. Both the bun and the burger have an area of 16 square inches.

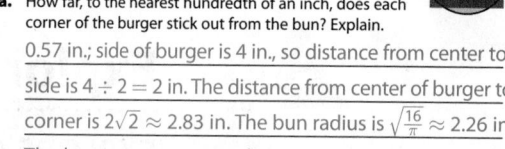

a. How far, to the nearest hundredth of an inch, does each corner of the burger stick out from the bun? Explain.

0.57 in.; side of burger is 4 in., so distance from center to side is $4 \div 2 = 2$ in. The distance from center of burger to corner is $2\sqrt{2} \approx 2.83$ in. The bun radius is $\sqrt{\frac{16}{\pi}} \approx 2.26$ in. The burger corner extends $2.83 - 2.26 \approx 0.57$ in.

b. How far does each bun stick out from the center of each side of the burger?

about $2.26 - 2 = 0.26$ in.

c. Are the distances in part **a** and part **b** equal? If not, which sticks out more, the burger or the bun? Explain.

No; the burger sticks out a little more than a half inch, and the bun sticks out about a quarter inch, so the corners of the burger stick out more.

© Houghton Mifflin Harcourt Publishing Company

EXTEND THE MATH PRE-AP

Activity available online ⏱ my.hrw.com

Activity A common right triangle is called the "3–4–5 triangle." This set of numbers is called a "primitive Pythagorean triple" because the side lengths have no factors other than 1 in common. If you multiply each length in a Pythagorean triple by a whole number like 2, 3, or 4, you will get another Pythagorean triple. So, 6–8–10, 9–12–15, and 12–16–20 are also Pythagorean triples. Find as many Pythagorean triples as you can. Remember—once you find a primitive triple, find whole-number multiples of the triple to get other triples! Hint: There are 50 Pythagorean triples where each length is less than 100, with 16 of them primitive triples.

Primitive Pythagorean Triples Less Than 100	
3–4–5	16–63–65
5–12–13	20–21–29
8–15–17	28–45–53
7–24–25	33–56–65
9–40–41	36–77–85
11–60–61	39–80–89
12–35–37	48–55–73
13–84–85	65–72–97

LESSON 20.2 Converse of the Pythagorean Theorem

 Florida Common Core Standards

The student is expected to:

 **Geometry—8.G.2.6**

Explain a proof of the Pythagorean Theorem and its converse.

Mathematical Practices

FL CC **MP.7.1** Structure

Engage

ESSENTIAL QUESTION

How can you test the converse of the Pythagorean Theorem and use it to solve problems?
Sample answer: Test whether triangles whose side lengths are a, b, and c satisfy $a^2 + b^2 = c^2$. You can use the converse of the Pythagorean Theorem to help you determine whether real-world triangles are right triangles.

Motivate the Lesson
Ask: How can you tell whether a triangle is a right triangle? Make a conjecture. Begin the Explore Activity to find out.

Explore

EXPLORE ACTIVITY

Talk About It
Check for Understanding

 Ask: How do you know if a triangle is a right triangle? If the sum of the squares of the lengths of the two shorter sides of a triangle is equal to the square of the length of the longest side, then the triangle is a right triangle.

Explain

EXAMPLE 1

Questioning Strategies Mathematical Practices
- In part A, how do you know which length should be the value of c in the equation $a^2 + b^2 = c^2$? The longest side length is always the value of c.
- Does the converse of the Pythagorean Theorem only apply to triangles with rational numbers as side lengths? No; the side lengths can be irrational numbers.

Focus on Math Connections Mathematical Practices
Point out that if $a^2 + b^2 > c^2$ or if $a^2 + b^2 < c^2$, then $a^2 + b^2 \neq c^2$, and the triangle made by the side lengths a, b, and c is not a right triangle. For part B of this example, $a^2 + b^2 > c^2$.

Avoid Common Errors
Students may be confused about when to use the Pythagorean Theorem and when to use its converse. Make sure that students understand that if they want to determine whether a triangle is a right triangle and have all three side lengths, they should use the converse of the Pythagorean Theorem. If they want to find a missing side length of a right triangle, they should use the Pythagorean Theorem.

YOUR TURN

Focus on Math Connections Mathematical Practices
Since the side lengths of the triangle in Exercise 3 have a common factor of 2, $16^2 + 30^2 = 34^2$ can be rewritten as $(2 \cdot 8)^2 + (2 \cdot 15)^2 = (2 \cdot 17)^2$. The converse of the Pythagorean Theorem shows that side lengths of 8 in., 15 in., and 17 in. also form a right triangle.

ADDITIONAL EXAMPLE 1
Tell whether each triangle with the given side lengths is a right triangle.

A 16 inches, 30 inches, 34 inches yes

B 14 feet, 49 feet, 51 feet no

Interactive Whiteboard
Interactive example available online

⏻ my.hrw.com

LESSON 20.2 Converse of the Pythagorean Theorem

FL CC 8.G.2.6
Explain a proof of the Pythagorean Theorem and its converse.

ESSENTIAL QUESTION How can you test the converse of the Pythagorean Theorem and use it to solve problems?

Math On the Spot
my.hrw.com

EXPLORE ACTIVITY FL CC 8.G.2.6

Testing the Converse of the Pythagorean Theorem

The Pythagorean Theorem states that if a triangle is a right triangle, then $a^2 + b^2 = c^2$.

The *converse* of the Pythagorean Theorem states that if $a^2 + b^2 = c^2$, then the triangle is a right triangle.

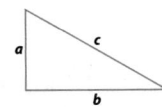

Decide whether the converse of the Pythagorean Theorem is true.

A Verify that the following sets of lengths make the equation $a^2 + b^2 = c^2$ true. Record your results in the table.

a	b	c	Is $a^2 + b^2 = c^2$ true?	Makes a right triangle?
3	4	5	yes	yes
5	12	13	yes	yes
7	24	25	yes	yes
8	15	17	yes	yes
20	21	29	yes	yes

B For each set of lengths in the table, cut strips of grid paper with a width of one square and lengths that correspond to the values of a, b, and c.

C For each set of lengths, use the strips of grid paper to try to form a right triangle. An example using the first set of lengths is shown. Record your findings in the table.

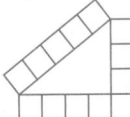

Reflect

1. **Draw Conclusions** Based on your observations, explain whether you think the converse of the Pythagorean Theorem is true.

Students should note that each set of lengths satisfies $a^2 + b^2 = c^2$ and forms a right triangle, and conclude that the converse is true.

Lesson 20.2 **645**

Identifying a Right Triangle

The converse of the Pythagorean Theorem gives you a way to tell if a triangle is a right triangle when you know the side lengths.

EXAMPLE 1 FL CC 8.G.2.6

Tell whether each triangle with the given side lengths is a right triangle.

A 9 inches, 40 inches, and 41 inches

Let $a = 9$, $b = 40$, and $c = 41$.

$$a^2 + b^2 = c^2$$
$$9^2 + 40^2 \stackrel{?}{=} 41^2 \qquad \text{Substitute into the formula.}$$
$$81 + 1600 \stackrel{?}{=} 1681 \qquad \text{Simplify.}$$
$$1681 = 1681 \qquad \text{Add.}$$

Since $9^2 + 40^2 = 41^2$, the triangle is a right triangle by the converse of the Pythagorean Theorem.

B 8 meters, 10 meters, and 12 meters

Let $a = 8$, $b = 10$, and $c = 12$.

$$a^2 + b^2 = c^2$$
$$8^2 + 10^2 \stackrel{?}{=} 12^2 \qquad \text{Substitute into the formula.}$$
$$64 + 100 \stackrel{?}{=} 144 \qquad \text{Simpify.}$$
$$164 \neq 144 \qquad \text{Add.}$$

Since $8^2 + 10^2 \neq 12^2$, the triangle is not a right triangle by the converse of the Pythagorean Theorem.

YOUR TURN

Personal Math Trainer
Online Assessment and Intervention
my.hrw.com

Tell whether each triangle with the given side lengths is a right triangle.

2. 14 cm, 23 cm, and 25 cm
not a right triangle

3. 16 in., 30 in., and 34 in.
a right triangle

4. 27 ft, 36 ft, 45 ft
right triangle

5. 11 mm, 18 mm, 21 mm
not a right triangle

646 Unit 9

PROFESSIONAL DEVELOPMENT

Integrate Mathematical Practices MP.7.1

This lesson provides an opportunity to address this Mathematical Practices standard. It calls for students to look for structure. Students determine whether triangle side lengths fulfill the Pythagorean Theorem. In Example 2 and in many of the exercises, students determine whether triangles in real-world situations are right triangles.

Math Background

Previously, students learned that if a triangle is a right triangle, then $a^2 + b^2 = c^2$, where a, b, and c are side lengths and c is the longest side. In this lesson, students learn that the converse of this statement is also true. When a conditional statement and its converse are both true, then the two statements can be combined to form a *biconditional* statement. For the Pythagorean Theorem and its converse, the biconditional statement can be stated this way: a triangle is a right triangle if and only if $a^2 + b^2 = c^2$, where a, b, and c are side lengths and c is the longest side.

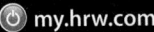
EXAMPLE 2

Questioning Strategies Mathematical Practices

• If the shortest edges of the garden must be 10 feet and 7 feet and the shape must be a right triangle, how long will the longest side be? 12.2 ft

• If the longest side of the garden must be 13 feet and the shape must be a right triangle, what are possible lengths for the other two sides? Sample answer: 5 ft and 12 ft

Engage with the Whiteboard

Have students sketch the triangle described in Example 2 in the margin of the page and then label the sides with the side lengths. Finally, label the sides a, b, and c.

YOUR TURN

Focus on Technology Mathematical Practices

Use geometry software to create the triangles in Exercises 6 and 7. Use the measurement tools of the software to find out if the triangle has an angle of 90°.

Elaborate

Talk About It
Summarize the Lesson

Ask: How can you use the converse of the Pythagorean Theorem to classify a triangle as a right triangle or not a right triangle? Find the sum of the squares of the two shortest sides of a triangle. If the sum is equal to the square of the longest side, the triangle must be a right triangle. Otherwise, it is not.

GUIDED PRACTICE

Engage with the Whiteboard

Have students sketch the triangles described in Exercises 2–3 in the margin and then label the sides with the side lengths. Then have them label the sides a, b, and c.

Avoid Common Errors

Exercises 1–3 Remind students to let c be the length of the longest side of the triangle. Also remind students to square the side lengths before adding.

Using the Converse of the Pythagorean Theorem

You can use the converse of the Pythagorean Theorem to solve real-world problems.

Math On the Spot
© my.hrw.com

EXAMPLE 2 (Real World)

FL CC 8.G.2.6

Katya is buying edging for a triangular flower garden she plans to build in her backyard. If the lengths of the three pieces of edging that she purchases are 13 feet, 10 feet, and 7 feet, will the flower garden be in the shape of a right triangle?

Use the converse of the Pythagorean Theorem. Remember to use the longest length for c.

Let $a = 7$, $b = 10$, and $c = 13$.

$a^2 + b^2 = c^2$

$7^2 + 10^2 \stackrel{?}{=} 13^2$ Substitute into the formula.

$49 + 100 \stackrel{?}{=} 169$ Simpify.

$149 \neq 169$ Add.

Since $7^2 + 10^2 \neq 13^2$, the garden will not be in the shape of a right triangle.

Math Talk
Mathematical Practices

To what length, to the nearest tenth, can Katya trim the longest piece of edging to form a right triangle?

approximately 12.2 feet

YOUR TURN

6. A blueprint for a new triangular playground shows that the sides measure 480 ft, 140 ft, and 500 ft. Is the playground in the shape of a right triangle? Explain.

Yes; $140^2 + 480^2 = 250{,}000$; $500^2 = 250{,}000$;

$250{,}000 = 250{,}000$

7. A triangular piece of glass has sides that measure 18 in., 19 in., and 25 in. Is the piece of glass in the shape of a right triangle? Explain.

No; $18^2 + 19^2 = 685$, $25^2 = 625$, $685 \neq 625$

8. A corner of a fenced yard forms a right angle. Can you place a 12 foot long board across the corner to form a right triangle for which the leg lengths are whole numbers? Explain.

No; there are no pairs of whole numbers whose

squares add to $12^2 = 144$.

Personal Math Trainer
Online Assessment and Intervention
© my.hrw.com

Guided Practice

1. Lashandra used grid paper to construct the triangle shown. (Explore Activity)

   a. What are the lengths of the sides of Lashandra's triangle?

      6 units,   8 units,   10 units

   b. Use the converse of the Pythagorean Theorem to determine whether the triangle is a right triangle.

   $a^2 + b^2 = c^2$

   $\boxed{6}^2 + \boxed{8}^2 \stackrel{?}{=} \boxed{10}^2$

   $\boxed{36} + \boxed{64} \stackrel{?}{=} \boxed{100}$

   $\boxed{100} \stackrel{?}{=} \boxed{100}$

   The triangle that Lashandra constructed **(is)/ is not** a right triangle.

2. A triangle has side lengths 9 cm, 12 cm, and 16 cm. Tell whether the triangle is a right triangle. (Example 1)

   Let $a = $ ___9___, $b = $ ___12___, and $c = $ ___16___.

   $a^2 + b^2 = c^2$

   $\boxed{9}^2 + \boxed{12}^2 \stackrel{?}{=} \boxed{16}^2$

   $\boxed{81} + \boxed{144} \stackrel{?}{=} \boxed{256}$

   $\boxed{225} \stackrel{?}{=} \boxed{256}$

   By the converse of the Pythagorean Theorem, the triangle **is /(is not)** a right triangle.

3. The marketing team at a new electronics company is designing a logo that contains a circle and a triangle. On one design, the triangle's side lengths are 2.5 in., 6 in., and 6.5 in. Is the triangle a right triangle? Explain. (Example 2)

   Yes; $2.5^2 + 6^2 = 42.25$, $6.5^2 = 42.25$, $42.25 = 42.25$

 **ESSENTIAL QUESTION CHECK-IN**

4. How can you use the converse of the Pythagorean Theorem to tell if a triangle is a right triangle?

   Test the side lengths in $a^2 + b^2 = c^2$, using the longest side for c.

   If the equation is true, the triangle is a right triangle. Otherwise, it isn't.

DIFFERENTIATE INSTRUCTION

Cooperative Learning

Have pairs of students create one real-world problem that can be solved using the Pythagorean Theorem and one real-world problem that can be solved using the converse of the Pythagorean Theorem. Have students find and justify their solutions.

Manipulatives

Have students make two triangles on a geometry board, one that is a right triangle and one that is not a right triangle. Then have them measure the lengths of the sides of each triangle to the nearest millimeter. Ask them to use the converse of the Pythagorean Theorem to verify that the right triangle is indeed a right triangle and the other triangle is not a right triangle. (Because the measurements are approximate, for the right triangle, $a^2 + b^2$ and c^2 may be close but not exactly the same.)

Additional Resources

Differentiated Instruction includes:

- Reading Strategies
- Success for English Learners **ELL**
- Reteach
- Challenge **PRE-AP**

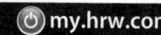
20.2 LESSON QUIZ

FL CC 8.G.2.6

Tell whether each triangle with the given side lengths is a right triangle.

1. 36 cm, 48 cm, 60 cm

2. 12 ft, 35 ft, 37 ft

3. 60.5 ft, 63 ft, 87.5 ft

4. A club at school designed a banner consisting of two congruent triangles surrounded by stripes. The lengths of the sides of each of the triangles were 1.5 feet, 2.0 feet, and 2.5 feet. Are the triangles right triangles? Explain.

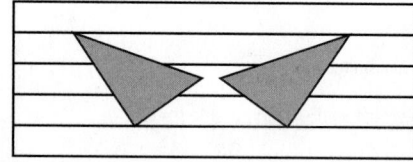

Lesson Quiz available online

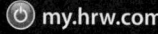
Answers

1. right triangle

2. right triangle

3. not a right triangle

4. Yes; $1.5^2 + 2.0^2 = 6.25 = 2.5^2$

Evaluate

GUIDED AND INDEPENDENT PRACTICE

FL CC 8.G.2.6

Concepts & Skills	Practice
Explore Activity Testing the Converse of the Pythagorean Theorem	Exercise 1
Example 1 Identifying a Right Triangle	Exercises 2, 5–14
Example 2 Using the Converse of the Pythagorean Theorem	Exercises 3, 15–17

Exercise	Depth of Knowledge (D.O.K.)	**FL CC** Mathematical Practices
5–14	**2** Skills/Concepts	**MP.5.1** Using Tools
15–17	**2** Skills/Concepts	**MP.4.1** Modeling
18–19	**3** Strategic Thinking **H.O.T.**	**MP.2.1** Reasoning
20–21	**3** Strategic Thinking **H.O.T.**	**MP.3.1** Logic
22	**3** Strategic Thinking **H.O.T.**	**MP.2.1** Reasoning
23	**3** Strategic Thinking **H.O.T.**	**MP.6.1** Precision

Additional Resources

Differentiated Instruction includes:

• Leveled Practice worksheets

20.2 Independent Practice

FL CC 8.G.2.6

Personal Math Trainer

Online Assessment and Intervention

my.hrw.com

Tell whether each triangle with the given side lengths is a right triangle.

5. 11 cm, 60 cm, 61 cm
right triangle

6. 5 ft, 12 ft, 15 ft
not a right triangle

7. 9 in., 15 in., 17 in.
not a right triangle

8. 15 m, 36 m, 39 m
right triangle

9. 20 mm, 30 mm, 40 mm
not a right triangle

10. 20 cm, 48 cm, 52 cm
right triangle

11. 18.5 ft, 6 ft, 17.5 ft
right triangle

12. 2 mi, 1.5 mi, 2.5 mi
right triangle

13. 35 in., 45 in., 55 in.
not a right triangle

14. 25 cm, 14 cm, 23 cm
not a right triangle

15. The emblem on a college banner consists of the face of a tiger inside a triangle. The lengths of the sides of the triangle are 13 cm, 14 cm, and 15 cm. Is the triangle a right triangle? Explain.
No; $13^2 + 14^2 = 365$, $15^2 = 225$, and $365 \neq 225$.

16. Kerry has a large triangular piece of fabric that she wants to attach to the ceiling in her bedroom. The sides of the piece of fabric measure 4.8 ft, 6.4 ft, and 8 ft. Is the fabric in the shape of a right triangle? Explain.
Yes; $4.8^2 + 6.4^2 = 64$, and $8^2 = 64$.

17. A mosaic consists of triangular tiles. The smallest tiles have side lengths 6 cm, 10 cm, and 12 cm. Are these tiles in the shape of right triangles? Explain.
No; $6^2 + 10^2 = 136$, $12^2 = 144$, and $136 \neq 144$.

18. **History** In ancient Egypt, surveyors made right angles by stretching a rope with evenly spaced knots as shown. Explain why the rope forms a right angle.
Sample answer: The knots are evenly spaced, so the side lengths are 3 units, 4 units, and 5 units. Since $3^2 + 4^2 = 5^2$, the sides form a right triangle.

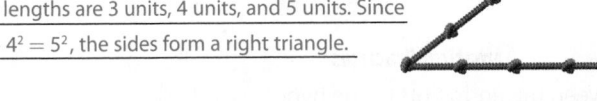

19. **Justify Reasoning** Yoshi has two identical triangular boards as shown. Can he use these two boards to form a rectangle? Explain.
Yes; since $0.75^2 + 1^2 = 1.25^2$, the triangles are right triangles. Adjoining them at their hypotenuses will form a rectangle with sides 1 m and 0.75 m.

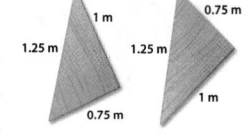

20. **Critique Reasoning** Shoshanna says that a triangle with side lengths 17 m, 8 m, and 15 m is not a right triangle because $17^2 + 8^2 = 353$, $15^2 = 225$, and $353 \neq 225$. Is she correct? Explain.
No, she did not use the longest length for c.
$8^2 + 15^2 = 17^2$, so it is a right triangle.

H.O.T. FOCUS ON HIGHER ORDER THINKING

21. **Make a Conjecture** Diondre says that he can take any right triangle and make a new right triangle just by doubling the side lengths. Is Diondre's conjecture true? Test his conjecture using three different right triangles.
Yes. His conjecture is true. Students' work will vary but should show that they've used the converse of the Pythagorean Theorem to test whether the new triangles are right triangles.

22. **Draw Conclusions** A diagonal of a parallelogram measures 37 inches. The sides measure 35 inches and 1 foot. Is the parallelogram a rectangle? Explain your reasoning.
Yes; 1 ft = 12 in. Since $12^2 + 35^2 = 37^2$, each half of the parallelogram is a right triangle. Therefore, the sides of the parallelogram meet at right angles, making the parallelogram a rectangle.

23. **Represent Real-World Problems** A soccer coach is marking the lines for a soccer field on a large recreation field. The dimensions of the field are to be 90 yards by 48 yards. Describe a procedure she could use to confirm that the sides of the field meet at right angles.
She could measure the diagonal of the field to see if the sides of the field and the diagonal form a right triangle. The diagonal should measure 102 yards if the sides of the field meet at right angles.

Work Area

EXTEND THE MATH PRE-AP

Activity available online my.hrw.com

Activity Draw three different acute triangles (triangles with all three angles less than 90°) and three different obtuse triangles (triangles with one angle greater than 90°). Label the longest side of each triangle c and the other two sides a and b. Measure each side of each triangle to the nearest millimeter and record the results in a table like the one shown here. Calculate a^2, b^2, and c^2 for each triangle. Compare c^2 to $a^2 + b^2$ for each triangle. Make a conjecture about the type of triangle that has $a^2 + b^2 > c^2$ and about the type of triangle that has $a^2 + b^2 < c^2$. Use your conjecture to predict whether a triangle with side lengths 12 cm, 60 cm, and 61 cm is acute, right, or obtuse.

Type of triangle	a	b	$a^2 + b^2$	c	c^2	$a^2 + b^2$ greater than or less than c^2
acute						
acute						
acute						
obtuse						
obtuse						
obtuse						

If the triangle is acute, then $a^2 + b^2 > c^2$. If the triangle is obtuse, then $a^2 + b^2 < c^2$; acute

20.3 Distance Between Two Points

 Florida Common Core Standards

The student is expected to:

 **Geometry—8.G.2.8**

Apply the Pythagorean Theorem to find the distance between two points in a coordinate system.

Mathematical Practices

 **MP.2.1** Reasoning

Engage

ESSENTIAL QUESTION

How can you use the Pythagorean Theorem to find the distance between two points on a coordinate plane? Sample answer: Draw a segment connecting the two points and a right triangle with that segment as the hypotenuse. Then use the Pythagorean Theorem to find the length of the hypotenuse.

Motivate the Lesson

Ask: How would you verify, without measuring, that three points on a coordinate plane form a right triangle? Take a guess.

Explore

To find the slope of a line on a coordinate plane, you can draw a horizontal line to represent the run and a vertical line to represent the rise. These two lines and the original line form a right triangle. Can you use the Pythagorean Theorem to find the distance between the two points on the hypotenuse? See also Explore Activity in student text.

Explain

EXAMPLE 1

Questioning Strategies Mathematical Practices

- What is the rise and run between the endpoints of the hypotenuse? rise = 4; run = 2
- What is the slope of the line segment that is the hypotenuse? 2

Focus on Math Connections Mathematical Practices

Remind students that they were drawing right triangles on the coordinate plane when they drew lines representing the rise and run between two points. Point out that the legs of the right triangle represent the rise and run between the endpoints of the hypotenuse.

YOUR TURN

Engage with the Whiteboard

Label the lengths of the legs. Label one leg *a* and the other leg *b* before substituting the values into the Pythagorean Theorem.

EXPLORE ACTIVITY

Questioning Strategies Mathematical Practices

- In the Distance Formula, what does $x_2 - x_1$ represent? the length of the horizontal leg
- The variable *c* in the Pythagorean Theorem is represented by what variable in the Distance Formula? *d*

Focus on Math Connections Mathematical Practices

Point out to students that finding the length of the hypotenuse of a right triangle is the same as finding the distance between the endpoints of the hypotenuse in the coordinate plane.

ADDITIONAL EXAMPLE 1

The figure shows a right triangle. Approximate the length of the hypotenuse to the nearest tenth without using a calculator. about 5.5 units

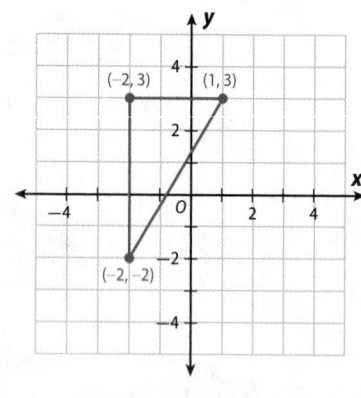

Interactive Whiteboard
Interactive example available online

ⓒ my.hrw.com

LESSON 20.3 Distance Between Two Points

FL CC 8.G.2.8
Apply the Pythagorean Theorem to find the distance between two points in a coordinate system.

ESSENTIAL QUESTION How can you use the Pythagorean Theorem to find the distance between two points on a coordinate plane?

Pythagorean Theorem in the Coordinate Plane

EXAMPLE 1

FL CC 8.G.2.8

Math On the Spot
my.hrw.com

The figure shows a right triangle. Approximate the length of the hypotenuse to the nearest tenth without using a calculator.

STEP 1 Find the length of each leg.

The length of the vertical leg is 4 units.

The length of the horizontal leg is 2 units.

STEP 2 Let $a = 4$ and $b = 2$. Let c represent the length of the hypotenuse. Use the Pythagorean Theorem to find c.

$$a^2 + b^2 = c^2$$

$$4^2 + 2^2 = c^2 \quad \text{Substitute into the formula.}$$

$$20 = c^2 \quad \text{Add.}$$

$$\sqrt{20} = c \quad \text{Take the square root of both sides.}$$

STEP 3 Approximate $\sqrt{20}$ by finding perfect squares close to 20.

$\sqrt{20}$ is between $\sqrt{16}$ and $\sqrt{25}$, or $\sqrt{16} < \sqrt{20} < \sqrt{25}$.

Simplifying gives $4 < \sqrt{20} < 5$.

Since 20 is about halfway between 16 and 25, $\sqrt{20}$ is about halfway between 4 and 5. So, $\sqrt{20} \approx 4.5$.

The hypotenuse is about 4.5 units long.

YOUR TURN

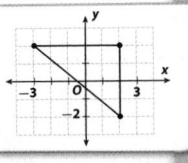

1. Approximate the length of the hypotenuse to the nearest tenth without using a calculator.

   6.5 units

Personal Math Trainer
Online Assessment and Intervention
my.hrw.com

© Houghton Mifflin Harcourt Publishing Company

EXPLORE ACTIVITY

FL CC 8.G.2.8

Finding the Distance Between Any Two Points

The Pythagorean Theorem can be used to find the distance between any two points (x_1, y_1) and (x_2, y_2) in the coordinate plane. The resulting expression is called the Distance Formula.

> **Distance Formula**
>
> In a coordinate plane, the distance d between two points (x_1, y_1) and (x_2, y_2) is
>
> $$d = \sqrt{(x_2 - x_1)^2 + (y_2 - y_1)^2}.$$

Use the Pythagorean Theorem to derive the Distance Formula.

A To find the distance between points P and Q, draw segment $\overline{PQ}$ and label its length d. Then draw horizontal segment $\overline{PR}$ and vertical segment $\overline{QR}$. Label the lengths of these segments a and b. Triangle PQR is a ___right___ triangle, with hypotenuse ___$\overline{PQ}$___.

B Since $\overline{PR}$ is a horizontal segment, its length, a, is the difference between its x-coordinates. Therefore, $a = x_2 - $ ___x_1___.

C Since $\overline{QR}$ is a vertical segment, its length, b, is the difference between its y-coordinates. Therefore, $b = y_2 - $ ___y_1___.

D Use the Pythagorean Theorem to find d, the length of segment $\overline{PQ}$. Substitute the expressions from **B** and **C** for a and b.

$$d^2 = a^2 + b^2$$

$$d = \sqrt{a^2 + b^2}$$

$$d = \sqrt{\left(x_2 - x_1\right)^2 + \left(y_2 - y_1\right)^2}$$

Math Talk
Mathematical Practices

What do $x_2 - x_1$ and $y_2 - y_1$ represent in terms of the Pythagorean Theorem?

They represent the lengths of the legs of the right triangle formed by P, Q, and R.

Reflect

2. Why are the coordinates of point R the ordered pair (x_2, y_1)?

   Since R lies on the same vertical line as Q, their x-coordinates are the same. Since R lies on the same horizontal line as P, their y-coordinates are the same.

PROFESSIONAL DEVELOPMENT

Integrate Mathematical Practices MP.2.1

This lesson provides an opportunity to address this Mathematical Practices standard. It calls for students to reason abstractly and quantitatively. Students connect the Pythagorean Theorem with finding the distance between two points in the coordinate plane and then derive the Distance Formula.

Math Background

The Distance Formula presented here is an application of the Pythagorean Theorem in two-dimensional space. In Lesson 8.1, the Pythagorean Theorem was used in two sequential operations to find the distance between opposite corners of a box of known length, width, and height. Points on a box or rectangular prism can be represented in a three-dimensional coordinate space using the (x, y, z) coordinate system. The distance between two points in three-dimensional space can be found by extending the Distance Formula to the (x, y, z) system:

$$d = \sqrt{(x_2 - x_1)^2 + (y_2 - y_1)^2 + (z_2 - z_1)^2}$$

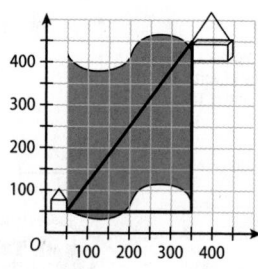
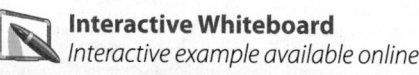
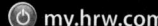
EXAMPLE 2

Questioning Strategies Mathematical Practices

• Why is $|280 - 10| = 270$? because the absolute value of a positive number is the number itself

• What would you get if you found $|10 - 280|$? Is it the same as $|280 - 10|$? Explain. 270; yes; because the absolute value of a negative number is the additive inverse (opposite) of the number.

Avoid Common Errors

The absolute value of the difference between coordinates is used here to emphasize that the length of a segment, or the distance between two points, is a positive number. If students subtract the larger coordinate from the smaller coordinate they may be confused by the negative number. Tell students to use the absolute value of the difference.

Integrating Language Arts ELL

Encourage a broad class discussion on the Math Talk. English learners will benefit from hearing and participating in classroom discussions.

YOUR TURN

Connect to Daily Life

Discuss with students why in real life the distance across the lake might be more easily calculated from the length of the legs of the triangle instead of directly. The distance over land can be measured with an odometer or a GPS device, or estimated by counting steps and measuring the length of a step. Only a GPS device could be used while crossing the lake, and only if a boat is available. Remind students that they have already learned another method to measure the length of inaccessible areas using similar triangles.

Elaborate

Talk About It
Summarize the Lesson

Ask: What are two ways you can find the distance between points (x_1, y_1) and (x_2, y_2) in the coordinate plane? Draw a segment connecting the two points and complete a right triangle with the segment as the hypotenuse. Then find the lengths of the sides of the triangle and use the Pythagorean Theorem to find the length of the hypotenuse. You can also find the distance between the two points directly by using the Distance Formula.

GUIDED PRACTICE

Engage with the Whiteboard

Sketch a graph for Exercise 2. Label the points, and then add vertical and horizontal segments that connect at (15, 7). Label the legs of the triangle with their length (horizontal leg is 12 units long; vertical leg is 5 units long).

Avoid Common Errors

Exercise 2 Watch for students who confuse the x- and y-coordinates. Have them write (x_1, y_1) and (x_2, y_2) over the given coordinates to help them substitute the correct values into the Distance Formula.

Exercise 3 Some students may be unsure what is meant by north and east. Help them to interpret the diagram.

Finding the Distance Between Two Points

The Pythagorean Theorem can be used to find the distance between two points in a real-world situation. You can do this by using a coordinate grid that overlays a diagram of the real-world situation.

Math On the Spot
my.hrw.com

EXAMPLE 2   Real World   FL CC 8.G.2.8

Francesca wants to find the distance between her house on one side of a lake and the beach on the other side. She marks off a third point forming a right triangle, as shown. The distances in the diagram are measured in meters.

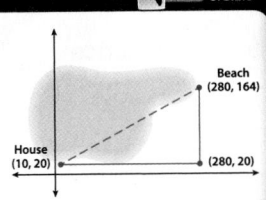

Use the Pythagorean Theorem to find the straight-line distance from Francesca's house to the beach.

STEP 1 Find the length of the horizontal leg.

The length of the horizontal leg is the absolute value of the difference between the x-coordinates of the points (280, 20) and (10, 20).

$$|280 - 10| = 270$$

The length of the horizontal leg is 270 meters.

STEP 2 Find the length of the vertical leg.

The length of the vertical leg is the absolute value of the difference between the y-coordinates of the points (280, 164) and (280, 20).

$$|164 - 20| = 144$$

The length of the vertical leg is 144 meters.

STEP 3 Let $a = 270$ and $b = 144$. Let c represent the length of the hypotenuse. Use the Pythagorean Theorem to find c.

$$a^2 + b^2 = c^2$$
$$270^2 + 144^2 = c^2 \quad \text{Substitute into the formula.}$$
$$72{,}900 + 20{,}736 = c^2 \quad \text{Simplify.}$$
$$93{,}636 = c^2 \quad \text{Add.}$$
$$\sqrt{93{,}636} = c \quad \text{Take the square root of both sides.}$$
$$306 = c \quad \text{Simplify.}$$

The distance from Francesca's house to the beach is 306 meters.

Math Talk
Mathematical Practices

Why is it necessary to take the absolute value of the coordinates when finding the length of a segment?

Sample answer: You take the absolute value because the length of a segment cannot be a negative number.

Reflect

3. Show how you could use the Distance Formula to find the distance from Francesca's house to the beach.

Let $(x_1, y_1) = (10, 20)$ and $(x_2, y_2) = (280, 164)$.

$$d = \sqrt{(280 - 10)^2 + (164 - 20)^2} = \sqrt{(270)^2 + (144)^2}$$
$$d = \sqrt{72{,}900 + 20{,}736} = \sqrt{93{,}636} = 306$$

Personal Math Trainer
Online Assessment and Intervention
my.hrw.com

YOUR TURN

4. Camp Sunshine is also on the lake. Use the Pythagorean Theorem to find the distance between Francesca's house and Camp Sunshine to the nearest tenth of a meter.

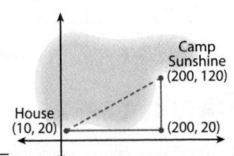

approximately 214.7 meters

Guided Practice

1. Approximate the length of the hypotenuse of the right triangle to the nearest tenth without using a calculator. (Example 1)   5.8 units

2. Find the distance between the points (3, 7) and (15, 12) on the coordinate plane. (Explore Activity)   13 units

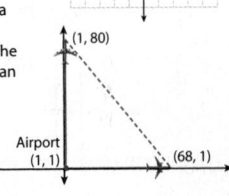

3. A plane leaves an airport and flies due north. Two minutes later, a second plane leaves the same airport flying due east. The flight plan shows the coordinates of the two planes 10 minutes later. The distances in the graph are measured in miles. Use the Pythagorean Theorem to find the distance shown between the two planes.

(Example 2)   103.6 miles

? ESSENTIAL QUESTION CHECK-IN

4. Describe two ways to find the distance between two points on a coordinate plane.

Sample answer: Draw a right triangle whose hypotenuse is the segment connecting the two points and then use the Pythagorean Theorem to find the length of that segment, or use the Distance Formula.

DIFFERENTIATE INSTRUCTION

Visual Cues

Show students how two points that do not form a vertical segment or a horizontal segment on the coordinate plane form a right triangle with a third point. Then lead them through the derivation of the Distance Formula using the points (x_1, y_1) and (x_2, y_2) as the endpoints of a nonvertical, nonhorizontal segment.

Cooperative Learning

Have groups of students graph various nonvertical, nonhorizontal segments in the coordinate plane. Have some students in the group find the length of each segment using the Pythagorean Theorem and other students find the length of the same segments using the Distance Formula. Ask them to compare and contrast their methods and solutions.

Additional Resources

Differentiated Instruction includes:

• Reading Strategies
• Success for English Learners **ELL**
• Reteach
• Challenge **PRE-AP**

20.3 LESSON QUIZ

 **FL CC** 8.G.2.8

1. Approximate the length of the hypotenuse of the right triangle to the nearest tenth of a unit.

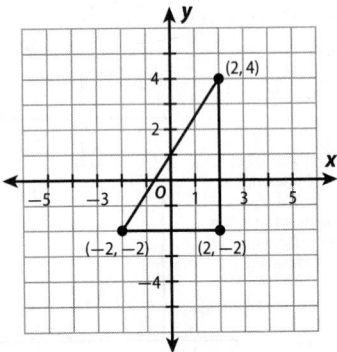

2. Find the distance between points (1, 3) and (9, 18) on the coordinate plane.

3. The coordinates of the vertices of a rectangle are $A(-4, 2)$, $B(2, 2)$, $C(2, -3)$, and $D(-4, -3)$. Plot these points on the coordinate plane and connect them to draw a rectangle. Connect points A and C. Find the exact length of the diagonal $\overline{AC}$.

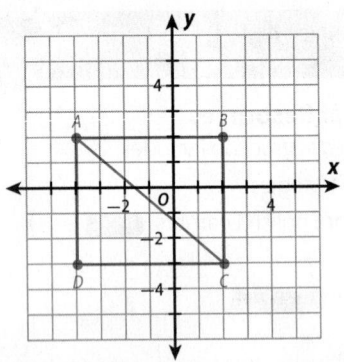

Lesson Quiz available online

⏻ my.hrw.com

Answers

1. 7.2 units

2. 17 units

3. $\sqrt{61}$ units

Evaluate

GUIDED AND INDEPENDENT PRACTICE

 **FL CC** 8.G.2.8

Concepts & Skills	Practice
Example 1 Pythagorean Theorem in the Coordinate Plane	Exercises 1, 5
Explore Activity Finding the Distance Between Any Two Points	Exercises 2, 7
Example 2 Finding the Distance Between Two Points	Exercises 3, 6, 7–8

Exercise	Depth of Knowledge (D.O.K.)	**FL CC** Mathematical Practices
5–6	**2** Skills/Concepts	**MP.4.1** Modeling
7	**2** Skills/Concepts	**MP.5.1** Using Tools
8	**2** Skills/Concepts	**MP.1.1** Problem Solving
9	**3** Strategic Thinking **H.O.T.**	**MP.8.1** Patterns
10	**2** Skills/Concepts	**MP.2.1** Reasoning
11	**3** Strategic Thinking **H.O.T.**	**MP.5.1** Using Tools
12	**3** Strategic Thinking **H.O.T.**	**MP.4.1** Modeling

Additional Resources

Differentiated Instruction includes:

• Leveled Practice worksheets

CLUSTER CONNECTION **Exercise 12** combines concepts from the Florida Common Core cluster "Understand and apply the Pythagorean Theorem."

20.3 Independent Practice

 FL CC 8.G.2.8

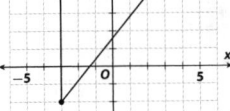
Personal Math Trainer

Online Assessment and Intervention

my.hrw.com

5. A metal worker traced a triangular piece of sheet metal on a coordinate plane, as shown. The units represent inches. What is the length of the longest side of the metal triangle? Approximate the length to the nearest tenth of an inch without using a calculator.

Accept any answer between 7.5 in. and 7.8 in.

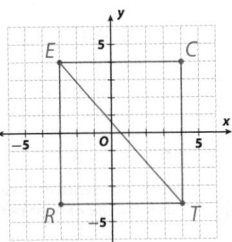

6. When a coordinate grid is superimposed on a map of Harrisburg, the high school is located at (17, 21) and the town park is located at (28, 13). If each unit represents 1 mile, how many miles apart are the high school and the town park? Round your answer to the nearest tenth.

13.6 miles

7. The coordinates of the vertices of a rectangle are given by $R(-3, -4)$, $E(-3, 4)$, $C(4, 4)$, and $T(4, -4)$. Plot these points on the coordinate plane at the right and connect them to draw the rectangle. Then connect points E and T to form diagonal $\overline{ET}$.

a. Use the Pythagorean Theorem to find the exact length of $\overline{ET}$.

$ET = \sqrt{113}$ units

b. How can you use the Distance Formula to find the length of $\overline{ET}$? Show that the Distance Formula gives the same answer.

Let $(x_1, y_1) = (-3, 4)$ and $(x_2, y_2) = (4, -4)$ and then substitute the coordinates into the Distance Formula.

$d = \sqrt{(x_2 - x_1)^2 + (y_2 - y_1)^2}$

$d = \sqrt{(4 - (-3))^2 + (-4 - 4)^2}$

$d = \sqrt{(7)^2 + (-8)^2} = \sqrt{49 + 64} = \sqrt{113}$

8. **Multistep** The locations of three ships are represented on a coordinate grid by the following points: $P(-2, 5)$, $Q(-7, -5)$, and $R(2, -3)$. Which ships are farthest apart?

the ships at points P and Q

9. **Make a Conjecture** Find as many points as you can that are 5 units from the origin. Make a conjecture about the shape formed if all the points 5 units from the origin were connected.

$(5, 0), (4, 3), (3, 4), (0, 5), (-3, 4), (-4, 3), (-5, 0), (-4, -3),$ $(-3, -4), (0, -5), (3, -4), (4, -3);$ The points would form a circle.

10. **Justify Reasoning** The graph shows the location of a motion detector that has a maximum range of 34 feet. A peacock at point P displays its tail feathers. Will the motion detector sense this motion? Explain.

Yes; the distance from the motion detector to the peacock is $\sqrt{30^2 + 15^2} \approx 33.5$ ft, which is less than 34 ft.

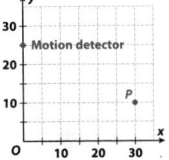

H.O.T. FOCUS ON HIGHER ORDER THINKING

Work Area

11. **Persevere in Problem Solving** One leg of an isosceles right triangle has endpoints (1, 1) and (6, 1). The other leg passes through the point (6, 2). Draw the triangle on the coordinate plane. Then show how you can use the Distance Formula to find the length of the hypotenuse. Round your answer to the nearest tenth.

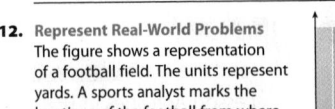

Let $(x_1, y_1) = (6, 6)$, and $(x_2, y_2) = (1, 1)$.

$d = \sqrt{(x_2 - x_1)^2 + (y_2 - y_1)^2} = \sqrt{(6 - 1)^2 + (6 - 1)^2}$

$d = \sqrt{(5)^2 + (5)^2} = \sqrt{25 + 25} = \sqrt{50}; d \approx 7.1$

12. **Represent Real-World Problems** The figure shows a representation of a football field. The units represent yards. A sports analyst marks the locations of the football from where it was thrown (point A) and where it was caught (point B). Explain how you can use the Pythagorean Theorem to find the distance the ball was thrown. Then find the distance.

A (40, 26) $\quad$ B (75, 14)

Create a right triangle with hypotenuse $\overline{AB}$. The vertex at the right angle is either (40, 14) or (75, 26), and the lengths of the legs of the triangle are 12 yards and 35 yards. The distance between A and B is about 37 yards.

EXTEND THE MATH PRE-AP

Activity available online my.hrw.com

Activity Draw and label a line segment from $A(0, 0)$ to $B(1, 1)$. Use the Pythagorean Theorem to find the length of $\overline{AB}$. Use a protractor with the compass point on A and the opening of the compass set to $\overline{AB}$. With the point of the compass on A, rotate the pencil point from B to a point on the x-axis. Label the point C. What are the exact coordinates of C? What is the length of $\overline{AC}$? What kind of number did you graph?

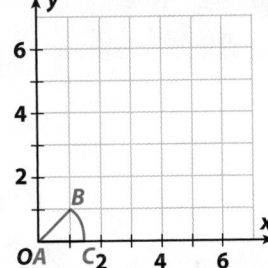

$AB = \sqrt{2}; C = (\sqrt{2}, 0); AC = \sqrt{2};$ irrational number

Ready to Go On?

....

Assess Mastery

Use the assessment on this page to determine if students have mastered the concepts and standards covered in this module.

 **RtI** ### Response to Intervention

Personal Math Trainer

Online Assessment and Intervention

⏻ my.hrw.com

Intervention	Enrichment

Access Ready to Go On? assessment online, and receive instant scoring, feedback, and customized intervention or enrichment.

Online and Print Resources

Differentiated Instruction
• Reteach worksheets
• Reading Strategies **ELL**
• Success for English Learners **ELL**

Differentiated Instruction
• Challenge worksheets **PRE-AP**
Extend the Math **PRE-AP** Lesson Activities in TE

Additional Resources

Assessment Resources includes
• Leveled Module Quizzes

Ready to Go On?

Personal Math Trainer

Online Assessment and Intervention

⏻ my.hrw.com

20.1 The Pythagorean Theorem

Find the length of the missing side.

1.

35 m

21 m

_____28 m_____

2.

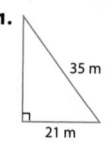

16 ft

30 ft

_____34 ft_____

20.2 Converse of the Pythagorean Theorem

Tell whether each triangle with the given side lengths is a right triangle.

3. 11, 60, 61 ____yes____

4. 9, 37, 40 ____no____

5. 15, 35, 38 ____no____

6. 28, 45, 53 ____yes____

7. Keelie has a triangular-shaped card. The lengths of its sides are 4.5 cm, 6 cm, and 7.5 cm. Is the card a right triangle? ____yes____

20.3 Distance Between Two Points

Find the distance between the given points. Round to the nearest tenth.

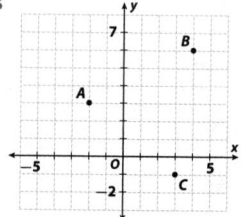

8. A and B ____6.7____

9. B and C ____7.1____

10. A and C ____6.4____

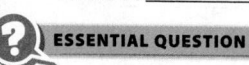 **ESSENTIAL QUESTION**

11. How can you use the Pythagorean Theorem to solve real-world problems?

Sample answer: You can use the Pythagorean Theorem to find missing lengths in objects that are right triangles.

Module 20 **657**

 ## Florida Common Core Standards

Lesson	Exercises	Common Core Standards
20.1	1–2	**8.G.2.6, 8.G.2.7**
20.2	3–7	**8.G.2.6**
20.3	8–10	**8.G.2.8**

PARCC Assessment Readiness

Assessment Readiness Tip Quickly sketching the problem situation can help students to organize information and solve correctly.

Item 3 Sketching the triangle and labeling the sides *a*, *b*, and *c* can help students to correctly use the Pythagorean Theorem to find the answer.

Item 5 Drawing a sketch of the flagpole, rope, and ground and labeling it with the given measurements can help students to see that they are finding the hypotenuse of a right triangle.

Avoid Common Errors

Item 4 Remind students to use the Distance Formula to find the distance between two points. Some students may try to count the boxes between *F* and *G*. Remind them that counting the boxes only works when a line is horizontal or vertical. If it is angled in any way, the Distance Formula must be used.

Additional Resources

Personal Math Trainer

Online Assessment and Intervention

my.hrw.com

 MODULE 20 MIXED REVIEW
PARCC Assessment Readiness

 Personal Math Trainer
Online Assessment and Intervention
my.hrw.com

Selected Response

1. What is the missing length of the side?

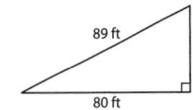
89 ft
80 ft

- Ⓐ 9 ft
- Ⓒ 39 ft
- Ⓑ 30 ft
- Ⓓ 120 ft

2. Which relation does **not** represent a function?

- Ⓐ (0, 8), (3, 8), (1, 6)
- Ⓑ (4, 2), (6, 1), (8, 9)
- Ⓒ (1, 20), (2, 23), (9, 26)
- Ⓓ (0, 3), (2, 3), (2, 0)

3. Two sides of a right triangle have lengths of 72 cm and 97 cm. The third side is **not** the hypotenuse. How long is the third side?

- Ⓐ 25 cm
- Ⓒ 65 cm
- Ⓑ 45 cm
- Ⓓ 121 cm

4. To the nearest tenth, what is the distance between point *F* and point *G*?

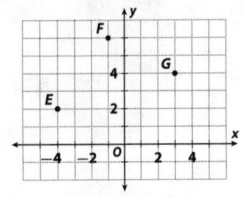

- Ⓐ 4.5 units
- Ⓒ 7.3 units
- Ⓑ 5.0 units
- Ⓓ 20 units

5. A flagpole is 53 feet tall. A rope is tied to the top of the flagpole and secured to the ground 28 feet from the base of the flagpole. What is the length of the rope?

- Ⓐ 25 feet
- Ⓒ 53 feet
- Ⓑ 45 feet
- Ⓓ 60 feet

6. Which set of lengths are **not** the side lengths of a right triangle?

- Ⓐ 36, 77, 85
- Ⓒ 27, 120, 123
- Ⓑ 20, 99, 101
- Ⓓ 24, 33, 42

7. A triangle has one right angle. What could the measures of the other two angles be?

- Ⓐ 25° and 65°
- Ⓒ 55° and 125°
- Ⓑ 30° and 15°
- Ⓓ 90° and 100°

Mini-Task

8. A fallen tree is shown on the coordinate grid below. Each unit represents 1 meter.

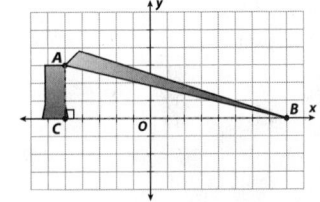

a. What is the distance from *A* to *B*?

13.3 meters

b. What was the height of the tree before it fell?

16.3 meters

© Houghton Mifflin Harcourt Publishing Company

Florida Common Core Standards

Items	Grade 8 Standards	Mathematical Practices
1	8.G.2.7	MP.4.1
2*	8.F.1.1	MP.6.1
3	8.G.2.7	MP.2.1
4	8.G.2.8	MP.2.1
5	8.G.2.7	MP.4.1
6	8.G.2.7	MP.4.1
7*	8.G.1.5	MP.2.1
8	8.G.2.7, 8.G.2.8	MP.4.1

* Item integrates mixed review concepts from previous modules or a previous course.

Volume

COMMON CORE

? ESSENTIAL QUESTION

How can you use volume to solve real-world problems?

You can use formulas to find the volumes of real-world objects shaped like cylinders, cones, and spheres.

© Houghton Mifflin Harcourt Publishing Company

Real-World Video

Many foods are in the shape of cylinders, cones, and spheres. To find out how much of the food you are eating, you can use formulas for volume.

⏻ my.hrw.com

GO DIGITAL

my.hrw.com

my.hrw.com
Go digital with your write-in student edition, accessible on any device.

Math On the Spot
Scan with your smart phone to jump directly to the online edition, video tutor, and more.

Animated Math
Interactively explore key concepts to see how math works.

Personal Math Trainer
Get immediate feedback and help as you work through practice sets.

Are You Ready?

Assess Readiness

Use the assessment on this page to determine if students need intensive or strategic intervention for the module's prerequisite skills.

 **Response to Intervention**

Intervention	Enrichment

Personal Math Trainer
Online Assessment and Intervention
my.hrw.com

Access Are You Ready? assessment online, and receive instant scoring, feedback, and customized intervention or enrichment.

Online and Print Resources

Skills Intervention worksheets
- Skill 12 Exponents
- Skill 16 Round Decimals
- Skill 52 Simplify Numerical Expressions

Differentiated Instruction
- Challenge worksheets **PRE-AP**
- Extend the Math **PRE-AP** Lesson Activities in TE

Are YOU Ready?

Complete these exercises to review skills you will need for this module.

 **Personal Math Trainer**
Online Assessment and Intervention
my.hrw.com

Exponents

EXAMPLE	$6^3 = 6 \times 6 \times 6$	Multiply the base (6) by itself the number of times indicated by the exponent (3).
	$= 36 \times 6$	Find the product of the first two terms.
	$= 216$	Find the product of all the terms.

Evaluate each exponential expression.

1. 11^2 __121__ 2. 2^5 __32__ 3. $\left(\frac{1}{5}\right)^3$ __$\frac{1}{125}$__ 4. $(0.3)^2$ __0.09__

5. 2.1^3 __9.261__ 6. 0.1^3 __0.001__ 7. $\left(\frac{9.6}{3}\right)^2$ __10.24__ 8. 100^3 __1,000,000__

Round Decimals

EXAMPLE	Round 43.2685 to the underlined place.	The digit to be rounded: 6
		The digit to its right is 8.
	$43.2685 \rightarrow 43.27$	8 is 5 or greater, so round up.
		The rounded number is 43.27.

Round to the underlined place.

9. 2.374 __2.37__ 10. 126.399 __126__ 11. 13.9577 __14.0__ 12. 42.690 __42.69__

13. 134.95 __135__ 14. 2.0486 __2.0__ 15. 63.6352 __63.64__ 16. 98.9499 __98.9__

Simplify Numerical Expressions

EXAMPLE	$\frac{1}{3}(3.14)(4)^2(3) = \frac{1}{3}(3.14)(16)(3)$	Simplify the exponent.
	$= 50.24$	Multiply from left to right.

Simplify each expression.

17. $3.14(5)^2(10)$ __785__ 18. $\frac{1}{3}(3.14)(3)^2(5)$ __47.1__ 19. $\frac{4}{3}(3.14)(3)^3$ __113.04__

20. $\frac{4}{3}(3.14)(6)^3$ __904.32__ 21. $3.14(4)^2(9)$ __452.16__ 22. $\frac{1}{3}(3.14)(9)^2\left(\frac{2}{3}\right)$ __56.52__

© Houghton Mifflin Harcourt Publishing Company

PROFESSIONAL DEVELOPMENT VIDEO

 Author Juli Dixon models successful teaching practices as she explores the concept of volume of curved-surface solids in an actual eighth-grade classroom.

 **Professional Development**
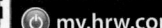 my.hrw.com

GO DIGITAL
my.hrw.com

 **Online Teacher Edition**
Access a full suite of teaching resources online—plan, present, and manage classes and assignments.

 ePlanner
Easily plan your classes and access all your resources online.

 Interactive Answers and Solutions
Customize answer keys to print or display in the classroom. Choose to include answers only or full solutions to all lesson exercises.

 Interactive Whiteboards
Engage students with interactive whiteboard-ready lessons and activities.

 Personal Math Trainer: Online Assessment and Intervention
Assign automatically graded homework, quizzes, tests, and intervention activities. Prepare your students with updated practice tests aligned with Common Core.

Reading Start-Up

Have students complete the activities on this page by working alone or with others.

Visualize Vocabulary

The chart helps students review the terms related to volume of three-dimensional figures. Students should write one or more review words in each box.

Understand Vocabulary

Use the following explanation to help students learn the preview words.

> A birthday hat with a pointed top is similar to a **cone**. A can of vegetables is a **cylinder**, and a basketball is a **sphere**. In this module, you will learn how to find the volume of all of these shapes.

Active Reading

Integrating Language Arts

Students can use these reading and note-taking strategies to help them organize and understand new concepts and vocabulary.

FL CC **LACC.68.RST.3.7** Integrate quantitative or technical information expressed in words in a text with a version of that information expressed visually (e.g., in a flowchart, diagram, model, graph, or table).

Additional Resources

Differentiated Instruction
- Reading Strategies **ELL**

Reading Start-Up

Visualize Vocabulary

Use the ✔ words to complete the empty columns in the chart. You may use words more than once.

Shape	Distance Around	Attributes	Associated Review Words
circle	circumference	r, d	radius, diameter
square	perimeter	90° corner, sides	right angle, length, width
rectangle	perimeter	90° corner, sides	right angle, length, width

Understand Vocabulary

Complete the sentences using the preview words.

1. A three-dimensional figure that has one vertex and one circular base is a ____cone____.

2. A three-dimensional figure with all points the same distance from the center is a ____sphere____.

3. A three-dimensional figure that has two congruent circular bases is a ____cylinder____.

© Houghton Mifflin Harcourt Publishing Company

Vocabulary

Review Words
- area (área)
- base (base, en numeración)
- ✔ circumference (circunferencia)
- ✔ diameter (diámetro)
- height (altura)
- ✔ length (longitud)
- ✔ perimeter (perímetro)
- ✔ radius (radio)
- ✔ right angle (ángulo recto)
- ✔ width (ancho)

Preview Words
- cone (cono)
- cylinder (cilindro)
- sphere (esfera)

Active Reading

Three-Panel Flip Chart Before beginning the module, create a three-panel flip chart to help you organize what you learn. Label each flap with one of the lesson titles from this module. As you study each lesson, write important ideas like vocabulary, properties, and formulas under the appropriate flap.

Module 21 **661**

Before	In this module	After
Students understand how to use formulas: • find the circumference of a circle • find the area of a circle • find the volume of rectangular prisms and pyramids, and of triangular prisms and pyramids	Students represent and solve for the volumes of three-dimensional curved figures: • describe the volume formula $V = Bh$ of a cylinder in terms of its base area and height • model the relationship between the volume of a cylinder and a cone having both congruent bases and height and connect that relationship to their volume formulas • solve problems involving the volume of cylinders, cones, and spheres	Students will connect: • the effect on volume when the dimensions of a solid change proportionally • capacity and volume

Unpacking the Standards

Use the examples on this page to help students know exactly what they are expected to learn in this module.

 Florida Common Core Standards

Content Areas

 **Geometry—8.G.3**

Solve real-world and mathematical problems involving volume of cylinders, cones, and spheres.

Go online to see a complete unpacking of the Florida Common Core Standards.

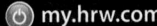 my.hrw.com

---

MODULE 21

Unpacking the Standards

Understanding the standards and the vocabulary terms in the standards will help you know exactly what you are expected to learn in this module.

FL CC 8.G.3.9

Know the formulas for the volumes of cones, cylinders, and spheres and use them to solve real-world and mathematical problems.

Key Vocabulary

volume *(volumen)*
The number of cubic units needed to fill a given space.

cylinder *(cilindro)*
A three-dimensional figure with two parallel, congruent circular bases connected by a curved lateral surface.

What It Means to You

You will learn the formula for the volume of a cylinder.

UNPACKING EXAMPLE 8.G.3.9

The Asano Taiko Company of Japan built the world's largest drum in 2000. The drum's diameter is 4.8 meters, and its height is 4.95 meters. Estimate the volume of the drum.

$$d = 4.8 \approx 5 \qquad V = (\pi r^2)h \qquad \text{Volume of a cylinder}$$
$$h = 4.95 \approx 5 \qquad = (3)(2.5)^2 \cdot 5 \qquad \text{Use 3 for } \pi.$$
$$r = \frac{d}{2} = \frac{5}{2} = 2.5 \qquad = (3)(6.25)(5)$$
$$= 18.75 \cdot 5$$
$$= 93.75 \approx 94$$

The volume of the drum is approximately 94 m³.

FL CC 8.G.3.9

Know the formulas for the volumes of cones, cylinders, and spheres and use them to solve real-world and mathematical problems.

Key Vocabulary

cone *(cono)*
A three-dimensional figure with one vertex and one circular base.

sphere *(esfera)*
A three-dimensional figure with all points the same distance from the center.

What It Means to You

You will learn formulas for the volume of a cone and a sphere.

UNPACKING EXAMPLE 8.G.3.9

6 in.

2 in.

Find the volume of the cone. Use 3.14 for π.

$$B = \pi(2^2) = 4\pi \text{ in}^2$$
$$V = \frac{1}{3} \cdot 4\pi \cdot 6 \qquad V = \frac{1}{3}Bh$$
$$V = 8\pi \qquad \text{Use 3.14 for } \pi.$$
$$\approx 25.1 \text{ in}^3$$

The volume of the cone is approximately 25.1 in³.

The volume of a sphere with the same radius is
$$V = \frac{4}{3}\pi r^3 \approx \frac{4}{3}(3)(2)^3 = 32 \text{ in}^3.$$

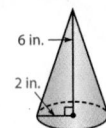 Visit my.hrw.com to see all Florida Common Core Standards unpacked.

my.hrw.com

662 Unit 9

© Houghton Mifflin Harcourt Publishing Company

Florida Common Core Standards	Lesson 21.1	Lesson 21.2	Lesson 21.3
FL CC 8.G.3.9 Know the formulas for the volumes of cones, cylinders, and spheres and use them to solve real-world and mathematical problems.			

LESSON
21.1 Volume of Cylinders

 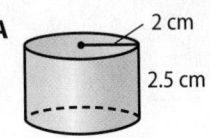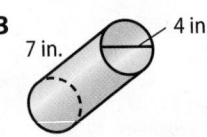

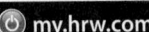

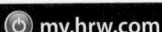
Engage

ESSENTIAL QUESTION

How do you find the volume of a cylinder? Sample answer: You multiply the area of the base by the height.

Motivate the Lesson

Ask: What three-dimensional objects with two congruent circular bases do you see around you in the classroom? What examples of this shape might you find in a kitchen? How could you find out how much food an object like this might hold?

Explore

EXPLORE ACTIVITY

Connect to Daily Life

Ask students to think of a circular pancake or cookie (*B*), and then to think of stacking up enough of these pancakes (*h*) to fill the cylinder. Relate this to the formula $V = Bh$.

Explain

EXAMPLE 1

Questioning Strategies Mathematical Practices

- Compare and contrast cylinders and prisms; how are they alike and how are they different? Both have two parallel congruent bases. For cylinders the bases are circles; for prisms the bases are polygons. The bases of a cylinder are connected by a curved surface; the bases of a prism are connected by faces that are polygons.

- Why do the steps in Example 1 use the symbol $\approx$ instead of $=$ after values are substituted in the formula? The value substituted for π is approximate, so the answer must also be approximate.

- Which will increase the volume by a greater amount, doubling the radius or doubling the height? Explain. Doubling the radius; the radius is squared when calculating the volume, so doubling the radius will increase the volume four-fold; doubling the height will double the volume.

Engage with the Whiteboard

Have students find the area of the circular base for each cylinder, and have a student label each base with its area. Complete the calculation of the volume by multiplying the area of the base by the height. Students should see that the volume calculations in the Examples could have included a step where the base area is found first and then multiplied by *h*. Point out that the final answer may differ slightly between the two methods if the area of the base is rounded before multiplying by the height.

LESSON
21.1 Volume of Cylinders

FL CC 8.G.3.9
Know the formulas for the volumes of...cylinders...and use them to solve real-world and mathematical problems.

? ESSENTIAL QUESTION

How do you find the volume of a cylinder?

EXPLORE ACTIVITY FL CC 8.G.3.9

Modeling the Volume of a Cylinder

A **cylinder** is a three-dimensional figure that has two congruent circular bases that lie in parallel planes. The volume of any three-dimensional figure is the number of cubic units needed to fill the space taken up by the solid figure.

One cube represents one cubic unit of volume. You can develop the formula for the volume of a cylinder using an empty soup can or other cylindrical container. First, remove one of the bases.

A Arrange centimeter cubes in a single layer at the bottom of the cylinder. Fit as many cubes into the layer as possible. How many cubes are in this layer?

Answers will vary. Check students' work.

B To find how many layers of cubes fit in the cylinder, make a stack of cubes along the inside of the cylinder. How many layers fit in the cylinder?

Answers will vary. Check students' work.

C How can you use what you know to find the approximate number of cubes that would fit in the cylinder?

Sample answer: Multiply the number of cubes in the bottom layer times the number of layers.

Reflect

1. **Make a Conjecture** Suppose you know the area of the base of a cylinder and the height of the cylinder. How can you find the cylinder's volume?

Multiply the area of the base times the height.

2. Let the area of the base of a cylinder be B and the height of the cylinder be h. Write a formula for the cylinder's volume V. $V = Bh$

Math On the Spot
my.hrw.com

Finding the Volume of a Cylinder Using a Formula

Finding volumes of cylinders is similar to finding volumes of prisms. You find the volume V of both a prism and a cylinder by multiplying the height h by the area of the base B, so $V = Bh$.

The base of a cylinder is a circle, so for a cylinder, $B = \pi r^2$.

Volume of a Cylinder

The volume V of a cylinder with radius r is the area of the base B times the height h.

$V = Bh$ or $V = \pi r^2 h$

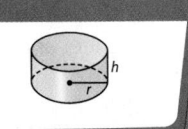

EXAMPLE 1 FL CC 8.G.3.9

Find the volume of each cylinder. Round your answers to the nearest tenth if necessary. Use 3.14 for π.

A

10 in.
3 in.

$V = \pi r^2 h$

$\approx 3.14 \cdot 3^2 \cdot 10$ Substitute.

$\approx 3.14 \cdot 9 \cdot 10$ Simplify.

≈ 282.6 Multiply.

The volume is about 282.6 in³.

B
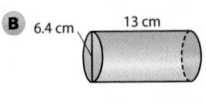
6.4 cm   13 cm

Since the diameter is 6.4 cm, the radius is 3.2 cm.

$V = \pi r^2 h$

$\approx 3.14 \cdot 3.2^2 \cdot 13$ Substitute.

$\approx 3.14 \cdot 10.24 \cdot 13$ Simplify.

≈ 418 Multiply.

> Recall that the diameter of a circle is twice the radius, so $2r = d$ and $r = \frac{d}{2}$.

The volume is about 418 cm³.

Reflect

3. **What If?** If you want a formula for the volume of a cylinder that involves the diameter d instead of the radius r, how can you rewrite it?

Write $\frac{d}{2}$ in place of r, so $V = \pi \left(\frac{d}{2}\right)^2 h$.

Animated Math my.hrw.com

My Notes

PROFESSIONAL DEVELOPMENT

Integrate Mathematical Practices MP.3.1

This lesson provides an opportunity to address this Mathematical Practices standard. It calls for students to construct viable arguments by making conjectures and building a logical progression of statements. Students explore ways to find the volume of a cylinder, working from descriptions or diagrams. Students then represent the volume in symbolic form as an equation.

Math Background

The general formula $V = Bh$ can be applied to all prisms and cylinders. However, the formula used to calculate B, the area of the base, will differ due to the shape of the base.

The cylinders in this lesson are *right cylinders* (with an axis perpendicular to the base) with circular bases. However, the same formula applies to *oblique* prisms and cylinders, based on Cavalieri's Principle: if two three-dimensional figures have the same height and the same cross-sectional area at every level, then they have the same volume.

YOUR TURN

Avoid Common Errors

Remind students to always consider the question, "Do I know the radius, *r*, or only the diameter?" In Exercise 4, students may try to use the diameter instead of the radius in the formula.

EXAMPLE 2

Questioning Strategies Mathematical Practices

• When is step 1 unnecessary? when you know the radius

• Why is 8 divided by 2? The formula calls for the radius, which is found by dividing the diameter by 2.

• Explain why you must square 4 before you multiply by 3.14. Sample answer: The correct order of operations (PEMDAS) requires evaluating the exponent before multiplying.

Talk About It
Check for Understanding

 Ask: Which words in the problem will you use to find the value of *r*? diameter of 8 feet Which words in the problem will you use to find the value of *h*? 4.5 feet deep

YOUR TURN

Focus on Critical Thinking

To calculate the answer for Exercise 6, Elsa multiplied 6^2 by 3.14 and then multiplied that product by 4. Tommie multiplied 6^2 by 4 and then multiplied that product by 3.14. Which process gives the correct answer? Explain. Both; factors can be multiplied in any order.

Elaborate

Talk About It
Summarize the Lesson

Ask: What measurements do you need to know in order to find the volume of a cylinder? What formula will you use? You need to know either the radius or the diameter of the bases and the height of the cylinder. $V = Bh$

GUIDED PRACTICE

Engage with the Whiteboard

In Exercise 3, have a student write the variables for the radius *r* and the height *h* next to the measurements on the cylinder. In Exercise 4, have a student draw and label a cylinder next to the statement of the problem.

Avoid Common Errors

Exercises 2–4 Ask students to predict the units they will write for the final answer before they begin the problem. Make sure students remember that volume requires cubed units.

Exercises 3–4 Have students circle the key words *radius* and *diameter* before they begin to substitute values into the volume formula. Students may carelessly use the diameter for the radius in Exercise 4.

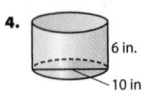

YOUR TURN

Find the volume of each cylinder. Round your answers to the nearest tenth if necessary. Use 3.14 for π.

4.

6 in.
10 in.

____471 in³____

5.

4 ft
12 ft

____602.9 ft³____

Finding the Volume of a Cylinder in a Real-World Context

The Longhorn Band at the University of Texas at Austin has one of the world's largest bass drums, known as Big Bertha.

EXAMPLE 2 Real World
FL CC 8.G.3.9

Big Bertha has a diameter of 8 feet and is 4.5 feet deep. Find the volume of the drum to the nearest tenth. Use 3.14 for π.

STEP 1 Find the radius of the drum.

$$r = \frac{d}{2} = \frac{8}{2} = 4 \text{ ft}$$

STEP 2 Find the volume of the drum.

$$V = \pi r^2 h$$

$\approx 3.14 \cdot 4^2 \cdot 4.5$ Substitute.

$\approx 3.14 \cdot 16 \cdot 4.5$ Simplify the exponent.

≈ 226.08 Multiply.

The volume of the drum is about 226.1 ft³.

YOUR TURN

6. A drum company advertises a snare drum that is 4 inches high and 12 inches in diameter. Find the volume of the drum to the nearest tenth. Use 3.14 for π.

____452.2 in³____

Personal Math Trainer
Online Assessment and Intervention
ⓜ my.hrw.com

Math On the Spot
ⓜ my.hrw.com

Personal Math Trainer
Online Assessment and Intervention
ⓜ my.hrw.com

Lesson 21.1 **665**

Guided Practice

1. Vocabulary Describe the bases of a cylinder. (Explore Activity)

two congruent circles that lie in parallel planes

2. Figure 1 shows a view from above of inch cubes on the bottom of a cylinder. Figure 2 shows the highest stack of cubes that will fit inside the cylinder. Estimate the volume of the cylinder. Explain your reasoning. (Explore Activity)

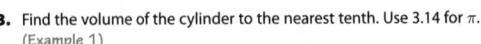

Sample answer: 427 in³; there are 61 cubes on

the bottom of the cylinder. The height is 7 cubes.

$V = 61 \times 7 = 427 \text{ in}^3$

Figure 1   Figure 2

3. Find the volume of the cylinder to the nearest tenth. Use 3.14 for π. (Example 1)

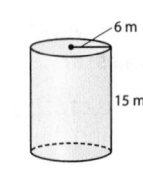

6 m
15 m

$V = \pi r^2 h$

$V = \pi \cdot \boxed{6}^2 \cdot \boxed{15}$

$\approx 3.14 \cdot \boxed{36} \cdot \boxed{15}$

$\approx \boxed{1695.6}$

The volume of the cylinder is approximately ___1695.6___ m³.

4. A Japanese odaiko is a very large drum that is made by hollowing out a section of a tree trunk. A museum in Takayama City hold three odaikos of similar size carved from a single tree trunk. The largest measures about 2.7 meters in both diameter and length, and weighs about 4.5 metric tons. Using the volume formula for a cylinder, approximate the volume of the drum to the nearest tenth. (Example 2)

The radius of the drum is about ___1.35___ m.

The volume of the drum is about ___15.5___ m³.

? ESSENTIAL QUESTION CHECK-IN

5. How do you find the volume of a cylinder? Describe which measurements of a cylinder you need to know.

You need to know the height and know or be able to

calculate the radius of the base. Then you can substitute

into the volume formula $V = \pi r^2 h$.

666 Unit 9

DIFFERENTIATE INSTRUCTION

Manipulatives

Help students understand the component parts of a cylinder by having them take a cardboard tube and cut it apart to see the the rectangle that forms the side, or lateral surface. Alternatively, have them build and tape together a cylinder from two circles and a rectangle. Have them label various measurements to discover and confirm that the width of the rectangle is the height of the cylinder and the length of the rectangle is the circumference of the circle.

Graphic Organizers

Use this web to help students see how various three-dimensional figures relate. Discuss why cylinders, cones, and spheres are not polyhedrons.

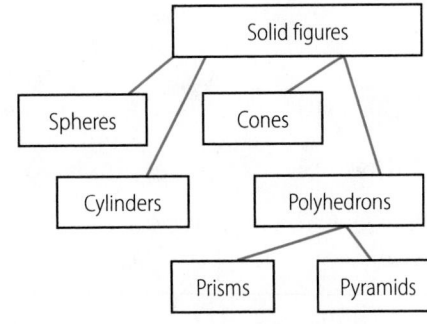

Additional Resources

Differentiated Instruction includes:

- Reading Strategies
- Success for English Learners **ELL**
- Reteach
- Challenge **PRE-AP**

Volume of Cylinders   **666**

Personal Math Trainer

Online Assessment and Intervention

Online homework assignment available

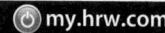 **my.hrw.com**

21.1 LESSON QUIZ

 **8.G.3.9**

Use 3.14 for π. Round answers to the nearest tenth if necessary.

1. A can of chili has a radius of 5.25 cm and a height of 13 cm. Find the volume.

2. A cylindrical carton of oatmeal has a diameter of 13 cm and is 24 cm tall. Find the volume.

3. Which has a greater volume?
Cylinder A: $r = 3$ m, $h = 1.2$ m
Cylinder B: $d = 4$ m, $h = 2.5$ m

4. Daren uses rice to fill a cylindrical glass measuring 6 inches high with a radius of 2.5 inches. He pours this rice into a cardboard cylinder that is 3.5 inches high with a diameter of 8 inches. Will he have enough rice to fill the cardboard cylinder? Explain.

Lesson Quiz available online

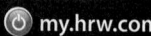 **my.hrw.com**

Answers

1. 1125.1 cm^3

2. 3184.0 cm^3

3. Cylinder A

4. The glass has a volume of 117.75 in^3. The cardboard cylinder has a volume of 175.84 in^3. He will not have enough rice to fill the cardboard cylinder, since 117.75 in^3 is less than 175.84 in^3.

Evaluate

GUIDED AND INDEPENDENT PRACTICE

 **8.G.3.9**

Concepts & Skills	Practice
Explore Activity Modeling the Volume of a Cylinder	Exercises 1–2
Example 1 Finding the Volume of a Cylinder Using a Formula	Exercises 3, 6–11
Example 2 Finding the Volume of a Cylinder in a Real-World Context	Exercises 4, 12–17

Exercise	Depth of Knowledge (D.O.K.)	FL CC Mathematical Practices
6–11	**2** Skills/Concepts	**MP.5.1** Using Tools
12–17	**2** Skills/Concepts	**MP.4.1** Modeling
18	**3** Strategic Thinking H.O.T.	**MP.3.1** Logic
19	**3** Strategic Thinking H.O.T.	**MP.6.1** Precision
20	**3** Strategic Thinking H.O.T.	**MP.3.1** Logic

Additional Resources

Differentiated Instruction includes:

• Leveled Practice worksheets

Name_____ Class_____ Date_____

21.1 Independent Practice

Personal
Math Trainer

Online
Assessment and
Intervention

my.hrw.com

FL CC 8.G.3.9

Find the volume of each figure. Round your answers to the nearest tenth if necessary. Use 3.14 for π.

6.

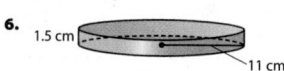
1.5 cm
11 cm

_____569.9 cm³_____

7.

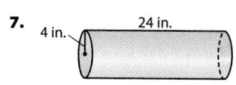
4 in.
24 in.

_____1205.8 in³_____

8.

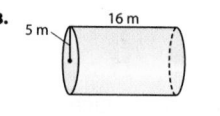
5 m
16 m

_____1256 m³_____

9.

10 in.
12 in.

_____942 in³_____

10. A cylinder has a radius of 4 centimeters and a height of 40 centimeters.

_____2009.6 cm³_____

11. A cylinder has a radius of 8 meters and a height of 4 meters.

_____803.8 m³_____

Round your answer to the nearest tenth, if necessary. Use 3.14 for π.

12. The cylindrical Giant Ocean Tank at the New England Aquarium in Boston is 24 feet deep and has a radius of 18.8 feet. Find the volume of the tank.

_____26,635.2 ft³_____

13. A standard-size bass drum has a diameter of 22 inches and is 18 inches deep. Find the volume of this drum.

_____6838.9 in³_____

14. Grain is stored in cylindrical structures called silos. Find the volume of a silo with a diameter of 11.1 feet and a height of 20 feet.

_____1934.4 ft³_____

15. The Frank Erwin Center, or "The Drum," at the University of Texas in Austin can be approximated by a cylinder that is 120 meters in diameter and 30 meters in height. Find its volume.

_____339,120 m³_____

Lesson 21.1 **667**

16. A barrel of crude oil contains about 5.61 cubic feet of oil. How many barrels of oil are contained in 1 mile (5280 feet) of a pipeline that has an inside diameter of 6 inches and is completely filled with oil? How much is "1 mile" of oil in this pipeline worth at a price of $100 per barrel?

_____184.7 barrels; $18,470_____

17. A pan for baking French bread is shaped like half a cylinder. It is 12 inches long and 3.5 inches in diameter. What is the volume of uncooked dough that would fill this pan?

_____57.7 in³_____

3.5 in.
12 in.

H.O.T. FOCUS ON HIGHER ORDER THINKING

18. **Explain the Error** A student said the volume of a cylinder with a 3-inch diameter is two times the volume of a cylinder with the same height and a 1.5-inch radius. What is the error?

Sample answer: The volumes are equal because a

cylinder with a 3-inch diameter has a 1.5-inch radius.

Work Area

19. **Communicate Mathematical Ideas** Explain how you can find the height of a cylinder if you know the diameter and the volume. Include an example with your explanation.

Divide the diameter by 2 to find the radius. Then

substitute the volume and radius in $V = \pi r^2 h$ and

solve for h. Sample example: For a cylinder with

volume 72 m³ and a diameter of 6 m, $72 = \pi \cdot 3^2 h$,

so $h = \frac{72}{9\pi} = \frac{8}{\pi} \approx 2.5$ m.

20. **Analyze Relationships** Cylinder A has a radius of 6 centimeters. Cylinder B has the same height and a radius half as long as cylinder A. What fraction of the volume of cylinder A is the volume of cylinder B? Explain.

$\frac{1}{4}$; for any height h, cylinder A has a volume of $36\pi \cdot h$.

Cylinder B has a volume of $9\pi \cdot h$. Since 9 is $\frac{1}{4}$ of 36, the

volume of cylinder B is $\frac{1}{4}$ the volume of cylinder A.

668 Unit 9

EXTEND THE MATH PRE-AP

Activity available online my.hrw.com

Activity When a three-dimensional figure and a plane intersect, the intersection is called a cross section. A three-dimensional figure can have many different cross sections. For example, when you cut a cylinder in half, the cross section that is exposed depends on the direction of the cut. Have students explore the cross sections of a right circular cylinder, either by using drawings or making a cylinder of clay or plastic foam, and cutting it in various ways to form a rectangle, a circle, or an ellipse (oval). Students may also obtain a partial ellipse if the cut enters the side and exits through a base.

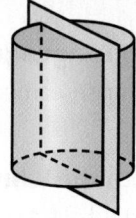

Florida Common Core Standards

The student is expected to:

 **Geometry—8.G.3.9**

Know the formulas for the volumes of cones, cylinders, and spheres and use them to solve real-world and mathematical problems.

Mathematical Practices

 **MP.4.1** Modeling

ADDITIONAL EXAMPLE 1
Find the volume of each cone. Round your answers to the nearest tenth. Use 3.14 for π.

A

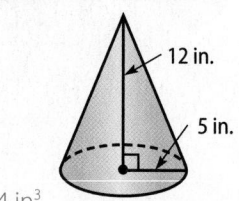

12 in.

5 in.

314 in³

B

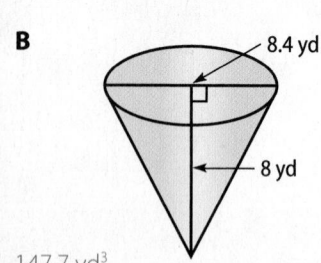

8.4 yd

8 yd

147.7 yd³

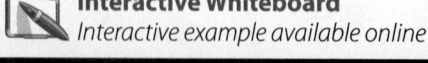 **Interactive Whiteboard**
Interactive example available online

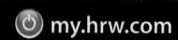 my.hrw.com

Engage

ESSENTIAL QUESTION

How do you find the volume of a cone? Sample answer: Find one-third of the product of the area of the circular base and the height of the cone.

Motivate the Lesson
Ask: If you had a paper cone and paper cylinder with the same base and height, which would hold more popcorn? How much more? Begin the Explore Activity to find out.

Explore

EXPLORE ACTIVITY

Avoid Common Errors
Some students may try to measure the height of a cone from the vertex to a point on the circumference of the base, which is the slant height. Point out that the height is a segment perpendicular to the base from the vertex to the center of the circular base.

Explain

EXAMPLE 1

Questioning Strategies 🖊 **Mathematical Practices**

• Compare and contrast a cone and a pyramid. A cone has one circular base and a curved lateral surface; a pyramid has one base that is a polygon and sides that are triangles.

• Compare and contrast a cone and a cylinder. A cone has one circular base and a curved lateral surface; a cylinder has two congruent circular bases and a curved lateral surface.

• If these cones were cylinders with the same base and height, how would you use the cone volumes to find the cylinder volumes? Multiply them by 3.

Integrating Language Arts ᴇʟʟ

Encourage English learners to use the active reading strategies as they encounter new terms and concepts.

Engage with the Whiteboard

🖊 In part B, have a student color the line that is labeled as 8 feet long, and then write the name of that part (either *d* or *diameter*). Have a student circle the 4 in the formula and explain the source of this value.

21.2 Volume of Cones

FL CC 8.G.3.9

Know the formulas for the volumes of cones...and use them to solve real-world and mathematical problems.

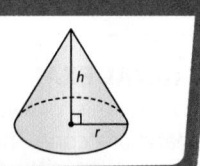
Math On the Spot
my.hrw.com

ESSENTIAL QUESTION

How do you find the volume of a cone?

EXPLORE ACTIVITY FL CC 8.G.3.9

Modeling the Volume of a Cone

A **cone** is a three-dimensional figure that has one vertex and one circular base.

To explore the volume of a cone, Sandi does an experiment with a cone and a cylinder that have congruent bases and heights. She fills the cone with popcorn kernels and then pours the kernels into the cylinder. She repeats this until the cylinder is full.

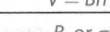

Sandi finds that it takes 3 cones to fill the volume of the cylinder.

STEP 1 What is the formula for the volume V of a cylinder with base area B and height h? _____ $V = Bh$

STEP 2 What is the area of the base of the cone? _____ B, or πr^2

STEP 3 Sandi found that, when the bases and height are the same,

_____ 3 times $V_{cone} = V_{cylinder}$.

STEP 4 How does the volume of the cone compare to the volume of the cylinder?

Volume of the cone: $V_{cone} = \boxed{\dfrac{1}{3}} \cdot V_{cylinder}$

Reflect

1. Use the conclusion from this experiment to write a formula for the volume of a cone in terms of the height and the radius. Explain.
 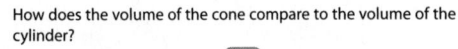
$V_{cylinder} = \pi r^2 h$, so $V_{cone} = \frac{1}{3}\pi r^2 h$

2. How are the formulas for the volume of a cone and a prism similar?

Both are one third the area of the base times the height.

Lesson 21.2 **669**

Finding the Volume of a Cone Using a Formula

The formulas for the volume of a prism and the volume of a cylinder are the same: multiply the height h by the area of the base B, so $V = Bh$.

In the **Explore Activity**, you saw that the volume of a cone is one third the volume of a cylinder with the same base and height.

Volume of a Cone

The volume V of a cone with radius r is one third the area of the base B times the height h.	
$V = \frac{1}{3}Bh$ or $V = \frac{1}{3}\pi r^2 h$	

My Notes

EXAMPLE 1 FL CC 8.G.3.9

Find the volume of each cone. Round your answers to the nearest tenth. Use 3.14 for π.

A
8 in.
2 in.

$V = \frac{1}{3}\pi r^2 h$

$\approx \frac{1}{3} \cdot 3.14 \cdot 2^2 \cdot 8$ Substitute.

$\approx \frac{1}{3} \cdot 3.14 \cdot 4 \cdot 8$ Simplify.

≈ 33.5 Multiply.

The volume is about 33.5 in³.

B Since the diameter is 8 ft, the radius is 4 ft.

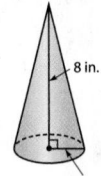
9 ft
8 ft

$V = \frac{1}{3}\pi r^2 h$

$\approx \frac{1}{3} \cdot 3.14 \cdot 4^2 \cdot 9$ Substitute.

$\approx \frac{1}{3} \cdot 3.14 \cdot 16 \cdot 9$ Simplify.

≈ 150.7 Multiply.

The volume is about 150.7 ft³.

Reflect

3. How can you rewrite the formula for the volume of a cone using the diameter d instead of the radius r?

$V = \frac{1}{3}\pi\left(\frac{d}{2}\right)^2 h$

670 Unit 9

PROFESSIONAL DEVELOPMENT

Integrate Mathematical Practices MP.4.1

This lesson provides an opportunity to address this Mathematical Practices standard. It calls for students to model with mathematics. Students use models to explore the relationship between the volume of a cone and a cylinder with congruent bases and heights. They use this activity to write a rule for the volume of a cone.

Math Background

A cone has two aspects that are referred to as *height*.

The *height* of the cone is the length of the segment from the vertex perpendicular to the center of the base. For a right circular cone, this height joins the vertex and the center of the base.

The *slant height* is the length of the segment from the vertex to any point on the circumference of the circular base. The slant height is used to find the lateral surface area of a cone.

YOUR TURN

Avoid Common Errors

If students use a calculator, remind them to enter 3.14 instead of using the π key.

Focus on Technology

Discuss the use of the π key if the instruction to use 3.14 were not given. Have students consider how much error is introduced by using 3.14 for π. Remind students that π is irrational, and even the value used by the calculator is inexact. When students are expected to use the π key, they will still need to round the answer to a specified precision.

ADDITIONAL EXAMPLE 2

A styrofoam model of a volcano is in the shape of a cone. The model has a circular base with a diameter of 48 centimeters and a height of 12 centimeters. Find the volume of foam in the model to the nearest tenth. Use 3.14 for π. 7234.6 cm³

 Interactive Whiteboard
Interactive example available online

⏻ my.hrw.com

EXAMPLE 2

Questioning Strategies Mathematical Practices

• Why is the first step to divide 12 by 2? The value of 12 is for the diameter; the formula uses the radius.

• After you substitute the values, what do you do first in the calculation? Explain. Begin by applying the exponent, following the PEMDAS rule for the order of operations.

Engage with the Whiteboard

Have a student draw and label a figure for this Example next to step 1.

YOUR TURN

Avoid Common Errors

Students may get arithmetic errors when calculating with large numbers. Before they solve the problem, have them estimate the answer. The radius is about 200 meters, so the radius squared is about 40,000 m². Multiplying this value by the height, which is about 400 meters, gives 16,000,000 m³. Multiplying by π and then multiplying by $\frac{1}{3}$ roughly cancel out. Since all the measurements in this estimate were rounded down, the volume should be larger than but within two-fold of 16,000,000 m³.

Elaborate

Talk About It
Summarize the Lesson

Ask: What step is similar when you find the volume of a cone, a cylinder, or a prism? You have to find the area of the base and multiply by the height. What do you think is the most important difference between a cone and a cylinder or prism when you need to find the volume? The volume for a cone is one-third of the product of the base area and height.

GUIDED PRACTICE

Engage with the Whiteboard

 Exercise 1 Have students draw both figures and label them. Note that they do not need to know the radius of the base for each figure because the base area is given.

Avoid Common Errors

Exercises 3–4 Have students, before they substitute or calculate, write the formula and write the value of the radius. This will help students who may use the diameter instead of the radius or who may forget to include the $\frac{1}{3}$ in the formula.

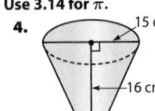

YOUR TURN

Find the volume of each cone. Round your answers to the nearest tenth. Use 3.14 for π.

4.

 15 cm, 16 cm

942 cm³

5.

 3 ft, 2 ft

12.6 ft³

Personal Math Trainer
Online Assessment and Intervention
my.hrw.com

Finding the Volume of a Volcano

The mountain created by a volcano is often cone–shaped.

EXAMPLE 2 Real World

FL CC 8.G.3.9

For her geography project, Karen built a clay model of a volcano in the shape of a cone. Her model has a diameter of 12 inches and a height of 8 inches. Find the volume of clay in her model to the nearest tenth. Use 3.14 for π.

STEP 1 Find the radius.
$r = \frac{12}{2} = 6$ in.

STEP 2 Find the volume of clay.

$V = \frac{1}{3}\pi r^2 h$

$\approx \frac{1}{3} \cdot 3.14 \cdot 6^2 \cdot 8$ Substitute.

$\approx \frac{1}{3} \cdot 3.14 \cdot 36 \cdot 8$ Simplify.

≈ 301.44 Multiply.

The volume of the clay is about 301.4 in³.

YOUR TURN

6. The cone of the volcano Parícutin in Mexico had a height of 410 meters and a diameter of 424 meters. Approximate the volume of the cone.

about 19,300,000 m³

Personal Math Trainer
Online Assessment and Intervention
my.hrw.com

Math On the Spot
my.hrw.com

Guided Practice

1. The area of the base of a cylinder is 45 square inches and its height is 10 inches. A cone has the same area for its base and the same height. What is the volume of the cone? (Explore Activity)

$V_{cylinder} = Bh = \boxed{45} \cdot \boxed{10} = \boxed{450}$

$V_{cone} = \frac{1}{3}V_{cylinder}$

$= \frac{1}{3}\boxed{450}$

$= \boxed{150}$

The volume of the cone is ___150___ in³.

2. A cone and a cylinder have congruent height and bases. The volume of the cone is 18 m³. What is the volume of the cylinder? Explain. (Explore Activity)

54 m³; the volume of a cylinder is

3 times the volume of a cone with

a congruent base and height.

Find the volume of each cone. Round your answer to the nearest tenth if necessary. Use 3.14 for π. (Example 1)

3.

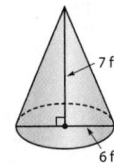 7 ft, 6 ft

65.9 ft³

4.

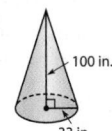 100 in., 33 in.

113,982 in³

5. Gretchen made a paper cone to hold a gift for a friend. The paper cone was 15 inches high and had a radius of 3 inches. Find the volume of the paper cone to the nearest tenth. Use 3.14 for π. (Example 2)

141.3 in³

6. A cone-shaped building is commonly used to store sand. What would be the volume of a cone-shaped building with a diameter of 50 meters and a height of 20 meters? Round your answer to the nearest tenth. Use 3.14 for π. (Example 2)

_13,083.3 m³_

? ESSENTIAL QUESTION CHECK-IN

7. How do you find the volume of a cone?

You can find one third of the volume of a cylinder with

the same base and height, or you can use the formula

$V = \frac{1}{3}\pi r^2 h$.

DIFFERENTIATE INSTRUCTION

Modeling

The tip of a sharpened pencil is shaped like a cone. How much of the pencil is lost after the tip is formed?

To answer this question, you should know that the volume of a cone is $\frac{1}{3}$ the volume of the cylinder from which it was formed.

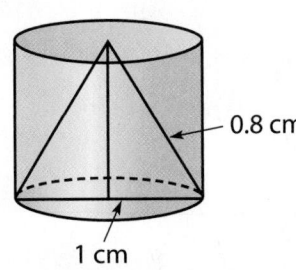 0.8 cm, 1 cm

The tip of this pencil was formed out of a cylinder with a height of 0.8 cm and a diameter of 1 cm.

The cylinder had a volume of approximately 0.63 cm³.

volume of cone $= \frac{1}{3} \cdot$ volume of cylinder

volume of cone $= \frac{1}{3} \cdot 0.63 = 0.21$

Since the tip of the pencil has a volume of 0.21 cm³, 0.42 cm³ was lost when the tip of the pencil was formed.

Additional Resources

Differentiated Instruction includes:

- Reading Strategies
- Success for English Learners **ELL**
- Reteach
- Challenge **PRE-AP**

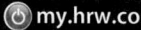
21.2 LESSON QUIZ

 **8.G.3.9**

Round your answers to the nearest tenth. Use 3.14 for π.

1. The volume of a cone is 20 cm³. What is the volume of a cylinder with the same base and height?

2. Find the volume of the cone.

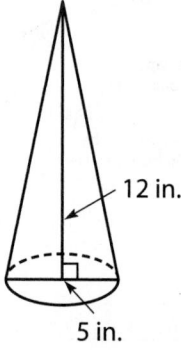

12 in.

5 in.

3. Find the volume of a cone with a radius of 20 inches and a height of 25 inches.

4. A paper cup in the shape of a cone has a diameter of 6 centimeters and is 7 centimeters high. Ken needs to add about 264 cm³ of water to his plaster mixture. How many paper cups of water will he need to use?

Lesson Quiz available online

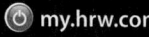

🔘 my.hrw.com

Answers

1. 60 cm³

2. 78.5 in³

3. 10,466.7 in³

4. 4 cups

Evaluate

GUIDED AND INDEPENDENT PRACTICE

 **8.G.3.9**

Concepts & Skills	Practice
Explore Activity Modeling the Volume of a Cone	Exercises 1–2
Example 1 Finding the Volume of a Cone Using a Formula	Exercises 3–4, 8–11, 16–17
Example 2 Finding the Volume of a Volcano	Exercises 5–6, 12–15

Exercise	Depth of Knowledge (D.O.K.)	Mathematical Practices
8–11	**2** Skills/Concepts	**MP.5.1** Using Tools
12–15	**2** Skills/Concepts	**MP.4.1** Modeling
16–18	**2** Skills/Concepts	**MP.2.1** Reasoning
19	**3** Strategic Thinking **H.O.T.**	**MP.3.1** Logic
20	**3** Strategic Thinking **H.O.T.**	**MP.2.1** Reasoning
21–22	**3** Strategic Thinking **H.O.T.**	**MP.3.1** Logic

Additional Resources

Differentiated Instruction includes:

• Leveled Practice worksheets

21.2 Independent Practice

FL CC 8.G.3.9

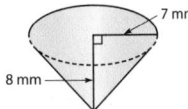

Personal Math Trainer

my.hrw.com

Online Assessment and Intervention

Find the volume of each cone. Round your answers to the nearest tenth if necessary. Use 3.14 for π.

8.

7 mm

8 mm

__410.3 mm³__

9.

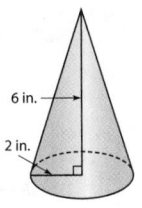

6 in.

2 in.

__25.1 in³__

10. A cone has a diameter of 6 centimeters and a height of 11.5 centimeters.

__108.3 cm³__

11. A cone has a radius of 3 meters and a height of 10 meters.

__94.2 m³__

Round your answers to the nearest tenth if necessary. Use 3.14 for π.

12. Antonio is making mini waffle cones. Each waffle cone is 3 inches high and has a radius of $\frac{3}{4}$ inch. What is the volume of a waffle cone?

__1.8 in³__

13. A snack bar sells popcorn in cone-shaped containers. One container has a diameter of 8 inches and a height of 10 inches. How many cubic inches of popcorn does the container hold?

__167.5 in³__

14. A volcanic cone has a diameter of 300 meters and a height of 150 meters. What is the volume of the cone?

__3,532,500 m³__

15. Multistep Orange traffic cones come in a variety of sizes. Approximate the volume, in cubic inches, of a traffic cone that has a height of 2 feet and a diameter of 10 inches. Use 3.14 for π.

__628 in³__

Find the missing measure for each cone. Round your answers to the nearest tenth if necessary. Use 3.14 for π.

16. radius = __4 in.__

height = 6 in.

volume = 100.48 in³

17. diameter = 6 cm

height = __6 cm__

volume = 56.52 cm³

18. The diameter of a cone-shaped container is 4 inches, and its height is 6 inches. How much greater is the volume of a cylinder-shaped container with the same diameter and height? Round your answer to the nearest hundredth. Use 3.14 for π.

__50.24 in³__

H.O.T. FOCUS ON HIGHER ORDER THINKING

Work Area

19. Alex wants to know the volume of sand in an hourglass. When all the sand is in the bottom, he stands a ruler up beside the hourglass and estimates the height of the cone of sand.

a. What else does he need to measure to find the volume of sand?

__either the diameter or the radius__

__of the base__

b. Make a Conjecture If the volume of sand is increasing at a constant rate, is the height increasing at a constant rate? Explain.

__No; the cone is tapered as it goes from top to bottom.__

__An equal volume of sand has a smaller radius and a__

__greater height as the sand rises.__

20. Problem Solving The diameter of a cone is x cm, the height is 18 cm, and the volume is 301.44 cm³. What is x? Use 3.14 for π.

__x = 8 cm__

21. Analyze Relationships A cone has a radius of 1 foot and a height of 2 feet. How many cones of liquid would it take to fill a cylinder with a diameter of 2 feet and a height of 2 feet? Explain.

__Since the radius and height of the cones and cylinder__

__are the same, it will take 3 cones to equal the volume__

__of the cylinder.__

22. Critique Reasoning Herb knows that the volume of a cone is one third that of a cylinder with the same base and height. He reasons that a cone with the same height as a given cylinder but 3 times the radius should therefore have the same volume as the cylinder, since $\frac{1}{3} \cdot 3 = 1$. Is Herb correct? Explain.

__No; the volume of the cone will be 3 times that of the__

__cylinder because the radius is squared in the formula.__

__For example, for a cylinder with radius 1 and height 5,__

__$V = \pi (1)^2(5) = 5\pi$. For a cone with radius 3 and height 5,__

__$V = \frac{1}{3}\pi (3)^2(5) = 15\pi$, or 3 times as much.__

EXTEND THE MATH PRE-AP

Activity available online ⊙ my.hrw.com

Activity The activity in the previous lesson explored the cross sections formed when a plane intersects a cylinder. The three shapes that can be obtained are a rectangle, a circle, and an ellipse.

Have students explore the cross sections of a right circular cone, either by using drawings or making a cone of clay or plastic foam, and cutting it in various ways. What two cross sections of a cylinder can also be obtained from a cone? circle, ellipse What shape cannot be obtained? rectangle What is the new shape obtained if the cut is through the vertex and perpendicular to the base? triangle Students will also find that they can generate curved shapes that are either parabolas or hyperbolas. Collectively, these cross sections are known as the *conic sections*.

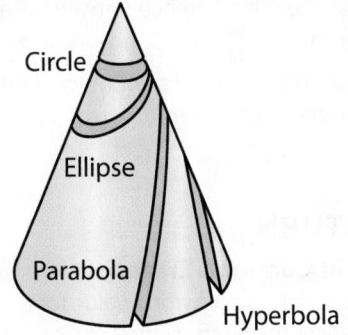

Circle

Ellipse

Parabola

Hyperbola

© Houghton Mifflin Harcourt Publishing Company

LESSON
21.3 Volume of Spheres

 Florida Common Core Standards

The student is expected to:

 **Geometry—8.G.3.9**

Know the formulas for the volumes of cones, cylinders, and spheres and use them to solve real-world and mathematical problems.

Mathematical Practices

 **MP.6.1** Precision

ADDITIONAL EXAMPLE 1

Find the volume of each sphere. Round your answers to the nearest tenth if necessary. Use 3.14 for π.

A

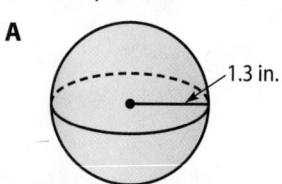 1.3 in.

9.2 in³

B

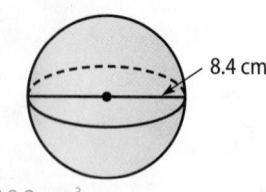 8.4 cm

310.2 cm³

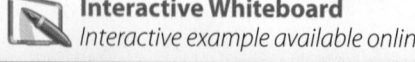 **Interactive Whiteboard**
Interactive example available online

⏻ my.hrw.com

Engage

ESSENTIAL QUESTION

How do you find the volume of a sphere? Sample answer: Find the product of $\frac{4}{3}$, the cube of the radius, and π.

Motivate the Lesson
Ask: What are some sports that are played with a ball? What is the mathematical name for this shape? How can you find the volume of a ball?

Explore

EXPLORE ACTIVITY

Engage with the Whiteboard
Have a student use a red marker to circle the height for each figure (to emphasize that h is the same for each). Then have a student use a blue marker to circle the three radii.

Explain

EXAMPLE 1

Connect Vocabulary ELL
Students may mispronounce *sphere* as *spere*. Remind them that the *ph* sound is an *f*, so this word is correctly pronounced *sfere*. Have them consider other examples of this sound, such as phone, graph and sphinx.

Questioning Strategies 🔲 Mathematical Practices
• How many variables are used when finding the volume of a sphere? one: the radius, r

• Describe the difference between the information in part A and that in part B. A shows the length of the radius; B shows the length of the diameter.

• What mathematical symbols change when you substitute values into the formula for the volume of a sphere? Numbers take the place of variables and, because the value for π is approximate, the = becomes ≈.

YOUR TURN

Avoid Common Errors
To avoid using the wrong value for the radius, have students circle the word *radius* or underline the word *diameter* twice in the problem before they substitute values.

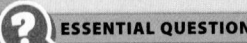

LESSON
21.3 Volume of Spheres

FL CC 8.G.3.9
Know the formulas for the volumes of...spheres and use them to solve real-world and mathematical problems.

? ESSENTIAL QUESTION

How do you find the volume of a sphere?

EXPLORE ACTIVITY FL CC 8.G.3.9

Modeling the Volume of a Sphere

A **sphere** is a three-dimensional figure with all points the same distance from the center. The **radius** of a sphere is the distance from the center to any point on the sphere.

You have seen that a cone fills $\frac{1}{3}$ of a cylinder of the same radius and height h. If you were to do a similar experiment with a sphere of the same radius, you would find that a sphere fills $\frac{2}{3}$ of the cylinder. The cylinder's height is equal to twice the radius of the sphere.

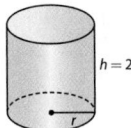 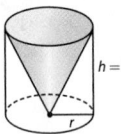 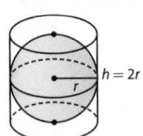

STEP 1 Write the formula $V = Bh$ for each shape. Use $B = \pi r^2$ and substitute the fractions you know for the cone and sphere.

Cylinder	Cone	Sphere
$V = \pi r^2 h$	$V = \frac{1}{3}\pi r^2 h$	$V = \frac{2}{3}\pi r^2 h$

STEP 2 Notice that a sphere always has a height equal to twice the radius. Substitute $2r$ for h. $V = \frac{2}{3}\pi r^2 (2r)$

STEP 3 Simplify this formula for the volume of a sphere. $V = \boxed{\frac{4}{3}}\pi r^3$

Reflect

1. **Analyze Relationships** A cone has a radius of r and a height of $2r$. A sphere has a radius of r. Compare the volume of the sphere and cone.

The cone's volume is $\frac{1}{3}$ of a cylinder with radius r and height 2r. The sphere's volume is $\frac{2}{3}$ of the volume of this cylinder.

So, the sphere's volume is twice the cone's volume.

Lesson 21.3 **675**

Math On the Spot
⊕ my.hrw.com

Finding the Volume of a Sphere Using a Formula

The Explore Activity illustrates a formula for the volume of a sphere with radius r.

Volume of a Sphere

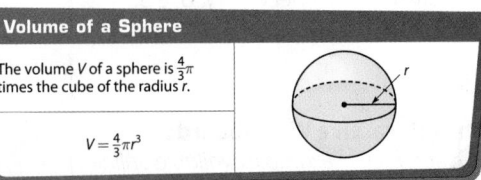

The volume V of a sphere is $\frac{4}{3}\pi$ times the cube of the radius r.

$$V = \frac{4}{3}\pi r^3$$

EXAMPLE 1 FL CC 8.G.3.9

Find the volume of each sphere. Round your answers to the nearest tenth if necessary. Use 3.14 for π.

A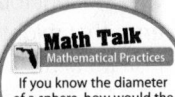

$V = \frac{4}{3}\pi r^3$

$\approx \frac{4}{3} \cdot 3.14 \cdot 2.1^3$ Substitute.

$\approx \frac{4}{3} \cdot 3.14 \cdot 9.26$ Simplify.

≈ 38.8 Multiply.

The volume is about 38.8 cm³.

B

Since the diameter is 7 cm, the radius is 3.5 cm.

$V = \frac{4}{3}\pi r^3$

$\approx \frac{4}{3} \cdot 3.14 \cdot 3.5^3$ Substitute.

$\approx \frac{4}{3} \cdot 3.14 \cdot 42.9$ Simplify.

≈ 179.6 Multiply.

The volume is about 179.6 cm³.

Math Talk
Mathematical Practices

If you know the diameter of a sphere, how would the formula for the volume of a sphere be written in terms of d?

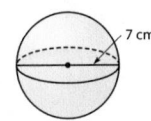

$V = \frac{4}{3}\pi\left(\frac{d}{2}\right)^3$

Personal Math Trainer
Online Assessment and Intervention
⊕ my.hrw.com

YOUR TURN

Find the volume of each sphere. Round your answers to the nearest tenth. Use 3.14 for π.

2. A sphere has a radius of 10 centimeters. ___4186.7 cm³___

3. A sphere has a diameter of 3.4 meters. ___20.6 m³___

676 Unit 9

PROFESSIONAL DEVELOPMENT

📋 Integrate Mathematical Practices MP.6.1

This lesson provides an opportunity to address this Mathematical Practices standard. It calls for students to communicate mathematics precisely. Students explore the relationship between the volumes of cylinders, cones, and spheres. Students learn to express the volumes through formulas and to explain the differences and similarities in the coefficients and variables in the formulas.

Math Background

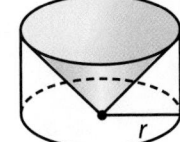 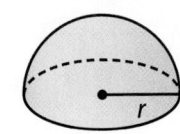

Archimedes derived the formula for the volume of a sphere by showing that a hemisphere with radius r and the solid remaining when the cone is removed from a cylinder with radius and height r have equal volumes.

$$(\pi r^2)r - \frac{1}{3}(\pi r^2)r = \frac{2}{3}(\pi r^2)r = \frac{2}{3}\pi r^3.$$

The volume of the sphere is thus twice that of the hemisphere, or $2\left(\frac{2}{3}\pi r^3\right) = \frac{4}{3}\pi r^3$.

Volume of Spheres **676**

EXAMPLE 2

Questioning Strategies Mathematical Practices

- Explain whether cubing the diameter first and then dividing by 2 would give the same answer. No; 11 cubed is 1331, but $22^3 = 10,648$, and half of that (5324) is much greater than 1331.

- How could you write the answer so that it is an exact value? $(1774\frac{2}{3})\pi$

Engage with the Whiteboard

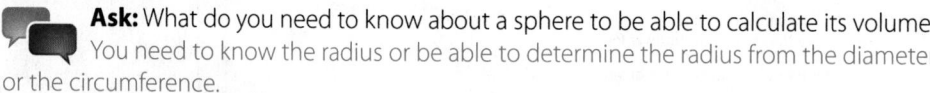 Have a student draw and label a sphere to represent the ball described.

YOUR TURN

Focus on Critical Thinking
One student found the volume to be 7234.6 in³ instead of the correct answer. Describe an error that might have led to this result. This answer could result from using the diameter instead of the radius to calculate the volume.

Elaborate

Talk About It
Summarize the Lesson
 Ask: What do you need to know about a sphere to be able to calculate its volume? You need to know the radius or be able to determine the radius from the diameter or the circumference.

GUIDED PRACTICE

Engage with the Whiteboard
In Exercises 5–8, draw diagrams of the spheres and label the diameter or radius as appropriate.

Avoid Common Errors
Exercise 8 Students may not find the radius correctly when given the circumference. Have students find the diameter first, and then find the radius from the diameter. Students should use a calculator when finding the radius. Answers may vary slightly, depending on how students choose to round the value found for the radius.

Finding the Volume of a Sphere in a Real-World Context

Many sports, including golf and tennis, use a ball that is spherical in shape.

Math On the Spot
© my.hrw.com

EXAMPLE 2 Real World   FL CC 8.G.3.9

Soccer balls come in several different sizes. One soccer ball has a diameter of 22 centimeters. What is the volume of this soccer ball? Round your answer to the nearest tenth. Use 3.14 for π.

STEP 1 Find the radius.

$r = \dfrac{d}{2} = 11$ cm

STEP 2 Find the volume of the soccer ball.

$V = \dfrac{4}{3}\pi r^3$

$\approx \dfrac{4}{3} \cdot 3.14 \cdot 11^3$ Substitute.

$\approx \dfrac{4}{3} \cdot 3.14 \cdot 1331$ Simplify.

≈ 5572.4533 Multiply.

The volume of the soccer ball is about 5572.5 cm³.

Reflect

4. What is the volume of the soccer ball in terms of π, to the nearest whole number multiple? Explain your answer.

1,775π; Sample answer: I multiplied $\dfrac{4}{3}$ and 11^3 and rounded.

5. Analyze Relationships The diameter of a basketball is about 1.1 times that of a soccer ball. The diameter of a tennis ball is about 0.3 times that of a soccer ball. How do the volumes of these balls compare to that of a soccer ball? Explain.

Basketball: about 1.3 times as big; tennis ball: about 0.03 times as big. The radius is cubed in the formula, so compared to the soccer ball, $1.1^3 \approx 1.3$, and $0.3^3 \approx 0.03$.

YOUR TURN

6. Val measures the diameter of a ball as 12 inches. How many cubic inches of air does this ball hold, to the nearest tenth? Use 3.14 for π.

904.3 in³

Personal Math Trainer
Online Assessment and Intervention
© my.hrw.com

---

1. Vocabulary A sphere is a three-dimensional figure with all points the same distance from the center. (Explore Activity)

2. Vocabulary The radius is the distance from the center of a sphere to a point on the sphere. (Explore Activity)

Find the volume of each sphere. Round your answers to the nearest tenth if necessary. Use 3.14 for π. (Example 1)

3. 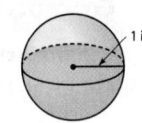 1 in.

4.2 in³

4. 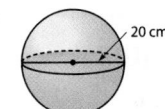 20 cm

4,186.7 cm³

5. A sphere has a radius of 1.5 feet. 14.1 ft³

6. A sphere has a diameter of 2 yards. 4.2 yd³

7. A baseball has a diameter of 2.9 inches. Find the volume of the baseball. Round your answer to the nearest tenth if necessary. Use 3.14 for π. (Example 2)   12.8 in³

8. A basketball has a radius of 4.7 inches. What is its volume to the nearest cubic inch? Use 3.14 for π. (Example 2)   435 in³

9. A company is deciding whether to package a ball in a cubic box or a cylindrical box. In either case, the ball will touch the bottom, top, and sides. (Explore Activity)

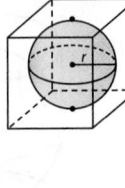

a. What portion of the space inside the cylindrical box is empty? Explain.
$\dfrac{1}{3}$; the ball takes up $\dfrac{2}{3}$ of the space, so $\dfrac{1}{3}$ is empty.

b. Find an expression for the volume of the cubic box. $(2r)^3 = 8r^3$

c. About what portion of the space inside the cubic box is empty? Explain.
Almost $\dfrac{1}{2}$; the empty space is $8r^3 - \left(\dfrac{4}{3}\right)\pi r^3$, or about $3.81r^3$, and $\dfrac{3.81}{8} \approx 0.48$.

? ESSENTIAL QUESTION CHECK-IN

10. Explain the steps you use to find the volume of a sphere.
Find the radius. Then substitute r into the formula $V = \dfrac{4}{3}\pi r^3$ and simplify.

DIFFERENTIATE INSTRUCTION

Modeling

The radius of a basketball is about 4.5 inches. To find the volume of a basketball, imagine the ball is sliced into two halves. Then find the volume of one half and multiply times 2.

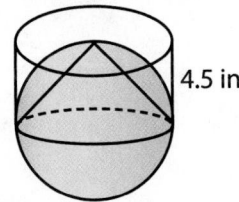 4.5 in.

The volume of a hemisphere is exactly halfway between the volume of a cone and the volume of a cylinder, which both have the same radius r as the hemisphere and a height equal to r.

Cognitive Strategies

Ask students in small groups to brainstorm which mnemonic devices they might use to remember the different formulas for the volumes of a cylinder, a cone, and a sphere. Invite them to create rhymes, raps, cartoons, etc. to help them remember these three different but related formulas and the shapes for which they apply.

Additional Resources

Differentiated Instruction includes:

- Reading Strategies
- Success for English Learners **ELL**
- Reteach
- Challenge **PRE-AP**

21.3 LESSON QUIZ

 **FL CC** 8.G.3.9

Round your answers to the nearest tenth if necessary. Use 3.14 for π.

1. A ball fits exactly into a cylinder as shown in the figure. The volume of the cylinder is 30 cm³. What is the volume of the sphere?

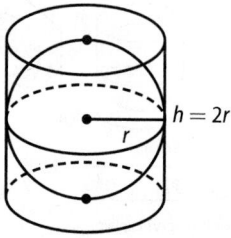

$h = 2r$

r

2. Find the volume of a sphere with a radius of 2.6 inches.

3. Find the volume of a sphere with a diameter of 8.2 meters.

4. Jen has a silver charm on her bracelet in the shape of a soccer ball with a radius of 1 centimeter. What is the volume of this charm?

5. A ball has a circumference of 37.68 inches. What is the volume of the ball?

Lesson Quiz available online

⏻ my.hrw.com

Answers

1. 20 cm³

2. 73.6 in³

3. 288.5 m³

4. 4.2 cm³

5. 904.3 in³

Evaluate

GUIDED AND INDEPENDENT PRACTICE

 **FL CC** 8.G.3.9

Concepts & Skills	Practice
Explore Activity Modeling the Volume of a Sphere	Exercises 1–2, 9
Example 1 Finding the Volume of a Sphere Using a Formula	Exercises 3–6, 11–16
Example 2 Finding the Volume of a Sphere in a Real-World Context	Exercises 7–8, 17–20

Exercise	Depth of Knowledge (D.O.K.)	**FL CC** Mathematical Practices
11–16	**2** Skills/Concepts	**MP.5.1** Using Tools
17–19	**2** Skills/Concepts	**MP.4.1** Modeling
20	**3** Strategic Thinking H.O.T.	**MP.1.1** Problem Solving
21	**2** Skills/Concepts	**MP.6.1** Precision
22	**3** Strategic Thinking H.O.T.	**MP.7.1** Using Structure
23	**2** Skills/Concepts	**MP.2.1** Reasoning
24	**3** Strategic Thinking H.O.T.	**MP.3.1** Logic
25	**3** Strategic Thinking H.O.T.	**MP.4.1** Modeling
26	**3** Strategic Thinking H.O.T.	**MP.2.1** Reasoning
27	**3** Strategic Thinking H.O.T.	**MP.3.1** Logic

Additional Resources

Differentiated Instruction includes:

• Leveled Practice worksheets

CLUSTER CONNECTION **Exercise 23** combines concepts from the Florida Common Core cluster "Solve real-world and mathematical problems involving volume of cylinders, cones, and spheres."

21.3 Independent Practice

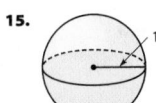
FL CC 8.G.3.9

Personal
Math Trainer
Online
Assessment and
Intervention
my.hrw.com

Find the volume of each sphere. Round your answers to the nearest tenth if necessary. Use 3.14 for π.

11. radius of 3.1 meters ___124.7 m³___

12. diameter of 18 inches ___3,052.1 in³___

13. $r = 6$ in. ___904.3 in³___

14. $d = 36$ m ___24,416.6 m³___

15.

11 cm

___5572.5 cm³___

16.

2.5 ft

___8.2 ft³___

The eggs of birds and other animals come in many different shapes and sizes. Eggs often have a shape that is nearly spherical. When this is true, you can use the formula for a sphere to find their volume.

17. The green turtle lays eggs that are approximately spherical with an average diameter of 4.5 centimeters. Each turtle lays an average of 113 eggs at one time. Find the total volume of these eggs, to the nearest cubic centimeter.

___5389 cm³___

18. Hummingbirds lay eggs that are nearly spherical and about 1 centimeter in diameter. Find the volume of an egg. Round your answer to the nearest tenth.

___0.5 cm³___

19. Fossilized spherical eggs of dinosaurs called titanosaurid sauropods were found in Patagonia. These eggs were 15 centimeters in diameter. Find the volume of an egg. Round your answer to the nearest tenth.

___1766.3 cm³___

20. **Persevere in Problem Solving** An ostrich egg has about the same volume as a sphere with a diameter of 5 inches. If the eggshell is about $\frac{1}{12}$ inch thick, find the volume of just the shell, not including the interior of the egg. Round your answer to the nearest tenth.

___6.3 in³___

21. **Multistep** Write the steps you would use to find a formula for the volume of the figure at right. Then write the formula.

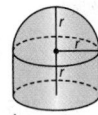

Find the volume of a sphere with radius r: $V = \frac{4}{3}\pi r^3$. Divide by 2 to find the volume of the hemisphere: $V = \frac{2}{3}\pi r^3$. Find the volume of the cylinder:

$V = \pi r^2 h = \pi r^3$. Note that $h = r$. Add the volume of the hemisphere and the volume of the cylinder: $V = \frac{2}{3}\pi r^3 + \pi r^3 = \frac{5}{3}\pi r^3$.

22. **Critical Thinking** Explain what happens to the volume of a sphere if you double the radius.

The volume is multiplied by 8 (or 2 cubed).

23. **Multistep** A cylindrical can of tennis balls holds a stack of three balls so that they touch the can at the top, bottom, and sides. The radius of each ball is 1.25 inches. Find the volume inside the can that is not taken up by the three tennis balls.

___12.3 in³___

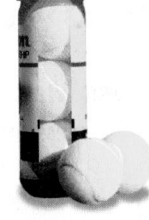

H.O.T. FOCUS ON HIGHER ORDER THINKING

Work Area

24. **Critique Reasoning** A sphere has a radius of 4 inches, and a cube-shaped box has an edge length of 7.5 inches. J.D. says the box has a greater volume, so the sphere will fit in the box. Is he correct? Explain.

No; the box has a greater volume, but it would need an edge length of 8 inches, the diameter of the sphere, for the sphere to fit inside the box.

25. **Critical Thinking** Which would hold the most water: a bowl in the shape of a hemisphere with radius r, a cylindrical glass with radius r and height r, or a cone-shaped drinking cup with radius r and height r? Explain.

The cylindrical glass; the cylinder has a volume of πr^3, while the hemisphere's volume is $\frac{2}{3}\pi r^3$, and the cone's volume is $\frac{1}{3}\pi r^3$.

26. **Analyze Relationships** Hari has models of a sphere, a cylinder, and a cone. The sphere's diameter and the cylinder's height are the same, $2r$. The cylinder has radius r. The cone has diameter $2r$ and height $2r$. Compare the volumes of the cone and the sphere to the volume of the cylinder.

The volume of the cone is one-third the volume of the cylinder. The volume of the sphere is two-thirds the volume of the cylinder.

27. A spherical helium balloon that is 8 feet in diameter can lift about 17 pounds. What does the diameter of a balloon need to be to lift a person who weighs 136 pounds? Explain.

About 16 feet; 136 is 8 times 17, so the volume must be 8 times as big. Because $2^3 = 8$, this means that the radius, and thus the diameter, must be twice as big.

EXTEND THE MATH PRE-AP
Activity available online my.hrw.com

Activity Use a sphere of clay or plastic foam, and intersect, or cut, it with a plane passing through the center of the sphere. The cross section formed is a *great circle* of the sphere, the largest cross section for that sphere. The distance along the edge of a great circle is the shortest distance between two points on the sphere. Examine a globe. What is the name for the special great circle on Earth from which latitude is measured? equator How many different intersections are possible that result in a cross section that is a great circle? infinitely many Are all great circles of a given sphere congruent? yes Examine a flat map of the world. What is the shortest route from New York to Beijing, China? Now look at a globe. Do you see a shorter route? Help students see that the shortest route from New York to Beijing is a great circle route that passes over the Arctic regions.

Ready to Go On?

Assess Mastery

Use the assessment on this page to determine if students have mastered the concepts and standards covered in this module.

Response to Intervention

Intervention	Enrichment
Access Ready to Go On? assessment online, and receive instant scoring, feedback, and customized intervention or enrichment.	

Personal Math Trainer
Online Assessment and Intervention

my.hrw.com

Online and Print Resources

Differentiated Instruction
• Reteach worksheets
• Reading Strategies **ELL**
• Success for English Learners **ELL**

Differentiated Instruction
• Challenge worksheets **PRE-AP**
• Extend the Math **PRE-AP** Lesson Activities in TE

Additional Resources

Assessment Resources include:
• Leveled Module Quizzes

MODULE QUIZ

Ready to Go On?

Personal Math Trainer
Online Assessment and Intervention
my.hrw.com

21.1 Volume of Cylinders

Find the volume of each cylinder. Round your answers to the nearest tenth if necessary. Use 3.14 for π.

1. 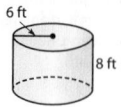 6 ft, 8 ft

904.3 ft³

2. A can of juice has a radius of 4 inches and a height of 7 inches. What is the volume of the can?

351.7 in³

21.2 Volume of Cones

Find the volume of each cone. Round your answers to the nearest tenth if necessary. Use 3.14 for π.

3. 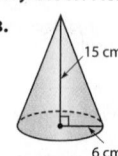 15 cm, 6 cm

565.2 cm³

4. 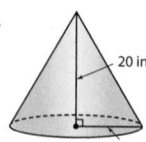 20 in., 12 in.

3014.4 in³

21.3 Volume of Spheres

Find the volume of each sphere. Round your answers to the nearest tenth if necessary. Use 3.14 for π.

5. 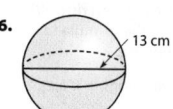 3 ft

113 ft³

6. 13 cm

1149.8 cm³

? ESSENTIAL QUESTION

7. What measurements do you need to know to find the volume of a cylinder? a cone? a sphere?

cylinder: radius of base and height; cone: radius of

base and height; sphere: radius

© Houghton Mifflin Harcourt Publishing Company

Module 21 **681**

Florida Common Core Standards

Lesson	Exercises	Common Core Standards
21.1	1–2	**8.G.3.9**
21.2	3–4	**8.G.3.9**
21.3	5–6	**8.G.3.9**

PARCC Assessment Readiness

Assessment Readiness Tip Students can use estimation to eliminate some of the answer choices.

Item 2 Students can round 11.4 down to 10, 10.7 down to 10, and 3.14 down to 3. This makes the estimate for the volume of the cylinder $3(5)^2(10) = 750$. Because all numbers were rounded down, the estimate is less than the actual volume. Answer choices A and B are less than the estimate, and D is several times larger than the estimate. C is the only reasonable answer.

Item 4 Students can round 17 to 20, 6 to 5, and 3.14 to 3, and then plug into the formula to find $\frac{1}{3}(3)(5)^2(20) = 500$. The only answer choice close to 500 is B, 640.6.

Avoid Common Errors

Item 3 Remind students that the volumes of both cylinders and cones are defined by radius and height, and they need to read the problem carefully to decide which formula to use. Some students may use the formula for the volume of a cylinder rather than the volume of a cone.

Item 6 Students may correctly find the volume of the sphere but forget to divide it by 2 to make it a half-sphere. Remind students to confirm that their numerical answer corresponds to the question that was asked.

Additional Resources

Personal Math Trainer
Online Assessment and Intervention
my.hrw.com

Selected Response

1. The bed of a pickup truck measures 4 feet by 8 feet. To the nearest inch, what is the length of the longest thin metal bar that will lie flat in the bed?

- (A) 11 ft 3 in.
- (B) 10 ft 0 in.
- (C) 8 ft 11 in.
- (D) 8 ft 9 in.

2. Using 3.14 for π, what is the volume of the cylinder below to the nearest tenth?

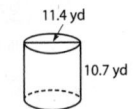
11.4 yd
10.7 yd

- (A) 102 cubic yards
- (B) 347.6 cubic yards
- (C) 1,091.6 cubic yards
- (D) 4,366.4 cubic yards

3. Rhett made mini waffle cones for a birthday party. Each waffle cone was 3.5 inches high and had a radius of 0.8 inches. What is the volume of each cone to the nearest hundredth?

- (A) 1.70 cubic inches
- (B) 2.24 cubic inches
- (C) 2.34 cubic inches
- (D) 8.79 cubic inches

4. What is the volume of a cone that has a height of 17 meters and a base with a radius of 6 meters? Use 3.14 for π and round to the nearest tenth.

- (A) 204 cubic meters
- (B) 640.6 cubic meters
- (C) 2,562.2 cubic meters
- (D) 10,249 cubic meters

5. Using 3.14 for π, what is the volume of the sphere to the nearest tenth?

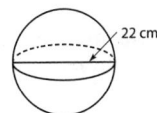
22 cm

- (A) 4,180 cubic centimeters
- (B) 5,572.5 cubic centimeters
- (C) 33,434.7 cubic centimeters
- (D) 44,579.6 cubic centimeters

Mini-Task

6. A diagram of a deodorant container is shown. It is made up of a cylinder and half of a sphere.

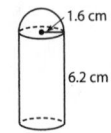
1.6 cm
6.2 cm

Use 3.14 for π and round answers to the nearest tenth.

a. What is the volume of the half sphere?

8.6 cubic centimeters

b. What is the volume of the cylinder?

49.8 cubic centimeters

c. What is the volume of the whole figure?

58.4 cubic centimeters

 ## Florida Common Core Standards

Items	Grade 8 Standards	Mathematical Practices
1*	8.G.2.7	MP.4.1
2	8.G.3.9	MP.4.1
3	8.G.3.9	MP.4.1
4	8.G.3.9	MP.2.1
5	8.G.3.9	MP.4.1
6	8.G.3.9	MP.4.1

* Item integrates mixed review concepts from previous modules or a previous course.

UNIT 9 Measurement Geometry

Study Guide Review

Additional Resources

Personal Math Trainer

Online Assessment and Intervention

my.hrw.com

Assessment Resources
- Leveled Unit Tests: A, B, C, D
- Performance Assessment

Vocabulary Development

Integrating Language Arts

Encourage students to practice using the unit vocabulary as they talk and write about mathematics. Understanding vocabulary will aid their understanding of the concepts.

FL CC   LACC.68.RST.2.4 Determine the meaning of symbols, key terms, and other domain-specific words and phrases as they are used in a specific scientific or technical context relevant to grades 6–8 texts and topics.

MODULE 19 Angle Relationships in Parallel Lines and Triangles

FL CC   8.G.1.5, 8.EE.2.6, 8.EE.3.7, 8.EE.3.7b

Key Concepts
- The alternate interior angles formed by transversal intersecting parallel lines are congruent as are the alternate exterior angles. Same–side interior angles are supplementary. *(Lesson 19.1)*
- The sum of the interior angle measures of a triangle is 180°. *(Lesson 19.2)*
- The measure of the exterior angle of a triangle is equal to the sum of its remote interior angles. *(Lesson 19.2)*
- If two angles of one triangle are congruent to two angles of another triangle, then the triangles are similar. *(Lesson 19.3)*

Study Guide Review

MODULE 19 Angle Relationships in Parallel Lines and Triangles

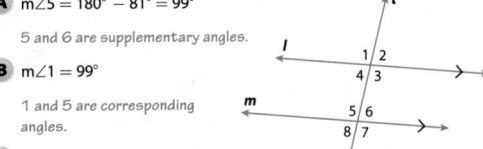

? ESSENTIAL QUESTION

How can you solve real-world problems that involve angle relationships in parallel lines and triangles?

Key Vocabulary

alternate exterior angles
(ángulos alternos externos)

alternate interior angles
(ángulos alternos internos)

corresponding angles
(ángulos correspondientes (para líneas))

exterior angle *(ángulo externo de un polígono)*

interior angle *(ángulos internos)*

remote interior angle
(ángulo interno remoto)

same-side interior angles
(ángulos internos del mismo lado)

similar *(semejantes)*

transversal *(transversal)*

EXAMPLE 1

Find each angle measure when m∠6 = 81°.

A m∠5 = 180° − 81° = 99°

5 and 6 are supplementary angles.

B m∠1 = 99°

1 and 5 are corresponding angles.

C m∠3 = 180° − 81° = 99°

3 and 6 are same-side interior angles.

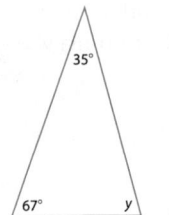

EXAMPLE 2

Are the triangles similar? Explain your answer.

$y = 180° − (67° + 35°)$

$y = 78°$

$x = 180° − (67° + 67°)$

$x = 46°$

The triangles are not similar, because they do not have 2 or more pairs of corresponding congruent angles.

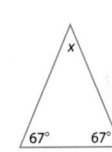

EXERCISES

1. If m∠*GHA* = 106°, find the measures of the given angles. (Lesson 19.1)

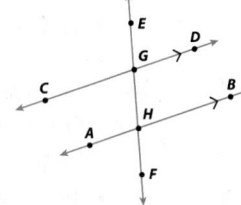

m∠*EGC* = ___106°___

m∠*EGD* = ___74°___

m∠*BHF* = ___106°___

m∠*HGD* = ___106°___

2. Find the measure of the missing angles. (Lesson 19.2)

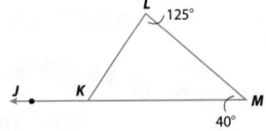

m∠*JKL* = ___165°___

m∠*LKM* = ___15°___

3. Is the larger triangle similar to the smaller triangle? Explain your answer. (Lesson 19.3)

The triangles are similar because all of their angles are congruent.

_____

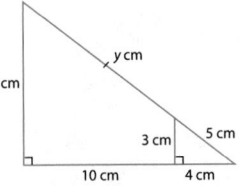

4. Find the value of *x* and *y* in the figure. (Lesson 19.3)

$x = 10.5$ cm and $y = 12.5$ cm

5. If m∠*CJI* = 132° and m∠*EIH* = 59°, find the measures of the given angles. (Lesson 19.1)

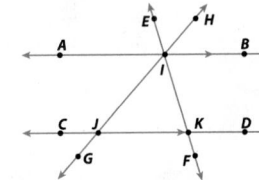

m∠*IKJ* = ___73°___

m∠*HIB* = ___48°___

m∠*EIJ* = ___121°___

m∠*AIK* = ___107°___

MODULE 20 The Pythagorean Theorem

 **FL CC** 8.G.2.6, 8.G.2.7, 8.G.2.8

Key Concepts
- If a triangle is a right triangle, the sum of the squares of the lengths of the legs is equal to the square of the length of the hypotenuse. *(Lesson 20.1)*
- If the sum of the squares of the lengths of the legs of a triangle is equal to the square of the hypotenuse, then it is a right triangle. *(Lesson 20.2)*
- The Distance Formula states that the distance d between two points (x_1, y_1) and (x_2, y_2) is $d = \sqrt{(x_2 - x_1)^2 + (y_2 - y_1)^2}$. *(Lesson 20.3)*

MODULE 21 Volume

FL CC 8.G.3.9

Key Concepts
- A cylinder is a three-dimensional figure with 2 congruent circular bases. To find the volume of a cylinder, use the formula $V = Bh$ or $V = \pi r^2 h$. *(Lesson 21.1)*
- A cone is a three-dimensional figure with 1 circular base and 1 vertex. To find the volume of a cone, use the formula $V = \frac{1}{3}Bh$ or $V = \frac{1}{3}\pi r^2 h$. *(Lesson 21.2)*
- A sphere is a three-dimensional figure with all points the same distance from the center. To find the volume of a cylinder, use the formula $V = \frac{4}{3}\pi r^3$. *(Lesson 21.3)*

Key Vocabulary
hypotenuse *(hipotenusa)*
legs *(catetos)*
Pythagorean Theorem
(teorema de Pitágoras)

? ESSENTIAL QUESTION
How can you use the Pythagorean Theorem to solve real-world problems?

EXAMPLE 1

Find the missing side length.
Round your answer to the nearest tenth.

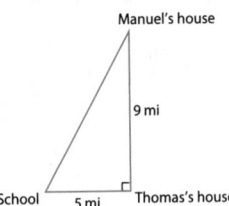

$a^2 + b^2 = c^2$

$7^2 + b^2 = 18^2$

$49 + b^2 = 324$

$b^2 = 275$

$b = \sqrt{275} \approx 16.6$

The length of the leg is about 16.6 inches.

EXAMPLE 2

Thomas drew a diagram to represent the location of his house, the school, and his friend Manuel's house. What is the distance from the school to Manuel's house? Round your answer to the nearest tenth.

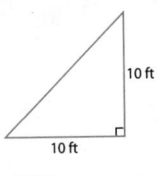

$a^2 + b^2 = c^2$

$5^2 + 9^2 = c^2$

$25 + 81 = c^2$

$c^2 = 106$

$c = \sqrt{106} \approx 10.3$

The distance from the school to Manuel's house is about 10.3 miles.

EXERCISES

Find the missing side lengths. Round your answers to the nearest hundredth. (Lesson 20.1)

1.

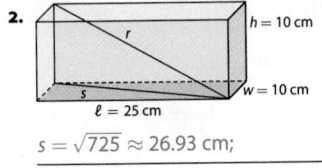

$\sqrt{200} \approx 14.14$ ft

2.

$h = 10$ cm
r
s
$\ell = 25$ cm
$w = 10$ cm

$s = \sqrt{725} \approx 26.93$ cm;
$r = \sqrt{825} \approx 28.72$ cm

---

3. Hye Sun has a modern coffee table whose top is a triangle with the following side lengths: 8 feet, 3 feet, and 5 feet. Is Hye Sun's coffee table top a right triangle? (Lesson 20.2)

   No, it is not a right triangle.

4. Find the length of each side of triangle *ABC*. If necessary, round your answers to the nearest hundredth. (Lesson 20.3)

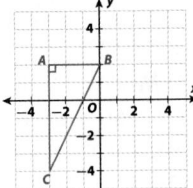

$\overline{AB}$ _____ 3 units _____

$\overline{BC}$ _____ $\sqrt{45} \approx 6.71$ units _____

$\overline{AC}$ _____ 6 units _____

Key Vocabulary
cone *(cono)*
cylinder *(cilindro)*
sphere *(esfera)*

? ESSENTIAL QUESTION
How can you solve real-world problems that involve volume?

EXAMPLE 1

Find the volume of the cistern. Round your answer to the nearest hundredth.

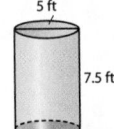

5 ft

7.5 ft

$V = \pi r^2 h$

$\approx 3.14 \cdot 2.5^2 \cdot 7.5$

$\approx 3.14 \cdot 6.25 \cdot 7.5$

≈ 147.19

The cistern has a volume of approximately 147.19 cubic feet.

EXAMPLE 2

Find the volume of a sphere with a radius of 3.7 cm. Write your answer in terms of π and to the nearest hundredth.

$V = \frac{4}{3}\pi r^3$

$\approx \frac{4}{3} \cdot \pi \cdot 3.7^3$

$\approx \frac{4}{3} \cdot \pi \cdot 50.653$

$\approx 67.54\pi$

$V = \frac{4}{3}\pi r^3$

$\approx \frac{4}{3} \cdot 3.14 \cdot 3.7^3$

$\approx \frac{4}{3} \cdot 3.14 \cdot 50.653$

≈ 212.07

The volume of the sphere is approximately 67.54π cm³, or 212.07 cm³.

Unit 9 Performance Tasks

The Performance Tasks provide students with the opportunity to apply concepts from this unit in real-world problem situations.

CAREERS IN MATH

Hydrologist In Performance Task Item 1, students can see how a hydrologist uses mathematics on the job.

SCORING GUIDES FOR PERFORMANCE TASKS

1. MATHEMATICAL PRACTICES 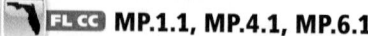 **MP.1.1, MP.4.1, MP.6.1**

Task	Possible Points (Total: 6)
a	**1 point** for explanation: Multiply the density, 1000 kg/m³, by the volume of the cylinder, $\pi r^2 h$, to find the mass. **2 points** for correct calculation and mass: 26,533,000 kg
b	**1 point** for correct answer: no **2 points** for explanation: The volume of the aquifer is 34,618.5 m³, which is 34,618,500 kg of water. Since the answer in **a** is less, the aquifer is not completely full.

2. MATHEMATICAL PRACTICES 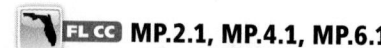 **MP.2.1, MP.4.1, MP.6.1**

Task	Possible Points (Total: 6)
a	**3 points** for correct diagram: 4 3 2 5 *Home*
b	**2 points** for correctly calculating that the total distance was 24 blocks. **1 point** for correctly calculating that the walk before the rain was 4 blocks longer than the walk home.

EXERCISES

Find the volume of each figure. Round your answers to the nearest hundredth. (Lessons 21.1, 21.2, 21.3)

1.

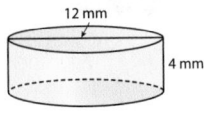
12 mm
4 mm

_____ 452.16 mm³

2.

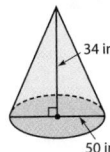
34 in.
50 in.

_____ 22,241.67 in³
_____ 19.85 in³

3. Find the volume of a ball with a radius of 1.68 inches.

4.

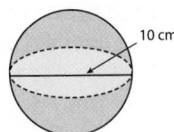
10 cm

_____ 523.33 cm³

5.

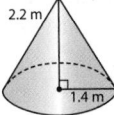
2.2 m
1.4 m

_____ 4.51 m³

6. A round above-ground swimming pool has a diameter of 15 ft and a height of 4.5 ft. What is the volume of the swimming pool?

_____ 794.81 ft³

7.

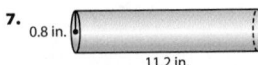
0.8 in.
11.2 in.

_____ 22.51 in³

8.

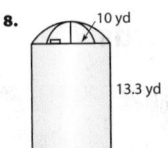
10 yd
13.3 yd

_____ 1,305.72 yd³

9. A paper cup in the shape of a cone has a height of 4.7 inches and a diameter of 3.6 inches. What is the volume of the paper cup?

_____ 15.94 in³

Unit 9 Performance Tasks

1. **CAREERS IN MATH** | Hydrologist A hydrologist needs to estimate the mass of water in an underground aquifer, which is roughly cylindrical in shape. The diameter of the aquifer is 65 meters, and its depth is 8 meters. One cubic meter of water has a mass of about 1000 kilograms.

a. The aquifer is completely filled with water. What is the total mass of the water in the aquifer? Explain how you found your answer. Use 3.14 for π and round your answer to the nearest kilogram.

Multiply the mass of one cubic meter of water by the volume

of the aquifer; $(3.14)(32.5^2)(8)(1000) = 26,533,000$ kg

b. Another cylindrical aquifer has a diameter of 70 meters and a depth of 9 meters. The mass of the water in it is 27×10^7 kilograms. Is the aquifer totally filled with water? Explain your reasoning.

No; if it were full of water, the mass would be 34,618,500 kg,

or 3.4×10^7 kg. Since the mass of the water is less than this,

the aquifer must not be full.

2. From his home, Myles walked his dog north 5 blocks, east 2 blocks, and then stopped at a drinking fountain. He then walked north 3 more blocks and east 4 more blocks. It started to rain so he cut through a field and walked straight home.

a. Draw a diagram of his path.

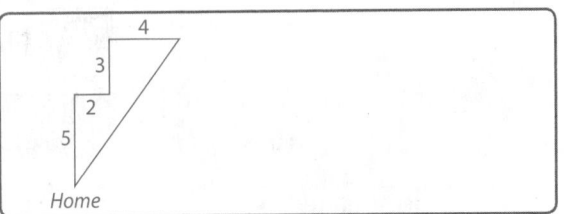
4
3
2
5
Home

b. How many blocks did Myles walk in all? How much longer was his walk before it started to rain than his walk home?

24 blocks; 4 blocks longer

MIXED REVIEW

PARCC Assessment Readiness

Assessment Readiness Tip Encourage students to draw a picture or diagram to organize information from the problem.

> **Item 5** Students can draw a right triangle to represent the situation in the word problem, which will help them plug the lengths into the Pythagorean Theorem correctly.

> **Item 7** If students draw a right triangle beside the problem with the legs and hypotenuse labeled, it may help them to put the numbers into the Pythagorean Theorem correctly, with the longest side always being the hypotenuse.

Avoid Common Errors

> **Item 2** Many students find x but forget to plug x back into the original expressions to find the smallest angle. Remind students to read carefully and double check that they have completely finished the problem before selecting an answer.

Florida Common Core Standards

Items	Grade 8 Standards	Mathematical Practices
1	8.G.1.5	MP.2.1
2	8.G.1.5	MP.2.1
3	8.G.3.9	MP.2.1
4*	8.NS.1.2	MP.6.1
5	8.G.2.7	MP.4.1
6	8.G.3.9	MP.2.1
7	8.G.2.6	MP.7.1
8*	8.EE.3.8a	MP.6.1
9	8.G.3.9	MP.2.1
10*	8.EE.3.8b	MP.2.1
11	8.EE.3.7b, 8.G.1.5	MP.2.1
12	8.G.1.5, 8.G.2.7	MP.1.1
13	8.G.3.9	MP.1.1

* Item integrates mixed review concepts from previous modules or a previous course.

PARCC Assessment Readiness

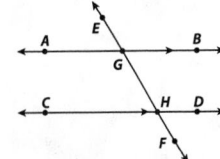

Personal Math Trainer
Online Assessment and Intervention
my.hrw.com

Selected Response

1. Which of the following angle pairs formed by a transversal that intersects two parallel lines are not congruent?

Ⓐ alternate interior angles

Ⓑ adjacent angles

Ⓒ corresponding angles

Ⓓ alternate exterior angles

2. The measures of the three angles of a triangle are given by $3x + 1$, $2x - 3$, and $9x$. What is the measure of the smallest angle?

Ⓐ 13°   Ⓒ 29°

Ⓑ 23°   Ⓓ 40°

3. Using 3.14 for π, what is the volume of the cylinder?

Ⓐ 200 cubic yards

Ⓑ 628 cubic yards

Ⓒ 1,256 cubic yards

Ⓓ 2,512 cubic yards

10 yd
8 yd

4. Which of the following is **not** true?

Ⓐ $\sqrt{36} + 2 > \sqrt{16} + 5$

Ⓑ $5\pi < 17$

Ⓒ $\sqrt{10} + 1 < \frac{9}{2}$

Ⓓ $5 - \sqrt{35} < 0$

5. A pole is 65 feet tall. A support wire is attached to the top of the pole and secured to the ground 33 feet from the base of the pole. Find the approximate length of the wire.

Ⓐ 32 feet   Ⓒ 56 feet

Ⓑ 73 feet   Ⓓ 60 feet

6. Using 3.14 for π, what is the volume of the sphere to the nearest tenth?

7 cm

Ⓐ 205.1 cm³

Ⓑ 1,077 cm³

Ⓒ 179.5 cm³

Ⓓ 4,308.1 cm³

7. Which set of lengths are **not** the side lengths of a right triangle?

Ⓐ 28, 45, 53   Ⓒ 36, 77, 85

Ⓑ 13, 84, 85   Ⓓ 16, 61, 65

8. Which statement describes the solution of a system of linear equations for two lines with different slopes and different y-intercepts?

Ⓐ one nonzero solution

Ⓑ infinitely many solutions

Ⓒ no solution

Ⓓ solution of 0

9. What is the side length of a cube that has a volume of 729 cubic inches?

Ⓐ 7 inches   Ⓒ 9 inches

Ⓑ 8 inches   Ⓓ 10 inches

10. What is the solution to the system of equations?

$$\begin{cases} x + 3y = 5 \\ 2x - y = -4 \end{cases}$$

Ⓐ no solution

Ⓑ infinitely many solutions

Ⓒ (2, 1)

Ⓓ (−1, 2)

Mini-Tasks

11. In the figure shown, $m\angle AGE = (5x - 7)°$ and $m\angle BGH = (3x + 19)°$.

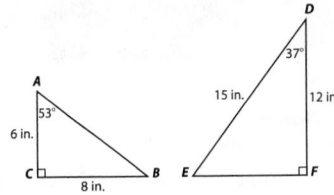

a. Find the value of x. _$x = 13$_

b. Find $m\angle AGE$. _58°_

c. Find $m\angle GHD$. _122°_

12. Tom drew two right triangles as shown with angle measures to the nearest whole unit.

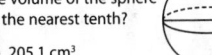

a. Find the length of $\overline{AB}$ in triangle ABC.

_10 in._

b. Find the length of $\overline{EF}$ in triangle DEF.

_9 in._

c. Are the triangles similar? Explain your answer.

yes; $m\angle B = 90° - 53° = 37°$, and $m\angle E = 90° - 37° = 53°$, so there are two pairs of corresponding angles with the same measure.

13. In the diagram, the figure at the top of the cone is a hemisphere.

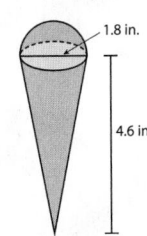
1.8 in.
4.6 in.

a. What is the volume of the cone? Round your answer to the nearest hundredth.

3.90 in³

b. What is the volume of the hemisphere on the top of the cone? Round your answer to the nearest hundredth.

1.53 in³

c. What would be the radius of a sphere with the same total volume as the figure? Explain how you found your answer.

About 1.09 in.; the total volume of the figure is about 5.43 in³. You can solve the equation $\frac{4}{3}\pi r^3 = 5.43$ to find r. You have to estimate the cube root of 1.30, which is about 1.09.

UNIT 10

Statistics: Bivariate Data

Contents

Unit Pacing Guide

45-Minute Classes

Module 22

DAY 1	DAY 2	DAY 3	DAY 4	DAY 5
Lesson 22.1	Lesson 22.1	Lesson 22.2	Lesson 22.2	Ready to Go On? PARCC Assessment Readiness

Module 23

DAY 1	DAY 2	DAY 3	DAY 4	DAY 5
Lesson 23.1	Lesson 23.1	Lesson 23.2	Lesson 23.2	Ready to Go On? PARCC Assessment Readiness

DAY 6				
Study Guide PARCC Assessment Readiness				

90-Minute Classes

Module 22

DAY 1	DAY 2
Lesson 22.1	Lesson 22.2 Ready to Go On? PARCC Assessment Readiness

Module 23

DAY 1	DAY 2	DAY 3	
Lesson 23.1	Lesson 23.2	Ready to Go On? PARCC Assessment Readiness	Study Guide PARCC Assessment Readiness

Program Resources

⏻ Plan

Online Teacher Edition

Access a full suite of teaching resources online—plan, present, and manage classes, assignments, and activities.

 **ePlanner** Easily plan your classes, create and view assignments, and access all program resources with your online, customizable planning tool.

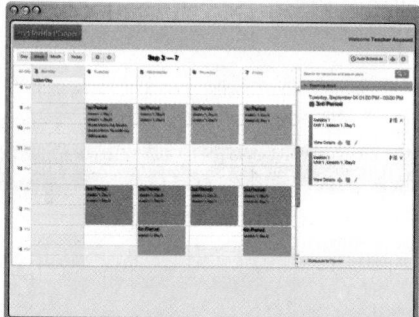

Professional Development Videos

Author Juli Dixon models successful teaching practices and strategies in actual classroom settings.

 **QR Codes** Scan with your smart phone to jump directly from your print book to online videos and other resources.

Teacher's Edition

Support students with point-of-use Questioning Strategies, teaching tips, resources for differentiated instruction, additional activities, and more.

⏻ Engage and Explore

Real-World Videos Engage students with interesting and relevant applications of the mathematical content of each module.

 **Animated Math** Online interactive simulations, tools, and games help students actively learn and practice key concepts.

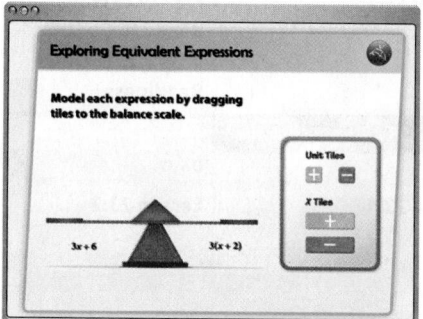

Explore Activities

Students interactively explore new concepts using a variety of tools and approaches.

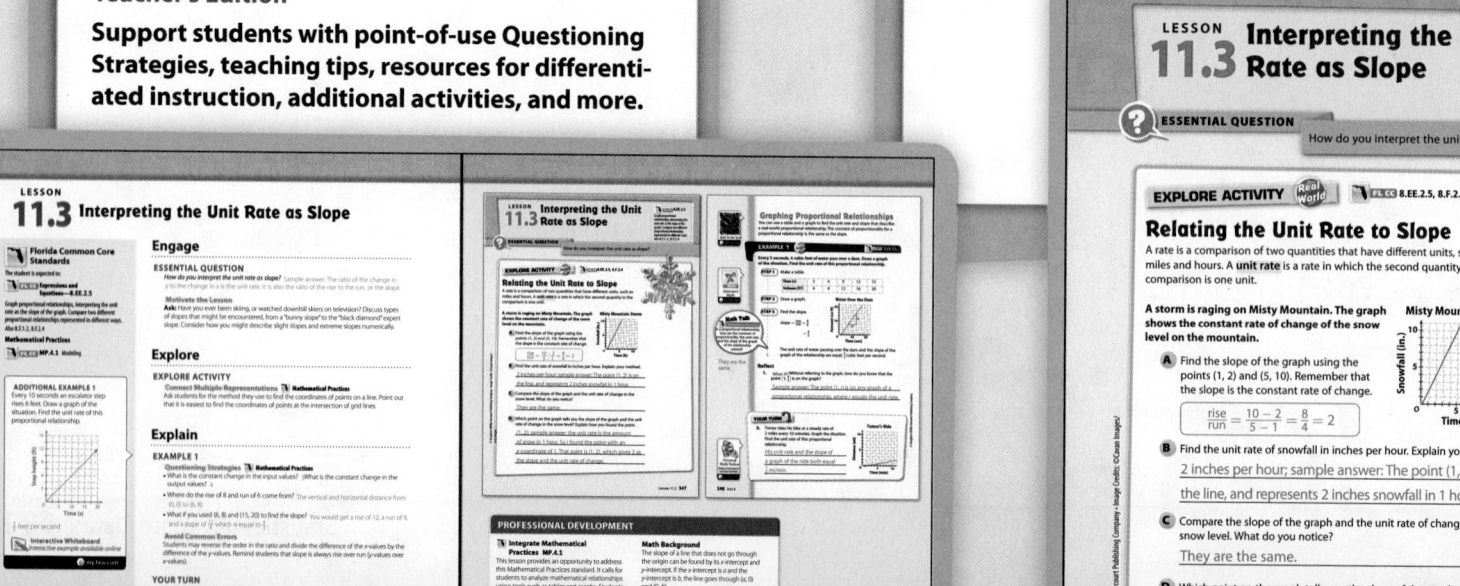

Teach

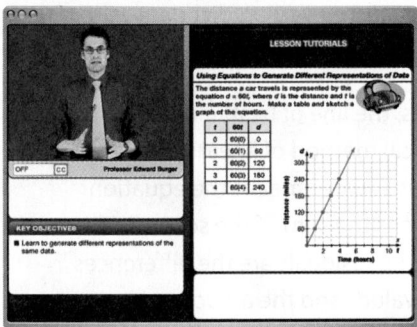

Math On the Spot video tutorials, featuring program authors Dr. Edward Burger and Martha Sandoval-Martinez, accompany every example in the textbook and give students step-by-step instructions and explanations of key math concepts.

Present engaging content on a multitude of devices, including tablets and interactive whiteboards.

Math Talk
Continually monitor and assess student progress with integrated formative assessment.

CLUSTER CONNECTION
Look for exercises indicated with this icon to build connections among standards within Florida Common Core clusters.

Differentiated Instruction Print Resources

Support all learners with Differentiated Instruction Resources, including

- **Leveled Practice and Problem Solving**
- **Reteach**
- **Reading Strategies**
- **Success for English Learners**
- **Challenge**

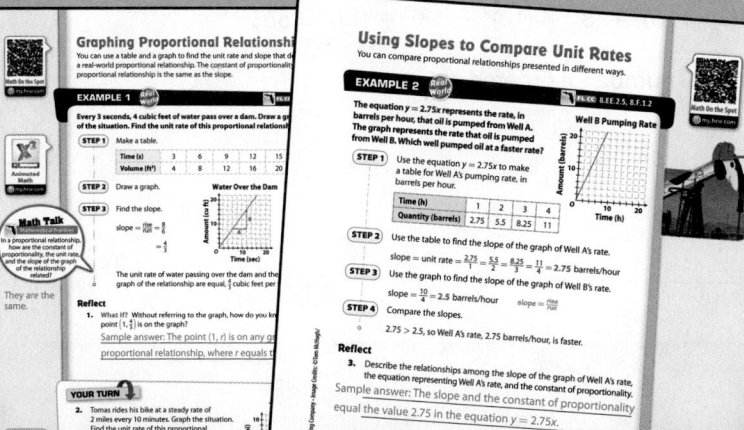

Assessment and Intervention

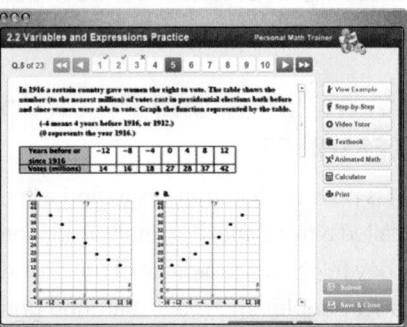

The **Personal Math Trainer** provides online practice, homework, assessments, and intervention. Monitor student progress through reports and alerts. Create and customize assignments aligned to specific lessons or standards.

- **Practice** – With dynamic items and assignments, students get unlimited practice on key concepts supported by guided examples, step-by-step solutions, and video tutorials.
- **Assessments** – Choose from course assignments or customize your own based on course content, standards, difficulty levels, and more.
- **Homework** – Students can complete online homework with a wide variety of problem types, including the ability to enter expressions, equations, and graphs. Let the system automatically grade homework, so you can focus where your students need help the most!
- **Intervention** – Let the Personal Math Trainer automatically prescribe a targeted, personalized intervention path for your students.

Raise the bar with homework and practice that incorporates higher-order thinking and mathematical processes in every lesson.

PARCC Assessment Readiness
Prepare students for success on the PARCC math test with practice at every module and unit.

Assessment Resources

Tailor assessments to meet the needs of all your classes and students, including

- **Leveled Module Quizzes**
- **Leveled Unit Tests**
- **Unit Performance Tasks**
- **Placement, Diagnostic, and Quarterly Benchmark Tests**

Math Background

Scatter Plots and Association 8.SP.1.1
LESSON 22.1

A scatter plot is a graph that shows *bivariate data*; that is, data for which there are two variables for each observation, such as height and weight. Each point on the scatter plot represents one data pair. Students are often tempted to connect points on a graph. It is essential that they understand that a scatter plot shows all the collected data and that, in general, it is meaningless to draw a jagged path connecting the points.

A scatter plot may suggest an association or a correlation between two variables. The terms *association* and *correlation* are often used interchangeably, but they do not mean exactly the same thing. An association can be linear or nonlinear, but a correlation always refers to a linear association. Associations and correlations may be negative or positive.

Trend Lines and Predictions 8.SP.1.3
LESSON 22.2

It is possible for students to find a line of best fit (also called a *trend line*) by purely visual methods. For example, they might place a piece of uncooked spaghetti on top of a scatter plot and move it around until about half of the data points lie above the line and half of the data points lie below the line. Or, they can use a ruler to draw a line on the scatter plot that has about half the data points above it and about half the data points below it.

A line of best fit may be used to interpolate and extrapolate data. You *interpolate* when you use a line of best fit to predict data values that lie between existing data values. You *extrapolate* when you use a line of best fit to predict data values that lie outside the range of existing data values. For example, a scatter plot might show the heights and weights of giraffes that are 15 ft, 16 ft, 18 ft, 20 ft, and 21 ft tall. You interpolate when you predict the weight of a giraffe that is 17 ft tall. You extrapolate when you find the weight of a giraffe that is 22 ft tall.

Note that data in a scatter plot may be highly correlated (in other words, there may be a strong relationship between the two variables), but the points on the scatter plot may not be well represented by a straight line. For example, if there is a quadratic relationship between the two variables, the data points can be approximated by a parabola. Nonetheless, in many situations, drawing a line of best fit offers a straightforward way to predict data values that may not be displayed on the graph.

In more advanced courses, the line of best fit is usually calculated using a statistical method of linear regression such as *least squares*. Least squares means the equation of the line chosen minimizes the sum of the squares of the *residuals* for the line. The residuals are the differences between the actual data values and the associated data values that fit the model. A graphing calculator automatically uses this method to give the line of best fit. To understand how to calculate the line of best fit by hand, it is best to see an example. Consider the data in the table.

x	2	4	5	8	9	11
y	3	5	8	10	13	14

Let x_{sum} = the sum of all x-values.
$$x_{sum} = 2 + 4 + 5 + 8 + 9 + 11 = 39$$

Let y_{sum} = the sum of all y-values.
$$y_{sum} = 3 + 5 + 8 + 10 + 13 + 14 = 53$$

Let xy_{sum} = the sum of the products $x_n y_n$.
$$xy_{sum} = (2)(3) + (4)(5) + (5)(8) + (8)(10) + (9)(13)$$
$$+ (11)(14) = 417$$

Let x^2_{sum} = the sum of the x-values squared.
$$x^2_{sum} = (2)^2 + (4)^2 + (5)^2 + (8)^2 + (9)^2 + (11)^2 = 311$$

Let y^2_{sum} = the sum of the y-values squared.
$$y^2_{sum} = (3)^2 + (5)^2 + (8)^2 + (10)^2 + (13)^2 + (14)^2 = 563$$

Let N = the total number of ordered pairs = 6.

Recall the equation for a line: $y = mx + b$. For the line of best fit for these data, find m and b using the following formulas.

$$m = \frac{(Nxy_{sum}) - (x_{sum}y_{sum})}{(Nx^2_{sum}) - (x_{sum})^2}$$

$$= \frac{(6 \cdot 417) - (39 \cdot 53)}{(6 \cdot 311) - (39)^2}$$

$$m = 1.2609$$

$$b = \frac{(y_{sum}) - m(x_{sum})}{N}$$

$$= \frac{53 - 1.2609(39)}{6}$$

$$b = 0.6375$$

The line of best fit is $y = 1.2609x + 0.6375$.

Two-Way Tables 8.SP.1.4
LESSONS 23.1 and 23.2

Two-way tables are used to show frequencies of data that is categorized two ways. The columns represent one categorization for the population and the rows represent a different categorization for the population. You can use relative frequencies in two-way tables to draw conclusions about whether or not there is an association between the two categories.

Two-way frequency tables can also be used to find other types of frequencies. A two-way relative frequency table can be created from a two-way frequency table. This table shows both joint relative frequency and marginal relative frequency. You can also find a conditional relative frequency from a two-way frequency table by dividing a frequency that is not in a total row or total column by the frequency's row total or column total. Conditional relative frequency can be used to see if there is an association between two variables.

UNIT 10
Statistics: Bivariate Data

CAREERS IN MATH

Psychologist A psychologist investigates the physical, mental, emotional, and social aspects of human behavior. Psychologists use math to evaluate and interpret data about human activities and the human mind. They create and use mathematical models to predict behavior of humans, both individually and in groups.

If you are interested in a career in psychology, you should study the following mathematical subjects:
- Algebra
- Trigonometry
- Probability and Statistics
- Calculus

Research other careers that require the analysis of data and use of mathematical models.

Unit 10 Performance Task

At the end of the unit, check out how **psychologists** use math.

© Houghton Mifflin Harcourt Publishing Company • Image Credits: ©Ron Levine/Getty Images

Careers in Math

Psychologist

A psychologist uses math to recognize correlations and patterns in how humans behave. You will learn more about analyzing psychological data in the Performance Tasks at the end of the unit.

For more information about careers in mathematics as well as various mathematics appreciation topics, visit the American Mathematical Society at www.ams.org

Vocabulary Preview

Use the puzzle to give students a preview of important concepts in this unit. Students may work individually, in pairs, or in groups.

Unit Resources

Go online to access all your unit resources.

my.hrw.com

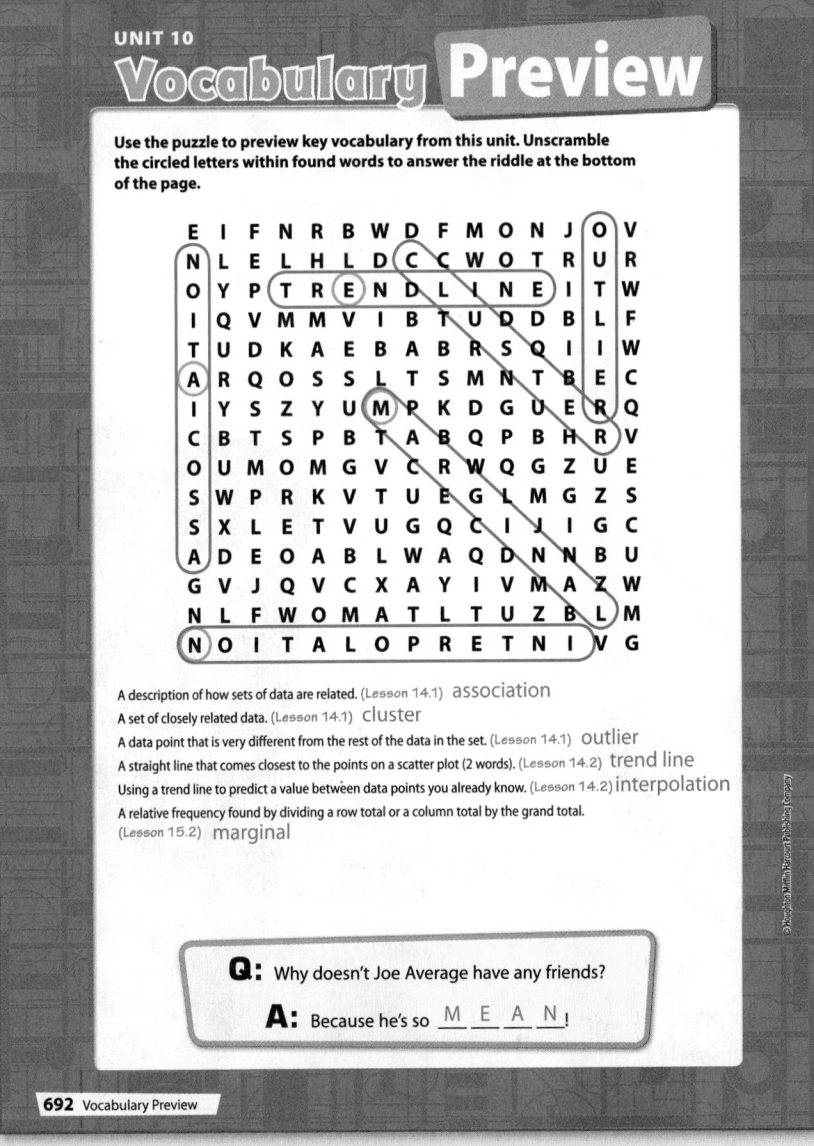

Before	In this Unit	After
Students understand: • how to interpret data • find the mean of a data set • solve problems using graphs of data	Students will learn about: • scatter plots and associations • trend lines and predictions • two-way frequency and relative frequency tables	Students will connect: • scatter plots and trend lines with linear equations • frequency and relative frequency

Scatter Plots

? ESSENTIAL QUESTION

How can you use scatterplots to solve real-world problems?

You can use scatterplots to find the relationships between two sets of real-world data.

LESSON 22.1

Scatter Plots and Association

FL CC 8.SP.1.1

LESSON 22.2

Trend Lines and Predictions

FL CC 8.SP.1.1, 8.SP.1.2, 8.SP.1.3

Real-World Video

An anthropologist measures dinosaur bones. To estimate a dinosaur's height based on the length of a bone, he can make a scatter plot comparing bone length and height of several dinosaurs.

🔘 my.hrw.com

© Houghton Mifflin Harcourt Publishing Company

GO DIGITAL

my.hrw.com

my.hrw.com

Go digital with your write-in student edition, accessible on any device.

Math On the Spot

Scan with your smart phone to jump directly to the online edition, video tutor, and more.

Animated Math

Interactively explore key concepts to see how math works.

Personal Math Trainer

Get immediate feedback and help as you work through practice sets.

Are You Ready?

Assess Readiness

Use the assessment on this page to determine if students need intensive or strategic intervention for the module's prerequisite skills.

Response to Intervention

Intervention	Enrichment

Personal Math Trainer

Online Assessment and Intervention

my.hrw.com

Access Are You Ready? assessment online, and receive instant scoring, feedback, and customized intervention or enrichment.

Online and Print Resources

Skills Intervention worksheets
- Skill 54 Evaluate Expressions
- Skill 60 Solve Two-Step Equations

Differentiated Instruction
- Challenge worksheets **PRE-AP**
- Extend the Math **PRE-AP** Lesson Activities in TE

Are YOU Ready?

Personal Math Trainer
Online Assessment and Intervention
my.hrw.com

Complete these exercises to review skills you will need for this module.

Evaluate Expressions

EXAMPLE

Evaluate $4x + 3$ for $x = 5$.

$4x + 3 = 4(5) + 3$ Substitute the given value for x.

$\quad\quad\quad = 20 + 3$ Multiply.

$\quad\quad\quad = 23$ Add.

Evaluate each expression for the given value of *x*.

1. $6x - 5$ for $x = 4$ 19
2. $-2x + 7$ for $x = 2$ 3
3. $5x - 6$ for $x = 3$ 9
4. $0.5x + 8.4$ for $x = -1$ 7.9
5. $\frac{3}{4}x - 9$ for $x = -20$ -24
6. $1.4x + 3.5$ for $x = -4$ -2.1

Solve Two-Step Equations

EXAMPLE

$5x + 3 = -7$

$\quad\quad\underline{-3 = -3}$ Subtract 3 from both sides.

$\quad 5x = -10$

$\quad \dfrac{5x}{5} = \dfrac{-10}{5}$ Divide both sides by 5.

$\quad\quad x = -2$

Solve for *x*.

7. $3x + 4 = 10$ 2
8. $5x - 11 = 34$ 9
9. $-2x + 5 = -9$ 7
10. $8x + 13 = -11$ -3
11. $4x - 7 = -27$ -5
12. $\frac{1}{2}x + 16 = 39$ 46
13. $\frac{2}{3}x - 16 = 12$ 42
14. $0.5x - 1.5 = -6.5$ -10

© Houghton Mifflin Harcourt Publishing Company

PROFESSIONAL DEVELOPMENT VIDEO

Author Juli Dixon models successful teaching practices as she explores the concept of scatterplots in an actual eighth-grade classroom.

 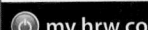

Professional Development

my.hrw.com

GO DIGITAL
my.hrw.com

 **Online Teacher Edition**
Access a full suite of teaching resources online—plan, present, and manage classes and assignments.

 **ePlanner**
Easily plan your classes and access all your resources online.

 Interactive Answers and Solutions
Customize answer keys to print or display in the classroom. Choose to include answers only or full solutions to all lesson exercises.

 Interactive Whiteboards
Engage students with interactive whiteboard-ready lessons and activities.

 Personal Math Trainer: Online Assessment and Intervention
Assign automatically graded homework, quizzes, tests, and intervention activities. Prepare your students with updated practice tests aligned with Common Core.

Reading Start-Up

Have students complete the activities on this page by working alone or with others.

Visualize Vocabulary

The content chart helps students review slope to prepare them to graph trend lines. Students should write one or more review words in the cells in the right column of the chart. As a class, review the process for finding slope and define each of the terms represented in the chart.

Understand Vocabulary

Use the following explanation to help students learn the preview words.

> In data analysis, a **cluster** is a set of closely grouped data. In a scatterplot, the dots showing a cluster are grouped close together. If they cluster in a linear fashion, you can draw a **trend line** to model the data. An **outlier** is a point that is very different from the others in the data set. On the scatterplot, an outlier is far away from the other dots and not close to the trend line.

Active Reading

Integrating Language Arts

Students can use these reading and note-taking strategies to help them organize and understand new concepts and vocabulary.

FL CC **LACC.68.RST.3.7** Integrate quantitative or technical information expressed in words in a text with a version of that information expressed visually (e.g., in a flowchart, diagram, model, graph, or table).

Additional Resources

Differentiated Instruction

• Reading Strategies **ELL**

Reading Start-Up

Visualize Vocabulary

Use the ✔ words to complete the right column of the chart.

Reviewing Slope	
Mathematical Representation	**Review Word**
$y = mx + b$	slope-intercept form of an equation, linear equation
y	y-coordinate
m	slope
x	x-coordinate
b	y-intercept

Understand Vocabulary

Match the term on the left to the correct expression on the right.

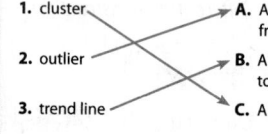

1. cluster
2. outlier
3. trend line

A. A data point that is very different from the rest of the data in a set

B. A straight line that comes closest to the points on a scatter plot.

C. A set of closely grouped data.

Active Reading

Two-Panel Flip Chart Create a two-panel flip chart, to help you understand the concepts in this module. Label each flap with the title of one of the lessons in the module. As you study each lesson, write important ideas under the appropriate flap. Include any sample problems or equations that will help you remember the concepts later when you look back at your notes.

© Houghton Mifflin Harcourt Publishing Company

Module 22 **695**

Vocabulary

Review Words
bivariate data *(datos bivariados)*
data *(datos)*
✔ linear equation *(ecuación lineal)*
✔ slope *(pendiente)*
✔ slope-intercept form of an equation *(forma pendiente-intersección)*
✔ x-coordinate *(coordenada x)*
✔ y-coordinate *(coordenada y)*
✔ y-intercept *(intersección con el eje y)*

Preview Words
cluster *(agrupación)*
outlier *(valor extremo)*
scatter plot *(diagrama de dispersión)*
trend line *(línea de tendencia)*

Before	In this module	After
Students understand: • ways to display data • ways to solve problems using graphs of data • ways to compare two sets of data	Students learn to: • represent data in a scatter plot • describe associations in data in scatter plots • represent bivariate data in a scatter plot with a trend line • make predictions from a scatter plot or trend line	Students will connect: • scatter plots and linear and nonlinear associations • scatter plots and positive and negative associations • scatter plots and trend lines • trend lines and linear equations

Unpacking the Standards

Use the examples on the page to help students know exactly what they are expected to learn in this module.

 Florida Common Core Standards

Content Areas

 **Statistics and Probability—8.SP.1**

Investigate patterns of association in bivariate data.

Go online to see a complete unpacking of the Florida Common Core Standards.

my.hrw.com

MODULE 22

Unpacking the Standards

Understanding the standards and the vocabulary terms in the standards will help you know exactly what you are expected to learn in this module.

FL CC 8.SP.1.1

Construct and interpret scatter plots for bivariate measurement data to investigate patterns of association between two quantities. Describe patterns such as clustering, outliers, positive or negative association, linear association, and nonlinear association.

What It Means to You

You will describe how the data in a scatter plot are related.

UNPACKING EXAMPLE 8.SP.1.1

The scatter plot shows Bob's height at various ages. Describe the type(s) of association between Bob's age and his height. Explain.

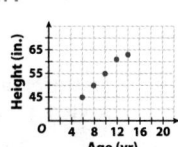

As Bob gets older, his height increases roughly along a straight line on the graph, so the association is positive and basically linear.

FL CC 8.SP.1.2

Know that straight lines are widely used to model relationships between two quantitative variables. For scatter plots that suggest a linear association, informally fit a straight line, and informally assess the model fit by judging the closeness of the data points to the line.

What It Means to You

You will use a trend line to show the relationship between two quantities.

UNPACKING EXAMPLE 8.SP.1.2

Joyce is training for a 10K race. For each of her training runs, she recorded the distance she ran and the time she ran. She made a scatter plot of her data and drew a trend line. Use the trend line to predict how long it would take Joyce to run 4.5 miles.

Distance (mi)	Time (min)
4	38
2	25
1	7
2	16
3	26
5	55
2	20
4	45
3	31

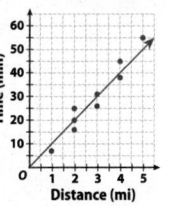

For a distance of 4.5 miles, the trend line shows a time of 45 minutes. So, it will take Joyce about 45 minutes to run 4.5 miles.

Visit my.hrw.com to see all Florida Common Core Standards unpacked.

my.hrw.com

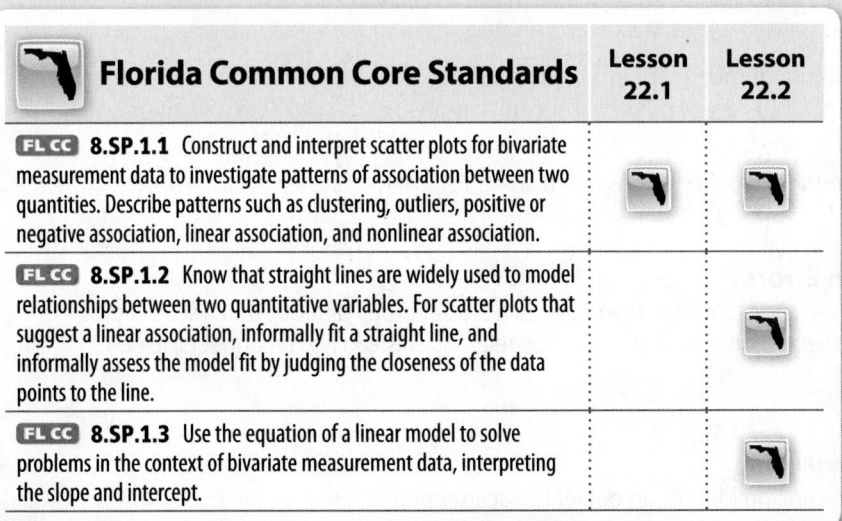

Florida Common Core Standards	Lesson 22.1	Lesson 22.2
FL CC **8.SP.1.1** Construct and interpret scatter plots for bivariate measurement data to investigate patterns of association between two quantities. Describe patterns such as clustering, outliers, positive or negative association, linear association, and nonlinear association.	✓	✓
FL CC **8.SP.1.2** Know that straight lines are widely used to model relationships between two quantitative variables. For scatter plots that suggest a linear association, informally fit a straight line, and informally assess the model fit by judging the closeness of the data points to the line.		✓
FL CC **8.SP.1.3** Use the equation of a linear model to solve problems in the context of bivariate measurement data, interpreting the slope and intercept.		✓

22.1 Scatter Plots and Association

 Florida Common Core Standards

The student is expected to:

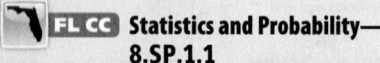 **Statistics and Probability—8.SP.1.1**

Construct and interpret scatter plots for bivariate measurement data to investigate patterns of association between two quantities. Describe patterns such as clustering, outliers, positive or negative association, linear association, and nonlinear association.

Mathematical Practices

 **MP.7.1** Structure

Engage

ESSENTIAL QUESTION

How can you construct and interpret scatter plots? Sample answer: Plot bivariate data on a coordinate plane, with one variable represented by each axis. Look for positive or negative association, clusters, and outliers to interpret the data.

Motivate the Lesson
Ask: Do you think the grade you get on a test is related to how long you study for the test? Take a guess. Begin the Explore Activity to find out.

Explore

EXPLORE ACTIVITY 1

Focus on Math Connections 🖊 Mathematical Practices
Emphasize that a scatter plot is used to investigate patterns of association between two quantities. This scatter plot shows hours spent studying as the independent variable and test grades as the dependent variable. Encourage students to discuss any trends they may see in the data in terms of these variables.

Explain

EXPLORE ACTIVITY 2

Questioning Strategies 🖊 Mathematical Practices
• What are some reasons there may be clusters in the data? When the variability of data is small, it tends to cluster. Multiple clusters may reflect the way a measurement was obtained or may indicate a relationship where a limited set of outcomes are more likely.

• What is the maximum number of points that could constitute a cluster of points? A cluster of points can be any number of points as long as they are grouped around a point or along a line.

• Name a new point that would be considered an outlier for this data set. Sample answer: A point at (30, 3) would be a clear outlier.

Avoid Common Errors
A common error is to try to connect the points of a scatter plot. Point out that a scatter plot shows all of the collected data, and that it is incorrect and misleading to connect the points in a jagged line.

Talk About It
Check for Understanding
Ask: How can you identify an outlier in a scatter plot? An outlier can be identified in a scatter plot as a point that is separated from all other data points. It does not fall within any cluster.

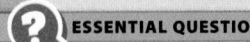

LESSON 22.1 Scatter Plots and Association

FL CC 8.SP.1.1
Construct and interpret scatter plots.... Describe patterns such as clustering, outliers, positive or negative association, linear association, and nonlinear association.

 ESSENTIAL QUESTION

How can you construct and interpret scatter plots?

EXPLORE ACTIVITY 1 Real World   FL CC 8.SP.1.1

Making a Scatter Plot

Recall that a set of bivariate data involves two variables. Bivariate data are used to explore the relationship between two variables. You can graph bivariate data on a *scatter plot*. A **scatter plot** is a graph with points plotted to show the relationship between two sets of data.

The final question on a math test reads, "How many hours did you spend studying for this test?" The teacher records the number of hours each student studied and the grade the student received on the test.

A Make a prediction about the relationship between the number of hours spent studying and test grades.

Sample answer: A greater number of study hours should be associated with higher test grades.

B Make a scatter plot. Graph hours spent studying as the independent variable and test grades as the dependent variable.

Hours Spent Studying	Test Grade
0	75
0.5	80
1	80
1	85
1.5	85
1.5	95
2	90
3	100
4	90

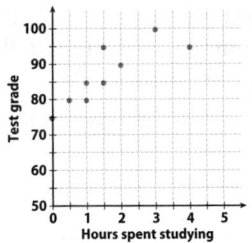

Reflect

1. What trend do you see in the data?

In general, test scores increase as the number of study hours increases.

2. **Justify Reasoning** Do you think that studying for 10 hours would greatly increase a student's grade?

No; the graph shows a general upward trend, but the grade cannot exceed 100.

Lesson 22.1 **697**

EXPLORE ACTIVITY 2 Real World   FL CC 8.SP.1.1

Interpreting Clusters and Outliers

A **cluster** is a set of closely grouped data. Data may cluster around a point or along a line. An **outlier** is a data point that is very different from the rest of the data in the set.

A scientist gathers information about the eruptions of Old Faithful, a geyser in Yellowstone National Park. She uses the data to create a scatter plot. The data show the length of time between eruptions (interval) and how long the eruption lasts (duration).

A Describe any clusters you see in the scatter plot.

There are clusters around the 50-minute and 80-minute intervals.

B What do the clusters tell you about eruptions of Old Faithful?

There are short wait times followed by short eruptions and longer wait times followed by longer eruptions.

C Describe any outliers you see in the scatter plot.

The point near (57, 3) appears to be an outlier because it does not fall into either cluster.

Math Talk Anno: Yes; because it would not fall near either cluster, it would satisfy the conditions for being an outlier.

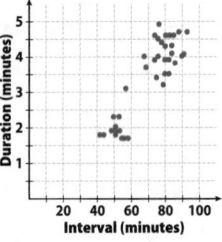

Math Talk
Mathematical Practices
If the point (20, 1) appeared on the scatter plot, would it be an outlier? Explain.

Reflect

3. Suppose the geyser erupts for 2.2 minutes after a 75-minute interval. Would this point lie in one of the clusters? Would it be an outlier? Explain your answer.

No, the interval was too long for the first cluster, and the duration was too short for the second cluster. It might be considered an outlier because it is not very close to the rest of the data.

4. Suppose the geyser erupts after an 80-minute interval. Give a range of possible duration times for which the point on the scatter plot would not be considered an outlier. Explain your reasoning.

Sample range: 3 to 5 minutes. The duration for other data points on the scatter plot that have an interval of 80 minutes are within this range.

698 Unit 10

PROFESSIONAL DEVELOPMENT

Integrate Mathematical Practices MP.7.1

This lesson provides an opportunity to address this Mathematical Practices standard. It calls for students to look closely to discern a pattern or structure. Students will look for patterns in scatter plots of bivariate data. They use a scatter plot to interpret clusters of data and identify any outliers. They also use scatter plots to identify how sets of data are associated.

Math Background

A scatter plot may suggest an association or a correlation between two variables. The terms *association* and *correlation* are often used interchangeably, but they do not mean exactly the same thing. An association can be linear or nonlinear, but a correlation always refers to a linear association. Like an association, a correlation can be negative or positive.

Scatter Plots and Association **698**

Animated Math
Scatter Plots and Association

Students model real-world data by creating scatter plots; students then engage in exploring associations in the data.

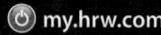 my.hrw.com

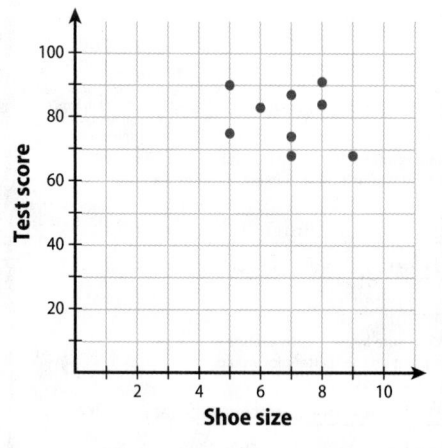

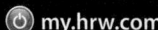

EXAMPLE 1

Questioning Strategies 🏴 Mathematical Practices

- **How are slope and association alike?** A positive association lies roughly along a line with a positive slope; a negative association lies roughly along a line with a negative slope.

- **What does it mean for bivariate data to have no association?** It means that changes in the values of one variable have no predictable effect on the values of the other variable.

- **What does it mean for bivariate data to have a nonlinear association?** It means that the data show a positive or negative relationship, but the points do not fall along a line.

Focus on Reasoning 🏴 Mathematical Practices

Point out to students that they cannot make any conclusions about data that show no association when graphed as a scatter plot. Emphasize that changes in one data set do not affect the other data set.

Integrating Language Arts **ELL**

Encourage English learners to ask for clarification on any terms or phrases that they don't understand.

YOUR TURN

Engage with the Whiteboard

Ask students if they see any clusters or outliers, and have them come up and circle them. They should not see any clusters in the data in Exercise 6, but the point (6, 45) should be recognized as an outlier.

Elaborate

. . . .

Talk About It
Summarize the Lesson

Ask: Which scatter plot shows a negative association? a positive association? no association? Label each plot with the correct type of association.

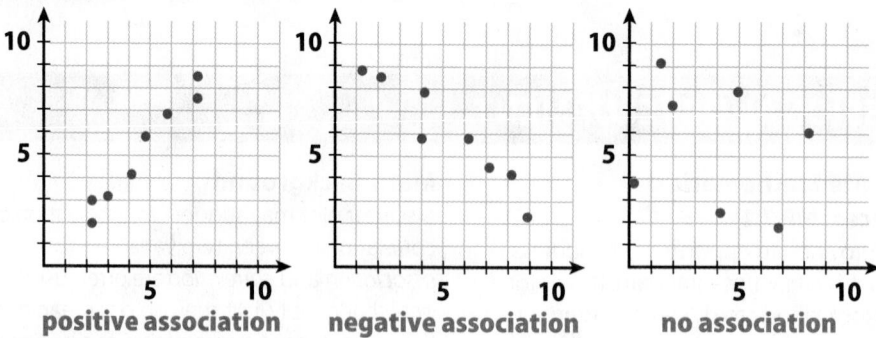

positive association   negative association   no association

GUIDED PRACTICE

Engage with the Whiteboard

 Ask student volunteers to complete Exercise 1. Discuss the type(s) of association between Bob's age in years and his height.

Avoid Common Errors

Exercise 3 Students may fail to identify the point at (35, 18) as an outlier because it fits the general trend of the data. Point out that if most of the data are clearly clustered, any point that lies outside the cluster or clusters is an outlier.

Determining Association

Association describes how sets of data are related. A *positive* association means that both data sets increase together. A *negative* association means that as one data set increases, the other decreases. *No* association means that changes in one data set do not affect the other data set.

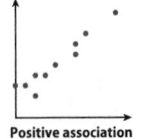 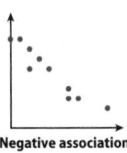 

Positive association   Negative association   No association

Data that show a positive or negative association and lie basically along a line exhibit a *linear* association. Data that show a positive or negative association but do not lie basically along a line exhibit a *nonlinear* association.

EXAMPLE 1   Real World   FL CC 8.SP.1.1

Susan asked 20 people if they would buy a new product she developed at each of several prices. The scatter plot shows how many of the 20 said "yes" at a given price. Describe the association between price and the number of buyers.

As price increases, the number of buyers decreases. So, there is a negative association. Because the data points do not lie along a line, the association is nonlinear.

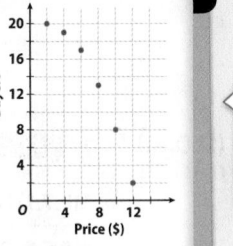

Reflect

5. **What If?** Based on the association shown in the scatter plot, what might happen if Susan increased the price to $14?

   It is likely that no one would buy the product.

YOUR TURN

6. The plot shows the reading level and height for 16 students in a district. Describe the association and give a possible reason for it.

   Positive and basically linear:

   Older students would be taller

   and read at a higher level.

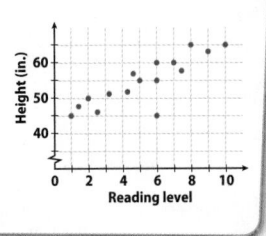

Guided Practice

Bob recorded his height at different ages. The table below shows his data.

Age (years)	6	8	10	12	14
Height (inches)	45	50	55	61	63

1. Make a scatter plot of Bob's data. (Explore Activity 1)

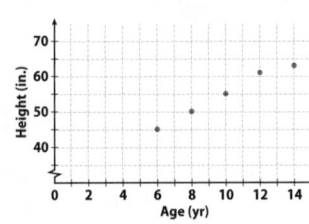

2. Describe the association between Bob's age and his height. Explain the association. (Example 1)

   Positive and basically linear; as Bob gets older, his height

   increases. But if the data continued for increasing age,

   we would see that Bob's height stops increasing.

3. The scatter plot shows the basketball shooting results for 14 players. Describe any clusters you see in the scatter plot. Identify any outliers. (Explore Activity 2)

   There is a cluster in the 20—23 shots attempted

   range, and a lesser one in the 7—14 shots

   attempted range. The point (35, 18) is an outlier.

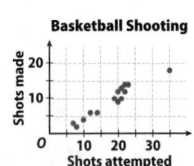

Basketball Shooting

ESSENTIAL QUESTION CHECK-IN

4. Explain how you can make a scatter plot from a set of bivariate data.

   Let the numbers on the *x*-axis represent one variable

   and the numbers on the *y*-axis represent the other

   variable. Then plot points (*x*, *y*) for each pair of numbers

   in the bivariate data set.

DIFFERENTIATE INSTRUCTION

Modeling

Ask students to make note cards showing graphs of scatter plots representing each type of association, positive, negative, and none, as well as linear and nonlinear. Tell them to include at least one scatter plot with clustering of data points and at least one scatter plot with one or more outliers. Have students circle any clusters and highlight any outliers.

Kinesthetic Experience

Clear space on the floor and make a large first quadrant coordinate plane using chalk or long strips of paper, with height as the vertical axis and age in months as the horizontal axis. Then ask the students to place themselves on the scatter plot according to their own ages and heights. Depending on space, you may need to divide the class into groups and have them take turns. Have students describe the type(s) of association shown in the human scatter plot.

Additional Resources

Differentiated Instruction includes:
- Reading Strategies
- Success for English Learners **ELL**
- Reteach
- Challenge **PRE-AP**

© Houghton Mifflin Harcourt Publishing Company

Personal Math Trainer

Online Assessment and Intervention

Online homework assignment available

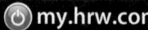 **my.hrw.com**

22.1 LESSON QUIZ

 **8.SP.1.1**

Use the table for Exercises 1–2.

Height (in.)	Weight (lb)	Height (in.)	Weight (lb)
50	83	60	98
53	90	65	97
56	86	65	103
57	92	68	100

1. Make a scatter plot of the data.

2. Describe the type(s) of association you see between the height and the weight. Explain.

For Exercises 3 and 4, use the scatter plot for annual movie attendance by age.

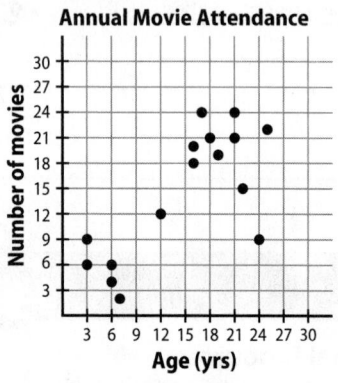

Annual Movie Attendance

3. Describe any clusters you see in the scatter plot.

4. Describe any outliers you see in the scatter plot.

Lesson Quiz available online

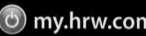 **my.hrw.com**

Evaluate

GUIDED AND INDEPENDENT PRACTICE

FL CC 8.SP.1.1

Concepts & Skills	Practice
Explore Activity 1 Making a Scatter Plot	Exercises 1, 10–11
Explore Activity 2 Interpreting Clusters and Outliers	Exercises 3, 8
Example 1 Determining Association	Exercises 2, 5–7, 9

Exercise	Depth of Knowledge (D.O.K.)	FL CC Mathematical Practices
5–9	**2** Skills/Concepts	**MP.7.1** Using Structure
10–11	**2** Skills/Concepts	**MP.6.1** Precision
12	**3** Strategic Thinking **H.O.T.**	**MP.7.1** Using Structure
13–14	**3** Strategic Thinking **H.O.T.**	**MP.3.1** Logic

Additional Resources

Differentiated Instruction includes:

• Leveled Practice worksheets

Answers

1.

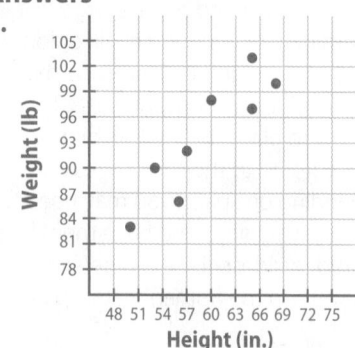

Height (in.)

2. Positive and linear; as the height increases, so does the weight.

3. There are clusters around the age of 6 and also around the age of 18.

4. There are outliers at (24, 9), and (12, 12).

22.1 Independent Practice

FL CC 8.SP.1.1

Personal Math Trainer

Online Assessment and Intervention

my.hrw.com

Sports Use the scatter plot for 5–8.

Olympic Men's Long Jump Winning Distances

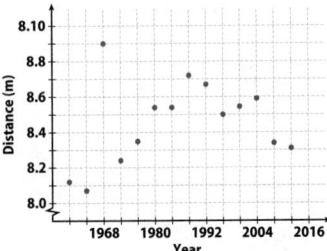

5. Describe the association between the year and the distance jumped for the years 1960 to 1988.

The data generally show a positive linear association. As the years increase, so does the winning distance.

6. Describe the association between the year and the distance jumped for the years after 1988.

Overall, the data from 1988 to 2012 generally show a negative association, even though the 8 year period from 1996 to 2004 looked at by itself shows a slight rise in distance jumped over time.

7. For the entire scatter plot, is the association between the year and the distance jumped linear or nonlinear?

Nonlinear; the data points first rise as the years increased from 1960 to 1988 and then fall as the years increase from 1988 to 2012, so there is no overall linear pattern.

8. Identify the outlier and interpret its meaning.

(1968, 8.9); the outlier represents a jump of 8.9 meters in 1968, a jump that far exceeds any jump made in prior or later years.

9. Communicate Mathematical Ideas Compare a scatter plot that shows no association to one that shows negative association.

Sample answer: A plot with no association has randomly scattered data points. There does not appear to be any pattern in the association. On a plot with negative association, the data points fall from left to right. As one data set increases the other decreases.

For 10–11, describe a set of real-world bivariate data that the given scatter plot could represent. Define the variable represented on each axis.

10.

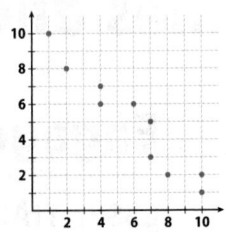

Sample answer: x-axis is number of people doing a job; y-axis is number of hours to do the job

11.

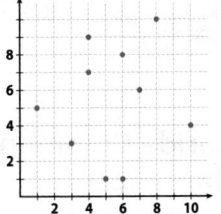

Sample answer: x-axis is miles student lives from school; y-axis is student's score on a 10-pt quiz

H.O.T. FOCUS ON HIGHER ORDER THINKING

Work Area

12. Multiple Representations Describe what you might see in a table of bivariate data that would lead you to conclude that the scatter plot of the data would show a cluster.

Sample answer: You would see a number of data items with x-values and y-values that are close to one another.

13. Justify Reasoning Is it possible for a scatter plot to have a positive or negative association that is not linear? Explain.

Yes; for example, the data points may appear to lie mostly along a rising or falling curve, or may generally rise or fall, but not in a way that suggests a linear association.

14. Critical Thinking To try to increase profits, a theater owner increases the price of a ticket by $25 every month. Describe what a scatter plot might look like if x represents the number of months and y represents the profits. Explain your reasoning.

Sample answer: Initially, the number of tickets sold might decline a little, but the price increase would offset the loss in sales. So, profits would increase, showing a positive association. When the price got too high, ticket sales would decline more rapidly, so profits would fall, giving a negative association.

EXTEND THE MATH PRE-AP

Activity available online my.hrw.com

Activity Use a graphing calculator to create a scatter plot of the height and points scored during the season for each player on the school basketball team. Then describe the type(s) of association you see between the height and number of points scored. There is no association in the data sets.

Height	Points
72, 68, 65, 73, 67, 78, 71, 72, 75, 77, 77, 78	85, 87, 62, 78, 78, 58, 24, 45, 52, 87, 79, 90

Press STAT and select "1: Edit" to enter the values for height and points into two lists L1 and L2. Press 2nd [STAT PLOT] Y=, choose "1:", select "On", then choose the scatter plot (first style), L1, and L2. Press ZOOM and choose "9: ZoomStat" to see the scatter plot.

LESSON
22.2 Trend Lines and Predictions

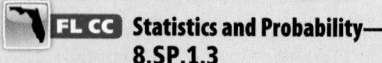

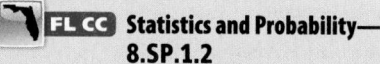

ADDITIONAL EXAMPLE 1

The scatter plot and trend line show the relationship between the number of customers that enter an electronics store in a day and the number of TVs sold. Write an equation for the trend line. Answers may vary; sample answer: $y = 0.05x$

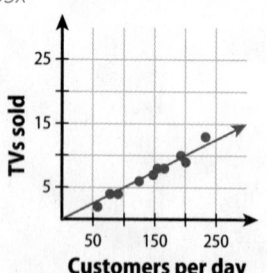

Customers per day

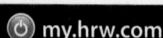 **Interactive Whiteboard**
Interactive example available online

⊙ my.hrw.com

Engage

ESSENTIAL QUESTION

How can you use a trend line to make a prediction from a scatter plot? Sample answer: Draw a trend line that fits the points as closely as possible. Then write an equation for that line, and use it to make predictions by substituting and solving.

Motivate the Lesson

Ask: Are you able to predict how far you can run in 5 minutes? in 30 minutes? Take a guess. Begin the Explore Activity to see how you could find out.

Explore

EXPLORE ACTIVITY 1

Focus on Patterns 📐 Mathematical Practices

Point out that trend lines should only be drawn if there is a clear linear association in the data once it is displayed in a scatter plot. Emphasize that you disregard the outliers when drawing a trend line because they do not fit the trend.

Explain

EXAMPLE 1

Questioning Strategies 📐 Mathematical Practices

- How can you use the slope to write an equation in the form $y = mx + b$ for the trend line? Select two points on the line, determine the coordinates of those points, and calculate the slope m. Substitute m and the coordinates of one of the points into $y = mx + b$. Solve for b.

- If chapters were on the vertical axis and pages were on the horizontal axis, what would be the value of the slope and what would it represent? The slope of the line would be $\frac{1}{10}$, and it would represent a rate of 0.1 chapter per page.

Focus on Modeling 📐 Mathematical Practices

Point out that drawing a trend line that goes through two data points makes finding the equation of the trend line easier if you know the coordinates of the points. However, it is not always possible to draw a good trend line that goes through two points.

Integrating Language Arts **ELL**

Encourage English learners to take notes on new terms or concepts and to write them in familiar language.

Avoid Common Errors

A common error is to attempt to use the trend line to connect as many points of a scatter plot as possible. Point out that this may not be the best trend line, however, because it may make other data points too far away from the line and, therefore, not give the best fit.

22.2 Trend Lines and Predictions

FL CC 8.SP.1.3

Use the equation of a linear model to solve problems in the context of bivariate measurement data, interpreting the slope and intercept. *Also 8.SP.1.1, 8.SP.1.2*

? ESSENTIAL QUESTION How can you use a trend line to make a prediction from a scatter plot?

EXPLORE ACTIVITY 1 *Real World*   FL CC 8.SP.1.2, 8.SP.1.1

Drawing a Trend Line

When a scatter plot shows a linear association, you can use a line to model the relationship between the variables. A **trend line** is a straight line that comes closest to the points on a scatter plot.

Joyce is training for a 10K race. For some of her training runs, she records the distance she ran and how many minutes she ran.

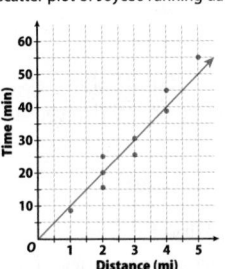

A Make a scatter plot of Joyce's running data.

Distance (mi)	Time (min)
4	38
2	25
1	7
2	16
3	26
5	55
2	20
4	45
3	31

B To draw a trend line, use a straight edge to draw a line that has about the same number of points above and below it. Ignore any outliers.

C Use your trend line to predict how long it would take Joyce to run 4.5 miles.

about 45 minutes

Reflect

1. How well does your trend line fit the data? Explain.

All the data points are close to the line. The data show a strong linear association, so the line should fit well.

Lesson 22.2 **703**

EXPLORE ACTIVITY 1 *(cont'd)*

2. Do you think you can use a scatter plot that shows no association to make a prediction? Explain your answer.

No; no association means that there is no relationship between the variables and the scatter plot shows no pattern.

Math On the Spot
my.hrw.com

Finding the Equation of a Trend Line

You can use two points on a trend line to write an equation in slope-intercept form for the trend line.

EXAMPLE 1 *Real World*   FL CC 8.SP.1.3

The scatter plot and trend line show the relationship between the number of chapters and the total number of pages for several books. Write an equation for the trend line.

STEP 1 Find the slope of the trend line. The line passes through points (5, 50) and (17, 170).

$m = \dfrac{y_2 - y_1}{x_2 - x_1}$ Use the slope formula.

$m = \dfrac{170 - 50}{17 - 5}$ Substitute (5, 50) for (x_1, y_1) and (17, 170) for (x_2, y_2).

$m = \dfrac{120}{12} = 10$ Simplify.

STEP 2 Find the y-intercept of the trend line.

$y = mx + b$ Slope-intercept form

$50 = 10 \cdot 5 + b$ Substitute 50 for y, 10 for m, and 5 for x.

$50 = 50 + b$ Simplify.

$50 - 50 = 50 - 50 + b$ Subtract 50 from both sides.

$0 = b$ Simplify.

STEP 3 Use your slope and y-intercept values to write the equation.

$y = mx + b$ Slope-intercept form

$y = 10x + 0$ Substitute 10 for m and 0 for y.

The equation for the trend line is $y = 10x$.

Math Talk
Mathematical Practices

Why are (5, 50) and (17, 170) the best points to use to draw the trend line?

Trend lines should have about the same number of points above the line as below it. By using (5, 50) and (17, 170), you get four points above the line and four points below it.

704 Unit 10

PROFESSIONAL DEVELOPMENT

Integrate Mathematical Practices MP.6.1

This lesson provides an opportunity to address this Mathematical Practices standard. It calls for students to communicate precisely to others. Students draw a trend line for a scatter plot of bivariate data with a positive linear association. Then students represent the trend line using an algebraic equation and use the equation to predict a value between data points that they already know or outside the data they know. In this way, students have used multiple representations, including symbols, graphs, and language, to communicate mathematical ideas precisely.

Math Background

A scatter plot may show a linear relationship between bivariate data. A line can be drawn to represent the data, called the trend line or the line of best fit. A trend line can be drawn by visualizing where a line would fall that best fits the data, usually with half the data points above the line and half below. The line of best fit is usually calculated using a statistical method of linear regression such as *least squares*. Least squares means the equation of the line chosen minimizes the sum of the squares of the *residuals* for the line. The residuals are the differences between the actual data values and the associated data values that fit the model. A graphing calculator automatically uses this method to give the line of best fit.

YOUR TURN

Avoid Common Errors
Suggest that students not pick two points that are close together to calculate the slope. Students may pick (0, 0) and (1, 1) and get a slope of 1. Point out that the line passes through (10, 9), which can be used with (0, 0) to get a more accurate value for the slope.

EXPLORE ACTIVITY 2

Questioning Strategies Mathematical Practices
• How can you use the equation of a trend line to make predictions? You can substitute a value for either x or y, and solve for the value of the other variable. Then interpret the meaning for the context.

• What is the difference between interpolation and extrapolation? Interpolation involves the prediction of values that fall between known data points. Extrapolation involves the prediction of values that lie above or below the known range of data.

Focus on Modeling Mathematical Practices
Point out to students that although extrapolation is generally less accurate than interpolation, any prediction about the future will involve extrapolation, so the technique is often necessary.

Engage with the Whiteboard
Invite a student volunteer to use the equation of the trend line for the data in Your Turn Exercise 6 to make predictions using interpolation and extrapolation. Discuss how they know whether they are using interpolation or extrapolation.

Elaborate

Talk About It
Summarize the Lesson
Ask students to fill in the blanks in the graphic organizer below to show the steps to find the equation of a trend line. Sample answers are shown.

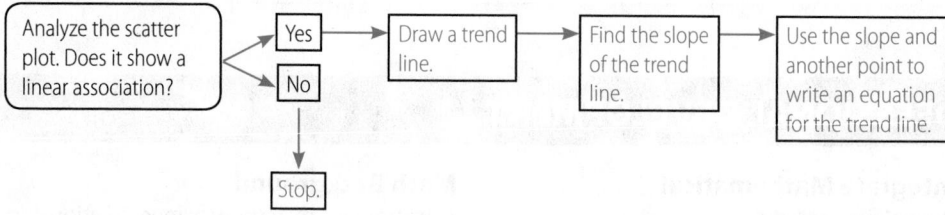

GUIDED PRACTICE

Engage with the Whiteboard
Ask a student to complete Exercise 1 at the board. Have them mark two points on the line and use them to calculate the slope and y-intercept for Exercise 3. Have a student mark a point on the line to check the reasonableness of their answer for Exercise 4.

Avoid Common Errors
Exercise 1 A common error is to try to connect the points of the scatter plot. Point out that this would not give a single straight line. Emphasize that they cannot find the equation of a jagged line, and therefore cannot make predictions using it.

Exercise 2 A common error is to assume a good fit for the line is if the trend line goes through as many data values as possible. Point out that this may place more values farther away from the line than if equal numbers of points lie above and below the line.

Reflect

3. What type(s) of association does the scatter plot show?

positive; linear

4. What is the meaning of the slope in this situation?

There is an average of 10 pages per chapter.

5. What is the meaning of the y-intercept in this situation?

the number of pages in a book with 0 chapters (0)

 **YOUR TURN**

6. The scatter plot and trend line show the relationship between the number of rainy days in a month and the number of umbrellas sold each month. Write an equation for the trend line.

Answers may vary.

Sample answer: $y = \frac{9}{10}x$

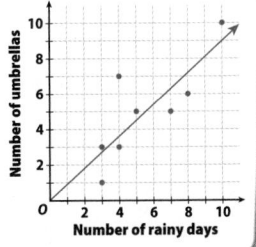

Number of umbrellas (y-axis) vs Number of rainy days (x-axis)

Personal Math Trainer
Online Assessment and Intervention
my.hrw.com

EXPLORE ACTIVITY 2 *Real World* FL CC 8.SP.1.3

Making Predictions

When you use a trend line or its equation to predict a value between data points that you already know, you *interpolate* the predicted value. When you make a prediction that is outside the data that you know, you *extrapolate* the predicted value.

Use the equation of the trend line in Example 1 to predict how many pages would be in a book with 26 chapters.

Is this prediction an example of interpolation or extrapolation? extrapolation

$y = \boxed{10x}$ Write the equation for your trend line.

$y = \boxed{10(26)}$ Substitute the number of chapters for x.

$y = \boxed{260}$ Simplify.

I predict that a book with 26 chapters will have _____260_____ pages.

EXPLORE ACTIVITY 2 (cont'd)

Reflect

7. **Make a Prediction** Predict how many pages would be in a book with 14 chapters. Is this prediction an example of interpolation or extrapolation?

140 pages; interpolation

8. Do you think that extrapolation or interpolation is more accurate? Explain.

Sample answer: Interpolation; the predicted value fits between known points where the trend is known. There is no guarantee that a trend will continue beyond the known data points.

Guided Practice

Angela recorded the price of different weights of several bulk grains. She made a scatter plot of her data. Use the scatter plot for 1–4.

Answers for 1–4 may vary slightly.

1. Draw a trend line for the scatter plot. (Explore Activity 1)

2. How do you know whether your trend line is a good fit for the data? (Explore Activity 1)

Most of the data points are close to the trend line and there is about the same number of points above and below the line.

3. Write an equation for your trend line. (Example 1) $y = 0.08x$

4. Use the equation for your trend line to interpolate the price of 7 ounces and extrapolate the price of 50 ounces.

(Explore Activity 2) $0.56; $4.00

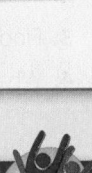

Price ($) vs Weight (ounces)

? ESSENTIAL QUESTION CHECK-IN

5. A trend line passes through two points on a scatter plot. How can you use the trend line to make a prediction between or outside the given data points?

Use the two points to write the equation of the line. Substitute in the equation the value of x for which you want to make a prediction. The value of y that you obtain is the prediction.

DIFFERENTIATE INSTRUCTION

Auditory Cues

Ask students to think of <u>inter</u>polation as using the trend line to predict values <u>in</u> between existing data values. They should think of <u>extra</u>polation as using the trend line to predict values outside existing values, like an <u>extra</u>terrestrial is outside Earth or an <u>extra</u>curricular activity is outside school.

Curriculum Integration

Ask students to work together to brainstorm some situations in science or social studies in which scatter plots and trend lines could be useful. For example, in social studies trend lines could be used to predict population growth, and in biology a scatter plot could show whether there is a relationship between average temperature and tree height.

Additional Resources

Differentiated Instruction includes:

• Reading Strategies
• Success for English Learners **ELL**
• Reteach
• Challenge **PRE-AP**

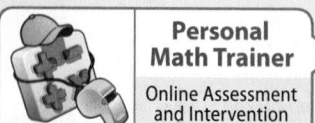
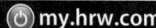
22.2 LESSON QUIZ

🔲 **FL CC** 8.SP.1.1, 8.SP.1.2, 8.SP.1.3

Marni recorded the cost of different weights of apples and made a scatter plot of her data. For Exercises 1–5, use the sample trend line drawn in the scatter plot.

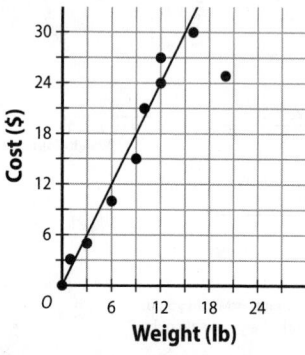

1. What type(s) of association does the scatter plot show?

2. Find the slope of the trend line.

3. Find the equation of the trend line.

4. What is the meaning of the slope in this situation?

5. **a.** Use the equation of the trend line to predict the cost of buying 5 pounds of apples.

   b. Is this prediction an example of interpolation or extrapolation?

Lesson Quiz available online

🔵 my.hrw.com

Answers

1. positive, linear

2. 2

3. $y = 2x$

4. The average cost of the price of apples is $2 per pound.

5. **a.** $10

   b. interpolation

Evaluate

GUIDED AND INDEPENDENT PRACTICE

🔲 **FL CC** 8.SP.1.1, 8.SP.1.2, 8.SP.1.3

Concepts & Skills	Practice
Explore Activity 1 Drawing a Trend Line	Exercises 1–2, 6, 11
Example1 Finding the Equation of a Trend Line	Exercises 3, 8, 12
Explore Activity 2 Making Predictions	Exercises 4, 9, 13

Exercise	Depth of Knowledge (D.O.K.)	 Mathematical Practices
6–14	**2** Skills/Concepts	**MP.4.1** Modeling
15–17	**3** Strategic Thinking **H.O.T.**	**MP.3.1** Logic

Additional Resources

Differentiated Instruction includes:

• Leveled Practice worksheets

CLUSTER CONNECTION **Exercises 11–14** combine concepts from the Florida Common Core cluster "Investigate patterns of association in bivariate data."

22.2 Independent Practice

FL CC 8.SP.1.1, 8.SP.1.2, 8.SP.1.3

Personal Math Trainer
Online Assessment and Intervention
my.hrw.com

Answers for 6–14 may vary slightly.

Use the data in the table for Exercises 6–10.

Apparent Temperature Due to Wind at 15 °F						
Wind speed (mi/h)	10	20	30	40	50	60
Wind chill (°F)	2.7	−2.3	−5.5	−7.9	−9.8	−11.4

6. Make a scatter plot of the data and draw a trend line.

7. What type of association does the trend line show?
_____negative; basically linear_____

8. Write an equation for your trend line. ___Sample answer: $y = -\frac{1}{4}x + 3$___

9. Make a Prediction Use the trend line to predict the wind chill at these wind speeds.
a. 36 mi/h ___about −6°F___   **b.** 100 mi/h ___about −22°F___

10. What is the meaning of the slope of the line?
The wind chill falls about 1 degree for every increase of 4 miles per hour in wind speed.

Apparent Temperature Due to Wind at 15 °F

(graph: Wind chill (°F) vs Wind speed (mi/h))

Use the data in the table for Exercises 11–14.

Apparent Temperature Due to Humidity at a Room Temperature of 72 °F						
Humidity (%)	0	20	40	60	80	100
Apparent temperature (°F)	64	67	70	72	74	76

11. Make a scatter plot of the data and draw a trend line.

12. Write an equation for your trend line.
Sample answer: $y = \frac{2}{15}x + 64$

13. Make a Prediction Use the trend line to predict the apparent temperature at 70% humidity. ___about 73°F___

14. What is the meaning of the y-intercept of the line?
At 0% humidity, the apparent temperature is 64°F.

Apparent Temperature at a Room Temperature of 72 °F

(graph: Apparent temperature (°F) vs Humidity (%))

© Houghton Mifflin Harcourt Publishing Company

H.O.T. FOCUS ON HIGHER ORDER THINKING

Work Area

15. Communicate Mathematical Ideas Is it possible to draw a trend line on a scatter plot that shows no association? Explain.
No; if the scatter plot shows no association, the data points have no relationship to one another. Unless there is a linear association you cannot draw a trend line.

16. Critique Reasoning Sam drew a trend line that had about the same number of data points above it as below it, but did not pass through any data points. He then picked two data points to write the equation for the line. Is this a correct way to write the equation? Explain.
No; although Sam drew the trend line correctly, he should use two points on the line to write the equation. Choosing two data points that are not on the line will result in an incorrect equation for the line.

17. Marlene wanted to find a relationship between the areas and populations of counties in Texas. She plotted x (area in square miles) and y (population) for two counties on a scatter plot:

Kent County (903, 808)   Edwards County (2118, 2002)

She concluded that the population of Texas counties is approximately equal to their area in square miles and drew a trend line through her points.

a. Critique Reasoning Do you agree with Marlene's method of creating a scatter plot and a trend line? Explain why or why not.
No; two points are not sufficient for creating a scatter plot or predicting a trend. Marlene should have plotted data points for many more counties.

b. Counterexamples Harris County has an area of 1778 square miles and a population of about 4.3 million people. Dallas County has an area of 908 square miles and a population of about 2.5 million people. What does this data show about Marlene's conjecture that the population of Texas counties is approximately equal to their area?
Sample answer: Marlene's conjecture is incorrect. Marlene chose counties whose areas are about equal to their populations. Harris and Dallas counties provide counterexamples for Marlene's original data.

© Houghton Mifflin Harcourt Publishing Company

EXTEND THE MATH   PRE-AP

Activity available online my.hrw.com

Activity Use a graphing calculator to find the equation of a trend line for a scatter plot of the data. Then use the trend line to predict the distance traveled in 12 hours.
701 mi

Time (h)	2	4	5.5	6	7	9	10
Distance (mi)	115	250	330	340	400	540	580

Follow the instructions given in Extend the Math for Lesson 14.1 to make a scatter plot of the data. Press **STAT**, select the "CALC" menu, then select "4: LinReg (ax+b)" and press **ENTER**. Press **Y=** and then press **VARS** and choose "5: Statistics". Select the EQ menu and choose "1: RegEQ". Press **ZOOM** and choose "9: ZoomStat" to see the trend line.

Ready to Go On?

Assess Mastery

Use the assessment on this page to determine if students have mastered the concepts and standards covered in this module.

RtI — **Response to Intervention**

Access Ready to Go On? assessment online, and receive instant scoring, feedback, and customized intervention or enrichment.

Personal Math Trainer
Online Assessment and Intervention
⏻ my.hrw.com

Intervention	Enrichment

Online and Print Resources

Differentiated Instruction	*Differentiated Instruction*
• Reteach worksheets	• Challenge worksheets
• Reading Strategies **ELL**	**PRE-AP**
• Success for English Learners **ELL**	Extend the Math **PRE-AP** Lesson Activities in TE

Additional Resources

Assessment Resources includes:
• Leveled Module Quizzes

MODULE QUIZ

Ready to Go On?

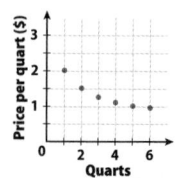

Personal Math Trainer
Online Assessment and Intervention
my.hrw.com

22.1 Scatter Plots and Association

An auto store is having a sale on motor oil. The chart shows the price per quart as the number of quarts purchased increases. Use the data for Exs. 1–2.

Number of quarts	1	2	3	4	5	6
Price per quart ($)	2	1.50	1.25	1.10	1	0.95

1. Use the given data to make a scatter plot.

2. Describe the association you see between the number of quarts purchased and the price per quart. Explain.
<u>Negative but nonlinear; as number of</u>
<u>quarts rises, price per quart decreases,</u>
<u>but the data appear to lie along a curve.</u>

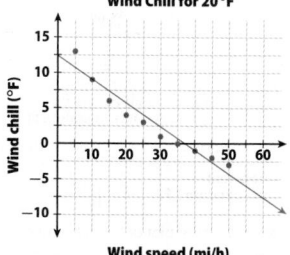

22.2 Trend Lines and Predictions

The scatter plot below shows data comparing wind speed and wind chill for an air temperature of 20°F. Use the scatter plot for Exs. 3–5. 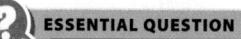 Answers may vary slightly.

3. Draw a trend line for the scatter plot.

4. Write an equation for your trend line.
Sample ans.: $y = -\frac{1}{3}x + \frac{37}{3}$

5. Use your equation to predict the wind chill to the nearest degree for a wind speed of 60 mi/h.
<u>−8°F</u>

? ESSENTIAL QUESTION

6. How can you use scatter plots to solve real-world problems?
<u>Sample answer: You can plot data points and draw trend lines</u>
<u>to make predictions.</u>

Module 22 **709**

 Florida Common Core Standards

Lesson	Exercises	🏴 Common Core Standards
22.1	1–2	**8.SP.1.1**
22.2	3–5	**8.SP.1.1, 8.SP.1.2, 8.SP.1.3**

PARCC Assessment Readiness

MODULE 22 MIXED REVIEW
PARCC Assessment Readiness

Personal Math Trainer
Online Assessment and Intervention
my.hrw.com

Selected Response

1. Which scatter plot could have a trend line whose equation is $y = 3x + 10$?

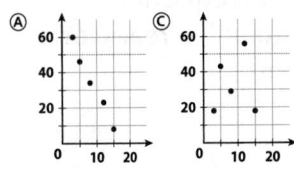

2. What type of association would you expect between a person's age and hair length?

Ⓐ linear   Ⓒ none
Ⓑ negative   Ⓓ positive

3. Which is **not** shown on the scatter plot?

Ⓐ cluster
Ⓑ negative association
Ⓒ outlier
Ⓓ positive association

4. A restaurant claims to have served 352,000,000 hamburgers. What is this number in scientific notation?

Ⓐ 3.52×10^6 Ⓒ 35.2×10^7
Ⓑ 3.52×10^8 Ⓓ 352×10^6

5. Which equation describes the relationship between *x* and *y* in the table?

x	−8	−4	0	4	8
y	2	1	0	−1	−2

Ⓐ $y = -4x$ Ⓒ $y = 4x$
Ⓑ $y = -\frac{1}{4}x$ Ⓓ $y = \frac{1}{4}x$

Mini-Task

6. Use the data in the table.

Temp (°F)	97	94	87	92	100	90
Pool visitors	370	315	205	135	365	240

a. Make a scatterplot of the data.

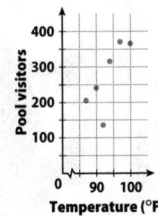

b. Which data point is an outlier?
(92, 135)

c. Predict the number of visitors on a day when the high temperature is 102°F.
about 410 visitors

© Houghton Mifflin Harcourt Publishing Company

Florida Common Core Standards

Items	🏴 Grade 8 Standards	🏴 Mathematical Practices
1	8.SP.1.2	MP.4.1
2	8.SP.1.1	MP.4.1
3	8.SP.1.2	MP.6.1
4*	8.EE.1.3	MP.4.1
5*	8.F.2.4	MP.4.1
6	8.SP.1.1, 8.SP.1.3	MP.4.1, MP.6.1

* Item integrates mixed review concepts from previous modules or a previous course.

Two-Way Tables

 **ESSENTIAL QUESTION**

How can you use two-way frequency tables to solve real-world problems?

You can use two-way frequency tables to organize and analyze real-world data that are paired and categorical.

....

LESSON 23.1

Two-Way Frequency Tables

FL CC **8.SP.1.4**

....

LESSON 23.2

Two-Way Relative Frequency Tables

FL CC **8.SP.1.4**

Real-World Video

Two-way tables can help identify and compare probabilities for non-numerical data, such as the probability that girls will like one of two sports teams more than boys will.

⏻ my.hrw.com

© Houghton Mifflin Harcourt Publishing Company • Image Credits: ©John Rowley/Getty Images

GO DIGITAL

my.hrw.com

my.hrw.com

Go digital with your write-in student edition, accessible on any device.

Math On the Spot

Scan with your smart phone to jump directly to the online edition, video tutor, and more.

Animated Math

Interactively explore key concepts to see how math works.

Personal Math Trainer

Get immediate feedback and help as you work through practice sets.

Are You Ready?

Assess Readiness

Use the assessment on this page to determine if students need intensive or strategic intervention for the module's prerequisite skills.

 **Response to Intervention**

Personal Math Trainer

Online Assessment and Intervention

my.hrw.com

Intervention	Enrichment

Access Are You Ready? assessment online, and receive instant scoring, feedback, and customized intervention or enrichment.

Online and Print Resources

Skills Intervention worksheets
- Skill 19 Simplify Fractions
- Skill 31 Fractions, Decimals, Percents
- Skill 46 Find the Percent of a Number

Differentiated Instruction
- Challenge worksheets **PRE-AP**

Extend the Math **PRE-AP** Lesson Activities in TE

Are YOU Ready?

Complete these exercises to review skills you will need for this module.

Personal Math Trainer
Online Assessment and Intervention
my.hrw.com

Simplify Fractions

EXAMPLE Simplify $\frac{18}{30}$.

$$\frac{1, 2, 3, 6, 9, 18}{1, 2, 3, 5, 6, 10, 30}$$

$$\frac{18 \div 6}{30 \div 6} = \frac{3}{5}$$

List all the factors of the numerator and denominator.
Find the greatest common factor (GCF). Divide the numerator and denominator by the GCF.

Write each fraction in simplest form.

1. $\frac{25}{30}$ $\frac{5}{6}$
2. $\frac{27}{36}$ $\frac{3}{4}$
3. $\frac{14}{16}$ $\frac{7}{8}$
4. $\frac{15}{45}$ $\frac{1}{3}$
5. $\frac{27}{63}$ $\frac{3}{7}$
6. $\frac{45}{75}$ $\frac{3}{5}$
7. $\frac{8}{27}$ $\frac{8}{27}$
8. $\frac{16}{28}$ $\frac{4}{7}$

Fractions, Decimals, Percents

EXAMPLE Write $\frac{13}{20}$ as a decimal and a percent.

$$20)\overline{13.00}$$
$$\underline{12\,0}$$
$$\quad 100$$
$$\underline{-100}$$
$$\qquad 0$$

$0.65 = 65\%$

Write the fraction as a division problem.
Write a decimal point and zeros in the dividend.
Place a decimal point in the quotient.
Write the decimal as a percent.

Write each fraction as a decimal and a percent.

9. $\frac{7}{8}$ 0.875; 87.5%
10. $\frac{4}{5}$ 0.8; 80%
11. $\frac{5}{4}$ 1.25; 125%
12. $\frac{3}{10}$ 0.30; 30%
13. $\frac{19}{20}$ 0.95; 95%
14. $\frac{7}{25}$ 0.28; 28%

Find the Percent of a Number

EXAMPLE 6.5% of 24 = ?

$6.5\% = 0.065$

$$\begin{array}{r} 24 \\ \times\ 0.065 \\ \hline 1.56 \end{array}$$

Write the percent as a decimal.

Multiply.

Find each percent of a number.

15. 4% of 40 __1.6__
16. 7% of 300 __21__
17. 4.3% of 1,200 __51.6__
18. 2.9% of 780 __22.62__
19. 1.6% of 75.20 __1.2032__
20. 3.56% of 3,200 __113.92__

© Houghton Mifflin Harcourt Publishing Company

PROFESSIONAL DEVELOPMENT VIDEO

Author Julie Dixon models successful teaching practices as she explores the concept of relative frequency in an actual eighth-grade classroom.

Professional Development

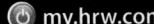 my.hrw.com

---

GO DIGITAL
my.hrw.com

 **Online Teacher Edition**
Access a full suite of teaching resources online—plan, present, and manage classes and assignments.

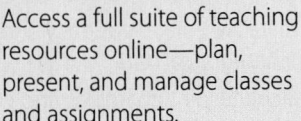 **ePlanner**
Easily plan your classes and access all your resources online.

 Interactive Answers and Solutions
Customize answer keys to print or display in the classroom. Choose to include answers only or full solutions to all lesson exercises.

 Interactive Whiteboards
Engage students with interactive whiteboard-ready lessons and activities.

 Personal Math Trainer: Online Assessment and Intervention
Assign automatically graded homework, quizzes, tests, and intervention activities. Prepare your students with updated practice tests aligned with Common Core.

Reading Start-Up

Have students complete the activities on this page by working alone or with others.

Visualize Vocabulary

The diagram helps students review vocabulary associated with scatter plots. Students should write one review word with its definition in each of the four rectangles.

Understand Vocabulary

Use the following explanations to help students learn the preview words.

Joint, marginal, and conditional relative frequencies all refer to different ratios between quantities found in a two-way table. A **joint relative frequency** is found by dividing the frequency of a cell in the body of the table by the grand total. A **marginal relative frequency** is the ratio of the total frequency of a row or column to the grand total. A **conditional relative frequency** is found by dividing the frequency of a cell in the body by a row or column total.

Active Reading

Integrating Language Arts

Students can use these reading and note-taking strategies to help them organize and understand new concepts and vocabulary.

FL CC LACC.68.RST.3.7 Integrate quantitative or technical information expressed in words in a text with a version of that information expressed visually (e.g., in a flowchart, diagram, model, graph, or table).

Additional Resources

Differentiated Instruction

• Reading Strategies **ELL**

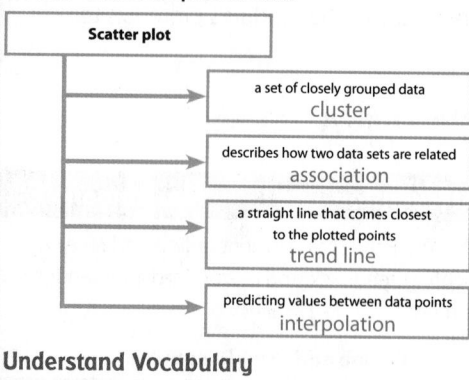

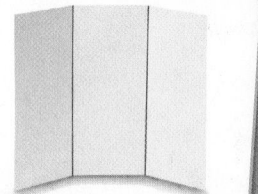

Reading Start-Up

Visualize Vocabulary

Use the ✔ words to complete the chart.

Scatter plot

→ a set of closely grouped data
cluster

→ describes how two data sets are related
association

→ a straight line that comes closest to the plotted points
trend line

→ predicting values between data points
interpolation

Understand Vocabulary

Complete the sentences using preview words.

1. The _____**frequency**_____ is the number of times an event occurs.

2. A ____**two-way table**____ shows the frequencies of data that is categorized two ways.

3. **Relative frequency** is the ratio of the number of times an event occurs to the total number of events.

Vocabulary

Review Words
- ✔ association *(asociación)*
- ✔ cluster *(grupo)*
- data *(datos)*
- ✔ interpolation *(interpolación)*
- extrapolation *(extrapolación)*
- outlier *(parte aislada)*
- scatter plot *(gráfico de dispersión)*
- ✔ trend line *(la línea de tendencia)*

Preview Words
- conditional relative frequency *(frecuencia relativa condicional)*
- frequency *(frecuencia)*
- joint relative frequency *(frecuencia relativa conjunta)*
- marginal relative frequency *(frecuencia relativa marginal)*
- relative frequency *(frecuencia relativa)*
- two-way table *(tabla de doble entrada)*
- two-way relative frequency table *(dos vías tabla de frecuencias relativas)*

Active Reading

Tri-Fold Before beginning the module, create a tri-fold to help you learn the concepts and vocabulary in this module. Fold the paper into three sections. Label the columns "What I Know," "What I Want to Know," and "What I Learned." Complete the first two columns before you read. After studying the module, complete the third column.

© Houghton Mifflin Harcourt Publishing Company

Before	In this module	After
Students understand:	Students will learn how to:	Students will connect:
• how to change a fraction into a decimal or percent	• create two-way frequency and relative frequency tables for categorical data	• frequencies and relative frequencies given as decimals or percents
• how to represent and analyze quantitative data	• calculate joint, marginal, and conditional relative frequencies given a two-way relative frequency table	• frequency tables and associations between variables
	• analyze a two-way table to discover any association between the variables	

Unpacking the Standards

Use the examples on the page to help students know exactly what they are expected to learn in this module.

 Florida Common Core Standards

Content Areas

 **Statistics and Probability—8.SP.1**

Investigate patterns of association in bivariate data.

Go online to see a complete unpacking of the Florida Common Core Standards.

my.hrw.com

 MODULE 23

Unpacking the Standards

Understanding the standards and the vocabulary terms in the standards will help you know exactly what you are expected to learn in this module.

FL CC 8.SP.1.4

Understand that patterns of association can also be seen in bivariate categorical data by displaying frequencies and relative frequencies in a two-way table. Construct and interpret a two-way table summarizing data on two categorical variables collected from the same subjects.

Key Vocabulary

two-way table *(tabla de doble entrada)* A table that shows the frequencies of data categorized in two ways.

What It Means to You

You will use two-way tables to find relative frequencies.

UNPACKING EXAMPLE 8.SP.1.4

Soojinn counted the vehicles in the school parking lot and recorded the data in the two-way table shown.

	During School Day	After School Day	Total
Cars	36	14	50
Trucks	19	6	25
Total	55	20	75

What percent of the vehicles parked after school were trucks?

$$\frac{\text{trucks after school}}{\text{total vehicles after school}} = \frac{6}{20} = 0.3, \text{ or } 30\%$$

30% of the vehicles in the school parking lot after school were trucks.

FL CC 8.SP.1.4

Understand … frequencies and relative frequencies in a two-way table. Construct and interpret a two-way table … . Use relative frequencies calculated for rows or columns to describe possible association between the two variables.

Key Vocabulary

conditional relative frequency *(frecuencia relativa condicional)* The ratio of a frequency by the given conditional total.

 Visit my.hrw.com to see all Florida Common Core Standards unpacked.

my.hrw.com

What It Means to You

You will use two-way tables to find conditional relative frequencies.

UNPACKING EXAMPLE 8.SP.1.4

Soojinn determined the gender of the driver for each of the 55 vehicles parked in the school parking lot during the day.

	Male	Female	Total
Cars	8	25	33
Trucks	15	7	22
Total	23	32	55

What is the conditional relative frequency that a driver is female given that the vehicle is a car?

$$\frac{\text{female car drivers}}{\text{total cars}} = \frac{25}{33} = 0.758, \text{ or } 76\%$$

There is a 76% likelihood that a driver is female given that the vehicle is a car.

© Houghton Mifflin Harcourt Publishing Company

Florida Common Core Standards	Lesson 23.1	Lesson 23.2
FL CC 8.SP.1.4 Understand that patterns of association can also be seen in bivariate categorical data by displaying frequencies and relative frequencies in a two-way table. Construct and interpret a two-way table summarizing data on two categorical variables collected from the same subjects. Use relative frequencies calculated for rows or columns to describe possible association between the two variables.		

LESSON
23.1 Two-Way Frequency Tables

 Florida Common Core Standards

The student is expected to:

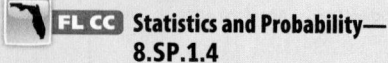 **Statistics and Probability—8.SP.1.4**

Understand that patterns of association can also be seen in bivariate categorical data by displaying frequencies and relative frequencies in a two-way table. Construct and interpret a two-way table .... Use relative frequencies calculated for rows or columns to describe possible association between the two variables.

Mathematical Practices

 MP.6.1 Precision

ADDITIONAL EXAMPLE 1
Determine whether there is an association between the events.

A Is there an association between having a car and having voted in the last election?

	Voted	Not Voted	TOTAL
Car	50	10	60
No Car	20	20	40
TOTAL	70	30	100

The relative frequency of having voted is 70%. The relative frequency of having voted among those that own a car is about 83%. The relative frequencies show that having a car makes it more likely that a person voted in the last election.

(Continued on page 453)

 Interactive Whiteboard
Interactive example available online

 my.hrw.com

---

 Animated Math
Create a Two-Way Frequency Table

Students create a two-way frequency table from a set of data and interpret the meaning of the results.

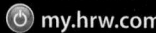 my.hrw.com

---

Engage

ESSENTIAL QUESTION

How can you construct and interpret two-way frequency tables? Sample answer: Make a table in which columns represent one set of categories for a population and the rows represent a different set of categories for the same population. You can compare the relative frequency of one event in a subpopulation to the frequency in the whole population to see if there is an association between categories.

Motivate the Lesson
Ask: How can you display and interpret data that is categorized in two ways? Begin the Explore Activity to find out.

Explore

EXPLORE ACTIVITY

Engage with Whiteboard
 Invite volunteers to complete the table and Parts A–E of the activity. Have them demonstrate the math used to arrive at their answers.

Explain

EXAMPLE 1

Connect to Vocabulary ELL
Compare *frequency* and *relative frequency*. Explain that frequency is the number of times an event occurs. Relative frequency is the *ratio* of the frequency of an event to the total number of events.

Questioning Strategies 🖊 Mathematical Practices
• How are relative frequencies useful? Relative frequencies can be used to help decide if there is an association between two variables or events.

• Why can't ordinary frequencies be used directly to discover an association between variables? In most cases, a population will not be evenly split between two characteristics. For example, in the data for part B, domestic flights are more common than international flights. To see whether international flights are late more often, we have to take into account that there are fewer international flights overall, which means we are using relative frequencies.

Focus on Math Connections
Students should recognize that relative frequency can be expressed as a fraction, a decimal, or a percent.

LESSON 23.1 Two-Way Frequency Tables

 FL CC 8.SP.1.4

Understand that patterns ... can be seen in bivariate categorical data by displaying frequencies in a two-way table. Construct and interpret a two-way table .... Use relative frequencies ... to describe possible association ....

? ESSENTIAL QUESTION How can you construct and interpret two-way frequency tables?

EXPLORE ACTIVITY *Real World*   **FL CC** 8.SP.1.4

Making a Two-Way Table

The **frequency** is the number of times an event occurs. A **two-way table** shows the frequencies of data that is categorized two ways. The rows indicate one categorization and the columns indicate another.

A poll of 120 town residents found that 40% own a bike. Of those who own a bike, 75% shop at the farmer's market. Of those who do not own a bike, 25% shop at the farmer's market.

	Farmer's Market	No Farmer's Market	TOTAL
Bike	36	12	48
No Bike	18	54	72
TOTAL	54	66	120

A Start in the bottom right cell of the table. Enter the total number of people polled.

B Fill in the right column. 40% of 120 people polled own a bike.

The remaining people polled do not own a bike.

C Fill in the top row. 75% of those who own a bike also shop at the market.

The remaining bike owners do not shop at the market.

D Fill in the second row. 25% of those who do not own a bike shop at the market.

The remaining people without bikes do not shop at the market.

E Fill in the last row. In each column, add the numbers in the first two rows to find the total number of people who shop at the farmer's market and who do not shop at the farmer's market.

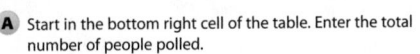

EXPLORE ACTIVITY (cont'd)

Reflect

1. How can you check that your table is completed correctly?

The last number in each row or column should be the sum of the other numbers in that row or column.

Math On the Spot
my.hrw.com

Animated Math
my.hrw.com

Deciding Whether There Is an Association

Relative frequency is the ratio of the number of times an event occurs to the total number of events. In the Explore Activity, the relative frequency of bike owners who shop at the farmer's market is $\frac{36}{120} = 0.30 = 30\%$. You can use relative frequencies to decide if there is an association between two variables or events.

EXAMPLE 1 *Real World*   **FL CC** 8.SP.1.4

Determine whether there is an association between the events.

A One hundred teens were polled about whether they are required to do chores and whether they have a curfew. Is there an association between having a curfew and having to do chores?

	Curfew	No Curfew	TOTAL
Chores	16	4	20
No Chores	16	64	80
TOTAL	32	68	100

Math Talk
Mathematical Practices
What is the difference between frequency and relative frequency?

Frequency is the number of times an event occurs. Relative frequency is the ratio of the frequency to the total number of events.

STEP 1 Find the relative frequency of having to do chores.

Total who have to do chores → $\frac{20}{100} = 0.20 = 20\%$
Total number of teens polled →

STEP 2 Find the relative frequency of having to do chores among those who have a curfew.

Number with a curfew who have chores → $\frac{16}{32} = 0.50 = 50\%$
Total number with a curfew →

STEP 3 Compare the relative frequencies. Students who have a curfew are more likely to have to do chores than the general population. There is an association. The relative frequencies show that having a curfew makes it more likely that a student will have to do chores.

PROFESSIONAL DEVELOPMENT

Integrate Mathematical Practices MP.6.1

This lesson provides an opportunity to address this Mathematical Practices standard, which calls for students to attend to precision. When constructing two-way tables, students need to be accurate with their computations and precise in their recording of the data. The row elements and column elements must be correctly placed in order for the totals to be calculated correctly. Relative frequencies will often not be whole percents, so students must choose to represent them with an appropriate degree of precision.

Math Background

In real-life statistical situations, relative frequencies will often vary somewhat due to chance even when there is no association between two variables. A statistical test called a *chi-squared test of independence* is able to evaluate whether two variables are associated, even when the data have a great deal of variation.

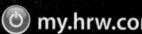
YOUR TURN

Focus on Reasoning Mathematical Practices
Discuss with students the different possible combinations of relative frequencies that could be found for this table. Two relative frequencies can be calculated for each column and for each row.

Avoid Common Errors
Encourage students to compare the relative frequency of all park visits to the relative frequency of park visits for high school students, rather than comparing the relative frequencies of park visits for middle school and high school students. Although the second comparison would arrive at the correct answer in this case, it would not necessarily work if the variables had more than two options.

Elaborate

Talk About It
Summarize the Lesson

Ask: How are relative frequencies determined and how do you know when there is an association between two variables? Relative frequency is found by writing a ratio comparing the frequency of an event to the total number of events. When the relative frequency of a variable within a subpopulation is significantly different than the relative frequency of the variable overall, there is an association between the variables.

GUIDED PRACTICE

Engage with the Whiteboard
For Exercise 1, have volunteers take turns completing the table. Have volunteers explain how to determine the value to write in each cell and have them show their arithmetic where necessary.

Avoid Common Errors
Exercise 2 Caution students to be careful in choosing the relative frequencies to calculate. For example, if they compare the relative frequency of being a boy with the relative frequency of being left-handed among those who are boys, they will arrive at the wrong answer.

B Data from 200 flights were collected. The flights were categorized as domestic or international and late or not late. Is there an association between international flights and a flight being late?

	Late	Not Late	TOTAL
Domestic	30	120	150
International	10	40	50
TOTAL	40	160	200

STEP 1 Find the relative frequency of a flight being late.

Total flights that are late → $\frac{40}{200} = 0.20 = 20\%$
Total number of flights →

STEP 2 Find the relative frequency of a flight being late among international flights.

Number of international flights that are late → $\frac{10}{50} = 0.20 = 20\%$
Total number of international flights →

STEP 3 **Compare the relative frequencies.** International flights are no more likely to be late than flights in general. There is no association. The relative frequencies show that international flights are just as likely to be late as any other flight.

YOUR TURN

2. Data from 200 middle school and high school students were collected. Students were asked whether or not they had visited at least one national park. Is there an association between being a high school student and visiting a national park? Explain.

	Have Visited a National Park	Have NOT Visited a National Park	TOTAL
Middle School	25	55	80
High School	80	40	120
TOTAL	105	95	200

Yes; relative frequency of visiting a park $= \frac{105}{200} =$
$0.525 = 52.5\%$; relative frequency of a high school
student visiting a park $= \frac{80}{120} \approx 0.667 = 66.7\%$;
$66.7\% > 52.5\%$, so being in high school improves the
likelihood that a student has visited a national park.

Personal
Math Trainer
Online Assessment
and Intervention
my.hrw.com

Guided Practice

1. In a survey of 50 students, 60% said that they have a cat. Of the students who have a cat, 70% also have a dog. Of the students who do not have a cat, 75% have a dog. Complete the two-way table. (Explore Activity)

	Dog	No Dog	TOTAL
Cat	21	9	30
No Cat	15	5	20
TOTAL	36	14	50

a. Enter the total number of students surveyed in the bottom right cell of the table.

b. Fill in right column.

c. Fill in top row.

d. Fill in second row.

e. Fill in last row.

2. The results of a survey at a school are shown. Is there an association between being a boy and being left-handed? Explain. (Example 1)

	Left-handed	Right-handed	TOTAL
Boys	14	126	140
Girls	10	90	100
TOTAL	24	216	240

No; the relative frequency of being left-handed (10%)
is the same as the relative frequency of being a
left-handed boy (10%).

? ESSENTIAL QUESTION CHECK-IN

3. Voters were polled to see whether they supported Smith or Jones. Can you construct a two-way table of the results? Why or why not?

No; the poll collected data on only one variable, voters.
A two-way table requires data on two variables, such
as men and women.

DIFFERENTIATE INSTRUCTION

Visual Cues

When they are testing an association using a two-way table, have students highlight the cells that they will need to find the total relative frequency in one color, and the cells they will need for the subpopulation relative frequency in another color. Point out that no cell should be highlighted twice, and some cells will not be highlighted.

Home Connection

Collect data from students in your class on whether or not they have a curfew on school nights and whether or not they have regular chores at home. Record the data for the students to see in a two-way table. Compare the relative frequencies of your class data to determine if there is an association between having a curfew and having to do chores. Compare your results to the data in part A of Example 1.

Additional Resources

Differentiated Instruction includes:
- Reading Strategies
- Success for English Learners **ELL**
- Reteach
- Challenge **PRE-AP**

23.1 LESSON QUIZ

 **FL CC** 8.SP.1.4

1. In a survey of 50 students, 40% said they mow lawns on Saturday. Of the students who mow lawns, 25% sleep until noon. Of the students who do not mow lawns, 70% sleep until noon. Complete the two-way table.

	Sleeps Until Noon	Does Not Sleep Until Noon	TOTAL
Mows	5	15	20
Does Not Mow	21	9	30
TOTAL	26	24	50

2. For the data in Exercise 1, is there an association between mowing lawns and sleeping until noon?

3. The results of a survey at a preschool are shown. Is there an association between being a boy and wearing a red shirt?

	Red	Not Red	TOTAL
Boys	10	15	25
Girls	5	15	20
TOTAL	15	30	45

Lesson Quiz available online

 my.hrw.com

Answers
1. Answers in the table above.

2. The relative frequency of mowing lawns is 40%. The relative frequency of mowing lawns among those who sleep until noon is about 19%. Yes, students who sleep until noon are less likely to mow lawns.

Evaluate

GUIDED AND INDEPENDENT PRACTICE

 **FL CC** 8.SP.1.4

Concepts & Skills	Practice
Explore Activity Making a Two-Way Table	Exercises 1, 4–6
Example 1 Deciding Whether There Is an Association	Exercises 2, 5–6

Exercise	Depth of Knowledge (D.O.K.)	**FL CC** Mathematical Practices
4	**2** Skills/Concepts	**MP.4.1** Modeling
5	**3** Strategic Thinking H.O.T.	**MP.4.1** Modeling
6	**3** Strategic Thinking H.O.T.	**MP.1.1** Problem Solving
7	**3** Strategic Thinking H.O.T.	**MP.2.1** Reasoning

Additional Resources
Differentiated Instruction includes:
• Leveled Practice worksheets

3. The relative frequency of wearing a red shirt is about 33%. The relative frequency of being a boy wearing a red shirt is 40%. Yes, boys are more likely to wear red shirts.

23.1 Independent Practice

FL CC 8.SP.1.4

Personal Math Trainer
Online Assessment and Intervention
my.hrw.com

4. Represent Real-World Problems One hundred forty students were asked about their language classes. Out of 111 who take French, only 31 do not take Spanish. Twelve take neither French nor Spanish. Use this information to make a two-way table.

	Take French	Do NOT Take French	TOTAL
Take Spanish	80	17	97
Do NOT Take Spanish	31	12	43
TOTAL	111	29	140

5. Represent Real-World Problems Seventh- and eighth-grade students were asked whether they preferred science or math.

a. Complete the two-way table.

	Prefer Science	Prefer Math	TOTAL
Seventh Grade	24	72	96
Eighth Grade	32	48	80
TOTAL	56	120	176

b. Is there an association between being in eighth grade and preferring math? Explain.

No; the relative frequency of being an eighth-grader who prefers math $\left(\frac{48}{80} = 60\%\right)$ is less than the relative frequency of preferring math $\left(\frac{120}{176} \approx 68\%\right)$.

6. Persevere in Problem Solving The table gives partial information on the number of men and women who play in the four sections of the Metro Orchestra.

a. Complete the table.

	Strings	Brass	Woodwinds	Percussion	TOTAL
Men	13	7	8	5	33
Women	42	9	10	4	65
TOTAL	55	16	18	9	98

b. Is there an association between being a woman and playing strings? Explain.

Yes; the relative frequency of being a woman who plays strings $\left(\frac{42}{55} \approx 76\%\right)$ is greater than the relative frequency of being a woman in the orchestra $\left(\frac{65}{98} \approx 66\%\right)$.

H.O.T. FOCUS ON HIGHER ORDER THINKING

Work Area

7. Multi-Step The two-way table below shows the results of a survey of Florida teenagers who were asked whether they preferred surfing or snorkeling.

a. To the right of the number in each cell, write the relative frequency of the number compared to the total for the *row* the number is in. Round to the nearest percent.

	Prefer Surfing	Prefer Snorkeling	TOTAL
Ages 13–15	52 40% ; 50%	78 60%; 74%	130 100%
Ages 16–18	52 65% ; 50%	28 35% ; 26%	80 100%
TOTAL	104 50% ;100%	106 50% ;100%	210 100%

b. Explain the meaning of the relative frequency you wrote beside 28.

It is the relative frequency of teenagers who are 16 to 18 years old and who prefer snorkeling to all 16- to 18-year-olds who were surveyed.

c. To the right of each number you wrote in part a, write the relative frequency of each number compared to the total for the *column* the number is in. Are the relative frequencies the same? Why or why not?

No; the total numbers in the last column (ages) are not the same as the total numbers in the last row (preferences), so the relative frequencies are different.

d. Explain the meaning of the relative frequency you wrote beside 28.

It is the relative frequency of teenagers who are 16 to 18 years old and who prefer snorkeling to all of those surveyed who prefer snorkeling.

EXTEND THE MATH PRE-AP

Activity available online my.hrw.com

Activity What could be concluded if the relative frequency of an event is equal to 1? What could be concluded if the relative frequency of an event is equal to 0?

In a two-way table, if there is one event in a column with a relative frequency of 1, what must the relative frequency be for the other event in that same column? Justify your answer.

A relative frequency of 1 or 100% means that all the observations had that outcome. A relative frequency of 0 or 0% means that none of the observations had that outcome.

The other event must have a relative frequency of 0. The sum of the two relative frequencies must be 1 or 100%.

LESSON
23.2 Two-Way Relative Frequency Tables

Engage

Florida Common Core Standards

The student is expected to:

 **Statistics and Probability— 8.SP.1.4**

Understand that patterns of association can also be seen in bivariate categorical data by displaying frequencies and relative frequencies in a two-way table. Construct and interpret a two-way table summarizing data on two categorical variables collected from the same subjects. Use relative frequencies calculated for rows or columns to describe possible association between the two variables.

Mathematical Practices

 **MP.8.1** Patterns

ESSENTIAL QUESTION

How can categorical data be organized and analyzed? Sample answer: You can use frequency tables and two-way frequency tables to show the frequency for each category or category pair. You can use relative frequency tables and two-way relative frequency tables to show what part of the whole data set is represented by each category or category pair. From these tables you can obtain joint relative frequencies, marginal relative frequencies, and conditional relative frequencies.

Motivate the Lesson
Ask: What is the sum of the relative frequencies in a frequency table? Take a guess. Begin the Explore Activity to find out.

Explore

EXPLORE ACTIVITY 1

Connect Vocabulary ELL
Remind students that the *frequencies* in a frequency table are the number of times events occur. The *relative frequency* table shows the ratio of frequency of an event to the total number of events. These ratios are most often written as decimals or percents.

Explain

EXPLORE ACTIVITY 2

Questioning Strategies 🏹 Mathematical Practices
• What is another way this data table could have been organized? The table could have been organized with the rows for Preferred Pet and the columns for Gender.

• What does it mean if you create a two-way frequency table and find that the sum of the row totals is different from the sum of the column totals? You have made an error in addition.

Focus on Critical Thinking 🏹 Mathematical Practices
Make sure students understand the difference between categorical and quantitative data. Categorical data refers to data that is defined by words or has a limited number of answer options, such as "What is the color of your backpack?" Quantitative data refers to data that numerically measures a particular characteristic, such as "How much does your backpack weigh?"

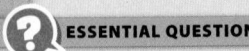

LESSON 23.2 Two-Way Relative Frequency Tables

 FL CC 8.SP.1.4

Understand that patterns ... can be seen in bivariate categorical data by displaying frequencies in a two-way table. Construct and interpret a two-way table ... . Use relative frequencies calculated for rows or columns to describe possible association ... .

? **ESSENTIAL QUESTION**

How can categorical data be organized and analyzed?

EXPLORE ACTIVITY 1 *Real World* **FL CC** 8.SP.1.4

Creating a Relative Frequency Table

The frequency table below shows the results of a survey that Maria took at her school. She asked 50 randomly selected students whether they preferred dogs, cats, or other pets. Convert this table to a *relative frequency* table that uses decimals as well as one that uses percents.

Preferred Pet	Dog	Cat	Other	TOTAL
Frequency	22	15	13	50

A Divide the numbers in the frequency table by the total to obtain relative frequencies as decimals. Record the results in the table below.

Preferred Pet	Dog	Cat	Other	TOTAL
Relative Frequency	$\frac{22}{50} = 0.44$	$\frac{15}{50} = 0.3$	$\frac{13}{50} = 0.26$	$\frac{50}{50} = 1$

B Write the decimals as percents in the table below.

Preferred Pet	Dog	Cat	Other	TOTAL
Relative Frequency	44%	30%	26%	100%

Reflect

1. How can you check that you have correctly converted frequencies to relative frequencies?

   The sum of the relative frequencies as decimals should be 1; the sum of the relative frequencies as percents should be 100%.

2. Explain why the number in the Total column of a relative frequency table is always 1 or 100%.

   To obtain a relative frequency from a frequency, you divide the frequency by the total. The total divided by itself will always equal 1 or 100%.

Lesson 23.2 **721**

EXPLORE ACTIVITY 2 *Real World* **FL CC** 8.SP.1.4

Creating a Two-Way Frequency Table

In the previous Explore Activity, the categorical variable was pet preference, and the variable had three possible data values: dog, cat, and other. The frequency table listed the frequency for each value of that single variable. If you have two categorical variables whose values have been paired, you list the frequencies of the paired values in a **two-way frequency table**.

For her survey, Maria also recorded the gender of each student. The results are shown in the two-way frequency table below. Each entry is the frequency of students who prefer a certain pet *and* are a certain gender. For instance, 10 girls prefer dogs as pets. Complete the table.

Preferred Pet / Gender	Dog	Cat	Other	TOTAL
Girl	10	9	3	22
Boy	12	6	10	28
TOTAL	22	15	13	50

A Find the total for each gender by adding the frequencies in each row.

B Find the total for each pet by adding the frequencies in each column.

C Find the grand total, which is the sum of the row totals as well as the sum of the column totals. Write this in the lower-right corner.

Reflect

3. Where have you seen the numbers in the Total row before?

   They are from the frequency table in the previous activity.

4. In terms of Maria's survey, what does the grand total represent?

   The number of students surveyed

EXPLORE ACTIVITY 3 *Real World* **FL CC** 8.SP.1.4

Creating a Two-Way Relative Frequency Table

You can obtain *relative* frequencies from a two-way frequency table:

722 Unit 10

PROFESSIONAL DEVELOPMENT

Integrate Mathematical Practices MP.8.1

This lesson provides an opportunity to address this Mathematical Practices standard, which calls for students to look for and express regularity in repeated reasoning. As students repeat calculations for each cell in a two-way relative frequency table, they become increasingly proficient in the process of calculating relative frequency. In addition, they generalize the process so they can apply the same calculations and reasoning to any categorical data set organized in a two-way frequency table.

Math Background

Theoretically, an unlimited number of variables can be displayed in a multiway table. The more variables, the more complicated it becomes to analyze relationships between them. Below is an example of a three-way table.

	Florida			Ohio		
	Green	Red	TOTAL	Green	Red	TOTAL
Male	30	40	70	15	45	60
Female	25	35	60	35	20	55
TOTAL	55	75	130	50	65	115

Two-Way Relative Frequency Tables **722**

© Houghton Mifflin Harcourt Publishing Company

EXPLORE ACTIVITY 3

Questioning Strategies Mathematical Practices

- If you are given a relative frequency table made from survey data, can you determine the number of people who were surveyed? Explain. No. The values in a relative frequency table are all percents. There is no way to tell what the original frequencies were from the table alone.

- What does it mean if you create a two-way relative frequency table and the sum of the row totals or the sum of the column totals is not 1? You have made an error, either in the calculation of the percents or in the addition of the columns and rows.

Engage with the Whiteboard

For Explore Activity 3, have volunteers demonstrate how to complete the table in part A and complete the equations in part B.

Avoid Common Errors

Some students may confuse joint relative frequency with marginal relative frequency. It may help them to think of the row and column totals as located in the margins of the table, and therefore the starting points for finding marginal relative frequency.

EXAMPLE 1

Questioning Strategies Mathematical Practices

- When dealing with conditional relative frequency problems, which word signals that a particular frequency should go in the denominator of the fraction? The word *given* signals this.

- How do you know which frequency goes in the numerator of the fraction? Two categories are mentioned in the problem. The frequency of belonging to both categories simultaneously goes in the numerator.

Avoid Common Errors

A question that asks for a conditional relative frequency is often of the form "What is the relative frequency that an item of data is in one category, given that the item is in another category?" By outlining or highlighting the "given" category, students should understand that this is the only part of the table that is relevant to the question and should therefore divide by the row or column total for that category.

YOUR TURN

Avoid Common Errors

To avoid errors in calculations with decimals within a fraction, suggest that students clear the decimals first by multiplying the numerator and denominators by the same power of 10. In this case, 0.18 and 0.44 can each be multiplied by 100 to arrive at the fraction $\frac{18}{44}$.

ADDITIONAL EXAMPLE 1
Use the frequency table shown below about preferred flavors of frozen yogurt. Express each answer as a decimal and as a percent.

Preferred Flavor / Gender	Vanilla	Chocolate	Other	TOTAL
Boy	1	6	4	11
Girl	3	4	2	9
TOTAL	4	10	6	20

A Find the conditional relative frequency that a student prefers vanilla yogurt, given that the student is a boy.

$\frac{1}{11} \approx 0.09$ or 9%

B Find the conditional relative frequency that a student surveyed is a boy, given that the student prefers vanilla frozen yogurt.

$\frac{1}{4} \approx 0.25$ or 25%

 Interactive Whiteboard
Interactive example available online

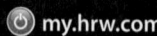 my.hrw.com

---

- A **joint relative frequency** is found by dividing a frequency that is not in the Total row or the Total column by the grand total.
- A **marginal relative frequency** is found by dividing a row total or a column total by the grand total.

A **two-way relative frequency table** displays both joint relative frequencies and marginal relative frequencies.

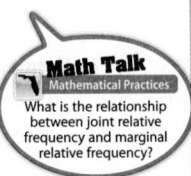

Math Talk
Mathematical Practices

What is the relationship between joint relative frequency and marginal relative frequency?

Create a two-way relative frequency table for Maria's data.

A Divide each number in the two-way frequency table from the previous Explore Activity by the grand total. Write the quotients as decimals.

Preferred Pet / Gender	Dog	Cat	Other	TOTAL
Girl	$\frac{10}{50} = 0.2$	$\frac{9}{50} = 0.18$	$\frac{3}{50} = 0.06$	$\frac{22}{50} = 0.44$
Boy	$\frac{12}{50} = 0.24$	$\frac{6}{50} = 0.12$	$\frac{10}{50} = 0.2$	$\frac{28}{50} = 0.56$
TOTAL	$\frac{22}{50} = 0.44$	$\frac{15}{50} = 0.3$	$\frac{13}{50} = 0.26$	$\frac{50}{50} = 1$

The sum of the joint relative frequencies in each row or column of a two-way relative frequency table must equal that row's or that column's marginal relative frequency.

B Check by adding the joint relative frequencies in a row or column to see if the sum equals that row's or column's marginal relative frequency.

Girl row: $0.2 + \underline{0.18} + \underline{0.06} = \underline{0.44}$

Boy row: $\underline{0.24} + \underline{0.12} + \underline{0.2} = \underline{0.56}$

Dog column: $0.2 + \underline{0.24} = \underline{0.44}$

Cat column: $\underline{0.18} + \underline{0.12} = \underline{0.3}$

Other column: $\underline{0.06} + \underline{0.2} = \underline{0.26}$

Reflect

5. A joint relative frequency in a two-way relative frequency table tells you what portion of the entire data set falls into the intersection of a particular value of one variable and a particular value of the other variable. What is the joint relative frequency of students surveyed who are boys and prefer cats as pets?

   0.12, or 12%

6. A marginal relative frequency in a two-way relative frequency table tells you what portion of the entire data set represents a particular value of just one of the variables. What is the marginal relative frequency of students surveyed who are boys?

   0.56, or 56%

Math On the Spot

my.hrw.com

My Notes

Calculating Conditional Relative Frequencies

One other type of relative frequency that you can obtain from a two-way frequency table is a *conditional relative frequency*. A **conditional relative frequency** is found by dividing a frequency that is not in the Total row or the Total column by the frequency's row total or column total.

EXAMPLE 1 Real World   FL CC 8.SP.1.4

From Maria's two-way frequency table you know that 22 students are girls and 15 students prefer cats. You also know that 9 students are girls who prefer cats. Use this to find each conditional relative frequency.

A Find the conditional relative frequency that a student surveyed prefers cats as pets, given that the student is a girl.

Divide the number of girls who prefer cats by the number of girls. Express your answer as a decimal and as a percent.

$\frac{9}{22} = 0.409$, or 40.9%

B Find the conditional relative frequency that a student surveyed is a girl, given that the student prefers cats as pets.

Divide the number of girls who prefer cats by the number of students who prefer cats. Express your answer as a decimal and as a percent.

$\frac{9}{15} = 0.6$, or 60%

Reflect

7. When calculating a conditional relative frequency, why do you divide by a row total or a column total and not by the grand total?

   The "given" in a conditional relative frequency restricts the discussion to a single row or column of a two-way frequency table. A conditional relative frequency is the portion of the data in just that row or column (not the portion of all data) that meets a certain criterion.

Personal Math Trainer

Online Assessment and Intervention

my.hrw.com

YOUR TURN

8. You can obtain conditional relative frequencies from a two-way relative frequency table. Find the conditional relative frequency that a student prefers cats as pets, given that the student is a girl.

   $\frac{0.18}{0.44} \approx 0.409$, or 40.9%

DIFFERENTIATE INSTRUCTION

Modeling

The results of Maria's survey from Explore Activity 2 are also used in Explore Activity 3, Example 1, and Example 2. Suggest that students copy this completed frequency table of data on one side of an index card. On the other side of the index card, have students copy the relative frequency table for Maria's data. They can then refer to their index cards when they need to extract data to answer questions.

Graphic Organizers

Have students complete a graphic organizer, such as the one shown below, to help them recall how to find each type of frequency from a two-way table.

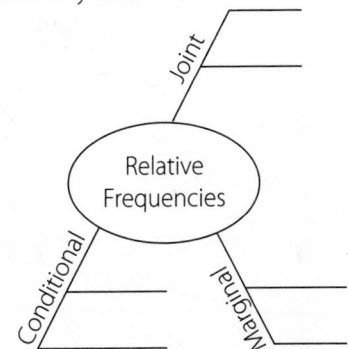

Additional Resources

Differentiated Instruction includes:
- Reading Strategies
- Success for English Learners **ELL**
- Reteach
- Challenge **PRE-AP**

EXAMPLE 2

Questioning Strategies Mathematical Practices

- If you know that a student prefers cats as pets, what prediction can you make about the student's gender given the conditional relative frequencies? The student is more likely to be a girl.

- If you know that a student prefers other pets, what prediction can you make about the student's gender given the conditional relative frequencies? The student is more likely to be a boy.

Connect to Daily Life

Discuss with students how surveys of this type might influence advertising. Point out that the use of surveys like this one allows advertisers to effectively target very specific populations.

YOUR TURN

Engage with the Whiteboard

 For Exercise 9 have volunteers calculate the percents and then explain how to analyze the data.

Elaborate

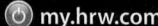

Talk About It
Summarize the Lesson

 Ask: What does it mean when all of the conditional relative frequencies for the rows of a table are similar or the same? It means that the variables are not highly associated with each other.

GUIDED PRACTICE

Engage with the Whiteboard

For Exercise 1, have volunteers explain the process of arriving at the correct value as they complete the table.

Avoid Common Errors

Exercise 1d Remind students that the data they used to complete the table in Exercises 1a–c will be needed to complete this table. Suggest students check their values by making sure the sum of the column totals and the sum of the row totals are the same.

Finding Possible Associations Between Variables

You can use conditional relative frequency to see if there is an association between two variables.

Math On the Spot
my.hrw.com

EXAMPLE 2
FL CC 8.SP.1.4

Maria conducted her survey because she was interested in the question "Does gender influence what type of pet people prefer?" If there is no influence, then the distribution of gender within each subgroup of pet preference should roughly equal the distribution of gender within the whole group. Use the results of Maria's survey to investigate possible influences of gender on pet preference.

STEP 1 Identify the percent of all students surveyed who are girls: 44%

STEP 2 Determine each conditional relative frequency.

Of the 22 students who prefer dogs as pets, 10 are girls.
Percent who are girls, given a preference for dogs as pets: 45%

Of the 15 students who prefer cats as pets, 9 are girls.
Percent who are girls, given a preference for cats as pets: 60%

Of the 13 students who prefer other pets. 3 are girls.
Percent who are girls, given a preference for other pets: 23%

STEP 3 Interpret the results by comparing each conditional relative frequency to the percent of all students surveyed who are girls.

The percent of girls among students who prefer dogs is close to 44%, so gender does not appear to influence preference for dogs.

The percent of girls among students who prefer cats is much greater than 44%, so girls are more likely than boys to prefer cats.

The percent of girls among students who prefer other pets is much less than 44%, so girls are less likely than boys to prefer other pets.

YOUR TURN

9. Suppose you analyzed the data by focusing on boys rather than girls. How would the percent in Step 1 change? How would the percents in Step 2 change? How would the conclusions in Step 3 change?

Step 1: 44% becomes 56%; Step 2: 45% becomes 55%, 60% becomes 40%, and 23% becomes 77%; Step 3: conclusions would not change.

My Notes

Personal Math Trainer
Online Assessment and Intervention
my.hrw.com

---

1. In a class survey, students were asked to choose their favorite vacation destination. The results are displayed by gender in the two-way frequency table. (Explore Activities 1–3)

Gender \ Preferred Pet	Seashore	Mountains	Other	TOTAL
Girl	7	3	2	12
Boy	5	2	6	13
TOTAL	12	5	8	25

a. Find the total for each gender by adding the frequencies in each row. Write the row totals in the Total column.

b. Find the total for each preferred vacation spot by adding the frequencies in each column. Write the column totals in the Total row.

c. Write the grand total (the sum of the row totals and the column totals) in the lower-right corner of the table.

d. Create a two-way relative frequency table by dividing each number in the above table by the grand total. Write the quotients as decimals.

Gender \ Preferred Pet	Seashore	Mountains	Other	TOTAL
Girl	0.28	0.12	0.08	0.48
Boy	0.2	0.08	0.24	0.52
TOTAL	0.48	0.2	0.32	1.00

e. Use the table to find the joint relative frequency of students surveyed who are boys and who prefer vacationing in the mountains.   0.08, or 8%

f. Use the table to find the marginal relative frequency of students surveyed who prefer vacationing at the seashore.   0.48, or 48%

g. Find the conditional relative frequency that a student surveyed prefers vacationing in the mountains, given that the student is a girl. Interpret this result. (Examples 1–2)

0.6, or 60%; girls are more likely than boys to prefer the mountains.

? ESSENTIAL QUESTION CHECK-IN

2. How can you use a two-way frequency table to learn more about its data?

You can find joint relative frequencies, marginal relative frequencies, conditional relative frequencies, and possible associations.

Personal Math Trainer

Online Assessment and Intervention

Online homework assignment available

 my.hrw.com

---

23.2 LESSON QUIZ

FL CC 8.SP.1.4

1. In a survey, 5 students prefer red, 9 prefer green, and 6 prefer blue. Create a relative frequency table of this data.

2. In the survey from Exercise 1, 2 boys prefer red, 5 girls prefer green, and 3 girls prefer blue. Use this information to complete the two-way frequency table below.

Preferred Color \ Gender	Red	Green	Blue	TOTAL
Boy	2	4	3	9
Girl	3	5	3	11
TOTAL	5	9	6	20

3. Create a two-way relative frequency table for the data in Exercise 2. Write the relative frequencies as decimals.

4. Find the conditional relative frequency that a student prefers the color red, given that the student is a boy.

5. Use the two-way frequency table from Exercise 2 to investigate the possible influence of gender on color preference.

Lesson Quiz available online

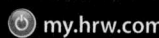 my.hrw.com

Answers

1.

Preferred Color	Red	Green	Blue	TOTAL
Relative Frequency	25%	45%	30%	100%

2. See answers in table in Exercise 2.

Evaluate

GUIDED AND INDEPENDENT PRACTICE

 **FL CC** 8.SP.1.4

Concepts & Skills	Practice
Explore Activity 1 Creating a Relative Frequency Table	Exercises 1a–b
Explore Activity 2 Creating a Two-Way Frequency Table	Exercises 1a–c, 3
Explore Activity 3 Creating a Two-Way Relative Frequency Table	Exercises 1d–f, 4–5
Example 1 Calculating Conditional Relative Frequencies	Exercises 1g, 5
Example 2 Finding Possible Associations Between Variables	Exercises 1g, 6

Exercise	Depth of Knowledge (D.O.K.)	**FL CC** Mathematical Practices
3	**3** Strategic Thinking H.O.T.	**MP.7.1** Using Structure
4	**2** Skills/Concepts	**MP.1.1** Problem Solving
5	**2** Skills/Concepts	**MP.4.1** Modeling
6	**3** Strategic Thinking H.O.T.	**MP.3.1** Logic
7	**3** Strategic Thinking H.O.T.	**MP.2.1** Reasoning
8	**3** Strategic Thinking H.O.T.	**MP.6.1** Precision

Additional Resources

Differentiated Instruction includes:

• Leveled Practice worksheets

 **CLUSTER CONNECTION**

Exercise 7 combines concepts from the Florida Common Core cluster "Investigate patterns of association in bivariate data."

3.

Preferred Color \ Gender	Red	Green	Blue	TOTAL
Boy	0.1	0.2	0.15	0.45
Girl	0.15	0.25	0.15	0.55
TOTAL	0.25	0.45	0.30	1

4. $\frac{2}{9} \approx 0.22$ or about 22%

5. Sample answer: Boys appear somewhat less likely to prefer red than girls and somewhat more likely to prefer blue.

23.2 Independent Practice

FL CC 8.SP.1.4

Personal Math Trainer

Online Assessment and Intervention

my.hrw.com

Stefan surveyed 75 of his classmates about their participation in school activities as well as whether they have a part-time job. The results are shown in the two-way frequency table. Use the table for Exercises 3–6.

Job \ Activity	Clubs Only	Sports Only	Both	Neither	TOTAL
Yes	10	12	20	9	51
No	5	6	10	3	24
TOTAL	15	18	30	12	75

3. a. Complete the table.

b. Explain how you found the correct data to enter in the table.

Sample answer: I worked backward from the given data, using the fact that the sum of the entries in each row and each column must equal the total for that row or column.

4. Create a two-way relative frequency table using decimals. Round to the nearest hundredth.

Job \ Activity	Clubs Only	Sports Only	Both	Neither	TOTAL
Yes	0.13	0.16	0.27	0.12	0.68
No	0.07	0.08	0.13	0.04	0.32
TOTAL	0.2	0.24	0.4	0.16	1.00

5. Give each relative frequency as a percent.

a. the joint relative frequency of students surveyed who participate in school clubs only and have part-time jobs _____13%_____

b. the marginal frequency of students surveyed who do not have a part-time job _____32%_____

c. the conditional relative frequency that a student surveyed participates in both school clubs and sports, given that the student has a part-time job _____about 40%_____

6. Discuss possible influences of having a part-time job on participation in school activities. Support your response with an analysis of the data.

Sample answer: There does not appear to be any influence. Within each category of school activity, the percent of students who have a part-time job is fairly close to 68%, the percent for the whole group.

H.O.T. FOCUS ON HIGHER ORDER THINKING

7. The head of quality control for a chair manufacturer collected data on the quality of two types of wood that the company grows on its tree farm. The table shows the acceptance and rejection data.

Wood \ Accept/Reject	Accepted	Rejected	TOTAL
White Oak	245	105	350
Redwood	140	110	250
TOTAL	385	215	600

Work Area

a. Critique Reasoning To create a two-way relative frequency table for this data, the head of quality control divided each number in each row by the row total. Is this correct? Explain.

No; each data value should have been divided by the grand total, 600, not by the row total.

b. Draw Conclusions Is any of the data the head of quality control entered into the two-way relative frequency table correct? If so, which is and which isn't? Explain.

Yes; the data in the Total row and Total column are correct. These entries were created by dividing each entry by 600, the grand total, which results in the correct marginal relative frequency. The joint relative frequencies are incorrect.

8. Analyze Relationships What is the difference between relative frequency and conditional relative frequency?

Relative frequency is the quotient of a frequency and the grand total. Conditional relative frequency is the quotient of a frequency and a column total or row total.

EXTEND THE MATH PRE-AP

Activity available online my.hrw.com

Activity Conduct your own survey using gender and a three-category variable of your choice. Organize your data in two-way frequency and relative frequency tables. Next, find conditional relative frequencies based on your calculations. Finally, use the conditional relative frequencies to analyze the data to investigate any possible influence of gender on the variable you have chosen.

Ready to Go On?

Assess Mastery

Use the assessment on this page to determine if students have mastered the concepts and standards covered in this module.

 **Response to Intervention**

Intervention	Enrichment

Personal Math Trainer
Online Assessment and Intervention
⏻ my.hrw.com

Access Ready to Go On? assessment online, and receive instant scoring, feedback, and customized intervention or enrichment.

Online and Print Resources

Differentiated Instruction
- Reteach worksheets
- Reading Strategies **ELL**
- Success for English Learners **ELL**

Differentiated Instruction
- Challenge worksheets **PRE-AP**
- Extend the Math **PRE-AP** Lesson Activities in TE

Additional Resources

Assessment Resources includes:
- Leveled Module Quizzes

Ready to Go On?

Personal Math Trainer
Online Assessment and Intervention
my.hrw.com

23.1 Two-Way Frequency Tables

Martin collected data from students about whether they played a musical instrument. The table shows his results. Use the table for Exercises 1–4.

	Instrument	No Instrument	TOTAL
Boys	42	70	112
Girls	48		88
Total	90	110	200

1. Of the students surveyed, how many played an instrument? ___90___

2. How many girls surveyed did NOT play an instrument? ___40___

3. What is the relative frequency of a student playing an instrument? Write the answer as a percent. ___45%___

4. What is the relative frequency of a boy playing an instrument? Write the answer as a decimal. ___0.375___

23.2 Two-Way Relative Frequency Tables

Students were asked how they traveled to school. The two-way relative frequency table shows the results. Use the table for Exercises 5–7. Write answers as decimals rounded to the nearest hundredth.

	Method			
School	Car	Bus	Other	TOTAL
Middle School	0.18	0.14	0.10	0.42
High School	0.38	0.12	0.08	0.58
TOTAL	0.56	0.26	0.18	1.00

5. What is the joint relative frequency of high school students who ride the bus? ___0.12___

6. What is the marginal relative frequency of students surveyed who are in middle school? ___0.42___

7. What is the conditional relative frequency that a student rides the bus, given that the student is in middle school? ___0.33___

 ESSENTIAL QUESTION

8. How can you use two-way tables to solve real-world problems?

You can use two-way tables to find frequencies, various types of relative frequencies, and possible associations.

 ## Florida Common Core Standards

Lesson	Exercises	🏳 Common Core Standards
23.1	1–4	**8.SP.1.4**
23.2	5–7	**8.SP.1.4**

PARCC Assessment Readiness

Assessment Readiness Tip Even if students do not remember the precise meaning of a vocabulary term, they can often use logic to arrive at the correct answer.

Item 2 If students do not immediately remember the difference between frequency and relative frequency, encourage them to look at the answer choices. The fact that the answers are all percents should lead them in the right direction.

Item 5 Students may not recall the meaning of the term *marginal relative frequency*. However, if they read the item carefully, they may note that only a single characteristic from the chart is mentioned—being female. Given this, the only relative frequency that could make sense is the frequency of female teachers to total teachers.

Avoid Common Errors

Item 3 If students choose answer B, point out that they found the joint relative frequency of male teachers who have taught for fewer than 10 years. For the relative frequency, they should ignore the female teachers.

Item 7 Remind students that to find the volume of a cone, they need to know the radius of the base.

Additional Resources

Personal Math Trainer
Online Assessment and Intervention
my.hrw.com

Selected Response

The table gives data on the length of time that teachers at Tenth Avenue School have taught. Use the table for Exercises 1–5.

	Fewer than 10 years	10 or more years	TOTAL
Male	9	6	15
Female	?	4	25
TOTAL	30	10	40

1. How many female teachers have taught for fewer than 10 years?
- Ⓐ 4
- Ⓒ 21
- Ⓑ 9
- Ⓓ 30

2. What is the relative frequency of teachers who have taught for 10 or more years?
- Ⓐ 10%
- Ⓒ 30%
- Ⓑ 25%
- Ⓓ 60%

3. What is the relative frequency of male teachers who have taught for fewer than 10 years?
- Ⓐ 0.09
- Ⓒ 0.6
- Ⓑ 0.225
- Ⓓ 1.50

4. What is the joint relative frequency of female teachers who have taught for more than 10 years?
- Ⓐ 4%
- Ⓒ 16%
- Ⓑ 10%
- Ⓓ 25%

5. What is the marginal relative frequency of teachers who are female?
- Ⓐ 0.16
- Ⓒ 0.4
- Ⓑ 0.25
- Ⓓ 0.625

6. A triangle has an exterior angle of $x°$. Which of the following represents the measure of the interior angle next to it?
- Ⓐ $(180 - x)°$
- Ⓒ $(90 - x)°$
- Ⓑ $(x - 180)°$
- Ⓓ $(x - 90)°$

7. What is the volume of a cone that has a diameter of 12 cm and a height of 4 cm? Use 3.14 for π and round to the nearest tenth.
- Ⓐ 25.12 cm^3
- Ⓒ 150.72 cm^3
- Ⓑ 602.88 cm^3
- Ⓓ $1,808.64 \text{ cm}^3$

Mini-Task

8. The table gives data on books read by members of the Summer Reading Club.

	Fewer than 25 books	25 or more books	TOTAL
Boys	7	21	28
Girls	9	27	36
TOTAL	16	48	64

a. Find the relative frequency of a club member reading fewer than 25 books.
$$\frac{16}{64} = 0.25 = 25\%$$

b. Find the relative frequency of a girl club member reading fewer than 25 books.
$$\frac{9}{36} = 0.25 = 25\%$$

c. Is there an association between being a girl and reading fewer than 25 books? Explain.

No; the relative frequencies show that girls are no more likely to read fewer than 25 books than members in general.

Florida Common Core Standards

Items	Grade 8 Standards	Mathematical Practices
1	8.SP.1.4	MP.4.1
2	8.SP.1.4	MP.4.1
3	8.SP.1.4	MP.4.1
4	8.SP.1.4	MP.4.1
5	8.SP.1.4	MP.4.1
6*	8.G.1.5	MP.7.1
7*	8.G.3.9	MP.4.1
8	8.SP.1.4	MP.3.1, MP.4.1

* Item integrates mixed review concepts from previous modules or a previous course.

Study Guide Review

Additional Resources

	Personal Math Trainer
⏻ my.hrw.com	Online Assessment and Intervention

Assessment Resources
- Leveled Unit Tests: A, B, C, D
- Performance Assessment

Vocabulary Development

Integrating Language Arts

Encourage students to practice using the unit vocabulary as they talk and write about mathematics. Understanding vocabulary will aid their understanding of the concepts.

FL CC LACC.68.RST.2.4 Determine the meaning of symbols, key terms, and other domain-specific words and phrases as they are used in a specific scientific or technical context relevant to grades 6–8 texts and topics.

MODULE 22 Scatter Plots
FL CC 8.SP.1.1, 8.SP.1.2, 8.SP.1.3

Key Concepts
- A scatter plot is a graph with points plotted to show the relationship between two sets of data. *(Lesson 22.1)*
- If two sets of data increase together, they show a positive association. If one set increases while the other decreases, they have a negative association. If changes in one data set have no effect on the other, they have no association. *(Lesson 22.1)*
- Data that have a linear association cluster along a line and can be modeled by a trend line. *(Lessons 22.1, 22.2)*

Study Guide Review

MODULE 22 Scatter Plots

Key Vocabulary
cluster *(agrupación)*
outlier *(valor extremo)*
scatter plot *(diagrama de dispersión)*
trend line *(línea de tendencia)*

ESSENTIAL QUESTION

How can you use scatter plots to solve real-world problems?

EXAMPLE 1

As part of a research project, a researcher made a table of test scores and the number of hours of sleep a person got the night before the test. Make a scatter plot of the data. Does the data show a positive association, negative association, or no association?

Sleep (hours)	Test score
4	30
5	40
6	50
6	70
8	100
9	90
10	100

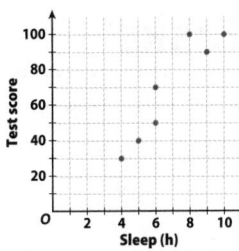

The data show a positive association. Generally, as the number of hours of sleep increases, so do the test scores.

EXAMPLE 2

Write an equation for a trend line of the data shown on the graph.

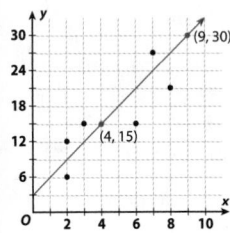

$m = \frac{30-15}{9-4} = 3$ Find the slope.

$15 = 3(4) + b$ Find the y-intercept.

$b = 3$

$y = 3x + 3$ Use the slope and y-intercept to write the equation.

EXERCISES

1. The table shows the income of 8 households, in thousands of dollars, and the number of televisions in each household. (Lesson 22.1)

Income ($1000)	20	20	30	30	40	60	70	90
Number of televisions	4	0	1	2	2	3	3	4

a. Make a scatter plot of the data.

b. Describe the association between income and number of televisions. Are any of the values outliers?

The data generally shows a positive association between income and number of televisions. As income increases, so does the number of televisions. There is an outlier at (20, 4).

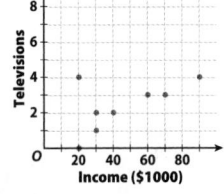

2. The scatter plot shows the relationship between the price of a product and the number of potential buyers. (Lesson 22.2)

a. Draw a trend line for the scatter plot.

b. Write an equation for your trend line.

Sample answer: $y = -2x + 24$

c. When the price of the product is $3.50, the number of potential buyers will be about ___Sample answer: 17___.

d. When the price of the product is $5.50, the number of potential buyers will be about ___Sample answer: 13___.

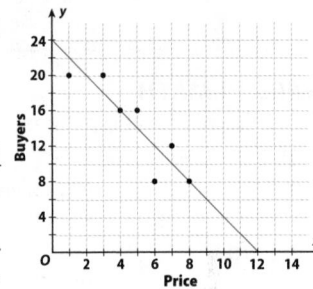

MODULE 23 Two-Way Tables

FL CC 8.SP.1.4

Key Concepts
- Two-way tables are used to display two types of categorical data for a single population at the same time. *(Lesson 23.1)*
- Frequency and relative frequency tables can be used to decide if there is an association between two variables. *(Lessons 23.1, 23.2)*

Unit 10 Performance Tasks

The Performance Tasks provide students with the opportunity to apply concepts from this unit in real-world problem situations.

CAREERS IN MATH

Psychologist In Performance Task Item 1, students can see how a psychologist uses mathematics on the job.

CAREERS IN MATH
For more information about careers in mathematics as well as various mathematics appreciation topics, visit the American Mathematical Society at www.ams.org

SCORING GUIDES FOR PERFORMANCE TASKS

1. MATHEMATICAL PRACTICES **FL CC** MP.4.1, MP.6.1, MP.7.1

Task	Possible Points (Total: 6)
a	**1 point** for correctly describing the graph as exhibiting a roughly linear association, or another correct description, and **1 point** for the correct answer of negative association.
b	**1 point** for a reasonable line, such as the line shown in the answer on the student page, and **1 point** for finding a reasonable slope of around −0.4 and explaining that it means test scores decrease by about 0.4 points per year of age.
c	**1 point** for noting that the line of best fit predicts a lower score, and **1 point** for any reasonable explanation, for example: the score for this woman was an outlier, or short-term memory tends to level off at ages after 65.

2. MATHEMATICAL PRACTICES **FL CC** MP.1.1, MP.2.1, MP.4.1, MP.7.1

Task	Possible Points (Total: 6)
a	**2 points** for correctly filling in the frequency table: from top to bottom, total column should 81, 67, 148; from left to right, total row should be 64, 84, 148
b	**1 point** for correctly finding the solution 57%
c	**1 point** for correctly finding the solution 56%
d	**1 point** for correctly answering no; and 1 point for a correct explanation, for example: The relative frequencies show that Big Red tomatoes are no more likely to have diameters greater than two inches than any of the tomatoes Kalila grew.

MODULE 23 · Two-Way Tables

❓ ESSENTIAL QUESTION

How can you use two-way tables to solve real-world problems?

EXAMPLE

A movie theater kept a record of patrons who bought tickets for a particular movie for two different times. The results are shown in the two-way frequency table. Create a two-way relative frequency table of these data.

	5:00 P.M. Showing	8:00 P.M. Showing	Total
Adults	22	39	61
Children	40	25	65
Total	62	64	126

Step 1: Divide each entry by the total number of patrons. Round to the nearest hundredth.

	5:00 P.M. Showing	8:00 P.M. Showing	Total
Adults	$\frac{22}{126} \approx 0.17$	$\frac{39}{126} \approx 0.31$	$\frac{61}{126} \approx 0.48$
Children	$\frac{40}{126} \approx 0.32$	$\frac{25}{126} \approx 0.20$	$\frac{65}{126} \approx 0.52$
Total	$\frac{62}{126} \approx 0.49$	$\frac{64}{126} \approx 0.51$	$\frac{126}{126} \approx 1.00$

Step 2: Convert decimals to percents.

	5:00 P.M. Showing	8:00 P.M. Showing	Total
Adults	17%	31%	48%
Children	32%	20%	52%
Total	49%	51%	100%

EXERCISES

Use the tables in the Example to answer each question. (Lessons 23.1, 23.2)

1. What is the joint relative frequency of patrons who are adults and attended the 8:00 P.M. showing?

    0.31, or 31%

2. What is the marginal relative frequency of patrons who went to the 8:00 P.M. showing?

    0.51, or 51%

3. What is the conditional relative frequency that a patron is an adult, given that the patron attends the 8:00 P.M. showing?

    0.61, or 61%

Key Vocabulary

conditional relative frequency *(frecuencia relativa condicional)*

frequency *(frecuencia)*

joint relative frequency *(frecuencia relativa común)*

marginal relative frequency *(frecuencia relativa marginal)*

relative frequency *(frecuencia relativa)*

two-way frequency table *(vector bidireccional de la frecuencia)*

two-way relative frequency table *(vector bidireccional de la frecuencia relativa)*

two-way table *(vector bidireccional)*

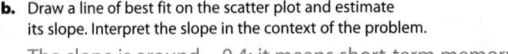

Unit 10 Performance Tasks

1. **CAREERS IN MATH** | Psychologist A psychologist gave a test to 15 women of different ages to measure their short-term memory. The test score scale goes from 0 to 24, and a higher score means that the participant has a better short-term memory. The scatter plot shows the results of this study.

    a. Describe the pattern in the data. Is there a positive or negative correlation?

    The graph exhibits a roughly linear association and shows a negative correlation.

    b. Draw a line of best fit on the scatter plot and estimate its slope. Interpret the slope in the context of the problem.

    The slope is around −0.4; it means short-term memory test scores decrease by about 0.4 points per year.

    c. In another test, a 70-year-old woman scored 8. Does your line of best fit predict a higher or lower score? What may have happened?

    The line of best fit predicts a lower score. Sample answer: The score for this woman is an outlier, or short-term memory tends to level off after 65.

2. Kalila has developed two different varieties of tomatoes, called Big Red and Sweet Summer, which she grows in her garden. When she harvests the tomatoes, she measures the diameters of each variety. The results are shown in the table.

	Diameter ≤ 2 in.	Diameter > 2 in.
Big Red	36	45
Sweet Summer	28	39

    a. Use the data to create a two-way frequency table.

	Diameter ≤ 2 in.	Diameter > 2 in.	Total
Big Red	36	45	81
Sweet Summer	28	39	67
Total	64	84	148

    b. What is the relative frequency of a tomato having a diameter that is greater than two inches? Round to the nearest percent.

    57%

    c. What is the relative frequency of a Big Red tomato having a diameter that is greater than two inches? Round to the nearest percent.

    56%

    d. Is there an association between Big Red tomatoes and diameters that are greater than two inches? Explain.

    No; the relative frequencies show that Big Red tomatoes are just as likely to have diameters greater than two inches as any other tomato.

Additional Resources

Personal Math Trainer

Online Assessment and Intervention

my.hrw.com

Assessment Resources
- Leveled Unit Tests: A, B, C, D
- Performance Assessment

PARCC Assessment Readiness

Assessment Readiness Tip Students should underline or highlight the word *not* when it appears in problem situations.

Item 7 Remind students to highlight the word *not* every time they see it, and it will tell them to find the opposite of what they would normally look for. In this problem, if they miss the word *not*, any of the three incorrect answers will appear to be correct.

Avoid Common Errors

Item 1 Students may calculate the percentage of only female voters that were between 18 and 62 years of age, rather than calculating the percentage of all voters that were female and between 18 and 62 years. Encourage students to double-check the question to see if they are supposed to find a percentage of a part, or a percentage of the whole.

Item 3 The formula for the volume of a sphere uses the radius, and this problem gives the diameter. Remind students to check to see if they have the correct values before substituting into the formula and solving.

 Florida Common Core Standards

Items	Grade 8 Standards	Mathematical Practices
1	8.SP.1.4	MP.1.1
2	8.SP.1.1	MP.6.1
3*	8.G.3.9	MP.2.1
4	8.SP.1.2	MP.6.1
5	8.SP.1.4	MP.1.1
6*	8.G.1.3	MP.2.1
7	8.SP.1.1	MP.2.1
8	8.SP.1.2, 8.SP.1.3	MP.4.1

* Item integrates mixed review concepts from previous modules or a previous course.

PARCC Assessment Readiness

Personal Math Trainer
my.hrw.com
Online Assessment and Intervention

Selected Response

1. A local election conducted an exit poll of the age and gender of its voters. The results are shown in the two-way frequency table.

	18–62 years old	63 years and older	Total
Female	142	22	164
Male	126	15	141
Total	268	37	305

What percent of the voters were female and 18 to 62 years old?

(A) 6.5%   (C) 53%

(B) 47%   (D) 87%

2. What type of association is there between the speed of a car and the distance the car travels in a given time at that speed?

(A) cluster

(B) negative association

(C) no association

(D) positive association

3. Using 3.14 for π, what is the volume of the sphere to the nearest tenth?

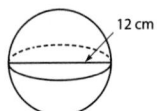

12 cm

(A) 508.7 cubic centimeters

(B) 678.2 cubic centimeters

(C) 904.3 cubic centimeters

(D) 2713 cubic centimeters

Hot Tip! Read graphs and diagrams carefully. Look at the labels for important information.

4. Which scatter plot could have a trend line given by the equation $y = -4x + 70$?

(A)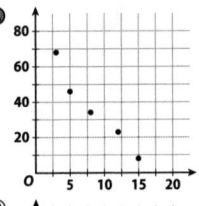

(B)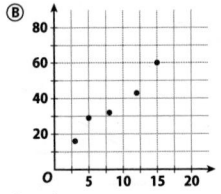

(C)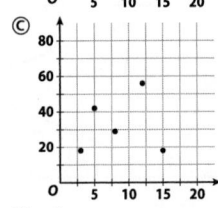

(D)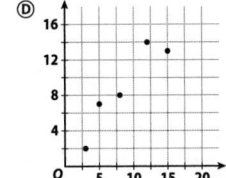

5. A group of middle school students were asked whether they prefer communicating with their friends by text message or email. The results are shown in the two-way frequency table.

	Text Message	Email	Total
Female	28	16	44
Male	31	18	49
Total	59	34	93

What is the conditional relative frequency that a student prefers email, given that the student is female?

(A) 17%   (C) 47%

(B) 36%   (D) 64%

6. The vertices of a triangle are (11, 9), (7, 4), and (1, 11). What are the vertices after the triangle has been reflected over the y-axis?

(A) (9, 11), (4, 7), (11, 1)

(B) (11, −9), (7, −4), (1, −11)

(C) (9, 11), (4, 7), (11, 1)

(D) (−11, 9), (−7, 4), (−1, 11)

7. Which of the following is **not** shown on the scatter plot below?

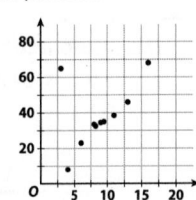

(A) cluster

(B) negative association

(C) outlier

(D) positive association

Mini-Task

8. A scatter plot and trend line of the weight of a Chihuahua puppy versus age is shown.

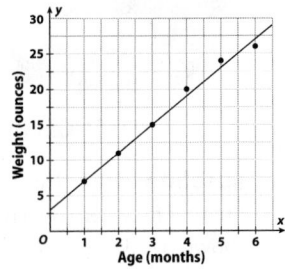

a. The trend line for these data is given by $y = 4x + 3$. What does the 3 represent in this context?

the weight of the puppy when it is 0 months old

b. If you use the trend line to predict the weight of the puppy after 60 months, the result is 243 ounces, or about 15 pounds. Is this a reasonable weight for the Chihuahua at 5 years old? Explain.

No, because the Chihuahua will stop growing at a certain point and its weight will level off.

Glossary/Glosario

ENGLISH	SPANISH	EXAMPLES
absolute value The distance of a number from zero on a number line; shown by | |.	**valor absoluto** Distancia a la que está un número de 0 en una recta numérica. El símbolo del valor absoluto es | |.	$\|-5\| = 5$
accuracy The closeness of a given measurement or value to the actual measurement or value.	**exactitud** Cercanía de una medida o un valor a la medida o el valor real.	
acute angle An angle that measures greater than 0° and less than 90°.	**ángulo agudo** Ángulo que mide mas de 0° y menos de 90°.	
acute triangle A triangle with all angles measuring less than 90°.	**triángulo acutángulo** Triángulo en el que todos los ángulos miden menos de 90°.	
Addition Property of Equality The property that states that if you add the same number to both sides of an equation, the new equation will have the same solution.	**Propiedad de igualdad de la suma** Propiedad que establece que puedes sumar el mismo número a ambos lados de una ecuación y la nueva ecuación tendrá la misma solución.	$\begin{aligned} 14 - 6 &= 8 \\ +6 \quad & +6 \\ \hline 14 &= 14 \end{aligned}$
Addition Property of Opposites The property that states that the sum of a number and its opposite equals zero.	**Propiedad de la suma de los opuestos** Propiedad que establece que la suma de un número y su opuesto es cero.	$12 + (-12) = 0$
additive inverse The opposite of a number.	**inverso aditivo** El opuesto de un número.	The additive inverse of 5 is -5.
adjacent angles Angles in the same plane that have a common vertex and a common side.	**ángulos adyacentes** Ángulos en el mismo plano que comparten un vértice y un lado.	
algebraic expression An expression that contains at least one variable.	**expresión algebraica** Expresión que contiene al menos una variable.	$x + 8$ $4(m - b)$
algebraic inequality An inequality that contains at least one variable.	**desigualdad algebraica** Desigualdad que contiene al menos una variable.	$x + 3 > 10$ $5a > b + 3$

ENGLISH	SPANISH	EXAMPLES
alternate exterior angles For two lines intersected by a transversal, a pair of angles that lie on opposite sides of the transversal and outside the other two lines.	**ángulos alternos externos** Dadas dos rectas cortadas por una transversal, par de ángulos no adyacentes ubicados en los lados opuestos de la transversal y fuera de las otras dos rectas.	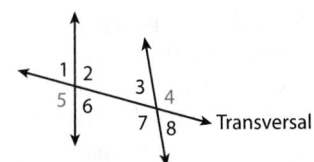 ∠4 and ∠5 are alternate exterior angles.
alternate interior angles For two lines intersected by a transversal, a pair of nonadjacent angles that lie on opposite sides of the transversal and between the other two lines.	**ángulos alternos internos** Dadas dos rectas cortadas por una transversal, par de ángulos no adyacentes ubicados en los lados opuestos de la transversal y entre de las otras dos rectas.	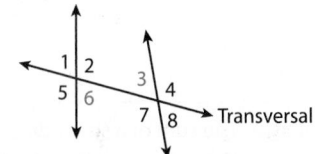 ∠3 and ∠6 are alternate interior angles.
angle A figure formed by two rays with a common endpoint called the vertex.	**ángulo** Figura formada por dos rayos con un extremo común llamado vértice.	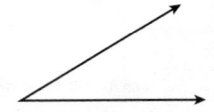
angle bisector A line, segment, or ray that divides an angle into two congruent angles.	**bisectriz de un ángulo** Línea, segmento o rayo que divide un ángulo en dos ángulos congruentes.	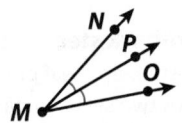 $\overrightarrow{MP}$ is an angle bisector.
arc An unbroken part of a circle.	**arco** Parte continua de un círculo.	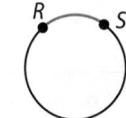
area The number of square units needed to cover a given surface.	**área** El número de unidades cuadradas que se necesitan para cubrir una superficie dada.	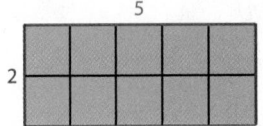
arithmetic sequence An ordered list of numbers in which the difference between consecutive terms is always the same.	**sucesión aritmética** Lista ordenada de números en la que la diferencia entre términos consecutivos es siempre la misma.	The sequence 2, 5, 8, 11, 14 ... is an arithmetic sequence.
association A description of how data sets are related.	**asociación** Descripción de cómo se relaciona un conjunto de datos.	
Associative Property (of Addition) The property that states that for all real numbers *a*, *b*, and *c*, the sum is always the same, regardless of their grouping.	**Propiedad asociativa (de la suma)** Propiedad que establece que para todos los números reales *a*, *b* y *c*, la suma siempre es la misma sin importar cómo se agrupen.	$a + b + c = (a + b) + c = a + (b + c)$

Glossary/Glosario

Associative Property (of Multiplication) The property that states that for all real numbers a, b, and c, their product is always the same, regardless of their grouping.

Propiedad asociativa (de la multiplicación) Propiedad que establece que para todos los números reales a, b y c, el producto siempre es el mismo, sin importar cómo se agrupen.

$$a \cdot b \cdot c = (a \cdot b) \cdot c = a \cdot (b \cdot c)$$

---

asymmetry Not identical on either side of a central line; not symmetrical.

asimetría Ocurre cuando dos lados separados por una línea central no son idénticos; falta de simetría.

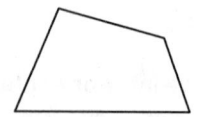

The quadrilateral has asymmetry.

---

average The sum of a set of data divided by the number of items in the data set; also called *mean*.

promedio La suma de los elementos de un conjunto de datos dividida entre el número de elementos del conjunto. También se llama media.

Data set: 4, 6, 7, 8, 10

Average: $\frac{4 + 6 + 7 + 8 + 10}{5}$

$= \frac{35}{5} = 7$

B

back-to-back stem-and-leaf plot A stem-and-leaf plot that compares two sets of data by displaying one set of data to the left of the stem and the other to the right.

diagrama doble de tallo y hojas Diagrama de tallo y hojas que compara dos conjuntos de datos presentando uno de ellos a la izquierda del tallo y el otro a la derecha.

Data set A: 9, 12, 14, 16, 23, 27
Data set B: 6, 8, 10, 13, 15, 16, 21

Set A		Set B
9	0	6 8
6 4 2	1	0 3 5 6
7 3	2	1

Key: |2| 1 means 21
7 |2| means 27

---

bar graph A graph that uses vertical or horizontal bars to display data.

gráfica de barras Gráfica en la que se usan barras verticales u horizontales para presentar datos.

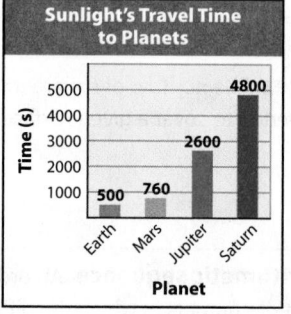

---

base When a number is raised to a power, the number that is used as a factor is the base.

base Cuando un número es elevado a una potencia, el número que se usa como factor es la base.

$3^5 = 3 \cdot 3 \cdot 3 \cdot 3 \cdot 3$; 3 is the base.

---

base (of a polygon or three-dimensional figure) A side of a polygon; a face of a three-dimensional figure by which the figure is measured or classified.

base (de un polígono o figura tridimensional) Lado de un polígono; cara de una figura tridimensional según la cual se mide o se clasifica la figura.

 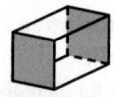

Bases of a cylinder   Bases of a prism

Base of a cone   Base of a pyramid

Glossary/Glosario

ENGLISH	SPANISH	EXAMPLES
biased question A question that leads people to give a certain answer.	**pregunta tendenciosa** pregunta que lleva a las personas a dar una respuesta determinada	
biased sample A sample that does not fairly represent the population.	**muestra no representativa** Muestra que no representa adecuadamente la población.	
binomial A polynomial with two terms.	**binomio** Polinomio con dos términos.	$x + y$ $2a^2 - 3$ $4m^3n^2 + 6mn^4$
bisect To divide into two congruent parts.	**trazar una bisectriz** Dividir en dos partes congruentes.	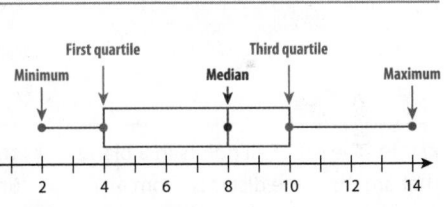 $\overrightarrow{JK}$ bisects $\angle LJM$.
bivariate data A set of data that is made of two paired variables.	**datos bivariados** Conjunto de datos compuesto de dos variables apareadas.	
boundary line The set of points where the two sides of a two-variable linear inequality are equal.	**línea de límite** Conjunto de puntos donde los dos lados de una desigualdad lineal con dos variables son iguales.	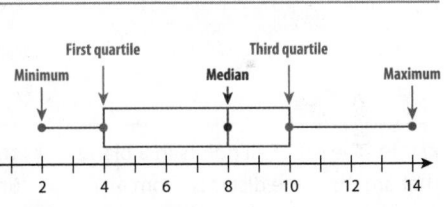 Boundary line
box-and-whisker plot A graph that shows how data are distributed by using the median, quartiles, least value, and greatest value; also called a *box plot*.	**gráfica de mediana y rango** Gráfica para demostrar la distribución de datos utilizando la mediana, los cuartiles y los valores menos y más grande; también llamado gráfica de caja.	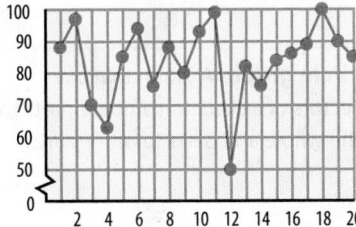
break (graph) A zigzag on a horizontal or vertical scale of a graph that indicates that some of the numbers on the scale have been omitted.	**discontinuidad (gráfica)** Zig-zag en la escala horizontal o vertical de una gráfica que indica la omisión de algunos de los números de la escala.	

ENGLISH	SPANISH	EXAMPLES
capacity The amount a container can hold when filled.	**capacidad** Cantidad que cabe en un recipiente cuando se llena.	A large milk container has a capacity of 1 gallon.
Celsius A metric scale for measuring temperature in which 0 °C is the freezing point of water and 100 °C is the boiling point of water; also called *centigrade*.	**Celsius** Escala métrica para medir la temperatura, en la que 0 °C es el punto de congelación del agua y 100 °C es el punto de ebullición. También se llama *centígrado*.	

ENGLISH	SPANISH	EXAMPLES
center (of a circle) The point inside a circle that is the same distance from all the points on the circle.	**centro (de un círculo)** Punto interior de un círculo que se encuentra a la misma distancia de todos los puntos de la circunferencia.	
center of dilation The point of intersection of lines through each pair of corresponding vertices in a dilation.	**centro de una dilatación** Punto de intersección de las líneas que pasan a través de cada par de vértices correspondientes en una dilatación.	
center of rotation The point about which a figure is rotated.	**centro de una rotación** Punto alrededor del cual se hace girar una figura.	
central angle An angle formed by two radii with its vertex at the center of a circle.	**ángulo central de un círculo** Ángulo formado por dos radios cuyo vértice se encuentra en el centro de un círculo.	
certain (probability) Sure to happen; having a probability of 1.	**seguro (probabilidad)** Que con seguridad sucederá. Representa una probabilidad de 1.	
chord A segment with its endpoints on a circle.	**cuerda** Segmento de recta cuyos extremos forman parte de un círculo.	
circle The set of all points in a plane that are the same distance from a given point called the center.	**círculo** Conjunto de todos los puntos en un plano que se encuentran a la misma distancia de un punto dado llamado centro.	
circle graph A graph that uses sectors of a circle to compare parts to the whole and parts to other parts.	**gráfica circular** Gráfica que usa secciones de un círculo para comparar partes con el todo y con otras partes.	
circuit A path in a graph that begins and ends at the same vertex.	**circuito** Una trayectoria en una gráfica que empieza y termina en el mismo vértice.	
circumference The distance around a circle.	**circunferencia** Distancia alrededor de un círculo.	

ENGLISH	SPANISH	EXAMPLES
clockwise A circular movement in the direction shown.	**en el sentido de las manecillas del reloj** Movimiento circular en la dirección que se indica.	
cluster A set of closely grouped data.	**agrupación** Conjunto de datos bien agrupados.	
clustering A condition that occurs when data points in a scatter plot are grouped more in one part of the graph than another.	**arracimando** Una condición que ocurre cuando los datos están apiñando en una parte de una diagrama de dispersión mas que en otras partes.	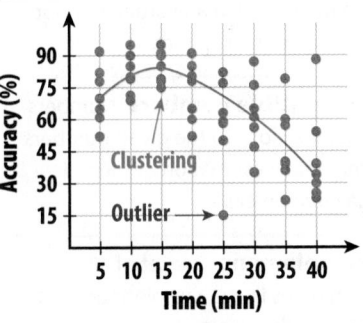
coefficient The number that is multiplied by the variable in an algebraic expression.	**coeficiente** Número que se multiplica por la variable en una expresión algebraica.	5 is the coefficient in 5*b*.
combination An arrangement of items or events in which order does not matter.	**combinación** Agrupación de objetos o sucesos en la que el orden no es importante.	For objects *A, B, C,* and *D,* there are 6 different combinations of 2 objects: *AB, AC, AD, BC, BD, CD.*
commission A fee paid to a person for making a sale.	**comisión** Pago que recibe una persona por realizar una venta.	
commission rate The fee paid to a person who makes a sale expressed as a percent of the selling price.	**tasa de comisión** Pago que recibe una persona por hacer una venta, expresado como un porcentaje del precio de venta.	A commission rate of 5% on a sale of $10,000 results in a commission of $500.
common denominator A denominator that is the same in two or more fractions.	**común denominador** Denominador que es común a dos o más fracciones.	The common denominator of $\frac{5}{8}$ and $\frac{2}{8}$ is 8.
common difference In an arithmetic sequence, the nonzero constant difference of any term and the previous term.	**diferencia común** En una sucesión aritmética, diferencia constante distinta de cero entre cualquier término y el término anterior.	In the arithmetic sequence 3, 5, 7, 9, 11, …, the common difference is 2.
common factor A number that is a factor of two or more numbers.	**factor común** Número que es factor de dos o más números.	8 is a common factor of 16 and 40.
common multiple A number that is a multiple of each of two or more numbers.	**común múltiplo** Número que es múltiplo de dos o más números.	15 is a common multiple of 3 and 5.
common ratio The ratio each term is multiplied by to produce the next term in a geometric sequence.	**razón común** Razón por la que se multiplica cada término para obtener el siguiente término de una sucesión geométrica.	In the geometric sequence 32, 16, 8, 4, 2, …, the common ratio is $\frac{1}{2}$.

ENGLISH	SPANISH	EXAMPLES
Commutative Property (of Addition) The property that states that two or more numbers can be added in any order without changing the sum.	**Propiedad conmutativa (de la suma)** Propiedad que establece que sumar dos o más números en cualquier orden no altera la suma.	$8 + 20 = 20 + 8; a + b = b + a$
Commutative Property (of Multiplication) The property that states that two or more numbers can be multiplied in any order without changing the product.	**Propiedad conmutativa (de la multiplicación)** Propiedad que establece que multiplicar dos o más números en cualquier orden no altera el producto.	$6 \cdot 12 = 12 \cdot 6; a \cdot b = b \cdot a$
compatible numbers Numbers that are close to the given numbers that make estimation or mental calculation easier.	**números compatibles** Números que están cerca de los números dados y hacen más fácil la estimación o el cálculo mental.	To estimate $7,957 + 5,009$, use the compatible numbers 8,000 and 5,000: $8,000 + 5,000 = 13,000$
complement The set of all outcomes in the sample space that are not the event.	**complemento** La serie de resultados que no están en el suceso.	Experiment: rolling a number cube Sample space: {1, 2, 3, 4, 5, 6} Event: rolling a 1, 3, 4, or 6 Complement: rolling a 2 or 5
complementary angles Two angles whose measures add to 90°.	**ángulos complementarios** Dos ángulos cuyas medidas suman 90°.	The complement of a 53° angle is a 37° angle.
composite figure A figure made up of simple geometric shapes.	**figura compuesta** Figura formada por figuras geométricas simples.	
composite number A number greater than 1 that has more than two whole-number factors.	**número compuesto** Número mayor que 1 que tiene más de dos factores que son números cabales.	4, 6, 8, and 9 are composite numbers.
compound event An event made up of two or more simple events.	**suceso compuesto** Suceso que consista de dos o más sucesos simples.	Rolling a 3 on a number cube and spinning a 2 on a spinner is a compound event.
compound inequality A combination of more than one inequality.	**desigualdad compuesta** Combinación de dos o más desigualdades.	$-2 \leq x < 10$
compound interest Interest earned or paid on principal and previously earned or paid interest.	**interés compuesto** Interés que se gana o se paga sobre el capital y los intereses previamente ganados o pagados.	If \$100 is put into an account with an interest rate of 5% compounded monthly, then after 2 years, the account will have $100\left(1 + \frac{0.05}{12}\right)^{12 \cdot 2} =$ \$110.49

conditional relative frequency The ratio of a joint relative frequency to a related marginal relative frequency in a two-way table.

frecuencia relativa condicional Razón de una frecuencia relativa conjunta a una frecuencia relativa marginal en una tabla de doble entrada.

---

cone A three-dimensional figure with one vertex and one circular base.

cono Figura tridimensional con un vértice y una base circular.

---

congruence transformation A transformation that results in an image that is the same shape and the same size as the original figure.

transformación de congruencia Una transformación que resulta en una imagen que tiene la misma forma y el mismo tamaño como la figura original.

---

congruent Having the same size and shape; the symbol for congruent is ≅.

congruentes Que tienen la misma forma y el mismo tamaño expresado por ≅.

$PQRS \cong WXYZ$

---

congruent angles Angles that have the same measure.

ángulos congruentes Ángulos que tienen la misma medida.

$\angle ABC \cong \angle DEF$

---

congruent figures See *congruent*.

figures congruentes Vea *congruente*.

---

congruent segments Segments that have the same length.

segmentos congruentes Segmentos que tienen la misma longitud.

$\overline{PQ} \cong \overline{SR}$

---

conjecture A statement believed to be true.

conjetura Enunciado que se supone verdadero.

---

constant A value that does not change.

constante Valor que no cambia.

$3, 0, \pi$

---

constant of variation The constant k in direct and inverse variation equations.

constante de variación La constante k en ecuaciones de variación directa e inversa.

$y = 5x$

↑

Constant of variation

---

continuous graph A graph made up of connected lines or curves.

gráfica continua Gráfica compuesta por líneas rectas o curvas conectadas.

Glossary/Glosario

convenience sample A sample based on members of the population that are readily available.

muestra de conveniencia Una muestra basada en miembros de la población que están fácilmente disponibles.

---

conversion factor A fraction whose numerator and denominator represent the same quantity but use different units; the fraction is equal to 1 because the numerator and denominator are equal.

factor de conversión Fracción cuyo numerador y denominador representan la misma cantidad pero con unidades distintas; la fracción es igual a 1 porque el numerador y el denominador son iguales.

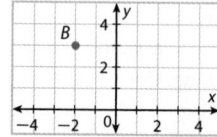

$\frac{24 \text{ hours}}{1 \text{ day}}$ and $\frac{1 \text{ day}}{24 \text{ hours}}$

---

coordinate One of the numbers of an ordered pair that locate a point on a coordinate graph.

coordenada Uno de los números de un par ordenado que ubica un punto en una gráfica de coordenadas.

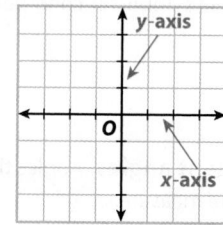

The coordinates of B are $(-2, 3)$.

---

coordinate plane A plane formed by the intersection of a horizontal number line called the *x*-axis and a vertical number line called the *y*-axis.

plano cartesiano Plano formado por la intersección de una recta numérica horizontal llamada eje *x* y otra vertical llamada eje *y*.

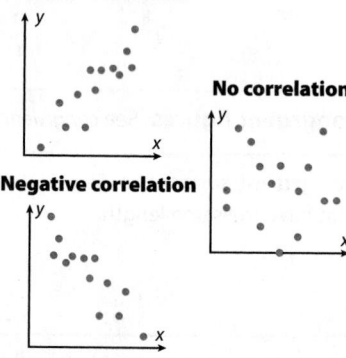

---

correlation The description of the relationship between two data sets.

correlación Descripción de la relación entre dos conjuntos de datos.

Positive correlation

No correlation

Negative correlation

---

correspondence The relationship between two or more objects that are matched.

correspondencia La relación entre dos o más objetos que coinciden.

$\angle A$ and $\angle D$ are corresponding angles.

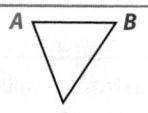

$\overline{AB}$ and $\overline{DE}$ are corresponding sides.

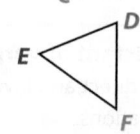

---

corresponding angles (for lines) For two lines intersected by a transversal, a pair of angles that lie on the same side of the transversal and on the same sides of the other two lines.

ángulos correspondientes (en líneas) Dadas dos rectas cortadas por una transversal, el par de ángulos ubicados en el mismo lado de la transversal y en los mismos lados de las otras dos rectas.

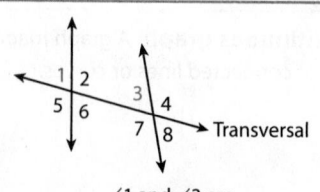

$\angle 1$ and $\angle 3$ are corresponding angles.

ENGLISH	SPANISH	EXAMPLES
corresponding angles (of polygons) Angles in the same relative position in polygons with an equal number of sides.	**ángulos correspondientes (en polígonos)** Ángulos en la misma posición formaron cuando una tercera línea interseca dos líneas.	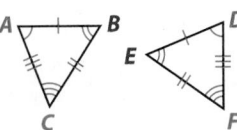 $\angle A$ and $\angle D$ are corresponding angles.
corresponding sides Matching sides of two or more polygons.	**lados correspondientes** Lados que se ubican en la misma posición relativa en dos o más polígonos.	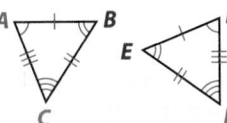 $\overline{AB}$ and $\overline{DE}$ are corresponding sides.
counterclockwise A circular movement in the direction shown.	**en sentido contrario a las manecillas del reloj** Movimiento circular en la dirección que se indica.	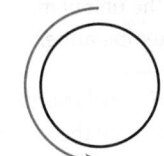
counterexample An example that proves that a conjecture or statement is false.	**contraejemplo** Ejemplo que demuestra que una conjetura o enunciado es falso.	
cross section The intersection of a three-dimensional figure and a plane.	**sección transversal** Intersección de una figura tridimensional y un plano.	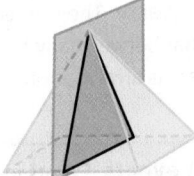
cube (geometric figure) A rectangular prism with six congruent square faces.	**cubo (figura geométrica)** Prisma rectangular con seis caras cuadradas congruentes.	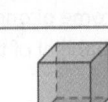
cube (in numeration) A number raised to the third power.	**cubo (en numeración)** Número elevado a la tercera potencia.	$2^3 = 2 \cdot 2 \cdot 2 = 8$ 8 is the cube of 2.
cube root A number, written as $\sqrt[3]{x}$, whose cube is x.	**raíz cúbica** Número, expresado como $\sqrt[3]{x}$, cuyo cubo es x.	$\sqrt[3]{8} = \sqrt[3]{2 \cdot 2 \cdot 2} = 2$ 2 is the cube root of 8.
cumulative frequency The sum of successive data items.	**frecuencia acumulativa** La suma de datos sucesivos.	
customary system of measurement The measurement system often used in the United States.	**sistema usual de medidas** El sistema de medidas que se usa comúnmente en Estados Unidos.	inches, feet, miles, ounces, pounds, tons, cups, quarts, gallons
cylinder A three-dimensional figure with two parallel, congruent circular bases connected by a curved lateral surface.	**cilindro** Figura tridimensional con dos bases circulares paralelas y congruentes, unidas por una superficie lateral curva.	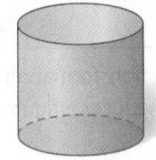

Glossary/Glosario

decagon A polygon with ten sides.

decágono Polígono de diez lados.

---

deductive reasoning Using logic to show that a statement is true.

razonamiento deductivo Uso de la lógica para demostrar que un enunciado es verdadero.

---

degree The unit of measure for angles or temperature.

grado Unidad de medida para ángulos y temperaturas.

---

degree of a polynomial The highest power of the variable in a polynomial.

grado de un polinomio La potencia más alta de la variable en un polinomio.

The polynomial $4x^5 - 6x^2 + 7$ has degree 5.

---

denominator The bottom number of a fraction that tells how many equal parts are in the whole.

denominador Número que está abajo en una fracción y que indica en cuántas partes iguales se divide el entero.

In the fraction $\frac{2}{5}$, 5 is the denominator.

Density Property The property that states that between any two real numbers there is always another real number.

Propiedad de densidad Propiedad según la cual entre dos números reales cualesquiera siempre hay otro número real.

---

dependent events Events for which the outcome of one event affects the probability of the other.

sucesos dependientes Dos sucesos son dependientes si el resultado de uno afecta la probabilidad del otro.

A bag contains 3 red marbles and 2 blue marbles. Drawing a red marble and then drawing a blue marble without replacing the first marble is an example of dependent events.

---

dependent variable The output of a function; a variable whose value depends on the value of the input, or independent variable.

variable dependiente Salida de una función; variable cuyo valor depende del valor de la entrada, o variable independiente.

For $y = 2x + 1$, y is the dependent variable.
input: x output: y

---

diagonal A line segment that connects two nonadjacent vertices of a polygon.

diagonal Segmento de recta que une dos vértices no adyacentes de un polígono.

---

diameter A line segment that passes through the center of a circle and has endpoints on the circle, or the length of that segment.

diámetro Segmento de recta que pasa por el centro de un círculo y tiene sus extremos en la circunferencia, o bien la longitud de ese segmento.

---

dilation A transformation that enlarges or reduces a figure.

dilatación Transformación que agranda o reduce una figura.

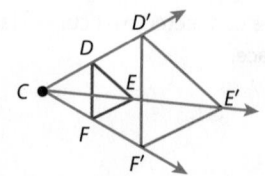

ENGLISH	SPANISH	EXAMPLES
dimensions (geometry) The length, width, or height of a figure.	**dimensiones (geometría)** Longitud, ancho o altura de una figura.	
dimensions (of a matrix) The number of horizontal rows and vertical columns in a matrix.	**dimensiones (de una matriz)** Número de filas y columnas que hay en una matriz.	
direct variation A linear relationship between two variables, x and y, that can be written in the form $y = kx$, where k is a nonzero constant.	**variación directa** Relación lineal entre dos variables, x e y, que puede expresarse en la forma $y = kx$, donde k es una constante distinta de cero.	$y = 2x$
discount The amount by which the original price is reduced.	**descuento** Cantidad que se resta del precio original de un artículo.	
discrete graph A graph made up of unconnected points.	**gráfica discreta** Gráfica compuesta de puntos no conectados.	
disjoint events See *mutually exclusive*.	**sucesos disjuntos** Vea *mutuamente excluyentes*.	
Distributive Property For all real numbers a, b, and c, $a(b + c) = ab + ac$, and $a(b - c) = ab - ac$.	**Propiedad distributiva** Dados los números reales a, b, y c, $a(b + c) = ab + ac$, y $a(b - c) = ab - ac$.	$5 \cdot 21 = 5(20 + 1) =$ $(5 \cdot 20) + (5 \cdot 1)$
dividend The number to be divided in a division problem.	**dividendo** Número que se divide en un problema de división.	In $8 \div 4 = 2$, 8 is the dividend.
divisible Can be divided by a number without leaving a remainder.	**divisible** Que se puede dividir entre un número sin dejar residuo.	18 is divisible by 3.
Division Property of Equality The property that states that if you divide both sides of an equation by the same nonzero number, the new equation will have the same solution.	**Propiedad de igualdad de la división** Propiedad que establece que puedes dividir ambos lados de una ecuación entre el mismo número distinto de cero, y la nueva ecuación tendrá la misma solución.	
divisor The number you are dividing by in a division problem.	**divisor** El número entre el que se divide en un problema de división.	In $8 \div 4 = 2$, 4 is the divisor.
dodecahedron A polyhedron with 12 faces.	**dodecaedro** Poliedro de 12 caras.	

Glossary/Glosario

ENGLISH	SPANISH	EXAMPLES
domain The set of all possible input values of a function.	**dominio** Conjunto de todos los posibles valores de entrada de una función.	The domain of the function $y = x^2 + 1$ is all real numbers.
double-bar graph A bar graph that compares two related sets of data.	**gráfica de doble barra** Gráfica de barras que compara dos conjuntos de datos relacionados.	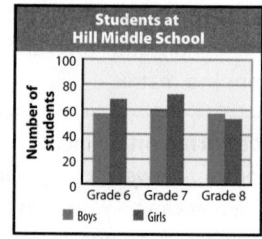
double-line graph A line graph that shows how two related sets of data change over time.	**gráfica de doble línea** Gráfica lineal que muestra cómo cambian con el tiempo dos conjuntos de datos relacionados.	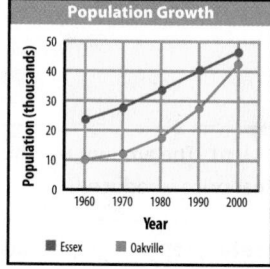

E

edge The line segment along which two faces of a polyhedron intersect.	**arista** Segmento de recta donde se intersecan dos caras de un poliedro.	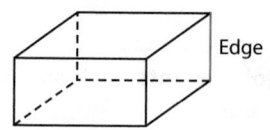
endpoint A point at the end of a line segment or ray.	**extremo** Un punto ubicado al final de un segmento de recta o rayo.	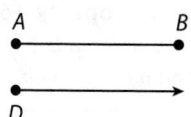
enlargement An increase in size of all dimensions in the same proportions.	**agrandamiento** Aumento de tamaño de todas las dimensiones en las mismas proporciones.	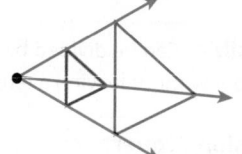
entries (of a matrix) Individual entries in a matrix.	**elementos (de una matriz)** Entradas individuales de una matriz.	
equally likely Outcomes that have the same probability.	**resultados igualmente probables** Resultados que tienen la misma probabilidad de ocurrir.	When tossing a coin, the outcomes "heads" and "tails" are equally likely.
equation A mathematical sentence that shows that two expressions are equivalent.	**ecuación** Enunciado matemático que indica que dos expresiones son equivalentes.	$x + 4 = 7$ $6 + 1 = 10 - 3$

© Houghton Mifflin Harcourt Publishing Company

Glossary/Glosario

G14 Glossary/Glosario

ENGLISH	SPANISH	EXAMPLES
equilateral triangle A triangle with three congruent sides.	**triángulo equilátero** Triángulo con tres lados congruentes.	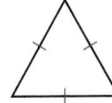
equivalent Having the same value.	**equivalentes** Que tienen el mismo valor.	
equivalent expressions Expressions that have the same value for all values of the variables.	**expresíons equivalentes** Las expresiones equivalentes tienen el mismo valor para todos los valores de las variables.	$4x + 5x$ and $9x$ are equivalent expressions.
equivalent fractions Fractions that name the same amount or part.	**fracciones equivalentes** Fracciones que representan la misma cantidad o parte.	$\frac{1}{2}$ and $\frac{2}{4}$ are equivalent fractions.
equivalent ratios Ratios that name the same comparison.	**razones equivalentes** Razones que representan la misma comparación.	$\frac{1}{2}$ and $\frac{2}{4}$ are equivalent ratios.
estimate (*n*) An answer that is close to the exact answer and is found by rounding or other methods. **(*v*)** To find such an answer.	**estimación (s)** Una solución aproximada a la respuesta exacta que se halla mediante el redondeo u otros métodos. **estimar (v)** Hallar una solución aproximada a la respuesta exacta.	500 is an estimate for the sum $98 + 287 + 104$.
evaluate To find the value of a numerical or algebraic expression.	**evaluar** Hallar el valor de una expresión numérica o algebraica.	Evaluate $2x + 7$ for $x = 3$. $2x + 7$ $2(3) + 7$ $6 + 7$ 13
event An outcome or set of outcomes of an experiment or situation.	**suceso** Un resultado o una serie de resultados de un experimento o una situación.	When rolling a number cube, the event "an odd number" consists of the outcomes 1, 3, and 5.
expanded form A number written as the sum of the values of its digits.	**forma desarrollada** Número escrito como suma de los valores de sus dígitos.	236,536 written in expanded form is $200,000 + 30,000 + 6,000 + 500 + 30 + 6$.
experiment (probability) In probability, any activity based on chance (such as tossing a coin).	**experimento (probabilidad)** En probabilidad, cualquier actividad basada en la posibilidad, como lanzar una moneda.	Tossing a coin 10 times and noting the number of "heads"
experimental probability The ratio of the number of times an event occurs to the total number of trials, or times that the activity is performed.	**probabilidad experimental** Razón del número de veces que ocurre un suceso al número total de pruebas o al número de que se realiza el experimento.	Kendra attempted 27 free throws and made 16 of them. Her experimental probability of making a free throw is $\frac{\text{number made}}{\text{number attempted}} = \frac{16}{27} \approx 0.59$.
exponent The number that indicates how many times the base is used as a factor.	**exponente** Número que indica cuántas veces se usa la base como factor.	$2^3 = 2 \times 2 \times 2 = 8$; 3 is the exponent.
exponential decay An exponential function of the form $f(x) = a \cdot r^x$ in which $0 < r < 1$.	**decremento exponencial** Función exponencial del tipo $f(x) = a \cdot r^x$ en la cual $0 < r < 1$.	

Glossary/Glosario

© Houghton Mifflin Harcourt Publishing Company

ENGLISH	SPANISH	EXAMPLES
exponential form A number written with a base and an exponent.	**forma exponencial** Se dice que un número está en forma exponencial cuando se escribe con una base y un exponente.	4^2 is the exponential form for $4 \cdot 4$.
exponential function A nonlinear function in which the variable is in the exponent.	**función exponencial** Función no lineal en la que la variable está en el exponente.	$f(x) = 4^x$
exponential growth An exponential function of the form $f(x) = a \cdot r^x$ in which $r > 1$.	**crecimiento exponencial** Función exponencial del tipo $f(x) = a \cdot r^x$ en la cual $r > 1$.	
expression A mathematical phrase that contains operations, numbers, and/or variables.	**expresión** Enunciado matemático que contiene operaciones, números y/o variables.	$6x + 1$
exterior angle (of a polygon) An angle formed by one side of a polygon and the extension of an adjacent side.	**ángulo extreno de un polígono** Ángulo formado por un lado de un polígono y la prolongación del lado adyacente.	

F

ENGLISH	SPANISH	EXAMPLES
face A flat surface of a polyhedron.	**cara** Superficie plana de un poliedro.	
factor A number that is multiplied by another number to get a product.	**factor** Número que se multiplica por otro para hallar un producto.	7 is a factor of 21 since $7 \cdot 3 = 21$.
factorial The product of all whole numbers except zero that are less than or equal to a number.	**factorial** El producto de todos los números cabales, excepto cero, que son menores que o iguales a un número.	4 factorial $= 4! = 4 \cdot 3 \cdot 2 \cdot 1$
Fahrenheit A temperature scale in which 32 °F is the freezing point of water and 212 °F is the boiling point of water.	**Fahrenheit** Escala de temperatura en la que 32° F es el punto de congelación del agua y 212° F es el punto de ebullición.	
fair When all outcomes of an experiment are equally likely, the experiment is said to be fair.	**justo** Se dice de un experimento donde todos los resultados posibles son igualmente probables.	When tossing a coin, heads and tails are equally likely, so it is a fair experiment.
Fibonacci sequence The infinite sequence of numbers (1, 1, 2, 3, 5, 8, 13,…); starting with the third term, each number is the sum of the two previous numbers; it is named after the thirteenth-century mathematician Leonardo Fibonacci.	**sucesión de Fibonacci** La sucesión infinita de números (1, 1, 2, 3, 5, 8, 13…); a partir del tercer término, cada número es la suma de los dos anteriores. Esta sucesión lleva el nombre de Leonardo Fibonacci, un matemático del siglo XIII.	1, 1, 2, 3, 5, 8, 13, . . .
first differences A sequence formed by subtracting each term of a sequence from the next term.	**primeras diferencias** Sucesión que se forma al restar cada término de una sucesión del término siguiente.	For the sequence 4, 7, 10, 13, 16, . . ., the first differences are all 3.

Glossary/Glosario

ENGLISH	SPANISH	EXAMPLES

first quartile The median of the lower half of a set of data; also called *lower quartile*.

primer cuartil La mediana de la mitad inferior de un conjunto de datos. También se llama *cuartil inferior*.

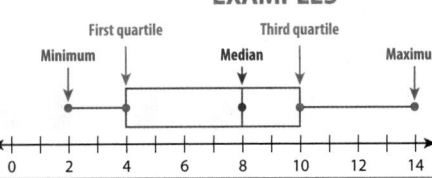

FOIL An acronym for the terms used when multiplying two binomials: the First, Outer, Inner, and Last terms.

FOIL Sigla en inglés de los términos que se usan al multiplicar dos binomios: los primeros, los externos, los internos, y los últimos (First, Outer, Inner, Last).

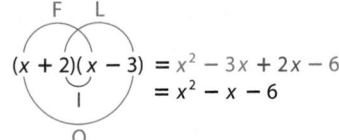

$$(x + 2)(x - 3) = x^2 - 3x + 2x - 6$$
$$= x^2 - x - 6$$

---

formula A rule showing relationships among quantities.

fórmula Regla que muestra relaciones entre cantidades.

$A = \ell w$ is the formula for the area of a rectangle.

---

fractal A structure with repeating patterns containing shapes that are like the whole but are of different sizes throughout.

fractal Estructura con patrones repetidos que contiene figuras similares al patrón general pero de diferente tamaño.

---

fraction A number in the form $\frac{a}{b}$, where $b \neq 0$.

fracción Número escrito en la forma $\frac{a}{b}$, donde $b \neq 0$.

$\frac{2}{3}$

---

frequency The number of times the value appears in the data set.

frecuencia Cantidad de veces que aparece el valor en un conjunto de datos.

Data set: 5, 6, 6, 7, 8, 9
The data value 6 has a frequency of 2.

---

frequency table A table that lists items together according to the number of times, or frequency, that the items occur.

tabla de frecuencia Una tabla en la que se organizan los datos de acuerdo con el número de veces que aparece cada valor (o la frecuencia).

Data set: 1, 1, 2, 2, 3, 5, 5, 5
Frequency table:

Data	Frequency
1	2
2	2
3	1

---

function An input-output relationship that has exactly one output for each input.

función Regla que relaciona dos candidates de forma que a cada valor de entrada corresponde exactamente un valor de salida.

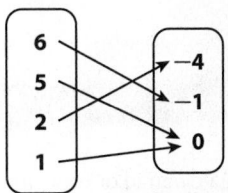

---

function notation The notation used to describe a function.

notación de función Notación que se usa para describir una función.

Equation: $y = 2x$
Function notation: $f(x) = 2x$

---

function table A table of ordered pairs that represent solutions of a function.

tabla de función Tabla de pares ordenados que representan soluciones de una función.

x	3	4	5	6
y	7	9	11	13

Fundamental Counting Principle If one event has m possible outcomes and a second event has n possible outcomes after the first event has occurred, then there are $m \cdot n$ total possible outcomes for the two events.

Principio fundamental de conteo Si un suceso tiene m resultados posibles y otro suceso tiene n resultados posibles después de ocurrido el primer suceso, entonces hay $m \cdot n$ resultados posibles en total para los dos sucesos.

There are 4 colors of shirts and 3 colors of pants. There are $4 \cdot 3 = 12$ possible outfits.

ENGLISH	SPANISH	EXAMPLES

geometric probability A form of theoretical probability determined by a ratio of geometric measures such as lengths, areas, or volumes. | **probabilidad geométrica** Método para calcular probabilidades basado en una medida geométrica como la longitud o el área. | 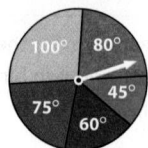
The probability of the pointer landing on red is $\frac{80}{360}$, or $\frac{2}{9}$.

geometric sequence An ordered list of numbers that has a common ratio between consecutive terms. | **sucesión geométrica** Lista ordenada de números que tiene una razón común entre términos consecutivos. | The sequence 2, 4, 8, 16 … is a geometric sequence.

graph of an equation A graph of the set of ordered pairs that are solutions of the equation. | **gráfica de una ecuación** Gráfica del conjunto de pares ordenados que son soluciones de la ecuación. |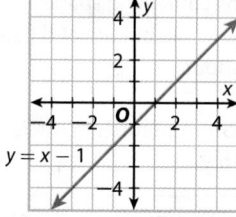

great circle A circle on a sphere such that the plane containing the circle passes through the center of the sphere. | **círculo máximo** Círculo de una esfera tal que el plano que contiene el círculo pasa por el centro de la esfera. |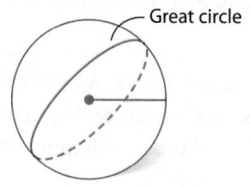

greatest common factor (GCF) The largest common factor of two or more given numbers. | **máximo común divisor (MCD)** El mayor de los factores comunes compartidos por dos o más números dados. | The GCF of 27 and 45 is 9.

height In a pyramid or cone, the perpendicular distance from the base to the opposite vertex. | **altura** En una pirámide o cono, la distancia perpendicular desde la base al vértice opuesto. |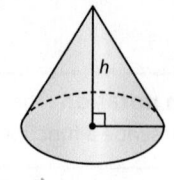

In a triangle or quadrilateral, the perpendicular distance from the base to the opposite vertex or side. | En un triángulo o cuadrilátero, la distancia perpendicular desde la base de la figura al vértice o lado opuesto. |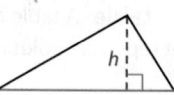

In a prism or cylinder, the perpendicular distance between the bases. | En un prisma o cilindro, la distancia perpendicular entre las bases. |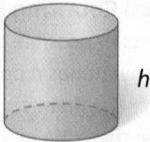

Glossary/Glosario

	ENGLISH	SPANISH	EXAMPLES

hemisphere A half of a sphere.

hemisferio La mitad de una esfera.

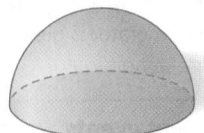

---

heptagon A seven-sided polygon.

heptágono Polígono de siete lados.

---

hexagon A six-sided polygon.

hexágono Polígono de seis lados.

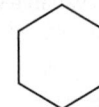

---

histogram A bar graph that shows the frequency of data within equal intervals.

histograma Gráfica de barras que muestra la frecuencia de los datos en intervalos iguales.

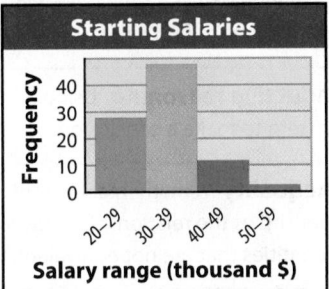

---

hypotenuse In a right triangle, the side opposite the right angle.

hipotenusa En un triángulo rectángulo, el lado opuesto al ángulo recto.

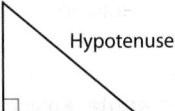

Identity Property (of One) The property that states that the product of 1 and any number is that number.

Propiedad de identidad (del uno) Propiedad que establece que el producto de 1 y cualquier número es ese número.

$4 \cdot 1 = 4$
$-3 \cdot 1 = -3$

Identity Property (of Zero) The property that states the sum of zero and any number is that number.

Propiedad de identidad (del cero) Propiedad que establece que la suma de cero y cualquier número es ese número.

$4 + 0 = 4$
$-3 + 0 = -3$

---

image A figure resulting from a transformation.

imagen Figura que resulta de una transformación.

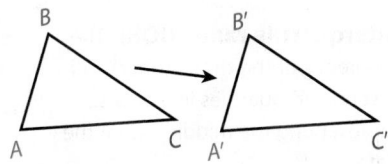

A'B'C' is the image of *ABC*.

---

impossible (probability) Can never happen; having a probability of 0.

imposible (en probabilidad) Que no puede ocurrir. Suceso cuya probabilidad de ocurrir es 0.

Glossary/Glosario (side tab)

ENGLISH	SPANISH	EXAMPLES
improper fraction A fraction in which the numerator is greater than or equal to the denominator.	**fracción impropia** Fracción cuyo numerador es mayor que o igual al denominador.	$\frac{17}{5}, \frac{3}{3}$
independent events Events for which the outcome of one event does not affect the probability of the other.	**sucesos independientes** Dos sucesos son independientes si el resultado de uno no afecta la probabilidad del otro.	A bag contains 3 red marbles and 2 blue marbles. Drawing a red marble, replacing it, and then drawing a blue marble is an example of independent events.
independent variable The input of a function; a variable whose value determines the value of the output, or dependent variable.	**variable independiente** Entrada de una función; variable cuyo valor determina el valor de la salida, o variable dependiente.	For $y = 2x + 1$, x is the independent variable. input: x output: y
indirect measurement The technique of using similar figures and proportions to find a measure.	**medición indirecta** La técnica de usar figuras semejantes y proporciones para hallar una medida.	
inductive reasoning Using a pattern to make a conclusion.	**razonamiento inductivo** Uso de un patrón para sacar una conclusión.	
inequality A mathematical sentence that shows the relationship between quantities that are not equivalent.	**desigualdad** Enunciado matemático que muestra una relación entre cantidades que no son equivalentes.	$5 < 8$ $5x + 2 \geq 12$
input The value substituted into an expression or function.	**valor de entrada** Valor que se usa para sustituir una variable en una expresión o función.	For the function $y = 6x$, the input 4 produces an output of 24.
inscribed angle An angle formed by two chords with its vertex on a circle.	**ángulo inscrito** Ángulo formado por dos cuerdas cuyo vértice está en un círculo.	
integers The set of whole numbers and their opposites.	**enteros** Conjunto de todos los números cabales y sus opuestos.	$\dots -3, -2, -1, 0, 1, 2, 3, \dots$
interest The amount of money charged for borrowing or using money.	**interés** Cantidad de dinero que se cobra por el préstamo o uso del dinero.	
interior angles Angles on the inner sides of two lines cut by a transversal.	**ángulos internos** Ángulos en los lados internos de dos líneas intersecadas por una transversal.	
interquartile range (IQR) The difference of the third (upper) and first (lower) quartiles in a data set, representing the middle half of the data.	**rango intercuartil (RIC)** Diferencia entre el tercer cuartil (superior) y el primer cuartil (inferior) de un conjunto de datos, que representa la mitad central de los datos.	Lower half — 18, (23), 28, First quartile; Upper half — 29, (36), 42 Third quartile; Interquartile range: $36 - 23 = 13$
intersecting lines Lines that cross at exactly one point.	**líneas secantes** Líneas que se cruzan en un solo punto.	m, n

interval The space between marked values on a number line or the scale of a graph.

intervalo El espacio entre los valores marcados en una recta numérica o en la escala de una gráfica.

---

inverse operations Operations that undo each other: addition and subtraction, or multiplication and division.

operaciones inversas Operaciones que se cancelan mutuamente: suma y resta, o multiplicación y división.

Addition and subtraction are inverse operations:
$5 + 3 = 8; 8 - 3 = 5$
Multiplication and division are inverse operations:
$2 \cdot 3 = 6; 6 \div 3 = 2$

---

inverse variation A relationship in which one variable quantity increases as another variable quantity decreases; the product of the variables is a constant.

variación inversa Relación en la que una cantidad variable aumenta a medida que otra cantidad variable disminuye; el producto de las variables es una constante.

$xy = 7, y = \frac{7}{x}$

---

irrational number A number that cannot be expressed as a ratio of two integers or as a repeating or terminating decimal.

número irracional Número que no se puede expresar como una razón de dos enteros ni como un decimal periódico o finito.

$\sqrt{2}, \pi$

---

isolate the variable To get a variable alone on one side of an equation or inequality in order to solve the equation or inequality.

despejar la variable Dejar sola la variable en un lado de una ecuación o desigualdad para resolverla.

$$x + 7 = 22$$
$$\underline{-7 \quad -7}$$
$$x \quad = 15$$

$$\frac{12}{3} = \frac{3x}{3}$$
$$4 = x$$

---

isometric drawing A representation of a three-dimensional figure that is drawn on a grid of equilateral triangles.

dibujo isométrico Representación de una figura tridimensional que se dibuja sobre una cuadrícula de triángulos equiláteros.

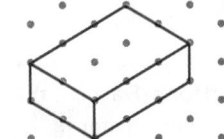

---

isosceles triangle A triangle with at least two congruent sides.

triángulo isósceles Triángulo que tiene al menos dos lados congruentes.

joint relative frequency The ratio of the frequency in a particular category divided by the total number of data values.

frecuencia relativa conjunta La razón de la frecuencia en una determinada categoría dividida entre el número total de valores.

lateral area The sum of the areas of the lateral faces of a prism or pyramid, or the area of the lateral surface of a cylinder or cone.

rango intercuartil (RIC) área lateral Suma de las áreas de las caras laterales de un prisma o pirámide, o área de la superficie lateral de un cilindro o cono.

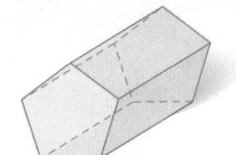

Lateral area = area of the 5 rectangular faces

Glossary/Glosario

	ENGLISH	SPANISH	EXAMPLES

lateral face In a prism or a pyramid, a face that is not a base.

cara lateral En un prisma o pirámide, una cara que no es la base.

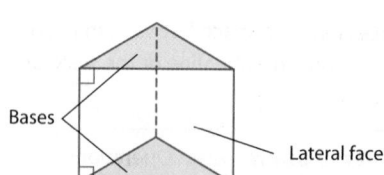

Bases — Lateral face

Right prism

---

lateral surface In a cylinder, the curved surface connecting the circular bases; in a cone, the curved surface that is not a base.

superficie lateral En un cilindro, superficie curva que une las bases circulares; en un cono, la superficie curva que no es la base.

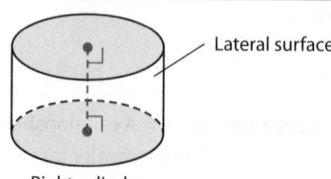

Lateral surface

Right cylinder

---

least common denominator (LCD) The least common multiple of two or more denominators.

mínimo común denominador (mcd) El mínimo común múltiplo más pequeño de dos o más denominadores.

The LCD of $\frac{3}{4}$ and $\frac{5}{6}$ is 12.

---

least common multiple (LCM) The smallest whole number, other than zero, that is a multiple of two or more given numbers.

mínimo común múltiplo (mcm) El menor de los números cabales, distinto de cero, que es múltiplo de dos o más números dados.

The LCM of 6 and 10 is 30.

---

legs In a right triangle, the sides that include the right angle; in an isosceles triangle, the pair of congruent sides.

catetos En un triángulo rectángulo, los lados adyacentes al ángulo recto. En un triángulo isósceles, el par de lados congruentes.

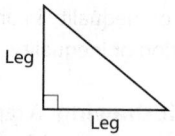

Leg

Leg

---

like fractions Fractions that have the same denominator.

fracciones semejantes Fracciones que tienen el mismo denominador.

$\frac{5}{12}$ and $\frac{7}{12}$ are like fractions.

---

like terms Terms that have the same variable raised to the same exponents.

términos semejantes Términos que contienen las mismas variables elevada a las mismas exponentes.

In the expression $3a^2 + 5b + 12a^2$, $3a^2$ and $12a^2$ are like terms.

---

line A straight path that has no thickness and extends forever.

línea Un trazo recto que no tiene grosor y se extiende infinitamente.

---

line graph A graph that uses line segments to show how data changes.

gráfica lineal Gráfica que muestra cómo cambian los datos mediante segmentos de recta.

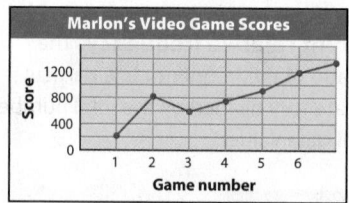

Marlon's Video Game Scores

---

line of best fit A straight line that comes closest to the points on a scatter plot.

línea de mejor ajuste La línea recta que más se aproxima a los puntos de un diagrama de dispersión.

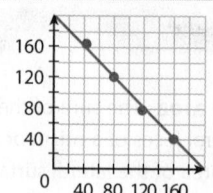

Glossary/Glosario

ENGLISH	SPANISH	EXAMPLES
line of reflection A line that a figure is flipped across to create a mirror image of the original figure.	**línea de reflexión** Línea sobre la cual se invierte una figura para crear una imagen reflejada de la figura original.	
line of symmetry A line that divides a figure into two congruent reflected halves.	**eje de simetría** Línea que divide una figura en dos mitades reflejas.	
line plot A number line with marks or dots that show frequency.	**diagrama de acumulación** Recta numérica con marcas o puntos que indican la frecuencia.	**Number of Pets**
line segment A part of a line consisting of two endpoints and all points between them.	**segmento de recta** Parte de una línea que consiste en dos extremos y todos los puntos entre éstos.	$\overline{GH}$
line symmetry A figure has line symmetry if one half is a mirror image of the other half.	**simetría axial** Una figura tiene simetría axial si una de sus mitades es la imagen reflejada de la otra.	
linear equation An equation whose solutions form a straight line on a coordinate plane.	**ecuación lineal** Ecuación cuyas soluciones forman una línea recta en un plano cartesiano.	$y = 2x + 1$
linear function A function whose graph is a straight line.	**función lineal** Función cuya gráfica es una línea recta.	$y = x - 1$
linear inequality A mathematical sentence using $<$, $>$, $\leq$, or $\geq$ whose graph is a region with a straight-line boundary.	**desigualdad lineal** Enunciado matemático en que se usan los símbolos $<$, $>$, $\leq$, o $\geq$ y cuya gráfica es una región con una línea de límite recta.	
linear relationship A relationship between two quantities in which one variable changes by a constant amount as the other variable changes by a constant amount.	**relación lineal** Relación entre dos cantidades en la cual una variable cambia según una cantidad constante y la otra variable también cambia según una cantidad constante.	
literal equation An equation that contains two or more variables.	**ecuación literal** Ecuación que contiene dos o más variables.	$d = rt$ $A = bh$

ENGLISH	SPANISH	EXAMPLES
lower quartile The median of the lower half of a set of data.	**cuartil inferior** La mediana de la mitad inferior de un conjunto de datos.	Lower half Upper half 18, (23,) 28, 29, 36, 42 Lower quartile

M

ENGLISH	SPANISH	EXAMPLES
major arc An arc that is more than half of a circle.	**arco mayor** Arco que es más de la mitad de un círculo.	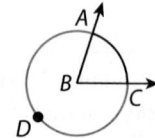 $\overset{\frown}{ADC}$ is a major arc of the circle.
marginal relative frequency The sum of the joint relative frequencies in a row or column of a two-way table.	**frecuencia relativa marginal** La suma de las frecuencias relativas conjuntas en una fila o columna de una tabla de doble entrada.	
matrix A rectangular arrangement of data enclosed in brackets.	**matriz** Arreglo rectangular de datos encerrado entre corchetes.	$\begin{bmatrix} 1 & 0 & 3 \\ -2 & 2 & -5 \\ 7 & -6 & 3 \end{bmatrix}$
mean The sum of a set of data divided by the number of items in the data set; also called *average*.	**media** La suma de todos los elementos de un conjunto de datos dividida entre el número de elementos del conjunto. También se llama *promedio*.	Data set: 4, 6, 7, 8, 10 Mean: $\frac{4+6+7+8+10}{5}=\frac{35}{5}=7$
mean absolute deviation (MAD) The mean distance between each data value and the mean of the data set.	**desviación absoluta media (DAM)** Distancia media entre cada dato y la media del conjunto de datos.	
measure of center A measure used to describe the middle of a data set; the mean, median, and mode are measures of center. Also called *measure of central tendency*.	**medida de tendencia dominante** Medida que describe la parte media de un conjunto de datos; la media, la mediana y la moda son medidas de tendencia dominante.	
median The middle number, or the mean (average) of the two middle numbers, in an ordered set of data.	**mediana** El número intermedio o la media (el promedio) de los dos números intermedios en un conjunto ordenado de datos.	Data set: 4, 6, 7, 8, 10 Median: 7
metric system of measurement A decimal system of weights and measures that is used universally in science and commonly throughout the world.	**sistema métrico de medición** Sistema decimal de pesos y medidas empleado universalmente en las ciencias y de uso común en todo el mundo.	centimeters, meters, kilometers, grams, kilograms, milliliters, liters
midpoint The point that divides a line segment into two congruent line segments.	**punto medio** El punto que divide un segmento de recta en dos segmentos de recta congruentes.	A B C B is the midpoint of $\overline{AC}$.

Glossary/Glosario

ENGLISH	SPANISH	EXAMPLES
minor arc An arc that is less than half of a circle.	**arco menor** Arco que es menor que la mitad de un círculo.	 $\overset{\frown}{AC}$ is the minor arc of the circle.
mixed number A number made up of a whole number that is not zero and a fraction.	**número mixto** Número compuesto por un número cabal distinto de cero y una fracción.	$4\frac{1}{8}$
mode The number or numbers that occur most frequently in a set of data; when all numbers occur with the same frequency, we say there is no mode.	**moda** Número o números más frecuentes en un conjunto de datos; si todos los números aparecen con la misma frecuencia, no hay moda.	Data set: 3, 5, 8, 8, 10 Mode: 8
monomial A number or a product of numbers and variables with exponents that are whole numbers.	**monomio** Un número o un producto de números y variables con exponentes que son números cabales.	$3x^2y^4$
multiple The product of any number and a nonzero whole number is a multiple of that number.	**múltiplo** El producto de cualquier número y un número cabal distinto de cero es un múltiplo de ese número.	
Multiplication Property of Equality The property that states that if you multiply both sides of an equation by the same number, the new equation will have the same solution.	**Propiedad de igualdad de la multiplicación** Propiedad que establece que puedes multiplicar ambos lados de una ecuación por el mismo número y la nueva ecuación tendrá la misma solución.	$3 \cdot 4 = 12$ $3 \cdot 4 \cdot 2 = 12 \cdot 2$ $24 = 24$
Multiplication Property of Zero The property that states that for all real numbers a, $a \cdot 0 = 0$ and $0 \cdot a = 0$.	**Propiedad de multiplicación del cero** Propiedad que establece que para todos los números reales a, $a \cdot 0 = 0$ y $0 \cdot a = 0$.	
multiplicative inverse A number times its multiplicative inverse is equal to 1; also called *reciprocal*.	**inverso multiplicativo** Un número multiplicado por su inverso multiplicativo es igual a 1. También se llama *recíproco*.	The multiplicative inverse of $\frac{4}{5}$ is $\frac{5}{4}$.
mutually exclusive Two events are mutually exclusive if they cannot occur in the same trial of an experiment.	**mutuamente excluyentes** Dos sucesos son mutuamente excluyentes cuando no pueden ocurrir en la misma prueba de un experimento.	When rolling a number cube once, rolling a 3 and rolling an even number are mutually exclusive events.

N

negative correlation Two data sets have a negative correlation if one set of data values increases while the other decreases.	**correlación negativa** Dos conjuntos de datos tienen correlación negativa si los valores de un conjunto aumentan a medida que los valores del otro conjunto disminuyen.	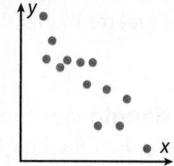

ENGLISH	SPANISH	EXAMPLES
negative integer An integer less than zero.	**entero negativo** Entero menor que cero.	−2 is a negative integer. 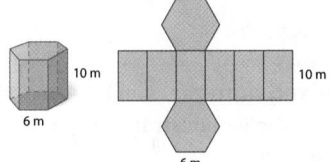 −4 −3 −2 −1 0 1 2 3 4
net An arrangement of two-dimensional figures that can be folded to form a polyhedron.	**plantilla** Arreglo de figuras bidimensionales que se doblan para formar un poliedro.	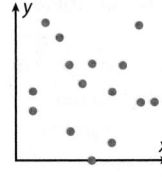 10 m 6 m 10 m 6 m
network A set of points and the line segments or arcs that connect the points.	**red** Conjunto de puntos y los segmentos de recta o arcos que los conectan.	
no correlation Two data sets have no correlation when there is no relationship between their data values.	**sin correlación** Caso en que los valores de dos conjuntos no muestran ninguna relación.	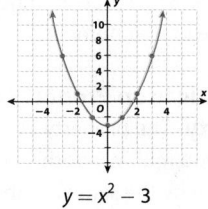
nonlinear function A function whose graph is not a straight line.	**función no lineal** Función cuya gráfica no es una línea recta.	$y = x^2 - 3$
nonlinear relationship A relationship between two variables in which the data do not increase or decrease together at the same rate.	**relación no lineal** Relación entre dos variables en la cual los datos no aumentan o disminuyen al mismo tiempo a una tasa constante.	
nonterminating decimal A decimal that never ends.	**decimal infinito** Decimal que nunca termina.	$0.\overline{3}$
numerator The top number of a fraction that tells how many parts of a whole are being considered.	**numerador** El número de arriba de una fracción; indica cuántas partes de un entero se consideran.	$\frac{4}{5}$ ← numerator
numerical expression An expression that contains only numbers and operations.	**expresión numérica** Expresión que incluye sólo números y operaciones.	$(2 \cdot 3) + 1$

0

obtuse angle An angle whose measure is greater than 90° but less than 180°.	**ángulo obtuso** Ángulo que mide más de 90° y menos de 180°.	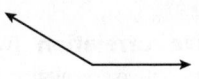
obtuse triangle A triangle containing one obtuse angle.	**triángulo obtusángulo** Triángulo que tiene un ángulo obtuso.	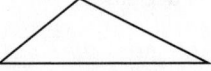

ENGLISH	SPANISH	EXAMPLES
octagon An eight-sided polygon.	**octágono** Polígono de ocho lados.	
odds A comparison of the number of ways an event can occur and the number of ways an event can *not* occur.	**probabilidades** Comparación del numero de las maneras que puede ocurrir un suceso y el numero de maneras que no puede ocurrir el suceso.	
odds against The ratio of the number of unfavorable outcomes to the number of favorable outcomes.	**probabilidades en contra** Razón del número de resultados no favorables al número de resultados favorables.	The odds against rolling a 3 on a number cube are 5:1.
odds in favor The ratio of the number of favorable outcomes to the number of unfavorable outcomes.	**probabilidades a favor** Razón del número de resultados favorables al número de resultados no favorables.	The odds in favor of rolling a 3 on a number cube are 1:5.
opposites Two numbers that are an equal distance from zero on a number line; also called *additive inverse*.	**opuestos** Dos números que están a la misma distancia de cero en una recta numérica. También se llaman *inversos aditivos*.	5 and −5 are opposites. 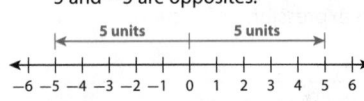
order of operations A rule for evaluating expressions: First perform the operations in parentheses, then compute powers and roots, then perform all multiplication and division from left to right, and then perform all addition and subtraction from left to right.	**orden de las operaciones** Regla para evaluar expresiones: primero se hacen las operaciones entre paréntesis, luego se hallan las potencias y raíces, después todas las multiplicaciones y divisiones de izquierda a derecha, y por último, todas las sumas y restas de izquierda a derecha.	$4^2 + 8 \div 2$ Evaluate the power. $16 + 8 \div 2$ Divide. $16 + 4$ Add. 20
ordered pair A pair of numbers that can be used to locate a point on a coordinate plane.	**par ordenado** Par de números que sirven para ubicar un punto en un plano cartesiano.	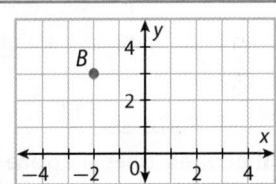 The coordinates of B are $(-2, 3)$.
origin The point where the *x*-axis and *y*-axis intersect on the coordinate plane; (0, 0).	**origen** Punto de intersección entre el eje *x* y el eje *y* en un plano cartesiano: (0, 0).	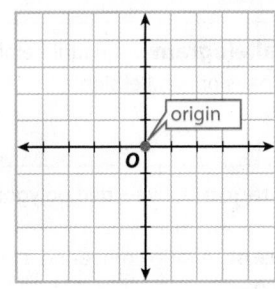

ENGLISH	SPANISH	EXAMPLES

orthogonal views A drawing that shows the top, bottom, front, back, and side views of a three-dimensional object.

vista ortogonal Un dibujo que muestra la vista superior, inferior, frontal, posterior y lateral de un objeto de tres dimensiones.

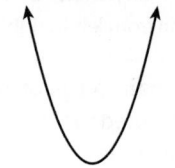

---

outcome (probability) A possible result of a probability experiment.

resultado (en probabilidad) Posible resultado de un experimento de probabilidad.

When rolling a number cube, the possible outcomes are 1, 2, 3, 4, 5, and 6.

---

outlier A value much greater or much less than the others in a data set.

valor extremo Un valor mucho mayor o menor que los demás valores de un conjunto de datos.

---

output The value that results from the substitution of a given input into an expression or function.

valor de salida Valor que resulta después de sustituir una variable por un valor de entrada determinado en una expresión o función.

For the function $y = 6x$, the input 4 produces an output of 24.

---

overestimate An estimate that is greater than the exact answer.

estimación alta Estimación mayor que la respuesta exacta.

100 is an overestimate for the sum $23 + 24 + 21 + 22$.

P

parabola The graph of a quadratic function.

parábola Gráfica de una función cuadrática.

---

parallel lines Lines in a plane that do not intersect.

líneas paralelas Líneas que se encuentran en el mismo plano pero que nunca se intersecan.

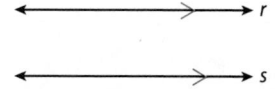

---

parallelogram A quadrilateral with two pairs of parallel sides.

paralelogramo Cuadrilátero con dos pares de lados paralelos.

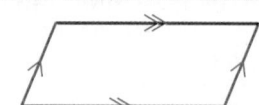

---

pentagon A five-sided polygon.

pentágono Polígono de cinco lados.

---

percent A ratio comparing a number to 100.

porcentaje Razón que compara un número con el número 100.

$45\% = \frac{45}{100}$

---

percent change The amount stated as a percent that a number increases or decreases.

porcentaje de cambio Cantidad en que un número aumenta o disminuye, expresada como un porcentaje.

---

percent decrease A percent change describing a decrease in a quantity.

porcentaje de disminución Porcentaje de cambio en que una cantidad disminuye.

An item that costs \$8 is marked down to \$6. The amount of the decrease is \$2, and the percent decrease is $\frac{2}{8} = 0.25 = 25\%$.

ENGLISH	SPANISH	EXAMPLES
percent increase A percent change describing an increase in a quantity.	**porcentaje de incremento** Porcentaje de cambio en que una cantidad aumenta.	The price of an item increases from \$8 to \$12. The amount of the increase is \$4, and the percent increase is $\frac{4}{8} = 0.5 = 50\%$.
perfect cube A cube of a whole number.	**cubo perfecto** El cubo de un número cabal.	$2^3 = 8$, so 8 is a perfect cube.
perfect square A square of a whole number.	**cuadrado perfecto** El cuadrado de un número cabal.	$5^2 = 25$, so 25 is a perfect square.
perimeter The distance around a polygon.	**perímetro** Distancia alrededor de un polígono.	 perimeter $= 18 + 6 + 18 + 6 = 48$ ft
permutation An arrangement of items or events in which order is important.	**permutación** Arreglo de objetos o sucesos en el que el orden es importante.	For objects *A*, *B*, and *C*, there are 6 different permutations: *ABC*, *ACB*, *BAC*, *BCA*, *CAB*, *CBA*.
perpendicular bisector A line that intersects a segment at its midpoint and is perpendicular to the segment.	**mediatriz** Línea que cruza un segmento en su punto medio y es perpendicular al segmento.	
perpendicular lines Lines that intersect to form right angles.	**líneas perpendiculares** Líneas que al intersecarse forman ángulos rectos.	
pi (π) The ratio of the circumference of a circle to the length of its diameter; $\pi \approx 3.14$ or $\frac{22}{7}$.	**pi (π)** Razón de la circunferencia de un círculo a la longitud de su diámetro; $\pi \approx 3.14$ ó $\frac{22}{7}$.	
plane A flat surface that has no thickness and extends forever.	**plano** Superficie plana que no tiene ningún grueso y que se extiende por siempre.	
point An exact location that has no size.	**punto** Ubicación exacta que no tiene ningún tamaño.	$P \bullet$
point-slope form The equation of a line in the form of $y - y_1 = m(x - x_1)$, where m is the slope and (x_1, y_1) is a specific point on the line.	**forma de punto y pendiente** Ecuación lineal del tipo $y - y_1 = m(x - x_1)$, donde m es la pendiente y (x_1, y_1) es un punto específico de la línea.	$y - 3 = 2(x - 3)$
polygon A closed plane figure formed by three or more line segments that intersect only at their endpoints (vertices).	**polígono** Figura plana cerrada, formada por tres o más segmentos de recta que se intersecan sólo en sus extremos (vértices).	

ENGLISH	SPANISH	EXAMPLES
polyhedron A three-dimensional figure in which all the surfaces or faces are polygons.	**poliedro** Figura tridimensional cuyas superficies o caras tiene forma de polígonos.	
polynomial One monomial or the sum or difference of monomials.	**polinomio** Un monomio o la suma o la diferencia de monomios.	$2x^2 + 3xy - 7y^2$
population The entire group of objects or individuals considered for a survey.	**población** Grupo completo de objetos o individuos que se desea estudiar.	In a survey about study habits of middle school students, the population is all middle school students.
positive correlation Two data sets have a positive correlation when their data values increase or decrease together.	**correlación positiva** Dos conjuntos de datos tienen una correlación positiva cuando los valores de ambos conjuntos aumentan o disminuyen al mismo tiempo.	
positive integer An integer greater than zero.	**entero positivo** Entero mayor que cero.	 2 is a positive integer.
power A number produced by raising a base to an exponent.	**potencia** Número que resulta al elevar una base a un exponente.	$2^3 = 8$, so 2 to the 3rd power is 8.
prediction Something you can reasonably expect to happen in the future.	**predicción** Algo que se puede razonablemente esperar suceder en el futuro.	
preimage The original figure in a transformation.	**imagen original** Figura original en una transformación.	
prime factorization A number written as the product of its prime factors.	**factorización prima** Un número escrito como el producto de sus factores primos.	$10 = 2 \cdot 5$, $24 = 2^3 \cdot 3$
prime number A whole number greater than 1 that has exactly two factors, itself and 1.	**número primo** Número cabal mayor que 1 que sólo es divisible entre 1 y él mismo.	5 is prime because its only factors are 5 and 1.
principal The initial amount of money borrowed or saved.	**capital** Cantidad inicial de dinero depositada o recibida en préstamo.	
principal square root The nonnegative square root of a number.	**raíz cuadrada principal** Raíz cuadrada no negativa de un número.	$\sqrt{25} = 5$; the principal square root of 25 is 5.
prism A polyhedron that has two congruent, polygon-shaped bases and other faces that are all parallelograms.	**prisma** Poliedro con dos bases congruentes con forma de polígono y caras con forma de paralelogramo.	
probability A number from 0 to 1 (or 0% to 100%) that describes how likely an event is to occur.	**probabilidad** Un número entre 0 y 1 (ó 0% y 100%) que describe qué tan probable es un suceso.	A bag contains 3 red marbles and 4 blue marbles. The probability of randomly choosing a red marble is $\frac{3}{7}$.

Glossary/Glosario

© Houghton Mifflin Harcourt Publishing Company

	ENGLISH	SPANISH	EXAMPLES

proper fraction A fraction in which the numerator is less than the denominator.

fracción propia Fracción en la que el numerador es menor que el denominador.

$\frac{3}{4}, \frac{1}{12}, \frac{7}{8}$

---

proportion An equation that states that two ratios are equivalent.

proporción Ecuación que establece que dos razones son equivalentes.

$\frac{2}{3} = \frac{4}{6}$

---

proportional relationship A relationship between two quantities in which the ratio of one quantity to the other quantity is constant.

relación proporcional Relación entre dos cantidades en que la razón de una cantidad a la otra es constante.

---

protractor A tool for measuring angles.

transportador Instrumento para medir ángulos.

---

pyramid A polyhedron with a polygon base and triangular sides that all meet at a common vertex.

pirámide Poliedro cuya base es un polígono; tiene caras triangulares que se juntan en un vértice común.

Pythagorean Theorem In a right triangle, the square of the length of the hypotenuse is equal to the sum of the squares of the lengths of the legs.

Teorema de Pitágoras En un triángulo rectángulo, la suma de los cuadrados de los catetos es igual al cuadrado de la hipotenusa.

13 cm
5 cm
12 cm

$5^2 + 12^2 = 13^2$
$25 + 144 = 169$

Pythagorean triple A set of three positive integers a, b, and c such that $a^2 + b^2 = c^2$.

Tripleta de Pitágoras Conjunto de tres números enteros positivos de cero a, b y c tal que $a^2 + b^2 = c^2$.

3, 4, 5 because $3^2 + 4^2 = 5^2$

Q

quadrant The x- and y-axes divide the coordinate plane into four regions. Each region is called a quadrant.

cuadrante El eje x y el eje y dividen el plano cartesiano en cuatro regiones. Cada región recibe el nombre de cuadrante.

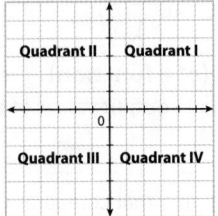

Quadrant II	Quadrant I
Quadrant III	Quadrant IV

---

quadratic function A function of the form $y = ax^2 + bx + c$, where $a \neq 0$.

función cuadrática Función del tipo $y = ax^2 + bx + c$, donde $a \neq 0$.

$y = x^2 - 6x + 8$

---

quadrilateral A four-sided polygon.

cuadrilátero Polígono de cuatro lados.

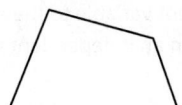

---

quarterly Four times a year.

trimestral Cuatro veces al año.

Glossary/Glosario

ENGLISH	SPANISH	EXAMPLES
quartile Three values, one of which is the median, that divide a data set into fourths.	**cuartil** Cada uno de tres valores, uno de los cuales es la mediana, que dividen en cuartos un conjunto de datos.	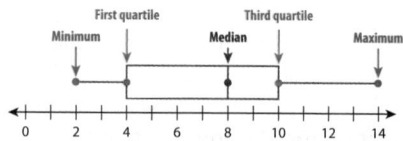
quotient The result when one number is divided by another.	**cociente** Resultado de dividir un número entre otro.	In $8 \div 4 = 2$, 2 is the quotient.

ENGLISH	SPANISH	EXAMPLES
radical symbol The symbol $\sqrt{\ }$ used to represent the nonnegative square root of a number.	**símbolo de radical** El símbolo $\sqrt{\ }$ con que se representa la raíz cuadrada no negativa de un número.	
radius A line segment with one endpoint at the center of the circle and the other endpoint on the circle, or the length of that segment.	**radio** Segmento de recta con un extremo en el centro de un círculo y el otro en la circunferencia, o bien se llama radio a la longitud de ese segmento.	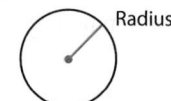
random numbers In a set of random numbers, each number has an equal chance of appearing.	**muestra aleatoria** Muestra en la que cada individuo u objeto de la población tiene la misma posibilidad de ser elegido.	
random sample A sample in which each individual or object in the entire population has an equal chance of being selected.	**números aleatorios** En un conjunto de números aleatorios, todos los números tienen la misma probabilidad de ser seleccionados.	
range (in statistics) The difference between the greatest and least values in a data set.	**rango (en estadística)** Diferencia entre los valores máximo y mínimo de un conjunto de datos.	Data set: 3, 5, 7, 7, 12 Range: $12 - 3 = 9$
range (of a function) The set of all possible output values of a function.	**rango (en una función)** El conjunto de todos los valores posibles de una función.	The range of $y = |x|$ is $y \geq 0$.
rate A ratio that compares two quantities measured in different units.	**tasa** Una razón que compara dos cantidades medidas en diferentes unidades.	The speed limit is 55 miles per hour or 55 mi/h.
rate of change A ratio that compares the amount of change in a dependent variable to the amount of change in an independent variable.	**tasa de cambio** Razón que compara la cantidad de cambio de la variable dependiente con la cantidad de cambio de la variable independiente.	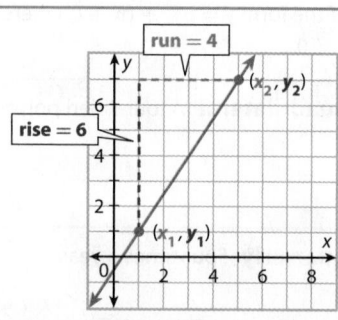

Rate of change $= \dfrac{\text{change in } y}{\text{change in } x} = \dfrac{6}{4} = \dfrac{3}{2}$

Glossary/Glosario

| --- | --- | --- |

rate of interest The percent charged or earned on an amount of money; see *simple interest*.

tasa de interés Porcentaje que se cobra por una cantidad de dinero prestada o que se gana por una cantidad de dinero ahorrada; ver *interés simple*.

---

ratio A comparison of two quantities by division.

razón Comparación de dos cantidades mediante una división.

12 to 25, 12:25, $\frac{12}{25}$

---

rational number Any number that can be expressed as a ratio of two integers.

número racional Número que se puede escribir como una razón de dos enteros.

6 can be expressed as $\frac{6}{1}$.

0.5 can be expressed as $\frac{1}{2}$.

---

ray A part of a line that starts at one endpoint and extends forever in one direction.

rayo Parte de una línea que comienza en un extremo y se extiende de manera infinitamente en una dirección.

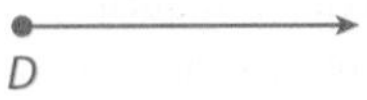

D

---

real number A rational or irrational number.

número real Número racional o irracional.

---

reciprocal One of two numbers whose product is 1; also called *multiplicative inverse*.

recíproco Uno de dos números cuyo producto es igual a 1. También se llama *inverso multiplicativo*.

The reciprocal of $\frac{2}{3}$ is $\frac{3}{2}$.

---

rectangle A parallelogram with four right angles.

rectángulo Paralelogramo con cuatro ángulos rectos.

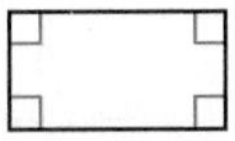

---

rectangular prism A polyhedron whose bases are rectangles and whose other faces are parallelograms.

prisma rectangular Poliedro cuyas bases son rectángulos y cuyas caras tienen forma de paralelogramo.

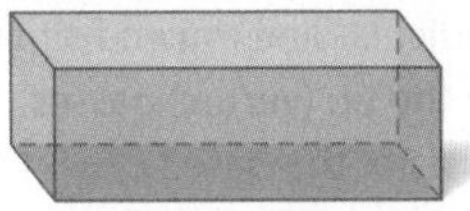

---

reduction A decrease in the size of all dimensions.

reducción Disminución de tamaño en todas las dimensiones de una figura.

---

reflection A transformation of a figure that flips the figure across a line.

reflexión Transformación que ocurre cuando se invierte una figura sobre una línea.

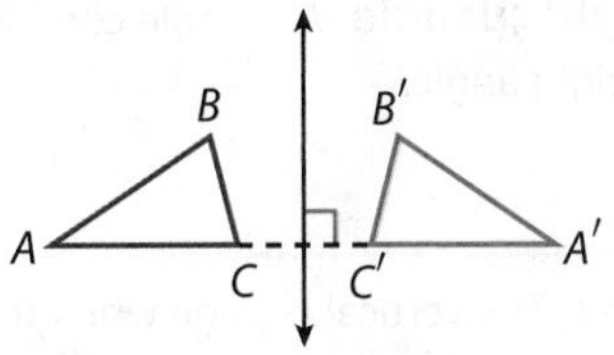

---

regular polygon A polygon with congruent sides and angles.

polígono regular Polígono con lados y ángulos congruentes.

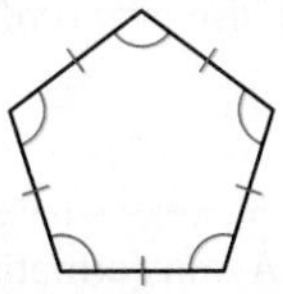

---

regular pyramid A pyramid whose base is a regular polygon and whose lateral faces are all congruent.

pirámide regular Pirámide que tiene un polígono regular como base y caras laterales congruentes.

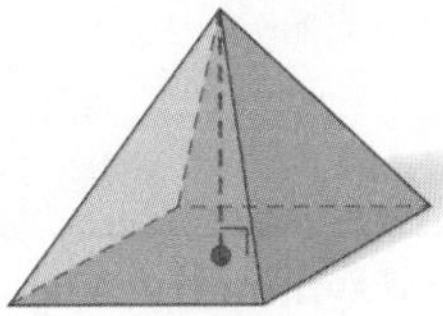

---

relation A set of ordered pairs.

relación Conjunto de pares ordenados.

(0, 5), (0, 4), (2, 3), (4, 0)

Glossary/Glosario

ENGLISH	SPANISH	EXAMPLES
relative frequency The frequency of a specific data value divided by the total number of data values in the set.	**frecuencia relativa** La frecuencia de un valor dividido por el número total de los valores en el conjunto.	
relatively prime Two numbers are relatively prime if their greatest common factor (GCF) is 1.	**primo relativo** Dos números son primos relativos si su máximo común divisor (MCD) es 1.	8 and 15 are relatively prime.
remote interior angle An interior angle of a polygon that is not adjacent to the exterior angle.	**ángulo interno remoto** Ángulo interno de un polígono que no es adyacente al ángulo externo.	
repeating decimal A decimal in which one or more digits repeat infinitely.	**decimal periódico** Decimal en el que uno o más dígitos se repiten infinitamente.	$0.757575\ldots = 0.\overline{75}$
rhombus A parallelogram with all sides congruent.	**rombo** Paralelogramo en el que todos los lados son congruentes.	
right angle An angle that measures 90°.	**ángulo recto** Ángulo que mide exactamente 90°.	
right cone A cone in which a perpendicular line drawn from the base to the tip (vertex) passes through the center of the base.	**cono regular** Cono en el que una línea perpendicular trazada de la base a la punta (vértice) pasa por el centro de la base.	Right cone
right triangle A triangle containing a right angle.	**triángulo rectángulo** Triángulo que tiene un ángulo recto.	
rise The vertical change when the slope of a line is expressed as the ratio $\frac{rise}{run}$, or "rise over run."	**distancia vertical** El cambio vertical cuando la pendiente de una línea se expresa como la razón $\frac{distancia\ vertical}{distancia\ horizontal}$, o "distancia vertical sobre distancia horizontal".	For the points $(3, -1)$ and $(6, 5)$, the rise is $5 - (-1) = 6$.
rotation A transformation in which a figure is turned around a point.	**rotación** Transformación que ocurre cuando una figura gira alrededor de un punto.	
rotational symmetry A figure has rotational symmetry if it can be rotated less than 360° around a central point and coincide with the original figure.	**simetría de rotación** Ocurre cuando una figura gira menos de 360° alrededor de un punto central sin dejar de ser congruente con la figura original.	90° 90° 90° 90°

Glossary/Glosario

ENGLISH	SPANISH	EXAMPLES
rounding Replacing a number with an estimate of that number to a given place value.	**redondear** Sustituir un número por una estimación de ese número hasta cierto valor posicional.	2,354 rounded to the nearest thousand is 2,000, and 2,354 rounded to the nearest 100 is 2,400.
run The horizontal change when the slope of a line is expressed as the ratio $\frac{rise}{run}$, or "rise over run."	**distancia horizontal** El cambio horizontal cuando la pendiente de una línea se expresa como la razón $\frac{distancia\ vertical}{distancia\ horizontal}$, o "distancia vertical sobre distancia horizontal".	For the points (3, −1) and (6, 5), the run is $6 - 3 = 3$.

sales tax A percent of the cost of an item that is charged by governments to raise money.	**impuesto sobre la venta** Porcentaje del costo de un artículo que los gobiernos cobran para recaudar fondos.	
same-side interior angles A pair of angles on the same side of a transversal and between two lines intersected by the transversal.	**ángulo internos del mismo lado** Dadas dos rectas cortadas por una transversal, par de ángulos ubicados en el mismo lado de la transversal y entre las dos rectas.	
sample A part of the population.	**muestra** Una parte de la población.	
sample space All possible outcomes of an experiment.	**espacio muestral** Conjunto de todos los resultados posibles de un experimento.	When rolling a number cube, the sample space is 1, 2, 3, 4, 5, 6.
scale The ratio between two sets of measurements.	**escala** La razón entre dos conjuntos de medidas.	1 cm : 5 mi
scale drawing A drawing that uses a scale to make an object smaller than (a reduction) or larger than (an enlargement) the real object.	**dibujo a escala** Dibujo en el que se usa una escala para que un objeto se vea menor (reducción) o mayor (agrandamiento) que el objeto real al que representa.	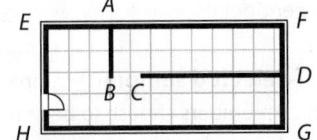 A blueprint is an example of a scale drawing.
scale factor The ratio used to enlarge or reduce similar figures.	**factor de escala** Razón empleada para agrandar o reducir figuras semejantes.	
scale model A proportional model of a three-dimensional object.	**modelo a escala** Modelo proporcional de un objeto tridimensional.	
scalene triangle A triangle with no congruent sides.	**triángulo escaleno** Triángulo que no tiene lados congruentes.	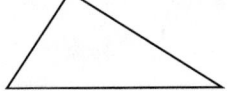

Glossary/Glosario

ENGLISH	SPANISH	EXAMPLES

scatter plot A graph with points plotted to show a possible relationship between two sets of data.

diagrama de dispersión Gráfica de puntos que muestra una posible relación entre dos conjuntos de datos.

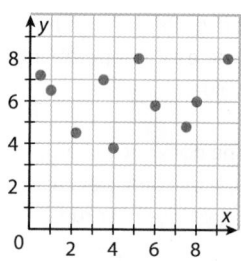

scientific notation A method of writing very large or very small numbers by using powers of 10.

notación científica Método que se usa para escribir números muy grandes o muy pequeños mediante potencias de 10.

$12{,}560{,}000{,}000{,}000 =$
1.256×10^{13}

second quartile The median of a set of data.

segundo cuartil Mediana de un conjunto de datos.

Data set: 4, 6, 7, 8, 10
Second quartile: 7

sector A region enclosed by two radii and the arc joining their endpoints.

sector Región encerrada por dos radios y el arco que une sus extremos.

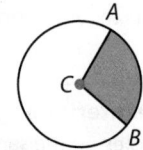

sector (data) A section of a circle graph representing part of the data set.

sector (datos) Sección de una gráfica circular que representa una parte del conjunto de datos.

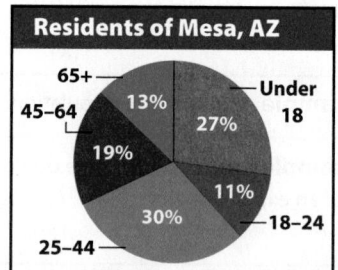

The circle graph has 5 sectors.

segment A part of a line between two endpoints.

segmento Parte de una línea entre dos extremos.

self-selected sample A sample in which members choose to be in the sample.

muestra auto-seleccionada Una muestra en la que los miembros eligen participar.

A store provides survey cards for customers who choose to fill them out.

sequence An ordered list of numbers.

sucesión Lista ordenada de números.

2, 4, 6, 8, 10, …

set A group of terms.

conjunto Un grupo de elementos.

side A line bounding a geometric figure; one of the faces forming the outside of an object.

lado Línea que delimita las figuras geométricas; una de las caras que forman la parte exterior de un objeto.

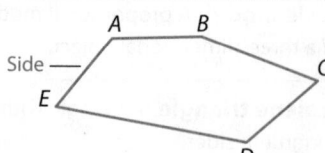

similar Figures with the same shape but not necessarily the same size.

semejantes Figuras que tienen la misma forma, pero no necesariamente el mismo tamaño.

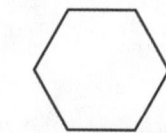

Glossary/Glosario

ENGLISH	SPANISH	EXAMPLES
similarity transformation A transformation that results in an image that is the same shape, but not necessarily the same size, as the original figure.	**transformación de semejanza** Una transformación que resulta en una imagen que tiene la misma forma, pero no necesariamente el mismo tamaño como la figura original.	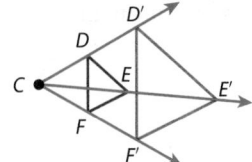
simple event An event consisting of only one outcome.	**suceso simple** Suceso que tiene sólo un resultado.	In the experiment of rolling a number cube, the event consisting of the outcome 3 is a simple event.
simple interest A fixed percent of the principal. It is found using the formula $I = Prt$, where P represents the principal, r the rate of interest, and t the time.	**interés simple** Un porcentaje fijo del capital. Se calcula con la fórmula $I = Cit$, donde C representa el capital, i, la tasa de interés y t, el tiempo.	$100 is put into an account with a simple interest rate of 5%. After 2 years, the account will have earned $I = 100 \cdot 0.05 \cdot 2 = \$10$.
simplest form A fraction in which the numerator and denominator have no common factors other than 1.	**mínima expresión** Una fracción está en su mínima expresión cuando el numerador y el denominador no tienen más factor común que 1.	Fraction: $\frac{8}{12}$ Simplest form: $\frac{2}{3}$
simplify To write a fraction or expression in simplest form.	**simplificar** Escribir una fracción o expresión numérica en su mínima expresión.	
simulation A model of an experiment, often one that would be too difficult or too time-consuming to actually perform.	**simulación** Representación de un experimento, por lo general, de uno cuya realización sería demasiado difícil o llevaría mucho tiempo.	
skew lines Lines that lie in different planes that are neither parallel nor intersecting.	**líneas oblicuas** Líneas que se encuentran en planos distintos, por eso no se intersecan ni son paralelas.	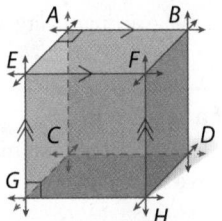 $\overleftrightarrow{AB}$ and $\overleftrightarrow{CG}$ are skew lines.
slant height (of a regular pyramid) The distance from the vertex of a regular pyramid to the midpoint of an edge of the base.	**altura inclinada (de una pirámide)** Distancia desde el vértice de una pirámide hasta el punto medio de una arista de la base.	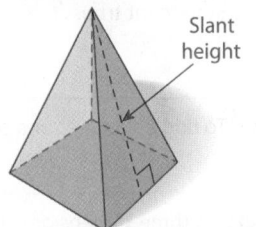 **Regular pyramid**
slant height (of a right cone) The distance from the vertex of a right cone to a point on the edge of the base.	**altura inclinada (de un cono recto)** Distancia desde el vértice de un cono recto hasta un punto en el borde de la base.	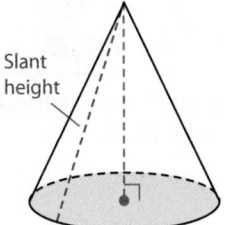

ENGLISH	SPANISH	EXAMPLES
slope A measure of the steepness of a line on a graph; the rise divided by the run.	**pendiente** Medida de la inclinación de una línea en una gráfica. Razón de la distancia vertical a la distancia horizontal.	Slope $= \frac{\text{rise}}{\text{run}} = \frac{3}{4}$ 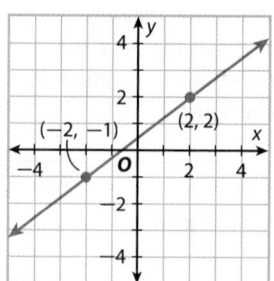
slope-intercept form A linear equation written in the form $y = mx + b$, where m represents slope and b represents the y-intercept.	**forma de pendiente-intersección** Ecuación lineal escrita en la forma $y = mx + b$, donde m es la pendiente y b es la intersección con el eje y.	$y = 6x - 3$
solid figure A three-dimensional figure.	**cuerpo geométrico** Figura tridimensional.	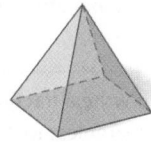
solution of an equation A value or values that make an equation true.	**solución de una ecuación** Valor o valores que hacen verdadera una ecuación.	Equation: $x + 2 = 6$ Solution: $x = 4$
solution of an inequality A value or values that make an inequality true.	**solución de una desigualdad** Valor o valores que hacen verdadera una desigualdad.	Inequality: $x + 3 \geq 10$ Solution: $x \geq 7$
solution of a system of equations A set of values that make all equations in a system true.	**solución de un sistema de ecuaciones** Conjunto de valores que hacen verdaderas todas las ecuaciones de un sistema.	System: $\begin{cases} x + y = -1 \\ -x + y = -3 \end{cases}$ Solution: $(1, -2)$
solution set The set of values that make a statement true.	**conjunto solución** Conjunto de valores que hacen verdadero un enunciado.	Inequality: $x + 3 \geq 5$ Solution set: $x \geq 2$ 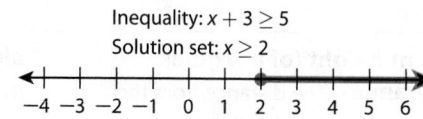
solve To find an answer or a solution.	**resolver** Hallar una respuesta o solución.	
sphere A three-dimensional figure with all points the same distance from the center.	**esfera** Figura tridimensional en la que todos los puntos están a la misma distancia del centro.	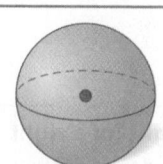
square A rectangle with four congruent sides.	**cuadrado** Rectángulo con cuatro lados congruentes.	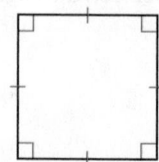

ENGLISH	SPANISH	EXAMPLES
square (numeration) A number raised to the second power.	**cuadrado (en numeración)** Número elevado a la segunda potencia.	In 5^2, the number 5 is squared.
square root A number that is multiplied by itself to form a product is called a square root of that product.	**raíz quadrada** El número que se multiplica por sí mismo para formar un producto se denomina la raíz cuadrada de ese producto.	A square root of 16 is 4, because $4^2 = 4 \cdot 4 = 16$. Another square root of 16 is -4 because $(-4)^2 = (-4)(-4) = 16$.
stem-and-leaf plot A graph used to organize and display data so that the frequencies can be compared.	**diagrama de tallo y hojas** Gráfica que muestra y ordena los datos, y que sirve para comparar las frecuencias.	<table><tr><td>Stem</td><td>Leaves</td></tr><tr><td>3</td><td>2 3 4 4 7 9</td></tr><tr><td>4</td><td>0 1 5 7 7 7 8</td></tr><tr><td>5</td><td>1 2 2 3</td></tr></table> *Key: 3|2 means 3.2*
straight angle An angle that measures 180°.	**ángulo llano** Ángulo que mide exactamente 180°.	$\longleftrightarrow$
subset A set contained within another set.	**subconjunto** Conjunto que pertenece a otro conjunto.	
substitute To replace a variable with a number or another expression in an algebraic expression.	**sustituir** Reemplazar una variable por un número u otra expresión en una expresión algebraica.	Substituting 3 for m in the expression $5m - 2$ gives $5(3) - 2 = 15 - 2 = 13$.
Subtraction Property of Equality The property that states that if you subtract the same number from both sides of an equation, the new equation will have the same solution.	**Propiedad de igualdad de la resta** Propiedad que establece que puedes restar el mismo número de ambos lados de una ecuación y la nueva ecuación tendrá la misma solución.	$$\begin{array}{rcl} 14 - 6 &=& 8 \\ -6 &=& -6 \\ \hline 14 - 12 &=& 2 \end{array}$$
supplementary angles Two angles whose measures have a sum of 180°.	**ángulos suplementarios** Dos ángulos cuyas medidas suman 180°.	30° 150°
surface area The sum of the areas of the faces, or surfaces, of a three-dimensional figure.	**área total** Suma de las áreas de las caras, o superficies, de una figura tridimensional.	12 cm 6 cm 8 cm Surface area $= 2(8)(12) + 2(8)(6) + 2(12)(6) = 432 \text{ cm}^2$
system of equations A set of two or more equations that contain two or more variables.	**sistema de ecuaciones** Conjunto de dos o más ecuaciones que contienen dos o más variables.	$\begin{cases} x + y = -1 \\ -x + y = -3 \end{cases}$
systematic sample A sample of a population that has been selected using a pattern.	**muestra sistemática** Muestra de una población, que ha sido elegida mediante un patrón.	To conduct a phone survey, every tenth name is chosen from the phone book.

© Houghton Mifflin Harcourt Publishing Company

Glossary/Glosario

term (in an expression) A part of an expression that is added or subtracted.

término (en una expresión) Las partes de una expresión que se suman o se restan.

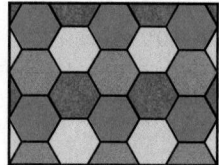
Term   Term   Term

---

term (in a sequence) An element or number in a sequence.

término (en una sucesión) Elemento o número de una sucesión.

5 is the third term in the sequence 1, 3, 5, 7, 9, …

---

terminating decimal A decimal number that ends, or terminates.

decimal finito Decimal con un número determinado de posiciones decimales.

6.75

---

tessellation A repeating pattern of plane figures that completely cover a plane with no gaps or overlaps.

teselado Patrón repetido de figuras planas que cubren totalmente un plano sin superponerse ni dejar huecos.

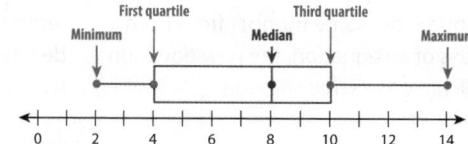

---

theoretical probability The ratio of the number of ways an event can occur to the number of equally likely outcomes.

probabilidad teórica Razón del número de las maneras que puede ocurrir un suceso al numero total de resultados igualmente probables.

When rolling a number cube, the theoretical probability of rolling a 4 is $\frac{1}{6}$.

---

third quartile The median of the upper half of a set of data; also called *upper quartile*.

tercer cuartil La mediana de la mitad superior de un conjunto de datos. También se llama *cuartil superior*.

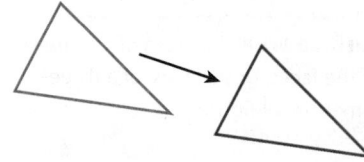

---

transformation A change in the size or position of a figure.

transformación Cambio en el tamaño o la posición de una figura.

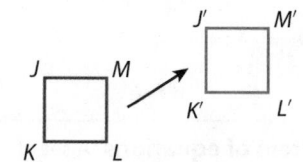

---

translation A movement (slide) of a figure along a straight line.

traslación Desplazamiento de una figura a lo largo de una línea recta.

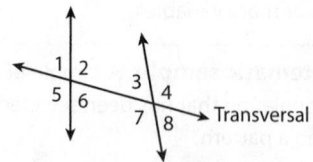

---

transversal A line that intersects two or more lines.

transversal Línea que cruza dos o más líneas.

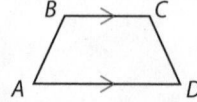

---

trapezoid A quadrilateral with exactly one pair of parallel sides.

trapecio Cuadrilátero con un par de lados paralelos.

Glossary/Glosario

ENGLISH	SPANISH	EXAMPLES

tree diagram A branching diagram that shows all possible combinations or outcomes of an event.

diagrama de árbol Diagrama ramificado que muestra todas las posibles combinaciones o resultados de un suceso.

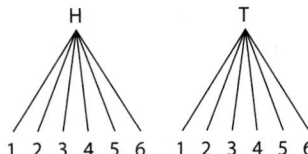

trend line A line on a scatter plot that helps show the correlation between data sets more clearly.

línea de tendencia Línea en un diagrama de dispersión que sirve para mostrar la correlación entre conjuntos de datos más claramente. *ver también* línea de mejor ajuste.

trial Each repetition or observation of an experiment.

prueba Una sola repetición u observación de un experimento.

When rolling a number cube, each roll is one trial.

Triangle Inequality Theorem The theorem that states that the sum of the lengths of any two sides of a triangle is greater than the length of the third side.

Teorema de Desigualdad de Triángulos El teorema dice que la suma de cualquier dos lados de un triangulo es mayor que la longitud del lado tercero.

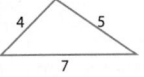

Can form a triangle   Cannot form a triangle

Triangle Sum Theorem The theorem that states that the measures of the angles in a triangle add up to 180°.

Teorema de la suma del triángulo Teorema que establece que las medidas de los ángulos de un triángulo suman 180°.

triangular prism A polyhedron whose bases are triangles and whose other faces are parallelograms.

prisma triangular Poliedro cuyas bases son triángulos y cuyas demás caras tienen forma de paralelogramo.

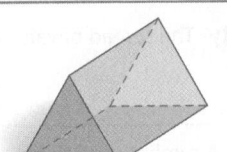

trinomial A polynomial with three terms.

trinomio Polinomio con tres términos.

$4x^2 + 3xy - 5y^2$

two-way relative frequency table A two-way table that displays relative frequencies.

tabla de frecuencia relativa de doble entrada Una tabla de doble entrada que muestran las frecuencias relativas.

two-way table A table that displays two-variable data by organizing it into rows and columns.

tabla de doble entrada Una tabla que muestran los datos de dos variables por organizándolos en columnas y filas.

		Preference		
		Inside	**Outside**	*Total*
Pet	**Cats**	35	15	50
	Dogs	20	30	50
	Total	55	45	100

underestimate An estimate that is less than the exact answer.

estimación baja Estimación menor que la respuesta exacta.

ENGLISH	SPANISH	EXAMPLES
unit conversion The process of changing one unit of measure to another.	**conversión de unidades** Proceso que consiste en cambiar una unidad de medida por otra.	
unit conversion factor A fraction used in unit conversion in which the numerator and denominator represent the same amount but are in different units.	**factor de conversión de unidades** Fracción que se usa para la conversión de unidades, donde el numerador y el denominador representan la misma cantidad pero están en unidades distintas.	$\frac{60\ min}{1\ h}$ or $\frac{1\ h}{60\ min}$
unit price A unit rate used to compare prices.	**precio unitario** Tasa unitaria que sirve para comparar precios.	Cereal costs $0.23 per ounce.
unit rate A rate in which the second quantity in the comparison is one unit.	**tasa unitaria** Una tasa en la que la segunda cantidad de la comparación es la unidad.	10 cm per minute
upper quartile The median of the upper half of a set of data.	**cuartil superior** La mediana de la mitad superior de un conjunto de datos.	Lower half Upper half 18, 23, 28, 29, (36,) 42 ↑ Upper quartile

V

variability The spread of values in a set of data.	**variabilidad** Amplitud de los valores de un conjunto de datos.	The data set {1, 5, 7, 10, 25} has greater variability than the data set {8, 8, 9, 9, 9}.
variable A symbol used to represent a quantity that can change.	**variable** Símbolo que representa una cantidad que puede cambiar.	In the expression $2x + 3$, x is the variable.
Venn diagram A diagram that is used to show relationships between sets.	**diagrama de Venn** Diagrama que muestra las relaciones entre conjuntos.	**Transformations** **Rotations**
vertex On an angle or polygon, the point where two sides intersect; on a polyhedron, the intersection of three or more faces; on a cone or pyramid, the top point.	**vértice** En un ángulo o polígono, el punto de intersección de dos lados; en un poliedro, el punto de intersección de tres o más caras; en un cono o pirámide, la punta.	C, A, B diagram. A is the vertex of $\angle CAB$.
vertical angles A pair of opposite congruent angles formed by intersecting lines.	**ángulos opuestos por el vértice** Par de ángulos opuestos congruentes formados por líneas secantes.	1, 2, 3, 4 angles. $\angle 1$ and $\angle 3$ are vertical angles.

© Houghton Mifflin Harcourt Publishing Company

Glossary/Glosario

ENGLISH	SPANISH	EXAMPLES

vertical line test A test used to determine whether a relation is a function. If any vertical line crosses the graph of a relation more than once, the relation is not a function.

prueba de la línea vertical Prueba utilizada para determinar si una relación es una función. Si una línea vertical corta la gráfica de una relación más de una vez, la relación no es una función.

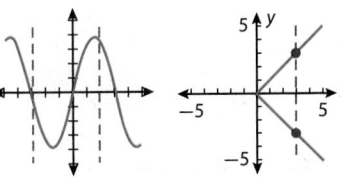

Function   Not a function

---

volume The number of cubic units needed to fill a given space.

volumen Número de unidades cúbicas que se necesitan para llenar un espacio.

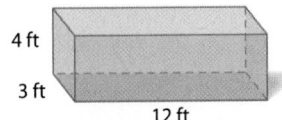

Volume $= 3 \cdot 4 \cdot 12 = 144 \text{ ft}^3$

weighted average A mean that is calculated by multiplying each data value by a weight, and dividing the sum of these products by the sum of the weights.

promedio ponderado Promedio que se calcula por multiplicando cada valor de datos por un peso, y dividiendo la suma de estos productos por la suma de los pesos.

If the data values 0, 5, and 10 are assigned the weights 0.1, 0.2, and 0.7, respectively, the weighted average is:
$$\frac{0(0.1) + 5(0.2) + 10(0.7)}{0.1 + 0.2 + 0.7} = \frac{8}{1}$$

x-axis The horizontal axis on a coordinate plane.

eje x El eje horizontal del plano cartesiano.

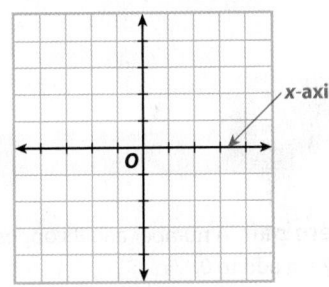

x-axis

---

x-coordinate The first number in an ordered pair; it tells the distance to move right or left from the origin (0, 0).

coordenada x El primer número de un par ordenado; indica la distancia que debes moverte hacia la izquierda o la derecha desde el origen, (0, 0).

5 is the x-coordinate in (5, 3).

---

x-intercept The x-coordinate of the point where the graph of a line crosses the x-axis.

intersección con el eje x Coordenada x del punto donde la gráfica de una línea cruza el eje x.

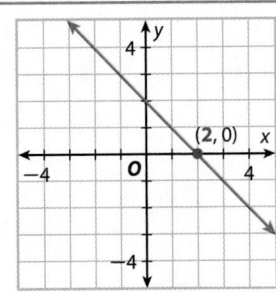

The x-intercept is 2.

Y

y-axis The vertical axis on a coordinate plane.

eje y El eje vertical del plano cartesiano.

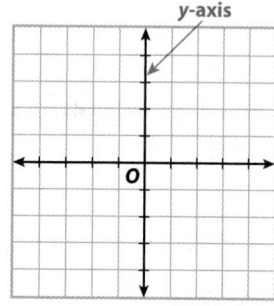

y-coordinate The second number in an ordered pair; it tells the distance to move up or down from the origin (0, 0).

coordenada y El segundo número de un par ordenado; indica la distancia que debes avanzar hacia arriba o hacia abajo desde el origen, (0, 0).

3 is the y-coordinate in (5, 3).

y-intercept The y-coordinate of the point where the graph of a line crosses the y-axis.

intersección con el eje y Coordenada y del punto donde la gráfica de una línea cruza el eje y.

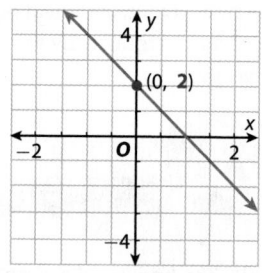

The y-intercept is 2.

Z

zero pair A number and its opposite, which add to 0.

par nulo Un número y su opuesto, cuya suma es 0.

18 and −18

Index

© Houghton Mifflin Harcourt Publishing Company

Index

Index

Index

© Houghton Mifflin Harcourt Publishing Company

Index

and surface area, 118–120
of trapezoids and quadrilaterals, 483

Persevere in Problem Solving, 12, 44, 104, 116, 122, 128, 208, 226, 238, 278, 302, 466, 483, 506, 572, 644, 656, 679, 719

Personal Math Trainer. *Personal Math Trainer is available online for every lesson.*

physical science, 314

pi (π), 105–106, 286

plane, intersection of three-dimensional figures and, 81–84

Pluto, 317

population, of largest countries, 315, 319

populations, 140, 144, 145
generating random samples from, 157–162
making inferences about, 151–156
and samples, 145–150
biased, 146–147
nonrandom, 145–146
random, 145–147, 151–156
statistical measures to compare, 181–186
differences in centers and variability, 181–182
with multiple samples, 183–184

Portland, Oregon, 452

positive integers, square of, 273

positive numbers
cube roots of, 273–274
square roots of, 273–274

positive variables, 2

powers
defined, 456
expressing products as, 301
patterns in, 297, 298
raising to a power, 298

powers of 10, 303
in equations involving decimals, 468–469
negative, 309–314
positive, 303–308

predictions, 222
with experimental probability, 211–212, 221–226
qualitative predictions, 222
quantitative predictions, 223
with linear equations, 404–405
from multiple samples, 183–184
from random samples, 151–160
with theoretical probability, 245–250
qualitative predictions, 246–247
quantitative predictions, 245–246
from trend lines, 705–708

preimage, 538, 543, 585, 586

prime numbers, 202

principal square root, 273

prisms
hexagonal, 127
rectangular
cross sections of, 81–82
height of, 44
surface area of, 117–122
volume of, 126
square, 125
surface area of, 117–122
trapezoidal, 124, 126, 128

triangular
cross sections of, 81
surface area of, 119–121
volume of, 123, 126
volume of, 123, 124, 126–128, 664

probability, 196, 201–208
of complements of events, 204–205
estimating, 210, 251–256
of events, 202–204
experimental, 210
calculating, 210–211
of compound events, 215–220
making predictions with, 211–212, 221–226
of simple events, 209–214
simulation of simple events, 251
theoretical
of compound events, 239–244
making predictions with, 245–250
of simple events, 233–238
simulations using technology, 251–256

Problem Solving, 41, 119, 223, 560, 674. *See also* Persevere in Problem Solving

problem solving. *Problem solving is a central focus of this course and is found throughout this book.*

problem-solving plan
making quantitative predictions, 223
surface area of composite solids, 119
using inequalities for negative elevations, 41

product, 12

properties
Addition Property of Inequality, 38, 39
Associative, 7
Commutative, 7, 572
Distributive, 7–10, 12, 473–478
Division Property of Inequality, 39–40
of equality, 479–482
Multiplication Property of Inequality, 39–40
Subtraction Property of Inequality, 38

proportional graphs, 438

proportionality
constant of, 336, 337, 348
dilations, 579–584
algebraic representations of, 585–590
functions
comparing, 431–436
describing, 425–430
identifying and representing, 417–424
linear equations
writing from situations and graphs, 391–396
writing from a table, 397–402
linear relationships and bivariate data, 403–410
in making quantitative predictions, 223–224
similar shapes and proportions, 71–76
in similar triangles, 627, 629
simulations, 251–256
trend lines on scatter plots, 703–708

proportional relationships, 2, 336
defined, 334
graphing, 348–349
interpreting unit rate as slope, 347–352
nonproportional relationships *vs.*, 377–384
comparing, 380–381
using equations, 378
using graphs, 377
using tables, 379

rates of change
finding, 341–342, 345–346
interpreting unit rate as slope, 347–352
representing, 335–340
with equations, 336
with graphs, 337
with tables, 335
slope
finding, 343–346
interpreting unit rate as, 347–352

proportions
making inferences from, 153
in making predictions
experimental probability, 221, 222
theoretical probability, 245, 247, 248
and similar shapes, 71–76

protractors, 78, 85, 544, 550, 556, 625

Proxima Centauri, 326

pyramids, 82–83, 199, 609

Pythagorean Theorem, 638–644
converse of, 645–650
for distance between two points, 651–656
proving, 639–640
in three dimensions, 641–642
using, 640–641

 Q

quadrilaterals
dilations of, 580
perimeter of, 483
rotations of, 563

qualitative predictions
with experimental probability, 222
with theoretical probability, 246–247

quantitative predictions
with experimental probability, 223
with theoretical probability, 245–246

quartiles, 152, 175

R

radius, 99
and area of circle, 105–106
finding, 101
finding circumference with, 100
of a sphere, 675
and volume, 664, 665, 666

random integers, 140

random numbers, 252–256
for simulating compound events, 252–253
for simulating simple events, 251, 252

random samples, 145–147
defined, 140, 144, 146
generating, 157–162
making inferences from, 151–156
using box plots, 152, 183–185
using dot plots, 151
using proportions, 153
multiple, 183–184

range
on box plots, 175–177
on dot plots, 171–174

© Houghton Mifflin Harcourt Publishing Company

Index

Index

ASSESSMENT REFERENCE SHEET

TABLE OF MEASURES

Length

1 inch = 2.54 centimeters

1 meter = 39.37 inches

1 mile = 5,280 feet

1 mile = 1,760 yards

1 mile = 1.609 kilometers

1 kilometer = 0.62 mile

Mass/Weight

1 pound = 16 ounces

1 pound = 0.454 kilograms

1 kilogram = 2.2 pounds

1 ton = 2,000 pounds

Capacity

1 cup = 8 fluid ounces

1 pint = 2 cups

1 quart = 2 pints

1 gallon = 4 quarts

1 gallon = 3.785 liters

1 liter = 0.264 gallons

1 liter = 1000 cubic centimeters

FORMULAS

Area

Parallelogram	$A = bh$
Circle	$A = \pi r^2$
Triangle	$A = \frac{1}{2} bh$

Volume

General Prisms	$V = Bh$
Cylinder	$V = \pi r^2 h$
Sphere	$V = \frac{4}{3} \pi r^3$
Cone	$V = \frac{1}{3} \pi r^2 h$

Circumference

Circle	$C = \pi d$ or $C = 2\pi r$

Other

Pythagorean Theorem	$a^2 + b^2 = c^2$